ANTIQUES
PRICE GUIDE 2003

ANTIQUES
PRICE GUIDE 2003

Judith Miller

DK PUBLISHING

LONDON, NEW YORK, MUNICH,
MELBOURNE, and DELHI

A joint production from DK
and THE PRICE GUIDE COMPANY

THE PRICE GUIDE COMPANY LIMITED

Publisher Judith Miller

Publishing Manager Julie Brooke

Editors Conor Kilgallon, Nicola Munro

Assistant Editors Megan Watson,
Sara Sturgess, Aislinn Mcivor

Editorial Assistants Chelsea Mannix,
Cara Miller, Kirsty Miller, Andrew Delve,
Kate James, Sarah Wainwright

Design and DTP Tim Scrivens, TJ Graphics

Marketing Consultant Richard Tidsall

Photographers Graham Rae, Bruce Boyajian,
John McKenzie, Mike Molloy,
Byron Slater, Elizabeth Field,
Dave Pincott, Jeremy Larkin

Indexer Hilary Bird

Workflow Consultant Edward MacDermott

DORLING KINDERSLEY LIMITED

Category Publisher Jackie Douglas

Managing Art Editor Heather McCarry

Managing Editor Julie Oughton

US Senior Editor Jill Hamilton

DTP Designer Mike Grigoletti

Senior Digital Librarian Scott Stickland

Jacket Designer Nicola Powling

Jacket Editor Beth Apple

Production Controller Joanna Bull

Production Manager Sarah Coltman

First American edition, 2002
00 01 02 03 04 05 10 9 8 7 6 5 4 3 2

Published in the United States by
DK Publishing, Inc.
375 Hudson Street
New York, New York 10014

The Price Guide Company (UK) Ltd
Studio 21, Waterside
44-48 Wharf Road
London N1 7UX
info@thepriceguidecompany.com

A CIP catalog record for this book is available from the Library of Congress.

ISBN 0-7894-8940-6

Color reproduction by Colourscan, Singapore
Printed and bound in Germany by MOHN media and Mohndruck GmbH

See our complete
product line at
www.dk.com

CONTENTS

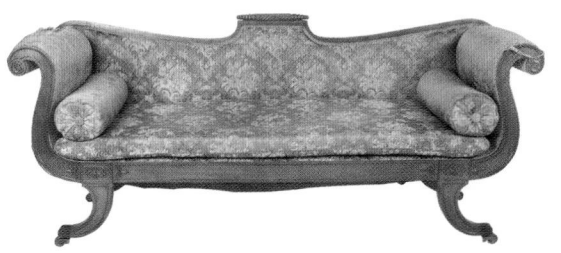

LIST OF CONSULTANTS

Overall Consultant

Paul Roberts
Freeman's
1808 Chestnut Street
Philadelphia PA 19111 USA

Furniture

Beau Freeman
Freeman's
1808 Chestnut Street
Philadelphia PA 19107 USA

Lee Young
Sloan's Washington DC
4920 Wyaconda Road
N Bethesda MD 20852 USA

Folk Art

Lynda Cain
Freeman's
1808 Chestnut Street
Philadelphia PA 19104 USA

Shaker

Willis Henry
Willis Henry Auctions Inc
22 Main Street
Marshfield MA 02050 USA

Clocks

Beau Freeman
Freeman's
1808 Chestnut Street
Philadelphia PA 19109 USA

Toys and Dolls

Bill Bertoia
Bertoia Auctions
2141 Demarco Drive
Vineland NJ 08360 USA

Decorative Arts

David Rago
Craftsman Auctions
333 North Main Street
Lambertville NJ 08530 USA

American Paintings

Alasdair Nichol
Freeman's
1808 Chestnut Street
Philadelphia PA 19103 USA

   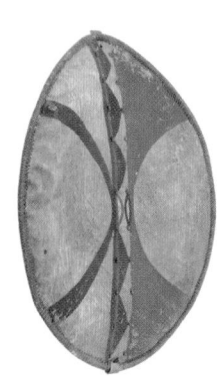

INTRODUCTION

Welcome to my first full-color antiques price guide, published in association with DK Publishing. I am very excited about this book and think we have managed to create the most useful reference book available, combining as it does, wonderful commissioned full-color photographs with researched information and price ranges.

The world of antiques has changed a great deal in the 25 years I have been writing about antiques, and I think that antiques price guides have to adapt too. All color pages are, of course, very beautiful to look at, but there is a serious point to them. It can be very misleading to look at antiques and not have a good color photograph. How can you tell what Sèvres "gros blue" looks like, or judge the quality of the vegetable dyes in a Caucasian rug? In many areas of antiques the color of the object can dramatically affect the value.

The antiques world has also become more global, and this has a great deal to do with the Internet. While I still attend auction sales every week and would miss terribly my visits to, and purchases from, specialist dealers, all I can say is if you haven't tasted the delights of buying on the Internet, now is the time to start. Further information about using the Internet and tips for buying online can be found on page 8.

There really never has been a better time to buy, particularly in the middle market. And my last thought is, that in all my years of antique buying, it is always the items I missed that plague me, not the ones I bought.

Happy hunting.

Judith Miller.

HOW TO USE THIS BOOK

Running head – Indicates the sub-category of the main heading.

Caption – The description of the item illustrated, including, when relevant, the period, the maker or factory, medium, the year it was made, dimensions, and condition. Many captions have **footnotes** which explain terminology or give identification or valuation information.

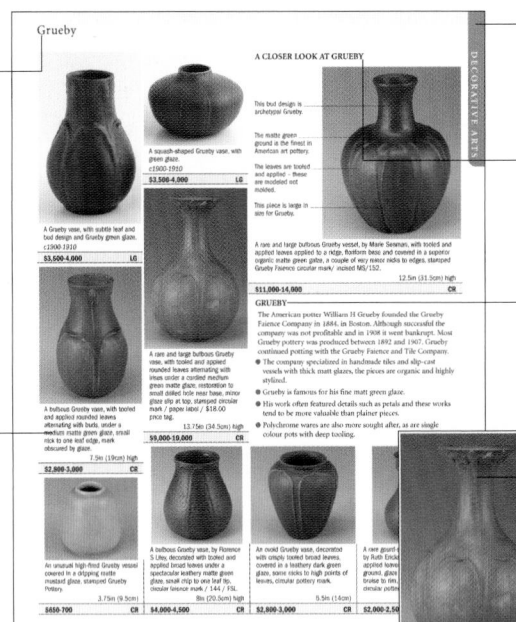

Page tab – This device appears on every spread and identifies the main category heading as indicated in the Contents List on page 5.

A closer look at – Does exactly that. This is where we show identifying aspects of a factory or maker, point out rare colors or shapes, and explain why a particular piece is so desirable.

Points of interest – about designers, makers, and factories, including biographical notes, themes and styles, particular pieces to look out for, and tips for spotting a fake.

The object – The antiques are shown in full color. This is a vital aid to identification and valuation. In many areas of antiques, a slight color variation can signify a large price differential.

The price guide – The price ranges in the Guide are there to give a ball-park figure of what you should pay for a similar item. The great joy of antiques is that there is not a recommended retail price. The price guides in this book are based on actual prices, either what a dealer will take or the full auction price. They are then checked by consultants. If you wish to sell an item you may be offered much less; if you want to insure your items the insurance valuation may be considerably more.

The source code – Every item in the Price Guide has been specially photographed at an auction house, a dealer's shop, an antiques market, or a private collection. These are credited by the code at the end of the caption, and can be checked against the Key to Illustrations on pages 724–6.

USING THE INTERNET

AS A METHOD OF PURCHASING ANTIQUES, many people have become hooked on Internet auctions. EBay, one of the market leaders, has 42 million registered users. The system is remarkably simple. You sign up, give your personal details, including credit card information, and you can begin. Prospective users should look for industry standard online security and trusted names to ensure that card details remain safe. There are three primary types of online auction:

ONLINE AUCTIONS – an item is offered for sale and bidding occurs over a fixed time period. At the end of that time period, the highest bidder wins the piece. These auctions can be frenzied and frustrating due to a large amount of last minute (or second!) bidding, so leave a maximum bid first and see what happens near the end.

ONLINE ABSENTEE BIDDING – rather than leave a bid in person or by fax, you can view a catalog and submit a bid straight away for submission into the auction by a clerk.

LIVE AUCTIONS – the most cutting edge service where bidders can bid in real time direct to the saleroom via the Internet, whilst witnessing and interacting with the bidding as it happens.

Not 100 percent reliable due to slowing/instability of the Internet, so it's wise to leave a covering online absentee bid before the sale.

Of course, you still have to decide what bid to leave and this is where I believe the Judith Miller/Dorling Kindersley antiques price guide reference library will become invaluable. Another good tip is to ask the right questions of the auction house or vendor, as you cannot examine the object first hand. Most sellers (private or trade) will want to realise the best price for their items so will be more than happy to help – if approached politely and sensibly.

Of course, auctions are not the only use of the Internet. Many dealers have websites – look these up and buy direct. For secure payment, use industry standard Escrow services, or well-known services such as Paypal, Bidpay, Billpoint, etc. These services create an e-paper trail, which can be handy if sellers claim "never to have received funds".

One cautionary note – as well as the e-hammer price there could be shipping, insurance and packing costs, and regional taxes to pay. And it is always worth considering how much to bid if that granite top table seating 12 happens to be in Paris, France.

PORCELAIN Berlin

THE IMMENSE VOLUME AND DIVERSITY OF DECORATIVE AND USEFUL WARES HAS MEANT THAT CERAMICS HAVE CONSISTENTLY PROVED TO BE ONE OF THE MOST COLLECTED TYPES OF ANTIQUE. The history of ceramics, with its fiercely guarded manufacturing secrets, shipwrecked cargoes and industrial espionage, serves only to increase its appeal.

Because it covers such a broad spectrum, it is always difficult to make sweeping generalizations about the state of the ceramics market but, generally speaking, it is relatively stable at the moment. However, there are trends and movements in specific areas that are of interest to the collector.

Rare pieces, as always, are selling extremely well, and provenance is always an important factor. While the top and lower end of the market are fairly buoyant, the middle section is relatively quiet. There is a premium for pieces in good condition, but as these are gradually becoming scarce, people are becoming more open to buying damaged wares.

There has been an increased appreciation for early ceramics. The more decorative pieces are doing better than plainer, simpler wares.

People continue to amass collections of chintz ware, blue and white pottery and porcelain and rustic stoneware, although lately there has been a move towards more classical taste.

The internet has brought about an increased awareness and availability of antiques, and many ceramics collectors are among those beginning to bid online. Although many buyers still prefer to visit a dealer or auction house so they can examine a piece before they buy, most auctioneers are surprised at the volume and value of internet bids.

BERLIN

A late 19thC Berlin painted porcelain plaque depicting a maiden and butterfly, impressed KPM scepter marks.

12.5in (31.8cm) high

$7,000-8,000   **SI**

A Berlin painted porcelain plaque, depicting the Three Theological Virtues, Faith with a chalice and a Bible, Charity with a child on her lap, and Hope with an anchor, all seated within a wooded landscape, impressed KPM and scepter marks.

c1870   13.5in (34.2cm) wide

$3,000-3,500   **SI**

A large Berlin painted porcelain plaque, depicting a gypsy girl, impressed KPM and scepter mark, in gilt frame.

c1880   12.5in (31.5cm) high

$4,500-5,000   **BonE**

A large Berlin painted porcelain plaque, depicting a young girl, KPM and scepter mark, in gilt frame.

c1880   12.5in (31.5cm) high

$4,500-5,000   **BonE**

A Berlin painted porcelain plaque, entitled "Solitude", depicting a nude, draped figure of woman, signed by Greiner, impressed KPM and scepter mark, incised 255 195, in gilt frame.

c1880   10in (25.5cm) high

$5,500-6,000   **BonE**

A KPM painted porcelain plaque, depicting Jesus in the temple among the scribes and pharisees, after a painting by H Hoffman, impressed KPM and scepter marks, inscribed "Jesus in Tempel", "nach H Hoffman" on the reverse.

1882   13in (33cm) wide

$4,500-5,000   **SI**

A Berlin painted porcelain plaque, entitled "Rebecca", signed by Hauterbach, impressed KPM and scepter marks on reverse, incised 255.195, in gilt frame.

c1890   10in (25.5cm) high

$2,500-3,000   **BonE**

A Berlin painted porcelain plaque, depicting a young girl perched on a tree branch, impressed KMP and scepter marks.

10 in (25.5cm) high

$3,000-3,500　　　SI

A late 19thC Berlin painted porcelain plaque, in the manner of Johannes Roisierse, depicting a peasant girl seated at a table holding an egg in front of a burner, impressed KPM and sword marks.

12.5in (32cm) high

$4,000-4,500　　　SI

A Berlin plate, decorated with the Iron Cross medal and date 1914 within a heavy wreath of oak and a burnished gilt rim band, KPM marks printed in red, scepter mark in blue and an iron cross in black.

1914　　　9.5in (24cm) dia

$150-200　　　Chef

Berlin Ceramic Marks

KPM

Orb mark. c1830　　　c1850

A Berlin porcelain plaque, depicting highland cattle in landscape, signed "J.J.HEROLD", marked KPM, in wood frame.

15.75in (40cm) wide

$3,000-3,500　　　SI

BOW

BOW PORCELAIN FACTORY WAS FOUNDED BY EDWARD HEYLYN AND THOMAS FRYE IN 1744. The factory, based in Stratford, east London, England, traded under the name of New Canton and became one of the largest porcelain factories in England in the mid-18th century.

Most of Bow's wares were influenced by Oriental styles, particularly those of blanc-de-Chine, famille rose and Japanese Kakiemon porcelain. However, inspiration was also drawn from Meissen figures and the Sèvres style. In 1775, the factory closed, and the molds and tools were passed on to Derby.

A rare early Bow coffee can, painted with the Cross-legged Chinaman and Fisherman patterns, willow fronds pendant from rim.

c1747-52

$1,800-2,200　　　GorL

An unusual Bow basket, softly painted with bamboo and peony, the reticulated border painted with foliage, repaired.

c1750-55　　　6.25in (15.5cm)

$600-700　　　WW

Bow Ceramic Marks

Early incised marks. c1750　　　Painted anchor and dagger mark. c1760-75　　　Underglaze blue mark. c1760

A Bow blue and white sauceboat, with scalloped rim, the fluted body painted with pagoda landscapes, 8 mark, hairline crack and chips to the foot.

c1755　　　5.75in (14.2cm) long

$400-500　　　WW

An unusual Bow saucer, painted in blue with a jumping boy and his mother, within a wavy border, some damage.

1755-60　　　4.5in (11.5cm) dia

$350-400　　　WW

A Bow plate, with prunus molding.

c1756

$700-800　　　SA

A Bow blue and white sauceboat, the fluted body painted with pagodas, trees and rockwork, some damage.

c1760　　　4.5in (11.5cm) long

$250-300　　　WW

Bow

A Bow white-glazed coffee can, applied with three prunus sprigs, tiny rim chips.

c1760   2.5in (6cm) high

$300-350   **WW**

A Bow two-handled cup, molded with a wide band of scales beneath a cell, 2 mark, cracked.

c1760   3in (7.5cm)

$300-350   **WW**

A Bow white-glazed coffee cup, with three applied molded prunus sprigs and a shaped handle.

c1755-60   2.5in (6cm)

$225-275   **WW**

A Bow blue and white sauceboat, of silver shape, molded with flowers, foliage and cartouche-shaped panels, painted with flowers and foliage, some damage.

c1760   7.75in (19.5cm) high

$350-400   **WW**

A Bow blue and white sauceboat, molded with fruit on matted panels, the interior painted with peony and a cell border, small chips, firing crack.

c1760-65   8in (20cm) high

$450-500   **WW**

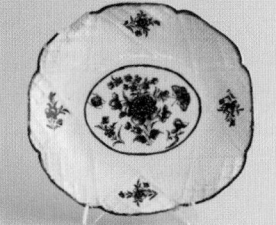

An Bow tea bowl and saucer, molded in the blanc-de-Chine style with prunus sprays,

1760

$120-180   **Chef**

A Bow hand-painted blue and white tea bowl and saucer, slight chips.

c1760   4.5in (11cm) wide

$140-200   **PC**

A Bow plate, of lobed form, painted with flowers and molded with basketwork patterns, some chips.

c1760   7.5in (19cm) dia

$200-250   **WW**

A Bow dish, of chamfered rectangular form, painted with peony, rockwork and willow tree, the border with panels of flowers, small chips.

c1760   **9.5in (24cm) wide**

$600-700   **WW**

A Bow plate, of octagonal form, painted with bamboo, flowers and rockwork, cracked.

c1760   9in (23cm) dia

$250-300   **WW**

A Bow blue and white sauceboat, of silver shape, molded with flowers and leaves and painted with figures, flowers and buildings, some cracks.

c1760   6.25in (16cm) high

$300-350   **WW**

A Bow blue and white butter tub, printed with flowers and foliage beneath a cell border, no marks, some damage.

c1760   4.5in (11cm) high

$140-180   **WW**

A Bow plate, of octagonal form, painted with Chinese riverscapes and flowers in central and alternating reserves against a blue ground, with mock Chinese four-character mark.

c1765   6.5in (16.5cm) dia

$400-450   **GorL**

An early Bow white-glazed model of Winter, sitting on firewood leaning over a brazier, no mark, one repaired chip to the edge of hood.

c1755   5in (12.5cm) high

$600-700   **WW**

An 18thC Bow figure, representing Summer, modeled as a lady in contemporary dress seated on a bushel of corn, raised on a rococo scroll base.

- Most early Bow pieces are unmarked, but after c1765 some colorful pieces were marked with an anchor and dagger painted in red enamel.
- Many pieces produced before c1755 were left in the white. Popular colors after this period were egg-yolk yellow, sky blue and deep puce.
- The pieces are prone to staining due to the large proportion of bone ash used in the porcelain mix.
- Figures were press-molded rather than slip-cast, which made them heavier than most other porcelain pieces from this period.

c1765   7in (17.5cm) high

$400-500   **BonS**

A Bow model of a nun, sitting reading from a large bible, no marks.

c1760   5.75in (14.5cm) high

$900-1,100   **WW**

A Bow model of a boy, in a theatrical pose sitting on a tree stump holding a letter, blue crescent and red anchor and dagger marks, repairs to hands and hat.

c1765   6in (15cm) high

$500-550   **WW**

◀ A Bow candlestick, modeled as a black lady kneeling and holding a sconce upon her head, raised on a scroll base, some restoration.

c1765   7in (18cm) high

$450-500   **WW**

◀ Two Bow figures of cherubs, each holding flowers, on flower encrusted bases, one with bocage, losses and restorations to flowers.

c1765   5in (12.8cm) high

$140-200   **HamG**

A pair of Bow figures, The New Dancers, with anchor and dagger mark in red, minor restoration to bocage and fingers of female.

c1770   9.5in (24cm) high

$5,000-6,000   **Gro**

A Bow sparrow-beak jug, of baluster form, molded with prunus and painted in Kakiemon style with scattered floral sprays, some stains and chips.

c1755   3in (7.5cm) high

$600-700   **DN**

A Bow mug, painted with flowers, leaves and rockwork, cracked and re-glued.

c1755   5.75in (14.3cm)

$400-450   **WW**

A Bow coffee cup and saucer, molded with scales and painted with enamel borders, gilded details, anchor and dagger marks to the saucer, some cracks.

c1760

$250-300   **WW**

A Bow plate, painted in the famille rose style with chrysanthemum, bamboo, foliage and rocks, within flower and leaf border, hairline crack through rim. Provenance: formerly in the Toppin Collection.

c1760   11.5in (29cm) dia

$600-700   **BonE**

A Bow plate, painted in the famille rose style with an insect above peony, rockwork and foliage, cracks.

c1760   9in (22.5cm) dia

$140-200   **WW**

A Bow porcelain coffee cup, with peony and rockwork enamel decoration.

c1760   2.5in (6cm) high

$250-350   **BonS**

A Bow frill vase and cover, of baluster shape, the spiral fluted body with pierced shoulder, painted with butterflies, applied with garlands of flowers and circle of leaves above foot, the mask handles beneath molded leaves, some chips.

c1765   10.75in (27cm) high

$900-1,200   **BonE**

CAUGHLEY

A POTTERY WAS ESTABLISHED IN CAUGHLEY, SHROPSHIRE, ENGLAND C1750. In 1772 Thomas Turner, previously from Worcester, took over the works, and began to produce transfer-printed porcelain, known as Salopian ware. Throughout its production period, much of

Caughley's ware was heavily influenced by the shapes and styles of Worcester, particularly in its Chinese style ware and it's use of leaf-molded jugs and mask-molded spouts.

In 1799 Turner sold Caughley to John Rose of the Coalport Porcelain Factory, who closed the works in c1812.

Caughley Ceramic Marks

S   So   Sx

*painted or printed 'S' marks
c1775*

*Painted or printed 'C' marks
c1775*

A Caughley blue and white miniature part tea service, each piece painted with the Island pattern, comprising globular teapot and cover, sucrier and cover, and a teabowl and saucer, C mark in underglaze blue.

c1770   max 3.25in (8cm)

$1,200-1,800   **BonE**

A Caughley blue and white transfer-printed saucer, in The Fisherman and Cormorant pattern, S mark.

c1775   4.75in (12cm) dia

$60-90   **PC**

A Caughley reeded tea bowl, printed to the interior with a blue cell diaper band.

                              2in (5cm)

$70-100   **BonS**

A set of three Caughley asparagus servers, printed in blue with the Fisherman pattern, S marks, one riveted.

c1780   3in (7.5cm)

$400-500   **WW**

● Although Caughley and Worcester can be difficult to distinguish, the blue pigment used in Caughley tends to be brighter than that of Worcester. When you hold a piece of Worcester to the light it tends to have a green tinge, whereas Caughley has an orange tinge.

● Caughley used a number of different marks including impressed SALOPIAN in upper or lower case letters (c1775-1799), blue printed or painted S, often followed by a small circle or cross (c1775-1795), and painted or printed C marks (c1775-1795).

A Caughley blue and white tankard, printed with the Pecking Parrot pattern, blue C mark.

c1780   4.5in (11.5cm) high

$450-550   **LC**

A Caughley sucrier and cover, with a flower knop, painted in bright enamels with flowers and foliage, no marks, the knop reapplied.

c1775   4.75in (12cm)

$450-550   **WW**

A late 18thC Caughley creamer, of Chelsea ewer form, spiral-molded with acanthus leaves, painted with flower sprays and a butterfly.

c1780   4.75in (12cm) long

$550-600   **WW**

Chelsea

A Caughley cabbage-leaf-molded mask jug, with C-scroll handle, decorated in enamels, probably in the Chamberlain's workshops, with garlands of flowers and leaves and with the monogram JC in gilt, with blue painted S mark.

c1785 7.5in (19cm)

$4,000-5,000 **AA**

A Caughley teapot and cover, the fluted globular body with foliate-molded high loop handle, the disc cover with bud finial, painted with Chantilly flower garlands over single Chantilly blooms, two small chips to cover, some wear to gilding.

The Chantilly pattern consists of sketchy sprigs or single "dotted" flowers. It was first used on Chantilly porcelain, and was used by several other French factories. In England it was copied at Derby and Caughley.

c1785 5.75in (14.5m)

$450-500 **BonS**

CHELSEA

The CHELSEA PORCELAIN FACTORY IN LONDON, ENGLAND, WAS FOUNDED BY NICHOLAS SPRIMONT IN c1745. It was the only 18thC English factory to concentrate exclusively on luxury porcelain for the aristocratic market. In 1769 the factory was sold to William Duesbury of Derby, who ran it until 1784, pieces from this period were very similar to Derby porcelain, and were sometimes referred to as Chelsea Derby.

A Caughley sucrier and cover.

c1785 4.75in (12cm) high

$450-500 **SA**

A Caughley tea canister and cover, of reeded barrel form, with gilded band, the disc cover with gilded mushroom finial, and a reeded Caughley cream jug.

c1790 max 4.3in (11cm) high

$150-200 **BonS**

A Caughley fluted coffee cup and saucer, painted with a Chantilly flower garland border about single flowers, minor wear to gilding.

c1785

$90-120 **BonS**

A Caughley teacup and saucer with flared barbed rims, with painted Sèvres-style decoration of vases of flowers interlinked with turquoise and gilt husk chains.

c1790

$225-275 **BonS**

A Chelsea figural salt or sweetmeat dish, modeled as a Turkish woman holding a scallop shell, red anchor mark, her fingers chipped, some flaking to the enamels.

c1755 6in (15cm) high

$1,500-2,000 **WW**

A small Chelsea figure of Summer, modeled as a barefoot peasant girl holding a corn sheaf, on a flat pad base, unmarked, the base repaired.

c1755 5.25in (13cm) high

$3,000-3,500 **WW**

Chelsea

COMMEDIA DELL'ARTE

This name refers to a type of improvised comedy found in 16thC Italy. Characters such as Pulcinella, Harlequin, Columbine and Pierrot provided the inspiration for many decorative wares during the 18thC, particularly in a series of figures produced by Meissen, which were widely copied throughout Europe.

A rare Chelsea figure of Scaramouche, from the Commedia dell'Arte series, after a Meissen original, depicted holding out a coin, the pad base with applied flowers and leaves, red anchor mark.

c1755   5.75in (14.5cm) high

$11,000-14,000   WW

A rare Chelsea figure of the Captain, from the Commedia dell'Arte series, after a Meissen model by Kändler, the base with applied flowerheads and leaves.

c1756   6.25in (16cm) high

$7,500-8,500   WW

A rare Chelsea figure of Bajazzo, from the Commedia dell'Arte series, after a Meissen original, depicted holding out a mask, the pad base with applied flowers and leaves, red anchor mark.

This figure is extremely rare and there are probably fewer than five in existence. It is also in exceptional condition, with little restoration. Many figures from this period are heavily restored.

c1755   6.25in (16cm) high

$25,000-30,000 WW

A rare Chelsea figure of Mezzetino, from the Commedia dell'Arte series, after a Meissen original, the base with applied flowers and leaves.

c1755   6in (15cm) high

$10,000-12,000   WW

A pair of Chelsea Derby figures, modeled as a shepherd and shepherdess, with dog and lamb at their sides, on floral encrusted bases.

7.5in (19cm)

$750-850   GorL

A rare pair of Chelsea models of Ranelagh Masqueraders, each wearing a spotted mask, he with a birdcage, she with a basket containing three fledgling birds, raised on scroll bases, he with gold anchor mark, she with brown anchor mark.

c1760   7.75in (19.5cm) high

$6,000-7,000   WW

A small Chelsea figure, modeled as a man with wicker basket, the scrolling base applied with flowers and leaves, gold anchor mark, chip to back of hat, section of basket re-glued.

c1760   5.5in (13.5cm) high

$1,500-2,000   WW

17

A Chelsea Derby figure, modeled as a shepherdess holding a posy of flowers, a lamb at her side, on a rococo base, with old paper label, The CR Stevens Collection, No.148.

7.5in (19cm)

$350-400	**GorL**

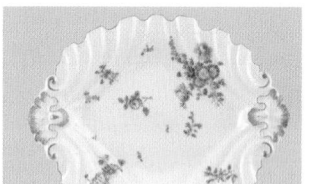

A pair of Chelsea silver-shape dishes.

c1758

$1,500-2,000 (pair)	**SA**

A Chelsea potpourri and cover.

c1760

$1,200-1,800	**SA**

A Chelsea beaker, of lobed form, painted in the Kakiemon palette with a bird, flowering branches and rockwork, the everted rim painted with flowerheads and leaves, red anchor mark.

c1752	2.75in (7cm) high	
$4,000-5,000		**AA**

A Chelsea plate, painted in enamels with scattered bouquets of flowers and insects, the border with four scroll cartouche of birds, red anchor mark, restored rim section.

c1755	13in (33cm) wide	
$450-550		**DN**

 (third image top right)

A Chelsea dish, of chamfered rectangular form, the border molded with a floral diaper design and painted with seven panels of flowers and one of butterflies, the center with scattered flowers, brown line rim, no mark.

c1755	12.5in (32cm) wide.	
$1,000-1,200		**WW**

CHELSEA

The history of the factory can be divided into four separate periods, distinguished by the four different marks used on the wares:

- Triangle period (c1744-49) – Most of the wares produced in this early period are white and inspired by silver design (Sprimont trained as a silversmith). Amongst the most well-known pieces are the "Goat and Bee" jugs, some dated 1747, and the white saltcellars shaped like crayfish. Pieces carry an incised triangle mark

- Raised anchor period (1749-52) – Wares were strongly influenced by Meissen, in particular the Kakiemon patterns and shapes it had been producing since the 1730s. The pastes were less glassy and the white glaze produced a more opaque surface. Pieces were marked with a raised anchor molded in shallow relief on an oval pad.

- Red anchor period (1752-56) – Wares continued to be influenced by Meissen. The period's most famous pieces were the "Hans Sloane" range. Sir Hans Sloane was a patron of the Royal Physic Gardens, Chelsea. Botanical subjects were copied from the Gardener's Dictionary by Philip Miller, published under Sloane's patronage.

- Gold anchor period (1756-1769) – The styles of Sèvres and Vincennes were most evident in the wares of this period; pieces were highly decorated with rich colored grounds and gilding, many were also based on the rococo-style. Pieces were marked with a thick gold anchor.

A Chelsea plate, decorated by Hans Sloane with stylized old roses, red anchor mark.

c1755

$7,000-8,000	**AA**

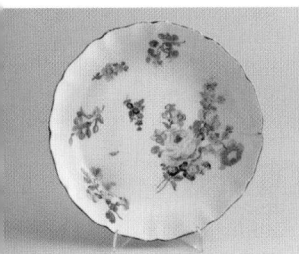

A Chelsea saucer dish, with fluted sides, painted with floral sprays and sprigs, red anchor mark, rubbed, hairline crack.

9in (23cm) dia

$225-275   **LC**

A Chelsea cup and saucer, gold anchor mark. c1765 saucer

5.25in (13cm) dia

$1,500-2,000   **AD**

A Chelsea teacup and saucer, painted in enamels with European flowers within scrolling turquoise and gilt oeil de perdrix borders, the cup with entwined handle, gold anchor marks.

Oeil de perdrix *(French: "pheasant's eye") is a circle motif with a bright central dot, used in a close repeat pattern as a ground decoration. It was first introduced at Sèvres in 1760.*

c1768

$2,500-3,000   **AA**

A Chelsea Derby mug.

c1775   4.25in (10.5cm) high

$1,200-1,800   **SA**

A small Chelsea bell-form mug, the twig handle with flowering vine terminals, painted with Deutsche blumen, chocolate brown line rim, red anchor painted mark.

First used at Meissen in from c1740, the Deutsche blumen pattern (German: "German flowers") consists of naturalistic flower motifs. It became highly fashionable throughout Europe. One of the main sources for the flowers was the Phytanthzia Iconographia, 1735-45, by JW Weinmann, which contained over 1,000 hand-colored botanical engravings.

c1775   2.5in (6cm)

$400-500   **BonS**

A Chelsea Derby dish, of scalloped lozenge form, centrally painted with a rose-garland-strewn vase, the scrolled border with a berried swag pendant, the rim scalloped in gilt, gilded D intersected by anchor mark, minor wear.

c1775   10.5in (26.5cm)

$300-350   **BonS**

A Chelsea coffee cup, painted with summer sprays, gold-plated D intersected by an anchor mark.

c1775   2.5in (6.5cm)

$225-275   **BonS**

A small Chelsea Derby bowl and cover, with flower and foliage finial, painted with a summer flower garland, gold-plated D intersected by anchor mark, bowl with hairline crack.

c1785   3.25in (8cm) high

$225-275   **BonS**

COALPORT

THE COALPORT FACTORY IN SHROPSHIRE ELNGLAND WAS FOUNDED BY JOHN ROSE IN THE 1790s. It produced table and decorative wares and after 1851 became known for its Sèvres-style vases, and from the 1870s for its flower-encrusted rococo pieces. Wares are still produced today in Stoke-on-Trent.

● Early Coalport pieces were not marked, but some later pieces carried the script "Coalport". Many of the flower-encrusted rococo vases were marked "Coalbrookdale". Pattern numbers were used after c1820

● Among the most popular decorations were Imari patterns, landscape views and Neo-classical designs. Apple-green, beige and dark blue featured largely as ground colors.

● Pieces before 1820 were made using a gray-colored hard paste and a grainy, dull glaze. After 1820, pieces were made using white bone china and a leadless feldspathic glaze, for which the factory became renowned.

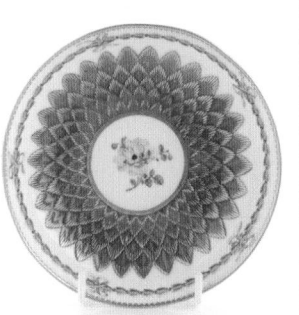

A Chelsea Derby saucer, with pineapple molding, slight crazing to rim.

5in (12.5cm) dia

$400-500   **AD**

A Coalport shell dish, decorated in the Imari style.

c1810   9.25in (23.5cm) wide

$300-400   **SA**

Coalport

A Coalport jug.

c1810 5.25in (10cm) high

$120-180 **SA**

A pair of Coalport sauce tureens, with covers and stands.

c1815-1820 5.75in (14.5cm) high

$850-950 (pair) **SA**

A pair of Coalport dishes.

c1815 9.25in (23.5cm) wide

$600-700 (pair) **SA**

A pair of Coalport ice pails and covers, after the Warwick vase shape.

c1820 14.25in (36cm) high

$8,500-9,500 (pair) **SA**

◄ A fine Coalport dessert service, richly gilded and with gadrooned borders, each piece brightly painted with luxuriant sprays of flowers and fruit, the borders decorated with gilt C-scrolls, flower sprigs and white leaf trails, comprising twenty-two plates, four rectangular, four oval and four shell-shaped dishes, a pair of sauce tureens, covers and stands and a tazza.

The price for this dessert service is based largely on its excellent condition. It is high Regency with superb painting and gilding. The decoration is in typical Coalport style, with delicate bouquets of fruit and flowers dominated by pink.

c1820-25

$18,000-22,000 **WW**

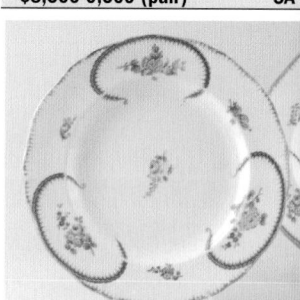

A set of five Coalport soup plates and five Coalport dinner plates.

c1825

$450-550 (set) **SA**

A Coalport scent bottle and stopper.

c1825 8in (20.5cm) high

$600-700 **Gro**

A Coalport vase, decorated with applied flowers, and painted with birds by Randall.

c1830 9in (23cm) high

$1,200-1,800 **Gro**

One of two Coalport flower-encrusted baskets, of flared form, the other with pink ground, some restoration to both.

c1830 8.5in (21.5cm)

$400-500 (pair) **DN**

► A Coalport vase and cover.

c1835 8in (20cm) high

$700-800 **Gro**

Coalport

An early Victorian Coalport quart mug, printed either side with views, one entitled "Ironbridge, Shropshire", the other "Buildwas Abbey, Shropshire", leaf-ribbed handle.

5.5in (14cm) high

$150-200   **Chef**

A 19thC Coalport plate, decorated with a central rose and panels of flowers on a gilt and pink ground, pattern no. 2/63.

9.5in (24cm) dia

$120-180   **WW**

A Coalport sugar bowl and cover, of lozenge shape with an ogee body, painted with floral sprays, the rim with beading and oval molding.

7.5in (19cm) wide

$240-300   **LC**

An early 19thC part tea service, probably Coalport, each piece decorated in gilt with a broad band of gilt flowers, comprising three tea cups, six coffee cups, one chipped, five saucers, two-handled sucrier and cover and milk jug, pattern no. 476, extensive chipping and cracks.

$400-500   **BonE**

A 19thC Coalport "named view" vase, signed by J H Plant, the ovoid body decorated with gilded foliate cartouches enclosing a vignette of Warwick Castle, a landscape to the reverse, on a cobalt-blue ground beneath gilded rams horn and laurel wreath handles, green printed mark, Warwick Castle and V.5501 in gilt.

11.45in (29cm) high

$550-650   **BonS**

A Coalport rococo vase, decorated with painted and applied flowers, with gilt scrolling handles, no mark.

This piece is a typical Coalport piece:

- The body, almost completely encrusted with flowers, is very similar to the style of Dresden. As a result such pieces were known as "English Dresden".
- The over-decorated style of these pieces was very popular during the rococo revival of the 1830s–1850s.
- Strong, conflicting colors were often used, which would not have been used in the 18thC.
- Due to the vast amount of detailing, the wares are prone to chips and fine cracks in the body.

c1850   9in (22.5cm) high

$400-500   **WW**

► A pair of late 19thC Coalport vases, decorated with turquoise jewels on a gold ground between gilded cream borders, green factory marks, pattern no. V6043/121.

6in (15cm) high

$700-800   **WW**

◄ A pair of Coalport cache-pots, each with molded scroll handles and with finely painted panels of flowers and fruit within heavily gilded scroll borders, printed marks.

1891-1919   4.25in (11cm) high

$1,000-1,500   **Clv**

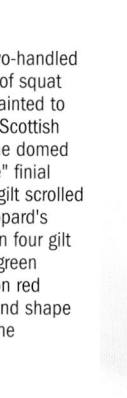

A small Coalport vase, painted with a landscape panel on a gilt and red patterned ground, gilt mask handles, green factory mark.

c1900   6in (15cm) high

| $300-350 | | WW |

A Coalport three-handled cup, painted with small landscape scenes within gilt-edged cartouches reserved on deep-blue and gilt ground, with scroll handles and knopped stem, pattern no. v5327, printed mark, stem restored.

c1900   8.75in (22cm) high

| $300-350 | | BonE |

► A Coalport two-handled vase and cover, of squat baluster form, painted to one side with a Scottish Loch vignette, the domed cover with "spire" finial above a pair of gilt scrolled handles with leopard's head capitals, on four gilt lion's paw feet, green printed mark, iron red painted marks and shape no. Y7019A, some damage.

c1905   10in (25cm) high

| $750-850 | | HamG |

DERBY

T HE EXACT DATE WHEN THE FIRST PORCELAIN FACTORY WAS SET UP IN DERBY, ENGLAND IS UNCERTAIN, but it is generally attributed to the arrival of André Planché in c1748-1750. Among the first wares of this period were chinoiserie figure groups. In 1756 William Duesbury and John Heath took over the factory, and began producing figures including shepherds, shepherdesses and actors of the day. The factory made more figures than any other and probably accounts for over 50% of all English 18thC figures.

A number of transfer-printed wares were also produced, including pieces to mark the coronation of George III and Queen Charlottein 1761. In 1786, Duesbury's son, also William, took over and began to produce "display wares" aimed at the affluent market. This was a particularly successful period for Derby and many great artist's were employed to decorate the pieces, including William Billingsley, Zachariah Boreman and George Complin. In 1797 the factory changed hands once again, and in 1848 the original factory closed, although other factories in the area carried on the name, including Royal Crown Derby.

A pair of small Derby figures, modeled as red squirrels, the bases applied with flowers and leaves.

Figures of animals attract avid bidding from collectors and hence always fetch high prices. These squirrels, which are in mint condition, are no exception. Earlier examples of Derby animals can sell for astronomical prices, some fetching up to $30,000. Chelsea and Bow animal figures are also highly desirable

c1760   2.5in (6.5cm)

| $2,200-2,800 | | WW |

A Derby figure, modeled as a bird perched on a stump applied with flowers and leaves, patch marks to the base, end of tail lacking, minor chips to the leaves.

c1760   6in (15cm)

| $1,500-2,000 | | WW |

A Derby figure, modeled as Neptune, standing above sea shells, sea weed and a river, with metal trident, no. 299 incised, chips to fingertips.

c1760-70   10.75in (27cm) high

| $1,200-1,500 | | WW |

Derby

A rare near pair of Derby figures, he modeled as David Garrick as Tancred from the play Tancred and Sigismunda, she as a street vendor, both on scroll bases, some restoration.

c1760-70   9in (22.5cm) high

$1,500-2,000   **WW**

A Derby figure, modeled as a stag recumbent before a flowering tree, no mark, some damage to antlers.

c1760-70   7.75in (19.5cm) high

$600-700   **WW**

A Derby figure, modeled as a gallant, holding a basket of flowers and with a dog at his feet, on a scrolling base, some repairs.

c1765   8.5in (21.5cm) high

$450-550   **WW**

A pair of Derby candlesticks, modeled as birds in branches, restoration to both sconces and one bird's tail.

c1765   9in (23cm) high

$2,000-2,400   **Gro**

A Derby figure, modeled as Minerva with a shield and owl at her side, on a scrolling base, right arm restored.

c1770   12in (30cm) high

$450-550   **WW**

A Derby figure, modeled as Falstaff, holding a sword and shield, on a scroll base, some damage.

c1770   8in (20.5cm) high

$300-350   **WW**

A pair of Derby candlesticks, modeled as birds in branches, each surmounted by pierced candle holders, on a scrolling base, some damage.

c1770   10in (25cm) high

$750-850   **WW**

A Derby candlestick, modeled as a shepherdess, standing before a flowering bocage and with a lamb at her feet, on a scrolling base, some restoration.

c1770   10.75in (27cm) high

$350-400   **WW**

A near pair of Derby figures, modeled as a man and young woman, each holding a cockerel and standing on a scrolling base, some repairs.

c1770   9in (23cm) high

$1,200-1,500   **WW**

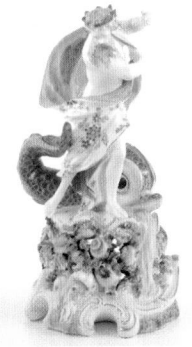

A Derby figure, modeled as Neptune standing before a stylized dolphin, the open scrollwork base encrusted with shells and seaweed, arm and dolphin tail restored.

c1775   8.5in (21.7cm) high

$300-350   **HamG**

A Derby figure, modeled as a gardener holding a bird's nest, on a scroll-molded flower-encrusted base, damage and restoration.

c1775   9in (23cm) high

$450-500   **DN**

A pair of Derby figures, modeled as a shepherd and companion, standing before flower-encrusted bocage, he with a hound at his side, she with a lamb at her feet, on pierced scroll bases, both restored.

c1775   8.75in (22cm) high

$600-700   **DN**

Two Derby figures, modeled as Mansion House dwarfs, both with pot bellies, outsized hats and brightly painted costumes, patch marks, incised no. 227, damage and restoration.

The original Chelsea "Dwarf" figures were probably based on a father and son who stood by Mansion House, wearing written advertisements on the large brims of their hats, announcing events such as auction sales. Since then the Derby factories have been well known for the production of these figures, although they were not the only factory to make them.

c1785   7in (18cm) high

$450-500	BonS

EARLY DERBY

- Most early Derby pieces are unmarked. After c1760 wares were fired on clay pads, and carry three small triangular patches on the bases.

- From c1770 onwards model numbers began to appear on the pieces.

- From c1780 onwards various marks were used. The common crown, crossed swords and "D".

1861-1935

A late 18thC Derby figure, modeled as the Madonna and Child, on a high molded plinth, N138 incised, base cracks and small chips.

8.75in (22cm) high

$300-350	WW

A Derby figure, modeled as a bagpiper, damage and restoration.
c1765   6.25in (15.5cm) high

$250-300	DN

A Derby figure group, The Shoemaker, modeled as a lady leaning on a tree stump, a kneeling cobbler fitting her shoe, inscribed no.78, both arms of the lady restored, part of shoe and bocage missing.
c1780   6.25in (16cmcm) high

$400-500	HamG

A late 18thC Derby figure, modeled as a recumbent doe sitting before flower-encrusted bocage, some damage and repairs.

6.25in (16cm)

$400-500	DN

A pair of Derby figures, modeled as Classical muses, each painted en grisaille with trophies of music, incised model nos 244 and 245, slight damage and losses.
c1790   9in (23cm) high

$750-850	DN

A late 18thC Derby figure, modeled as Milton wearing a gilt-trimmed jacket and robe, his left arm supported on three books, the plinth molded with classical figures, painted mark and incised no. 261.

10in (25.5cm) high

$280-340	Chef

A late 18thC Derby figure, modeled as Shakespeare, wearing a gilt decorated jacket, his right arm leaning on three books, the plinth molded with mask heads, incised no. 305.

10in (25cm) high

$220-280	Chef

► A Derby figure, modeled as a shepherdess, playing a mandolin, a lamb to one side before a bocage, on rococo pierced scroll-work base, her skirt with che-quered Indianische Blumen deco-ration, restoration.

Indianische blumen (German: Indian flowers) describes a design of fanciful botanical motifs, taken from Oriental porce-lain.

9in (23cm) high

$220-280		BonS

A late 18thC Derby figure group, Music, modeled as a female flautist standing before a truncated column, two putti flanking, one holding a furled manuscript the other a violin, on rockwork base with applied florets, incised N217 over 2, restored.

c1790

| $300-350 | | **BonS** |

A pair of Derby figures, modeled as a shepherd and shepherdess, he with a dog at his feet, she with a sheep, each standing before a bocage, on scroll base, incised no. 60, each with one arm and hat repaired.

5.5in (14cm)

| $400-500 | | **BonE** |

A set of four Derby figures, representing the Seasons, comprising Spring, a young girl with garland of flowers, Summer, a young boy carrying a sheaf of corn, Autumn, a young boy with a basket of grapes and Winter, a young girl wearing a fur-lined cloak, slight chips.

max 8.75in (22cm)

| $3,000-3,500 | | **BonE** |

A Derby figure, modeled as a piper with a dog at his feet, seated against a bocage, on a scroll base, slight chips to bocage, dog's ear missing.

8.75in (22cm)

| $400-450 | | **BonE** |

A pair of early 19thC figural candlesticks, possibly Derby, modeled as lady and gallant wearing 18thC dress, standing before tree trunks entwined with applied flowers and supporting the candle nozzles, blue crossed swords mark.

10in (25cm) high

| 700-800 | | **Chef** |

A pair of Derby figures, modeled as a Scotsman and companion, he with a plumed bonnet, she carrying a basket of flowers, both with incised numeral to base N378, chips to his fingers, her arms repaired.

man 11.75in (30cm)
lady 10.25in (26cm)

| $1,000-1,200 | | **BonE** |

A 19thC Derby figure, modeled as a young girl in 18thC dress, carrying a basket of fruit, painted mark in iron-red, incised no. 123, one arm replaced.

7in (17.5cm)

| $150-200 | | **BonE** |

A Derby tureen and cover, modeled as a pigeon.

This piece is quite rare because it is modeled as a squab rather than an adult pigeon, which are more commonly portrayed. The inside is decorated with naturalistic flower sprays. This tureen may have been used to serve quails eggs.

c1760   6.75in (17cm) long

| $4,500-5,000 | | **SA** |

A Derby stand.

c1770

| $1,000-1,200 | | **SA** |

A small Derby blue and white sauceboat, of silver shape, molded with a fruiting vine panel over fine fluting, a fruit and nut swag panel on the reverse, the interior painted with a floral spray, chip to spout.

c1770   4.5in (11.5cm)

| $750-850 | | **BonS** |

A pair of Derby fan-shaped asparagus servers, each painted in underglaze blue with a Chinese landscape, beneath a cell diaper band.

c1775   3in (8cm) long

| $1,500-2,000 | | **AA** |

Derby

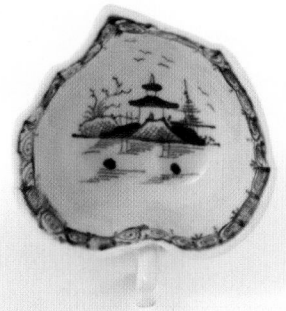

A Derby pickle leaf dish, of heart form with angular handle, on three molded "leaf" pad feet, painted with a pagoda on an island within a sworl and pendant border.

c1780   2.5in (6.5cm)

$400-500   **BonS**

A pair of Derby two-handled chocolate cups and covers, with wrythen and fern molded decoration, overpainted with summer flower garlands, the rims scalloped in gilt, ball finial to cover, blue painted mark.

c1780   4in (10cm)

$1,500-2,000   **BonS**

A Derby mug, of globular body with grooved neck, the wavy strap handle with trefoil finial, painted with Deutsche blumen and bands of cobalt with gilded decoration, blue painted mark.

c1780   5.25in (13.5cm)

$400-500   **BonS**

A Derby coffee cup and saucer, of fluted form, painted with a Chantilly flower swag suspended from a gilded chain and ribbon band, puce painted mark and pattern no.109.

c1785

$120-180   **BonS**

A Derby cream jug, with sparrow beak spout and wishbone handle, internally painted with a landscape vignette attributed to Boreman, puce painted mark and pattern no. 86, and a conforming coffee cup, hairline crack.

c1785   max 3in (7.5cm) high

$1,000-1,500   **BonS**

A Derby custard cup and cover, of bell form, with domed cover and loop finial, gilded with foliate and dotted meanders, puce painted mark, pattern no. 61, impressed D, finial restored.

c1785

$400-500   **BonS**

A late 18thC Derby plate, the center painted with a landscape panel in the manner of Boreman, the border with flowerheads joined by a gilt wave, inscribed "Near Coxbench, Derbyshire", blue mark, pattern no.178.

8.5in (21.5cm)

$300-350   **WW**

A late 18thC Derby plate, entitled "Pansies or Heart's Ease", painted in the manner of Quaker Pegg, painted blue mark and pattern no. 212, slight rubbing to gilt.

$450-500   **WW**

A pair of Derby kidney-shaped dishes, the centres painted with a rose sprig, probably by William Billingsley, puce mark and no. 232.

c1795 10in (25cm) wide

$1,000-1,500 (pair)   **DN**

A late 18thC Derby teapot and cover, painted and gilt-decorated with the 552 pattern of cornflower and foliate guilloche, puce marks.

c1795

$400-500   **Chef**

A Derby porcelain cup and saucer, puce mark.

c1795   3.25in (8cm) high

$400-500   **SA**

A Derby teapot, cover and stand, puce mark.

c1795   5.75in (14.5cm) high

$2,500-3,000   **SA**

A Derby mug, modeled as Ariadne, with vine leaves and grapes tied in the maiden's hair, red crown and crossed batons marks, repair to the handle.

c1800   3.5in (9cm)

| $120-180 | WW |

An early 19thC Derby plate, entitled "Near Udolpho, Italy", painted with figures and a castle on a cliff, within a gilt scrolling border, red painted mark.

8.75in (22cm) dia

| $225-275 | WW |

An early 19thC Derby soup plate, painted with a view of the Harbour of Leghorn, titled on the reverse, factory mark, pattern no. 321, some rubbing.

| $300-350 | WW |

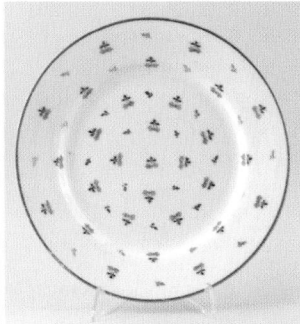

A set of six Derby plates.

c1810   8.75in (22cm) dia

| $500-600 (set) | SA |

An early 19thC Derby part dinner service, comprising fourteen plates, two sauce tureens, covers and stands, two ice pails and covers, a two-handled dish, two kidney-shaped dishes and four square dishes.

c1810

| $2,200-2,800 (set) | Chef |

A Derby saucer dish, painted in the Imari style.

c1815   8.5in (21.5cm) dia

| $120-180 | SA |

A rare trout's head stirrup cup, possibly Derby, the rim inscribed The Fisher's Delight in gilt, unmarked, some small scratches to the enamel.

c1820   5in (13cm) high

| $2,200-2,800 | WW |

WILLIAM PEGG. Known as "Quaker" Pegg, took over from William Billingsley at Derby. Pegg was outstanding in the field of botanical painting. In 1800 he joined The Society of Friends and subsequently developed a religious mania that caused him to reject his own botanical works as idolatry. He returned to Derby as a decorator in 1813, but by 1820 the delusions had returned and he left the factory for good.

● William Pegg's painting is on a par with the best botanical painters of his day. People said they could touch the flowers he painted.

● He is renowned for painting across the entire width of a piece, rather than in the center or at random, as other artists did.

● His use of enamels was so skilled he gave his botanical subjects an intensity and three-dimensional quality.

● Named, signed pieces by Pegg are rare and desirable.

One of a pair of Derby botanical plates, Orange Lily and Morandia, and Spathia Poppy and Passion Flower, by Quaker Pegg.

c1813 and c1813-15

| $23,000-26,000 (pair) | AA |

A pair of Derby potpourri vases, with applied gilt masks to the rims, decorated with gilt scrollwork, printed red marks.

c1820   5.25in (13cm) high

$350-400   **WW**

A pair of Derby potpourri urns and covers, each of squat urn form on paw feet, the pierced upper rims applied with pan masks, the covers with acanthus bud finials, painted with Neo-classical urn motifs, red painted marks, damage and loss.

c1820   6in (15cm)

$400-500   **BonS**

A Derby jardinière, the bucket bowl with bowed gilt handles with foliate terminals, painted with summer flowers, red painted mark, wear and discoloration to interior.

c1825   6.25in (16cm)

$300-350   **BonS**

An early Victorian Derby cabinet cup and saucer, painted with two reserves each of two figures in landscapes, with gilt eagle-neck handles and paw feet, the saucer with gilt foliage decoration, marks in red.

$100-150   **Chef**

A pair of mid-19thC Derby urns, each painted with floral panels in the Imari style, with gilt serpentring handles and socle feet, marks in red.

6.5in (16.5cm) high

$450-550   **Chef**

A Derby "View" plate, painted with a Welsh view of a riverside ruined building and a tree-lined track, the broad border enriched with gilt, iron-red crowned baton mark.

9in (23cm) dia

$300-350   **LC**

A Derby Crown Porcelain vase, of bottle form with flared rim, the horn-shaped handles with mask terminals, decorated in a Japan pattern in Imari colors, red printed mark.

6in (15cm)

$200-250   **BonS**

A Derby dessert service dish, of shell form, painted in the Imari palette, iron-red crown, with baton mark.

8in (20.5cm) dia

$180-220   **LC**

A large Derby Japan pattern bowl, painted in the center with a tulip and Oriental foliage, within paneled border and gilt rim, painted D, crown and batons mark in iron-red.

13.5in (34.5cm)

$400-450   **BonE**

A pair of Derby Crown Porcelain Company two-handled vases, of flattened globular body with short cylindrical neck and circular foot, the horn-shaped handles with mask terminals, richly decorated with tube-lined gilding of birds amid verdant foliage, red printed marks, one of the pair restored, wear to gilding.

c1890   3.5in (9cm)

$225-275   **BonS**

Dresden

DRESDEN

DRESDEN REFERS TO FIGURES AND WARES THAT WERE PRODUCED IN AND AROUND THE AREA OF DRESDEN, Saxony, during the mid-19thC onward. The factories producing the better copies of Meissen, included Carl Thieme of Potschappel, Helena Wolfsohn and the Dresden Porcelain Factory.

The pieces, modeled in the style of 18thC Meissen, can be difficult to distinguish from the originals, however the following tips can help to differentiate:

- Dresden figures generally used a paste which was less sophisticated and white than that of Meissen.
- Decoration on Dresden pieces tends to be more elaborate and over-stylized than Meissen pieces. The paintwork, is usually of a lower standard and uses a more gaudy palette.
- Some factories used a similar mark to that of the Meissen crossed swords. Beware of pieces that carry an unglazed patch on the base or back; markings may have been scratched off to disguise origins.

A late Dresden figure, modeled as a pug, some restoration to leg.

c1860   6.75in (17cm) high

$600-700   **RdeR**

A large Dresden tobacco jar, modeled as a pug, restoration to paint on front chest.

c1870   7.25in (18.5cm) high

$750-850   **RdeR**

A pair of Dresden figures, modeled as pugs, the male with remodeling on two bells and tail, the female with remodeling on bow and one bell repainted.

c1870   5in (12.5cm) high

$750-850   **RdeR**

A large Dresden figure, modeled as a pug, restoration to tail.

c1870   5.25in (13cm) high

$450-500   **RdeR**

A late Dresden figure, modeled as a pug.

c1890   4in (10cm) high

$150-200   **RdeR**

A late Dresden figure, modeled as a pug.

c1900   6in (15cm) high

$150-200   **RdeR**

A 19thC Dresden box and cover, painted with romantic courting figures within gilt borders, canceled underglaze blue marks.

5in (12.5cm) high

$225-275   **BonS**

▶ A pair of Dresden four-branch figural candelabra, each support modeled as a mother holding a young child and sitting, the removable top section with three floral-encrusted scrolling branches, stylized leaf drip trays, underglaze blue painted marks.

20.5in (52cm) high

$3,000-4,000   **L&T**

A late 19thC Dresden quatrefoil bowl, cover and stand painted with Watteausque scenes, the domed cover with lemon finial, minute chips to finial.

9.5in (24cm) high

$700-800   **DN**

Limoges

A late 19thC Dresden figure group, representing Art, modeled as two putti seated side by side with attributes, Berlin-type scepter mark, some small chips.

6in (15cm) wide

$70-100   **DN**

One of a pair of late 19thC Continental Empire-style porcelain écuelles, probably Dresden, of tapered cylindrical form and painted with figures of rustics in landscapes, covers and stands, painted blue Nyon-style fish marks.

c1890

$600-700 (pair)   **DN**

A Dresden six-light chandelier, in the Meissen style, the central section modeled as overlapping leaf forms with gilt highlights and decorated with floral sprigs, the lower part has six branches, each with applied flowers and leaves and hung with floral bouquets.

23.5in (60cm) high

$1,800-2,200   **SI**

A Dresden plaque, depicting Vestalin as a young girl holding a lit oil lamp, in original gilt-brass and enamel frame, inscribed "Dresden" and "Vestalin/ A. Kauffman"

c1900   8in (20cm) high

$3,000-4,000   **SI**

LIMOGES

A Limoges tray and set of 12 custard cups, lids and saucers marked Decoré pour MW Beveridge Washington DC.

c1889 cups   5.5in (14cm) dia

$2,200-2,700   **Gro**

Eight Limoges oyster plates, each molded with five scallop shells and decorated with gilt seaweed and rim, with green and red printed "T&V/FRANCE" marks, also ten Limoges game plates, each decorated with animals, the cobalt rims highlighted with gilt geometric, floral and foliate motifs, with green printed Charles Field Haviland marks. oyster plates

7.5in (18.5cm) dia

$11,000-15,000 (2 sets)   **SI**

Six early 20thC Limoges dinner plates, with transfer printed floral reserve, marked T&V Limoges France.

10in (25.5cm) dia

$225-275 (six)   **SI**

An early 20thC Haviland Limoges charger, painted in the center with a draped female nude, signed J. Soustre, red printed Theodore Haviland/Limoges/ FRANCE/ Patent applied for.

17.5in (45cm) dia

$900-1,100   **SI**

An early 20thC Haviland Limoges charger, painted with Cupid whispering in the ear of Psyche, signed J. Soustre, red printed Theodore Haviland/ Limoges/ FRANCE/ Patent applied for.

17.5in (45 cm)

$900-1,100   **SI**

Liverpool

LIVERPOOL

Liverpool, England, was a major center for ceramics production during the 18th and 19th centuries. Much of the porcelain produced was decorated with blue and white chinoiserie and inky black cobalt. The grayish appearance of the pieces is similar to early Worcester, as is much of the enamel decoration. One of the largest and well-known factories was Richard Chaffers, established in 1756. Wares produced at this factory are very white and translucent in appearance. They also have a green tinge when strong white light is applied to them.

A Richard Chaffers & Co Liverpool coffee can, decorated with the Jumping Boy pattern.

c1756-58

$4,000-5,000	**AA**

White body is typical of Chaffers.

Dark cobalt-blue color is associated with most Liverpool factories.

Pattern is derived from Chinese porcelain, but is very loosely painted.

Peppering was a problem, caused by air bubbles in the glaze.

A Richard Chaffers & Co Liverpool coffee can, decorated with Chinese scenes.

c1758

$1,500-2,000	**AA**

A Richard Chaffers & Co Liverpool saucer, hand-painted with a Chinese scene.

c1760   4.75in (12cm)

$80-120	**PC**

A Liverpool teapot and cover, of globular form, painted in the Imari palette with a fence, bamboo and rockwork, hairline crack to body.

c1760   5.5in (13.5cm) high

$450-500	**WW**

A Liverpool bust of Milton, after the model by Schneemaker, on shell and C-molded tapering plinth, probably Richard Chaffers & Co.

c1760   8.5in (21.6cm) high

$15,000-18,000	**AA**

A Liverpool blue and white sauceboat.

c1765   3.5in (9cm) high

$1,500-2,000	**SA**

LONGTON HALL

Longton Hall had a very short production period of ten years. Founded in Staffordshire, England, in 1750, the factory produced many soft paste porcelain figures, similar to those of Meissen. The company went bankrupt in 1760. When the site was excavated in 1955, quantities of kiln waste were found, which showed that they had problems making the porcelain.

A small Longton Hall bowl, of rare conical form, painted with Chinese scenes.

c1755-56

$3,000-3,500	**AA**

Lowestoft

A pair of Longton Hall figures, modeled as musicians, he with a lyre, she with a tambourine, each decorated in colored enamels, on scroll-molded bases.

These are the largest figures known to have been produced at Longton Hall.

c1758   11.75in (30cm) high

$15,000-20,000   **AA**

A Longton Hall tea bowl and saucer, painted with European flowers and leaves.

The Meissen-style flowers are attributed to an artist known as the "trembly rose painter", although many artists painted in this manner.

c1758

$1,800-2,200   **AA**

A Longton Hall strawberry-leaf-molded plate, painted with exotic birds, minor chip and stress mark.

c1760

$2,000-2,500   **SA**

A pair of Longton Hall leaf dishes.

c1760

$6,000-7,000 (pair)   **SA**

LOWESTOFT

L OWESTOFT, ESTABLISHED IN 1757, WAS PROBABLY THE SMALLEST PORCELAIN FACTORY IN ENGLAND, and yet it produced one of the finest examples of soft paste. The wares were often decorated with views of Lowestoft and portraits of ships along with popular Oriental styles. The pieces are thick-bodied, with a heavy bubbled glaze. Some early pieces have relief-molded decoration with panels in underglaze blue. Enamel colors were introduced after c1770. The factory closed by 1800. Lowestoft is highly collectable, not only because it is difficult to find, but also for its whimsical charm; many pieces recorded the name and date of the birth of local children.

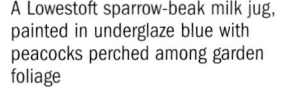

A Lowestoft sparrow-beak milk jug, painted in underglaze blue with peacocks perched among garden foliage

c1765

$1,000-1,500   **GorL**

A Lowestoft leaf-shaped pickle dish, painted in underglaze blue with fruiting vines.

c1770

$700-800   **GorL**

A Lowestoft gravy jug, painted in underglaze blue with foliage, within leaf-molded reserves.

c1770   6.75in (17cm)

$300-350   **GorL**

A Lowestoft gravy jug, painted in underglaze blue with foliage, within leaf-molded reserves, cracked.

c1770   6in (15cm)

$225-275   **GorL**

Four 18thC Lowestoft blue and white coffee cups and one saucer, each painted with chinoiserie decoration, the handles with a kick to the lower terminal.

c1770

$700-800   **Chef**

A Lowestoft bowl, painted with the Dragon pattern.

c1770   4in (10cm) dia

$1,500-2,000   **BonS**

A pair of Lowestoft blue and white baskets.

c1775   8in (20cm) wide

$3,000-3,500 (pair)   **SA**

Meissen

A Lowestoft sparrow-beak cream jug, with loop handle, decorated with two houses on an island, a small vignette of rockwork on the reverse, hairline crack.

c1775	3.5in (8.5cm)
$300-350	**BonS**

A Lowestoft dolphin ewer creamboat, painted in enamels.

c1775	3in (7.5cm)
$750-850	**WW**

MEISSEN

THE FIRST TRUE EUROPEAN PORCELAIN WAS THE RESULT OF EXPERIMENTS BY THE ALCHEMIST JOHANN FRIEDRICH BÖTTGER (1682-1719) and the scientist Ehrenfried Walter Von Tschirnhausen (1651-1708) at the court of Augustus the Strong, Elector of Saxony. They discovered the basic formula c1706-7 and by 1708 had made a hard paste porcelain.

Meissen was founded by royal decree in Dresden in 1710, later moving to Meissen. Early pieces included bowls, teapots, and figures. Most early pieces (c1710-1720) were creamy-yellow in color, with a thick glaze often with trapped bubbles, many were kept in the white, although some carried floral or molded leaf borders.

As a result of technical advances, porcelain after c1720 was whiter in color, and the glaze was thinner giving a more even appearance. Decoration consisted mainly of chinoiserie-style scenes, although the first European landscapes began to appear in the mid 1720s. Developments in enamel production allowed for a wider range of colors to be used.

Figures produced at Meissen, from the late 1720s onward, were by far the best from the period and as a result were widely copied throughout Europe. Early pieces used strong bold colors, such as yellow, black and red, whereas later ones favored a more pastel palette. Meissen also produced a wide range of tablewares, most notably that of the "Swan" service, commissioned in 1736 by the factory's director Count Heinrich von Brühlo.

A large Meissen model of a swan, by JJ Kändler, marked with a small crossed swords to the back of the base, restoration to one of the rushes.

JOHANN JOACHIM KÄNDLER (1706-1775) was the chief modeler at the Meissen factory from 1733 to 1775. During his time there he produced some of the finest figures and groups ever made at the factory including the Commedia dell' Arte figures, armorial dinner services and the Monkey Band series. Figures made by Kändler will always fetch high prices. This is a large and impressive piece in good condition. Life-sized animals by Kändler can fetch up to $300,000.

c1750	10.5in (27cm) high
$10,000-12,000	**WW**

A pair of late 18thC Meissen monkey band figures, after originals by JJ Kändler, one modeled as a flautist, the other with a pair of drums on its back, each wearing 18thC dress, Pressnummern 54 & 58, blue crossed swords marks, flautist's instrument restored, other figure lacks tail, small chips.

	5.5in (14cm) high
$2,000-2,500	**DN**

A large Meissen figure group, modeled as a sleeping 18thC youth by a floral encrusted tree, his adoring suitor sitting attentively with a child and dog, all on a naturalistic plinth, painted underglaze marks and impressed numerals.

	9.5in (24cm) high
$3,000-4,000	**L&T**

Meissen

A large pair of mid- to late 19thC Meissen pagoda figures, with nodding heads and rocking hands and tongues, gilded details, crossed swords and incised marks.

12.5in (31.5cm) high

$20,000-25,000	WW

A 19thC Meissen figure group, modeled as a dancing couple in period costume, on rococo base, inscibed C.75.

6.25in (16cm) high

$550-650	GorL

A Meissen porcelain mantel clock, with floral twin-handled surmount over a circular enamel dial,flanked by a man holding a lyre and a Roman maiden with a shield, the plinth encrusted with summer flowers on flower-clasped feet, the movement striking on single bell.

17.75in (45cm) wide

$2,500-3,000	L&T

A 19thC Meissen figure group, modeled as a winged putto holding a letter and riding a fox, on a naturalistic base, underglaze blue crossed swords mark, incised S.109, impressed Y and painted 17.

6in (15cm) long

$1,500-2,000	SI

A Meissen figure, modeled as a pug ,with blue bow and bells, marked.

c1870   4.75in (12cm) high

$1,200-1,800	RdeR

It is thought that the ancestors of the pug began to arrive in the West from China in the 16th and 17th centuries and first became popular in the Dutch Court. The vogue for pugs eventually spread across Europe, and by the 18thC they were seen as a fashion appendage. During the 19thC several factories produced models of pugs, notably Meissen and Dresden. At a glance the figures from these two factories look very similar, but a closer look reveals the superior quality of the Meissen pugs. The modeling is more naturalistic, with the contours of the animal's body sensitively defined. The faces too are more expressive, and the painting more detailed and accurate.

A large Meissen figure, modeled as a pug, after JJ Kändler.

c1830   9.5in (24cm) high

$1,500-2,000	RdeR

A Meissen clock, with white enamel dial, the timepiece movement contained in a drum, surmounted by artistic emblems and draped with cloth upon which a youth reclines to one side, the plinth painted with florets, blue crossed swords mark, some damage.

9.75in (25cm) wide

$1,500-2,000	LC

A late 19thC Meissen figure, modeled as a Bolognese hound, underglaze blue crossed swords mark and scratched numerals C26.

6in (15cm) high

$1,000-1,400	BonS

► A late19thC Meissen figure group, representing Spring, modeled as a youth and his companion in 18thC dress, she playing a recorder, a basket of flowers at her feet, the base with Greek key decoration, underglazed blue crossed swords mark and impressed numerals V25, 123 and painted 44.

6in (15cm) high

$1,200-1,500	BonS

Meissen

A late 19thC Meissen figure group, representing Spring, modeled as a youth and his companion in 18thC dress, she playing a lute, a bushel of corn at their feet, the base with foliate moldings, underglaze blue crossed swords mark and painted 65, losses.

6.25in (16cm)

$1,100-1,500 **BonS**

A late19thC Meissen figure, modeled as a gentleman wearing frock coat and flower-decorated waistcoat, underglaze blue cross swords mark, inscribed model no.2425, chips to hat and coat.

5.25in (13cm) high

$400-500 **HamG**

A pair of late 19thC Meissen figures, modeled as a shepherd and his companion, both in rustic dress, he leaning on a tree-stump, attaching a love letter to a dove, a lamb at his feet, she with the caged dove on her shoulder, holding the letter in her hand, a recumbent lamb at her feet, incised F73, blue crossed swords marks, Pressnummern, small chips and losses.

7.5in (19cm) high

$1,600-2,000 **DN**

A late 19thC Meissen figure, representing Hearing, from a series of The Senses, modeled as a woman at a harpsichord, her Watteau dress painted with sprays of flowers, the base with an egg and dart frieze, blue crossed swords mark, Pressnummern, minor chips.

5in (12.5cm)

$900-1,200 **DN**

A CLOSER LOOK AT MEISSEN

A late 19thC Meissen figure group, modeled as a lady and gentleman beside a classical marble column, a crouching man at their side, with two doves.

12.5in (32cm) high

$3,000-3,500 **GorL**

Meissen figure groups like this were extremely popular in the 19th century, and many were reissued using earlier molds.

Generally, a close look will reveal the differences; later pieces have slightly harsher colors and are not so finely detailed.

This is a particularly fine piece, although the poses are rather static. Here, it is the base that provides the most obvious clue to the date. Early Meissen figures stand on a simple mold base with delicately applied flowers. From the 1750s the scrolls and gilding on the bases were much more complex.

A late 19thC Meissen figure, Sentiment, after the original by Schoenheit, modeled as a young woman in 18thC dress, seated beside a table with a birdcage, underglaze blue crossed swords mark, impressed 127, inscribed E4 and 22 in overglaze brown, restorations, losses.

6in (15.5cm) high

$550-650 **SI**

A late 19thC Meissen figure group, modeled as a lady playing a harp, accompanied by gentleman and boy with flute, on pierced and gilded rococo base.

8in (20.5cm) high

$1,800-2,200 **GorL**

A late 19thC Meissen white-glazed figure, modeled as a cherub playing the pipes, the base molded with scrolls, blue crossed swords mark, impressed numerals.

4.5in (11cm) high

$225-275 **Chef**

► A late 19thC Meissen figure group, The Lovers Surprised, modeled as a lady in bed drinking coffee, Cupid behind her pillow, the husband looking over the end of the bed, crossed swords mark and D64 incised, a chip to her toe, the separately modeled lover missing.

7.25in (18.5cm) high

$2,000-2,500 **WW**

Meissen

A Meissen figure, modeled as a woman with a book in one hand and a feather muff in the other, on a scroll-molded base, blue crossed swords mark, Pressnummern, damage and restoration.

c1900   8.75in (22cm) high

| $400-500 | DN |

A Meissen hausmalerie schwartlot-decorated tea bowl and saucer, probably decorated in the Auffenwert workshop in Augsberg, the tea bowl painted with a band of a hound disturbing two foxes, within gilt line borders, the interior with and and a gilt border decoration, the saucer painted with a sleeping cowherd within a gilt border, the saucer with blue crossed swords mark, some wear, porcelain c1725, decoration c1730.

Hausmalerie, *German for "house painter", is a term used to describe a freelance painter who decorated porcelain left "in the white" by the factory. Some of the work of these painters is highly regarded, particularly that of Ignaz Bottengruber of Breslau, F.J. Ferner and Johann and Sabina Auffenwerth.*

c1725

| $1,200-1,500 | DN |

A late Meissen figure, modeled as Minerva, decorated in enamels and gilt, on a square base, blue crossed swords mark.

4.4in (14cm) high

| $180-220 | GorL |

Two Meissen waste bowls, each painted with chinoiserie figures in reserve within gilt quatrelobe cartouches, underglaze blue crossed swords mark, one bearing Johanneum mark N=240/W.

c1725   5.25in (13.5cm) dia

| $10,000-12,000 | SI |

A Meissen Dot period plate, painted with a Tichenmaester pattern.

Also known as the Academic period, because much of the factory's output lacked originality, the Dot period ran from 1763-1774 and was characterized by a dot between the familiar crossed swords.

9.5in (24cm) dia

| $100-150 | LC |

A 19thC Meissen figure, modeled as a bewigged Cupid kneeling on a rococo-style footstool, with gilt highlights, underglaze blue crossed swords mark.

8in (20cm) high

| $800-900 | SI |

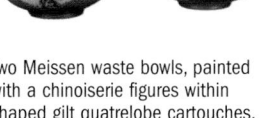

Two Meissen waste bowls, painted with a chinoiserie figures within shaped gilt quatrelobe cartouches, each embellished with gilt scrollwork and two gilt cockerels, underglaze blue crossed swords marks, one with Johanneum mark N=503/ W, the other with Johanneum mark N-239/W.

c1725   5.25n (13.5) dia

| $12,000-15,000 | SI |

A Marcolini Meissen charger, with later decoration, molded with scrolls and flowers, painted in the center with a peony and floral sprays, underglaze blue crossed swords and star mark, impressed 13.

15.25in (38.5cm) dia

| $1,000-1,200 | SI |

An early 20thC Meissen figural salt, modeled as a girl in 18thC dress, holding a bird and sitting between two oval baskets, the wells scattered floral sprigs, the scrollwork base heightened in gilt, underglaze blue crossed swords mark.

5.5in (14cm) high

| $450-550 | SI |

A Meissen box, with a gold-mounted hinged lid, the interior painted with a view of the Schloss Albrechtsburg and the town of Meissen on the river Elbe, the exterior and base painted with spiralling flower garlands and scalework borders, unmarked.

c1765   3.25in (8cm) wide

| $10,000-12,000 | WW |

A Marcolini Meissen part tea and coffee service, each piece painted with fruit and flowers within a ribbon spiral, comprising eleven tea cups, three coffee cups, fourteen saucers, spoon tray, waste bowl and tea caddy, coffeepot, tea pot, sugar pot and milk jug, all with covers.

c1780

| $8,000-10,000 | Chef |

Meissen

Two of six Marcolini Meissen coffee cans and saucers, each painted with a basket of flowers held by a blue ribbon, the square bracket handles edged in ocher line, crossed swords and star marks.

c1800

$1,700-2,000 (six)   **Chef**

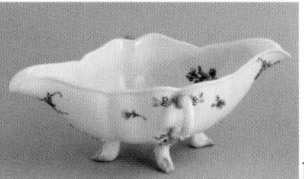

A Marcolini Meissen double-spouted sauceboat, painted with Deutsche blumen, of silver shape, the double-scroll handles with floret terminals, on four volute twig feet, blue crossed swords and star mark.

c1810   9.25in (23.5cm) wide

$300-400   **BonS**

A 19thC Meissen cup and saucer, modeled as a pink rose, the saucer as green leaves, the interior gilded, crossed swords mark.

c1850

$350-400   **WW**

A 19thC Meissen potpourri vase and cover, painted with panels of birds and scattered flowers, canceled crossed swords mark.

6.25in (15.5cm) wide

$400-500   **WW**

A Meissen Schneeballen -covered game tureen, the floral-encrusted dome cover with stag's head pelt, the body with scrolled foliate handles and rococo-style cartouches depicting stag with herd, the reverse depicting huntsman with dog and death of the stag, losses to stag's antlers, chips to lid rim and tureen rim, hairline cracks on body.

15in (38cm) high

$12,000-15,000   **SI**

A pair of Meissen Documentary Period coffee cups and saucers, possibly hausmaler-decorated, painted with rose sprays and insects, within osier-molded borders and gilt rims, the cups with applied wishbone handles, underglaze blue crossed swords mark, one cup chipped and cracked.

5.5in (13.5cm) dia

$300-400   **HamG**

A 19thC Meissen plate, decorated with a stag in a landscape within floral sprigs and turquoise chequer band, canceled crossed swords mark.

9.25in (23.5cm) dia

$60-80   **Chef**

A Meissen two-handled chocolate cup and saucer, each painted with a harbor scene within quatrefoil cartouche, surrounded by elaborate scrolls and a small Chinese figure on either side, within iron-red and gilt scroll and dot border, crossed swords mark.

3.75in (9.5cm) high

$1,500-1,800   **BonE**

A set of five 19thC Meissen tea cups and saucers, painted with birds and various insects, within turquoise and gilt brocade border.

c1850

$1,500-2,000   **L&T**

A Meissen flower-encrusted cup and saucer, of fluted form, painted with scattered flowerheads, on small feet, crossed swords mark, two feet chipped.

2.75in (7cm) high

$600-700   **BonE**

A 19thC Meissen cabinet cup and saucer, hausmaler-decorated with a garland of flowers within gilt borders, the Etruscan-shaped cup inscribed "Immer Lustig!", bearing special underglaze blue crossed swords and "I" date mark. 1814-15. 5.25in (13.5cm) dia

$300-400   **HamG**

A 19thC Meissen potpourri vase and cover, the basket-molded pear-shaped body painted with flowers, the base strewn with flowers and leaves and with a hound stalking two partridges, crossed swords mark, some damage.

8.25in (21cm) high

$550-650	WW

A Meissen tureen and cover, the double-walled body with handles of female busts in feathered headdresses and figures of putti holding pendant garlands, with small panels of figures on a quayside, the cover bearing the coats of arms of Saxony and Poland, supported by two putti and surmounted by a crown, crossed swords mark, incised no. B136, chips to rim, three putti and one handle repaired, damage to crown finial. After the model made for the wife of Augustus the Strong.

10.25in (26cm) wide

$5,000-6,000	BonE

A late 19thC Meissen cabinet cup and saucer, of ovoid lappeted form with applied bifurcated handles, painted to the interior with white flower sprays and insects, the exterior encrusted with flowers, on five stump feet, underglaze blue crossed swords mark, losses to flowers.

5.25in (13cm) dia

$180-220	HamG

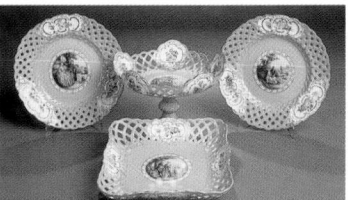

A late 19thC Meissen part dinner service, comprising eleven dinner plates, painted to the center with Deutsche blumen bouquets within osier-molded borders, decorated with insect panels and gilt rims, underglaze blue crossed swords mark, impressed no.s and painted decorators nos, two plates chipped to foot rim.

10in (25.5cm) dia

$1,000-1,400 (set)	HamG

An early 20thC Meissen fruit service, comprising twenty-four plates, a pair of square dishes and a pair of tazzas with spirally fluted domed circular plinths, all with lattice pierced scalloped border, the projecting scroll panels painted with sprays of summer flowers to both interior and exterior of larger pieces, the central roundel with romantic couples in idyllic landscapes, blue painted crossed sword mark, one plate with hairline crack, most with very minor rubbing.

plates 9.5in (24cm) dia

$4,000-5,000	L&T

An early 20thC Meissen Onion pattern tray, underglaze blue crossed swords mark with a dot and four strikes running through it, inscribed No. 18, and underglaze 26.

17.25in (44 cm) wide

$1,000-1,500	SI

► An early 20thC Meissen porcelain vase, the central gilt cartouche depicting a bird among flowering branches, underglaze blue crossed swords mark

5.25in (13.5cm) high

$350-400	SI

► A 20thC Meissen iron-red Onion pattern plate, underglaze blue crossed swords mark, impressed R2, with the Meissen mark enclosed in the lower part of the bamboo cane within the decoration.

9in (23cm) dia

$100-150	SI

Minton

MINTON

MINTON, ESTABLISHED IN 1798 BY THOMAS MINTON, undoubtedly produced some of the finest English porcelain during the 18th and 19th centuries. Initially producing earthenware and soft-paste porcelain, imitating the Meissen style, the factory soon moved on to decorative and useful wares in bone china. Under

Thomas's son, Herbert, Minton began to produce first-rate copies of 18th century pieces in high-quality porcelain. These copies were so good, that Sèvres even offered them their old casts. Minton are renowned for Majolica wares, both in Renaissance and Art-Nouveau styles, and also for their figures and busts in parian ware.

Minton Ceramic Marks

1800-30, found on early porcelain

MINTONS
ENGLAND

1891-1912, basic mark

A Minton biscuit porcelain model of William Wilberforce, sitting in an armchair and reading a book, raised on a scrolling base, no. mark.

c1840 7.25in (18.5cm) high

$300-400 **WW**

A Minton biscuit porcelain model of a girl, wearing a lacy dress and sitting beside a sheaf of corn, no. mark, some chips.

c1840 5.5in (14cm) high

$70-100 **WW**

A mid-19thC white-glazed Minton candlestick, with a satyr seated between the two candle branches, impressed marks, with some repairs.

11.25in (28.5cm) high

$100-150 **WW**

A good pair of mid-19thC Minton figures of a shepherd and sheperdess, he with a sheep and a dove, she with a lamb, each on circular Greek key base, crossed swords mark, with minor repairs.

8in (20cm) high

$1,000-1,500 **WW**

A Minton "Celadon" figural table centerpiece, modeled with two putti supporting a scallop-shell, on a coral-encrusted shaped oval base, impressed marks, shape no. 365 and date code, some small chips to the interior of the shell dish.

1868 10.25in (26cm) wide

$450-550 **DN**

A Minton dessert plate, painted with the A3082 pattern of a lady before a church within a gilt arcade border pierced with pairs of florettes, impressed marks, date code.

1857 9in (23cm) dia

$150-200 **Chef**

◄A pair of early Victorian spill vases, possibly Minton, the cylindrical bodies painted with a green leaf diaper centered by colored flowers.

3.5in (9cm) high

$150-200 **Chef**

▶ A Minton dessert plate, painted with the A3082 pattern of a lady before a church within a gilt arcade border pierced with pairs of florettes, impressed marks, date code.

1857 9in (23cm) dia

$150-200 **Chef**

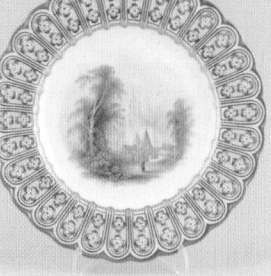

Seven English porcelain dessert plates, probably by Minton, well painted with a spray of roses, the gilded scalloped rim pierced with foliate roundels interspersed with swags of summer flowers, impressed marks, some damage.

c1860   9.25in (23.5cm) dia

$400-500 (set)   **BonS**

A 15-piece Minton dessert service, retailed by John Mortlock.

c1860   largest plate 9in (23cm) dia

$3,000-3,500 (set)   **Gro**

A large pair of Minton vases and covers, with pierced gilt side handles, painted with garden flowers and butterflies, no marks, with restoration to the covers and some glaze crazing.

c1870   14.75in (37.5cm) high

$1,500-2,000   **WW**

One of a pair of Minton tureens, covers and stands, each of oval bombe shape, delicately painted with floral sprays and insects beneath puce, turquoise and gilt feueulle de choux. stands

9.5in (24cm) wide

$900-1,100 (pair)   **LC**

A scarf-ring painted by Antonin Boullemier, probably Minton, painted with a bust profile of Mercury in the manner of an antique cameo, within a "jeweled" turquoise border, signed Boullemier, slight wear, glued section.

c1875   0.75in (2cm) wide

$500-600   **DN**

A pair of Minton circular white and gilt plates, painted with chinoiserie scene of three figures and a see-saw with a flower and rock decorated border, blue painted Sèvres style mark and pattern no. 539.

8.75in (22.5cm) diam

$500-600   **L&T**

A Minton vase and cover, with elaborate gilt handles and a circular socle base, decorated with roses and floral swags, printed and impressed marks, pattern no. A1359, with the knop re-glued and repaired through the stem.

12.25in (31cm) high

$180-220   **WW**

A late 19thC Minton bone china plate, with reticulated border, the center painted with a bird perched on a leafy branch, titled "Brantail", impressed marks.

9.5in (24cm) dia

$225-275   **WW**

A Minton oval vase and cover, with gilt handles and a tall stem, decorated with a plate panel of Cupid and Venus, gilded details, gilt mark, one handle well repaired.

c1900   8.5in (21.5cm) wide

$400-500   **WW**

A Minton double dahlia ink stand.

c1830　　　9.5in (24cm) wide

$1,000-1,500　　　**Gro**

A Minton flower-encrusted teapot.

c1835　　　2.25in (6cm) high

$600-700　　　**Gro**

A Minton flower plate, with forget-me-nots painted on the underside.

These often had forget-me-nots applied on the underside. Forget-me-nots were given as a token of affection and so placing them on the underside of a piece avoided any embarrassment on the part of the giver or the receiver.

c1830　　　6.25in (16cm) dia

$1,500-2,000　　　**Gro**

A pair of English pot pourri vases and covers, probably Minton, the two-handled campana vase shaped bodies painted in polychrome colors with summer flowers within molded foliate C-scrolls picked out in gilt, the pierced cover surmounted by a spire of applied flowers, very damaged – both covers badly broken and glued, losses and cracks to both bodies.

c1830　　　10.5in (26.5cm) high

$300-350　　　**BonS**

A Minton vase and cover, encrusted with flowers.

c1835　　　10.25 (26cm) high

$1,500-2,000　　　**Gro**

A Minton miniature part tea service, comprising a teapot and cover, a milk jug and a teacup and saucer, all heavily encrusted with flowers, blue crossed swords marks, minor damage and restoration.

c1840

$1,000-1,500　　　**DN**

NANTGARW

NANTGARW FACTORY WAS FOUNDED IN 1813 IN SOUTH WALES BY WILLIAM BILLINGSLEY, RENOWNED FOR HIS EXCEPTIONAL FLOWER PAINTING. His aim was to rival the quality of French porcelain, but the factory was dogged by firing problems. Up to 90% of their wares were destroyed in the kiln. After one year at Nantgarw the business was moved to Swansea, but the problems continued. The Nangarw factory re-opened in 1820. Output was never large and despite the superb quality of the finely painted porcelain it never made a profit. The factory mostly made plates, cabinet cups, dishes and some services. Billingsley went to work at Coalport in 1819 and the remaining stock was painted by Thomas Pardoe until the factory closed in 1822.

A Minton flower-encrusted miniature teapot and cover, with fruit finial, and a sugar bowl ensuite, both flower-encrusted, teapot with blue crossed swords mark, minor chips and damage.

c1840

$600-700　　　**DN**

A mid-19thC miniature Minton bone china teapot and cover, with a green handle and spout, encrusted with flowers, cover damaged.

3.75in (9.5cm) wide

$140-200　　　**WW**

A pair of Nantgarw plates, one with impressed Nantgarw CW mark.

1813-23　　　9.5in (24cm) dia

$1,000-1,500　　　**WW**

Nantgarw

This magnificent, unrecorded Nantgarw vase is the subject of much debate and controversy. Although it is the most spectacular piece of Welsh porcelain to emerge in many years, experts are divided as to whether the piece was made during the first period of production at Nantgarw (1814-15), or fired at Swansea and transported there for decoration by the founder of the Nantgarw pottery, William Billingsley. However, connoisseurs are in no doubt as to its rarity and value. Billingsley is considered the greatest English flower painter - it is often said of his rose paintings that you can almost smell them - and the 14.5in (37cm) vase is lavishly decorated with a band of roses, morning glory and foliage. The quality of the brushwork and depth of detail alone are exceptional, but it is a testament to the prized nature of the vase that he also decorated the interior with a superb border of gilt and enamel scrollwork and an extraordinary Catherine wheel of flowers and foliage. The small quantities of Regency porcelain from the Swansea and Nantgarw factories are highly coveted. Only one other vase of this kind is known to exist, a kiln-damaged, undecorated model in the National Museum of Wales. This vase reached $45,000 at auction - a world record for a piece of Welsh porcelain. However, if it could have been proved exactly when and where the vase had been made, the price would undoubtedly have been higher.

A fine and rare Welsh campana vase, painted by William Billingsley, with molded acanthus and applied beads to the rim, each side with gilded and bronzed satyr masks and raised on a fluted stem and circular foot, the exterior painted with flowers, the interior with a gilt and enameled scrollwork border and with a whorl of foliage inside, marked 'NANTGARRW' painted in red.

1813-23   10.75in (27.5cm) high

$45,000-50,000   **WW**

A Nantgarw plate, decorated in London, the center painted with four doves perched on the edge of a bowl within a band of flowers, the molded C-scroll and foliate border painted with sprays of roses on a seeded ground, impressed Nantgarw CW.

1814-23   10in (25cm) dia

$12,000-15,000   **WW**

A Nantgarw plate, painted with flower sprays in overglaze blue enamel, with leaf and scroll-molded borders and with gilt rim, impressed Nant-Garw C.W mark, a section of the rim glued.

1813-20   10in (25.5cm) dia

$250-300   **WW**

A Nantgarw plate, the center painted with a large flower spray, the gilt-decorated border molded with scrolls and flowers and painted with rose sprays, impressed Nantgarw C.W. mark, slight scratching and re-touching to the gilt.

c1820   8.75in (22cm) dia

$1,200-1,500   **WW**

A Nantgarw plate, the center painted with a wild rose spray.

c1825   9.5in (24cm) dia

$1,000-1,300   **SA**

NEW HALL

A New Hall sucrier and cover.

c1795	5.25in (13cm) high

$450-550 SA

A New Hall helmet-shaped jug.

c1795	5.25in (13cm) high

$300-350 SA

An unusual New Hall lozenge-shaped spoon tray, painted with flower sprays and ribbon borders.

c1800	5.75in (14.5cm) dia

$1,000-1,500 WW

A New Hall fluted milk jug, pattern no.195.

c1800	5in (12.5cm) high

$400-500 WW

A New Hall teapot.

c1800	6in (15cm) high

$70-100 SA

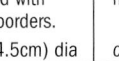

◀1 A Newhall sucrier and cover, Warburton's patent.

c1805

$900-1,100

◀2 A Newhall teapot, Warburton's patent.

Warburton, a partner in Newhall factory, patented the technique of gilt bat prints. These pieces are marked in red on the base Warburton's Patent.

c1805	6.25in (15.5cm) high

$1,500-2,000 SA

PARIS

Three Newhall tea bowls and four saucers, decorated with the Boy at the Window pattern.

c1800

$200-250 (7 items) Chef

DURING THE 1780s, PARIS BECAME AN IMPORTANT CENTER OF PORCELAIN PRODUCTION. After the discovery of kaolin in the Limoges area in 1768, hard-paste porcelain was produced in large quantities. When the laws restricting porcelain decoration in order to maintain the monopoly of the Sèvres factory were relaxed, the Parisian factories were swift to take advantage. 19th century European fashion was heavily influenced by French taste and the porcelain industry in France was thriving. There were over 160 factories and decorating establishments in Paris including the Dihl factory, the Nast factory, the Darte factory and the Dagoty and Honore factories.

A New Hall coffee can, pattern number 1305.

c1820	2.5in (6.5cm) high

$140-180 AD

A Continental coffee can and saucer, possibly Paris.

c1795	2.75in (7cm) high

$500-550 SA

A Paris coffee can and saucer.

c1810	3in (7.5cm) high

$180-220 SA

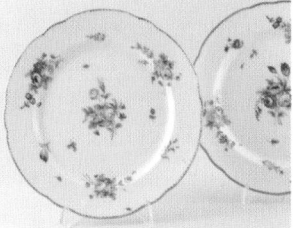

Twelve Paris dessert plates.

c1810	8.75in (22cm) dia

$900-1,100 (set) SA

A Paris cup and saucer, from a Sèvres design, the saucer with retailer's mark for Rihouet a Paris.

c1820   *saucer* 5in (12.5cm) dia

$400-500   **Gro**

A mid-19thC Paris tea and coffee service, comprising a coffeepot, teapot, creamer, sugar bowl, six cups and six saucers, each piece decorated in gilt with a grape and vine pattern and interlocking ovals, sugar bowl missing lid. Coffeepot

10in (26cm) high

$1,200-1,500   **SI**

A pair of Paris dishes, marked Feuillet.

c1820   6in (15cm) high

$4,000-5,000 pair   **Gro**

A Paris pastille burner.

c1830   4.75in (12cm) high

$800-1,200   **Gro**

▶ A Paris jardinière and stand, painted with figures in a landscape within gilt arched panels, with a frieze of shells and sea scrolls, signed Pouchin, dated, firing cracks to the foot, wear to the gilding.

1834   7.5in (19cm) high

$1,500-2,000   **DN**

- Paris porcelain tends to be even and pure white, made of hard-paste with a clear glaze.
- Classical motifs and scattered flowers, painted scenes with colored and gilt grounds and borders, painted imitations of hard stones and lacquer are all typical decorations.
- Biscuit figures of children and allegorical subjects were popular in Paris.

Paris Ceramic Marks

Dagoty. c1785   *Dihi. 1817-29*   *Jacob Petit.*   *Limoges.*   *Entrined 'S'.*
                                        1830-62   *c1855*   *c1845 onwards*

A set of six Paris plates, decorated with lemon, pear, redcurrant, peach, plum and walnut.

c1840   8in (20.5cm) dia

$1,500-2,000   **Gro**

A Paris vase, retailer's mark for FR Bronté Fournisser du Roi. Footnote: This design won a gold medal at the 1844 Exposition, the king in question was Louis Phillipe.

c1845   13.5in (34cm) high

$1,000-1,500   **Gro**

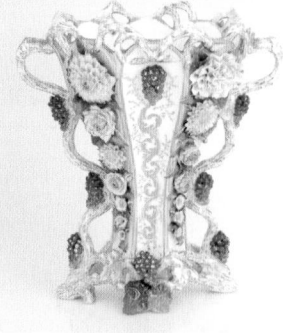

A 19thC Paris flower-encrusted vase, by Jacob Petit, with knarled vine rim, handles and feet, restored feet.

11.5in (29cm) high

$400-500   **DN**

A mid-19thC ormolu-mounted Paris lamp, the body painted with oval panels of flowers between scrolling vine handles of ormolu, the socle on pierced, gadrooned and beaded foot.

21in (53cm) high

$1,200-1,500   **Chef**

A pair of Paris vases, each finely painted with hunting scenes within gilded borders, the twin-handles with mask head terminals, raised on a square plinth base.

13.25in (33.5cm) high

$500-550   **Chef**

Samson et Cie

A late 19thC Continental box, reserved in a rococo cartouche depicting a gallant couple on a cobalt blue ground, the whole with gilt scrolls and diaperwork, bearing overglaze crossed arrows mark of La Coutille, Paris.

3.5in (9cm) dia

$200-250 **SI**

A pair of Paris urn-shaped twin-handled vases, painted with romantic landscape frieze and gilt decoration, with opposed sphinx handles, on plinths with rectangular blocks.

10in (25cm) high

$450-550 **L&T**

A late 19thC Paris sucrier and cover, painted with gambolling putti, the foot and cover enriched with gilding. Provenance: The Society of the Cincinnati.

5.25in (13cm) high

$450-550 **SI**

A Paris inkstand, the central handle flanked by a pounce pot and an ink receiver, the sides molded in low relief with classical motifs on a solid gilt ground, one cover replaced.

5.5in (14cm) wide

$225-275 **LC**

A Paris inkstand, modeled as a lady reclining and inscribing on a gilt pedestal with a cherub by her side.

5.5in (14cm) high

$400-500 **LC**

A Paris plaque, painted with two ladies in a verdant landscape, signed HP, reverse inscribed Pelier 136 Vardon, dated.

1902   11in (28cm) high

$1,500-2,000 **SI**

A Paris La Courtille plate, painted with a pair of billing doves, the rim with fruiting vine, rubbing.

9in (23cm) dia

$70-100 **LC**

An early 20thC. Paris cabinet plate, painted with a classical goddess.

$70-100 **HamG**

SAMSON ET CIE

THE SAMSON ET CIE FACTORY WAS ESTABLISHED IN PARIS, FRANCE, BY EDMÉ SAMSON WHO BEGAN IN THE 1830S by making replacements for broken pieces of dinner services. He went on to make reproductions of Meissen, Sèvres, Worcester, Chelsea, and Chinese porcelain, and some of the copies were of extremely high quality. The pieces are usually highly decorative and are much sought after today. The firm closed in 1970.

▶ A mid-to late 19thC Samson figure group, modeled as Cupid in disguise, advising three maidens in the art of love, cross mark and S, the chair back re-glued.

9in (23cm) wide

$400-450 **WW**

A late 19thC Samson figure, modeled as a young man, painted blue anchor mark.

8in (20cm) high

$60-80 **Chef**

A late 19thC Samson Gold Anchor figure, modeled as an man in 18thC dress, holding a violin.

6.75in (17cm) high

$60-80 **Chef**

A late 19thC Samson Gold Anchor figure, modeled as a bagpipe player before a flowering bush with a dog at his side.

9in (23cm) high

$70-100	Chef

A 19thC ormolu-mounted figure of Pu Tai, painted in famille-verte style, probably Samson.

Provenance: The Society of the Cincinnati.

9in (23cm) wide

$1,200-1,500	SI

A pair of associated Samson figures, modeled as hounds.

12in (30.5cm) wide

$2,000-2,500	SI

A pair of late 19thC Samson chocolate cups and covers, painted with armorials in the famille rose style, with berry knops.

3.25in (8cm) high

$300-350	WW

A late 19thC Samson jardinière, painted in famille rose palette with alternating floral and scrolling scale panels within gilt lines.

5.5in (14cm) high

$120-180	Chef

A pair of late 19thC gilt-metal mounted Sèvres-style urns and covers, the bodies of ovoid form painted with reserves of courting couples on a bleu celeste ground, gilded with foliate C-scrolls.

18.25in (46cm) high

$1,500-2,000	BonS

A pair of late 19thC Samson vases, in Chinese export style, each of waisted hexagonal form, painted with an armorial amid scattered borders, iron-red pseudo-Chinese mark.

12in (30.5cm) high

$700-1,000	SI

A late 19thC Samson armorial plate, painted in the Compaigne des Indes style, the silver-shaped rim pierced with trelliswork.

9.5in (24cm) dia

$80-120	LC

SÈVRES

THE SÈVRES FACTORY WAS ESTABLISHED C1740 IN THE CHÂTEAU OF ORRY DE FULVY. In Vincennes outside Paris but moved to Sèvres in 1756. The factory had the support of Louis XV who banned any foreign porcelain imports and even forbade other factories from decorating in more than one color. The earlier wares were of soft-paste porcelain and decorated in Rococo style, until kaolin was discovered in 1768 enabling the factory to make hard-paste porcelain. In the late 1770s Neo-classical taste became popular in France and Sèvres porcelain became more restrained and classically inspired. Motifs including arabesques, garlands, palmettes, and festoons were popular as were "jeweled" enamel decoration and grisaille medallions. Sèvres lost its aristocratic custom and royal patronage during the French Revolution, however the new government looked upon the factory as an asset and Sèvres porcelain still flourishes today.

A Sèvres hard-paste coffee cup and saucer, decorated in gold and platinum with anthemion borders, the cup with an armorial, printed and painted marks. c1826

$225-275	WW

An 18thC Sèvres-style vase, with 19thC gilt-metal mount, the ovoid body painted with reserves of children, with gilt vine meander and oiel de perdrix pattern.

7.25in (18.5cm) high

$225-275   **BonS**

A pair of Paris vases, the ovoid bodies decorated in Empire style with tooled gilt on a leaf-green ground, red painted M Imple de Sèvres mark, damage and repair.

c1870   8in (20cm) high

$225-275   **BonS**

► A Sèvres two-handled chocolate cup and cover, painted on one side with a woman beside a baby in a crib, the other with the woman feeding the baby, inscribed on base Le Bonheur Du Menage and L'Enfant Cheri, within gilt-bordered cartouche reserved on bleu celeste ground, gilt scrollwork border, interlaced Ls mark, date code S and initial m c, small repair to rim of cup.

Bleu celeste *is a turquoise glaze used as a ground color. It was introduced in 1752 at the Sèvres factory and developed by Jean Hellot.*

5.5in (14cm) high

$450-500   **BonE**

Sèvres Ceramic Marks

Date letter within two Ls. 1753

R.F
Sevres

First Republic. 1793-1804

Charles X. 1824-28

S 1912 DA	S 1912 DN

20thC marks and dates.

A pair of late 19thC Continental Sèvres-style plates, painted with flower sprays, gilt rims, with interlaced L marks.

10.25in (26cm) dia

$120-180   **WW**

A Sèvres teapot and cover, painted on one side with a portrait of Louis XV, the other with a spray of flowers, reserved on bleu celeste ground, interlaced Ls mark.

8.75in (22cm) high

$300-350   **BonE**

A pair of late 19thC gilt-metal mounted Sèvres-style urns and covers, the bodies of ovoid form painted with reserves of courting couples on a bleu celeste ground, gilded with foliate C-scrolls.

18.25in (46cm) high

$1,500-2,000   **BonS**

A pair of late 19thC Sèvres-style cabinet plates, centrally painted with a cartouche bust portrait, one titled Mmme. Elizabeth, within a "jeweled" gros bleu border interspaced by three panels painted with flowers, pseudo marks and title in gilt. Max

10in (25cm) dia

$1,500-2,000 (pair)   **BonS**

A late 19thC Sèvres-style ormolu-mounted centerpiece, the bleu du roi ground with gilding, signed Lebrun. Provenance: The Society of the Cincinnati.

Bleu de Roi *is a royal blue glaze first introduced at Vincennes in 1749 and later at Sèvres.*

9.5in (24cm) dia

$450-550   **SI**

A late 19thC gilt-metal mounted Sèvres-style vase and cover, of urn shape, painted on one side with a woman in classical dress with a putto, the reverse with a landscape, with gilt-metal goat mask handles and pinecone knop.

11.75in (30cm) high

$750-850   **BonE**

A late 19thC Sèvres-style covered box, painted with reserves of flowers.

Provenance: *The Society of the Cincinnati.*

9.5in (20cm) wide

$450-500   **SI**

Sitzendorf

A late 19thC trembleuse cup, cover and saucer, painted with medallions of flowers and a portrait of Marie Antoinette on a bleu celeste ground, with a pomegranate finial, Sèvres mark.

Provenance: *The Society of the Cincinnati. Footnote: A trembleuse saucer has a pierced gallery in the center to hold the cup steady.*

6in (15cm) high

$550-650	SI

A pair of gilt-metal mounted Sèvres-style lamps, the urn-shaped bodies painted with cherubs in a garden landscape, on acanthus fluted base and square pedestal foot, signed Claire Rochette, converted to electric.

c1900   11.5in (29cm) high

$700-800	BonS

A 20thC Sèvres cabinet plate, decorated with a portrait of Madame de Pompadour, the cobalt rim profusely decorated with gilt crown, fleur-di-lis, the Sèvres mark and inscribed M de Pompadour, illegibly signed, underglaze blue Sèvres mark, CHATEAU/DE/VERSAILLE printed in a red circle surmounted by a banner and crown, impressed MR in circle and 25.

10in (5.5cm) dia

$300-350	SI

SITZENDORF

Sitzendorf factory was founded in Thuringia, Germany in 1850 by the Voigt brothers. The factory made large quantities of decorative porcelain, typically encrusted with cupids and flowers in pastel shades. The factory is still in production today.

▶ A late 19thC Sitzendorf centerpiece, the detachable bowl with pierced and floral encrusted decoration, the central pillar modeled as a tree stump design pillar with two amorini figures, on an oval foot.

14in (35.5cm) high

$550-600	Clv

A late 19thC Sitzendorf figure group, modeled as a boy and girl with a garland of flowers and a nest of chicks, underglaze blue cross hatch mark, small chip to base.

6in (15cm) high

$300-350	HamG

A late 19thC Sitzendorf figure group, modeled as a wood-cutter and a girl, he seated on a bundle of wood on a sledge, underglaze blue cross hatch mark, chip to wood.

5.5in (13.5cm) high

$300-350	HamG

A late 19thC Sitzendorf centerpiece, the detachable bowl with pierced and floral encrusted decoration, the central pillar modeled as a tree stump with two amorini figures, on a scroll-decorated foot.

14in (35.5cm) high

$450-550	Clv

SPODE

JOSIAH SPODE (1733-1797) PRODUCED GOOD QUALITY PORCELAIN AND POTTERY FROM 1776 at the factory at Stoke-on-Trent in Staffordshire, England. Spode is generally attributed with the invention of bone china around 1796-97. The majority of the porcelain produced was table wares and ornamental wares, derived from Etruscan or Roman forms. Decorative techniques included bat-printing, which involved the application of tiny dots on to the porcelain using bats of soft glue. This was then dusted over with colored powder to form the design. Spode also produced a wide range of Imari patterns and wares decorated with botanical subjects, topographical views and copies of Old Master paintings.

Spode Ceramic Marks

SPODE	Spode	COPELAND & GARRETT	
c1774 onwards	c1790-1880	c1833-47	
			c1894-1910
SPODE Spode	COPELAND & GARRETT LATE SPODE	COPELAND	Spode ENGLAND
c1790-1820	c1833	1851-85	c1970

An early 19thC Spode coffee cup and saucer, pattern 4018.
c1810
$45-55 — **BonS**

A Spode sucrier and cover, pattern no. 2214.
c1812 — 4.5in (11cm) high
$450-500 — **Gro**

A Spode part dessert service, comprising a pair of sauce tureens, stands and a cover, a two-handled serving dish (pictured), a pair of similar and smaller serving dishes, four shell-shaped dishes, a pair of lozenge-shaped dishes, four smaller dishes and seventeen plates, each painted with a band of roses within gilt-lined borders, pattern no. 2573, iron red marks, minor damage.
c1815
$7,500-8,500 (part service) — **DN**

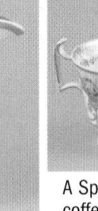

A Spode jug, decorated in gilt and enamel.
c1815 — 3.5in (9cm) high
$250-300 — **SA**

A Spode trio, comprising teacup, coffee cup and saucer, the outside decorated with flower and gilt scroll decoration, the inside with gilt swag and pendant border, wear to gilding.
c1815 — 2.5in (6cm) high
$140-200 — **SA**

► A Spode trio, painted with figures in a landscape, with gilded and scalloped rim, red painted pattern no. 1926.
c1815
$140-200 — **BonS**

A Spode sauce tureen, cover and stand, with gilt foliate and floral decoration, the cover with gilded knop.
c1825 — 6.5in (16cm) high
$500-550 — **SA**

A 19thC porcelain bourdalou, possibly Spode, painted with flowers in monochrome on a gilt ground.
9.5in (24cm)
$130-180 — **BonS**

► A Spode trio, painted with specimen flowers within Imari borders, pattern no. 2782, wear to gilding.
c1815
$50-80 — **BonS**

SWANSEA

S WANSEA PORCELAIN FACTORY WAS ESTABLISHED IN THE 1760S BY WILLIAM COLES and produced soft-paste porcelain. The delicate translucent paste was an ideal ground for flower painting, and realistic botanical designs are typical of Swansea porcelain. The painter William Billingsley was influential at the Swansea works, taking inspiration from the French style of decoration that was at the height of fashion in London. Later decoration includes landscapes, figures and birds.

A pair of small Swansea plates, decorated with gilt sprigs, with spiral and ozier-molded borders and and gilt-line rims, both faintly marked Swansea in red.

c1814-22   7in (18cm) dia

$200-250   **WW**

A pair of Swansea square dishes, each decorated with gilt sprigs, the borders molded with scrolls and flowers, one with a hairline crack.

c1814-22   8.25in (21cm) dia

$200-250   **WW**

◀ An unusual Swansea pottery plate, printed with three figures before a mill house with a church beyond, impressed Dillwyn & Co. Swansea.

Although Swansea owes its reputation to its fine hand-decorated porcelain, earlier wares included Staffordshire-type pottery with printed decoration, such as this plate.

c1815   10in (25cm) dia

$1,200-1,500   **WW**

A Swansea "London" shape part tea service, comprising a teapot, cover and stand, a sugar box and cover, a milk jug, a slop bowl, a sandwich plate, twelve tea cups and eleven coffee cups and saucers, painted with roses issuing from urns and scattered sprays of flowers, printed iron-red mark, painted iron-red pattern no. 411, slight damage.

● Swansea porcelain is extremely fine and translucent known as "glassy", "duck egg" and "trident."
● Swansea's paste was closer to Sévres than Staffordshire.
● Wares were typically decorated with painted flowers.
● Dinner and dessert services, tewares, flatwares, ice pails and cabinet cups are the most common wares.

c1820

$10,000-12,000 (part service)   **DN**

◀ A Swansea-style urn-shaped vase, painted with flowers and with gilt foliage, with gilt swan side handles, unmarked.

c1820   8.25in (21cm) high

$450-550   **WW**

A pair of shell-shaped Swansea dishes, decorated in the Mandarin palette with Chinese figures, the borders with birds in panels, marked Swansea in red, each riveted.

c1820   8.5in (21.5cm) dia

$700-800   **WW**

American porcelain

THE TUCKER PORCELAIN FACTORY

THE TUCKER PORCELAIN FACTORY WAS THE FIRST AMERICAN WORKS TO ENJOY COMMERCIAL SUCCESS. The company was established by William Ellis Tucker in Philadelphia in 1827 and produced hard-paste porcelain which initially copied English and French pieces but soon started to incorporate American subjects such as President Jackson and views of Philadelphia. The decoration tends to be sparse and can include floral sprays or simple landscapes in polychrome or sepia with the characteristic gold band. The company won a number of prizes for its work within the first year and was patronized by people such as President Jackson who used pieces in the White House. Tucker is rarely signed but can be identified by the form, style of painting and the gold bands. Some individual pieces can also be attributed to the chief decorator Thomas Tucker (1812-1890), brother of William.

In 1828 Thomas Hulme became a partner in the company and items made during that year are marked "Tucker and Hulme China Manufactures, Philadelphia, 1828" or "Tucker and Hulme, Philadelphia, 1828". Hulme retired the year after and in 1832 Alexander Hemphill joined the firm, but the following year William Tucker died at the age of 32, leaving the company in disarray. Hemphill continued to run the company with his father who took a keen interest and brought over a number of artists from Europe. As a result pieces produced during this time are very similar to Sèvres porcelain. During 1833 and 1834, pieces were marked "Manufactured by Jos. Hemphill, Philad".

The company changed its name to The American Porcelain Co. in 1835, but by 1838 Hemphill had sold the company and the factory was closed.

An early 19thC Tucker-type porcelain footed punch bowl, with a thin gold band to the rim and edge of the foot and a band of yellow and gilt vine with leaves about the top.

11in (27.9cm) dia

$350-450   **FRE**

A Tucker porcelain circular tureen, the tapering body and conforming flat-topped lid with grisaille reserves of architectural landscapes, with turned gilt handles between triangular bracket supports, and on a low spreading foot with a gilt rim. Museum repair to lid and finial.

c1826-1838   9.2in (23.3cm) dia

$2,000-4,000   **FRE**

A Tucker porcelain tea service, the border decorated with gilt tulips and leaves and thin bands. Consisting of a hot water pot, three straight-sided cups with handles, seven inverted bell-form tea cups with handles, eight saucers, ten individual fruit dishes, twelve cake plates, one cake plate differs slightly in decoration; age cracks to sugar bowl, and a star crack to one saucer.

c1830

$10,000-12,000 (service)   **FRE**

▶ A pair of Tucker porcelain pitchers, of urn form with reeded bases, with loop handles and molded spout. Decorated with two polychrome reserves of summer flowers in a wreath of gilt flowers and leaves.

Pitchers of all shapes and sizes were a speciality of the Tucker factory. This vase-shaped pitcher with an arched handle is a shape unique to Tucker.

c1830   9.5in (24.1cm) high

$10,000-12,000 (pair)   **FRE**

A Tucker porcelain tea and coffee service. Comprising a baluster-form coffee pot, a pair of ovoid teapots, a covered sugar bowl, a cream jug, a waste bowl (each with wide flaring rims and domed lids), twelve cups with flaring sides and twelve saucers, eleven small plates, and a serving plate, all decorated with gilt rims enclosing black painted reserves of Philadelphia views.

c1830

$30,000-40,000   **FRE**

Two Tucker porcelain whimsies, one in the form of a heart with polychrome floral decoration gilt neck. 1.5in (3.8cm) high and a blue and white decorated pipe bowl with turned wood shaft and grip.

c1830-1835   8in (20.3cm)

$600-650   **FRE**

Vienna

VIENNA

IN 1718 THE FIRST AUSTRIAN PORCELAIN FACTORY WAS FOUNDED BY CLAUDIUS DU PAQUIER (d1751). Du Paquier sought the expertise of Meissen arcanist Cristoph Conrad Hunger (active c1717-1748) as he endeavored to find the secret of making porcelain. His success was limited until 1719 when he enlisted the help of another defector from the Meissen factory, Samuel Stolzel (d1737), and the factory produced its first successful hard-paste porcelain.

During the Du Paquier period from 1719-1744, the factory produced porcelain wares similar to those of the Meissen factory, copied from baroque silver in symmetrical form and embellished with scrollwork. From c1730 the Vienna factory pioneered the use of European flower decoration on porcelain. It also introduced the use of black, iron-red or puce monochrome for hunting or battle scenes and chinoiserie.

Du Paquier sold the factory to the State in 1744, and during the First State Period 1744-1841 the factory initially shows Baroque influence, and later that of Sèvres. The wares were made in the fashionable rococo style.

Konrad Sörgel von Sorgenthal was appointed director 1784 following financial problems at the factory. He brought success to the company, introducing Neo-classical styles, combining geometric forms with urn and amphora shapes copied from pieces found at Pompei and Herculaneum. The factory began to decline by 1830 and was closed by the Emperor Francis Joseph in 1864. However, other Viennese factories such as Augarten, Bock and Goldscheider used forms of the Vienna banded shield mark well into the 20thC.

► A large pair of urn-shaped Vienna vases, each with ornate gilt scroll and jeweled frieze over flared-waisted neck, the body decorated with figural frieze, one depicting "Karl VI befreit die christlichen sclaven in Tunis" and "Petrarch and Laura am Hase des Papstres in Avignon", the other inscribed "Kaiser Rudolph II bei seinem Alchemisten", and "Die Verhorstung der Sohne des Konigs Manfred", blue printed Vienna FD Austria mark.

c1910	50.75in (129cm) high
$30,000-35,000	**L&T**

A pair of 18thC Vienna plates, painted with butterflies, flowers and insects, brown line rims, shield marks, each with a rim chip.

A large Vienna saucer, decorated with blue linked cartouches set with gilt urns and shaded paterae, reserved on a solid gilt ground, beehive mark and impressed date number, some rubbing to center.

	9.5in (24cm) dia	1805	
$150-200	**WW**	**$70-100**	**LC**

A painted Vienna plaque, by Laurent, depicting a gypsy fortune-teller holding the palm of a young boy, bears Aitken Dott paper label, signed in ink, in an ebonized and gilt frame.

A mid-19thC Royal Vienna cabinet plate, decorated with scene of a fisherman and water nymph, the rim with raised gilt foliate decoration and panels containing allegorial scenes of animals in classical landscapes, signed Wagner, the back of the plate inscribed Fischer und Nixe, with underglaze blue shield mark.

A late 19thC Vienna porcelain plaque, painted with central roundel "Der Gebrochene Krug", depicting a girl standing by a swagged urn clasping flowers, the border with gilt-jeweled scroll and floral decoration, pattern no. D202.

A Vienna plate, painted to the center with "Et in Arcadia Ego", after Poussin, within deep border of scrolls and vases in panels, on tooled gilt ground, painted beehive mark, hairline crack through rim.

1842	23in (58cm) high		9.5in (24cm) dia		14.25in (36cm) dia	c1890	9.75in (24.5cm) dia
$14,000-17,000	**L&T**	**$600-700**	**SI**	**$4,000-4,500**	**L&T**	**$300-350**	**BonE**

Worcester

WORCESTER

Worcester porcelain factory was founded in 1751 by Dr John Wall and William Davis. Soon after it was established, Worcester also acquired the Bristol Porcelain factory, allowing access to large quantities of soapstone. The use of soapstone in Worcester's porcelain made pieces very hard-wearing and able to withstand hot liquids, this was particularly suitable for the tea and coffee wares produced in large quantities in the early years. Sauceboats, decorated in underglaze blue were also popular during the first few years, as were pieces that copied Chinese imports of the time.

- In the mid-18thC Worcester pioneered the process of over-glaze and later under-glaze transfer printing on porcelain.

- In 1783 Thomas Flight and his sons took over the factory and led Worcester through one of its most successful periods. Inspired by contemporary Paris porcelain, Flight began to produce wares in the French Neo-classical style.

- In 1792, Martin Barr joined Joseph Flight and the company began trading under Flight & Barr 1792-1804, changing to Barr, Flight & Barr 1804-13, and later Flight, Barr & Barr 1813-1840 when Barr's son joined. During this period, the factory concentrated on quality designs for the top end market, producing Regency designs with fine gilding, beautifully hand-painted work and "rich Japan" styles based on the Imari patterns.

- In 1840 the company joined forces with the Chamberlain family, and began producing under Chamberlain & Co. In 1863 become the Worcester Royal Porcelain Co. which it continues to trade under today.

A Worcester bowl, painted in underglaze blue with a version of the Tambourine pattern, workman's mark. Provenance: Dr. Bernard Watney Collection.
1754-1755

$7,000-8,000 **AA**

A Worcester teacup and saucer, with particularly fine decoration, "pencilled" in black with the Boy and Buffalo pattern, workman's mark.
c1756

$1,500-2,000 **AA**

A Worcester bell-shaped mug, with ridged loop handle, painted in underglaze blue with the Walk in the Garden pattern, workman's mark.
1756-58   5.25in (13.5cm)

$4,500-5,000 **AA**

A Worcester guglet, hand-painted with chinoiserie scenes of a fisherman on a bridge, damage to neck.
c1755-60   10.25in (26cm) high

$1,500-2,000 **PC**

A rare Worcester eggcup, decorated with three applied flower sprays and painted in underglaze blue with trailing flowers beneath a trellis band, the foot applied and painted with flowers, workman's mark.
c1758   2.25in (6cm) high

$3,500-4,000 **AA**

A Worcester bowl, printed in black by Robert Hancock with Britannia, naval trophies, women and waifs, and inscribed "For the service of our country", and "Marine Society", the interior with a portrait of George II, after Thomas Worlidge. The Marine Society, a sea school for boys, was founded by Sir John Fielding, Jonas Hanway and others in 1756.
c1758   6in (15cm) dia

$6,000-7,000 **AA**

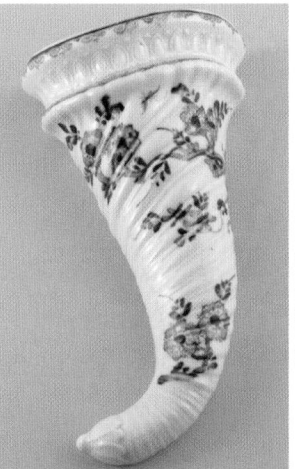

A pair of Worcester First Period wall pockets, painter's marks.
1758-60   8.75in (22cm) high

$5,000-6,000 (pair) **SA**

A Worcester sparrow-beak jug, printed with two vignettes, one depicting a lady and a gentleman seated at a tripod table taking chocolate, the other with a lady escorted by her servant, hairline crack.
c1760   3.5in (8.5cm) high

$450-550 **DN**

A Worcester teacup, hand-painted with the Two Quails pattern, crescent mark.

c1760   2.5in (6cm) high

$220-280   **PC**

A Worcester bowl, printed with The Man in the Pavilion pattern, chips to foot.

c1760   6in (15.2cm) dia

$200-250   **BonS**

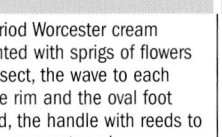

A First Period Worcester cream boat, painted with sprigs of flowers and an insect, the wave to each side of the rim and the oval foot gadrooned, the handle with reeds to each side, crescent mark.

c1760   4.5in (11.5cm) long

$300-350   **Chef**

A First Period Worcester coffee can, the sides painted with island landscape of pine and prunus by a hut.

c1760   2.5in (6.5cm) high

$150-200   **Chef**

A Worcester coffee can, painted with the Fisherman and Willow Pavilion pattern, press-molded with C-scroll mirror cartouches over strap flutes with C-scroll handle.

c1760   2.5in (6.5cm) high

$900-1,100   **BonS**

A Worcester coffee cup, painted with the Gazebo pattern, plain-thrown with loop handle, workman's mark to base.

c1760   2.25in (6cm) high

$1,200-1,800   **BonS**

A Worcester porcelain tea bowl, decorated with the Feather Mold Floral pattern, workman's mark.

c1760   1.75in (4.5cm) high

$40-60   **BonS**

A Worcester coffee cup, painted with the Fisherman and Willow Pavilion pattern, press-molded with C-scroll mirror cartouches over strap flutes, workman's mark to base.

c1760   2.5in (6cm) high

$1,200-1,800   **BonS**

A Worcester pickle leaf dish, painted with the Pickle Leaf Daisy pattern, press-molded with twig handle and leaf exterior, workman's mark.

c1760   3.25in (8cm) dia

$400-500   **BonS**

A First Period Worcester shallow bowl, with molded foliate scrolls and basketweave, transfer-printed decoration.

c1760   9.5in (24cm) dia

$400-500   **Clv**

A First Period Worcester basket, cover and stand, printed with gooseberries, flowerheads and fruit, the rustic handles with applied floral terminals, the cover and stand pierced with lappets, each filled with two blue florets, the quatrefoil section sides of the basket molded with hexagonal diaper and florettes, scrolling W mark.

c1760   11in (28cm) wide

$2,800-3,200   **Chef**

Worcester

A First Period Worcester basket, printed with the Pine Cone pattern within diamond lattice-pierced sides, the rope handles terminating in applied florets, crescent mark.

8.5in (21.5cm) wide

$650-750 **Chef**

A Worcester mug, decorated with the Plantation pattern .

1760-70 3.5in (8.5cm) high

$500-550 **AD**

A Worcester bowl, hand-painted with a dragon pattern.

c1765 7in (18cm) dia

$700-800 **PC**

A First Period Worcester wavy-edge plate, the scalloped body transfer-printed in the Pine Cone pattern, crescent mark.

8in (20.5cm) dia

$150-200 **GorL**

A Worcester teapot and cover, of globular form, painted with the Mansfield pattern, W mark, metal repair to the handle.

1760-70 6in (15cm) high

$400-450 **WW**

A Worcester First Period salt spoon.

c1765 3.75in (9.5cm) long

$1,200-1,800 **SA**

A pair of Worcester pickle dishes, painted in underglaze blue in the Pickle Vine pattern, crescent marks.
c1765

$550-600 **GorL**

A Worcester Blind Earl design dish, decorated with "dry blue" flowers, bud chipped.

c1770 6.25in (15.5cm) wide

$1,000-1,500 **AD**

● According to myth, this raised design was created when a blind Earl commissioned Worcester to mold dishes so that he could feel the pattern..

● The blue and white floral decoration on this early piece shows the influence of Chinese export porcelain.

● The dish has an unusual gilt dentil edge.

● Molded rose leaves cover the surface

An 18thC Worcester two-handled baluster vase, with underglaze decoration of flowers and butterflies.

11.75in (30cm) high

$1,200-1,500 **GorL**

An 18thC Worcester cabbage-leaf-molded mask jug, decorated in underglaze blue with large floral spray.

7.25in (18.5cm) high

$700-1,000 **GorL**

A Worcester tea bowl, with unusual transfer-print of two oxen on a sampan.

c1770 1.75in (4.5cm) high

$80-120 **PC**

A Worcester tapering cylindrical mug, printed with two moths and two large flower sprays, crescent mark, cracked and riveted.

1770-80 6in (15cm) high

$70-100 **WW**

Worcester

A Worcester globular teapot and cover, printed and painted with the Orchid pattern, some restoration to the spout and cover.

c1760   7.25in (18.5cm)

$300-350   WW

A Worcester globular teapot and cover, painted in enamels with scattered flower sprays, gilt line rims.

c1760   7.5in (19cm) long

$1,000-1,300   WW

A small Worcester teapot and cover, printed with Chinese figures in various pursuits, with a loop handle, no mark, minor damage and repairs, knop possibly replaced.

c1760   6.25in (16cm) long

$250-300   WW

A small molded Worcester cream jug, hand painted with English flowers.

c1760   3.25in (8cm) high

$700-800   PC

A Worcester "High Chelsea Ewer" cream jug, painted with the Putai pattern, in Chinese famille verte style, the interior with an iron-red and gilt looped band.

c1760   3.25in (8cm) high

$2,800-3,200   AA

A Worcester coffee cup, finely painted in Chinese famille rose style with the Valentine pattern.

c1760   2.25in (6cm) high

$1,500-2,000   AA

A pair of flared Worcester baskets, painted in enamels in Rogers style, with a spray of European flowers and leaves and scattered flowers, the exterior with flowerheads, one with small restoration.

c1760   5.25in (13.5cm) dia

$5,500-6,000   AA

A Worcester sucrier and domed cover, painted in enamels in Rogers style, with European flowers and leaves, with flower knop.

c1760   4.25in (11cm) high

$2,800-3,200   AA

A twin-handled Worcester basket, the interior freely painted with summer flowers, the exterior with flowerhead cast decoration and flower and leaf cast rustic handles, riveted restorations on base, handles and large part of one side.

c1765   8.75in (22cm) wide

$250-300   L&T

A Worcester dolphin ewer creamboat, of silver shape, with a lamprey handle, decorated in enamels.

c1765   3.5in (8.5cm)

$2,200-2,800   WW

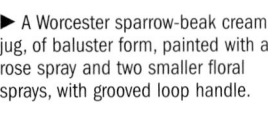

▶ A Worcester sparrow-beak cream jug, of baluster form, painted with a rose spray and two smaller floral sprays, with grooved loop handle.

c1765   3.5in (8.5cm) high

$450-500   BonS

A Worcester oval sauceboat, both sides painted in enamels with an exotic bird within puce scroll cartouche, on a scale-molded ground, with C-scroll handle.

c1765   6.5in (16.5cm) long

$2,800-3,200   **AA**

A Worcester Chelsea ewer cream jug, molded with foliage and painted with flowers in enamels.

c1765

$550-600   **GorL**

A Worcester faceted teabowl and saucer, boldly painted in famille verte palette with a chequered tent, flowering branches and birds in flight, blue fret marks.

Although attributed to the Giles atelier by Gerald Coke, the pattern is now accepted as factory decoration.

c1768

$2,000-2,500   **AA**

A Worcester sparrow-beak milk jug and cover, of baluster form, painted in the Kakiemon style with flowering branches alternating with flowers and leaves on a blue ground, with loop handle and flower knop, blue fret marks.

c1768   5.25in (13.5cm) high

$2,500-3,000   **AA**

A Worcester tea bowl and saucer, decorated with the Queen Charlotte pattern.

c1770   saucer 4.75in (12cm) dia

$330-380   **AD**

A Worcester tea bowl and saucer.

c1770   saucer 4.5in (11.5cm) dia

$1,000-1,300   **AD**

A Worcester trio, decorated with the Bengal Tiger pattern, slight rubbing.

c1770 saucer 5.25in (13.5cm) dia

$700-800   **AD**

A Worcester teacup, hand-painted in over-glaze enamels.

c1770   2.5in (6cm) high

$200-250   **PC**

A pair of Worcester baskets, with applied flowerheads, the exteriors with puce leaf details.

c1768   8.75in (22cm) dia

$5,500-6,500   **WW**

A Worcester coffee cup, painted in enamels with three Chinese figures in a garden, with a grooved loop handle.

c1770   2.5in (6.5cm) high

$280-320   **WW**

▶ A Worcester teacup, hand-painted in over-glaze enamels.

c1770   2.5in (6cm) high

$200-250   **PC**

Worcester

A Worcester teacup, hand-painted in enamels, with scalloped rim, badly cracked.

c1770   2.5in (6cm) high

$150-200   **PC**

A Worcester teacup and saucer, painted in the London atelier of James Giles, with European flowers within leaf scroll and brown line bands, crossed swords and numeral 9 marks.

This pattern is now given the name "Sheridan". The written "Sheridan" is recorded in the Giles workshop client accounts.

c1770

$2,000-2,500   **AA**

A rare Worcester claret ground globular teapot and cover, painted in the London atelier of James Giles, with European flowers within gilt flower and scroll cartouches on a claret ground.

Provenance: Dr. Harold Schenberg Collection.

c1770   5.5in (14cm) high

$15,000-18,000   **AA**

A Worcester plate, painted in enamels with two agitated birds on a branch within a flower garland border, gilt line rim. This pattern is unrecorded by HR Marshall.

c1770   9in (23cm) dia

$1,200-1,500   **AA**

A pair of Worcester plates, painted in enamels in the London atelier of James Giles, with a spray of European flowers and leaves, the rim with an entwined leaf and brown line band.

c1770   8.5in (21.5cm) dia

$4,200-4,800 (pair)   **AA**

A Worcester basket, painted in enamels with European flowers and leaves within a gilt cartouche, on a blue scale ground, the exterior with applied flowerheads, blue fret mark.

c1770   7.25in (18.5in) dia

$2,800-3,200   **AA**

A Worcester teacup and saucer, painted in enamels in the London atelier of James Giles, with flowers and fruit on turquoise ground, blue crossed swords and numeral 9 marks.

c1770

$10,000-13,000   **AA**

A Worcester milk jug, of ovoid shape and painted with Mandarin figures and foliage.

c1770

$600-700   **GorL**

A Worcester bowl, decorated in colored enamels with chinoiserie figures, butterflies and insects, within gilt cartouches, on a blue scale ground.

The exceptional quality of decoration to this bowl is tempting to attribute to the Giles atelier, although there is no documented comparison.

c1770   5.25in (13.5cm) dia

$5,500-6,000   **AA**

A First Period Worcester cup and saucer.

c1770   saucer 5in (13cm) dia

$600-650   **Gro**

Worcester

A Worcester coffee cup and saucer, decorated with panels of exotic birds in parkland within rococo gilt scroll borders and smaller panels of birds in flight, all reserved on an apple-green ground.

Tea wares often have borders of apple-green known as "The Marchioness of Huntley" pattern, but the all-over ground is rare.

c1770

$2,000-2,500   **AA**

A Worcester reeded ovoid tea caddy, decorated in the Holly Berry pattern, painted with swags of green hops pendant from pink cherron borders.

c1770-1775   6.75in (17cm) high

$2,800-3,200   **AA**

A Worcester reeded barrel-shaped teapot, decorated in the Pink Hop Trellis pattern, with ogee handle.

c1770-1775   5.5in (14cm) high

$5,500-6,500   **AA**

A Worcester reeded barrel-shaped teapot, decorated in the Holly Berry pattern, painted with swags of green hops pendant from pink cherron borders, with ogee handle, the flat cover with molded flower finial.

c1770-1775   5.5in (14cm) high

$5,500-6,500   **AA**

A Worcester First Period teacup and saucer.

c1770   2.5in (6cm) high

$1,200-1,800   **SA**

A Worcester porringer and cover, painted with flowers and leaves within gilt cartouches on a blue scale ground, with scroll handles and flower knop, blue fret mark.

Provenance: *Dr. Harold Schenberg Collection.*

c1770   5in (13cm) high

$4,000-5,000   **AA**

A Worcester kidney-shaped dish, in Sèvres style, from the Mrs. Arthur James service, decorated with exotic pheasant-like birds and insects within an irregular border.

There was only one tea service and one dessert service made in this pattern. This service was produced at the very end of the Dr Wall period. Mrs. Arthur James was a celebrated London hostess of the Edwardian era but it is not known how long the service was in her possession.

c1775   10in (25.5cm) wide

$7,000-8,000   **AA**

A Worcester trio, decorated with flower sprays.

c1775   saucer 5.25in (13cm) dia

$1,200-1,500   **AD**

A Worcester First Period teapot.

c1775   5.25in (13cm) high

$850-950   **SA**

▶ A pair of Worcester partridge tureens and covers, each with a nesting bird on a basket, with molded base, applied with leaves, with gilt highlights.

c1775   6.5in (16.5cm) wide

$7,500-8,500   **AA**

A Worcester First Period flared vase.

c1775   5.75in (14.5cm) high

$1,200-1,800   **SA**

A Worcester First Period gros bleu coffee cup and saucer, decorated with exotic birds.

c1775   2.75in (7cm) high

$700-800   **SA**

A Worcester trio, fluted with scalloped rim, painted in black with a Neo-classical husk chain and medallions about a gilded vitruvian scroll roundel and flower spray.

c1775

$280-320	**BonS**

A Worcester teapot and stand, each decorated in the Dalhousie pattern, with circular panels of landscapes enclosed within narrow turquoise husk and gilt line borders flanked by bouquets of European flowers and scattered insects within narrow royal-blue and gilt borders, the pot of reeded barrel shape with ogee handle and the flat cover with flower finial, the stand hexagonal with fluted sides, crescent marks.

The Dalhousie pattern is distinguished by flower sprays instead of fruit clusters that usually accompany these patterns.

c1777   pot 5.5in (14cm) high

$6,000-7,000	**AA**

A Barr Worcester sucrier and stand, decorated with orange bands and gilt scrolling foliage, incised B marks.

1792-1807   7.25in (18.5cm) high

$400-500	**WW**

A Worcester globular teapot, decorated with sprigs of flowers, the cover with knop finial, some restoration to handle.

5.25in (13.5cm) high

$200-250	**GorL**

A pair of Worcester Flight & Barr coffee cans, richly decorated with gilt scrollwork and foliage on an orange ground, incised B marks.

c1800

$400-500	**WW**

A Worcester mug, by Chamberlain's.
c1805   4.5in (11.5cm) high

$900-1,100	**SA**

A Worcester prow-fronted teapot, cover and stand, by Flight, Barr & Barr, bat-printed with floral sprays within gilt-line borders, the cover with flame finial, impressed mark, finial restored.

c1810

$400-450	**DN**

A rare Worcester plate, by Chamberlain's, from the Duke of Cumberland's service, the central armorial with uninscribed blue ribbon, the rim with pairs of garden reserves between four iron-red rosettes on gilt-diapered rotal blue grounds, printed marks, old paper labels.

This plate is suggested, by the old lot description, to be a trial piece differing from the completed service and is probably unique, it came from the C Wentworth Wass collection and is thought to have been given to him by RW Binns out of the works collection.

c1806   9.5in (24cm) dia

$750-850	**Chef**

◄ An early 19thC Worcester vase, by Flight, Barr & Barr, painted with The Monk from Sterne Rubbing his Horn Box upon the Sleeve of his Tunic, on a deep turquoise-green ground, with interlacing gilt snake handles, the socle on square foot, painted marks and address London House, 1 Coventry Street.

7.75in (19.5cm) high

$280-320	**Chef**

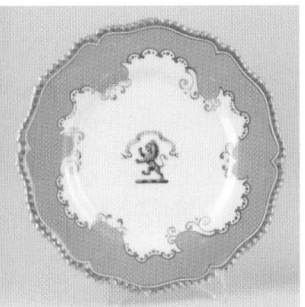

Six Worcester plates, by Flight, Barr & Barr, with crest.

c1815-20   9in (22.5cm) wide

$600-650 (set)   **SA**

Twelve Worcester plates, by Flight, Barr & Barr.

c1815-20   8.75in (22cm) wide

$1,000-1,500   **SA**

A Worcester "Named View" cabinet cup and saucer, by Flight, Barr & Barr, painted with a view of Malvern within a gilded foliate scroll cartouche ,the tulip-shaped cup with gilded butterfly-form handle, the rim interspersed with florets, the stand of similar design with plain well, red hand-painted script mask, minor wear to gilding.

c1820   2.75in (7cm) high

$700-1,000   **BonS**

A small Worcester two-handled vase, by Flight, Barr & Barr, painted with a panel of flowers and trees on a green ground, painted mark, some restoration.

c1820   4.5in (11cm) dia

$450-550   **WW**

A Worcester potpourri vase and cover, by Flight, Barr & Barr, painted with a panel of flowers and trees on a green ground, raised on a square base, painted mark, the knop restored.

c1820   4.5in (11cm)

$1,200-1,800   **WW**

A Worcester cabinet cup, by Chamberlain's, tiny stress cracks.

c1820   3.75in (9.5cm) high

$280-320   **AD**

A very large Worcester ashet, by Flight, Barr & Barr, printed with the Japan pattern and decorated with flowers and leaves in typical palette, impressed mark.

22in (56cm) wide

$500-600   **BonE**

A large Worcester punch bowl, by Grainger's.

c1820   12in (30.5cm) dia

$450-500   **SA**

A Worcester plate, by Flight, Barr & Barr, printed and painted in the Imari palette with floral sprays, impressed and printed marks.

8.25in (21cm) dia

$30-50   **LC**

A Worcester dish, by Flight, Barr & Barr, with central painted panel of figures in a landscape with pagoda, within a gold-painted seaweed border, gilded shaped edge, the reverse with printed marks and painted title Virginia Water.

9in (23cm) dia

$280-320   **Clv**

A Worcester vase, by Grainger Lee & Co, decorated with all-round landscape design and applied flowers.

c1835   15in (38cm) high

$900-1,100   **Gro**

A Worcester scent bottle, by Chamberlain's, with gilt-metal mount and stopper.

c1840   9.25in (23.5cm) high

$850-950   **Gro**

A pair of Worcester dessert dishes, by Flight, Barr & Barr, small chips.

c1825

$280-320   AD

A Chamberlain Worcester oval sugar box and cover, spiral-molded and decorated with blue and gilt border, gilt script mark inside cover.

5.5in (14cm) high

$200-250   WW

A pair of Worcester plates, by Chamberlain's, each painted in the center with a rose within a deep border of flowers and leaves, gilt line rim, script mark on base.

10.25in (25.5cm) dia

$150-200   BonE

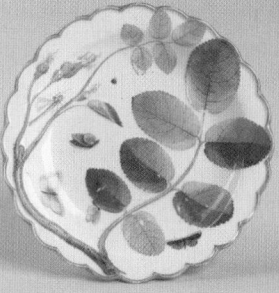

A Worcester Blind Earl design plate, with leaf and insect relief decoration and gilt border, impressed Grainger's mark.

8in (20.5cm) dia

$400-450   L&T

A Grainger Worcester loving cup, of cylindrical shape with two scroll handles, painted with a floral spray within a gilt-edged panel, the reserve with RT monogram, printed mark.

5.75in (14.5cm) high

$220-280   BonE

A late 19thC Grainger Worcester mug, decorated with a view of Worcester, with gilt line rims, printed mark.

4.5in (11.5cm) high

$200-250   WW

A Worcester glazed ivory inkstand, cover and liner, by Kerr & Binns, the compressed ovoid body molded with grotesque masks supported by three caryatid monopodia and lion's paw feet, on a triform plinth base, the domed cover with cupid finial, printed shield mark and date code, base and finial broken and restored.

1858   6in (15cm) high

$200-300   HamG

A late 19thC Grainger Worcester vase, the ovoid shape molded with poppies, shaded green and gilt details, gilt handles, printed marks and pattern no. 2693.

8in (20cm) high

$150-200   WW

A Worcester reticulated bottle vase, by Grainger and Co, the neck and body pierced with scrolling foliage, the ivory ground with gilded scrolled sprays, the centers of the flowers jeweled in turquoise, printed shield mark, shape 469 over G3585, minor wear.

c1890   10.25in (26cm) high

$280-320   BonS

► A pair of Grainger Worcester vases, decorated with roses on an ivory ground, the side handles with flower terminals, factory marks.

c1900   10.25in (26cm) high

$450-550   WW

OTHER BRITISH FACTORIES

A Bradley white glazed table centerpiece, formed as a large leaf supported by three cherubs all on a tri-form base, with impressed mark.

c1876-96	10.25in (26cm) wide	
$180-220		WW

A Bristol saucer dish, painted in enamels with a couple in a wooded landscape, gilt line rim, crossed swords and dot mark in underglaze blue.

Provenance: The Peter Stephens Collection.

c1775	7in (17.75in) dia
$2,800-3,200	AA

A Bristol sweetmeat dish, of saucer shape, painted in enamels with European flowers within a gilt leaf cartouche on a marbled blue ground, the rim with a gilt scroll paneled band, blue painted X mark.

c1775	
$2,000-2,500	AA

A Bristol teacup and saucer, finely painted with swags and C-scrolls with radiating gilded lines, blue painted crossed swords mark and underglaze gilded 3.

c1775	
$700-800	BonS

A Bristol cup and saucer.

c1775	2.75in (7cm) high
$1,000-1,300	SA

COPELAND & GARRETT

In 1833 W T Copeland and T Garrett took over the Spode factory in Stoke-on-Trent, Staffordshire, and began trading under Copeland and Garrett, later changing to W.T.Copeland. During the mid-19th century the factory produced a number of ornate table services and Parian ware figures. The factory, now known as Spode Ltd, remains one of the most productive in England.

A 19thC Copeland and Garrett 22-piece dessert service, each with individual painted botanical center within a gilt and pale-blue vine leaf and scroll border, comprising two-handled sucrière with cover and stand, four oval dishes, a pair of rectangular-shaped dishes and ten dessert plates.

c1840	
$2,800-3,200 (service)	Clv

A Copeland Parian figure of Sabrina, depicted sitting on a rock beside a river, Copeland impressed and Marshall Fect incised, repaired through neck.

c1840	12in (30cm) high
$150-200	WW

A pair of Copeland figures, modeled as cupids holding turquoise and gilt torches, the socles similarly colored, impressed marks, dated.

1872	10.75in (27cm) high
$280-320	Chef

A mid-19thC Copeland Parian bread plate, molded with the arms and motto of William of Wykham, small chip to the reverse.

	13in (33cm) dia
$200-250	WW

A pair of H&R Daniel shell dishes.

c1830	9.5in (24cm) wide
$500-550 (pair)	SA

Other British factories

A Factory Z trio, decorated with a basket of flowers and fruit, minor wear to gilding.

c1795

$120-180   **BonS**

A Factory Z trio, gilded and painted en grisaille with a Neo-classical urn with ivy swag.

c1795

$120-180   **BonS**

A Herculaneum jug.

c1810   4.5in (11cm) high

$120-180   **SA**

A Miles Mason coffee can and saucer.

c1810   3in (7.5cm) high

$200-250   **SA**

A Miles Mason teacup and saucer, painted with landscapes within thickly gilded oval reserves.

c1810

$40-60   **BonS**

A Pinxton cup and saucer.

c1800   2.5in (6.5cm) high

$400-450   **SA**

A Pinxton part tea service, each piece painted with scattered sprigs of flowers within gilt leaf and line border, comprising teapot, cover and stand, sucrier and cover, milk jug, slop basin and tea bowl, teapot cracked.

c1800

$4,000-4,500   **L&T**

▶ A pair of early 19thC Ridgway dishes, printed and overpainted with the 400 pattern of flowers and the shaped rim with muslin band, printed marks.

Job Ridgway set up the Ridgways factory in Staffordshire, in 1802. Rare porcelain marked "Ridgway and son" dates from 1808-1814.

10.25in (26cm) wide

$30-50 (pair)   **Chef**

A Plymouth mug, of baluster form, with notched loop handle, painted in enamels with exotic birds in a wooded landscape, beneath a gilt trellis band, numeral 4 mark in red. Provenance: The Alfred Trapnell Collection, The Peter Stephens Collection.

The distinctive style of Plymouth bird decoration is attributed to the French painter Mons Soqui.

c1770   5.25in (13.5cm) high

$4,000-4,500   **AA**

A Ridgway trio, painted with Japan pattern no. 487.

c1810

$50-80   **BonS**

A Ridgway sucrier and cover, with applied C-scroll handles and gilt decoration.

c1815   5.75in (14.5cm) wide

$450-500   **SA**

Staffordshire

A mid-Victorian dessert service, possibly Ridgway, comprising four comports, two square dishes, a tall comport, an oval comport and fourteen plates, each piece printed and painted with bunches of flowers within shaped rims and gilt cerise borders.

c1850

$400-500 (service) **Chef**

An extremely rare Vauxhall rococo-molded cream boat, adapted from a silver shape, each side painted with colorful birds with a smaller panel beneath the spout, richly gilded with scrolls and insects on a deep gros bleu ground.

c1760-65 5.5in (14cm) long

$4,500-5,000 **WW**

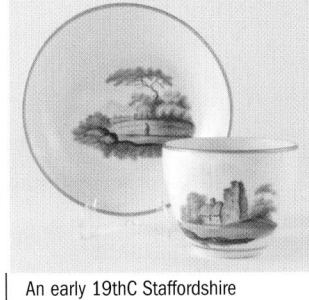

An early 19thC Staffordshire porcelain teacup and saucer, painted with landscapes.

c1810

$30-40 **BonS**

A Staffordshire porcelain bat-printed milk jug, probably New Hall, printed in puce and painted after Adam Buck, with two vignettes of a woman seated on chaise lounge, her child at her side, each holding a small racket, the child with a shuttlecock, and two vignettes of fruit, blue line rims, small hairline crack to rim.

c1820 5.5in (14cm) high

$180-220 **DN**

A Staffordshire porcelain spill vase, painted with a panel of a girl holding a flower garland, slight wear to gilt rim.

c1830 4.5in (11.5cm) high

$180-220 **WW**

A Staffordshire porcelain flower-encrusted miniature kettle and cover, together with two similar milk jugs, kettle handle glued, other minor chips.

c1840

$700-800 **DN**

A three-piece Staffordshire porcelain Hollandaise vase.

c1845 10.25in (26cm) high

$750-850 **Gro**

An early 19thC cider mug, painted with puce scrolled leaves within gilt-banded reserves and the initials C J, with applied wreath-molded scroll handle, crack to base, wear to gilding.

4in (10cm) high

$225-275 **HamG**

An 18thC hunting bowl, the exterior printed in black with an extensive and continuous fox hunting scene, the interior decorated with five hunting subjects.

11in (28cm) dia

$700-800 **Clv**

A porcelain plaque, painted with a view of Melrose Abbey, with a richly gilded integral frame.

c1820 7.5in (23cm) wide

$900-1,100 **BonE**

65

British porcelain

A campana vase, with gilt loop handles, painted with flowers on a gilt-decorated ground, no mark, slight wear.

c1825   6.5in (16.5cm)

$400-450   **WW**

A three-handled vase, the body decorated with flowers and gilt scrolls, no mark.

c1830-40   8.25in (21cm) high

$300-350   **WW**

An19thC mug, with painted scene.

c1835   3.5in (9cm) high

$500-550   **AD**

A mid-19thC letter stand, modeled as a castle with a spill vase tower at each end, the center panel painted with colorful birds, gilded details, some good restoration to the top of one tower.

6.75in (17cm) wide

$450-500   **WW**

A large 19thC two-handled loving cup, painted with two landscape panels on a gilded cerise ground, gilt borders and details, no marks.

8.75in (22cm) wide

$450-550   **WW**

A 19thC small triple spill vase, modeled with three birds with yellow baskets on their backs, raised on a triform base, unmarked,

4.5in (11cm) high

$200-250   **WW**

An ice pail, cover and liner, the cover with an upstanding rim and central scroll handle, printed and painted with floral swags, some restoration.

3.75in (22cm) dia

$280-320   **LC**

A mid-19thC biscuit porcelain figure, modeled as man carrying a basket, no marks, the figure reattached to the base, the basket handle restored.

7.25in (18.5cm) high

$80-120   **WW**

A 19thC milk jug, painted with roses on a blue and gilt ground.

6.25in (16cm) long

$200-250   **WW**

A pair of twin-handled rococo-style vases and covers, the knops with elaborate floral-encrusted decoration above pierced domed lids.

17.5in (44cm) high

$1,000-1,500   **L&T**

 ▶ A late 19thC cache pot and stand, painted with a broad band of roses on a black ground, stand cracked.

5.25in (13.5cm) high

$120-180   **LC**

An English porcelain part dinner service, painted in the Imari palette, comprising twin-handled soup tureen, cover and stand, large rounded rectangular ashet, two other smaller ashets, 21 meat plates, 12 soup plates, eight fish plates, some damage.

Largest ashet 21in (53cm) wide

$5,000-6,000 (service)   **L&T**

An 18thC Chantilly custard cup and cover, painted with stylized blue flower sprays, painted and incised marks.

c1750

$280-320 **WW**

Two 19thC French biscuit porcelain busts, one modeled as Louis XVI, the other as Marie Antoinette. largest

15.75in (40cm) high

$700-800 each **CdK**

A 19thC French inkstand, with lift-out well and sander, the sides painted with birds and pagodas, no mark, rubbed, small chip to sander.

6.25in (15.5cm) high

$150-200 **WW**

Part of an early 20thC French dessert service, comprising a large oval serving plate and nine plates, painted with birds in woodland settings, the cobalt-blue borders printed in gilt with foliate lambrequins, printed retailer's mark.

largest 18.25in (46cm) dia

$1,000-1,500 (service) **BonS**

A late 18thC Frankenthal figure, modeled as a shepherdess in 18thC-style dress, her apron holding flowers, with a lamb at her feet, on a floral encrusted C-scroll base, underglazed blue crown and interlocking C and T mark of Carl Theodor of the Frankenthal factory.

6.25in (16cm) high

$550-600 **SI**

A 19thC figure group, modeled as five putti musicians in 18thC attire, on a scrollwork mound with applied flowers, puce enamel crown and interlocking C's marks.

8.5in (21.5cm) high

$800-900 **SI**

A late 19thC figural compote, modeled as a peasant man and woman under a flower-encrusted bower, printed mark C.G. Schierholz Porcelain Manufactory.

17.25in (44cm) high

$1,000-1,500 **SI**

A Ludwigsburg part tea and coffee service, comprising a teapot and cover, coffeepot and cover, hot water jug and cover and a sugar bowl with associated cover, each piece painted with Deutsche blumen, blue marks, two covers restored, one finial lacking.

c1765

$800-900 (part service) **DN**

◄ A19thC Nymphenburg 13-piece dessert set, comprising a teapot, two creamers, two scallop-edged oval dishes, five cups and two demitasse, each decorated with a finely painted floral spray, the basketweave-molded rims edged in a Greek key pattern, underglaze green printed crown, shield mark and Nymphenburg.

Dishes 12in (30.5cm) wide

$850-950 (set) **SI**

A charger, painted with three maidens and a peacock, in a giltwood frame.

c1880-1901 11.5in (29cm) dia

$400-500 **SI**

◀ A 19thC 59-piece Nymphenburg "Named Views" part dinner service, comprising thirty-seven dinner plates, sixteen salad plates, a reticulated bowl, an octagonal dish, one reticulated dessert plate, a twelve-sided dish, one shaped tray and one demitasse, each piece finely painted with landscape or architectural scenes en grisaille, within gilt and blue ribbon-tied frames surrounded by gilt trailing foliage, the rims with molded beading, the plates and serving pieces entitled in black script on the reverse.

Largest tray 13in (33cm) wide

$15,000-20,000 (service)   **SI**

A late 19thC Helena Wolfsohn box and cover, with gilt-metal mounted edge, the reserves decorated with romantic figures in landscapes, underglaze blue Augustus Rex marks.

7.5in (19cm) wide

$600-700   **BonS**

A late 19thC centerpiece, the oval twin-handled pierced basket encrusted and painted with flowers, supported on a leaf-molded pedestal, the base modeled with embracing cherubs.

11.75in (29.5cm)

$225-300   **Chef**

A late 19thC cabinet cup and saucer, the central portrait medallion of a woman in 19thC-style gown, the whole scattered with polychrome floral sprigs and highlighted with gilt foliate pattern, applied C-shaped scroll handle terminating in a falcon head, underglazed red L and crown mark of Ludwigsburg.

Cup 4.5in (11.5cm) high

$400-500   **SI**

An early 20thC blue and white plate, painted with the Onion pattern, crossed swords mark, damaged.

14.25in (36cm) wide

$120-150   **LC**

An early 20thC Rosenthal vase, of baluster form, the central cartouche depicting two putto seated on a grassy knoll, with scattered floral sprigs, the rim and foot banded with gilt.

10in (25.5cm) high

$200-250   **SI**

An early 20thC Pirkenhammer centerpiece, the scroll-molded bowl modeled with masks and encrusted with lavender flowers and vines, the baluster form standard modeled with a putto and a monkey among vines, the base with applied flowers, foliage and putto in cartouches, green underglaze mark of double headed eagle in a shield.

17.75in (44.4cm) high

$1,000-1,300   **SI**

A Continental figure, modeled as a putto with a bumblebee, set on a circular socle, underglazed blue R and 1762 marks.

5.75in (15cm) high

$750-950   **SI**

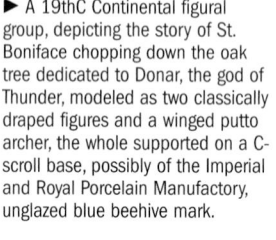

▶ A 19thC Continental figural group, depicting the story of St. Boniface chopping down the oak tree dedicated to Donar, the god of Thunder, modeled as two classically draped figures and a winged putto archer, the whole supported on a C-scroll base, possibly of the Imperial and Royal Porcelain Manufactory, unglazed blue beehive mark.

9.75in (25cm) high

$600-800   **SI**

European porcelain

A 19thC Continental bust of Apollo, raised on a plinth with "Apollo" in gilt lettering, the whole supported by a socle foot and decorated with gilt banding.

8in (20cm) high

$300-350   **SI**

A 19thC German figure, modeled as a young peasant girl holding her skirt, supported on square pedestal, bearing the blue interlocked AR monogram of Augustus Rex.

4.75in (12cm) high

$450-550   **SI**

A late 19thC bust, representing Autumn, modeled as a young lady with fruiting vines to the head and shoulders, raised on a gilded oval base.

8.75in (22cm) high

$180-220   **Chef**

A pair of late 19thC figures, modeled as a young gallant and his female companion, each wearing 18thC style floral decorated dress, standing upon gilded C-scroll and shell-molded circular bases.

7.5in (19cm) high

$200-250   **Chef**

A 20thC Continental porcelain figure, modeled as a gentleman in 18thC attire, holding a rose and a book and seated next to an inkwell, a plume and a letter resting on an elaborate hoof-footed table, blue enamel psuedo-Meissen mark, incised 417.

9.25in (23.5cm)

$900-1,100   **SI**

A pair of Plaue on Havel figural candelabra, representing The Seasons, each modeled with two children beneath five rose-encrusted branches, the bases painted with insects and supported on four scroll feet, marks in blue.

18in (45.5cm) high

$400-450 (pair)   **Chef**

A Russian two-handled urn, probably Gardner, with reticulated upper and lower sections, the mid-section painted with various floral sprays, losses to one handle.

c1830   22in (55.8cm) high

$15,000-20,000   **SI**

A First Period Belleek dish, modeled as a conch-type shell with the broad lip forming the bowl, the oval foot modeled as lapping waves, black printed mark.

5.5in (14cm) wide

$200-250   **Chef**

► A mid- to late 19thC Russian teapot and cover, painted with Sirin, green mark for the Imperial Porcelain Factory, blue hammer and sickle mark, decoration with date mark for 1921, knop restored.

Sirin is a fabled bird woman in Russian folklore

$700-900   **WW**

A 19thC Capo di Monte serpentine casket, molded in low-relief with figures of Venus and Neptune and decorated in polychrome enamels and gilt.

5.5in (14cm) wide

$150-200   **GorL**

Commemorative ceramics

A rare bone china mug, made to commemorate Queen Victoria's Diamond Jubilee.

1897 3.25in (8.5cm) high

$800-900   **H&G**

A dual commemorative earthenware mug, with one side commemorating the coronation of Edward VII, the other commemorating peace in the Boer War.

1902   3in (8cm) high

$80-120   **H&G**

▶ A rare Staffordshire earthenware beaker, made for the proposed Coronation of Edward VIII, printed with his portrait within a garter reserve, with oak leaves and flags, crazed.

4.5in (11.5cm) high

$50-80   **HamG**

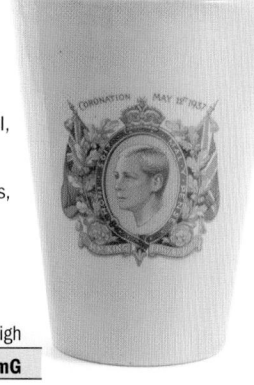

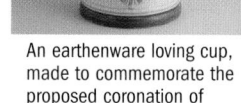

An earthenware loving cup, made to commemorate the proposed coronation of Edward VIII.

Edward VIII was going to be crowned in 1937 but he abdicated in 1936.

1936   6in (15cm) h

$150-200   **H&G**

A bone china mug, with E-handle, made to commemorate the proposed coronation of Edward VIII.

1936   3.25in (8.5cm) h

$200-250   **H&G**

A Copeland earthenware mug, for Thomas Goode, made for the proposed coronation of Edward VIII.

3.75in (9.5cm) high

$70-100   **H&G**

A Crown Derby mug, made to commemorate the coronation of George VI, the sides printed with portrait roundels of the Royal couple, and with their ciphers within gilt wreaths, printed marks and dated.

1937 3.75in (9.5cm) high

$70-100   **Chef**

A Crown Ducal earthenware mug, depicting a young Princess Elizabeth on the occasion of her parents' coronation.

1937   2.75in (7cm) high

$200-250   **H&G**

A Crown Ducal earthenware mug, depicting a young Princess Margaret on the occasion of her parents' coronation.

Mugs featuring Princess Margaret are rarer.

1937   2.75in (7cm) high

$220-280   **H&G**

A Crown Devon earthenware musical mug, made to commemorate the coronation of George VI.

1937   5in (12.5cm) high

$280-320   **H&G**

A Minton bone china loving cup, designed by Wadsworth, made to commemorate the coronation of Queen Elizabeth II.

4in (10cm) high

$220-230   **H&G**

A Burleighware earthenware mug, made to commemorate the coronation of Queen Elizabeth II.

1953 3.25in (8.5cm) high

$60-80   **H&G**

A Stanley bone china loving cup, made to commemorate the coronation of Queen Elizabeth II.

1953   3.5in (9cm) high

$80-120   **H&G**

A Spode bone china tankard, made to commemorate the Silver Jubilee of Queen Elizabeth II.

1977   4in (10cm) high

$70-100   **H&G**

▶ A Caverswall bone china lion-head beaker, made to commemorate the birth of Prince William.

This mug was limited edition of 1000.

1982 4.5in (11.5cm) high

$80-120   **H&G**

An Aynsley small bone china loving cup, made to commemorate the birth of Prince Henry.

1984   2.25in (6cm) high

$80-120   **H&G**

A gold luster earthenware coach teapot, made to commemorate the coronation of Queen Elizabeth II.

1953   5in (13cm) high

$220-280   **H&G**

A Chiswick Ceramics earthenware teapot, made to commemorate the Silver Jubilee of Queen Elizabeth II.

This teapot was made in a limited edition of 100.

1977   7.75in (20cm) high

$280-320   **H&G**

A Carltonware spitting image teapot, designed by Luck and Flaw, depicting Margaret Thatcher.

1980   8.5in (22cm) high

$280-320   **H&G**

A Carltonware spitting image teapot, designed by Luck and Flaw, depicting Ronald Reagan.

1981   10.5in (27cm) high

$380-420   **H&G**

An Exile eathenware teapot, depicting Queen Elizabeth II.

1981   8.25in (21cm) high

$200-250   **H&G**

An earthenware teapot by Richard Parrington, depicting "Princess Di". Limited edition of 100.

1981   8.25in (21cm) high

$450-500   **H&G**

A Kiln Cottage Pottery earthenware teapot, made to commemorate the wedding of Prince Charles and Lady Diana Spencer.

1981   6.75in (17.5cm) h

$200-250   **H&G**

▶ A rare buff stoneware jug, made to commemorate the coronation of George IV, of ovoid form, the rose, thistle and shamrock-molded neck applied with a handle in the shape of a climbing lion, the body applied with a sprigged bust of the King against a molded medallion, flanked by two winged angels, on a circular foot, spout chipped.

8.75in (22cm) high

$220-280   **HamG**

A stoneware jug, made to commemorate the birth of Edward, Prince of Wales.

1841   9.75in (25cm) high

$820-880   **H&G**

A parian jug, made to commemorate the death of Prince Albert.

1861   9.5in (24cm) high

$650-750   **H&G**

A Staffordshire plate, made to commemorate William IV, with the motto "William the Fourth King of Great Britain".

c1831   6.25in (16cm) dia

$220-280   **AD**

A Wedgwood & Co bone china plate, made to commemorate Queen Victoria's Diamond Jubilee.

1897   9in (22.5cm) high

$150-200   **H&G**

An Aynsley bone china deluxe plate, made to commemorate the coronation of Queen Elizabeth II.

1953   10.25in (26cm) high

$350-400   **H&G**

A bowl, made to commemorate the Golden Jubilee of George III, printed in black in the base with a medallion inscribed "A King Revered, a Queen Beloved, G III C", framed with laurel leaves and with a ribbon at the base inscribed "Long May They Live", the inside rim printed with a chinoiserie border, the outsides printed in black with cupid scenes, unmarked, rim cracks.

c1809   7.5in (19cm) dia

$450-500   **DN**

A rare Doulton earthenware jardinière, made to commemorate the Australian Federation.

1901   4.75in (12cm) high

$1,300-1,500   **H&G**

A Royal Crown Derby bone china 5-petal dish, made to commemorate the wedding of Prince Charles to Lady Diana Spencer.

1981   4.25in (11cm) dia

$60-80   **H&G**

◀ A Sèvres vase, by the artist A Duduzeaus.

This is one of a pair of vases exhibited at the 1851 Great Exhibition at the Crystal Palace by the French government.

1851   10.75in 27(cm) high

$4,500-5,000   **H&G**

Creamware

▲1 A creamware plate, with pierced border.

c1765   8.75in (22cm) dia

▲2 A Liverpool-printed (Sadler and Green) creamware plate, probably Wedgwood, printed in black with vignettes of peafowl, some minute rim chips.

9.25in (23.5cm) dia

A Staffordshire creamware pineapple-molded coffeepot and cover, the knobs and handle re-glued, a rim chip and hairline crack.

c1765   9.25in (23.5cm) high

$1,000-1,500	WW

A creamware figure, of Whieldon type, modeled as a seated cat, painted with a streaked brown glaze, one paw glued.

3.75in (9.5cm) high

$450-500 (both)	DN

$1,300-1,500	DN

A creamware toy figure, of Whieldon type, modeled as a squirrel eating a nut, on a pad base, painted in colored glazes.

1.5in (3.5cm) high

$750-850	DN

A creamware toy figure, of Whieldon type, modeled as a frog on a pad base, painted in shades of green glaze.

1.5in (4cm) long

$750-850	DN

A mid- to late 18thC creamware plate, painted in Holland with a portrait of a man above an inscription, with feather-molded rim, some flaking to the enamels.

10in (25cm) dia

$380-420	WW

A Wedgwood creamware punch bowl, with central en grisaille transfer print of a ship and figures with "Jenny's Farewell" and "Jenny's Return" on the exterior.

11.25in (28.5cm) dia

$1,500-2,000	L&T

A creamware sugar bowl and cover, painted with a stiff leaf band, the applied entwined handles with flowerhead terminals, the cover with a flower finial.

c1780

$360-400	DN

A creamware two-handled sugar bowl and cover, Yorkshire or Staffordshire, painted with scattered floral sprigs, with applied swagged ornament, the spiral handles with floret terminals, the cover with floret finial, some small chips, large chip to finial.

c1780   5.5in (13.5cm)

$1,200-1,800	DN

A creamware two-handled sugar bowl and cover, Staffordshire or South Yorkshire, painted with sprays of flowers, cracked.

c1780

$150-200	DN

A creamware sugar box and cover, possibly Derbyshire, painted with sprays of flowers, with applied foliate twist handles with flowerhead terminals, the cover with flowerhead finial, cover cracked.

c1780

$150-200	DN

Creamware

A Wedgwood Liverpool-printed creamware dinner plate, printed in black with exotic birds, with silver-shape molded rim, unmarked. Provenance: bears label for the Williams-Wood collection.

c1760-90

$280-320 DN

A creamware plate, possibly Melbourne pottery, printed with classical ruins, within a leaf-molded border, small rim chips.

c1780 10in (25cm) dia

$400-450 DN

A creamware figural spill vase, modeled as a putto supporting a cornucopia, partially painted in colored glazes, rim chip.

c1780 7.5in (19cm) high

$550-650 DN

A Leeds creamware tea bowl and saucer, small chips.

c1785 saucer 5in (12.5cm) dia

$220-280 AD

An 18thC creamware plate, painted with four insects.

9in (23cm) dia

$80-120 WW

An 18thC Neale creamware armorial two-handled cup and cover, decorated in in black and iron-red enamels, with border designs and an armorial for Ferrier-Williams to one side, no mark.

4in (10cm) wide

$450-500 WW

An English creamware teapot, decorated with overglaze enamels, with molded spout and crab handle, damage to cover.

c1790 4.25in (10.5cm) high

$1,000-1,200 PC

A Leeds creamware mug, with sentimental motto.

c1790 2.5in (6.5cm) high

$220-280 PC

An 18thC creamware plate, painted with three insects and a fruit spray.

8in (20cm) dia

$100-150 WW

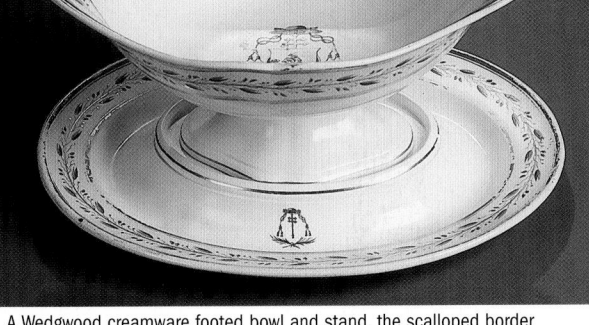

A Wedgwood creamware footed bowl and stand, the scalloped border painted with continuous wheatsheaf sprig frieze and gilt line decoration, with central painted heraldic device and the initials E e Y Fr s M Y P, on an oval stand with opposed simplified heraldic devices, gilt border and line decoration rubbed, base with chip to inner border. bowl

7in (18cm) high

$600-700 L&T

An 18thC Wedgwood creamware part dinner service, comprising two soup plates, one meat plate, large ashet and smaller ashet, each bearing the Black Watch crest, the center with painted sword, feathered hat and tartan plaid, for the Scottish regiment, the rim with painted sphinx opposing oval device with motto Nemo Me Impune Lacessit, impressed mark, chips and scratching.

soup plates 9.5in (24cm)

$1,000-1,500 (part service) L&T

A late 18thC creamware figure, modeled as a clown, possibly from the Commedia del'Arte, repaired foot.

5.75in (14.5cm) high

$300-350 DN

Creamware

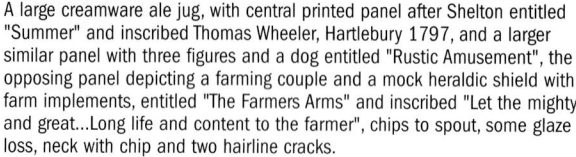

A large creamware ale jug, with central printed panel after Shelton entitled "Summer" and inscribed Thomas Wheeler, Hartlebury 1797, and a larger similar panel with three figures and a dog entitled "Rustic Amusement", the opposing panel depicting a farming couple and a mock heraldic shield with farm implements, entitled "The Farmers Arms" and inscribed "Let the mighty and great...Long life and content to the farmer", chips to spout, some glaze loss, neck with chip and two hairline cracks.

c1797   13.5in (34cm) high

$1,500-2,000   **L&T**

A creamware coffeepot and cover, painted with a figure in an Oriental garden, the domed lid with knop finial, the baluster body with entwined strap handle and reeded spout, on a circular foot.

c1800   10in (25.5cm) high

$500-550   **BonS**

An early 19thC Liverpool creamware mug, decorated with black transfer printed allegorical scene of Love and Obedience, with molded base and strap handle.

       6.25in (16cm) high

$300-350   **SI**

An early 19thC creamware basket, possibly Spode, printed with Chinese figures fishing from a boat in front of castle towers and ruins.

       9.75in (24.5cm)

$250-300   **Chef**

▶ A large Staffordshire creamware jug, transfer printed in iron-red with engravings of Admiral Nelson's ship, a lady and two children in a garden and The World in Planisphere, over-enameled with a flower border, inscribed J H Holt 1812 to the spout, and with two verses "We carpenters always prove true, both to our King and country two", and "When this you see, remember me, tho many miles we distant be", body cracked at handle join.

A rare mid-18thC Dutch Delft ware model of a slipper, painted with three flowers and a zigzag band toward the toe.

c1812   10.5in (26.5cm) high

       3.75in (9.5cm)

$2,800-3,200   **HamG**

$700-800   **WW**

A pair of mid-18thC Dutch Delft ware plates, painted with a flowering plant and fence within a floret and chain border, feathered edge rim, losses.

9in (23cm)

$225-275 (pair) | **BonS**

An 18thC Dutch Delft ware tankard, of fluted baluster form, painted with chinoiserie frieze of figures in a garden, with embossed pewter lid and thumbpiece and plain loop handle, with minor glaze losses, the handle with slight glaze rubbing.

8in (20cm)

$700-800 | **L&T**

An 18thC Dutch Delft ware dish, polychrome decorated with a bird perched on a leafy branch, rim chip, some glaze flaking.

14.5in (36.5cm)

$600-650 | **WW**

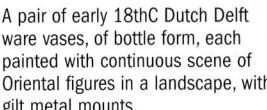

A pair of early 18thC Dutch Delft ware vases, of bottle form, each painted with continuous scene of Oriental figures in a landscape, with gilt metal mounts.

Provenance: *The Society of the Cincinnati 150-250.*

27in (67.5cm) high

$4,500-5,000 | **SI**

A Dutch Delft ware dish, boldly painted with flowering plants and fence, usual frittings.

12.25in (31cm) dia

$150-200 | **LC**

DUTCH DELFT

- Delft ware was produced from the 17thC in Holland.
- Dutch Delft is finely potted with a thick, white and sometimes pitted glaze. It is usually painted with indigo blue or bright colors.
- The body of Dutch Delft ware is usually yellow-buff in color, with a sandy, gritty texture that resembles sand or brick.
- Air bubbles trapped in the glaze often causes "peppering" or discoloured spots pitting the surface of the glaze. This is never found in English delftware.

A pair of 18thC Dutch Delft ware bowls, each depicting three musicians in a pastoral scene, the deep border with naturalistic floral sprays, one with repaired rim chip forming hairline and another hairline, minor rim fritting, slight crazing to central panel, the other similar but with one hairline to rim.

13.5in (34.5cm) dia

$700-800 (pair) | **L&T**

A Dutch Delft ware saucer dish, with painted chinoiserie decoration of an island scene, usual chippings.

9in (23cm) dia

$250-300 | **LC**

A 19thC Dutch Delft ware vase, of flattened baluster form, with molded C-scroll cartouche enclosing a painted view of a village with clock tower, damaged.

9.5in (24cm) high

$200-250 | **BonS**

A 19thC Dutch Delft ware oval box, the hinged lid painted with lovers beneath a tree, the sides with flowers and foliage, marked HL.S.

3.75in (9.5cm)

$220-280 | **WW**

A mid-19thC Dutch Delft ware trencher salt, the shaped oval sectioned sides and the well painted with flowers, blue lined rim.

3.5in (9cm) wide

$300-350 | **Chef**

A 19thC Dutch Delft ware tile picture of a clock, in rococo style, decorated in manganese and orchre glazes on a white ground, the twelve tiles mounted on a wood backing covered with plaster.

20.75in (54cm) high

$650-750 | **SI**

A late 19thC Dutch Delft ware vase, mounted as a lamp.

15in (38cm) high

$450-500 | **SI**

A rare early English delftware armorial plate, painted in blue, yellow and ocher with the initial letters P, M & A, dated, broken into eight pieces and riveted.

c.f. Lipski & Archer, Dated English Delftware, No. 101 for a molded dish with these arms, initial and this date in the British Museum. The arms may be those of the Makers of Playing Cards or Pasteboard Makers.

1653   9in (22.5cm) dia

$16,000-18,000	WW

ENGLISH DELFT

- English delftware is thicker and less finely potted than Dutch Delftware. The glaze is often tinged slightly blue or occasionally pink.
- The colors are more muted than those on Dutch Delft. The colors sink into the surface because the tin-glaze is absorbent. English delftware potters often used a soft blue, sage green and red. The red tends not to sink into the glaze but stands prominent. However the majority of delftware is blue and white and painted in Chinese style.
- English delftware tends to have a pinkish tinge unlike the much whiter Delft.
- The foot-rim on delftware tends to be thinner with a flare.
- It is highly unusual to find undamaged delftware as these wares were intended to be used. If a piece is smooth and unchipped it may be a fake.
- Wares include large dishes or chargers, plates, mugs, puzzle jugs, punch-bowls and commemorative wares.

A Bristol delftware "Farmyard" plate, painted in shades of iron-red, ocher and blue with a peacock between sponged trees, small rim chips, some with old restoration.

c1730   9in (23cm) dia

$4,000-4,500	DN

An English delftware posset pot and domed cover, London or Bristol, painted with peafowl amongst flowering plants, loop handles, restored, replacement sections.

c1730   9.25in (23.5cm) high

$2,300-2,800	DN

A Liverpool delftware plate, with painted chinoiserie decoration of two Oriental figures seated on rockwork beneath a tree, the border with sprigs of flowering shrubs, the reverse with initials ST and dated, repaired section.

1737   8.75in (22cm) dia

$900-1,000	DN

A mid-18thC English delftware plate, painted with a stylized floral sprig within a leaf lappet border, some rim chips.

9in (23cm) dia

$100-150	DN

An 18thC delftware dish, probably Bristol, painted in blue, green and iron-red with stylized leaves and flowers, blue line rim.

13.75in (35cm)

$650-750	WW

Two mid-18thC English delftware square tiles, transfer printed in black, one with five figures drinking and smoking pipes, the other with a man riding on another man's back with a windmill beyond.

5in (12.5cm) wide

$450-550	WW

An unusual 18thC English delftware dish, painted with a peacock between sponged trees with five geese flying over, the border with a geometric pattern, riveted crack.

12in (30.5cm)

$850-950 WW

A mid-18thC English delftware ewer, of ovoid form, painted with stylized flowers, with applied loop handle, small rim chips.

5in (12.5cm) wide

$400-450 DN

A mid-18thC English delftware slop bowl, painted with scrolling foliage, hairline crack.

7in (17.5cm) dia

$150-200 DN

An English delftware punch bowl, possibly Bristol, with painted chinoiserie decoration of stylized flowers, insects and lappets, the interior with a floral spray, some small rim chips.

c1760 10in (25.5cm) dia

$850-950 DN

A Liverpool delftware plate, painted with a jumping Chinese boy, marked 3. Provenance: From the Louis Lipski collection, No. 102.

c1760 9.25in (23.5cm)

$750-850 PC

An English delftware flower brick, possibly London, the sides painted with a band of meandering foliage, the pierced top section with all-over pattern, cracked.

c1760 5in (12.5cm) long

$500-550 DN

An English delftware soup bowl, possibly Liverpool, painted in the Fazackerly style with sprays of flowers, two restored rim chips.

c1760 9in (23cm) dia

$1,000-1,500 DN

A Liverpool delftware plate, painted with a vignette of a keep by a lake in a parkland setting, rim chips.

c1760 8.5in (21.5cm) dia

$450-500 DN

► An English delftware plate, probably Liverpool, painted with a Chinese figure seated beside a house, within a stylized foliate border and iron-red rim, minor overpainted rim chips.

c1760 8.75in (22cm) dia

$550-600 DN

◄ An English delftware charger, probably London, with painted chinoiserie decoration of a stylized fence section issuing sprays of flowers, within a similar foliate border, minor rim chips.

c1760 13.5in (34cm) dia

$750-800 DN

A Bristol delftware plate, painted in the Chinese style with a landscape, chips to rim. Provenance: From the Louis Lipski collection, No. 737.

c1765 9in (22.5cm) dia

$300-350 PC

A London delftware punch bowl, painted in shades of blue, green, ocher and red with a band of flowers pendant from the rim, restored rim chips.

c1770   9.25in (23.5cm) dia

$400-450   **DN**

► An English delftware blue charger, possibly Liverpool, with painted chinoiserie decoration of a figure and houses in an Oriental landscape, within a diaper band border with panels of leaves, brown-line rim, small rim chips.

12in (30cm) dia

$300-350   **DN**

A Liverpool delftware plate, painted with a vignette of a keep by a lake in a parkland setting, rim chips.

c1760   8.5in (21.5cm) dia

$450-500   **DN**

A set of eight late 18thC French faience plates, possibly Moustiers, each painted with central stylized acorn and leaf spray, with continuous scroll, the swag border hung with garlands of fruit, the back of each with blue printed initials D D S, with two matching oval ashets and two stands.

c1790

$1,000-1,500 (12 pieces)   **L&T**

A faience dish, the central boss painted with a half-length figure of a man with a halberd, damaged.

c1810   14in (36cm) dia

$180-220   **LC**

A 19thC French faience Imari charger, the rim decorated with panels of lions and birds.

16in (40.5cm)

$150-200   **GorL**

A late 19thC French faience inkwell, of concave square shape, the lid and sides painted with swags of flowers, on scroll feet.

4.25in (10.5cm)

$50-80   **Chef**

◄ A late 19thC faience Toby jug, modeled as a gallant, dressed in finery and resting upon a rococo-style bench, losses, cracks.

13.5in (34cm) high

$2,500-3,000   **SI**

An unusual Italian Castelli maiolica socketed saucer, signed by Carmine Gentile (1678-1763), probably dating from 2nd decade of the 18thC, painted on the broad rim with views of a shore with ships and figures, the outer and inner rim edged with thin bands in brown and orange, the reverse inscribed "GENTILI.P", attached torn label "T G and Co", rim cracked in two sections and rivited (on the reverse).

Signed pieces by this decorator (who nevertheless worked at Castelli over a long period) are rare. A signed roundel dated 1716 in the FitzWilliam Museum, Cambridge is almost identical to this piece in size and style of decoration. This saucer was probably also copied from a print by the engraver Gabriel Perelle (1603-1677). Other Castelli saucers of this shape are known, mostly attributed to CA Brue. They may have been the inspiration when this shape of saucer was first introduced in porcelain in France at Sèvres in 1759, and described as "soucoupes enfonces".

7in (17.8cm) dia

$1,000-1,200   **L&T**

Maiolica

An 18thC Castelli maiolica rectangular plaque, painted with Christ, the Virgin Mary and John the Baptist, a few minor rim chips.

The Castelli potteries were a group of factories that grew up near Teramo, in the former kingdom of Naples, in the 17thC and 18thC. They were famous for their istoriato wares, which were inspired by religious and mythological prints after Baroque artists. Their products are distinct from other Italian makers of maiolica as they used lighter, more subtle colors, including a pale gray-blue, buff, brown and olive-green.

10.75in (27cm) wide

$850-950   **WW**

An 18thC Italian maiolica tin glazed albarello, with narrow flared neck above bellied frieze painted with blue scrolls, similar footed base with central frieze painted in dark puce latters, "El diaraidolir", neck with chips, chips and crazing to the foot and lower body.

7.75in (19.5cm)

$450-550   **L&T**

A 19thC Italian maiolica vase, the ovoid body painted with a fishing scene and figures with guns approaching a village, with double loop handles, dated to the reverse.

21in (53.5cm) high

$750-800   **Chef**

An Italian maiolica two-handled drug jar, in the Venetian style, inscribed DIALACCADIMES within a scroll cartouche and reserved on a typical foliate ground, large foot rim chip, other small chips to leading edges.

9in (23cm) high

$500-550   **DN**

A Cantagalli maiolica basin, of shell-shaped form with a dolphin handle, painted in the Urbino style with grotteschi of animals and scrolling foliage, painted black cockerel mark, handle broken off and re-glued.

c1900   14.25in (36cm) wide

$850-950   **DN**

A 19thC Italian maiolica vase, of ovoid body and trumpet neck, decorated in Deruta style, with mirror-shaped reserves of putti desporting on an ornate dolphin, or with a bird, the grotesque serpent handles with mask terminals, typical colors, damage and staple repairs to foot.

21.75in (55cm) high

$400-450   **BonS**

A mid-to late 19thC Cantagalli maiolica ewer, painted in the istoriato style with five warriors to one side and a castle to the reverse, painted cockerel mark.

Istoriato (Italian: "story-painted") refers to a painting which tells a story, usually historical, mythological, allegorical or biblical, and is often found on Italian maiolica. It was popularized in the early 16th century, and the style was later copied by other Italian potters, notably Ulisse Cantagalli (1839-1901).

11.5in (28.5cm)

$450-550   **WW**

Three Portuguese majolica Palissy-style vases, each of ovoid form with crimped rim, molded in relief with insects, supported on a foliate stem and dome foot, each impressed T.S, one with a small restored chip and losses.

c1900   4.5in (11cm) high

$220-280   **DN**

Pearlware

▲**1** A pearlware plate, molded in relief with a bird with outstretched wings, crazing.

4in (10cm) wide

▲**2** A creamware toy model of a jelly on a plate, spirally molded and painted with brown-glazed spots, cracked and stained.

c1770   2.75in (7cm) wide

$300-350 (both)	DN

A late 18thC pearlware jug, printed in black to one side with a girl entitled Market Lass, the reverse with three figures in conversation beneath a tree, a faint hairline crack and rim chip.

5.5in (14cm)

$120-180	WW

A pearlware platter, decorated with a Chinese figure before a landscape with pagoda.

c1790   16.5in (41.5cm) wide

$650-750	AD

A pair of pearlware figures, modeled as a ewe and a ram, each with textured coat and standing on hollow grassy base, ram repaired to back leg, ewe with chip to one ear.

4.5in (11cm)

$1,000-1,500	BonE

A pearlware Ralph Wood style figure group, "Roman Charity", modeled as a woman with a child in her arms, a child and old man flanking left and right, the man chained to a rock impressed title.

c1790   7.5in (19cm) high

$550-650	DN

An English pearlware sparrow-beak jug.

c1800   2.75in (7cm) high

$350-400	AD

A pearlware group, "The Dame School", modeled as the seated pedagogue, together with four charges, set in a brick arched bower of fruiting vine, some damage.

6.25in (16cm) high

$3,000-3,500	LC

A pearlware "Macaroni Figures" tea canister and cover, typically molded with a caricature of a gentleman and his servant and a lady and her attendant, painted in Pratt-type colors, small firing crack to neck, finial restored.

c1800   6in (15cm) high

$600-700	DN

A pearlware figure, "Age", modeled as an old woman wearing a cape, a stick in one hand, a basket in the other, standing on a square plinth.

c1820   8in (20.5cm) high

$200-250	BonS

Two pearlware mugs, painted in enamels with sprays of summer flowers flanking iron-red monograms, blue line rim, dash decoration to the loop handles, each dated to base.

1823   3.25in (8cm)

$1,000-1,500	BonS

A pearlware honeypot and cover, modeled as a straw hive.

5in (12.5cm) dia

$220-280	LC

Pearlware

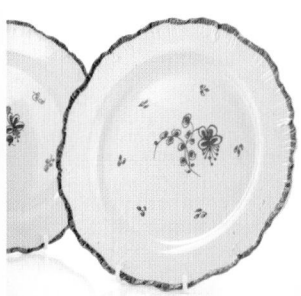

A pair of pearlware plates, with blue and white feather edge.

10in (25cm) dia

$300-350   AD

A pair of Masons Cambrian Argus pearlware plates, painted with sprigs and sprays of flowers, the rim with molded with swags of flowers, impressed marks.

8.25in (21cm) dia

$140-200   Chef

▶ A 19thC pearlware puzzle jug, of squat baluster form, painted with summer flowers and WH monogram, the pierced neck with three applied griffin head spouts and hollow strap handle, chip to foot.

6.25in (15.5cm)

$500-600   BonS

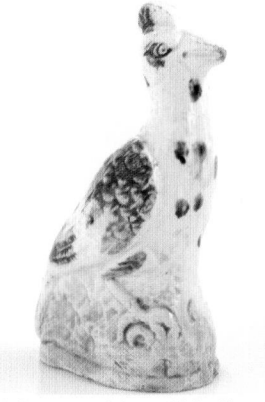

A Prattware miniature bird, with minute chip.

c1790   3.25in (8cm) high

$500-600   AD

A Prattware-style Military Review jug, molded with cavalrymen and artillerymen beside a cannon, painted in a typical palette, minor foot rim chips.

c1790   7in (18cm) high

$1,300-1,500   DN

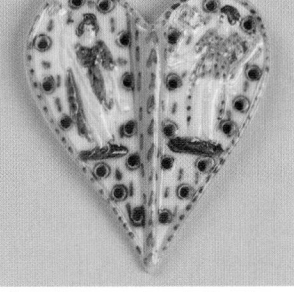

A rare Prattware plume holder, of heart shape with central tapered cylindrical spine, flanked by allegorical figures with pierced holes.

c1800   3.5in (9cm) high

$1,000-1,500   L&T

A Prattware tripod spill holder, modeled as a figure group, depicting three musical putti around central flower, on turned column and circular plinth, one figure with minor toe chips.

c1810   4.75in (12cm)

$650-750   L&T

◀ A Prattware Bacchus mug, with hairline crack.

c1810   4.5in (11cm) high

$300-350   AD

▶ A small Prattware mug, modeled as a satyr's head, with plain loop handle, hairline crack extending from rim to mid-ear.

c1810   3.25in (8cm)

$400-450   L&T

A Toby jug, in the manner of Ralph Wood.

c1780-90   10in (25cm) high

$1,500-2,000   Gro

An Toby jug and lid, in the manner of Ralph Wood, the hat and lid with sponge-painted decoration, with caryatid cast handle, restored breaks to spout and part of rim, some damage to body and plinth.

10in (25cm) high

$950-1,250   L&T

A small Prattware Toby jug.

c1800   7in (17.5cm) high

| $1,200-1,800 | Gro |

A Prattware-type Toby jug, modeled as a seated toper, some damage.

7.5cm (19cm) high

| $180-220 | LC |

◄ A 19thC English salt-glazed relief-molded Toby jug, depicting Admiral Nelson, bearing inscribed medals, one with Nile 1798, the circular plinth inscribed Trafalgar 1805.

1805   11.75in (29.5cm) high

| $550-650 | L&T |

An American salt-glazed teapot, of shaped oval form molded with paneled sides, one side with a central relief of a putto riding an eagle on a cloud, the other with the arms of America, below a scalloped edge and hinged domed cover, the panel edges, rims and handle picked out with blue borders. Loss to part of cloud relief, chip to end of spout.

c1790   5.5in (13.9cm) high

| $300-400 | FRE |

A rare mid-late18thC English slipware model of a mansion, probably intended as a nightlight.

6.5in (16.5cm)

| $3,000-3,500 | WW |

An English earthenware child's part tea set, comprising of a teapot, a two-handled sucrier and cover, a waste bowl and four cups and saucers, printed with chinoiserie figurative scenes, within flower and scroll borders, teapot chipped to spout, two cups chipped, one saucer cracked.

c1835-40   7in (17cm) high

| $220-280 | HamG |

A Whieldon ware domino tea caddy.

4.75in (12cm) high

| $1,000-1,500 | LC |

A German stove tile, of square shape, molded in low relief with acanthus foliage around a central boss, the corners with floret set bosses, minor glaze chips.

8.25in (21cm) square

| $120-180 | LC |

► A19thC pottery head-and-shoulder bust of Napoleon.

11.5in (29cm) high

| $1,000-1,500 | L&T |

Ironstone

IRONSTONE

MASON'S PATENT IRONSTONE

Mason's Patent Ironstone China was made at the Staffordshire factory of Charles James Mason (1791-1856) from 1813. The wares produced ranged from dinner plates to chimney pieces, and were often decorated in rich, bright colors in the Japanese style. Wares are marked MASON, or MASON'S PATENT IRONSTONE CHINA or MASON'S CAMBRIAN ARGIL, impressed or printed in blue.

Although small, this piece reached a high price at auction because the shape is rare. It is also in good condition, apart from some slight rubbing to the gilt, the pattern is well-defined and the colors are fresh and bright.

An Ironstone part dinner service, comprising an ashet, a tureen stand, ten meat plates, eight fish plates, four side plates, four soup plates and five dessert plates, each with printed and clobbered Imari decoration, depicting a pavilion landscape, pattern no 212, puce printed mark "Red ron stone china",

$1,800-2,200 (part service) L&T

Ironstone is a heavy, dense, grayish-white ware.

This piece is decorated in the typical Imari pattern

The thickly applied cobalt blue underglaze gives a deep, rich color

The lighter, more patchy blue was created by thinly applying the underglaze in a wash

The wares were mass-produced and the blue was often applied too quickly, which resulted in dribbling and blurring.

A Mason's Patent Ironstone China card rack, painted in Imari colors with a Japan pattern of rockwork and peonies, the rims molded with foliate scrolls terminating in scrolled corners, with lustrous ocher glaze, wear to gilding.

c1820   5in (13cm)

$1,500-2,000   **BonS**

A pair of Mason's Ironstone pottery plates.

c1820   9.5in (24cm) dia

$450-500 (pair)   **SA**

A pair of early 19thC Ironstone vases and covers, possibly Masons, decorated in all-over pattern of birds and flowers, with ball knop and wolf masks, some restoration.

22in (56cm)

$7,000-8,000 (pair)   **GorL**

A pair of Mason's Patent Ironstone China vases, of ovoid form, painted in Imari colors with a Japan pattern of rockwork and peonies, the applied shell-topped loop handles with leaf terminals, circular impressed mark, wear to gilding.

c1815   4.5in (11.5cm)

$600-700   **BonS**

A pair of Mason's Patent Ironstone China cylindrical spill vases, circular impressed mark.

c1815   5.25in (13cm)

$450-500   **BonS**

Ironstone

A Masons Patent Ironstone China part dinner service, comprising large soup tureen and cover, three smaller tureens and covers, six meat plates, a bowl, a drainer, two sauce tureens and covers, two sauceboats, twenty-four dinner plates, ten soup plates and three side plates, each printed in blue with the Indian Grasshopper pattern and decorated with polychrome hand coloring, all with early blue printed mark without crown and patent ironstone china warranted marks, staple repairs, minor chips.

c1820   dinner plate 10in (25cm) dia

$6,500-7,000 (part service)	BonS

◄ A Mason's Ironstone plate, printed with figures walking beneath a Gothic building, printed marks.

10in (25.5cm)

$80-120	WW

LUSTERWARE

► An early 19thC commemorative lusterware jug, relief-molded with General Hill and Lord Wellington between flags, each with an impressed title, chip and hairline crack.

5.25in (13cm)

$120-180	WW

LUSTERWARE

● The commercial production of luster pottery started in Sunderland, England, in 1805.

● The effect was first used in the Middle East around the 7thC and was perfected in Spain in the 15thC.

● Lusterwares became a huge export market for Britain and so potteries at ports flourished; the main centers were Sunderland, Newcastle and Hull but the technique spread to many British factories.

● Oxides of silver, gold, platinum or copper are dissolved in acid, mixed with an oily medium and painted onto the glazed ground. The the ware is fired to produce a metallic or iridescent surface.

● When buying, condition is important. White small chips are acceptable but cracks are less so. Good enamel decoration is another plus.

● Marks are rare as most potters sold through retailers and warehouses who did not want their customers to buy direct, and so discouraged marking.

● English colors include yellow (silver), ruby (gold), silver (platinum), and red to pinkish copper.

An early 19thC Sunderland pink luster jug, printed and painted with verses either side of the handle, and with the iron bridge below the spout.

9in (23cm) high

$150-200	Chef

◄ An early 19thC copper luster jug, possibly made for a Royal occasion, printed and overpainted with a crown scepter and sword below the spout and flanked by figures on one side and objects on the other, both representing the world.

6in (15cm) high

$200-250	Chef

◄ A copper and pink luster jug, with the initials MR, dated.

1830   6in (15cm) high

$200-250	Chef

Lustreware

A Dixon Austin & Co creamware water jug, in armorial pink and Sunderland luster, inscribed Edwd & Elizth Feltham, Bakers Arms Breamore, and printed with a view of the Sunderland iron bridge, some damage.

Dixon, Austen & Co *(1800-1865) was the most important of all the Sunderland potteries. The factory specialized in jugs and bowls decorated in pink marbled luster, often depicting local views. Sunderland wares are usually impressed with the name of the factory.*

	9in (23cm)
$150-200	GorL

An early 19thC luster mug, one side printed and painted with The Mariner Arms, the other with The Sailor's Farewell.

	5in (13cm) high
$80-120	Chef

A splashed pink luster plaque, with transfer print of three masted ship, copper luster border.

c1860-80	8.75in (22cm) wide
$120-180	PC

A late 19thC gold luster jug, with stylized floral decoration to brown banded body, with trumpet foot.

	8in (20.5cm)
$70-100	GorB

A Grays pottery blue luster cream jug, one side printed with a poem by Sir Philip Sidney, damaged.

	4in (10cm) high
$20-30	AS&S

▶ A 19thC Davenport Sunderland luster part tea and coffee service, comprising twelve teacups and saucers, a teapot and cover and a matched cream jug, each printed in black with the Durham pattern, with a man fishing and a woman and child before a river view of the city of Durham, washed in a pink luster glaze; black printed pattern name within a foliate cartouche above DAVENPORT, slight damage.

$1,000-1,500 (part service)	BonS

◀ A silver luster candy box and cover, made in Stoke on Trent.

c1900	4in (10cm) wide
$40-60	PC

▶ A large First Period Belleek two-handled luster basket, with three strand base, the lattice border applied with roses, dandelion buds, shamrocks and a pair of thorny stem handles, applied strap impressed Belleek Co Fermanagh, one handle possibly re-stuck, one leaf lacking,

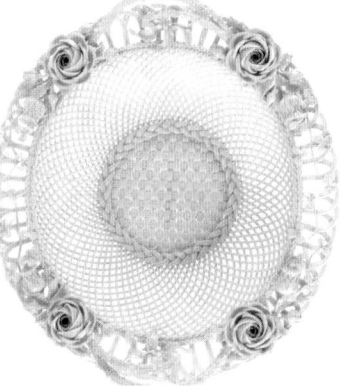

	11.5in (29cm) wide
$450-500	HamG

Staffordshire

STAFFORDSHIRE

For centuries, the five towns of the English Staffordshire Potteries – Stoke, Burslem, Hanley, Longton and Tunstall - were the heart of British ceramic production. Early wares were simple, functional household items such as drinking vessels, jugs and bottles. The first notable decorative pottery to be produced in Staffordshire was the slip-decorated earthenware of Thomas Toft (d.1689), whose name appears on pieces dating from 1680 to 1690. As the potteries expanded, the variety and quality of the wares increased. Thomas Whieldon (1719-95) is among the most revered of all the early potters. His small factory at Little Fenton produced colorful tea and coffee pots, toys and chimney ornaments.

From the end of the 18th century and throughout the 19th century, huge quantities of decorative Staffordshire figures were made. During the 19th century there were 1,000 firms working in the region, including the great potting families of Wedgwood, Spode and Ridgway, and countless others whose names have been lost over the years. It can be very difficult to attribute Staffordshire pottery to specific makers as much of it is unmarked.

A good quality pair of Staffordshire figures, modeled as Bacchus and Venus, Bacchus re-attached and cup restored.

c1790   9in (23cm) high

$2,500-3,000   AD

A Staffordshire pearlware figure, modeled as Andromache, standing beside an urn and weeping over the ashes of Hector, raised on a rectangular base, one thumb lacking, slight flaking to enamel.

c1800   9.5in (24cm) high

$280-320   WW

A Staffordshire figure, modeled as a bagpiper, mouthpiece restored.

c1800   8.75in (22cm) high

$850-900   AD

A Staffordshire pottery figure, modeled as Iphegenia, minor chips.

c1810   8in (20cm) high

$1,000-1,500   AD

A Staffordshire pottery figure, modeled as a himney sweep, perfect condition.

c1810   6.75in (17.5cm) high

$600-700   AD

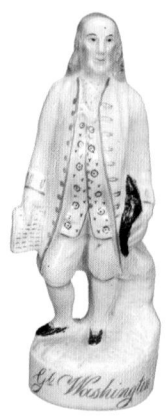

An early 19thC Staffordshire porcelain figure, modeled as Benjamin Franklin, the figure is misidentified as G. Washington in gold script.

10in (25.5cm) high

$850-950   SI

A Staffordshire pottery figure, modeled as a maid at a well, with distinctive combed paint effect.

c1820   6.25in (16cm) high

$1,000-1,500   PC

A good quality Staffordshire figure, modeled as a girl with a guitar, repair to arm and part of guitar.

c1840   5.25in (13cm) high

$350-400   AD

Staffordshire

A pair of Staffordshire porcelain groups, each modeled as a lady with a male attendant, on pierced scroll bases, some repairs.

c1840   8in (20cm) high

$140-200   **WW**

STAFFORDSHIRE FIGURES

- Ceramic portrait figures were popular from the 18thC and throughout the 19thC.
- Subjects include pastoral and romantic scenes, statesmen, politicians, actors, sportsmen, criminals, soldiers and sailors, preachers and animals.
- Many of the figures were "flatbacks" designed to stand on the mantelshelf, these are highly collectable
- Pairs will always be more valuable than a single piece
- Staffordshire figures have been frequently copied, faked and reproduced
- Be aware of the original range of colors used by the manufacturers, as modern copies tend to be paler and less detailed than the originals.
- Fakes will sometimes have a network of cracks over the surface to make them look old, but the effect is often over-emphasized
- Fake figures are made using a pure white porcelain which has been stained to imitate age, and do not have earthenware bodies.
- Very few Staffordshire figures are marked.

A Staffordshire figure, modeled as a shepherdess, slight staining.

c1840-45   4in (10cm)

$300-350   **AD**

A pair of Staffordshire quill holder groups, modeled as a man and a woman, he with a dog, she with a lamb, he with both hands and dog's paw restored, chip to hat, she with chips to hands, neck, foot and nose.

c1840

$650-750   **AD**

A pair of 19thC Staffordshire figural spill vase groups, each modeled as a seated figure and a donkey before a tree, a few tiny chips.

9in (23cm) high

$550-650   **WW**

A pair of Staffordshire porcellanous figures, modeled as a milkmaid and a cowherd, each standing beside a cow, on oval bases molded with meadow and stream, the cows dappled in iron red-orange, gilded highlights, some damage.

6.5in (16.5cm) high

$300-350   **BonS**

A Staffordshire double figure group, modeled as a man and woman holding hands, he with his arm around her waist.

c1845   7in (18cm) high

$400-450   **AD**

A Staffordshire figure, modeled as a boy with a poodle, nose chip restored.

c1845   6.25in (16cm) high

$250-350   **AD**

A Staffordshire Wellington jug, small restored chip to rim.

c1845-50   6.5in (16.5cm) high

$300-400   **AD**

A Staffordshire figure, modeled as Louis Phillipe, slight flaking.

c1845-50   9in (22.5cm) high

$400-450   **AD**

Staffordshire

A 19thC Staffordshire portrait bust of Shakespeare.

8.5in (21.5cm) high

$250-300   Clv

A 19thC Staffordshire figure of Shakespeare, leaning on a pillar with books.

18.5in (47cm) high

$300-350   Clv

A 19thC Staffordshire spill vase, modeled as a horse standing before a tree and a recumbent foal, on an oval base.

11.25in (28.5cm) high

$450-500   WW

A mid-19thC Staffordshire figure, modeled as a lady, standing on a rocky base applied with moss.

8.5in (21.5cm) high

$60-80   WW

A pair of mid-19thC Staffordshire flatback figures, modeled as a boy and girl riding horses.

7.75in (19.5cm) high

$300-350   WW

A 19thC Staffordshire equestrian model of the Prince of Wales, the green and brown base applied with moss, hairline cracks to the base.

10.75in (27cm) high

$200-250   WW

A mid-19thC Staffordshire tobacco jar and cover, modeled as a seated man, some restoration.

8in (20cm) high

$300-350   WW

A pair of mid-19thC Staffordshire figures, one modeled as a man wearing a turban and holding a colorful bird, the other as a sailor boy.

8in (20.5cm) high

$220-280   WW

A 19thC Staffordshire figure, modeled as a girl riding a donkey, on a rocky base applied with moss.

8.25in (21cm) high

$250-300   WW

A 19thC Staffordshire jar and cover, modeled as a black shoeshine boy.

11in (28cm) high

$750-850   WW

A Staffordshire spill holder, modeled as a man and his dog, crack to base.

c1850   6in (15cm) high

$350-400   AD

Staffordshire

A Staffordshire miniature figure, modeled as a man seated on a chair, slight loss of color.

c1850-60   3.25in (8cm) high

$100-150   **AD**

A Staffordshire watch stand, modeled as three women in colorful dress, perfect condition.

c1850-60   11in (28cm) high

$300-350   **AD**

A 19thC Staffordshire figure, modeled as Uncle Tom and Eva, the base inscribed "Eva gaily laughing was hanging a wreath of roses round Tom's neck", slight flaking, Eva's hand reglued.

8.25in (21cm) high

$150-200   **WW**

A mid-19thC Staffordshire figure, modeled as Androcles and the Lion, the rockwork base applied with moss.

10.25in (26cm) high

$300-350   **WW**

A mid-19thC Staffordshire flatback figure group of the orange sellers, modeled as a man and woman each with a basket of oranges, titled to the base.

13.75in (35cm) high

$280-320   **WW**

A 19thC Staffordshire equestrian group, some damage.

8.25in (21cm) high

$120-180   **WW**

A 19thC large Staffordshire figure, modeled as the Prince of Wales, titled in gilt, rubbing to gilt.

17.75in (45cm) high

$350-400   **WW**

A 19thC Staffordshire equestrian group, modeled as King William III on his horse, titled in gilt, rubbing to gilt.

10.25in (26cm) high

$100-150   **WW**

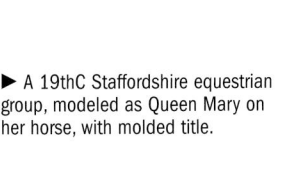

▶ A 19thC Staffordshire equestrian group, modeled as Queen Mary on her horse, with molded title.

10.25in (26cm) high

$100-150   **WW**

◀ A 19thC Staffordshire clock group, modeled as a girl and boy flanking a bridge, with a swan beneath.

8in (20cm) high

$100-150   **Chef**

89

Staffordshire

A Staffordshire figure group, modeled as a girl and boy with deer, she with repair to neck.

c1860   6.75in (17cm) high

$150-200   **AD**

A Staffordshire figure, modeled as Jimmy Wood.

c1860   8in (20cm) high

$400-450   **AD**

A Staffordshire figure, modeled as David Garrick as Richard III.

c1860   9.5in (24cm) high

$400-450   **AD**

A Staffordshire clock group, modeled as two girls sitting beneath a fruiting vine, with two birds.

c1860   11.5in (29cm) high

$350-400   **AD**

A Victorian Staffordshire Pottery spill vase, modeled as a seated maiden with a harp, a recumbent lamb at her feet.

13in (33cm) high

$150-200   **J&H**

A small mid-to late 19thC Staffordshire figure group, modeled as musicians, he with a lyre, she with a mandolin.

7.5in (19cm) high

$120-180   **WW**

A Victoria Staffordshire watch holder, modeled as a young man and woman, each with an exotic bird, with a keyless wind pocket watch.

10.75in (27cm) high

$200-250   **J&H**

A Victorian Staffordshire figure, modeled as a fisherman.

c1870   10in (25cm) high

$400-450   **AD**

A Victorian Staffordshire Martha Gunn jug, she stands holding glass and bottle.

9.75in (24.5cm) high

$120-180   **Chef**

▶ A pair of late 19thC large Staffordshire figures, modeled as a man and woman selling fish.

13.75in (35cm) high

$300-350   **WW**

90

Staffordshire

STAFFORDSHIRE DOGS

- Staffordshire dogs were produced from c1840 through the turn of the century, probably inspired by Queen Victoria's King Charles Spaniel, Dash.

- Also known as "Comforter Spaniels", the name deriving from the Elizabethan era when women kept spaniels in their skirts for added warmth during the winter. Another tale is that Staffordshire spaniels were sold outside drinking establishments and were bought by husbands who had spent too long in the tavern to give to their wives to comfort them.

- They were made in pairs in several sizes and with "flatbacks".

- Types include jugs, spaniels with flower baskets, and "Disraeli spaniels" after Benjamin Disraeli, the Prime Minister, with a distinctive curl on the forehead.

- Later dogs were produced with inset glass eyes.

- Colors include red and white, black and white, white with copper luster patches, white with gold highlighting and liver and white. After Prince Albert's death in 1861 all-black spaniels became popular.

A pair of Staffordshire models of pugs, restoration to one front leg.

c1840   10.75in (27cm) high

$1,000-1,500   **RdeR**

◀ A Staffordshire model of a "judge's wig" poodle, stained.

c1845   6in (15cm) high

$400-450   **AD**

A pair of 19thC Staffordshire standing Spaniel comforter dogs, with glass eyes and gilt highlights.

7.25in (18cm) high

$120-180   **Clv**

An unusual pair of Staffordshire models of King Charles spaniels, with a boy and a girl riding on their backs, the bases molded with leaves and bunches of grapes, the dogs decorated with feathered iron-red patches, probably mid-19thC, some damage.

9.5in (24cm) high

$1,000-1,500   **WW**

A Staffordshire model of a spaniel, decorated with feathered iron-red patches, slight flaking.

c1850   7.25in (18.5cm) high

$400-450   **AD**

A Staffordshire model of spaniel, decorated with feathered black patches.

c1850   6in (15cm) high

$520-580   **AD**

A Staffordshire model of a spaniel and puppy, very small chips repaired.

c1850   3.25in (8cm) high

$600-700   **AD**

A pair of 19thC Staffordshire models of spaniels, each decorated with feathered iron-red patches, with gilt details.

8.75in (22cm) high

$380-420   **WW**

Staffordshire

A pair of 19thC Staffordshire models of spaniels, each decorated with black patches, with gilt and enamel details.

10.25in (26cm) high

$300-350 WW

A mid-19thC Staffordshire porcelain model of a poodle with puppies, enhanced with coleslaw and frit chips, on a scrolling rococo-style base, with gilt details.

5.25in (13.5cm) high

$450-500 SI

A pair of Staffordshire models of poodles, each with crusty decoration, with gilt details.

c1850   7.5in (19cm) high

$600-700 RdeR

Two mid-19thC Staffordshire models of spaniels, each decorated with black patches.

13in (33cm) high

$650-750 SI

Two mid-19thC Staffordshire models of spaniels, each decorated with feathered brown patches.

8.5in (21.5cm) high

$550-600 SI

A pair of 19thC Staffordshire models of spaniels, with gilt highlights, some wear.

12.5in (32cm) high

$550-600 SI

A pair of Staffordshire models of spaniels, some restoration, hairline crack on back.

c1860   **11in (28cm) high**

$650-750 RdeR

A pair of Staffordshire models of spaniels, each decorated with black patches, with gilt details.

c1860   10.25in (26cm) high

$400-450 RdeR

A pair of Staffordshire models of spaniels, with blue eyes.

c1860   10in (25cm) high

$600-700 RdeR

A Staffordshire model of a spaniel and puppy, the dog decorated with feathered iron-red patches, the puppy with black patches, on a blue cushion base.

c1870   6.25in (16cm) high

$350-400 AD

A pair of Staffordshire jugs, modeled as spaniels, each decorated with feathered iron-red patches, with molded fruit and leaf decoration to the rim.

c1860   10.25in (26cm) high

$650-750 RdeR

A pair of mid-Victorian Staffordshire models of King Charles spaniels, each decorated with copper luster patches, with gilt padlocked collars and chains.

12.5in (32cm) high

$400-450 Chef

A pair of large Staffordshire models of spaniels, each decorated with yellow spots, with gilt details.

c1870   13in (33cm) high

$400-450 RdeR

A small pair of mid-to late 19thC Staffordshire models of poodles, the ears, shoulders and tails decorated with clay chippings.

4.5in (11.5cm) high

$150-200 WW

A pair of Staffordshire models of spaniels, each decorated with feathered iron-red patches, one with damage to the base.

7.5in (19cm) high

$300--350 WW

A pair of Staffordshire models of spaniels, each decorated with feathered iron-red patches, with gilt details.

13in (33cm) high

$150-200 Chef

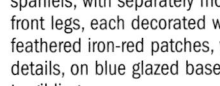

A pair of Staffordshire models of spaniels, with separately molded front legs, each decorated with feathered iron-red patches, with gilt details, on blue glazed bases, wear to gilding.

8in (20.5cm) high

$2,000-2,500 BonS

A Staffordshire figure, modeled as a seated stag, perfect condition.

c1810   7in (18cm) high

$1,000-1,500 AD

An early 19thC Staffordshire porcelain figure, modeled as a lamb, recumbent on a grassy knoll.

6.5in (16.5cm) long

$180-220 SI

A Staffordshire figure, modeled as a deer, with unusual floral bocage, ears restored.

c1825   5.5in (13.5cm) high

$750-850 AD

A Staffordshire porcelain figure, modeled as an eagle, the base with gilt highlights, stress crack.

c1840   7.5in (19cm)

$400-450 AD

A pair of Staffordshire models of spaniels, each with a paw resting on a dead bird, slight rubbing.

c1845   2.75in (7cm) high

$650-750 AD

A pair of 19thC Staffordshire figures, modeled as Zebras, one nose re-glued.

6.5in (16.5cm) high

$400-450 WW

A pair of Staffordshire pearlware figures, of Walton type, each modeled as a cow and calf, before a flowering bocage, the rockwork base with applied mosswork, one cow sponged in iron-red, the other in black, losses.

6in (15cm) high

$650-750 BonS

A mid-19thC Staffordshire figure, modeled as a zebra, standing four square on a naturalistic base.

4.75in (12cm) high

$250-300 Chef

A mid-19thC Staffordshire inkwell, modeled as a greyhound, reclining on a blue oval base with a quill holder to one side.

6.75in (17cm) long

$80-120 Chef

Staffordshire

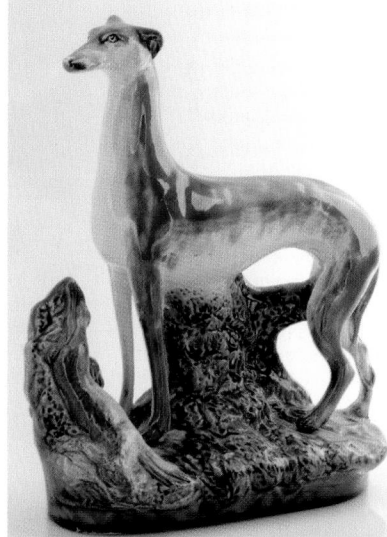

A pair of Staffordshire flatback spill vases, each modeled as a zebra, with coiled serpent about its body, standing before a tree trunk, on oval gilt line bases, one leg re-glued, losses to enamels.

8in (20cm) high

| $450-500 | BonS |

A 19thC Staffordshire figure, modeled as a zebra being attacked by a snake, standing on a shaped base.

10.75in (27cm) high

| $520-580 | BonS |

A 19thC Staffordshire figure, modeled as a standing greyhound, a hare at his feet, supported by a rocky outcrop issuing from an oval base with majolica-style glaze.

10.75in (27cm) high

| $300-350 | BonS |

A pair of Staffordshire figures, each modeled as a cow and calf, with iron-red patches, supported by a stump and standing on an oval base molded with meadow and stream, gilded highlights.

5in (12.5cm) high

| $300-350 | BonS |

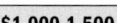 A pair of 19thC Staffordshire pottery candlesticks, each modeled as a recumbent gryphon, the bell form nozzle decorated with a Greek key motif in ocher and held between the upraised wings, the looped tails forming handles, damage and restoration.

4.5in (11.5cm) high

| $1,000-1,500 | BonS |

- Lions are an unusual subject for Staffordshire figures and this pair, surrounded by their cubs, are a very attractive subject matter.
- The moss applied to the trees and the base is typical of mid-19th century figures.
- This pair are in good condition: common damage includes chips and flaking and crazing to the glaze.
- The gilding is a rich, deep color typical of earlier Staffordshire figures and is not rubbed. Later gilding appears silvery or brassy and rubs off easily.
- The vibrancy of the colors, fine painted detail, and the crispness of the molding denote quality.

A pair of mid-19thC Staffordshire flatback figures, modeled as goats above sleeping figures of a boy and a girl, minor damage.

11in (28cm) high

| $350-400 | WW |

A Staffordshire figure, modeled as a Roc bird, a man hanging from its claws, perfect condition.

c1860   13in (33cm) high

| $850-950 | AD |

A pair of mid-19thC Staffordshire spill vase groups, each modeled as a lion and lioness and their cubs, recumbent before a knarled flowering tree entwined with a green snake.

11in (28cm) high

| $2,000-2,500 | WW |

A chalkware poodle, with paint decoration, made in Pennsylvania, repair to base.
c1840-50

$500-700 **BCAC**

A 19thC chalkware lamb and ewe, all over golden rod paint, hairline crack and minor paint loss.

$380-420 **BCAC**

A 19thC chalkware parrot, with old repair.

$220-280 **BCAC**

CHALKWARE

Chalkware was made in America from plaster of Paris, which was set in a mold then brightly painted. These pieces typically copied more expensive Staffordshire or other porcelain figures. The Staffordshire copies, which were popular from 1860-1890, were usually sold by door-to-door salesmen. In the early 20thC, chalkware was re-introduced to produce cheap carnival prizes.

A chalkware dog bank.
c1910

$180-220 **BCAC**

A pair of late 19thC Staffordshire figures, modeled as birds, the rockwork bases applied with mosswork.

9.75in (24.5cm) high

$820-880 **WW**

A Staffordshire figure, modeled as a running deer, before a tree, slight rubbing.

3.25in (8cm) high

$200-250 **AD**

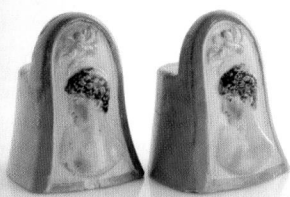

A pair of 19thC Staffordshire window stops, each relief molded with a Romanesque bust, a putto flying above, damage and restoration.

4.5in (11cm) high

$200-250 **BonS**

A rare 19thC Staffordshire sign language mug, printed in brown with the alphabet and corresponding hand signs, unmarked.

2.75in (7cm) high

$520-580 **WW**

A Staffordshire mug, with chinoiserie decoration.
c1810 3.5in (8.5cm) high

$120-180 **AD**

An early 19thC "Gaudy Welsh" Staffordshire footed bowl.

$20-30 **GorL**

An early 19thC Staffordshire "Gaudy Welsh" cream jug.

$30-50 **GorL**

An early 19thC Staffordshire "Gaudy Welsh" lidded cream jug.

$30-50 **GorL**

An early 19thC Staffordshire "Gaudy Welsh" teapot and cover.

$50-80 **GorL**

An early 19thC Staffordshire "Gaudy Welsh" cup.

$20-30 **GorL**

American Stoneware

AMERICAN STONEWARE

STONEWARE IS A NON-POROUS FORM OF POTTERY THAT WAS ORIGINALLY DEVELOPED IN CHINA DURING THE SHANG PERIOD (c1500-1028BC). It re-emerged in Germany during the Middle Ages and from there it spread to the rest of Europe. Huguenot Anthony Duche probably introduced it to America in the 1720s when he arrived in Philadelphia. In this period it seemed to be used mainly in the manufacture of chamberpots.

The non-porous property of stoneware makes it ideal for storing acidic foodstuffs such as pickled vegetables, beer and vinegar and so pieces tend to be utilitarian in design with minimal decoration. As a result pieces with even minimal decoration are more desirable.

The most prolific producers of stoneware in America were the Norton Family of Bennington, Vermont, established by Captain John Norton in 1785. Typical pieces include the "Bennington crock", covered pots, spittoons and jugs. Early examples are very plain with little decoration. In the 1850s and 60s the decoration became more elaborate with bold, usually blue, designs and pieces from this period are highly prized.

By the end of the 19thC, stoneware in America had been largely replaced by English and other functional pottery.

A Penn or Ohio three gallon ovoid jug, with blue slip bird design on one side and flower on the other side, impressed No3 mark.
c1820

$1,400-1,700　　　**BCAC**

A flower pot, probably Fulper, Flemington NJ.
c1870-1880

$300-350　　　**BCAC**

A stoneware crock, decorated with a vivid peacock on an elaborate stump.

$4,200-4,700　　　**BCAC**

A stoneware crock by Littleworth, 10th Street, with blue flower decoration, impressed mark and No 2.
c1850

$350-450　　　**BCAC**

Three New York stoneware pitchers.

$120-180 (each)　　　**BCAC**

A redware glazed storage jar.

$60-100　　　**BCAC**

A blue and white decorated stoneware pitcher.

$180-220　　　**BCAC**

A brown granite ware coffee pot.
c1893

$100-150　　　**BCAC**

A rare late 19thC redware pepperpot with manganese glaze.

$700-1,000　　　**BCAC**

A redware pitcher, incised, by Jason Medinger.

$1,200-1,900　　　**BCAC**

▲1 A Minton "Society of Arts" relief-molded jug, in light grey stoneware, molded marks including inscription, maker's initials, model number 302 and registration diamond for 26th May 1846.

7.25in (18cm) high

$100-150

▲2 A William Ridgway, Son & Co. Eglinton relief-molded jug, in light blue stoneware, impressed publication mark dated September 1st 1840.

9.5in (24cm) high

$120-180

▲3 A graduated pair of Thomas Furnival & Co. Falstaff relief-molded jugs, in blue stoneware, each in the form of a seated figure of Falstaff with one arm forming the handle, larger jug with handle glued and crack to rim. Largest

9.75in (25cm) high

$120-180

▲4 A "York Minster" relief-molded jug possibly by Charles Meigh, in white stoneware, the Britannia metal lid with thistle knop and marked T. Booth, Hanley.

8.75in (22cm) high

$150-200

▲5 An "Arabic" relief-molded jug, possibly by Samuel Alcock & Co., in white stoneware, with a Britannia metal lid, black-printed title mark only.

c1840-50   10in (25.5cm) high

$60-80

▲6 An ornate relief-molded ewer, in white stoneware, with ovoid body on a slender pedestal foot, with a narrow neck, broad leaf-molded spout and rim, and a prominent leafy-scroll handle, the body encircled by a deep applied band of grapes and vine leaves, unmarked, minor faults.

c1835-50   12.5in (32cm) high

$60-80

▲7 A Charles Meigh & Son Four Season relief-molded jug, in white stoneware, molded registration diamond for 25th August 1852.

10.25in (26cm) high

$150-200

▲8 An Apostle relief-molded jug possibly by Charles Meigh, in white stoneware, unmarked.

11.25in (28.5cm) high

$150-200   **DN**

A 19thC brown-glazed stoneware ball or toy rattle, probably Nottingham, pierced with geometric patterns within pierced band borders.

3.25in (8cm) dia

$900-1,000   **DN**

TRANSFER PRINTED POTTERY

PRINTING PROCESSES ALLOWED CERAMICS TO BE DECORATED AND MASS-PRODUCED WITHOUT THE NEED FOR SKILLED AND EXPENSIVE HAND PAINTING. Two methods developed: transfer-printing (mid-18th century), and lithographic printing (late 19th century). Transfer-printing involves inking an engraved copper plate which is then transferred either onto a sheet of paper, or a sheet ("bat") of glue (a type of transfer-printing called bat-printing). These sheets are then pressed onto the surface of the object and the design is fixed by firing.

The lithographic process involves laying a paper-backed print on the object's surface. The paper is sponged off leaving the pattern, which is formed by tiny dots.

Designs are usually in monochrome, although polychrome printing became possible as the processes improved.

▲1 A well-and-tree meat dish, possibly Richard Woolley, printed with the Ornate Pagodas pattern, unmarked.

c1810-20   20.25in (51.5cm) wide

$420-480

▲2 A meat dish, printed with the Temple with Panel, with inner and outer geometric borders, unmarked, repairs to small rim chips.

c1790-1800   18.75in (48cm) wide

$150-200

▲3 A pair of meat dishes (one shown), printed with the Long Bridge pattern, unmarked.

c1800-15   20.75in (52.5cm) wide

$450-500

▲4 A well-and-tree meat dish, printed with the Net pattern, with scenic vignettes on a sheet floral ground with a net center, unmarked.

c1810-20   18.5in (47cm) wide

$220-280

▲5 An octagonal meat dish, printed with the Two Figures pattern, with typical geometric border, unmarked except for a printed small eight-petal flower, restoration to rim.

c1790-1805   20.25in (51.5cm) wide

$150-200

▲6 A meat dish, printed with the Spotted Deer pattern , with a border of stylized flowers and geometric panels, unmarked.

c1810-20   20.75in (52.5cm) wide

$500-600   **DN**

A pearlware meat plate, printed with Gorhambry, Hertfordshire, crowned impressed mark for John Meir.

c1820   16.75in (42.5cm)

$1,000-1,500   **WW**

Two Pineapple Border Series plates, the dinner plate with Roche Abbey, Yorkshire, cracked, the tea plate with Caefilly Castle, Glamorganshire, broken and riveted, each with appropriate printed title cartouche. Provenance: Blyton Blue collection nos 34 and 55

c1820-30   dinner plate 10.25in (26cm) dia

$60-80   **DN**

A Wedgwood Blue Rose Border Series tea plate, printed with a country scene, within the usual series border, impressed mark.

c1824-35   6.5in (16.5cm) dia

$150-200   **DN**

A pearlware meat dish, printed with the Colossal Sacrcophagus near Castle Rosso, unmarked.

c1825   19in (48cm)

$1,000-1,500   **WW**

A J&W Ridgway pearlware well-and-tree platter, printed with a view of the Capitol, Washington, within a rose-leaf border, the view identified in underglaze blue, old staple repair.

Made for the American market.

c1825   20.5in (52cm) long

$1,800-2,200   **SI**

A J&W Ridgway Rural Scenery Series dessert plate, printed with a rural scene, within the usual border of flowers and hops, printed series mark with maker's initials, hairline crack. Provenance: Blyton Blue collection no. 38

c1825-30   8.25in (21cm) dia

$150-200   **DN**

A William Smith & Co bowl, printed with the Napoleon pattern, within a broad geometric floral scroll border with reserves of Napoleon Empereur, Passage du Pont de Lodi and Bataille d'Iena, printed leafy scroll mark with inscription Napoleon/J.B. Cappellemans/Aine, W. Smith & Cie./Bruxelles.

c1830-50   4.5in (11.5cm) dia

$150-200   **DN**

A Joseph Stubbs pearlware platter, printed with a view of Fairmount, near Philadelphia, within a border of eagles, scrolls and flowers, the view identified in underglaze blue.

Made for the American market.

c1830   21in (53.5cm) long

$2,000-2,500   **SI**

A cake or cheese stand, attributed to Robert May, printed with the Bird Fountain pattern, within a floral border, unmarked, fine hairline crack. Provenance: Blyton Blue collection no. 120

c1830   11.5in (29cm) dia

$80-120   **DN**

A transfer-printed and hand-painted Staffordshire platter, made by William Ridgway & Co., Hanley for the American market, printed in underglaze-black with View of the Capitol at Washington, the border with over-glaze decoration of four eagles over crossed American flags and shield, the view identified in underglaze black, impressed maker's mark, old mends.

This view was derived from American Scenery by N.P. Willis, 1840.

c1840   18.75in (47.5cm) wide

$750-850   **SI**

Two William Ridgway, Son & Co. Humphrey's Clock Series dessert plates, printed with a rural scene with Dicken's characters, within a border of scrolls and flower swags, one with printed clock cartouche with series title and maker's initials, the other with printed title only, minor chips behind one rim.

c1840-48 — largest 8.25in (20.9cm) dia

$80-120 — **DN**

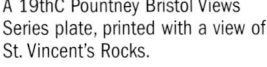

A 19thC Pountney Bristol Views Series plate, printed with a view of St. Vincent's Rocks.

10in (25.5cm) dia

$150-200 — **Clv**

A 19thC Spode pearlware plate, printed with a maid at a water pump.

9.75in (24.5cm) dia

$50-80 — **WW**

An19thC ashet, printed with a chinoiserie scene, the floral frieze with oval panel.

18.5in (47cm) wide

$350-400 — **L&T**

A meat dish, by S Barker & Son, printed with an English country scene, rare griffon mark.

1850 — 18in (46cm) wide

$120-180 — **AS&S**

An early 19thC Staffordshire serving plate, printed with the Willow Pattern, no marks except impressed 3 and 83.

17.75in (45cm)

$120-180 — **AS&S**

A Copeland and Garrett late Spode meat plate, printed with the Venice pattern.

19in (48.5cm) wide

$220-280 — **Clv**

A J Jamieson and Co, Boness scalloped ashet, printed in sepia with the Scottish National Gallery with Edinburgh Castle in the distance, impressed factory mark.

15.5in (39cm) wide

$300-350 — **L&T**

A J&W Ridgway ashet, printed with the Rural Scenery pattern, restored top left rim.

16.5in (42cm) wide

$150-200 — **L&T**

A pair of soup dishes, printed with a view of Kincardine Castle Perthshire, within an oak-leaf border, one with small chip to rim.

9.75in (24.5cm) dia

$150-200 (pair) — **BonE**

A plate, printed with a Chinese pavillion and river scenery, within continuous scene border.

9.75in (24.5cm) dia

$50-80 — **BonE**

 ◀ A small Davenport plate, printed with the Tudor Mansion pattern, within foliage border, impressed mark.

8in (20.5cm) dia

$50-80 — **BonE**

 ▶ A J&R Riley plate, printed with The Girl Musician pattern, within floral border, impressed and printed mark.

9.5in (24cm) dia

$80-120 — **BonE**

A J&W Ridgway plate, printed with Christ Church Oxford. within flower and panel border, printed mark.

10in (25.5cm) dia

$80-120 **BonE**

A plate, printed with figures and sheep in landscape, within leaf and scroll border.

10in (25.5cm) dia

$50-80 **BonE**

A plate, printed with figures in landscape, within a leaf border.

9.75in (24.5cm) dia

$30-50 **BonE**

A soup plate, printed with The Piping Boy pattern.

9.75in (25cm) dia

$80-120 **LC**

An Eastern Port pattern covered supper dish, of quadrant shaped from a set, probably Ridgway, printed in blue with the port scene and the usual border of roses, other flowers and crowns, unmarked, firing tear to rim of base, fine hair crack to cover.

c1815-25   11.75in (30cm) wide

$220-280 **DN**

A Pineapple Border Series meat dish, printed with a view of Furness Abbey, Lancashire, within the usual border of flowers and scrolls, printed title mark, cracked.
Provenance: Blyton Blue collection no. 107

c1820-30   16.75in (42.5cm) long

$100-150 **DN**

Three Staffordshire black transfer-printed plates, by Job and John Jackson, and Clews, the first a dinner plate printed in underglaze black with scalloped floral border enclosing a view of the President's house in Washington, the view identified in underglaze, together with two Clews dessert plates with molded scalloped edge, floral scroll and bird border enclosing Hudson river views of West Point and Sandy Hill.

Made for the American market. The Jackson brothers produced at least forty different American views, most derived form the 1830 publication of "The History and Topography of the United States."

c1835   largest 10.25in (26cm) dia

$550-650 **SI**

A Staffordshire transfer-printed platter, by Thomas Godwin, the scalloped rim with morning glory and nasturtium border enclosing a view of T. Godwins Wharf Baltimore, view identification and maker printed in underglaze green, imperfections.

Made for the American market. This platter shows one of the fourteen patterns in Godwin's American Views Series. The views were derived from prints published in the 1840 American Scenery by N P Willis.

c1840

$480-520 **SI**

A transfer-printed Staffordshire platter, by James and Ralph Clews, Cobridge, England, the molded scalloped border printed with scrolls, flowers and birds enclosing a view of Newbergh, Hudson River, unmarked.

Made for the American market. This scene was derived from a collection of prints published by Henry I. Megany, New York, entitled Hudson River Portfolio.

17.5in (45cm) wide

$520-580 **SI**

A pair of Spode Caramanian Series oval sauce tureen stands, printed with the Necropolis or Cemetery of Cacamo, within the usual border of Indian Sporting animals, impressed marks, one with tiny rim chip, the other with small chip beneath rim.
Provenance: Burgan collection nos 608 and 609; also previously the Amos collection nos S29 and S30

c1810-20   7.5in (19cm) wide

$650-750 **DN**

Transfer-Printed

A London shape teapot, printed with the Palladian Temple pattern, with floral border to shoulder and cover, unmarked, minor chips to spout and inner rim.

c1820-30   9.75in (25cm) long

$150-200   **DN**

A London shape teapot, printed on either side with a Gleaners pattern, a border of running flowers to the shoulder and cover, unmarked, hairline crack across handle, restoration to spout and cover.

c1820-1830   10.75in (27cm) long

$225-275   **DN**

An Enoch Wood & Sons teapot, of ornate shape, printed on either side with a scene of abbey ruins, within a cusped oval frame surrounded by flowers, the floral border with a lace ground, cover lacking, cracks to body.

c1820-30   10in (25.5cm) long

$80-120   **DN**

A teapot, with wavy-edged gallery and angular molded handle, printed on either side with a scene featuring a man with greyhounds talking to a kneeling lady gardener, with borders of prominent flowers and leaves, unmarked, crack to body, spout tip broken, other minor faults.

c1820-1830   11in (28cm) long

$120-180   **DN**

A teapot, with scroll molded spout and wavy-edge gallery, printed with the Imperial pattern, printed title on a floral scroll, body crack, minor chips.

c1830-1840   11in (28cm) long

$100-150   **DN**

A Dutch shape jug, printed with the Horn Blower pattern, beneath a border of stylized flowers, unmarked, restoration to spout and rim crack.

c1800-1810   6.75in (17cm) high

$150-200   **DN**

A Dutch shape jug, possibly by Harley of Lane End, printed with a panoramic rural scene featuring a large thatched cottage beneath a border of flowers, birds and scenic vignettes, unmarked, cracks to base and spout, chips to spout and rim.

c1805-15   5.5in (14cm) high

$100-150   **DN**

A Wedgwood Dutch shape jug, printed with the Peony pattern and with the usual stringing of idealized flowerheads, gilding to rim and sides of handle, impressed mark, chip to spout, gilding rubbed.

c1807-20   5in (12.5cm) high

$100-150   **DN**

An early 19thC pearlware jug, printed with a goldfinch among flowers, fruit and foliage, flat rim chip.

                    7in (18cm) high

$300-350   **WW**

A Swansea Dutch shape jug, printed with the Pulteney Bridge pattern beneath a floral border, unmarked, chips to spout, hairline crack to handle.

c1810-25   5in (13cm) high

$150-200   **DN**

A Dutch shape jug, with ocher edging to rim and handle, printed with a panoramic scene of a country house with long orangery, beneath a border of grapes and vine leaves, unmarked, star crack to body, hairline cracks to rim and base.

c1810-20   5.75in (14.5cm) high

$150-200   **DN**

An Opaque China Dutch shape jug, with a wavy rim and shaped strap handle, printed with the Ladies with Bird and Cage pattern, beneath a leafy flower border, printed mark Opaque China in an oval frame, rim chips.

c1815-35   4.75in (12cm) high

$120-180   **DN**

▶ A Dutch shape jug, with ocher edging to rim and handle, covered with a sheet pattern of twinning passionflowers, unmarked, cracked.

c1815-30   4.75in (12cm) high

$120-180   **DN**

▶ A Dutch shape jug, printed with the Grazing Rabbits pattern, with the usual floral border inside and out, unmarked, small rim chips.

1815-30   5in (13cm) high

$280-320   **DN**

A Clews Dutch shape jug, with molded handle and wavy-edged rim to neck, printed on either side with the Water Girl pattern, within an octagonal frame surrounded by large flowers, a similar floral border inside and outside the neck, printed crown cartouche with title and Clews Manufacturer, cracked.

c1818-1834   5.5in (14cm) high

$280-320   **DN**

A Dutch shape jug, possibly by J&W Ridgway, printed on one side with a view identified as Wanstead House in Essex, the reverse with a rustic scene of gleaners, beneath a border of roses, unmarked, small chip to top, "kick" on handle.

c1820-30   5.5in (14cm) high

$150-200   **DN**

A jug, printed with the Sheep Shearer pattern, beneath a floral scroll border, unmarked.

c1820-35   6.25in (15.5cm) high

$650-750   **DN**

A monumental presentation or exhibition pitcher, of baluster form on a molded circular foot, with C-scroll handles, printed with sprays of exotic animals and flowers and Oriental scenes of exotic buildings, old mends, repairs.

Made for the American market. The pattern is identified in underglaze-blue as Chinese Marine/Opaque China. According to family tradition, this pitcher was brought to the United States before World War II for safe-keeping.

c1830   26.5in (67.5cm) high

$3,500-4,000   **SI**

A jug, attributed to William Copestake junior, of ornate bulbous shape with molded handle and spout, gadrooning around the shoulder and rim, printed with the Oriental pattern, depicting a Middle Eastern-style romantic scene, printed scroll cartouche with title, maker's initials W.C. Jr, L.P, tiny chips to rim and foot.

c1835-50   7.25in (18.5cm) high

$220-280   **DN**

An octagonal jug, with molded angular scroll handle, each face printed with a different figure in Chinese costume, the neck with a border of a butterfly catcher in scroll reserves, unmarked.

c1835-50   6.75in (17cm) high

$150-200   **DN**

A John Meir & Son Northern Scenery Series Dutch shape jug, printed with a view of Dunolly Castle, near Oban, with the usual border of flowers and scrolls inside and outside the rim, printed pseudo-arms marks, titles and maker's initials, rim chip.

c1836-50   4.75in (12cm) high

$200-250   **DN**

A Victorian Brownfield & Sons water jug, printed with scene of dogs hunting.

12in (30.5cm)

$80-120   **GorL**

An early tankard and a custard cup, the tankard of silver baluster shape with ornate scroll-molded handle, printed outside with the Buffalo pattern and with a chinoiserie-type border featuring swans around the inner rim, unmarked, restored rim chip, the custard cup of footed form with everted rim and scroll handle, printed outside with two floral sprays and with a line border inside the rim, unmarked, small rim chip.

c1790-1810
tankard 5.25in (13.5cm) high

$220-280   **DN**

A Wedgwood large mug, printed with the Water Lily pattern, with the usual cut-reed border stringing inside the rim and down the handle, impressed mark, star crack to base.

c1811-20   5in (13cm) high

$400-450   **DN**

A pair of tea bowls and saucers, printed with the Tea Party pattern, within a floral border, unmarked.

c1815-30
saucers 5.5in (13.5cm) dia

$250-300   **DN**

A Copeland Spode milk jug, printed with the Italian pattern, marked.

c1890   3.5in (9cm) high

$50-80   **PC**

Transfer-Printed

A pair of sauceboats, with blue lining to rims and handle edges, the outsides printed with the Zebra pattern, the inside rims with a chinoiserie-style cellular ground floral-scroll border, unmarked, small chip to one spout.

Although the main scene on these sauceboats corresponds closely with the popular Rogers version, the border is completely different and suggests an earlier date.

c1805-15   6.5in (16.5cm) long

$300-350   **DN**

A Spode knife rest, printed with the floral ground and one figure panel taken from the border of the Greek Series, unmarked, small chip beneath one corner.

c1810-15   4in (10cm) long

$200-250   **DN**

A pair of knife rests, possibly Spode, printed with the border from the Net pattern, unmarked.

c1810-20   4in (10cm) long

$220-280   **DN**

Acruet stand, probably by Spode, printed with clippings from the Gothic Castle pattern, the rim with the the usual vignette border, unmarked, small chip to one container, covers lacking.

c1810-20   5.5in (13.5cm) dia

$80-120   **DN**

A pair of Rogers knife rests, printed with border flowers and stringing from the Zebra pattern, impressed marks, one with small corner chip.

c1810-20   3.5in (9cm) long

$400-450   **DN**

A rare pair of Wedgwood dish lifters, of slightly concave wedge shape, printed with flowers and edge stringing from the Peony pattern, impressed marks.

c1815-30   2.5in (6cm) long

$200-250   **DN**

A set of four knife rests or dish lifters, probably Davenport, of unusual curved shape, printed with the border from the Tudor Mansion pattern, unmarked, small areas of restoration to two corners.

c1810-15   3in (7.5cm) long

$150-200   **DN**

A pair of Spode knife rests, printed with part of the border from the Lucano pattern, printed marks, one with restored chips.

c1815-30   4in (10cm) long

$150-200   **DN**

A British Views Series toilet box and cover, printed with the Series border, the lid with a detail of the water dog, unmarked, lid cracked, small chips.

c1815-30   8in (20.5cm) long

$150-200   **DN**

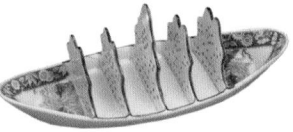

A Spode toast rack, of boat shape, printed at each end with a fragment of the Woodman pattern and narrow borders, impressed mark, one end divider broken off.

c1815-25   10in (25.5cm) long

$350-400   **DN**

A Rural Scenery Series covered toilet box, attributed to Bathwell & Goodfellow, the cover printed with a bridge landscape framed by a border of flowers and foliate scrolls, repeated inside the base, unmarked, minor chips beneath cover.

c1818-23   7.5in (19cm) long

$400-450   **DN**

A Semi-China basket-molded dessert comport, of ornate rectangular shape with twig handles, printed with a rural scene within an open floral border, the outer sides with further scenes, one apparently of St. Albans Abbey, printed mark SEMI/CHINA in a double line octagonal panel, one handle restored.

c1815-25   10in (25.5cm) long

$400-450   **DN**

▶ A Clews cheese cradle, of typical scroll form on an oval pedestal foot, printed with the Willow pattern and standard border, impressed maker's mark, broken and glued, other damage.

c1818-30   15.75in (40cm) long

$350-400   **DN**

A Staffordshire pearlware footbath, by Andrew Stevenson, Cobridge, printed to the exterior with romantic vistas of ruins, bridges, rivers and cottages under a floral-scroll border, the interior repeats floral border, the base printed with a view of country estate with deer , molded handles at rim, old restoration.

c1816-1836

$3,500-4,000   **SI**

An infant feeding bottle, printed with a romantic scene of figures in a country house landscape, unmarked.

c1830-50   6.5in (16.5cm) long

$600-650   **DN**

A pair of knife rests, of ornate molded shape, printed with sheet pattern of leaves and flowerheads, unmarked, one with small chip to base.

c1835-50   3.25in (8cm) long

$200-250   **DN**

A mid-19thC English pottery child's tea set, possibly Burgess and Leigh, comprising teapot and cover, milk jug, covered sugar bowl, three cups and saucers and two side plates, printed with the Forest pattern, beehive marks in blue.

c1850

$180-220   **Chef**

A mid-19thC twin-handled footbath, printed on the base interior with ornate cottage scene with two figures by a lake with mountainous landscape, with flower decorated apron, the interior and exterior sides with shaped panels of an urn issuing flowers and a fence with pavillions to one side, impressed crown mark to one side below handle, chip to base rim and frieze above, hairline crack, some glaze loss to exterio, handles with minor glaze chips and fritting, minor scratching to lower body.

19.75in (50cm) wide

$1,800-2,200   **L&T**

A late 19thC Adams Union Border Series plant holder, of cylindrical form on three knob feet, the outer surface with two narrow engine-turned decorative bands, printed with a rural scene, the inside rim with the Series border of roses, thistles and shamrocks, impressed ADAMS/TUNSTALL, cracks, rim chip, one foot re-glued.

c1890

$80-120   **DN**

A pearlware bourdalou, probably Staffordshire, with printed decoration, extensively restored.

If perfect value would be approx $1,000-1,300.

c1820   9.25in (23.5cm) wide

$300-350   **PC**

A Semi-China twin-handled footbath, with ribbed sides and scroll cast handles, printed with all-over pattern of looose floral sprays, the interior with panel of vase issuing exotic summer flowers.

21in (53cm) wide

$3,000-3,500   **L&T**

Two pepper pots, of different vase shapes, both printed in with versions of the standard Willow pattern and border, unmarked, one with crack to sprinkler.

c1825-50   largest 4.5in (11.5cm) h

$150-200   **DN**

A Staffordshire jar and cover, with scroll handles, printed with the Cattle River pattern, no marks, small chip to the foot rim, chips to the flange beneath the cover.

11in (27.5cm) high

$900-1,000   **WW**

Wedgwood

WEDGWOOD

A Wedgwood black basalt oil lamp and cover, known as "Reading", originally from a pair including "Vestal", thought to be modeled by William Keeling, of navette form with fluted upper section and similar domed foot, a classical maiden seated on the upper section, damaged and repaired.

c1773   7.75in (20cm) wide

$650-750   **DN**

A large Wedgwood black basalt mug, the contemporary silver-mounted rim above a cylindrical body molded in relief with trailing oak leaves and berry molded scroll handle, impressed lower case mark, one side cracked.

c1780-98   7.25in (18.5cm) high

$300-350   **HamG**

A Wedgwood black basalt bust of Shakespeare, on footed plinth, incised marks "Shakespeare" and Wedgwood.

13in (33cm) high

$900-1,000   **L&T**

A rare pair of early 19thC black basalt figures of Lord Rodney and Admiral Hood, one impressed "Ld. Rodney", the other inlaid "Ad. Hood", metal swords lacking.

12in (30.5cm)

$15,000-18,000   **WW**

A Wedgwood black basalt vase, of ovoid form with flared neck, painted in colored enamels with sprays of Oriental flowers, impressed marks, dated.

1861   4.75in (12cm) high

$280-320   **DN**

A late 19thC Wedgwood black jasper tobacco jar and domed cover, typically molded and modeled in white relief with classical figures, impressed mark.

8in (20.5cm) high

$450-500   **DN**

SPRIGGING

- Clay is pressed into a mold to form a "sprig" which is then removed.
- The sprig is attached to the surface of an unfired vessel, in a process called "luting" using water or slip.
- Usually a sprig of one color is applied onto a ground of a different colorSprigging is most commonly associated with Wedgwood

A Wedgwood pale-blue jasper cup and saucer, sprigged with scrolling foliate and classical ornament, impressed mark.

$1,000-1,500   **DN**

An early19thC Wedgwood pale-blue jasper bowl, sprigged with an ozier band in white and ocher, impressed mark.

11.5in (29cm) wide

$2,000-2,500   **DN**

An early 19thC Wedgwood pale-blue jasper custard cup and cover, with an engine-turned band of flowerheads on a chequerboard ground, impressed mark, handle re-glued, cup cracked.

Size?

$1,400-1,600   **DN**

A late 19thC dark blue jasper cheese bell and stand, in the manner of Wedgwood, sprigged in white with Neo-classical figures and putti, the base edged in a garland of oak leaves.

10.25in (26cm) dia

$300-350   **BonS**

An English relief molded Wedgwood-style lozenge decorated baluster jug, with continuous leaf sprig border and brightly painted lemon and orange lozenge body.

5.25in (13cm) high

$400-450   **L&T**

A Wedgwood caneware game pie tureen and cover, typically molded with game. Marked with date code.
1874

8.75in (22.5cm) wide

$250-300   **DN**

WEMYSS

WEMYSS POTTERY WAS PRODUCED BY THE FIFE POTTERY IN KIRKCALDY, SCOTLAND, FROM THE 1880s. Quirky and highly original, Wemyss ware has a special place in the history of ceramics.

Production began when Robert Methven Heron, the son of a successful pottery factory owner, inherited his father's business in 1887. He and Karel Nekola, a gifted Bohemian painter hired by Heron Snr., began working on a new range of high quality wares. Nekola produced botanically accurate and boldly rendered floral decoration, such as cabbage roses and other flowers, berries and fruits.

The popularity of Wemyss grew both in Scotland and England, aided by the appointment of Thomas Goode & Co., London, as the sole distributor in England. His backstamp can be seen on many of the pieces he sold.

After Nekola's death in 1915, Edwin Sandland became chief decorator, but as public taste changed, so the fortunes of the factory waned, despite the introduction of new designs. The factory closed in 1930, but the Wemyss name was kept alive throughout the 20th century.

Today, Wemyss wares are a popular collectible, known for their distinctive style and superb painting.

- Pieces produced before 1930 have an impressed Wemyss mark, and often "R Heron & Son" and "T. Goode & Son" retailers mark.
- After 1930, wares are painted "Wemyss" or stamped "PLINCHTA LONDON ENGLAND".
- Pieces are rarely signed, but some by Nekola are. Any work by him, particularly if signed, is highly sought after.
- Early pieces are more desirable and have a pink rim. Later pieces have a green rim.
- Look for unusual subjects such as nasturtiums, gorse or pink flamingos.
- Be wary of unmarked pieces, these could be copies or factory rejects.

A small Wemyss black and white sponged pig, restoration to one ear.

c1890   6.25in (16cm) long

$450-500   **RdeR**

A Wemyss black and white sponged pig, with soft wrinkles.

c1900   10.5in (27cm) high

$2,200-2,800   **RdeR**

An English Wemyss black and white sponged pig, restoration to trotter, tail and tummy.

c1930   10.5in (27cm) high

$2,000-2,500   **RdeR**

A Wemyss preserve pot, painted with trees, bees and hive, small chip to base.

c1900   5in (12.5cm) high

$400-500   **RdeR**

A Wemyss honeycomb box and lid with dish, Thomas Goode design.

c1930   box 5.5in (14cm) wide

$600-700   **RdeR**

▶ A large Wemyss preserve pot, painted with blackberries, brambles and autumn leaves, minor restoration to rim.

c1890   6.25in (16cm) high

$500-550   **RdeR**

A pair of small Wemyss early morning plates, painted with blackberries.

This is a very good example of quality Wemyss; the piece is beautifully painted with fine detail.

c1900   5.5in (14cm) dia

$250-300 (pair)   **RdeR**

A large Wemyss jam pot, painted with blackcurrants.

c1890   6in (15cm) high

$420-480   **RdeR**

Wemyss

A rare small Wemyss plate, finely painted with buttercups.

c1900   4.75in (12cm) dia

$420-480   **RdeR**

A rare Wemyss basket, painted with buttercups, marked T. Goode and Co. South Aldley's London.

c1900   8.25in (21cm) high

$2,200-2,800   **RdeR**

A Wemyss mug, painted with cherries, restoration to chips on base rim.

c1890   5.75in (14.5cm) high

$420-480   **RdeR**

A Wemyss basket, painted with cherries, minor chips to rim.

c1890   15.75in (40cm) wide

$800-900   **RdeR**

A Wemyss mug, painted with flowering clover.

c1890   5.5in (14cm) high

$500-600   **RdeR**

A Wemyss pig, painted with flowering clover by Joseph Nekola, with minor restoration to ear.

c1930   10.5in (27cm) high

$2,200-2,800   **RdeR**

A Wemyss bullet teapot, painted with black cockerels, restoration to spout and handle.

c1890   4in (10cm) high

$600-700   **RdeR**

A small Wemyss pin tray, painted with cockerels by Karel Nekola, impressed mark of T.Goode & Co.

c1890   4.5in (11.5cm) wide

$250-300   **RdeR**

A small Wemyss plate, painted with brown cockerels and the words Bon Jour, restoration to chips on rim.

c1900   4.75in (12cm) dia

$200-250   **RdeR**

A Wemyss dolphin inkwell, painted with wild dog roses, replacement lids and minor restoration to tails.

c1890   8in (20cm) wide

$600-700   **RdeR**

A rare Wemyss gypsy pot, painted with mallard ducks, some restoration.

c1900   9.75in (25cm) high

$2,800-3,200   **RdeR**

A rare small Wemyss plate, beautifully painted with hairy gooseberries by Karel Nekola.

c1900   5.5in (14cm) dia

$550-600   **RdeR**

A rare large Wemyss fruit bowl, beautifully painted with grapes, minor restoration.

c1890   5.25in (13cm) high

$1,500-2,000   **RdeR**

A rare Wemyss early morning plate, painted with greengages.

c1900   5.5in (14cm) dia

$400-450   **RdeR**

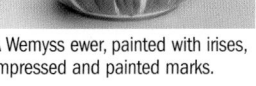

A Wemyss ewer, painted with irises, impressed and painted marks.

9.75in (25cm) high

$1,300-1,500   **L&T**

A small Wemyss Grosvenor vase, painted with irises, restoration to chips on base.

c1900   5.5in (14cm) high

$400-450   **RdeR**

Wemyss

A rare Wemyss loving cup tyg, painted with lilacs, some restoration to interior.

c1890   9in (23cm) high

$2,200-2,800   **RdeR**

A large Wemyss preserve pot, painted with oranges.

c1900   6in (15cm) high

$400-450   **RdeR**

A Wemyss Gordon plate, painted with oranges, restoration to crack.

c1900   8.25in (21cm) dia

$300-350   **RdeR**

A large Wemyss jam pot and cover, painted with plums, minor scratches to top rim.

c1890-1900   6.25in (16cm) high

$400-450   **RdeR**

A Wemyss small gypsy pot, painted with plums, restored chip to foot.

c1900   5.25in (13cm) high

$600-700   **RdeR**

A Wemyss powder bowl and cover, painted with plums, minor restoration to lid, stain to base.

c1930   3.25in (8cm) high

$250-300   **RdeR**

A fine large Wemyss tyg, painted with roses, with impressed mark RH & S, minor stain inside.

9in (23cm) high

$750-850   **RdeR**

A Wemyss small pig, painted with roses, slight re-touching to one foot, small scratch to one ear.

c1890   6.25in (16cm) long

$600-700   **RdeR**

A Wemyss double Victoria inkwell, painted by Karel Nekola, restoration to one of the knops, hair crack and chip to base.

c1890   10.25in (26cm) wide

$450-550   **RdeR**

A Wemyss fern pot, painted with roses, minor restoration to rim chips.

c1900   4.75in (12cm) high

$250-300   **RdeR**

An unusual Wemyss biscuit barrel, painted with roses by Karel Nekola, with cane handle, restoration to lid and pot rim.

c1900   6in (15cm) high

$500-600   **RdeR**

A small Wemyss three-handled tyg, painted with roses, a rare piece in perfect condition.

A tyg is a large mug with three or more handles, which allows several people to drink from it. They were very popular during the 16th & 17th centuries and were mostly made in Wrotham in Kent and the Staffordshire potteries

c1900   4in (10 cm) high

$500-600   **RdeR**

108

ORIENTAL Chinese Ceramics

GOOD 19TH CENTURY CHINESE PORCELAIN IS INCREASINGLY COLLECTABLE. Late Imperial pieces which were thought of as garish are now fetching good prices because of their high quality. When buying, ensure the piece has the appropriate reign mark for the period when it was made.

Today people are putting aesthetic value above historical value. A dull, monochrome piece of 12th century celadon will not sell unless it is top quality. The market for South-east Asian pots is in a similar position.

Ming furniture continues to command very high prices, but 19thC heavily carved dark pieces imported to the West are not to current taste and hard to sell.

The market for fine Japanese lacquer remains strong, particularly for quality pieces with a known provenance. High quality Chinese cinnabar lacquer still commands good prices, but later, poorer quality pieces are harder to sell.Good quality Japanese carvings, both in wood and ivory, continue to do well, but this is specialist market. Beware of fakes, particularly netsukes.

The market for earlier Japanese pieces depends on the Japanese economy. If there is a crisis then prices will suffer. However, this does not apply so much to Satsuma and later wares which have a strong market in the West.

As ever, spend $500 on one good piece rather than $100 on five poor ones and always buy from reputable sources.

CHINESE

A Chinese Neolithic vase, Gansu or Quinghi province, Majiayao culture, second or third milleniumBC.

$1,500-2,000	OG

A Chinese Neolithic vase, second or third millenium BC.

15.5in (39cm) high

$1,000-1,500	OG

A silver-green glazed vase, Han Dynasty (206BC-AD220).

17.75in (45cm) high

$1,500-2,000	OG

A glazed vase, Han Dynasty (206BC-AD220).

17.75in (45cm) high

$80-120	OG

A pair of pottery soldiers, Han Dynasty (206BC-AD220).

17.5in (44cm) high

$1,500-2,000	OG

A large cocoon vase, Han Dynasty (206BC-AD220), some repairs.

15.5in (39cm) high

$1,000-1,500	OG

A Chinese gray pottery model of a pig house, Han Dynasty (206BC-AD220).

9in (23cm) high

$750-850	SI

◄ A Chinese polychrome gray pottery bowl and cover, Han Dynasty (206BC-AD220).

9in (23cm) diam

$280-320	SI

Chinese Blue and White

A Chinese gray pottery granary, Han Dynasty (206BC-AD220).

12in (30.5cm) high

$280-320	SI

A Chinese pottery figure of a camel, Tang Dynasty.

12in (30.5cm) high

$400-450	SI

A Chinese red pottery figure of a horse, Tang Dynasty (618-907).

11in (28cm) high

$400-450	SI

A pair of Chinese Ming porcelain hand-painted blue and white stem cups, Hongzhi Dynasty.

1.5in (4cm) high

$400-450	PC

A 16thC Chinese provincial bowl with everted rim, decorated in underglaze blue with a band of grape vines, the interior with a vine medallion and a cell border, four characters Da Ming mark.

5.5in (14cm) diam

$120-180	DN

A CLOSER LOOK AT WANLI

Irregular, dark speckling is caused by uneven cobalt. On most early pieces you find spots of the "heaped and piled" effect where the cobalt has come through the glaze during firing and turned black.

The thick glaze tended to pool creating a green/blue ring inside bowls, etc.

Most decoration was floral and featured strong brushwork with spacious, carefully painted patterns.

You can often see a ring of reddish brown on unglazed foot-rims where the iron in the clay has oxidized during firing.

Reign marks tend to be blurred because of the thick glaze, which was filled with air bubbles.

A small Chinese blue and white Ming porcelain teapot and cover, Wanli Dynasty.

Porcelain was produced at Jingdezhen and later at Chenghua, from the late 14thC. Porcelain makers received encouragement from the Ming emperors and vessels were often given a reign mark, which was the royal seal of approval. Due to demand, from both the royal courts and the export market, quality declined after c1520.

c1580   4.5in (11cm high)

$400-500	PC

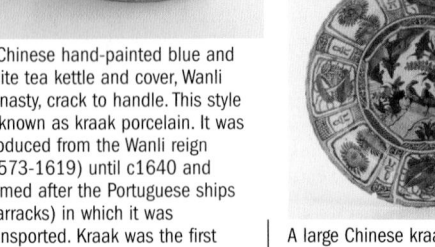

A Chinese hand-painted blue and white tea kettle and cover, Wanli Dynasty, crack to handle. This style is known as kraak porcelain. It was produced from the Wanli reign (1573-1619) until c1640 and named after the Portuguese ships (carracks) in which it was transported. Kraak was the first Chinese export ware to arrive in Europe in large quantities.

7.5in (19cm) high

$1,400-1,800	PC

A large Chinese kraak porcelain hand-painted blue and white dish, Wanli Dynasty, crack and chip.

13.75in (35cm) diam

$1,200-1,800	PC

A Chinese Ming porcelain vase, of lobed oval form, with floral and foliate decoration, Wanli period.

7in (18cm) high

$1,500-2,000	SI

A late 16thC Chinese blue and white hand-painted kraak porcelain guglet vase, Wanli Dynasty, badly damaged neck.

10.5in (26.5cm) high

$1,500-2,000	PC

Blue and White

A Chinese Ming kraak porcelain kendi, with tall waisted neck and narrow mouth, the globular body with mammiform spout, painted with panels of flower sprays, Wanli period (1573-1619).

7.5in (19cm) high

| $800-900 | SI |

A Chinese kraak ware dish, with Islamic-style design of figures in a landscape, with tulip and pomegranate borders, Transitional Period.

13.75in (35cm) diam

| $2,200-2,800 | R&GM |

A Chinese Ming kraak porcelain charger, the shaped central medallion with flowering branches and birds, the cavetto with alternating panels of precious objects and floral sprays, Chingzhen period.

14in (35.5cm) diam

| $1,400-1,800 | SI |

A Chinese blue and white beaker vase, painted in underglaze blue enamel with a bird perched on a branch, Transitional period.

8in (20cm) high

| $600-700 | SI |

A Chinese porcelain hand-painted box and cover, with liner, the glaze on exterior of box affected by sea water. A piece without its original Christies label as shown above) is worth 50 percent less.

Provenance: From the Hatcher Junk collection sold at Christies Amsterdam June 1984, with original label.

c1645

3.25in (8cm) diam

| $400-450 | PC |

SHIPWRECKED CARGOES

Many countries have lost ships over the centuries, but it is Chinese ships and artefacts that have made the news in recent years.

The Hatcher Collection of thousands of pieces of Chinese porcelain was recovered from an un-named junk that sunk between 1643 and 1646. When it was sold over two auctions at Christies Amsterdam in 1983 and 1984, it created interest among serious collectors and dealers.

Captain Mike Hatcher was also responsible for the discovery of the Nanking cargo from the Dutch Geldermalsen, which sank in 1752. This sale, also held at Christies Amsterdam, in 1986 raised US$10.1 million.

The latest treasure was found in the South China seas, again by Hatcher, when he found the wreck of the Tek Sing, or True Star, lost in 1822. This huge collection of over 350,00 pieces was the largest hoard of Chinese porcelain found to date. When it was auctioned in Germany in 1999 in a mammoth eight-day sale, it fetched US$14.5 million. Some of the rarer pieces went to the British Museum and the Gallery of New South Wales, Australia.

A pair of hand-painted Chinese porcelain miniature tapering vases.

Provenance: From the Hatcher Junk collection sold at Christies Amsterdam June 1984 with original label.

c1645   4.5in (11.5cm) high

| $750-850 | PC |

A hand-painted Chinese miniature vase.

Provenance: From the Hatcher Junk collection sold at Christies Amsterdam June 1984 with original label.

c1645   4.75in (12cm) high

| $300-350 | PC |

A hand-painted Chinese stem cup.

Provenance: From the Hatcher Junk collection sold at Christies Amsterdam June 1984 with original label.

c1645   3in (7.5cm) high

| $300-350 | PC |

A Chinese hand-painted blue and white porcelain bowl and cover.

Provenance: From the Hatcher Junk collection sold at Christies Amsterdam June 1984 with original label.

c1645   3.25in (8cm) diam

| $400-450 | PC |

Chinese Blue and White

A hand-painted Chinese porcelain kendi.

Provenance: *From the Hatcher Junk collection sold at Christies Amsterdam June 1984 with original label.*

A kendi is a Persian drinking vessel with a bulbous body, a side spout and a waisted cylindrical neck which acts as a handle. These vessels were made for the Persian market in China, Korea, Japan and the Middle East.

c1645   5.5in (13.5cm) high

$450-500   **PC**

A pair of hand-painted Chinese reticulated bowls.

Provenance: *From the Hatcher Junk collection sold at Christies Amsterdam June 1984, with original labels.*

c1645   3.5in (9cm) diam

$1,000-1,500   **PC**

A Chinese hand-painted blue and white porcelain teapot, lacking lid.

Provenance: *From the Hatcher Junk collection sold at Christies Amsterdam June 1984 with original label.*

c1645   4.5in (11cm) high

$750-850   **PC**

A small hand painted Chinese porcelain tea bowl.

Provenance: *From the Hatcher Junk collection sold at Christies Amsterdam June 1984 with original label.*

c1645   2.5in (6cm) diam

$220-280   **PC**

A small Chinese porcelain white teabowl, with simple blue line.

Provenance: *From the Hatcher Junk collection sold at Christies Amsterdam June 1984 with original label.*

c1645   2.5in (6cm) diam

$180-220   **PC**

A small Chinese hand-painted porcelain mustard pot and cover, slight chip to lid.

Provenance: *From the Hatcher Junk collection sold at Christies Amsterdam June 1984 with original label.*

c1645   1.5in (4cm) high

$400-450   **PC**

A tall Chinese hand-painted porcelain vase, with painted decoration including a rabbit and grasshoppers, chip to rim.

Provenance: *From the Hatcher Junk collection sold at Christies Amsterdam June 1984 with original label.*

c1645   9.25in (23.5cm) high

$650-750   **PC**

A small Chinese hand-painted porcelain box and cover, with landscape scene on lid.

Provenance: *From the Hatcher Junk collection sold at Christies Amsterdam June 1984 with original label.*

c1645   2in (5cm) diam

$300-350   **PC**

A pair of small Chinese hand-painted porcelain cups.

Provenance: *From the Hatcher Junk collection sold at Christies Amsterdam June 1984 with original label.*

c1645   1.5in (4cm) high

$300-350   **PC**

Blue and White

A Chinese hand-painted ginger jar, painted with a dignitary on a mythical beast, Transitional period, lacking cover.

c1650   7in (18cm) high

$450-500   **PC**

A late 17thC Chinese hand-painted ginger jar, with wooden cover.

7.5in (19cm) high

$450-500   **PC**

A CLOSER LOOK AT BLUE AND WHITE

The rare gilt mounts on the ewer are original and increase the value of the piece, especially as they are intact

It is remarkable that this piece has survived in such good condition, particularly when you look at the slender spout, which is extremely susceptible to damage.

Most Chinese export pieces were intended for the European market. The Middle Eastern shape of this ewer, with its long neck and globular body is very rare.

A Chinese export underglazed blue and white wine ewer, for the Middle Eastern market, the star-shaped neck rim with white metal mount and scroll handles, slender neck and spout, the slightly fluted baluster bar with six alternative flower spray and objects panels, Kong Hsi, with amusing paper label, date around 1650-70, made by a Chinese monk in Indian Persia.

This ewer would originally have been one of a pair. However this has not detracted from the value of the piece because it is of such interest in its own right.

10.25in (26cm) high

$40,000-45,000   **L&T**

A Chinese vase, decorated with figures in a landscape and scroll design, Transitional Period, small rim chips.

c1650   7in (18cm) high

$850-950   **R&GM**

A large Chinese hand-painted vase and cover, decorated with courtiers, Transitional period.

The Transitional Period marks the change from the Ming Dynasty to the Qing Dynasty c1620-50. The blue and white ware typically has images of flowers, foliage, animals and figures as well as scenes from Chinese Classical literature and are usually of a high quality with a natural style. The bases are usually flat and unglazed.

c1650   13in (33cm) high

$1,000-1,500   **PC**

A mid-to late 17thC Chinese blue and white pear-shaped vase, with tall neck and globular mouth, decorated with butterflies and foliage.

7in (17cm) high

$650-750   **WW**

A mid-to late 17thC Chinese blue and white stem cup, decorated with insects and prunus, some restoration to the foot.

3.5in (8.5cm) high

$300-350   **WW**

A Chinese hexagonal baluster vase, each panel decorated in underglaze blue with figures in a river landscape, Kangxi period, neck lacking.

11.75in (29.5cm) high

$750-850   **DN**

Chinese Blue and White

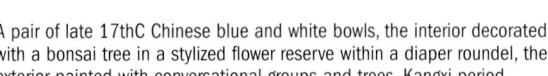

A pair of late 17thC Chinese blue and white bowls, the interior decorated with a bonsai tree in a stylized flower reserve within a diaper roundel, the exterior painted with conversational groups and trees, Kangxi period.

It is very rare to find Chinese piece with Japanese bonsai decoration.

8.25in (21cm) diam

$2,200-2,800 (pair)	BonS

A Chinese mallet-shaped vase, decorated with the Hundred Antiques pattern, Kangxi period, with well restored chip.

1662-1722   8in (20.5cm) high

$500-600	WW

A Chinese molded tea kettle and cover, decorated with flower sprays, Kangxi period, the silver spout a replacement .

6.75in (17cm) high

$400-500	WW

◄ A pair of Chinese baluster vases and covers, decorated with panels of flowers and foliage, Kangxi period, one with a very faint hairline crack to the rim.

$1,400-1,800	WW

A Chinese rouleau vase, decorated in underglaze blue with lotus and prunus within lappet bands, reduced and now with white metal neck, Kangxi period.

12.25in (31cm) high

$500-600	DN

A pair of Chinese ginger jars, each decorated in underglaze blue with lobed panels of antiques on a prunus and cracked-ice ground, with wood covers, Kangxi period.

8in (20cm) high

$1,000-1,500	DN

A Chinese porcelain vase, the high-shouldered body painted with a broad composite floral scroll below a ruyi band, Kangxi period.

5in (12.75cm) high

$300-350	SI

► A pair of Chinese Qing porcelain vases, the triple gourd body painted with quatrefoil medallions enclosing flowers, the lower section with a café-au-lait glaze, Kangxi period.

10in (25.5cm) high

$1,000-1,500	SI

A Chinese brush pot, decorated in underglaze blue with figures in a pavilion by a fenced garden with a plantain, with wood stand, Kangxi period, cracked.

6.5in (16.5cm)

$1,000-1,500	DN

A Chinese hand-painted plate, Kangxi period.

9in (23cm) diam

$220-280	PC

A Chinese porcelain jar, of ovoid form, with stylized bird decoration, Kangxi period.

4in (10cm) high

$120-180	SI

A Chinese vase, decorated with a landscape, from the Vung Tau Cargo, Kangxi period.

5.5in (14cm) high

$600-700 **R&GM**

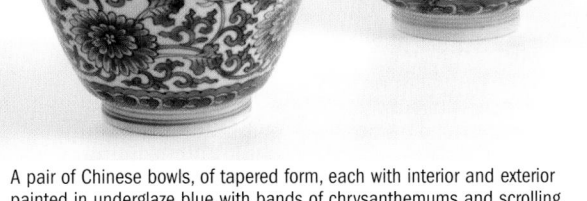

A pair of Chinese bowls, of tapered form, each with interior and exterior painted in underglaze blue with bands of chrysanthemums and scrolling tendrils, within foliate borders, bearing Kang Hsi marks, small abrasion to one rim, one bowl broken and poorly repaired.

5in (13cm) diam

$100-150 **HamG**

A pair of early 18thC Chinese blue and white vases, the square-section baluster bodies painted with garden panels, the flared necks with landscapes.

13.25in (33.5cm) high

$650-750 **Chef**

A Chinese bottle vase, painted in underglaze blue with flowers issuing from rockery and two flying birds, Yongzheng period.

5in (12.75cm) high

$150-200 **SI**

18TH C BLUE & WHITE

By the 18th century the demand from the West for Chinese porcelain was so great that standards declined.

- The 18thC wares have a sketchiness about the decorationand much of the painting follows standard guidelines and patterns
- Imported cobalt tended to give a blotchy look to the painting.
- Most of the foot-rims are crudely trimmed.
- Black flecks on neck or foot-rims are evidence of dirt in the kiln or impurities in the paste.

A set of four 18thC Chinese blue and white plates, decorated with birds in a trelised garden, the octagonal rims with diamond diaper bands.

8.75in (22cm) diam

$120-180 (set) **Chef**

A small 18thC Chinese tureen and cover, decorated with flowers and foliage, small chip.

7in (18cm) wide

$280-320 **WW**

A set of five 18thC Chinese blue and white plates, each centrally painted with a stem of two peonies within elaborate border and petal edged rims.

9in (23cm) diam

$280-320 (set) **Chef**

A pair of 18thC Chinese blue and white plates, each painted with figures by islands within four sprays of flowers.

10in (25.5cm) diam

$120-180 (pair) **Chef**

An 18thC Chinese tureen cover and stand, the sides of the tureen and the center of the stand painted with islands and pavilions within lappet and flower rim bands, the tureen with beast head handles.

Stand 14.5in (37cm) wide

$1,200-1,800 **Chef**

An 18thC Chinese blue and white soup tureen and cover, painted with bridges and island reserves within scroll frames, with mythical beast handles and pomegranate finial.

13.75in (35cm) wide

$1,000-1,500 **Chef**

Chinese Blue and White

An 18thC Chinese deep dish, painted with a man fishing from a boat between two islands, the 12-sided edge with a diaper and pendant trefoil band.

14.5in (37cm) wide

| $300-350 | Chef |

An 18thC Chinese deep dish, painted with three quails eating in a garden another in the air.

14.75in (37.5cm) wide

| $350-400 | Chef |

A pair of 18thC Chinese platters, painted with bridges between islands with pagodas, the rim with butterflies and diaper lappets.

14.25in (36cm) wide

| $350-400 | Chef |

An 18thC Chinese platter, painted with a willow tree on top of a rock, with peonies and trellis scrolls and diaper.

18.5in (47cm) wide

| $500-600 | Chef |

A pair of 18thC Chinese dishes, the wells painted with long Elizas, the a border with chrysanthemum and peony sprays within a gently barbed rim, six character mark.

8.25in (21cm) diam

| $400-450 | BonS |

An 18thC Chinese blue and white porcelain Meiping vase, painted with white prunus clusters reserved on a blue "cracked ice" ground, Qing Dynasty.

6.5in (16.5cm) high

| $220-280 | SI |

An 18thC Chinese Ming-style porcelain Meiping vase, painted with scrolling foliage and flowerheads, Qing Dynasty.

7in (18cm) high

| $1,500-2,000 | SI |

▶ A Chinese soup dish, decorated with rockwork, peony and willow, from the Nanking Cargo, Qianlong period.

c1752   9in (23cm) diam

| $200-250 | R&GM |

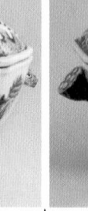

◀ A Chinese teapot and cover, decorated with figures on bridges in pagoda landscapes, Qianlong period, the cover rim chipped.

9in (23cm) high

| $100-150 | WW |

A Chinese chamfered rectangular tureen and cover, with a scroll knop and animal handles decorated with figures in a watery landscape, Qianlong period, the cover perhaps related.

14.25in (36cm) long

| $800-900 | WW |

A Chinese chamfered rectangular tureen and cover, decorated with a pagoda landscape, with a pomegranate knop and lotus seed pod handles, Qianlong period, one leaf chipped.

1736-95   13.5in (34.5cm) long

| $800-900 | WW |

Blue and White

A pair of Chinese export porcelain sauceboats, each of silver shape with barbed rims and loop handles, painted with a bird above a peony and pine tree, the oval foot decorated with lambrequins, Qianlong period, one handle restuck.

9.75in (24.5cm) wide

$420-480   **BonS**

A Chinese export deep meat plate, painted with an extensive river landscape within a cell diaper border, the rim decorated with foliate scroll lambrequins and further panels of cell diaper work, Qianlong period, chipped to rim.

14.75in (37.5cm) wide

$120-180   **BonS**

A Chinese export porcelain oval meat plate, decorated in blue with a river landscape within a cell diaper border, Qianlong period, gilding worn.

17.5in (44cm)

$300-350   **BonS**

A Chinese porcelain jar, painted with flowerheads alternating with calligraphy below a band of ruyi heads, Qianlong period.

8.5in (21.5cm) high

$300-350   **SI**

Three Chinese porcelain brush washers, each of ovoid form, one painted with a horse and a man under a pine tree beside a bridge, one painted with boys at play, a fence, a scholar and a pine tree, and one with a Qianlong mark painted with a flying phoenix amongst clouds and bats, Qing Dynasty.

Largest 2.25in (6cm) high

$650-750   **SI**

A large Chinese export porcelain meat dish, painted with pagodas in landscape within a cracked ice border, the rim with foliate scrolls, cell diaper panels and peony flowers, Qianlong period.

20in (50.5cm) wide

$600-700   **BonS**

A pair of Chinese porcelain vases, each decorated with flower-filled cartouches on all-over floral ground.

19.5in (49.5cm) high

$4,500-5,000   **SI**

A Chinese export ware octagonal tureen, the sides painted with a water landscape, with rabbit's head handles, Qianlong period, lacking cover.

13.75in (35cm) wide

$150-200   **BonS**

A Chinese export porcelain tureen and cover, the tureen painted with pagodas in extensive landscapes, with foliate S-scroll handles, the cover decorated with foliate lambrequin design within diaper borders, with lotus blossom strap handle.

$1,000-1,500   **BonS**

◀ A Chinese Canton porcelain tureen and cover.

12in (30.5cm) wide

$1,200-1,800   **SI**

A Chinese Ming-style porcelain bottle vase, painted with flower heads and scrolling foliage, Qing Dynasty.

15in (38cm) high

$1,000-1,500   **SI**

Chinese Celadon

A pair of 20thC Chinese Canton porcelain hexagonal jardinières and undertrays, decorated with riverscapes.

11.25in (18.5cm) high

$1,000-1,500   **SI**

▶ A 12thC Chinese Qingbai ware bowl, with carved twin fish design, Southern Song Dynasty.

In the 11thC and 12thC, Qingbai was made from petsune (porcelain stone) and by the 13thC kaolin (china clay) had been added. This was covered with a glassy pale-blue glaze, which was prone to pooling.

3in (7.5cm) diam

$750-850   **R&GM**

A CLOSER LOOK AT CELADON

Luminous, thick, pale gray-green color, with a slightly bubbly appearance

Celadon wares are typically of a simple shape

Minimal, low relief decoration, with flower, bird or fish motifs. Later pieces are more flamboyant

In areas of wear or chips you can see the slightly off white body underneath the glaze

A 13thC Chinese celadon dish, with twin fish molded design, Southern Song or Yuan Dynasty.

The Celadon glaze was made to imitate nephrite jade. The translucent, gray-green or blue-green color is achieved by heating iron oxide in a reducing atmosphere. This ware was at its finest during the Song Dynasty (960-1279) when bowls, vases, ewers, censers and large dishes were made with simple, elegant shapes and molded or carved low-relief decoration.

8in (20cm) diam

$1,300-1,500   **R&GM**

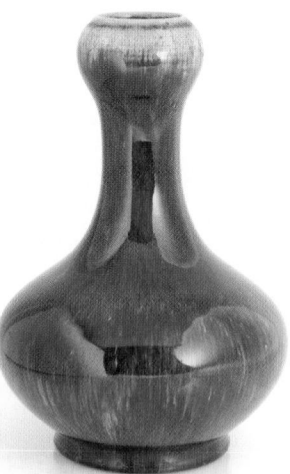

A Chinese bottle vase, with onion neck, the thick flambé glaze falling over the unglazed foot, cracked.

13in (33cm) long

$650-750   **DN**

A Chinese ovoid bottle vase, covered in a white crackled glaze, the slightly reduced rim mounted in silver, with wood stand.

6.25in (16cm) high

$100-150   **DN**

A Chinese bottle vase, with an even glaze of rich liver-red tone shading to grayish pink at the edge of the white glazed mouth rim, Qianlong mark.

11.5in (29.5cm) high

$1,800-2,200   **SI**

A Chinese porcelain saucer dish, with a deep liver-red glaze, with Daoguang six character and of the period.

7in (18cm) diam

$1,000-1,500   **SI**

A 19thC Chinese flambé vase, of globular form with slender flared neck, the thick phosphatic glaze falling short of the foot, reduced.

12in (30.5cm) high

$100-150   **DN**

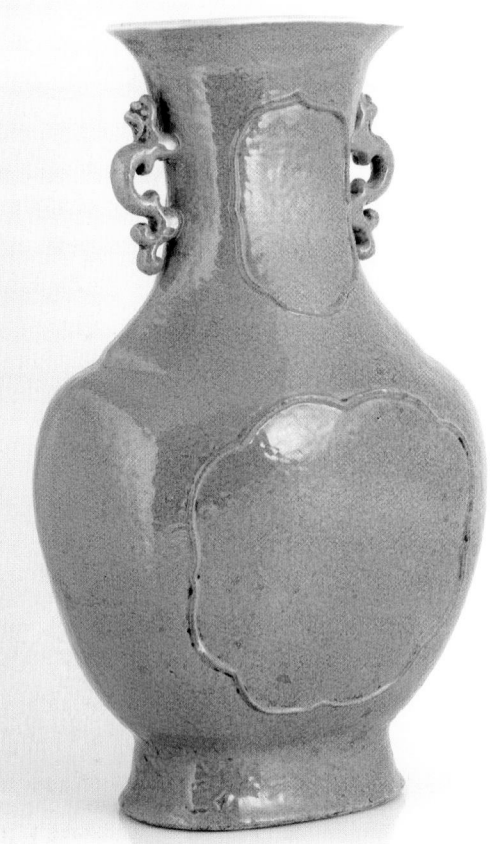

A 19thC Chinese sang-de-boeuf ovoid vase, the thick glaze falling over the foot, on a carved wood stand.

The stand has the remains of a label suggesting a loan exhibition in October 1894.

6.5in (16.5cm)

| $200-250 | DN |

A late 19thC Chinese sang-de-boeuf vase, of tapering square-section, chipped.

Sang-de-boeuf (trans: bull's blood) is found in monochromatic Chinese wares from the Kangxi period. It can be bright red or a darker plum color. It often has pale green or pink streaks, usually around the foot and shoulder, where the glaze has run.

10.25in (26cm) high

| $60-80 | DN |

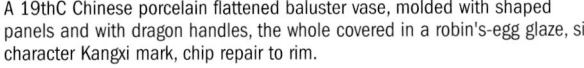

A 19thC Chinese porcelain flattened baluster vase, molded with shaped panels and with dragon handles, the whole covered in a robin's-egg glaze, six character Kangxi mark, chip repair to rim.

Robin's-egg glaze *is more typically found on Chinese porcelain archaic wares from c1720 and is an opaque pale blue or turquoise glaze.*

16in (40.5cm)

| $500-550 | DN |

A late 19thC Chinese hexagonal section tapering vase and cover, with free-running phosphatic glaze.

7.25in (18.5cm)

| $60-80 | DN |

A late 19thC Chinese porcelain garden seat.

15.5in (39cm) high

| $400-450 | OG |

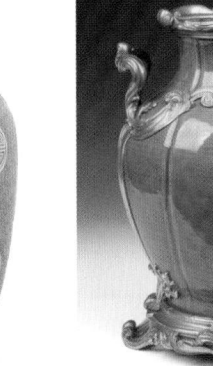

A Chinese export baluster vase, incised with Zhou medallions in gilt on a blue key fret ground, on original ceramic stand.

15in (38cm) high

| $220-280 | DN |

A Chinese turquoise glazed and ormolu-mounted vase, the profuse mounts of acanthus and C-scroll design, all on scrolling feet.

15.25in (38.5cm) high

| $3,500-4,000 | L&T |

A Chinese celadon vase, decorated with four barbed reserves of flowers, with further flowers molded beneath the crackled green glaze, Song Dynasty.

11in (28cm) high

| $400-450 | Chef |

A Chinese copper-red bottle vase, covered with an even glaze, Qing Dynasty.

6in (15.5cm) high

| $400-450 | SI |

FAMILLE VERTE

Famille verte (green family) was developed from the Wucai (five color) style and was adopted during the Kangxi period (1662-1722). The predominant colors are a bright, apple green and iron red but also yellow and aubergine which are then covered with a thin and glassy glaze. Typical designs include rocky gardens or landscapes, figures, the Eight Precious Things and the Eight Buddhist Emblems.

A Chinese famille verte porcelain brush pot, painted with children at play and a woman holding a ruyi scepter, Kangxi period.

5in (12.5cm) high

$1,400-1,800 SI

A Chinese famille verte porcelain teapot, of ovoid form with floral decoration, Kangxi period.

8in (20cm) high

$350-400 SI

Three late 17thC Chinese famille verte dishes, later painted with the coats of arms of Vlaanderen, Nameur and Groeningen within alternating lappets painted with sages and Buddhist objects.

13.75in (35cm) diam

$2,200-2,800 (three) Chef

A pair of Chinese famille verte porcelain vases, of double gourd form, with elongated neck, painted with lappet and floral decoration, Kangxi period.

9.5in (24cm) high

$1,800-2,200 SI

A pair of 18thC Chinese famille verte biscuit porcelain joss stick holders, modeled as a pair of Fu lions in mirror image, one with his paw resting on a brocaded ball.

6.5in (16.5cm) high

$2,000-2,500 SI

▶ A Chinese coffee can, the café au lait ground painted in the famille verte palette with a crest between two five-clawed dragons amid scrolled clouds, Jiaqing period.

c1815   2.5in (6.5cm) high

$150-200 HamG

A famille verte brush pot, each side painted to a reserve with a bird perched in a tree, against a faux shagreen ground, painted with iron-red dragons and foliate scrolls.

5.25in (13.5cm) high

$500-600 HamG

A Chinese famille verte plate, centrally decorated with birds flying over large-scale lotus, the rim with a band of butterflies and flowers, artemisa leaf mark, cracked.
Provenance: *Liddell Collection no.107*

13.75in (35cm) diam

$1,000-1,500 DN

Two Chinese famille verte porcelain figural groups, one with a man on a Fu dog, the other with a man on an ox, Qing Dynasty.

Tallest 4.75in (12cm) high

$1,800-2,200 SI

Two Chinese famille verte porcelain baluster vases and covers, decorated with alternating figural and landscape reserves.

25in (63.5cm) high

$4,000-4,500 SI

Famille Rose

A set of three Chinese famille rose small cruet bottles and covers, each painted with a butterfly between flower and leaf sprays, the handles and the one spout decorated in iron red, Yongzheng period (1723-35), the tip of one handle missing.

5in (12.5cm)

$1,000-1,500	WW

A Chinese famille rose porcelain teapot, molded with flowering branches trailing from the branch-form handle and spout, Yongzheng period.

4in (10cm) high

$600-700	SI

A pair of 18thC Chinese famille rose plates, centrally painted with bamboo supporting chrysanthemums, the scrolling border interrupted by four florets.

9in (23cm) diam

$200-300 (pair)	Chef

A set of six mid-18thC Chinese famille rose plates, each centrally painted with peony, chrysanthemum and prunus by rockwork, the octagonal rims with four sprays of flowers.

9in (22.75cm) wide

$1,000-1,500 (set)	Chef

A late 18thC Mandarin palette bowl, painted with two reserves of figures on terraces against a coral-red Y-diaper ground.

10.5in (26.5cm) diam

$600-700	Chef

An 18thC famille rose dish, painted with two exotic birds on pomegranate branches, the pierced rim painted to simulate a bamboo trellis.

8.75in (22cm) diam

$1,200-1,800	Chef

A set of six 18thC Chinese famille rose plates, each painted with sprigs and sprays of flowers within double red line on the rim.

9in (22.5cm) diam

$1,000-1,500 (set)	Chef

A set of six 18thC Chinese famille rose plates, each with central pink peony and other flowers within a lappet rim band painted with flower heads on an iron-red scrolling ground.

9in (23cm) diam

$600-700 (set)	Chef

A set of six mid-18thC Chinese famille rose plates, each centrally painted with peony, chrysanthemum and prunus beside rockwork, the octagonal rims with four sprays of flowers.

9in (23cm) diam

$600-700 (set)	Chef

An 18thC Chinese Mandarin palette bowl, painted with figures on terraces in two reserves on a gilt scroll ground, the interior with rim band and central flower spray.

10.5in (26.5cm) diam

$600-700	Chef

An 18thC Chinese famille rose dish, the cavetto sides trellis pierced, the center painted with peonies, rockwork and a zigzag fence.

12in (30cm) diam

$1,000-1,500	Chef

◄ A pair of 18thC Chinese export porcelain famille rose covered butter tubs, decorated with flowers and foliage, chips.

5.5in (14cm) diam

▶ An 18thC Chinese export porcelain famille rose bourdalou, painted with flowers and foliage, with gilt highlights.

9in (23cm) long

$700-800 (pair)	SI	$750-850	SI

Chinese Famille Rose

A pair of 18thC Chinese export porcelain famille rose platters, painted with a central scene of a boatman ferrying a woman in courtly dress through a tunnel overhung with trees, flowers and foliage, the well edged in gilt decoration, the rim with rockwork, bamboo, flowers and foliage.

11.5in (29cm)

$1,000-1,500   SI

An 18thC Chinese export porcelain famille rose chocolate pot, decorated with flowers, vines and peacocks, restorations.

9.5in (24cm) high

$500-600   SI

An 18thC Chinese export porcelain rose Mandarin platter, enameled with a scene of courtly figures engaged in various whimsical pursuits, the scalloped rim with cartouches containing sepia landscapes and floral sprays on a ground of iron-red cellwork and purple diaperwork.

14.75in (37.5cm) long

$2,000-2,500   SI

A Chinese lotus-shaped famille rose dish, decorated with peony, Qianlong period.

c1750   9in (23cm) diam

$800-1,200   R&GM

A Qianlong famille rose armorial dish, painted to the center with a flower bouquet, birds and insects, within gilt chain-link band and ribbon-tied flower swag border and an elaborate shield-shaped crest with feathered cartouche surmounted by a bat and motto "Prudentia" for Wakefield impaling Christie, rim chips and hair crack, some wear to decoration.

c1760   11in (28cm) diam

$1,000-1,500   HamG

A Chinese famille rose tea pot and cover, Qianlong period, some chips.

$220-280   HamG

A Chinese export famille rose meat dish, decorated with a river landscape within brocade scroll borders, some rubbing and degrading, Qianlong period.

14.75in (37.5cm) long

$400-450   DN

► A Chinese famille rose oval meat dish, in tobacco-leaf pattern, centrally decorated with leaves, trees and rockwork within a border of scattered flowers, Qianlong period, minor rim chips.

11.75in (30cm) wide

$1,000-1,500   DN

A Chinese famille rose saucer dish, with basket pierced band, decorated with ladies and children in an interior, the rim with scattered flowers, Qianlong period.

10.75in (27cm) diam

$1,200-1,800   DN

A Chinese famille rose sauceboat, decorated with two exotic birds and a peony, Qianlong period.

8.75in (22cm) long

$800-1,200   WW

◄ A pair of Chinese famille rose octagonal plates, centrally decorated with a phoenix and antiques with flowers within a shaped border of flowers, Qianlong period, cracked.

8.25in (21cm) diam

$400-450   DN

Famille Rose

A Chinese famille rose plate, decorated with two deer beneath flowering rockwork, the border with three flower sprays, Qianlong period (1736-95).

9in (23cm) diam

$400-450 **WW**

Three rare Chinese famille rose mythological subject tea bowls and saucers, after Albani representing Earth, painted with Cybele, Flora, Ceres and Bacchus with winged putti beneath trees, Qianlong period, two saucers with short, tight hairline cracks.

c1765

$7,000-8,000 **WW**

A Chinese Mandarin palette porcelain mug, painted with a central medallion depicting a court scene, flanked by two smaller medallions and floral clusters, Qianlong period.

5.5in (14cm) high

$220-280 **SI**

A rare Chinese famille rose mythological subject teapot and cover, after Albani representing Earth, painted with Cybele, Flora, Ceres and Bacchus representing Spring, Summer and Autumn, the reverse with winged putti, Qianlong period.

c1736-95 7in (18cm)

$3,000-3,500 **WW**

A Chinese famille rose porcelain teapot, painted with ducks among aquatic plants and rockery, Qianlong period.

5in (12.5cm) high

$500-600 **SI**

A Chinese export porcelain octagonal armorial plate, painted with the arms of Pringle of Whitbank with motto Spero et Progreditor to the rim, painted with sprays of Deutsche Blumen in the famille rose palette, bordered by a gilded, black and iron-red lozenge chain, Qianlong period, small chip to rim, star crack to center.

c1765 9.75in (24.5cm) diam

$220-280 **BonS**

A Chinese export famille rose armorial tureen and cover, decorated with the arms of Gibbes of Tackley, the cover with pomegranate knop, Qianlong period, slight rubbing to gilt.

Chinese armorial wares are rare and have always been highly collectable and prices usually reflect this. They were made from c1700 until the late 18thC. They were not mass-produced, but were ordered by families or nobles for special occasions such as marriage. Drawings of the family's coat-of-arms would be sent to China to be painted on to the service. They were then shipped back to England. Rarer and particularly lavish wares will be of more value.

14in (35.5cm) wide

$6,000-7,000 **WW**

A Chinese famille rose hexagonal reticulated vase and cover, decorated with panels of figures in interiors, Qianlong period, restored knop.

13.5in (34cm) high

$500-600 **WW**

An impressive Mandarin-style export porcelain punch bowl, the interior and exterior richly painted with Chinese figure subject panels set in a complex diaper pattern ground, some wear to gilding.

c1775   14.25in (36cm) diam

$4,000-4,500   HamG

A Chinese export Mandarin palette mug, with double strap handle, decorated with figural cartouches on a diaperwork ground, with gilt highlights.

c1780   4.25in (10.5cm) high

$600-700   SI

A Chinese export porcelain side plate, painted in the famille rose palette with the seated figure of Minerva resting on a scrolled cartouche bearing the initials J G S, within foliate banded borders, slight rim chips.

c1790   6.25in (16cm) diam

$80-120   HamG

A late 18thC Chinese Mandarin palette mug, painted with figures in a country landscape, with a slender dragon molded handle.

5.25in (13cm) high

$200-250   Chef

A large pair of 18thC Chinese famille rose baluster vases and covers, each painted with scrolling foliage, scattered flowerheads and butterflies, with a band of leaf decoration to base, the covers with lion finials, both extensively damaged and repaired.

25in (63cm) high

$1,200-1,800   BonE

FAMILLE ROSE

As with famille verte (which it virtually replaced), famille rose (pink family) uses predominately rose-pink or purple and green colors and was popular from c1720.

This palette was developed from a combination of Eastern and Western enamels including the pink color derived from gold chloride, which was introduced to China from Europe by Jesuit missionaries. This was to be the only advancement in ceramics made by the Europeans rather than the Chinese.

These new enamels were of a higher quality than earlier Chinese enamels and provided brighter colors with more opacity and artists could employ a much wider range of styles than previously.

Typical decoration features panels of figures, landscapes or interior scenes and motifs such as rockwork, branches, flowers and birds.

Famille rose was exported to Europe in vast quantities during the 18th and 19thC. It was particularly fashionable for wealthy families to have large dinner services decorated with armorial designs.

A late 18thC Chinese export porcelain famille rose teapot, decorated with rockwork, chrysanthemums and foliage, with molded angular handle, the spout molded as a rooster head.

$700-800   SI

A Chinese famille rose plate, painted with chrysanthemums, flower panels sprays, rim chips, Qianlong period.

$50-80   HamG

A Chinese famille rose standing figure, some damage.

c1800   9.5in (24cm) high

$180-220   WW

Two late 18th/early 19thC Chinese export porcelain mugs, painted in famille rose and iron-red with an intricate pattern of interlocking mirror-shaped cartouches, some enclosing birds and prunus, others decorated with cell diaper, the strap handles with applied scrolled heart-shaped motif, one cracked across base, gilding worn.

Tallest 5.25in (13cm) high

$500-600   BonS

Famille Rose

A pair of Chinese famille rose porcelain figures, modeled as elephants, each with an elaborate saddle cloth and saddle supporting a beaker vase, Qing Dynasty.

6.5in (16.5cm) high

$6,000-7,000 **SI**

A pair of 18thC Chinese export porcelain rose Mandarin covered vases, of paneled baluster form, the cover surmounted with a Fu dog, the neck applied with serpents and painted with scenes of birds perched in branches, the body with scenes of courtly figures in a landscape, the ground densely patterned with cellwork, chips, wear to gilt.

12.75in (32.5cm) high

$3,000-3,500 **SI**

A large Chinese famille rose baluster vase, painted with a continuous scene of dignitaries seated on a terrace surrounded by warriors and entertainers, the neck with kylin handles.

34.25in (87cm) high

$3,000-3,500 **BonE**

A Chinese armorial plate, painted with the arms of Stewart, Earl of Galloway, within a gilt medallion, the trellis border decorated with the crest and motto Virescit Vulnere Virtus, rubbing to gilt, hairline crack.

9in (23cm) diam

$350-450 **BonE**

A Chinese export porcelain Mandarin palette mug, with spreading foot and an angular strap handle, decorated with figural cartouches on a diaperwork ground, with smaller cartouches containing birds, flowers and landscape scenes.

c1800   5.25in (13.5cm) high

$600-700 **SI**

A Chinese famille rose porcelain bowl, decorated with floral swags and sprays.

10in (25.5cm) diam

$1,40-1,800 **SI**

An early 19thC Chinese Canton dish, painted with a figure scene within a fret-pierced border.

$600-700 **HamG**

A Chinese famille rose porcelain jardinière, painted to depict flowering branches, Jiaqing period.

9.75in (25cm) high

$750-850 **SI**

◄ An early 19thC Chinese export famille rose porcelain charger, depicting scholars, brilliantly enameled in a vivid palette, the gilt border densely decorated with bats, scrolls and flowers and panels with butterflies and flowers in reserve.

14.75in (37.5cm) diam

$400-450 **SI**

◄ An early 19thC Chinese export famille rose porcelain charger, the center painted with a floral basket, butterflies and scattered fruit and flowers, the rim with flowers, insects, butterflies and fruit.

13.75in (35cm) diam

$500-550 **SI**

A Chinese export rose Mandarin porcelain mug.

5in (12.5cm) high

$1,800-2,200 **SI**

A pair of 19thC Chinese famille rose chargers, each painted with pink peony and other flowers, within floral lappet and scroll rim bands.

14.25in (36cm) diam

$150-200 **hef**

Chinese Famille Rose

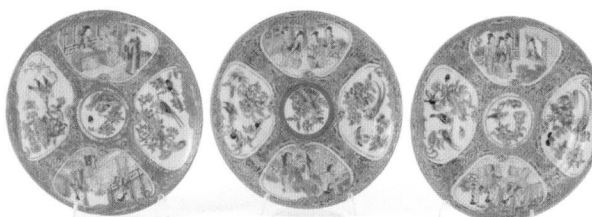

Nine Chinese Canton famille rose side plates, rim chips, wear to gilding.
c1840   8in (20cm) diam

$400-450   **AS&S**

A mid-19thC Chinese Canton onion-shaped porcelain vase, decorated with floral and domestic scenes.

19.75in (50cm) high

$350-450   **AS&S**

A 19thC Bencharong famille rose porcelain bowl and cover, painted with shaped cartouches enclosing a figure with flowers on an iron-red ground alternating with flower heads and scrolling foliage on a rose ground.

The word Bencharong comes from the Thai benja, meaning five, and rong, meaning color.

8in (20cm) high

$600-700   **SI**

A Chinese Canton famille rose part dinner service, comprising a well and tree platter, a tureen, a covered vegetable dish, two sweatmeat dishes, five dinner plates, five dessert plates, four small side plates, one lobed saucer, two small sweatmeat dishes, two soup bowls, five plates, three cups, two square vegetable dish covers, an oval mazarin and an oval platter.
c1840   Platter 16.5in (42cm) wide

$6,000-7,000   **SI**

A Chinese famille rose porcelain jardinière, painted with birds perched on flowering branches, late Qing Dynasty.

14in (35.5cm) diam

$500-600   **SI**

A pair of 19thC Chinese export rose medallion porcelain Gu vases, each decorated with floral and figural reserves on a gilt scrollwork ground with flowers.

13in (33cm) high

$1,800-2,200   **SI**

A large pair of mid-19thC Chinese Canton famille rose vases and covers, one vase with small rim chip and hairline crack, one cover with small re-glued chip.

These types of large decorative vases were mass-produced and decorated in Canton, in China and then exported to Europe. During the first half of the 19thC wares were elaborately and brightly painted but by the end of the century the quality of the decoration had deteriorated.

24.5in (62cm)

$9,000-10,000   **WW**

A Chinese export rose mandarin porcelain teapot.

8in (20cm) high

$1,200-1,800   **SI**

A Chinese famille rose porcelain mug, cylindrical with floral spray decoration.

5in (12.5cm) high

$00-900   **SI**

▶ A Chinese export famille rose porcelain reticulated dish, decorated with figures in garden.

9.25in (23.5cm) wide

$1,500-2,000   **SI**

Famille Rose

A pair of similar 19thC Chinese export rose medallion candlesticks, each decorated with alternating floral and figural reserves.

6in (15.5cm) high

$600-700   **SI**

A pair of 19thC Chinese export rose medallion porcelain candlesticks, each decorated with figural and floral cartouches with birds, the shaft applied with entwined gilt dragons.

8in (20cm) high

$800-900   **SI**

A pair of 19thC Chinese export rose medallion porcelain vases and covers, each decorated with floral and figural reserves, the gilt ground embellished with scrollwork and flowers, the domed cover with a gilt Fu dog finial.

18.25in (46.5cm) high

$2,500-3,000   **SI**

Twelve 19thC Chinese export famille rose porcelain plates, each decorated with alternating reserves of flowers and landscapes, the gilt ground with flowers, butterflies and fruits, with gilded reticulated rims.

8in (20cm) diam

$1,500-2,000   **SI**

A 19thC Chinese export famille rose porcelain soap dish and small barrel-form jar and cover, the dish decorated with reserves of birds perched on flowering branches on a gilt ground with green scrollwork, bats and flowers; the jar with figural and floral panels on a similar ground decorated with butterflies. dish.

5.75in (14.5cm) wide

$350-400   **SI**

A large 19thC Chinese rose medallion porcelain punch bowl, decorated with floral and figural reserves on a gilt scrollwork ground, the rim with panels of flowers and foliage.

13.25in (33.5cm) diam

$2,200-2,800   **SI**

A 19thC Chinese export rose medallion pitcher and wash basin, each decorated with floral and figural reserves on a gilt scrollwork ground with flowers, fruits and butterflies. basin.

15.75in (40cm) wide

$1,300-1,500   **SI**

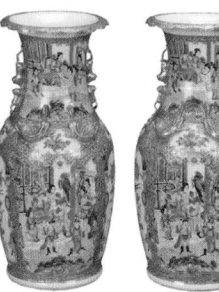

A pair of 19thC Chinese export rose medallion porcelain vases, decorated with floral and figural reserves on a gilt scrollwork ground with butterflies and flowers, the neck applied with gilt Fu dogs, the shoulders applied with gilt qilins.

A qilin is a mythical Chinese creature similar to a unicorn. It represents grandeur, happiness and joy.

18.5in (47cm) high

$2,200-2,800   **SI**

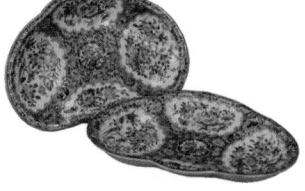

A pair of 19thC Chinese export famille rose porcelain dishes, each of kidney form, decorated with floral reserves, the gilt ground densely enameled with flowers, butterflies and fruit.

11in (28cm) diam

$650-750   **SI**

Two similar 19thC Chinese export rose medallion porcelain bottle vases, decorated with floral and figural reserves on a gilt scrollwork ground, restorations.

Tallest 17.5in (44cm) high

$1,200-1,800   **SI**

▶ A 19thC Chinese export famille rose porcelain footed dish, the well decorated with a scene of courtly figures, the ground scattered with flowers, birds and fruits.

14in (35.5cm) diam

$1,200-1,800   **SI**

A 19thC Chinese export rose medallion porcelain large vase and associated cover, decorated with alternating floral and figural reserves, the gilt ground profusely decorated with flowers, fruits and butterflies, the shoulders with applied gilt qilin, the cover with a gilt Fu dog finial.

26in (66cm) high

$1,800-2,200   **SI**

Two similar mid-19thC Chinese export rose medallion porcelain tazzas, each decorated with figural reserves alternating with reserves of flowers and birds surrounding a central medallion of a flower and a bird, the gilt ground with green scrollwork and scattered flowers, the underside of each with scattered flowers, the foot banded with scrollwork and flowers on a gilt ground.

Largest 9.5in (24cm) diam

$500-550   **SI**

A Chinese Wucai square-section bowl, with flared rim, decorated with a band of figures, Wanli mark and period, damaged.

Wucai is a type of decoration using five colors.

4.5in (11.5cm)

$150-200 **DN**

A pair of clobbered slender ovoid vases, with mask and ring handles and decorated with ladies in an interior beneath later enamels with flowers and birds, Kangxi period (but later enameled), damaged.

12in (30cm) high

$120-180 **DN**

A Chinese yellow ground green dragon bowl, decorated with two dragons in pursuit of flaming pearls over breaking waves, six character mark of Kangxi and of the period (1662-1722), rim frits and hairline crack.

6in (15.5cm)

$1,000-1,500 **WW**

A rare Chinese famille noire porcelain teapot, molded with four large open flower heads, the gilt centers reticulated with overlapping lotus petals, the black ground decorated with flowers, with a Buddhist lion-form spout and handle, the cover reticulated and with a hen-form finial, Yongzheng period.

5.75in (14.5cm) high

$2,500-3,000 **SI**

A Chinese armorial plate, decorated in iron-red, gilt and en grisaille, with the arms of Braithwaite of High Wray, Lancashire impaling Tayleur to the center, the cavetto with red and gilt flowers and scrolls, the rim with floral sprays and butterflies within reserves against a ground of peonies and foliage, Yongzheng period, two chips to rim.

9in (23cm) diam

$350-450 **BonE**

A Chinese small teapot and cover, decorated in sepia and gilt with panels of scrolling foliage, Qianlong period.

7in (18cm) long

$800-900 **WW**

A pair of rare and important Chinese export figures, modeled as hawks, Qianlong period, both broken in half across body.

These are some of the most valuable Chinese export animal figures ever sold. In 1981 a similar pair sold at Sotheby's for $48,000, and another pair sold at Christie's for $63,000. Although neither were as good as this pair, the provenance has much to do with the high price that was reached. The highest price ever achieved for a Chinese export animal was for a tiger, which fetched $600,000 at Sotheby's.

Provenance: *4th Duke of Newcastle.*

c1740   20.5in (52cm) high

$450,000-500,000 **WW**

An 18thC Chinese plate, with a shaped rim, painted with flower sprays within iron-red and gilt borders, small rim flakes.

9in (23cm) diam

$120-180 **WW**

A Chinese famille jaune porcelain bottle vase, painted with shaped medallions enclosing flower-filled basket within flower heads and scrolling foliage, Qianlong mark.

9.5in (24cm) high

$800-1,200 **SI**

Export

A pair of Chinese porcelain barbed dishes, painted with a central medallion enclosing a bouquet and floral sprays within an iron-red and gilt ring, the cavetto with floral clusters, Qianlong period.

9in (23cm) diam

$400-450 (pair)   **SI**

A Chinese coffee cup and saucer, decorated with the marriage arms of two European families, Qianlong period.

c1770   Saucer 5in (12.5cm) diam

$750-800   **R&GM**

Two Chinese mugs, each of cylindrical shape with reeded interlacing strap handles, with blue Fitzhugh type rim band, inscribed within a green oval Ed Pytts Middleton To His Niece Miss Mary Ford 1784.

6in (15.5cm) diam

$800-900   **Chef**

A Qianlong porcelain side plate, of octagonal form, painted in polychrome enamels with the crest and initials J E M, for General Mansell who led the attack on Havana in 1762, within a green and puce foliate scroll border.

c1785   6in (15.5cm) diam

$150-200   **HamG**

A late 18thC Chinese export tea caddy, initialled NEP in an oval held by blue ribbons.

4.75in (12cm) high

$200-250   **Chef**

A late 18thC Chinese export porcelain mug, of bell form, painted in black with an urn and single flower between two ram's horns flanked by two sprays of flowers beneath a band of lotus flowers, fabulous beasts and C-scrolls, gilded highlights, the strap handle with heart-shaped terminal, some wear.

5.5in (13.5cm) high

$250-350   **BonS**

A Chinese coffee cup and saucer, painted in enamels and gilding with the arms of Haworth within floral motif banded borders, hair cracks, one restored, chip to foot rim, Qianlong period.

c1795   Plate 5.5in (14cm) diam

$80-120   **HamG**

A China export porcelain plate, painted to the center with a bird of prey on an anchor, the rope forming the initials J H, within an unusual blue enamel banded and gilt foliate scroll decorated border.

The naval theme probably related to a London merchant who either traded or controlled ships to Canton.

c1800   7.75in (19.5cm)

$100-150   **HamG**

A large Chinese rouge-de-fer painted circular charger, the central roundel depicting a five-clawed dragon chasing the pearl, the deep frieze and border with two similar dragons.

20in (51cm) diam

$2,500-3,000   **L&T**

A Chinese ogee baluster vase, the duck-egg blue ground decorated with a lady and attendant with a crane by rockwork, bats above, Qianlong seal mark, but probably 19thC.

16.25in (41cm) high

$6,500-7,500   **DN**

 A pair of large mid-19thC Chinese Canton twin-handled baluster vases, each with the neck painted with bat and scroll frieze, the inner neck with butterflies and peonies, the body with shield-shaped panels of warriors above two larger similar panels, the pale celadon ground with profuse bird, butterfly and peony decoration with scrolling tree branch, with twin gilt pierced handles, one with two repaired rim cracks, both with areas of glaze flaking.

24in (61cm) high

$2,200-2,800   **L&T**

Ceramics

A Chinese ridge tile figure, modeled with a pigs head and standing on a cloud scroll, Ming Dynasty, restored, part of the base lacking.

11.5in (29cm) high

$400-500	DN

A 19thC pair of Chinese joss stick figures, depicting of dogs of Fo, each with a pup.

8in (20cm) high

$60-80	DN

A pair of Chinese lead-glazed censers, in Han style, each with five legs and paw feet issuing from dragon masks, with wood covers and stands.

3.25in (8cm) high

$225-275	DN

A rare Chinese blanc-de-Chine figure of Li Tieguai, modeled seated cross-legged, his crutch over his knee and right shoulder, a gourd in his right hand, Kangxi period, fingers and crutch damaged.

Li Tieguai – iron-crutch Li – was one of the Eight Immortals and his spirit was able to leave his body to travel. Once, he asked a student to look after his body while he was away, telling him to burn it if he was not back in seven days. On the sixth day the student had a family emergency and so he burned the body immediately and left a day early. When Li Tieguai returned he was forced to take the body of a crippled beggar who had recently died. He kept this form forever, and was forced to walk with the iron crutch which gave him his name.

3.5in (9cm)

$500-600	DN

A Chinese earthenware Koro and cover, decorated with an ocher and aubergine lead glaze, the cover with agate knop.

A Koro is an earthenware incense burner.

4.75in (12cm) high

$60-80	DN

A Cizou-type vase, the short neck applied with four simple loop handles, the sides covered in a cream glaze and decorated with a carp and an inscription, possibly Ming Dynasty.

10in (25.5cm) high

$300-350	DN

An 18thC Chinese blue and copper-red porcelain Meiping vase, painted with three butterflies, Qing Dynasty.

6.25in (16cm) high

$700-800	SI

A pair of Chinese porcelain bowls and covers, each decorated with lotus, now with gilt metal mounts and set up as censer and cover, with vine knop and pierced border, some damage.

7in (18cm) high

$500-600	DN

A Chinese export baluster vase, incised with Zhou medallions in gilt on a blue key-fret ground, on original ceramic stand.

15in (38cm) diam

$225-275	DN

An early Ming Tzuchou vase, painted in deep brown with flowers on a white slip ground.

9.5in (24cm) high

$250-300	Chef

Japanese Blue and White

SYMBOLISM IN ORIENTAL ART

Oriental art has a rich heritage of symbolism, in which plants, animal, characters and objects have specific meanings, both singularly and in combination. Many of these come from religions such as Confucianism, Taoism and Buddhism, which were introduced in the Far East and shared, between countries. Hinduism has many images represent the balance or cycle of life and death.

Foliage and flowers

- Chrysanthemum - Autumn as well as happiness and a life of ease.
- Wild plum - Winter and longevity.
- Peony - Spring, love and good luck.
- Lotus - Summer and purity.
- In combination, the prunus (sweetness), pine (longevity) and bamboo (uprightness) are called the Three Friends and represent the characteristics of an honorable man.

Animals

- Fish are common motifs, often in pairs, which represent tenacity and fertility.
- The crane, which represents longevity.
- Horses, which represent speed and perseverance.
- Mythical creatures also feature. The dragon symbolizes the Emperor, the phoenix is linked to the sun, the harvest and fertility and is emblematic of the Empress and the Chinese unicorn or "qilin" stands for grandeur, happiness and joy.

Colors

- In Chinese art, colors are linked with the elements and directions of the universe.
- Yellow represents the center of the universe, the earth and the Emperor.
- Red is associated with the south, fire and birth and marriages.
- Black is for the north and water, white is linked with the west and metal, and is the traditional color of mourning.
- Blue represents the east, and wood.

Historical and Legendary Characters

- From Daoism come the Eight Immortals, three of who are historical characters, the rest come from mythology and each has an attribute by which they are identified.
- Zhungli Quan is the chief of the immortals (fan).
- He Xiangu is the Patroness of Housewives (lotus).
- Lan Zaihe is Patron Saint of Florists and Protector of Horticulture (basket of flowers).
- Zao Guozhui is Patron Saint of the Theater (castanets).
- Li Tieguai is the Sage of Magicians and Patron of the Sick (gourd).
- Lu Dongbai is Patron Saint of Barbers (sword).
- Han Xianzi is Patron Saint of Musicians (flute).
- Zhang Gualao is Patron of Old Men (fish drum).

CERAMICS - JAPANESE

A Japanese sake kettle and cover, decorated with panels of prunus and peonies.

c1680   6.75in (17cm) high

$1,500-2,000   **BD**

A CLOSER LOOK AT NABESHIMA

- Practically flawless, off-white body
- Subtle, gray/blue glaze
- Fine potting with an even thickness and shape
- Stylized decoration, typically of flowers and foliage

A Japanese porcelain dish, decorated with a floral arabesque design, the exterior with groups of jewels and ribbons, Nabeshima.

Nabeshima was a feudal lord who controlled production of the kilns at Okawachiyama village in Imari from the mid-1600s. The wares produced at this factory were tightly regulated to a high quality and most sub-standard pieces were destroyed. Production ended in the mid-18thC. The usual palette of iron red, green, yellow, manganese and black was similar to "wucai" which makes this particular piece rare, due to its blue and white decoration. These superior wares were not allowed to be sold but were destined for the Shogun or other lords or high-ranking officials. Many are still retained in Japan where they are treasured, only a few pieces have reached the West.

8in (20cm) diam

$25,000-30,000   **BD**

An early 18thC Japanese Arita mug, decorated with birds and insects amid flowers and foliage, crack to base.

6.75in (17cm) high

$550-650   **WW**

A pair of Japanese hexagonal cups, of conical form, decorated with a paulownica design spreading to the interior, Nabeshima.

c1700   4.5in (11.5cm) wide

$22,000-25,000   **BD**

An 18thC Japanese Arita bottle vase, decorated with foliage.

12.5in (32cm) high

$225-275   **WW**

Japanese Imari

A CLOSER LOOK AT IMARI

The cockerel finial on these vases is rare, as animal motifs are not typically used as finials.

It is very unusual to find a pair of these vases in such good condition.

The paintwork is very intricate and exhibits the skill of the Japanese painters.

The most striking aspect of these pieces is the sheer size – they are almost a meter tall.

A pair of late 17th/early 18thC Japanese Imari octagonal section baluster vases and covers, each decorated with alternate panels of underglaze blue flowers with dense foliage and panels of peony sprays, the shoulders decorated with Karashishi, the domed lids with four Karashishi and with cockerel and chick surmount.

Karashishi *(trans: "Chinese lion")* are *Japanese stone lions or dogs, based on Chinese Fu dogs, and are often found guarding Buddhist temples.*

35in (88.5cm) high

A pair of late 17thC/early 18thC Japanese Imari beaker vases, each painted with a reserve of figures on a pavilion terrace watching frolicking horses, the reverse with a reserve of flowers in a vase.

13in (33cm) high

$24,000-28,000	**L&T**	**$700-800 (pair)** **Chef**

A set of five late 17th/early 18thC Japanese Imari plates, each molded as a gunnera leaf within barbed rims, painted with pine prunus and bamboo with a trellis.

9in (23cm) diam

$300-400 (set)   **CH**

A rare Arita porcelain Imari shallow bowl, the reticulated border painted with a reclining bijin smoking a pipe and reading a scroll, with gilt highlights, the underside with Prunus branch sprays and typical spur mark.

Bijin *is Japanese for "beautiful lady".*

c1700   10.5in (26.5cm) diam

$6,500-7,500   **BD**

An early 18thC Imari plate, painted with a vase of flowering plants, the rim with stylized foliage and floral cartouches enclosing birds.

9.5in (24cm) diam

$225-275   **LC**

A Japanese Imari dish, of peach form, decorated with fish in a stream.

c1720

$1,000-1,300   **BD**

A set of nine early 19thC Japanese Imari plates, decorated in underglaze blue and enamels with a central chrysanthemum, barbed panels and scrolling foliage, gilt rims, with six-character Chinese Chenghua mark, two riveted, minor chips.

9.75in (24.5cm)

$1,000-1,300 (set)   **DN**

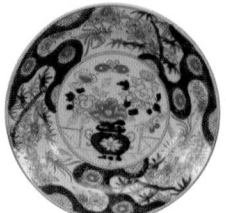

A Japanese Imari porcelain charger, decorated with a central medallion depicting a flower-filled vase and a butterfly, the cavetto and border with shaped reserves with birds and flowering branches, Edo period.

12in (30.5cm) diam

$1,200-1,400   **SI**

A 19thC Japanese Imari deep bowl, centrally decorated with birds in underglaze blue and trailing prunus in iron red, green and yellow, the exterior with a band of boys, with a six-character pseudo-Chinese mark.

6in (15.5cm) diam

$150-200   **DN**

A 19thC Japanese Imari wine pot, the sides decorated with panels of lotus and characters, with chrysanthemum cover.

6.25in (16cm) high

$225-275   **DN**

Japanese Imari

A CLOSER LOOK AT IMARI

IMARI WARE is named after the port of Imari near Arita, Japan from which it was shipped. This ware was developed in the late 17thC and was copied in China, and in Europe by Meissen, Derby and Delft.

These are typically large, display pieces

Blue under-glaze

Iron red and gilt decoration

Densely decorated

Colors sit proud of the surface and can be felt if you run your finger over the piece

Designs were often based on textiles

Typical contrasting area of decoration with panels containing figures, flowers or animals over a background of flowers or flowering branches

◄ A large pair of Japanese Imari bottle vases, each with the neck painted with stylized flowerhead mon and radiating leaf scrolls, the body with alternate opposed circular and quatrefoil panels, one painted with pine tree the other with prunus blossom and exotic birds amid dense mon flowerheads, signed on the base, minor glaze scratching.

30.75in (78cm) high

$9,000-12,000   **L&T**

A pair of 19thC Japanese Imari octagonal bowls, centrally decorated with a floral medallion within a paneled border, the exterior with alternate geometric and diaper ground panels, one with minor chip.

4.75in (12cm) diam

$400-450   **DN**

A 19thC Japanese Imari bowl, decorated with a bird in a pine tree and panels of dragons.

5.75in (14.5cm) diam

$100-140   **DN**

A 19thC Japanese Imari lobed bowl, the interior unusually decorated with gourds and a dragon, the exterior with gourds and flowers, six-character Wanli mark.

7.5in (19cm) diam

$250-300   **DN**

A set of three 19thC Japanese Imari dishes, each decorated with a vase of flowers on a terrace, characters to the corners.

13.5in (34cm) wide

$1,500-2,000 (set)   **DN**

A 19thC Japanese Imari barbed plate, decorated with a dragon within a band of peony.

10.75in (27cm) diam

$150-200   **DN**

A pair of 19thC Japanese Imari plates, with central underglaze blue medallion within radiating panels of flowers, lobed border.

6.75in (17cm) diam

$70-80 (pair)   **DN**

A Japanese Imari mukozuke-type dish, molded and shaped in the form of a duck, seal mark, possibly 19thC.

A mukozuke is a small serving dish

7in (1 8cm) diam

$300-350   **DN**

A 19thC Imari bleeding bowl, centrally decorated with a vase of flowers within a band of iron-red stiff leaves, damaged.

10in (25.5cm) diam

$225-275   **DN**

▶ A pair of Japanese Imari saucer dishes, decorated with central underglaze blue medallions within a border of Zhou medallions and shaped panels of vases and prunus, six character Chinese Chengua mark but 19thC.

8.5in (21.5cm) diam

$120-150 (pair)   **DN**

◄ A pair of late 19thC Japanese Imari bottle vases, each decorated with panels of prunus on a flowering ground.

11.75in (30cm) high

$250-300   **DN**

Japanese Imari

A Japanese Imari double gourd vase, decorated with stylized panels of flowers and foliage, Meiji period, hairline crack to base.

12.25in (31cm) high

$80-100 **WW**

A Japanese Imari porcelain vase and cover, of ovoid form, painted with shaped cartouches containing flower-filled vases, Meiji period.

20in (51cm) high

$1,100-1,300 **SI**

A pair of Japanese Imari porcelain bottles, of square form with short neck, painted with floral and foliage decoration, Meiji period.

8.5in (21.5cm) high

$1,700-2,000 **SI**

A Japanese Imari bottle vase, the globular ribbed body with elongated neck, decorated with shaped medallions enclosing phoenix alternating with bird on flowering branches, with gilt highlights, Meiji period.

19in (48.5cm) high

$1,600-2,000 **SI**

A Japanese Imari pail, decorated in underglaze blue with brocade panels over crashing waves, with high arched handle.

15.5in (39.5cm) high

$110-1300 **DN**

A graduated set of three Japanese Imari barbed dishes, each quartered with lobed panels on a cell ground around an underglaze blue medallion, pseudo Chinese marks.

Largest 8.5in (21.5cm) diam

$400-450 (set) **DN**

A pair of Japanese Imari saucer dishes, decorated with three green ground panels about a central underglaze blue and gilt medallion, pseudo Chinese four character marks.

3.25in (8cm) diam

$150-200 (pair) **DN**

A 20thC Japanese Imari bowl, decorated with panels of flowers within cell borders, with wood cover.

3.25in (8cm) diam

$15-25 **DN**

A Japanese Fukagawa-style fish bowl, the exterior painted with two shaped medallions of fish and flowering blossom, reserved on a paneled ground of dragons, geometric designs and flowers, with gilt highlights, the interior with a large fish, signature to base.

The Fukagawa Porcelain Manufacturing Company was founded in 1894 and still makes high quality contemporary Imari.

11.25in (28.5cm) diam

$600-700 **BonE**

A pair of 20thC Japanese bronze-mounted Imari porcelain jars, each with a pierced basketweave cover, the jar decorated with flowers, foliage and birds highlighted with gilt, the trifid pedestal with scrolling legs and masks.

24.5in (62cm) high

$1,500-2,000 (pair) **SI**

A pair of Japanese Imari baluster vases and covers, decorated with scattered foliage, with shaped bands to the rims, one vase and cover glued, one cover chipped.

c1900 10.5in (26.5cm) high

$60-80 **DN**

Japanese Kakiemon

A CLOSER LOOK AT KAKIEMON

Fine, milky-white body with an almost transparent glaze

Non-circular bodies - tradition has it that Japanese potters were not capable of making round pieces

Bright colors such as iron-red, sky blue, turquoise, pale manganese, dirty yellow and black were used sparingly. Unlike the Imari pattern it was used mostly on smaller pieces

Delicate, free flowing decoration

Iron brown edges were added to protect against chipping

▲1 A Japanese Kakiemon dish, with foliate rim, painted in bright enamels with a butterfly and a chrysanthemum spray, no mark.

c1680	8.25in (21cm) diam

$5,500-6,500

▲2 A rare Japanese Kakiemon tankard, of European form, molded with panels of dragons and chrysanthemums on an unglazed "fish roe" ground and birds in flight above unglazed waves, with a Karakusa scroll to the handle.

Only four other examples of this form have been recorded, a pair noted in the 1688 inventory at Burghley House and a pair that sold at Sotheby's in the late 1960s, c.f. G.Lang, 1983, No. 83, New York, Japan Society, 1986, No. 98.

c1670	5.5in (14cm) high

$35,000-45,000   **WW**

Another product of the Arita area, Kakiemon porcelain reached its peak in the 1680s. It takes its name from legendary porcelain maker and painter, Sakaida Kakiemon, who is credited with inventing the enameling process. Kakiemon was highly prized in Europe and had an influence on factories such as Meissen, Chelsea, Worcester and Samson.

A Japanese Kakiemon plate, with underglaze blue and overglazed enamels of rockwork and flowers.

c1700	8in (20cm) diam

$1,500-2,000   **R&GM**

A set of five Japanese Kakiemon shaped dishes, each painted to the center with a floral bouquet, the border with relief molded decoration and a brown rim, one with gold lacquer repair, another with hairline crack.

	4.75in (12cm) wide

$450-500   **BonE**

A 19thC Japanese Kutani square section tokuri, decorated with figures on a red ground.

Kutani *wares are copies of "Ko Kutani" or old Kutani, which was made during the 17thC and was characterized by bright and plentiful decoration. A Tokuri is a bottle for holding sake.*

	8in (20.5cm) high

$120-180   **WW**

A pair of 19thC Japanese hexagonal slim baluster vases, decorated with prunus, one with a small rim chip.

	9in (23cm)

$225-275   **WW**

► A 19thC Japanese polychrome coffeepot and cover, decorated with birds and foliage.

	9.5in (24cm) high

$200-250   **WW**

A late 19thC Arita green and red plate, the center painted with a plant issuing from rockwork, the sides with variously diapered panels.

	8.25in (21cm) diam

$280-340   **LC**

An early 20thC Kutani figure of Kwannon, depicted wearing beads and robes, decorated in bianco-sopra-bianco with clouds.

Kwannon *was the Japanese Buddhist goddess of Mercy. The term bianco-sopra-bianco (trans: white-on-white) is used to describe white decoration on an off-white ground.*

	12.25in (31cm) high

$140-180   **Chef**

Japanese Satsuma

A Japanese Kutani bowl, the interior decorated with flowering branches, the exterior with scrolling peony.

c1900   6in (15.5cm) diam

$45-60	DN

A Japanese wine cup, decorated with prunus, together with three Oriental paste jars and covers and a small wine pot.

$75-95	DN

Two Japanese Kutani iron-red wine pots and covers, with side handles.

$45-60	DN

A Japanese Kutani footed bowl, the interior decorated with a bird and clouds within iron-red borders, the exterior with a continuous band of ducks and water plants, a leaf band to the foot.

7.5in (19cm) diam

$225-275	DN

SATSUMA

Korean potters in the late 16thC established the first kilns in the Satsuma region of Kyushu. Early wares have a finely crackled slightly yellowish glaze and are typically simple in design, featuring flowers or the occasional phoenix or dragon. These were highly prized by the Japanese nobility and were noted by early Western visitors.

In the 19thC, Satsuma Province exhibited at a number of international exhibitions including the Paris Exposition of 1867 and demand from the West increased. This resulted in more elaborate decoration such as landscapes and figural panels and the introduction of enamels from Kyoto at the end of the 18thC. However, quality was often sacrificed as a result.

The Seikozan studio, and Kinkozan IV (1824-84) and Yabu Meizan (1853-1934) of Kyoto are considered some of the finest producers of Satsuma.

A 19thC Satsuma bowl, the interior decorated with scene of a lady with children crossing a bridge, the exterior with floral sprays, signed Kozan.

6in (15.5cm) diam

$3,500-4,500	BD

A 19thC Satsuma earthenware bowl, decorated with many tiny butterflies in colored enamels and gilt, signed Koshida.

4.75in (12cm) diam

$1,500-2,000	BD

A Satsuma vase, of baluster form with short ring foot, short neck and flared rim, decorated with a dragon chasing flaming pearls through waves and clouds, the shoulders with band of ho-ho and kiri motifs, the neck with brocade design, signed "Satsuma Yaki Rokuzan Sei" and with Kakihan.

A Kakihan is an artist's seal, which is usually made up from kanji characters and is used in conjunction with the impressed seal or signature.

Dragons are a common motif in Oriental art. They are generally considered a benevolent creature and are often used to symbolize royalty. If the dragon represents the Emperor, it will have five claws, a prince, four and a high official, three. They are also considered to guard the spirits of ancestors and have connections to the Spring and rain. You will often see a dragon, or a pair of dragons chasing the flaming pearl wisdom, which symbolized the constant cycle of birth and death.

c1865   12.25in (31cm) high

$8,000-10,000	BD

A Satsuma earthenware dish, decorated with a view of Itsukushima, signed with seal mark of Yabu Meizan.

Itsukushima is one of the most beautiful scenic locations in Japan, situated southwest of Hiroshima, it is also known as Miyajima or Shrine Island. The shrine is still home to the treasures dedicated by the Heishi family, who worshipped a guardian deity there and the entrance to the sacred grounds is marked by the largest torii (gateway to a shine) known. The artist, Yabu Meizan (1853-1934), set up his own workshop in Osaka in 1880 and by the late 1880's was successfully exporting fine earthenware to the West. His great skill brought him fame at domestic and International exhibitions, such as Paris in 1889, Chicago in 1893 and London in 1910. Although well known for his designs incorporating small figures and landscapes with lakes and mountains around the Osaka area, it is rare to find an identifiable location as in this example. Yabu Meizan was considered the most important "modern" decorator of Satsuma. His work is highly prized among collectors and prices are continuing to escalate.

c1880   8.25in (21cm) diam

$9,000-11,000	BD

Japanese Satsuma

An earthenware Kogo, the box and cover painted with a central medallion of children playing games, painting and reading within a border of adjacent petal panels enclosing dense clusters of morning glory and white plum blossoms, the sides similarly decorated with overlapping chrysanthemum blossoms, the interior painted with three small brown birds on twisted vines of purple wisteria on a cream crackle glaze ground, in original fitted wood box, bearing paper label on the underside of the lid Yabu Meizan Of The Finest Satsuma Porcelain, no. 197, Naka, Ni-chrome, Dojima, Osaka, Japan, signed Yabu Meizan.

A kogo is an incense case.

c1880   3.5in (9cm) diam

$7,000-8,000   **BD**

A Satsuma jar and cover, decorated with panels depicting a snow scene, birds in flight among blossom and figural scenes, the cover with flowers and butterflies and panels of boys, monkeys and a sparrow, signed Yabu Meizan.

c1880   4.75in (12cm) high

$9,000-11,000   **BD**

A Satsuma earthenware bowl, of deep tapering cylindrical form, the exterior decorated with group of women and children with kiku and butterflies overhead, the lip and base with patterned designs, the interior depicting a mountainous snow scene, with dwellings amongst pine and willow, the base painted with bijin and children, signed Yabu Meizan.

c1880   3.75in (9.5cm) high

$4,500-5,500   **BD**

▶ A Satsuma earthenware bowl, decorated with a continuous band of three groups of figures meeting on the shore before Mount Fuji, the foot and rim of diaperwork, the interior with travelers and mothers and children in a landscape above a central medallion of birds perched in trees, signed Seikozan.

c1880   6in (15.5cm) diam

$12,000-15,000   **BD**

A small slender ovoid Satsuma vase, decorated in colored enamels with trailing maple leaves, two shaped handles, signed Yabu Meizan.

c1880   4.75in (12cm) high

$2,200-2,600   **BD**

A 19thC Satsuma earthenware vase, of trumpet form, decorated with birds amongst branches, signed Yabu Meizan.

8.25in (21cm) high

$6,000-8,000   **BD**

A Japanese Satsuma vase, decorated with a peacock and other birds among foliage, with gilt seal mark, on a wooden stand, Meiji period.

7.5in (19cm) diam

$400-500   **WW**

A late 19thC Satsuma dish, decorated with figures on a boat before a bridge in a mountainous landscape, the border decorated with chrysanthemum's within a key pattern rim, signed Hankinzan'do.

6in (15.5cm) wide

$5,000-6,000   **BD**

A Japanese Satsuma vase, decorated with figures, Meiji period.

12.5in (32cm) high

$70-80   **WW**

A Japanese Satsuma vase, decorated with figures, Meiji period.

$50-60   **WW**

Japanese Satsuma

A CLOSER LOOK AT SATSUMA

This is a stunning piece of Satsuma ware, made by one of the greatest studios.

Very fine details particularly in the faces, clothing and trees

Delicate borders

Subtle colors

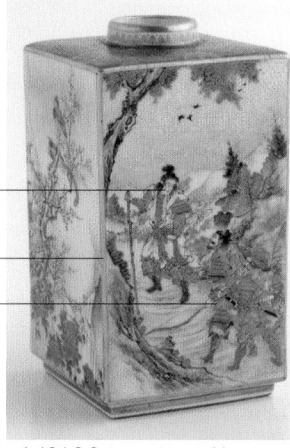

Although it resembles the piece on the left, even a cursory glance reveals the poor quality

Harsh colors

Stiff and unnatural poses

Lack of detail

Poor quality painting

Roughly painted borders

A 19thC Satsuma tea caddy, decorated with scenes of warriors, landscapes and fowl, signed Seikosan Zo.

5in (13cm) high

| $7,500-9,500 | BD |

A Japanese Satsuma vase, Meiji period, decorated with figures.

| $30-40 | WW |

A pair of Japanese square section vases, each decorated with figures in a landscape beneath Mount Fuji, with gilt marks, Meiji period, one with damage to rim.

6.25in (16cm) high

| $160-190 | WW |

A Japanese Satsuma bowl, the interior decorated with a landscape scene of ladies accompanying a group of young boys, bordered by a wide band of flowerheads, the exterior with cascading flowers, signed Seikozan, Meiji period.

c1890   4.75in (12cm) diam

| $4,500-5,500 | BD |

A late 19thC Satsuma dish, decorated with a lobed central cartouche of karako at play on a riverbank, the ground with a multitude of sparrows in flight above buildings in a river landscape, signed Nakamura Baikei.

7.25in (18.5cm) diam

| $12,000-14,000 | BD |

A Satsuma earthenware plate, by Nakamura Baikei, with a shaped and pierced rim, decorated with a city scene depicting a procession including an elephant surrounded by dancing karako, within bands of fans and tennin on dragons over waves.

| $15,000-18,000 | BD |

A pair of Satsuma vases, the bodies of globular form, each decorated with four overlapping panels, one depicting figures in a boat, a geisha playing with a puppet, figures in a tea shop and two ladies reading, the other depicting a watashibune with travelers aboard, ladies dressed in kimonos, figures at a festival by a lake and a lady and young boy by a flower arrangement, the necks decorated with morning glory and with mythical animal handles, signed Nakamura Baikei.

c1885   4.25in (11cm) high

| $18,000-22,000 | BD |

An early 20thC Satsuma jar and cover, the sides painted with warriors and with a dignitary with children, the knop in the form of a boy, indistinct impressed seal marks.

9.75in (25cm) high

| $225-275 | Chef |

A pair of early 20th century Satsuma vases, the cylindrical shapes hollowed out and modeled with bears in caves.

10.25in (26cm) high

| $120-150 | Chef |

A Satsuma vase, of paneled baluster form, painted and gilded with immortals resting on clouds on a dotted ground, the shoulder decorated with fan and star motifs, seal mark to base, late Meiji period.

9.75in (24.5cm) high

| $225-275 | BonS |

Japanese Satsuma

A Satsuma vase, of baluster form, decorated with Samurai warriors, the reverse with birds amid peonies, with applied pierced demi-mon handles, probably late Meiji period.

15.25in (39cm)

$500-600	BonS

A large Satsuma koro and cover, the body delicately decorated in the style of a Japanese painting, depicting an early morning scene of the Imperial Palace, Mount Fuji and other mountains in the distance, the irregular border with scrolling flowers in gilt, the cover with decorated with millefleur reserved among scrolling flowers, with kiku finial, the reverse with peonies and butterflies, signed Kinkozan zo, with his stamped mark.
The Kinkozan factory (1645-1927) produced some of the most collectable Satsuma wares. The factory was made the offical potter for the Tokugawa shogunate in 1756.

c1910   9.5in (24cm) high

$15,000-18,000	BD

▶ A Japanese Satsuma earthenware vase, of ovoid form with a short, waisted neck and everted rim, decorated in enamels and gilt with four rectangular panels, depicting a Chinese style landscape, performers among cherry trees, a flock of sparrows and two ladies in an Autumn garden, all on an iron-red ground overlaid with gilt key-fret pattern and scattered with chrysanthemum, signed Kinkozan.

5.75in (14.5cm) high

$3,000-3,500	BD

A Japanese Satsuma Kinkozan square-section reticulated vase, two sides with pierced roundels and decorated with spring blossom with circular, the others with pierced Moorish-type panels with figural decoration.

5in (13cm) high

$900-1,100	L&T

A mid-20thC Satsuma bowl, painted in gray and gilt with pagoda and pavilion below Mount Fuji, the cinquefoil rim with chevron band.

6in (15.5cm) diam

$40-50	Chef

A Japanese Satsuma vase, painted with a bijin standing in front of a flowering blossom by a lake, within a scrolling gilt border, signed, hairline crack to neck, damaged.

7.5in (19cm) high

$225-275	BonE

A pair of Japanese Satsuma vases, each painted with females standing in front of a pagoda, with mountain and lake landscape, signed.

8.75in (22cm) high

$120-150	BonE

A Japanese Satsuma hexagonal vase, decorated with a prunus tree on a stylized cloud-filled ground within geometric border bands, black and gilt character seal mark to base, signed Kinkozan, late Meiji period.

7.5in (19cm) high

$700-800	BonS

A pair of Satsuma vases, of ovoid shape and painted with processions, three leaf mons on the shoulder bands below the hexagonal rims.

9.75in (24.5cm) high

$700-800 (pair)	Chef

◀ A large pair of Japanese Satsuma vases, decorated with two panels depicting warriors, reserved on a brocade ground, one vase cracked, rubbing to gilt.

24.25in (61.5cm) high

$450-550	BonE

▶ A fine Japanese Satsuma vase, the tapering oviform body painted with a landscape panel, Mount Fujiama in the distance, the reverse depicting immortals and a dragon, reserved on a blue ground with gilt trailing foliage, signed, possibly Seizan.

8in (20cm) high

$1,000-1,300	BonE

Japanese Earthenware

A Japanese Satsuma vase, the ovoid body and pleated neck rim painted with four roundels depicting exotic birds, flowers and a kylin, reserved on a scrolling foliate ground.

12in (30.5cm) high

$700-800	BonE

Two Japanese Satsuma saucer dishes, one painted with a group of bijin resting by a lake, within a floral and brocade border, signed Dai Nippon Kizan, with remains of paper label, the other painted with a group of scholars crossing a bridge in front of a pavillion, Mount Fujiama in the background, signed Dai Nippon Tsuruyama, both with slight rubbing to gilt.

6in (15.5cm) diam

$2,500-2,800	BonE

A late 19thC Japanese group of three earthenware Lohans, one standing, one seated with a scroll, the other with beads, each with a bowl, all inscribed and with seal marks.

Tallest 5.5in (13.5cm) high

$260-300	DN

A late 19thC Japanese earthenware jar, the sides decorated with flowerheads and scrolling tendrils, with bronze rim and pierced wood cover, bearing seal mark.

4.5in (11cm) high

$225-275	DN

A pair of late 19thC Japanese earthenware buckets, each decorated with panels of flowers on a brocade ground, one handle damaged.

6in (15.5cm) high

$300-400	DN

A Japanese Kutani earthenware vase, Meiji period.

10in (25.5cm) high

$600-700	SI

A late 19thC Japanese earthenware bottle vase, decorated with flowering branches of prunus and chrysanthemum within decorative border, with pierced and carved wood stand.

7.5in (19cm) high

$450-500	DN

A Japanese earthenware wine pot and cover, decorated with an exotic bird, knop restored.

2.5in (6.5cm) high

$110-140	DN

A miniature pair of Japanese earthenware baluster vases, decorated with shaped panels of figures on a brocade ground, stained crackle.

3in (7.5cm) high

$700-800	DN

A Japanese earthenware bowl, in the form of a half bundle of cloth tied at each end, covered in a crackled gray glaze with gold lacquer highlights, impressed seal mark, repair.

7.5in (19cm) long

$400-450	DN

Three Japanese earthenware miniature teapots, in unusual shapes, each enameled with brocade panels.

$225-275	DN

A Japanese earthenware bowl, decorated with a band of fruiting branches.

4.75in (12cm) diam

$75-100	DN

◀ A Japanese earthenware two-tier box and cover, pierced with swastika panels and decorated with lotus, possibly lacking a tier.

5.25in (13.5cm) high

$600-700	DN

The term "**swastika**" in Sanskrit translates as a state of well-being. It occurs at the beginning and end of many Buddhist texts to emphasize the words and in Chinese and Japanese it represents the number 10,000 and more generally symbolizes timelessness or immortality. Chinese and Japanese Buddhas are often depicted with a swastika on their chests.

A Japanese earthenware box and cover, with Kylin finial, the feet modeled as crouching figures.

4.75in (12cm) high

$150-200	DN

Japanese Earthenware

A pair of Japanese earthenware vases, of slender baluster form, each decorated with panels of figures on a brocade ground, both damaged.

6in (15cm) high

$75-95   **DN**

A pair of Japanese earthenware baluster vases and covers, decorated with panels of figures and flowers.

10.25in (26cm) high

$500-600   **DN**

A pair of Japanese earthenware oval dishes, decorated in Chinese famille rose style, each with an exotic bird amongst prunus within lappet and cell borders.

10in (25.5cm) long

$150-200 (pair)   **DN**

A 19thC Japanese porcelain table screen, in the form of a crescent moon resting on rocks with two tortoises, the moon covered in a thick blue glaze molded and reserved in white with bats among the clouds, one tortoise restored.

6.25in (16cm)

$100-140   **DN**

A Japanese green glazed brush-washer, in the form of a shell, signed.

c1900   2.75in (7cm) long

$30-40   **DN**

A Japanese conical ash-glazed bowl, with three enameled dancing figures, seal mark and paper labels.

c1900   5.25in (13cm) diam

$150-200   **DN**

A late 19th/early 20thC Japanese porcelain group, depicting two naked boys wrestling, with wood stand.

3in (7.5cm)

$225-275   **DN**

A late 19th/early 20thC Japanese stoneware conical bowl, in Chinese Song Dynasty style, the thick green glaze falling short of the unglazed carved foot, signed.

4.5in (11.5cm) high

$220-250   **DN**

A Japanese Soma ware bowl, the interior sprigged with a horse, the exterior with a horse by a tree, seal mark.

Soma ware typically has a clear, glassy glaze with a green tinge, similar to celadon. It is common to find general crazing.

c1900   4in (10cm) diam

$100-140   **DN**

A Japanese pottery bowl, the ribbed body with molded overlapped edges, the cream glazed ground decorated with grass sheaves and flower pods, on unglazed circular foot, signed Ogata Kenzan.

8in (20cm) wide

$300-350   **BonE**

CERAMICS - OTHER NATIONS

▶ A Thai red-painted earthenware vessel, of ovoid form with a two ring waisted foot, with geometric decoration, Ban Chiang culture. Ban Chiang was a Bronze Age village in North Eastern Thailand whose ruins were first excavated in 1967. Among the remains found was a highly distinctive and varied type of ceramics characterized by red-painted decoration on a buff ground.

3rdC BC-AD 2ndC   8in (20cm) high

$550-650   **SI**

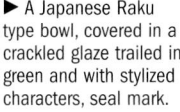

▶ A Japanese Raku type bowl, covered in a crackled glaze trailed in green and with stylized characters, seal mark.

5.25in (13.5cm) diam

$75-95   **DN**

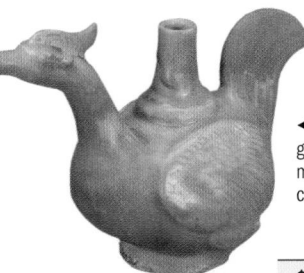

◀ A 14th/15thC Thai Sawankhalok glazed stoneware figural kendi, modeled to depict a bird with a celadon bluish glaze.

6.25in (16cm) high

$300-350   **SI**

A 15thC Vietnamese dish, with bird design, from the Hoi An shipwreck.

8.75in (22cm) diam

$1,000-1,300 **R&GM**

A 15thC Vietnamese water dropper, in the form of a spotted frog, from the Hoi An shipwreck.

2.5in (6.5cm) wide

$500-550 **R&GM**

A 15th/16thC Iznik faience tile, painted in Armenian blue and green on a white ground with a large serrated leaf amid flowering branches.

Trade between China and the Middle East was established by the Tang Dynasty (618-906AD), and together with spices, one of the popular exports was ceramics. By the 16thC, the Middle East were making their own versions of Chinese blue and white ware, in particular in the Iznik region, east of Istanbul, which was on the trade route from the East. Early Iznik is typically blue and white, with the introduction of turquoises and greens from c1525-35 and decoration typically includes the use of flowers such as tulips, carnations and bluebells. Next came the addition of "Armenian bole" (sealing-wax red) and brighter blues and the production of dishes, jugs, mosque lamps and tiles for Istanbul's mosques and palaces. Iznik pottery was also exported to Europe at this time, often with the addition of silver-gilt mounts, and in turn, influenced the look of Italian maiolica.

8in (20cm) wide

$650-750 **SI**

An 18thC Korean celadon wine pot, of double gourd form with loop handle, Chosen Dynasty (1392-1910).

8.5in (21.5cm) high

$1,000-1,300 **SI**

A 19thC Persian polychrome pottery bowl and cover, with floral decoration.

11in (28cm) high

$600-700 **SI**

An Indian glazed terracotta surahi.
c1880

$300-400 **AM**

A western Indian pottery Bombay jar, Maharashtra.
c1880   8.75in (22.5cm) high

$225-275 **AM**

A Thai Sawankhalok stoneware kendi, of globular form with elongated neck, bulbous spout.

Sawankhalok *ware is characterized by its greenish transparent glaze.*

8in (20cm) high

$1,500-1,800 **SI**

A Korean celadon porcelain double gourd vase, inlaid with flowerheads, Koryo Dynasty.

12in (30.5cm) high

$650-750 **SI**

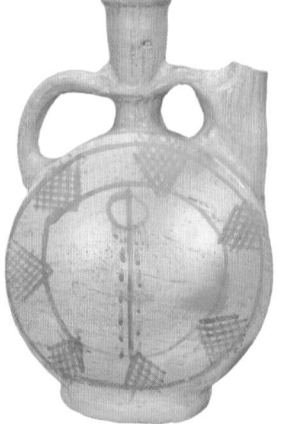

An Islamic pottery pilgrim flask, of flattened circular form, with elongated neck and cylindrical handles, the body painted in brown with a band enclosing geometric motifs.

10.5in (26cm) high

$350-400 **SI**

An Islamic pottery pilgrim flask, of flattened circular form with elongated neck and loop handles, the body painted with square reserves enclosing geometric decoration.

8.75in (22.5cm) high

$400-450 **SI**

BOXES

A quantity of mostly 19thC Chinese export mother-of-pearl gaming counters, in wooden box.

$75-95   DN

One of a pair of 19thC Chinese food baskets.

29.25in (74cm) high

$1,100-1,300 (pair)   OG

A 19thC Indian turned wood spice box, polychrome painted, from Kerala.

5.75in (14.5cm) diam

$200-240   AM

An Indian sewing box, from Manghyr, Bengal.

c1850   12.25in (31cm) wide

$1,200-1,400   AM

An Indian alloy bidri pan box, in the form of a flowerhead, inlaid with silver, from Deccan.

c1860   3.75in (9.5cm) wide

$500-550   AM

A collection of approximately 68 mid- to late 19thC Chinese export mother-of-pearl gaming counters, in fabric-covered box.

$320-380   DN

An Indian Koftgari casket, from Punjab.

Koftgari is gold inlaid into steel.

c1870   6.25in (16cm) wide

$1,000-1,300   AM

A Japanese iron kodansu, with a single door opening to reveal five drawers, the exterior worked in nunomezogon (damascene work) in fine gold sheet with fruiting vines and lobed panels depicting the torii gate of the Itsukushima shrine in Hiroshima, the stage of the Kiyomizu temple in Kyoto, the Toshogu temple in Nikko and a distant view of Mount Fuji in Shizuoka, the drawer fronts decorated with birds among flowers, cranes and pine trees, and phoenix and dragons, signed Dai-Nihon Kyoto-shi Okuno sei.

A late 19thC Chinese Mandarin's bamboo hat box.

11.5in (29cm) high

$225-275   OG

A late 19thC Chinese painted rice barrel.

13.75in (35cm) high

$180-220   OG

An Indian painted box, from Kashmir.

c1900   5in (12.5cm) wide

$300-350   AM

c1880   7in (18cm) high

$30,000-35,000   BD

A late 19thC sandalwood sewing box, decorated with inlaid ivory, sadeli work and metal micro mosaic, with brass handles and claw feet, from Bombay, western India.

12.5in (32cm) wide

$650-750   AM

An Indian octagonal box, from Kashmir.

c1900   3.75in (9.5cm) wide

$350-400   AM

An early 20thC Chinese wooden food box.

22.75in (57.5cm) high

$95-110   OG

An early 20thC Chinese wooden food box.

21in (53cm) high

$95-110   OG

An early 20thC Chinese painted wooden food box.

$95-110   OG

An early 20thC Chinese food basket.

16.5in (42cm) high

$150-180   OG

A pair early 20thC Chinese painted wood food containers.

25.25in (64cm) high

$1,000-1,300 (pair)   OG

A Chinese cinnabar-covered box, decorated with figures in a landscape, containing an eight-piece famille rose porcelain sweetmeat set.

12in (30.5cm) square

$750-850   SI

CARVINGS

A Japanese carved boxwood miniature Noh mask, depicting a frowning man, with pierced eyes and mouth.

2in (5cm) high

$100-150   Clv

A Japanese carved wood miniature Noh mask, depicting a man sticking out his tongue.

2.5in (6.5cm) high

$120-150   Clv

NOH MASKS

Noh theater's origins lie in various forms of rustic, folk entertainment, which by the 14thC, had been combined into a formalized performing art.

All parts are acted by men. The lead actor and his companions may wear a mask if they are playing any character other than an adult man, but boy actors or extras do not.

They are typically made from wood, usually cedar, and are then gessoed and sometimes painted. There are a number of different and specific types of mask such as the "okina" mask for gods, the "jo" mask for old men, and masks for demons, ghosts and women. They are considered to be sculptural works of art.

A Japanese carved wood miniature Noh mask, depicting a snarling man.

2in (5cm) high

$120-150   Clv

A Japanese carved wood miniature Noh mask, signed.

2.5in (6.5cm) high

$130-160   Clv

A Japanese carved wood miniature Noh mask, with pierced mouth, signed.

2.5in (6.5cm) high

$150-180   Clv

A Japanese carved wood miniature Noh mask, with pierced eyes.

2in (5cm) high

$150-180   Clv

▶ A Japanese miniature Noh mask, with gilt lacquer decoration.

2.5in (6.5cm) high

$225-275   Clv

▶ A Japanese carved wood miniature Noh mask, depicting a lady, with pierced eyes and mouth.

2.5in (6.5cm) high

$120-150   Clv

Works of Art

A Japanese wood figure of a Buddha, depicted seated in Lotus position, on a two-tier lotus pedestal, Momoyama period.

22in (56cm) high

$5,000-6,000   **SI**

A Chinese carved wood Ruyi, carved in high relief to depict leafy branches.
*The **Ruyi** scepter is a symbol of rank, authority and achivement.*

20in (50.75cm) long

$1,800-2,200   **SI**

A pair of Chinese gilt wood figures of Fu lions, each depicted surrounded by cubs.

14.5in (37cm) wide

$1,800-2,200   **SI**

► A 19thC Cambodian gilt lacquered wood figure of Buddha, depicted Shan style, seated in dhyanasana on a plinth, his right hand in bhumisparsa mudra and his left hand in dhyana mudra wearing a sanghati, jewelry and a domed crown with elongated finial.

Shan-style refers to the Shan states, Burma, in the late 18thC to early 19thC.

Bhumisparsa is the mudras or 'attitude' for touching the earth and is the most common in Buddhist art. The right hand touching the ground represents the Buddha's signal to the Earth Goddess (Mae Toranee) to witness his resistance to the Mara – the demoness of desire.

26in (66cm) high

$800-900   **SI**

A pair of 19thC Burmese wooden lion dogs.

15.5in (39cm) high

$900-1,200 (pair)   **OG**

A set of four Indian wooden figures, depicting young devotees, with traces of painted decoration, from Calcutta.

c1900   10in (25.5cm) high

$1,500-1,800   **AM**

A 19thC Cambodian gilt lacquered wood figure of Buddha, depicted Shan style, seated in dhyanasana on a plinth, his right hand in bhumisparsa mudra and his left hand in dhyana mudra wearing a sanghati, jewelry and a domed crown with elongated finial.

22.5in (57cm) high

$500-600   **SI**

An Indonesian polychrome wood mask.

16.75in (42.5cm) high

$120-150   **SI**

An Indonesian polychrome wood mask.

19in (48cm) high

$120-150   **SI**

A 18thC Nepalese polychrome wood figure of Bhairava, depicted standing in alidhajana and trampling a victim lying on the base, the face with fierce expression and stylized flaming eyebrows, wearing a wide jeweled collar with incised foliate motifs, a naga around his neck, large beaded disk earrings ornamented with serpents, with foliate diadem fronted by a naga.

49in (124.5cm) high

$2,200-2,600   **SI**

An 18thC carved wood figure, depicting a seated monk with inlaid glass eyes, the robes in black lacquer, the shawl decorated with leaves in gesso and gilding.

6.25in (16cm) high

$650-750   DN

A Buddhistic carved wood figure, possibly depicting Vajrakila, seated on the back of a recumbent bull, with a flaming Mandorla behind, probably 19thC.

9.5in (24cm) high

$800-900   DN

A stained wood and ivory figure, depicting a man in a pointed hat, the tunic and pantaloons with applied ivory and mother-of-pearl mon decoration, a small creel at his waist and holding a broom, on naturalistic plinth, signed on red inset tablet.

17.75in (45cm) high

$3,500-4,000   L&T

A 10th/11thC Indian sandstone carving of an elephant.

10.25in (26cm) high

$600-700   OG

A 10th/11thC Indian sandstone carving of an elephant.

10.25in (26cm) high

$600-700   OG

An 18th/19thC Nepalese polychrome wood phur-pa, depicting three heads with ferocious expressions, with a triangular blade.

*A **phur-pa** (trans: ritual tent stake) is a Tibetan ritual dagger which is used symbolically to conquer evil spirits or negative emotional states, as well as to avert obstacles.*

9in (23cm) high

$900-1,300   SI

An 11thC Indian sandstone carving of an incarnation of Vishnu.

12.25in (31cm) high

$1,500-2,000   OG

An 11thC Indian sandstone Kali head.

12in (30cm) high

$1,500-2,000   OG

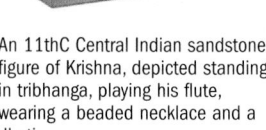

An 11thC Central Indian sandstone figure of Krishna, depicted standing in tribhanga, playing his flute, wearing a beaded necklace and a dhoti.

Tribhanga or "three bends" is a standing posture following an "S" curve.

15in (38cm) high

$1,000-1,300   SI

An Indian sandstone bust.

9th-12thC   14.25in (36cm) high

$1,500-2,000   OG

▶ An 11th/12thC Indian stone bust of a woman, depicted wearing a high chignon and holding attributes in her raised hands.

7.5in (19cm) high

$600-700   SI

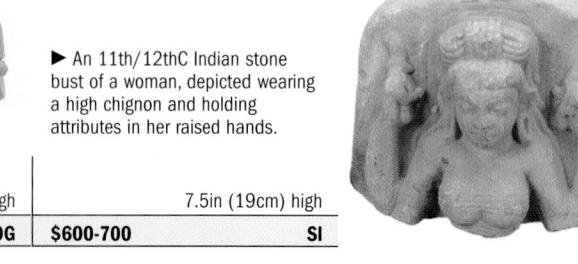

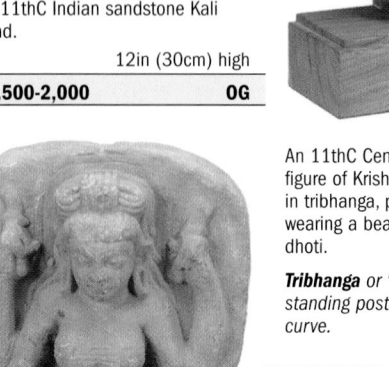

Works of Art – Stone

An Indian red sandstone figure of a woman, depicted standing with her right leg flexed, her two hands behind her head, wearing beaded jewelry, the face with smiling expression.

11thC   14.5in (35.5cm) high

$2,000-2,400   **SI**

An 11th/12thC Indian stone figure of a woman and duck.

10.5in (26.5cm) high

$750-850   **SI**

An 18th/19thC Indian schist carving.

26.75in (68cm) high

$1,100-1,300   **OG**

A 12thC Indian red sandstone bust of a goddess.

10in (26cm) high

$225-275   **SI**

A 2nd/3rdC Indian sandstone hand of Vishnu, from Kushan.

The Kushan people originated from the Turkistan region of China and had settled in northern India by the 1stC BC.

5in (12.5cm) long

$1,200-1,500   **AM**

An Indian Gandharan gray schist figure of Bodhisattva, depicted wearing long robes, a high chignon and jewelry.

3rd-4thC   7.5in (19cm) high

$350-450   **SI**

An Indian sandstone torso of a female divinity, depicted standing in samapada and wearing a short dhoti, a central sash falling between her legs. Samapada means "equal feet".

10thC   19.5in (32cm) high

$1,800-2,200   **SI**

A 9thC North Central Indian head of Vishna, from Uttar Pradesh, wearing an elaborate crown, the face with smiling expression and features in low relief.

This kind of tall conical crown is known as a kiritamukata. It is characteristic of several more fully preserved Vishnu images in the Kanauj district Uttar Pradesh.

8.5in (22cm) high

$2,000-2,300   **SI**

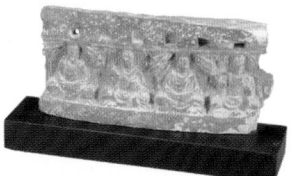

An Indian Gandharan gray schist freize, carved to depict the life of Buddha.

3rd-4thC   10in (25.5cm) long

$700-800   **SI**

► A Japanese granite lantern, of five sections, decorated with calligraphy, Meiji period.

$2,000-2,300   **SI**

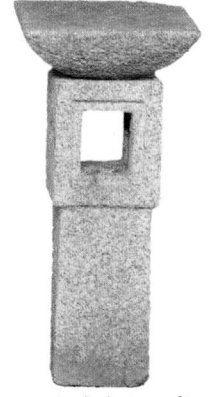

A Japanese granite lantern, of two sections, the flat top above two rectangular and two circular openings, Edo-Meiji period.

$1,000-1,300   **SI**

A Japanese granite lantern, of four sections, the upper section carved with figures in high relief, Edo-Meiji period.

$2,000-2,300   **SI**

A Japanese granite lantern, of five sections, the domed top above hexagonal sections carved with animal lotus panels, the central section with a ring, the base with lotus panels, Meiji period.

$1,800-2,200   **SI**

A Japanese stone figure of a monk, depicted seated in dhyanasana on a rectangular plinth, his hands in namaskara mudra, Edo-Meiji period.

Dhyanasana *is a meditation pose and namaskara is a prayer gesture.*

26in (66cm) high

$1,500-1,800   **SI**

A Japanese stone figure of a monk, depicted seated in dhyanasana on a rectangular plinth, holding a mala in his hands, Edo-Meiji period.

Mala are prayer beads used to aid with meditation and to count the number of times a chant has been repeated.

26in (66cm) high

$1,200-1,500   **SI**

A Japanese stone figure of a monk, depicted seated in dhyanasana on a rectangular plinth, his hands in dhyana mudra holding a bowl with offerings, Edo-Meiji period.

25.5in (65cm) high

$1,100-1,300   **SI**

A late 12thC Thai Khmer brown glazed stoneware figure of an elephant, modeled kneeling with two men on his back, from Angor Wat, Bayon period.

10.5in (26.5cm) high

$600-700   **SI**

Two 14th-15thC Sukhothai stoneware roof tiles, depicting mythical beasts.

Largest 16in (40.5cm) high

$800-900   **SI**

A 17thC Chinese white jade carving of a Fu lion and cub, the white stone with russet inclusion.

2.25in (5.75cm) long

$750-850   **SI China**

An 18thC Chinese white jade carving of two rabbits, depicted holding a lingzhi branch in their mouths.

3in (7.5cm) long

$2,700-3,000   **SI**

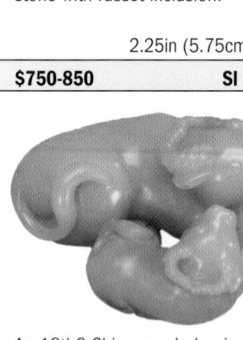

An 18thC Chinese celadon jade carving of a water buffalo and young, the stone with an even tone.

4in (10cm) long

$3,500-4,000   **SI**

A 19thC Persian jade bottle and cover, of flattened ovoid form, with a domed cover and jeweled band on the neck and base.

5.75in (15cm) high

$1,200-1,400   **SI**

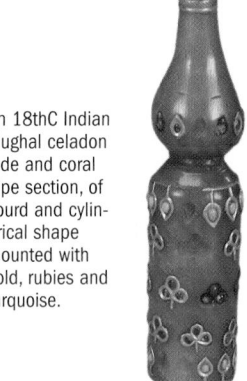

An 18thC Indian Mughal celadon jade and coral pipe section, of gourd and cylindrical shape mounted with gold, rubies and turquoise.

4in (10cm) long

$1,800-2,400   **SI**

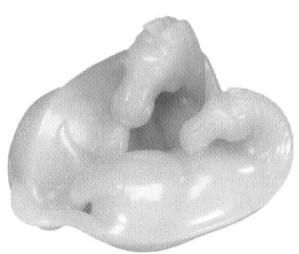

◄ An 18thC Chinese light celadon jade carving of two horses, depicted in recumbent pose looking back over their shoulders.

5in (13cm) long

$3,500-4,000   **SI**

A pair of Chinese "spinach" jade bowls, each carved with rounded sides and slightly everted mouthrim, raised on a slayed footrim, the well-polished stone with green striations and suffused throughout with darker green black speckles, Qing Dynasty.

7.75in (20cm) diam

$2,000-2,500	SI

A pair of Chinese Mughal-style "spinach" jade covered bowls, each finely carved with numerous lotus panels radiating from a central chrysanthemum medallion, Qing Dynasty.

4.5in (11.5cm) diam

$4,000-5,000	SI

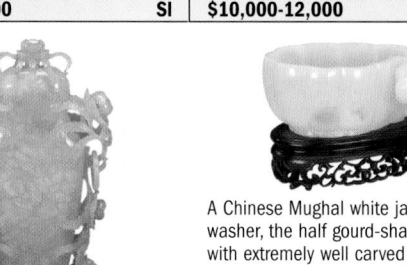

A 19thC Chinese carved jadeite figure of a meiren, depicted wearing flowing robes and ribbons, holding a flowering branch and a vase, the pale mottled stone with apple-green inclusions.

10.75in (27.5cm) high

$1,600-1,900	SI

A 19thC Chinese carved celadon jade figural group, depicting Guanyin seated on a Fu lion, the hands held in dhyanasana supporting a vessel, the voluminous outer robe falling in folds, the inner robe revealing the bare chest adorned with beaded jewelry.

11.5in (29cm) high

$10,000-12,000	SI

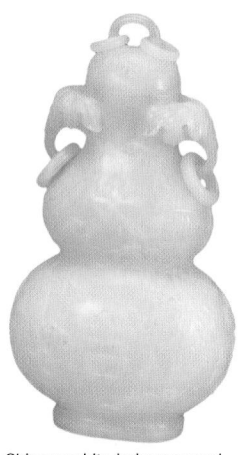

A Chinese Mughal jade covered vase, of flattened ovoid form, the sides and finial carved with flowering branches in high relief, the pale mottled stone with apple-green inclusions, Qing Dynasty.

5.5in 14cm high

$3,000-3,500	SI

A Chinese Mughal white jade brush washer, the half gourd-shaped bowl with extremely well carved ram's head handle, the stone of even white tone, with brownish yellow spots, the base carved with lotus panels.

A similar brush washer is included in the special exhibition of Hindustan jade in the National Palace museum, Taipei.

6in (15.5cm) long

$15,000-18,000	SI

A Chinese white jade vase and cover, of flattened double gourd form, carved with calligraphy and scrolling foliage, with foliate loop and ring handles and finial, Qing Dynasty.

7in (18cm) high

$4,500-5,000	SI

A Chinese white marble stele, carved in the Wei Dynasty style, depicting Buddha standing on a plinth with a frieze of Buddha.

72in (183cm) high

$4,000-4,500	SI

CLOISONNÉ AND ENAMEL

A Chinese white marble head of Guanyin, depicted wearing a headdress and high chignon.

15in (38cm) high

$400-450	SI

A Burmese gilt marble head of Buddha, the face with divine countenance, the gilt hair arranged in rows, surmounted by a unisa.

13.5in (35cm)

$1,800-2,200	SI

A pair of 19thC Japanese Kawano Yoshitaro-style cloisonné vases, decorated with a garden scene with floral sprays and fence on a blue ground.

4.75in (12cm)

$3,500-4,000	BD

A 19thC Japanese silvered-copper-mounted hexagonal cloisonné koro and cover, the five panels decorated with birds and flowers, the sixth with a butterfly and flowers, the shoulders with scrolling foliage and butterflies, the cover pierced with heart designs, with kiku knop.

4.5in (11cm)

$3,500-4,000	BD

A 19thC Japanese cloisonné vase, the front decorated with three Manchurian cranes, another preening itself on the reverse, on a midnight-blue ground, worked in silver wire, signed on the base Aichi Hayashi saku, with stamped lozenge-seal of Hayashi Kodenji.

9.5in (24cm)

$7,500-8,500   **BD**

A 19thC Japanese cloisonné enamel tray, by Kawade Shibataro, decorated with a cockerel, hen and chick on a graduated blue ground within a foliate border.

11.5in (29.5cm) diam

$6,000-7,000   **BD**

A Japanese ivory and silver filigree tray, the central ivory panel with inlaid decoration depicting cockerels and hens amongst flowering branches, surrounded by four shaped gold lacquer panels with inlaid floral decoration, within a silver filigree border, each corner with a cloisonné enamel and silver foliate detail, signed on a mother-of-pearl tablet to base, possibly Masai.

11in (27.5cm)

$6,500-7,500   **BonE**

A CLOSER LOOK AT CLOISONNÉ

The cloisonné technique was introduced into China from Western Asia and wares were first produced in China in the 14th century. Cloisonné was first produced in Japan in the 17th century. The Donin family began making cloisonné medallions as decoration for sword fittings. Chinese cloisonné was exported to Europe in the 19th century.

Soft glass pastes, colored by the addition of minerals and metallic oxides, are applied within the spaces or "cloisons" formed by thin wire, which is soldered to a metal surface. Firing melts the enamel and fuses it to the metal, after which it is ground flush with the surface.

A Japanese silver and enamel vase, the fluted ovoid body embossed and applied with cloisonné flowerheads and copper and silver leaves and branches, reserved on a matt ground, the long trumpet neck and shaped feet with scrolled floral cloisonné details, signed plaque to base, slight denting to neck.

10.5in (26.5cm) high

$600-700   **BonE**

Wares typically have a simple range of colors with a turquoise background, with dark green, cobalt blue, yellow, red and white.

During the Qing dynasty (1644-1911) animals and birds became common motifs

Rose-pink was added to the range of colors in the 18thC

A 19thC Japanese cloisonné enamel vase, decorated wth pigeons among foliage and morning glory, the rim with geometric designs, early Namikawa Sosuke.

12.25in (31cm) high

$4,500-5,000   **BD**

▶ A Japanese cloisonné enamel ovoid vase, with waisted neck and slightly everted mouth, decorated with a sparrow rendered in wireless enamels among a cluster of narcissus in enamels within silver wires, the foot and mouth rimmed in shakudo (an alloy of copper and gold), signed Namikawa Sosuke (1847-1910).

Along with Hayashi Kodenji and Namikawa Yasuyuki, Namikawa Sosuke is one of the most famous and highly sought after names in cloisonné, with prices reflecting the esteem in which his work is held.

c1880   12in (30cm) high

$25,000-30,000   **BD**

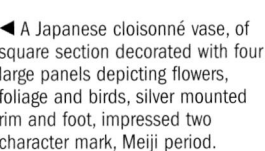

◀ A Japanese cloisonné vase, of square section decorated with four large panels depicting flowers, foliage and birds, silver mounted rim and foot, impressed two character mark, Meiji period.

9.5in (24cm) high

$1,500-2,000   **WW**

150

Works of Art – Cloisonné

A pair of Japanese cloisonné baluster vases, with narrow flared necks, the duck-egg blue ground decorated with hydrangea blossom and birds, one with slight hairline crack to neck.

9.75in (24.5cm) high

$350-450   **L&T**

A pair of small Japanese cloisonné square section tapered baluster vases, the royal blue ground decorated with bamboo shoots, blossom and birds, both with slight bruising to shoulders.

6.25in (15.5cm) high

$180-240   **L&T**

A pair of small Japanese cloisonné hexagonal section tapered baluster vases, the black ground decorated with pigeons on a maple tree above irises and spring flowers.

6in (15cm) high

$200-240   **L&T**

A Japanese green wireless cloisonné ovoid vase, with trumpet neck and everted rim, decorated with a paler green band of chrysanthemum, metal rims, in original wooden box, impressed Tamura seal to base.

10in (25.5cm) high

$500-600   **BonE**

A pair of Japanese cloisonné enamel bottle vases, decorated with animals on a goldstone ground, Meiji period.

4in (10cm) high

$600-650   **SI**

A pair of Japanese Namikawa cloisonné vases, of hexagonal form, decorated with a flowering tree decoration on a yellow-ocher ground, Meiji period, signed.

6in (15cm) high

$4,500-5,000 (pair)   **SI**

A Japanese cloisonné enamel vase, decorated with peony buds, blossoms and foliage on a dark blue ground, Meiji period.

14in (35.5cm) high

$400-450   **SI**

A Japanese cloisonné vase, with floral decoration, Meiji period.

9in (23cm) high

$330-390   **SI**

A pair of Japanese cloisonné vases, with polychrome floral decoration, Meiji period.

7in (18cm) high

$600-650   **SI**

Three Japanese cloisonné enamel vases, a pair of globular vases and an ovoid form vase, all with red enamel and silver mounts, Meiji period.

Tallest 7.25in (18.5cm) high

$350-400   **SI**

A Japanese cloisonné vase, the all-over red enamel decorated with flowering prunus branch, Meiji period, slight damage.

7in (18cm) high

$120-150   **SI**

A Japanese cloisonné vase, the red ground decorated with a flying crane and wave, Meiji period.

6in (15cm) high

$225-275   **SI**

A large Japanese cloisonné enamel vase, decorated with irises on blue ground, Meiji period.

17.5in (44.5cm) high

$1,000-1,400 **SI**

A pair of Japanese cloisonné baluster vases, decorated with birds on a buff ground.

c1900 15.75in (40cm) high

$150-180 **DN**

The Japanese established the art of wireless cloisonné or musenjippo. The Imperial Household of Japan appointed Namikawa Sosuke (1847-1910), an Imperial Craftsman, to perfect the technique. This involves removing the wires that separate the different colors of enamel before firing. Taking out or covering up the wires of the piece concealed the mechanics of the cloisonné and allowed the artist to create enamel decoration that had all the subtlety of a Japanese painting.

A Japanese wireless cloisonné vase, by Gonda Hirosuke (1865-1937), with blue, purple and white iris decoration on rose ground.

3.5in (9cm) high

$1,100-1,300 **SI**

A pair of Chinese cloisonné small bowls, each with in-turned rims and carved wooden tops, decorated with four bats below a linked jui scroll, standing on three bronze elephant head feet, both damaged.

4in (10cm) wide

$250-300 **WW**

An 18thC Chinese gilt bronze and cloisonné vase, of archaic bronze form, decorated with flowerheads and scrolling foliage decoration, with gilt dragon's head handles.

17.25in (44cm) high

$14,00-16,000 **SI**

A Chinese gilt bronze and cloisonné enamel kylin censor, standing four-square on four clawed feet, the broad head with open mouth, horn and mane, on hexagonal cloisonné plinth, Qianlong period.

11in (28cm) high

$3,500-4,000 **SI**

A Chinese cloissonné incense burner, with floral decoration and upright loop handles, Qing Dynasty.

6in (15cm) high

$300-350 **SI**

A pair of Chinese cloisonné enamel partridges, each on a gilt-bronze stand and clutching in its beak a gilt bronze prunus branch terminating in two candle holders.

c1800 9.5in (24.5cm) high

$5,500-6,500 **SI**

▶ A 19thC Chinese small cloisonné jardinière, decorated with roundels of dragons.

8in (20cm) wide

$160-200 **WW**

A cloisonné bowl and bronze stand, the shallow bowl decorated with dragons reserved on a scrolling cloud ground, the stand with similarly intertwined beasts.

8in (20.5cm) diam

$250-300 **BonE**

A cloisonné enamel model of a peacock, with g ld wire.

c1900 8in (20cm) high

$8,000-9,000 **BD**

A cloisonné baluster vase, the faceted body decorated with dragons in compartments reser ed on a blue ground.

14.25in (36cm) high

$90-120 **BonE**

An 18thC Chinese enamel jar, for the Mughal market, slight damage.

The Mughals inhabited North India from the 16th to 18th century. This is an unusual piece because it was made in the Mughal style in China and exported to India. Most Mughal works were made in India.

2.25in (6cm) high

$2,400-2,800	AM

A Chinese Peking enamel double gourd vase, decorated with famille rose enamels on yellow ground, Qianlong mark and period.

10.5in (26.5cm) high

$4,000-5,000	SI

A Chinese famille rose Canton enamel Gu beaker vase, decorated with Shou symbols on a blue flower-strewn ground within gilt borders, six character Qianlong mark and of the period, base drilled.

12.75in (32.5cm) high

$1,500-2,000	WW

A Chinese cloissonné enamel cache pot, of conical form, decorated with flowering branches within rectangular reserves, on three figural feet, Qianlong period.

10.5in (26.5cm) high

$3,000-3,500	SI

A pair of Chinese enamel and silver filigree boxes, of lobed cylindrical form with foliate and bud decoration.

c1800 7in (18cm) high

$1,500-1,800	SI

▶ A Chinese Peking enamel bowl, of shallow shaped form, the center decorated with men on horseback, the cavetto with a dragon chasing the flaming pearl of wisdom, Qing Dynasty (1644-1912).

8.5in (21.5cm) diam

$180-240	SI

◀ A pair of late 19thC Chinese Canton enamel jardinières, each decorated with panels of figures and flowers and raised on lappet feet.

7.5in (19cm)

$225-275	DN

A late 18thC Chinese Peking enamel box and cover, of circular form, with floral medallions.

3in (7.5cm) diam

$750-950	SI

Two Chinese champlevé enamel and bronze umbrella stands.

26in (66cm) high

$270-320 (each)	SI

A 19thC Chinese Canton enamel wine pot and cover, reserved with barbed panels of figures on a scrolling ground beneath yellow border to the neck, some damage.

6in (15.5cm)

$225-275	DN

A pair of 20thC Chinese Canton enamel wine pots, each with arched handle, the rectangular section bodies paneled with figures in landscapes, covers damaged, some dents.

7in (18cm) high

$270-300	DN

INRO

A four-case lacquer inro, the roiro ground decorated in silver, gold and red hiramakie, gold takamakie and details in mother-of-pearl, with a design of segments of water melon in a bowl beside a cleaver, the remainder of the fruit lying under a cloth, signed Hasegawa Shigeyoshi.

c1780   3in (7.5cm) long

$4,500-5,000   **BD**

A late 18thC three-case inro, the hirame ground worked in stained ivory inlays, the front depicting one of the rokkasen seated, enveloped in a voluminous cloak, the reverse with tea ceremony implements, signed beneath with the ritsuo seal.

The Rokkasen were six Immortal poets.

3.25in (8.5cm) long

$3,000-3,500   **BD**

A CLOSER LOOK AT INROS

Inros were introduced in Japan from the mid-16thC. Made up of separate compartments, and typically decorated with lacquer, they were used as a type of purse to carry money, tobacco or herbs. They would be hung from a kimono using a netsuke as a toggle.

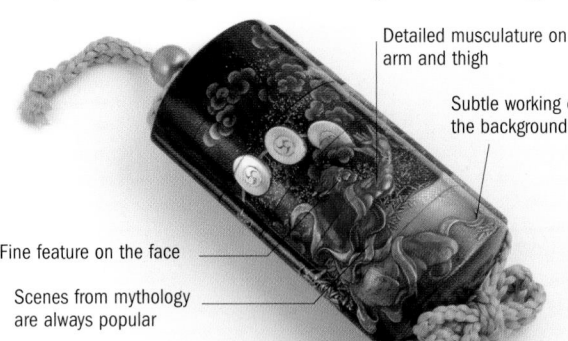

Detailed musculature on arm and thigh

Subtle working of the background

Fine feature on the face

Scenes from mythology are always popular

A 19thC five-case lacquer inro, decorated to the front with Kintaro holding an axe standing on a rock before a waterfall, the scene continues onto the reverse, depicting Raiden with his drums before clouds, the details worked in gold, black, red and rogin takamaie, hiramakie and togidashi, signed on the base in gold lacquer characters Toju, with red lacquer kakihan, Tokyo School.

Kintaro is a popular figure in Japanese folklore. He is a boy who appears in a legend of the 11th century. He was a prodigy of Herculean strength who wrestled with bears and other beasts. Raiden was the god of thunder and lightening.

4in (10cm) long

$15,000-20,000   **BD**

A four-case inro, the brown ground with black lacquer onlays depicting leaves and a broken wheel.

c1850   3in (8cm) long

$1,500-2,000   **BD**

A 19thC five-case laquer inro, the roiro ground with a gilt dragon among swirling clouds in high relief with details in mura nashiji and kirikane, the interior of nashiji, signed Yoyusai with kakihan.

4.75in (12cm) long

$1,500-2,000   **BD**

A Japanese four-case inro, signed, decorated in gold hiramakie with flowering branches, nashiji interior, ivory ojime, Meiji period.

3.5in (9cm) high

$2,000-2,500   **SI**

A Japanese lacquer inro, the nashiji ground embellished in gold hiramakie and laque burgautee inlay depicting butterflies, Meiji period.

3.25in (8.5cm) high

$2,000-2,500   **SI**

A Japanese lacquer two-case inro, the lustrous roiro ground embellished in gold and silver hiramakie decoration of a horse under a pine tree, with a nut ojime, Meiji period.

2.5in (6.5cm) high

$1,000-1,300   **SI**

A Japanese lacquer and shibyama inro, decorated with flowering vine set on a bamboo fence, on nashiji ground and interior, with ivory ojime, Meiji period, signed.

3in (7.5cm) high

$1,500-2,000   **SI**

A Japanese four-case lacquer inro, the gold hiramakie and mother-of-pearl decoration depicting shi shi among flowering branches, with a turquoise glass ojime, Meiji period.

3.5in (9cm) high

$2,200-2,600   **SI**

A Japanese Shibayama ivory inro, signed Shibayama, the inlaid decoration depicting a bird perched on a flowering prunus tree, the reverse with a flowering branch below butterflies, with an ivory ojime, Meiji period.

3.25in (8.5cm) high

$4,000-4,500   **SI**

A Japanese laquer burgautee five-case inro, the center in gold hiramakie with a mon decoration surrounded by floral and foliate decoration, the gilt-silver ojime with filigree floral decoration, Meiji period.

2.25in (5.5cm) high

$1,200-1,500   **SI**

A Japanese gilt lacquer inro, with imperial mon decoration on nashiji ground, Meiji period.

4in (10cm) wide

$900-1,200   **SI**

A Japanese gold and black lacquer four-case inro, with nashiji interior, a bone carved netsuke and a frog-form bronze ojime, Meiji period.

3.5in (9cm) high

$2,000-2,500 SI

A Japanese wood four-case inro, carved to depict a riverscape and architectural decoration, with a wood figural netsuke and an agate, Meiji period.

3.25in (8cm) high

$8,000-9,000 SI

A Japanese gold lacquer three-case inro, decorated with a dignitary wearing a red lacquered robe surrounded by four samurai, the reverse with mountainous riverscape nashiji ground, the coral and gilt-bronze netsuke depicting a shi shi in a niche, the red and black lacquer ojime carved to depict a man and scrolls, Meiji period.

4in (10cm) high

$9,000-11,000 SI

A Japanese gold lacquer four-case inro, the nashiji ground with cart and floral decoration, Meiji period.

3.5in (9cm) high

$1,200-1,500 SI

A Japanese wood three-case inro, carved to depict figures under a pine tree, with a pierced netsuke and a white jade ojime, Meiji period.

3.5in (9cm) high

$500-600 SI

A three case inro, decorated with cranes, signed Kajikawa.

2.75in (7cm) long

$1,500-2,000 BD

IVORY

Ivory has been used in China since the Neolithic period, when the tusks of mammoths were used. Japanese ivory production has always been dependant on imported supplies. The ivory trade is now heavily regulated worldwide. Hong Kong still remains the principle center for ivory carving, although much ivory is now substituted with camel bone.

Cracks in ivory emerge with age, however these are not considered imperfections. Beware of artificial cracking or ageing.

An 18thC Chinese carved ivory figure, depicting a woman wearing a traditional costume, standing on a circular plinth.

7in (18cm) high

$2,250-2,750 SI

A 19thC Indian carved ivory figure, depicting a woman holding a pitcher on her shoulder, on a lotus base.

4.75in (12cm) high

$600-700 SI

A 19thC Chinese carved ivory figure of a "medicine lady", depicting recumbent nude woman on her side.

8in (20cm) long

$1,000-1,300 SI

▶ A 19thC Chinese carved ivory figure of a boy.

4.5in (11.5cm) high

$1,800-2,200 SI

A mid-19thC Indian ivory figure of an Akali Sikh.

5in (13cm) high

$700-800 AM

A Chinese carved bone figure, depicting an acrobat, with articulated joints.

c1870   2.5in (6.5cm) high

$120-150 MB

An Indian ivory figure of Krishna, southern India.

c1900   5.5in (14cm) high

$600-700   **AM**

An early 20thC carved ivory figure, depicting a standing hippopotamus.

5in (12.5cm) long

$120-150   **HamG**

Two early 20thC Chinese carved ivory figures, depicting fishermen holding bamboo sticks and fish.

7in (18cm) high

$350-400   **SI**

An early 20thC Chinese carved ivory figural group, depicting four female musicians seated and standing on rockery.

7in (18cm) high

$500-600   **SI**

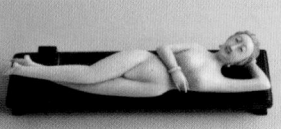

A Japanese carved ivory figure, depicting a reclining nude female, with hardwood stand.

8in (20cm) high

$850-950   **Clv**

A Japanese carved ivory figure, depicting a bear with a crab attacking his back foot, the base with engraved signature.

4in (10cm) long

$1,000-1,300   **Clv**

A Nepalese carved ivory figure of Bhairava, depicted seated, wearing a garland of human heads and a five-skull crown, his face with fierce expression, short curly beard, bulging eyes and flaming eyebrows, holding attributes.

6in (15.5cm) high

$750-850   **SI**

A pair of Chinese ivory figures of meiren, each depicted standing against a pavillion wall with pierced windows, one holding a mirror, the other a musical instrument.

12.25in (31cm) high

$1,100-1,300   **SI**

A pair of Chinese ivory figures of emperor and empress, she holding a ruyi scepter and wearing a high chignon, he holding a sword and wearing a beaded necklace and a hat carved with a dragon.

12in (30.5cm) high

$800-900   **SI**

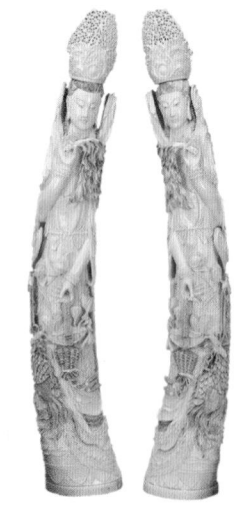

A pair of large Chinese figures of Meiren, each depicted wearing long robes and holding a flower-filled basket and a leafy branch, a high pierced diadem around the well-coiffed hair.

24.5in (62.5cm) high

$3,000-3,500   **SI**

▶ A Chinese carved ivory figure of a meiren, depicted nude, wearing a chignon and holding a shawl on her back.

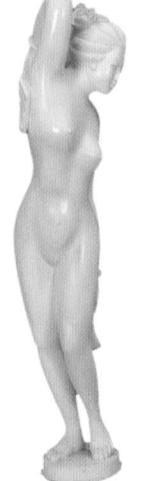

12.25in (31cm) high

$1,000-1,200   **SI**

A pair of Chinese carved ivory figures of emperor and empress, each depicted wearing elaborate robes, jewelry and crown.

9.75in (25cm) high

$600-700   **SI**

▶ A Chinese carved ivory figure of a "medicine" lady, depicting a woman with her head on a pillow.

8in (20cm) high

$350-400   **SI**

Works of Art – Ivory

A Chinese carved ivory figural group, depicting an elephant playing with tigers and leopards.

13in (33cm) long

$500-600 SI

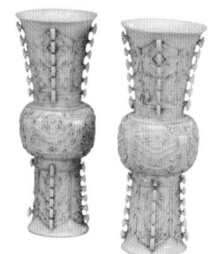

A pair of 18th-19thC Chinese ivory guform vases, of archaic bronze form with taotie masks carved in low relief separated by notched flanges, Qing Dynasty.

6in (15.5cm) high

$3,000-3,500 SI

The hard surface of ivory makes it ideal for carving together with its dense structure which prevents splintering.

Hollow tusks are often fashioned into vases, figures or brush-pots.

Handling and polishing will darken the patina.

Ivory absorbs oils and therefore can be colored.

An 18th-19thC Chinese polychrome ivory vase, of baluster form, with kylin and bat decoration in high relief.

6in (15.5cm) high

$750-850 SI

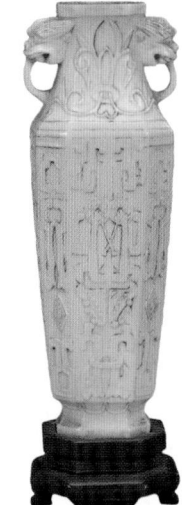

A 19thC Chinese ivory vase, of flattened ovoid form, carved in the archaic style, the waisted neck with two fu dog masks and ring handles.

4in (10cm) high

$750-850 SI

A Japanese ivory tusk vase, finely carved and inlaid in shells and gilt lacquer depicting birds and flowering branches, the black lacquer wood base decorated in hiramakie with flowers and foliage, Meiji period.

10.5in (27cm) high

$600-700 SI

A pair of Japanese ivory vases, carved with floral decoration on stippled ground, Meiji period.

4in (10cm) high

$1,500-2,000 SI

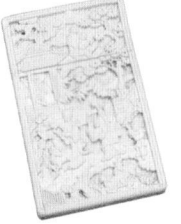

A pair of Japanese Shibayama-style tusk vases, each decorated with a continuous scene of a hen and cockerel beneath boughs of prunus blossom, on integral gilt lacquer stands.

7in (18cm) high

$600-700 L&T

A Chinese ivory vase, of ovoid form, the waisted neck carved to depict two taotie masks within key fret borders, with a dragon finial.

16in (41cm) high

$900-1,100 SI

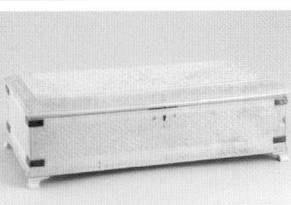

An 18thC ivory Mughal scribe's box, with silver mounts, the interior with pen-tray and secret compartment, from northern India.

11.5in (29.5cm) wide

$6,000-7,000 AM

A Chinese ivory box, carved to depict figures in a landscape, Qing Dynasty.

c1820   3.75in (9.5cm) long

$1,600-2,000 SI

A Chinese ivory card case, carved to depict figures in a courtyard on a key fret ground.

c1840   4.5in (11.5cm) high

$900-1,100 SI

A Chinese carved ivory card case, with figural decoration.

c1840　　4.5in (11.5cm) wide

$1,300-1,600　　**SI**

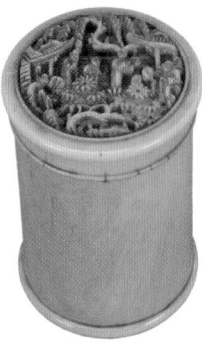

A 19thC Chinese ivory box and cover, the cover depicting figures in a courtyard.

2.5in (6.5cm) high

$400-500　　**SI**

A Chinese Canton ivory export jewelry container, the hinged lid carved in deep relief with a procession of figures, one on horseback, the sides shaped with panels of figures.

5.75in (15cm) wide

$900-1,100　　**L&T**

A 17thC Indian ivory panel, from a box (probably a pen box).

9.75in (25cm) long

$2,000-2,500　　**AM**

An 18thC Indian carved ivory plaque, depicting an erotic couple in an elaborate architectural surrounding, wood frame.

3in (7.5cm) high

$1,200-1,400　　**SI**

A Chinese rhinoceros horn libation cup, of lotus form, the exterior delicately carved in low relief with a continuous large band enclosing a profusion of flowering branches.

c1700　　3in (7.5cm) diam

$3,000-3,500　　**SI**

▶ A large Chinese rhinoceros horn libation cup, finely carved with fruiting and flowering branches and a kylin clambering on the exterior, the interior with an immortal carved in high relief.

Libation cups *were originally used as ritual vessels to offer wine to the gods and those made of rhinoceros horn were additionally considered to protect against poison and confer long life.*

c1700　　8in (20cm) high

$15,000-18,000　　**SI**

A Chinese ivory pocketwatch rest, decorated with figures in a landscape.

c1820　　4in (10cm) long

$1,200-1,400　　**SI**

A pair of Chinese ivory cricket cages, of pierced double gourd form with prunus branches carved in high relief.

c1840　　5in (13cm) high

$2,000-2,400　　**SI**

An 18thC Chinese ivory brush pot, of hexagonal form, with foliate, floral and calligraphy decoration.

4in (10cm) high

$500-600　　**SI**

A Chinese carved ivory pomander, of shaped lozenge form, each side carved in low relief with a central raised medallion with a kylin surrounded by flowering branches on a pierced brocade ground, Qianlong period.

3.5in (9cm) long

$1,800-2,200　　**SI**

A Chinese ivory fan, the pierced decoration depicting a court scene.

c1840　　7.5in (19cm) high

$750-850　　**SI**

A Chinese ivory fan, the pierced decoration depicting a courtyard scene.

c1840　　7.5in (19cm) high

$1,200-1,400　　**SI**

Front

A small late 17thC suzuribako, the cover decorated with an irregular panel depicting a scene of cormorant fisherman, in gold and silver takamakie with e-nashiji and kirigane details, and a corresponding irregular panel of scrolling karakusa and kiku heads in kirigane on a roiro ground (probably later re-lacquering), the interior shows an irrigation trough in the same techniques, with later fitted case.

7in (17.5cm) high

$7,000-8,000   **DN**

LACQUER BOXES

SUZURIBAKO

A Suzuribako is a writing box containing brushes, a water dropper, an ink stick, an inkstone and a water pot.

The art of calligraphy came to Japan with the Buddhist priests of China in the 5th and 6thC. The oldest known piece of Japanese calligraphy is the "Commentary on the Lotus Sutra", attributed to Prince Shotoku (574-622 AD).

The tools of calligraphy have changed little over the centuries and generally consist of two kinds of brushes, thick (futofude) and narrow (hosofude). Ink (sumi) is stored as a stick and is usually made from soot mixed with glue from hides and then dried. This stick is rubbed on an inkstone (suzuri), which has a small, sloping well into which water is poured using a metal or ceramic dropper (suiteki).

Lid inside

Inside

▶ An 18thC suzuribako, the nashiji ground richly decorated with kiku beneath a full moon amid bands of clouds, in silver and shades of gold takamakie with gold foil, kirigane, mother-of-pearl and shakudo details, the inside cover with maple and kiri amid rocks by a river, the sides with similar decoration, the interior fitted with two trays decorated with further maples, a shakudo and gilt mizuire of unusual form, lacking suzuri, with fitted case.

9.5in (24cm) high

$3,000-3,500   **DN**

Front

Lid inside

Inside

▶ An 18thC suzuribako, the kinji ground decorated in silver and gold takamakie with kirigane details, depicting a flowering plum tree within borders of gyobu-nashiji, the inside cover with a landscape of trees beside a lake beneath a cloud-shrouded moon, all similar techniques on a nashiji ground, ink stone and mizuire, with fitted case.

Provenance: *Ex Tomkinson Collection No. 289*

9.75in (25cm) high

$5,000-5,500   **DN**

Front

Lid inside

Inside

Works of Art – Lacquer Boxes

Lacquer is produced from the sap of the Rhus vernicifera tree, which is native to China, Japan and Korea. A Japanese myth states that about 1,600 years ago, Yamato Takeru no Mikoto, a member of the Imperial Family, (referred to as Japan's Odysseus), was fighting for the unification of Japan. While on the battlefield, he broke off a branch of a tree whose leaves had turned brightly red. Beautiful transparent sap began to flow from the broken branch. The prince ordered his retainers to collect the juice and when this was applied to his favorite utensils, they began to glow with a magnificent radiance.

● Lacquer ware has many purposes, it is hard enough to be carved, can withstand heat and is resistant to water.

● Initially used in China as a protective coating, it was developed for decorative purposes during the Han period (206 BC-AD 220).

● During the 13th and 14thC cinnabar was added to create red lacquer.

● During the Ming period (1368-1644), carved scenes in polychrome lacquer with mother-of-pearl inlay were popular.

● From the 16thC Chinese lacquer ware was exported to Europe.

● Lacquer ware has often been restored or re-lacquered. It is sometimes possible to tell the age of a piece by the damage. Song period (960-1279) pieces often have hairline cracks. Yuan period (1279-1368) wares sometimes show signs of deeper cracks. More recent Negoro wares sometimes simulate age. However these wares are not intended to deceive, the makers simply copy the old style out of respect.

● Lacquer wares are frequently marked with an artists name, seal mark or reign; however, these are not always reliable markers of age. Successive generations of artists may have used the same name and also signatures may be forged.

A Japanese suzuribako, decorated in gold hiramakie with a village scene under a full moon and a flying bird, the interior with water dropper and inkstone, Meiji period.

8.5in (21.5cm) high

$800-900	SI

A Japanese suzuribako, decorated in gold hiramakie with flying cranes, the interior with water dropper and inkstone, Meiji period.

9in (23cm) high

$1,000-1,300	SI

▲ A 19thC Chinese tortoiseshell card case.

$90-110	DN

▲ A 19thC Japanese ivory and shibayama purse.

$90-110	DN

▲ A late 19thC Japanese card case, the gilt metal case mounted with rosewood and shibayama decoration of baskets of fruit and vases of lotus.

4in (10cm)

$150-200	DN

A Japanese suzuribako, decorated in gold hiramakie with flying cranes, the interior with a silver crane form water dropper and an inkstone, the cover decorated with three tortoises, Meiji period.

9in (23cm) high

$3,000-3,500	SI

◄ A Japanese lacquer bunko, the interior with a tree on a black and nashiji ground, Meiji period.

12in (30.5cm) wide

$3,500-4,000	SI

◄ A Japanese lacquer suzuribako, the nashiji interior with a stone and fan-shaped brush washer, Taisho period.

6in (15.5cm) wide

$800-900	SI

◄ A Japanese lacquer suzuribako, the interior fitted with a circular ink stone among flowering prunus branches on a nashiji ground, mixed metal brush washer, Meiji period.

9in (23cm) high

$3,000-3,500	SI

Works of Art – Lacquer

A Japanese black and gilt lacquer storage trunk, with hinged top, the gilt-bronze mounts with foliage and mon decoration, the top and sides with gold hiramakie foliage and mon decoration, Meiji period.

35in (89cm) long

$6,000-6,500 **SI**

A Korean lacquer and mother-of-pearl box, the cover decorated with a hunting scene, Yi Dynasty.

19in (48cm) high

$1,800-2,200 **SI**

A 15th/16thC Japanese tanto, in aikuchi mounts, in a black lacquer saya textured to form a stream with waterplants and a tree in gold and brown hiramakie and takamakie, carved with egrets and swallows, the blade signed Kuniyoshi.

A tanto is a dagger with a blade less than 12in (30cm) long. Hirazukuri means a flat blade without a ridge line. Saya is a scabbard.

13.75in (35cm) long

$10,000-12,000 **BD**

A Chinese lac burgaute table screen, finely inlaid with figures by a pavilion in a garden to one side and an inscription to the other, with a carved wood stand, Qianlong period.

Lac burguate means inlaid with mother-of-pearl.

9in (23cm) high

$1,000-1,300 **DN**

A set of three late 18th/early 19thC Chinese lac burgaute small trays, each finely decorated with figures in landscapes, some damage.

4.25in (11cm)

$350-400 **DN**

An 18thC Chinese cinnabar lacquer tray, carved with a scholar and boy in a mountainous river landscape within key fret band, the rim paneled with prunus, on a cell ground.

16.25in (41cm) wide

$1,500-1,800 **DN**

▶ A late 19thC Japanese lacquered tortoiseshell leaf-shaped dish, decorated with three carp, flakes to lacquer.

11in (28cm)

$280-360 **DN**

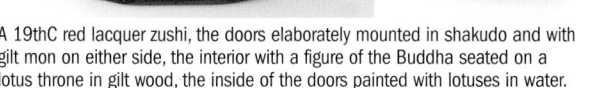

A 19thC red lacquer zushi, the doors elaborately mounted in shakudo and with gilt mon on either side, the interior with a figure of the Buddha seated on a lotus throne in gilt wood, the inside of the doors painted with lotuses in water.

4.25in (11cm)

$1,100-1,400 **DN**

A pair of Japanese shibayama and gilt lacquer vases, each of bamboo form, decorated with butterflies and flowering prunus tree, Meiji period.

6.75in (16.5cm) high

$4,500-5,000 **SI**

A Japanese shibayama and lacquer vase, of ovoid form with a waisted neck, decorated with a woman on a dragon's back, a dove and flowering branches, Meiji period.

7.5in (19cm) high

$1,500-1,800 **SI**

Metalware

An eastern Indian bronze Pala figure, depicting Padmapani seated on a lotus flanked by devotees, with silver inlay, the finial set with a ruby, Pala period

Padmapani means "lotus in hand" and is another name for Avalokiteshvara, the Bodhisattva of Compassion who is always depicted with a lotus. This is a good quality example of the figures being produced at the time, although the iconography is fairly standard. This particular style influenced much Tibetan art in the centuries to follow.

7.75in (20cm) high

$22,000-26,000 AM

A 16thC Indian brass figure of Ambika, from Gujarat.

Ambika is a personification of Parvati, consort of Shiva.

4.25in (11cm) high

$900-1,100 AM

A 16thC western Indian brass figure of Ganesha.

2.25in (6cm) high

$750-850 AM

A 16th/17thC southern Indian bronze figure of Balakrishna.

This figure represents the story of the mischevious baby (bala) Krishna who stole a ball of butter from his mother.

3.5in (9cm) high

$1,200-1,500 AM

A 16th/17thC southern Indian bronze figure of Vithoba.

Vithoba is an incarnation of Krishna and was worshipped in Pandharpur, in western Maharashtra.

5.5in (14cm) high

$700-800 AM

A 16th/17thC southern Indian brass Vijayanagar figure of Yashoda.

4.75in (12cm) high

$1,100-1,400 AM

A 17thC southern Indian brass figure of a dancing Krishna, from Nayaka.

3.25in (8cm) high

$400-450 AM

A North Indian bronze figure of a dancing boy, depicted holding a ball and standing on a lotus pedestal, probably 18thC.

7in (18cm) high

$300-350 DN

An 18thC western Indian bronze figure of Shiva.

4.5in (11.5cm) high

$800-900 AM

An 18thC southern Indian bronze figure of Dipa-Lakshmi.

8.25in (21cm) high

$400-450 AM

An 18thC western Indian brass figure of a Shiva lingham.

This figure represents the god Shiva. The lingham is the phallic symbol representing the male force. Many of these figures were designed to be carried around at processions. This piece is slightly more valuable than similar ones as it carries the head of Shiva, others have no face at all.

6in (15.5cm) high

$2,000-2,500 AM

Metalware

An 18thC southern Indian brass figure of Ganesha, from Deccan.

Ganesha, or Ganesh, is one of the most important gods in Hinduism. He is the son of Shiva and is depicted as an elephant. He is the god of education, knowledge and wisdom, literature and the fine arts. He is also the destroyer of obstacles.

3.25in (8.5cm) high

$600-700   **AM**

▶ An 18thC northwest Indian brass figure of Vishnu and Lakshmi.

Vishnu, also known as Narayana, is one of the greatest gods of Hinduism. Vishnu has many incarnations including Matsya (the fish), Kurma (the tortoise), Varaha (the boar), Narasimha (the man-lion), Vamana (the dwarf), Parashurama (Rama with the axe), Rama, Krishna, Buddha and Kalkin. Vishnu is usually portrayed crowned and bearing in his four hands his emblems; the discus, mace, conch and lotus.

4in (10cm) high

$800-900   **AM**

A 19thC Indian bronze figure of Krishna, from Bengal.

6.25in (16cm) high

$1,200-1,600   **AM**

A 19thC western Indian brass figure of Durga.

3.5in (9cm) high

$1,000-1,300   **AM**

A 19thC southern Indian bronze figure of Vamana.

Vamana the Dwarf is the fifth avatar or manifestation of the Hindu god Vishnu.

4.5in (11.5cm) high

$800-900   **AM**

A 19thC southern Indian brass figure of Garuda.

The half man and half vulture, Garuda the Devourer, was originally an ancient Hindu sun symbol, lived on a diet of snakes and served as a transport for the god Vishnu and his wife, Lakshmi.

3.25in (8.5cm) high

$600-700   **AM**

An Indian bronze figure of Ganesha, depicted dancing with four hands holding attributes, wearing tiered conical crown.

21in (53.5cm) high

$500-600   **SI**

A 19thC (or earlier) central Indian bronze votive figure.

5.75in (14.5cm) high

$1,500-1,800   **AM**

A southern Indian bronze figure of Shiva Nataraja, dancing on a dwarfish demon.

The dancing lord Shiva represents the constant process of creation, preservation and destruction of the universe. He treads on the dwarf, symbol of ignorance, which must be eliminated if a believer is to attain release from the eternal cycle of birth and death.

35.5in (90cm)

$600-700   **SI**

A 17thC southern Indian alloy bidri bowl, with silver inlay, from Deccan.

5in (13cm) diam

$1,000-1,200   **AM**

A 17thC northern Indian brass bowl, with incised floral decoration.

2.75in (7cm) high

$300-400   **AM**

A southern Indian 17thC brass bottle, of bulbous form, with ridged flared neck, from Deccan.

6.25in (16cm) high

$650-750   **AM**

Metalware

A 17th/18thC southern Indian bronze bowl, from Deccan.

4.5in (11.5cm) diam

$500-550   **AM**

An 18thC southern Indian brass jar, with traces of tin, decorated with incised chevron design, from Deccan.

3.5in (9cm) high

$500-550   **AM**

An 18thC Indian bronze bottle, from Sirahi.

7in (18cm) high

$500-550   **AM**

An 18thC southern Indian brass surahi, from Deccan.

Surahi vases were used to keep wine or water, they were luxury items found in the palaces of kings and emperors.

5.5in (14cm) high

$400-450   **AM**

A 15th/16thC southern Indian bronze model temple.

4.5in (10.5cm) high

$2,000-2,500   **AM**

◀ A 16th/17thC bronze southern Indian Makara finial, with Tamil inscription translated as: "O the greatest of great Lord Muruga, you have permeated in all the things of this world, this work is my humble offer to you", from Tamil Nadu.

This finial probably came from a Palaquin pole on a sedan chair. The inscription increases the value of the piece.

Provenance: *Collection of George & Verna Lazarnik, San Diego (purchased at Spink & Son., 1990)*

8.5in (21.5cm) long

$3,500-4,500   **AM**

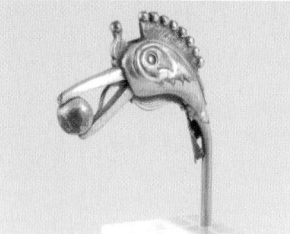

A 17thC southern Indian brass inkpot, of architectural form, with hinged lid, from Deccan.

3.25in (8.5cm) high

$400-450   **AM**

▶ A 17thC southern Indian brass ritual spoon, with makara finial, from Deccan.

In Hindu temples offerings such as saffron, rose, water, honey, milk and ghee were often made in spoons such as this one. If the ritual was not offered correctly, the spoon was discarded and would then be used domestically.

$500-550   **AM**

A 17thC Indian Mughai copper-gilt peacock head.

2.75in (7cm) high

$750-850   **AM**

◀ A 17thC southern Indian brass leopard vyala finial, from Deccan.

*A **vyala** is a mythical, lion-like creature, often featured with horns and a variety of different heads. It is a sun symbol representing the triumph of spirit over matter.*

$350-400   **AM**

A 17thC Indian brass temple lamp, in the form of an elephant standing on a low table supporting a lotus Deccan.

11.5in (29cm) high

$750-850   **AM**

Metalware

A southern Indian brass incense burner, from Deccan.

c1700   5.5in (14cm) high

$500-550   **AM**

An Indian bidri lid, from Deccan.

c1700   8.75in (22cm) diam

$1,200-1,400   **AM**

An 18thC southern Indian bronze temple lamp.

6in (15cm) high

$500-550   **AM**

An 18thC southern Indian brass shrine, mounted.

8.75in (22.5cm) high

$1,000-1,300   **AM**

An 18thC southern Indian bronze ritual spoon, from Deccan.

10.5in (27cm) long

$400-450   **AM**

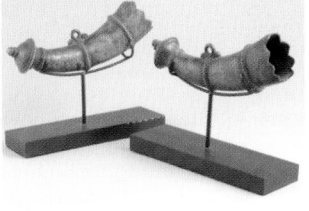

A pair of 18th/19thC western Indian bronze buffalo horns.

7.5in (19cm) long

$200-250   **AM**

An 18thC southern Indian brass dagger hilt, from Deccan.

6.25in (16cm) high

$750-850   **AM**

A 19thC northern Indian silver pendant, with glass inlay.

4in (10cm) long

$400-450   **AM**

METALWARE - JAPANESE

An 18th-19thC Indian repoussé gilt-copper plaque, depicting the head of Shiva, the face with serene expression, the headdress with lotus buds, wearing ear ornaments, a vertical third eye in the forehead.

Together with Brahma and Vishnu, Shiva is one of the three principal gods of Hinduism and his name translates as "auspiciousness, welfare". He is the god of destruction and re-creation. Hinduism teaches that life follows death and, therefore, Shiva is seen as a reproductive power, restoring to life that which has been destroyed. He is always depicted with a third eye in his forehead, which is opened only to destroy evil.

7.25in (18.5cm) high

$900-1,200   **SI**

A 19thC Japanese bronze slender ovoid vase, inlaid in gold and silver colored metals and molded in relief with birds in flowering branches, with two mask handles, some degrading and a dent.

14.5in (37cm) high

$700-800   **DN**

A 19thC Japanese bronze vase, overlaid and lacquered with cranes among lotus and reeds.

9in (23cm) high

$1,500-2,000   **DN**

Metalware

A 19thC Japanese bronze vase, decorated with mallards in various metals, by Chokichi.
Susuki Chokichi (1848-1919) was Imperial Court Artist and Director of the cast metalwork department of the Kiritsu Kosho Kaisha (the first Japanese manufacturing and trading company).

11in (27.5cm) high

$45,000-55,000 **BD**

A Japanese metalwork vase and cover, the body of drum form with two panels depicting Raiden (god of thunder and lightening) and Futen (god of wind), raised on a waisted foot, the cover with kirin finial, the two handles of high flattened form, worked in various metals, signed Motonobu, with Ozeiki seal.

c1880   15.75in (40cm) high

$45,000-50,000 **BD**

A 19thC Japanese tapering ovoid vase, with elongated flared neck, the body with medallions of scrolling foliage, a dragon and ho-ho bird, with two shaped panels with carp, wysteria branches, kiku and waterlillies overhead, tthe neck with stylized wysteria, worked in nikubori and kebori and inlaid in silver and gilt takazogan, signed Ozecki, with fitted box (not shown).

Nikubori *is a type of carving, kebori is line carving, takazogan is raised inlay.*

9.5in (24cm) high

$40,000-50,000 **BD**

A Japanese bronze vase, on a high foot, inlaid and onlaid in silver, gilt and copper, with two shaped panels, one depicting a maiden in a landscape, the other with two ducks in a watery landscape, Meiji period.

9in (23cm) high

$1,300-1,600 **WW**

A pair of Japanese mixed metal vases, each with an ovoid form body with four shaped panels depicting floral scenes, the long flared filigree neck with two shaped enamel panels at the top, worked in silver, shakudo, shibuichi, gold, copper and colored enamels, with stylized handles, signed on a rectangular gold plaque Inshi, Yamada Motonobu for the Ozeki Company.

Yamada Motonobu *is a renowned metalwork artist appointed by the Ozeiki Company which produced the finest works of art of the Meiji period, his artist name (go) is Inshi Motonobu.*

The metalwork of Asian countries is usually of a high quality, both technically and artistically, and through the centuries styles and technical knowledge have passed from country to country. This particularly fine piece is an excellent example of the metalworker's art. Japanese craftsmen often used many different metals to create one item. These included silver, iron and lead and alloys such as copper, pewter, "shibuichi" or "rogin" (which is four parts copper to one part silver and silver-gray in color) and "shakudo" (copper and gold mixed to produce a blue-black alloy).

A pair of late 19thC Japanese silver and shakudo vases, each with bulbous ovoid form body, the neck of slim trumpet design decorated with cockerel and hen in applied metals, signed Hasagawa Issei, Meiji period.

8.75in (22cm) high

$25,000-30,000 **BD**

9in (23cm) high

$150,000-200,000 **BD**

A Japanese hexagonal shibayama vase, the body with shaped panels depicting flowers and birds surrounded by filigree, the long slender neck flared at the rim, the foot and upper part with enameled floral sprays, signed Sadayoshi Koku, Meiji period.

c1880   15in (38cm) high

$12,000-14,000 **BD**

Metalware

A pair of Japanese gold lacquer and silver vases, the bodies decorated with butterflies and flowers, the silver bases and trumpet necks applied with enameled floral cartouches, signed Masayuki on a red lacquer tablet, damage to silver and lacquer.

7in (18cm) high

$900-1,100 **BonE**

A large Japanese bronze baluster vase, cover and stand, decorated in relief with two eagles, one standing on a rocky outcrop, the other diving above waves, smaller birds in the distance, all below a broad band of hanging blade decoration and a Greek key border, the cover modeled with a windswept figure standing in the water surrounded by a dragon, the circular stand with wave and bird decoration, seal mark to base.

35in (89cm) high

$3,500-4,000 **BonE**

A pair of Japanese tetsubin, each cast with panels of stylized birds within formal surrounds, raised on three stub feet, the handle with silver nunome kiku blossoms, the lacquered wood cover depicting cranes over waves, with agate and silver knop.

6.5in (16.5cm)

$225-275 **DN**

A 19thC Japanese iron tetsubin, applied on either side with scenes of Chorio and Kosekiko, one with the shoe riding on a dragon, with gold nunome and soft metal inlays, marbled bronze cover, the handle with gold and silver nunome scrolling foliage.

Nunome decoration *involves cutting a cross-hatched pattern in to metal and then pressing a contrasting colored metal into the grooves.*

Tetsubin are iron teapots whose use seems to coincide with the change in tea-drinking habits in 18thC Japan. As tea drinking became less formal and leaves were used instead of powdered tea, the emphasis moved away from ceremony toward medicine and the simple act of sharing a drink with friends and family. As the traditional utensils were too costly for most people a more affordable teapot was needed and the tetsubin was adapted from simple kitchen equipment. By the 19thC, tetsubin had become symbols of status and many were made with high-relief decoration and inlaid with copper, gold and silver.

9in (23cm) high

$750-850 **DN**

A 19thC Japanese iron tetsubin, the sides cast with scattered cherry blossoms, a stylized character and a maple tree within a snowflake reserve, the signed bronze cover with clove knop.

9in (23cm) high

$90-120 **DN**

▶ An 18thC Japanese Goto School Kogai, the gilt cat-scratched ground with a panel depicting a warrior amid waves by a bridge, unsigned.

7.5in (19cm)

$1,000-1,200 **DN**

▶ A Japanese Hamono School copper split Kogai, carved and inlaid in silver and gold with a spray of kiku and a sake cup, signed Toryusai Noriyuki.

$600-650 **DN**

▶ An 18thC Japanese iron Shoami School Kozuka and Kogai set, decorated in relief and gilding with a spray of flowering prunus, Kozuka and blade.

$650-750 **DN**

A bulbous globular Japanese tetsubin, the textured ground cast with stylized characters and a spray of kiri leaves, with gilt details, the copper handle formed as bamboo, with mottled bronze cover.

8in (20cm) high

$400-500 **DN**

A 19thC Japanese bronze censer and cover, in the form of a mythological Buddhistic beast clutching an entwined base.

4.75in (12cm) high

$750-850 **DN**

▶ A 19thC black lacquered Japanese zushi, with four folding doors at the front, the exterior decorated in gold hiramakie with swirling waves and crane mon, the elaborate gilt copper mounts with scrolling karakusa and kiku, the gilt interior painted with lotuses amid waves, Deity missing.

A zushi *is a miniature shrine.*

6in (15.5cm) high

$140-180 **DN**

Metalware

An 18thC Chinese gilt-bronze figure of Buddha, depicted seated in dhyanasana, the face with serene expression, wearing a foliate crown.

8.5in (21.5cm) high

$1,100-1,400   **SI**

A 19thC Chinese bronze figure of a warrior, depicted standing with billowing robes on a carved wood lacquer lotus base, covered overall in gold and red lacquer.

12in (30.5cm) high

$800-900   **DN**

A Chinese bronze figure of Buddha, depicted seated in dhayanasana, his primary hands in namaskara mudra, the remaining six hands radiating around him and holding attributes, wearing a foliate crown, Qing Dynasty.

10in (25.5cm) high

$350-400   **SI**

On the left, a Chinese bronze figure of Lohan, depicted seated with a rui sceptre, together with three other small Oriental bronzes.

Tallest 4in (10cm) high

$250-300   **DN**

A CLOSER LOOK AT CHINESE BRONZES

Representations of Guanyin always have a small figure of the Amida Buddha in the headdress.

The figure is modeled naturalistically, which is common in Buddhist art of this period.

Guanyin is sitting in a relaxed and natural pose as she waits compassionately to provide comfort and guidance to those in need.

A Chinese gilt-bronze figure of Guanyin, depicted sitting in lalitasana with a child on her knee, flanked by two attendants, Ming Dynasty.

Guanyin is the Chinese name for the Bodhisattva Avalokiteshvara and represents mercy and compassion.

13.5in (33.5cm) high

$14,000-16,000   **SI**

An 18thC Chinese bronze figural incense burner, cast to depict a three-legged toad.

5.5in (14cm) long

$225-275   **SI**

An 18thC Chinese gold splashed bronze ku-form vase, of archaic style, with a rich brown patina with splashed gold.

9.5in (24cm) high

$3,300-4,000   **SI**

A Chinese enamel and filigree silver basket, with a domed cover and swing handle.

c1800   9in (23cm) long

$4,000-4,500   **SI**

A late 19thC Chinese bronze figure of a Fu dog, depicted resting on its haunches with his paw on a ball.

Fu dogs are an ancient, Oriental breed that was originally used as a working dog for hunting and protection. In China they are call "Dogs of Fo" where Fo means Buddha. It is also possible that the name comes from the city of Foochow.

5in (13cm) long

$225-275   **SI**

A late 19thC Chinese bronze brush pot, cast with figures in a continuous landscape.

3.5in (9cm)

$1,500-2,000   **DN**

A pair of late 19thC Chinese bronze censers, each with pendant lappet bands and four feet.

4.5in (11cm) high

$150-200 (pair)   **DN**

A pair of late 19thC Chinese silver colored wine goblets, the rounded bowls on molded bamboo stems, Shanghai.

5in (12.5cm) high

| $120-160 | WW |

A Chinese archaic bronze dagger, the blade with a green patina, animal finial, Eastern Zhou Dynasty.

9in (23cm) high

| $1,300-1,600 | SI |

A Chinese silver punch bowl, on spreading foot, embossed and chased with a continuous mountainous landscape, with figures and pavillions and plain shield, the liner with reeded border, marks to base, slight bruising to interior and liner.

11in (28cm) diam

| $3,000-3,500 | BonE |

A pair of Chinese bronze vases, each cast with flying birds on a brocade ground.

18in (46cm) high

| $750-850 | SI |

METALWARE - TIBET

A 16th/17thC Tibetan gilt-bronze Lama, depicted with the hands in dharmacakra mudra, the flaming sword and jewel emblem on a lotus at either shoulder. Dharmachakra mudra is the gesture of teaching.

6.75in (17cm) high

| $5,000-5,500 | AM |

A Tibetan gilt-bronze figure, depicted in full robes, wearing a crown and seated in contemplation, probably 17thC.

4in (10cm)

| $3,500-4,500 | DN |

A pair of 17thC eastern Tibetan gold damascened steel scroll finials.

1.75in (4.5cm) high

| $450-500 | AM |

An 18thC Sino-Tibetan gilt-bronze figure of Buddha, depicted seated in dhyanasana, the hands in bhumisparsa and dhyanamudra, wearing a sanghati delicately decorated with incised foliate designs, the hair arranged in rows of snail-shell curls.

12in (30.5cm) high

| $12,000-13,000 | SI |

Amid prayers to the various Buddhas and Bodhisattvas of Tibetan Buddhism, is the central figure of Tara, mankind's savior and protector across the ocean of existence. She is said to have been born from a single tear of Avoloketshevara, the Boddhisatva of eternal compassion, and as such, she is seen as a symbol of understanding and compassion. Her love for living beings and her desire to save them from suffering on their journey to enlightenment is said to be stronger than a mother's love of her child.

An 18thC Sino-Tibetan gilt bronze figure of Tara, depicted seated in Lalitasana with her hands in varada and vitarka mudras, a padma rising above her shoulders, wearing a close fitted dhoti and foliate tiara. Tara is any of a group of twenty-one female deities or symbolic figures used as supports during meditation. Lalitasana is a relaxed meditaion pose, varada mudra is the gesture of compassion and vitarka is the gesture of debating. A dhoti is a Hindu loincloth.

4.5in (11.5cm) high

| $1,100-1,300 | SI |

An 18thC Sino-Tibetan gilt bronze figure of Buddha, depicted seated in dhyanasana on a waisted lotus pedestal with hands in dhyanamudra, wearing a sanghati, the face with soft contours framed by tight curls rising to the usnisa.

4in (10cm) high

| $800-900 | SI |

A Sino-Tibetan gilt-bronze figure of Buddha, depicted seated in dhyanasana on a double lotus base, the left hand in dhyanamudra, wearing sanghati, composed facial features framed by snail curls.

7in (18cm) high

| $1,500-1,800 | SI |

Metalware

A Sino-Tibetan silver hand and shrine of Buddha, Amitabha, depicted seated in dhyanasana on beaded double lotus throne, his hands resting in dhyana mudra and supporting a patra, wearing a sanghati, his face with contemplative expression, a numbus behind him with scrolling flames.

Amitabha *is a prominent Buddhist figure.*

3.5in (9cm) high

$600-700   **SI**

A Tibetan gilt-bronze figure of Buddha, depicted seated in dhyanasana with hands in bhumisparsa and dhyana mudras wearing a dhoti.

8in (20cm) high

$400-450   **SI**

A Tibetan gilt-bronze figure of Buddha, depicted seated in dhyansana, hands in dhyana mudra, wearing a dhoti, bracelets, necklaces and crown.

12.5in (32cm) high

$300-350   **SI**

A Tibetan gilt-bronze figure of Manjusri.

Manjusri is the Bodhisattva of Wisdom.

16in (40.5cm) high

$600-700   **SI**

METALWARE - THAI

A 16th/17thC Thai bronze head of Buddha.

3.25in (8.5cm) high

$700-800   **AM**

A 19thC Thai bronze hand of Buddha, from a figure of the divinty, of graceful and elongated form and depicted raised in abhaya mudra, traces of gilding, from Sukhotai.

8in (20.5cm) high

$1,100-1,400   **SI**

An 8thC Thai bronze bust of Vishnu, from Srivijaya.

3in (7.5cm) high

$3,000-3,500   **AM**

A Tibetan gilt bronze figure of Acala, depicted stepping in pratyalidhasana, the right hand holding a flaming sword, the left in karana mudra. 10in (25.5cm) high

Acala is a Bodhisattva who has attained the state of being unperturbed. Here he is pictured in pratyalidhasana, the warrior pose. Buddhist deities are often depicted with their hands forming a ritualized and stylized pose called a mudra, they may also be holding a symolic object and each of these singly and in combination have a specific meaning. For exampe, the karanda mudra is the gesture of Banishing.

10in (25.5cm) high

$500-600   **SI**

A Thai gilt-bronze figure of Buddha, depicted seated in dhyanasana on a lotus throne, his hands in dhyana mudra, wearing a sanghati and elaborate jewelry, Bangkok period.

9.5in (24cm) high

$900-1,100   **SI**

A Thai gilt-bronze figure of Buddha with the Naga, depicted seated in dhyanasana, his hands in dhyana mudra, wearing a sanghati with floral decoration, his face with serene expression, his hair in rows of tight curls, Bangkok period.

10.5in (26.5cm) high

$400-450   **SI**

A Thai gilt lacquered bronze figure of Buddha, depicted with hands raised vitarka mudra, wearing robe, broad belt and collar, with bud-shaped earrings and crown, Bangkok period.

19in (48cm) high

$600-700   **SI**

Metalware

An 18thC Nepalese brass scent bottle.

3.25in (8.5cm) high

$150-175	AM

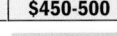

A 19thC Nepalese bronze figure of a female deity.

3.5in (9cm) high

$450-500	AM

▶ A pair of bronze tripod censers and pierced covers, the loop branch handles with flowerhead decoration molded in relief, the pierced covers with similar decoration, on matching bronze stand, slight damage to one cover.

8in (20cm) high

$400-450	BonE

An 18th/19thC Nepalese gilt-bronze figure of Inora, depicted seated in lalitasana, wearing a dhoti decorated with stippled rosettes, a meditation cord across her chest, with foliate armbands, jeweled collar, large beaded disk earrings and tall crown with central quatrefoil ornament.
Inora is the goddess of winter snows.

10in (25.5cm) high

$1,300-1,600	SI

NETSUKE

DESPITE BEING HIGHLY DECORATIVE AND SYMBOLS OF STATUS, NETSUKE ARE ALSO PRACTICAL OBJECTS. Originally, Japanese kimonos were made without pockets, so small, personal items would have to be carried in a bag or box that would be attached by strings to the obi (belt or sash) that fastened the kimono. The strings would be passed through the two holes in the netsuke, which acted as a toggle, to stop the bag or box slipping off the obi.

- Most netsuke are made from wood and ivory, although some are made from silver, tortoiseshell, pottery and stone.
- Look out for pieces with high quality carving, which convey depth and a realistic representation as well as an appealing subject matter.

- The material used does not have a great effect on the value.
- Famous artists carved and signed netsuke, however unsigned pieces are not necessarily less valuable.
- Early netsuke are usually round and flat (manju).
- Later pieces form shallow bowls with a metal lid (kagamibuta) or figures (katabori) such as animals, mythological or legendary characters, ghosts and supernatural beings or masks (men).
- Netsuke were produced from the 17th to the 20thC. The most prolific period being during the first half of the 19thC.
- Fakes are on the market. These are usually made of ivory or plastic or resin made to look like ivory or wood. The carving is usually crude and the poses are unnatural.

▶ An 18thC Japanese ivory netsuke of triangular section, depicting a sennin, standing on one foot, a rice cake in one hand, a sheaf of rice stalks across his shoulders, unsigned.

A sennin is a hermit or wizard.

2.5in (6cm) long

$270-330	DN

An 18thC Japanese wood manju netsuke, carved in relief with kiku blooms and leaves.

1.5in (3.5cm)

$150-175	DN

An 18thC ivory netsuke, depicting a cat scratching, the hairwork marked with patches, the eyes inlaid in dark horn.

2in (5cm) high

$6,000-7,000	BD

An 18thC Japanese ivory netsuke, depicting the story of the blind men and the elephant, the five figures and animal on a rectangular base bearing a key-fret frieze, unsigned.

Five blind men were instructed by their king to describe an elephant by touch. Each man touched a different part and described a different object; the trunk was a giant snake, the tail was a rope, a leg was a tree trunk, an ear was a fan and the body was a wall. An argument started as each man believed he had accurately described the elephant, unable to accept his description only represented a particular perspective.

1.25in (3cm) long

$300-350   **DN**

An 18thC Japanese flat ivory netsuke, carved as a Tartar archer, with a rich amber patina, unsigned.

3.25in (8cm) long

$250-300   **DN**

An 18thC Japanese stagshorn netsuke, depicting a monkey holding a large chestnut and seated on a rock, unsigned.

2.5in (6cm) high

$150-175   **DN**

An 18thC Japanese stagshorn netsuke, depicting a Dutchman holding a crane before him, wearing a crowned hat and an elaborately carved robe, unsigned.

3.75in (9.5cm) high

$250-300   **DN**

A 18thC wood netsuke of a wolf and crab, the eyes inlaid, signed Tomotada.

2in (5cm) long

$2,200-2,600   **BD**

An 18thC Japanese ivory netsuke, depicting two shi shi perched on a ball.

2in (5cm) long

$700-800   **SI**

An 18thC Japanese ivory manju netsuke, carved to depict a melon.

2.5in (6cm) diam

$700-800   **SI**

An 18thC Japanese ivory netsuke, depicting a man seated on a water buffalo's back, on a rectangular plinth.

2in (5cm) high

$750-850   **SI**

A late 18thC Japanese wood netsuke of a rat, the eyes inlaid in tortoiseshell, unsigned.

1.5in (4cm) high

$700-800   **DN**

An late 19thC Japanese wood netsuke, depicting a monkey holding a giant chestnut and seated on a rock.

2in (5cm) high

$120-160   **DN**

An ivory netsuke of a grazing horse, the eyes inlaid in dark horn, unsigned.

c1800   2.75in (7cm) high

$1,500-1,700   **BD**

An early 19thC Japanese ivory netsuke of a rabbit, with double inlaid eyes, signed Tomokazo.

2in (5cm) long

$750-850   **SI**

▶ A 19thC Japanese rogin lacquer hako netsuke, decorated in fundame and nashiji with kiku and kiri mon, with nashiji, unsigned.
Hako netsuke are boxes usually decorated with lacquer or inlay.

1.5in (4cm) high

$450-550   **DN**

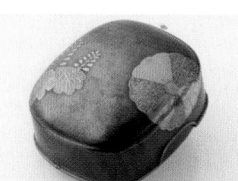

A wood netsuke, depiciting a turtle within its carapace, signed Tomokazu.

Tomokazu worked only with wood, usually boxwood which was then stained a rich medium brown. He often depicted animals, especially those from the zodiac, both singularly and in pairs, and had a very naturalistic style.

c1820   2in (5cm) high

$9,000-10,000   **BD**

A 19thC Japanese ivory netsuke of a sage, depicted standing holding a whisk, unsigned, some damage.

3.5in (9cm) long

$100-140   **DN**

Netsuke

A 19thC Japanese ivory netsuke, depicting an Oni mask, stained and crackled.

An Oni is a traditional Japanese devil mask used by Ninjas to scare superstitious onlookers.

2in (5cm) high

$150-175   **DN**

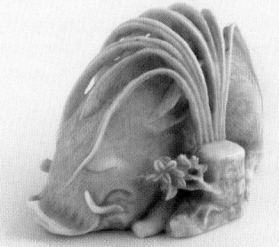

A 19thC ivory netsuke, depicting a sleeping boar among grasses, signed Ryumin, Kyoto.

$6,000-7,000   **BD**

A 19thC ivory netsuke of a clam, with interior scene, signed Kagetoshi.

2in (5cm)

$3,000-3,500   **BD**

A 19thC ivory netsuke of a wickerwork bird cage, opening to reveal a hen, cockerel and chicks, their eyes inlaid, signed Kagatoshi.

1.5in (4cm) high

$3,000-3,500   **BD**

A 19thC wood netsuke, depicting a Nio mending a sandal, signed Takanori.

Originally Hindu gods, the Japanese Buddhists adopted these aggressive guardian deitites in order to justify the use of physical force for the protection of beliefs and values in an otherwise pacifist religion.

1.5in (4cm) high

$2,200-2,800   **BD**

A wood netsuke of a carp and namazu, each biting the tail of the other, the eyes of gilt and black enamel, unsigned and inscribed Sanjin, Nagoya School.

c1850   2in (5.5cm) long

$7,500-8,000   **BD**

A wood netsuke of pumpkin, with snail and aubergine, signed Shigemasa (1739-1820).

c1850   1.75in (4.5cm) high

$6,000-7,000   **BD**

A 19thC ivory netsuke, depicting five frogs clambering on a discarded straw sandal, signed Seimin.

1.5in (4cm) high

$3,000-3,500   **BD**

A 19thC coral netsuke, carved as a biwa fruit, signed Kinma.

2in (5cm) long

$1,100-1,400   **BD**

A wood netsuke, depicting the san sukuni grabbing the leg of a frog as it tries to jump free, the eyes inlaid with horn, signed Haramitsu.

c1850   1.5in (4cm) long

$5,000-6,000   **BD**

A 19thC wood ittobori netsuke of a bat, signed Sukesada.

Ittobori translates as "every stroke counts" and indicates that the craftsman's full attention has into making this piece.

2.25in (5.5cm) high

$1,000-1,400   **BD**

A 19thC wood netsuke, depiciting loquats on a leafy branch.

1.75in (4.5cm) long

$1,200-1,400   **BD**

A 19thC ivory manju netsuke, depicting a dragon among clouds.

Manju netsuke are round and flat and take their name from the popular manju bean paste confection of the same shape.

2.25in (5.5cm) diam

$1,100-1,400   **BD**

A 19thC ivory and metal kagamibuta netsuke, decorated with a standing figure and flowers, unsigned.

1.75in (4.5cm) diam

$750-850   **BD**

A wood netsuke, depiciting a frog on a lotus pod, unsigned.

c1860   1.5in (3.5cm) wide

$1,000-1,300   **BD**

A 19thC ivory netsuke, depicting frogs on a lotus leaf carrying a bucket, drum, batons and rolled leaf, the reverse depicting a small frog trapped under a fold, signed Seimin.

Murata Seimin (1761-1837) was a famous metal artist working in the late Edo period.

2in (5cm) high

$1,100-1,400   **BD**

Netsuke

A late 19thC Japanese bone netsuke, depicting a Noh drama character, signed Gyokko.

1.5in (4cm) high

$100-140   **DN**

A late 19thC ivory netsuke of a seated tiger, the eyes inlaid with pale horn, signed Hakuryu.

1.25in (3cm) high

$450-550   **BD**

A Japanese ivory netsuke, depicting two men seated in a boat, signed, Meiji period.

2in (5cm) long

$600-700   **SI**

A Japanese ivory netsuke depicting a smiling child kneeling over a bowl, signed Keimin, Meiji period.

1.25in (3cm) long

$750-850   **SI**

A Japanese ivory two-section manju netsuke, carved to depict a running figure holding a banner, signed Kogetsusai, Meiji period.

2in (5cm) diam

$650-750   **SI**

A Japanese staghorn kagamibuta netsuke, with shibuichi disc depicting a crane under a flowering tree, Meiji period.

1.5in (4cm) diam

$550-650   **SI**

A Japanese wood netsuke, depicting Chinese coins, Meiji period.

2in (5cm) high

$750-850   **SI**

A Japanese cinnabar lacquer manju netsuke, with foliate scrolling decoration, Meiji period.

1.5in (4cm) square

$450-550   **SI**

A Japanese lacquer kagamibuta netsuke, with shibuichi disc depicting a gilt bird under a flowering tree, Meiji period.

Kagamibuta *means "mirrored lid" and is a special type of netsuke with a metal lid or bowl.*

1.25in (3cm) diam

$600-700   **SI**

A Japanese lacquer netsuke of a double gourd, carved with flowers and waves, Meiji period.

1.5in (4cm) high

$600-700   **SI**

A Japanese ivory netsuke, depicting a boy hiding under a large hat, Meiji period.

2in (5cm) diam

$750-850   **SI**

A Japanese wood netsuke, depicting a shi shi holding a brocade ball, Meiji period.

1.5in (4cm) high

$750-850   **SI**

A Japanese wood and copper netsuke, depicting a crab in a shell, Meiji period.

2in (5cm) long

$650-750   **SI**

A Japanese ivory netsuke of a shi shi, Meiji period.

1.5in (4cm) long

$900-1,100   **SI**

A Japanese ivory netsuke, depicting a snake and toad perched on rockery, with shibiyama inlay, signed Masa Haru, Meiji period.

2in (5cm) high

$500-600   **SI**

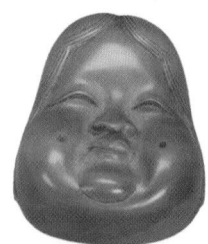

A Japanese wood netsuke of a mask, the smiling female face with a serene expression, signed Tokuto, Meiji period.

1.5in (4cm) high

$600-700   **SI**

Netsuke

A Japanese netsuke, depicting a monkey holding a large mushroom, signed, Meiji period.

2.75in (7cm) long

$800-900   **SI**

A Japanese wood netsuke of a recumbent boar, Meiji period.

2in (5cm) long

$600-700   **SI**

A Japanese ivory netsuke, depicting a rat perched on a rope, with inlaid eyes, Meiji period.

2.5in (6cm) long

$750-850   **SI**

A Japanese ivory netsuke of a man, depicted leaning against a bell, Meiji period.

1.5in (3.75cm) high

$550-600   **SI**

A Japanese wood netsuke of a cicada on a nut, Meiji period.

1.5in (4cm) long

$750-800   **SI**

A Japanese wood netsuke of a shi shi head, Meiji period.

Provenance: *The Society of the Cincinnati*

$450-500   **SI**

Eleven ivory netsuke, carved as various animals including a mouse, ape and rabbit.

$250-300   **Clv**

A Japanese ivory and white metal manju netsuke, cast in relief with a chrysanthemum head, multiple chains attached to an embroidered tobacco pouch, decorated with floral sprays and a white metal clasp in the form of a chrysanthemum.

$650-750   **BonE**

A wood netsuke, in the form of a mask box, Asakura Jo depicted on the lid, inscribed "Nibaku gyonen shichiju-ni saku".

Asakura Jo was a member of the Asakura family that ruled the Echizen area of Japan over 500 years ago.

1.25in (3cm) long

$500-600   **BD**

A Japanese ivory netsuke of a rabbit, with inlaid eyes.

1.5in (4cm) high

$900-1,100   **SI**

A Japanese ivory netsuke of Buddhist emblems, signed.

2.5in (6cm) long

$700-800   **SI**

A Japanese ivory manju netsuke, carved to depict a man and a fish, signed.

2in (5cm) diam

$700-800   **SI**

A Japanese wood netsuke of an elephant, standing on a cartouche-form plinth.

1.5in (4cm) high

$600-700   **SI**

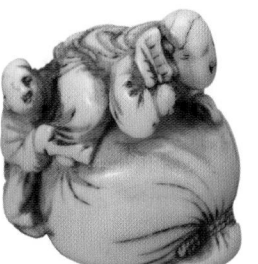

A Japanese ivory netsuke, depicting two men on a sack holding a fan.

1.5in (4cm) high

$750-850   **SI**

A Japanese ivory netsuke of a rabbit gnawing on a stalk, signed.

1.75in (4.5cm) long

$750-850   **SI**

Okimono

OKIMONO

USING SIMILAR THEMES TO THE SMALLER NETSUKE, Okimono are decorative carvings on a larger scale, often depicting intricately worked figurative and animal designs carved from ivory or wood. They were usually made by netsuke carvers and were intended to stand inside a tokonoma or alcove.

The Meiji period was the most prolific period of production. As the Japanese adopted Western clothing, netsuke became obsolete and carvers turned their skills to making okimonos, which were popular with Western collectors.

A 19thC wood okimono of a crouching ratcatcher, an octopus emerging from under his basket, the eyes inlaid with horn, signed Jiun on an ivory plaque.

4in (10cm) high

$3,000-3,500   **BD**

An ivory okimono of a fisherman, depicted seated mending his nets, his son playfully grasping his arm and presenting him with a grasshopper, signed Joei, Meiji period.

c1880   3.75in (9.5cm) high

$4,500-5,000   **BD**

A CLOSER LOOK AT OKIMONO

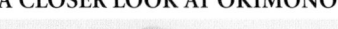

People at work are common subjects for Okimono groups

Japanese carved pieces often have striking poses and flowing lines

Export pieces tend to have a smooth surface without chisel marks which was preferred by the West

A 19thC ivory okimono, depicting a farmer seated on a pile of faggots.
Okimonos were in great demand in the West, which resulted in the production of some poor quality pieces. However, some artists maintained the traditional high standards and produced some wonderful examples.

3.5in (8.5cm) high

$5,000-6,000   **BD**

◀ A Japanese ivory okimono of a basket seller, Meiji period.

3in (7.5cm) long

$1,100-1,400   **SI**

A Japanese ivory okimono, depicting a falcon attacking a wolf, Meiji period.

6.75in (17cm) high

$1,600-1,900   **SI**

▶ An ivory okimono, depicting the young Yoshitusne and Kurama-tengu fighting against Benkei.

Yoshitsune was the child of Yoshitomo, Commander-in-Chief of the Genji family. He trained to become an esoteric priest and educated himself in martial arts. Benkei, who thought himself the strongest man in the world, challenged the samurai to fight. He battled with Yoshitsune but was beaten, and then became a loyal follower of the young master.

c1880   5.25in (13cm) high

$12,000-15,000   **BD**

A 19thC okimono, depicting a lady carrying a basket of fruit, signed Godo.

12.75in (32.5cm) high

$6,000-7,000   **BD**

A Japanese ivory okimono, depicting a monkey clambering on a lantern, Meiji period.

7.5in (19cm) high

$1,800-2,200   **SI**

A Japanese ivory okimono, depicting a hermit and a young boy with puppy, Meiji period.

7in (18cm) high

$3,500-4,000 SI

A Japanese ivory okimono, depicting a farmer with a hoe, a pipe and a basket of vegetables, Meiji period.

8in (20.5cm) high

$1,100-1,400 SI

A Japanese ivory okimono, depicting a mask seller with a musical instrument, Meiji period.

9.5in (24cm) high

$650-750 SI

A Japanese ivory okimono, depicting a man carrying wood and a gourd on his back, Meiji period.

4.5in (11cm) high

$350-400 SI

A Japanese ivory okimono, depicting a woman with two children, Meiji period.

7in (18cm) high

$1,100-1,400 SI

A Japanese ivory okimono, depicting a man with a basket of fruits, Meiji period.

6in (15.5cm) high

$400-500 SI

A Japanese ivory okimono of a Rakan, depicted holding a stick and a model of a pagoda, signed, Showa period.

A Rakan is a disciple of Buddha.

8in (20.5cm) high

$650-750 SI

A Japanese ivory okimono of a seated woodworker, Meiji period.

2in (5cm) high

$180-240 SI

From left: A netsuke in the form of a dog of Fo and a ball, damaged; a Japanese pierced ivory netsuke in the form of a table screen, with a tiger beneath a tree; an okimono carving of a figure seated on a log, damaged.

$250-300 DN

SNUFF BOTTLES

A Chinese white jade snuff bottle, the flawless white stone of flattened ovoid form, set on a neatly finished footrim, one side carved in low relief with a lady holding a mirror, the other with a cartouche enclosing calligraphy, well hollowed, Qianlong period.

$1,200-1,500 SI

A Chinese amber snuff bottle, of pebble form, carved in low relief with a kylin on waves below a fruiting branch, very well hollowed, Qianlong period.

$1,200-1,500 SI

A Chinese enamel snuff bottle, of shield form, decorated with a medallion with bat border enclosing flowering branches, Qianlong period.

$1,800-2,200 SI

A Chinese enamel snuff bottle, of flattened ovoid form, decorated with a deer under a pine and flowering trees and bats, Qianlong mark and period.

$4,500-5,000 SI

Snuff Bottles

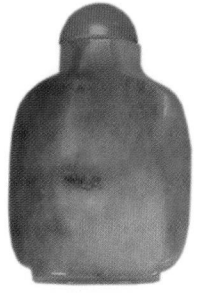

A 19thC Chinese celadon jade snuff bottle, the stone with russet inclusions, well hollowed.

$180-220   **SI**

A 19thC Chinese hair crystal snuff bottle, of flattened rectangular form, resting on a neatly finished footrim, the translucent stone suffused with black crystallines, very well hollowed.

Hair crystal is a form of rock crystal with prisms of black tourmaline. It is brittle with a tendency to split, which makes it difficult to carve.

$250-300   **SI**

A 19thC Chinese yellow jade snuff bottle, the flattened body with relief carving of two birds perched on a flowering prunus branch, well hollowed.

$250-300   **SI**

A 19thC Chinese rock crystal snuff bottle, of hexagonal form, painted inside with a mountainous landscape and calligraphy, well hollowed.

$250-300   **SI**

A 19thC Chinese agate snuff bottle, of flattened rectangular form, the shoulders carved with Fu lion mask and ring handles, the stone of light gray color suffused with ocher inclusions of varied tones, very well hollowed.

$450-500   **SI**

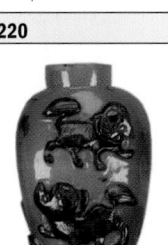

A 19thC Chinese jade snuff bottle, of flattened ovoid form, the stone of honey tone, well hollowed.

$180-220   **SI**

A 19thC Chinese celadon jade snuff bottle, of rectangular form, on neatly finished footrim, carved with four cartouches, well hollowed.

$1,000-1,300   **SI**

A 19thC Chinese agate snuff bottle, of flattened ovoid form, set on a neatly finished footrim, the stone of gray tone with russet inclusions, well hollowed.

$150-175   **SI**

A 19thC Chinese celadon jade snuff bottle, of pebble form, the stone of light celadon tone with russet inclusions.

$400-500   **SI**

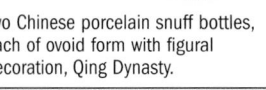

A 19thC Chinese agate snuff bottle, of flattened ovoid form, carved in high relief with two Fu lions, the stone of gray tone with chocolate inclusions, very well hollowed.

$180-220   **SI**

A 19thC Chinese smoked crystal snuff bottle, of flattened rectangular form, set on a neatly finished foot rim, well hollowed.

$120-160   **SI**

A 19thC Chinese agate snuff bottle, of flattened ovoid form, set on a neatly finished footrim, the stone of pale gray tone with white and chocolate inclusions, very well hollowed.

$1,500-2,000   **SI**

A 20thC Chinese lapis lazuli snuff bottle, of flattened ovoid form, carved in high relief with a boy on a carp's back.

$75-100   **SI**

Two Chinese porcelain snuff bottles, each of ovoid form with figural decoration, Qing Dynasty.

$250-300   **SI**

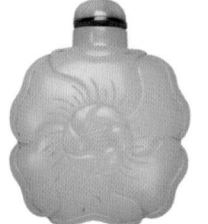

A Chinese white jade snuff bottle, of flattened flowerhead form, the stone of a glossy white tone, well hollowed, Qing Dynasty.

$2,000-2,500   **SI**

A Chinese white jade snuff bottle, of flattened ovoid form, carved with a dragon in high relief, well hollowed, Qing Dynasty.

$3,000-3,500   **SI**

Snuff Bottles

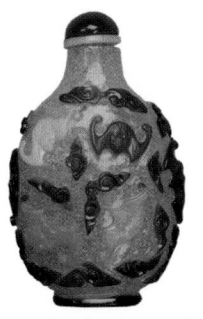

A Chinese six-color glass overlay snuff bottle, of flattened ovoid form rising to a short neck, supported on an oval footring, the overlay over the white "snowflake" ground carved with bats and clouds, Qing Dynasty.

$3,000-3,500   **SI**

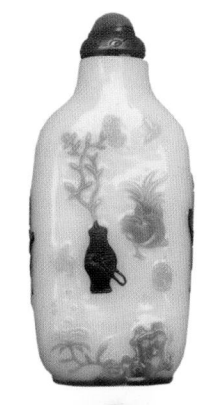

▶ A Chinese five-color overlay glass snuff bottle, of flattened rectangular form, the opaque white body overlaid with blossoming flowers springing from rockwork and precious vessels, a bat and butterfly in flight above, Qing Dynasty, Yangzhou School.

Yangzhou school was situated the Jiangsu district of China, which supported a prosperous artist community during the 19thC. Snuff bottles from this school are typically carved in low relief and with great delicacy.

$1,300-1,600   **SI**

A Chinese jadeite snuff bottle, the ovoid body carved to depict a duck among lotus, set on an oval footrim, the stone of an apple green tone with a darker inclusion, well hollowed, Qing Dynasty.

$900-1,200   **SI**

A Chinese four-color overlay snuff bottle, of flattened ovoid form, the opaque white ground overlaid with continuous scene of duck, lotus and foliage.

$250-300   **SI**

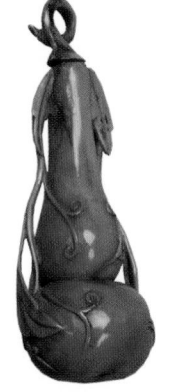

A pair of Chinese ivory snuff bottles, of double gourd form.

$650-750 (pair)   **SI**

A Chinese root amber snuff bottle, of flattened shield form, carved utilizing the ocher inclusions to depict a pine tree issuing from rockery, the reverse with Lui Hai tempting the toad with a child behind him, well-hollowed, Qing Dynasty.

$1,200-1,500   **SI**

A Chinese agate snuff bottle, of flattened form, carved utilizing the russet inclusions against the light gray ground to depict a kylin, a bat and a flaming pearl, very well hollowed, Qing Dynasty.

$500-600   **SI**

● Snuff was introduced to China from the West in the 17th century.

● The Chinese already used small bottles for storing medicine and these early pieces were easily adapted to snuff bottles in the early 18thC.

● Glass , jade and amber were the principle materials, although ivory, porcelain, amber and lacquer were also used.

● Decorative techniques include enameling, carving and cloisonné. During the 18th century the Chinese experimented with carved overlay glass.

● Snuff bottles are highly collectable and even the absence of a stopper will not detract from its value. Some have been adapted from pendants and so may have threading holes. Again this will not detract from the value.

● Snuff bottles are occasionally marked with reigns of dynasties or personal names.

A Chinese shadow agate snuff bottle, of flattened rectangular form, carved utilizing the darker markings to depict a monkey under a pine tree, the reverse with a leaf, very well hollowed, Qing Dynasty.

$750-1,000   **SI**

A Chinese ivory snuff bottle, of shield form, delicately carved with men with a horse and a water buffalo under a willow tree, the shoulders with a ruyi and floral motif, well-hollowed, Qing Dynasty.

$1,200-1,500   **SI**

A Chinese ivory snuff bottle, of flattened ovoid form, exquisitely carved with a dragon chasing the flaming pearl of wisdom on a concentric wave ground, the reverse with two fish with inlaid eyes swimming among aquatic plants, well hollowed, Qing Dynasty.

$800-900   **SI**

A Chinese agate snuff bottle, of flattened square form, carved in low relief with a flying eagle, the stone of gray tone, very well hollowed, Qing Dynasty.

$1,300-1,600   SI

A Chinese ivory snuff bottle, of shield form, carved in low relief with children at play among bamboo issuing from rockery and butterflies, Qing Dynasty.

$800-900   SI

A Chinese agate snuff bottle, of flattened circular form tapering to an oval footrim, carved utilizing the natural inclusions to depict a landscape with trees and pavilion, very well hollowed, Qing Dynasty.

$700-800   SI

A Mughal white jade snuff bottle, embellished with gold and precious stones.

$2,200-2,800   SI

Two Chinese Peking glass snuff bottles, each painted inside to depict warriors on horseback.

$600-700   SI

A Chinese Peking glass double snuff bottle, painted inside to depict birds perched on flowering branches, signed.

$600-700   SI

A Chinese gourd snuff bottle, carved to depict a tiger and palm trees.

Provenance: *The Society of the Cincinnati*

$1,200-1,500   SI

TSUBA

Tsuba are the hand guards on Japanese katana and tachi swords. They protect the hand from the blade and also provide balance. Early tsuba were practical. They were made by the sword-maker himself, from leather with an iron or wooden frame

During the feudal wars of the Muromachi (1338-1573) period, tsuba developed into a status symbol. As tsuba became more highly decorated and specialized, artists began to produce them and schools such as Goto, Hirata, Omori and Nara appear, each with their own distinct style.

Popular materials were iron (tetsu-tsuba) and soft metals (kinko-tsuba) including brass, copper, shaduko, sentoku and shibuichi. Elaborate pieces were pierced and inlaid and decorated with filigree.

During the Edo (1603-1867) period, Tokugawa Ieyasu brought unity and peace to Japan. The Samurai became involved in areas other than fighting and so the production of swords, and therefore tsuba, was reduced. Today few are found that were made after this period.

Tsuba are highly collectible, as they are small and very decorative with a rich history.

An 18thC Japanese iron tsuba, pierced and decorated in gold nunome to represent kenjo-style fans, hitsu-ana plugged in shakudo, unsigned.

3.25in (8.5cm) diam

$800-900   DN

A Japanese iron tsuba, the plate carved and inlaid with a samurai under a flowering prunus tree, the details in gold takazogan and silver, Edo period.

2.25in (6cm) diam

$650-750   SI

A Japanese iron tsuba, of circular quatrefoil form with rope border, the plate with scrolling foliage, Edo period.

3in (8cm) diam

$450-500   SI

A Japanese iron tsuba, of octagonal form, the plate decorated with a shi shi, a dragon and bamboo, with gilt highlights, Edo period.

3.25in (8.5cm) diam

$450-500   SI

Tsuba

A Japanese iron Kenjo Shoami tsuba, pierced and carved with screens in marubori and inlaid with floral designs in gilding, signed Baishige with seal "Ryu".

Marubori means "carving in the round".

3in (8cm) diam

$2,200-2,500   DN

A Japanese Yamagane Tsuba, of octagonal form, perforated with eight rectangular apertures inlaid with lines of blue enamel, the body scattered with cloisonné enamel emblems, early Hirata School.

Yamagane is unrefined copper.

3in (8cm) diam

$1,200-1,500   DN

A Japanese iron tsuba, pierced to depict a flying crane above a pine tree, Edo period.

2.5in (6.5cm) high

$300-350   SI

A Japanese Shakudo Tsuba, decorated on one side with a stag and doe among autumn grasses in kebori and katakiri with gilt inlay, signed Hogen Ichijo, the reverse similarly decorated with two bats among clouds, signed Isshi Hashimoto.

A katakiri is a blade with one flat side and one ridged side.

2.75in (7.5cm) diam

$2,200-2,500   DN

A Japanese Goto School tsuba, the shakudo nanako with plain rim, the body decorated with a dragon in high relief and gilding, pierced with a single hitsu-ana

Nanako means "raised dimpling". A hitsu-ana is a piercing in the handle from which accessories can be hung.

The history of the Goto School spans over five centuries. It was a family of artists who produced an unequalled body of work in the production of soft metal (kodogu). They made sword fittings and also operated the National mint, which produced the majority of the gold coins produced over this period. Theirs were the only fittings allowed to be worn at court functions. They were the height of good taste, reflecting the lifestyles and interests of the Samurai.

3in (8cm) diam

$1,500-1,800   DN

A Japanese iron tsuba, well cast with pavillion and trees, the reverse with a harvest scene, signed Bushu Ju Masatoshi, Edo period.

2.5in (7cm) diam

$500-600   SI

A Japanese iron tsuba, of pierced floriform, with a circle of stylized flowers, Edo period.

3.25in (8.5cm) diam

$350-400   SI

A Japanese iron tsuba, with insect decoration, Edo period.

2.25in (6.5cm) wide

$350-400   SI

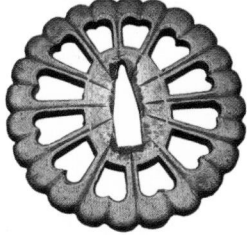

A Japanese iron tsuba, of oval form, pierced to depict a flower, Edo period.

3.25in (8.5cm) diam

$300-350   SI

◄ A Japanese bronze tsuba, of shaped circular form, cast to depict a shi shi mask and kylins on a pierced ground, Edo period.

3in (8cm) diam

$700-800   SI

◄ A Japanese iron tsuba, of circular form, with gilt foliage decoration, Edo period.

3.25in (8.5cm) diam

$300-350   SI

FURNITURE

A Chinese wooden baby chair.

c1800   37.5in (95cm) high

$450-550	**OG**

A 19thC Chinese carved elmwood ladies' chair.

30.75in (78cm) high

$600-700	**OG**

A mid-19thC Chinese yoke-back chair.

43in (109cm) high

$450-550	**OG**

A mid-19thC Chinese folding chair.

36.25in (92cm) high

$350-400	**OG**

A 19thC Chinese elmwood baby chair.

23.25in (59cm) high

$450-550	**OG**

A mid-19thC Chinese carved blackwood chair.

38.25in (97cm) high

$500-600	**OG**

A pair of Chinese stained wood armchairs, each with elaborately carved and pierced frames, the back and arms composed of entwined serpents above serpentine seat with Greek key fret, the legs with winged dragon terminals.

$900-1,200	**L&T**

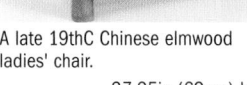

▲1 A 19thC Chinese walnut recessed table.

41in (104cm) wide

$750-850	

▲1 A 19thC Chinese elmwood side chair, with rectangular S-curved splat, Qing Dynasty.

$350-400	**SI**

A late 19thC Chinese elmwood ladies' chair.

27.25in (69cm) high

$220-280	**OG**

CHINESE FURNITURE is typically made from elmwood of which there are two main types.

Northern elm is the most common and as the name suggests, is found mostly in the northern regions. It is chestnut brown and although it is not particularly strong it is resistant against rot and is easy to work with.

Elmwood from the south is a finer wood and is also stronger and denser and can be found with yellow, red or "blood" tones.

A late 19thC Chinese elmwood ladies' chair.

24.5in (62cm) high

$220-280	**OG**

Furniture – Tables

A late 19thC Chinese cypress and elmwood chair.

36in (91cm) high

$300-350   **OG**

An early 20thC Chinese bamboo farmer's chair.

$100-130   **OG**

An early 20thC Chinese bamboo recliner.

42.75in (108.5cm) long

$200-250   **OG**

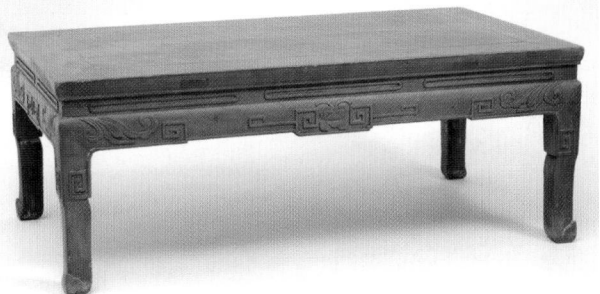

A Chinese yellow elmwood low table.

c1800   31in (78.5cm)

$750-850   **OG**

A Chinese yellow elmwood painting table.

c1800   38in (96.5cm) long

$110-140   **OG**

A 19thC Chinese elmwood small table.

22in (58cm) high

$300-350   **OG**

A 19thC Chinese square table, with rattan top.

25.5in (64.5cm) long

$500-600   **OG**

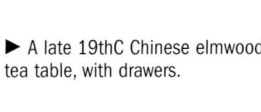

▶ A late 19thC Chinese elmwood tea table, with drawers.

29.25in (74cm) high

$250-300   **OG**

A late 19thC Chinese elmwood tea table, with drawers.

30.5in (77cm) high

$250-300   **OG**

A late 19thC Chinese elmwood tea table with drawers.

30in (76cm) high

$250-300   **OG**

Furniture

A late 19thC Chinese elmwood table, with rattan top and five legs.

25.75in (65.5cm) high

$350-400   **OG**

A late 19thC Chinese elmwood tea table.

30.5in (77.5cm) high

$220-280   **OG**

A 19thC Chinese book cupboard, gilded wood.

14.25in (36cm) long

$350-400   **OG**

A 19thC Chinese red lacquer cabinet, Qing Dynasty.

69in (175.5cm) high

$800-900   **SI**

A Chinese hardwood lacquered cabinet, with pierced foliate galleries and cupboards arranged within a frame of open shelves, carved with painted bone mounts depicting birds within stylized tree and floral landscapes, on a carved base.

41.75in (106cm) wide

$2,200-2,800   **BonE**

A late 19thC Chinese dressing stand.

52in (132cm) high

$450-550   **OG**

A late 19thC Chinese ladies' dressing table.

71.25in (181cm) high

$1,000-1,400   **OG**

An early 20thC Chinese small elmwood cabinet.

29.75in (75.5cm) high

$450-650   **OG**

A late 19thC southern Chinese Kang cabinet.

A Kang cabinet is used for storing blankets and is typically low with a flat top.

42in (106.5cm) long

$350-400   **OG**

An early 20thC Chinese wooden chest.

23.75in (60cm) high

$220-280   **OG**

A pair of Chinese rosewood cabinets, inlaid with hardstones to depict flowering trees, Republic period.

40.5in (95cm) wide

$3,500-4,500 (pair)   **SI**

Furniture

An 18thC Chinese elmwood stool, with rattan top.

17.5in (44cm) high

$300-350　　**OG**

An 18thC Chinese red elmwood stool.

41.5in (105cm) wide

$500-550　　**OG**

An 18th/19thC Chinese elmwood stool.

$200-250　　**OG**

An early 20thC Chinese Congo wooden throne.

$300-350　　**OG**

An early 20thC Chinese yellow elmwood stool.

23.75in (60cm) high

$100-130　　**OG**

A Chinese rosewood jardinière stand, with pink marble inset top above profusely carved apron and legs, the ball and claw feet connected by stretchers.

17.75in (45cm) high

$220-280　　**BonE**

A late 19thC Chinese washing bowl stand.

32in (81cm) high

$150-175　　**OG**

A pair of Chinese hardwood jardinière stands, each with lobed circular tops relief carved with a band of peony and with beaded edge, above an elaborate pierced and carved frieze, the leaf-carved cabriole legs linked by a lower tier and terminating in claw and ball feet.

32.75in (83cm) diam

$2,500-3,000　　**L&T**

An early 20thC Chinese wooden washing bucket.

22.5in (57cm) high

$75-95　　**OG**

▶ A large 19th/20thC Chinese wooden washing bowl.

14.75in (37.5cm) high

$450-550　　**OG**

A 19thC Chinese cypresswood baby cradle.

37.75in (96cm) high

$450-550　　**OG**

A late 19thC Chinese carved wood screen, with porcelain panels.

66.5in (169cm) high

$1,100-1,400　　**OG**

185

Beds

THE MARKET FOR AMERICAN FURNITURE HAS BECOME MORE SOPHISTICATED OVER THE PAST TEN YEARS. SO MUCH RESEARCH HAS BEEN PUT INTO THE COUNTRY'S FURNITURE MAKERS that collectors are becoming increasingly discerning. As a reult there is little interest in mediocre pieces while buyers are willing to pay top prices for the best they can find; a trend which is likely to continue. Condition is paramount, especially that of the surface and the brasses.

Regionalism is very important, with buyers concentrating on furniture from areas such as Boston, Philadelphia, New England, New Hampshire and Baltimore. Prices have never been stronger for items originating in the German areas of Pennsylvania. Plus, a piece of furniture which can also be identified as being made a particular craftsman has much added appeal.

The market for English furniture from the reigns of King George II and King George III continues to be strong and, as always, smaller pieces command higher prices because they are better suited to modern homes.

Dining room furniture is selling well as more and more households emulate the formal dining style of the 19thC upper classes, buying sets of dining chairs, tables and cellarets. Library furniture is another growth area, with desks, globes, and library chairs appealing to a wider market. Away from specialist buyers, fashion and decorators are influencing the market. This has contributed to a decline in demand for furniture in the French taste.

Top quality is desirable in every field and poor quality pieces, or those which are over restored, are extremely difficult to sell.

BEDS

A fine George III-style satinwood four-poster bed, the canopy with a domed molded cornice painted with floral trails, surmounted by urns painted with swags of flowers and with a painted lambrequin border, on turned reeded supports carved with leafage, and painted with swags, including a silk hanging and lace frills and side curtains.

An extremely similar period bed is illustrated by Percy MacQuiod, The Age of Satinwood, p.144; as the resemblance is so close and the arms coincide, it would seem reasonable that this was made as a pair to the bed illustrated by MacQuoid, and the present one may once have been part of the Assheton Smith collection.

c1890	109in (277cm) high
$22,000-25,000	**WW**

A pair of late 19thC turned-brass single bedsteads, each open headboard incorporating a row of finialled and annulated posts on turned feet, the footboard similar but lower and with curved ends.

59.5in (151cm) high

$2,000-3,000 (pair)	**SI**

A late 19thC French Louis XV-style ivory-painted carved beechwood lit d'alcove.

Provenance: *The Society of the Cincinnati.*

43in (109cm) wide

$700-800	**SI**

A Classical tiger maple bed with tester, the baluster-turned and "tassle" carved posts on block and ring-turned legs and tapering feet, metal tester.

c1830	88in (223.5cm) high
$2,000-2,500	**SI**

BONHEURS DU JOUR

A mid-19thC crossbanded walnut bonheur du jour, the double galleries over ogee-gabled doors, flanking four central drawers, the base with single frieze drawer on cabriole legs, the whole with gilt-metal mounts.

56.75in (144cm) wide

$3,000-3,500 **L&T**

A late 19thC French bonheur du jour, rosewood-veneered with gilt-brass mounts, the serpentine top with a superstructure fitted with a shelf and two drawers, the drawer with a tooled leather inset slide, on slender cabriole legs, serpentine top split.

28.5in (72cm)

$1,100-1,400 **WW**

A late 19thC Louis XVI-style ormolu and porcelain-mounted part-ebonized thuya wood bonheur du jour, the upper section with a tall central mirror-backed open display cabinet with a three-quarter gallery flanked by similar but lower cabinets, each door cencenteredd by a porcelain plaque painted with a French courtly lady, the canted stiles mounted with free-standing ormolu figures of Shakespeare and Milton, the outset lower section with an entrelac frieze incorporating three drawers, the center drawer with a hinged leather-lined adjustable writing slope, raised on turned tapered and fluted legs supporting open mirror-backed shelves and raised on turned feet with casters, inlaid throughout with thuya wood panels on an ebonized ground and mounted with gilt-bronze moldings and "Sèvres" floral plaques.

58.75in (149cm) high

$6,000-7,000 **SI**

BOOKCASES

A late 19thC French Louis XV-style rosewood and marquetry bonheur du jour, the superstructure with a central cupboard surmounted by an arched cornice with a shell-cast crest flanked by flame finials, the front with a glazed door opening to a velvet-lined interior rised on low galleried pedestals, each incorporating a drawer, the outset lower section with a serpentine top over a shaped frieze with a drawer, continuing into square-section cabriole legs, bronze-dore-mounts and floral marquetry panels throughout.

52.25in (133cm) high

$3,000-3,500 **SI**

▶ A Regency satinwood library bookcase, the arcaded cornice over glazed double-lancet arched doors, the base with oval-banded inset panel doors, on plinth.

37in (94cm) wide

$10,000-12,000 **L&T**

A French walnut and burr-walnut bonheur du jour, the top with a gallery and three drawers with turned wood handles, above a fall enclosing a fitted interior with leather inset and a drawer on cabriole legs.

27.5in (69.5cm) wide

$900-1,100 **DN**

A Regency mahogany break-front bookcase, the projecting molded-cornice above twin central astragal-glazed doors flanked by two further doors, each enclosing adjustable shelves, above a base with four paneled doors raised on a plinth.

114.5in (291cm) high

$7,000-8,000 **L&T**

A Regency oak break-front bookcase, the molded cornice above glazed doors enclosing adjustable shelves on deeper base with paneled doors incorporating ogee-gothic moldings enclosing drawers and shelves, on plinth base.

Provenance: Property of the Clan Mackay Association.

100.5in (255cm) wide

$10,000-12,000 **L&T**

Bookcases

An early 19thC mahogany bookcase, the molded cornice above a pair of astragal-glazed doors enclosing adjustable shelves, on deeper base with pair of reeded panel doors and splayed bracket feet.

95.25in (242cm) high

$5,000-6,000   **L&T**

A Regency-style satinwood and mahogany-veneered cabinet bookcase, the upper section with astragal-glazed doors enclosing adjustable shelves, surmounted by gothic-arcaded cornice with balustrade and finials, the base with paneled doors enclosing cupboard flanked by reeded columns with leaf-carved capitals on turned feet.

54.5in (138cm) wide

$7,000-8,000   **L&T**

A late Regency mahogany library bookcase, the molded cornice over two lancet Gothic doors, with roundels, enclosing shelves, the base with two paneled cupboards flanked by columns on plinth base.

56in (142cm) wide

$5,000-6,000   **L&T**

A late Regency mahogany break-front cabinet bookcase, the upper section with a molded cornice, the outset central-section with a pair of eight-pane astragal doors opening to adjustable shelves, the recessed sides similar but with single doors, the conforming lower section with four paneled doors opening to shelves, raised on a molded plinth base.

c1825   87.5in (222.5cm) high

$6,000-7,000   **SI**

A William IV mahogany bookcase, the molded cornice above three glazed doors enclosing adjustable shelves, with deeper base and three frieze drawers above three recessed paneled cupboard doors flanked by waisted pilasters on plinth base.

103.5in (263cm) high

$4,000-5,000   **L&T**

A William IV mahogany reverse break-front secrétaire bookcase, the molded cornice above two open adjustable shelves divided by pilasters, the deeper base centered by a secrétaire drawer with paneled doors below, flanked by frieze drawers and pedestals of five graduated drawers with hinged locking-flaps, on plinth base.

88.5in (225cm) high

$10,000-12,000   **L&T**

An early Victorian mahogany break-front bookcase, the molded cornice with plain central pediment above four doors with arcaded astragals enclosing adjustable shelves, the deeper base with paneled doors and plinth base.

100.5in (255cm) wide

$9,000-11,000   **L&T**

A 19thC mahogany secrétaire bookcase, double-door glazed top having four adjustable shelves above frieze-fitted secrétaire drawer, double door cupboard to base.

$2,000-2,500   **BW**

A Victorian burr-walnut break-front bookcase, the molded cornice above three pinned arched doors enclosing adjustable shelves, framed by flat pilasters with tulipwood crossbanding, raised on deeper base with rounded angles and corresponding arched paneled doors, the central door flanked by ring-turned columns and enclosing drawers with sunken handles, on plinth base, stamped Holland & Sons.

71in (180cm) wide

$20,000-25,000   **L&T**

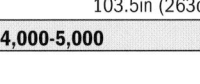

▶ A 19thC walnut break-front bookcase, possibly French, the raised central door with applied cusped moldings enclosing shelves with later lateral dividers, flanked by corresponding doors with lower panels divided by ring-turned columns with octagonal turrets and finials, on deeper corresponding base, the central door with applied circular-cusped panel flanked by doors with arched paneling on plinth base.

109in (277cm) high

$7,000-8,000   **L&T**

A Victorian mahogany bookcase, the molded cornice above a pair of doors with arched glazed panels enclosing adjustable shelves, raised on deeper base with frieze drawer above corresponding doors on plinth base and bun feet.

94.5in (240cm) high

$3,000-4,000   **L&T**

Bookcases

► An Edwardian William and Mary-style walnut break-front bookcase, with seaweed-marquetry and crossbanding, the molded cornice with cushion-molded frieze above three astragal-glazed doors enclosing adjustable shelves, the base with three-quarter veneered paneled doors on molded plinth and bun feet.

93in (236cm) high

$9,000-11,000	L&T

◄ An Edwardian six-door oak break-front library bookcase, with deep-molded cornice above glazed doors enclosing adjustable shelves, on deeper base with stepped paneled doors flanked by plain paneled pilasters, on plinth base, by J & T Scott, Edinburgh.

141.75in (360cm) wide

A mahogany cabinet, the top with inlaid and banded corners above adjustable shelves with glazed tracery doors, the cupboard base with a sliding tray enclosed by veneered doors with inlaid circles, on bracket feet.

49in (124.5cm) wide

$3,000-3,500	WW

An Edwardian mahogany break-front secrétaire bookcase, the dentil pediment over four lancet-glazed doors, the base with central fitted secrétaire bounded by cupboards and drawers on a solid plinth, brass drop-handles.

96in (244cm) wide

$7,500-8,500	L&T

$7,000-8,000	L&T

A CLOSER LOOK AT BUREAU BOOKCASES

Check that all the elements of the bureau bookcase conform. Sometimes a bureau will have a later bookcase put with it. It is usually quite easy to notice as the furniture will not be in proportion. This piece is clearly all original. The bureau and bookcase are of the same color and type of wood, with good patination.

This bureau has its original handles. Replacements are usually visible as the old handle will have left a darkish outline where it used to be.

When you pull out the drawers of this piece you can see the handmade dovetail joints, the oak drawer lining and the thick mahogany hand-cut veneer. These are all typical of Georgian furniture.

An early 20thC satinwood break-front bookcase, with painted Neo-classical decoration in the manner of Seddon and Sons, the molded cornice with central arched tablet and urn finials above four glazed doors with interlacing astragals enclosing adjustable shelves, the deeper base with three frieze drawers above cupboards with decorative panels, with shaped apron and splayed bracket feet.

83.75in (213cm) high

$30,000-40,000	L&T

A Queen Anne-style crimson-lacquer and chinoiserie bureau bookcase, the upper section with an arched and molded cornice over a pair of arched and molded doors opening to a fitted interior, the lower section with a molded fall front opening to a further fitted interior, the front with four pairs of molded and graduated drawers, on compressed bun feet, gilt-chinoiserie figural landscapes throughout.

90.5in (230cm) high

$6,000-8,000	SI

A George III mahogany bureau bookcase, the dentilled cornice above diamond-pattern astragal-glazed doors enclosing adjustable shelves, the bureau base with fall-front enclosing interior fitted with central door flanked by pilasters, drawers and pigeon-holes above four long graduated drawers, lopers and shaped bracket feet.

43.5in (110cm) wide

$4,500-5,500	L&T

► A George II mahogany bureau bookcase, the molded cornice above a pair of astragal-glazed doors enclosing adjustable shelves and pigeon-holes, and a pair of candle slides, raised on bureau with fall-front enclosing fitted interior, above four long graduated drawers and lopers, on shaped bracket feet.

87.75in (223cm) high

$4,000-5,000	L&T

Bookcases

A George III burled walnut secretary desk, the double-arched crest surmounted by finials over two arched cupboard doors with beveled mirrors opening to reveal a series of document drawers, shelves and pigeonholes, the case beneath with slant lid opening to fitted interior over five graduated drawers on straight bracket feet, losses to veneer, minor chips/cracks, interior with old dealer label of "Frank Partridge, New York".

c1730- 50 86.5in (219.5cm) high

$20,000-25,000   **FRE**

A Chippendale curly maple secretary-desk, Massachusetts, in two parts, the stepped cornice with dentil molding overhanging two cupboard doors on a molded based, the case with hinged slant-lid opening to six valanced pigeonholes over seven drawers centering a pillard prospect door enclosing two fan-carved drawers, all above four graduated thumb-molded drawers on ball and claw feet; brasses are old replacements, loose bookcase moldings, the interior painted red and yellow.

A note accompanying the desk states, "This desk descended in the Richmond family of Brockton mass. Purchased Ruth Isgro, dealer Pemberton"; another note explains a partial lineage "1) Horace Richmond, Brockton Massachusetts 2) Edward A. Richmond, owners of curly Maple secy".

c1770 36in (91.5cm) wide

$30,000-40,000   **FRE**

A Federal walnut secretary bookcase, possibly Shenandoah Valley, the upper case with molded cornice over recessed panel doors opening to five shelves over lower case with molded hinged lid opening to an interior with prospect door flanked by eight valanced pigeonholes and six drawers, the case below with four graduated long drawers, all above shaped apron and splayed bracket feet, original brasses.

c1790 42in (106.5cm) wide

$17,000-20,000   **SI**

An early 18thC (and associated) walnut-veneered bureau cabinet, feather-banded, the broken-arch pediment with turned ebonized urn-finials and a central panel inlaid with a parquetry star, the fitted interior with concave cupboard-door, gilt corinthian stop-fluted pilasters, drawers and folio compartments, a pair of doors with beveled glass, formerly mirrored, above candle-slides, the fall-flap with a stepped fitted interior with cupboard door and pilasters, secret compartments, a sliding door-cover to the well, a girdle molding above two long oak-lined drawers with engraved brass plate-handles and escutcheons, on replaced bun feet.

40in (102cm) wide

$9,000-11,000   **WW**

A late Victorian mahogany and marquetry-inlaid bureau cabinet, with ribbon-tied husk swags, urns and rosettes, the broken pediment with Greek key frieze above pair of doors enclosing shelves, the cylinder bureau centered by musical trophy above drawer and kneehole flanked by deeper drawers, on leaf-carved reeded tapering bulbous legs.

40.25in (102cm) wide

$4,500-5,500   **L&T**

A Southern Federal inlaid walnut secretary bookcase, the associated, slightly later upper section with a cavetto cornice over a pair of 13-pane astragal doors enclosing pigeon-holes and adjustable shelves, the outset lower section with a secretaire drawers opening to a fitted interior, over three graduated drawers, all cockbeaded, with stringing and raised on splayed bracket feet, indecipherable pencil inscription, secondary woods poplar and yellow pine.

c1800 43.25in (110cm) wide

$8,000-7,000   **SI**

Bookcases

A George III mahogany secrétaire bookcase, the upper section with chinoiserie-style fretwork supporting two graduated shelves, the base with six drawers, the top two opening to reveal a secrétaire with a fitted interior of pigeonholes and drawers, standing on bracket feet, repairs and restorations.

30in (76cm) wide

$9,000-11,000	HamG

A George III mahogany secrétaire bookcase, the dentilled cornice above a pair of gothick-astragalled glazed doors enclosing adjustable shelves, on deeper base with fluted frieze above twin panel-fronted secrétaire drawer and three long graduated drawers, on shaped bracket feet.

95.25in (242cm) high

$8,500-9,500	L&T

▶ A George III mahogany secrétaire bookcase, the arched cornice with fluted pedestals and ball finials above a pair of astragal-glazed doors enclosing adjustable shelves, the base with false-fronted fitted secrétaire drawer above three long graduated drawers on shaped apron and splayed bracket feet, bears label to its first drawer and rear: "Mant, Upholder & Cabinet Maker, High Street, Winchester, NB. Goods appraised and sold by Auction on the most reasonable terms".

103.5in (263cm) high

$60,000-70,000	L&T

A matched pair of George III mahogany secrétaire bookcases, each with molded cornice above astragal-glazed doors, enclosing adjustable shelves, raised on deeper base with false-fronted drawer above paneled doors, on plinth with cut-down bracket feet, one with secretaire drawer and cupboard drawers, one with sliding trays.

96.5in (245cm) high

$11,000-13,000	L&T

A Sheraton mahogany secrétaire bookcase, the molded detachable cornice above a pair of carved, glazed tracery doors, the fall-front fitted drawer with inlaid stringing above three long drawers with oval brass plate-handles, on splay feet.

93in (236cm) high

$10,000-11,000	WW

A Regency mahogany-veneered secrétaire bookcase, the cornice with a sycamore band, the adjustable shelves enclosed by glazed gothic-arch tracery doors, the base inlaid with stringing and banded, the fall-front fitted drawer above three drawers, on splay feet.

43in (109cm) wide

$4,000-5,000	WW

A Regency Gothic oak bookcase cabinet, the molded cornice carved with rose, thistle, shamrock and leaves, surmounted by cusped destiny, above pair of open gothic traceried-doors flanked and divided by paneled buttresses, enclosing adjustable shelves, on deeper base with similar solid traceried doors and plinth base.

The bookcase is very much in the Gothic manner popularized in the 1820s by the publications of George Smith and particularly Ackermann's Repository of Arts.

77.25in (196cm) high

$18,000-20,000	L&T

A Regency mahogany and brass-inlaid bookcase cabinet, the leaf-carved cornice above inlaid frieze centered by parcel-gilt framed tablet, the open shelves with tripartite mirror to lower half flanked by inlaid paneled pilasters, the deeper base with arched open kneehole flanked by cross-banded drawers and folio compartments and projecting spirally reeded, turned and leaf-carved columns to the corners terminating in larger corresponding feet, the sides with crossbanded brass-strung panel.

73.5in (187cm) high

$6,000-7,000	L&T

An early 19thC mahogany secrétaire bookcase, the associated bookcase top with molded cornice above four gothic astragal-glazed doors, with reeded plinth, raised on a chest of drawers with top veneered in two sections above crossbanded and ebony-lined secrétaire drawer, fitted with drawers and pigeonholes and three long graduated drawers with ivory escutcheons, on turned feet, shelves lacking.

91.25in (232cm) high

$3,000-3,500	L&T

A CLOSER LOOK AT A HIGHBOY

Highboys were first made in England at the end of the 17thC, but by 1730 the style was almost exclusive to the Americas, where the colonists favored designs with a compact vertical emphasis. Highboys were typically made in two sections: the upper with graduated drawers and the lower with a case standing on cabriole legs.

The carved pediment and finial are common to pieces of this time. The graceful shell carvings here and at the base incorporate drawer handles.

The fluted chamfered corners and lamb's tongue terminals add refinement.

The mellow patination of the figured walnut adds to the appeal.

Although the sections were not made together, they are a happy marriage as the skirt is in keeping with the pediment. The later addition of the lower shell drawer adds to this impression.

$20,000-25,000 FRE

A Queen Anne figured walnut highboy, in two parts, the upper section with swan's neck pediment and floral carved terminals centering an urn/flame finial above shell-carved drawer and series of seven drawers, all flanked by fluted chamfered corners with lamb's tongue terminals, the lower section with single long drawer above three smaller drawers, the center one being shell-carved and flanked by similarly chamfered corners, a shaped skirt beneath and cabriole legs ending in bold ball and claw feet, upper and lower case married, pediment and finial replaced, lower shell drawer later, shop of Samuel Harding, Philadelphia.

Provenance: *by descent to the present generation in the family of James Kerney (1873-1934), owner and publisher of the Trenton Times. Given to the Kerneys by Mrs. Kerney's parents, the Mullens, the highboy stayed in the board room until 1976 at which time, after the sale of the paper, it was removed by the current owner's grand-mother and given to his parents.*

c1740-50   38in (97cm) wide

A Chippendale Centennial highboy, swan neck pediment with carved rosettes, flame finials, all over a straight front with a centering shell carved drawer flanked by two small over four wide graduated thumb molded drawers, the lower section having one wide thumb molded drawer over shell carved center drawer and twin drawers, the apron with acorn drops, cabriole legs terminating on claw and ball feet.

39in (99cm) wide

$7,000-10,000 FRE

A New Hampshire Queen Anne maple highboy, with flat cove-molded cornice over straight front, single top drawer with mock twin drawer facing over three wide thumb-molded drawers with mock triple drawer facing, center having shell carving, brass bail handles, escutcheons and lockplates, shaped apron, cabriole legs and pad feet.

c1750   38.5in (97.5cm) high

$9,000-11,000 FRE

A New Hampshire Queen Anne maple highboy, with flat cove-molded cornice over straight front, single top drawer with mock twin drawer facing over three wide thumb-molded drawers with mock triple drawer facing, center having shell carving, brass bail handles, escutcheons and lockplates, shaped apron, cabriole legs and pad feet.

c1750   38.5in (97.5cm) high

$20,000-30,000 FRE

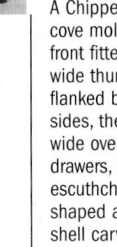

A Chippendale cherry highboy, flat cove molded cornice over straight front fitted with five small and three wide thumb-molded drawers, flanked by quarter fluted column sides, the lower section having one wide over two small thumb molded drawers, brass bail handles, escutcheons and lock plates, shaped apron, cabriole legs with shell carved knees, claw and ball feet terminating on casters.

1760s   46in (117cm) wide

$20,000-30,000 FRE

A Queen Anne-style walnut flat top high chest of drawers, the upper section with an overhanging cornice above three short drawers and three graduated long drawers, the lower section with one drawer, the shaped apron below on cabriole legs ending in bold "Spanish" feet, replaced knee returns and brasses, Delaware River Valley.

41.5in (105.4cm) wide

$25,000-30,000 FRE

An early 18thC oak tallboy, the molded cornice with cushion drawer over two short and three long graduated drawers, the base with a single long drawer on short cabriole legs, the whole with chevron-stringing and pierced brass handles, adapted.

43.5in (110cm) wide

| $3,500-4,500 | L&T |

An early 19thC mahogany tallboy, the domed paneled frieze above two short and three long drawers, mahogany-lined with brass shell-ring handles, on front scroll feet.

88.25in (224cm) high

| $6,000-7,000 | WW |

BUREAUX

A Queen Anne-style herringbone-banded walnut bureau, of unusually narrow proportions, the arched mirrored door beneath a parcel-gilt fluted cornice enclosing vertical compartments and drawers over a writing slant and three further long drawers on bracket feet.

26in (66cm) wide

| $4,500-5,500 | GorL |

An early Georgian oak bureau, the fall-front with bookrest enclosing fitted interior with well above two short and two long graduated drawers, on shaped bracket feet.

27.25in (69cm) wide

| $2,500-3,000 | L&T |

A George II mahogany bureau, the top over a molded and hinged slope opening to an interior fitted with 12 small drawers, the front with four long cockbeaded and graduated drawers, the molded base on bracket feet.

c1750   41in (104cm) high

| $3,000-3,500 | SI |

▶ A Louis XV bronze-dore-mounted kingwood and tulipwood bureau encoignure, the top with a pierced three-quarter gallery, the shaped tapering hinged slope opening to an interior fitted with a shelf, convex drawer and velvet-lined writing-surface, the front with two shaped doors opening to an interior with an arrangement of one long drawer over two small drawers divided by a small arch, raised on three square-section tapering legs with foliate-scroll sabots, foliate encadrements throughout, the back similarly finished.

37.25in (94.5cm) high

| $11,000-13,000 | SI |

A Scottish George III mahogany bureau, the chequer-strung fall-front with flame-veneered oval panel enclosing fitted interior with marquetry and chequer-strung pigeon-holes and drawers, above two short and three long graduated cockbeaded drawers with ivory escutcheons, flanked by reeded clasping pilasters, on ogee bracket feet.

47.25in (120cm) wide

| $3,000-3,500 | L&T |

A George III mahogany bureau, the sloping fall opening to reveal an interior fitted with drawers and pigeon-holes, above four long graduated drawers on bracket feet.

42in (106.5cm) wide

| $1,500-2,000 | L&T |

A North Italian Neo-classical style kingwood and marquetry lady's secrétaire, decorated to all sides with pictorial and floral panels, the canted rectangular top surmounted by stage with six drawers, secrétaire frieze drawer above tambour door enclosing further drawers, on cabriole legs joined by undershelf.

40.25in (102cm) high

| $3,000-3,500 | L&T |

An early 19thC oak writing chest, the sloping top with central hinged-lid bearing a book rest and opening to reveal a well, above four long graduated drawers flanked by eight short graduated drawers, with paneled sides on bracket feet.

42.5in (108cm) high

| $850-950 | L&T |

A mid-19thC French brass-inlaid rosewood and Vernis Martin-paneled bureau-de-dame, the fitted single drawer opening to activate a tambour sliding top on fluted legs.

27in (68.5cm) wide

| $1,200-1,500 | GorL |

A late 18thC American Chippendale mahogany slant front desk, slant top opens to fitted interior over four graduated thumb-molded drawers on molded base with ball and claw feet, restored.

43.75in (109cm) wide

$1,500-2,500 **SI**

◀ An American Pennsylvania, Chippendale curly-maple slant front desk, the hinged lid opening to an interior with eight valanced pigeonholes above eight stacked drawers centering a tombstone-carved prospect door flanked by document drawers carver with wheat sheaves, the case with four graduated drawers on spurred ogee bracket feet, minor repairs to feet, missing brass hardware.

c1780 41in (104cm) wide

$30,000-35,000 **FRE**

An early 19thC New England Sheraton cherry wood and maple slant-lid desk, the rectangular hinged lid opening to a curly maple interior wtoh four document drawers centering two sets of four drawers and a prospect door, the case beneath wtih four graduated drawers on replaced ogee bracket feet, new handles.

44in (111.5cm) high

$1,500-2,000 **FRE**

A third quarter 18thC American Chippendale walnut slant-front secretary, probably Virginia, with a fitted interior, five graduated drawers and bracket feet, secondary wood yellow pine.

43.5in (110.5cm) high

$3,000-4,000 **SI**

An American Chippendale tiger maple fall front writing desk, with fitted interior over straight front fitted with four graduated thumb-molded drawers, oval brass bail handles, eagle estucheons and oval lock plates, straight bracket feet.

c1780 41in (104cm) high

$7,000-10,000 **FRE**

A Federal maple and tiger-maple slant-front desk, New England, with molded slope front, fitted interior, four long graduated drawers and molded base with French feet, secondary wood white pine.

c1800 44in (112cm) high

$2,200-2,800 **SI**

A CLOSER LOOK AT A SLANT FRONT DESK

The architecturally filled interior adds to the value.

Secret drawers add to desirability.

Original brasses and good original condition make this a very desirable piece.

A Philadelphia Chippendale slant front desk, of walnut with architecturally fitted interior composed of eight serpentine fronted drawers, eight pigeonholes with scalloped molding, a central serpentine door flanked by fluted half columns enclosing three small drawers, entire compartment pulls out to reveal secret drawers behind, lower portion with four wide thumbmolded graduated drawers, original butterfly brasses, ogee bracket feet, some losses and replacements to feet.

c1770-1780 41in (104cm) wide

$25,000-30,000 **FRE**

◀ A George III-style satinwood and marquetry cylinder desk, the paneled cylinder front with floral diaperwork opening to a leather-lined sliding writing-surface, the square-section tapering legs with block feet and similar inlay, stringing and cross-banding throughout.

33in (84cm) wide

$3,500-4,000 **SI**

CABINETS

A George II bow-fronted Norfolk cabinet.

c1730   48.5in (123cm) high

$3,000-4,000   **CdK**

An early George III mahogany corner cupboard, the shallow swan-neck pediment above a raised and fielded paneled door with brass H-hinges, opening to reveal an interior of three shaped shelves.

23in (59cm) wide

$1,000-1,400   **HamG**

A late 18thC French walnut corner cupboard, with variegated black marble top, with a crossgrain mould frame, above a serpentine-shaped door opening to reveal a single shelf, standing on shaped stile feet with a shaped apron.

36.25in (92cm) high

$1,500-2,000   **HamG**

A George III oak bow front hanging corner cupboard, with Greek key frieze and fluted pilasters.

28in (71cm) wide

$850-950   **GorL**

A George III mahogany-banded oak hanging corner cupboard, with dentil cornice and paneled door and serpentine shelves.

30in (76cm) wide

$600-700   **GorL**

A George III mahogany corner cabinet, the molded dentil cornice above frieze inlaid with shell paterae, the arched twin-doors with chequer-strung panels enclosing shaped and fitted shelves, the whole enclosed within molded surround.

54.5in (138cm) high

$900-1,100   **L&T**

▶ A large George III mahogany corner cupboard, the concave-dentilled cornice above fluted frieze with inlaid paterae and pair of paneled doors with boxwood and ebony-framing enclosing shaped shelf and hanging rail, flanked by fluted pilasters, the base with fluted frieze above pair of corresponding oval-paneled doors on plinth and shaped bracket feet.

89in (226cm) high

$3,500-4,000   **L&T**

A Sheraton mahogany double standing corner cupboard, with a satinwood-banded frieze above shaped shelves enclosed by outline panel doors with ivory escutcheons, the canted corners on bracket feet, some damage.

42in (107cm) wide

$3,000-4,000   **WW**

A small Italian painted corner cabinet.

c1810   30in (76cm) high

$1,800-2,200   **SS**

A pair of 19thC rococo-style lacquered corner cabinets, each of pronounced serpentine-form with molded breche d'alep marble top above pair of doors decorated with landscape scene and gilt-brass mounts, shaped apron and squat cabriole legs with sabots.

29.5in (75cm) wide

$5,000-6,000   **L&T**

Cabinets

A 19thC bow-fronted hanging corner cupboard, the molded cornice above two doors enclosing shelves and painted with figures and a horse.

23in (58cm) wide

$450-500　　　　　　　**DN**

A late Victorian inlaid rosewood corner cabinet, with mirrored superstructure over two doors and alcove.

22in (56cm) wide

$400-450　　　　　　**GorL**

A Regency mahogany side cabinet, with brass stringing, the top with rounded angles above pair of glazed doors enclosing shelf flanked by spirally and ring-turned columns, on corresponding feet.

34.75in (88cm) wide

$4,000-4,500　　　　　**L&T**

A 19thC George II-style mahogany bow-front corner cabinet, the molded and projecting cornice above twin glazed doors with shaped and molded gilt-gesso slips enclosing two shelves, the lower section with two similar glazed doors enclosing single shelf, raised on a plinth.

81.5in (207cm) high

$4,000-4,500　　　　　**L&T**

▶ A black and gold laquer-decorated corner cupboard, on an open stand, the interior with an arched frieze and stop-fluted pilasters and shaped shelves, a pair of paneled doors decorated with figures and summer palaces, canted corners, the base with shaped frieze and square-channeled legs.

44in (112cm) wide

$2,200-2,800　　　　　**WW**

A pair of Regency rosewood side cabinets, with inlaid molded-brass banding, each with rectangular top above a pair of glazed doors enclosing shelves flanked by gilt-wood carved monopodiae with anthmion and palmette decoration on a plinth base.

Savoy Croft was built by the architect James A Morris for his own use in 1893. He furnished it with a combination of contemporary and antique furniture, of which this pair of cabinets was the highlight. The house and collection remained intact until sold by his daughter Sarah's executors. The cabinets are closely based on a Thomas Hope design, the monopediae in particular being virtually identical to those on the literary table illustrated by Frances Collard in Regency Furniture, 1985, pg. 95. This is derived from pm. 32 of Hope's Household Furniture and Interior Decoration 1807

41.75in (106cm) wide

$45,000-55,000　　　　　　　　　　　　　**L&T**

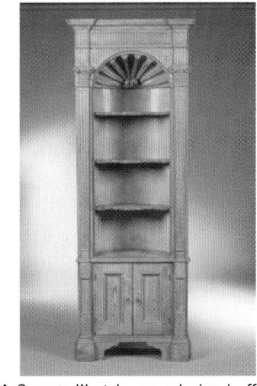

A George III-style waxed-pine buffet niche, the reverse break-front dentil cornice above a fluted frieze and arched alcove, enclosing shaped open shelves with a shell carved to the arch, enclosed by fluted pilasters above twin door below, raised on a plinth.

2.25in (209cm) high

$2,500-3,000　　　　　**L&T**

A mid-Victorian burr-walnut and ebonized corner cabinet, the surmount with two mirror-backed open shelves, supported by gilt-incised turned columns, the stepped and shaped top above a central panel door flanked by velvet-covered and mirror-backed open shelves, raised on turned tapering legs, gilt-brass mounts.

64.25in (163cm) high

$2,500-3,000　　　　　**L&T**

A late 19thC mahogany standing corner cupboard, a dentil cornice, the plush interior with shelves, a glazed tracery door above pagoda fluting and blind fret, the door with applied carving, canted corners, on bracket feet.

32in (81.5cm) wide

$1,200-1,500　　　　　**WW**

Cabinets

A Victorian walnut and mahogany credenza, the boxwood frieze with gilt-brass beading, the reverse break-front top with molded edge above adjustable open shelves at center flanked by glazed cupboards with lined shelves, on corresponding plinth base.

78.25in (199cm) wide

$5,000-5,500   L&T

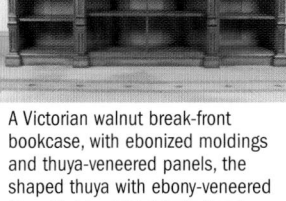

A Victorian walnut break-front bookcase, with ebonized moldings and thuya-veneered panels, the shaped thuya with ebony-veneered top with boxwood stringing and brass-balustraded three-quarter gallery above four frieze drawers and adjustable open bookshelves divided by deep Mannerist pilasters, on plinth base.

122in (310cm) wide

$9,000-10,000   L&T

An Edwardian oak reverse break-front bookcase, the top above ogee frieze carved with grotesques and centered by a strapwork panel, the central open and adjustable shelves with tooled dust-flaps flanked by glazed cabinet with adjustable shelves and flanking fluted pilasters, raised on molded square-section feet.

96.75in (246cm) wide

$1,200–1,500   L&T

A CLOSER LOOK AT A CHIFFONIER

A Regency rosewood chiffonier, the top with mirror-back and shelf with scrolling console supports and palmette gallery, above frieze drawer and door with brass lattice and gathered fabric flanked by free-standing columns on plinth base.

50.5in (128cm) high

$4,000–4,500   L&T

The shelves with enclosed cupboards beneath are typical of this type of cabinet, made from c1800. They were often used as a sideboard.

Rosewood and mahogany were the most popular woods used to make chiffoniers.

The rectangular door panels are typical of the Regency period. Victorian chiffonier panels are usually arched.

This piece boasts original pleated silk panels. These are often replaced.

A Regency Brazilian-rosewood chiffonier, the two-tier back with a three-quarter Grecian gallery, above a white-line inlaid base, with a pair of pleated silk doors opening to an interior with two adjustable shelves, standing on ring-turned toupie feet.

36in (91cm) wide

$3,500-6,000   HamG

A Regency mahogany bow-front chiffonier, the two open graduated shelves supported by tooled-brass columns with mirror-back, raised on cabinet with pair of gothic arched paneled doors, each supporting later fittings for cocktail glasses, on shaped bracket feet.

51.25in (130cm) high

$2,500-3,000   L&T

A William IV mahogany chiffonier, the raised arch-shaped back panel fitted one shelf on tapered column supports, a cushion-shaped drawer with cupboard below enclosed by a pair of paneled doors flanked by pilasters on turned bun feet.

35.5in (90cm) wide

$1,000-1,200   Clv

A Regency mahogany chiffonier, the shelved upper stage with turned supports over single drawer and two paneled cupboards with canted and fluted corners on short curved square-section legs.

30in (76cm) wide

$6,000-7,000   L&T

▶ A Regency mahogany chiffonier, the brass gallery above two open shelves, the top with molded edge above twin doors, with brass-wire lattice panels, enclosing an interior fitted with pigeonholes and sliding shelves raised on turned supports with pot casters.

57.5in (146cm) high

$1,800-2,200   L&T

A William IV rosewood chiffonier, the two-tier shelves with "S"-scrolls and turned supports above a frieze with three short drawers over a pair of silk-lined doors with reel-and-bobbin molding, flanked by a pair of turned columns standing on a plain plinth base.

57.5in (146cm) high

$2,500-3,000   HamG

Cabinets

A Victorian mahogany miniature chiffonier, the pedimented back above a serpentine-shaped top and single frieze drawer over a pair of paneled cupboard doors flanked by split-turned columns, possibly an apprentice piece.

10in (25.5cm) wide

$600-800	HamG

A late Victorian Rio-rosewood side cabinet, the mirror-backed top with shelf supported on carved and turned columns, above a bow front drawer with a pair of classically inlaid bow-fronted doors opening to reveal a pair of shelves with floor-level lower tier, stamped "Jas. Shoolbred and Co".

24in (61cm) wide

$900-1,100	HamG

A French Napoleon III brass-inlaid, bronze-dore-mounted and ebonized-marble top meuble d'hauteur d'appui, the rectangular top with outset front-corners over a conforming frieze mounted with a band of acanthus-foliage, the front with two glazed doors opening to adjustable shelves and flanked by canted and paneled stiles, the shaped skirt centered by a Bacchic mask and continuing into block feet profusely decorated with bronze-dore-mounts and brass stringing.

55in (140cm) wide

$5,500-6,500	SI

A third-quarter 19thC porcelain-mounted, ebonized and parcel-gilt credenza, the molded top with rounded ends and outset corners, the front with a frieze inlaid with Vitruvian waves and centered by a Jasperware panel depicting putti at play, the front with a central section with two arched and glazed doors opening to a velvet-lined interior with shelves and flanked by paired free-standing fluted Corinthian columns, all with Jasperware roundels, the convex end sections similar, raised on a conforming plinth base, gilt-metal mounts throughout.

72in (183cm) long

$5,500-6,500	SI

An American Victorian Renaissance Revival marble top side cabinet, New York City, possibly Kimball and Cabus, burgundy variegated stepped marble top over griffin decorated single drawer and maskhead, urn and floral marquetry paneled cabinet door, flanked by angled paneled marquetry doors, all flanked by gilt decorated ebonized column sides.

c1870   64in (162.5cm) wide

$7,000-9,000	FRE

► A late Victorian ebony, ebonized and ivory-inlaid credenza, bearing label of Howard & Sons, London, the shaped top with quadrant ends above dentilled triglyph frieze and pair of glazed doors enclosing shelves, flanked by open mirror-backed shelves, on plinth and flattened bun-feet.

57in (145cm) wide

$1,200-1,500	L&T

A Victorian burr-walnut credenza, with gilt-brass mounts, the shaped top above frieze centered by floral marquetry spray and pair of doors with floral marquetry panels flanked by open quadrant shelves, on plinth base, with shaped apron.

72.5in (184cm) wide

$5,500-6,500	L&T

A Victorian ebony and tortoiseshell boulle credenza, with gilt-brass mounts, the shaped top above frieze and central door flanked by glazed quadrant doors divided by half-columns with figural capitals, on plinth base with shaped apron.

77.5in (197cm) wide

$1,500-2,000	L&T

An Edwardian mahogany Neo-classical bow-front credenza, the shaped rectangular top with pierced gallery above fluted frieze centered by a cartouche, above pair of doors centered by fan medallions flanked by glazed doors with oval astragals, on turned legs.

63in (160cm) wide

$2,000-2,500	L&T

A Regency burr-elm side cabinet, the stepped top supported on projecting columns with acanthus capitals, the doors with false panels with carved frames, on plinth base.

65in (165cm) wide

$3,000-3,500	L&T

Cabinets

A William IV yew-wood side cabinet, the top with ledge back and reeded edge above frieze and pair of doors with fabric panels enclosing shelved interior flanked by columns with brass capitals and bases, on plinth and turned feet with casters.

35in (89cm) high

$4,500-5,000	L&T

A Victorian walnut serpentine pier cabinet, crossbanded and inlaid in tulipwood, satinwood and ebony and enclosed by an arched glazed door, with gilt-metal mounts and on plinth base.

31in (79cm) wide

$1,400-1,800	GorB

A Victorian walnut and marquetry pier cabinet, inlaid with Prince of Wales feathers and flowers, with single glazed door.

31in (79cm) wide

$2,200-2,500	GorL

A mahogany cabinet, with two paterea-inlaid doors, on bracket feet.

39in (99in) wide

$700-800	GorL

An 18thC Dutch walnut display cabinet, the molded and shaped cornice with carved central mythical beasts over two glazed doors on a bombé base with three long shaped drawers and claw-and-ball feet.

59.5in (151cm) wide

$3,000-4,000	L&T

▶ A George III carved mahogany breakfront cabinet-on-stand, the cabinet surmounted by a molded swan-neck fretted dentil cornice mounted with rose-carved terminals and centered by a platform over an outset front with a pair of doors, each with diamond-form tracery over a panel simulating a cockbeaded drawer front, enclosing molded adjustable shelves, the recessed end sections similar but with single doors, the molded conforming out-set stand with a central frieze drawer, flanked on each side by a smaller drawer, the drawer fronts cockbeaded, raised on baluster-turned reeded legs headed by paterae.

77.5in (197cm) high

$7,500-9,000	SI

A Regency small painted display cabinet, grained as oak with "ebony" lines, the glazed top enclosing three tray shelves faced with painted scrolling leaves, the base fitted with two long projecting drawers on ring-turned legs.

25in (63cm) wide

$2,500-3,000	BonS

A 19thC ebonized and boulle two-door vitrine, the arched pediment and paneled frieze above two glazed and paneled doors, plain plinth and with disc feet, the whole with gilt-metal mounts.

80.75in (205cm) high

$3,000-3,500	L&T

A late 19thC gilt and painted vitrine, in the 18thC French manner, the arched pediment with pierced rococo gilt-metal crest above twin-arched glazed doors and painted Vernis Martin-style figural panels, revealing interior with mirror-back and glass shelves, pink velvet-lined cupboard, the sides similarly decorated, all on short cabriole legs, the whole with gilt-metal rococo mounts.

40.25in (102cm) wide

$4,000-4,500	L&T

A large late 19thC Louis XV-style rosewood and floral marquetry vitrine, with reeded serpentine top with shell-cresting over two shaped glazed doors with floral marquetry panels flanked by four shaped glass panels, with glass shelves and with a damask back all on short cabriole legs the whole with rococo gilt-metal mounts on scroll feet.

71.75in (182cm) wide

$15,000-18,000	L&T

A Louis XV-style kingwood vitrine, of serpentine-form with gilt-metal mounts, the tapering ogee top with central cartouche above a pair of serpentine-glazed doors and similar sides enclosing mirrored interior with glass shelves, above single central door with Vernis Martin bombé panel of lovers flanked by corresponding panels, on serpentine legs.

80in (203cm) high

$10,000-13,000	L&T

Cabinets

An Edwardian mahogany satinwood-banded and boxwood-inlaid display cabinet, the molded cornice with chequer-inlaid frieze above a single astragal-glazed door flanked by canted astragal-glazed panels and enclosing fitted shelves, the lower section with single drawer above turned and bracket supports linked by a lower shelf, bears makers label "Reynolds & McCulloch, Charing Cross, Glasgow".

56.5in (143cm) wide

$4,000-4,500   **L&T**

An Edwardian mahogany-canted display cabinet, with boxwood and ebony stringing, the dentilled cornice above inlaid scalloped frieze with oval panels, the central astragal-glazed panel flanked by similar bow-fronted doors enclosing a unified interior with glass shelves, raised on square-section tapering legs with spade feet, the whole with canted sides to fit into an alcove.

75in (190cm) wide

$4,000-4,500   **L&T**

An Edwardian inlaid mahogany Adam-style side cabinet by Gillows, with satinwood banding, the consoled reverse break-front cornice above central beveled mirror flanked by cupboards with grotesque inlaid doors, raised on deeper base with three frieze drawer central glazed door flanked by open shelves with inlaid drawers below, on bracket feet, stamped to drawer front.

69.75in (177cm) high

$4,500-5,000   **L&T**

A CLOSER LOOK AT A DISPLAY CABINET

These cabinets tend to be on a narrower scale than 18thC originals, this was so that they would fit the smaller Edwardian interiors.

The figured satinwood veneers and elaborate glazing bars are all signs of quality.

The top part of the cabinet would have been used to display books or ceramics. Leader to shelf

The legs on the piece are long and slender, but the galleried tray provides strength.

An Edwardian painted satinwood display cabinet, with ebony and boxwood stringing, the molded break-front cornice with central arch surmounted by carved ribbons and swags enclosing oval painted with Diana the Huntress, above a single astragal-glazed door painted with ribbon-bound swags and flanked by two bowed panels enclosing glass shelves, raise on base painted with frieze of rose garlands above turned and tapering legs joined by shaped undershelf on toupie feet.

81in (206cm) high

$15,000-20,000   **L&T**

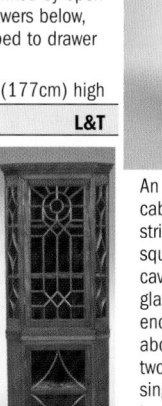

An Edwardian mahogany corner display cabinet, of deep-canted form, the molded dentilled cornice above single glazed door with elaborate astragals enclosing velvet-lined shelved interior, raised on corresponding base.

80.75in (205cm) high

$1,200–1,600   **L&T**

An Edwardian rosewood and marquetry side cabinet, the raised back with an arrangement of mirrors and spindle galleries on inlaid square-supports united by a shelf, the base with a door having an inlaid panel of a lady playing a lute, flanked by glazed doors above an open spindle gallery on square supports.

54in (137cm) wide

$3,000-3,500   **L&T**

An Edwardian satinwood display cabinet, with boxwood and ebony stringing, the ogee-domed top with square-molded surmount above cavetto frieze and single astragal-glazed door and glazed sides enclosing fitted glass shelves, above reciprocal cavetto frieze with two crossbanded drawers above a single door, on square-section tapering legs terminating in spade feet.

68.5in (174cm) high

$6,000-6,500   **L&T**

A George III mahogany serpentine commode, probably adapted from a side table, the shaped and hinged top opening to reveal a fitted interior, above a fluted frieze with central panel applied with oval leaf-carved paterae and leaf-swag over paneled door, flanked by two deep drawers, enclosing divided interiors and with dummy drawer fronts, raised above deeply fluted square tapering legs terminating in block feet.

35.75in (91cm) high

$6,500-7,500   **L&T**

Cabinets

A Regency amboyna demi-lune cabinet, with three-quarter brass gallery and applied beaded frieze over superstructure of two coromandel crossbanded cupboard doors enclosing small drawers, the base with two central drawers similarly decorated, flanked by bowed cupboard doors on square-section tapered legs with applied anthemion capitals.

37in (94cm) wide

$4,000-4,500	L&T

An early 19thC japanned cabinet on later stand, the cabinet painted with figures in oriental landscapes, with two doors enclosing seven drawers with turned handles.

44in (112cm) high

$700-800	DN

A late George III mahogany night table, the three-quarter galleried top with pierced carrying-handles, satinwood banding and spandrel inlay, above a single door with similar decoration standing on tapered legs with spade feet.

33.75in (86cm) high

$600-650	HamG

A 19thC Dutch mahogany marquetry-inlaid side cabinet, the tray top above twin doors and a single drawer below, raised on square-section tapering legs.

21.5in (54.5cm) wide

$1,000-1,200	L&T

A 19thC French sycamore, kingwood and floral marquetry small table, with a mid-19thC French Sevres-style porcelain plaque painted with a basket of fruit and flowers inset to the top, a pierced brass gallery and mounts, with three drawers, square tapering legs and a shelf, stamped "G. DESTER JVE".

16.25in (41cm) high

$50,000-60,000	DN

A 19thC French mahogany kidney-shaped table with gilt-metal mounts, in Louis XVI-style, the royal-red marble top with a mounted edge, the front and back with marquetry birds and baskets of flowers, the ends with musical trophies, with a concave drawer and door flanked by pilasters, on square-tapering legs with gilt-metal terminals.

27.5in (70cm) high

$2,200-2,800	DN

A 19thC Dutch walnut cabinet on stand, in the 17thC manner, the deeply molded stepped cornice containing cartouche with figure of a goddess, above door with shaped fielded panel flanked by carved pilasters centered by putti, enclosing shelves, on stand with four stained and simply turned column supports joined by shaped X-stretcher on bun feet, incorporating earlier elements.

65.75in (167cm) high

$1,800-2,400	L&T

A pair of Louis XVI-style marble-top mahogany tables de chevet, each rouge-royal top with convex sides and a pierced three-quarter gallery, the front with a paneled drawer over a paneled door flanked by fluted stiles, the convex sides similarly paneled, the baluster-turned brass fluted legs with toupie feet joined by a rectangular undertier, bronze-dore encadrements throughout.

c1860   33.5in (85cm) high

$1,200-1,500	SI

► A late 19thC French bedside cabinet, with a faux bookcase front.

14.5in (37cm) wide

$400-450	CdK

◄ A late 19thC French-style rosewood bedside table, the shaped top inset with marble over a single cupboard on carved cabriole legs, with intersecting undershelf.

15.5in (39cm) wide

$900-1,100	L&T

A late 19thC kingwood and satinwood transitional-style table a ecrire, with foliate marquetry decoration, the oval top with pierced three-quarter brass gallery above three drawers and shaped apron raised on cabriole legs joined by kidney-shaped undershelf inlaid with book and inkwell motif, the feet with brass sabots.

31in (79cm) high

$2,200-2,800   **L&T**

A French Louis XV-style walnut bedside cabinet.

1910-20   15.75in (40cm) wide

$225-275   **CdK**

A late Victorian inlaid rosewood music cabinet, with shallow-shaped top vase inlaid back panel over twin foliate-inlaid panels above glazed section door enclosing shelved interior, on plinth base.

21.25in (54cm) wide

$500-550   **BAR**

A late Victorian ebonized and amboyna-inlaid music cabinet, the top with pierced brass gallery and beaded edge above twin doors, each with shaped panels centered by a circular ceramic panel and with guilded incised decoration, enclosing shelves, the base with two drawers, the whole raised on plinth with casters.

46.75in (119cm) high

$2,500-3,000   **L&T**

An Edwardian mahogany, boxwood and ebony-strung music cabinet, the rectangular quarter-veneered top with molded edge, above two drawers, inlaid with foliate scrolls, raised on turned fluted supports with shelves below for music, on pierced lyre sides, toupie feet.

40.25in (102cm) high

$1,800-2,200   **L&T**

An Edwardian mahogany music cabinet, with rosewood cross-banding and boxwood stringing, the two-tier galleried superstructure with one drawer and hinged brass candle arm to one side, the base with sliding rest to one side and five graduated drawers on tapering feet with brass caps and casters.

53.25 (147cm) wide

$1,400-1,800   **L&T**

A Regency burr-oak pedestal cabinet, in the style of George Bullock, with ebony inlay and ebonized moldings, the top with bowed and hinged ends, above deep-paneled frieze converted to drawers to one side, raised on pedestals with inlaid paneled doors and corresponding spandrels, on turned feet, the ends also paneled (adapted).

78.5in (199cm) wide

$6,000-7,000   **L&T**

An early 19thC rosewood and brass-inlaid table cabinet, decorated to the top and front with a brass frieze of meandering flowering foliage, the single glazed door enclosing single shell, the brass-lined sides with brass swing carrying-handles, beaded base.

23.25in (59cm) high

$1,000-1,300   **L&T**

CANTERBURIES

An early 19thC Dutch mahogany two-door table cabinet, inlaid with conch shells and bat's-wing spandrels.

23in (58.5cm) wide

$280-340   **GorL**

A late 19thC walnut tabletop collector's cabinet, the top with cyma edge above four drawers locking by side pilaster above plinth foot.

16.25in (41cm) wide

$850-950   **Chef**

▶ An early 19thC mahogany canterbury, the two-division top with carrying handle, ring-turned supports and a single full width drawer with original ebonized handles, standing on toupie feet with brass casters.

$1,500-2,000   **HamG**

A Regency mahogany three-division music canterbury, having concave top and fitted drawer to base on turned supports.

20in (51cm) wide

$1,400-1,800   GorB

A CLOSER LOOK AT A CANTERBURY

This piece has nicely concave top rails which enhance the value.

It has its originally turned wooden knob handles on the drawer.

Canterburies are relatively delicate, especially around the legs which have often been damaged or replaced. It is a good idea to turn the piece upside down as repairs can be more easily seen.

It has good quality turned wooden legs.

A Regency mahogany canterbury, the dished top with three divisions, turned and block-stretchered frame with turned finials and turned knob handles to the frieze drawers, the turned legs on brass casters.

9.5in (49.5cm)

$2,500-3,000   WW

An early 19thC mahogany music canterbury, with swept top, four divisions and a double-fronted drawer on turned legs with brass casters.

18.25in (46cm) wide

$2,500-3,000   DN

A Regency inlaid rosewood canterbury, with three spindle divisions, the box base with a drawer, the turned legs with casters.

21.75in (55cm) wide

$3,500-4,000   SI

A Regency mahogany Canterbury, of rectangular outline, the slatted dividers with concave tops above a single panel drawer, raised on turned and tapering legs with brass caps and casters.

21.25in (54cm) wide

$2,000-2,500   L&T

A William IV rosewood canterbury, the three compartments with open crossed dividers centered by wreaths to each side and united by ring-turned rails above a single drawer with applied leaf decoration, on turned feet with brass caps and casters.

$2,000-2,500   L&T

A 19thC and later mahogany canterbury, having three X-shaped open divisions fronted by a carved wreath fitted one drawer with carved knob on four tapered turned supports with brass terminals and casters.

23in (58cm) high

$1,000-1,200   Clv

A Victorian walnut-finished three-tier canterbury, turned spindle supports above two frieze fitted drawers raised on turned supports with ceramic casters.

$750-850   BW

A Victorian rosewood canterbury, of rectangular form with bowed ends, the three open compartments with turned supports and pierced scrolling side panels, above single drawer and turned feet with brass caps and casters.

21.75in (55cm) wide

$4,500-5,000   L&T

WINE COOLERS

A George II mahogany cellaret, with boxwood stringing and hinged lid enclosing lead interior raised on square-section legs with caps and casters.

25in (63cm) wide

$5,500-6,000   L&T

A George III mahogany cellaret, with brass loo-handles on square-tapered legs, fitted brass casters.

17in (43cm) wide

$2,200-2,800   GorL

Wine Coolers

A George III mahogany and brass-bound wine cooler, the hinged top enclosing a lined and fitted interior for bottles, with brass side-handles, on square-tapering legs with brass terminals and casters.

18.25in (46cm) wide

$4,000-5,000	DN

A George III mahogany cellarette, the hinged top enclosing a six-bottle interior with brass carrying-handles, raised on square-chamfered legs with casters.

16.5in (42cm) wide

$1,800-2,400	Chef

A George III mahogany and brass-bound wine cooler, the tapered body with a fitted interior on square-section tapered fluted and stopped legs.

23in (58cm) high

$4,000-4,500	L&T

An mahogany open wine cooler, brass-bound with cast lion-mask Irish-style ring handles and zinc liner, on a serpentine base, with cabouchon-carved edge, foliage-carved cabriole legs with scroll toes.

27in (68.5cm) wide

$4,500-5,000	WW

A CLOSER LOOK AT A WINE COOLER

The sarcophagus shape is typical of the Regency period.

The ebony stringing is another early 19thC feature.

This piece has a very high quality veneer.

The fact that this piece has retained some of its original lead lining increases its value.

Ebonized moldings, here in the form of a sphinx, were extremely popular at that time. Lion's paw feet were also a common motif.

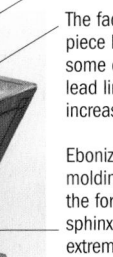

A Regency mahogany-veneered open wine cooler, with remains of a lead lining, inlaid ebony stringing, the reeded frieze resting on ebonized sphinx supports to a rectangular plinth on later brass casters.

A design attributable to Thomas Hope, a related cistern in George Smith's Collection of Designs for Household Furniture and interior decoration.

43.5in (110.5cm) wide

$10,000-12,000	WW

A early 19thC mahogany cellaret, the hinged top with satinwood and rosewood crossbanding and cushion-molded edge, enclosing divided interior, above corresponding body and plinth on ring-turned tapering legs with brass caps and casters.

22.75in (58cm) high

$1,200–1,500	L&T

A Regency mahogany celleret cabinet, the hinged lid enclosing deep-divided interior above pair of cupboard doors and shallow side drawers, on paw feet and casters.

22in (56cm) wide

$4,000-5,000	L&T

A Regency mahogany cellaret, the hinged lid with rosewood cross-banding, ropework-molding and corresponding brass-stringing enclosing divided interior above single drawer raised on spirally and ring-turned feet with brass caps and casters.

26.5in (67cm) high

$4,000-4,500	L&T

A late George III mahogany cellaret, coopered with two brass bands with later-added lid (now missing), with original tapered leg stand.

25in (62cm) high

$1,000-1,300	HamG

A late Regency mahogany wine cooler, the top decorated with knulled moldings, opening to reveal a lead-lined interior the tapered sides above turned bun feet and original casters.

22in (56cm) wide

$3,000-3,500	HamG

A late Regency mahogany cellaret, with ebony and brass-stringing, with stepped hinged lid enclosing divided lead-lined interior, the tapering body on shallow plinth and ebonized paw feet with sunken casters.

26.5in (67cm) wide

$3,000-3,500	L&T

CHAIRS

A pair of William and Mary walnut open armchairs, the pierced S-scroll crests with central shell motifs above caned backs, later arms and embossed leather seats, raised on turned front legs united by H-shaped stretchers.

$1,000-1,300 (pair)   **Chef**

A George II walnut elbow chair, with yolk-shaped toprail, solid vase splat and outscrolled arms above a drop-in needlework seat on cabriole legs united by stretchers.

$1,300-1,600   **BonS**

A George II mahogany-framed love seat, the shaped upholstered back with open outscrolled arms above bow-fronted drop-in seat and shaped apron raised on simply carved cabriole front legs with pad feet.

$6,000-7,000   **L&T**

A George III mahogany ladder-back elbow chair, with pierced waved splat, shaped arms, on square-chamfered legs.

$300-400   **GorB**

A pair of Regency faux-bamboo painted open armchairs, with spindle-filled toprails, squab cushions and caned seats, on turned legs with stretchers.

$1,100-1,400 (pair)   **BonS**

A Regency armchair, with caned seat and brass inlay, on sabre legs.

c1815   30.75in (78cm) high

$450-500   **CdK**

A Regency ebonized and gilt-painted and decorated elbow chair, with pierced lozenge splat over silk-upholstered seat and simulated bamboo supports.

32.5in (82.5cm) high

$900-1,100   **GorL**

A pair of Regency mahogany library chairs, each with hoop back with brass slot to rear, above Gothic-pierced splat and spreading seat, for reverse seating, on leaf-carved baluster legs with brass caps (casters lacking), by Morgan and Saunders.

$25,000-30,000   **L&T**

A Regency bamboo elbow chair, with a later rattan seat, on stretchered legs. Footnote: Taken from the 1802 pattern for the Royal Pavilion Brighton.

$3,000-3,500   **WW**

A George IV mahogany rail-back elbow chair, the back set with two turned spheres, with reeded down-swept arms, turned supports, a padded seat and ring-turned legs.

$1,000-1,200   **DN**

A 19thC Sheraton-style cream and floral-painted elbow chair, with pierced X-splat above bowed cane seat and squab cushion, on turned tapering legs, all-over decorated with trailing flowers.

$2,000-2,500   **BonS**

Chairs

A pair of 19thC Hepplewhite-style Consulate satinwood elbow chairs, with arched triple-splat shield backs, open down-swept arms and serpentine-fronted seats, on tapered turned legs, later restorations.

$1,200-1,500 (pair)   **BonS**

A set of six 19thC George III-style painted armchairs, the backs with interlaced splats above open arms with vase-turned supports, the padded seats, raised on slender turned front legs.

$2,200-2,800 (set)   **Chef**

▶ A mid-18thC George III carved mahogany open armchair, the slightly splayed rectangular back with a leaf-carved tri-arched crest rail centered by a flowerhead over a pierced Gothick splat, the outcurved arms with acanthus-carved scroll terminals on back-curved supports, the padded drop-in seat with molded and shaped rails raised on square section tapering legs with chamfered inner corners, modifications.

39.25in (99.5cm) high

$2,200-2,800   **SI**

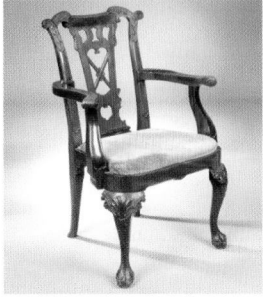

A pair of Victorian George I-style open armchairs, each with carved and pierced fan-backs, serpentine arms with acanthus-carved supports and scroll terminals, the overstuffed needlework seats above acanthus cabriole legs with claw-and-ball feet.

This pattern is copied from the celebrated set at Stourhead, Wiltshire, commonly attributed to Giles Grendey.

$7,500-8,500   **L&T**

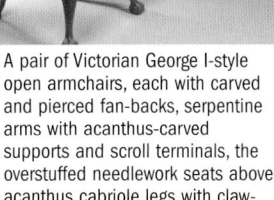

A matched pair of late 18thC Derbyshire-type fruitwood open armchairs, with pierced crestings, spindle-filled backs, outscrolled arms and drop-in seats, on square section legs united by stretchers, restorations.

$1,000-1,300 (pair)   **BonS**

A late 19thC Sheraton Revival satinwood elbow chair, painted overall with flowers and leaves, the shield-shaped back with pierced splat, with down-swept arms, padded seat on turned tapering legs, with an ivorine plaque for Edwards and Roberts, Wardour Street, London.

$3,000-3,500   **DN**

A late Victorian rosewood open elbow chair, the oval back with pierced splat brass-inlaid foliage and a swan with outspread wings, raised on cabriole legs.

40.25in (102cm) high

$650-700   **GorL**

An Edwardian mahogany George II-style carver armchair, the scrolled and carved toprail above pierced splat and paneled uprights, outscrolled open arms and drop-in shaped seat, the cabriole front legs shell-carved with claw-and-ball feet.

$750-850   **L&T**

A William IV mahogany elbow chair, with curved crest-rail and lappet-carved back, downswept arms, a padded seat and reeded turned tapering legs.

$800-1,000   **DN**

A set of six Scottish early 20thC Restoration-style oak chairs, including two larger open armchairs, each with tall back centered by carved panel with scrolling frame and thistles, the toprail carved with crown flanked by thistles and framed by baluster and blocked uprights, with further thistles and finials, the spreading carved seat with relief-carved rails raised on leaf-carved scrolled legs joined by scrolled crown and thistle apron and turned and blocked H-stretcher.

$4,000-5,000   **L&T**

Chairs

A set of 12 early 20thC George I-style open armchairs, each with shaped solid vase splat, serpentine arms with scroll terminals, drop-in seat and cabriole legs with pad feet.

$5,000–6,000	L&T

An 18thC French beech-wood fauteuil, the back with carved roses and outswept padded arms, the wide serpentine-fronted seat with carved apron, raised on turned and reeded legs terminating in toupie feet.

$750-850	HamG

A mid-18thC Gainsborough chair, probably Irish, the square cresting with padded arms and profusely carved acanthus supports, the elegantly carved cabriole legs with shell, C-scroll and claw-and-ball decoration, having later H-stretchers, original color, restorations.

$4,500-5,500	HamG

A set of four Neo-classical open armchairs, possibly 18thC, each with husk and rosette-carved paneled frame, the square back with upholstered panel, the open arms with serpentine uprights and squabs, stuff-over seat raised on turned and leaf-carved legs with spiral fluting.

$1,200-1,600	L&T

A pair of George III fauteuils, in the manner of John Linnell, the molded frames with upholstered oval backs united by an anthemion, above padded arms with stylized ball-and-foliate terminals, on fluted supports, the serpentine stuff-over seats on anthemion-headed fluted inverted baluster legs, restored, lacking gilding.

$4,500-5,500	BonS

A George III mahogany Gainsborough-type armchair, with padded back, seat and arms, upholstered in tapestry fabric on square legs with H-stretcher.

$2,500-3,000	DN

A set of six French-style George III fauteuils, each with scrolling rails, arms and legs, two upholstered with needlework covers, the others with distressed silk.

$6,000-7,000	L&T

An early 19thC French walnut fauteuil, the oval-shaped back with carved roses and outswept padded arms, the wide serpentine-fronted seat with carved apron, raised on turned, reeded and fluted front legs.

$300-350	HamG

A Regency walnut fauteuil, with arched upholstered padded back, manchettes with shell-and-foliate scroll supports and stuff-over seat, on foliate-carved cabriole legs and shell centered apron.

$2,200-2,600	BonS

A pair of Scottish Regency oak open armchairs, each with oak leaf-clasped corner to the spreading concave back, enclosing upholstered panel, the arms with scrolling uprights issuing from the seat rail, on turned and reeded tapering front legs with toupie feet .

$7,500-8,500	L&T

A Regency mahogany bergère armchair, the back with reeded frame and arms, with turned terminal supports and corresponding front legs with brass caps and casters, the seat with leather squab.

$5,000-6,000	L&T

A large George IV gilt-framed armchair, in the manner of Gillows, the carved scrolling reeded frame with acanthus and flower motifs, upholstered back panel, armrests and drop-in seat, the top rail and seat rail centered by rocaille cartouches, on cabriole legs with scroll toes.

$3,000-3,500   **L&T**

A 19thC French Hepplewhite-style beech fauteuil, with upholstered cartouche back, manchettes on spiral-carved supports and stuff-over serpentine seat, on carved cabriole legs.

$750-850   **BonS**

A 19thC Louis XVI-style giltwood fauteuil, with rectangular needlework-upholstered back, manchettes with foliate-carved baluster supports and stuff-over seat, on paterae-headed tapered fluted legs.

$3,000-3,500   **BonS**

A 19thC Colonial carved oak open armchair, with hide upholstered back and seat cushion on tapered legs with paw feet.

$700-800   **BonS**

A pair of 19thC Anglo-Indian ebony armchairs, each with scrolling reeded uprights and bar-back enclosing caning, similar down-swept arms with reeded baluster supports, reeded seat rails (seat with later boarding) on ring-turned and tapering reeded legs.

Ebony is doing well on the market at the moment. Despite being "his and hers" chairs they are a pair, which adds to the value.

$18,000-22,000   **L&T**

A pair of 19thC rosewood Louis XV-style fauteuils, each molded and shaped upholstered back, open arms and serpentine seat on cabriole legs.

$3,000-3,500 (pair)   **L&T**

A Victorian Gothic-style mahogany and parcel-gilt open armchair, the arched back with upholstered panel, above down-swept arms and stuff-over seat, on cabriole legs united by turned stretchers.

$1,200-1,500   **BonS**

A Victorian walnut lady's parlor armchair, the upholstered scalloped buttoned back and circular seat flanked by molded and carved scrolling open arms, raised on similar cabriole front legs and casters.

$2,500-3,000   **L&T**

A large late Victorian carved oak-framed armchair, with leopard-skin effect upholstery, on swept supports.

$400-450   **GorB**

A pair of late French 19thC Louis XIV-style beechwood and needlework fauteuils, with down-swept, molded scroll arms on back-curved scroll supports, the stuff-over seats raised on back-curved legs with shaped block feet, the wavy H-stretcher centered by a floral basket, upholstered in old needlework panels,

$5,000-6,000   **SI**

A set of four Louis XVI-style giltwood fauteuils, each with leaf-carved molded frame, the back with shaped gadrooned rail and fluted uprights with leaf-carved finials, open arms raised on baluster supports, bow-fronted overstuffed seat with carved seat rail on stop fluted turned legs.

$4,000-5,000   **L&T**

Chairs

A pair of George II-style mahogany library armchairs, each with shaped upholstered rectangular back and serpentine open arms with rocaille-carved curved supports terminating in animal heads, the stuffover rectangular seat with scrolling acanthus-carved aprons to front and sides centered by cartouches, cabriole legs with hairy paw feet and lion masks to the front, ancanthus leaves to the rear, sunken casters.

These chairs are of identical design to the celebrated suite now divided amongst some of the world's finest public and private collections. A single chair is in the Philadelphia Museum of Art. There is also a pair of chairs in the Metropolitan Museum of Art, New York, of identical pattern but slightly different proportions which were acquired in 1964.

$45,000-50,000	**L&T**

▲**1** A George III mahogany Raeburn chair, the open arms with floral-carved down-swept supports, on fluted square section legs, joined by H-stretcher.

$3,000-3,500	**L&T**

▲**2** A George III mahogany Raeburn chair, with upholstered serpentine-back and seat, the open arms with leaf-carved down-swept supports, on, fluted square section legs joined by H-stretcher.

$3,000-3,500	**L&T**

A Regency Napoleon armchair, the upholstered back with outscrolled arms of different heights, on simulated rosewood legs, of bulbous beehive form to the front, with brass caps and casters. Napoleon was painted sitting in a chair of this form, an image which in turn inspired the architect Edwyn Lutyens to design related chairs for his own use. The chair appears to have Scottish origins, as the beehive leg used is a common Scottish form.

37in (94cm) wide

$7,000-8,000	**L&T**

A CLOSER LOOK AT A WING ARMCHAIR

The deep wings were designed to protect the sitter from drafts.

Early household inventories have shown that these chairs were more likely to be used in bedrooms than parlors.

The vertical rolls arm supports on this chair are a common feature of New England wing chairs.

When buying a wing chair it is important to check the legs are solid as they are the only visible part of the frame. Buyers should look for reasonable wear and skilled carving.

An American Classical Revival wing armchair, with leaf-carved arm supports with rosette blocks ribbed and acanthus carved tapering legs. *c1825*

$50,000-70,000	**FRE**

A mid-18thC George II mahogany wing-back armchair, the back flanked by outcurved deep wings, the padded over-scroll arms flanking a loose-cushion seat, the square section legs joined by H-stretcher, upholstered in close-nailed leather.

$4,000-4,500	**SI**

A Louis XV bergère.
c1760   36.75in (93cm) high

$ 4,000-4,500	**CdK**

A Regency mahogany-framed library armchair, possibly Scottish, the curved scroll-over back and arms with charged scrolling terminals enclosing morocco button-upholstered base on baluster-turned legs terminating in brass caps and casters.

$4,000-5,000	**L&T**

A late Regency mahogany-framed leather armchair, the outscrolled back and lower arms with scrolled facings, raised on turned, tapering octagonal front legs with rosette terminals and brass caps and casters.

$7,000-8,000	**L&T**

A CLOSER LOOK AT AN ARMCHAIR

The chair is in fantastic, untouched original condition, if very tired which actually appeals to collectors.

The exceptionally large size is unusual and attractive.

Original leather and squab upholstery adds to the value.

A Regency mahogany Napoleon armchair, with scratched leather buttoned upholstery and seat squab, outscrolled back and arms, one low and one high, on lotus leaf-carved tapering legs with brass caps and casters, one seat rail inscribed in pencil "Mrs Gilmour of the Inch, 1829".

41.75in (106cm) wide

$40,000-45,000	L&T

A William IV rosewood armchair, foliate scroll-carved arms, the seat rail with a central flowerhead on urned and lappet-carved legs with brass casters.

$3,000-3,500	DN

A large early Victorian mahogany-framed armchair, with leather upholstery, the back with molded and carved scrolling frame, low open arms with pads and console terminals, above cushion-molded seat rail and squat-carved sabre legs with leaf-carved capitals.

$2,000-2,500	L&T

A pair of 19thC George II-style mahogany armchairs, each with back and arms truncating in outscrolled lion's heads, the overstuffed seat with concave rail raised on shell-carved cabriole front legs with scroll toes.

$3,500-4,000 (pair)	L&T

A pair of mid-19thC rococo-style mahogany parlor chairs, with C- and S-scrolls, acanthus leaves and auricular decoration, each with waisted-back with pierced cartouche surmount, shaped down-swept sides and serpentine seat rail, cabriole legs with scroll toes and casters.

$3,500-4,000	L&T

A pair of Victorian easy armchairs, the backs, scrolled arms and serpentine seats covered in a figured buttermilk fabric, raised on ebonized and gilt-metal mounted cabriole legs.

$1,500-2,000	Chef

A Louis XVI-style bergère.

c1900   41.5in (105cm) high

$2,200-2,800	CdK

COUNTRY CHAIRS

A 17thC oak settle, the four-panel back with hinged glazed toprail and arms with baluster supports above hinged seat and two panel front, reconstructed, by Muirhead Moffat & Co., Glasgow.

62.25in (158cm) wide

$1,800-2,400	L&T

An early 18thC oak chair, the yoke-shaped back with a raised and fielded panel, with flat arms and a paneled seat, raised on turned supports and front stretcher.

$750-850	HamG

Two early 19thC yew-and elm-wood Windsor bow-back armchairs, the first north Midlands, with a vasiform pierced splat flanked by six rods, the arms on back-curved supports, the dished slab seat raised on turned tapering splayed legs joined by an incurved stretcher; the second similar, Suffolk.

$1,500-2,000	SI

Chairs

A pair of Victorian elm and beech stick-back kitchen elbow chairs, on turned underframes.

$225-275 (pair) **GorB**

An early 19thC ash and elm Windsor elbow chair, with saddle-shaped seat, ring-turned supports on stretcher base.

39.5in (100cm) high

$500-600 **Clv**

A set of five 19thC ash Lancashire chairs, each with turned spindle-back above rush seat and club legs joined by stretchers.

$900-1,100 (set) **L&T**

An early 19thC ash wing armchair, the shaped toprail above three rows of turned spindles and a rush seat, raised on club legs united by stretchers.

$350-450 **Chef**

A 19thC ash and elm Windsor wheel-back elbow chair, on turned and tapered front supports with stretcher base.

35in (89cm) high

$450-550 **Clv**

◄ A Windsor ash-wood, yew-wood and elm-wood bow-back high chair, the back with eight tapering rods, the arms joined at the terminals by a restraining rod, the dished slab seat with a scribed edge, the turned tapering splayed legs supporting a pegged foot rest and joined by a turned tapering splayed legs supporting a pegged foot rest and joined by turned H-stretcher. c1800

$2,400-2,800 **SI**

A 19thC yew and elm Windsor elbow chair, with pierced splat above a saddle seat on cabriole legs united by a crinoline stretcher, with restorations.

$1,500-2,000 **BonS**

A set of four 19thC ash and elm gothic chairs, the lancet-backs over pierced splats and shaped seats on cabriole legs and hoop stretcher.

$2,400-2,800 **L&T**

A pair of Georgian yew Windsor armchairs, each with hoop-back and arms, Gothick-pierced splat and spars, elm saddle seat and cabriole front legs with pad feet joined by hoop stretcher.

$4,500-5,500 **L&T**

A 19thC ash and elm Windsor armchair, the hoop-back and arms above hollow seat and baluster-turned legs joined by stretchers.

$350-450 **L&T**

A late 19thC satin-birch Darvel chair, the comb-back above hooped rail with outscrolled terminals, the serpentine-fronted seat above baluster-turned legs joined by similar H-stretcher.

$1,500-1,800 **L&T**

Chairs

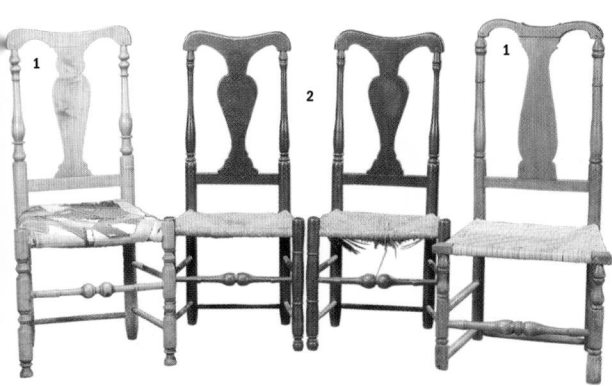

1 Two late 18thC Queen Anne turned maple side chairs, probably Connecticut, each with shaped crest, turned stiles enclosing a vasiform splat, raised on turned legs joined by baluster-turned front stretcher; the first with an over-rail "Crazy Quilt" covered seat, the second with a splint seat, (refinished, imperfections).

Highest 40.5in (103cm) high

| **$500-600** | SI |

An early 19thC American rush seat ladder back side chair, with turned finials to posts and five arched rungs.

| **$200-300** | FRE |

A reproduction parcel-gilt and painted banister-back side chair, the back with an arched and beveled crest rail over a stick splat flanked by split-banister splats, the trapezoidal, woven-bark seat raised on ring-turned legs joined by a turned double-box stretcher, painted with red and gilt highlights on an indigo ground, inscribed C & B/1763.

| **$300-400** | SI |

2 A pair of 18thC grain-painted country Queen Anne side chairs, New England, possibly Connecticut, the shaped crest rail over vasiform splat, turned stiles and trapezoidal rush seat raised on tapering back legs and turned front legs joined by a baluster-turned front stretcher (old breaks and wear).

39in (99cm) high

| **$900-1,200** | SI |

A CLOSER LOOK AT A LADDERBACK CHAIR

The original paint on these chairs is highly desirable to collectors. To check whether paint is original, check worn areas where remnants of old paint might be visible.

Few rush seats are original as they wear our relatively quickly and are replaced.

The turning on the front stretcher and tops of the front legs are evidence of good craftsmanship.

One of a set of six ladderback chairs, all with original grained salmon and yellow paint, with graduated, arched slats.

Ladderback chairs were first introduced in the 17thC and continued to be made in the 18thC, when the form became lighter. Although it was a popular form after the Revolution, it is unusual to find an authentic set of early chairs. Many sets are harlequins, made up from different sets, and so a true set has a high value.

When looking at such a simple design it is important to consider the subtle details, such as the turning of the wood.

c1785

| **$12,000-18,000 (set)** | BCAC |

An early banister-back rush seat side chair, having turned finials and posts with four banister splats, turned legs and stretchers, arched crestrail repaired.

| **$250-300** | FRE |

A fancy slat-back grain-painted and stencilled arm chair, the turned rolled-back crest rail above a shaped upper slat and arched lower slat with spindle-shaped incised seat on splayed turned legs, rosewood grained with yellow highlights and gilt stencilling.

c1820   32.5in (82.5cm) high

| **$450-550** | SI |

A first half 19thC ladderback painted and decorated side chair, the turned finials on cylindrical posts, three arched slats and woven rush seat, cylindrical front legs, double box seat, cylindrical front legs, double box stretcher, painted black and heightened with gilt floral and foliate motifs, feet extended.

43.5in (110.5cm) high

| **$800-1,000** | SI |

A pair of fancy side chairs, probably Baltimore, scrolled and rolled back crest rails over vase-turned styles enclosing shaped splat above a caned seat and tapering legs, rosewood grained with gilt and green highlights, wear.

c1825   31.25in (79.5cm) high

| **$400-600** | SI |

Chairs

AMERICAN WINDSOR CHAIRS

Windsor chairs originated in England early in the 18th century, and by 1730 American craftsmen had taken the form and adapted it to create their own distinctive variations. For the next 100 years they produced classic models, until the mid-19thC when these were superseded by the mass-produced versions and copies which are still being made today. These sturdy, all-wood, chairs were inexpensive and easy to make and lend themselves to all manner of design interpretations.

There are six basic variations of Windsor Chair:

Low-back or captain's chair: shorter back spindles and a top rail that doubles as an armrest.

Hoop-back: similar to the low-back, but with an arched addition to the central portion of the back.

Comb-back: similar to the low-back, but the row of spindles extends above the arm rail and fits into a serpentine top rail.

Fan-back side chair: similar to the comb-back, but with no arm rail and heavier turned stiles at either side of the back.

Continuous arm: the arms and arched top rail are made from a single piece of bentwood and with no mid-rail.

Loop-back: a side chair, with long spindles set into an exaggerated, hooped back rail.

High-chairs, stools, settees and writing chairs with an adapted arm were other popular styles.

Windsors were made from several types of wood: pine for the seat as it was soft to work with, hickory, ash or birch for spindles and rails as they provide flexibility, maple for the legs for its strength. The resulting mix of colors and grains was both disguised and protected using paint. Common colors included solid yellow, black, white, green and red.

An early 19thC New England painted square-back Windsor side-chair, rod-turned rail and stiles enclose bamboo-turned spindles in a shaped seat and bamboo-turned splayed legs, joined by similar stretchers.

32in (81cm) high	
$300-400	SI

An early 19thC square-back Windsor highchair, with bamboo-turned stiles, arms supports, legs and stretchers (refinished, imperfections).

30in (76cm) high	
$300-400	SI

An early 19thC bamboo-turned slat-back rocker Windsor armchair, New England, turned stiles enclose rod-turned spindles above turned arms and arm supports, shaped seat over turned, splayed legs and rockers, painted black, old repairs.

$300-400	SI

An early 19thC pair of Windsor birdcage-back side chairs. with seven bamboo-turned spindles, shaped seat on bamboo-turned legs and stretchers.

$500-600	FRE

One of a pair of 18thC seven-spindle Windsor chairs, with old green paint preserved by varnish.

$2,500-3,000 (pair)	BCAC

A Pennsylvania fan-back Windsor side chair, rounded ears on arched crest above ring-and-vase turned stiles enclosing seven spindles over a saddle seat and splayed ring-and-vase turned legs.

c1800	37.5in (95.5cm) high
$600-700	SI

A bamboo-turned square back Windsor armchair, with a shaped seat.

c1810	36in (91.5cm) high
$350-450	SI

A butterfly Windsor armchair, chrome-yellow paint and black line decoration.

c1810

$2,000-2,400	BCAC

▲**1** A fan-back Windsor side chair, Pennsylvania, rounded ears on arched crest above ring-and-vase turned stiles enclosing seven spindles over a saddle seat and splayed ring-and-vase turned legs.

37.5in (95cm) high

$600-700	SI

2 A fan-back Windsor side chair, Connecticut or Rhode Island,

c1800	35.5in (90cm) high
$400-500	SI

A Connecticut or Rhode Island fan-back Windsor side chair, arched crest with shaped ears on vase and ring-turned stiles and ring-turned legs, with imperfections

c1800	35.5in (90cm) high
$350-400	SI

A child's fan-back Windsor side chair, with a shaped crest rail with carved ears above baluster-turned stiles and seven spindles, saddle seat on splayed baluster-turned legs joined by bulbous-turned stretchers and vasiform and spool-turned medial stretcher, branded "A. Coeser," PA.

26in (66cm) high

$2,000-3,000	SI

American Chairs

A mid-18thC Queen Anne walnut side chair, probably Rhode Island, yoked crest above a vasi-form splat and trapezoidal seat, with shaped skirt on frontal cabriole legs ending in pad feet and chamfered rear legs joined by block, vase-and-ring turned stretchers, repairs.

38in (96.5cm) high

$1,500-1,800   **SI**

A Queen Anne transitional white cedar side chair, Northern Coastal States, the shaped peaked crest with carved volutes above a vase form splat flanked by curved stiles, continuing to square rear legs, a trapezoidal seat frame with shaped apron on cabriole front legs ending in pad feet joined by block vase-turned side and rear stretchers and flat curved medial stretcher.

An analysis of a wood sample extracted from the chair, determined that the chair is made of Atlantic white cedar native to an American species occurring in a relatively narrow belt from southern Maine to northern Florida, and from Florida westward to Louisiana along the Gulf Coast. The wood does not grow in Bermuda.

c1750

38.5in (98cm) high

$5,000-6,000   **SI**

QUEEN ANNE STYLE

The Queen Anne style brought a greater delicacy and sophistication in furniture making. This period, which ran from 1725 to 1750, saw the first regional variations in American furniture making. Wood – mainly walnut, along with cherry, maple and mahogany – was carved and given a rich finish.

A CLOSER LOOK AT A QUEEN ANNE CHAIR

Scalloped shells and volutes (scrolls) were one of the carved designs most favored by Queen Anne furniture makers in Pennsylvania.

This chair has superb patination.

The rectangular seat support is a part American feature. It has been cut from the solid frame and therefore additional corner supports are not needed.

The claw and ball feet, although not exuberant, have immense elegance, as do the carved cabriole legs with volutes. The cabriole leg was first introduced in the Queen Anne period, giving the furniture a wonderfully human scale

The Queen Anne style reached its high point in Philadelphia in the mid-18thC when this chair was made.

The proportions of the chair are exactly what collectors look for.

The chair also has a superb provenance which adds tremendously to the value.

A Philadelphia walnut Transitional arm chair, with serpentine crest rail with urn back splat, flaring arm on spooned supports with scroll and scroll-carved grips, slip-seat with straight seat rail, on shell-carved cabriole legs, claw-and-ball feet.

c1760

$9,500-10,000   **FRE**

A rare Philadelphia Queen Anne Transitional side chair, of walnut with shell carved crest rail with double scrolled volutes, continuing to carved rounded styles centering a vasiform splat, balloon fitted slip seat supported by two shell carved cabriole legs with two volutes, terminating in claw and ball feet. The front seat rail is inscribed with two strokes, indicating that the chair is number two of a set of six or more. The balloon slip seat frame is inscribed with IIIII, indicating that it had originally belonged to chair number five of the set. It is interesting to note that the back edge of the slip seat is constructed to fit between the edges of the stiles which extend a bit more than one inch into the back seat rail. Below, on the back seat rail, the letters SM are inscribed in white chalk. These chalk letters are similar to those found on the chair advertised in "Antiques" April issue 1988, page 766. Therefore we believe this chair to be from the same set which was owned by Samuel Morris, one of twenty-eight men who formed the First City Troop of Light Horse. He became captain of this troop, served with George Washington in the battles of Princeton and Trenton and in The Revolutionary War. He was a member of the Committe of Safety, The Pennsylvania Assembly and the colony in Schuylkill, in 1776 he became its Governor, a post he held untill his death. He was an ardent patriot and strongly supported Colonial artisans as opposed to importing manufactured goods from England.

c1750-1760

41in (104.1cm) high

$350,000-400,000   **FRE**

A Philadelphia carved walnut side chair, with serpentine crest rail with carved shell, flanked by scroll volutes over solid vasiform back splat, slip-seat, straight aproon, cabriole legs with shell-carved knees terminating on claw-and-ball feet.

c1760

$6,000-6,500   **FRE**

An 19thC New England Queen Anne rush seat side chair, having a yoke crest rail, solid vase splat back, rush seat, turned legs and stretchers. Arched crestrail repaired.

$350-400   **FRE**

A Chippendale mahogany side chair.
c1770

$2,200-2,500	**FRE**

A Chippendale Philadelphia mahogany side chair, the pad feet with unusual turning, the seat rail incised with Roman numeral "IIII."
1740-1770

$9,000-11,000	**FRE**

A Chippendale carved walnut side chair, probably Philadelphia PA, serpentine shell-carved crest with scrolled terminals above a volute-carved strapwork splat over the trapezoidal slip seat within molded frame with shaped apron on cabriole legs ending in ball and claw feet, restorations.

c1760   40in (101.5cm) high

$1,200-1,800	**SI**

A third quarter 18thC pair of Philadelphia walnut side chairs. Having serpentine crest rails with pierced flaring splats, off-white floral embroidered linen seats, straight seat rails, plain cabriole legs, claw & ball feet.

$10,000-12,000	**FRE**

A Chippendale walnut side chair, Philadelphia. Shell carved crest rail with scrolled ears, pierced splat with scoll carving, shaped front and side rails, cabriole legs with boldly carved knees terminating in ball and claw feet, marked with Roman numerals "V" on front rail. Provenance: From the Estate of Letitia Martin Pittman.

c1760-1780   39.75in (101cm) high

$2,500-3,500	**FRE**

A CLOSER LOOK AT A CHIPPENDALE CHAIR

The crest rail with a carved shell in the center flanked by scrolls and carved ears is typical of the form.

The pierced splat back is relatively plain for a Chippendale chair, which would usually be carved as well.

The shell on the crest rail is echoed by an inverted shell carved on the shaped skirt.

The cabriole legs have C-scrolls at the top and claw-and-ball feet. The feet are typical of American Chippendale.

A Chippendale walnut side chair, Philadelphia, front marked with Roman numerals "I", bottom 2 inches of both rear legs replaced. Provenance: From the Estate of Letitia Martin Pittman.
c1760-1780   40in (101.5cm)

$4,500-5,500	**FRE**

A pair of Queen Anne walnut side chairs, each with serpentine crest rail, flared ears and shaped stiles centering a solid vasiform splat, the trapezoidal slip seat and shaped skirt beneath resting on cabriole legs and drake feet, raked rear legs, joints reworked, includes two remade seats, Delaware Valley, .

Lot accompanied by a period silhouette of James Fausett, Sr. (1800-1833) who inherited the chairs through the Green family Trenton.
c1765   Chairs 21in (53.5cm) wide

$12,000-15,000	**FRE**

A Chippendale curly maple tilt-top candlestand, Philadelphia, the circular dish top tilting above an oak block and ring-turned standard with suppressed ball on peaked downswept legs ending in snake feet, retains an old alligatored finish, old repairs to block and ankle.
c1770   20.25in (51.5cm) diam

$6,000-8,000	**FRE**

A pair of second half 18thC Chippendale carved walnut side chairs, possibly New Jersey or Maryland, serpentine crest centered by a carved shell over a pierced vasi-form splat, the padded drop-in seat with molded rails on cabriole legs with claw-and-ball feet.

          39.25in (99.5cm) high

$5,500-6,500	**SI**

A late 18thC Delaware Valley set of six walnut side chairs. Plain serpentine crest rails, thin pierced splats, slip seats on straight seat rails with square grooved and chamfered leg with H-stretched. Numbered I through VI. Some glue blocks replaced and some missing.

$4,000-5,000 (set)	**FRE**

A Chippendale walnut side chair, probably Pennsylvania, yoked crest with rounded ears over pierced splat and trapezoidal slip seat within a molded conformingly shaped seat frame, square legs joined by stretchers.

37.5in (95cm) high

$1,800-2,400   **SI**

A Philadelphia walnut side chair, having a flat crest rail with pointed and carved volutes, Gothic pierced splats, slip seat, staring seat rail, on plain cabriole legs with claw-and-ball feet, lacking glue blocks.

$3,000-4,000   **FRE**

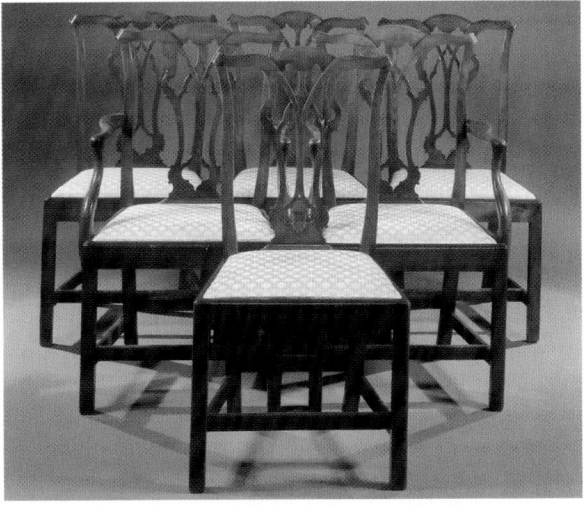

A set of six George III yew-wood dining chairs, comprising of two arm and four side chairs, each with shaped crest rail, scolled ears and shaped stiled centering a Gothic-pierced splat, trapezoidal slip seat on square straight legs, two crest rails repaired, various other repairs.

c1780   37.75in (96cm) high

$10,000-15,000   **FRE**

A pair of Hepplewhite mahogany side chairs, with shoaed crest rail over pierced urn and floral swag-carved back splat, supported by flat spindles, with carved fruit basket base, upholstered seat molded tapering legs, conjoined by stretcher, attributed to Benjamin Frothingham, Charlston and carved by Samuel McIntire, Salem, Mass.

Provenance: John S Walton, New York, May 1965.

c1780

$23,000-25,000   **FRE**

A third quarter 18thC Chippendale carved walnut side chair, probably Philadelphia, PA, with a carved serpentine crest centered by acanthus spray over a pierced Gothick strapwork splat, the trapezoidal drop-in slip seat with molded rails raised on square section molded legs chamfered on the inside and joined by an H-stretcher.

22.25in (56.5cm) wide

$1,000-1,500   **SI**

A pair of Chippendale mahogany ribbon back side chairs, Philadelphia, each with serpentine crestrail being the first of four pierced and ribbon-carved slats joined by molded and shaped stiles, the slip seat with serpentine front rail on molded and tapered legs joinging the rear raked legs by an "H" stretcher, scuffs to front legs, reblocked.

c1785   20.5in (52cm) wide

$6,000-8,000 (pair)   **FRE**

A late 18thC New England maple side chair, having a yoke crestrail with slightly curved volutes, slender pierded splat, old needlepoint covered slip seat, straight seat rail on angular cabriole legs with pad feet and turned H-stretcher, new glue blocks.

$700-1,000   **FRE**

Four 19thC carved mahogany centennial chairs, a pair of side chairs and armchair, each with serpentine crest rail above a pierced splat over a molded and shell-carved seat rail and acanthus-carved cabriole legs with ball and claw feet, the fourth armchair of similar form.

40in (51cm) high

$1,000-1,500   **SI**

A set of six late 19thC Chippendale-style carved mahogany dining chairs, comprising four side chairs and two armchairs, each open rectangular back with a pierced gothic splat, the stuff-over seat on square-section, molded legs with an H-stretcher.

$2,500-3,000   **SI**

A pair of late 19th/early 20thC Chippendale style carved mahogany side chairs, each open rectangular back with a tracery splat, the padded drop-in seat, shell-carved rails, leaf-capped cabriole legs on claw-and-ball feet.

$1,000-1,500   **SI**

Chairs

A set of nine George III mahogany dining chairs, each back with pierced splat-carved with patera and garrya, with padded seats on square-tapering molded legs, two with arms, three of a later date.

| $5,000-6,000 (set) | DN |

A set of six George III-style elm dining chairs, the shaped toprails above pierced vertical splats and drop-in seats, raised on square-chamfered legs united by H-shaped stretchers.

| $750-850 (set) | Chef |

A set of six George III mahogany dining chairs, the backs with pierced vertical leaf-capped splats above drop-in seats raised on square-tapering legs united by H-shaped stretchers.

| $1,800-2,400 (set) | Chef |

A set of eight Sheraton-period dining chairs, possibly Irish, the backs with wheatsheaf decoration and trailing garrya husks with a pierced splat, carvers with outswept arms and carved decoration, with blue upholstered drop-in seats on panel-molded and tapered kick-out front legs.

| $2,000-3,000 (set) | HamG |

A set of ten Scottish George III Sheraton-style mahogany dining chairs, each with corner rosette paterae, above stuff-over seat on turned tapering front legs (recently restored and prepared for final upholstery).

Despite being refinished, which often detracts from value, these are attractive because of their compact size, and sophisticated style. Also their provenance increases their worth.

Provenance: *The Duke of Hamilton's apartments, Holyroodhouse, Edinburgh. The Dukes of Hamilton are hereditary Keepers of Holyroodhouse, and have long held apartments there, This set of chairs is understood to have always been in the Palace and bears inventory labels accordingly. The Edinburgh cabinet makers Young, Trotter and Hamilton famously furnished the apartments at Holyrood occupied by the dethroned French Princes in 1797, and the Hamilton's are known to have been clients of William Hamilton of Young, Trotter and Hamilton, who prepared an inventory of Hamilton Palace in 1784.*

| $27,000-35,000 (set) | L&T |

A set of ten Regency beechwood dining chairs, the reeded curved shoulder rails with scroll-end turnings, the horizontal bifurcated splats centered by oblong-lobed paterae with drop-in seats on sabre legs, including a pair of elbow chairs.

| $6,500-7,500 | BonS |

A Regency painted and decorated dining chair, with padded seat and turned splayed legs with cross-stretchers.

| $75-125 | BonS |

A set of four Regency beech and brass-mounted dining chairs, the backs with X-splats, cane seats and sabre legs.

| $700-800 (set) | BonS |

A set of six Regency mahogany dining chairs, and two matched carvers, each with paneled mid-rail above drop-in seat and reeded seat rail on sabre legs.

| $3,000-4,000 (set) | L&T |

A set of six Regency rosewood dining chairs, with caned seats.

33.5in (85cm) high

$4,000-5,000 (set)   **CdK**

A set of six early 19thC mahogany dining chairs, each with a serpentine crest and pierced splat, a saddle seat and square-tapering legs with H-stretcher, repairs and replacements.

$1,100-1,600 (set)   **DN**

A pair of Regency mahogany dining chairs, with scroll-over crest rails, shaped pierced spars, on front sabre supports.

$250-300 (pair)   **GorB**

A set of four Regency mahogany and brass-lined dining chairs, each back between scrolled uprights continuing as seat rail and front sabre legs, caned seat and squab.

$2,600-3,200 (set)   **L&T**

A set of ten Regency mahogany dining chairs, including two carvers, each back with paper-scrolled surmount and sprially reeded and turned mid-rail between scrolling uprights, stuff-over seat and turned tapering legs.

$8,500-9,500 (set)   **L&T**

A set of eight Scottish Regency mahogany dining chairs, including two carvers, each back and pierced mid-rail with central tablet above drop-in seat and molded seat rail on ring-turned octagonal front legs with toupie feet.

$7,000-8,000 (set)   **L&T**

A pair of Regency Sheraton-style mahogany dining chairs, the flame-veneered bar-back and curved X-splat centered by a rosette, between reeded uprights, the stuff-over seat and reeded rail raised on carved and ring-turned tapering front legs, stamped "Thos Williamson, maker, Boston".

A Joshua, John and Ann Williamson are listed in the Dictionary of English Furniture Makers as working in Boston in the 1830s.

$1,300-1,600   **L&T**

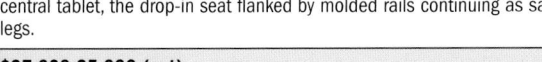

A matched set of fourteen Scottish Regency mahogany dining chairs, comprising two carvers and six chairs and a further six chairs of virtually identical design, each with serpentine yoke-back incorporating anthemion motifs and surmounted by a paper-scroll, above corresponding mid-rail with central tablet, the drop-in seat flanked by molded rails continuing as sabre legs.

$27,000-35,000 (set)   **&T**

A set of four late George III elm dining chairs, the backs with diamond splats above drop-in seats on square-tapered legs united by stretchers.

$600-700 (set)   **BonS**

A set of six late George III mahogany dining chairs, each with a shaped crest, pierced interlaced splat, a drop-in seat and straight-molded legs with H-stretchers, one with, one without arms.

$2,000-2,500 (set)   **DN**

Two from a set of six late Regency dining chairs, the backs with carved lumber rail, with moire overstuffed seats, standing on turned front legs.

$1,500-2,000 (set)   **HamG**

A set of William IV mahogany dining chairs, each with a shaped crest rail and a leaf and shell-carved back, a drop-in seat on turned and lappet-carved legs, two from the set.

$1,500-2,000 (set)   **DN**

A set of eight William IV mahogany dining chairs, each with outswept floral-carved yoke-back over upholstered seat and turned lappet legs, stamped "James Winter, 101 Wardour Street, Soho, London".

$10,000-12,000 (set)   **L&T**

A set of nine William IV dining chairs, including one larger, each with scrolled toprail and upholstered back above stuff-over seat and turned and reeded tapering front legs.

$4,500-5,500 (set)   **L&T**

A pair of mid-19thC walnut campaign dining chairs, with shaped and cared lumbar rails with black-oiled canvas seats and turned front legs, with a metal plate "Ross and Co, manufacturers 9, 10, and 11 Ellis's quay, Dublin".

$550-650 (pair)   **HamG**

A set of ten 19thC mahogany dining chairs, each with a shaped crest, a pierced vase-shaped splat carved with garrya, a drop-in seat on square-tapering legs with H-stretcher, two with arms, two of a later date.

$4,500-5,500 (set)   **DN**

A set of six late Victorian mahogany Sheraton-style dining chairs, each back with three pierced splats above stuff-over serpentine nailed leather seat raised on molded square section tapering legs with spade feet.

$4,000-5,000 (set)   **L&T**

A set of six mid-Victorian walnut dining chairs, with pierced scroll spars, on acute cabriole legs.

$550-650 (set)   **GorB**

A set of eight Victorian oak dining chairs, the S-sroll and foliate-carved toprails above interlaced and quatrefoil vertical splats flanked by turned uprights with finials, the leather overstuffed seats raised on block-turned baluster legs united by H-shaped stretchers.

$1,500-2,000 (set)   **Chef**

A set of eight late 19thC mahogany dining room chairs, each with serpentine toprail above a pierced splat and nailed stuff-over leather seat, carved cabriole front legs on pad feet.

$6,000-7,000 (set)   **L&T**

A set of twelve Chippendale-style mahogany dining chairs, including two carvers each with molded rail and uprights with pierced splat centered by a tassel, overstuffed seat and acanthus-carved cabriole front legs with claw-and-ball feet, by Jas Shoolbred & Co, of London.

$25,000-30,000 (set)   **L&T**

A set of ten Edwardian mahogany dining chairs, with leather upholstery, including two larger carvers, each with upholstered back on fluted supports above corresponding seat on carved, turned and fluted tapering legs.

$3,000-4,000 (set)   **L&T**

A set of eight Edwardian mahogany Sheraton-style dining chairs, including two carvers, each with satinwood-banded chamfered bar-back with pierced and rosette-carved mid-rail between reeded uprights, the overstuffed seat on turned tapering front legs.

$6,000-7,000   **L&T**

A set of eight Edwardian mahogany Chippendale-style dining chairs, including two carvers, each with serpentine toprail above pierced interlaced splat, stuff-over seat and cabriole legs, stamped "J & T Scott, Edinburgh".

$6,000-7,000   **L&T**

A set of eight early 20thC mahogany Hepplewhite-style dining chairs, including two carvers, each with arched molded back with pierced and carved splat centered by an urn, drop-in seat and square section tapering legs with spade feet joined by H-stretcher.

$3,000-4,000 (set)   **L&T**

A set of eight early 20thC Queen Anne-style walnut dining chairs, including two carvers, each with relief-carved toprail and a vase splat above waisted drop-in seat and shaped seat rail on cabochon and acanthus-carved legs with claw-and-ball feet.

$7,500-8,500 (set)   **L&T**

A set of Chippendale-style mahogany dining chairs, each with scrolling toprail over pierced splat and upholstered seat on carved cabriole front legs.

$7,500-8,500 (set)   **L&T**

A set of twelve Sheraton-style mahogany dining chairs, the backs with carved pillars over drop-in seats on square section tapered and molded front supports, comprising two armchairs and ten singles.

$7,500-8,500 (set)   **L&T**

A matched set of ten mahogany dining chairs, the serpentine-shaped cresting rails with carved volutes to the ears, having gothic-shaped pierced splats, with drop-in seats and ovolo-molded seat rails standing on chamfered straight legs united by H-stretchers.

c1765

$12,000-14,000 (set)   **HamG**

A set of eight Queen Anne-style mahogany dining chairs, each with shaped open-back centered by waisted splat above drop-in leather seat and reeded rail with cabriole legs joined by shaped H-stretcher.

$3,500-4,500 (set)   **L&T**

A set of six early George III-style mahogany dining chairs, including two carvers, each with shaped and carved toprail above pierced interlacing splat, drop-in seat and cabriole front legs with claw-and-ball feet.

$1,200-1,500 (set)   **L&T**

Chairs

A set of four George III mahogany hall chairs, with wide slightly dished seats on tapered legs.

$7,500-8,500 (set)   **GorL**

A pair of Regency mahogany hall chairs, the shaped solid backs with sunken oval cartouches below a gadrooned surmount and C-scrolls applied with roundels, on molded sabre legs, restorations.

$600-800   **BonS**

A George III mahogany hall chair, attributed to Thomas Chippendale, the back with central circular panel and molded waved rim enclosing radiating arched spokes, above a waisted and incised support with fluted collar, the shaped seat with molded rim above a stop-fluted frieze on square section tapering legs with block feet.

This chair can be compared closely with various hall chairs supplied by Chippendale to, among other houses, Normanton Hall, Harewood and Nostell Priory. Particularly distinctive features include the wheel back with its paneled and fluted shoe, and the form of the front leg.

This is an attractive piece, attributed to Chippendale, which increases its value. If it had been a pair they would be worth $15,000+.

$5,000-6,000   **L&T**

A set of eight solid oak country Georgian hall chairs, each seat on quatrefoil pierced trestle supports.

$4,500-5,500 (set)   **L&T**

A pair of Regency mahogany hall chairs, in the Grecian taste, the molded paneled tapering square-backs on scroll supports, the solid seats on molded sabre legs.

$1,800-2,200   **BonS**

A Regency mahogany hall chair, with back centered by a painted heraldic crest over a wood seat and reeded sabre legs.

34.5in (87.5cm) high

$450-550   **GorL**

A set of three 19thC painted armchairs, the pierced toprails above caned backs and seats, raised on ring-turned and tapering front legs.

$850-950 (set)   **Chef**

A near pair of late George III mahogany hall chairs, each back with C and S-scrolled frames containing carved crest with garter star enclosing Irish harp and crown surmounted by hand and sword surmount, above fan medallion and spreading bow-fronted seat with paneled tapering legs.

$1,100-1,400   **L&T**

A pair of mid-Victorian mahogany hall chairs, with shaped scrolled backs centered by armorials over solid seats and baluster turned legs.

33in (84cm) high

$600-700   **GorL**

Chairs

A set of four Victorian oak hall chairs, the backs carved and pierced in the form of grotesque masks above solid seats, raised on foliate-carved and turned front legs.

$650-750 (set)   **Chef**

A pair of late 19thC Robert Adams-style mahogany hall chairs, the backs with pierced medallions and central brass-mounted oval tablets, the dished seats on fluted seat rails with turned and fluted legs united by turned cross-stretchers.

$3,500-4,000 (pair)   **BonS**

A Victorian carved walnut nursing chair, on turned tapering legs.

$225-275   **GorL**

A Victorian carved walnut-framed nursing chair, covered in cut velvet, on cabriole legs.

$350-450   **GorB**

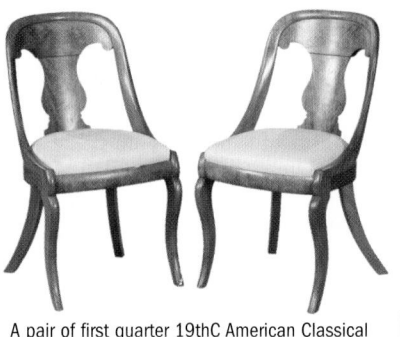

A pair of first quarter 19thC American Classical mahogany gondola-form chairs, each arched curved back with a vasiform splat, the crest rail continuing into shaped sabre-form front legs, padded seat slip.

33.5in (85cm) high

$1,500-2,000   **SI**

A pair of second half 19thC carved walnut American Rococo Revival parlor chairs, of gondola form, each arched curved and pierced back centered with a floral panel beneath an acanthus crest, each upholstered seat raised on cabriole legs with castors.

39in (99cm) high

$700-1,000   **SI**

An American Gothic Revival carved walnut armchair, the carved and pierced crest over a padded back flanked by spiral spindles and similarly turned stiles, the padded upholstered and ring-turned arms meet spiral-turned supports ending in ball-turned hand-holds, the upholstered seat raised on spiral-turned legs.

46.5in (118cm) high

$500-700   **SI**

A CLOSER LOOK AT A GEORGE I CHAIR

The solid splat was often veneered only to the front, leaving the back plain.

The toprail is susceptible to damage and has sometimes been repaired or strengthened by a metal brace at the back. You can see the repairs on this chair by the different tone of wood used.

The "ears" or spandrels on the knee of the leg have often been replaced or repaired and the cabriole legs are vulnerable to damage. It is therefore always advisable to check for repairs or replacements which will detract from the value.

A George I walnut side chair, with solid splat, shaped supports and drop-in seat on leaf-carved cabriole legs, with claw-and-ball feet, stamped "IM", some repairs.

$1,200-1,500   **DN**

Two mahogany side chairs, one George II, the other of a later date, each with leaf-carved cabriole legs and pad feet, one stamped "TB".

$6,000-7,000   **DN**

A Louis XV walnut side chair, the back and seat upholstered in floral needlework, with carved and shaped rails standing on stiff cabriole legs.

$1,000-1,300   **HamG**

Chairs

A Louis XVI gilt side/hall chair.
c1770   35.5in (90cm) high

$600-700 (set)   CdK

A George III mahogany side chair, with pierced vase-shaped splat, a drop-in seat on straight chamfered legs with H-stretcher.

$225-275   DN

A pair of Regency mahogany side chairs, the ebony-strung board toprails above a narrow horizontal splat and drop-in seat, raised on sabre legs.

$600-700 (pair)   Chef

A William IV mahogany single carver chair, the gadrooned carved cresting rail with a carved and pierced lumber rail, the down-swept double reed-molded arms with stuff-over seat, the reeded front and side rails supported on turned and reeded legs, distressed.

$225-275   HamG

A pair of 19thC early George III-style mahogany side chairs, each seat raised on pierced fretwork front legs.

$4,500-5,000   L&T

A Victorian carved walnut side chair, the back with floral cresting above a needlework panel of a Centurion with stuff-over seat, on cabriole legs and casters.

$300-400   BonS

A pair of Victorian Sheraton-revival painted satinwood side chairs, each back centered by an oval portrait of a girl, with caned seat on turned tapering.

$3,000-3,500 (pair)   DN

A late 19thC mahogany side chair, the back with garrya, patera, and a central palmette, with a padded seat and square-tapering legs with spade feet.

$200-250   DN

▲1 A late 19thC/early20thC mahogany-framed Cockpen armchair, with cut-floral marquette upholstery, the arched back above hollow seat, scrolling arms with pads, on typical splayed legs with bead to leading edge joined by H-stretcher.

$1,200-1,500   L&T

▲2 A 19thC mahogany Cockpen armchair, the back above curved square open arms and hollow seat on typical splayed legs with leading bead.

$1,200-1,500   L&T

A former pair of 19thC mahogany Cockpen chairs, one with altered back, the other with typical chinoiserie lattice above hollow upholstered seat and curved front legs linked by stretchers.

$1,000-1,400 (pair)   L&T

A Louis XV painted commode provincial chair, in beech and cane with curved arms and legs and floral decoration.

c1760   35.5in (90cm) high

$2,500-3,500   CdK

Chairs

A CLOSER LOOK AT A VICTORIAN CHAIR

These chairs would have been placed in the sitting room or bedroom.

This type of chair was also known as a "showframe".

Walnut was commonly used to make furniture during the Victorian era.

A Victorian walnut-framed drawing room chair, the back with heavily carved foliate design crest, conforming apron on carved cabriole front supports.

9in (99cm) high

$450-500		Clv

A Victorian walnut-framed drawing room chair, the back panel on scroll supports with casters.

31.5in (80cm) high

$350-400		Clv

A pair of Victorian papier-mâché drawing room chairs, the backs with painted floral decoration and gilt highlights, upholstered serpentine seats all on cabriole legs, stamped "Jennens and Bettridge, Birmingham, London".

$1,000-1,400		L&T

An Edwardian mahogany open arm drawing room chair, with boxwood string inlay with pierced scroll-decorated panel back with marquetry panel, padded seat on front cabriole supports.

41in (104cm) high

$750-850		Clv

A Regency mahogany library chair, the scrolling back rail over leather-upholstered back, seat and arm pads, with turned and fluted arm supports and legs with brass caps and casters.

$3,000-3,500		L&T

A George IV mahogany library armchair, with two buttoned squabs and turned legs with brass casters, the caned seat worn.

$1,000-1,400		DN

A matched pair of early Victorian Gothic Revival inlaid-oak library chairs, a gentleman's armchair and a lady's chair, the stop-chamfered frames with pointed arch-backs and arcaded rails, above stuff-over seats with shaped rails and turned tapering front legs with casters.

$2,000-2,500		L&T

◄ A Victorian mahogany rosewood library armchair, the buttoned outscrolled back framed between molded uprights, the overstuffed arms with lion's head terminals raised on molded cabriole legs with scroll toes and casters.

$1,200-1,500	L&T

A set of six Victorian mahogany parlor chairs, the backs with central upholstered panel and leaf-carved panel, the serpentine-upholstered seat above scroll-carved rails on molded cabriole legs and casters.

$2,500-3,500 (set)	L&T

A 19thC walnut prie-dieu chair, possibly Italian, with open arms, padded back and serpentine seat, on X-frame supports and casters.

$500-550	BonS

Chairs

A Victorian dark-stained beech prie-dieu, with petit point upholstery, on turned underframe with molded stretchers.

$150-200   **GorL**

A Victorian walnut and tapestry-upholstered prie-dieu, the back flanked by twist columns on turned supports.

39in (99cm) high

$150-200   **GorL**

A pair of 19thC Continental oak smoker's chairs, the hinged box tops above backs carved with ribbon-tied pipes and pouches flanked by flowerhead-turned uprights, the shaped upholstered seats raised on spiral-turned legs united by conforming X-shaped stretchers.

$400-500 (pair)   **Chef**

A Victorian elm and beech smoker's bow chair, with spindle-turned back, on turned underframe.

$250-300   **GorB**

A George I walnut corner chair, the curved arm surmounted by a over-scroll crest block and ending in rounded terminals, the vasiform splats interspersed with columnar supports, the padded drop-in seat with molded shaped rails raised on a square section front leg, the other legs turned, all joined by a cross-stretcher.   *c1720*

$2,500-3,000   **SI**

A George II mahogany corner chair, the ring-turned columnar supports with vasiform splats, the cabriole legs with pad feet.

c1740

$2,500-3,000   **SI**

A Louis XVI leather tub desk chair.

32.25in (82cm) high

$1,800-2,400   **CdK**

A late Victorian ebonized tub-shaped corner chair, with pierced lyre splats over a rush seat and turned underframe.

$120-180   **GorL**

▶ An American Queen Anne mahogany commode chair, the curved continuous arm and backrest surmounted by a shaped crest block and terminating in outcurved scroll grips, raised on baluster-turned supports interspersed by pierced vasiform splats, the padded drop-in seat with molded rails and deep semi-circular skirts, the front leg of cabriole form with a pad foot, the side and back legs turned and tapering with similar pads, secondary woods yellow pine and mahogany.

c1750

$4,000-5,000   **SI**

▶ An American walnut Queen Anne corner arm chair, plain three piece crest rail terminating in volutes, solid vasiform back splats, deep scalloped skirt, short cabriole legs, trifid fore foot.

c1740-1760   31.7in (80.5cm) high

$25,000-30,000   **FRE**

Chairs/Chests

A pair of French Directoire chairs, with musical instrument brass inlay.

c1795   (81cm) high

$900-1,100	Cdk

An early 19thC occasional chair, satinwood with painted detail.

c1815

$180-240	PC

A Victorian walnut show-frame chair, with upholstered back and serpentine-padded seat on cabriole legs with ceramic casters.

$800-900	DN

A Victorian walnut lady's chair, the frame with rocaille and cabochon carving, the waisted open-back with upholstered splat above bow front stuff-over seat on splayed legs with casters, woolwork upholstery.

$450-550	L&T

CHESTS

A George I walnut chest-on-stand, the top with molded frieze above two short and three later crossbanded drawers with brass handles, the later stand with shaped apron on cabriole legs with pad feet.

39.75in (101cm) wide

$1,800-2,400	DN

A late George II oak chest-on-stand, the shallow-molded cornice above an arrangement of two short and three long, graduated drawers with later pierced brass handles, the original base with three further drawers supported on cabriole legs.

36in (91.5cm) wide

$1,500-2,000	HamG

A George III mahogany shaving table, the divided hinged top enclosing interior fitted for large and small bowls with lifting mirror at rear, above dummy frieze drawer and pot cupboard with two long drawers below, on square section legs.

21.75in (55cm) wide

$1,000-1,400	L&T

A Georgian mahogany pot cupboard.

14.25in (36cm) wide

$375-450	CdK

A Georgian walnut-veneered chest-on-stand, the molded cornice above two short and three long graduated drawers with feather banding, the stand with single drawer raised on cabriole legs and terminating in pointed pad feet.

54.5in (138cm) high

$2,000-2,500	L&T

An early 19thC mahogany washstand, the fold-out tray top above a false drawer and a black line-inlaid cupboard, opening to a void over two full-width drawers standing on slightly tapered legs with side carrying-handles.

17in (43cm) wide

$400-450	HamG

A Regency mahogany pot cupboard, with three-quarter galleried top on slender-turned tapered legs with uniting tier.

14in (35.5cm) wide

$600-700	GorL

A 19thC Dutch walnut and marquetry bedside cupboard, with floral-inlaid top and tambour compartment over a drawer, on fluted square-tapered legs.

20in (51cm) wide

$1,500-2,000	GorL

Chests

A Pennsylvania Queen Anne walnut chest-of-drawers, the rectangular-molded top over three drawers over four graduated drawers on straight bracket feet, retains original cast brass hardware.

c1760   40.5in (102.5cm) wide

$5,000-7,000   **FRE**

A Pennsylvania Chippendale walnut chest-on-chest, rectangular flat top with molded cornice, three drawers over seven graduated drawers, all thumb-molded, molded skirt ending in ogee bracket feet (all feet replaced), drawer fronts are highly figured walnut, poplar and cedar secondary woods.

c1750-1780   41.5in (105.5cm)

$12,000-15,000   **FRE**

A Delaware Valley walnut chest-on-chest, having a flat-molded crest rail, with five small varisized and two graduated wide lip-molded drawers in the upper section, three graduated wide lip-molded drawers in base, both sections with quarter-round fluted corners, on bracket feet, old batwing brasses.

42.5in (108cm) wide

$8,000-10,000   **FRE**

A Chippendale walnut tall chest of drawers, straight front fitted with five small over three wide graduated thumb-molded drawers, brass bail handles and escutcheons, sides inset with arched carved panels, terminating on straight bracket feet (replaced).

c1770   39.5in (100cm) wide

$6,000-8,000   **FRE**

An early George III mahogany chest-on-chest, the upper section with an outset dentil cornice surmounting an arrangement of two short over three molded and graduated drawers, flanked by reeded canted stiles, the lower section with three further molded and graduated drawers on braket feet.

75.5in (192cm) high

$2,000-3,000   **SI**

A George III mahogany chest-on-chest, with a molded cornice above three short and three graduated long cockbeaded drawers, retaining the original gilded drop handles and rococo-style escutcheons, the lower part fitted with three long drawers raised upon bracket feet.

40.5in (103cm) wide

$4,000-5,000   **J&H**

◄ A New England cherrywood top of a chest-on-chest, with flat cove-molded cresting, five small drawers, the centermost being fan-carved, and four graduated wide drawers below, all with lip molding, on later tall logical bracket feet.

37.5in (95cm) wide

$2,500-3,000   **FRE**

► A Philadelphia Chippendale carved cherrywood chest-on-chest, flat cove-molded cornice over straight front fitted with three small over four wide graduated thumb-molded drawers, the lower section having two wide thumb-molded drawers, brass bail handles and oval lockplates, appears to retain original brasses, the upper and lower chest flanked by quarter-fluted column sides, terminating on ogival bracket feet.

c1770   41in (104cm) wide

$12,000-15,000   **FRE**

An American Chippendale mahogany chest-on-chest, the upper section with a molded swan-neck pediment centered by a flaming urn over a front with two short and three long drawers, the lower section with three long drawers, drawer fronts graduated and cockbeaded throughout, on a molded base with bracket feet, secondary wood white pine.

82.5in (209.5cm) high

$8,000-12,000   **SI**

Chests

A Federal polychrome lift-lid blanket chest, brown feather-painted technique, front with twin incised painted panels, lion and flat tulip motif after Heinrich Otto, the side panels with flat tulip and parrot substitution, red polychrome straight bracket feet.

c1800 44in (112cm) wide

$7,000-10,000	FRE

A first half 19thC Pennsylvania painted pine blanket chest, with hinged paneled lid, candle till and molded base, the front and sides painted with floral sprays, inscribed "F.L. 1.8.4.3.".

52.5in (138.5cm) wide

$1,000-1,500	SI

A 19thC Pennsylvania German painted "Dower" or blanket chest, rectangular molded edge lift lid, front painted with an American eagle with shield for a body, blue ground.

50in (127cm) wide

$1,000-1,500	FRE

A 19thC Pennsylvania German painted lift-lid pine blanket chest, front and side with stencil floral tulip decoration, inside strapwork, wrought iron hinges.

The interior of the chest was papered with Reform Church Record, Lebanon, PA..

Dated Nov. 5, 1891. 54in (137cm) long

$3,000-5,000	FRE

A mid-17thC oak chest of drawers, the top with molded edge above three drawers of differing depths, the middle one deepest, each with twin-paneled front of different patterns, paneled sides and molded base raised on stile feet.

37.75in (96cm) wide

$3,000-3,500	L&T

A late 17thC oak chest, the top with molded edge, above a stained dentil cornice, three long drawers with a raised yew-wood veneered panels.

43.5in (110cm) wide

$2,000-2,500	DN

A George I walnut and parquetry chest of drawers, the mirror-veneered top with a crossbanded border and ogee-molded edge, the front with an arrangement of three short over three long graduated drawers, all similarly veneered and banded, the outset base on bracket feet.

c1720 40.5in (103cm) wide

$3,500-4,000	SI

A George I oak chest of drawers, the molded top above an arrangement of two short and two long drawers with double-bead molding to the carcass and petition rails, standing on still feet, with later ring handles, paneled ends, and supported on stile feet.

34in (87cm) wide

$1,800-2,200	HamG

A George I oak commode, in the form of a small chest of drawers, the molded top rising to reveal a void interior, the fronts with three false graduated drawers with double-bead decoration, standing on low bracket feet, with metal carrying-handles (one missing).

20in (51cm) wide

$450-500	HamG

A George II mahogany bachelor's chest, the top with molded edge above brushing slide and four long graduated drawers on shaped ogee bracket feet (possibly later).

31.75in (81cm) high

$6,000-7,000	L&T

Chests

A George II mahogany bachelor's chest, the top with molded edge above brushing slide and four graduated drawers on ogee bracket feet.

33in (84cm) wide

$6,000-7,000   L&T

An 18thC small oak chest of drawers, the molded top above two short and two long graduated drawers on shaped bracket feet.

30.75in (78cm) wide

$1,000-1,500   L&T

A walnut and feather-banded chest, the two short and three long drawers with brass handles, flanked by fluted canted corners on bracket feet, originally the top part of an 18thC chest-on-chest, adapted.

40.25in (102cm) wide

$900-1,200   DN

An 18thC mahogany and walnut chest, the top with reeded edge above an arrangement of three short and four long crossbanded drawers with later brass handles on bracket feet, adapted.

36.75in (93cm) wide

$750-850   DN

A Dutch 18thC walnut chest of drawers, of serpentine block-fronted form, the shaped top with molded edge above four long graduated drawers flanked by canted consoles with correspondng ogee feet.

1in (79cm) wide

$4,500-5,500   L&T

An early George III mahogany chest of drawers, with molded top, two short over three long graduated drawers, bracket feet.

41.5in (105.5cm) wide

$3,000-4,000   SI

A Scottish George III mahogany serpentine chest-of-drawers, with boxwood chequer stringing, the shaped top above four long graduated drawers flanked by reeded pilasters with roundel terminals on bracket feet.

48in (122cm) wide

$3,000-4,000   L&T

A George III mahogany serpentine chest-of-drawers, the shaped top above three long graduated drawers on shaped apron and bracket feet.

43.5in (110cm) wide

$1,300-1,600   L&T

A George III mahogany bow front chest, of two short and three long graduated drawers with later brass handles on splayed bracket feet.

39in (99cm) wide

$1,500-2,000   Clv

A late 18thC Milanese Italian chest, in kingwood-veneered wood, walnut with original ormolu handles.

46.5cm (118cm) wide

$7,500-10,000   CdK

Chests

An 18thC Philadelphia mahogany four-drawer chest, with rectangular lip-molded top with notched corners, graduated wide drawers with lip-molded edges with early batwing brasses, on cut down carved feet. **Provenance:** *There is a paper notation affixed to the back listing the provenance of the piece, including the name Fisher, 18thC.*

35in (89cm) wide

| $15,000-20,000 | FRE |

A Pennsylvania Chippendale mahogany dresser, the rectangular molded top rests atop four graduated cockbeaded drawers, case flanked by fluted quarter on ogee bracket feet, period brass bail handles and oval key escutcheons, secondary wood cedar.

c1750-1780   40.5in (103cm) wide

| $10,000-12,000 | FRE |

A Philadelphia Chippendale carved walnut chest-of-drawers, with rectangular-molded top over straight front fitted with four graduated thumb-molded drawers, brass bail handles, escutcheons and lock plates of a later date, flanked by quarter-reeded columnar sides terminating on ogival bracket feet.

c1765   33.5in (85cm) wide

| $20,000-30,000 | FRE |

A Philadelphia Chippendale carved cherrywood chest-of-drawers, rectangular molded top over straight front fitted with four wide graduated cockbeaded drawers, brass bail handles and lockplates, flanked by quarter-fluted columnar sides terminating on ogival bracket feet, appears to retain original brasses.

c1770   38.5in (98cm) wide

| $15,000-20,000 | FRE |

A Pennsylvania Chippendale mahogany chest of drawers, molded top (highly figured crochwood) over four thumb-molded, graduated drawers flanked by fluted quarter columns, molded base rests on ogee bracket feet. minor repairs to feet and case, brasses possibly replaced, secondary wood cedar, carved initials "BL" on underside of case and faint chalked inscription.

c1760-1780   42in (106.5cm) wide

| $9,000-12,000 | FRE |

A Connecticut Chippendale cherry chest of drawers, rectangular top above a case fitted with four graduated long drawers, flanked by fluted stiles and fluted chamfered corners with lambs tongue moldings, the molded base below on spurred ogee bracket feet, dark brown color.

c1780   45in (114.5cm) wide

| $9,000-12,000 | SI |

A rare Boston Chippendale figured mahogany serpentine-front chest of drawers, Massachusetts, the oblong-molded, serpentine and block-fronted top above a conformingly shaped case with four graduated drawers, on straight bracket feet, appears to retain its original cast brass hardware, shrinkage to top, chip to right foot bracket.

c1780   37.25in (94.5cm) wide

| $75,000-100,000 | FRE |

A Massachusetts Chippendale mahogany serpentine front chest-of-drawers, with rectangular-molded top having applied undermolding, over serpentine front fitted with four graduated drawers, brass bail handles, ogival bracket feet.

c1780   32.25in (82cm) high

| $60,000-80,000 | FRE |

A last quarter 18thC Baltimore Chippendale walnut chest of drawers, molded rectangular top over case with four molded and graduated drawers, molded base continuing into ogee-molded bracket feet, repairs, inscribed in chalk on one drawer base "David Wilson/Cabinet maker/Baltimore".

34.75in (88cm) wide

| $6,000-8,000 | SI |

A mid-18thC Chippendale mahogany chest of drawers, with molded rectangular top, four graduated and scribed drawers and bracket feet, secondary wood white pine, feet replaced.

38in (96.5cm) high

| $2,000-3,000 | SI |

A third quarter 18thC New England Chippendale mahogany chest of drawers, with molded rectangular top over a front with four long graduated drawers with overlapping molding, the canted stiles with boxwood stringing, the molded base raised on ogee-molded bracket feet, secondary wood maple.

40in (101.5cm) wide

| $2,000-3,000 | SI |

Chests

An early Federal mahogany chest of drawers, with outset rectangular top with stringing, the front with three short over three long graduated and cockbeaded drawers raised on bracket feet, secondary wood white pine.

44in (112cm) wide

$2,000-3,000 — **SI**

A Federal mahogany chest of drawers, with crossbanded top, two short over three long graduated drawers, a shaped skirt and bracket feet, the drawer fronts cockbeaded, secondary wood white pine.

c1800 45in (114.5cm) high

$2,000-3,000 — **SI**

A Federal inlaid mahogany chest of drawers, Baltimore MD, the overhanging rectangular top with crossbanded edge over front with four graduated cock-beaded drawers, shaped skirt continuing into bracket feet, pencil inscription: "Done up by Mr. Kraft/Balto.MD./ Oct.1917".

c1800

$3,000-5,000 — **SI**

A Federal inlaid cherrywood serpentine chest of drawers, possibly Virginia, the dramatic serpentine top with inlaid edge above a conforming case with four graduated inlaid drawers on flaring French bracket feet, replaced brass hardware.

c1800 43.75in (111cm) wide

$7,000-10,000 — **FRE**

A George III mahogany serpentine front chest of drawers, the figured top with serpentine front and sides and conforming case beneath with tray table and three graduated drawers flanked by bowed corners, the scalloped skirt below on flaring bracket feet, signed "Wagner" in pencil on the base.

c1800 41.5in (105.5cm) wide

$25,000-30,000 — **FRE**

A late Federal stained birch and tiger maple chest of drawers, with rectangular top, two short and three long graduated drawers between split-spindle stiles, on turned short legs, secondary wood poplar.

c1820 52.5in (133.5cm) high

$3,000-4,000 — **SI**

An early 19thC late Federal tiger-maple chest of drawers, rectangular top, four graduated drawers, turned feet.

41.25in (105cm) wide

$3,000-4,000 — **SI**

An early 19thC country Federal curly and wavy birch chest of drawers, rectangular top over case with four drawers and applied bracket-footed base.

39.5in (100.5cm) wide

$1,300-1,800 — **SI**

A Federal Southern states mahogany chest of drawers, rectangular top with line inlaid veneered edge above case with two cockbeaded short drawers and three cockbeaded long drawers, each with an ivory escutcheon, on a shaped skirt and French feet (imperfections).

c1810 42.5in (108cm) wide

$2,500-3,500 — **SI**

A Federal mahogany and mahogany veneer bowfront chest of drawers, rectangular bowed top with outset corners above a case with four cockbeaded drawers and shaped skirt flanked by ring-turned and reeded stiles, with vasiform legs ending in peg feet (age crack and imperfections).

c1815 41.5in (105.5cm) wide

$2,500-3,500 — **SI**

A late Federal tiger maple chest of drawers, rectangular top over case with projecting drawer and three recessed drawers, flanked by inlaid stiles on ring-turned feet.

c1820 43.25in

$2,500-3,500 — **SI**

A Federal Mid-Atlantic states mahogany bow-fronted chest of drawers, the rectangular top with a convex front and cross-banded edge, the conforming front with four graduated and cross-banded drawers, the shaped skirt continuing into splayed bracket feet.

41.75in (106cm) wide

$4,000-5,000 — **SI**

Chests

A George III mahogany chest, the top with a molded edge above a slide and two short and three long drawers with later brass handles, on bracket feet, lacking some molding.

30.75in (78cm) wide

$2,200-2,800   DN

A George III mahogany chest, the top with an edge-molding above a slide to one side, two short and three long drawers feet, the top patched, one leg detached.

29in (73.5cm) wide

$4,500-5,000   DN

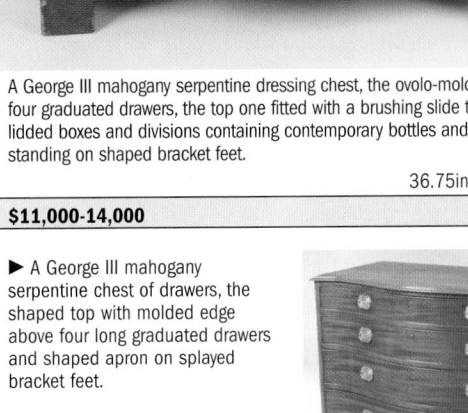

A George III mahogany serpentine dressing chest, the ovolo-molded top above four graduated drawers, the top one fitted with a brushing slide to reveal various lidded boxes and divisions containing contemporary bottles and an easel mirror, standing on shaped bracket feet.

36.75in (93.5cm) wide

$11,000-14,000   HamG

A late 18thC Dutch walnut-veneered chest, with sycamore banding, the molded edge top above four graduated long drawers to the swelling front and sides, banded angled corners on later bracket feet.

37.5in (95cm) wide

$2,200-2,800   WW

A late 18thC mahogany chest, of narrow and low proportions, the two short and three long drawers with brass swan-neck handles, on bracket feet.

36in (92cm) wide

$1,300-1,600   WW

▶ A George III mahogany serpentine chest of drawers, the shaped top with molded edge above four long graduated drawers and shaped apron on splayed bracket feet.

41.75in (106cm) wide

$7,000-8,000   L&T

A George III mahogany chest of drawers, the top with molded edge above two short and three long cockbeaded drawers with ivory escantheons and turned handles, flanked by quarter-engaged fluted columns, on shaped bracket feet.

38.5 (98cm) wide

$4,500-5,500   L&T

A George III mahogany serpentine chest of drawers, the shaped molded top above four long graduated drawers enclosed by canted angles on shaped bracket feet.

94.5in (86cm) wide

$12,000-14,000   L&T

A small Sheraton-period faded mahogany-veneered chest, the top banded and inlaid stringing, the four long graduated drawers with brass oval plate-handles, on swept French feet, one side with a burn mark.

32.75in (83cm) wide

$1,000-1,300   WW

A Regency faded mahogany-veneered bow front commode chest, inlaid stringing, three long graduated drawers with later brass plate-handles, oak-lined on front splay French feet.

43.5in (110cm) wide

$4,500-5,500   WW

Chests

▶ An American late Classical mahogany and mahogany veneer chest of drawers, rectangular top above two ogee-shaped short drawers, surmounted by two Gothic supports mounted with candle sconces which flank an ogee-molded framed mirror, the base with ogee-shaped frieze drawer and three recessed drawers, enclosed by scrolled-stiles, raised on scrolled feet.

c1825   77in (195.5cm) high

$1,000-1,500   SI

An American second quarter 19thC Empire carved mahogany and mahogany veneer chest of drawers, molded rectangular top over three outset short drawers, leaf-carved attached columns flanking four recessed drawers, on leaf-capped hairy-paw feet, stamped "Wm Palmer/Cabinet Maker/Catherine St./New York".

48.5in (123cm) wide

$2,000-2,500   SI

An early 19thC mahogany secrétaire chest of drawers, the top with molded edge above shallow crossbanded frieze and false-fronted paneled secrétaire drawer fitted with drawers and pigeonholes, three long graduated drawers below and shaped apron with splayed bracket feet.

47.25in (120cm) wide

$1,500-2,000   L&T

An early Victorian rosewood specimen chest, the top with waved moldings above a plain frieze with ripple moldings, the twin hinged and locking uprights with scrolled brackets enclosing two banks each of 17 drawers with glazed covers, the whole raised on a plinth.

45in (114cm) wide

$5,000-6,000   L&T

A 19thC mahogany-veneered bow front chest, with floral marquetry to the corners, chequer-banding and stringing, two short and four long graduated drawers with replaced brass ram's-head swag plate swing-handles.

43in (109cm) high

$1,800-2,400   WW

An American late Classical mahogany secretary chest, the rectangular top above projecting drawer opening to a writing surface and an interior fitted with curly maple drawer fronts above three recessed drawers flanked by scrolled stiles and arched feet.

44in (112cm) high

$1,500-2,000   SI

A pair of Victorian pitch-pine and faux bamboo-decorated tall chest of drawers, each top with molded edge, above six drawers, raised on a plinth, each stamped to top drawer "Howard and Sons, Berners Street' and bearing makers label.

45in (114.5cm) high

$3,500-4,000   L&T

A late 19thC Dutch Empire-style walnut and marquetry tall chest of drawers, the molded top with outset frieze drawer.

Provenance: *The Society of the Cincinnati.*

41in (104cm) wide

$3,000-3,500   SI

An Edwardian mahogany breakfast gentleman's compactum, by James Hicks, Dublin, the three-quarter ledge back above a rectangular top with projecting dentil cornice and blind fretwork frieze, the central section with twin doors having oval panels and enclosing sliding shelves, flanked by two banks of six graduated drawers, the angles with stop-fluted quarter columns, the whole raised above a plinth, bears makers labels, stamped marks to five drawers.

107.5in (273cm) wide

$4,000-5,000   L&T

A George I-style feather-banded walnut bachelor's chest, with folding top and two short drawers over three graduated long drawers, on ogee feet.

30in (76cm) wide

$4,000-4,500   GorL

A CLOSER LOOK AT A WELLINGTON CHEST

Wellington chests were popular from 1820.

This piece is in excellent condition and is very well constructed.

The high quality veneers are exceptionally attractive.

Wellington chests are locked by means of a hinged flap which runs down one side and locks over the drawers.

They can have up to 12 drawers.

A mid-19thC figured maple Wellington chest, of seven graduated drawers, the locking flap with applied scroll-leaf decoration.

8.75in (22cm) wide

$5,000-6,000   **L&T**

A small 19thC mahogany-finished Wellington chest, of seven drawers with turned wooden handles, the whole standing on plinth base.

41.5in (105.5cm) high

$450-550   **BW**

A Victorian oak Wellington chest, fitted with seven drawers with side-locking bar, on plinth foot.

19in (48.25cm) wide

$750-850   **GorL**

A Victorian mahogany Wellington chest, with spindle three-quarter gallery above two drawers fitted with indexed stationery compartments, above six drawers, two with hinged covers, raised on a plinth base.

28.5in (72cm) wide

$6,000-7,000   **BonS**

A mid-Victorian mahogany secrétaire Wellington chest, the thumb-molded top over a crossbanded frieze, the pilasters with carved corbels and an arrangement of seven graduated drawers with original turned wooden handles, including a full front secretaire with an interior of pigeonholes and drawers veneered in maple.

24.5in (62cm) wide

$2,000-3,000   **HamG**

COMMODES

A late 19thC French rosewood chest of drawers, the canted corner carrera marble top above an arrangement of six molded edged drawers with original knob handles, standing on a molded plinth.

16.25in (41cm) wide

$400-450   **HamG**

An Edwardian kingwood semainiere, by W.J. Mansell, London, with gilt-brass mounts, the marble top with molded edge above seven quarter veneered drawers with leaf-cast molding, flanked by canted angles with scrolled consoles, on shaped plinth.

46in (117cm) high

$4,000-5,000   **L&T**

A mid-18thC mahogany French commode, the serpentine ogee-molded top with geometric rosewood inlay, above three bombé-shaped drawers with elaborate panel-molded front, with original bronze door handles, the bombé-shaped sides also paneled standing on stile feet.

53in (135cm) wide

$18,000-24,000   **HamG**

An 18thC mahogany serpentine bombé commode, the shaped top with molded edge above three long graduated drawers with pierced and cast handles, shaped apron and splayed bracket feet.

41.25in (105cm) wide

$8,000-9,000   **L&T**

A late 18thC Southern States walnut hanging corner cupboard, arched molded crest above conforming raised panel tombstone door opening to interior with three shaped shelves, molded stiles and base.

39.5in (100.5cm) high

$3,000-4,000   **SI**

A late 18thC Southern States yellow pine corner cupboard, molded cornice above fluted frieze and paneled 'tombstone' upper door opening to interior with two shelves and lower paneled door opening to interior with single shelf, on molded base with spurred bracket feet.

36.5in (92.5cm) wide

$3,000-5,000   **SI**

A Pennsylvania Classical cherrywood corner cupboard, probably, molded cornice above two glazed doors opening to an interior with three shelves over two recessed panel doors opening to an interior with single shelf, shaped apron and bracket feet.

c1800   86in (218.5cm) high

$3,000-4,000   **SI**

A Pennsylvania cherrywood corner cupboard, the step-molded cornice above single glazed door enclosing four shelves and flanked by chamfered sides, a molded divider above two cupboard doors, scalloped apron and bracket feet.

c1825   38in (96.5cm)

$12,000-15,000   **FRE**

An American Renaissance Revival carved walnut cabinet, with rectangular variegated red marble top over carved chamfered corners centering two cupboard doors, each with bronze panel of a classical maiden framed by carving.

c1870   38in (96.5cm) wide

$5,000-6,000   **FRE**

A late 18th/early 19thC Pennsylvania Chippendale walnut corner cupboard, in two sections: the upper section with cove-molded projecting cornice over glazed doors opening to a painted interior with two shelves; the lower section with three short drawers over recessed panels opening to single shelf, on straight bracket feet.

84in (213.5cm) high

$3,000-5,000   **SI**

An 18th/19thC cherrywood corner cabinet in two parts, having a molded top above a single glazed door, the base having two recessed panel doors, on bracket feet.

40.5in (103cm)

$7,000-8,000   **FRE**

A small red-painted yellow pine corner cupboard, possibly Lynnhurst, Virginia. projecting top over a door with open upper section and paneled lower section opening to two shelves, bracket feet at back and sides (imperfections).

38in (96.5cm) high

$1,500-2,500   **SI**

A late Chippendale Southern inlaid mahogany corner cabinet, the upper section with an outset molded cavetto cornice with canted sides over a tracery door opening to three shelves and flanked by similarly canted stiles, the conforming base with a pair of doors with raised and fielded panels, the shaped skirt continuing into splayed bracket feet.

45in (114.5cm) wide

$8,000-10,000   **SI**

A pine two-part corner cabinet, having a slightly arched and flat molded cresting, single glazed arched door with Pennsylvania molded "keystone" above and reeded panels beside, base with two drawers and two recessed panel doors on bracket feet, feet of a later date.

47in (119.5cm) wide

$2,500-3,000   **FRE**

American Cupboards

CUPBOARD

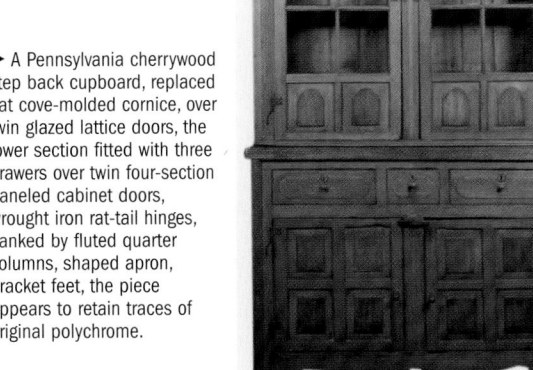

▶ A Pennsylvania cherrywood step back cupboard, replaced flat cove-molded cornice, over twin glazed lattice doors, the lower section fitted with three drawers over twin four-section paneled cabinet doors, wrought iron rat-tail hinges, flanked by fluted quarter columns, shaped apron, bracket feet, the piece appears to retain traces of original polychrome.

c1780 53in (135.5cm) wide

$7,000-10,000   **FRE**

A late federal mahogany desk bookcase, in two parts, the upper with a three-quarter gallery and a reeded top, over a pair of six-pane doors and three cockbeaded short drawers, the lower section with a hinged writing-flap over a similarly cockbeaded drawer on reed legs with ovoid feet, repairs, Baltimore, MD.

c1780   37in (94cm) wide

$3,500-4,500   **FRE**

A 19thC brown-painted yellow pine cupboard on stand, Scottsville, Virginia area, the top section with hinged door, opening to three shelves over base with projecting top above a single drawer, open shelf with cross bracing above demilune cut-out ends (imperfections).

64in (162.5cm) high

$1,000-1,500   **SI**

A 19thC Southern states red-painted step-back pine cupboard, , rectangular top over two open shelves and projecting lower section with tongue-and-groove doors opening to a single shelf, raised on bracket base with shaped ends (replacements and repairs).

73in (185.5cm) high

$2,000-3,000   **SI**

A 19thC red-painted step-back pine cupboard, rectangular top over two open shelves and projecting lower section with tongue-and-groove doors opening to a single shelf, raised on bracket base with shaped ends (replacements and repairs).

41.5in (105.5cm) wide

$2,000-3,000   **SI**

A 17thC oak court cupboard, the upper part with carved frieze above two panel doors, centering two further panels with lozenge carving and flanked by baluster-turned supports, the lower part with scroll-carved frieze above two carved and panel doors upon stile feet, alterations.

61in (155cm) wide

$750-900   **J&H**

◀ A French provincial Transitional Louis XV/XVI walnut and oak bonnetière, with arched cavetto cornice, a conforming paneled upper door over a drawer and further drawer, the rounded stiles continuing into short cabriole legs.

c1775   89.25in (226.5cm) high

$1,700-1,900   **SI**

▶ An American Empire-style mahogany display cabinet on stand, with ogee-molded cornice, a pair of 13-pane astragal doors, three small drawers and cabriole legs with ball-and-claw feet, (the cabinet formerly the upper section of a secretary bookcase).

68.5in (174cm) high

$2,000-2,500   **SI**

Chests/Desks

An 18thC New England red-painted pine chest-over-drawers, molded hinged top above a case with two false drawers and two working drawers, straight front skirt with side shaping, imperfections, old surface.

38in (96.5cm) wide

$1,500-2,000	SI

A New England red-painted pine and poplar chest-over-drawers, molded hinged lid on case with two false drawers and three working drawers with a molded based and shaped bracket feet, old surface, imperfections.

c1800   42.75in (108.5cm) long

$1,200-1,800	SI

A poplar blanket chest-over-drawers, New England, the molded hinged lid over case with two false drawers and three working drawers on molded base with shaped bracket feet, refinishd, loss of height.

c1810

$900-1,200	SI

A miniature walnut and poplar chest of drawers, rectangular top with rounded corners over case with four drawers, shaped skirt and bracket feet (losses).

c1850   14in (35.5cm) high

$300-400	SI

A miniature mahogany and poplar chest of drawers, rectangular top over case with two short cockbeaded drawers and two long cockbeaded drawers, raised on shaped skirt continuing to bracket feet.

c1825   14.5in (37cm) high

$900-1,100	SI

A late 18th/early 19thC grain-painted poplar and pine chest over drawers, molded, hinged and cleated lid on case with applied molding over a single drawer, molded base with shaped sides continuing to form feet, restoration.

38.5in (98cm) wide

$1,000-1,500	SI

A miniature chest of drawers, molded rectangular top over case with two short drawers and three large drawers raised on turned feet (losses).

13in (33cm) high

$250-350	SI

DESKS

A William & Mary burr-walnut dwarf kneehole desk, the adapted top, quarter-veneered and crossbanded with molded edge, above long drawer and six short drawers flanking arched recess with inset cupboard door, molded plinth and later shaped bracket feet.

32.75in (83cm) wide

$5,000-6,000	L&T

A George I walnut dwarf kneehole desk, the crossbanded quarter-veneered top with molded edge above feather-banded long drawer and six short drawers flanking kneehole with frieze drawer and cupboard door, on plinth base and shaped bracket feet, restored.

27.25in (69cm) wide

$10,000-14,000	L&T

An oak kneehole desk, the top with molded edge, above eight drawers with brass handles, arranged around a kneehole with a door on bracket feet, in part George II.

32.5in (82.5cm) wide

$1,500-2,000	DN

▶ A George III mahogany pedestal desk, the crossbanded molded top with gilt-tooled leather-insert above frieze drawer and twin pedestals with three graduated drawers and opposing dummy drawers, on plinth base.

55.25in (140cm) wide

$10,000-14,000	L&T

Desks

A Victorian mahogany pedestal desk, having leather-lined molded top over nine short drawers.

41in (104cm) wide

$900-1,100	GorB

A Victorian elm partners' desk, the tooled leather skriver inset to a molded top, with reverse break-front, raised above two pedestals of six opposed and graduated panel drawers, the canted angles set with carved brackets depicting garlands of fruiting foliage, the whole raised on plinths.

54in (137cm) wide

$6,000-8,000	L&T

A late 19thC walnut partners' desk, with burr-walnut veneered paneled drawers, the top with molded edge and tooled leather skiver above three shallow frieze drawers to each side, one with hinged gilt-tooled leather writing slope, raised on twin pedestals each with three graduated drawers to one side and corresponding false-fronted cupboard with pigeonholes to the other, on plinth bases.

60in (152cm) wide

$9,000-11,000	L&T

A late 19thC painted satinwood kidney desk, the crossbanded and leather-lined top above an arrangement of nine drawers with Neo-classical painted decoration, with further painted panels all round, standing on short tapered legs.

48in (122cm) wide

$4,000-5,000	HamG

A CLOSER LOOK AT A PARTNER'S DESK

A mahogany partners' desk, the molded top with canted angles, inset with tooled leather skiver, above three oppposing frieze drawers over twin pedestals of three graduated drawers opposing cupboard doors raised on a plinth, stamped "James Winter & Son, Soho, London".

59.75in (152cm) wide

$18,000-24,000	L&T

From the reign of George II onward, pedestal desks are usually made from mahogany.

Desks with drawers or cupboards fitted to both sides are called partners' desks.

These large pedestal desks were introduced into Britain in the first half of the 18thC and were a reaction to the small and somewhat cramped kneehole desks that had been popular since the late 17thC.

Desks are usually constructed in three parts, a top with three frieze drawers and two pedestals also containing drawers.

The tooled leather tops are often replaced and original leather is very rare and desirable even when stained.

A late Regency mahogany gentleman's writing desk, with astragal cockbeading and paneling, the stage-back containing three sprung locking drawers above desk with counter sliding top and fall front secretaire drawer, containing rosewood fitted interior, above three long lockable drawers, one fitted, raised on reeded, fluted and turned legs.

51.5in (131cm) wide

$3,000-4,000	L&T

An early 20thC gentleman's oak washstand, modeled as a desk, the hinged top opening to reveal an arrangement of recesses for washbasin etc, the whole on barley-twist supports and stretcher base.

$300-400	BW

A George III-style burr-yew wood Carlton House desk, with galleried superstructure, leather-lined top, three frieze drawers and square section tapering legs.

61.25in (155.5cm) wide

$4,500-6,000	SI

An early 19thC French mahogany clerk's desk, with a three-quarter gilt-metal gallery and leather-inset slope top, the gilt-metal mounted frieze with a drawer above a grille door and sides with folio divisions, flanked by turned columns above a platform with square supports, on bun feet.

36.5in (93cm) wide

$3,000-4,000	DN

An early 20thC Adam-style inlaid lady's mahogany writing desk, the top with pierced brass three-quarter gallery above marquetry fall-front centered by medallion, enclosing fitted interior, pair of frieze drawers with swagged inlay, on square-tapering legs with brass capital, united by shaped X-stretcher.

37in (94cm) high

$1,500-2,000	L&T

DRESSERS

An 18thC oak dresser base, the projecting top with associated spice rack, above three graduated central drawers flanked projecting drawers and cupboards raised on stile feet.

71.25in (181cm) wide

$3,500-4,500	L&T

A Georgian oak and mahogany crossbanded dresser, the later dentilled cornice above shaped frieze and three open shelves flanked by cupboard doors with inlaid Prince of Wales feathers, medallions and small doors below, the base with molded rim and three drawers above corresponding shaped apron on squared cabriole legs.

78in (198cm) high

$4,500-5,500	L&T

A mid-18thC oak dresser, the associated corniced plate rack with later back above molded rectangular top and pair of fielded drawers, raised on cabriole front legs with claw-and-ball feet.

62in (157cm) wide

$1,500-2,000	L&T

A Georgian oak dresser, the corniced and framed three-shelf plate rack with later back and shaped rests raised on break-front base with four central drawers flanked by quarter columns and drawers with cupboards below, on shaped bracket feet, with ivory escutcheons.

67.5in (171cm) wide

$5,000-6,000	L&T

▶ An early 19thC oak housekeepers' cupboard, the molded and projecting dentil cornice above two paneled doors enclosing a central panel, the lower section flanked by two pairs of drawers on block feet.

67.5in (171cm) wide

$6,000-7,000	L&T

An George III mahogany dresser base, the top with molded edge above arrangement of nine short drawers around flat arched recess enclosing paneled door framed by quarter-engaged fluted columns with blind fretwork bases and arch, raised on ogee bracket feet.

84.25in (214cm) wide

$4,500-5,500	L&T

DUMB WAITERS

A CLOSER LOOK AT A DUMB WAITER

The proportions of this example are perfect, the quality and originality of this piece makes it a superb example

Dumb waiters were invented in Britain around 1725 and were designed to partly replace waiters so that diners could help themselves to condiments.

The most commonly used wood is mahogany. This example has superb figuring and patina.

The carving on the claw-and-ball feet, legs and stem are signs of a high quality piece

▶ A George II mahogany two-tier dumb waiter, each circular tray with spindle-turned balustraded gallery raised on pedestals with spirally turned knops and tripod base with cabriole legs boldly carved with acanthus leaves and claw-and-ball feet.

26.5in (67cm) dia 38.25in (97cm) h

$160,000-190,000	L&T

LOWBOYS

A William and Mary oak dressing-table, the rectangular top with molded edge above a frieze with applied beaded molding and single long drawer over a carved, shaped apron on cabriole legs ending in trifid feet, now fitted with a marble top, old repairs, losses, possibly Virginia.

c1700   40.5in (103cm) wide

$1,200-1,500   **SI**

◄ ***Provenance:*** *This dressing table is said to have descended in the family of Lord Thomas Fairfax, 1693-1781. Fairfax inherited territory between the Potomac and Rappahannock Rivers, amounting to an area of more than 5 million acres. Though born in England, Lord Fairfax immigrated to this country in 1747, and lived in the Shenandoah Valley in a hunting lodge called Greenway Court. The dressing table descended through his family for generations to sisters Lillian Fairfax and Gwendolind Fairfax Moncure, and stood in their home in Washington, D.C., until their deaths in the 1940's. The house and its contents, including the table, were acquired by Mary Fineran. The Boswell's acquired the table from Miss Fineran in the 1950s.*

A Queen Anne carved walnut dressing table, New England, possibly Conneticut, the rectangluar molded top with long drawer over three drawers, the central one having sunburst carving, the shaped apron below with acorn drop finials on cabriole legs and pad feet, replaced brass hardware, split to back of one leg, signed "Andrew".

c1750   33.25in (84.5cm) wide

$40,000-50,000   **FRE**

A CLOSER LOOK AT A LOWBOY

The top, with its chamfered fluted corners, is in proportion to the body.

The apron's high arch and fishtail center serve to lighten the design.

The cabriole legs have skilfully carved lambrequin knees and trifid feet.

Lowboys were used as dressing or writing tables and were often made to match a highboy. This example has an excellent provenence, which for collectors is an added attraction.

A Philadelphia Queen Anne lowboy, attributed to William Savery and possibly owned by Benjamin Franklin, two piece curly maple top with notched corners on maple case with one wide over two small drawers, scalloped apron, butterfly brasses.

c1750-1760   35.5in (90cm) wide

$600,000-700,000   **FRE**

From George Vaux's journal, dated December 28, 1900. "This small ancient table now in Molly's room at 1715 Arch St. appears to be made of maple. It has three drawers in it with brass handles. It was bought by brother William at the Sanitary Fair in 1863 and he seemed to be satisfied with the account given to him that it originally belonged to Franklin". At the Fair William Vaux was employed as treasurer of Relics, Curiosities and Autographs. It is conceivable that Vaux bought the piece from within his department. In terms of who may have been the donor, several of Franklin's great grandsons were the Vice President of the United States Sanitary Commission. R. Meade Beche, Dallas' brother, was a Philadelphian and on the editorial committee of "Our Daily Fair", a journal produced by the Sanitary Fair. Finally, there is the death of Dr. Franklin Bache, the eldest Bache brother and a prominent Philadelphia physician. He passed away in March 16 immediately prior to the Fair. In reading the account of the dispersal of Dr. Bache's property, it is not possible to determine if the dressing table currently for sale was owned by him. Several pieces of furniture are mentioned but no specific connection can be made with the Vaux table.

► An early 18thC walnut veneered lowboy, the rectangular top with molded edge and featherbanding, above one short flanked by two deep drawers enclosing kneehole, raised by slender cabriole legs terminating in pad feet.

28.75in (73cm) wide

$3,000-4,000   **L&T**

◄ A George III mahogany lowboy, the crossbanded top with molded edge and rounded corners, the two short and one long drawers with brass handes, on chamfered straight legs.

30.5in (77.5cm) wide

$2,000-2,500   **DN**

Miniature Furniture

A 17thC Spanish walnut and marquetry miniature chest, the front with a hinged fall-front opening to an arrangement of six drawers with paneled front, all profusely inlaid with foliate arabesques and geometric banding.

17in (43cm) wide

$2,000-3,000   SI

An 18thC walnut-veneered "Meuble de Maitrise" miniature desk, possibly French.

16.5in (42cm) high

$1,300-1,200   CdK

An American miniature mahogany and poplar chest-of-drawers, rectangular top over case with two short cockbeaded drawers and two long cockbeaded drawers, raised on shaped skirt and bracket feet.

c1825   12.5in (31.75cm) wide

$900-1,200   SI

A "Meuble de maitrese" miniature chest.

c1830   13in (33cm) wide

$300-350   CdK

A 19thC miniature Dutch display cabinet, the shaped domed top with central carved cartouche, above a single glazed and molded door opening to reveal a shaped shelves, the bombé section base with three long drawers, original brass handles and escutcheons, standing on stylized lion's paw feet and shaped and carved frieze.

27.25in (69cm) wide

$4,000-4,500   HamG

▲1 A 19thC miniature mahogany chest-of-drawers, the rectangular top above two short and three long graduated drawers with turned handles on plinth base and bun feet.

11in (28cm) wide

$750-850   L&T

▲2 A 19thC mahogany tea caddy, in the form of a miniature sideboard, the reverse breakfront hinged top with molded edge and plain frieze enclosing satinwood-lined interior with pair of lidded compartments flanking divided well, the body with false arched cupboards on plinth base.

14.5in (37cm) wide

$1,500-1,800   L&T

A 19thC miniature Dutch marquetry walnut display cabinet, the serpentine-molded cornice above single astragal glazed door enclosing a shelf, the side with glazed panels above a base of bombe outline with three long graduated drawers, on claw-and-ball feet.

119in (48cm) wide

$3,000-3,500   L&T

A Victorian mahogany miniature cabinet, with swan neck cresting above two arched glazed doors and shelves, above a bow-front base with a hinged top and having four graduated drawers, flanked by turned columns to the top and base, raised on turned and tapering feet, broken handle and middle bauble.

15in (38cm)

$1,200-1,500   BonS

A Victorian miniature chest, of two short and three long drawers, with molded edge top over turned bone handles flanked by pilaster uprights, on plinth base.

13in (33cm) wide

$500-600   BAR

◀ A Victorian mahogany miniature chest, of two short and three long drawers with molded edge top over turned ebonized handles and on bun feet.

9.5in (24cm) wide

$120-180   BAR

A "Meuble de Maitrese" mahogany-veneered miniature chest.

11in (28cm) wide

$750-850   CdK

MIRRORS

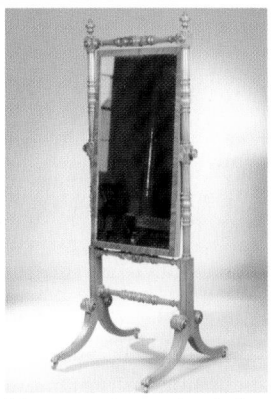

A Regency mahogany cheval mirror, with ebonized decoration, the rectangular frame enclosed by a ring of turned and blocked frame, surmounted by turned finials and raised above block paneled supports linked by turned and blocked stretcher on inlaid sabre legs with turned boss decoration terminating in cast brass paw feet and casters.

$4,000-5,000　　　**L&T**

A 19thC mahogany and marquetry inlaid cheval mirror, the rectangular frame with swan-neck pediment inlaid with meandering flower border, supported by square section uprights, similarly inlaid and surmounted by urn finials, the trestle base with square section curved legs terminating in brass caps and casters.

30.75in (78cm) wide

$4,000-5,000　　　**L&T**

A Victorian Regency-style satinwood cheval mirror, the rectangular beveled plate enclosed by molded frame with architectural pediment, supported by paneled uprights and raised on trestle base, with elaborate scroll-carved anthemion brackets, linked by a stretcher.

33.5in (85cm) wide

$2,200-2,800　　　**L&T**

A late 19thC Georgian-style mahogany cheval mirror, the oval beveled glass panel having carved and pierced pediment on tapered molded supports with central stretcher having blind fret decoration, the four scroll-shaped feet carved with acanthus leaves and having brass terminals and casters.

75in (190.5cm) high

$1,800-2,200　　　**Clv**

A George III mahogany toilet mirror, the box plateau fitted three small drawers, on ogee bracket feet.

15.5in (39.5cm) wide

$300-350　　　**GorB**

A George III satinwood dressing mirror, with chequer stringing, the oval plate with scrolling supports and serpentine base with three drawers, on shaped bracket feet.

16.25in (41cm) wide

$1,500-1,800　　　**L&T**

▶ A George III mahogany and satinwood toilet mirror, the rectangular plate within a conforming swing frame between square-section tapering posts with ormolu urn form finials, the serpentine front box base incorporating three drawers, raised on ogee-molded bracket feet, chevron banding and satinwood crossbanding throughout.

20.25in (51.5cm) wide

$1,500-2,000　　　**SI**

A George III mahogany toilet mirror [sic]

A Regency mahogany rectangular swing toilet mirror, the frame with an arc d'arbelet cresting, ring-turned supports with ivory finials, a barrel front base, with stringing and a tulipwood band, the three drawers with brass knob handles, on ivory ball feet.

25.5in (64.5cm) wide

$1,100-1,400　　　**WW**

◀ A William IV mahogany dressing mirror, the rectangular plate within molded frame supported by scrolling anthemion consoles on base with cushion-molded frieze drawers and carved scrolled feet, bears label Guthrie and Wells, Glasgow.

A Georgian mirror, with drawers and ivory escutcheons.

c1810　　14.25in (36cm) wide

$350-400　　　**CdK**

19.75in (50cm) wide

$450-550　　　**L&T**

A early 19thC labeled Federal carved giltwood looking glass, the pediment with outset corners and hung with spherules, the frieze with carved rosettes above a white, gold and blue eglomise panel depicting a towered building in a landscape, all above a rectangular plate flanked by beaded colonettes on a molded base with outset corner blocks, printed paper label from the Philadelphia Shop of C.P.Wayne and Son, Looking Glass Manufactory.

39in (99cm) high

$2,500-3,000   SI

An mahogany Federal shaving stand, having a rectangular frame swing-mirror with turned supports and acorn finials, slightly swelled band-inlaid base with three small drawers on ball feet, ebony and brass pulls.

19.5in (49.5cm) wide

$250-300   FRE

A Classical carved and giltwood eglomise looking glass, labeled James Todd, Portland, ME, the molded cornice with spherules above molded and beaded columnar supports centering a polychrome eglomise panel.

c1820   27.75in (70.5cm) high

$5,000-6,000   FRE

A Classical giltwood and eglomise looking glass, the molded cornice hung with spherules over an eglomise panel decorated with a bowl of fruit, the rectangular mirror plate flanked by baluster-turned pilasters, plate replaced.

c1830   24.5in (62cm) high

$900-1,300   SI

A late Classical maple looking glass, corner blocks joined by half-round balusters with gilt-molded ends.

c1835   33.75in (85.5cm) wide

$700-900   SI

A Swedish rococo giltwood pier glass, branded with the initials "NM" followed by an indecipherable stamp in black ink incorporating the date, the beveled and divided rectangular plate with re-entrant upper corners within a similarly beveled conforming mirror border applied with raised gilt floral sprays, the pierced rocaille crest carved with floral sprays, the pendant skirt similar.

1772   22.5in (57cm) wide

$6,000-7,000   SI

A late 18thC George III mahogany and parcel gilt wall mirror, the beveled rectangular plate within a molded, petal-carved frame surmounted by a pierced foliate crest and suspending a similar skirt.

20.75in (52.5cm) wide

$2,000-2,500   SI

Two small 19thC looking glasses, each with an eglomise panel depicting a building over mirror plate (losses).

largest 22in (56cm) high

$250-300   SI

► A 19thC Classical mahogany and carved giltwood looking glass, architectural pediment above tablet with carved eagle with wheat, and mirror plate flanked by colonettes with carved capitals and bases, (losses, replacements).

47in (119.5cm) high

$1,500-2,000   SI

A Regency giltwood and gesso framed triptych overmantel mirror, with three rectangular plates, each enclosed within a reeded and ebonized slip and framed by boldly fluted half columns with leaf rococo-scrolled clasps, the surmount frieze central with an applied shell and scrolling foliate moldings below fluted frieze with applied lion's heads.

80.75in (205cm) wide

$6,000-7,000   L&T

A 19thC Florentine giltwood mirror, the oval frame carved with foliate scrolls, some damage.

8.75in (22cm) wide

$225-275	DN

A large 19thC giltwood and gesso mirror, of oval outline with laurel wreath cresting centered by a putto and lyre, the central oval beveled plate with beaded frame enclosed by a further beveled plate border, in a bound rope molded frame with applied shell cartouches and laurel pendant.

43in (109cm) wide

$4,000-4,500	L&T

A 19thC French Louis XIV-style brass repousse wall mirror, the beveled rectangular plate within a canted mirror border in a conforming frame chased with a band of morning glory vine, the corners applied with foliate clasps, the crest centered with a floral urn flanked by mythological birds.

26in (66cm) wide

$1,500-2,000	SI

A 19thC-style giltwood wall mirror, the shaped oval plate with rocaille frame and open C-scroll surround with Ho-Ho bird cresting and floral sprays.

26.75in (68cm) wide

$3,000-4,000	L&T

A large Victorian giltwood overmantel mirror, the rectangular plate within ogee-molded and acanthus-carved frame centered by a mask cabochon with ribbon-tied fruit and flower swags and drops.

76in (193cm) wide

$6,000-7,000	L&T

A late 19thC French Louis Philippe gilt-gesso wall mirror, the arched rectangular plate within a frame cast over-all with scrollwork, feuillage and coquillage, the crest centered by female bust.

30.75in (78cm) wide

$2,200-2,800	SI

PRESSES

A part 17thC oak joined press cupboard, with carved frieze and panel doors, acanthus and rib-turned baluster supports, gadrooned frieze above a pair of panel cupboards and panel sides.

46in (117cm) high

$1,500-2,000	WW

A George II mahogany linen press, the dentilled cornice with inlaid scrolling foliate frieze above a pair of flat arched fielded panel doors with matched veneers enclosing four sliding trays, raised on bases with two short over two long graduated drawers and molded ogee bracket feet.

52in (132cm) wide

$9,000-11,000	L&T

An 18thC oak press cupboard, the molded and projecting cornice above twin paneled doors enclosing hanging space, the paneled base raised on stile supports.

53.5in (136cm) wide

$3,000-4,000	L&T

A George III mahogany linen press, the molded cornice with a crossbanded frieze over a pair of flame-fronted oval paneled doors, opening to a void interior with hanging rail above an arrangement of two short and two long drawers with oval handles, standing on a shaped apron with bracket feet,

49in (125cm) wide

$1,800-2,400	HamG

A George III mahogany linen press, the molded cornice above boxwood paneled frieze and pair of paneled doors with crossbanded flame-veneered ovals enclosing hanging space, the base with two long drawers on splayed bracket feet, the upper drawer fixed and cut to provide deeper hanging space.

51.25in (130cm) wide

$3,000-3,500	L&T

A George III mahogany bowfront linen press, with boxwood stringing, arched cornice with satinwood crossbanding above a pair of doors with oval crossbanded panels, the base with three long graduated drawers and shaped apron with splayed bracket feet.

49in (124cm) wide

$4,500-5,500	L&T

A Pennsylvania Chippendale cherrywood linen press, with overhanging dentil-molded cornice, twin arched paneled doors flanked by chamfered fluted corners enclosing four shelves, the lower section with three wide graduated drawers, replaced batwing brasses, ogee bracket feet.

c1770-1800 48.75in (123.5cm) w

$15,000-20,000   **FRE**

A Federal inlaid cherrywood linen press, possibly New Jersey, in two parts, the top with molded and band inlaid cornice overhanging a line inlaid frieze with swag tassels centering two cupboard doors with band inlaid ovals, the base with molded edge over three inlaid graduated drawers on an inlaid and scalloped skirt resting on tapered bracket feet; appears to retain the original ovel brass hardware, patched repairs to feet.

c1800   42.5in (108cm) wide

$15,000-20,000   **FRE**

An early 19thC mahogany linen press, of narrow proportions, the corniced top above pair of paneled doors enclosing sliding trays, two only, the base with two short and two long drawers, on turned feet.

34.25in (87cm) wide

$7,500-8,500   **L&T**

A late Regency mahogany and ebony-lined linen press, the molded and projecting cornice above twin panel doors flanked by reeded panels and enclosing interior with sliding trays, the lower section with two short over two long drawers on cast-iron hairy paw feet.

55.5in (141cm) wide

$4,500-5,000   **L&T**

A 19thC oak press, the molded cornice with crossbanded walnut frieze above a pair of ogee arched paneled doors enclosing shelves, on a similar base with stile feet.

53.25in (135cm) wide

$2,200-2,800   **L&T**

A North German 18thC limed oak armoire, the projecting molded cornice above a cushion frieze and twin doors with ogee arched panels flanked by similar paneled flanks, the sides with inlaid paneled, above molded base with frieze drawer and plinth.

84in (213cm) wide

$4,500-5,000   **L&T**

A mid-18thC Provincial Louis XV walnut two-door armoire, the outset cavetto-molded cornice with rounded front corners, the front with a be-swagged and paneled frieze over a pair of bi-paneled doors, each panel with floral sprays carved in the spandrels, flanked by rounded and fluted stiles, the shaped and carved apron centered by a quatrefoil and raised on stile feet.

60.75in (154.5cm) wide

$3,000-4,000   **SI**

A Regency mahogany inverted breakfront wardrobe, the molded cornice centered by a pediment above pair of paneled doors at center enclosing sliding trays with four graduated drawers below, flanked by full length paneled and pilastered doors enclosing hanging and drawers on plinth base.

113.75in (289cm) wide

$13,000-15,000   **L&T**

▶ An early 19thC Continental oak wardrobe incorporating 17thC carving, the molded cornice with carved frieze incorporating two crest, above pair of paneled doors centered by cherubs divided by a central male figure standing on a fluted column, flanked by correponding fluted columns, above drawer carved with the date flanked by lion masks on carved leaf scroll feet.

1835   66.25in (168cm) wide

$8,000-10,000   **L&T**

▶ An early Victorian elm and burr gentleman's wardrobe, the reverse breakfront-molded cornice above a pair of doors with lancet arched gothic panels above egg-and-dart molded panels enclosing an interior fitted with drawers and sliding shelves, flanked by similar panels with leafy scrolling bracket supports and sides with opposing paneled doors enclosing hanging space, raised on a plinth with flattened bun feet.

81in (205.5cm) wide

$3,000-3,500   **L&T**

A Victorian mahogany wardrobe, in style of Alexander "Greek" Thomson, the shallow pedimented cornice above frieze with rounded spacers, central mirror door flanked by paneled doors enclosing drawers, shelves and hanging space, on plinth base.

This wardrobe bears similarities with several pieces associated with Greek Thomson, particularly the celebrated cabinet at Kelvingrove Art Gallery and Museum, Glasgow. Thomson created his own unique Neo-classical architecture in the mid-19thC and is increasingly acknowledged as a visionery of international stature, although he built little outside Glasgow. The extent of his furniture designing is unclear, but it has been possible to identify a style which might be considered his.

81in (206cm) wide

$8,000-10,000   **L&T**

SCREENS

A mid-18thC mahogany polescreen, with gilt-pineapple finial, the molded edge panel with early 18thC woolwork fragment and a later 18thC chinoiserie silk panel to the reverse, the turned stand with shaped swept legs.

$450-500   **HamG**

A Victorian burr ash breakfront wardrobe, the deep-molded cornice with inlaid panels and central segmental pediment above three doors centered by circular panels, enclosing hanging space and drawers, on plinth base.

84.25in (214cm) wide

$2,200-2,800   **L&T**

An Edwardian mahogany bedroom suite, with linenfold panels and copper strap hinges and handles, comprising a triple door wardrobe, a dressing chest, with swing mirrors and drawers, a washstand, a pot cupboard and an associated bed, by R Strahan & Co, Cabinet Makers and Shopfitters, Dublin.

wardrobe: 69.75in (177cm) wide

$1,500-2,000   **L&T**

A mahogany firescreen, the adjustable banner inset with an 18thC tapestry panel of flowers, flanked by channeled supports on cabriole legs with pad feet.

44.75in (114) high

$1,000-1,300   **DN**

A ten piece Adam-style Edwardian inlaid mahogany bedroom suite, by Mackintosh, Kirkcaldy, with rosewood crossbanding and boxwood stringing, comprising a three door wardrobe centered by a mirror with arched cornice and arabesque panels, a dressing table, with arched cheval glass at center flanked by three drawer pedestals on deep single drawer base, a washstand with marble top above two cupboard doors on legs, a pot cupboard, three single chairs, a twofold towel airer, a double bed and a single bed. wardrobe:

91.5in (232cm) wide

$9,000-11,000   **L&T**

▶ A French Louis XVI-style bronze-dore-mounted marble top mahogany vitrine, the white marble rectangular top with outset front corners, the front with a paneled frieze over two glazed doors opening to adjustable shelves and flanked by ionic pilasters headed by paterae, the outset molded base raised on toupie feet, bronze-dore encadrements moldings and cannelures.

33.5in (85cm) wide

$2,500-3,000   **SI**

A Regency Gillows-style firescreen, the rectangular rising and pull-out screen with floral-painted decoration, standing on trestle-ended supports with reeded and swept legs.

40in (102cm) wide

$500-600   **HamG**

An Edwardian mahogany wardrobe, with Neo-classical marquetry decoration, the molded cornice with central stepped arch above a pair of paneled doors enclosing shelves and two short over three long drawers, flanked by mirror doors enclosing hanging space and drawers, on a plinth base with bracket feet and later casters.

79.5in (202cm) wide

$2,200-2,800   **L&T**

A Regency mahogany cheval firescreen, fitted with three sliding panels with inset floral pink damask on splayed end standards.

$400-450   **GorL**

A French painted firescreen, the frame with urn finials and carved with ribbons inset with a 19thC Aubusson-type panel of flowers and scrolls, on cabriole legs.

40.5in (103cm) high

$500-600	DN

A Victorian ebonized chinoiserie firescreen, with mother-of-pearl and ivory inlay.

c1890 34.5in (88cm) high

$900-1,100	CdK

A Victorian japanned polescreen, painted with gilt flowers on a black ground, the banner with re-entrant corners and two exotic birds, on a turned column and triform base.

$450-500	DN

A Regency ebonized and parcel-gilt polescreen, the adjustable shield-shaped banner worked in silk with an oval panel depicting a young lady within a ribbon-tied floral border, raised on a leaf-carved and turned support with vitruvian scroll feet.

56in (142cm) high

$650-750	Chef

A large Victorian rosewood firescreen, the oval woolwork panel enclosed within molded frame, the baluster pedestal with tripod base and carved cabriole legs.

45.25in (115cm) high

$350-450	L&T

A late 19thC Louis XV-style six-fold giltwood and gesso draught screen, each graduated screen with shaped beveled glass panel above an embroidered panel below, each enclosed within elaborately scrolling leaf-carved and rocaille work frames, largest fold

74.5in (189cm) high

$3,000-3,500	L&T

SHELVES

A mid-17thC joined oak court cupboard, the top with thumbcut frieze, on baluster-turned block front-carved supports with a central tier with scroll brackets, the pot board base on block feet, worm damage and some restoration.

43in (110cm) high

$2,000-3,000	WW

A set of mid-18thC cherrywood hanging wall shelves, comprising four tiers united by turned baluster supports.

35in (89cm) wide

$500-600	HamG

A late Regency mahogany two-tier buffet, each rectangular tier with carved three-quarter gallery and thumbnail rim, linked by rectangular section supports with linenfold carved panels and leafy capitals, the whole raised on trestle ends with acanthus-carved brackets and scroll-carved feet, brass casters.

54in (137cm) wide

$4,500-5,000	L&T

A set of William IV rosewood hanging wall shelves, with pierced cresting and four tiers united by turned and carved barley-sugar supports with original mirrored backs and shaped fronts.

22in (56cm) wide

$600-700	HamG

A pair of 19thC painted and gilded bow-fronted encoignures, the scrolling mirrored superstructure with veined marble tops over three open shelves on scroll feet.

51.25in (130cm) high

| $4,500-5,000 | L&T |

A pair of Victorian carved oak buffets, of Irish design, the tops with mask and foliage crest, open scrolls and carved finials, front putti supports to a galleried undertier, with acanthus to the front cabriole legs, and paw feet.

52in (132cm) high

| $1,200-1,500 (pair) | WW |

A Victorian three-shelf bird's-eye maple wall bracket, with fret-cut scrollwork sides and spiral-twist dividing pillars.

27in (68.5cm)

| $900-1,100 | GorB |

SIDEBOARDS

A mid-17thC oak standing livery cupboard, the dentil and block cornice frieze above fielded panel doors with a carved bordered panel, doric capital ringed vase supports, a ribbed and fluted frieze drawer on front ringed vase supports to a potboard base, with ivory trade label for Frank Partridge, Works of Art, 26 King Street St James & New York.

50.5in (128cm) wide

| $1,500-2,000 | WW |

A George III mahogany sideboard, with boxwood stringing and lion mask handles, the crossbanded D-shaped top above frieze drawer and inset underdrawer with arched spandrels, flanked by a cupboard and deep drawer, raised on ring-turned tapering legs.

66.25in (168cm) wide

| $4,500-5,500 | L&T |

A George III satinwood bowfront sideboard, with later decoration, the crossbanded top with central fan medallion above frieze drawer and recessed arched kneehole drawer, flanked by deeper drawers on square section tapering legs.

54in (137cm) wide

| $6,500-7,500 | L&T |

A George III mahogany serpentine sideboard, the whole decorated with rosewood crossbanding and panels, boxwood and chequer stringing, the shaped top above bowed frieze drawer with apron below, flanked by concave drawers, one a cellaret, with cabinets below, raised on tapering legs with splayed feet, modern back.

69.5in (176cm) wide

| $5,500-6,500 | L&T |

A George III Scottish mahogany sideboard, with chequer and boxwood stringing, the raised stage with applied brass rail, having four frieze drawers below, the stepped D-shaped top above three central drawers flanked by two short and two deep drawers with false fronts, raised on square section tapering legs with spade feet.

90.25in (229cm) wide

| $5,500-6,500 | L&T |

A George III mahogany serpentine sideboard, the crossbanded and boxwood inlaid top with brass rail above central drawer flanked by two deep drawers inlaid with paterae, raised on square section tapering legs terminating in spade feet.

60.25in (153cm) wide

| $9,000-11,000 | L&T |

▶ A George III bowfront mahogany sideboard, with rosewood-crossbanded shaped top above a central drawer and arched brackets flanked by two further drawers with two deep drawers below, the whole raised on square section tapering legs terminating in spade feet.

66.5in (169cm) wide

| $7,500-8,500 | L&T |

Sideboards

An Irish Regency mahogany sideboard, the reverse breakfront rectangular top with heavily molded and carved scrolling anthemion backboard, three frieze drawers divided by panels, a dropped paneled cupboard at center with paneled door flanked by similar anthemion consoles, the whole raised on four boldly carved console legs with paw feet and a pair of paneled rear supports.

80.5in (204cm) wide

$12,000-14,000   L&T

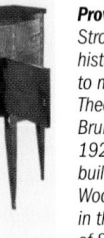

Provenance: By descent in the Strong family. According to family history " This old sideboard was left to me by the will of my father, Theodore Strong, who died at New Brunswick, N J on December 24, 1928. It is believed to have been built for Colonel Benjamin Ruggles Woodbridge, of the Continental Army in the Revolution. He was a A native of South Hadley, Mass.

A Federal inlaid mahogany sideboard, Mid-Atlantic states, the rectangular top with ovolo corners and conforming case of three drawers above four cupboard doors, all with line inlay, six square-tapered legs inlaid with strings of bell flowers and line panels, some damage to lower legs, replaced brasses.
c1800   69in (175cm) wide

$8,000-10,000   FRE

A Federal inlaid mahogany sideboard, possibly from the workshop of John and Thomas Seymour, Boston, MA, rectangular top with turret corners and outset front with lunette-inlaid edge over conforming case with reeded supports ending in tapering vasiform reeded legs, enclosing band-inlaid cupboard doors, two bottle drawers and five short drawers.

c1800   69in (175cm) wide

$2,000-3,000   SI

A Regency mahogany buffet, the rectangular top with ledge back above reeded frieze and reeded and lotus leaf-carved tapering legs joined by shaped undershelf.

45in (114cm) wide

$4,500-5,000   L&T

A pair of New York Federal figured mahogany demi-lune sideboards, each with pie-section veneered top over two graduated drawers flanked by cabinet doors on tapered diamond legs ending on spade feet, split to one top, some replaced hardware.

c1800   50in (127cm) wide

$8,000-10,000 (pair)   FRE

A Regency mahogany breakfront sideboard, the shaped top above later fitted false fronted drawer with recessed kneehole drawer below, flanked by false front cellaret drawer and two corresponding drawers, all with cupboards below, divided by turned leaf-carved and reeded columns with stump feet, stamped "T. Wilson, 68 Great Queen Street".

73.25in (186cm) wide

$4,500-5,000   L&T

An American Classical mahogany and bird's-eye maple sideboard, the rectangular top with a scrolled and paneled backboard, the front with three outset frieze drawers raised on free-standing columns flanking three paneled drawers interspersed with pilasters, raised on foliate lion-paw feet, secondary wood poplar and white pine.
c1815   72.5in (184cm) wide

$5,000-6,000   SI

An American second quarter 19thC Empire carved mahogany Baltimore sideboard, the molded rectangular top with a three-quarter gallery, the outset frieze with three cockbeaded drawers interspersed with four gothic-arch panels, the front with a pair of doors with ogee-form panels opening to a shelf, flanked on each side by a door with a gothic panel opening to a further panel, all interspersed with free-standing ionic columns raised on bun feet; secondary wood poplar. LITERATURE: For a related example, see figure 143 page 118, "Classical Maryland 1815-1845, Fine and Decorative Arts From the Golden Age," (1993), the Maryland Historical Society.

73in (185.5cm) wide

$3,000-4,000   SI

An early Federal inlaid mahogany breakfront New York sideboard, the rectangular top with inset convex front corners, the conforming case with an outset center section with a drawer over two doors, each convex end with a frieze drawer over a cupboard door, raised on square section tapering legs inlaid with pendant bell flowers and cuffs, stringing throughout.

63.5in (161.5cm) wide

$5,000-6,000   SI

A late 19thC mahogany demi-lune sideboard, the central fluted frieze drawer flanked by two pairs of two cupboards with oval stringing on square section fluted and stopped legs, stamped "Waring and Gillow, London".

85.5in (217cm) wide

$6,000-7,000 **L&T**

A mahogany bowfronted sideboard in George III-style, with turned brass rail, above two paneled drawers, with brass handles, flanked by a door and a deep drawer, on square tapering legs with spade feet.

65.25in (165.5cm) wide

$1,800-2,400 **DN**

A walnut sideboard, the rectangular crossbanded top above central relief-carved cupboard door flanked by burr-walnut faced doors, on shaped legs with molded feet, by Whytock & Reid of Edinburgh.

71.75in (182cm) wide

$1,500-2,000 **L&T**

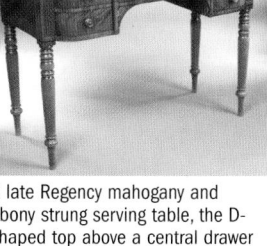

A late Regency mahogany and ebony strung serving table, the D-shaped top above a central drawer and arched brackets, enclosed by two pairs of curved drawers and reeded panels, the whole raised on ring-turned and tapering legs terminating in toupie feet.

41.75in (106cm) wide

$2,800-3,400 **L&T**

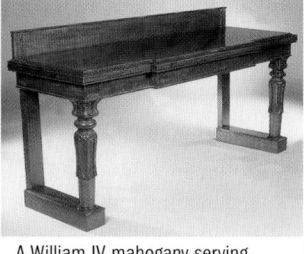

A William IV mahogany serving table, the breakfront rectangular top with molded edge and ledge back, frieze with paneled terminals, raised on turned and lotus leaf-clasped front legs and plain rear pilasters joined by sled bases.

84.75in (215cm) wide

$7,500-8,500 **L&T**

A 19thC mahogany serpentine serving table, in the Neo-classical manner, the shaped top with canted angles above a fluted frieze centered by tablet with applied urn and scrolling folite decoration raised above square section stop-fluted tapering legs terminating in spade feet.

66.25in (168cm) wide

$7,500-8,500 **L&T**

▶ A George III-style carved mahogany serving table, the shaped rectangular top with a serpentine front edge, conforming frieze, square section tapering legs, carved with foliate motifs.

c1900   69in (175.5cm) wide

$2,000-3,000 **SI**

SOFAS AND SETTEES

A George I walnut-framed two-seater sofa, the upholstered rectangular back above outscrolled arms and seat raised on shell-carved mahogany cabriole legs with pad feet, restorations.

55.5in (141cm) wide

$4,500-5,500 **L&T**

A George II style two-seater settee, of generous proportions, the woolwork-upholstered square back and outscrolled arms above seat with separate squab and leaf carved mahogany cabriole legs with claw-and-ball feet.

53.25in (135cm) wide.

$6,000-7,000 **L&T**

A George III faux bamboo caned settee, the rectangular back and downswept arms raised on legs with open brackets, separate seat squab.

73in (185cm) wide

$2,200-2,800 **L&T**

▶ A George III mahogany-framed sofa, with serpentine back and outscrolled arms, the square section legs joined by stretchers.

82in (208cm) wide

$3,000-3,500 **L&T**

A Regency mahogany settee, with scroll-crested reeded top rail, scroll arms, carved seat rail and sabre legs, fitted brass cups and casters.

$3,000-4,000 **GorL**

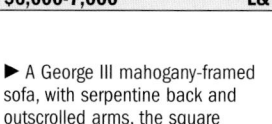

A CLOSER LOOK AT A CAMEL BACK SOFA

This sofa gets its name from the serpentine shape of its upholstered back.

Horizontal rolls serve as armrests and the arm supports slope elegantly forward and down to the tops of the corner legs.

The overall design is typical of late Chippendale-style furniture. Beware of reproductions which have lighter proportions and evidence of modern tools, such as circular saws, on the inner framework.

The square front legs and square, sloping back legs, and plain rectangular stretcher are typical of Chippendale seat furniture.

A Chippendale mahogany camelback sofa, with serpentine crest flanked by outscrolled arms on downswept supports centering a rectangular upholstered seat on square legs with corbels and joined by stretchers.

c1780   59in (150cm) wide

$6,000-7,000   **FRE**

A Federal carved mahogany sofa, the downcurved arms with reeded baluster-turned supports, the bow-fronted seat raised on turned tapered and reeded legs with castors.

Provenance*: The Society of the Cincinnati.*

79in (200cm) long

$3,500-4,500   **SI**

A Federal inlaid mahogany sofa, incorporating period components, the padded rectangular back with padded downswept arms with reeded baluster-form supports, the stuff-over padded seat raised on similarly turned legs headed by flame mahogany panels with chevron-banded borders.

70in wide (177.5cm) wide

$5,500-6,500   **SI**

A first quarter 19thC Empire carved mahogany sofa, with padded over-scroll back and arms, loose-cushion seat, molded rails and lion paw feet.

93in (231cm) long

$2,000-2,500   **SI**

A Classical carved mahogany sofa, New England, rounded scrolling crest rail above shaped upholstered back and seat flanked with scrolling arms ending in molded terminals over bolection-molded seat rail on leaf-carved legs with paw feet.

c1825   85in (216cm) wide

$500-800   **SI**

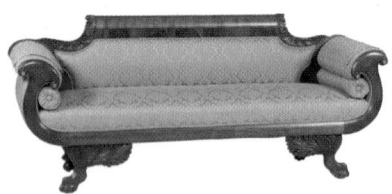

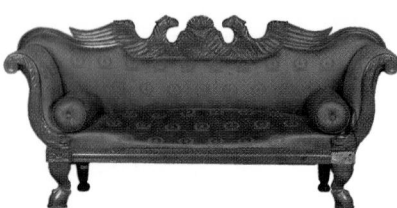

An Empire carved mahogany sofa, the padded rectangular back surmounted by a convex crest rail with leaf-capped ends, the stuff-over seat flanked by padded, overscroll arms, the convex rails raised on lion-paw feet with leaf-carved brackets.

c1830   82in (211cm)

$1,500-2,000   **SI**

A Classical mahogany sofa, curving asymmetrical rail over conforming upholstered back continuing to cornucopia-shaped arms, upholstered seat on stepped molded rail, scrolled feet.

c1830   77.5in (197cm) wide

$1,500-2,000   **SI**

A mid-19thC Empire-style carved mahogany sofa, the crest rail carved with a pair of eagles with outstretched wings and centered with a foliate basket, the overscroll arms with facings carved as leaf-capped dolphins.

Provenance*: The Society of the Cincinnati.*

92in (234cm) long

$5,000-7,000   **SI**

Sofas

An early 19thC mahogany Biedermeier day bed, the rectangular overstuffed seat with outscrolled end and splayed feet, the frame decorated with applied moldings to each face.

61in (155cm) wide

$1,800-2,400	L&T

A Regency mahogany window seat, the turned and scrolled panel ends flanking paneled seat with fluted frieze, on splayed legs.

63in (160cm) wide

$10,000-12,000	L&T

A Regency mahogany sofa, wth reeded and scrolled back rail and outscrolled arms incorporating bolsters, the reeded seat rail with bead and reel panels above the ring-turned tapering legs.

84.75in (215cm) wide

$3,000-4,000	L&T

A pair of early Victorian oak conversation sofas, upholstered in buttoned velvet, each of lobed L-shape with three-quarter stuffover back, molded seat rail and carved scrolling arm raised on fluted and gadrooned square section tapering legs and casters.

These sofas are believed to have come from Taymouth Castle, Perthshire, the home of the Marquesses of Breadalbane. Taymouth was extravagantly rebuilt in the 1840s and 50s and much furniture was supplied by the firms of William Trotter and Thomas Dowbiggin.

$6,000-7,000	L&T

A 19thC bobbin-turned oak hall settee, the galleried four section back above open arms on a rush seat and corresponding base.

59in (150cm) wide

$900-1,100	L&T

A late 19thC mahogany Empire Revival settee, with Neo-classical gilt-brass applied moldings, upholstered back and seat on turned legs.

$4,500-5,500	L&T

An Edwardian walnut tub-shaped settee, with pierced back on turned legs with fitted casters.

$900-700	GorL

A CLOSER LOOK AT SETTEES AND SOFAS

When buying an antique settee or sofa the condition and quality are important. However, certain signs of wear are inevitable and actually provide confirmation of authenticity.

There will be a certain amount of shrinkage in the joints. There will be evidence of wear, especially along the seat rail. The color of the carving will vary as certain areas will have been handled more or been more exposed to sunlight. Legs and feet will show signs of wear that would be difficult to reproduce artificially. The vast majority of settees will have been reupholstered. These are to be expected and will not greatly affect the value.

An Edwardian carved giltwood loveseat in the Louis XV-style, the shaped back and arms carved with leafy C-scrolls and with three caned panels above kidney-shaped caned seat raised on rose-carved cabriole legs with scrolled feet.

35.5in (90cm) wide

$750-850	L&T

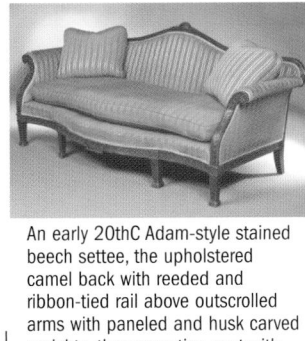

An early 20thC Adam-style stained beech settee, the upholstered camel back with reeded and ribbon-tied rail above outscrolled arms with paneled and husk carved uprights, the serpentine seat with loose squab and cushions, anthemion-carved seat rail centered by tablet, on tapering fluted legs.

82.75in (210cm) wide

$2,200-2,800	L&T

A small mahogany framed Chippendale-style sofa, the upholstered serpentine back and outscrolled arms raised on square section legs united by H-stretcher, with brass casters.

69in (175cm) wide

$1,500-2,000	L&T

Sofas/Stands

A Louis XVI-style giltwood canapé, the slightly bowed buttoned upholstered back with gadrooned rail and ribbon-tied surmount, flanked by fluted column and open arms, on turned and fluted legs.

51.25in (130cm) wide

$1,800-2,400	**L&T**

A Victorian rosewood chaise lounge, with buttoned upholstery and scrolling frame on cabriole legs and pot castors.

72.5in (184cm) wide

$1,200-1,500	**L&T**

A Regency stained beech chaise lounge, the reeded frame with outscrolled ends and turned tapering legs with brass caps and casters, separate seat cushion and bolsters, formerly ebonized.

84.75in (215cm) wide

$4,000-4,500	**L&T**

STANDS

A George III mahogany metamorphic music stand, the adjustable lifting boxwood, satinwood ebony strung and rosewood crossbanded top with rounded angles and reeded edge, fitted with retracting brass music rests, raised on telescopic reeded and ring-turned pedestal and tripod base with reeded sabre legs and ball feet.

29.25in (74cm) high

$4,500-5,500	**L&T**

▶ A George IV mahogany hat stand, with four tiers each with three serpentine hooks, supported by baluster-turned column with urn finial and concave quadriform base with flattened bun feet.

68.5in (174cm) high

$2,200-2,800	**L&T**

A matched pair of Regency walnut torchère stands, the circular tops raised on scrolled supports and triform bases with flattened bun feet, one of a later date.

28in (72cm) high

$1,000-1,500	**Chef**

A Regency mahogany bookcase, the molded and dished square top above two adjustable open shelves flanked by lotus-capped columns to each corner, raised on a plinth base with casters.

$2,000-2,500	**Chef**

A late Regency mahogany duet stand, the lattice work double-sloping top, supported on an adjustable ring-turned and ebonized stem, with three swept legs with black line inlaid, supported on ball feet, candle arms missing.

50in (127cm) high

$2,200-2,800	**HamG**

◀ A 19thC padouk wood stand, with marble inset top above carved frieze, the whole raised on carved supports.

36in (91.5cm)

$220-280	**BW**

254

A Napoleon III ebonized and bronze-dore-mounted jardinière, of inverted urn form, the stand with three in-curved legs, the triangular stretcher surmounted by a vase, hung with chairs and spherules.

53in (134.5cm) high

$1,500-2,000   **SI**

A pair of Napoleon III ebonized "boulle" marble top pedestals, each white marble rectangular top with canted front corners, the conforming cavetto frieze over a tapering paneled square section shaft raised on an ogee-molded plinth, all with bronze-dore moldings, encadrements and mounts, the front inlaid with Berainesque "boulle", work panels on a tortoiseshell ground.

47in (119.5cm) high

$7,000-8,000   **SI**

A Victorian oak torchère, the turned column carved with scrolling acanthus foliage, on square plinth.

38in (96.5cm) high

$220-280   **GorB**

A late 19thC Continental macassar ebony gueridon, the hexagonal top with rising mechanism on a triangular platform base with shaped feet.

16.25in (41cm) wide

$150-200   **HamG**

A mahogany stick stand.

c1890   33in (84cm) high

$400-500   **SS**

A late 19thC mahogany hexagonal-topped torchère, on twist column and shaped legs.

36in (91.5cm) high

$150-200   **GorL**

▶ A pair of late 19thC French Louis XVI-style marble top ormolu gueridons, each gray-veined white marble top raised on an urn-form standard flanked by three square section supports in the form of monopodi hung with floral garlands and tassled lambrequins, the triangular base with concave sides each centered by a female mask, guilloche molding, beading, paterae and other Classical motifs throughout.

25in (63.5cm) high

$10,000-12,000 (pair)   **SI**

STOOLS

A Continental walnut easel, the shaped supports carved with swans heads, with an adjustable rest, some damage.

74.5in (189cm) high

$2,200-2,800   **DN**

A mid-17thC carved oak joined bench, the molded rectangular top over a molded frieze carved with an acanthus-filled arcade and raised on splayed gun-barrel-turned legs with bun feet.

77.75in (197.5cm) long

$2,500-3,000   **SI**

▶ A George III oak joint stool, the molded rectangular top above plain frieze on ring-turned and blocked supports united by stretchers.

17.75in (45cm) wide

$400-450   **L&T**

A George III oak joint stool, the overhanging molded rectangular top above plain frieze on turned and blocked supports united by stretchers.

19.5in (50cm) high

$300-400   **L&T**

A Regency Gothic Revival stool, in the early style of AWN Pugin, over-painted in gold and black, the stuffover rectangular top with molded rail and arched frieze raised on turned octagonal tapering legs with leafy capitals.

19in (49cm) wide

$3,000-4,000   **L&T**

Stools

A pair of Regency japanned and caned window seats, each with raised scrolled ends, concave serpentine front and square section tapering legs with brass caps and casters.

53in (135cm) long

$13,000-15,000　　　**L&T**

A Regency simulated rosewood window seat, of spreading form with raised scroll-over sides and brass strung rail, on ring-turned legs with brass caps and casters.

59in (150cm) wide

$2,200-2,800　　　**L&T**

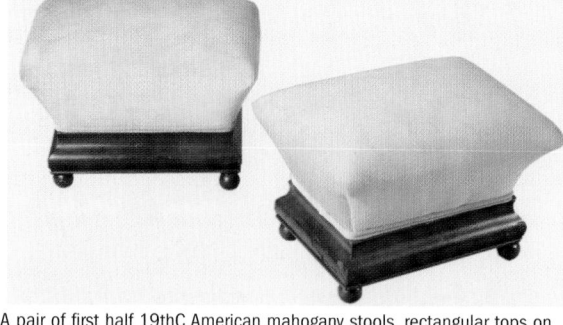

A pair of first half 19thC American mahogany stools, rectangular tops on ogee apron, upholstered in pale green velvet, ball feet.

$900-1,000　　　**FRE**

A pair of needlepoint stools.

1840　　　17.75in (45cm) high

$1,800-2,200 (pair)　　　**SS**

A tortoise-shaped footstool.

1840　　　18.5in (47cm) long

$1,300-1,600　　　**SS**

A William IV rosewood ottoman of concave form, with padded seat, upholstered sides and scroll-carved frieze on cabriole legs.

17.5in (44cm) wide

$700-800　　　**DN**

A large 19thC walnut stool in the French taste, the gold-colored upholstered top with brass stud nailing, having C-scroll shaped frieze carved with bouquets of flowers, the French cabriole legs terminating in scrolled toes.

29in (74cm) wide

$1,000-1,400　　　**HamG**

A 19thC French foliate-carved walnut X-frame stool, with watered silk upholstery.

$500-600　　　**GorB**

A 19thC Carolean-style walnut low stool, covered in tapestry, on scrolled supports.

21in (53.5cm) wide

$250-300　　　**GorB**

A mid-19thC walnut window seat, with upholstered scroll ends and seat, the frame carved to both sides with foliate scrolls on cabriole legs.

$1,000-1,400　　　**DN**

A mid-19thC Louis XV-style carved giltwood banquette, the top with serpentine sides, each shaped and pierced frieze centered by a foliate rocaille, the molded cabriole legs with scroll feet, the foliate X-stretchers joined by posies.

43.75in (110cm) long

$5,000-6,000　　　**SI**

A pair of Victorian walnut round footstools, each with a wool and beadwork top, gilt-brass studs and sycamore straps with shaped apron.

11in (28cm) dia

$450-550 (pair)　　　**DN**

A late 19thC inlaid rosewood piano stool, with revolving circular seat upholstered in velvet, the four inlaid turned and tapered supports and central pillar united by a ring turned 'X'-shaped stretcher.

17.25in (44cm) high

$500-600　　　**Clv**

An Edwardian mahogany piano stool, with incised ivory inlay, the adjustable overstuffed seat raised on four cabriole legs joined by X-stretcher, by Jas Shoolbred & Co.

$750-850　　　**L&T**

An Regency-style ebonized and gilt-japanned rectangular stool, with caned seat on ring-turned tapering legs with X-stretcher.

19in (48cm) high

$700-800　　　**DN**

Tables

TABLES

A George III mahogany writing table, with ebony stringing, the top with lifting slope and baize lining, above dummy drawers and two drawers below, on square section tapering legs with brass caps and casters.

38.25in (97cm) wide

$2,000-2,500   **L&T**

An early19thC mahogany writing table, the rectangular top with astragal edge and cusped corners, inset writing surface, above three cockbeaded frieze drawers to each side, the central one false-fronted to one side, raised on reeded square section tapered sabre legs with lion mask terminals and brass casters.

60.25in (153cm) wide

$20,000-25,000   **L&T**

► A George III mahogany lady's writing tale, firescreen to rear, the rectangular top with rosewood crossbanding and molded edge above dummy drawer and secret drawer to side, raised on square section tapering legs united by shaped undershelf with three quarter gallery, stamped "Gillows, Lancaster".

28in (71cm) high

$2,200-2,800   **L&T**

An early 19thC mahogany writing table, with boxwood stringing, the rectangular crossbanded top with molded angles above frieze drawer and opposing dummy, on square section tapering legs with spade feet.

28.75in (73cm) high

$2,200-2,800   **L&T**

A William IV mahogany and rosewood crossbanded writing table, the drop-leaf top with rounded angles above two drawers and opposing dummies, raised on bulbous square section pedestal and concave quadriform base with carved paw feet casters.

33in (84cm) wide

$1,500-2,000   **L&T**

A French Empire mahogany and gilt-brass mounted writing desk, the rectangular top with inset tooled skiver above an arrangement of five drawers around an arched kneehole raised on turned tapering legs with cast capitals and bases on cup feet.

51.25in (130cm) wide

$4,500-5,500   **L&T**

A William IV mahogany writing table, the rectangular-molded top with adjustable central panel, inset with tooled skiver, above a plain panel to the front and drawer to the side, the whole raised on scrolling ogee-shaped supports linked by an arched stretcher on molded sabre legs terminating in brass caps and casters.

30.75in (78cm) high

$3,000-4,000   **L&T**

A mid-19thC kidney-shaped writing table, veneered in figured walnut with banding and marquetry foliage to the leather inset top, with a mahogany-lined frieze drawer, and gilt-bronze mounts to the cabriole legs.

44.5in (113cm) wide

$5,000-6,000   **WW**

A mid-19thC bureau plat, veneered in tulipwood and rosewood, with inlaid stringing, the serpentine top with a chased brass molding, cast spray handles to a central frieze drawer, chased bronze mounts to cabriole legs.

42.5in (108cm) wide

$2,200-2,800   **WW**

A Victorian mahogany writing table, fitted with two frieze drawers, on turned tapering legs.

33in (84cm) high

$150-200   **GorL**

A Victorian mahogany French-style writing table, the rectangular top with rounded angles and molded edge, flame-veneered border and leather writing surface, above shaped frieze drawer with C-scrolled moldings, on carved and molded cabriole legs.

39in (99cm) wide

$2,200-2,800   **L&T**

Tables

A Victorian French-style burr-walnut writing table, with kingwood crossbanding, the kidney-shaped top with tooled leather panel and molded crossbanded edge above shaped frieze with concealed drawer and molded cabriole legs with gilt-brass mounts.

49.25in (125cm) wide

$4,500-5,500   **L&T**

A Victorian Louis XV-style bur-walnut writing table, the shaped rectangular top with matched veneer and kingwood crossbanding above shaped frieze with single drawer and slender cabriole legs with gilt-brass mounts and sabots.

(97cm) wide

$1,500-2,000   **L&T**

▶ A Louis XVI-style mahogany writing table, with gilt-brass mounts, the oval top with plum pudding veneer above paneled frieze with leaf-cast beading and spring-loaded drawer to the front, raised on tapering fluted octagonal legs with cast mounts joined by an interlaced stretcher, with spirally turned cast feet, by Henry Dasson, stamped.

28.25in (72cm) wide

$5,000-6,000   **L&T**

A Victorian walnut writing table, in the Louis XV-style, the top with pierced brass three-quarter gallery, the hinged central section flanked by oval marquetry panels, above shaped frieze centered by drawer with compartments and drawers, raised on cabriole legs with gilt-brass mounts.

37.75in (96cm) wide

$3,500-4,500   **L&T**

A late Victorian mahogany traveling writing table, the folding action with a bottle-green leather-fitted interior, on X-legs and fluted and plain stretchers.

4in (61cm) high

$1,200-1,800   **WW**

A late 19thC Louis XV-style kingwood and floral marquetry lady's writing desk, the shaped serpentine top with leather inset skiver above three frieze drawers, each with shaped scroll marquetry fronts, the sides of serpentine outline and similarly decorated on slender cabriole legs, the whole with rococo gilt-ormolu mounts.

37.25in (94.5cm) wide

$6,000-7,000   **L&T**

A late 19thC French parquetry kingwood escritoire, with gilt-brass mounts, the rectanguar top with rounded angles and brass-bound edge above frieze drawer and writing slide to side with gilt-tooled leather skiver, raised on cabriole legs with mask terminals and beaded edge with hoof sabots.

28in (71cm) high

$3,500-4,500   **L&T**

An Edwardian mahogany and marquetry writing desk, the D-shaped top with leather skiver, with slight reverse breakfront and three drawers, on square section tapered legs with brass caps and casters, the drawers, sides, back and legs inlaid with Neo-classical marquetry.

42.25in (107cm) wide

$4,500-5,500   **L&T**

▶ A Louis XV-style cherrywood lady's writing table, with gilt-brass mounts, the rectangular parquetry top with brass edge, above drawer and opposing writing slide to the sides, raised on cabriole legs united by undershelf with pierced brass gallery, stamped GARMS.

27.5in (70cm) high

$4,500-5,500   **L&T**

◀ An early 19thC German mahogany center table, the crossbanded quarter veneered circular tilt-top with scalloped frieze and ball pendants, raised on octagonal pedestal with columns at each angle and corresponding massive stepped plinth.

30.75in (78cm) high

$5,000-6,000   **L&T**

Tables

A CLOSER LOOK AT A REGENCY TABLE

An early 19thC West Indian center table, the circular tilt-top inlaid with a Catherine wheel design in exotic woods, with a central parquetry star and an outer diamond-patterned border banded in palm and mahogany, the reverse segment veneered in four different woods, the block with a locking device, the canted triform base veneered in thuya wood, acanthus-carved scroll terminals to an egg and dart molding, the carved winged tulip and paw feet with sunken casters, attributed to Ralph Turnbull, Kinston, Jamaica.

The fact that this piece is West Indian makes it more interesting than other colonial furniture from, say, China or India.

52.5in (133cm)

$35,000-40,000   **WW**

This piece has an unusual veneer on the top.

The stem is beautifully turned, adding to its value

A Regency small center table, the circular tilt-top with painted scagliola pastoral scene within a border of laburnum veneer and a gadroon edge, the triform stem veneered in rosewood with molded corners to scroll-leaf terminals, a gadroon molding to the base, on leaf-carved scroll-ribbed feet on brass casters, stamped "C Hope patent".

34in (86cm) dia

$20,000-25,000   **WW**

A Scottish Regency pollard elm center table, the top with lappet moldings and shallow frieze with bead-and-reel molding raised on fluted column with saucer plinth, the circular base with corresponding lappet molding and three projecting spars with scroll feet and casters, possibly by William Trotter.

This table displays various particular characteristics of William Trotter, notably the common sunken bead-and-reel molding to the frieze, a variety of Grecian molding to the rim, and particularly the scroll feet. The latter in particular can be compared with the scroll feet used on the magnificent circular table in the Signet Library, Edinburgh, supplied by Trotter in 1820 for the Faculty of Advocates.

29.5in (75cm) high

$10,000-12,000   **L&T**

A Scottish Regency pollard elm center table, the segmental-veneered and banded circular top with central panel above faceted baluster column and concave triform base with bun feet, one replaced.

52.75in (134cm) dia

$12,000-14,000   **L&T**

An early Victorian walnut octagonal center table, the tilt-top with satinwood panel, elaborate marquetry and specimen wood decoration, on triangular pedestal with carved columns and strapwork decoration on tripod base.

48.5in (123cm) wide

$15,000-18,000   **L&T**

▶ An early Victorian rosewood and parquetry inlaid center table, the rectangular top inlaid with a panel of exotic specimen woods enclosed within a coromandel border, the parquetry frieze above profusely scrolling supports on a trestle base with leaf-carved cabriole legs, linked by twin-turned stretchers and raised on bun feet.

29in (74cm) high

$3,000-4,000   **L&T**

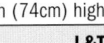

A William IV mahogany center table, the circular tilt-top with burr-oak banding raised on reeded and turned pedestal and concave quadriform base with bead and reel molding and carved paw feet with casters.

28.75in (73cm) high

$6,000-7,000   **L&T**

A 19thC Anglo-Indian mahogany center table, the serpentine-sided rectangular top with ribbon-tied reeded edge, raised on leaf-carved baluster pedestal with four molded cabriole legs terminating in paw feet.

28.75in (73cm) high

$5,000-6,000   **L&T**

A 19thC colonial center table, the circular tilt-top with radiating segmental veneering centered by sunburst, coromandel crossbanding and deep rosewood crossbanded edge, raised on spirally carved and stylized leaf-clasped column with concave crossbanded triform base, with turned roundels and paw feet with casters.

49in (125cm) dia

$4,000-5,000   **L&T**

A Victorian coromandel and mahogany center table, the lobed top with burr-walnut crossbanding and molded edge above shallow frieze, raised on bulbous reeded pedestal and four molded cabriole legs with scroll toes and casters.

58.25in (148cm) wide

$4,000-5,000   **L&T**

Tables

A Victorian rosewood center table, with rounded rectangular top and twin column end standards, on trestle feet.

45in (114.5cm) wide

$350-450   GorL

A Victorian Louis XV-style marquetry center table, of serpentine form, with gilt-brass mounts, the shaped top above shaped apron with frieze drawer to one side, on cabriole legs with female mask mounts and sabots.

53in (135cm) wide

$7,500-8,500   L&T

◀ A late 19thC shaped rosewood floral marquetry center table, with oval serpentine top with central floral marquetry sprays within cartouche, serpentine walnut frieze and ebonized scroll border with bird and flower panels, over-shaped frieze drawer and sides on cabriole legs with gilt-metal female caryatid figures, cast feet and cast-metal mounts.

60in (152cm) wide

$9,000-11,000   L&T

A late 19thC French drop-flap center table, the shaped top profusely inlaid with amboyna and exotic woods, on an ebony groundwork with an ormolu molded edge, the base with a single drawer and grotesque mask mounts, on turned tapered legs united by wavy stretchers centered by an ormolu urn.

42in (107cm) wide

$1,500-1,800   HamG

A late 19thC Irish mahogany Chippendale-style center table, the rectangular top with rounded angles and molded edge above deep shaped frieze centered by shells to each side, raised on four shell-carved cabriole legs with claw-and-ball feet.

64.25in (163cm) wide

$6,000-7,000   L&T

An Edwardian plum pudding mahogany center table, the quarter veneered top with gilt-metal rope-twist border with applied cherubs masks and husk swags all on slender legs, turned feet, linked by a cross-stretcher, by Morison & Company, Edinburgh, stamped.

31.25in (79.5cm) dia

$5,000-6,000   L&T

An Edwardian mahogany circular center table, with pierced frieze, raised on multi-triple column legs to the platform under-stage.

36in (91.5cm) wide

$400-450   GorB

▶ A Scottish Regency rosewood console table, the rectangular top with bead-and-reel molded edge and corresponding shelf with mirror back above frieze drawer centered by rosette tablet, raised on leaf-carved truss legs and concave plinth base.

45.5in (116cm) high

$7,500-8,500   L&T

▶ A mid-to late 18thC Italian Rococo giltwood marble-top console table, the shaped rectangular and molded Egyptian marble top with serpentine front and sides, the shaped and pierced conforming frieze raised on canted, double C-scroll legs with scroll feet joined by a C-scroll cross-stretcher, carved throughout with coquillage, feuillage and flowerheads.

37.5in (95.5cm) wide

$6,000-7,000   SI

A Scottish Regency stained oak lobby table, the later rectangular mahogany top with ledge back above ogee frieze, raised on two flat-paneled consoles with scroll toes on bun feet.

33.85in (86cm) wide

$750-850   L&T

◀ An early Victorian mahogany console table, the rectangular top with leaf-carved reeded edge above ogee frieze, on leaf-carved scrolling supports with rear pilasters, on shaped plinth with bun feet.

40.25in (102cm) wide

$3,500-4,000   L&T

Tables

A pair of American Classical stencil-decorated figured mahogany marble top pier tables, the rectangular marble tops above a stencil-decorated frieze supported by marble columns with gilt mountings, centering a rectangular mirror; all on a shaped base with stencil decoration and lobed feet, new glass and marble tops possibly replaced.

c1820   35.7in (90.5cm)

$25,000-35,000   **FRE**

A pair of Regency Revival gilt console tables, the inverted composite marble tops with panel friezes, ebonized anthemion motifs, on ebonized and gilt lion monopodia supports, paneled back supports, the incurved bases decorated to simulate marble.

42.75in (109cm) high

$9,000-11,000   **WW**

An Italian-style giltwood console table, the rectangular marble top above molded leaf-carved frieze raised on auricular C-scrolled supports joined by similar X-stretcher with central pedestal.

50in (127cm) wide

$3,000-4,000   **L&T**

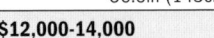

A George III mahogany breakfast table, the rounded rectangular snap-top with coromandel crossbanding, raised on ring-turned baluster column and four sabre legs with brass lion's paw feet.

56.5in (143cm) wide

$12,000-14,000   **L&T**

A Regency mahogany breakfast table, with brass inlay, the rectangular top with rounded corners and a veneered frieze, the pineapple cup and turned stem on a quatreform platform with splay legs and brass sabots and caster.

55in (140cm) wide

$3,000-4,000   **WW**

An over-painted giltwood rococo-style console table, the marble serpentined top raised on fluted carved scrolling frame, with cabriole legs joined by pierced strapwork stretcher.

48in (122cm) wide

$2,200-2,800   **L&T**

A mahogany breakfast table, the banded rectangular altered top with bowed ends, on a Regency base with ribbed and petal-carved stem with a gadroon collar, the quatreform base on paw feet on casters.

67in (170cm) wide

$2,200-2,800   **WW**

► A Scottish Regency mahogany breakfast table, the rectangular drop-leaf top with molded edge above frieze drawer and turned and reeded tapering leg with brass caps and casters, bears label to drawer, by James Mein of Kelso.

46.75in (119cm) wide

$3,000-4,000   **L&T**

A Regency mahogany and burr-elm inlaid breakfast table, with boxwood and ebony stringing, the rectangular top with rounded angles above a plain frieze with beaded edging, raised above a turned and reeded column and quadreform base on molded sabre legs with turned knees, terminating in brass paw caps and casters.

58.25in (148cm) wide

$7,000-8,000   **L&T**

► A French Louis Philippe walnut demi-lune fold-over breakfast table, with hinged flush-paneled top, molded frieze and baluster-turned legs.

30in (76cm) high

$1,400-2,000   **SI**

◄ A William IV rosewood circular breakfast table, over column with applied leaf-carving on platform base with four scroll-under feet.

52in (132cm) dia

$3,000-4,000   **L&T**

Tables

A rectangular mahogany breakfast table, the tilt-top with rounded angles and reeded edge raised on beehive pedestal and four shaped reeded sabre legs with brass paw caps and casters.

60in (152cm) wide

$2,200-2,800   **L&T**

An American Federal walnut drop-leaf table, the rectangular top with rounded inset corners, the frieze with a drawer, on square section tapering legs, secondary woods white pine and poplar.

c1800   39.25in (99.5cm) wide

$1,500-2,000   **SI**

A George III mahogany triangular-topped drop-leaf table, on pole-turned tapered legs ending in pad feet, with later top.

28in (71cm) wide

$450-550   **GorL**

An Irish George III mahogany wake table, the oval drop-leaf top raised on six square section legs with beaded angles.

82.5in (210cm) long

$10,000-12,000   **L&T**

A George III mahogany drop-leaf table, the oval top with chamfered edge supported on four club legs with pad feet.

35.5in (90cm) wide

$1,500-2,000   **L&T**

A large George III mahogany drop-leaf table, the oval top with chamfered edge supported on six club legs with pad feet.

49in (124cm) wide

$15,000-18,000   **L&T**

An Edwardian mahogany and satinwood-banded Sutherland table, with canted corners on pierced end standards.

27in (68.5cm) wide

$300-350   **GorL**

A large 17thC oak refectory table, the rectangular-planked top above a stop-fluted frieze on turned and blocked supports linked by stretchers.

109in (277cm) long

$4,500-5,500   **L&T**

A 17thC oak refectory table, the rectangular-planked top above a plain frieze on ring-turned and blocked supports linked by lower stretchers.

80in (203cm) long

$3,000-4,000   **L&T**

A late 17thC oak refectory table, the later cleated top above plain frieze rails with shaped corner brackets standing on bottle-turned legs united by peripheral stretchers.

92in (234cm) long

$1,500-2,000   **HamG**

An 18thC oak oval gateleg table, with one drawer and turned legs, on bun feet.

51.25in (130cm) wide

$600-700   **DN**

▶ A George III mahogany D-end dining table, with drop-leaf center section, and plain frieze and square section tapering legs.

(extended) 111.5in (283cm) long

$4,500-5,500   **L&T**

A George III Gillows-style mahogany D-end dining table, with central gateleg table, the molded top over beaded frieze on turned reeded and tapering legs, with two drop leaves and two further leaves.

157.5in (400cm) long extended

$12,000-15,000   **L&T**

Tables

An American Classical two-part carved walnut dining table, each section having a rectangular top with rounded corners and a hinged leaf over a frieze with acanthus-carved tablets at center and at corners, on tapering ring and spirally turned legs on ball feet.

c1825   47in (119.5cm) wide

$3,000-4,000   **SI**

An early 19thC country Federal walnut drop-leaf table, the oblong top with molded edge and D-shaped leaves above eight square section legs and plain frieze.
The table was called a "coffin" table by the owners in that its substantial proportions could hold a casket.

88.5in (225cm) long

$4,000-6,000   **SI**

A Federal mahogany extending dining table in two parts, probably Baltimore, MD, the rectangular top with rounded corners and a reeded edge, the molded conforming frieze raised on ring-turned and reeded legs, each part with a drop-leaf.

85.5in (217cm) long

$10,000-14,000   **SI**

▶ An early 19thC Federal mahogany two-part dining table, Southern states, each with demi-lune top with rectangular leaf above a conforming frieze with molded edge and three molded square section legs.

45in (114.5cm) wide

$4,000-6,000

▶ An Empire low center table, having a circulate rope-carved top on a floral carved and glided pedestal with claw-caved feet.

41in (35.5cm) dia

$2,000-3,000   **FRE**

A Classical carved and brass-inlaid mahogany and mahogany veneer drop-leaf dining table, rectangular top with double elliptical leaves above a beaded and brass-bound apron with drawer at one end and inlaid corner blocks with pendants over ring-turned pedestal on arched knees with brass stringing continuing to reeded legs ending in paw feet on brass casters (losses, surface scratches).

c1825   56in (142cm) wide

$2,000-3,000   **SI**

A Federal carved mahogany drop-leaf breakfast table, the rectangular top with rounded corners and reeded edges, the frieze with a drawer, the reeded baluster-form standard with leaf-capped downswept legs.

46.75in (119cm) long

$4,500-6,500   **SI**

A pair of early 19thC D-end tables, the plain frieze above square block-tapered supports.

60in (152.5cm) wide

$1,000-1,300   **BW**

An early 19thC mahogany pedestal dining table, comprising pair of tripod pedestal ends with turned pillar and square section sabre legs with brass caps and casters and central double-gate leg section with ring-turned legs with brass caps and casters, and three leaves, the top with rounded angles and reeded edge.

28.25in (72cm) high

$6,000-7,000   **L&T**

▶ A Regency mahogany metamorphic dumb waiter, the rectangular top with rounded angles and molded edge, raised on paneled trestles joined by turned stretcher, on sled bases with roundel terminals and bun feet with casters, the three-part top lifting and falling to give three tiers.

48in (122cm) wide

$3,000-4,000   **L&T**

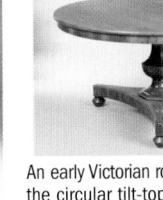

An early Victorian rosewood loo table, the circular tilt-top with plain frieze raised on octagonal baluster pedestal.

8.75in (73cm) high

$4,500-5,500   **L&T**

Tables

A 19thC mahogany telescopic pedestal dining table, the molded D-end top over deeply carved and turned divided baluster column on four scrolling carved legs with casters.

123in (312cm) long

$7,500-8,500   L&T

A Victorian inlaid figured walnut oval snap-top loo table, having four tapered turned pillars with central finial and four carved scroll supports with claw terminals with casters.

46in (117cm) dia

$900-1,100   Clv

A large Victorian oak and bur-walnut banded extending dining table, including eight leaves, the rectangular top with rounded angles above a fluted frieze with applied divided rosettes, with carved bracket supports raised above eight turned and tapering legs carved with lion-head grotesques and scrolling.

217in (553cm) long (extended)

$12,000-15,000   L&T

A late 19thC satinwood table, the walnut, kingwood and tulipwood banding incorporating a bullrush border over a shaped column and an ogee platform base with scrollunder feet, hinges stamped "HS".

52in (132cm) long

$7,500-9,500   L&T

An Edwardian George II-style mahogany telescopic dining table, with two leaves, the rectangular top with ribbon molding above deep frieze with carved border raised on cabriole legs with claw-and-ball feet.

118in (300cm) long

$4,500-5,500   L&T

An early 20thC large mahogany dining table, the mahogany rectangular top with rounded angles and molded edge, above molded crossbanded frieze, supported by carved cabriole legs with pad feet and casters to each corner, and four further similar central legs, the six later leaves, each with full frieze, by Whytock and Reid, Edinburgh.

228in (579cm) long

$9,000-11,000   L&T

An Elizabethan-style oak refectory table, the top with draw leaves to each end above anthemion frieze and carved bulbous cup and cover legs joined by stretcher.

143in (363cm) long fully extended

$2,200-2,800   L&T

A Regency-style two-pillar mahogany dining table, with molded edge and rounded angles raised on turned pedestals with molded tripod sabre legs, brass paw caps and casters, with two leaves.

64in (163cm) long

$4,500-5,500   L&T

A Jacobean-style carved oak refectory table, the rectangular top with gadroon molding, the frieze with a drawer at each end, the baluster-turned legs with a box stretcher, profusely carved with foliate arabesques.

31.5in (80cm) high

$3,000-4,000   SI

A Regency-style inlaid mahogany extending dining table, the top with slightly rounded ends and a satinwood crossbanded border, each pedestal on a tripod base with downswept molded legs, lion paw caps and casters, one leaf.

96in (244cm) long

$3,000-4,000   SI

A George I mahogany fold-over tea/games table, the hinged, molded rectangular top over an arched frieze with a central pendant, the cabriole legs with pointed pad feet.

28.75in (73cm) high

$2,200-2,800   SI

A mahogany tea table, the hinged top above a frieze drawer on turned tapering legs, with pad feet, in part 18thC, but adapted.

35in (89cm) wide

$1,200-1,600   DN

A small George III mahogany tea table, the rectangular flame-figured folding top over a plain frieze with painted chamfered square legs.

29in (74cm) wide

$800-900   **HamG**

A late George III mahogany tea table, the demi-lune shaped folding top with tulipwood banding above a plain frieze supported on tapered legs.

29.5in (75cm) high

$1,000-1,300   **HamG**

A George III oak tea table, with circular tilt-top and cannon-barrel stem on cabriole tripod.

31in (79cm) dia

$500-600   **GorL**

A George III mahogany circular tilt-top tea table, with "bird cage" and reduced wrythen-carved pillar and tripod cabriole base.

26in (66cm) wide

$450-550   **GorB**

A George III mahogany drop-leaf supper table, raised on chamfered supports linked by concave plateau.

29.25in (74cm) wide

$300-400   **GorB**

A Scottish George III mahogany demi-lune tea table, with boxwood stringing, the fold-over top above frieze drawer on square section tapering legs and spade feet.

37in (94cm) wide

$1,200-1,400   **L&T**

A George III mahogany and boxwood strung fold-over tea table, the stepped D-shaped hinged top above a single drawer flanked by parrot inlaid patera and paneled sides, the whole raised on square section tapering legs terminating in brass caps and casters.

44.5in (113cm) wide

$1,500-2,000   **L&T**

A Regency rosewood fold-over tea table, the hinged top opening to reveal a baize-lined interior, above beaded rim and paneled sides raised on a tapering faceted column with gadrooned collar on quadruped base with reeded sabre legs, brass paw caps and casters.

36.5in (92.5cm) wide

$3,000-4,000   **L&T**

An early 19thC Continental mahogany and rosewood crossbanded tea table, with a hinged folding top and two hinged legs, a later frieze drawer, on reeded and ring-turned legs headed by roundels.

38in (96.5cm) wide

$1,500-2,000   **DN**

A Regency rosewood fold-over tea table, with boxwood and ebony stringing, the rounded rectangular top with satin-birch banding, above a frieze inlaid to all sides with drawer to one end, on canted square column and quadriform base, with sabre legs terminating in brass caps and casters.

41in (104cm) wide

$4,000-5,000   **L&T**

A Scottish late Regency mahogany fold-over tea table, the rosewood crossbanded top with beaded edge over turned and gadrooned column on quadruped base with sabre legs and brass lion paw caps and casters.

38.5in (98cm) wide

$4,500-5,500   **L&T**

▶ A Regency mahogany fold-over tea table, the rectangular top with reeded edge and rounded angles above plain frieze, raised on turned pedestal and four reeded sabre legs with carved paw feet and casters.

29.5in (75cm) high

$2,200-2,800   **L&T**

Tables

An American late Queen Anne mahogany tea table, the rectangular top with cyma-recta-molded edges and re-entrant corners, the shaped frieze with a molded drawer, the molded cabriole legs terminating below in voluted trifid feet, secondary wood and white pine.

c1740-50   36in (91.5cm) wide

$4,000-5,000   **SI**

A Louis XV-style mahogany, rosewood and kingwood tea table, the quarter veneered top with shell and floral marquetry decoration and gilt-metal mounts, the square top with serpentine-shaped drop leaves to each side, on square section cabriole legs with sabot.

37.5in (95cm) wide (extended)

$2,200-2,800   **L&T**

An Italian burr-walnut fold-over tea table, the shaped top above plain frieze and shaped apron on square section cabriole legs.

31in (79cm) high

$2,200-2,800   **L&T**

A George III mahogany snap-top supper table, the lobed circular top with central dish surrounded by eight smaller dishes with flowerheads and reeded fans to the spaces, raised on birdcage and spirally reeded and knopped pedestal with three carved cabriole legs terminating in claw-and-ball feet.

32in (81cm) dia

$10,000-12,000   **L&T**

A George III mahogany snap-top supper table, on central vase-shaped pillar and triple scroll supports.

33in (83.5cm) reduced

$750-950   **Clv**

An American Renaissance Revival carved walnut library table, with molded top and and Greek key inlaid border, twin supports below with carved griffins on a fitted base. **Provenance:** From Oaks Cloister, home of Joseph M Huston.

c1880-1890   71in (180cm) wide

$50,000-70,000   **FRE**

A William IV mahogany library table, the rounded rectangular leathered top over single drawer on carved trestle supports and sledge base with turned and fluted ball feet and brass casters.

49.25in (125cm) dia

$4,500-5,500   **L&T**

A 19th C walnut library table, the molded top on trestle supports with pierced decoration with sledge bases and barley-twist stretcher.

47.75in (121cm) wide

$2,200-2,800   **L&T**

A pair of late 19thC Italian Renaissance-style carved walnut intarsia library tables, the tops with geometric strapwork in walnut, ebony and bone, the pierced end supports carved as be-swagged, stallion-form monopodia.

Provenance: *The Society of the Cincinnati*

28in (71cm) wide

$6,000-7,000   **SI**

A 19thC French kingwood and marquetry occasional table, the shaped rectangular crossbanded top with gilt-metal rim inlaid with scrolling foliage above frieze drawer, raised on slender cabriole legs.

24.5in (62cm) wide

$1,500-2,000   **Chef**

Tables

A Victorian rosewood occasional table, the square tilt-top raised on Chippendale-style mahogany base, the stop-fluted pedestal with leaf-carved knop and similar cabriole legs with claw-and-ball feet.

8.25in (72cm) high

$1,000-1,400   **L&T**

An Edwardian circular-shaped topped mahogany two-tier occasional table, on slender cabriole legs.

34in (86.5cm) dia

$250-350   **GorL**

An Edwardian mahogany, satinwood-banded and floral marquetry inlaid occasional table, on square-tapered supports with shaped uniting stretchers.

26in (66cm) dia

$1,000-1,300   **GorL**

An Edwardian rosewood-banded and bat's wing inlaid occasional table, on square-tapered legs and X-uniting platform.

32in (81.5cm) wide

$600-800   **GorL**

A Federal inlaid mahogany New York Pembroke table, the rectangular top having shaped drop-leaves with ovolu corners above a single inlaid drawer flanked by inlaid paterae above square-tapered legs inlaid with bellflowers and lines ending in cuffs.

c1800   20in (50cm) wide

$10,000-15,000   **FRE**

A Sheraton faded mahogany Pembroke table, with a frieze drawer and dummy drawer, the turned stem on four splay legs with brass sabots on casters, trade label for Druce & Co, Baker St, London W, repaired.

32in (81cm) high

$1,000-1,300   **WW**

A George III mahogany Pembroke table, with boxwood and ebony stringing, the oval crossbanded top with matched veneers above crossbanded frieze drawer and opposing dummy raised on butterfly-molded square section tapering legs with brass caps and casters.

45.5in (116cm)

$7,500-8,500   **L&T**

A Regency mahogany pembroke table, the crossbanded top with rounded angles above frieze drawer and dummy, raised on turned and reeded tapering legs with brass caps and casters.

$1,200-1,500   **L&T**

A George IV mahogany Pembroke table, with two rounded flaps of real and dummy drawers on square-tapered legs, with fitted brass casters.

20in (51cm) wide

$1,500-2,000   **GorL**

A George IV mahogany and ebony strung Pembroke table, the top with shaped corners above a drawer opposing a false drawer with lion mask handles, on turned column and four reeded splayed legs with brass terminals and casters.

44in (111.5cm) wide

$900-1,100   **DN**

Tables

A Regency mahogany, boxwood and ebony strung sofa table, the crossbanded rectangular top with tulipwood banding, above two drawers opposing two false drawers on end supports with a high stretcher and splayed legs with brass paw feet and casters, some damage.

58.75in (149.5cm) wide expended

$3,000-4,000   **DN**

A Scottish Regency William Trotter-style rosewood sofa table, the rectangular top with rounded angles above two frieze drawers with bead-and-reel molding, opposing dummy drawers raised above four scrolling supports with applied rosette terminals on quadriform base with square legs, terminating in oak leaf-cast brass caps and casters.

open 63.5in (161.5cm) wide

$10,000-12,000   **L&T**

A 19thC nest of four satinwood tables, with ebony stringing and beaded rim, each with rectangular crossbanded top with paired ring-turned trestle supports on down-scrolled sled bases.

27.25in (69cm) high

$5,500-6,500   **L&T**

An American Federal mahogany drop end sofa table, probably Baltimore, having a rectangular top and D-shaped drop ends with double-reeded edge, two cockbeaded apron drawers on two flat pinched pedestals with fluted cabriole legs, brass caps and casters.

c1810   59in (150cm) wide

$4,000-4,500   **FRE**

A George IV mahogany, ebony and boxwood strung sofa table, the rosewood crossbanded top with rounded corners above two frieze drawers opposing two false drawers, with gilt-brass handles on turned end supports and stretcher, and splayed legs with brass paw feet and casters.

23.75in (162cm) wide

$4,500-5,500   **DN**

A 19thC mahogany sofa table, the rectangular top with rounded angels and reeded edge above a pair of frieze drawers opposing false drawers on pierced leaf-carved lyre supports and reeded sabre legs joined by carved and reeded stretchers.

56in (142cm) wide (open)

$7,500-8,500   **L&T**

▶ A late Regency nest of three rosewood crossbanded tables, each with turned trestle supports with scrolling feet and turned intersecting stretchers.

15.5in (39cm) wide

$2,200-2,800   **L&T**

A Regency mahogany sofa table, the rectangular top with rounded drop-flat ends and purplewood banding above frieze with opposing drawers, raised on scrolled trestle supports with turned roundels joined by turned stretcher, on sabre legs with brass caps and casters.

57in (145cm) wide

$4,000-4,500   **L&T**

A late Regency mahogany sofa table, the drop-flap top crossbanded in partridge wood, above a pair of opposing frieze drawers with later brass handles, the trestle end supports with a pair of high knee-swept legs decorated with inlaid arrows, united by a later turned stretcher, possibly later.

54in (137cm) wide

$3,000-4,000   **HamG**

An Edwardian nest of three mahogany tables, with sunburst pattern and checkered banding.

19in (48cm) wide

$1,500-2,000   **L&T**

Tables

A nest of four Edwardian mahogany occasional tables, the rectangular tops with fine banding, on ring-turned twin-end supports with stretchers and splay feet. largest

19in (48cm) wide

$1,800-2,200   **WW**

A nest of four occasional tables, the papier-mâché tops painted with flowers to a golden ground, on gilt-sprayed turned wood twin-end supports with stretchers, on splay scroll feet. largest

21.5in (54.5cm) high

$600-700   **WW**

A nest of three rosewood tables, each with cockbeaded rectangular top, ring-turned legs with sled feet and broad stretcher to rear.

28.75in (73cm) high

$4,000-5,000   **L&T**

A 17thC Dutch oak side table, the top with shaped edge and thumbnail molding, above single drawer and shaped apron, raised on turned and tapering faceted supports, linked by wavy X-stretchers on turned feet, replacements and restorations.

39.75in (101cm) wide

$4,000-5,000   **L&T**

A 17thC oak side table, the rectangular-planked top above a single drawer on bobbin-turned and blocked legs linked by similar stretchers on turned feet, some restoration.

27in (69cm) high

$3,000-4,000   **L&T**

An early George II mahogany fold-over side table, the rectangular top with ovolo edge above single drawer on square section tapering legs with cusped panels and ogee block feet and casters.

30in (76cm wide)

$2,200-2,800   **L&T**

A George II-style side table, in the style of William Kent, stained a dark mahogany color with rectangular verde antico marble top, the base with egg and dart cornice above Vitruvian scroll frieze with central foliate mask issuing suspended cornucopiae swags, raised on four bold acanthus-carved cabriole front legs with paw feet and drapery swags and flat rear legs with corresponding paw feet.

84.25in (214cm) wide

$30,000-40,000   **L&T**

A George II mahogany side table, the top with rounded angles, above a single frieze drawer raised on cabriole legs with lappet-clasped knees and terminating in pad feet.

33in (84cm) wide

$4,000-5,000   **L&T**

An George II Irish mahogany side table, the later marble top with molded edge above frieze with shaped apron, centered with shell molding, the whole raised on cabriole legs with acanthus-carved knees and terminating in shaped and molded pad feet, wooden casters.

50.75in (129cm) wide

$40,000-50,000   **L&T**

A Louis XV French fruitwood small table, the serpentine-shaped gray marble top with a raised gallery, floral marquetry sides and a frieze drawer, on slender cabriole legs with a shelf, damage to marble, the legs retipped.

28in (71.5cm) high

$5,000-6,000   **DN**

Tables

A George III table, with serpentine front and marquetry top.

c1780   12.5in (32cm) wide

$4,000-5,000   **CdK**

A George III mahogany side table, the shaped serpentine top with molded edge above deep frieze with drawers to each side and lambrequin molding, raised on French cabriole legs.

63.5in (161cm) wide

$4,500-5,500   **L&T**

▶ One of a pair of George III Pierre Langlois-style oval tables, each crossbanded in kingwood and decorated in parquetry with a trellis and flower design on a sycamore ground, with a mahogany central oval panel and a marquetry spray of flowers with a ribbon, with conforming shaped parquetry frieze on slender cabriole legs with pendant garrya marquetry, some restoration.

65.5cm wide

$20,000-25,000 (pair)   **DN**

A William and Mary yew-wood side table, the molded rectangular top over a molded frieze incorporating a drawer, the bobbin-turned legs with compressed bun feet joined by a wavy cross stretcher.

28.25in (86cm) wide

$3,000-4,000   **SI**

A George III mahogany and satinwood demi-lune sidetable, the fan-inlaid crossbanded top inlaid with yew-wood and harewood, above a plain frieze raised on square section tapering legs with boxwood angles and collared feet.

Provenance: *Bonython Maner, Cornwall.*

32.5in (83cm) high

$3,000-4,000   **L&T**

An early 19thC laburnum table, the planked top with rounded angles raised on square section tapering legs joined by H-stretchers.

Provenance: *Woodcote, Rhu*

24in (61cm) wide

$600-800   **L&T**

A Regency banded mahogany side table, with one fitted long drawer on rectangular end standards.

24in (61cm) wide

$750-850   **GorL**

A Regency Gillows-style mahogany side table, the top with molded edge above two frieze drawers on turned and reeded legs with brass caps and casters.

48in (122cm) wide

$2,200-2,800   **L&T**

A Regency mahogany and boxwood line-inlaid side table, fitted one long drawer, on square-tapered legs.

31in (79cm) wide

$500-600   **GorB**

▶ A George IV mahogany side table, the rectangular top with quadrant angles and stepped front above deep fluted frieze with paneled tablets to the center and above the bold reeded and turned tapering legs.

78in (199cm) wide

$7,500-8,500   **L&T**

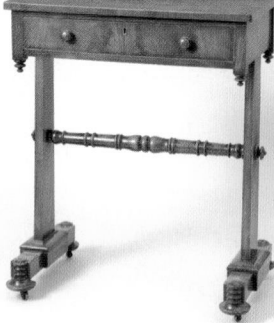

A pair of Scottish Regency pollard oak side tables, attributed to William Trotter, each top with banded and paneled veneers and egg-and-dart molding to the edge, above three frieze drawers with sunk bead and reel panels, the projecting canted front legs of scrolling truss form carved with palmette and anthemion motifs with reeded scroll toes, rectangular section paneled rear legs, extended to the back and the rear legs possibly later.

These tables use the "truss" leg commonly identified with William Trotter, and a Grecian molding to the edge of the rim. The form used here bears close comparison with that used on the circular center table in the Lower Signet Library, Edinburgh, as well as on the tables at Paxton House in particular.

76in (193cm) wide

$40,000-45,000   **L&T**

Tables

An early Victorian rosewood lamp table, the veneered rectangular top with a frieze on open scroll-end supports, with a roundel, a turned and petal-carved stretcher, the plinth on splay feet.

22in (56cm) wide

$2,000-2,500 **WW**

A late 19thC inlaid rosewood two-tier corner table, with foliate decoration on two ring-turned supports.

26.75in (68cm) wide

$500-600 **Clv**

A 19thC painted sidetable, the rectangular top with green-painted ground work and floral swag decoration, above a single drawer standing on tapered legs, profusely decorated.

31in (79cm) wide

$1,200-1,600 **HamG**

A Victorian burr-walnut oval Sutherland table, the quarter veneered top over twin-carved baluster uprights issuing well-carved cabriole supports with ceramic casters, with turned stretcher and single swing-action to each side.

36in (91cm) wide

$700-800 **BAR**

A 19thC George III-style over-painted mahogany side table, the scagliola top with molded edge above carved fluted frieze with foliate medallions heading the husk-paneled tapering legs with acanthus-scrolled tops and molded feet, with similar side returns and rear legs.

72in (183cm) wide

$12,000-15,000 **L&T**

A late 19thC mahogany side table, the top with molded edge above a frieze drawer, with brass handles on square tapering legs.

32.25in (82cm) wide

$500-600 **DN**

A late 19thC French Louis XIV-style carved giltwood marble-top center table, the molded frieze carved with guilloches and palmettes.

Provenance: *The Society of the Cincinnati*

27in (68.5cm) wide

$7,500-8,500 **SI**

A late Victorian Sutherland table, with japanned top and turned legs.

1890-1900   22in (56cm) wide

$300-350 **CdK**

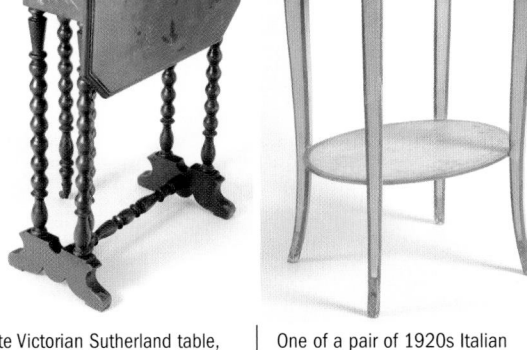

One of a pair of 1920s Italian painted bedside tables.

25.5in (65cm) high

$1,000-1,300 (pair) **SS**

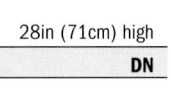

A walnut side table, the top with yew oyster-veneers and boxwood stringing in the form of two bees, above a frieze drawer on shell-carved cabriole legs and scrolled pad feet.

42.5in (108cm) wide

$1,400-1,800 **DN**

► A Continental fruitwood small table, the scagliola inset top with raised border and a frieze drawer on slender cabriole legs.

28in (71cm) high

$1,400-1,800 **DN**

A George II mahogany kettle stand, the octagonal top with solid gadrooned gallery raised on spirally fluted knopped pedestal and tripod base, with acanthus-carved cabriole legs terminating in claw-and-ball feet.

24in (61cm) high

$18,000-22,000	L&T

An early George III mahogany tripod table, the circular single plank top above a birdcage block and a wrythen-carved baluster stem, raised on shaped swept legs profusely carved on the knee with acanthus and garrya husk decoration, terminating in pad feet.

28.25in (72cm) high

$2,000-2,500	HamG

A George III mahogany circular tilt-top wine table, on baluster-turned pillar and carved cabriole base with pad feet.

19in (49cm) wide

$1,000-1,300	GorL

A George II mahogany kettle stand, the circular top with brass-lined spindle gallery, above a fluted column with leaf-carved baluster knop on a tripod base with cabriole legs termintaing in claw-and-ball feet and carved to the knees with leafy cartouches.

23in (58.5cm) high

$35,000-45,000	L&T

An early George III mahogany tripod table, the figured circular top above a birdcage block, with a baluster-turned stem, supported on three swept legs.

21in (53.25cm) dia

$2,000-3,000	HamG

A Victorian mahogany-topped wine table, on slender turned pillar and tripod platform base.

20in (51cm) dia

$300-400	GorL

A mid-18thC oak tripod table, the two-part circular top with primitive tilt mechanism, supported on a gun barrel stem with three diminutive swept legs, repairs and restorations.

19in (48cm) dia

$600-800	HamG

A George III mahogany tripod table, the circular crossbanded top over a baluster-shaped stem on three swept legs, repairs and restorations,

30in (77cm) dia

$700-800	HamG

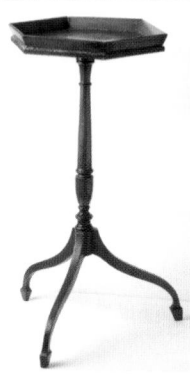

A George III mahogany tripod table, the hexagonal-galleried top raised on a slender vase-shaped column and umbrella tripod base with spade feet, restored.

31in (78.5cm) wide

$700-800	BonS

A CLOSER LOOK AT A TILT-TOP TABLE

The dished top is a sure sign of a sophisticated table. This was achieved by carving away a solid board of wood to create a neat raised edge.

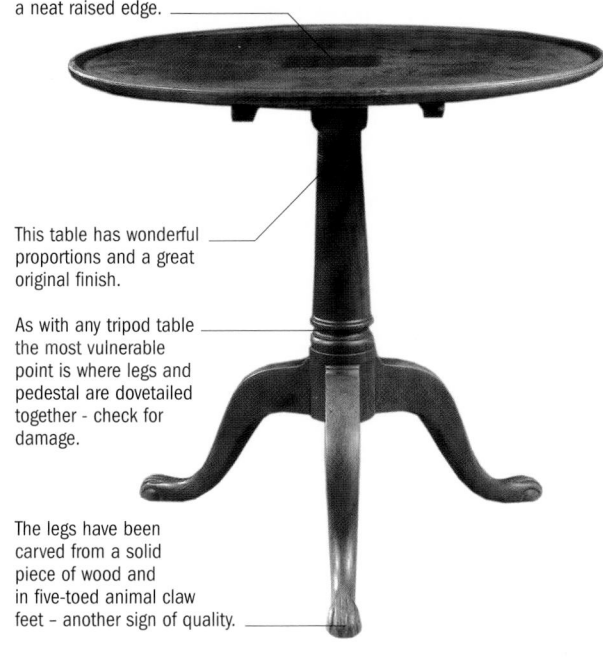

This table has wonderful proportions and a great original finish.

As with any tripod table the most vulnerable point is where legs and pedestal are dovetailed together - check for damage.

The legs have been carved from a solid piece of wood and in five-toed animal claw feet – another sign of quality.

A Chippendale carved mahogany tilt-top tea table, Newport, Rhode Island, the circular dished top of one solid board, hinged on a fixed block supported by a ring-turned standard on downswept legs ending in five-toed animal claw feet, bleached finish, tiny patch to top.

c1760	31.5in (80cm) wide
$25,000-30,000	**FRE**

A Delaware Valley mahogany Queen Anne candlestand, a circular tilting dish-molded top, birdcage tilting and revolving mechanism, turned pedestal with beaded suppressed ball base, cabriole legs, snakehead feet.

$8,000-10,000	**FRE**

A Federal mahogany rectangular candle stand, New England, the rectangular top with urn-form standard on three cabriole legs ending in slipper feet.

c1800	26in (66cm) high
$1,500-2,500	**SI**

A Chippendale tilt-top tea table, the circular tilting top on a fluted columnar shaft with urn standard on peaked downswept legs ending in snake feet.

c1780	32in (81.5cm) dia
$4,000-5,000	**FRE**

A Federal mahogany candlestand, square top with shaped corners above an urn-form standard and cabriole legs ending in snake feet.

c1800	26.75in (68cm) high
$3,000-4,000	**SI**

A first quarter 19thC Federal birch tripod candlestand, rectangular top with shaped corners, baluster-turned supports on arched legs.

28in (71cm) high

$600-800	**SI**

A early 19thC Federal maple candle stand, circular top above urn-form standard on arched legs ending in snake feet (cracked top, old repairs).

25.25in (64cm) high

$700-1,000	**SI**

▶ An 18thC cherrywood tea table, circular dish top, birdcage tilting and revolving mechanism on fluted pedestal on leaf-and-vine-carved cabriole legs, claw-and-ball feet, one foot repaired.

30.25in (76.5cm) wide

$3,500-4,500	**FRE**

Tables

A Georgian mahogany wine table, the tilt-top with thumbnail rim raised on carved and turned pedestal and three cabochon-carved cabriole legs terminating in pad and claw feet.

16.25in (41cm) dia

$3,000-4,000	**L&T**

A Regency satinwood-banded rosewood work table, with canted angles and hinged top, on turned column and tripod base.

16in (40.5cm) wide

$600-800	**GorL**

A William IV mahogany table, the round tilt-top inlaid with a rosewood and satinwood star, on an octagonal column, the triform base with scroll feet.

24in (61cm) dia

$900-1,100	**DN**

A George III mahogany and boxwood-strung adjustable snap-top table, the oval-molded top enclosing a floral silkwork panel above a facetted baluster support, adjustable for height, the whole raised on triform base with square-shaped legs terminating in spade feet.

18in (46cm) wide

$1,000-1,300	**L&T**

A 19thC mahogany wine table, the shaped rectangular top over turned and carved column on a scrolling tripod base.

21.75in (55cm) wide

$2,000-3,000	**L&T**

A 19thC oak circular snap-top occasional table, turned column and tri-form base.

30.5in (77.5cm) dia

$400-500	**BW**

◄ A 19thC Italian giltwood marble-topped table, the circular back slate-inlaid with floral spray, set into carved and molded table, the turned and knopped pedestal with applied rosettes, the base with three scrolling cabriole legs.

30in 76cm) high

$7,500-8,500	**L&T**

A Victorian walnut occasional table, the shaped circular top on turned fluted column and tripod base.

21in (53.5cm)

$250-300	**GorB**

A Victorian mahogany occasional table, with fitted single drawer on a bulbous-turned pillar and quadruple cabriole base.

$1,000-1,300	**GorL**

Tables

A Victorian faded mahogany occasional table, the drop-leaf top with a frieze drawer and dummy drawer with turned wood knob handles, the turned and ogee petal-carved stem to a quatreform veneered base with bun feet on casters.

20.5in (52cm) high

$750-850	WW

A Victorian walnut occasional table, the figured circular fixed top with a carved rim raised on a turned carved column and cabriole legs.

19.75in (50cm) dia

$450-550	Chef

A mid-Victorian tripod table, the parquetry-decorated top with carved molded edge on a fluted turned and carved stem, supported on three acanthus-decorated legs with scroll toes and original brass casters, stamped "Holland and Son".

22in (56cm) dia

$1,300-1,600	HamG

A Victorian satinwood George II-style kettle stand, the serpentine square top with molded edge and cusped angles, raised on pedestal with two tiers of clustered columns and tripod base with molded cabriole legs terminating in cabochon-carved scroll toes.

28.75in (73cm) high

$3,500-4,500	L&T

A George II mahogany card table, the rectangular fold-over top with lobed angles enclosing a baize-lined interior with inset guinea wells and candle stands to the angles, the shaped apron with central carved shell, raised on shell-carved cabriole legs terminating in webbed pad feet.

33.75in (86cm) wide

$5,000-6,000	L&T

A George II mahogany demi-lune tea and card table, the two fold-top with plain interior and baize-lined games surface with wells, raised on four club legs with pad feet.

29.56in (75cm) wide

$3,500-4,500	L&T

A late 18thC Dutch demi-lune card table, the top inlaid with butterflies, cornucopia and a basket of flowers, opening to reveal further floral marquetry decoration, the frieze with a pair of pivoting drawers similarly decorated standing on inlaid tapered legs headed by guttae decoration.

35in (89cm) wide

$1,800-2,200	HamG

▶ A George II mahogany card/tea table, the shaped double-folded top with a baize lining and an adjustable writing slope on slender legs and pad feet.

31in (79cm) wide

$9,000-11,000	DN

An 18thC Dutch mahogany-veneered card table, with inlaid marquetry detail.

29.75in (75.5cm) wide

$4,000-5,000	CdK

A Federal inlaid mahogany serpentine-front card table, Middle Atlantic states, possibly Philadelphia, the rectangular serpentine top with line inlay on a conformingly shaped frieze with inlay framed panels centering a marquetry shell, the crossbanded skirt on four square-tapered legs with diamond-inlaid dies, line inlay the length ending in crossbanded cuffs.

c1790   36in (91.5cm) wide

$12,000-15,000   **FRE**

A Federal inlaid mahogany fold-over tea/card table, the hinged rectangular top with inset rounded corners, the conforming frieze centered by a tablet, the square-section legs tapered, chequer banding throughout.

c1800   36in (91.5cm) wide

$2,500-3,500   **SI**

A Philadelphia Federal mahogany card table, the rectangular top with bowed front, ovolo corners and reeded edge on a conforming frieze, inlaid dies above the tapered and reeded legs ending in ball/ring turnings.

c1805   34.5in (87.5cm) wide

$1,500-2,000   **FRE**

A Federal mahogany fold-over card table, probably Baltimore, MD, the hinged rectangular top with rounded corners over a conforming cockbeaded frieze raised on ring-turned and reeded legs ending in ball feet.

c1810   37in (94cm) long

$5,000-6,000   **SI**

A late 19thC Federal-style inlaid rosewood serpentine-fronted fold-over card table, Mid-Atlantic States, the serpentine hinged top with an edge with double stringing, opening to a polished surface outlined with further stringing, the conforming frieze with oval reserves and edged with chequer banding, the square-section tapering legs inlaid with stringing and pendant bell-flower and headed with oval reserves inlaid with floral sprays, the cuffs with ebony stringing, secondary woods oak and poplar.

36in (91.5cm) wide

$2,500-3,500   **SI**

A Classical carved mahogany or mahogany-veneered card table, attributed to Isaac Vose (1767-1823) or Isaac Vose, Jr (1794-1872), Boston, the rectangular top with rounded corners and carved and paneled frieze above paneled and leaf-carved molded pedestal on a curving platform raised on carved feet and castors; refinished, some losses.

1819- 24 35.75in (91cm) wide

$2,000-3,000   **SI**

A Classical part-ebonized mahogany fold-over pedestal card table, Baltimore, the hinged , molded rectangular top opening to a polished surface above a molded frieze and reel-turned, lobed urn-form pedestal on ringed base and four reeded legs with cast brass hairy paw feet on casters.

c1825   29.5in (75cm) high

$4,000-6,000   **SI**

A pair of first half 19thC Empire mahogany folding top game or card tables, the rectangular tops with rounded corners, half-round molded frieze, columnar and square pedestals with rope carving on four leaf-carved paw feet.

36in (91.5cm) wide

$3,500-4,000 (pair)   **FRE**

A George III mahogany folding top card table, with fitted small drawer, on square-chamfered supports.

25in (63.5cm) wide

$500-600   **GorB**

A Regency mahogany card table, with ebony inlaid D-shaped top, on ring-turned tapered legs.

35in (88.9cm) wide

$800-1,000   **GorL**

A Scottish Regency rosewood fold-over card table, the rectangular top with rounded angles and crossbanded edge above frieze with central tablet, raised on acanthus-clasped and ring-turned pedestal with gadrooned plinth and concave quadriform base with leaf-carved shaped and reeded sabre legs with cast-brass caps and casters.

36.25in (92cm) wide

$4,500-5,500   **L&T**

A Regency mahogany fold-over card table, the rounded rectangular top enclosing tooled leather interior above a beaded entablature frieze on turned column and quadruped base with reeded sabre legs terminating in cast brass paw feet and casters.

Provenance: *Bonython Manor, Cornwall.*

29in (74cm) high

$2,000-3,000   **L&T**

Tables

A Victorian brass-mounted mahogany coaching card table, with baize top, inset corner wells and vesta pockets on folding X-frame and pad feet.

30in (76cm) wide

$1,500-2,000   **GorL**

A William and Mary-style walnut card table, with a baize-lined feather banded fold-over top, the arcaded front with turned leg gates, and side frieze drawer.

30in (76cm) wide

$1,500-1,800   **WW**

A matched pair of early 20thC George I-style walnut card tables, each with crossbanded lugged rectangular fold-over top above plain frieze and concertina action cabriole legs with leaf carving and claw-and-ball feet.

27.5in (70cm) high

$7,500-8,500 (pair)   **L&T**

▶ A Victorian rosewood card table, the rectangular fold-over top with rounded angles and inlaid strapwork border, enclosing baize-lined interior, above frieze with scrolling bracket terminals, raised on turned pedestal with carved knop base and four leaf-carved cabriole legs with scroll toes and casters.

30in (76cm) high

$3,000-4,000   **L&T**

A pair of Edwardian Adam-style inlaid mahogany card tables, with satinwood crossbanding and boxwood stringing each with fold-over demi-lune top with fan medallion and ribbon-tied husk decoration above paneled frieze and square section tapering legs with husk drops and spade feet.

28.75in (73cm) high

$3,500-4,500   **L&T**

An early 19thC West Indies games table, veneered in Thuya wood, the top banded in braziletta with mahoe wood, the reversible central sliding cover inlaid with a chequerboard, reveals a lift-out backgammon tray and a parquetry panel underneath of specimen woods (with chart), two small frieze drawers for counters and dice shakers and dummy drawers, fitted ebony knob handles, an ebonized reed and dart molding, a canted stem to quatreform platform, with tulip-carved scroll feet on casters, by Ralph Turnbull of Kingston, Jamaica.

This table was sold with a chart naming all the specimen woods used in its construction, making it more interesting to collectors and historians.

33in (84cm) wide

$14,000-16,000   **WW**

An Edwardian mahogany folding top card table, of serpentine outline, on swept beaded legs with uniting under-tier.

24in (61cm) wide

$180-240   **GorB**

A Queen Anne walnut triple-top games table, the molded rectangular hinged top with outset corners, opening to an inlaid backgammon and chess board, the second top opening to a felt-lined playing surface with guinea wells, the third top opening to a fitted writing-surface, the well containing the backgammon frame, the conforming crossbanded frieze raised on bracketed cabriole legs with pad feet.

31.75in (80.5cm) wide

$6,000-7,000   **SI**

An early 19thC penwork pedestal games table, the square concave-sided top with a chequerboard and scrolling foliage, a frieze drawer, the stem with classical figures and motifs to a petal bowl, foliage-decorated quatreform base on turned feet.

23.5in (60cm) high

$3,500-4,500   **WW**

Tables

A William IV rosewood veneered games table.

c1835   19.25in (49cm) wide

$500-600	CdK

A mid-19thC rosewood games/work table, the inlaid chessboard top opening to reveal a fitted interior over a shaped polygonal column with shaped platform base and scrolling feet.

18.25in (46cm) wide

$3,000-4,000	L&T

► An American late Federal mahogany drop-leaf work table, New England, with a rectangular over-hanging top over three drawers raised on twist-turn legs with castors.

c1820   36in (91.5cm) wide

$2,000-3,000	SI

A Victorian rosewood and bird's-eye maple chequer-topped games table, on tapered octagonal pillar on platform base with scrolled toes.

22in (56cm) wide

$400-450	GorL

A Victorian mahogany-veneered swivel-top games table, the fold-over top reveals inlaid chequer and backgammon boards, the faceted stem with molded collar to the quatreform base, on flattened bun feet.

19in (48cm) wide

$500-600	WW

An American mahogany Empire sewing stand, the rectangular top over two varisized drawers, three-quarter round corners on octagonal pedestal with four scroll feet.

$600-800	FRE

An Amrican 19thC cherrywood work stand, the top with three-quarter splash back, apron drawer, and shelf below on turned feet.

$500-600	FRE

A Victorian walnut and burr-walnut veneered games table, the hinged serpentine top opening to reveal interior inlaid with backgammon, cribbage and chess boards, above single drawer and wool bin on turned baluster supports and trestle base with relief-carved scrolling feet.

28.5in (72.5cm) high

$1,200-1,500	L&T

A late Victorian mahogany bridge table, with inlaid stringing, the swivel flap-top baize-lined and inlaid with a garland of bellflowers, satinwood-banded, the well frieze on tapering legs with stretchers.

21in (53.5cm) high

$600-700	WW

◄ An early 19thC Federal mahogany sewing stand, the rectangular top with demi-lune hinged lid, material compartments at the ends, two varisized drawers with brass and glass knob pulls, on an urn-turned pedestal with four reeded splayed legs with brass caps and casters, veneer loss.

top 28in (71cm) wide

$2,000-2,500	FRE

Tables

A William IV rosewood veneered lady's reading table, the easel-hinged top above a frieze drawer, with wood knob handles, the side supports with a turned stretcher, on plinths, with turned feet with casters.

18.5in (47cm) wide

| $2,000-2,500 | WW |

An early Victorian rosewood reading table, with compartmented racheted top on an octagonal pillar with circular platform base with scrolled toes.

22in (56cm)

| $750-850 | GorL |

A George III satinwood writing/work table, with ebony stringing, leather-lined lectern top, two candle slides and fitted drawer over a wool box, on square-tapered legs.

22in (56cm) wide

| $2,000-2,500 | GorL |

A late George III mahogany work table, the crossbanded rectangular top with rounded corners above a double-fronted drawer and another drawer, flanked by two candle arms, with a narrow drawer to one side, on square tapering legs with brass terminals and casters.

29in (74cm) high

| $3,500-4,500 | DN |

A William IV Anglo-Indian rosewood work table, the top with egg and dart molded edge above carved frieze drawer with pierced brackets, the tapering pierced wool bin on pierced and carved trestle supports joined by a similar stretcher.

30.75in (78cm) wide

| $2,000-3,000 | L&T |

A Regency mahogany sewing table, the round-cornered rectangular crossbanded top above a single frieze drawer with ebony shield-shape escutcheon and similar false drawers all round, with a hanging bag frame, with oval ebony escutcheon, supported on reeded sabre legs terminating in brass casters, hanging bag lacking.

29.5in (75cm) high

| $1,000-1,400 | HamG |

A Regency mahogany Pembroke worktable, fitted with two short drawers with opposing dummy drawers, on turned supports.

20in (51cm) wide

| $1,000-1,400 | GorB |

◀ A near pair of early Victorian rosewood sewing tables, each with molded single drawer and wood bin, raised on hoop supports and tapering hexagonal pedestal and concave quadriform base with saucer feet and casters.

28.25in (72cm) high

| $3,500-4,500 | L&T |

An 1820s lacquer sewing table.

28.5in (72cm) high

| $1,500-2,000 | SS |

Tables

A late Regency Brazilian rosewood work table, the rectangular top opening to reveal a later fitted tray and void interior, above a pleated and tapered silk work bag, supported on a turned central column with triple S-scroll supports on a concave triangular base with brass mounts.

17in (43cm) wide

$1,200-1,600   HamG

An early Victorian rosewood games and work table, the fold-over top enclosing chequerboard above fitted drawer and wool bin on pierced scrolling trestle supports, with sled bases joined by turned stretcher raised on scroll feet.

22in (56cm) wide folded

$2,000-2,500   L&T

▶ A Victorian figured walnut sewing table, the hinged cover with inlay enclosing a fitted interior on a tapered octagonal central column and triple scroll support.

28in (71cm) high

$800-1,200   Clv

A George IV mahogany sewing table, fitted with two real and two dummy drawers with turned handles on a hexagonal central pillar, the shaped platform base with four bun feet.

27.5cm (70cm) high

$800-900   Clv

A 19thC mahogany sewing table, the hinged rectangular top with reeded edge and floral marquetry panel centered by a bird, enclosing divided interior above similar frieze with false front and single drawer, on curved supports joined by undershelf with scrolled feet, wool bin lacking.

19.25in (49cm) wide

$1,500-2,000   L&T

A William IV blond tortoiseshell work table, with hinged top, silk-pleated box and square stem, on saltire base, fitted with brass casters.

14in (35.5cm) wide

$1,800-2,200   GorL

A mid-Victorian walnut sewing table, the top with geometric inlay, opening to reveal an interior of sewing compartments with fret-work lids to the inlaid hanging box, standing on carved and turned supports united by a turned stretcher with carved swept legs ending in volutes.

28in (71cm) high

$1,000-1,300   HamG

A William IV rosewood work table, inlaid in mother-of-pearl with filate bands, the rectangular top with a drawer, on octagonal tapering column carved with stylized leaves and a concave-sided base the turned and reeded feet with recessed brass casters, some damage to the top.

51cm wide

$3,500-4,500   DN

A mid-Victorian combination card or sewing table, the rectangular burr-walnut top with floral marquetry, opening to reveal a baize-lined and gilt-tooled interior, above three frieze drawers and pull-out sewing basket, on trestle end supports with shaped and scrolled feet united by a turned and carved stretcher.

33in (84cm) wide

$1,000-1,300   HamG

◀ A Victorian Sheraton Revival painted satinwood drop-leaf work table, the top with rounded corners, decorated with a lady and sheep within a floral cartouche with sprays and a foliate scroll border, above two drawers on square tapering legs.

24.75in (63cm) wide

$6,000-8,000   DN

Tables

A Victorian Sheraton Revival painted satinwood work table, the oval hinged top decorated with putti, flowers, ribbons and bows above a drawer on turned tapering legs with X-stretchers, possibly altered.

19.25in (49cm) wide

$2,000-2,500	DN

A Victorian Jennens & Bettridge papier-mâché work table, decorated with mother-of-pearl buildings, on hexagonal stem with triangular foot and scroll feet.

17in (43cm) high

$2,000-2,500	GorL

A Victorian burr-walnut and birds-eye maple-banded sewing table, with canted angles over a fitted drawer and pull-out silks basket, on tapered supports.

28in (71cm) wide

$1,000-1,400	GorL

A Victorian burr-walnut veneered sewing and games table, the shaped serpentine fronted fold-over top, enclosing backgammon, chequer and cribbage boards, above a frieze drawer and sliding wool bin, on baluster-turned trestle supports joined by paired stretcher, on cabriole feet

21.75in (55cm) wide

$2,000-2,500	L&T

A French late 19thC fruitwood and rosewood work table, the oval top with central musical trophy motif inlaid in various exotics, opening to reveal a mirrored interior of burr maple and purple heart, the base supported on four straight legs with cabriole lower sections, with ormolu mounts, united by a wavy center stretcher with an ormolu flambé urn.

20in (50cm) wide

$1,500-2,000	HamG

A Sheraton Revival painted satinwood work table, with hinged octagonal top and silks box, on turned figured legs with fitted brass casters.

21in (53.5cm) high

$3,500-4,500	GorL

A French walnut work table.

20in (51cm) wide

$400-450	CdK

▶ A Louis XV-style kingwood and rosewood-veneered petit table des dames, with gilt-brass mounts and quarter veneered panels, the shaped rectangular top above leather-lined writing slide and concealed frieze drawer to the side all on square section cabriole legs with sabots.

14.5in (37cm) wide

$2,200-2,600	L&T

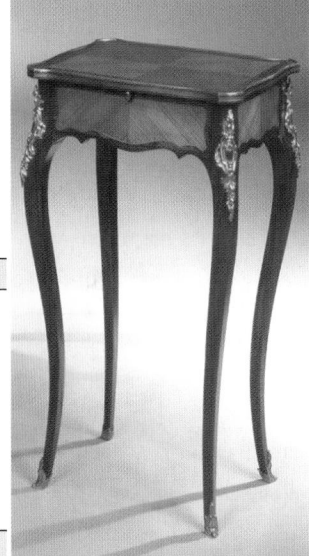

◀ A late 19thC mahogany bijouterie cabinet, the circular hinged top with inset bevel-glazed panel revealing lined interior with four glass panels on slender cabriole legs with pierced gilt-brass leaf-cast pendant mounts terminating in hoof feet, united by shaped stretcher.

30.25in (76.5cm) high

$2,000-2,500	L&T

▶ A late Victorian George III-style inlaid satinwood bijouterie table, the hinged and glazed rectangular top with canted angles enclosing velvet-lined interior, on square section tapering legs with splayed feet joined by arched cross-stretcher supporting shaped tray.

26in (66cm) wide

$4,500-5,500	L&T

Tables

A Louis XV-style kingwood-veneered bijouterie table, with gilt-brass mounts, the hinged shaped rectangular top with beveled glass enclosing lined interior with glass sides, raised on square section cabriole legs with sabots.

31.5in (80cm) wide

$1,200-1,600	L&T

An early 20thC French bijouterie table, the hinged serpentine top with a beveled glass panel enclosing a damask-lined interior, standing on French cabriole legs with brass sabots and espagnolettes, with brass paneled sides.

23.25in (59cm) high

$750-850	HamG

An 18thC oak cricket table, on chamfered triangular legs, cut down.

25in (63cm) wide

$400-500	GorL

A George III mahogany architect's table, the rectangular top above single fitted drawer and square section legs with molded angles enclosing turned columns on bun feet, adapted.

29.5in (75cm) high

$3,000-4,000	L&T

An 1860s large Indian mother-of-pearl Moorish table.

23.25in (59cm) high

$750-850	SS

An 1870s three-tier bamboo table.

28.25in (72cm) high

$200-250	SS

A Victorian folding table, with painted top.

15.75in (40cm) dia

$450-550	CdK

A Victorian mahogany bagatelle table, with a folding baize top, with balls and scoring board, the stand on turned legs.

42in (107cm) long

$750-850	WW

◄ A marble specimen table, the rectangular Carara marble top inlaid with grid of specimen squares within a border, raised on ebonized stand with square section tapering legs with gilt-brass mounts.

36in (91cm) wide

$6,000-7,000	L&T

TEAPOYS

A Regency elm teapoy, surmounted by floral knop and coffered lid revealing a fitted interior, on square spreading column and shaped platform base with turned feet.

17.75in (45cm) wide

| $4,000-5,000 | L&T |

A Regency mahogany and ebony-lined teapoy, the crossbanded caddy top opening to reveal an interior fitted with two lidded boxes for tea, two compartments for mixing and teaspoon apertures, the tapering inlaid sides raised above a lyre support on quadruped base with square cabriole legs terminating in brass caps and casters.

15in (38cm) wide

| $3,500-4,500 | L&T |

An early Victorian rosewood teapoy, the molded edge-hinged lid with canted corners over deep ogee-molded frieze and spiral-turned knop to the baluster upright, on four double C-scroll supports with brass casters.

20.5in (52cm) wide

| $450-550 | BAR |

An early Victorian rosewood teapoy, the stepped, hinged rectangular top enclosing four removable lidded rosewood canisters and two crystal mixing bowls, the tapering body raised on tapering octagonl pedestal and concave quadriform base with bun feet and casters.

33in (84cm) high

| $1,500-2,000 | L&T |

A mid-19thC pollard elm teapoy, of casket form with turned carved column on platform base with paw feet.

19.5in (49cm) wide

| $3,000-4,000 | L&T |

A Victorian burr-walnut circular-topped teapoy, with four division interior, raised on wrythen-fluted column and tripod cabriole base.

19in (48.5cm) dia

| $1,000-1,300 | GorL |

WASHSTANDS

▶ A George III mahogany washstand-night table, the flame mahogany veneered bi-fold top opening to reveal an interior with a rising mirror and cut outs for bowls and jars, with a pot cupboard and a full-width drawer, standing on square-chamfered legs with block feet and original casters.

19in (48cm) wide

| $1,000-1,300 | HamG |

One of a pair of George III mahogany washstands, with galleried square tops, mid-tier drawers and squared legs.

| $750-850 (pair) | GorL |

A Sheraton-period mahogany cheveret, the open top above two short and one long drawer, sycamore and purpleheart-banded, a baize easel flap, above an open incurved compartment, on square-tapering legs to brass casters.

17.25in (44cm)

| $3,000-4,000 | WW |

American Tables

An early 19thC Federal red-washed birch tavern table, rectangular top with breadboard ends raised on base with single drawer and square tapering legs.

45.25in (115cm) long

$1,500-2,000	SI

A Pennsylvania German maple-framed slant-topped table, the top on splayed block and spool-turned legs, one deep drawer, box stretcher, shaped apron on two sides, missing two boards, drawer carved H A and 1790 on the front.

c1790   27.5in (70cm) high

$2,500-3,000	FRE

An early 19thC Federal cherrywood stand, with a rectangular overhanging top, frieze with a drawer and square-section tapering legs.

20in (51cm) wide

$1,200-1,600	SI

An English Regency mahogany washstand, the three-quarter galleried top over two small drawers, on ring-turned supports.

45in (114.5cm) wide

$300-400	GorB

An early 19thC Federal cherry drop-leaf table, with cross-stretcher.

c1810

$900-1,200	SI

A side table, with original paint and turned legs.

c1850-60

$600-800	BCAC

A Federal-style green-painted country pine sideboard, overhanging rectangular top over single drawer with turned knob, raised on tapering, square section legs.

49.5in (125.5cm) wide

$800-1,000	SI

A Regency mahogany washstand, with three-quarter galleried top over two small drawers, on turned supports.

46in (117cm) wide

$200-300	GorB

A Regency mahogany dressing table, the top with a gallery, the four drawers with brass star knob handles, on square tapering legs.

34in (86.5cm) wide

$600-800	WW

A Victorian mahogany washstand, with three-quarter galleried top over two small drawers, on turned legs.

39in (99cm) wide

$250-300	GorB

A late 19thC French rosewood ladies poudereuse, with a cube-inlaid and crossbanded top, the central portion opening to reveal a mirror with side flaps with void interiors, frieze with three drawers and a slide, standing on tapered and inlaid legs, with brass feet.

9in (48cm) high

$500-600	HamG

A late 19thC side table, on inside of left-hand drawer, stamped "Heal, London".

35.5in (90cm) wide

$650-700	CdK

Whatnots

WHATNOTS

A late Regency mahogany whatnot, the three rectangular tiers with shaped aprons supported by ring-turned and blocked columns, with a single drawer to the base and corresponding legs with brass caps and casters.

19.5in (49cm) wide

$2,000-2,500	L&T

A CLOSER LOOK AT A WHATNOT

Whatnots are freestanding shelves, generally of two or three tiers.

Rosewood and mahogany are typically used in their construction.

This whatnot is of high quality, shown by the pierced brass gallery and brass tubular supports. It exudes the quality of late Regency.

A George IV rosewood and brass three-tier whatnot, the top tier with a pierced border, the brass tubular supports with lobed finials, on brass casters, the top tier repaired.

14.5in (37cm) wide

$6,000-7,000	DN

A 19thC rosewood whatnot, the tapering square base with brass stringing canted angles and open sides with brass wire lattice, including a door to the front enclosing shelved interior raised on brass paw feet with plinths, surmounted by two open tiers with lyre supports raised on plinths with ball spacers.

45.25in (115cm) high

$3,000-3,500	L&T

A pair of mid-Victorian walnut-veneered whatnots, each with three shaped oval tiers, with beveled rim, linked by pierced and scroll-carved side supports, the lower tier with single drawer, the whole raised on boldly turned legs, on pot casters.

43in (109cm) high

$7,500-8,500	L&T

A late Victorian satin-wood two-tier étagère, the detachable oval tray top with brass carrying handles raised on chequer-inlaid scrolled supports united by an X-shaped stretcher.

27.5in (70cm) high

$2,000-2,500	Chef

▶ A Victorian figured walnut three-tier whatnot, the pierced three-quarter gallery above a central shelf fitted with a drawer raised on spiral-twist supports and later turned feet with brass caps and casters.

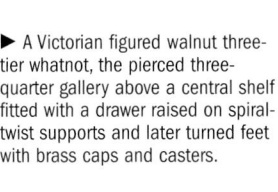

22.5in (57cm) high

$1,000-1,300	Chef

A Victorian inlaid figured walnut four-tier graduated corner whatnot, with turned pillars on casters.

54in (137cm) high

$1,000-1,400	Clv

A Victorian inlaid walnut four-tier whatnot, decorated with urns and foliage divided by turned pillars.

24in (61cm) wide

$600-800	GorL

MISCELLANEOUS

An early 19thC American walnut quilt stand, turned finials to vase-shaped posts on scroll feet with shelf stretcher, two turned rungs.

45.5in (115.5cm) wide

$300-400	**FRE**

◄ A Frank Furness oak church pew, each side with rear support having chamfered corners and a large roundel standard, the molded armrest with turned supports and applied geometric design, all enclosing a plank seat and back.

Frank Furness (1839-1912), was an architect and designer from Philadelphia. He is best known for his American Gothic Revival furniture of the so-called "Reformed" Gothic type.

$4,000-5,000	**FRE**

An American Classical brass-inlaid mahogany and mahogany veneer pianoforte, brass plate engraved, 'A. Babcock Boston'; the brass inlaid rectangular top with hinged front section, rounded corners above frieze and three drawers on eight tapering, reeded legs ending in peg feet with casters, and pencil inscription on underside of case, 'C Chas...' and brass plate inscribed, "Hugo Worch..1110 G Washington DC Vitrolas; Worch Pianos".

c1830   66in (167.5cm) wide

$3,000-4,000	**SI**

PROVENANCE: Hugo Worch was a scholar and collector of, and dealer in, keyboard and instruments in Washington D.C. Between 1914 and 1921 Hugo Worch donated nearly 175 pianos to the Museum of American History of the Smithsonian Institution forming the nucleus of the present keyboard collection. From 1921 to 1938 he held the title of Honorary Curator of Musical Instruments at the Smithsonian Institution. He is listed in the New Grove Dictionary of American Music, page 562. This pianoforte was purchased from Worch in 1928. The Boswell family recounts how he delivered it to the Capitol Hill house himself in a horse-drawn wagon. As with all his instruments, Hugo Worch wanted to see the family and home to which his instruments were placed.

A Frank Furness carved walnut library, attributed to the workshop of Daniel Pabst, in twelve pieces, comprised of a mantel, over-mantel mirror, and ten bookcases units; the mantelpiece with carved catlike support, stippled intaglio panels and shell-carved base; the mirror with turned columnar supports and chamfered standards flanking a mirror glass surmounted by a frieze with carved and turned decoration and central shield having carved griffin head, all above a reeded panel. The bookcase each connected and having adjustable shelves enclosed by a glazed door flanked by turned columnar supports with carved and chamfered standards, the whole capped by a reeded pitched roof.

early 1870s   total length of cabinets and mantelpiece 437in (1109.9cm)

$70,000-100,000	**FRE**

A small late 18thC beech and birch spinning wheel, with turned decoration, with some losses and need of restoration.

$225-285	**HamG**

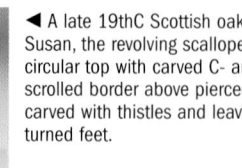

◄ A late 19thC Scottish oak lazy Susan, the revolving scalloped circular top with carved C- and S-scrolled border above pierced apron, carved with thistles and leaves, on six turned feet.

24in (61cm) wide

$4,500-5,500	**L&T**

▶ A pair of Victorian Renaissance Revival carved walnut and ebonized sculpture stands, square top inset with rouge-variegated marble over a tapering standard, decorated with egg and dart carved C-scroll and portrait medallion, acanthus-carved lower section on burlwood and ebonized stepped base, partial molding loss to one panel.

c1880   44.5in (113cm) high

$4,500-5,500	**FRE**

A giltwood and painted blackamoor, holding a gilt-metal oval tray, the square section plinth with stepped foot.

63.75in (162cm) high

$2,500-3,000	**DN**

A Louis Vuitton trunk, with brass-mounted leather-banded LV covering, leather loop handles, wooden slatted front and two internal trays, no.183958.

44in (111.75cm) wide

$4,000-5,000	GorL

TRAYS

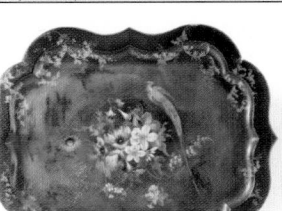

A George III mahogany cutlery tray, the molded rectangular tray with a deep gallery pierced on all four sides with heart-shaped carrying-holes, raised on a folding stand.

25.5in (65cm) high

$1,500-2,000	SI

A 19thC mahogany butler's tray, the three-quarter gallery with a low front, pierced carrying handles and a typical folding stand.

37.75in (96cm)

$300-400	HamG

A 19thC papier-mâché rectangular tray, painted in black and gilt with Chinese buildings, on a later simulated bamboo and ebonized stand.

17.75in (45cm) high

$1,500-2,000	DN

A late 19thC mahogany oval tray, with raised chequer border and two brass handles, decorated overall with marquetry flowers and leaves.

23in (58.5cm) wide

$300-400	LFA

A Victorian papier-mâché tray.

32in (81cm) wide

$450-550	CdK

A Victorian tole-ware tray.

26.5in (67cm) wide

$450-550	CdK

A CLOSER LOOK AT A PAPIER-MÂCHÉ TRAY

A Victorian papier-mâché tray, of serpentine-form, painted with an urn of flowers and birds with shaped border.

This piece is in very good condition, and the gilt decoration is not too worn.

Less brightly colored trays are not as popular with collectors. The most desirable trays have well painted landscapes and are by known makers.

25in (63cm) wide

$700-800	DN

A Victorian printed and gilt papier-mâché tray, of curvilinear-shaped outline, the deep concave rim decorated with gilt penwork leaves, the main panel painted with mountain landscape containing figures crossing a waterfall, stamped B. Walton & con warranted, and inscribed "Himalayan Mountains 3391".

24.5in (62cm) wide

$2,200-2,800	L&T

FOLK ART Metalware

THE FLOURISHING MARKET FOR AMERICAN FOLK ART IS NOT JUST AN EMOTIONAL REACTION TO THE TERRORIST ATTACKS OF SEPTEMBER 2001, BUT THE result of increased scholarship and the arrival of a new generation of collectors. There is no question that in the past year there has been a renewed enthusiasm for American icons such as the flag, eagles and items connected with any of the founding fathers. The successful sale of American flags from the collection of Tom Connelly at Sotheby's New York in May 2002 proved just how strong the market has become. Needlework, miniature portraits and American school paintings are also bringing in big figures at auction.

Folk Art has always had an appealing quality. However, the research scholars and enthusiasts have invested in Folk Art means collectors are becoming better informed.

Over the past decade much has been written about makers and pieces and this has inspired more people to start collecting. The opening of the new American Folk Art Museum in New York has also led to an increased appreciation of decorative and practical objects from America's past, whether they be paintings, samplers, furniture or tools. There is no longer any question that Folk Art can be bought as a long term investment, and new, younger collectors are coming into the marketplace and building up collections.

Collectors look for pieces in good condition, with the original surface – it is important that a piece has not been cleaned – and with a provenance and/or known maker if at all possible. Good pieces can stand on their own, but information about the history of a piece, especially about the maker, is what collectors are always looking for.

METALWARE

A rare 18thC bird spit with penny feet.

$1,000-1,300   BCAC

Three 18thC/19thC iron ladles, one decorated with circles and half circles on the flattened handle.

16.5in (42cm) long

$350-400   SI

A three-legged long-handled cooking pan.

6.5in (16.5cm) dia

$100-150   JDJ

A wrought iron peel, with decorative scroll handle, two holes in blade.

A bait bucket, marked "EV Butler, Boston".

$400-500

Maker's mark on bait bucket.

BCAC

A camp stove.

$800-900   BCAC

A salesman's sample flatiron, with trivet.

$30-50   BCAC

A early 19thC New England brass hinged warming pan, with turned wooden handle, the cover decorated with punch work.

45in (114.3cm) long

$150-200   SI

◄ A wrought iron peel, with decorative scroll handle, two holes in blade.

40in (101.5cm) long

$70-100   JDJ

Metalware/Wood

A 19thC brass warming pan, the cover chased with scrolls, circles and pierced with moon and L-shaped devices, with turned applewood handle, imperfections.

41in (104cm) long

$500-550 SI

◀ Three brass pails.

largest 10in (25.5cm) dia

$80-150 (each) BCAC

Seven 19thC tin candle-moulds, ranging from a single to a 12-candle mold.

tallest 12in (30.5cm) high

$750-800 SI

▶ A 19thC punchwork-decorated tin lantern, with conical top and strap ring handle.

15in (38cm) high

$100-150 SI

A coffee pot, attributed to Peter Derr.

Peter Derr *(1793-1868) was a prolific ironworker, coppersmith and pewterer of Tulpehocken Township, Berks Country, PA.. He is best known for his copper, brass and iron standing and hanging fat lamps.*

$2,000-3,000 BCAC

Twenty-five late 19thC tin plate cookie-cutters, a few later.

The most desirable cookie-cutter shapes are hearts and animals.

$200-250 (set) BCAC

A miniature copper kettle, possibly Philadelphia.
c1810

$900-1,000 BCAC

A candlemaker, consisitng of pewter moulds in a wooden frame.

$1,300-1,700 BCAC

A 19thC tin anniversary whisk-broom holder.

The 10th wedding anniversary is traditionally celebrated with gifts made from tin. Neighbors often made items from tin to give the couple celebrating the anniversary.

$250-300 BCAC

WOOD

Two late 18th-19thC burlwood mortars, each of tapering cylindrical form, one with moulded foot.

7.5in (19cm) high

$450-500 SI

A large 19thC painted burlwood chopping bowl, old iron repair at rim.

19.75in (50cm) long

$500-600 SI

One of a pair of late 18th-19thC burlwood mortars, of tapering cylindrical form, with moulded foot.

7.5in (19cm) high

$450-500 (pair) SI

A 19thC turned burl bowl, the interior decorated with incised lines, together with a darning egg, a turned rolling pin and a hand plane, some early 20thC.

12.5in (31.5cm)

$250-300 (set) SI

◀ A bird's-eye maple bowl, marked "Munising".

$80-120 BCAC

Wood

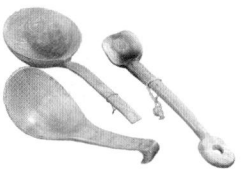

Three 18thC-19thC wooden scoops or ladles.

11.5in

$300-350   **SI**

Four 19thC wooden ladles and a wooden skimmer.

longest 21in (53.5cm) long

$200-250   **SI**

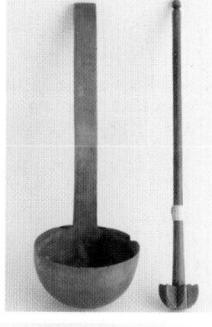

◄ A carved wood dipper, with strainer holes, together with a carved wood swizzle stick.

both 16in (40.5cm) long

$60-80   **JDJ**

A 19thC pierced walnut foot warmer, probably Pennsylvania, square-form pierced with heart pattern at sides and diamond pattern at front, sliding panel and back, wire bail handle.

9in (23cm) wide

$350-450   **SI**

A wooden foot warmer, with decorative design of holes on top and sides and coal tray, some old repairs, initialed "M.C".

9in (22.5cm) wide

$200-250   **JDJ**

A round wood and tin foot warmer, the hinged door opens to reveal tin insert, wood rim on top and bottom, pierced holes on sides and top.

9in (22.5cm) dia

$350-400   **JDJ**

A heart-shaped mold.

$250-300   **BCAC**

Two 19thC turned wooden lamp stands.

For a similar example see Beatrice B. Garvan, The Pennsylvania German Collection.

tallest 10.75in (27.5cm) high

$500-600   **SI**

An 18thC pantry box.

$250-300   **BCAC**

A double-sided cake board, formed as a man and woman in costume, some worm holes.

33in (83.5cm) high

$600-700   **JDJ**

A wooden whirligig, polychrome-painted flat wood cut-out of a rooster with spinning wings.

18.5in (47cm) high

$350-400   **SI**

A late 19th/early 20thC red-painted pantry box, with fitted cover, straight nailed laps.

9.5in (24cm) dia

$250-300   **SI**

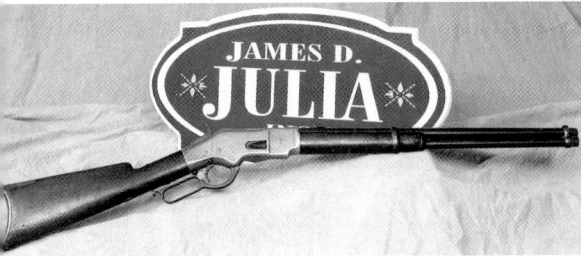

Boxes

A wallpaper-covered hat box, decorated with a landscape scene centering a large classical building. **Provenance:** The Society of the Cincinnati.

c1835   11in (39cm) high

$2,800-3,500	**SI**

A 19thC cardboard trinket box, reverse-painted with a woman feeding a rooster, interior mirror on lid, dated inside June 1841.

$700-800	**BCAC**

A decorated box, of dovetailed construction.
c1840

$450-500	**BCAC**

An early spice box, of dovetailed and square-nailed construction, found on the eastern shore of Maryland.

$200-250	**BCAC**

A stained one-drawer pipe box, constructed with rose-head nails, shaped top with hanging hole, the drawer with ring handle and dovetails.

18in (45.5cm) high

$4,500-5,000	**JDJ**

Three 19thC mid-Atlantic and Southern states painted yellow-pine and poplar wall boxes, two with shaped backboards, painted ochre and green, the third with arched back, painted red.

largest 6.5in (16.5cm) wide

$850-950	**SI**

A 19thC American painted and decorated tinware box, with hinged domed lid, asphaltum surface, decorated with swags, foliage and flowerheads, scattered floral flourishes on base.

6.5in (16.5cm) long

$800-900	**SI**

A 19thC paint-decorated wood canteen, decorated with red and white striping enclosing similarly coloured star, leather strap nailed at sides, carved "J R" at back.

$500-600	**SI**

A 19th painted and decorated tinware box, with hinged domed cover, decorated with stylized flowerheads, leaves and feathery flourishes.

9.25in (23.5cm) long

$9,500-10,000	**SI**

A 19thC mahogany knife box, with carved heart-shaped handle.

$600-650	**BCAC**

◄ A late 19thC hanging wall box, with heart cut-out, red and cream paint, from the Delaware Valley.

$400-500	**BCAC**

► A late 19thC/early 20thC tin candlebox, with hinged lid and pierced tapering straps for hanging.

10.75in (27.5cm) long

$250-300	**SI**

Baskets/Eagles

A 20thC Nantucket purse basket, with a wooden swing handle, the lid centered with an ivory whale on an oval medallion, ivory pin and knobs, base impressed, "NANTUCKET ISLAND/M.F.DIAS".

5.5in (14cm) high

$750-850 SI

Nantucket baskets were first made in the 19thC by sailors living on Nantucket Island's lightships – floating lighthouses which warned mariners of danger.

A ship and its crew could be at sea for six to eight months at a time and so the men began basket weaving to pass the time.

The result was intricately made baskets which, by the early 20thC, had become a popular souvenir with visitors to the Nantucket area. Today, collectors seek both antique and contemporary versions.

A Nantucket lightship pocketbook, with swing handle, leather hinges and clasp, the lid plaque engraved with a scene of Nantucket harbour, branded Barlow.

c1960   8.75in (22cm) wide

$350-400 SI

A three-color painted basket.

$300-400 BCAC

A covered Indian basket.

$200-300 BCAC

A birch bark basket.

$150-200 BCAC

A field basket.

$50-100 BCAC

A late 19th/early 20thC painted and carved eagle plaque, with shield and crossed flags in gold, red, white and blue.

27.75in (70.5cm) long

$3,500-4,000 SI

m A carved mahogany eagle plaque, carved in the half-round with spread wings and applied pennants above an American shield, by John Haley Bellamy (1836-1914) Kittery, Maine.

Provenance: Originally owned by Admiral George Dewey.

33 in (83.5cm) wide

$800-900 SI

A 19thC gilt-painted cast iron eagle. **Provenance:** First National Bank, Camden, New Jersey.

13.5in (10.25cm) high

$2,000-2,500 SI

Two late 19thC stamped copper eagles, one clutching oak leaves (imperfections).

largest 8.5in (21.5cm) high

$150-200 SI

Two stamped gilt-brass eagles, each with adjustable wings and originally used for patriotic displays, marked "Patented September 15, 1891, N.Y." (splits).

$600-700 SI

▶ A cast eagle, with original red surface.

c1910

$900-1,000 BCAC

Duck Decoys/Scrimshaw

A CLOSER LOOK AT A DUCK DECOY

This duck is branded with the name of the gunning boat it was floated from, which adds to its value.

Duck decoys were probably first made by Native Americans around 2,000 years ago using reeds, cattail and bulrush. Centuries later the settlers used carved and painted wooden ducks to lure waterfowl to roosting areas. Today, collectors look for examples bearing their original paint and made by known makers.

This duck has its original gunning paint, something prized by collectors.

The bird is nicely carved.

This weight helped to float the decoy in the water.

A drake duck decoy, with early gunning paintwork and canvas back, from Maryland and branded with the name of the gunning boat "Reckless".

The name of a gunning boat adds to the value of a decoy.

c1900

$650-750		BCAC

A drake eider duck decoy, with "turtle back-style" pegged head, carved bill and old gunning paintwork, made by Captain William Rowling, Musquodoit Harbor.

c1920

$150-200	BCAC

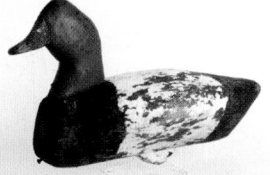

An oversized North Carolina drake duck battery decoy, with canvas back and old gunning paintwork.

$200-300	BCAC

A pair of carved and painted whistling swans, one in preening position, both with glass eyes, signed and dated Russell V. Brown, 1984, Virginia.

largest 25in (63.5cm) long

$1,000-1,500	SI

A carved and painted Canada goose decoy, with solid body, original paintwork with touch ups, damage to tip of bill, by Elmer A Crowell, oval impressed stamp to base "Pequaw Honk Club".

23in (58.5cm) long

$3,500-4,000	JDJ

A carved and painted black breasted plover, with carved split tail and typical squarish head, by George Boyd.

10.5in (26.5cm) long.

$12,000-15,000	JDJ

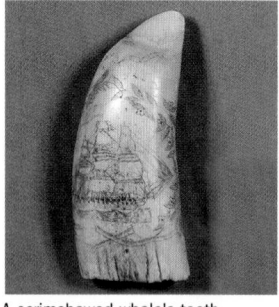

A scrimshawed whale's tooth, decorated with a three-masted warship surrounded by a floral wreath, the reverse with an American eagle, shield and cannon above the date.

1801

$2,500-3,000	FRE

An early to mid-19thC scrimshawed whale's tooth, decorated with a three-masted whaling vessel flying the American flag on one side, whale's tails in the water, the reverse with similar ship and whaleboat about to harpoon a victim.

6in (15cm) long

$900-1,000	FRE

▶ A superb scrimshawed whale's tooth, depicting the ship "COURIER OF NEW BEDFORD," a three-masted vessel with various hand-colored flags flying, an eagle hovering above with spyglass and the 24 stars of the union, the reverse depicting the "Capture of the William Tell" naval engagement.

In the 19thC craftsmen and sailors from the east coast of North America decorated whale and walrus teeth and tusks to make decorative objects known as scrimshaw. Popular subjects included whaling scenes and ships. These examples are exceptional and genuine pieces, but there are many replicas on the market – for every genuine piece there may be 100 reproductions.

c1821-1836 *7in (18cm) long*

$30,000-40,000	FRE

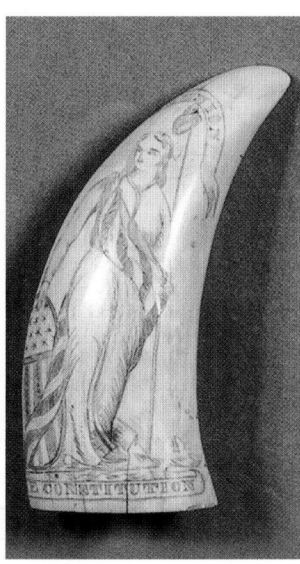

A mid-19thC scrimshawed whale's tooth, decorated with Columbia on one side holding hand-colored flag/shield, staff and cap, "THE UNION' and "THE CONSTITUTION" on scrolled mottoes, the reverse with anchor and star "WE LIVE IN HOPES", and signed "WT."

4.75in (12cm) long

$2,000-2,500   **FRE**

A late 19thC American copper and zinc horse weathervane, in the form of the trotter, Dexter, retains traces of gilding, splits, attributed to L.W. Cushing, Waltham, MA.

31in (78.75cm) long

$2,500-3,000   **SI**

A large late 19thC/early 20thC painted dough box on legs, the overhanging top above tapering rectangular box raised on splayed legs with shaped skirt.

$700-750   **SI**

A superb mid-19thC scrimshawed walrus tusk, decorated the length with a three-masted sailing ship, compass, an American eagle, a whaling scene and the tip with the likeness of a barracuda's head, the name "Alice" appears within scrolls near the ship (possibly the ship's name or the woman for whom this was made).

19.5in (49.5cm) long

$1,500-2,500   **FRE**

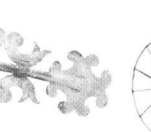

A late 19thC copper arrow bannerette weather vane, the shaft ornamented with scrolls and devices.

21.5in (54.5cm) long

$1,000-1,500   **SI**

A pierced and appliquéd Baltimore Album bedspread, comrised of twenty-five blocks of muslin appliquéd with floral sprays, wreathes, vases of flowers and an American eagle with stars within a zig-zag and flower bud border, all worked with a variety of printed and solid cotton pieces, some losses and discoloration, Baltimore, Maryland.

Provenance: *Probably worked by Emma Kate Parrish, of Baltimore, MD. Parrish was related to the prominent Merryman and Horton families of Baltimore. She married John Rouzer and moved to Frederick County, MD.*

c1855   101 x 100 in

$2,000-3,000   **SI**

A mid-19thC scrimshawed whale's tooth, decorated on one side with a large sperm whale being harpooned by a whaleboat crew, the reverse with numerous sperm whales and whaleboats, a masted whaling vessel in the background flying the American flag, highlighted in black and red ink.

9.25in (23.5cm) long

$25,000-30,000   **FRE**

A copper weather vane, in the form of horse and sulky.

33.5in (85cm) long

$250-300   **SI**

A 19thC horse weather vane, with original surface.

$3,000-3,500   **BCAC**

An early 19thC Pennsylvanian cherrywood cradle, with tapering arched ends, shaped sides pierced with handle holds, on shaped rockers.

40in (101.5cm) wide

$1,400-1,600   **SI**

A Windsor stool, with early surface.

$200-250   **BCAC**

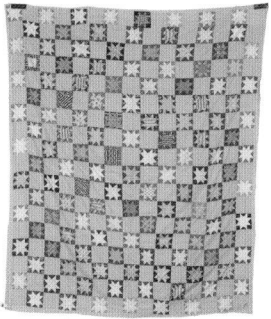

A cotton patchwork quilt, with various printed patches arranged in a square and star pattern, hand and machine stitching, dated.

Provenance: *Made by Ivy Stanford, an African-American woman, of Brooklyn, New York.*

1873   80 x 68in

$300-500   **SI**

Miscellaneous

A pin cushion, fastened to a cherry turned-leg stool-like base, pieced silk top cover with earlier cover beneath it

c1840-1860

| $100-150 | | BCAC |

▶ An American nickel-plated brass presentation lantern, the pierced domed top with swing handle over pear-shaped globe, etched with floral swags enclosing the inscription "W.H. Smith" with a wirework mid-section, domed base below, by Westlake and Co., New York; Patent December 12, 1865.

The lantern has been associated with General William H. (Baldy) Smith (1824-1903). A West Point graduate of 1845, Smith worked as a military topographical engineer. During the Civil War he rose to the rank of Major General. He became infamous for an incident during the Civil War when he condemned to death a Private Scott, who was found sleeping on sentry duty. The sentence was commuted by President Abraham Lincoln.

9.25in (23.5cm) high

| $900-1,000 | | SI |

▶ A nickel-plated brass and etched glass presentation lantern, the cylindrical pierced top with swing handle above a wirework mid-section enclosing oblong globe, the front engraved with "General P.H. Sheridan", enclosed by swags of olive and oak leaves; the obverse engraved with an eagle with outspread wings over a shield, crossed American flags and cannonballs, cylindrical base with domed foot, stamped Kelly & Co., Rochester, New York.

Sheridan, (1831-1888), a fierce and determined fighter, was one of Abraham Lincoln's most valued Generals. He graduated from West Point in 1853 and served in the frontier. He rose through the ranks becoming a Major General in 1862. He is buried in Arlington Cemetary.

c1870 12in (30.5cm) high

| $4,000-5,000 | | SI |

A 19thC painted leather fire bucket, with a wooden band above straight, tapering form and inscribed "S. Cornell" in yellow.

14.25in (36cm) high

| $500-550 | | SI |

A 19thC ebonized poplar spool holder.

7.5in (19cm) high

| $70-100 | | SI |

▶ A late 19thC painted and decorated tin and mirrored-glass container, stencilled "American Can Co", with projecting top with mirrored plate, inscribed "Hyson," supported by free standing colonettes, flanking recessed mirrored plate above a sliding door, painted black and stencil-decorated with yellow and red scrolls and stylized flowers and leaves.

20 1/2 (32cm) high.

| $550-600 | | SI |

A late 19thC peanut warmer/roaster, copper with brass manufacturers label "E Taunay, 226 Hudson Street NY".

| $800-1,200 | | BCAC |

▲1 A late 19thC sailor's valentine, in a hinged hardwood case with shellwork designs of flowers, hearts and "HOME AGAIN" motto.

8.5in (21.5cm) dia

| $4,000-5,000 | | FRE |

▲2 A late 19thC sailor's valentine, in a hinged hardwood case with shellwork decoration including floral designs and a bird.

10.25in (26cm) dia

| $9,000-10,000 | | FRE |

Two folk art display boxes.

c1940-50

| $200-250 | | BCAC |

SHAKER Furniture

THE SHAKERS WERE A RELIGIOUS GROUP FORMED IN MID-18THC LANCASHIRE, ENGLAND. UNDER THE LEADERSHIP OF AN ENGLISH BLACKSMITH'S DAUGHTER, Ann Lee – known as Mother Ann – a small group emigrated to America in 1774 following a revelation that their faith would flourish there. They carried out preaching journeys across New York State and New England and Shakerism became established in New York, Connecticut, Maine, New Hampshire, Massachusets, Ohio, Kentucky and Indiana.

They were initially called the United Society of Believers in Christ's Second Appearing, but became known as "Shaking Quakers" and then Shakers because of their practice of shaking and trembling to rid themselves of evil. Shaker Brothers and Sisters practiced celibacy, separation from the world, communal ownership of property, pacifism and the confession of sin. Women were seen as equal to men and God was celebrated as both Father and Mother. By the first half of the 19thC there were 19 principle communities with around 5,000 members. However, by the middle of the century allegiance had started to wane and by the mid-20thC only three villages remained: Hancock, Massachusets; Canterbury, New Hampshire; and Sabbathday Lake, Maine, which is the only one which exists today.

The Shaker's emphasis on simplicity, harmony and perfection within the community led to the development of a distinctive arts and crafts tradition which has been appreciated by collectors since the 1930s. The top end of the market is very strong at the moment, with collectors looking for pieces in exceptional condition. The middle continues to hold steady, as it has for the last three or four years, while the bottom end also remains good.

FURNITURE

An Elder's rocking chair, tiger maple, original varnish finish, beige taped seat, curvilinear arms, tall finial, New Lebanon, NY.

c1840   44in (112cm) high

$3,500-4,500   WH

A pair of children's maple chairs, with cane seats, made in Enfield, New Hampshire.

c1850   26.5in (67.5cm) high

$2,500-3,500   WH

A birch side chair, with original staining, cane seat and tilters, made in Enfield, New Hampshire.

Provenance: Ex. Courcier/Wilkins '78.
Tilters are unique to Shaker chair-making and allow the sitter to lean back in the chair, without the risk of falling over, and are typical of the ingenuity of Shaker craftmanship. Chairs with tilters were made solely for use within Shaker communities. Tilters are rounded feet, which are tied with thongs within the chair to cups, which can then rotate so that they stay flat on the floor when the legs are tilted.

c1840   41in (104cm) high

$5,000-6,000   WH

A 19thC Shaker child's arm rocker, oval-pointed finials to posts, hemispheric turning to arms, turned legs and double stretchers, blue and white woven cloth tape seat and back, label affixed to the inside of one rocker "Shaker's no. 1/Trade Mark/MT. Lebanon, N Y".

29in (73.6cm) high

$800-1,000   FRE

A maple side chair, with original stained finish and taped seat, stamped "FW" on front stile.

Provenance: Ex. Jean Peterson, Pittsfield-1973."

"FW" is Brother Freegift Wells (1785-1871).

39.5in (100.5cm high)

$3,500-4,500   WH

A maple child's rocking chair, with dark walnut stain, shawl bar, transfer decal on back of bottom slat, original tape seat and trade label for "No 1 Mount Lebanon Shaker Rocker".

28in (71cm) high

$2,000-3,000   WH

A cherry-wood candlestand, with dark stained finish, round top, rectangular-chamfered cleat, turned shaft with original tin plate at base of post, from New Lebanon, New York, labeled "14".

The underside of the table is marked with the number 14. This was the room it was made for and meant it could easily be returned to its proper place. This is a common feature of items made for Shaker dwellings.

c1825-40   24.75in (62.5cm) high

$28,000-32,000   **WH**

A chest of drawers, butternut, poplar and pine secondary wood, original varnish finish, finely double beveled top board, inset paneled ends, six dovetailed and lipped drawers, cherry wood threaded knobs, arched feet.

43in (109cm) wide

$20,000-25,000   **WH**

SHAKER BOXES

Shaker boxes are sought by specialist box and Shaker collectors. They are often displayed in stacks of decreasing size. As the smallest (3in [7cm] long) tend to be the hardest to find they therefore command a premium. Condition and provenance also add to a box's desirability.

A CLOSER LOOK AT A SHAKER WORK STAND

Shaker furniture is simple but elegant with a purity of line.

The Shaker's exacting craftsmanship can be seen throughout the furniture, in joints and handles and the fit of the drawers.

Characteristically it has no decorative turning, carving or painting.

A birch work stand, with dovetailed and thumbnail molded single drawer with turned wood knob, finely turned legs.

25in (63.5cm) high

$3,500-4,500   **WH**

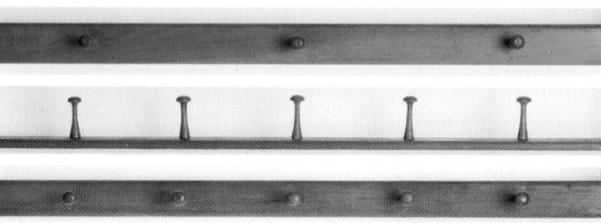

Two pegboards, pine with maple pegs, smaller one signed on back in red script "The 3 Loft under the Eaves".

60in (152.5cm) and 70in (178cm) long

$1,000-1,500   **WH**

▶ A four-finger Shaker box.

$2,000-2,500   **BCAC**

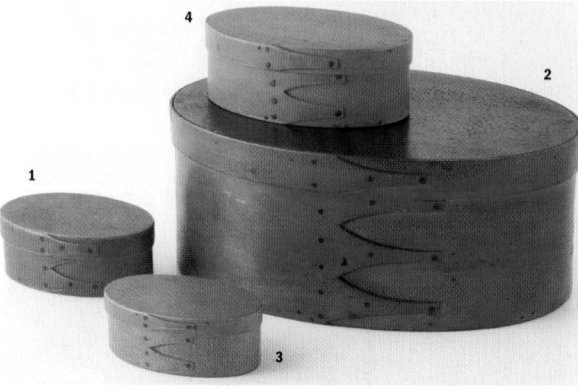

A maple and cherry-wood sewing case, with breadboard top, over single drawer and two-door cupboard, on canted square legs, original varnish finish, by Hancock, MA.

Provenance: *Ex. Belfit collection.*
c1840

$37,000-42,000   **WH**

A three-step stool, butternut, natural varnish finish.

This is a classic Shaker form. This piece was once owned by a Mrs McKuerley who worked for the Shakers at Canterbury, NH, and was purchased from her in 1951.

23in (58.5cm) high

$18,000-23,000   **WH**

▼**1** An oval pine three-finger box, with original finish.

3.5in (9cm) diam

$28,000-32,000   **WH**

▼**2** An oval pine and maple four-finger box, with original stain and varnish, initialed "EH" in pencil under lid.

8.75in (22.5cm) diam

$3,000-4,000   **WH**

◀**3** An oval pine and maple three-finger box, with original stain and copper rivets.

c1830-40   3.25in (8cm) long

$8,500-9,500   **WH**

◀**4** An oval pine and maple three-finger box, with original painted finish and iron rivets, signed in blue ink script on bottom, "Grace E. Tyler".

c1830-40   4.5in (11.5cm) long

$10,500-11,500   **WH**

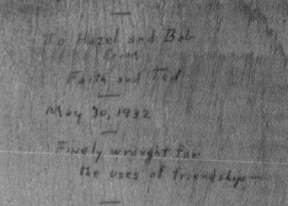

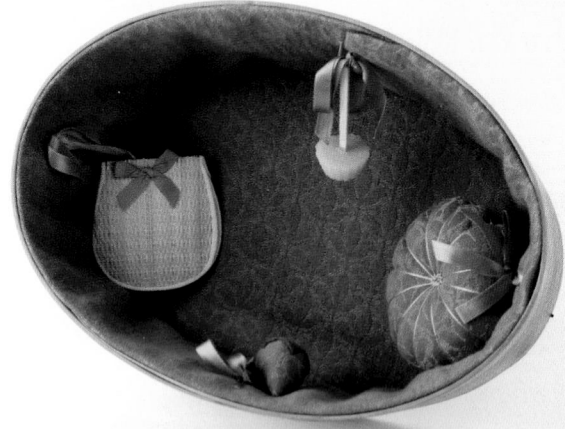

An oval maple and pine four-finger box, maple and pine, with original chrome yellow finish, later blue cloth fitted interior with sewing items, tomato pincushion, poplar woven needlecase, strawberry emery and beeswax cake, signed in pencil on bottom "To Hazel and Bob From Faith and Ted" "May 30, 1932" and "Finely wrought for the uses of friendship".

This box was a gift from Shaker collectors and authors Faith and Edward Denning Andrews to fellow collectors and authors Hazel and Robert Belfit and so has an excellent provenance. The inscription also adds to its value. Gift giving was important to the Shakers, and handmade gifts were often exchanged by Brothers and Sisters. So, this gift from the Andrews to the Belfits was a continuation and acknowledgement of this tradition.

$20,000-25,000		WH

A pine seed box, with label "Shaker's Choice Vegetable Seeds", "D.M. Mount Lebanon, NY".

Provenance: *Ex. Edward Case Collection.*
The Shakers were successful farmers and took advantage of their success by selling surplus seeds.

22in (55.5cm) wide

$2,000-3,000	WH

A walnut and pine desk box, with original stained finish, breadboard hinged lid with attached interior hinged and dovetailed paper holder with handmade iron clasp, interior till for pens and inkwell, full-length drawer in front with original turned knobs.

18in (45.5cm) wide

$10,000-12,000	WH

A basket, black ash, rectangular base to oval top, carved inset side handles, initialed "JH" in red on base, Shirley, MA.

c1840   30.5in (77.5cm) high

$8,500-9,500	WH

A rare four-handled woven basket, to be carried by two Sisters, probably from the laundry.

20.5 in (52cm) diam

$2,000-3,000	WH

A gathering basket, black ash, carved side handles, open weave bottom, three notched runners to reinforce base.

c1840   21.5in (54.5cm) wide

$2,000-3,000	WH

A pine and cherry-wood carrier, with natural varnish finish, tall canted sides, fixed hoop handle and pine base.

12in (30.5cm) long

$2,000-3,000	WH

A tiger maple and silk pincushion, with three maple turned spools in the apple core shape, in original painted finish.

6.5in (16.5cm) diam

$1,000-1,300	WH

A walnut and maple string holder, with original varnish finish, made by Bro. Thomas Fisher, Enfield, CT.

c1880

$10,000-15,000	WH

A walnut thread chest, with original varnish finish, two wooden hinged pullout compartments, each with 12 pins for spools, front holes for thread over a drawer, signed on back of drawer "T. Fisher 1889", Enfield, CT.

It is often possible to identify the maker of Shaker items as pieces were sometimes signed. Although Shaker objects are typically simple in design, the name of the craftsman or the community can also be distinguished by specific design elements, for example, the way a Brother or group of Brothers joined pieces of wood or fashioned handmade locks. The use of locks might seem unusual in a community committed to communal ownership. However, when the Shakers started giving homes to orphans and the destitute they sometimes found that the community's new members did not share its values.

8.25in (21cm) wide

$3,000-4,000	WH

A watercolor by Sister Cora Helena Sarle, entitled "Under the Maples", depicts the road, stone wall and maples on the road to the Canterbury, New Hampshire, Shaker village.

c1950   5.5in (14cm) wide

$1,800-2,200	WH

A woven straw poplar-work bonnet, with silk net covering.

This fancy bonnet would have been worn on special occasions.

$2,000-3,000 **WH**

A Sister's bonnet mold and three poplarware Sister's bonnets, the pine mold with eight drilled holes for holder, Canterbury, NH.

$400-600 **WH**

A maple dipper, with original chrome yellow painted finish.

Provenance: *Ex. Belfit collection.*

Chrome yellow is the quintessential Shaker color and so pieces with their original paint are highly sought after by collectors.

$25,000-30,000 **WH**

A maple dipper, with original paint.

Provenance: *Ex. Belfit collection.*

$17,000-22,000 **WH**

A pill drier, pine board with 74 round head, thin nails for drying rolled and cut pills, Mt Lebanon, New York.

12.5in (32cm) long

$700-1,000 **WH**

A pill roller, two pieces, cherry, walnut and brass, top with carved handles and brass bearings, base with 24 brass grooves corresponding on top and bottom.

12in (30cm) long

$150-200 **WH**

A sander, very finely turned maple, with original chrome-yellow paint, punched star design for sand and green paper covered bottom.

3.25in (8cm) high

$450-550 **WH**

A maple, iron and brass sewing awl and holder, with original paint, maple holder in the shape of an apple core, brass-cuffed iron awl with wood turned knob handle.

4in (10cm) high

$800-1,000 **WH**

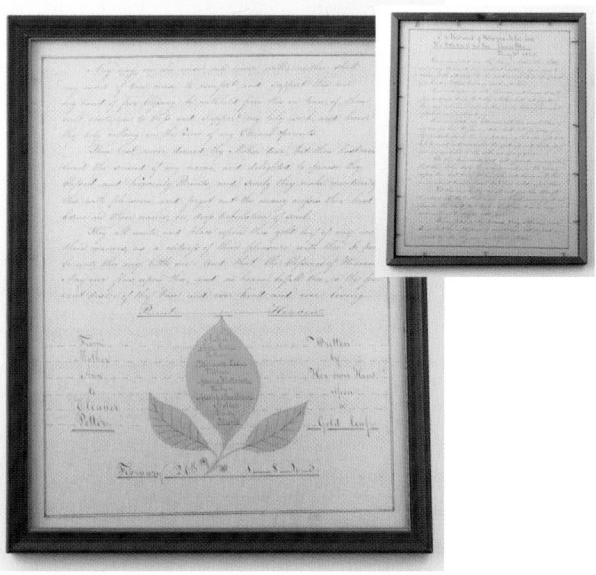

A spirit message, inscribed "A Short word of Notice from Mother Ann, To a Little One of her Love, Eleanor Potter, February 20, 1845".

The Shakers set great store by visions and prophecies and these "gifts" were recorded in decorated documents. From 1837 the group experienced an intense religious revival known as the "Era of Manifestations" or "Mother's Work" which saw a boom in the number of visions experienced by members. These messages of encouragement from God were often given as gifts to other members of the community.

$140,000-180,000 **WH**

A framed photograph of Sister Neale, inscribed "Sister Sadie Neale, Church Family of Shakers, Mt. Lebanon, N.Y." and "W.F. Winter, Photographer".

By William Winter, who was a photographer for Time magazine in the 1930s and 40s.

20in (50.5cm) high

$700-1,000 **WH**

BOXES APPEAL TO COLLECTORS ON A NUMBER OF DIFFERENT LEVELS. As well as being both functional and decorative, they come in a wide variety materials and have many different uses. Consequently, they cover a very broad area of interest, from tea caddies to sewing accessories, ivory to ebony, fine art to folk art.

For this reason the market for boxes is always fairly buoyant, but those made in the early 19th century, which are usually of particularly fine quality, have the best investment potential. Another area that has seen a marked increase in interest from collectors in recent years are the 19th century novelty boxes, modeled or painted to resemble miniature cottages.

▲1 A 17thC Indo-Portuguese miniature barguena, the mahogany, tortoiseshell and ivory case with wrought iron carry handles, the fall front enclosing drawers with turned handles.

8.75in (22cm) wide

$2,200-2,500

▲2 A George II satinwood tea caddy, with purplewood banding, inlaid with fan patera to the top and tulip to the front, lidded interior.

5in (3cm) high

$600-650

▲3 A George III tortoiseshell pounce pot, in the form of a four pointed star, the concave top incised and pierced.

2.75in (7cm) high

$1,800-2,200   **L&T**

A George II tea chest, veneered in burr yew, the oak interior with divisions, the cover with a brass swing handle and brass escutcheon.

9.5in (24cm) wide

$1,400-1,800   **WW**

A George III stained tortoiseshell-veneered caddy, with pewter stringing and ivory edging, lacking interior.

2.75in (7cm) high

$7,000-8,000   **BonS**

A George III mahogany tea chest, with Oriental-style gilt japanning, the hinged cover with brass swan-neck handle, the front with pierced brass escutcheon.

9.75in (25cm) wide

$1,000-1,200   **WW**

A George III tea chest, mahogany-veneered with inlaid stringing, the hinged lid with chased brass swing handle, the oak interior with divisions.

9.25in (23.5cm) wide

$200-250   **WW**

A late 18thC harewood-veneered tea caddy, inlaid stringing with later oval panels of flowers and other painted decoration.

6.75in (17cm) wide

$2,500-3,000   **WW**

A late 18thC tea chest, with canted corners, veneered in burr yew within chain circlets, feather-banded inlaid stringing and fluting, the interior with two lidded compartments.

10.5in (27cm) wide

$2,000-2,500   **WW**

Tea Caddies

A late 18thC tortoiseshell tea caddy, with bright cut silver borders, the front with a miniature of the Goddess of Love with cherub, the hinged cover with silver handle, lidded interior.

4.5in (11.5cm) wide

$5,000-5,500   **WW**

A Regency tea caddy, with floral penwork decoration.

c1810   5in (12.5cm) high

$1,200-1,500   **WW**

A Regency papier-mâché tea caddy, with painted stripe decoration, a paperwork urn to the front, the cover with garlands of foliage, with brass Dutch drop handle.

4.75in (12cm) high

$4,000-5,000   **WW**

A Regency mahogany tea caddy, with boxwood and chequer stringing, the hinged top enclosing lead-lined interior.

6.5in (16.5cm) wide

$550-600   **L&T**

A Regency acajou tea caddy, with boxwood stringing and mahogany crossbanding, the hinged top centered by inlaid fan patera, the body with inlaid panels and faux flutes to the angles.

***Acajou** is a type of mahogany from the cashew, a tropical American tree.*

6.5in (16.5cm) wide

$550-600   **L&T**

A Regency satinwood tea caddy, with mahogany crossbanding and ebony and boxwood stringing, the hinged lid enclosing lined interior.

4in (10cm) wide

$800-900   **L&T**

A Regency mahogany tea caddy, the hinged lid opening to reveal a lidded compartment, the front painted with dummy drawers, with applied bone handles.

6in (15cm) wide

$450-500   **L&T**

A Regency satin mahogany tea caddy, with boxwood stringing and mahogany crossbanding, the hinged top inlaid with scrolling brass motif, enclosing divided interior, the body with inlaid panels centered by snakewood ovals.

8in (20cm) wide

$1,000-1,200   **L&T**

An early 19thC tortoiseshell tea caddy, the domed, hinged lid divided into panels by wire fillets and centered by an ivory knop, the interior with two lidded compartments.

6.75in (17cm) wide

$750-850   **Chef**

An early 19thC Dutch tole tea caddy, with chinoiserie decoration to an ogee rectangular body, the hinged cover with brass finial, on ball feet.

***Tole** is a term used to describe painted, laquered or jappaned tinware.*

5.25in (13.5cm) wide

$300-350   **WW**

An early 19thC hexagonal tea caddy, the canted sides veneered in satinwood with mahogany banding and panels of burr yew, the hinged cover with fan inlay and brass finial.

5.5in (14cm) wide

$1,300-1,600   **WW**

An early 19thC tea chest, veneered in blonde tortoiseshell with ivory stringing, the interior with two lidded compartments.

6.5in (16.5cm) wide

$1,800-2,200   **WW**

Tea Caddies

An early 19thC sarcophagus-shaped tea chest, veneered in burr yew with stringing, a bone escutcheon, the divided interior with lids, on bun feet.

8.25in (21cm) wide

$450-500   **WW**

An early 19thC tortoiseshell-veneered silver-mounted tea caddy, with ivory stringing, the hinged cover enclosing two compartments, the front with an oval cartouche engraved with a monogram, on ball feet.

6.5in (16.5cm) wide

$1,800-2,200   **BonS**

$3,000-3,500

A William IV tortoiseshell tea caddy, of pagoda form with inverted front and pewter stringing, the hinged cover revealing two lidded compartments with ivory handles, on brass ball feet.

8in (20.5cm) wide

WW

A William IV rosewood tea caddy, the lid with stickwork inlay in a tumbling block pattern.

Stickwork is a technique in which rods of colored wood are glued together and then sliced across to form a patterned veneer.

8in (20.5cm) wide

$450-550   **MB**

A coco-de-mer tea caddy, with ivory-inlaid teak interior.

Coco-de-mer, also known as the double coconut, is the large nut of the Seychelles palm.

c1830   11.75in (30cm) high

$1,200-1,500   **MB**

An early Victorian rosewood veneered cottage tea chest, with hinged roof, the front with mother-of-pearl inlaid door and windows.

7.5in (19cm) wide

$900-1,000   **WW**

An early Victorian tortoiseshell-veneered tea chest, with scrolling front, mother-of-pearl raised panel and ivory border, the hinged cover opening to reveal two lidded compartments, on bun feet.

8in (20cm) wide

$2,000-2,500   **WW**

A Victorian rosewood veneered cabin tea chest, with a hinged roof, the front with mother-of-pearl inlaid door and windows.

5.5in (14cm) wide

$1,500-2,000   **WW**

A Victorian figured walnut tea caddy, with brass mounts, the divided interior with domed covers, plates engraved "Black" and "Green" and "J.J. Nechi, 112 Regent Street, London".

8.5in (21.5cm) wide

$400-500   **Clv**

Tea Caddies

A 19thC blond tortoiseshell-veneered tea caddy, with inlaid pewter stringing, on ball feet.

5in (12.5cm) high

$1,600-2,000   **BonS**

Left: A Victorian burr walnut tea caddy, with boxwood and ebony stringing, the interior with pair of lidded removable boxes, the waisted body inlaid with crossed Union Jack flags, on plinth base.

11.45in (29cm) wide

Right: A Victorian specimen wood sewing box, with satinwood banding, the hinged rosewood lid centered by octagonal specimen panel enclosing fitted lifting tray and parquetry stationery compartment, kingwood sides, on rosewood plinth and saucer feet.

13in (33cm) wide

$1,200-1,500   **L&T**   **$600-700**   **L&T**

A mid-19thC papier-mâché tea caddy, with gilt decoration, the lid inset with mother-of-pearl, and the interior with two compartments.

9.5in (24cm) wide

A 19thC papier-mâché tea chest, with shell and mother-of-pearl Oriental scenes and foliage, fitted interior, mixing bowl missing.

11in (30.5cm) wide

A 19thC Regency blond tortoiseshell tea caddy, the sarcophagus body with white metal stringing, enclosing two caddies with retailer's label "Dunnetts, Toy and Tunbridgeware repository, No3 Cheapside , London" and velvet-lined mixing bowl compartment, with gilt-brass lion ring handles and claw feet.

12in (30.5cm) wide

$300-350   **Chef**   **$550-600**   **WW**   **$5,200-5,800**   **B**

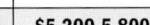

A pair of 19thC tea caddies, veneered in satinwood with painted flowers, the hinged covers with a paterae fan and banded in laurel.

5in (12.5cm) high

A 19thC rosewood-veneered novelty cheroot box, used as a tea chest, in the form of a kennel with a metal terrier, the hinged roof with mother-of-pearl inlay.

8.5in (21.5cm) wide

A Kashmir lacquer caddy.

c1860   15.5in (39cm) wide

A late Victorian tin tea caddy, painted as a cottage.

8.25in (21cm) high

$4,500-5,000 **WW**   **$800-1,000** **WW**   **$1,000-1,200** **SS**   **$2,700-3,000** **WW**

PAPIER MÂCHÉ Snuff Boxes

Papier-mâché was used by European craftsman as an alternative to the Oriental lacquer that became fashionable during the second half of the 18th century. It was used to make a variety of items, including furniture, but was most popular for small pieces, especially snuff-boxes. Early examples are generally round and decorated with painted portraits or landscapes. In the 19th century more novelty shapes were introduced, and mother-of-pearl and metal inlays became fashionable.

When buying papier-mâché check the piece all over, paying particular attention to corners, as they are most vunerable to damage. Decoration should be crisp and bright. Sometimes quite large areas of painted decoration has flaked away, so be sure that everything is intact – restoration involving overpainting will considerably reduce value.

A CLOSER LOOK AT STOBWASSER

The crowded scene is remarkably detailed and accurate

The sensitive paintwork rivals the work of the best miniaturists

Stobwasser's work often had a humorous element

A German papier-mâché snuff-box, signed by Stobwasser and inscribed Pinching the cats tail after Wilkie.

c1790	3.75in (9.5cm) diam
$2,700-3,000	**RdeR**

JOHANN HEINICH STOBWASSER

Collectors often prize the work of one particular maker above all others, and in the field of painted papier-mâché snuff-boxes Johann Heinrich Stobwasser (1740-1820) is just such a name. Stobwasser was a German japanner who began producing snuff-boxes in Lobenstein, Germany in 1757, opening a factory in Braunschweig in 1763. He specialized in exquisitely made and finely decorated boxes, and it is easy to see why his work is so coveted. Popular subject matter included portraits and caricatures, satirical scenes, historical events, mythology, theater and famous people. These were often executed by famous artists of the day, such as PJF and FGM Weitsch, HC Brüning, F Barthel and HHJ Brandes. Some of the rarest and most desirable feature erotic images – often concealed on the inside of the lid. However, the most valuable and highly sought after are those painted in the late 18th and early 19th centuries, depicting city scenes. Most were signed by Stobwasser, but those of a lesser quality were occasionally sold unsigned. His boxes were so popular other factories began to produce imitations. Although these are nowhere near as fine as the genuine article, it is always advisable to proceed with caution when buying.

A papier-mâché snuff-box, with a painting of a gentleman taking snuff.		A papier-mâché snuff-box, with a painting of Character of the Day.	
c1790	3.5in (9cm) diam	c1790	3.5in (9cm) diam
$420-450	**RdeR**	**$400-500**	**RdeR**

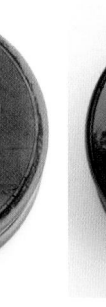
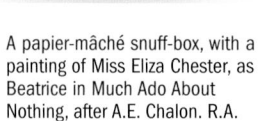

A French papier-mâché box, with erotic print "Le L'avement D'air Inflamable". *The value of this piece is lower as the picture is a print, not a painting.*		A papier-mâché snuff-box, with a painting of Miss Eliza Chester, as Beatrice in Much Ado About Nothing, after A.E. Chalon. R.A.		▶ A papier-mâché snuff-box, painted and signed by Raven.	
c1800	3.25in (8.5cm) diam	c1800	4.5in (11.5cm) diam	c1790	4in (10cm) diam
$200-300	**RdeR**	**$550-650**	**RdeR**	**$600-700**	**RdeR**

Snuff Boxes

A French painted papier-mâché table snuff-box.

c1800   2.5in (6.5cm) diam

$150-200	**MB**

A Regency papier-mâché snuff-box, with a painting of a lady in a rose garden.

c1820   4in (10cm) diam

$420-480	**RdeR**

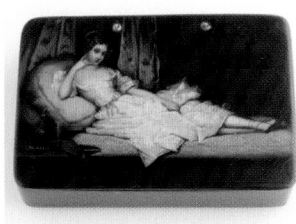

A German papier-mâché snuff-box, signed by Stobwasser, with a painting of a lady reclining and the motto Elle Attend (She Waits).

c1830   3.75in (9.5cm) wide

$2,000-2,500	**RdeR**

A Victorian papier-mâché shaped snuff-box, with a painted print of a man knuckling his eye.

c1860   3in (8cm) wide

$600-700	**RdeR**

A German papier-mâché snuff-box with pounce painting, "Running Fox" mark inside lid.

*A **pounce painting** is where an outline of the picture is printed onto a surface and then painted in afterwards.*

c1840   3.5in (9cm) wide

$300-350	**RdeR**

A painted papier-mâché double-sided blotter, Scottish hunting scene to one side.

c1850   12in (30cm) wide

$400-450	**MB**

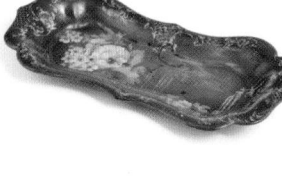

A Victorian papier-mâché painted tray.

c1850   10in (25.5cm) wide

$140-180	**MB**

A Victorian papier-mâché shaped snuff-box, with a painted print of a man with a cap over his eye.

c1860   3in (7.5cm) wide

$400-450	**RdeR**

A Victorian shaped papier-mâché snuff-box, with a painted print of a cat's face.

c1860   3.5in (8.5cm) wide

$450-500	**RdeR**

A 19thC German Stobwasser-type papier-mâché circular snuff-box, painted with a portrait of a man.

    3.5in (9cm) diam

$180-220	**BAR**

A Russian papier-mâché tobacco box, with painted lid.

c1915   6in (15cm) wide

$100-150	**MB**

A Victorian papier-mâché inkstand, painted with landscapes within gilt scroll borders, with two square section cut glass wells.

    10.5in (26.5cm) wide

$100-150	**LFA**

TREEN Boxes

THE BROAD DEFINITION OF THE WORD "TREEN", MEANING "FROM THE TREE", IS ANYTHING MADE FROM WOOD, but it is usually applied to small turned items that were made from Medieval to Victorian times for use around the home or farm. Since most treen objects were intended to be functional, many bear no superfluous decoration; their beauty lies in their simplicity and the form, feel and figuring of the wood. However, some craftsmen embellished their wares with carved and turned decoration, and these examples are particularly sought after.

The market for treen has changed dramatically in the last 30 years. Today it is almost impossible to find good quality early pieces from the 17thC. Items from the 19thC are easier to come by but the popularity of collecting treen means prices are increasing every year.

WHAT TO LOOK FOR

Since most treen objects are unique, having been hand crafted, it can be difficult to attribute age, origin and sometimes even use. People often say it is difficult to learn about different woods, but collectors quickly develop an eye, and a feel, for the diversity of native and imported timber.

- ✦ Condition and patination are important, as is original carved decoration, dates, initials, mottoes etc.
- ✦ Look for well-proportioned forms and figured wood.
- ✦ The best pieces of treen were made from around 1720 to the end of the 18thC.
- ✦ Many early pieces were hollowed by hand and gouge marks can easily be seen.
- ✦ The most popular woods in use in the early 17thC were beech, elm and chestnut.
- ✦ In the late17thC yew, sycamore, alder and fruitwoods were also used.
- ✦ In the early 18thC pine, boxwood and maple became popular.
- ✦ By the second quarter of the 18thC exotic timbers such as lignum vitae, ebony, teak and mahogany were more prevalent.

![A French coquilla nut snuff-box]

A French coquilla nut snuff-box with fine carving of Napoleon with his marshals on the lid, the reverse depicts the widow and her son.

A **coquilla** is a Brazilian palm tree nut. It has a thick, hard shell, which is often used for carving.

c1815   3.5in (8.5cm) wide

$600-650	RdeR

An important mid-18thC English treen fruitwood snuff-box, shaped as a double-headed man, depicting good and evil.

3.5in (8.5cm) high

$2,000-2,500	PC

A French coquilla nut snuff-box, carved in the shape of a man, restoration to feet.

c1790   3in (8cm) high

$600-650	RdeR

A 19thC Tunbridgeware novelty snuff-box, modelled as a boot with half-square mosaic top, the hinged sole missing a sliver of welt.

3.5in (9cm) long

$650-700	B

A mahogany shoe-shaped snuff-box, decorated with studs.

c1840   5in (12.5cm) long

$370-450	RdeR

A 19thC treen shoe-shaped Masonic snuff-box, with nail decoration of sun, dividers and set square, crown, trowel, eye, purse, moon etc.

4.5in (11cm) long

$400-450	BAR

A treen shoe-shaped snuff-box, with brass pique decoration and a sliding cover.

3.75in (9.5cm) long

$200-250	WW

An English treen mahogany mid-19thC pacifier (or cosh), with weighted brass head.

8in (20.5cm) long

$100-150   PC

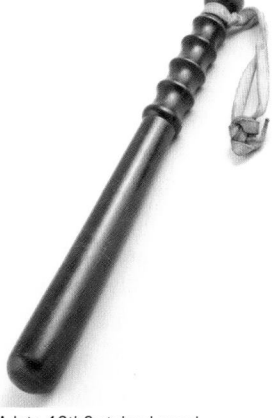

A very rare treen fruitwood apple corer.

c1770   6.5in (16.5cm) high

$400-450   RdeR

A late 18thC English lignum vitae bilboquet.

***Lignum vitae** is a tropical American hardwood.*

7in (17.5cm) high

$200-250   PC

A 19thC turned rosewood cup and ball, a bilboquet.

5.75in (14.5cm) long

$200-250   BonS

A late 19thC stained wood truncheon, with turned handle and leather strap.

15.5in (39cm) long

$30-60   DN

A late 19thC English "Brighton Bun" boxwood traveling candlestick, with snuffer.

4.5in (11cm) diam

$180-220   PC

A boxwood pipe tamper.

c1740   4in (10cm) high

$600-650   RdeR

An English treen mahogany and grospoint pin-cushion on turned feet.

From the W.J. Shepherd Collection (no. NW1037)

c1860   7in (17.5cm) wide

$300-350   PC

A 17thC English oak collection box, with contemporary painted scene.

From the W.J. Shepherd Collection (no. CH2110)

10in (26.5cm) high

$225-250   PC

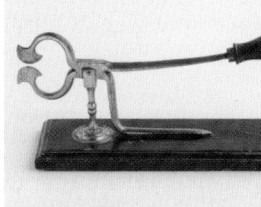

A late 18thC English fruitwood turned goblet, cracked and stapled.

From the W.J. Shepherd Collection (no. D1890)

7in (18cm) high

$400-450   PC

An early 19thC English rosewood spill holder.

10in (25.5cm) high

$180-220   PC

18thC treen, steel and brass sugar nippers, with turned wooden handle, on a wooden stand.

In the 18thC sugar was sold in cone-shaped blocks which had to be broken with a sugar hammer or axe and then with sugar nippers.

$250-300   PC

An early 19thC treen mahogany trivet.

***Trivets** are three- or four-legged stands that were used to support cooking vessels in front of an open fire.*

$90-120   PC

MAUCHLINEWARE Snuff Boxes

auchlineware is the name given to the wooden souvenir items made in Scotland from the early 1800s until the 1930s. Mauchlinware, named after the Ayrshire town where it was made, is characterized by its simplicity, usually decorated only with a decal-like painting or transfer of a familiar scene. Mauchlinewares have their origins in a series of high-quality wooden snuff-boxes and tea caddies made in the late 18th and early 19th centuries, which incorporated an ingenious hidden hinge. They were initially produced by Charles Stiven of Laurencekirk, Kincardineshire, but demand was so great that craftsmen elsewhere in Scotland, especially Mauchline, began to make them. As tourism increased they rapidly diversified their output, producing a vast range of decorative wooden objects.

Entry level prices for Mauchlinewares start at around $30 for simple transfer-printed wares, rising to four figures for rarer, early penwork or hand-painted examples. Over the last five years, prices for Mauchlinewares in general have have kept pace with, or slightly exceeded inflation. However, during the last year there has been a surge of interest from American collectors, some of whom are prepared to pay a great deal for good pieces. Because the decorative finishes were protected by numerous coats of varnish, many Mauchlinewares have survived in excellent condition. Consequently, damaged or worn examples are worth 30-70 percent less than near-pristine equivalents.

JAMES SANDY (1766-1819) was the inventor of the integral wooden hinge as applied to Mauchlineware snuff-boxes and tea caddies. His invention was exploited by Charles Stiven from Laurencekirk, a town roughly half-way between Dundee and Aberdeen. In the early 19th century, a French nobleman, who was staying at the Old Cumnock home of Sir Alexander Boswell, accidentally broke his snuff-box, probably one made by Stiven (snuff-boxes and tea caddies carrying the "Stiven" stamp are among the finest made anywhere). His host took the box to the local blacksmith, William Crawford, for repair. At first, Crawford did more harm than good – solder seeped into the hinge rendering the box useless. But Crawford persevered and managed to produce some tools to file out the solder. In so doing, he discovered exactly how the hinge was made. The secret eventually spread to other Ayrshire locations, including Mauchline. It was from these beginnings that the vast range of Mauchlineware products owe their origin.

A Scottish Mauchlineware penwork boxwood snuff-box, with grape motif.

c1820-30   3.25in (8cm) wide

$350-400   **RdeR**

▶ A Scottish Mauchlineware boxwood snuff-box, with penwork study of seated lady, slight damage to varnish under base.

c1840   3in (7.5cm) wide

$500-550   **RdeR**

The practice of taking snuff was well established in Scotland by the early 17th century and continued well into the Victorian era, although it was falling out of fashion. However, Scottish snuff was renowned as being particularly pure, and the habit continued longer there. Edward Pinto, a great authority on treen advanced the opinion that "burrs are notoriously difficult to identify", but most of these boxes seem to be formed from trees commonly found in Scotland, particularly elm, which produces very good burrs. This box is stamped "George Sinclair Bonnington", a recorded maker who worked in Angus so can be associated with the Stiven's of Laurencekirk.

A Scottish Mauchlineware penwork and brushwork spectacle case of sycamore wood. c1820-1830, containing Georgian silver spectacles that have "wig" extensions.

c1820   4.75in (12cm) wide

$1,200-1,500   **RdeR**

A 19thC Scottish burr elm snuff mull, stamped Geo Sinclair, of kidney-shaped form, the hinged split lid bearing silver plaque inscribed "Col. Robert Ross to George Ross of Pitcalnie 1835", together with an elm coaster of reciprocal auricular form within S and C scroll border, on brass and leather castors.

9in (23cm) wide

$5,000-5,500   **L&T**

Snuff Boxes

A 19thC Mauchlineware burr elm snuff mull, of shaped lozenge form, the hinged split sycamore lid with transfer print of "Tam O'Shanter's Orgy", the underside decorated with thistles.

7in (18cm) wide

$1,500-1,800   L&T

A large Scottish 19thC Mauchlineware burr walnut tea caddy, of oval form, the split hinged lid with erotic print of a lady and maid in her boudoir within penwork background.

$1,800-2,200   L&T

A 19thC Mauchlineware burr maple snuff mull, the hinged split sycamore lid bearing transfer print of the Scott Monument with thistles enclosing a pair of hands below the legend "For Auld Lang Syne".

5.5in (14cm) wide

$1,200-1,500   L&T

A large 19thC Mauchlineware burr snuff mull, the hinged split lid bearing color print of a family in a cottage interior.

8.25in (21cm) wide

$3,000-3,500   L&T

A19thC Mauchlineware burr maple snuff mull, the hinged split lid decorated with greyhounds chasing a hare.

6.75in (17cm) wide

$600-650   L&T

A 19thC burr elm snuff mull, the hinged split sycamore lid decorated in penwork with the crown, thistle and rose.

5.5in (14cm) wide

$1,200-1,500   L&T

Boxes

A 19thC burr elm snuff mull, the hinged split sycamore lid bearing painting of a cockerel and a hen.

6in (15cm) wide

$750-850   L&T

A 19thC Mauchlineware burr elm snuff mull, the split hinged lip bearing print of a Highlander and the words "Made of Wood Grown on Sheriff Muir, where a battle was fought On 13th Novr. 1715 etc", the underside bearing card of Commander F.G. Crofton inscribed "to J.H. Wallace...wishing him another £1000 [$1,500] a year".

7.5in (19cm) wide

$1,000-1,200   L&T

19thC Robert Burn's Trysting Thorn: a large thorn bearing a silver metal mount inscribed "To Lady Mackinnon from Archd. Munro Burn's Trysting Thorn".

7in (17cm) long

$300-350   L&T

A Mauchlineware sycamore napkin ring, with transfer print of Caerphilly Castle.

c1880   2in (5cm) diam

$30-60   MB

A sycamore and larch medicinal tumbler holder, the lid with transfer print view of "Happy Valley, Llandudno", with steel tumbler.

c1880   3in (7.5cm) high

$80-100   MB

A Mauchlineware tower money box, printed with a view of Great Yarmouth from the sea.

4in (10cm) high

$60-80   Chef

A late 19thC tubular Mauchlineware bodkin case, with photographic print of Gun Hill, Southwold.

9in (23cm) long

$30-60   DN

A Mauchlineware sycamore box, with a picture of Dunkeld Cathedral.

c1870   4in (10.5cm) wide

$75-100   MB

A Mauchlineware sycamore box, with print of "Auld Brig O'Doon".

c1850   4.25in (10.5cm) wide

$90-120   MB

Fernware/Tartanware

FERNWARE IS A TYPE OF MAUCHLINEWARE IN WHICH, INSTEAD OF LANDSCAPES OR TARTAN, ANOTHER SCOTTISH motif – the fern – was used as a motif. Impressions of different types of fern were hand-stippled onto a piece, which was then varnished and polished. The finished result is a restrained and intriguing form of decoration, the subtly colored layers of foliage against the dark glossy ground giving an unusual impression of depth. Fernware has become a very popular variation of Mauchlineware over the last few years. As with other types of Mauchlineware, size adds value, unusual shapes are highly sought after, and good condition is crucial.

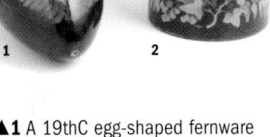

A 19thC fernware sewing box, the interior of the domed cover with buttoned red silk lining.

9in (23cm) wide

$270-300   B

▲**1** A 19thC egg-shaped fernware string box.

4.5in (11cm) high

$150-200

▲**2** A cylindrical fernware powder box.

3in (8cm) high

$60-80   B

Two 19thC fernware vestas with match stands.

2.5in (6cm) and 1.5in (4cm) high

$270-320   B

A pair of 19thC fernware tulip vases, one with damage to scalloped mouth.

9in (23cm) high

$300-350   B

TARTANWARE

FOLLOWING QUEEN VICTORIA'S 1837 ASCENSION TO THE THRONE AND SUBSEQUENT POPULARIZING OF ALL THINGS Scottish, there was a huge demand for souvenirs from Scotland. Tartans came into vogue not only for fashionable clothing and upholstery fabrics, but also as decorative finishes on wooden souvenir wares. Early tartanware was decorated by hand-ruling and penwork applied directly to the wood. However, from c1853, machines were used to apply colored inks to paper, which was then glued to the item.

In the last decade or so there has been a renewed interest in these simple woodenware items. Their popularity peaked in the early 1990s, when a number of top fashion and interior designers began to incorporate tartans into their ranges. Collectors look for pieces that are unusual, either in terms of size – the larger the better – or shape. Novelty items such as cottage or clock-shaped boxes are particulary sought after. Condition is crucial, as tartanware is difficult to restore, and some collectors will only consider a piece if it appears never to have seen the light of day.

A McBeth tartanware hat-shaped thimble holder, with metal thimble inside.

c1870

1.25in (3.5cm) high

$400-450   RdeR

A rare miniature Robertson tartanware box, with hand-painted picture of Balmoral, signed Lamme Cumnock inside lid.

This unusual painting shows Balmoral before Prince Albert made his additions.

c1850

1in (3cm) wide

$950-1,100   RdeR

Tartanware

A McFarlane tartanware note case, with metal clasp.

c1870   2.75in (7cm) long

$400-450   **RdeR**

A McBeth tartanware match holder.

c1870   4.5in (11.5cm) high

$520-580   **RdeR**

A McDonald tartanware book, "The Lady of The Lake" by Sir Walter Scott, with hand-painted cartouche of "The Monarch of the Glen".

1870   5in (13cm) high

$1,300-1,500   **RdeR**

A Prince Charlie tartanware glove stretcher.

c1870   5.75in (14.5cm) long

$300-350   **RdeR**

A Stuart tartanware jewel box, with metal clasp, slight damage to hinge.

c1870   5in (13cm) wide

$450-500   **RdeR**

A McFarlane tartanware circular pillbox.

c1870   1.75in (4.25cm) wide

$120-150   **MIB**

A beehive-shaped tartanware thimble and needle-holder.

c1870   1.75in (4.5cm) high

$250-300   **MIB**

A late 19thC tartanware rouge pot.

2in (5cm) high

$60-80   **MIB**

A tartanware knife-box-shaped needle case.

c1870   2in (5.5cm) high

$150-200   **MIB**

A Caledonian tartanware standing match striker.

c1870   2in (5.5cm) high

$180-220   **MIB**

A late 19thC large cylindrical tartanware standing container.

3.75in (9.5cm) high

$150-200   **MIB**

An extremely rare glazed tartanware chessboard, in mahogany frame, with photographs of European heads of state and their tartans

c1900   19.25in (49cm) wide

$2,500-3,000   **RdeR**

Tunbridgeware

Tunbridgeware is the name given to the decorative souvenir and gift wares made in and around Tunbridge Wells, in Kent, England from the 17th century until the late 1930s. The most appealing aspect of Tunbridgeware is the ingenuity and skill used in its construction and decoration. Craftsmen exploited the natural colors of local woods to create vivid and complex designs incorporating three dimensional geometrics, flora and fauna and pictorial patterns. Until the 19th century they used the traditional techniques of marquetry and parquetry, but from the late 1820s these were supplanted by the faster techniques of stick work, tessellated mosaic and half-square mosaic.

Since much was bought in the 19th century by Americans, it can turn up unrecognized at antiques fairs and garage sales.

WHAT TO LOOK FOR

When buying Tunbridgeware, collectors look for tessera marquetry in good condition – it is extremely difficult to repair. Views and pieces by named makers will always attract strong interest.

- Avoid pieces that have suffered significant loss or damage.
- Make sure the mosaic is not lifting.
- Check that the lids of boxes close properly, warping is impossible to rectify.
- Beware of cheaper imported versions. Sorrento ware and German strapwork are often mistaken for Tunbridgeware.
- Look for detailed designs and a variety of different woods with good contrasting colors.
- Pieces with their original label are highly sought after.

An early 19thC Tunbridgeware tea caddy, the rectangular body with perspective cube decoration and Vandyke waisted top, the interior with bright perspective cube lid and mahogany mixing bowl surround, with brass ring handles and gilt brass ball feet stands.

12.5in (32cm) wide

$600-650   **B**

A whitewood Tunbridgeware sycamore box, with painted lid.

c1820   4in (10.5cm) wide

$100-150   **MB**

An early Tunbridgeware pin poppet beehive, with pincushion concealed, turned white wood with painted decoration.

c1820   4in (10.5cm) high

$350-400   **RdeR**

◄ An early 19thC whitewood sewing clamp, the circular body painted with a laurel wreath, printed label "A Trifle from Tunbridge Wells" the latter scratched but lettering clearly legible, some paint damage.

6in (15cm) long

$350-400   **B**

Boxes

A 19thC Tunbridgeware burr sycamore box by Robert Russell, bearing the almost unique label of "R. Russell, Tunbridgeware Manufacturer and Inventor of 'Tunbridge Wells Marquetry'".

This glove box was sold for $1,500 in May 1997. This piece is unusual due to its domed top, and features Russell's signature stylized oak-leaf marquetry and a label.

10in (25.5cm) wide

| $3,300-3,600 | B |

A 19thC Tunbridgeware burr sycamore glove box by Wise, the lid with marble cover and tessera cross banding, some damage to front left and back right corners.

A burr or burl is a growth on a tree that when cut reveals complex figuring that lends itself to decorative veneering.

9.5in (24cm) wide

| $450-500 | B |

A 19thC Tunbridgeware rosewood and marquetry box, the domed cover with tessera dog and butterflies, the interior with green silk lining.

8in (20cm) wide

| $450-500 | B |

A 19thC Tunbridgeware rosewood and marquetry box, the domed cover with tessera dog and butterflies, the interior with green silk lining.

8in (20cm) wide

| $450-500 | B |

A 19thC Tunbridgeware rosewood glove box, the domed cover with perspective cube and tessera crossbanding, the interior with marbled papers, restored condition.

10in (25cm) wide

| $450-500 | B |

A 19thC Tunbridgeware rosewood glove box, with floral tessera lid and banded walls.

10.75in (27cm) wide

| $400-450 | B |

A 19thC Tunbridgeware rosewood box, the cover with tessera flower spray on a blond ground.

9in (23cm) wide

| $400-450 | B |

A 19thC Tunbridgeware rosewood stamp box, depicting the head of the young Queen Victoria, said to contain some 1,000 pieces of inlay.

1.5in (4cm) wide

| $300-350 | B |

Left: A 19thC Tunbridgeware mahogany matchbox cover with perspective cube design.

2.5in (6cm) wide

| $150-180 | |

Right: A 19thC Tunbridgeware mahogany matchbox cover by Green, with accompanying notes.

2.5in (6cm) wide

| $250-300 | B |

A 19thC Tunbridgeware rosewood vesta, the octagonal stem with tessera mosaic.

2.5in (6cm) high

| $200-250 | B |

Boxes

A 19thC Tunbridgeware novelty mahogany book-shaped box, having three spine drawers, the cover with perspective cube and tessera mosaic crossbanding.

3.75in (9.5cm) wide

$200-250   **B**

A 19thC Tunbridgeware rosewood box, the cover with tessera flower spray.

4.5in (11cm) wide

$140-180   **B**

A 19thC Tunbridgeware rosewood scent-bottle box, the dome cover with tessera stag, the velvet lined interior missing its two bottles.

5in (13cm) wide

$700-800   **B**

A 19thC Tunbridgeware mahogany box, the cover with tessera Berlin-work panel

Berlinwork *involved copying patterns from Berlin woolwork designs. Many books of patterns were produced in Berlin and these were printed on a grid corresponding with the mesh of the canvas, which enabled the Tunbridgeware manufacturers to reproduce them easily.*

4.5in (11.5cm) wide

$200-250   **B**

A 19thC Tunbridgeware bird's-eye maple tea caddy, the dome top with tessera view of Eridge Castle, the interior with two lidded divisions, the swept sides with broad band of tessera roses, standing on bun feet, restoration right-front and back corners.

10in (26cm) wide

$825-900   **B**

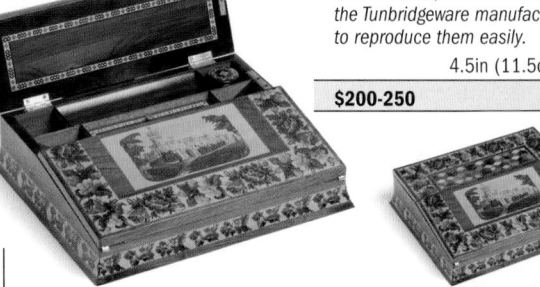

A 19thC Tunbridgeware rosewood writing slope, with tessera view of Eridge Castle and perspective cube lid opening to reveal inkwell and pen box.

13in (33cm) wide

$2,000-2,400   **B**

A rosewood Tunbridgeware snuff-box, with unusual mosaic inlay.

3.5in (8.5cm) diam

$140-170   **MB**

A Tunbridgeware rosewood handkerchief box, with specimen wood lid of tumbling block design.

c1880   6in (15.5cm) wide

$240-280   **MB**

Above: A 19thC Tunbridgeware ruler, with tessera flower band.

6in (15.5cm) long

$90-120   **B**

Below: A 19thC Tunbridgeware ruler, with tessera flower band.

9in (23cm) long

$90-120   **B**

A 19thC Tunbridgeware rosewood desk stand, housing a glass ink bottle with perspective cube lid, the stand with canted edges inlaid with tessera banding, minor damage to all four corners.

4.75in (12cm) wide

$380-420   **B**

A 19thC Tunbridgeware rosewood desk stand, housing a rectangular glass ink bottle between a pair of pen rollocks, the stand with canted front edge inlaid with tessera band of roses, on bun feet

4.75in (12cm) wide

$320-380   **B**

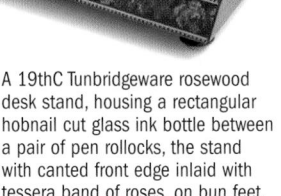

A 19thC Tunbridgeware rosewood desk stand, housing a rectangular hobnail cut glass ink bottle between a pair of pen rollocks, the stand with canted front edge inlaid with tessera band of roses, on bun feet.

5in (12.5cm) wide

$330-390   **B**

GLASS Wine glasses

THE VAST RANGE OF GLASSWARE AVAILABLE, DATING FROM 3000BC TO THE 20TH CENTURY offers enormous scope to collectors. Diversity of shape, color and decorative detail are found in pieces from all periods. Some collectors concentrate on specific types of glass such as potash, lead crystal, or soda, or focus on shape, color, decoration or techniques of manufacture. Unlike silver or porcelain, glass is still relatively undervalued, with an 18th century decanter perhaps costing the same as a modern equivalent. However a modern decanter will only be worth around one tenth of its cost price, whereas an antique will hold or even increase its value over time.

French glass made before the mid-18thC is not widely available. However, after the establishment of the major glasshouses – Baccarat, St. Louis and Clichy, high quality glass was mass-produced, and this is more easily obtainable. Bohemian glass is also abundant, and the beauty of its engraved and colored glass make it highly desirable. Paperweights are often considered to be works of art, and tend to fetch high prices.

The glass market has remained relatively stable over recent decades, although the past year has seen a 20–30 percent rise in value in certain areas, particularly colored enamel twist stem glasses and early baluster wine glasses, Jacobite glass, early bottles and 18th century Dutch engraved glass. Late 19th/early 20thC American glass with deep cutting is becoming more desirable, particularly from the Brilliant period. In certain areas, prices have increased directly due to a collection coming onto the market, which results in raised awareness among collectors. This is certainly true of Dutch engraved glass and the colored enamel twists.

When buying glass it is advisable to spend more on a single good quality piece than to amass a large collection of cheaper wares. In the long run it will be a better investment and will bring greater pleasure to the owner.

A balustroid wine glass, the ovoid bowl engraved with rosebuds over a stem with central swelling knop and folded foot.

c1730   6in (15.5cm) high

$300-350   **JH**

A drawn trumpet wine glass, with multi-spiral air-twist stem and plain foot.

c1745   6.75in (17cm) high

$300-400   **JH**

A balustroid wine glass, the round funnel bowl over a double knop stem containing a tear and folded foot.

c1730   5.5in (14cm) high

$400-420   **JH**

► A composite wine glass, the bell bowl over a beaded knop and shoulder-knopped multi-spiral air-twist stem, with a domed foot.

This glass is extremely rare.

c1745-50   7in (18cm) high

$1,500-1,800   **JH**

A wine glass, the bell bowl over a plain stem and folded foot.

c1730   6in (15cm) high

$150-200   **JH**

A drawn trumpet wine glass, the stem with tear and folded foot.

c1730   6in (15.5cm) high

$180-220   **JH**

A reproduction early to mid-18thC heavy baluster wine glass with a funnel-shaped bowl over a tiered knopped stem.   5in (13cm) high

$650-750   **WW**

Wine glasses

A baluster wine glass, the bowl engraved with shells, flowers and scrolling tendrils, over a knop stem and domed foot, two flat chips beneath the foot.

c1750   6in (15.5cm) high

$300-350   **WW**

A mid-18thC Jacobite wine glass, the bowl engraved with a rose, a bud and an oak leaf, over a knopped air-twist stem and circular foot.

6.75in (17cm) high

$1,300-1,500   **WW**

A wine glass, the bell bowl over a multi-spiral air-twist stem with vermicular collar and plain foot.

c1750   6.25in (16cm) high

$700-800   **JH**

A wine glass, the bell bowl over a mercury air-twist stem and plain foot.

The stem does not contain mercury, but it is so called because of the way that the glass sparkles.

c1750   6.5in (16cm) high

$450-500   **JH**

▶ A late 18thC English commemorative naval wine goblet, engraved with Admiral Howe's flagship titled "Queen Charlotte", and the Clinton crest above a "J.C." monogram and "June 1 1794" within a circle of stars, on a lemon squeezer base.

6.5in (16.5cm) high

$2,500-3,000   **WW**

A wine glass, the round funnel bowl over a double-series air-twist stem and with a plain foot.

This type of glass is sometimes described as a semi-cordial.

c1750   6.75in (17cm) high

$550-650   **JH**

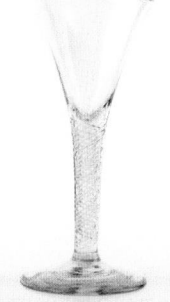

A set of six late 18thC wine glasses, the cylindrical bowls engraved with flowers above fluting to the conical bases and tapering into the double-helix opaque-twist stems on circular feet.

6in (15cm) high

$2,000-2,500 (set)   **Chef**

A wine glass, the plain bowl over an opaque-twist stem.

c1760   5.5in (14cm) high

$300-350   **WW**

A wine glass, the part-molded bowl over a double-series opaque-twist stem.

c1760-70   5.5in (14cm) high

$250-300   **WW**

A wine glass, the funnel-shaped bowl over an opaque-twist stem.

c1760-70   5in (13cm) high

$250-300   **WW**

A wine glass, the tapering conical bowl over an air-twist stem.

c1760   6.25in (16.5cm) high

$200-300   **WW**

Wine glasses

A green tulip-shaped wine glass,

c1830   4.75in (12cm) high

$50-70   **JH**

A ruby-cased wine glass, the petal-cut bowl over a hollow sliced-cut stem.

c1840   5in (13cm) high

$55-85   **JH**

A pale-green wine glass, with ribbed bowl.

c1840   4.25in (11cm) high

$55-70   **JH**

A mid-19thC amber wine glass, with slice-cut bowl and stem.

5in (13cm) high

$60-80   **JH**

A late 19thC wine glass, possibly Lowenstein, an armorial engraved below the gilt rim, tears at the top and below the knop of the stem, the foot folded. This is a revival of an 18thC style.

7in (18cm) high

$120-160   **Chef**

A ruby wine glass, made by J. Powell of Whitefriars.

c1870   4.5in (11.5cm) high

$40-55   **JH**

A G.T. Jackson wine glass, made by J. Powell of Whitefriars.

c1870   5in (12.5cm)

$85-110   **JH**

A ruby-cased and diamond-cut wine glass.

c1890   5in (13cm) high

$40-55   **JH**

A wine glass, the bowl machine acid-etched in gilt over a plain stem.

c1890   5in (13cm) high

$30-35   **JH**

Five Stourbridge blue overlay, clear and amber-tint hock glasses, intaglio-cut with stylized flowers, two with minute footrim chips.

c1900

$4,000-4,500   **DN**

A large Victorian wine glass.

7in (8cm) high

$30-40   **PC**

A baluster "mead" glass, the bowl engraved at a later date, stem with annular knop above an invented baluster, on domed foot. Without engraving this glass would be twice the value.

The traditional belief that this form of glass was used for mead is now discredited and it is generally accepted that they were used for champagne.

c1725   5in (13cm) high

$600-650   **BonE**

A ruby-cased champagne glass, with lens and slice cutting, and a cut stem.

c1820   5in (12.5cm) high

$70-100   **JH**

A G.T. Jackson champagne glass, made by J. Powell of Whitefriars.

c1870   4.75in (12cm) high

$100-170   **JH**

An ale glass, the bell bowl over a plain stem and folded foot.

c1730   7.5in (19cm) high

$280-320   **JH**

An ale glass, with an elongated round funnel bowl, engraved with hops and barley, with a plain stem and folded foot.

c1740   6in (15cm) high

$200-250   **JH**

An 18thC ale glass, the narrow round funnel bowl engraved with hops and barley over a double-knopped air-twist stem and conical foot.

8in (20.5cm) high

$550-600   **BonE**

A flammiform dwarf ale glass.

c1740   4.25in (11cm) high

$300-400   **JH**

An ale glass, the large round funnel bowl over a double-series opaque-twist stem and plain foot.

c1765   7.5in (19cm)

$400-500   **JH**

A pair of late 19thC Stourbridge glass goblets, the ovoid bowls engraved with exotic birds between applied rope swags over rope-ring stems, the rib-edged circular feet engraved with bead band.

6.25in (16cm) high

$180-220   **Chef**

◄ A Scottish presentation goblet, the cup-shaped bowl engraved on either side with monograms WR and IC, flanked by ribbon-tied wreaths of thistles over a knopped stem containing a silver threepenny piece dated 1874, on folded circular foot.

9.25in (23.4cm) high

$300-400   **BonE**

Decanters

A pair of plain glass decanters, with triple neck rings and bull's-eye stoppers.

Neck rings evolved toward the end of the 18thC, both for decoration and ease of handling.

c1800   10.75in (27cm) high

$450-500   **WW**

A decanter of tapering shape, with slice-cut neck and shoulders, the neck rings formed by cutting away from the body, with cut bull's-eye stopper.

c1800   10.25in (26cm) high

$250-300   **JH**

A three neck ring decanter, with bull's-eye stopper.

c1800   10.75in (27cm) high

$250-300   **JH**

A rare Bristol glass decanter, the mallet-shaped body decorated with a gilt suspended octagonal label "Rum", inscribed on base in gilt I. Jacobs Bristol 8, lacking stopper.

Isaac Jacobs *was a second generation German immigrant. In 1806 he presented George III with a purple and gilt "dessert set".*

c1800

$750-850   **BonE**

A decanter, the slice-cut neck having three neck rings, with fruit-cut base and mushroom stopper.

c1810   10in (25.5cm) high

$250-300   **JH**

A decanter, with step-cut neck, the body decorated with cut diamonds, pillars and slices, with pillar-cut mushroom stopper.

c1825   10in (25cm) high

$250-300   **JH**

A square spirit decanter, the diamond-cut canted corners between diamond fruit cutting, with stopper.

c1825   9.5in (24cm) high

$200-250   **JH**

A pair of early 19thC decanters, the step-cut necks above wide diamond-cut bands and flutes, with stoppers, small rim chips.

9in (22.5cm) high

$450-500   **WW**

A pair of decanters, the mallet-shaped bodies cut with a broad band of shallow relief diamonds between prism-cut borders, with stoppers, chips.

c1830   9.75in (25cm) high

$600-700   **BonE**

A pair of glass decanters, with split-cut sides and three steps to the shoulders, with stoppers.

c1835   11.75in (29.5cm)

$150-200   **WW**

An unusual pair of Richardson's translucent glass decanters, decorated with comical figures spelling "Rum" and "Gin" bordered by vine leaves and grapes, marked "Richardson's Vitrified", the silver-gilt stoppers hallmarked for 1835.

c1835   14in (36.5cm) high

$1,300-1,600   **WW**

A CLOSER LOOK AT ENGLISH REGENCY DECANTERS

Regency decanters show the much sought-after skills of English glass-cutters at the beginning of the 19thC when the gilded and engraved styles of the previous century were replaced by heavily cut examples such as this one.

Early Regency decanters feature horizontal bands or panels of deeply cut motifs such as relief or strawberry diamonds. Pillar cutting – the most expensive type of cut glass at the time – was introduced c1820. It was costly because the technique involved cutting away glass from the body of the decanter to create rounded pillars, which required a lot of glass to begin with.

Stoppers are usually variations of the mushroom design, although other shapes include ball and bull's-eye. These are often cut.

WHAT TO LOOK FOR:

- A Regency decanter should feel heavy for its size.
- Matched pairs are worth up to three times the value of a single decanter.
- It is rare to find matching sets of more than four decanters.
- Check the proportions, Regency decanters have a large body and a short neck which makes them easy to handle.
- Good quality cutting adds to the value of Regency glass.
- The glass should have a soft gray tone. Brown or yellow tints are the result of impurities in the glass and are undesirable.
- Continental copies of Regency decanters can be distinguished by a brown tint to the glass. They may also have heavily cut bases and be lighter in weight.
- The style was revived in the 1880s and the 1930s. Copies are often uncomfortable to handle, the color of the glass is too bright and the neck rings are molded from the body rather than applied to it. Examples from the late 19thC are highly collectable, whereas those from the 20thC are not.

The style of decoration should be the same on the stopper and the body.

Neck rings should have been applied to the outside of the decanter.

The decoration should be cut heavily into the glass.

The base should be worn through use.

A decanter, with three neck rings, slice and diamond shoulders and alternate panels of fine diamond cutting, with mushroom stopper.

c1830   9.25in (23.5cm) high

$200-250   **JH**

A decanter with three neck rings, slice-cut shoulders and flute-cut panels, with stopper.

c1835   10.25in (26cm) high

$120-180   **JH**

Two 19thC amber flagons, the ovoid bodies with loop handles and cork stoppers.

9.25in (23.5cm) high

$150-200   **WW**

A pair of 19thC decanters, each of mallet form, the tapering neck with three rings, with a three-mold blown stopper.

10in (25.5 cm) high

$375-450   **SI**

A pair of mid-19thC mallet-shaped decanters, with wrythen-molded bodies and bull's-eye stoppers.

$500-550 (pair)   **BonS**

Decanters

A wine carafe, engraved with fruit and vines.

c1860   8.25in (21cm) high

$150-200   **JH**

▶ An early acid-etched shaft and globe decanter, decorated with fruit and vines, by Richardsons.

Invented around 1830, acid-etching is the frosted or matt finish on glass when it has been exposed to hydrofluoric acid. Jugs, decanters and goblets are the most desirable examples of acid-etched wares.

c1860   11.5in (29cm) high

$300-400   **JH**

One of a pair of shaft and globe decanters, with scallop, miter and lens cutting.

Pairs of these decanters are three times the value of a single.

c1870   13ins (33cm) high

$350-400 (pair)   **JH**

One of a pair of spiral pillar-cut spirit flagons.

8.25in (21cm) high

$375-425 (pair)   **JH**

A pale-green English decanter and stopper, cut with deep swags, in emulation of drapery.

Similarly shaped and colored decanters were produced in Continental Europe during this period, but tend to be much lighter than their heavy, lead glass English equivalents.

c1840-50

$300-400   **JH**

A late 19thC Stourbridge engraved ewer, of globular form with slender cylindrical neck and pinched spout, supported on a domed foot, intaglio-engraved and polished in the rock crystal style, with exotic birds and foliage.

Stourbridge glasshouses *were established in the early 17thC near Stourbridge in the West Midlands. They initially produced flat glass but began to specialize in decorative and colored glass in the mid-18th century.*

$2,000-2,500   **DN**

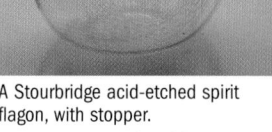

A Stourbridge acid-etched spirit flagon, with stopper.

9in (23.5cm) high

$350-400   **JH**

A pair of late Victorian bell-shaped red glass decanters, with hand-decorated oval cameos and gilt borders.

9.5in (24cm) high

$280-340   **AS&S**

An American-Scottish whisky flagon, engraved with thistles and marked "Libby".

c1900   8.25in (21cm) high

$500-650   **JH**

A 19thC Continental molded yellow glass decanter, together with a "sandwich-type" molded yellow glass spoon holder.

13.5in (34cm) high

$1,000-1,400 (both)   **SI**

A pair of Victorian ruby flash decanters, with grape and vine, decoration, color-rubbed, chipped.

14in (35cm) high

$200-300   **AS&S**

Claret jugs

An Edwardian oak tantalus, with silver-plated handle and mounts, fitted with three cut-glass glass decanters with stoppers and three silver decanter labels.

*A **tantalus** is a wooden frame, often silver-plated, fitted with two to three spirit decanters. The frame could be locked to prevent theft.*

15in (38cm) wide

| $600-650 set | | Clv |

An Edwardian four-division glass ovoid liqueur decanter, with engraved labels, "Starboard Light Crème de Menthe", made for Humphrey Taylor, London, with four silver-plated mounted titled corks.

12in (30.5cm) high

| $150-200 | | Clv |

A pair of Edwardian glass decanters, of cylindrical waisted and tapering form, having bulbous hobnail-cut stoppers, swollen hobnail-cut stem and starburst base, with silver collars made in Sheffield.

1902   14in (36cm) high

| $700-800 | | BonS |

A sliced and flute-cut claret jug, with ball stopper.

c1800   11.5in (29cm) high

| $500-550 | | JH |

A claret jug, with horizontal pillar-cut neck and vertical pillar-cut body, stick-dome handle, and pillar-cut mushroom stopper.

c1820   9in (23cm) high

| $400-500 | | JH |

RICHARDSONS

- W.H., B. & J. Richardson established in 1829 by William Haden Richardson, and his brothers, Benjamin and Jonathan, in Worsley, near Stourbridge, England.

- In c1850 became Henry G. Richardson & Sons

- They produced cut glass as well as many patented techniques, including Bohemian-style glass with color-flashed, clear, and engraved panels. Amber is the most usual color, but red, green and purple were also made.

- Items made in another Richardsons patent, "Vitrified Colors", were displayed at the Great Exhibition of 1851. The process involved firing a transfer-print pattern onto the glass body. Occasionally the enamels were hand-painted.

- Richardsons also made cameo glass vases and scent bottles – many designed by Joseph Locke (1846–1936) before he emigrated to America in 1882 and joined the New England Glass Company.

An early acid-etched claret jug, by Richardsons of Stourbridge, decorated with exotic birds, flowers and butterflies.

c1860   10in (25cm) high

| $850-1,000 | | JH |

A claret jug, with flat-cut flutes and pillar-cut neck rings, with stick-down handle, and mushroom stopper.

c1830   10.5in (26.5cm) high

| $300-400 | | JH |

A claret jug, with slice-cut neck, pillar-cut body and stick-down handle, with stopper.

c1850   12.5in (32cm) high

| $250-300 | | JH |

A waterjug, by Richardsons of Stourbridge, with stylized leaf decoration, frosted inside and miter-cut, with rope-twist handle.

c1860   9.5in (24cm) high

| $280-320 | | JH |

A 19thC glass claret jug and cover, the ovoid body engraved with grasses, with a rope-twist handle and knop.

13in (33cm) high

$400-450   **WW**

Two late 19thC silver-mounted American Brilliant Period cut glass pitchers, each cut vertically with fluting and beading.

12.5in (31.5cm) high

$200-300   **SI**

Two late 19thC silver-mounted American Brilliant Period cut glass pitchers, each cut vertically with fluting and beading.

Much American cut glass made between 1876 and 1914 features deep cutting and was highly polished, giving it a brilliant finish which has given its name to the period. The reflective quality of the glass is enhanced by bold and detailed patterns.

12.5in (31.5cm) high

$850-950   **SI**

A late 19thC silver-mounted American Brilliant Period cut glass pitcher, finely cut with a motif of hobstars and fluting, fitted with an elaborate collar and spout and bordered with beading and shellwork.

13.5in (34.5cm) high

$1,000-1,300   **SI**

A claret jug, the body with acid-etched floral decoration and rope-twist handle.

c1875   11.5in (29cm) high

$350-400   **JH**

A shaft and globe claret jug, the body with lens cutting and stick-down handle, with stopper.

c1880   12.5in (32cm) high

$250-300   **JH**

A champagne jug, of baluster form, engraved with exotic sunflowers.

c1890   10.25in (26cm) high

$250-300   **JH**

A lemonade jug, engraved all over with foliage and berries.

c1890   10in (25.5cm) high

$100-150   **JH**

An early 20thC ruby glass jug, with clear glass handle.

6in (15cm) high

$70-100   **AS&S**

A claret jug, with diamond and miter-cut decoration.

c1900   11.75in (29.5cm) high

$150-200   **JH**

A small lemonade jug, engraved with panels including a stork in an oasis.

c1900   5.5in (14cm) high

$70-100   **JH**

Two 18thC Continental glass rectangular section flasks, the larger painted with two birds, both with flowers and leaves.

7.75in (20cm) high

$500-550   **WW**

Bottles

A French engraved and enameled "cloisonné" bottle marked GF, probably for George Fouquet.

c1800   7.5in (19cm) high

$3,500-4,500   **AL**

A French Charles X extremely rare "gorge de pigeon" perfume bottle, with three-color gold mount.

"Gorge de pigeon" refers to the pale-pink color of a pigeon's throat which this glass copies.

c1815-1825   2.5in (6cm) high

$4,000-6,000   **AL**

A French Charles X Palais Royal turquoise opaline perfume bottle.

c1825   5in (13.5cm) high

$1,000-2,000   **AL**

A French opaline tall cylindrical scent bottle or flacon, in overlaid glass, with Gothic brass stand.

c1835-40   10.76in (27cm) high

$1,000-2,000   **AL**

A French Palais Royal original casket, with three opaline perfume bottles.

c1840-60   5in (13.5cm) high

$1,500-2,000   **AL**

A French ormolu-mounted ruby-glass overlay perfume casket, complete with two bottles key.

c1860   4.75in (12cm) high

$2,500-3,000   **AL**

A late 18thC canoe-shaped pedestal bowl, probably Irish, cut and polished with a husk band beneath a waved rim, on a plain stem and square-molded foot, minute rim chips.

The canoe shape is typical of bowls made as luxury items in Ireland in the late 18thC.

10in (25.5cm) wide

$750-800   **DN**

A pair of serving bottles, of shaft and globe form, each decorated with a sand-blasted bust of Robert Burns and the inscription "Burn's Decanter, Tak'a cup o' kindness yet, for auld Lang Syne".

8.5in (21.5cm) high

$400-450   **BonE**

A set of three George III salts, the oval bowls with petal-edge tops and cut with diamond bands, the diamond-shaped feet on oval serrated-edge plinths.

4in (10cm) wide

$350-450 (set)   **Chef**

A U-shaped sugar bowl and cover, with a short flared foot.

c1800   5.5in (14cm) high

$200-250   **WW**

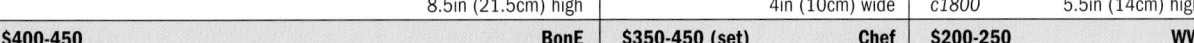

327

Bowls

A pair of piggins, each with large fan-cut handles and serrated rims above a diamond band, some small chips.

Glass piggins were used as drinking vessels or as dippers for milk and cream. They may also be made from ceramic or silver.

A U-shaped sugar bowl and cover, with a short flared foot.

c1800	5.5in (14cm) diam
$200-250	**WW**

c1825	6in (15cm) diam
$700-800 pair	**DN**

A late 19thC Regency Revival cream jug and matching bowl, each cut with bands of diamonds.

5.25in (13.5cm) diam

$150-200	**WW**

A silvered footed glass bowl.

Silvered glass is created by lining glassware with silver, creating a mirror effect. The gap in the base is then sealed and marked. It is important that the seal is intact beacause the piece will deteriorate if it is not airtight.

c1850	6.75in (17.5cm) diam
$300-400	**AL**

▶ A 19thC centerpiece, the central lift-out trumpet engraved with flowers and foliage, the circular bowl similarly decorated and raised on a flared foot.

14.5in (37cm) high

$150-200	**WW**

◀ Two early 19thC American blown cut-glass footed vases, attributed to the Pittsburgh Glass Works, Pittsburgh, each trumpet-form body cut with stylized leafy upper border above a strawberry and fan border over a knopped stem and round base, chip.

8in (20cm) high

$375-425	**SI**

An extremely rare pair of French Charles X vases, in gorge de pigeon opaline glass and bronze.

c1825	10in (25.5cm) high
$12,000-15,000	**AL**

A 19thC American cut-glass vase, the rim of the bowl cut with urns and diamond-filled rectangular reserves, the body cut with flutes on faceted stem and octagonal base.

7.25in (18.5cm) high

$300-350   **SI**

A 19thC American gilt and grisaille-decorated opaline glass vase, in urn-form with a view of the US Capitol, and inscribed in gold to reverse "Capitol of the US, Washington," chip to rim.

9.5in (24cm) high

$1,200-1,500   **SI**

A French turquoise opaline vase, in exceptional condition, probably St Louis.

Opaline is colored opaque glass. The St. Louis glassworks were founded in the mid-18th century and became well known manufacturers of lead crystal glass.

c1850-60   10in (25.5cm) high

$1,500-2,500   **AL**

A French yellow opaline glass vase, with red and white spiral cable torsade, by St. Louis or Clichy.

c1850-60   5.5in (14cm) high

$1,000-1,500   **AL**

A pair of Victorian pink overlay glass vases, of slender baluster shape with tulip rim, the opaque white body painted with gilt leaves.

15.75in (40cm) high

$300-350   **BonE**

A French "rock crystal" vase, engraved with marine life and with fine quality enamel work, unmarked.

"Rock crystal" is glass engraved in rock crystal style.

c1880   8.75in (22cm) high

$4,000-5,000   **AL**

A pair of black opaline glass vases.

c1880   10.5in (27cm) high

$400-500   **SS**

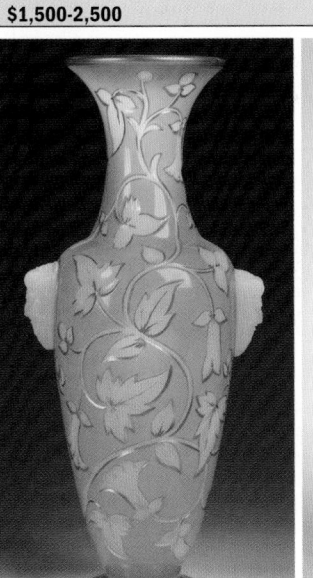

A French opaline vase, of baluster shape, the white opaline body cased in pink with cut and gilt white lilies, the shoulders with applied moulded masks of Pan.

c1880   15.5in (39.5cm) high

$300-350   **BonE**

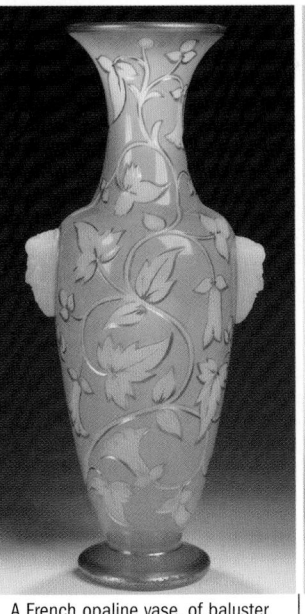

A large ruby glass vase, of baluster shape, the white overlay cut with flowers and foliage.

c1880   16.5in (42cm) high

$300-350   **BonE**

A 19thC cranberry glass epergne, the four trumpets with clear crimped rim and applied with clear spiral-pincered decoration, the three clear crook-shaped rope-twist arms suspending baskets, on circular base with clear crimped rim.

Epergnes *are table centerpieces, produced from the 18thC.*

$1,000-1,300	BonE

A 19thC seven-branch glass epergne, the borders shading from red and opaque white through clear glass.

20in (51cm) high

$800-900	WW

A 19thC vaseline glass epergne, with three spiralling clear glass canes, the four trumpets and base applied with crimped yellow borders.

21.75in (55cm) high

$600-800	WW

A 19thC cranberry glass seven-branch epergne, with wavy edges.

19.75in (50cm) high

$900-1,200	WW

A pair of 19thC cut glass lusters, the baluster stem with bands of diamond cutting, the scalloped rim hung with prism-cut drops.

6.75in (17cm) high

$700-800	BonE

A pair of Victorian pink overlay glass lusters, of globular shape with knopped stem, painted with flowers and leaves in colors and gilt, with prism-cut drops.

14in (35.5cm) high

$700-800	BonE

A pair of Victorian lusters, the star-cut bases supporting tapering octagonal stems and spiral-cut sconces with prism drops.

8.25in (21cm) high

$420-450 pair	Chef

A late 19thC table luster, with a faceted stem and circular base.

9.5in (24cm) high

$200-250	WW

A pair of early 20thC cut glass lusters, the fan-cut rims hung with beads and drops (replaced), the hexagonal tapering vase stems on star-cut feet.

6in (15cm) high

$150-200	Chef

Bohemian goblets

THE AREA OF EASTERN AND CENTRAL EUROPE KNOWN AS BOHEMIA BEGAN PRODUCING GLASS AS EARLY AS THE 5TH CENTURY. During the 16th and 17th centuries glassmakers began to experiment with making colored glass by adding minerals to the batch. However, it was not until the early 19th century that there were significant developments.

Three Bohemian chemists, Friederich Egermann and the Counts Buquoy and Harrach made discoveries that led to the mass production of affordable, fine quality colored glass. Buquoy invented a dense opaque glass called "Hyalith", or flashed glass, usually in dark red or black, and Engermann patented "Lithyalin", or stained glass, a polished opaque glass that was then brushed with metal oxides to resemble veining. By the 1860s there were around 100 factories and Bohemian glass manufacturing had become a well-established industry, exporting worldwide.

Ruby, cranberry, amber, blue, green and violet were the most sought-after colors, and pieces were often engraved with views of spa towns and civic buildings. Other popular decorations were woodland scenes with stags, dogs and huntsmen.

Today Bohemian glass is generally more affordable than Venetian glass, which retains its popularity due to the flourishing tourist trade. The earlier, better cut Bohemian wares are stronger and of more value than later pieces which tend to be thinner and weaker. The quality of the color and overall condition of the glass are the main determinants of worth.

WHAT TO LOOK FOR

- Overall condition. With colored glass, especially when it is heavily cut and engraved, it can be difficult to detect small chips or cracks, so be extremely vigilant when checking for damage. Goblets were often made with covers, so make sure that this is not missing.
- High quality decoration. Overlay glass has a greater depth and quality of decoration than flashed or stained glass. Feel for varying degrees of relief in the engraved surface and examine the depth of the cuts.
- Good, strong colors. Stained glass is always duller than overlay glass, but sometimes it is also blotchy and uneven. Unlike overlay glass, stained glass was not generally given an all-over color, many pieces were only partially stained. Blue stained glass is susceptible to fading and this will affect the value.
- Identification. Two of the three main types of glass, potash and lead, are used in the manufacture of Bohemian glass. They can be identified by color, weight, and the "ping" they make if you tap them with a fingernail. Potash glass gives a dull ring, whereas lead glass is heavier and gives a clear ring.

A pair of late 19thC Bohemian cut to clear glass covered amber goblets, the cover with a faceted spire finial, the bowl etched with a scene of a deer in a landscape, the stem with a faceted knop, the whole set upon a scalloped foot.

13.5in (34.5cm) high

| $800-900 | | SI |

A Bohemian alabaster glass goblet and cover, with gilt engraved spa views, with English initials and coronet, dated.

1860   9.5in (24cm) high

| $700-1,000 | | AL |

A Bohemian amber flash goblet and cover, engraved with stags in a woodland setting.

c1840   16.75in (42.5cm) high

| $1,000-1,700 | | AL |

A two-color Bohemian stained flash goblet and cover.

Staining involves the application of metal oxides to clear glass, which is then fired to fix the color. Flashed glass is similar to overlay glass but has a much thinner layer of colored glass applied over the clear body.

c1850   16.75in (42.5cm) high

| $2,000-3,000 | | AL |

A mid-19thC Bohemian overlay glass vase of baluster shape, the seaweed gilt white overlay cut with onion topped lappet panels through to sky-blue glass below.

11.5in (29cm) high

$300-350 Chef

A mid-19thC Bohemian glass vase, the serrated rim above alternating white overlay panels of flowers and diamond cutting, repeated on the baluster body, the socle foot cut with six panels in gilt with scrolling rinceaux.

17.25in (44cm) high

$500-600 Chef

A mid-19thC Bohemian glass vase and cover, of classical form on a spreading circular base, with all-over gilt leafy scrollwork, the sides with two overlay panels, painted on one side with a bust portrait of a young woman, the other with a bouquet of flowers.

17in (43cm) high

$1,000-1,200 BonS

A pair of late 19thC Bohemian glass vases, of baluster form, with clear glass overlaid with rose in a leaf pattern veined with gold, highlighted in gilt, both later mounted as lamps.

24in (61 cm) high

$450-550 SI

A mid-19thC Bohemian flashed and engraved glass vase, the cylindrical body cut with a scrolling pattern, the center of the scrolls decorated with raised medallions, one with heart, one with cornucopia, one with cross and the other inscribed "E.M".

6in (15cm) high

$300-400 SI

A pair of modern Bohemian enameled glass vases, opaque-white cut to cranberry, each of ovoid form and set on a broad disc foot, the whole decorated with polychrome floral sprigs and highlighted with gilt.

12.25in (31cm) high

$300-400 SI

A Bohemian overlay trumpet-shaped vase.

Overlay glass, sometimes known as "cased glass" consists of a clear body covered with one or more relatively thick layers of colored glass. The design is then cut through the top layers.

c1865   19.75in (50cm) high

$900-1,400 AL

A pair of 19thC Bohemian amber flashed etched glass trumpet vases, each tall paneled vessel with floriform knop and foot, engraved with grapevines, chips to bases.

21.5in (54.5cm) high

$1,800-2,200 SI

A pair of white-on-ruby overlay Bohemian vases.

One of the pair would be only one third of the value of the pair.

c1868   11.75in (30.5cm) high

$1,100-1,700 AL

A footed Bohemian overlay vase, with hand-painted panels of flowers and a rabbit.

c1870   8.75 (22cm) high

$350-500 AL

▶ A pair of mid-19thC Bohemian white overlaid glass vases, decorated with panels cut with diamonds and painted with flowers on a gilt scrolling ground, one damaged.

8.75in (22cm) high

$250-300 WW

Bohemian vases

A pair of late 19thC Bohemian tulip-shaped vases, each on a knopped stem, with opaque-white ruby overlay panels, decorated in gilt.

15.25in (39cm) high

$1,000-1,200	BonE

A late 19thC Bohemian cranberry glass vase, of paneled cylindrical shape, painted in enamels with central crest within a ribbon-tied wreath, the reverse with a titled cartouche-shaped scrolling panel.

8.75in (22cm) high

$150-200	Chef

A late 19thC Bohemian baluster vase, white cut to green, cut in a Gothic pattern, the whole highlighted with gilt strippling and floral and foliate motifs, converted to a lamp.

11.25in (29cm) high

$400-500	SI

A Bohemian ruby flash glass vase, engraved with a stag and scrolls.

c1940   4.75in (12cm) high

$75-100	BonE

A pair of 20thC Bohemian vases engraved with bird scrolls, one damaged.

6in (15.5cm) high

$30-55	BonE

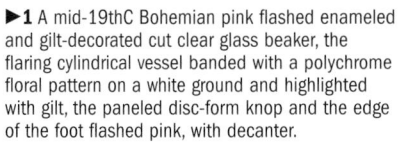

A Bohemian overlay glass jug, cut through to clear with roundels enclosing polychrome-enameled flower sprays and single blooms, the shoulder and spout with gilded acanthus leaves, together with two conforming drinking glasses.

c1875   11.5in (29cm) high

$800-900	BonS

- The shape of this decanter is interesting, the hookah form being based on the Turkish "hubbly-bubbly" pipes.
- The piece is rare – due to the turbulent situation in the Middle East in the last 150 years there is little surviving Bohemian glass of this form.
- It is particularly unusual to find a pair of decanters of this type with both stoppers intact.
- Always check that the stopper is right for the piece, sometimes they are numbered, and this should correspond with the number on the main body of the piece.
- Check that the stopper and top rim show signs of age and wear. If not, it may have been ground down to disguise damage.

▶1 A mid-19thC Bohemian pink flashed enameled and gilt-decorated cut clear glass beaker, the flaring cylindrical vessel banded with a polychrome floral pattern on a white ground and highlighted with gilt, the paneled disc-form knop and the edge of the foot flashed pink, with decanter.

▶2 A mid-19thC Bohemian pink flashed enameled and gilt-decorated cut clear glass decanter, decorated with a polychrome floral spray centered with a cobalt blue medallion inscribed in German, the neck banded with grapes and vines, highlighted with gilt, chips.

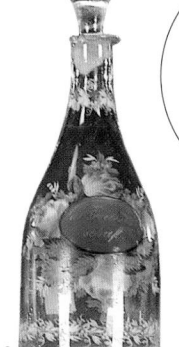

Decanter 11.5in (29cm) high

$250-350 (both)	SI

One of a pair of Bohemian overlay decanters, of hookah form, made for the Islamic market.

c1865   13.5in (34.5cm) high

$2,500-3,500 pair	AL

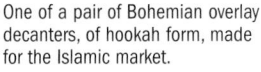

An 18thC Bohemian glass beaker, the tapering cylindrical sides wheel-engraved and cut with birds, foliage and ovals.

6.75in (17.5cm) high

$150-200	Chef

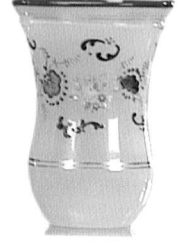

A Bohemian turquoise opaline beaker.

c1845   5.25in (13.5cm) high

$900-1,300	AL

A pink double-overlay Bohemian beaker.

c1845   5.5in (14cm) high

$550-850	AL

A mid-19thC Bohemian ruby flashed and enameled clear glass beaker, the paneled vessel with ocher and ivory scroll and foliage enamel work, the whole highlighted with gilt.

5in (13cm) high

$500-600	SI

A mid-19thC Bohemian enameled glass beaker, decorated with ocher and beige scrolling motifs and highlighted with gilt.

5in (13cm) high

$200-300	SI

A mid-19thC Bohemian enameled yellow vaseline glass beaker, the waisted flaring vessel painted with flowers with gilt foliage and silver scrolls, the lip cased in cobalt.

4.75in (12cm) high

$250-300	SI

An overlaid Bohemain clear cut glass mug, with clear handle and gilt rim, cut in a diaper pattern, together with a mid-19thC Bohemian pink and white overlaid clear cut glass beaker. A metal mount indicates a damaged rim.

5in (13cm) high

$150-200 (both)	SI

Two mid-19thC Bohemian flash cut glass beakers, the paneled vessels both flashed pink at the ribs, some chips, gilding worn.

5in (13cm) high

$150-250 set	SI

A Bohemian ruby flash tankard, sides engraved with buildings, the cover with a stag. This therefore combines the two most popular subjects.

c1845   5in (12.8cm) high

$600-800	AL

A 20thC Bohemian cranberry glass beaker, decorated in gilt and silver with a band of scrolled and "jeweled" flowers and foliage, within scale pattern borders, damaged.

4in (10cm) high

$30-50	HamG

► A Bohemian ruby flash two-footed beaker, with a view of a spa town, inscribed "La Fontaine Elise".

Made for sale in France, this piece is unusual as it depicts a foreign spa town.

c1875

$200-300	

5in (13cm) high

	AL

Bohemian lusters

A mid-19thC Bohemian engraved yellow vaseline glass mug, the ovoid vessel centered with a raised octagonal panel engraved with a classical building among tall trees, entitled in German.

4.5in (11.5cm) high

$150-200 SI

A Bohemian enameled humpen, with historismus decoration dated 1645.

*The term **historismus** refers to 19thC glass made in styles from earlier centuries. It was mainly made in Germany and was particularly popular after the reunification of Germany in 1871 when, in an attempt to create a sense of national unity, glasses were produced with enameled decoration of fictional coats of arms.*

c1865 6.5in (16.7cm) high

$200-350 AL

A 19thC Bohemian luster. The value of a single luster is considerably less than half that of a pair.

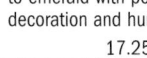

12.25in (31cm) high

$450-500 Chef

A pair of 20thC Bohemian glass overlaid lusters, opaque white-cut to emerald with polychrome floral decoration and hung with prisms.

17.25in (43.8cm) high

$1,500-2,000 SI

A pair of Bohemian ruby flash wine glasses, engraved with grape and vine pattern.

c1865 5.75in (14.5cm) high

$200-400 AL

A pair of modern Bohemian enameled white overlaid green glass lusters, each baluster-form standard with floriform pan hung with prisms, surmounted by a campana-form vase, decorated with polychrome floral sprays and gilt highlights, mounted as lamps.

$1,000-1,300 SI

A pair of Bohemian ruby glass lusters, the scalloped bowl decorated with white overlay medallions painted with portraits and flowers, on straight stem and domed foot with similar medallions, on gilt-decorated ground, hung with non-original, replaced drops, halving the value of the pair.

12.25in (31cm) high

$900-1,200 BonE

A pair of ruby flash lusters, on baluster stem cut with ovals, the scalloped rim hung with prism-cut drops.

The term "luster" refers to the glass drops that are hung from the drip pan of candlesticks. The hanging glass rods are faceted to catch and reflect the light and the attached beads help them to hang more easily and give a little movement.

$300-350 BonE

An unusual early Bohemian perfume bottle, with chinoiserie decoration and a reducing lens stopper.

c1845 8.75in (22cm) high

$700-1,000 AL

A mid-19thC Bohemian enameled yellow vaseline glass perfume bottle and jar, the jar (shown) of paneled cylindrical form with deeply scalloped rim and foot, each enameled in white, rose, deep blue, orange, red and gilt with floral sprays and scrolling flourishes, jar with chips.

Jar 5.5in (14cm) high

$200-300 SI

Bohemian bottles

A pair of mid-19thC Bohemian green glass perfume bottles, each originally centered with reserves surrounded by gilt beading and rocaille, with gilt spherical stoppers.

6in (15cm) high

$250-300	SI

A cobalt-blue Bohemian perfume bottle, overlaid in white.

c1860   5in (13cm) high

$250-350	AL

A Bohemian overlaid opaline glass casket, for sugar, tea or jewelry.

Opaline *is a translucent milky-white glass which, by the addition of various metallic oxides can be colored. It was originally discovered in France c1810, but was later made by Bohemian factories. The Bohemian pieces tend to be thicker and heavier.*

c1845   5in (13cm) high

$2,500-3,500	AL

A Moser (Karlsbad) Bohemian ruby polychrome-enameled casket, for tea, sugar or jewelry.

c1850   4.5in (11.5cm) high

$900-1,300	AL

A mid-19thC Bohemian vaseline glass bowl with undertray, the bowl of paneled form with flaring tab-shaped handles, the undertray with a deeply scalloped rim, both decorated with silver scrolling vines and foliage. The missing cover reduces its value by 50 percent.

6.25in (16cm) diam

$350-400	SI

A mid-19thC Bohemian glass and gilt metal mounted iron, modeled as a coal heated iron and fitted with a drawer, the whole decorated with gilt and silver flowers and foliage.

6in (15cm) long

$1,000-1,300	SI

A Bohemian ruby flash engraved perfume bottle, with rare "umbrella" stopper.

c1870   8.75in (22cm) high

$1,000-1,300	AL

A Bohemian amber-flashed glass stand, the decagonal bowl engraved with deer beneath trees and vines, over a faceted knopped stem and octagonal foot.

7in (18cm) diam

$400-450	WW

A three-color double-overlay Bohemian perfume bottle, probably Harrach.

c1880   8in (20.2cm) high

$850-1,100	AL

A late 19thC Bohemian footed jar and cover, cylindrical-molded with two rings, a cushion base and shoulder, cut with circle and oval decoration, the domed cover with shaped knop.

15.5in (39.5cm) high

$200-250	SI

Paperweights

A Baccarat multi-cane scatter glass paperweight.

1847　　　2.75in (7cm) diam

$1,300-1,500　　　**GorL**

A 19thC Baccarat-style faceted pansy paperweight, the petals about a pink and white star center, with five leaves and star-cut base, "Juin 1890 H D Tour Eiffel" etched to outer rim.

Baccarat made weights in various sizes and specialized in brightly colored carpet grounds. Rare weights include those featuring a snake, lizard or butterfly.

1.75in (4.5cm) diam

$400-500　　　**BonE**

A 19thC Baccarat close millefiori paperweight, the colored canes including a silhouette of a butterfly.

3.25in (8.5cm) diam

$1,000-1,300　　　**BonE**

A 19thC Clichy scrambled cane paperweight.

2.5in (6.5cm) diam

$700-800　　　**GorL**

An unusual pair of 19thC American paperweight mantle ornaments, each composed of a globe with a central white, blue and pink crystalline trumpet enclosing an air bubble surrounded by three similar trumpets, on a separate baluster-form base with enclosed bubble decoration.

$700-850　　　**SI**

A Clichy patterned millefiori paperweight, the clear glass set with a central pink and green rose cane surrounded by a trefoil garland composed of multi-colored composite florets.

c1845　　　3.25in (8cm) diam

$1,200-1,600　　　**SI**

A St. Louis faceted dahlia paperweight, the clear glass set with a flower composed of fifteen overlapping cobalt-blue pointed and ribbed petals around a blue and white star-form stamen with four green leaves and a stem, on a latticinio ground.

c1845　　　3.25in (8cm) diam

$800-900　　　**SI**

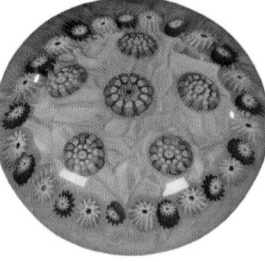

A mid-19thC St. Louis faceted garland and posy paperweight, the clear glass set with a central bouquet of five millefiori canes in shades of blue, ocher, yellow, pink and white over six green leaves and surrounded by a garland of pink, green and white floret canes.

3in (7.5cm) diam

$750-800　　　**SI**

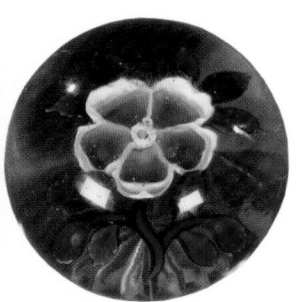

A 19thC Baccarat dog-rose paperweight, the clear glass set with a flower formed with five petals edged in white around a white stardust stamen and red-whorl cane center, on a green stem with eleven leaves, with a star-cut base.

2.5in (6.5cm) diam

$750-800　　　**SI**

A 19thC faceted millefiori glass paperweight, on latticinio ground, the clear glass set with a central green, white, yellow and pink composite cane surrounded by scattered star canes.

2.75in (7cm) diam

$750-800　　　**SI**

A 19thC New England paperweight, the hollow glass pear shaded from pinkish-red to yellow, on a clear glass circular base.

2.75in (6.5cm) diam

$400-450　　　**SI**

A small 19thC millefiori glass paperweight, on latticinio ground, the clear glass set with a central pink, blue, green and white composite floret and star cane, star and whorl canes within a garland of alternating coral, blue and white pastry mold canes, on an upset muslin ground.

2.25in (5.5cm) diam

$450-550　　　**SI**

A 19thC St. Louis paperweight, the clear glass set in the center with a pink, yellow and white composite star cane, on a blue and white jasper ground.

2.5in (6cm) diam

$750-850	SI

A 19thC St. Louis paperweight, with two central concentric rings reserved on a blue and white japser ground.

St. Louis produced paperweights from the 1840s.

2in (5.5cm) diam

$400-450	BonE

PAPERWEIGHTS

The Venetian glassmaker Pietro Bigaglia produced paperweights from 1843 and this is probably where they originated. Although not an immediate success in Venice, they became popular in France, where Baccarat, St. Louis and Clichy were the dominant producers. The technique involves placing tiny sections or "set-ups" of colored canes or rods on a decorative ground in a mold. This is then covered with a dome of clear glass which magnifies the pattern, which often includes flowers, fruit and insects.

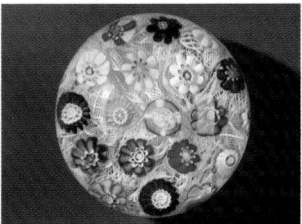

A Clichy millefiori weight, the spaced concentric canes reserved on a tossed muslin ground.

The Clichy glassworks was established in 1837, first in Billancourt, and then at Clichy-la-Garenne, in Paris.

c1850   2in (5cm) diam

$500-550	BonE

A Baccarat-style red and white primrose weight, the flower with five green leaves showing behind, the stalk with six further leaves.

2in (5cm) diam

$300-350	BonE

A 19thC clematis paperweight, the yellow, blue and white centered flower with two layers of deep blue petals, against four green leaves.

1.5in (3.5cm) diam

$150-200	BonE

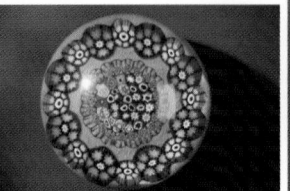

A Monart millefiori weight, the center with colored canes within a pink cane border, with an outer ring of blue, pink and white canes on a blue ground, with paper label.

2.75in (7cm) diam

$700-800	BonE

A late 19thC English millefiori glass ink bottle and stopper, the bell-form base and mushroom-form stopper set with concentric rings of star canes in shades of cobalt-blue, yellow, lavender, white, pink and mint green.

6in (15cm) high

$600-700	SI

A Paul Ysart butterfly paperweight, the blue insect encircled by purple and pink canes.

Paul Ysart was born in Barcelona of Bohemian parents and produced some of the finest British paperweights in Scotland. Many of his designs feature millefiori decoration.

2.75in (7cm) diam

$600-700	WW

A 19thC Baccarat-style pansy weight, the petals about a pink and white star center, with a bud and leaves, star-cut and faceted base, small chip and scratching to surface.

3.5in (8.5cm) diam

$450-550	BonE

An late 19thC "end of the day" paperweight.

1.25in (3cm) diam

$90-120	BonE

A miniature paperweight, with a spray of three colored flowerheads with green leaves.

1.5in (3.5cm) diam

$150-200	BonE

A Perthshire scattered millefiori weight, the canes on a tossed muslin ground, including silhouettes, a kangaroo and an elephant.

2in (5cm) dia

$150-200	BonE

Miscellaneous

A French Charles X opaline snuff or pill box, in verte absinthe color.

1815-1825   2in (5cm) diam

$1,800-2,500   AL

A 19thC French turquoise opaline glass box and cover, with gilt metal mounts, on scroll and figure cast supports and shaped rectangular base with loop feet.

7.5in (19cm) high

$750-850   DN

A glass tazza, with an eight-sided molded pedestal stem and a domed, folded foot.

c1750   11.75in (30cm) diam

$350-400   JH

A late 18thC small glass tazza, with a multi-ribbed, molded pedestal stem and a domed fold-over foot.

6.25in (16cm) diam

$250-300   JH

Two early 19thC American blown and cut-glass compotes, attributed to the Pittsburgh Glass Works, Pittsburgh, each cut with geometric devices in a diamond and fan pattern, the bowl raised on a single knopped stem and circular base, surface scratches.

11in (28cm) high

$2,000-2,500   SI

Three mid-19thC American clear pressed glass celery glasses, first possibly Sandwich, two of the same pattern with thumbprints, the third with a ruffled lip.

9.75in (25cm) high

$150-200   SI

A pair of late 19thC Venetian glass figural compotes, each shell-form bowl of clear glass mottled with rose and gilt, with applied dragon-form handles.

10in (25.5cm) high

$850-950   SI

Six early 20thC enameled Bohemian glass sorbet dishes and liners, each banded with deep-green leaves on a pale-green ground, the lip edged in gilt.

3.5in (9cm) high

$150-200 set   SI

Two American free-blown witch balls. The first ball solid blue, the second clear ball with red, white and blue loops.

Witch balls *date from the late 17th century, and were popular in England, Europe and America. They were believed to protect from evil spirits.*

8in (20cm) diam

$500-550   SI

A French "Bristol" blue glass serpent with gilded scales.

Bristol glass *was originally made in Bristol, England from the end of the 18th century, but the term came to be used generically for similar Continental glass.*

c1840   4in (10cm) diam

$900-1,200   AL

▶ A French enameled glass curio, in Persian taste, signed JP Imberton and dated.

It is unclear if this piece was intended to be this unusual shape or whether it was an accident that was allowed through.

1882   3.75in (9.5cm) high

$1,100-1,500   AL

◀ Three Clarkes "fairy" glass night-lights, with wrythen cranberry shades, stencilled S Clarke's Patent, the glass bases with similar molded marks.

4.75in (12cm) high

$250-300   Chef

Miscellaneous

A pair of Continental cut clear crystal and cobalt crystal three-arm candelabra, on a square-molded brass plinth with four spherical feet.

24in (70cm) high

$10,000-13,000	SI

Three 19thC American blown and pressed-glass fluid lamps, various patterns, with burners.

Tallest 11in (28cm) high

$400-500	SI

▶ A 19thC American fluted-glass candlestick with silvered interior, along with a similar candlestick.

8.75in (22cm) high

$85-110	GorL

A large glass whisky dispenser, of ovoid shape on knopped-stem and domed-foot and engraved "DUNVILLE'S OLD IRISH WHISKY, BELFAST", chipped and lacking cover.

20in (51cm) high

$550-600	BonE

▶ A large whisky dispenser and cover, engraved and inscribed in gilt BALDERSON'S Special JG's BEST, chipped. Beware of modern copies when buying.

28.75in (73cm) high

$600-700	BonE

◀ A Regency cut-glass urn and cover, the body covered with a wide band of diamonds.

11.5in (29cm) high

600-700	BonE

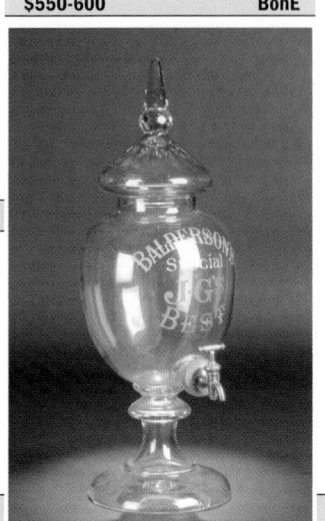

A late 19thC Continental glass wine funnel on stand, the handled funnel etched with grape clusters and vines and supported on a silver-plated stand, the S-scroll arm cast with grapes and leaves, the scalloped base engraved with rococo scrolls, with floral and foliate motifs.

22.5in (57cm) high

$400-500	SI

COFFEEPOTS

A George III silver coffeepot, marks rubbed, probably London, of tapering cylindrical form, decorated with repoussé work with flowers and leaves on fine stippled ground, the bombe hinged cover with bud finial, the leaf-capped spout issuing from foliage, with multi-scroll wooden handle.

1753-54   10.25in (26cm) high

$1,200-1,500   **SI**

A George III Irish silver coffeepot, by William Homer, of baluster shape on circular foot with gadrooned decoration, the hinged bombe cover with flame finial, with scrolled wooden handle.

c1770   10 .75in (27.5cm) high

$2,000-3,000   **SI**

A George III silver coffeepot, by William Grundy, London, of baluster shape on reeded and beaded foot, the leaf-capped spout issuing from foliage, the bombe cover with beaded rim and baluster finial, with scrolled wooden handle, engraved with a crest.

1776-77   10.75in (27cm) high

$3,000-4,000   **SI**

A George III silver traveling coffeepot, marked "I.H.", London, of tapering cylindrical form, with flat detachable cover and folding handle.

1784   5.5in 14cm high

$1,000-1,500   **SI**

A French silver coffeepot, the spout modeled as an animal head and the feet as animal feet.

c1820   11.5in (29cm) high

$1,500-2,000   **JBS**

A silver coffeepot, by Emes and Barnard, London.
Rebecca Emes and Edward Barnard (a. 1808-1829) were important Regency silversmiths who supplied silver to Royal jewelers and silversmiths Rundell, Bridge and Rundell.

1825   8.75in (22.5cm) high

$1,000-1,500   **JBS**

Four pieces from a Victorian silver tea and coffee service, by E Barton, London, comprising a coffeepot, teapot, two-handled open sugar and creamer.

1839-40   Coffeepot 9.75in (25cm) high

$4,500-5,000   **SI**

A silver coffeepot, by Hayne and Cater, London.

1846   10.5in (26.5cm) high

$1,000-1,500   **JBS**

◀ A silver teapot, coffeepot, milk jug and sugar bowl, by Hayne and Cater, London.

1850 Coffeepot 11.5in (29cm) high

$3,000-4,000   **JBS**

A silver coffeepot, by Edward Hutton, London.

1883   9in (23 cm) high

$800-1,000   **JBS**

An 18thC Alexander Gordon, New York, sterling teapot, oval, canted corners, bright cut foliate band at the foot and shoulder, monogrammed cartouche flanked by garlands, hinged cover, pear finial, straight spout, ebonized handle.

1795-1803 21oz 7in (18cm) high

$2,000-2,500 SI

Three pieces from a 19thC Shepherd & Boyd, Albany, NY coin silver tea service, teapot (unmarked), two-handled cover sugar and creamer; oval, lobed lower body, a foliate and floral band at the shoulder, bombe cover, bud finial, multi scroll handle.

1810-30 65oz (4dwt) teapot 9.75in (25cm) high

$2,000-3,000 SI

A 19thC E. Cole, New York State, coin silver tea & coffee service, coffeepot, teapot, two handle cover sugar and creamer; shaped rectangular, berries and foliate band at the shoulder, the rims applied with palmettes, bombe cover, angular handle.

1818-26 Coffeepot 8.5in (21.5cm) h

$2,500-3,500 SI

A silver tea pot and covered sugar, Samuel Kirk, Baltimore, Maryland, each of bombe form on circular foot, two vacant cartouches flanked by scrolls, foliage and flowers, leaf-capped handle and spout, hinged cover, bud finial, engraved on the underside of each foot "Presented to M.A. Hatch by F.A. Clifton", marked "S. Kirk 10.15".

c1840 Coffeepot 8.75in (22.25cm)

$500-600 SI

A five piece 19thC S.Kirk. Baltimore, MD sterling repousse tea and coffee service, marked "Sterling SK", coffeepot, teapot, kettle on stand, two handled covered sugar and creamer; baluster shape on circular foot, the body repousse with castle, architectural design in landscape within repousse flowers and foliage on fine stippled ground, hinged cover and foot with similar decoration, foliage and floral finial, foliate and floral angular handle capped with ram's head; kettle on stand with conforming decoration, swing handle capped with two ram's heads, two floral and foliate supports on circular base with conforming decoration.

c1830-46 Kettle 16.5in (42cm) high

$13,000-18,000 SI

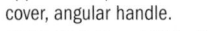

Six piece Tuttle Silversmiths, Boston sterling tea and coffee service, coffee pot, teapot, kettle on stand, two handle covered sugar, creamer and waste bowl, ovoid form, fluted lower body on square base and partly fluted circular foot, loop handle, leaf-capped spout, partly fluted bombe hinged cover; kettle with conforming decoration, fixed handle on circular stand with burner, four foliate supports, engraved with a crest.

1929-1933 kettle 15in (38cm) h

$4,000-4,500 SI

A three-piece Gorham sterling demi-tasse coffee service, no.2311, baluster shape with canted corner on oval foot, angular handle, swan neck spout.

Coffeepot 11in (28cm) high

$700-800 SI

◄ Three pieces from a sterling demi-tasse coffee service, Old Newbury crafters, coffeepot, two handle open sugar, creamer; baluster shape, waisted reeded band, on molded foot, dome cover, ball finial, monogrammed.

Coffeepot 8.5in (22cm) high

$500-600 SI

► A coffeepot, marked "sterling", ovoid on circular foot, applied at the shoulder with grapevines, foliate rims, floral and foliate capped handle, swan neck spout capped and issuin g from foliage, hinged cover, bud finial.

11.5in (29cm) high

$1,500-2,500 SI

Nine pieces Towle Manufacturing sterling tea & coffee service, "Lady Constance" pattern, coffee pot, chocolate pot, teapot, two handle covered sugar, 2 creamers, waste bowl and two handle tray; ovoid, foliate and beaded band at the shoulder, on reeded circular foot with beaded decoration, leaf-capped spout and handle issuing from foliage, dome cover, bud finial; two handle tray, border applied with foliate band, flowers and scrolling foliage at intervals, two foliate handles.

245oz tray 27in (69cm) long

$5,500-6,000   **SI**

A three piece W. Gale & Son for Dominick & Haff sterling bachelor tea service, teapot, two handle open sugar and creamer, oval canted corners, bright cut decoration of scrolls and foliage centering two vacant cartouches, angular handle, teapot with bombe hinged cover, bud finial.

16oz (2dwt) teapot 6in (15cm) high

$600-800   **SI**

A three piece American sterling coffee service, Eatson Company, reproduction of a Georgian coffee service, c. 1735, coffeepot, two handle open sugar and creamer; coffeepot: lighthouse form, multi scroll handle, bud finial, monogrammed: "E du P B", 29 oz.

Coffeepot 10 in (25.5) cm high.

$600-800   **RP**

A six-piece French silver coffee service, by Mon Odiot, Paris, comprising a coffeepot, teapot, chocolate pot, two handled covered sugar, creamer and waste bowl, engraved with armorials.

Coffeepot 9.5in (24cm) high

£2,600-2,800   **SI**

A German silver tea and coffee service, custom designed and made by Eugen Fehrer, comprising a coffeepot, teapot, two-handled covered sugar and creamer and a silver-plated two-handle tray.

Tray 24.5in (62cm) long

£1,000-1,500   **SI**

SILVER - TEA

An 18thC French silver teapot, marked "A" below a crown and "P" below a crown, repoussé-decorated with pastoral scenes within scrolls and floral swags, the bombe hinged cover with scrolling foliage and floral decoration and foliate finial, the spout issuing from scrolls and foliage, with ebonized handle, engraved underneath "Elizabeth".

6in (15cm) high

£450-500   **SI**

A George III silver hot water urn, by John Robins, London, with beaded decoration and a vacant cartouche flanked by foliate garland, with beaded loop handles.

1780   14.25in (36cm)

£1,900-2,100   **SI**

A George III silver teapot, by George Smith, London, with bright cut foliate decoration at the foot and rim and wooden handle.

1780-81   5in (12.5cm) high

£1,000-1,200   **SI**

▶ A silver teapot, by John Emes, London, with engraved Greek key design.

1805   6.25in (16cm) high

£700-900   **JBS**

A silver teapot, marked as made in London by Thos, Ullivant but overstruck P&W Bateman.

1792   6in (15cm) high

£1,200-1,600   **JBS**

An assembled George III silver tea service, comprising a teapot, with two vacant cartouches and stylized foliate band at the rim, the hinged cover with pineapple finial; a kettle on stand, by AF Pairpoint, London, with conforming decoration 1916-17; a two-handled sugar; a creamer by Ann, Peter and William Bateman, London, 1800.

1800	Tallest 14in (35.5cm) high

$2,000-2,500 SI

A three piece Georgian silver tea service, made in London, comprising a teapot, a two-handled open sugar and a creamer, all repoussé-decorated with foliage, flowers and fruits, with crested cartouche, on four floral, foliate and beast feet, handles with similar decoration, gilt interior.

The "Georgian" period covers the period 1714 to 1811 and is typified by elegance and refinement. A key influence was Classical architecture though other themes also came through, this led to the following motifs in silverware.

● Early Georgian (1714-1730s) is dominated by the Palladian style with its Classical Greek and Roman influence.

● The Rococo style is much lighter and arrived in Britain c1740. It is characterized by shell, flower and fruit motifs.

● The Neo-classical style was encouraged by important archaeological discoveries c1740 and lead to Classical motifs retaining their popularity when George III came to the throne in 1760. Guilloche, Greek Key and Vitruvian scrolls are common in all areas of decorative arts at this time.

● Elegant, classic lines with the addition of lavish and exotic French-inspired decoration are the signatures of the Regency style, which was in accordance with the personal taste of the Prince Regent, who became George IV in 1820.

1822-23	Teapot 6.5in (16.5cm) high

$1,800-2,200 SI

A silver teapot, by EK Reid, London.

A silver teapot, by Walter and John Barnard, London, engraved "Empingham July 1888 from the choir".

1868 5.25in (13.5cm) high	*1876* 6in (15.5cm) high
$1,000-1,500 JBS	**$1,500-2,000** JBS

▶ A silver small oval teapot, by Charles Stuart Harris, London, embossed with birds, flowers and C-scrolls, the spout with bird's-head terminal, with ebonized handle, on three mask and pad feet.

1902 5.25in (13.5cm) high

$200-300 LFA

A silver teapot, sugar bowl and milk jug, by Mappin and Webb, London.

A silver teapot, with composition handle and knop, made in Birmingham.

1920 Teapot 6.25in (16cm) high	*1930*
$500-750 JBS	**$250-300** LFA

A silver tea kettle, by William Hutton and Sons Ltd, London.

A German silver tea caddy, of quatrefoil form, repoussé-decorated with figures dancing below flowers and cherub's head, the detachable cover with floral and scroll decoration.

A silver tea caddy, by Thomas Bradbury and Son, Sheffield.

A silver tea caddy, by William Hutton & Sons, Sheffield, of compressed rounded rectangular form with hinged cover and vase-shaped finial.

1907 15in (38cm) high	4in (10cm) high	*1911* 4in (10cm) high	*1913* 3.75in (9.5cm) high
$1,000-1,500 JBS	**$200-300** SI	**$200-300** JBS	**$150-220** Chef

Chocolate Pots/Bowls

CHOCOLATE POTS

A 19thC French silver bachelor chocolate pot, of inverted pear shape, the partly swirled fluted body with foliate decoration, a vacant cartouche flanked by scrolling foliage, with straight ebonized handle, on scroll feet, gross weight 5oz, 8dwt.

6in (15cm) high

$450-500 **SI**

A George III silver saucepan with cover, by R Emes & E Barnard, London, circular, with hinged spout, the cover with ivory finial, the handle part silver and part wood, the cover and side engraved with a crest.

1813-14 5in (22.5cm) high

$3,000-4,000 **SI**

A four piece Continental silver bachelor chocolate set, comprising chocolate pot, covered sugar and two creamers, two pieces bearing additional marks SR below a crown within a shield, the chocolate pot and one creamer each with partly fluted body, with foliate swags and vacant cartouche, and with ebonized handle on both.

Chocolate pot 6.5in (17cm) high

$600-1,000 **SI**

BOWLS, DISHES & TRAYS

An early George II silver punch bowl, by Thomas Farren, London, the plain body with applied molded rim and engraved with an armorial for the Smith family anciently of Stoke Prior, Worcs., and the Smyth family of Upton, Essex, on a stepped circular spreading foot with molded edge, 22.5oz.

1729 8.5in (21.7cm) diam

$1,000-1,200 **HamG.**

An 18thC Italian silver bowl, of circular form with beaded rim, the handles in the form of cherubs, the circular foot with tongue and dart decoration.

5.5in (14cm) diam

$300-400 **SI**

A 19thC Russian silver two-handled covered sugar bombe, the body decorated with a geometrical design.

5.25in (13cm) high

$350-450 **SI**

A silver bowl, by Henry Wilkinson, Sheffield.

1874 4.25in (11cm) diam

$400-500 **JBS**

A late Victorian sugar bowl, the semi-spherical ostrich egg body within a wire pattern frame, on button feet.

6in (15cm) diam

$300-400 **BonS**

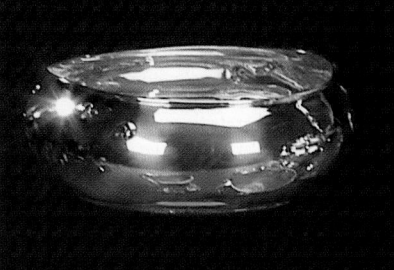

An Italian silver bowl, by Calderoni Gioielli, with foliate decoration.

9.7in (25cm) diam

$250-300 **SI**

A late 18thC silver footed bowl, by Joseph Lownes, Philadelphia, PA, circular form on flaring foot and square base, bright-cut engraved with various banding under rim, leafy swags enclosing an oval cartouche with initials "L A B," bright-cut engraved leaves at foot.

5in (12.5cm) high

$1,000-2,000   SI

A silver covered sugar bowl, oval-lobed form, with domed cover with urn finial, beaded rim and engraved swags and dense diamond pattern at shoulder, strap handles.

c1810   8in (20.5cm) high

$350-450   SI

A coin silver covered sugar, probably John Richardson, Philadelphia, oval on square base, datachable cover, baluster finial, reeded rims, monogrammed "ER" flanked by foliage, marked "J.R." in rectangular shield.

1793-1831   14 oz 11in (28cm) high

$2,000-2,500   SI

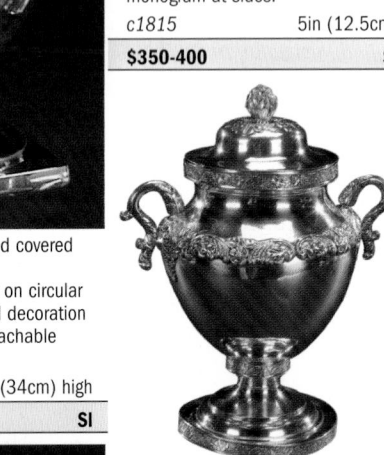

A silver open sugar bowl, maker's mark, William Thomson, New York, of rounded rectangular form with beaded edge on rim and foot, the shoulders bright-cut engraved with oak leaf sprays and oval cartouches with flowerheads at corners, die-rolled vine on handles, on ball feet, monogram at sides.

c1815   5in (12.5cm)

$350-400   SI

A coin silver two-handled covered sugar, by Harvey Lewis, Philadelphia, cylindrical on circular molded foot, gadrooned decoration at the rim and foot, detachable cover, acorn finial.

1811-1826   9.5in (34cm) high

$1,000-1,500   SI

A silver footed bowl, Maker's mark, William Thomson, New York, circular lobed form on a molded flaring foot-everted rim with die-rolled oak leaves, gadrooning at stem and foot.

c1815   7.5in (19cm) diam

$450-550   SI

Silver covered sugar bowl, urn form on a stepped circular foot, domed cover with greyhound finial, cast scrolling handles, engraved initials at shoulders.

c1830   9.25in (23.5cm) high

$450-500   SI

A Black, Tompkins & Black sterling porringer, circular, flat pierced handle, also marked Marouand & Co.

c1839   5.5in (14cm) diam

$800-1,200   SI

A silver covered sugar bowl, unmarked, urn form with stepped circular foot, domed cover with flower form knop, die-rolled grapevine at neck, stem and foot, applied leaves and flowers at shoulders leafy cast scrolled handles.

c1840   10.5in (26.5cm) high

$450-550   SI

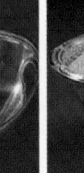

A Tiffany & Co. sterling bowl, 17066/9584, oval, two pierced handles flanked by stylized foliage, molded rim, monogrammed "E du P B".

1907-08   8.75in (12cm) long

$500-600   SI

A Gorham sterling footed bowl, "Marie Antionette" pattern, circular, the sides and border repousse with floral garlands, upper body with floral panel, monogrammed.

1927   10in (25.5cm) diam

$500-600   SI

Trays

A 19thC S.Kirk & Son, Baltimore, MD sterling tray, shaped rectangular, repousse border with flowers and foliage on fine stippled ground on four ball and claw feet, the field with trellis centering vacant cartouche flanked by foliage.

1880-90   35oz 16in (41cm)

$2,000-2,500   **SI**

A Tiffany & Co. sterling tray, 11903A/14270. Shaped square with scalloped corners, reeded rim on four ball feet, monogrammed "EB".

1907-38   6in (15cm) wide

$200-250   **SI**

A nickel-silvered tray, Albert Rich and Companies, Bridgeport, Conn, oblong form with gadrooned rim and cast handle, engraved with four stars and "U.S.N.".

1920-27   18in (46cm) wide

$400-600   **SI**

A sterling platter, Gorham, "Cinderella" pattern, the border applied with foliate and floral decoration at intervals, foliate rim.

1927   18in (46cm) wide

$600-800   **SI**

An American sterling dish, Gorham, "Cinderella" pattern, oval.

1927   11.25in (28.5cm) wide

$150-200   **SI**

A sterling dish, Towle, "Lady Constance".

13.75in (35cm) wide

$150-200   **SI**

A sterling platter, Towle, "Lady Constance" pattern.

14.5in (37cm) diam

$400-500   **SI**

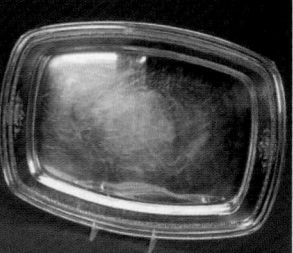

A Towle sterling dish, "Lady Constance" pattern.

11in (26cm) wide

$300-500   **SI**

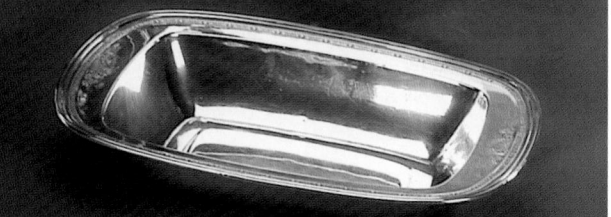

A Towle sterling platter, "Lady Constance" pattern, border applied with foliate band, flowers and scrolling foliage at intervals.

17.5in (44cm) wide

$550-650   **SI**

Five Towle Manufacturing Co. sterling compotes, circular openwork border with scrolls on shaped circular foot with conforming decoration, monogrammed.

Tallest 5.75in (14.5cm) high

$1,500-2,000   **SI**

A set of 18 Towle Manufacturing Co. sterling place plates, also marked "PR", with molded rim with shell at intervals.

29oz 10in (25.5cm) diam

$3,500-4,000 (set)   **SI**

347

Silver – Trays and Baskets

A silver dish, by Calderoni Giorelli, with clear liner, two glass holders and glasses, foliate decoration to the sides.

7in (18cm) diam

$200-250   **SI**

An Italian silver soup tureen, by Calderoni Gioielli, with foliate decoration to the sides and cover.

12in (31 cm) long

$750-1,000   **SI**

A Continental silver dish.

c1900   12.75in (32.5cm) wide

$300-450   **JBS**

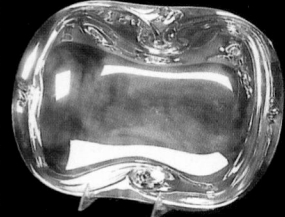

A silver dish, with scroll and foliate decoration.

13.5in (34cm) long

$250-300   **SI**

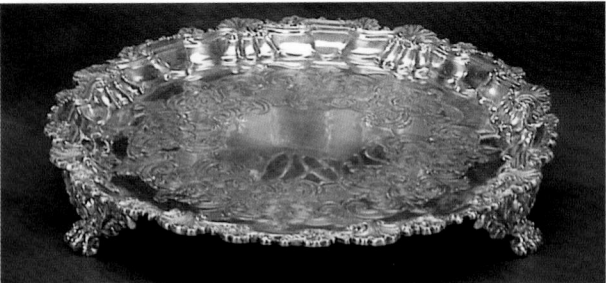

A George III silver salver, by Jonathan Alleine, London, engraved with scrolls and foliate decoration with vacant cartouche, with circular shell and scrolling foliate border, on three foliate and paw feet.

9.25in (23.5cm) diam

$700-800   **SI**

A George III silver card tray, by G Smith & T Hayter, London, engraved with armorials.

6.25in (16cm) long

$600-800   **SI**

A George III silver two-handled tray, by William Fountain, London, with reeded rim and handle, engraved with armorials.

1797   21in (54cm) long

$6,000-7,500   **SI**

An embossed silver tray, by William Comyns, London.

1901   8in (20.5cm) long

$200-250   **JBS**

A French silver basket and glass liner, the sides pierced with floral garlands and foliage, the foliate swing handle pierced with bird, on paw feet, probably 18thC.

4.75in 12cm diam

$400-450   **SI**

A George III silver sugar basket, by Robert Hennell, London, engraved with initials within a panel, with bright cut ground and oval foot.

1789   6in (15cm) wide

$800-1,000   **LFA**

A George III silver swing-handle basket, by Robert Hennell, London, decorated with bright cut stylized flowers below pierced panels and engraved with armorials, with reeded rims and a swing handle, the pierced foot with reeded rim.

Robert Hennell I was active between 1763 and 1811 and was known for his good-quality domestic silver. Both his father David and his sons Samuel and David were silversmiths.

1792-93   14.5in (27cm) long

$2,500-3,500   **SI**

A German silver basket, for fruit or bread.

c1880   10in (25cm) high

$1,500-1,800   **JBS**

A Dutch silver basket, London import mark for 1896.

1896   10.25in (26cm) long

$700-1,000   **JBS**

Salts

SALTS

A French silver salt, with original blue glass liner, some damage.

c1760   7.75in (20cm) high

$1,500-2,000   **JBS**

A George III oval cauldron salt and glass liner, with leaf molded rim, on four flower feet, together with an associated spoon engraved D.W.A.1764, maker's mark indistinct, London, possibly 1762.

c1760

$400-500   **BonS**

A pair of George III silver salt cellars, by Alexander Johnston, London, each with shaped gadrooned rim and blue cobalt glass liner, the three paw feet issuing from foliage.

1762-63   2.75in (7cm) diam

$500-750   **SI**

A pair of silver salts, by William Skeen, London.

1772   3.5in (9cm) wide

$500-700 (pair)   **JBS**

A silver salt, by Robert Hennell, London.

1782   6in (15cm) high

$1,000-1,500   **JBS**

A set of four silver salts, by Robert Hennell, London.

1783   3in (8cm) high

$1,500-1,800   **JBS**

Four George III silver salt cellars, by Hester Bateman, London, each with pierced sides and bright cut decoration with vacant cartouche, on claw and ball feet.

HESTER BATEMAN AND WIDOW SILVERSMITHS

In 18thC England, silversmithing was traditionally a family business and when a man died his widow often took over the running of the family firm and registered her own mark. This explains why there are a number of female silversmiths at that time, despite the fact that is was very rare for women to work in the arts then.

One such widow was Hester Bateman. Despite being more or less illiterate, she registered her own mark in 1761 and ran the workshop of her chain-maker husband John Bateman.

She ran the company for 30 years and in her hands, it thrived, going from a small family concern to one of the most successful workshops in London. Among the other Batemans employed there were her sons John, Peter and Jonathan, and later Jonathan's wife Anne and their son William and grandson William II.

Today, Hester's work is highly sought after and is typically elegant with attractive engraving.

Among the Huguenots refugees who fled France at the end of the 17thC were established silver and goldsmiths who set up workshops in England. These included a number of women including Anne Tanqueray, Louisa Courtauld and Elizabeth Godfrey, who was named "Goldsmith, Silversmith, and Jeweler to his Royal Highness the Duke of Cumberland".

Other women to look out for are mother-and daughter Mary and Eliza Sumner, who specialized in flatware, and Margaret Binley, who made wine labels.

A pair of George III silver salt cellars, maker's mark rubbed, London, the pierced sides with foliate medallions, with blue colbalt glass liner, on claw and ball feet.

1783-84   3in (7.5cm) long

$400-450   **SI**

A silver salt and spoon, by Robert and David Hennell, London.

1795   2.25in (6cm) high

$700-1,000   **JBS**

1786-87   3.25in (8cm) long

$1,000-1,500   **SI**

One of a set of four Scottish silver salts, by J McKay, Edinburgh.

c1820   3.5in (9cm) wide

$1,000-1,350 (set)   JBS

A pair of William IV Gothic Revival salts, by Henry Wilkinson & Co, Sheffield, each with pierced lancet panels and stiff leaf frieze, with double-scroll leaf-capped handle, the plain hinged cover with scroll thumb-piece.

Henry Wilkinson & Co *were major producers of plated wares and made a number of pieces in the Gothic Revival style. The Gothic Revival style of the 19thC was promoted by designers such as AWN Pugin and W Burgess. It drew its influence from 12thC-15thC ecclesiastical architecture and is characterized by motifs such as trefoils, quatrefoils and cinquefoils, grotesque imagery and heraldic devices.*

1836   3in (7.5cm) diam

$600-750   BonS

A pair of silver salts, by William Skeen, London.

1772   3.5in (9cm) wide

$600-800 (pair)   JBS

A pair of silver salts, by Haseler and Haseler, London, with blue glass liners.

1912   4in (10cm) high

$300-450   JBS

A pair of French silver salts.

1880   4.25in (11cm) high

$600-800   JBS

A pair of German .800 silver salt cellars, each in the form of a shell with a seated putti playing a musical instrument, the base repoussé-decorated with reptiles, frogs, flowers and rushes, the stem modeled as unicorn with armorial shield.

6.5in (16.5cm) high

$650-800   SI

A pair of Russian silver and enamel kovsh, each with a flat handle, enameled with colorful birds on white ground, the roped rim applied with white beads.

3in (7.5cm) long

$3,000-4,500   SI

An Italian silver pepper and salt shaker, by Buccellati, in the form of two mushrooms, a fixed mushroom at the base.

3in (7.5cm) high

$350-450   SI

A silver cruet set by Mappin and Webb, Birmingham, comprising salt, pepper pot, mustard pot and tray.

1933   tray 6.75in (17.5cm) wide

$800-1,000 (set)   JBS

CREAMERS AND JUGS

An 18thC American creamer, by Thomas Byrnes, Wilmington, Delaware, of helmet shape on square base, with MJ monogram, 7oz, 2dwt.

7in (18cm) high

$1,800-2,200   SI

Two French silver creamers, probably 18thC, each repoussé-decorated and with ebonized handles, one bearing Paris marks for 1785.

Largest 3.5in (9cm) high

$300-400   SI

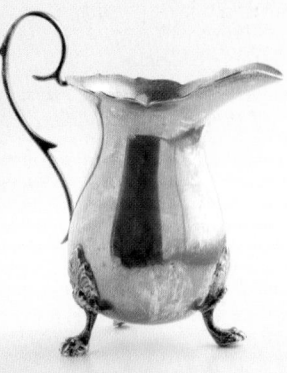

A silver cream jug, marks indistinct.

c1780

$120-180   PC

A George III silver creamer, maker's mark partly rubbed, London, of helmet shape, chased with floral and foliate garlands and crested cartouche, with reeded loop handle, on a square base.

6in (15cm) high

$800-1,000   SI

Creamers and Jugs

An 18thC coin silver sterling water pitcher, bombé, egg and dart decoration on foot and at the shoulder, multi scroll handle by Brower, 17 Camp St., New Orleans.

9.5in (24cm) high

$1,500-2,000   **SI**

A silver creamer, probably, Samuel Richards, Jr., Philadelphia, PA, dated "1803". Oval lobed form with chased gadrooning at shoulders and foot, strap handle with spur, engraved "John Keen, Jr./Hannah Foster/married November 10th, 1802," also monogrammed.

5.75in (14.5cm) high

$500-600   **SI**

A silver creamer, possibly Ward and Bartholomew, Hartford, Connecticut, of rounded rectangular form with molded shoulder, bright-cut engraved with band of flower buds and cross-hatching, the sides engraved with wreath cartouche with square reeded handle, on ball feet, marked.

c1805   6.5in (16.5cm) high

$450-550   **SI**

A silver creamer and covered sugar, maker's mark, Edward Lownes, Philadelphia, each of urn form with spreading circular foot with a square base, with gadrooned borders enclosing chased grapevines, the shoulders with applied water leaves and acorn sprays, cast scroll handles, the covered sugar with flame knopped domed cover.

c1815   10.25in (26cm) high

$800-1,000   **SI**

A silver creamer, Maker's mark. William Thomson, New York, of lobed baluster form with applied die-rolled shell border at spout, stem and foot, a die-rolled oak leaf band at the shoulder, cast scrolling handle.

c1815   7in (18cm) high

$400-500   **SI**

A rare J.D. Shepper, Philadelphia, sterling ewer, circular on sqaure base on four ball and claw feet issuing from scrolls and foliage, applied floral and foliate band at the shoulder above stylized foliage, ovolo rim, leaf-capped foliate and scroll handle.

1818-1819   11.5in (29cm) high

$4,500-5,500   **SI**

Three coin silver creamers and a covered sugar, three pieces unmarked: two creamers, one chased with grapevines centring inscribed cartouche, the other with foliate band at the shoulder; two-handle covered sugar, lower lobed body on circular foot; one creamer marked "R & W.W.", with a grapevine band at the foots and shoulder.

c1825   Sugar 9.5in (24cm) high

$550-650   **SI**

A silver creamer, James M. Bennett and J. Elliott Caldwell, Philadelphia, PA, of baluster form on a stepped circular foot, the shoulders chased with scrolling cartouches and flowers, die-rolled leaf banding below neck, stem and foot, cast leaf scrolled handle.

1843-48   8.25in (21cm) high

$500-600   **SI**

An American sterling silver jug.

c1920   6.5in (16.5cm) high

$800-1,000   **JBS**

A water pitcher, Towle, "Lady Constance" pattern.

9.5in (24cm) high

$550-600   **SI**

A ewer, marked "sterling", ovoid on circular foot with stylized foliate decoration, beaded rims, multi-scroll scrolling foliate handle capped by figural mask, vacant cartouche flanked by chased foliage, weighted foot.

15in (38cm) high

$1,000-1,500   **SI**

Silver – Creamers and Jugs/Drinking Vessels

An early 19thC American silver creamer, by Joseph Lownes, Philadelphia, of oval paneled form, with reeded rim and strap handle.

6in (15cm) high

$600-700 | **SI**

A silver sugar bowl and cream jug, by Mappin and Webb, London.

1897 — Jug 4in (10cm) high

$350-450 | **JBS**

A silver sugar bowl and cream jug. by William Aitken, Chester.

1899 — Bowl 3in (7.5cm) high

$300-400 | **JBS**

An unmarked Colonial silver jug.

c1850 — 2.25in (5.5cm) high

$180-240 | **JBS**

A silver jug, by Savory and Savory, London.

1836 — 4.25in (11cm) high

$500-600 | **JBS**

A silver cream jug, by Elkington and Co, Birmingham, of plain baluster shape raised on four masked scroll feet, with leaf-capped scrolled handle.

1929 — 6.25in (16cm) high

$350-400 | **Chef**

DRINKING VESSELS

An 18thC Russian silver beaker, by Stopa, Assayer Shagin, Moscow, repoussé-decorated with bird, lion and cherub within scrolling foliage.

3.5in (9cm) high

$400-600 | **SI**

An 18thC Russian silver beaker, by Andre Wekman, Assayer Al'derman K.A., Moscow, repoussé-decorated with birds and foliate and floral garlands.

1762-91 — 3.25in (8cm) high

$600-700 | **SI**

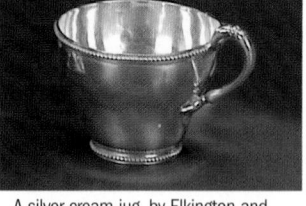

A silver cream jug, by Elkington and Co, Birmingham, of plain baluster shape raised on four masked scroll feet, with leaf-capped scrolled handle.

1929 — 6.25in (16cm) high

$350-450 | **Chef**

A John B. Jones & Co. Boston coin silver beaker, tulip form, lower bopdy repousse with stylized flowers and leaves, on circular foot.

c1838 — 3.75in (9.5cm) high

$520-580 | **SI**

► A 19thC Russian silver gilt beaker, by Orlov, Moscow, the fluted body with guilloche decoration, the rim with stylized flowers.
Guilloche is an ornamental border formed of two or more interlacing bands with the gaps often filled with floral motifs.

1869 — 4.75in (12cm) high

$750-850 | **SI**

◄ An Irish silver goblet, made in Dublin.

1770 — 5.5in (4cm) high

$1,500-2,000 | **JBS**

FLATWARE

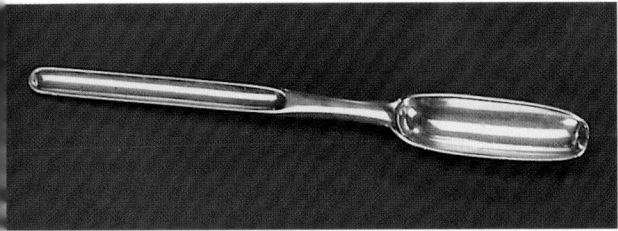

An Irish marrow spoon, by William Suttons, with TS monogram.

1740   7.75in (30cm) long

$500-600   **SI**

► Two large silver-gilt spoons, bearing French marks, imported to England by John George Smith in 1898, the terminals depicting Louis XVI and Marie-Antionette, the bowls, one with the armorials of Louis XVI and Marie-Antionette, the other with the armorials of Louis XVI, King of France and Navarre, flanked by scrolls and foliage below a fleur-de-lys and the letter "L" for Louis.

1762-68   10.75in (27.5cm)

$700-800   **SI**

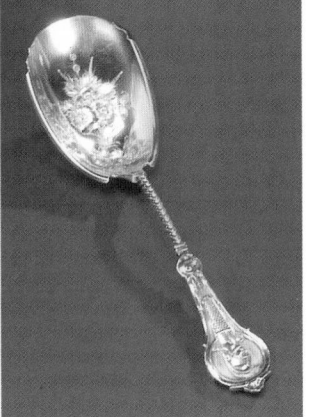

A 19th century sterling silver spoon, Wood & Hughes, "Medallion" pattern, large gilded bowl repousse with flower spray.

2oz (6 dwt) 9in (23cm) long

$450-500   **SI**

A 19thC sterling soup ladle, Wood & Hughes, "Medallion" pattern.

8oz (2dwt) 12in (31cm) long

$550-650   **SI**

A George III silver caddy spoon, probably by John Shea, London, in the Fiddle, Thread and Shell pattern.

$150-220   **LFA**

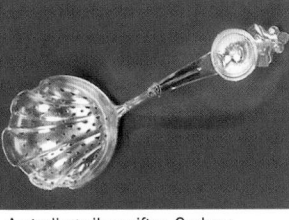

A sterling silver sifter, Gorham, "Medallion" pattern, also marked "H. Richardson & Co.", pierced fluted gilded bowl.

2oz 7.5in (19cm) long

$220-280   **SI**

▲1 A George III silver caddy spoon, in the form of a leaf, no maker's mark, London.

1798-99

▲2 A George III silver caddy spoon, by Matthew Linwood, Birmingham, the oval bowl repoussé-decorated with grapevine.

1807-08

▲3 A pair of Georgian silver caddy spoons, each in the form of a leaf, no marks.

$800-1,000 (four items)   **SI**

A 19thC sterling soup ladle, "Medallion" pattern.

5oz (4dwt) 12.5in (32cm) long

$250-300   **SI**

A 19thC sterling punch ladle, Bailey & Co., 1848-78, "Medallion" pattern.

5oz (4dwt) 12.5in (32cm) long

$550-650   **SI**

A silver serving spoon, large oval bowl applied with flowers and foliage, ivory handle, monogrammed "E.B", by Whiting Manufacturing Company, and a large shell serving spoon, the handle as a shell attached to bowl with silver plated form of a bug.

Larger 9.5in (24cm) long

$600-700   **SI**

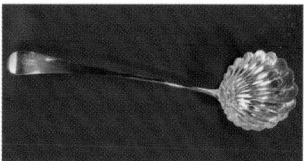

A George III silver punch ladle, by John Wren, London, in the Old English pattern, with M monogram.

1785	12.5in (32cm) long
$400-500	**SI**

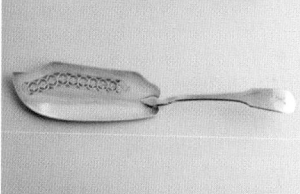

A George III silver crested Fiddle pattern fish slice, by Emes and Barnard, London, the blade pierced with a leaf and roundel band.

1814

$200-300	**LFA**

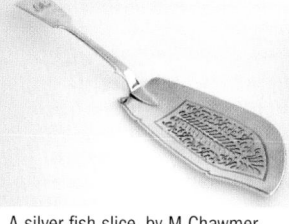

A silver fish slice, by M Chawmer, London.

1828	12in (30.5cm) long
$200-300	**JBS**

A silver stilton scoop, by James Dicks, London.

1820	8.75in (22.5cm) long
$450-550	**JBS**

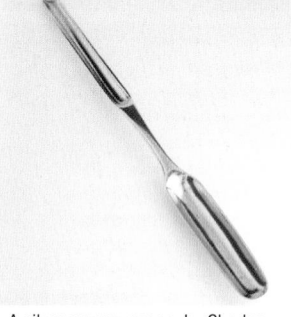

A silver marrow scoop, by Charles Hougham, London.

1782	9in (23cm) long
$180-220	**JBS**

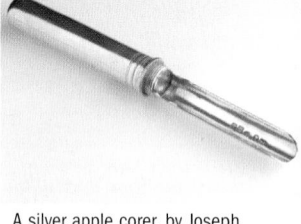

A silver apple corer, by Joseph Willmore, Birmingham.

1835

$600-700	**JBS**

CANDLESTICKS

A pair of silver candlesticks, by John Carter, London.

John Carter *was a prolific candlestick maker.*

1770	10.5in (26.5cm) high
$4,500-5,500	**JBS**

A pair of George IV silver drip pans from candlesticks, cast with flowers and leaf scrolls, made in Sheffield.

1825

$60-100	**LFA**

A pair of George III silver candlesticks, by John Carter, London, each with a stepped weighted base with beaded rim rising to a fluted column with foliate sconce, the detachable bobeches with scalloped gadrooned rims.

1768-69	12.5in (32cm) high
$2,500-3,500	**SI**

▶ One of a pair of 18thC silver on copper three-light candelabra, each with two multi-scrolled branches and one fixed branch, with floral and beaded drip pans and vasiform sconces, detachable bobeches, convertible to candlestick, by either Roberts, Smith & Co, 1828 or Smith, Sissons & Co, 1848.

	20.75in (53cm) high
$1,800-2,200 (pair)	**SI**

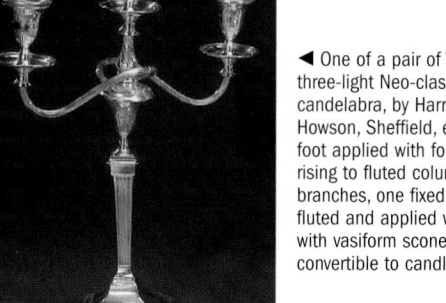

◀ One of a pair of Victorian silver three-light Neo-classical candelabra, by Harrison Bros & Howson, Sheffield, each with square foot applied with foliate garlands rising to fluted columns, two reeded branches, one fixed branch, partly fluted and applied with garlands, with vasiform sconces and drip pans, convertible to candlesticks.

1899-1900	19in (48cm) high
$1,800-2,200 (pair)	**SI**

◀ A pair of silver candlesticks, by James Dixon and Sons, Sheffield.

James Dixon and Sons were founded in 1806. They made Sheffield Plate, Britannia wares (an alloy of tin with antimony and copper), silver and electro-plate. They were also responsible for developing the technique of electro-plating Britannia metal.

1902	10.25in (26cm) high
$1,500-2,000	JBS

▶ An important silver and glass cruet set, by JE Terry and Co, London.

It is now very rare to see a set of this size. As well as size, condition is very important when looking at cruet sets - the feet and handles are usually the most vulnerable to damage.

1835	11.5in (29cm) high
$10,000-13,000	JBS

◀ A silver and cut glass cruet set, by Urquhart and Hart, London.

1789	9.5in (24cm) high
$2,000-2,500	JBS

CRUETS AND CASTERS

A George III Warwick cruet, by Samuel Wood, London, the cinquefoil base and frame with central turned handle, the base with C-scroll and fan feet, the front with an ornate Rococo shield with engraved crest showing the arms of TROTTER (second son) impaling STUART of Allan Bank Berwickshire, the five divisions with two bottles with silver caps with flame finials, foliate engraving and a crest, the three baluster casters with similar engraving, engraved with a scratch weight 72 – 15 2217gm of weighable silver.

Samuel Wood was an important caster maker.

Crests are found instead of coats-of-arms on smaller pieces. Both crests and coats-of-arms, if they are contemporary, can be used to identify the original owner of a piece and this information can be useful for dating un-hallmarked pieces and may increase interest. Look out for pieces that have had engraving, such as crests, removed as this can leave an area of thin metal that is more liable to get damaged.

1754	
$6,000-10,000	L&T

A 19thC American sterling soup tureen, the oval, foliate rim within beads on foot and body, two handles in the form of a deer's head, bombé cover, and standing deer finial, by Ball, Black and Co., New York.

c1865	17in (43cm) long
$6,500-7,500	SI

A South American .925 silver two handled tureen, the bombé vessel with lobed and domed cover surmounted by a berry finial, chased with bands of leafage, on four leaf capped ball and claw feet.

118oz (4dwt)	16in (40.5cm) long
$4,000-4,500	SI

A 19thC Gorham sterling tureen, oval on oval foot, dart and foliate rim, two handles in the form of a deer's head, bombe cover, lying deer finial, also marked J.W. Tucker & Co., San Francisco, CA.

	43oz (2dwt) 13.5in (34cm) long
$5,000-5,500	SI

Silver – Miscellaneous

A silver and glass vase, by WJ Myatt, Birmingham.

1902   9in (23cm) high

$800-1,000   **JBS**

A silver vase, by Walker and Hall, Sheffield.

1914   10.5in (27cm) high

$1,500-2,000   **JBS**

A Victorian silver heart-shaped photograph frame, pierced and embossed with flowers and leaf scrolls, made in Birmingham.

1895   5.75in (14.5cm) high

$300-350   **LFA**

A Victorian silver photograph frame, by William Comyns, London, pierced and embossed with putti and leaf scrolls.

1900   7.75in (19.5cm) high

$350-450   **LFA**

A 'sterling' silver cow creamer.

c1910   4.25in (11cm) long

$700-750   **JBS**

A 'sterling' silver oil lamp.

c1920   5.25in (13cm) wide

$150-200   **JBS**

▶ A George III silver argyle, by Andrew Fogelberg, London, engraved with an armorial, with gadrooned edges and opposite filling and pouring spouts, hinged cover and cane-clad handle, pourer repaired at base.

An argyle is a gravy server with a lid. The gravy is kept warm by a central conical section filled with hot water and is reputed to have been invented by the Duke of Argyle.

c1770   5in (13cm) high

$800-1,000   **Chef**

A silver sauceboat, by Benjamin West, London.

1747   4.25in (10.5cm) high

$800-1,000   **JBS**

A silver toast rack, by Atkins Bros, Sheffield.

1900   4.5in (11.5cm) high

$300-400   **JBS**

A silver toast rack, by Goldsmiths and Silversmiths Co Ltd, London.

1904   4.75in (12cm) high

$200-300   **JBS**

A silver toast rack, by Richard Comyns, London.

1932   3.5in (9cm) high

$100-150   **JBS**

▶ A pair of South American .925 silver two-light sconces, each shaped oval wood backplate faced with repousse silver depicting a robed figure standing under a cartouche and a shell amid scrolling floral vines and birds, within a C-scroll and gadrooned border, mounted with two scrolling foliate candle arms terminating in foliate chased candle cups and fluted drip pans.

21.5in (54.5cm) high

$3,500-4,500   **SI**

▶ A Tiffany & Co. sterling ring holder, 28666, in the form of a hand on circular base.

3.25in (8.5cm) high

$200-250   **SI**

Miscellaneous

A George III Adam-style silver gilt epergne, by William Holmes, London, profusely pierced and embossed with bell husk swags, decorated with beaded borders throughout, the oval central basket supported by a swept platform with four stiff leaf cast pillars and a circular frame with central vase-shaped finial, issuing four foliate cast scrolled arms surmounted by four baskets, on four scrolled legs and leaf-cast feet suspended with cast berry and laurel leaf swags, each basket engraved with the crest of the arms of Hall of Devonshire with a shield probably for law in pretence, minor losses to the large basket.

1781   17in (43.5cm) high

$15,000-20,000   **HamG**

A silver tea infuser with telescopic handle, by G.E.W.L.D, Birmingham.

1895

$400-500   **JBS**

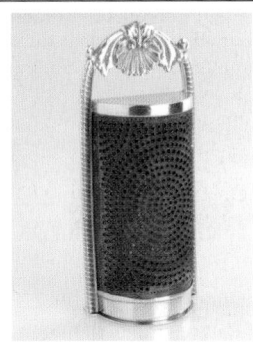

A silver nutmeg grater, by Philips and Robinson, London.

1810   4.75in (12cm) long

$2,000-3,000   **JBS**

A George III silver pap-boat, by Hester Bateman, London.

1784-85   4.75in (12cm) long

$800-1,000   **SI**

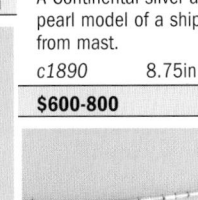

A George III silver cream pail, maker's mark indstinct, London, of tapering cylindrical form, with a beaded bail handle.

1777   10.5cm high

$600-1,000   **Chef**

A silver candle snuffer, maker's mark IB, London.

1778   6.25in (10.5cm) high

$500-800   **JBS**

A four-piece Victorian condiment set, in the form of owls, comprising an unmarked silver shaker, a silver-plated mustard pot and two shakers.

Mustard pot 4in (10cm) high

$400-600   **SI**

A Continental silver and mother-of-pearl model of a ship, flag missing from mast.

c1890   8.75in (22.5cm) high

$600-800   **JBS**

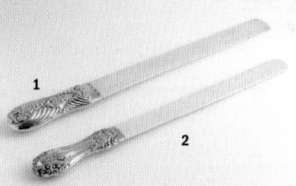

▲1 A silver and ivory paper knife, made in London.

1891   16.5in (42cm) long

$200-300   **JBS**

▲2 A silver and ivory paper knife, made in Birmingham.

1900   15.25in (39cm) long

$300-400

A silver napkin ring in original box, by Mappin and Webb, London.

1899   1.5in (4cm) diam

$150-200   **JBS**

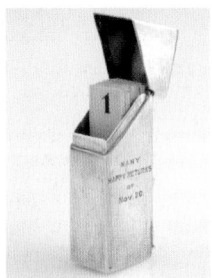

A silver butt selector box, by S. Clifford and Co, London, containing ivory markers labeled one to six.

1911   2in (5.5cm) wide

$200-300   **JBS**

A silver easel-shaped menu holder, embossed with putti flanking a cartouche, made in Birmingham.

1900   3.5in (9cm) high

$200-250   **LFA**

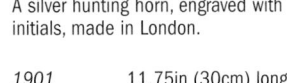

A silver hunting horn, engraved with initials, made in London.

1901   11.75in (30cm) long

$250-350   **LFA**

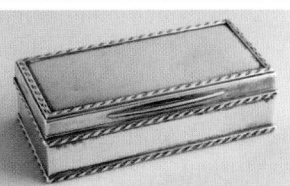

A silver rectangular box and hinged cover, with entwined borders, made in London.

4in (10cm) wide

$150-200   **LFA**

SILVER PLATE

SILVER PLATE

LEGEND HAS IT THAT IN 1742, WHILE REPAIRING A KNIFE IN HIS WORKSHOP, Thomas Bolsover (1705-1788) found that melted silver would adhere to copper. He realized that this accidental discovery could be of commercial use and began to make small items that looked like silver but were largely made of a cheaper metal. This form of plating is called Sheffield Plate after Bolsover's birthplace.

At first, Bolsover made small items only, but the demand for affordable silverware from the new merchant classes meant that larger, domestic pieces such as entrée dishes and soup dishes were soon being manufactured.

By the 1770s Sheffield Plate was being mass-produced.

Despite its popularity Sheffield Plate took time to manufacture, was labor intensive and was not always suitable for hot foods as the heat was prone to melt the lead solder used to attach feet to serving dishes.

Electroplating was much more practical. Discovered by Italian chemist Luigi V. Brugnatelli in 1805 and patented by 1840, it was a much simpler process and the silver could be laid down in any desired thickness. Ten years later, production of Sheffield Plate production had virtually halted.

A George III silver-plated dish, by Matthew Boulton, with silver-plated liner.

c1794   9in (19cm) diam

$700-1,000   **SI**

A Victorian silver-plated meat dish cover, with leaf-cast handle and gadrooned border.

13in (33cm) long

$100-150   **LFA**

A Victorian silver-plated meat dish cover, with beaded handle.

12.75in (32.5cm) long

$100-150   **LFA**

A silver-plated serving dish, by Hulkin and Heath, with removable internal divider.

c1880   12.25in (31cm) diam

$200-300   **JBS**

A large silver on copper three-tier dish.

24.5in (62cm) high

$200-250   **SI**

A pair of silver-plated entrée dishes, each with beaded decoration and detachable foliate and beaded handle.

14in (35.5cm) long

$1,000-1,500   **SI**

A Continental silver-plated centerpiece, the lower part applied with a foliate garland, with two bifurcated angular handles and reeded paw feet, liner lacking.

21.5in (55cm) long

$700-1,000   **SI**

A Continental silver-plated centerpiece, the sides pierced with ogives above foliage and floral garland with vacant cartouche, the loop handles with reeded and scrolling foliate decoration, with liner.

23in (59cm) long

$300-400   **SI**

▶ A Continental silver-plated mirror plateau, with scroll and foliate border and two bifurcated foliate and floral handles.

A mirror plateau is a flat glass stand that held a centerpiece or epergne and reflected the light.

22in (56cm) long

$600-800   **SI**

A massive Continental silver on copper centerpiece, the sides applied with foliate garlands and two vacant cartouches, with bifurcated scroll and foliate handles, the cut glass liner with partly scalloped rim and stylized foliage.

30in (66cm) wide

$1,500-2,500   **SI**

Silver Plate

A pair of silver-plated compotes, each with a cut glass bowl, the base cast with swirled scrolled foliage.

10.5in (27cm) diam

$300-400　　　　**SI**

A 19thC silver-plated rectangular two-handled tray, the center with engraved foliate design, the gadrooned border with vine leaf and grape decoration, on four ball feet.

26in (66cm) wide

$400-600　　　　**Clv**

An Old Sheffield Plate covered bowl, with handles by Matthew Boulton.

Matthew Boulton *was the first major producer of Sheffield Plate, manufacturing it in a factory he set up in 1762. Although Sheffield Plate was popular, silversmiths were unhappy with the legal implications of hallmarking plated silver. In 1773 an act of Parliament banned the use of hallmarks on plated silver following a movement led by Boulton. The same act of Parliament granted Birmingham its own Assay office and Boulton was its first Assay Master.*

c1810　　　　　　　　　　　　6.25in (16cm) wide

$700-1,000　　　　**JBS**

A 19thC silver-plated two-handled soup tureen and cover, of lobed oval form, with flower and scroll cast border, and four-leaf scroll feet.

16.5in (42cm) wide

$500-800　　　　**LFA**

An Old Sheffield Plate candlestick and snuffer.

c1810　　　　4.75in (12cm) wide

$70-100　　　　**JBS**

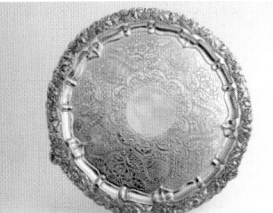

An Old Sheffield Plate salver on three legs.

c1860　　　14.25in (36cm) diam

$200-300　　　　**JBS**

An Old Sheffield Plate rococo-style sauce tureen, with applied decoration.

1820　　　7.75in (20cm) wide

$1,000-1,500　　　　**JBS**

▶ A pair of Old Sheffield Plate candlesticks, each with a knopped fluted baluster stem supporting extended campana-shaped sockets with detachable nozzles.

c1825　　　11.5in (29cm) high

$300-500　　　　**Chef**

A pair of silver-plated three-light candelabra, each with detachable bobeches, convertible to candlestick.

19in (48cm) high

$600-800　　　　**SI**

A pair of Victorian silver-plated Corinthium column candlesticks, each on square stepped base.

11.75in (29.5cm) high

$300-500　　　　**LFA**

A pair of silver-plated candle sticks.

c1890　　　6in (15cm) high

$300-500　　　　**JBS**

Silver Plate

A pair of silver-plated two-branch candelabra, each with central flame finial and gadrooned borders.

11.25in (28.5cm) high

$300-500 (pair)   **LFA**

A pair of silver-plated three-light candelabra, each with detachable bobeches, convertible to candlestick.

19in (48cm) high

$700-1,000   **SI**

A pair of Sheffield silver on copper Neo-classical candlesticks, each with a square base applied with deer's heads between drapery, rising to a fluted stem with foliate sconce, the detachable bobeches with scalloped beaded rims.

12.5in (32cm) high

$1,500-2,000   **SI**

A Victorian electroplate on copper tea urn and cover.

13.75in (35cm) high

$200-250   **Chef**

A pair of massive bronze silver-plated eight-light candelabra, each on a tripod base cast with foliage and grapevines, the stem modeled as a cherub holding a branch with grapevines, with foliate openwork drip pans and vasiform sconces with similar decoration.

24in (74cm) high

$3,000-3,500   **SI**

An engraved silver-plated tea kettle and stand.

c1890   14.5in (37cm) high

$700-1,000   **JBS**

A silver-plated tea kettle and stand.

c1900   9.75in (25cm) high

$200-250   **JBS**

A silver-plated half fluted tea-kettle, with ebonized handle, on stand with lamp.

12.25in (31cm) high

$150-200   **LFA**

▶ A Sheffield silver on copper urn, engraved with armorials, with leaf-capped spigot, loop handles and beaded rims, the cover with urn finial, the interior with vertical copper tube, the base with ball feet.

22in (56cm) high

$1,500-2,000   **SI**

Three pieces of Sheffield silver on copper, by J Dixon & Son, comprising a kettle on stand, a two-handled covered sugar and a creamer, each repoussé-decorated with foliage, scrolls and flowers with two vacant cartouches.

Kettle 18.5in (47cm) high

$700-1,000 **SI**

A Victorian silver-plated folding biscuit box, the two bowls with pierced scrolling liners, the fluted body with scrolling foliate decoration.

11in (27.5cm) high

$500-600 **SI**

A silver-plated vase, with blue glass liner.

c1890 14.25in (36cm) high

$600-800 **JBS**

A George III Sheffield Plate boat-shaped double tea caddy, the pair of hinged covers with locks at each end, the swing handle with slight damage.

8.7in (22cm) wide

$700-1,000 **WW**

A 19thC silver-plated box and hinged cover, embossed with putti, on four turned feet.

4.5in (11.5cm) wide

$100-150 **LFA**

A pair of silver-plated baluster vases, with foliate and floral waisted band.

12.5in (32cm) high

$100-150 **SI**

A set of eight Victorian silver-plated knife rests, each in the form of two cranes flanking entwined branches.

3.5in (9cm) wide

$400-500 **LFA**

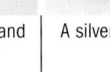

A 19thC silver-plated tea caddy and hinged cover, with lion-mask ring handles, on bun feet.

3.25in (13.5cm) high

$100-150 **LFA**

A massive Continental silver on copper two-handled urn, upper body applied with a vacant cartouche flanked with flowers, foliage and scrolls within a reeded band, the reeded foot applied with cast scroll and foliate decoration.

24.5in (62cm) high

$400-600 **SI**

A pair of Victorian silver-plated fish servers, with scroll and shell embossed handles.

$80-120 **LFA**

A silver-plated biscuit box.

c1860 8.5in (22cm) wide

$800-1,200 **JBS**

A Continental silver on copper two-handled urn, the upper body repoussé-decorated with two vacant cartouches flanked by beads, scrolls and openwork foliage, with leaf-capped reeded loop handles, the foot with reed and tie decoration.

15.75in (40cm) high

$150-200 **SI**

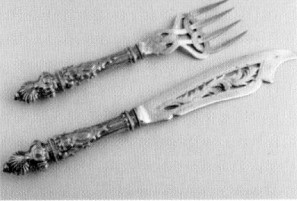

A pair of Victorian silver-plated fish servers, with scroll embossed handles.

$60-100 **LFA**

A French cast bronze hinged top box, by Auguste-Nicholas Cain (1822-1894), molded as a pheasant on a berry, acorn, vine and branch encrusted box, with relief scene of rabbits within cartouche, the reverse with relief scene of guinea fowl in cartouche, signed CAIN.

10in (25.5cm) long

$2,500-3,000	SI

A pair of Continental gilt-bronze and cut crystal graduated triple tier tazzas.

24in (60.5cm) high

$12,000-14,000	SI

A pair of Continental cast bronze "Grande Tour" urns, each cast with eight classical busts in relief, with entwined handles.

5in (12.5cm)

$750-850	SI

A Continental bronze tazza, with figural relief decoration of a young boy, signed "Henri Ple".

13.25in (33.5cm)

$500-600	SI

WINE ANTIQUES

CORKSCREWS

Corkscrews are becoming increasingly collectable. The early history of corkscrews is unclear, but inspiration probably came from the "worm" found on gun-barrel cleaning rods and early corkscrews appear to have been made by gunsmiths. These first models would have consisted of a simple metal worm attached to a plain wooden handle.

The 18thC saw many technological advances and the Reverend Samuel Henshall won the first corkscrew patent in 1795, but its greatest period of development was the mid-19thC, which coincided with the industrial revolution in Great Britain.

There are two basic types of corkscrew: the helix type and the Archimedian type.

The helix type has a smooth metal screw and has two variations: the grooved helix and the double helix, which has a second worm part way down the shaft. The Archmedian type is based on the Archimedes water-screw and is popular in Germany and America.

▶ A Wier's 1885 American patent "Peerless" corkscrew, with two-fold concertina action, two of the arms marked "Peerless", two others marked "Pat. Nov. 10, 1885".

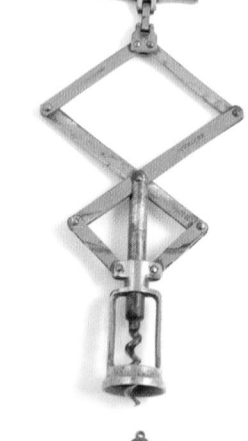

$1,200-1,500	DN

An early 19thC Thomason-type varient corkscrew, with wire helix, turned brass barrel with applied label marked "Josh. Rodgers / & Sons / Sheffield", the main handle of turned lignum vitae, the upper handle of plated metal (dusting brush missing).

$1,000-1,200	DN

An early 19thC Thomason-type corkscrew, with stained turned wood handle and grooved wire helix, the turned brass barrel with applied label marked "patent" supported by a lion and unicorn (hanging ring missing).

$300-350	DN

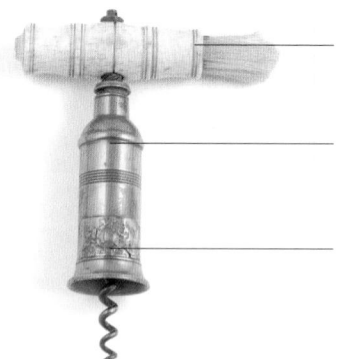

A replaced handle will not affect the value greatly.

Early versions have an open frame and later ones are closed.

This is a standard version of the Thomason-type, decorated or embellised barrels are much more sought after.

An early 19thC Thomason-type corkscrew, with turned bone handle and wire helix, the turned brass barrel with applied label bearing the royal arms and "Ne plus Ultra" (replacement brush, hanging ring missing, extreme tip of helix broken off).

Patented by Edward Thomason in 1802.

$300-350	DN

Wine Antiques

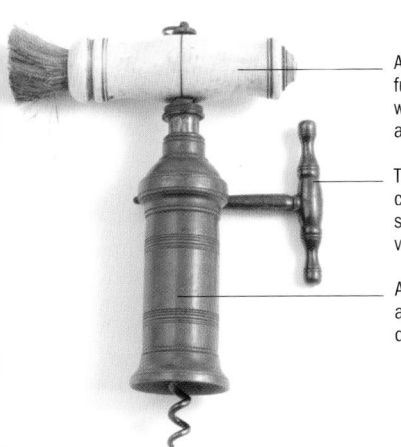

As corkscrews are fuctional items, general wear does not tend to affect the value greatly.

These are still practical corkscrews, but care should be taken as the value is set to rise.

An example marked with a maker's name is more desirable.

An English 19thC King's Screw-type narrow rack corkscrew, with brass barrel, wire helix, shaped bone handle complete with brush, hanging ring, and turned steel side handle (tip of helix broken).

$500-600   DN

A Weir's 1884 English patent corkscrew, by Heeley & Son, with four-fold concertina action, brass neck and ring handle, and wire helix, the steel frames marked "Heeley & Son, Makers", "Patent", and "Weir's Patent / 12804 / 25 Septr. 1884".

$300-350   DN

A Lund's Patent London Rack corkscrew, with copper-bronze washed steel frame, rosewood steel frame, rosewood handle, steel side handle, and wire helix, unmarked (dusting brush missing, some rust pitting).

$150-200   DN

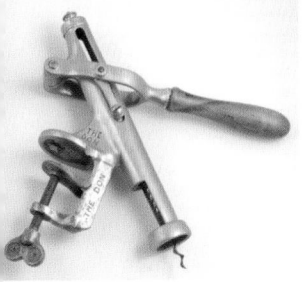

A brass bar corkscrew, with turned fruitwood handle and steel mounting clamp, both body and clamp marked " The Don", barrel length.

11.5in (29.5cm) long

$450-550   DN

This is an elegant example of a "double-lever" type.

There is little variation in the design of this model and so the price is quite set.

Damage to the helix will reduce the value.

A Heely "A1" double-lever corkscrew, with copper-bronze washed frame and levers, wire helix, and steel handle marked "James Heely & Sons Ld. / A1 Double Lever".

$200-300   DN

A simple straight-pull corkscrew, with wire helix, rosewood handle with dusting brush, and hanging ring.

$75-95   DN

A silver-plated and cut glass claret jug.

c1880   11.25in (28.5cm) high

$450-550   JBS

A silver-plate and cut glass claret jug, the finial modeled as a cherub with baskets of flowers.

c1880   10.25in (26cm) high

$750-850   JBS

A silver-plated and cut glass claret jug.

c1890   11.5in (29cm) high

$450-550   JBS

A silver and ribbed glass claret jug, by Heath and Middleton, Birmingham, the glass decorated with roses and engraved Judel 1485, the lid with a crest.

1893   10.5in (27cm) high

$2,000-3,000   JBS

A silver and glass claret jug, by Mappin and Webb, Sheffield.

1898   7.5in (19cm) high

$900-1,100   **JBS**

A silver and glass decanter, by Horace Woodward, Sheffield.

1911   9.5in (24cm) high

$450-500   **JBS**

A Continental .800 silver and cut glass claret jug.

c1920   11.5in (29.5cm) high

$900-1,100   **JBS**

A George III silver wine funnel, by Hester Bateman, London, with beaded rim and pierced interior.

1781   5in (13cm) high

$900-1,100   **SI**

A silver wine funnel, by Joseph Wyatt, London.

1790   4.75in (12cm) high

$900-1,100   **JBS**

A silver wine funnel, by S.A., London.

1810   5.75in (14.5cm) high

$1,200-1,500   **JBS**

A silver wine funnel, by Emes and Barnard, London.

1816   6.25in (16cm) high

$1,200-1,500   **JBS**

A Danish silver drinking horn, engraved with Nordic designs including a warrior and Cupid, the lid made in Copenhagen with finial modeled as sea nymph blowing a shell horn, the feet modeled as porpoises.

1870   11.75 (30cm) high

$3,000-4,000   **JBS**

A Russian silver kovsh, by B.O. Kurlyukov, decorated with applied scrolls and fruits, each side with an enameled cartouche, one depicting a lady presenting the bread and salt to the newlywed couple, the other with blossoms, the loop handle engraved and applied with scrolls.

A kovsh is a Russian wine tasting vessel. Orest Kurlyukov's Moscow-based factory made fine silverware and enamels between 1884-1916 and was well known for its fine silverware and other wares. Tiffany & Co. of New York were retailers and there is a permanent collection in the State Museum of History in Moscow.

     6in (15.2cm) long

$4,500-5,500   **SI**

A pair of 19thC Sheffield silver on copper wine coolers, each of campana shape with fluted lower body and foliate branch form handles, the border with gadrooned foliate and floral decoration, engraved with armorials of Baskerville-Mynords Mynords, with detachable liner and collar.

     10.25in (26cm) high

$4,000-5,000   **SI**

A silver ice bucket, by Calderoni Giorelli, with foliate decorations to the shoulder and detachable cover.

     9.5in (24cm) high

$500-600   **SI**

A Victorian silver wine cooler, maker's mark partly rubbed, London, of campana shape, the lower body applied with acanthus below fluted decoration, the upper body chased with flowers and leaves, with two reeded handles issuing from masks, both cartouches replaced.

12.25in (31cm) high

$750-850   **SI**

A French silver wine taster, with serpent loop handle, the round bowl embossed with flowers and vines beneath a scratched inscription.

4.75in (12cm) diam

$300-400   **LFA**

A pair of silver coasters, by John Grinsell & Son, Birmingham.

1913   4.5in (11.5cm) diam

$1,000-1,200   **JBS**

A silver punch ladle, by James Goodwin, London, with wooden handle.

1724   12.5in (31.5cm) long

$750-850   **JBS**

A silver "sherry" wine label, made in London.

1844   3in (7.5cm) wide

$250-350   **JBS**

BRASS

An 18thC Dutch brass oblong box, embossed with a half-length portrait of Frederick the Great, with emblems and inscriptions.

6.5in (16.5cm) long

$400-500   **LFA**

A Victorian brass mounted iron, the scroll handle with turned mahogany grip.

6.25in (16cm) high

$220-280   **LFA**

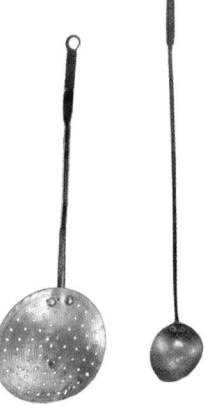

An 18th/19thC brass and iron skimmer, the bowl engraved with concentric circles, together with a brass and iron ladle.

25.5in (64.5cm) long

$450-550   **SI**

▶ A late 19thC brass adjustable book stand, the hinged front cast with urns and foliate scrolls, on bun feet.

9.75in (25cm) wide

$400-500   **DN**

A 19thC brass shot flask, embossed with a basketwork design.

8.25in (21cm) long

$220-280   **LFA**

An mid-19thC brass barber's bowl, the bulbous bowl with rolled edge on a flaring rim.

13.5in (34cm) diam

$600-700   **SI**

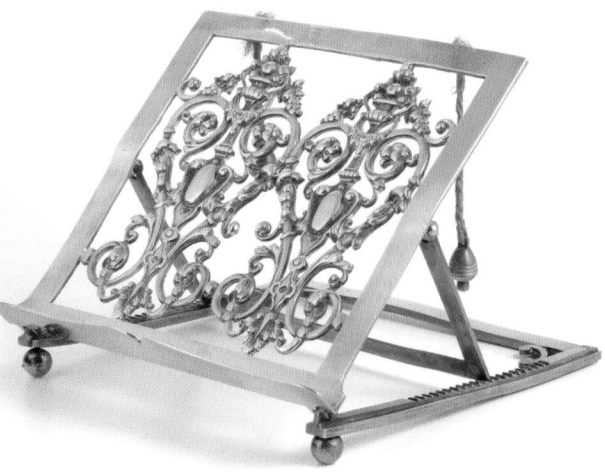

A mid-to late 19thC American brass postage scale, with shaped openwork stand, mounted on a rosewood veneer base with velvet-lined receptacles for weights, the plaque engraved with the initials "M A P."

10.5in (26.5cm) wide

| $150-250 | | SI |

A brass door stop, the spiral twist column with loop handle, on round base.

11.75in (20cm) high

| $75-100 | | LFA |

A 19thC American Standing Indian sculpture, bronze, gold patina.

23in (58.5cm) high

| $700-1,000 | | SI |

MISCELLANEOUS

A three-piece early to mid-19thC pewter tea service, by James Dixon & Son, comprising a teapot, a two-handled covered sugar and a creamer, each of ribbed baluster-form with swelled bellies and set upon stepped vasiform feet, the sugar and creamer with cast reeded C-scroll handles, the teapot with an ebonized wood handle and a scrolling spout, teapot with repair to handle.

Teapot 10in (25.5cm) high

| $300-350 | | SI |

A collection of twenty-seven 18thC and 19thC pewter plates, some with shallow reeding inside the wide rims, mainly by Jno Watts and B Foster, London.

9.5in (24cm) diam

| $800-1,000 | | CH |

An early 19thC pewter flagon, inscribed Heringham Friendly Society July 3 1802, with William IV capacity verification marks.

13in (33cm) high

| $750-850 | | DN |

A George III two-handled copper tea urn, the domed cover with urn shaped knop, the body fitted with a brass tap, standing on a square base with pierced panels to the sides and bun feet.

21in high

| $180-220 | | Clv |

A Regency copper tea urn, with brass moldings and ram's head ring side handles, the reeded brass tap with green stained ivory handle, with brass stem and bell metal plinth, on brass bun feet.

17in (43cm)

| $200-300 | | WW |

A 19thC French gilt-metal and cloisonné garniture set, comprising a central potpourri vase and cover with putti supports, and two cylindrical vases with molded stem and flowerhead handles.

11.75in (30cm) high

| $1,500-2,000 | | BonS |

Marble

A 16thC Italian marble portrait of a boy, Venetian School.

6.5in (16.5cm) high

$1,500-2,000   SI

A 19thC marble figure of Psyche, after Antonio Canova.

14.5in (35cm) high

$4,000-5,000   SI

A 19thC marble figure of Eros, after Antonio Canova (It. 1757-1822)

15in (37.5cm) high

$5,000-6,000   SI

A 19thC marble sculpture of a bird of prey, Continental School.

44in (111.5cm) high

$1,000-1,400   SI

A Carara marble statue of Caro, the Countess of Breadalbane's Italian greyhound, by Peter Turnerelli (1774-1839), inscribed P. Turnerelli.

Turnerelli was one of the most eminent sculptors of his age. He was born in Belfast and educated in Dublin before moving to London and enrolling at The Royal Academy. In 1797 he was appointed to teach the Royal Princesses and in 1801 became Sculptor in Ordinary to the Royal Family; he subsequently became sculptor to HRH the Princess of Wales, as well as the kings of France, Russia and Portugal. Over this period Turnerelli carved portraits of most of the Royal family, including the Jubilee bust of George III in 1809, of which over 80 copies were made, a companion bust of the Queen, and a full-length statue of the King in state robes. This latter was exhibited at the Royal Academy in 1811, his only other submission that year being this statue of Cara. Turnerelli exhibited extensively at the Academy throughout his career and carved portrait busts of may of the most eminent characters of his time, including William Pitt, Lord Melville, Lord Palmerston, Daniel O'Connell (of which 10,000 plaster copies are alleged to have been made), the Duke of Wellington, Lady Caroline Lamb and Robert Burns, for the memorial in Dumfries. He twice refused a knighthood from the Prince of Wales, later George IV.

25.5in (65cm) high

$60,000-80,000   L&T

A 19thC marble model of the ruin of the Temple of Vespasian, comprising three fluted Corinthian columns on a rusticated plinth with a section of cornice inscribed "Estitver", and carved frieze to the return.

18in (45.5cm) high

$6,000-8,000   L&T

A 19th/20thC marble relief plaque, entitled Allegory of Life and Love, signed T. Malpieri.

Overall 23.5in (59.5cm) high

$1,800-2,200   SI

A marble study of a seated hound, by Henri Vallette (1877-1962), signed on the base.

41.5in (105cm) high

$25,000-30,000   L&T

A French terracotta sculpture of the Contesse de Sabran, after Jean-Antoine Houdon (1741-1828), on a variegated marble socle.

21.5in (54.5cm) high

$3,000-3,500   SI

THE MARKET FOR ANTIQUE CLOCKS HAS REMAINED STRONG IN THE LAST YEAR. Many buyers are choosing to buy an antique clock rather than invest in the stock market or pension funds as it is likely to appreciate in value, can be enjoyed as part of their home and be sold at a future date to raise funds if necessary.

Prices for fine furnishing clocks (those which are bought for their decorative rather than their technical aspects) have risen more strongly than any other type over the last 30 years, but more recently have remained relatively stable. Buyers should look for a good moon-phase painted dial and a high quality mahogany case. Thirty-hour clocks, at around $4,000 fully restored, remain relatively inexpensive and, because of their small size, are suitable for most modern homes, and the best quality eight-day clocks are increasing in value.

The market for fine and rare collectors' clocks is stronger, and with fewer of them coming onto the market, this trend looks sent to continue. It is worth noting that these clocks – particularly rare examples – are highly sought after by collectors and sell quickly and at a premium.

Prices are rising for good carriage clocks, particularly rare ones and those with fine porcelain panels and engraved cases are always in demand.

American clocks in original condition dating from the 18th century and from the main centers of production – New York, Philadelphia and Boston – continue to demand a permium price. However, at the lower end of the market, mass-produced 19th century New England clocks, from manufacturers such as the Ansonia Clock Company, offer a good investment at a reasonable price.

A japanned Queen Anne eight-day longcase clock, the associated twin-train movement with anchor escapement, later decoration, adapted.

99.75in (253cm) high

$2,200-2,800   L&T

A George I walnut eight-day longcase clock, the twin-train movement with anchor escapement striking on a bell, the brass dial with moon phase, inscribed silvered chapter ring, seconds dial and date aperture, by George White of Bristol.

88.5in (225cm) high

$8,500-9,500   L&T

A George II japanned eight-day longcase clock, the twin-train movement with anchor escapement striking on a bell, the brass dial with strike/silent lever, subsidiary seconds dial and date aperture, inscribed Tho. Stones, Lothbury.

85.5in (217cm) high

$1,500-2,000   L&T

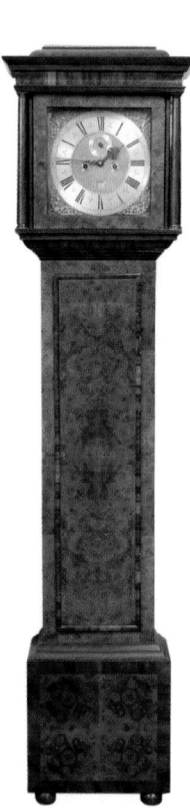

A mid-18thC burr walnut longcase clock, the brass dial with silvered chapter ring, seconds and calendar apertures with eight-day movement, and signed Salom Michel, London.

82.75in (210cm) high

$2,200-2,800   J&H

An 18thC longcase clock, with 30-hour movement, the engraved brass square dial signed John Batt, Petersfield.

76in (193cm) high

$1,500-2,000   J&H

Longcase

An 18thC 30-hour oak longcase clock, the striking movement with a brass dial, the chapter ring inscribed P. Bower Redlinch, old restoration to plinth.

78.75in (200cm) high

$4,500-5,000   WW

A figured mahogany pagoda-top longcase clock, the five-pillar movement striking the hours on a bell, by John Hubbard, Southwark.

c1770 90in (229cm) high

$18,000-22,000   DR

A mid- to late 18thC Provincial George III oak longcase clock, the dial with brass chapter ring, subsidiary seconds dial and date aperture, by Richard Upjohn, Exeter.

86.5in (220cm) high

$2,500-3,000   SI

An brass-faced moon-phase longcase clock, the eight-day, five-pillar movement striking and repeating the hours on a bell, by Thomas Iles, London.

c1780 96in (244cm) high

$20,000-25,000   DR

A longcase automaton clock, with five-pillar movement striking the hour on a bell, the brass dial with a seconds ring below 12 o'clock, a date aperture and a silvered brass strip bearing the maker's signature, by Samuel Toulmin, London.

This is an extremely rare automaton longcase clock, depicting in the arch of the brass dial a couple playing tennis, knocking the ball to and fro with their rackets.

c1770 88in (223.5cm) high

$35,000-40,000   DR

A Victorian mahogany, eight-day longcase clock, the twin-train movement with anchor escapement striking on a bell, the painted dial with subsidiary seconds and date dials, by Young, of Dundee.

83in (211cm) high

$3,500-4,000   L&T

► A George III mahogany eight-day longcase clock the fitted three-train movement striking and chiming on six bells, made in London by B. Hutchinson.

$4,000-5,000   GorB

A Georgian oak eight-day longcase clock, the twin-train movement with anchor escapement striking on a bell, the brass dial with subsidiary seconds and date dials.

81.5in (207cm) high

$2,500-2,800   L&T

A George III mahogany eight-day longcase clock, the twin-train movement with anchor escapement striking on a bell, the engraved silvered dial with subsidiary seconds dial and date aperture, inscribed Lancaster, Plymo. Dock.

82in (208cm) high

$3,500-4,000   L&T

An early 19thC Dorset oak 30-hour longcase clock, with striking movement, the engraved brass dial inscribed Arnold Child Ockford.

79.25in (201cm) high

$1,200-1,500　　**WW**

An early 19thC mahogany eight-day longcase clock, painted to the arch with the Burns Mausoleum at Dumfries, by Alex Black, Kirkcaldy.

85in (216cm) high

$2,200-2,400　　**L&T**

An early 19thC mahogany moon-phase longcase clock, the eight-day twin-train movement striking on a bell, the painted dial with subsidiary seconds and date dials, escapement and plinth lacking.

84in (213cm) high

$5,500-6,000　　**L&T**

An early 19thC mahogany eight-day longcase clock, the twin-train movement with anchor escapement striking on a bell, the painted dial with subsidiary date and seconds dials, by D. Duff, Paisley.

98.5in (250cm) high

$2,800-3,200　　**L&T**

A William IV Dorset mahogany longcase clock, with eight-day striking movement, the painted dial with a subsidiary seconds dial and calendar, inscribed Norman, Sherborne.

Matthew Norman is recorded at Sherborne c1830

87in (221cm) high

$1,300-1,500　　**WW**

A mid-19thC mahogany eight-day longcase clock, the twin-train movement with anchor escapement striking on a bell, the enameled dial painted to the arch with the Pass of Killiecrankie and to the spandrels with the Continents, by P. Whytock, Dundee.

83.5in (212cm) high

$4,000-5,000　　**L&T**

A 19thC eight-day mahogany longcase clock, the twin-train movement with anchor escapement striking on a bell, by Wn Anderson, St Andrews.

91in (231cm) high

$2,400-2,800　　**L&T**

A 19thC mahogany eight-day long case clock, the twin-train movement with anchor escapement, the enamel dial with subsidiary dates and seconds dial, painted to the angles with portraits of Reynolds, Rubens, Hogarth & Morland, painted to the arch with " Thunder Storm in Harvest", by W.M. Dobbie, Falkirk.

85.5in (217cm) high

$3,500-4,000　　**L&T**

A mid-19thC mahogany eight-day longcase clock, painted to the arch with a two-masted yacht and other boats.

84.75in (215cm) high

$900-1,000　　**L&T**

A Victorian mahogany eight-day longcase clock, the twin-track movement with anchor escapement striking on a bell.

85.5in (217cm) high

$2,000-2,500　　**L&T**

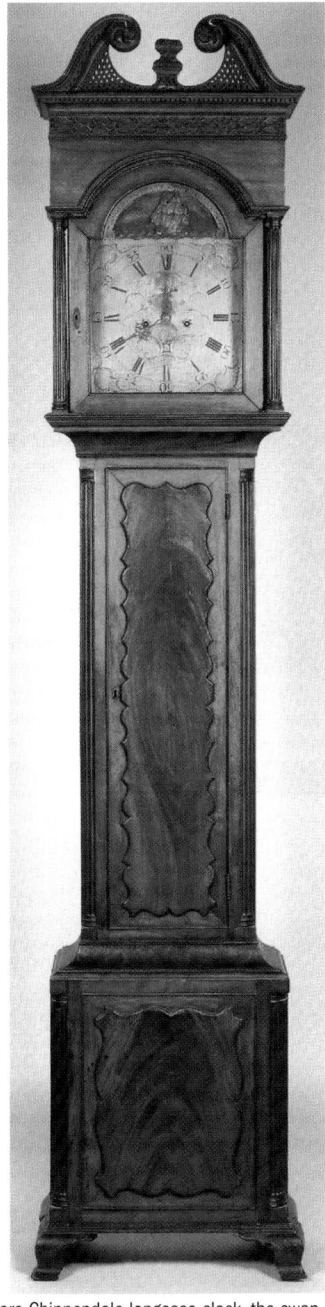

▶ A mid-18thC high-style Philadelphia Chippendale mahogany longcase clock, the swan-neck pediment with carved applied rosettes and flame finials, applied scrolling detail above arched door flanked by columnar supports, applied "Chinese" fret work above pendulum door flanked by fluted quarter columns, ogee-paneled base flanked by fluted corner columns, ogee bracket feet, silvered brass face with phases of the moon by James Warne, London, missing center cartouche, losses to rosettes and applied scrollwork, face resilvered and paint touched up, loose fret work, holes drilled through back of case.

c1760 100.5in (255.2cm) h

$80,000-100,000   FRE

A Pennsylvania Chippendale cherrywood tallcase clock, the swan-neck pediment with carved rosettes over brass face with calendar dial and painted phases of the moon, flanked by cylindrical columnar sides, over shaped pendulum door, straight bracket feet, signed "Thomas Wagstaffe, London."

c1770 88in (223.5cm) h

$12,000-15,000   FRE

A Philadelphia Chippendale cherrywood tallcase clock, the swan-neck pediment with carved rosettes, over arched brass and steel face with calendar dial, signed and painted phases of the moon, flanked by cylindrical columnar sides over shaped columnar sides over shaped pendulum door with ring-turned quarter columnar sides, the shaped paneled base terminating on stepped platform, by John Wood.

c1770 100in (254cm)

$55,000-60,000   FRE

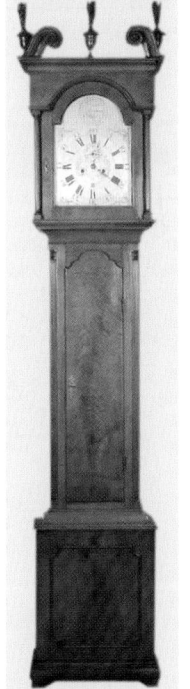

An American Chippendale carved walnut tall case clock, engraved steel face with calendar dial.

c1770 99.5in (253cm)

$50,000-60,000   FRE

An American cherrywood tall case clock, face signed Aaron Willard, Boston.

c1800 93in (236.5cm)

$7,500-8,000   FRE

A Delaware Chippendale longcase clock, the swan-neck pediment with carved rosettes centering unique finial, over arched engraved brass face with painted rocking ship which moves with the pendulum, column supports, ogival-paneled pendulum door flanked by fluted quarter columns, ogival paneled lower section flanked by fluted quarter columns, ogee bracket feet, works by Duncan Beard, walnut case attributed to John Janvier Sr., dial signed Duncan Beard, Appoquinimink, case inscribed in chalk on paneled door "Made at Cantwell's Bridge Delaware 1779," right swan neck with hair crack, small piece missing from right ogee foot, broken pendulum, general wear to painted ship.

c1779 97in (246cm) high

$450,000-500,000   FRE

371

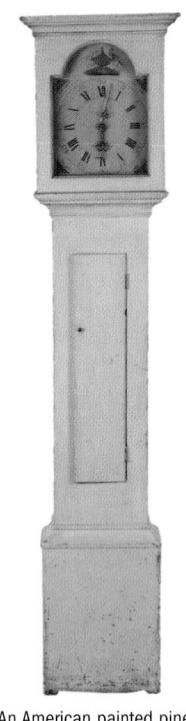

An early 19thC American Federal inlaid cherrywood tallcase clock, the white painted dial with chapter ring with Roman numerals and subsidiary second dial and date aperture, spandrels and arch painted with floral sprays, the hood with a swan-neck pediment over arched door flanked by turned colunettes with bronze capitals and bases, the case with mounted rectangular door flanked by fluted columnar stiles, the plinth raised on a moulded bracket base, maple and ebony stringing throughout, possibly Pennsylvania.

88.5in (225cm) high

| **$6,000-7,000** | **SI** |

An American painted pine tallcase clock, the hood with flat-molded cornice painted over an arched glazed door enclosing a painted wooden dial decorated with bird and urn at arch and fans at spandrels in red, green and gold, the waist with thumb-molded door, all raised on short bracket feet, loss of height, New England.

c1820 81in (206cm) high

| **$2,500-3,000** | **SI** |

A Federal mahogany tallcase clock, the bonnet with swan-neck pediment having pierced trelliswork and bull's-eye rosettes, painted dial below with moon phases, parcel gilt spandrels, the case with chamfered corners flanking a figured door and panel at bottom, on French bracket feet, the calendar and seconds register inscribed "John J Parry, PHILADa," inscribed in white chalk.

c1800 97in (246cm) high

| **$6,000-7,000** | **FRE** |

A Federal inlaid maple tallcase clock, the arched bonnet with pierced and fret-carved crest surmounted by inlaid dies and urn finials, above chinoiserie painted dial flanked by inlaid columns, the case beneath with inlaid door, fluted quarter columns, with brass capitals and inlaid lower case on French feet, New England.

c1800 94.5in (240cm) high

| **$8,500-9,500** | **FRE** |

An American grain-painted pine tallcase clock, the shaped scrolling crest over a glazed door enclosing a painted wooden dial, on boxed base with cut-out feet and scrolled skirt, red and black graining simulating rosewood, with 30-hour wooden gear movement, weight-drive with strike, the retouched painted wooden dial inscribed R. Whiting Manchester.

c1820 87in (220cm) high

| **$3,500-4,000** | **SI** |

▶ An American Victorian Renaissance Revival carved walnut tallcase clock, with architectural plume cartouche over arched pediment inset with carved portrait bust, arched pendulum, glazed door enclosing circular brass-mounted enamel face, steel-engraved pendulum, case embellished with burl walnut panels, stepped base, by George A Jones, Courtland St, NY.

c1870 106in (269.5cm)

| **$10,500-12,000** | **FRE** |

WALL

A Regency rosewood brass-inlaid wall timepiece, the single-train fusee movent with silvered dial, by Ritchie and Son, Edinburgh.

26.5in (67cm) high

| **$1,100-1,200** | **L&T** |

A William IV mahogany wall clock, with eight-day striking fusee movement, the convex dial indistinctly signed, probably M. Bartley, Bristol.

11in (28cm) diam

| **$3,000-3,350** | **Clv** |

Wall/Bracket

A 19thC mahogany wall clock, with single-fusee movement, the enamel dial inscribed W Bradley, Petersfield.

17.5in (44cm) diam

$900-1,200 | **J&H**

A 19thC French tortoiseshell boulle wall clock, the twin-train movement striking on a gong, the pendulum cast with Apollo's mask.

Boulle *is a type of decorative marquetry developed by the great French ebéniste André-Charles Boulle (1642-1732). Sheets of tortoiseshell or turtleshell and brass were glued together, then cut into patterns with a fretsaw to produce either shell inlaid with brass, or brass inlaid with shell.*

55in (140cm) high

$4,500-5,000 | **L&T**

A 19thC French gilt-metal cartel clock, in the late 18thC style, the twin-train movement with enamel dial.

27in (69cm) high

$2,200-2,800 | **L&T**

A 19thC Louis XV-style gilt-bronze cartel clock.

21in (35cm) high

$1,200-1,500 | **SI**

A Continental giltwood cartel clock.

28in (71cm) high

$1,500-2,000 | **SI**

An early 19thC mahogany tavern clock by Gadsby, Leicester.

54.25in (138cm) high

$22,000-24,000 | **DR**

A veneered walnut multi-dial wall regulator, with spiral drive to lunar calendar showing phases of the moon depicted successively by four faces – a child then a young, middle and old aged man, by Arthur Kinder.

Arthur Kinder was probably a gifted amateur horologist. He made this clock when he was 74 years old.

1899 | 67in (170cm) high

$30,000-33,000 | **DR**

BRACKET

► A small ebonized bracket clock, the dial with fast/slow regulation in the arch, the six-pillar movement with verge escapement and pull-quarter repeat on three bells, the engraved backplate bearing the maker's signature, by Fromanteel, London.

The Fromanteels were an English family of clockmakers of Dutch or Flemish origin. Ahasurus Fromanteel worked in Smithfield, London, from c1620-90 and was one of the earliest makers of pendulum clocks in England.

c1720 | 15.5in (39cm) high

$19,000-23,000 | **DR**

► An ebonized verge bracket clock, with moon phases, the twin-fusee movement with verge escapement and pull-quarter repeat on six bells, the dial with subsidiary fast/slow and strike/silent dials, the engraved backplate featuring Diana the Huntress with her dogs, by Claudius du Chesne.

c1730 | 18.5in (47cm) high

$28,000-32,000 | **DR**

A George II bracket clock, the five-pillar bell-striking movement with engraved backplate, the original verge escapement beneath false pendulum aperture, with subsidiary strike/silent dial, the brass break-arch dial with silvered plaque signed Jno. Pepys, London.

c1740   17.75in (45cm) high

$6,000-7,000   **BAR**

A mid-18thC ebonized and panel-gilt bracket clock, with associated case, the later brass dial signed to the arch above silvered chapter ring pendulum and date apertures, the single-fusee movement with verge escapement and pull-repeat striking bells, the engraved backplate signed John May Witney, restorations and alterations.

20.5in (52cm) high

$3,500-4,000   **BonS**

This clock has a five-pillar three-train movement with anchor escapement.
The pillars hold the two wheels of the movement together. On a clock of this period they are usually made out of brass.
The train, an interconnected series of wheels and pinions, transmits power from the mainspring or weights to the escape mechanism and the hands.
The escapement regulates the clock. The anchor-shape of this clock's escape mechanism engages with the toothed escape wheel at precise intervals. The anchor allows the use of a pendulum (visible here) and gives greater accuracy than was previously possible. It was supposedly invented c1670.

JOHN ELLICOT (1703-1772) was one of the foremost English clockmakers of the 18th century. He worked with his son Edward from 1760, taking him into partnership in 1769, from which time they were known as John Ellicot & Sons. Ellicot worked extensively for the export market and particularly for King Ferdinand VI of Spain; it seems likely that this clock was made with such a client in mind. There is a magnificent walnut-cased clock in the Victoria and Albert Museum, London, with silver-gilt mounts, possibly by George Michael Moser, which are directly comparable to the mounts on this clock. Moser made exceptional watch cases for Ellicot, and although he is not known to have made clock mounts these are attributable to him by association.

A George III ebonized and ormolu-mounted table clock, the five-pillar three-train movement with anchor escapement, bell striking and quarter chiming on eight bells, the later painted dial with subsidiary enamel strike/silent calender dials and with name plate below, the engraved backplate signed Ellicot, London, later sound panels to the sides.

30in (74cm) high

$20,000-23,000   **L&T**

The bell on this clock strikes and quarter chimes on eight bells. On most antique clocks, the bell is made out of a copper-tin alloy known as "bell metal".

Bracket

An unusual spring clock by John Holmes, London.

c1780   15.25in (38.5cm) high

$20,000-23,000   **DR**

A George III mahogany triple-pad top-bracket clock, with five-pillar, twin-fusee bell-striking movement and anchor escapement, the finely engraved backplate signed Muckarsie, Holborn.

c1800   10.75in (42.5cm) high

$6,000-7,000   **BAR**

An unusual musical bracket clock with automaton scene in arch and playing one of two tunes on the hour, employing eight bells and fifteen hammers, the very fine six-pillar three-train movement with verge escapement, by Stephen Rimbault, London.

c1780   21.75in (55.5cm) high

The dial has a large cutout to the top in the form of a stage. A painted scene depicts a couple playing cards while automaton figures move across from either side to serve them at the hour, one with a loaf and the other with fish.

$35,000-40,000   **DR**

A Georgian mahogany bracket clock with enameled dial, by Eardley Norton, London.

$25,000-30,000   **DR**

◄ A Regency mahogany and cut-brass-inlaid bracket clock, with enamel dial, the twin-train fusee movement striking on a bell.

16.5in (42cm) high

$1,000-1,500   **BonS**

A small moon-phase bracket clock, in mahogany case, by J.N. Stirling, London.

c1790   13.5in (34.5cm) high

$15,000-18,000   **DR**

A late 18th/early 19thC mahogany and gilt-metal-mounted bracket clock, the brass dial with silvered chapter ring and strike/silent to the arch, the twin-fusee movement striking a bell, the engraved backplate signed William Edwards, London, restorations.

25in (64cm) high

$5,000-5,500   **BonS**

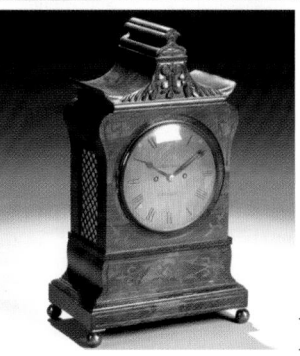

A George III ebonized bracket clock, the twin-train five-pillar fusee movement striking the hour on a steel bell, the dial with silvered chapter ring and subsidiary date aperture, with strike/silent and seconds dials to the arch, profusely engraved blackplate, by Andrew Dickie, Edinburgh.

19in (48cm) high

$7,000-8,000   **L&T**

An early 19thC bracket clock by James McCabe, Royal Exchange, London.

16.45in (41.5cm) high

$4,500-5,500   **DR**

◄ An early 19thC rosewood and brass-inlaid bracket clock, with twin-train fusee movement, by Muirhead, Glasgow.

20in (51cm) high

$1,500-1,800   **L&T**

A Regency ebonized bracket clock with trip repeat, the eight-day striking twin-fusee five-pillar movement with anchor escapement, the engraved backplate signed Tho's Pace, London.

c1820   18.5in (47cm) high

$2,000-2,500   **BAR**

▲**1** A Regency mahogany and brass-inlaid bracket clock, with enameled dial, the twin-train movement striking on a bell, inscribed to the dial and backplate Tupman of Charles St, Grosvenor Square, London.

17in (43cm) high

$3,000-3,500   **L&T**

▲**2** A Regency ebonized bracket clock, with inscribed enameled dial, the twin-train movement striking on a bell, with side repeater, by William Nicoll, Great Portland Street, London.

13.75in (35cm) high

$2,700-3,000   **L&T**

A long duration mahogany table regulator, by Collas à Paris.

This table regulator has a beautifully executed convex enameled dial 5.75in (14.5cm) in diameter with a counter-balanced center-sweep seconds hand and a date hand, both in blued steel. The minute and hour hands are fire-gilt. The blued center to the dial is bordered with gilt-edged lobes interspersed with tiny green stones. Surrounding the dial is a delicately engine-turned gilded bezel. The movement has two very substantial gong barrels, external pin-wheel escapement and an excellent nine-rod gridiron pendulum with knife-edge suspension. There is count-wheel strike on a bell with the count-wheel mounted externally. The clock bears repair marks for the 21st September 1828 and 28th May 1897.

c1815   19in (48cm) high

$58,000-62,000   **DR**

A 19thC burr walnut eight-day bracket clock, the twin-train movement with anchor escapement striking on a gong, with rectangular bracket on shaped consoles, by Brysons of Edinburgh.

clock 20.5in (52cm) high
bracket 6.25in (16cm) high

$2,500-3,000   **L&T**

A small, rosewood-veneered bracket clock, with elaborate cast foliate fretwork, the two-chain fusee movement striking the hours on a bell, the pendulum with regulating nut above the bob, by Alabone, Newport, Isle of Wight.

c1850   11.5in (29cm) high

$9,000-10,000   **DR**

A 19thC brass-mounted ebonized wood bracket clock, with enameled dial, the subsidiary dial inscribed strike/silent, the rectangular movement with anchor escapement striking on a bell, engraved J. Barwise, St Martin's Lane, London.

15.5in (39.5cm) high

$3,200-3,800   **SI**

▶ A 19thC brass-mounted rosewood bracket clock, with bell-striking movement.

13.25in (33.5cm) high

$800-1,200   **SI**

A Victorian pollard oak-cased bracket clock, the three-train movement striking on a gong and bell, the chased silvered dial with subsidiary slow/fast dials, engraved Barraud & Lunds, 14 Bishopsgate, St Within, Cornhill, London 6364.

25in (63cm) high

$2,700-3,000   **L&T**

A late 19thC French gilt-bronze and ebonized wood bracket clock, the pendulum impressed 8017, silvered metal chapter ring, the bell-striking square movement with anchor escapement impressed with Japy Frères mark and BEST RACK/8017/55.

15.25in (39cm) high

$550-600   **SI**

Bracket/Mantel

A late 19thC French Louis XIV-style ormolu-mounted stained tortoiseshell and brass-inlaid bracket clock, the movement stamped Grohe/Wigmore Street/London.

12in (30.5cm) high

$750-950   **SI**

An Edwardian rosewood-cased bracket clock, the three-train chiming movement striking the quarters, the gilt-brass dial with silvered chime/silent and slow/fast dials.

22.5in (57cm) high

$2,000-2,500   **L&T**

A George III-style mahogany bracket clock, the brass dial with signed silvered chapter ring, the twin-fusee movement striking a bell, by Swindon & Sons, Birmingham.

c1900   17.75in (45cm) high

$1,000-1,200   **BonS**

A late Victorian/early Edwardian inlaid rosewood Westminster chiming table clock, the eight-day three-train movement with anchor escapement, each train with fusee, striking the hour and chiming the quarters on five gongs or eight bells, the brass dial with silvered chapter ring beneath three subsidiary dials for chime/silent, slow/fast running and Westminster chimes/chime on eight bells, the dial with retailer's plaque for RH Halford & Sons, 43 Fenchurch Street, London.

21.75in (55cm) high

$3,000-4,000   **DN**

▶ A late 19thC Tiffany & Co. mahogany and brass bracket clock, the arched top wtih embossed foliate and figural decoraton, within a pierced brinze gallery, below is an arched moon-faced dial with silver chaptering and foliate pierced spandrels, flanked by reeded turned pilasters on ornate cast bracket feet.

28in (71cm) high

$3,800-4,200   **SI**

MANTEL

A French mahogany and gilt-metal-mounted mantel clock, retailed by Charles Frodsham, 27 South Molton Street, London, the signed enamel dial with twin-train movement striking a gong and stamped Vincenti 3077.

c1900   11in (28cm) high

$800-900   **BonS**

An early 19thC French rosewood-cased drum timepiece, with enamel dial.

6.75in (17cm) high

$300-350   **J&H**

A rosewood and glass-cased fusee timepiece, with anchor escapement and waxed silver dial, by Vogt.

9.25in (23.5cm) high

$6,000-7,000   **DR**

An early 19thC mahogany mantel timepiece, with enamel dial and single fusee movement, restored.

13in (33cm) high

$300-350   **BonS**

▶ An early 19thC mahogany mantel regulator, with detached escapement and mercury pendulum, the movement striking on gong, the silvered dial with large minute chapter ring and subsidiary hours and seconds ring, signed Dalgety's patent.

19in (49cm) high

$10,000-12,000   **LC**

◄ A late Victorian black slate mantel clock, the eight-day three-train movement striking the hours on a coiled gong and chiming the quarters on eight bells, with brass presentation plaque bearing date 1883.

c1880   17in (43cm) high
$700-800   **DN**

An early Victorian maple-cased mantel timepiece, the single-train movement with engraved brass dial, by James McCabe, London.

9in (22.5cm) high
$4,000-5,000   **L&T**

A late 19thC French walnut mantel timepiece, with porcelain dial.

6.75in (17cm) high
$180-220   **J&H**

A late 19thC rosewood and marquetry mantel timepiece, the eight-day single-train movement with anchor escapement, the backplate stamped Ht. Marc, Paris.

9in (23cm) high
$450-500   **DN**

An 18thC-style mahogany and gilt-metal-mounted mantel clock, the silvered dial with twin-train movement striking a gong, retailed by FINNIGANS LTD, MANCHESTER & LIVERPOOL.

c1900   15.75in (40cm) high
$450-500   **BonS**

An Edwardian mahogany and pale-wood-banded lancet mantel clock, the eight-day two-train movement striking on gongs, some wear to the dial.

15in (38cm) high
$550-600   **DN**

An Edwardian rosewood and inlaid lancet mantel clock, the eight-day two-train movement with anchor escapement striking the hours and the quarters on two gongs, the brass dial inscribed for the retailers Russells Ltd, Liverpool, beneath a subsidiary slow/fast dial, the case set with presentation plaque dated 1911, soldered repair to hands.

14.25in (36cm) high
$700-800   **DN**

An early 20thC ebonized and walnut-cased mantel clock, the drum movement striking on a bell, some chipping to enamel dial.

12in (30.5cm) high
$120-180   **LC**

Mantel

A mid-19thC French ormolu and bronze mantel clock, the eight-day movement striking on a bell and stamped Butte, 1426.

16.5in (42cm) high

$900-1,200   **J&H**

A mid-19thC French ormolu mantel clock, the movement with count-wheel strike on a bell and fast/slow regulation, backplate numbered 1092, by Costain, Galerie de la Madeleine, Paris.

13.5in (34cm) high

$1,500-2,000   **DR**

A mid-19thC French Empire-style bronze and gilt-metal-mounted mantel clock, the eight-day two-train movement with outside countwheel strike on a bell, the bronze case surmounted with an equestrian figure of a Mameluk.

22in (56cm) high

$1,000-1,400   **DN**

A 19thC French gilt-bronze and marble mantel clock, with bell striking circular movement, the pendulum with Medusa weight and impressed 6204, the dial inscribed Roque A Paris, movement impressed Roque a Paris N,1282.

19in (48.5cm) high

$2,800-3,200   **SI**

A 19thC gilt bronze Empire-style mantel clock, the twin-train movement with anchor escapement striking with two hammers on a bell.

13.5in (34cm) high

$2,800-3,400   **L&T**

A mid-19thC Empire-style gilt and patinated bronze clock, with cast bronze figure of Orpheus with lyre.

35.5in (90.5cm) high

$6,000-7,000   **SI**

A 19thC French bronze and ormolu Louis XV-style mantel clock, the movement stamped E P 5010 and striking on a single gong, with cast chinoiserie figure over a drumhead with enamel dial, on cast bronze elephant.

24.4in (62cm) high

$5,000-5,500   **L&T**

A 19thC French marble mantel clock, the eight-day two-train movement striking on a bell, inscribed F. BARBEDIENNE FONDEUR, marble damaged, bell lacking, repaired, losses.

28in (71cm) high

$4,000-4,500   **DN**

A late 19thC French onyx-mounted mantel timepiece, the eight-day movement with a bronzed metal pendulum cast as a girl on a swing, case damaged and repaired.

9.75in (24.5cm) high

$120-150   **DN**

A late 19thC Louis XVI-style ormolu mantel clock, the case set with Sèvres-style plaques, the drum movement striking on a bell and stamped R M 647.

13.5in (34cm) high

$450-500   **LC**

A late 19thC French bronze and rouge marble mantle clock, with cast bronze figure of Mercury, signed by Jean de Bologne.

36in (91.4cm) high

$1,200-1,500   **SI**

A Belle Époque bronze-patinated metal and black iron figural mantel clock, depicting Abraham Lincoln.

18in (46cm) high

$1,500-2,000   **SI**

Mantel

An early 20thC French gilt-bronze mantel clock, with mercury pendulum, retailed by Theodore Starr.

13.5in (34cm)

$400-450	SI

An elaborate 20thC gilt-bronze mantel clock, the movement with German maker's mark.

24in (61cm) high

$600-700	SI

A French champlevé enamel and gilt-metal-mounted mantel clock, the twin-train movement striking a gong and stamped L Marti et Cie.

c1889   18.25in (46cm) high

$900-1,200	BonS

A late 19thC mantel clock, the silvered dial with engine-turned center, signed GOLDSMITHS ALLIANCE LTD.

$750-850	BonS

A late 19thC Louis XV-style stained tortoiseshell cut brass and gilt-metal-mounted mantel clock, the eight-day movement striking on a bell, the dial and backplate signed W M JOHNSON, 54 THREADNEEDLE ST, ROYAL EXCHANGE, LONDON.

12.25in (31cm) high

$1,400-1,800	BonS

A late 19thC French gilt-metal mantel clock, the two-train movement with outside count wheel striking on a bell, chips to dial.

7in (18cm) high

$350-400	DN

A late 19thC French gilt-metal-mounted Sèvres-style mantel clock, the eight-day two-train movement with outside count wheel striking on a bell.

12.5in (31.5cm) high

$200-250	DN

A late 19thC French gilt-metal-mounted mantel timepiece, the eight-day single-train movement with enameled dial, by Leroy à Paris.

10.25in (26cm) high

$120-180	DN

A late 19thC gilt-metal and onyx-mounted four glass clock, the annular dial with exposed escapement, the drum movement striking on a gong.

15.5in (39cm) high

$700-800	LC

A 19thC French gilt-metal and Sèvres-style porcelain-mounted mantel clock, the twin-train movement striking on a coiled gong, by Lewis P. Muirhead & Co, Paris.

19.5in (49.5cm) high

$2,000-2,500   L&T

A 19thC ormolu-mounted and Sèvres-style porcelain mantel clock, works stamped B.R/271/38100, plinth stamped 38100.

16.75in (42.5cm) high

$2,500-3,000   SI

A porcelain mantel clock, the movement with counter wheel striking on a bell, silk suspension, signed Raingo Freres, Paris no. 832.

c1860   11.25in (28cm) high

$3,000-4,000   DR

A porcelain mantel clock, by Beguin, Paris.

c1860   14.5in (37cm) high

$2,500-3,000   DR

A Second Empire Paris porcelain-cased mantel clock, the eight-day movement with outside count wheel striking on a bell, the backplate stamped SCHULLER A PARIS, blue JP marks for Jacob Petit, some cracks to enamel dial.

13.75in (35cm) high

$2,800-3,200   DN

A late 19thC French gilt metal and champlevé enamel-cased mantel clock, with Sèvres-style porcelain panel, the movement striking on a gong.

16.5in (42cm) high

$2,500-3,000   L&T

An French ormolu and porcelain mantel clock, the movement striking on a bell, by Richard et Cie, Paris no. 2083.

c1870   15in (38cm) high

$2,500-3,000   DR

A giant French porcelain-paneled gorge-cased mantel clock, the movement striking the hours and half hours on a bell and bearing the stamp of Marti et Cie.

c1870   15.5in (39cm) high

$8,000-9,000   DR

◄1 A French ormolu and Sèvres-style porcelain-mounted mantel clock, the two-train brass movement by Japy Frères with anchor escapement striking half hourly on a bell, founder's mark S. Tilmourey 69.

5.5in (39cm) high

$750-850   HamG

◄2 A late 19thC French bronze ormolu and black marble mantel clock, surmounted by a patinated bronze figure group of a crusader on horseback fighting a Persian foot soldier, the brass two-train drum movement striking on a bell.

4.5in (62cm) high

$400-500   HamG

A late 19thC French gilt-metal-mounted Sèvres-style mantel clock, the eight-day two-train movement with outside count wheel striking on a bell.

12.5in (31.5cm) high

$200-250   DN

▲1 An early 20thC French gilt-bronze and Carara marble mantel clock, the twin-train movement with painted enamel dial.

25in (63cm) high

$1,200-1,500 **L&T**

▲2 A late 19thC French Transitional style gilt-bronze mantel clock, the twin-train movement with painted porcelain dial, slight damage to case.

19.25in (49cm) high

$1,100-1,400 **L&T**

An American Federal mahogany pillar-and-scroll mantel clock, the white-paneled gilt-decorated wood dial above reverse-painted glazed tablet depicting garden scene, by Eli Terry & Sons, Plymouth, Connecticut, imperfections.

c1825 31.5in (80cm) high

$2,000-2,500 **SI**

A Classical painted, stenciled and mahogany veneered shelf clock, the shaped crest painted black and stenciled with basket of flowers above the painted wood dial decorated with gilt at spandrels over the glazed reverse-painted panel depicting a woman at a well, all flanked by engaged colunettes painted black and stenciled with foliate devices, New England.

c1820 30.5in (77.5cm) high

$800-1,000 **SI**

A Classical mahogany, giltwood and mahogany veneer shelf clock, carved eagle cresting above glazed door opening to white painted wood dial embellished with gilding, over a recessed mirrored plate and second glazed door reverse-painted with romantic scene, all flanked by half-round and free-standing colunettes, carved claw front feet, manufactured by Atkins & Downs for George Mitchell; Bristol Connecticut, paint loss to reverse-painted panel, retouched.

c1825 37in (94cm) high

$1,000-1,400 **SI**

A late Federal stencil-decorated mahogany shelf clock, the lower panel of the glazed door with a reverse-painted panel of a European monarch, possibly Charles X of France, labeled "Hopkins and Alfred, Harwinton, CT."

Provenance: *The Society of the Cincinnati.*

c1830 17.5in (44.5cm) wide

$550-750 **SI**

A Classical carved mahogany and mahogany veneer shelf clock, "Patent Clock" by Eli Terry, made and sold by Seth Thomas, Plymouth, Connecticut. The cresting with carved bowl of fruit over glazed door opening to painted wood dial decorated with berry sprays at spandrels above a door with mirrored plate flanked by three-quarter round colonnettes with carved capitols and feet, (imperfections).

c1830 37.25in (94.5cm) high

$500-700 **SI**

A Classical mahogany and veneer shelf clock, white-painted wood dial with raised gilt decoration above a recessed mirror plate and reverse-painted glazed tablet depicting a large house, flanked by half-round and free-standing colonettes raised on turned feet, Birge Case & Co, Bristol, Connecticut, loss to reverse painting, some restoration.

c1835 36in (91.5cm) high

$700-900 **SI**

A 19thC monumental clock, with French twin-train movement, by Sorly, Glasgow.

38.5in (98cm) high

$3,000-3,500   L&T

A late 19thC Atmos clock, of conventional form, by Jaeger le Coultre.

8.75in (22.5cm) high

$900-1,100   LC

A late 19thC ebonized mantel clock, the rectangular backplate striking on two gongs.

23in (59cm) high

$400-500   LC

A late 19thC American mahogany clock/perpetual calendar, by Seth Thomas, patented February 15th 1876, with white enamel dials, in chamfered arched case with plinth base.

20in (51cm)

$900-1,200   J&H

GARNITURES

A 19thC black slate and brass clock garniture, the clock with twin-train movement, inscribed F Aizblin, and retailed by Tiffany & Co, New York, with attendant urns.

clock 20.25in (51.5cm) high

$1,000-1,300   L&T

A French 19thC gilt and champlevé enamel clock garniture, the clock with mercurial pendulum.

clock 19in (48.5cm) high

$4,000-5,000   L&T

A late 19thC French gilt-brass and Sèvres-style porcelain clock garniture, the clock with cylinder movement striking single bell, with attendant urns.

clock 22.5in (57cm) high

$2,200-2,800   L&T

A 19thC gilt brass and champlevé enamel clock garniture.

clock 17in (43cm) high

$2,400-2,800   L&T

A late 19thC French gilt-metal and Sèvres-style porcelain garniture, the clock with twin-train movement stamped SR1472, striking on a bell, the candelabra restored.

clock 14.5in (37cm) high

$1,500-2,000   BonS

A late 19thC brass and silvered French Aesthetic-style clock garniture, the twin-train movement with enameled dial inscribed Howell James & Co, to the Queen, London Paris.

clock 19.75in (50cm) high

$2,800-3,400   L&T

Carriage

CARRIAGE & TRAVEL

◀ A giant carriage clock, no. 4148, four gongs chime and are mounted on a standard behind the backplate, between the plates are five pin barrels for the quarters and hours with massive spring barrel below, regulating lever in the base for hours and quarters, attributed to Achille Brocot.

ACHILLE BROCOT (1817-78) was a French clockmaker who invented the Brocot escapement and the Brocot suspension, a method of regulating a clock by using a key to adjust the length of the pendulum spring.

c1885   9.25in (23.5cm)

$13,000-15,000	**DR**

A champlevé enamel carriage clock with an Anglaise Riche case, the lever escapement movement striking and repeating the hours and half hours on a gong, the enamel signed Chaudot Emailler Paris.

c1885   6.5in (16cm) high

$8,000-10,000	**DR**

A carriage clock, in Anglaise Riche case, with fine Limoges enamel panels, petite sonnerie striking movement, no. 2726.

c1885   5.75in (14.5cm) high

$8,000-9,000	**DR**

A late 19thC French carriage timepiece, in brass and champlevé enamel case, with eight-day cylinder movement, the silvered dial inscibed H. Greaves, Birmingham.

6in (15.5cm) high

$120-150	**LFA**

A late 19thC French gilt-metal carriage clock, with push repeat, the platform-lever escapement movement striking on a gong, stamped E M & Co.

6in (15.5cm) high

$700-800	**BonS**

A late 19th French gilt-metal carriage clock with push repeat, the enamel mask signed by retailers Gaydon & Sons, Norwood, Purley & Hull, the platform lever escapement movement striking a gong and stamped E.G.L.

6.25in (16cm) high

$550-600	**BonS**

A French late 19thC brass-cased carriage clock, the eight-day two-train movement with lever escapement and striking on a coiled gong, repeat button.

6.75in (17cm) high

$600-700	**DN**

A late 19thC small brass-cased repeating carriage clock, the twin-train movement with lever platform escapement, striking the half hours on a gong.

$700-800	**L&T**

A miniature French eight-day gilded carriage timepiece, with enamel panels.

c1900   2.25in (5.5cm) high

$3,500-4,000	**DR**

▶ A late 19th/early 20thC French brass-cased carriage clock, the eight-day twin-train movement with lever escapement and striking on a coiled gong, with repeat button.

7in (17.5cm) high

$450-550	**DN**

A mid-19thC petit sonnerie repeating carriage clock, the twin-train movement with lever platform escapement, alarm and slow/fast guage, striking on two gongs, the chased silvered brass dial with subsidiary alarm dial.

A late 19th/early 20thC French brass-cased carriage timepiece, with lever escapement, the enameled dial inscribed for the retailer JOHN WALKER 77 CORNHILL LONDON.

6.5in (16cm) high

A French (R & Co) 20thC brass-cased carriage clock, the twin-train movement with lever escapement and striking the hours and half-hour pass strike on coiled gong.

6in (15cm) high

6.25in (16cm) high

$200-250	DN	$500-550	DN	$3,000-3,500		L&T

SKELETON AND MYSTERY

JEAN EUGÈNE ROBERT-HOUDIN (1805-1871) was a French clockmaker, conjurer and magician, who was celebrated for his optical illusions and mechanical devices. He transformed magic in the mid-19th century from a circus side-show to an elegant stage performance. His shows so mesmerized audiences that the American magician Eric Weiss took his stage name, Harry Houdini, as a tribute to the Frenchman. These clocks by Robert-Houdin are intriguing because there are no visible means by which the hand is carried round and there is no apparent connection between the dial and the movement concealed within the base. The conundrum is explained by having an outer stationary glass column that supports the dial assembly and an inner rotating glass column with gears applied to the top and bottom, which provides a link between the movement below and the bezel above. Concealed within the bezel is a very fine wheel, which is cemented to the edge of a circular glass plate on which the hour hand is mounted and thus carried around. The movement is stamped La Compte A Paris no.77.

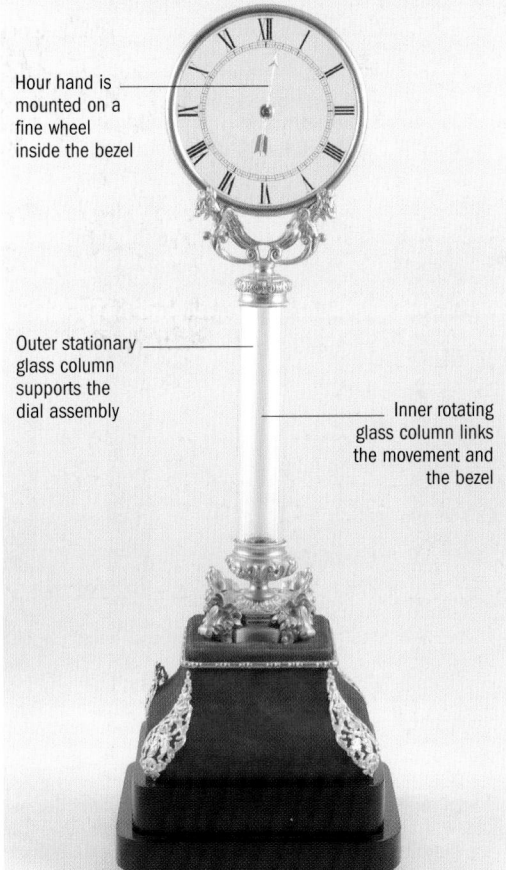

Hour hand is mounted on a fine wheel inside the bezel

Outer stationary glass column supports the dial assembly

Inner rotating glass column links the movement and the bezel

A rare example of a glass-dialled mystery clock with a glass column, by Robert-Houdin, Paris.

c1845　21in (53cm) high

$30,000-35,000		DR

A 19thC brass skeleton clock, with silvered metal chapter ring, in a glass dome.

11in (28cm) high

$550-600	SI

A 19thC skeleton clock, with silvered metal pierced chapter ring, in a glass dome.

15.25in (38.5cm) high

$1,200-1,500	SI

BAROMETERS

A 19thC French skeleton clock in glass dome, with silk suspension, anchor escapement and a striking bell in base, the chapter ring inscribed PIERRET A PARIS.

9.5in (24cm) high

$1,200-1,500   **SI**

A late 19th/early 20thC Gothic tracery lancet skeleton timepiece, the eight-day single-train movement with anchor escapement and fusee, the base of the case with retailer's plaque for Wolff, Gunson and O'Meara Ltd, Manchester.

24in (61cm) high

$1,600-2,000   **DN**

LANTERN

◄ A late Victorian brass lantern clock, in the 17thC style, the eight-day single-train fusee movement with anchor escapement and single pass strike on a bell.

14.25in (36cm) high

$1,200-1,500   **DN**

A winged lantern clock, by Thomas Dyde.

15.75in (40cm) high

$12,000-15,000   **DR**

A winged lantern clock, by Henry Hotham at Ye Black Spread Eagle.

c1680   15.75in (40cm) high

$12,000-15,000   **DR**

BAROMETERS

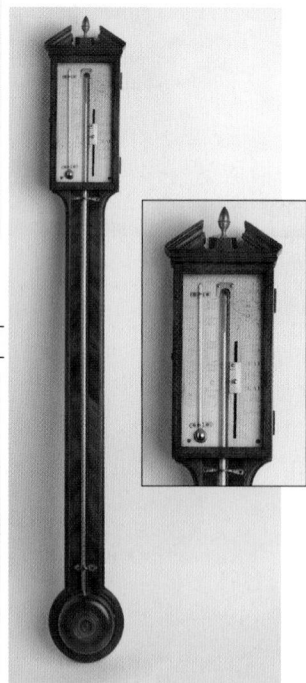

An 18thC mahogany stick barometer, the feather-veneered case with chequer feather stringing, the silvered register plate signed Joseph Somalvico & Co. 256 Holburn, London.

37.5in (95cm) high

$2,000-2,400   **LC**

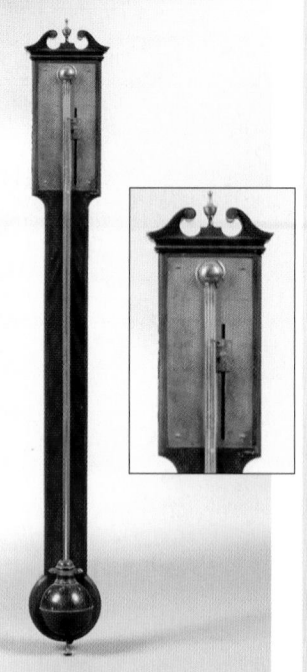

A George III mahogany stick barometer, with inscribed brass vernier scale above long rectangular trunk and circular domed reservoir cover, signed Cary, London.

$4,000-5,000   **L&T**

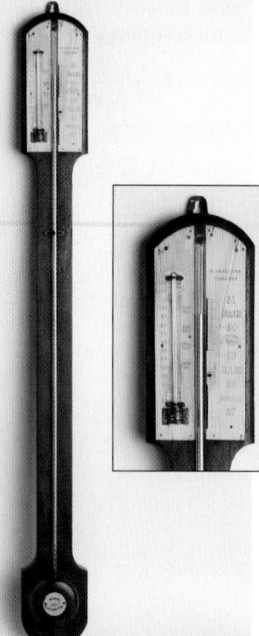

A 19thC rosewood stick barometer, the cistern set with an ivory tablet inscribed Model Barometer, the ivory register plate with mercury thermometer signed W Carleton, Torquay, ivory cracked.

37.5in (95cm) high

$450-550   **LC**

A George III mahogany and boxwood-strung wheel barometer, the baluster case inset with shell and flower patera, with silvered dial and thermometer, signed C Somalvico, 41 Kirsty Street, Hatton Garden, London.

38.5in (98cm) long

$900-1,000 L&T

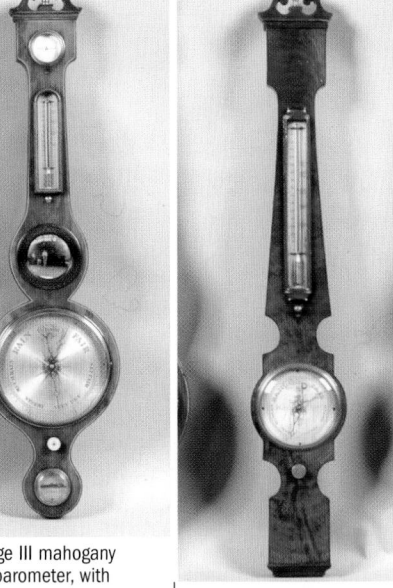

A George III mahogany wheel barometer, with boxwood and ebony stringing, the case fitted with dry/damp dial, thermometer, silvered dial, convex mirror and spirit level, signed D Balerna.

38.25in (97cm) long

$700-800 L&T

A George III mahogany and ebony-strung wheel barometer, the case inset with thermometer and small silvered dial, signed Huntley, London.

38.5in (98cm) long

$2,000-2,500 L&T

A 19thC rosewood wheel barometer, with silvered dial, the case set with a mirror, alcohol thermometer, hygrometer and spirit level, signed Kendrick of Droitwich.

38in (96.5cm) high

$600-700 LC

A 19thC mahogany wheel barometer, the onion terminal case set with convex mirror, alcohol thermometer, hygrometer and spirit level.

37.75in (96cm) high

$600-700 LC

A 19thC rosewood wheel barometer, the case set with a convex mirror, mercury thermometer, hygrometer and spirit level, signed Panton & Co, Glasgow.

38.5in (98cm) high

$450-550 LC

A 19thC rosewood wheel barometer, the case set with a convex mirror, alcohol thermometer, hygrometer and spirit level, signed Norman Sherbourne.

37.5in (95cm) high

$450-550 LC

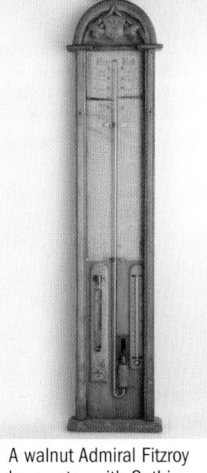

A walnut Admiral Fitzroy barometer, with Gothic cresting.

Admiral Fitzroy *(1805-1865) was a pioneering English meteorologist. He was the commander of HMS Beagle in the Darwin expedition of 1834-36.*

47in (120cm) high

$350-400 LC

A late 19thC aneroid barometer, with silvered dial and mercury thermometer, the banjo-shaped walnut case inlaid with stringing and floral sprays.

32.75in (83cm) high

$300-350 LC

A late 19thC cast-iron wall clock, the foliate case set with an enameled dial, the neck with a mercury thermometer beneath an aneroid barometer.

26in (66cm) high

$150-200 LC

387

Watches

WRISTWATCHES

A 1920s 9ct gold Rolex with cushion case, sub seconds and arabic numerals, movement and dial signed Rolex.

$1,000-1,200   **TEM**

A 1920s 9ct pink-gold Rolex with cushion case, sub seconds, arabic numerals and watersilk dial, movement and dial signed Rolex.

$1,000-1,200   **TEM**

A 1920s 9ct pink-gold ladies Rolex for retail by Mappin & Webb, with original box.

$800-1,000   **TEM**

A Rolex with large silver cushion case, sub seconds, arabic numerals and white enamel dial, movement and dial signed Rolex.

1927

$1,500-2,000   **TEM**

A 9ct gold Rolex with oblong case, engine-turned decoration, Arabic numerals and watersilk dial, movement and dial signed Rolex.

The oblong shaped case is very popular and typical of the 1920s and 30s.

1928

$2,500-3,000   **TEM**

A silver Rolex with oblong case, sub seconds and watersilk dial, signed Rolex on the movement and dial.

1928

$1,500-1,800   **TEM**

A 9ct gold Rolex with cushion case, sub seconds, applied gold numerals and white dial, movement and dial signed Rolex.

1938

$1,000-1,200   **TEM**

A Rolex Precision, with twisted lugs and 9ct gold center seconds, movement and dial signed Rolex.

1957

$1,000-1,200   **TEM**

A 1960s 18ct gold Rolex Precision, with associated 18ct gold mesh-bracelet, with center seconds, movement and dial signed Rolex.

$2,000-3,000   **TEM**

A 1960s 9ct gold Rolex Precision, with center seconds and baton numerals, movement and dial signed Rolex.

$1,000-1,200   **TEM**

A 9ct gold Rolex Precision, with applied numerals and batons, movement and dial signed Rolex.

1966

$1,000-1,200   **TEM**

▶ A 1920s 18ct gold Longines wristwatch, with enamel dial, sub seconds and Roman numerals.

Enamel dials are rarer, but are more easily damaged. The red numeral "12" is typical of the 1920s.

$1,200-1,800   **TEM**

A 1920s 9ct gold Longines wristwatch, with sub seconds and unusual concentric numerals.

$500-800   **TEM**

Watches

A 1920s large silver Longines wristwatch for retail by Mappin & Webb, with stylized and elongated concentric numerals.

$1,000-1,200   **TEM**

A 1920s silver Longines wristwatch with cushion-shaped case, white dial, sub seconds and Roman numerals.

$400-500   **TEM**

A 1930s 18ct gold Longines wristwatch, with oblong case, sub seconds and Arabic numerals.

This is a small size for a gentleman's watch which is typical of early watches.

$1,000-1,200   **TEM**

A 1940s 14ct gold Longines wristwatch marked New York on the inside back cover, signed Longines New York.

14ct gold Longines were made for the US market.

$700-1,000   **TEM**

A 1920s large silver Omega wristwatch, with cushion case, enamel dial, sub seconds and Arabic numerals.

$400-600   **TEM**

A 1920s silver Omega wristwatch, with oblong case, sub seconds and Arabic numerals.

$1,000-1,300   **TEM**

A 1930s steel Omega wristwatch, with black dial, luminous hands and numerals and center seconds.

Luminous hands and numerals are found on watches from the 1930s and 40s.

$300-400   **TEM**

An unusual waterproof wristwatch for retail by JW Benson, Jewellers, screw bezel movement hinges out with solid back, rainproof winder with seals and enamel dial.

$450-550   **TEM**

A silver wristwatch for retail by Harrods, with oblong case, two-tone dial brushed in two directions and fancy Arabic numerals.

$500-600   **TEM**

A Harwood automatic wristwatch with watersilk dial.

This was the first successful automatic wristwatch
c1928-32

$800-1,000   **TEM**

A Cartier cocktail-watch, with square dial enclosed by a border of circular-cut diamonds flanked by further lines of diamonds, with a cut-diamond winder and a flexible pearl bracelet with gold mounts.

Face 1.25in (3cm) long

$25,000-28,000   **Duk**

A gold Jaeger Le Coultre gentlemans wristwatch, the enamel dial with numerical batons inscribed "Asprey Automatic" on link bracelet.

8.5in (21.5cm) long

$650-850   **Duk**

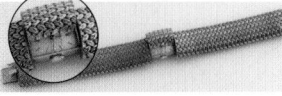

A French Tiffany woven-gold bracelet with concealed watch and hinged section.
c1960   7.5in (19cm) long

$3,500-4,000   **NBloom**

An Art Deco cocktail-watch, set with circular and baguette-cut diamonds, with a fine-link safety chain.

6in (15cm) long

$2,000-3,000   **Duk**

An Art Deco sapphire and diamond cocktail-watch, with six rows of calibre-set rectangular-cut sapphires on a ground of circular-cut diamonds, with a cabochon sapphire winder and a textile strap.

2in (5.2cm) long (excluding strap)

$4,500-5,500   **Duk**

JEWELRY

JEWELRY AND GEMSTONES HAVE ALWAYS BEEN A TRADITIONAL COLLECTIBLE DUE TO THEIR INTRINSIC VALUE AND, UNLIKE OTHER WORKS OF ART, many pieces can be worn as well as admired. Jewelry was often given as a gift, or was worn to display wealth or grief, and so it was well looked after and passed through the family. As a result, much survives today.

The market for jewelry has seen a shift away from 19th century pieces in the past year. Prices for 19thC jewelry set in silver or gold are now similar to what they were eight to ten years ago and, as such, represent good value for money.

Diamonds, and jewelry set with them, remain one of the securer, more stable sectors of the market. Better color diamonds are relatively scarce and have generally been performing well at auction. Buyers of colored stones are more selective, usually wanting certificates to prove origin and lack of artificial treatments.

In the past year, there has been more demand for early 20th century jewelry set in platinum. Signed jewelry is also performing well, although there are a lot of fakes in circulation and collectors should ensure they are buying from a reputable source.

The recent popularity of Art Deco jewelry continues. One new collecting trend is for pieces from the 1950s and 60s. Buyers are taking an interest in pieces which are indicative of the era, rather than classic or timeless styles which happen to have been made then.

There is always a market for subtle pieces which are wearable and this is unlikely to change. The fact that pins are back in fashion is also expected to have an effect on the market in the coming year.

RINGS

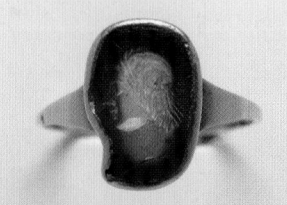

An 18thC gold ring set with an ancient cornelian intaglio of Alexander.

$1,200-1,800 JHB

▶ An American pink gold ring, the oval-form bordered by seed pearls enclosing interwoven locks of hair.

Note attached "26 seed pearls with interlocking locks of hair. Benjamin Lincoln and his wife Mary Cushing Lincoln, to their daughter-in-law to be Hannah Mayhew, 10 days prior to her marriage to Theodore Lincoln, May 6, 1794."

$200-300 SI

A Georgian gold garnet and split-pearl ring.

$600-800 JHB

A Georgian single stone amethyst ring.

$300-400 JHB

A Georgian ring set with an amethyst and two garnets.

$800-1,100 JHB

A Georgian ring, set with hair under rock crystal.

$300-400 JHB

A Georgian gold ring.

$300-400 OACC

An early 19thC rose cut diamond and ruby cluster ring.

$1,000-1,500 JHB

An early 19thC gold and enamel ring, set with diamonds and cabochon rubies.

$2,000-2,500 JHB

A gold-set turquoise and split-pearl cluster ring.
c1840

$200-300 JHB

A 19thC 18ct gold three-stone diamond (est 2.8ct) ring.

$6,000-7,000 JHB

390

Rings

A 19thC old brilliant-cut solitaire diamond (est 2.96ct) ring.

$12,000-17,000   JHB

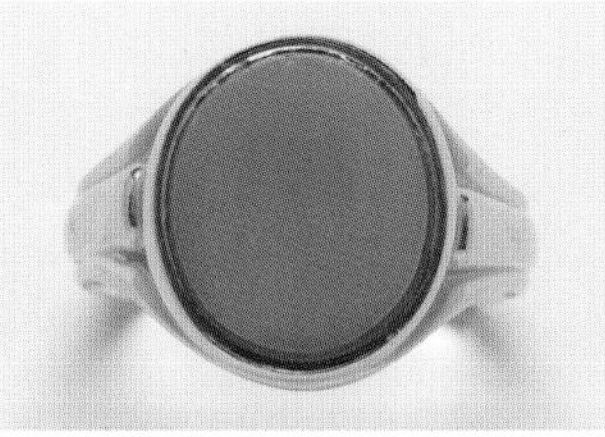

A 19thC 18ct gold signet ring set with sardonyx.

$400-450   JHB

A 19thC 18ct gold five stone diamond ring with diamond points, diamond 4.71cts

$10,000-15,000   JHB

A 19thC 18ct gold 12 stone, two row diamond ring.

$1,000-1,200   JHB

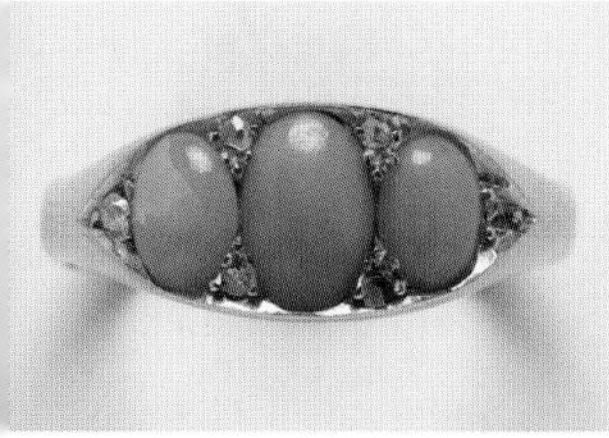

A 19thC gold and coral ring with diamond sparks.

$300-400   JHB

A Victorian marquise ring, set with rose cut diamonds and rubies.

$2,000-2,500   JHB

A Victorian ruby (2.07cts) and diamond oval cluster ring.

$6,000-7,000   JHB

A Victorian 18ct gold set bloodstone signet ring, Birmingham hallmarks.
1887

$500-600   JHB

An 18ct gold oval cluster diamond-set ring.
c1870

$1,000-1,200   JHB

A gold and turquoise enamel ring, set with split pearls.
c1880

$300-400   JHB

An 18ct gold double-cluster emerald and diamond-set ring.

c1880

$4,500-5,500   JHB

A sapphire and diamond set cluster ring.
c1880   sapphire 3.7cts

$7,000-8,000   JHB

An 18ct gold three-stone "gypsy" ring set with opal and spilt pearls, London hallmarks.
1886

$200-300   JHB

A late 19thC diamond-set "marquise" ring.

$2,200-2,700   JHB

An 18ct gold and enamel "MIZPAH" ring, Birmingham hallmark.
Mizpah is the Hebrew word for watchtower and implies "God watch over you". It is typically found on 19thC sentimental jewelry.
1888

$350-450 JHB

A 19thC three-stone diamond ring, set with three principal mine-cut diamonds graduating from the center, interspersed with four diamond chips, on a chased yellow gold shank.
Setting 0.75in (2cm) wide

$8,000-10,000 Duk

A late 19thC 18ct gold-set demantoid garnet and diamond five-stone ring.

$1,000-1,200 JHB

A late 19th sapphire and diamond cluster ring.

$2,000-3,000 JHB

An 18ct gold ring, set with an old-cut diamond and two Ceylon sapphires, Birmingham hallmarks.
1890

$400-600 JHB

An 18ct gold "keeper" ring, Chester hallmarks.
1892

$400-500 JHB

A 15ct gold ruby and split-pearl ring.
c1900

$350-450 JHB

An emerald (est 1.21ct) and diamond (est 1.71ct) three-stone ring.
1900

$7,000-8,000 JHB

A three-stone sapphire and diamond ring with carved settings.
c1900

$700-1,000 JHB

A Ceylon sapphire and diamond cluster ring.
c1900

$1,800-2,200 JHB

A three-stone diamond-set ring, with diamond sparks.
c1900

$4,000-6,000 JHB

An old cut diamond cluster ring with white gold bezels.
c1900

$2,000-3,000 JHB

An old brilliant-cut diamond and emerald three-stone ring.
c1900

$4,000-5,000 JHB

A 15ct gold mourning ring set with enamel and split pearls, Chester hallmarks.
1908

$300-400 JHB

An 18ct gold-set garnet and diamond ring, London hallmarks.
1910

$1,200-1,300 JHB

An Edwardian gold, enamel and amethyst ring.

$1,000-1,200 JHB

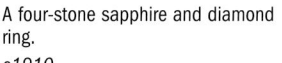

A four-stone sapphire and diamond ring.
c1910

$400-500 JHB

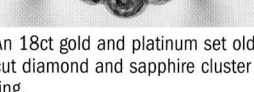

An 18ct gold and platinum set old cut diamond and sapphire cluster ring.

$1,800-2,200 JHB

Rings

A jade and diamond dress ring, with a central oval panel of jade surrounded by brilliant-cut diamonds, the scrolling shoulders set with diamonds, on a white gold shank.

Setting 0.5in (1.5cm)

$800-1,000   **Duk**

A "fire-opal" and diamond cluster ring, the central cushion-shaped "fire opal" surrounded by a border of mine-cut diamonds, on a yellow gold shank.

Setting 0.75in (2cm)

$2,000-3,000   **Duk**

A sapphire and diamond ring, claw-set with a central oval-cut sapphire, flanked by three brilliant-cut diamonds on an 18ct white gold shank.

0.5in (1.5cm)

$500-1,000   **Duk**

A three-stone diamond ring, on an 18ct yellow gold and platinum shank.

Setting 0.5in (1.5cm)

$3,000-3,500   **Duk**

A ruby and dimaond cluster ring, claw-set with a central oval-cut ruby surrounded by a petal-shaped border of brilliant-cut diamonds, on an 18ct white gold shank.

Setting 0.75in (2cm)

$2,500-3,500   **Duk**

A solitaire diamond ring, claw-set with a central cushion-shaped diamond, each shoulder set with three small diamonds, on a white-metal shank.

Stone 0.25in (1cm)

$7,000-8,000   **Duk**

A ruby and diamond cluster ring, with a central oval-cut ruby surrounded by ten brilliant-cut diamonds, on a yellow gold shank.

Setting 0.75in (2cm)

$1,800-2,200   **Duk**

An emerald-cut diamond ring, on a white gold shank.

Sold with a report from the Gem Testing Laboratory of Great Britain (Lon 0093361), which states that the diamond weights 0.97 cts and is color graded as "K tinted white" and clarity VS1.

0.05in (0.5cm) (stone)

$2,000-3,000   **Duk**

PINS

A Georgian silver, gold and rose diamond "Trophy" pin.

1.5in (4cm) wide

$1,000-1,500   **JHB**

A Georgian gold locket pin, set with a double portrait of two ladies.

$800-1,000   **JHB**

A Georgian garnet pin.

1in (2.5cm) wide

$300-400   **OACC**

A Georgian seed-pearl pin.

1in (2.5cm) wide

$200-250   **OACC**

An early 19thC French pink gold friendship pendant/pin, the navette shape enclosing gold openwork in the form of crossed flags, anchor, laurel leaves and the inscription "L'Amitie" on ivory.

$80-100   **SI**

An early 19thC gold and foiled topaz pin.

2in (5cm) long

$800-1,200   **JHB**

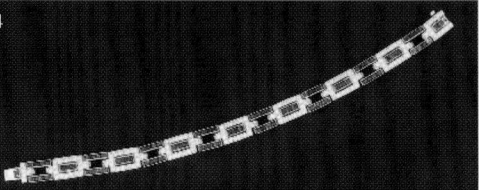

Pins

A Mortimer and Hunt cross pin and drop earrings, set with amethysts and diamonds.

c1840 2.5in (6.5cm) long

$10,000-12,000 **NBlm**

A gold and silver pin, with central amethyst and French paste border.

c1840 1in (2.5cm) wide

$200-250 **JHB**

A rose diamond-set pin, with locket back.

c1840 2in (5cm) wide

$8,000-10,000 **JHB**

A gold cannetille work pin, set with chalcedony and turquoise.

c1840 1.25in (3cm) long

$300-500 **JHB**

A 19thC diamond button pin, the principal cushion-shaped diamond surrounded by numerous mine-cut and cushion-shaped diamonds in a closed setting.

0.75in (2cm) wide

$5,000-8,000 **Duk**

A rose-cut bohemian garnet butterfly pin, with split-pearl eyes.

c1850 1.5in (4cm) wide

$300-500 **JHB**

A 15ct gold and cabochon garnet "Vine" pin.

c1850 2.25in (5.5cm) long

$1,000-1,300 **JHB**

A 19thC old cut diamond and cabochon sapphire pin.

2.25in (5.5cm)

$8,000-10,000 **JHB**

A 19thC Indian gold pertabghar-work pin.

$200-300 **JHB**

A gold-mounted hairwork pin and earrings.

c1857 Pin 1.5in (4cm) diam

$800-1,000 **JHB**

An Audoard Philibert-Honore chased and enameled pin, set with rubies and diamonds.

c1860 2in (5cm) long

$10,000-14,000 **NBlm**

A gold almandine garnet and seed-pearl pin.

c1860 2in (5cm) wide

$800-1,000 **JHB**

A gold-set banded onyx and diamond pin, with concealed locket on hinged pendant loop.

c1860 2.25in (5.5cm) long

$1,000-1,500 **JHB**

A gold and citrine pin.

c1860 2in (5cm) wide

$300-500 **JHB**

A silver double-horseshoe pin.

c1870 1.5in (4cm)

$80-120 **JHB**

Pins

A gold and enamel pin, set with old-cut diamonds and black enamels-on-pearl and diamond-set pendant loop.

c1860

$10,000-15,000 JHB

A diamond-set star pin (center stone 0.97ct).

c1870 1.5in (4cm) diam

$4,000-7,000 JHB

 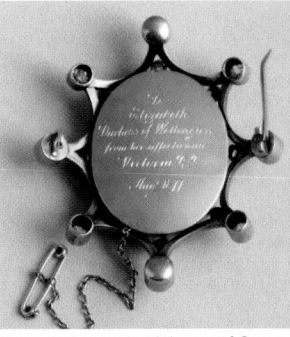

A gold diamond and pearl pin, inset with an oval portrait miniature of Queen Victoria, on a gold ground within an undulating border set with eight diamonds and eight pearls, the reverse inscribed "To Elizabeth, Duchess of Wellington from her affectionate Victoria RI, Aug. 1877", with a fine link safety chain.

2in (5.5cm) long

$5,000-8,000 Duk

A Victorian gold and garnet pin.

c1880

$200-250 PC

A flowerspray pin, set with diamonds.

c1880 2.5in (6cm) long

$1,000-1,500 JHB

A 15ct gold pin, set with a sapphire.

c1885 1.75in (4.5cm) long

$200-300 JHB

A pin set with opal and rose-cut diamonds.

c1885 1.75in (4.5cm) long

$700-1,000 HB

A winged Medussa-head pin, with a hairpin attachment.

c1890 4.25in (11cm) wide

$5,000-8,000 NBlm

A Victorian cut steel work and garnet pin.

Cut steel jewelry was made by riveting faceted steel studs onto plates to imitate gems and was used extensively in England in the 18thC and 19thC. The best-known maker was Matthew Boulton, who produced jewelry and accessories. The main areas of manufacture were London, Birmingham and Woodstock in Oxfordshire.

$350-450 PC

A diamond plaque pin, of rectangular form, mille grain set throughout with old-cut diamonds.

$700-1,000 LFA

A late 19thC French ruby, pearl and diamond-set pin.

1.25in (3cm) diam

$700-1,000 JHB

An important 19thC emerald and diamond pin/pendant, set with a central rectangular cushion-shaped emerald enclosed by an inner border of sixteen old-cut diamonds, and an outer border composed of eight principal diamonds divided by eight lines of two smaller diamonds.

1.25in (3.5cm) wide

$20,000-30,000 Duk

Pins

A late 19thC 15ct gold pin, set with small diamonds.

1.5in (4cm) long

$200-300　　　　　　JHB

A late 19thC 9ct gold pin, set with small diamonds.

1.75in (4.5cm) long

$200-250　　　　　　JHB

A turquoise and pearl-set bug pin.

c1890　　　　1.5in (4cm) long

$150-250　　　　　　JHB

A late 19thC silver bug pin, set with tiger's-eye and split pearl.

2in (5cm) long

$100-200　　　　　　JHB

A late 19thC 9ct gold citrine and split-pearl pin.

1.25in (3cm) wide

$400-500　　　　　　JHB

A belle époque diamond and pearl-set pin.

1.75in (4.5cm) wide

$3,500-4,500　　　　JHB

A Belle époque diamond and pearl-set pin.

1.75in (4.5cm)

$1,000-1,500　　　　JHB

A gold, amethyst and seed pearl pin, hallmarked.

1900　　　1.75in (4.3cm) long

$200-300　　　　　　PC

A cabochon sapphire and rose-cut diamond set pin.

c1900　　　1.5in (4cm) wide

$700-1,000　　　　　JHB

A 15ct gold new moon pin, set with split pearls.

c1900　　　1.25in (3cm) diam

$200-300　　　　　　JHB

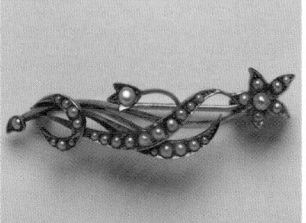

A 15ct gold and seed pearl spray pin.

c1900　　　1.5in (4cm) long

$150-250　　　　　　JHB

A gold prospector's pin.

c1900　　　2.25in (5.5cm) long

$350-450　　　　　　JHB

A gold chrysoprase and enamel Egyptian Revival pin.

c1900　　　1.25in (3cm) wide

$1,200-1,800　　　　JHB

A signed watercolor-on-ivory, set in silver pin.

c1900　　　2in (5cm) wide

$150-200　　　　　　OACC

An Edwardian amethyst and split-pearl pin, set in matte gold.

$300-400　　　　　　LFA

A 15ct gold aquamarine and seed-pearl bar pin.

c1905　　　2in (5cm) long

$200-300　　　　　　JHB

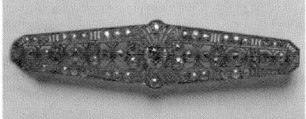

An Edwardian pin, set with old brilliant-cut diamonds (est 3.40ct).

2.75in (7cm) wide

$4,000-5,000　　　　JHB

An Edwardian 18ct gold, pearl and ruby-set spray pin.

1.75in (4.5cm) long

$600-1,000　　　　　JHB

A Tiffany and Co. pin, with a central oval-cut green peridot surrounded by a band of topaz and an outer border of green enamel, signed on a plaque Tiffany & Co.

2in (5cm) wide

$5,000-7,000　　　　Duk

397

Pins

An early 20thC sapphire and half-pearl circle pin.

0.75in (2cm) diam

$400-600   **JHB**

A white gold bar pin, set with aquamarine and diamonds.

c1910   2in (5cm) long

$500-700   **JHB**

A 1920s silver and French paste bow pin.

2.25in (5cm)

$150-250   **JHB**

A French platinum diamond and pearl-set pin.

c1915   1in (2.5cm) diam

$2,000-3,000   **JHB**

A low grade silver (gold-washed) and enamel Egyptian pin.

c1925   2in (5cm) long

$100-150   **JHB**

A 1940s French mixed-cut diamond-set double clip pin

3in (7.4cm) long

$20,000-30,000   **NBlm**

A 1940s 16.6ct diamond pin.

$20,000-30,000   **JHB**

A 20thC "leaf hand" pin, with red enamel nails, designed by Salvador Dali and made by Alemany & Ertman.

$4,000-6,000   **NBlm**

A Cartier carved ivory rose, with a coral leaf and a square diamond at center.

1956   2in (5.5cm) long

$15,000-20,000   **NBlm**

A Paillard large iris clip, set with sapphires and diamonds, Paris.

c1970   4in (10cm) long

$15,000-18,000   **NBlm**

A Botsward silver-mounted agate pin, of linked circlet form.

1970

$30-60   **LFA**

NECKLACES

An 18thC Iberian gold necklace, set with topaz and pearls.

16.5in (42cm) long

$3,500-4,500   **JHB**

An early 19thC gold necklace, set with topaz and pearls.

15in (38cm) long

$5,000-7,500   **JHB**

A French necklet set with emeralds and split pearls.

c1845   15.75in (40cm)

$1,000-1,500   **JHB**

A 19thC gold bead necklace.

c1870   76.25in (193.5cm) long

$4,000-6,000   **NBlm**

Necklaces

A gold necklace, set with red spinel diamonds and split pearls.

c1870   15.75in (40cm) long

$1,800-2,200   **JHB**

A Bohemian garnet necklace.

c1870   15in (38cm) long

$800-1,200   **JHB**

A 14ct gold fancy-link collar.

c1870   19in (48cm) long

$1,000-1,500   **JHB**

A 19thC gold-leaf necklace.

$300-400   **PC**

A Indian necklace from Bikaner, with kundun-set native-cut diamonds and rubies on one side, and green, red and white enamel on the other, with pearl tassles.

Kundan jewelry was made in India using 24ct gold. The technique involved inserting gold foil between a stone and its mount. It was popular during the Mughal period (1526-1857).

c1890   6in (15cm) wide

$6,000-7,000   **NBlm**

A French 1940s diamond-set necklace, of graduated half bows.

$6,000-7,000   **NBlm**

A 1960s French textured gold necklace, with graduated fringe.

16.25in (41cm) long

$3,000-3,500   **NBlm**

An amethyst, cultured pearl and gold bead-twist necklace, by Van Cleef & Arpels, separates to form two bracelets.

c1970   15.75in (40cm) long

$10,000-13,000   **NBlm**

A flat "Gaspipe" crossover necklace, with diamond detail and a cabochon emerald and ruby at either end.

c1970   17.5in (44cm) long

$4,000-5,000   **NBlm**

An 18ct yellow gold necklace, with Byzantine links.

52.75in (48cm) long

$700-1,000   **Duk**

A faceted amethyst bead necklace, with gold wire links.

$100-150   **LFA**

A 1960s all platinum set marquise, brilliant and baguette cut diamond set necklace, est. 42.62cts

$100,000-120,000   **JHB**

A diamond-set suite, comprising bangle, pin and earrings, from the Abbatucci cargo.

The French steamship "General Abbatuuci" was sunk off the northern coast of Corsica in May 1869. Her cargo included gifts for Pope Pius IX. The wreck was discovered in May 1996 and much of the recovered cargo was later sold at Christies.

Locket 1.75in (4.5cm) wide

$3,000-4,000   **JHB**

A late Georgian gold cannetille work foiled quartz parure, comprising necklace, pin, cross pendant and pair of bracelets.

Cannetille goldwork *is produced from gold wire, which is worked into elaborate scrolls, spirals, flowers, coils and beads on a filigree core. It was used extensively in England and France during the early 19thC, often used in combination with aquamarine, amethyst and topaz.*

$15,000-18,000   **JHB**

BRACELETS AND BANGLES

A late Georgian seed-pearl bracelet, on garnet and split-pearl-set clasp.

8.25in (21cm) long

$1,000-1,200   **JHB**

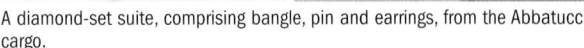

A gold garnet and split-pearl bracelet, in original case.
c1855   6.75in (17cm) long

$1,800-2,300   **JHB**

A gold and baroque-pearl bracelet.

c1860   7.25in (18.5cm) long

$200-300   **JHB**

An Etruscan Revival broad gold bangle, in original case.
c1860

$1,000-1,500   **JHB**

A bloomed gold bangle, set with three cabochon garnets and rose-cut diamonds.
Bloomed gold has a matt finish achieved by applying a solution of saltpeter, acid and water.
c1860

$1,000-1,500   **JHB**

An "anchor" link gold bracelet, with garnet-set padlock.

c1860   8.25in (21cm) long

$1,000-1,500   **JHB**

An 18t gold bangle, set with diamonds, split pearls and enamels with concealed locket front.
c1865

$5,000-7,000   **JHB**

A 19thC chased gold bracelet, with a buckle motif at center.
c1870   7.75in (20cm) long

$1,500-2,200   **NBlm**

▶ A twin bangle, with removable sapphire, ruby and diamond-set clusters with ring fittings.

c1870   2.5in (6cm) diam

$6,500-7,500   **JHB**

A pair of platinum and 14ct gold arrow-hinged bangles.
c1890

$3,000-4,000   **NBlm**

Bracelets and Bangles

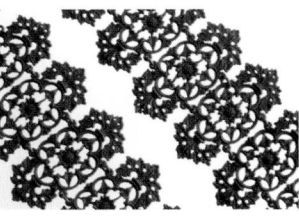

A pair of late 19thC Berlin ironwork bracelets, some rust and one link missing on one bracelet.

7.5in (19cm) long

$100-150   **PC**

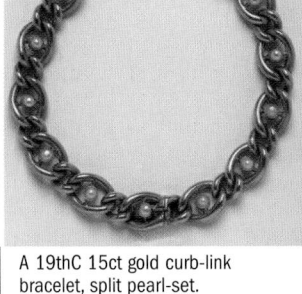

A 19thC 15ct gold curb-link bracelet, split pearl-set.

7in (18cm) long

$700-1,000   **JHB**

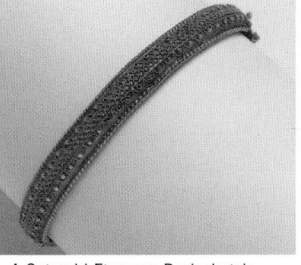

A 9ct gold Etruscan Revival-style bangle, Birmingham 1890.

$300-500   **JHB**

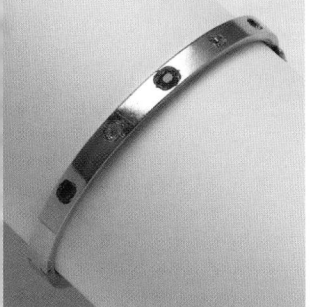

A 15ct gold ruby and diamond-set five-stone bangle.

c1895

$800-1,000   **JHB**

A 9ct pink gold curb bracelet, with original padlock.

c1896   8in (20cm) long

$300-500   **JHB**

A 15ct gold split-pearl and turquoise-set bracelet.

c1900   7.75in (19.5cm) long

$800-1,200   **JHB**

An early 20thC gold bracelet.

$350-450   **PC**

An early 20thC 14ct gold and silver rose-cut diamond-set bangle.

$2,000-2,700   **JHB**

An early 20thC 9ct gold fancy-link gate bracelet.

7in (18cm) long

$700-1,000   **JHB**

An early 20thC platinum and water-opal bracelet.

$5,000-6,000   **JHB**

A French mabe pearl and enamel bracelet, with chased rose motifs.

***Mabe pearls** are composite pearls with a mother-of-pearl back.*

c1930   7.5in (19cm) long

$5,000-6,000   **NBlm**

A 1940s three-color gold circular panel bracelet, each panel with a floral motif at center, set with rubies and diamonds.

7.5in (19cm) long

$3,000-4,000   **NBlm**

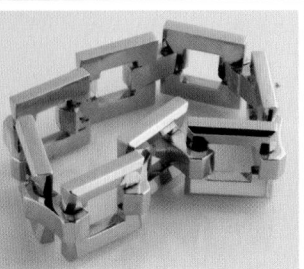

A 1940s large open-square 18ct gold bracelet.

8in (20.5cm) long

$1,800-2,200   **NBlm**

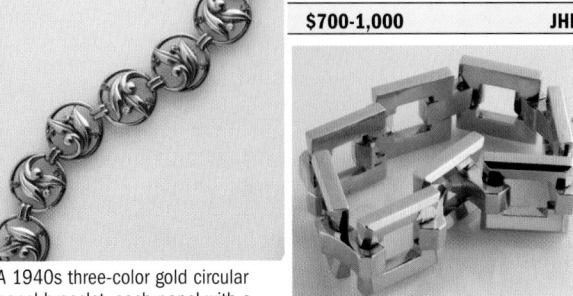

A 1940s French hinged bangle, with diamond-set flowers at terminals, the flowers detach to form a pair of clips.

2.25in (6cm) wide

$12,000-13,500   **NBlm**

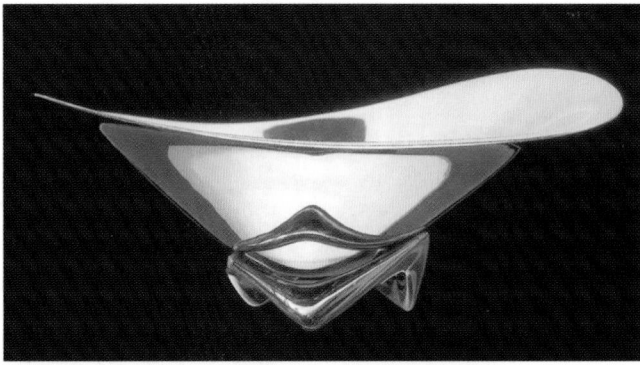
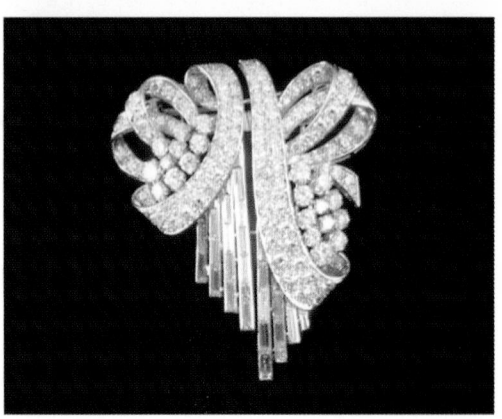
402

A 1950s "belt buckle" hinged bangle, set with diamonds and calibré rubies,

4.5cm wide

$15,000-22,000   **NBlm**

A 16-row cultured pearl twist bracelet, with a ruby-set bow clasp.

c1950   8.25in (21cm) long

$1,500-2,200   **NBlm**

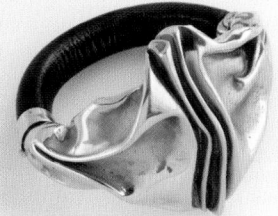

A diamond-shaped folded gold bracelet, by Balbinot, possibly Swiss.

c1965   3in (8cm) diam

$4,500-6,000   **NBlm**

A 1970s wide gold cuff bracelet, with a chevron pattern throughout.

$1,500-2,200   **NBlm**

An unusual seven-section bracelet, with carved white agate and emerald-set dividers.

c1970   2.75in (7cm) diam

$3,000-3,500   **NBlm**

A 1970s diamond-set open-work rectangular panel bracelet.

7.25in (18.5cm) long

$4,000-6,000   **NBlm**

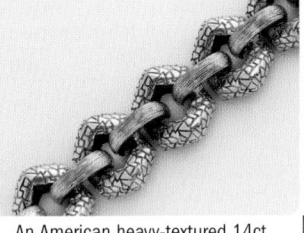

An American heavy-textured 14ct gold link bracelet, by "Arc de Triomphe".

7.5in (19.5cm) long

$3,500-4,500   **NBlm**

An 18ct yellow gold charm bracelet, with eleven various attahced charms including a boot, "Cock & Bull story" and a steering wheel.

9in (23cm) long

$450-600   **Duk**

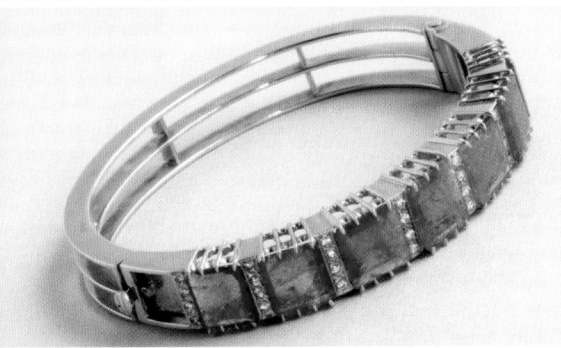

An emerald and diamond bangle, set in 18ct yellow gold with seven graduated rectangular-cut emeralds, divided by eight lines each containing four circular-cut diamonds.

2.25in (6cm) diam

$3,000-4,500   **Duk**

EARRINGS

An early 19thC gold and blue chalcedony pendant earrings.

3.5in (9cm) long

$1,200-1,600   **JHB**

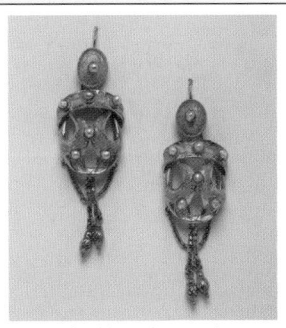

A pair of gold pendant earrings, set with split-pearls.

c1840   2.25in (5.5cm) long

$1,500-2,200   **JHB**

A 1940s pair of baguette and brilliant-cut diamond earclips, with emerald drops in white gold mounts.

2.25in (5.5cm) long

$10,000-13,000   **JHB**

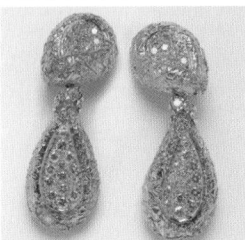

A pair of earrings, signed Kutchinsky, diamond-set, removable drops, in orignal case.

c1970   2.25in (5.5cm) long

$10,000-13,000   **JHB**

A pair of Continental silver and paste pendant earrings.

$50-80   **LFA**

A pair of diamond floral cluster earrings, set in 18ct yellow gold with numerous brilliant-cut diamonds and central oval-cut diamonds.

1in (3cm) wide

$1,500-2,200   **Duk**

SCOTS AGATE

An early 19thC gold-set moss agate pin.

2.5in (6cm) long

$800-1,300 **JHB**

A silver set-banded agate and quartz pennanular pin.

1860 2.75in (7cm) diam

$700-1,000 **JHB**

A silver and Aberdeen granite garter pin.

c1860 1.75in (4.5cm) diam

$400-500 **JHB**

A silver and Scots agate pin.

1865 2in (5cm) wide

$700-1,000 **JHB**

A silver-mounted Scots agate bracelet.

c1865 8in (20cm) long

$700-1,000 **JHB**

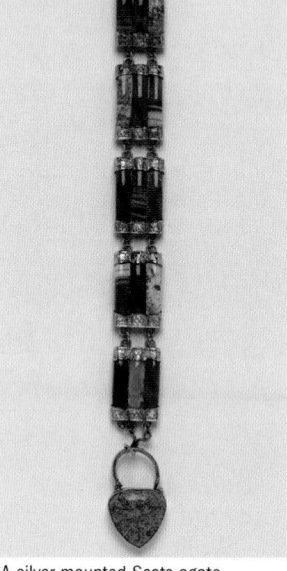

A silver-mounted Scots agate bracelet, with "Padlock" clasp.

c1865 8in (20cm) long

$800-1,200 **JHB**

A gold-mounted Luckenbooth pin, set with citrine, granite and split pearls, registration marks.

1866 1.75in (4.5cm) wide

$700-1,000 **JHB**

A silver and Scots agate kilt pin, with registration marks.

1880 2.5in (6.5cm) long

$200-300 **JHB**

A silver quartz-set kiltpin, hallmarked Edinburgh.

1891 3.25in (8cm) long

$400-500 **JHB**

A 9ct gold agate-set spinning fob.

c1900 1.5in (4cm) wide

$150-200 **JHB**

Cameos

CAMEOS

A 17thC hardstone three-layer agate cameo pendant, depicting Bacchus, in a 19thC mount.

2in (5.5cm) long

$3,000-4,000   **NBlm**

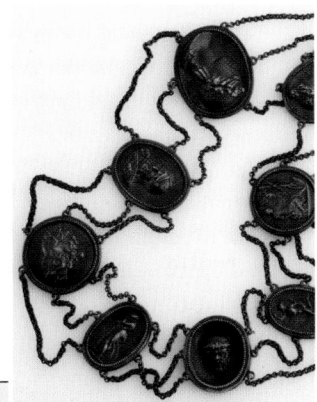

▶ A Berlin ironwork necklace, with eight oval cameo plaques, each depicting a classical figure.

Berlin Ironwork was produced in Berlin and Silesia from the early to the mid-19thC. It was first made to replace the jewelry wealthy Prussian women had donated to help fight the Napoleonic wars.

c1820   16.5in (42cm) long

$4,500-5,500   **NBlm**

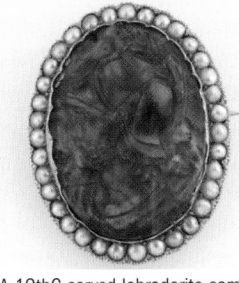

A 19thC carved labradorite cameo, depicting Mars in a half-pearl surround.

Labradorite is a mineral common in Newfoundland and Labrador, Canada. It is typically blue and green, but can also be red, gold and yellow.

1.25in (3.5cm) long

$1,500-2,200   **NBloom**

A 19thC rectangular-banded agate cameo plaque, by Jean Louis-Francois, depicting the birth of Venus, after Botticelli.

Jean Louis Francois worked between 1841-1896.

2.5in 6.5cm long

$7,000-8,000   **NBlm**

A 19thC shell cameo pin, of a classical lady with grapes in her hair, mounted in an 18ct frame.

c1870   2.25in (6cm) long

$800-1,200   **NBlm**

A carved coral cameo of Flora.

c1870   2in (5cm long)

$2,000-3,000   **NBlm**

A hardstone cameo pin/pendant, signed "C Fuchs", in gold mount.

c1870   2in (5cm) long

$2,000-3,000   **JHB**

A gold-set shell cameo pin/pendant.

c1870   3in (7.5cm) long

$1,000-1,200   **JHB**

A cameo pin, depicting St. George and the Dragon.

2.5in (6cm) long

$250-350   **OACC**

MOURNING

▶ An American gold mourning ring, the navette-shape enclosing strands of woven hair, bordered by black enamel bearing the inscription "OH Williams OBIT 15 July 1794 age 45", the reverse engraved "M Williams OB Nov 19th 1796 Age 35".

c1795

$100-150   **SI**

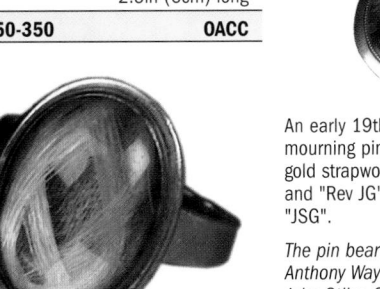

▶ An American gold mourning ring, of simple form, enclosing woven strands of hair, with a note accompanying the ring inscribed "The ring with the hair of Elizabeth Judson Canfield (1732-1801) wife of Samuel Canfield Col In the Rev War, ancestor of Mrs. Northrup."

Provenance: *The Society of the Cincinnati*

$300-400   **SI**

An early 19thC American gold mourning pin, with locks of hair and gold strapwork, inscribed "Gen AW" and "Rev JG", the reverse inscribed "JSG".

The pin bears the hair of General Anthony Wayne and the Reverend John Stiles Gano.

$100-150   **SI**

An early 19thC locket mourning ring, set with French "jet" and inscribed "Mrs Calder died 19th Nov 1827".

Mourning jewelry was at its most popular during the 18thC and 19thC. 19thC examples are typically black enamel, engraved with the deceased's name and containing a lock of their hair.

$800-1,200   **JHB**

COSTUME JEWELRY Joseff of Hollywood

THE TERM COSTUME JEWELRY GENERALLY REFERS TO PIECES OF JEWELRY MADE FROM NON-PRECIOUS MATERIALS AND DESIGNED TO EMBELLISH PARTICULAR (AND CURRENTLY FASHIONABLE) OUTFITS. The definition also applies to the numerous pieces of non-precious jewelry produced by civilizations both ancient and modern prior to the 20th century. There is, for example, a thriving trade in 18th- and 19th-century pieces, made from materials as diverse as gold plate, paste (crystal or glass cut to resemble gemstones), seed-pearls, jet (fossilized coal), bone, copper, cut-steel, and pinchbeck (an alloy of zinc and copper with the appearance of gold).

Over the last five years or so the intrinsic worth of 20th-century costume jewelry (which resides in its design and provenance, rather than the materials used) has begun to be fully appreciated by collectors – the upshot of the latter being that prices for many pieces are still very reasonable, and should only rise in the forseeable future.

Costume jewelry embraces all the major stylistic movements of the 20th century. However, many collectors focus on individual designers and manufacturers. Miriam Haskell's work has increased steadily in value over the past few years, and both Joseff of Hollywood and Stanley Hagler are tipped to follow her lead. There continues to be a buoyant market for pieces designed by or for leading couturiers such as Coco Chanel, Elsa Schiaparelli and Christian Dior, and up-market pieces by designers and makers such as Trifari, Eisenberg, Hobé, Coro(craft), Boucher & Cie, Weiss, Mazer Bros., Napier, Hattie Carnegie and, since the 1980s, Butler & Wilson. Pieces by all these designers are likely to appreciate in value in future.

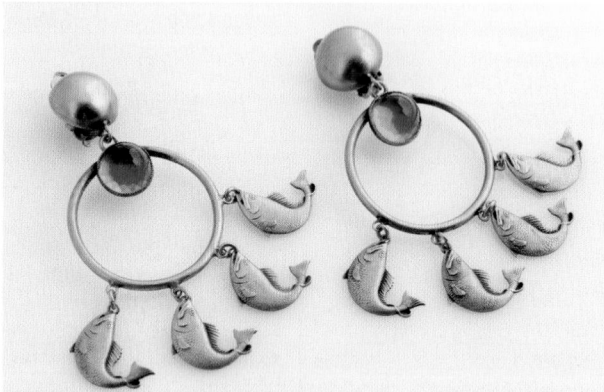

Earrings by Joseff of Hollywood, decorated with fish and topaz cabouchons.

1940s	3.5in (9cm) long
$140-170	**Cris**

A large hand-cut aquamarine crystal pin, by Joseff of Hollywood.

1940s	6in (15cm) long
$800-850	**Cris**

A kitty cat pin, by Joseff of Hollywood, with emerald crystal and rhinestone eyes.

1940s	3in (7.5cm) wide
$200-250	**Cris**

A wolf pin, by Joseff of Hollywood, decorated with colored cabouchons.

	2.5in (6cm) long
$140-170	**Cris**

A camel chatelaine pin, by Joseff of Hollywood, set with multicolored cabouchons on a filigree backing.

1940s	1.25in (3cm) long
$300-350	**Cris**

A pin, by Joseff of Hollywood, decorated with basket set crystals.

1940s	4in (10cm) wide
$140-200	**Cris**

Joseff of Hollywood

JOSEFF OF HOLLYWOOD

Joseff of Hollywood leased costume jewelry to the major film studios and used the resulting publicity to promote his retail line. As a result its founder Eugene Joseff's (1905-1948) distinctive designs are as sought after today by collectors as they were by the cinema-goers who saw them on the silver screen in the 1930s, 40s and 50s. Prices have risen an average 10–12% per annum over the last 10 years and this is likely to continue. The company continued to produce jewelry well into the 1960s.

✦ Joseff of Hollywood's jewelry appeared in films including *A Star is Born* (1936); *The Wizard of Oz* and *Gone With The Wind* (both 1939); *Casablanca* (1942); *Anchors Aweigh* (1945); *Easter Parade* (1949); *Singing in the Rain* (1952); *To Catch a Thief* (1955); *Ben Hur* (1959); *Breakfast at Tiffany's* (1961); *Cleopatra* (1963); and *My Fair Lady* (1964).

✦ It was worn by stars such as Greta Garbo, Vivian Leigh, Bette Davis, Marlene Dietrich and Grace Kelly, as well as Douglas Fairbanks Jnr, Clark Gable, Errol Flynn and Tony Curtis.

✦ There is a diverse range of styles: numerous "historical" styles inspired by costume dramas; major 20th-century styles such as Art Nouveau, Art Deco and 1940s "Retro" and 'Romantic-Historical', as well as "Oriental" and "Middle-Eastern" styles, astrological motifs and animal, fish, bird and insect imagery.

✦ Russian-gold-plated pieces are either plain, or augmented with faux pearls and/or clear or colored crystal highlights – the latter hand-cut, rather than pressed, on the best pieces. You will also find a number of Bakelite pieces – either black, ivory-colored or, very occasionally, red.

✦ All pieces are stamped either Joseff or Joseff of Hollywood – the exception being some one-off examples made for celebrity clients, which are rarely seen on the market.

✦ The subtle, semi-matte finish of the Russian-gold-plating gradually acquires a darker, more mellow patina over time. Avoid overly bright Russian-gold-plating – the result of polishing them with a proprietory metal cleaner which renders the piece worthless.

A collection of bees by Joseff of Hollywood.

1940s   Largest 1.75in (4.5cm) long

l $70-100,m $50-80,s $30-40 Cris

A bee on flower pin with matching earrings by Joseff of Hollywood.

1940s   Pin 2.75in (7cm) diam

Pin $300-350, ear's $180-220 Cris

Snake earrings, by Joseff of Hollywood.

1940s   3.5in (8.5cm) long

$220-280   **Cris**

A pin by Joseff of Hollywood decorated with ruby glass stones in basket settings.

1940s   5.5in (14cm) long

$900-1,000   **Cris**

A tassel, by Joseff of Hollywood, necklace.

1940s   41.5in (105cm) long

$200-250   **Cris**

An Art Deco amethyst three pendant necklace and earrings, by Joseff of Hollywood.

1940s   Earrings 3.5in (9cm) long

$750-800   **Cris**

Joseff of Hollywood

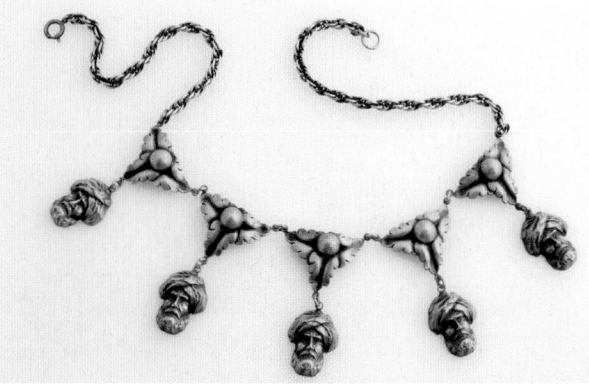

A necklace, by Joseff of Hollywood, decorated with turbaned men.

1940s — 18.5in (47cm) long

$200-300 — **Cris**

A pin and necklace, by Joseff of Hollywood, decorated with oak leaves.

A necklace similar to this one was worn by the actress Carol Lombard. Designed in 1939, the pin can be clipped onto the necklace as a pendant.

1940s Pin — 2.75in (7cm) long

$550-600 — **Cris**

A lily of the valley pin, by Joseff of Hollywood.

1940s

$300-350 — **Cris**

A retro design chatelaine pin, by Joseff of Hollywood, decorated with basket set crystals.

1940s — 4.75in (12cm) wide

$780-820 — **Cris**

A chatelaine pin, by Joseff of Hollywood, decorated with multicolored cabouchons and charms.

1940s — 7.25in (18.5cm)

$250-300 — **Cris**

A chatelaine pin, by Joseff of Hollywood.

1940s — 2.75in (7cm) diam

$250-300 — **Cris**

Three zodiac pins, by Joseff of Hollywood.

2.25in (5.5cm) diam

$150-200 each — **Cris**

A crab and pearl pin, by Joseff of Hollywood.

2in (5.5cm) diam

$70-100 — **Cris**

A shell and dolphin necklace decorated with pearls, by Joseff of Hollywood.

This piece was worn by the actress Pia Angeli.

1940s — Shell motif 6in (15.5cm)

$300-350 — **Cris**

A crescent moon pin, by Joseff of Hollywood.

1940s — 1.25in (4cm) long

$70-100 — **Cris**

► A pair of Moon God earrings, by Joseff of Hollywood, Russian gold set with trembling rhinestone eyes.

*Joseff's **Moon Gods**, and their Sun God cousins, are among his most distinctive pieces. Featured on earrings, necklaces and pins the clear rhinestone eyes sway with the movement of the wearer. If the eye stones were missing the value of this piece would be reduced by up to 80 percent.*

Mid-1940s	3in (8cm) long
$300-350	**Cris**

A Moon God necklace by Joseff of Hollywood with trembling rhinestone eyes.

1940s	17.5in (44cm) long
$600-650	**Cris**

TRIFARI

Trifari are one of the most successful costume jewelry designers and manufacturers of the 20th century. The company produces highly convincing imitations of fashionable precious jewelry and has also conceived many innovative pieces.

✦ Founded in 1918 by the "Diamanté kings" Gustavo Trifari and Leo Krussman, the company became known as K.F.T. after Carl Fishel joined them in 1925.

✦ Helped to make costume jewelry an acceptable accessory with society women after Mamie Eisenhower wore specially commissioned Trifari parures at the Presidential Inaugurations of 1952 and 1956.

✦ The company's most famous designer is Alfred Philippe, who joined Trifari after the Wall Street Crash in 1929, having previously worked for William Scheer, Inc. (who manufactured for jewellers Cartier and Van Cleef and Arpels).

✦ All pieces are marked, and those made after 1952 include a copyright symbol. Until that time Trifari and its rival Coro produced many almost identical pieces. Trifari took Coro to court and obtained a judgment which established jewelry design as a work of art and something that could be copyrighted.

A large pavé and citrine sunflower pin, by Trifari, with a rhodium plated backing.

1930	3.5in (9cm) diam
$550-650	**Cris**

A retro style necklace with matching pin, by Trifari, rose gold-plated setting with multiple shaped emerald and sapphire stones and crystal rhinestones, in original box.

1940s	Pin 2.5in (6cm) long
N'lace $400-500, pin $140-200	**Cris**

A Jewels of India style pin with matching earrings, by Trifari, in original box.

This set was worn by the singer Madonna in the film Evita. The green crystal cabouchons and multi-color rhinestones set in "vermeil" silver (silver plated or washed with yellow gold) were inspired by the carved (rather than faceted) Indian Mughal jewels first popularized by Cartier in the 1920s.

1950s	Pin 2.5in (6cm) long
$300-350	**Cris**

A necklace, by Trifari, handset with crystals.

1940s	
$350-400	**Cris**

A snail fur clip, by Trifari, cold enamel over gold plate.

This model is exceedingly rare and therefore very desirable.

1940s	3.5in (8.5cm) wide
$1,300-1,400	**Cris**

Trifari

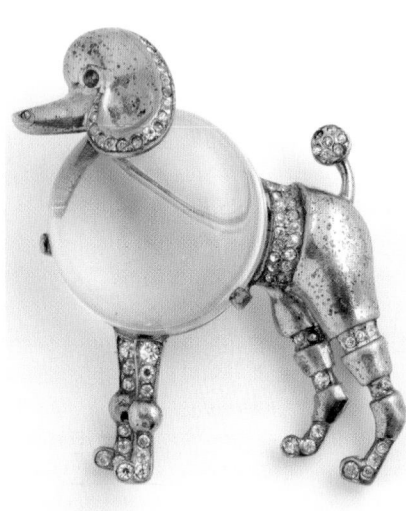

A poodle "jelly belly" pin, by Trifari.

▶ **Jelly bellies** *are one of Trifari's most collectable styles – a series of highly distinctive, clear lucite-centered animals. This example, which also features sterling silver head, flippers and tail, and an aquamarine-colored stone ball. However, the "jelly-bellies" that Trifari continued to produced after the 1940s are less desirable, and therefore command commensurately lower prices.*

1940s 2in (5cm) long

$650-700 **Cris**

A seal "jelly belly" pin, by Trifari, sterling silver with a clear lucite belly.

1940s 2.5in (6.5cm) long

$550-600 **Cris**

A rooster "jelly belly" pin, by Trifari.

1940s 2.5in (6.5cm) long

$500-550 **Cris**

A hyacinth pin, by Trifari, decorated with cold enamel and pavé-set stones.

4.5in (11cm) long

$580-620 **Cris**

A rose pin, by Trifari, desgined by Alfred Philippe, gold-plated with fruit salad stones set to imitate a flower pot and trailing plant.

1940s 2.25in (5.5cm) long

$350-400 **Cris**

A wheelbarrow-shaped pin and earrings, by Trifari, designed by Alfred Philippe for Trifari, featuring pavé-set fruit salad stones.

This exceedingly rare design imitates those created in the 1920s and 30s by jewelers such as Cartier. They were inspired by the Tree of Life, an ancient Egyptian fertility symbol. Egyptian symbolism became a popular design motif after the opening of Tutankhamun's tomb.

Pin 3.25in (8cm) wide

$1,300-1,400 **Cris**

A pin, by Trifari, with glass pendant drop.

1950s 3in (7.5cm) long

$70-100 **Cris**

An imitation ruby and diamond poinsettia pin, by Trifari, designed by Alfred Philippe.

The way the stones are set imitates the "invisible setting" developed by jewelers Van Cleef and Arpels.

1950s 3in (7cm) long

$400-500 **Cris**

A pin, by Trifari, decorated with hand enameling and faux pearls.

1950s 2.5in (6.5cm) long

$140-200 **Cris**

A parrure of necklace, bracelet and earrings, by Trifari.

1950s

$400-500 **Cris**

Christmas Tree Pins

CHRISTMAS TREE PINS

Many well-known manufacturers and designers have created new limited edition Christmas tree pin designs every year for decades, which means there is now a healthy market in signed and unsigned pieces. Names to watch include Stanley Hagler, Weiss, Eisenberger Ice, Boucher, Hattie Carnegie, Hobé, Trifari and Vendome. However, there are many unsigned pieces from the 1940s onwards which are highly collectible.

A pin set with diamanté, ruby cabouchon and green baguette stones.

This pin, designed by Cristobal, was made in a limited edition of 100.

	4.5in (11cm) long
$100-150	**Cris**

An Eisenberg Ice pin.

1980s	2.5in (6cm) long
$30-40	**Cris**

An unsigned Austrian pin set with multicolored crystal rhinestones and clear baguettes for candles.

1950s	3in (7.5cm) long
$40-60	**Cris**

An Eisenberg Ice pin, set with aurora borealis stones and red and green crystal rhinestones.

1980s	2.5in (6cm) long
$30-60	**Cris**

A Stanley Hagler pin, set with aurora borealis stones, ruby red glass beads and emeralds and a glass angel pendant.

	2.5in (6cm) long
$70-100	**Cris**

A pin, by Stanley Hagler, set with red baguette and green glass cabouchons.

1960s	3.5in (8.5cm) long
$140-200	**Cris**

A pin, by Stanley Hagler, set with mother of pearl, green and red glass stones.

1960s	3.5in (8.5cm) long
$200-250	**Cris**

A pin, by Stanley Hagler, set with hand-wired Czechoslovakian glass beads.

c1970	4in (10cm) long
$140-200	**Cris**

A pin, by Stanley Hagler, decorated with Murano glass fruit and beads.

c1970	2.75in (7cm) long
$100-150	**Cris**

Miscellaneous

A pin, by Stanley Hagler, decorated with Murano glass beads.

c1970   2in (5.5cm) long

$100-140   **Cris**

A pin, by Lawrence Verba set with topaz baguette stones.

4.5in (11.5cm) long

$140-200   **Cris**

A pin, by Lawrence Verbaset, with blue, ruby red and clear crystal stones.

1990   4.5in (11.5cm) long

$140-200   **Cris**

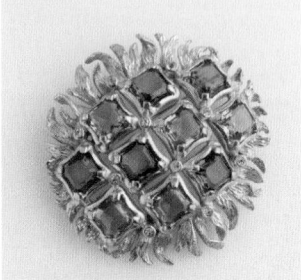

A flower pin, by Marcel Boucher.

1950s   2in (5.5cm) dia

$70-100   **Cris**

An stylized African pin, by Hattie Carnegie, made from bakelite and metal.

1950s   3.5in (8.5cm) long

$250-300   **Cris**

A bracelet, by Corocraft, decorated with crystal cabochons, pavé crystal rhinestones and gold plate.

1940s   3in (8cm) diam

$800-900   **Cris**

A handset crystal, glass and faux pearl necklace, by Christian Dior.

Christian Dior *costume jewelry is unusual in that most pieces are dated on the back.*

1959   13.75in (35cm) long

$500-550   **Cris**

A necklace with matching earrings and pin, by Kramer for Christian Dior, featuring French glass drops and hand-set clear crystal marquise on a rhodium plated setting.

Late 1950s   Pin 2in (5cm) long

$550-600   **Cris**

A Russian dancer sterling pin by Eisenberg.

1940s   3.5in (9cm) long

$1,000-1,500   **Cris**

A necklace, attributed to Goossens, with gilded stampings and glass coral cabouchons, crystals and faux pearl drops.

1940s   14in (36cm) long

$550-600   **Cris**

A necklace with matching earrings, by Stanley Hagler.

Mid-1960s Motifs 1.25in (3.5cm) diam

$700-800   **Cris**

Miscellaneous

A necklace and earrings, by Stanley Hagler, set with mother of pearl and cushion pearls.

Mid-1960s   1.5in (3.5cm) diam

$550-600   **Cris**

A necklace with matching earrings, by Stanley Hagler.

Mid-1960s Earrings 1.75in (4.5cm)

$500-550   **Cris**

A necklace with matching earrings, by Stanley Hagler.

Late 1960s Earrings 1.75in (4.5cm)

$500-550   **Cris**

A leaf pin, by Stanley Hagler, set with pressed Murano glass and bakelite leaves.

Mid 1960s   4in (10cm) long

$140-200   **Cris**

A necklace, bracelet and earrings, by Miriam Haskell, featuring handwired seed pearls and clear crystal stones.

These seed pearls were specially produced by Miriam Haskell in Japan. The secret of their production was lost when she died.

1940s   1.75in (4.5cm) long

$1,000-1,500   **Cris**

A French glass necklace, with matching earrings, by Miriam Haskell.

This is an unusual style for Miriam Haskell. She used French glass during the war years when she was prevented from obtaining her signature pearls from Japan.

1940s   Earrings 1.25in (3cm) long

$650-700   **Cris**

A necklace with matching bracelet by Miriam Haskell.

1940s   Bracelet 8.25in (21cm) long

$500-550   **Cris**

A bib collar necklace, with matching earrings, by Miriam Haskell.

1950s Earrings 1.25in (3cm) diam

$650-700   **Cris**

A faux baroque pearl necklace, by Miriam Haskell, with a flower clasp lined with handwired seed pearls.

1950s   16.5in (42cm) long

$350-400   **Cris**

Miscellaneous

A black baroque pearl necklace with a flower motif clasp, by Miriam Haskell.

1950s   15in (38.5cm) long

$650-700   **Cris**

A Hobé pin, sterling silver-plated with rose gold.

1940s   6in (15.5cm) long

$800-900   **Cris**

A rhinestone bib necklace, by Hollycraft.

1955   18in (46cm) long

$350-400   **Cris**

A poured glass bead necklace with matching earrings, by Maison Gripoix.

1990   Earrings 1.5in (4cm) diam

$1,300-1,800   **Cris**

A necklace with matching earrings, by Maison Gripoix.

1990 Earrings 1.75in (4.5cm) diam

$1,400-2,000   **Cris**

A necklace with matching earrings, by Maison Gripoix, featuring hand poured French glass beads with gilded frames studded with rhinestones.

1990s

$1,200-1,800   **Cris**

A sterling chrome crown pin, by Mazer, with amethyst cabouchons and multicolored crystal.

1940s   2.5in (6cm) long

$350-400   **Cris**

A sterling silver pin, decorated with a rose gold wash and pink baguette stones, designed by Pennino Brothers.

                    2.75in (7cm) long

$550-600   **Cris**

A pin with matching earrings, designed by Pennino Brothers.

1940s   Pin 3in (7.5cm) long

$850-900   **Cris**

A bracelet, by Schiaparelli, set with "black diamond" octagon pear-shaped rhinestones.

1950s   7.25in (18.5cm)

$550-600   **Cris**

An early Schiaparelli woven chain necklace, with hand cut crystal drops.

c1930-40   17in (43cm) long

$650-700   **Cris**

Miscellaneous

A gold plated bracelet, by Schiaparelli, with matching earrings, decorated with ruby red cabouchons and aurora borealis stones.

1950s   Bracelet 7.5in (19cm) long

$500-550   **Cris**

A disc bracelet and earrings, by Schiaparelli, with amethyst and aurora borealis stones.

1950s   Bracelet 7in (18cm) long

$550-600   **Cris**

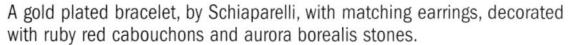

A pearl and shell bracelet, by Schiaparelli, set with aurora borealis stones.

1950s   7in (18cm) long

$400-500   **Cris**

A fruit pin with matching earrings, by Schiaparelli, set with crystal aurora borealis stones and yellow bakelite cabouchons.

1950s   Pin 2.5in (6cm) long

$300-350   **Cris**

A pin designed, by Henry Schreiner, with jonquille keystone crystals surrounding a claw set matrix glass cabochon.

      3in (7.5cm) long

$400-500   **Cris**

A necklace, by Henry Schreiner.

1950s   17in (43cm) long

$500-550   **Cris**

A bow pin, by Larry Verba, gun metal plated settings filled with crystal stones.

1990s   5in (13cm) wide

$140-200   **Cris**

An enameled silver gilt necklace.

1910   17in (43cm) long

$350-400   **Cris**

A poured glass heart-shaped pin, with matching earrings.

This set is reputed to have been made for Coco Chanel. However, as it is unmarked and undocumented the value is relatively low. If it was Chanel the value would triple.

1920s   Pin 3.25in (8cm) long

$300-350   **Cris**

Miscellaneous

WHAT TO LOOK FOR WHEN BUYING

✦ Top-quality, more up-market pieces by the better-known designers and makers in good condition.

✦ Provenance of manufacture. Many pieces are marked or signed, but just as many are unsigned. With some very plausible forgeries, notably of Schiaparelli, in circulation, it is best to familiarize yourself with the marks and buy from reputable sources.

✦ Pieces originally designed for, or advertised by, famous Hollywood film stars are especially desirable (see Joseff of Hollywood).

✦ There is a premium on complete parures – matching sets or suites (usually consisting of a necklace, bracelet, pin and earrings) – and demi-parures (two matched pieces, such as a pin and earrings).

✦ Unmarked pieces can be as collectable as marked ones – look for good quality materials and attractive designs.

A very high quality silver bracelet, galleried with handset crystals.

1920s	7in (18cm) long

$800-850   **Cris**

A silver bracelet, galleried with handset crystals.

1920s	7.25in (18.5cm) long

$700-800   **Cris**

A pin in the form of a palm tree, sterling silver with channel-set crystal and emerald glass, unmarked.

1920s	2in (5cm) long

$500-550   **Cris**

A bird of paradise pin, silver set with marcasite.

1920	3.5in (9cm) long

$400-500   **Cris**

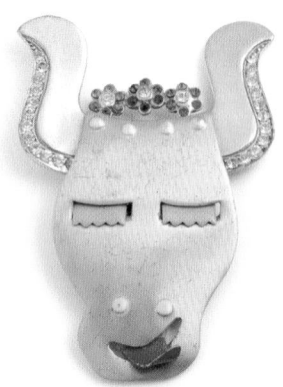

A cartoon cow fur clip, unmarked but bearing a patent number.

1930s	3.5in (8.5cm) long

$500-550   **Cris**

A gold and black geometric necklace.

1930s	17.5 in (44cm) long

$400-500   **Cris**

A cocktail bracelet, decorated with scenes from the Marriage of Figaro, unmarked.

1940s	8in (20cm) long

$1,000-1,500   **Cris**

An unsigned necklace with matching bracelet, decorated with enameled leaves and petals.

1950s	Necklace 14in (35.5cm) long

$180-220   **Cris**

An unsigned retro design necklace, featuring gold plated snake chain and falling tassel.

1940s	15.75in (40cm) long

$100-140   **Cris**

A necklace with matching earrings, rhodium-plated backings decorated with baguette clear crystal rhinestones and pear-shaped and hexagonal emerald-cut crystal rhinestones, unmarked but in heart-shaped box marked 'James Walker, London Jeweller'.

Earrings 1.75in (4.5cm) long

$400-500   **Cris**

BOXES Visiting Card Cases

The practice of leaving a calling card to request visits or introductions became popular among polite society in the early 19th century. It was a custom born out of the strict etiquette rules of the time, and was largely practiced by women, who were involved in visiting. There were a number of discreet ways to indicate the intention of your visit through these cards; turning up the bottom right hand corner of the card suggested you were inquiring about the health of an individual, while turning up all four corners indicated that you would like to visit all members of the household.

Although the earliest visiting cards date back to the late 18th century, the special cases to hold them did not start to appear until the 1830s. Initially they were made from silver, but soon they began to appear in a variety of materials, including leather, tortoiseshell, lacquered papier mâché, mother-of-pearl, and different types of wood, such as walnut, mahogany, olivewood and aromatic sandalwood.

While most cases were rectangular in form, some had scrolled edges or rounded corners. Men's cases were generally smaller and more curved than ladies', allowing them to fit easily into waistcoat pockets.

The popularity of visiting cards, and subsequently their cases, began to decline in the 1930s, and today the tradition remains only in the business world.

The market for collecting visiting card cases has only emerged in the past five to ten years, and it has been growing since. This is expected to continue over the next few years, with prices rising steadily. However, compared to the majority of antiques on the market, they are still moderately priced.

The price of a visiting card case very much depends on the rarity and value of the materials used, the quality of the decoration and overall condition. However, as a rule, tortoiseshell and ivory are particularly desirable, especially now that they are controlled areas and cannot be imported or exported without a license. Prices for these items are kept high by the competition from Far Eastern collectors of ivory and tortoiseshell. Japanese ivory cases decorated with shibayama work are probably the most sought-after, and are priced accordingly. Due to these unique conditions, prices of these particular cases are expected to rise dramatically in the next 10 years.

Although the market for silver castle-top cases can be unpredictable, the growing demand from specialist collectors means that prices for these should also increase with time.

Visiting card cases made of unusual materials, such as hardstone and porcelain are highly prized, mainly due to their rarity.

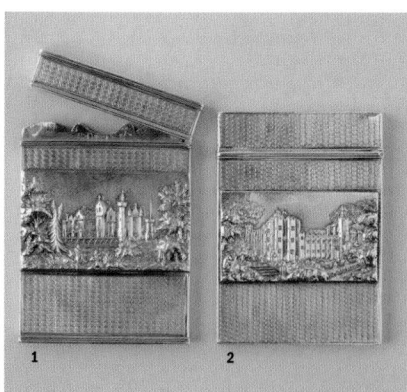

▲1 A silver castle-top visiting card case, showing Abbotsford House, by Gervase Wheeler, Birmingham.
1838   3.75in (9.5cm) high

$900-1,000	BM

▲2 A silver castle-top visiting card case, showing Windsor Castle and Kenilworth Castle, engine turning above and below, M.N. Birmingham.
1838   3.75in (9.5cm) high

$900-1,000	BM

▲1 A silver castle-top visiting card case, showing Windsor Castle and Warwick Castle, by Taylor & Perry, Birmingham.
1839   3.75in (9.5cm) high

$900-1,000	BM

▲2 A silver castle-top visiting card case, showing Windsor Castle and Kenilworth Castle, bordered by pierced and chased scrolling leaves and flowers, by Nathaniel Mills, Birmingham.
1839   3.75in (9.5cm) high

$1,000-1,500	BM

▲3 A silver castle-top visiting card case, with applied relief of Windsor Castle and Abbotsford House, by Nathaniel Mills, Birmingham.
1842   4in (10cm) high

$900-1,300	BM

▲1 A silver visiting card case, with high relief of Houses of Parliament as seen from River Thames, with case (not shown), M.N. Birmingham.
1844   4in (10cm) high

$2,200-2,800	BM

▲2 A silver castle-top visiting card case, with original case (not shown), by David Petiffer, Birmingham.
1852   4in (10cm) high

$1,000-1,500	BM

Visiting Card Cases

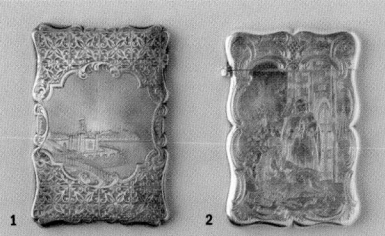

▲1 A silver visiting card case, the front with a sea and fort scene, bordered and to the reverse with engaved geometric pattern, Birmingham.

1858   3.75in (9.5cm) high

| $200-250 | BM |

▲2 A silver visiting card case, engraved with two figures and deer before a church, reverse with foliate cartouche, by Charles Riley & George Storer, London.

1845   3.75in (9.5cm) high

| $400-450 | BM |

▲1 A Chinese silver visiting card case, with filigree.

c1880   4in (10cm) high

| $100-150 | BM |

▲2 A Chinese silver visiting card case, with filigree.

c1880   3.5in (9cm) high

| $100-150 | BM |

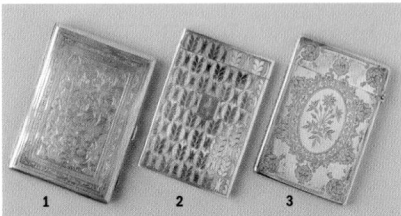

▲1 A silver visiting card case, with side opening, original case by Rankin (not shown), blue interior, C.C. Birmingham.

1882   4in (10cm) long

| $180-220 | BM |

▲2 A silver visiting card case, finely machine-engraved, with shield and crest to front, original box (not shown), by Taylor & Perry, Birmingham.

1856   3.75in (9.5cm) high

| $180-220 | BM |

▲3 A silver visiting card case, with engraved foliate and stylized decoration, and case (not shown), by Thomas Johnson, London.

1869   3.75in (9.5cm) long

| $180-220 | BM |

▲1 An American silver visiting card case, showing Battle Abbey, reverse embossed with floral pattern.

c1880   3.75in (9.5cm) high

| $500-550 | BM |

▲2 An American silver visiting card case, the reverse with chased flowers, by Leonard and Wilson, Philadelphia.

1854   3.5in (9cm) high

| $500-550 | BM |

▲1 A silver visiting card case, engraved with the Scott Monument, flanked by foliage, Birmingham.

1861   4in (10cm) high

| $300-350 | BM |

▲2 A silver visiting card case, engraved with the Scott Monument, by Naysmith, Edinburgh.

1886   3.75in (9.5cm) high

| $600-650 | BM |

▲1 A silver visiting card case, with floral filigree sides and applied enamel decoration of houses beneath trees.

c1870   3.75in (9.5cm) high

| $350-400 | BM |

▲2 A silver visiting card case, with chased decoration of Egyptian heads, side opening, blue silk interior, with original pencil, retailer's mark for Purcell & Co, Cork, by Samuel Mordan, London.

1874   4.5in (11cm) high

| $200-250 | BM |

▲1 A silver castle-top visiting card case, possibly showing Hampton Court, reverse with central medallion, D.P. Birmingham.

1855   3.75in (9.5cm) high

| $1,000-1,500 | BM |

▲2 A silver castle-top visiting card case, showing the Scott Monument, very high relief, reverse with scrollwork decoration, F&P Birmingham.

1870   4in (10cm) high

| $1,200-1,800 | BM |

▲3 A silver-gilt castle-top visiting card case, showing St Paul's Cathedral, reverse with scrolls and cartouche, by Hilliard & Thomasson, Birmingham.

Castle-tops *are embossed or engraved silver visiting card cases, snuff-boxes or vinaigrettes, with views of well-known landmarks, such as castles and historic houses. They were made from the 1830s, mainly in Birmingham. One of the most renowned makers was Nathaniel Mills.*

1870   3.75in (9.5cm) high

| $1,000-1,500 | BM |

A silver visiting card case, depicting four putti with sheep in landscape, hinged top, Elkington.

1870   4in (10cm) high

| $350-400 | BM |

Visiting Card Cases

A silver visiting card case, decorated with bamboo and birds, by Deakin & Francis, Birmingham, with original retailer's case by John C. Jacob.

1883 3.75in (9.5cm) high

$250-300 **BM**

A silver visiting card case, engraved with flowers, gold center panel, by Hilliard & Thomasson, Birmingham, with original case.

1887 3.75in (9.5cm) high

$250-300 **BM**

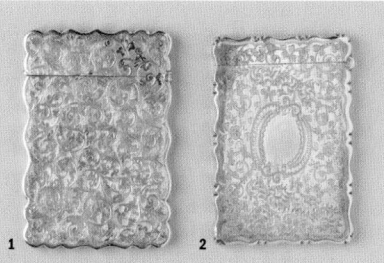

▲1 A silver visiting card case, with engraved scrollwork decoration, Birmingham, with original case (not shown).

1896 4in (10cm) high

$250-300 **BM**

▲2 A silver visiting card case, with floral and foliate scroll engraving, oval center each side, with original leather case (not shown), George Unite, Birmingham.

1897 3.75in (9.5cm) high

$200-250 **BM**

▲1 A silver visiting card case, with cherubs, H.M. Birmingham, and original retailer's case by Mappin & Webb (not shown).

1899 4in (10cm) high

$300-350 **BM**

▲2 A silver visiting card case, with embossed profile of a lady, shield to the reverse.

1904 3.75in (9.5cm) high

$180-220 **BM**

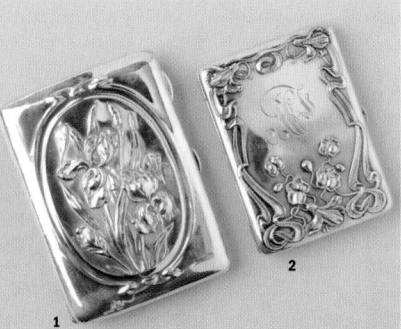

▲1 A silver Art Deco visiting card case, with embossed irises in central oval, the reverse with plain oval, green silk interior, original ivory leaf and silver pencil, by H. Matthews, Birmingham.

1904 4in (10cm) high

$200-250 **BM**

▲2 A sterling silver Art Deco visiting card case, with embossed design, replacement white silk interior.

1900 3.5in (9cm) high

$150-200 **BM**

▲1 A silver gentleman's visiting card case, W.H.S. Birmingham.

1903 3.25in (8.5cm) high

$150-200 **BM**

▲2 A silver gentleman's visiting card case, with engine-turned decoration, S.I.L. Ltd. Chester.

1919 3.25in (8.5cm) high

$80-120 **BM**

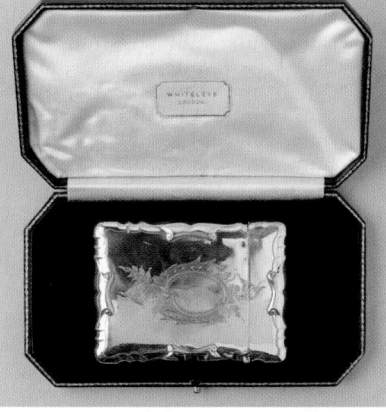

▲1 A silver visiting card case, depicting a cathedral scene, possibly Salisbury, with cart and horses in foreground, original purple silk-lined box, J.D./W.D. E.S.N. Birmingham.

1906 3.75in (9.5cm) high

$300-350 **BM**

▲2 A silver visiting card case, embossed with a knight and lady on horseback, by W.M. Hayes, Birmingham.

1903 3.75in (9.5cm) high

$350-400 **BM**

A silver visiting card case, with scrolled edges, cartouches front and back, by Richard Pike, Chester, with original retailer's box by Whiteleys.

1904 4.25in (10.5cm) high

$200-250 **BM**

▲1 A silver visiting card case, the front showing The Kiosk at Philae, Egypt, the reverse with foliate scrollwork decoration and cartouche, by Crisford & Norris, Birmingham, with original box (not shown).

1905 4in (10cm) high

$350-400 **BM**

▲2 A silver visiting card case, the overall engraved decoration with shield to front, W.H. Birmingham, with original retailer's box (not shown).

1901 3.75in (9.5cm) high

$200-250 **BM**

Visiting Card Cases

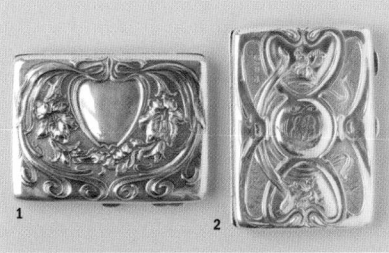

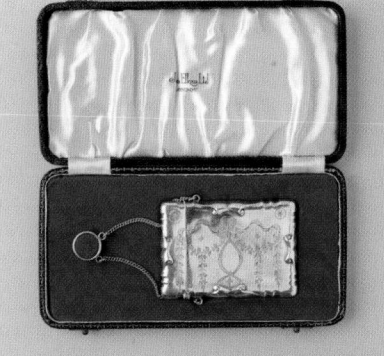

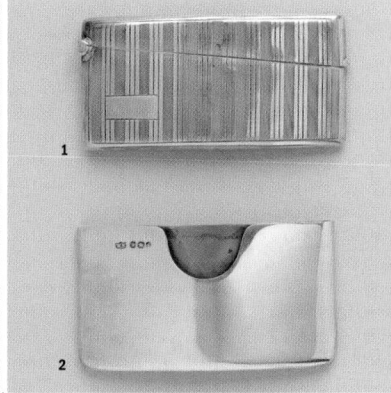

▲**1** A silver Art Nouveau visiting card case, with heart-shaped shield, foliate scrolls, leather interior and ivory tablet, W.N. Chester.

1904   4in (10cm) high

$200-250	BM

▲**2** A silver Art Deco visiting card case, with irises in heart-shaped reserves, side opening, leather interior, ivorine leaf and ivory pencil, W.N. Chester.

1905   4in (10cm) high

$200-250	BM

A silver visiting card case, with scroll edges, floral engraving to front, chain, by John Elkan, T&S Chester, with original retailer's case.

1909   3.75in (9.5cm) high

$200-250	BM

▲**1** A silver gentleman's visiting card case, engraved with lines, curved hip, by D. Bros, Birmingham.

1930   3.25in (8.5cm) high

$80-120	BM

▲**2** A silver gentleman's visiting card case, with plain curved hip, open top, W.N. Sheffield.

1923   3.25in (8.5cm) high

$80-120	BM

▲**1** A tortoiseshell visiting card case, with inlaid mother-of-pearl flowers, gold fittings and gold top plate.

c1820   3.5in (9cm) high

$450-500	BM

▲**2** A tortoiseshell visiting card case, with mother-of-pearl flowers and catch mount, hinged top, no lining.

c1820   3.25in (8.5cm) high

$200-250	BM

▲**1** A tortoiseshell visiting card case, the front with central silver star motif, side opening, blue fan interior.

c1860   4.25in (10.5cm) high

$450-500	BM

▲**2** A tortoiseshell visiting card case, the front inlaid with silver trellis and vine decoration, central shield, side opening, blue fan interior.

c1860   4.25in (10.5cm) high

$450-500	BM

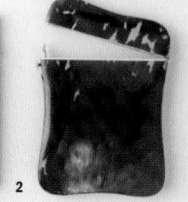

▲**1** A curved tortoiseshell visiting card case, the top inset with two metal strips, red interior, small piece of ivory missing.

c1860   4in (10cm) high

$120-180	BM

▲**2** A dark tortoiseshell visiting card case, of waisted shape, with silver top plate, red interior, repair to edge above hinge, large chip below clip, interior separating at top.

c1860   4in (10cm) high

$100-150	BM

▲**1** A tortoiseshell visiting card case, with silver piqué and inlaid decoration of ho ho birds in trees and pagoda, chipped above catch.

c1860   4.25in (10.5cm) high

$350-400	BM

▲**2** A tortoiseshell visiting card case, with silver piqué and inlaid decoration of Oriental figures in a garden, unmarked silver plate.

c1860   4.25in (10.5cm) high

$350-400	BM

▲**1** A tortoiseshell visiting card case, with pewter stringing and gem painting of the Crystal Palace, part of ivory strip missing.

c1870   3in (8cm) high

$450-500	BM

▲**2** A tortoiseshell visiting card case, with a gem painting of Westminster Cathedral, top plate missing.

c1870   3in (8cm) high

$450-500	BM

▲**1** A tortoiseshell visiting card case, the top inset with two metal strips, unmarked top plate, bright red interior.

c1870   4in (10cm) high

$180-220	BM

▲**2** A tortoiseshell visiting card case, unmarked top plate, red interior.

c1870   4in (10cm) high

$180-220	BM

Visiting Card Cases

▲**1** A tortoiseshell visiting card case, with silver piqué and inlay depicting herons and stylized Oriental foliage, blue fan interior.

c1890   4in (10cm) high

$400-450	BM

▲**2** A tortoiseshell visiting card case, with inlaid silver panel of birds at fountain, plain to reverse.

c1870   4.25in (10.5cm) high

$300-350	BM

▲**1** A tortoiseshell visiting card case, with regular all-over piqué decoration, unmarked silver top plate, red interior.

c1870   4in (10cm) high

$400-450	BM

▲**2** A tortoiseshell visiting card case, with silver piqué crosses, bright red interior.

c1870   4.25in (10.5cm) high

$350-400	BM

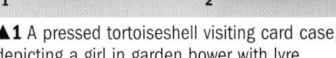

▲**1** A pressed tortoiseshell visiting card case, depicting a girl in garden bower with lyre.

c1870   4in (10cm) high

$400-500	BM

▲**2** A pressed tortoiseshell visiting card case, depicting Gothic arches.

c1870   4.25 (10.5cm) high

$400-500	BM

▲**1** A tortoiseshell visiting card case, the carved decoration depicting Chinese family scenes, with gilded highlights.

c1870   4.5in (11cm) high

$700-800	BM

▲**2** A tortoiseshell visiting card case, with finely carved domestic scenes.

c1870   3.75in (9.7cm) high

$350-400	BM

▲**1** A tortoiseshell and mother-of-pearl visiting card case.

c1870   4.25in (10.5cm) high

$100-150	BM

▲**2** A mother-of-pearl visiting card case, the central tortoiseshell panel decorated with piqué trees and birds.

c1870   4in (10cm) high

$100-150	BM

▲**1** A tortoiseshell visiting card case, inset with silver wire.

c1880   4in (10cm) high

$350-400	BM

▲**2** A tortoiseshell visiting card case, inset with mother-of-pearl flowers.

c1870   3.75in (9.5cm) high

$200-250	BM

▲**1** A tortoiseshell visiting card case, both sides inlaid with mother-of-pearl, with very fine basket of flowers in center, unmarked silver plaque to top, bright red interior.

c1880   4.25in (10.5cm) high

$450-500	BM

▲**2** A tortoiseshell visiting card case, with edged mother-of-pearl floral sprays, unmarked shield to front.

c1880   4in (10cm) high

$450-500	BM

▲**1** A mother-of-pearl visiting card case, with pierced enameled metal fretwork decoration to front.

c1850   4.25in (10.5cm) high

$120-180	BM

▲**2** A mother-of-pearl visiting card case, with mercury silvered glass panel of roses.

c1860   4in (10cm) high

$100-150	BM

▲**1** A mother-of-pearl visiting card case, with deep carved decoration of a bouquet of flowers.

c1860   3.5in (9cm) high

$100-150	BM

▲**2** A mother-of-pearl visiting card case, with deep carved portrait of William Shakespeare.

c1860   3.5in (9cm) high

$450-500	BM

Visiting Card Cases

Two mother-of-pearl visiting card cases.

c1850   4.25in (10.5cm) high

$70-100 (each)   **BM**

Two mother-of-pearl visiting card cases, with haliotis decoration.

c1860   4in (10cm) high

$70-100 (each)   **BM**

▲**1** A mother-of-pearl visiting card case, with tortoiseshell serpentine edge and green silk fan interior.

c1860   4.25in (10.5cm) high

$100-150   **BM**

▲**2** A mother-of-pearl visiting card case, with side opening and blue silk fan interior.

c1860   4.25in (10.5cm) high

$100-150   **BM**

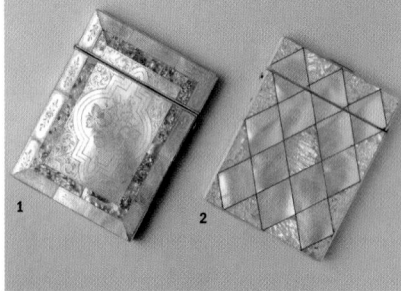

▲**1** A mother-of-pearl hand-engraved visiting card case, with abalone border.

c1870   4.25in (10.5cm) high

$100-150   **BM**

▲**2** A mother-of-pearl and abolone visiting card case.

c1870   4in (10cm) high

$100-150   **BM**

▲**1** A mother-of-pearl silver visiting card case, with haliotis and tortoiseshell decoration.

c1870   4.25in (10.5cm) high

$100-150   **BM**

▲**2** A mother-of-pearl and haliotis visiting card case, with machine-engraved silver center panel.

c1860   4.25in (10.5cm) high

$200-250   **BM**

Two machine-engraved mother-of-pearl visiting card cases, with hand-engraved spray of flowers, silver engraved center panel.

c1860   4.25in (10.5cm) high

$70-100 (each)   **BM**

▲**1** An ivory visiting card case, carved in high relief with figures among pavilions, lotus and willow trees, with boat on one side.

c1860   3.5in (9cm) high

$200-300   **BM**

▲**2** An ivory visiting card case, deeply carved with domestic scenes, pull-off top.

c1860   3.75in (9.5cm) high

$300-350   **PC (BM)**

▲**3** An ivory visiting card case, with deep carved domestic scenes, gold plaque coronet, brass inner sleeve.

c1850   3.75in (9.5cm) high

$400-450   **BM**

▲**1** An ivory visiting card case, with sprung hinged top.

c1870   4in (10cm) high

$150-200   **BM**

▲**2** An ivory visiting card case, with side opening, silver clasp, ivory tablet and silver pencil.

c1880   4in (10cm) high

$150-200   **BM**

▲**3** An ivory visiting card case, with silver crest in center and red interior.

c1850   4in (10cm) high

$120-180   **BM**

▲**1** An ivory visiting card case, with coarse heavily pierced geometric pattern and slide-off top.

c1860   3.5in (9cm) high

$120-180   **BM**

▲**2** An ivory card case, with heavily pierced decoration and slide-off top, slight crush damage.

c1870   3.5in (9cm) high

$150-200   **BM**

THE MARKET FOR ANTIQUE TEXTILES CONTINUES TO THRIVE AS IT APPEALS TO BOTH SPECIALIST COLLECTORS AND FASHION ENTHUSIASTS. While the retail market had a slow start to the year there have not been any dramatic changes. The textile market is always relatively stable. Despite being dictated partly by fashion trends, the serious collectors of early costume, shoes, hats and later originals tend to maintain the balance.

At the moment clothes from the 1960s and 70s are doing extremely well, particularly originals with labels by big names such as Ossie Clark.

The fashion for gypsy-style clothing has meant that Edwardian whites, camisoles, petticoats and undergarments are selling well. 1950s print dresses are popular and this may be an indication of future fashion trends. Chiffon is not fairing as well this season as it has over the past few years.

CLOTHING

A micro-beaded purse, with floral decoration, intricate fringe and heavy silver frame.

11in (27.5cm) high

$700-750   **FLA**

A purse, with unusual all-over hand embroidery, with mixed stitches including trapunto, chain and French knots, with rose-embroidered gold frame.

$375-425   **FLA**

A beaded purse, the black jet ground with roses grapes and a bird, very early plastic chain link handle.

12in (30cm) high

$700-800   **FLA**

An early 20thC floral beaded bag, the elaborate gilt-metal clasp set with faux rubies, moonstones and turquoise.

8.25 x 6in (21 x 15cm)

$80-120   **SCT**

A beaded purse, with colored flower garlands on a black irridescent ground, black-looped fringe, sterling frame and chain.

12in (30cm) high

$600-800   **FLA**

A "puffy" beaded purse, with geometric design and blue silk lining.

6in (15cm) high

$400-450   **FLA**

A 1920s gold and silver lamé and tambour embroidered bag, with chain handle and gilt metal clasp.

7.25 x 7.5in (18.5 x 19cm)

$80-120   **SCT**

A German beaded purse, decorated on both sides with a peacock and roses, with ornate fringe and embossed silver frame, leather interior.

$700-750   **FLA**

◀ A 1920s gold lamé bag, with gilt-metal paste-set clasp.

6.5 x 7.25in (16 x 18.5cm)

$30-50   **SCT**

▶ A needlework bag, hand-stitched with winter landscape, in engraved silver frame, the clasp set with marcasites, with chain handle, mint condition.

c1935

$600-750   **SC**

Clothing

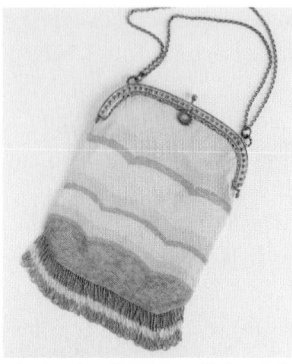

A micro-beaded purse, with beaded fringe and gold-toxed chain.

10in (25cm) high

$600-700   FLA

A 1940s French Lucite purse, with gold beading.

7in (18cm) wide

$200-300   CRIS

A 1940s "guild creations" wool bag, with zip opening, the wave-shaped decorative metal top engraved with small flowers and set with paste stones.

$250-350   SC

A 1950s Lucite purse, in the shape of a basket, with wavy ruff and gold filigree.

Plastic Lucite was created by DuPont in the 1950s and was used to make purses in a variety of shapes, textures and shades throughout the decade. They were sold in high-end department stores and were popular with actresses and showgirls. Later manufacturers catered for the lower end of the market and made purses out of lighter and more fragile plastics.

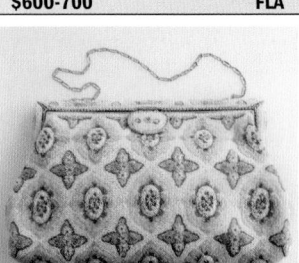

A 1940s French beaded purse.

9.25in (23.5cm) wide

$300-400   CRIS

A 1950s green wicker purse, in the shape of a frog.

14in (36cm) wide

$450-600   CRIS

A 1960s Gucci clutchbag, of patent white leather with large gilt interlocking G-clasp, stamped inside Gucci of Italy.

11 x 6.75in (28 x 17.2cm)

$100-200   SCT

$300-400   CRIS

An American hand-painted wooden box bag, by Enid Collins of Texas, with plastic handle and leather fastening, set with pearls and white plastic flowers, one petal damaged, copyright 1966.

$200-300   SC

An American hand-painted wooden box bag, by Collins of Texas, with black plastic handle, gold colored fastening and colored plastic beads.

In 1959 Edith Collins founded the Collins Company, in Medina, Texas. She designed and produced two main types of handbags: wooden box bags and canvas bucket-style bags. The bags were designed around themes and were hand-painted and embellished with sequins and rhinestones and are usually marked with their theme. Early pieces are often signed "Edith Collins" with the year of production, otherwise they are marked "ec" or "c".

The Tandy Leather Corporation purchased the company in 1970 and added new designs to the existing ones. Bags produced after 1970 are marked "Collins of Texas" or "C".

$175-225   SC

An 1840s hat, made of staw on a wire frame, possibly European.

$500-600   **SC**

An 1860s Native American hat, made for the Scottish market.

$500-600   **SC**

A late 19thC man's velvet embroidered tasseled smoking hat, with original box.

$250-300   **SC**

A 1940s black felt hat, by Howard Hodge of New York, with large fishnet veil set with red felt flowers.

$200-250   **SC**

A 1940s straw hat, by Jingo.

$300-400   **SC**

A 1940s Ma Be of New York brown straw "wet look" hat, with large velvet flowers.

$150-250   **SC**

A 1950s egret feather hat, by Madame Fausta.

$150-250   **SC**

A 1940s Jersey hat, in pale-blue wool pleats, with feathers to top.

$150-250   **SC**

A 1940s red felt hat, by Mabel Elsworth of New York, with feathers and red veil.

$150-250   **SC**

A 1960s cream feather hat, by Swan and Edgar of Piccadilly Circus, with gold feathers.

$150-250   **SC**

An Eastern European embroidered cotton cap, with silk ribbon to back, together with a matching blouse.

$600-700   **SC**

Clothing

A pair of early 19thC ladies velvet shoes, embroidered with silver thread, with small buckles to front, some wear.

$150-200 SC

A pair of Victorian burgundy silk velvet shoes, embroidered with gold thread and sequins, with ribbon bows to front, moth damage to both heels. *c1870*

$450-500 SC

A pair of Edwardian glacé leather kid shoes, by Lord and Taylor of New York, with eyelet and ribbon fastening, unworn.

$250-300 SC

A pair of 1920s gold and polychrome lamé shoes, with louis heel with ribbon laces and rosettes.

$250-300 SC

A pair of 1920s lamé shoes, with louis heel and rosettes to front.

$250-300 SC

A pair of Native American children's shoes, in white leather with turquoise and pink beads.

$150-200 SC

A 19thC "Turkish" cape, with gold embroidered thread on black wool and deep gathered hem.

$400-450 SC

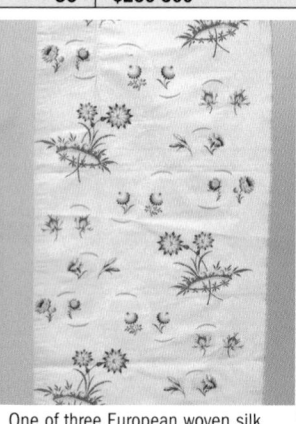

One of three European woven silk panels, originally from an 18thC dress, with abstract flowers and floral wreaths.

$1,500-2,000 (set) SC

An early 19thC man's cotton waistcoat, embroidered with flowers, with embroidered buttons, alterations to neck, some fading to embroidery.

$400-450 SC

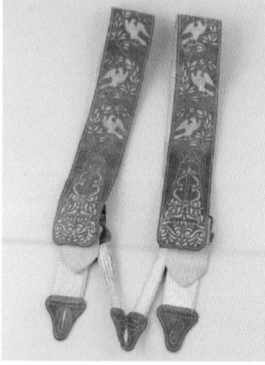

A pair of 1820s leather and kid men's braces, embroidered with decorative stitching depicting birds, leaves and a cello motif, possibly European.

$400-450 SC

▶ An 1850s ensemble, comprising a blouse, jacket and skirt, in cotton pique with embroidered motifs.

$1,500-2,000 SC

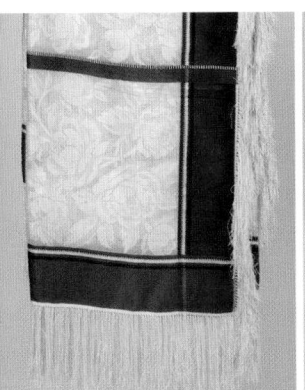

A late 19thC gauze shawl, in cream glazed fabric, with large flowerheads contained within bands of bright-blue and yellow silk, possibly French.	An Egyptian-style shawl, in orange cotton net with hammered silver design. *c1920*	A 1930s square lamé shawl, with Oriental design, the long fringing shaded from black to red.	A 1930s striped lamé stole.
$700-800 SC	$600-700 SC	$800-1,000 SC	$300-400 SC

CURTAINS AND HANGINGS

A woven silk panel, in polychrome striped paisley pattern.

137 x 70in (348 x 178cm)

$200-300   GorL

A 17thC Flemish tapestry, depicting an extensive landscape with exotic fowl.

78 x 96in (198 x 244cm)

$9,000-10,000   SI

An early 18thC tapestry, possibly Aubusson or Oudenaarde, the scene depicting figures (possibly Piranes and Thisbe) in court dress with an attending page, on the steps of a classical terrace, within a tree and flower surround, with attached border.

Aubusson carpets and rugs began to be produced in 1740, when the Savonnerie workshop was unable to cope with the increased demand. Aubusson, in central-southern France, was already famed for its tapestries, although the quality had previously been mediocre. Aubusson carpets were often copies of Oriental carpets. They were produced in the Savonnerie style, but were typically less skilled and detailed than their forerunner.

139in (353cm) wide

$20,000-30,000   DN

An early 18thC Brussels tapestry, woven with classical figures representing Juno seated on a dias, beneath a tasseled canopy, with peacocks, hounds and child attendants, flanked by farming implements and vines, the field with rabbits, parrots, masks and fruit, with two smaller panels of peasants gathering fruit, within a border of comical faces, rabbits, masks, flowers and shells.

This tapestry is related in its design to Berain's Grotesques series at Beauvais.

149.5in (380 cm) wide

$20,000-30,000   DN

▶ A 19thC Brussels tapestry panel, worked with exotic bird and two foxes beside a river in a wooded landscape, the inner border worked with a signature.

100 x 72in (254 x 182cm)

$6,000-8,000   GorL

An early 19thC Continental tapestry, decorated with a landscape with a house and gardens with bears, a river with boats and fishermen, above an encampment, the inner border with Middle Eastern and European figures, with hunting parties and encampments, some stains and rucking.

$40,000-50,000 DN

A pair of 19thC silk chinoiserie curtains, woven with exuberant Oriental scenes depicting figures and birds in exotic landscapes, lined and interlined with fixed gathered headings.

132in (335.3cm) high

$1,000-1,200 SCT

A late 19thC embroidered Turkish mosque pelmet, the satin ground embroidered in couched metal threads, applied with calligraphic cartouches, lined with glazed saffron cotton and edged with metal lace trimming.

A cartouche is an inscription panel on a carpet. It usual refers to the person who commissioned it, the maker, or the date of production.

82 x 21in (208 x 53cm)

$300-450 SCT

A late 19thC Turkish mosque hanging, the ivory cotton ground densely embroidered in couched metal and polychrome silk threads, depicting a hanging basket within columned mirhab arch, the border with calligraphic inscriptions.

70 x 50.5in (178 x 128cm)

$150-300 SCT

An 18thC-style silk wall hanging, brocaded in colored silks with naturalistic large-scale flowers and feathers, against a self-colored spriged and zig-zagged ground.

c1860   89.75in (228cm)

$500-600 SCT

An early 20thC Continental needlework panel, depicting a landscape with Cavaliers and a stagecoach.

46 x 61in (117 x 155cm)

$600-750 SI

A late 19th/early 20thC Continental tapestry, depicting a maiden and a knight on horseback.

80 x 63in (203 x 160cm)

$1,000-1,200 SL

A 20thC French tapestry panel, depicting garden flowers.

62 x 51in (157 x 129.5cm)

$800-1,000 SI

LACE

A group of French Chantilly lace, comprising a scalloped edge triagular shawl, a skirt flounce, a silk scalloped edge shawl, six different trims and a headpiece, all finely worked with flowers and scrolling foliage.

c1845　　　　　　　　　　　　largest 100in (254cm) long

$600-800 (10 pieces)　　　　　　　　　　　　**SI**

A net on net Brussels lace shawl.
c1860-70　　　　　　　　79.5in (202cm)

$300-500　　　　　　　　　　**SCT**

TOILE AND OTHER FABRICS

A late 19thC stole of black blonde machine-woven lace, with large flowers to field and scalloped leaf border.

104 x 33.5in (264 x 85cm)

$40-60　　　**SCT**

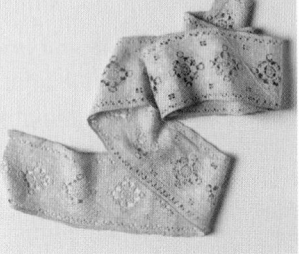

A length of early 20thC reticella-style cutwork.

96 x 4.25in (244 x 11cm)

$40-70　　　**SCT**

A length of 18thC crimson silk damask, woven with large scale stylized fruiting flowerheads sprouting from stylized foliage, with flourishes and pairs of pomegranates.

108 x 21in (274 x 53cm)

$300-400　　　**SCT**

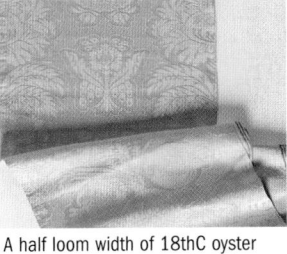

A half loom width of 18thC oyster silk damask, woven with flowering sprigs and fruiting flowerheads against a self colored striped ground.

99.5 x 10.5in (253 x 26.5cm)

$70-120　　　**SCT**

A late 18thC square panel of toile, printed with scenes of the naval battle of Gibraltar of 1782, showing the victory of Captain Elliot and his garrison.

29.25 x 30in (74 x 76cm)

$300-400　　　**SCT**

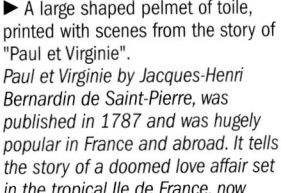

A quilted panel of toile, printed with pattern entitled L'Art d'Aimer, depicting idyllic country scenes with classical ruins, fishing boats, courting couples.
Manufactured by Petitpierre Freres who had factories at Nantes and Bourdeaux. Attribution varies between the factories.

36.25 x 42.5in (92 x 108cm)

$150-250　　　**SCT**

▶ A large shaped pelmet of toile, printed with scenes from the story of "Paul et Virginie".
Paul et Virginie by Jacques-Henri Bernardin de Saint-Pierre, was published in 1787 and was hugely popular in France and abroad. It tells the story of a doomed love affair set in the tropical Ile de France, now Mauritius.

Toile *is cotton cloth with a single-color design printed onto it. In 1759, Christophe-Phillipe Oberkampf, a French textiles designer, set up his factory in Jouy-en-Josas, near Versailles. Here he produced some of the best-known toiles called "toiles de jouy" using engraved copper plates and Indian cotton.*

c1804 84in x 26.75in (213 x 68cm)

$300-500　　　**SCT**

◀ A mid-19thC panel of toile, printed with country scenes of animals and children playing, with watermill and boat, with the inscription "Fque d'A HENRY a Rouen".

49.25 x 28.5in (125 x 72cm)

$120-180	SCT

▶ A late 19th/early 20thC joined coverlet, of crimson silk damask in 18thC style, woven with large scale fruiting flowerheads and stylized foliage, with flourishes and pairs of pomegrantes, trimmed with self-coloured silk fringe.

83 x 95in (211 x 241cm)

$450-550	SCT

RUGS AND CARPETS

Tʜᴇ ᴛᴇʀᴍ Oʀɪᴇɴᴛᴀʟ ʀᴜɢ ᴜꜱᴜᴀʟʟʏ ʀᴇꜰᴇʀꜱ ᴛᴏ ʜᴀɴᴅ-ᴋɴᴏᴛᴛᴇᴅ ʀᴜɢꜱ ᴍᴀᴅᴇ ɪɴ ᴛʜᴇ Eᴀꜱᴛ. As they are hand-made they are considered to be unique works of art that appreciate in value like any other.

The main areas of production are Turkey, Persia, the Caucasus and Turkestan, and to a lesser degree Afghanistan, Pakistan, Nepal, India and China.

Flatweaves, such as kilims, are made up of warp threads, which are stretched vertically on a loom; weft threads are then woven through them horizontally to create a design. There is no pile and these carpets are often made in panels that are sewn together.

Pile weaves are made by stretching the warp threads on a loom, weaving through a weft thread and knotting the pile threads to it. Once a row of knots is complete the next weft thread is woven through and another row of pile added. When the rows are complete, the pile is clipped. A good quality rug will have densely packed, tight knots (up to 500-1,000 knots per sq in or 2.5cm)

which create a clear image that will be closely clipped.

The design of a carpet can often be used to work out when and where it was made as each region can be characterized by its own unique patterns and designs.

The rugs market fluctuates like any other. At the moment good quality rugs are doing extremely well, while more mediocre examples are struggling, although they are selling. The modern trend for geometric shapes and forms has meant that tribal rug and carpets are appealing to a younger market as the bold colors and strong lines are perfectly suited to contemporary décor. Persian Ziegler rugs and Indian Agra carpets are also doing well. It is worth noting that modern Persian rugs, made in present-day Iran, are well priced. In general antique rugs in good condition will command good prices, particularly if they come from an area respected for its quality of manufacture and design. A high knot count is also a determining factor.

PERSIAN

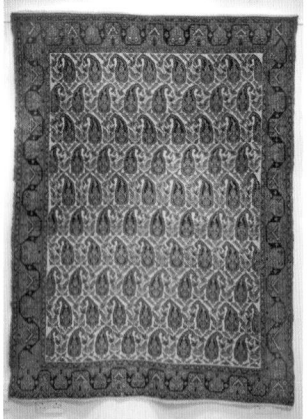

A southern Persian Afshar rug.
c1900
80.75 x 60in (205 x 152cm)

$1,200-1,500	GH

A late 19thC south Persian Afshar rug.
65 x 53in (165 x 134.5cm)

$3,000-3,500	SI

A Bidjar rug, from north-west Persia.
c1860
87.75 x 49.25in (223 x 125cm)

$5,000-6,000	GH

A Bidjar rug.
c1890
86.75 x 56.25in (220 x 143cm)

$11,000-13,000	GH

► A Bidjar carpet.

It is rare to find a carpet of this size from this region.

160 x 106in (406 x 269cm)

$10,000-12,000   SI

A Bidjar rug.
c1920   80 x 54in (203 x 137cm)

$4,000-5,000   SI

A northwest Persian Bidjar rug.
c1925

132 x 93in (335.5 x 236cm)

$4,500-5,500   SI

◄ A Bakhtiari rug, from south Persia.

The western Iranian Bakhtiari tribe is known for rugs designed as compartments filled with brightly colored garden motifs. Bakhtiari village rugs have single cotton weft threads; Bakhtiari nomadic rugs have double wool weft threads. Other Bakhtiari rug designs include bold central medallions and vertical stripes filled with small botehs.

78 x 50in (198 x 124cm)

$1,500-2,000   GH

A Bidjar rug.

c1945   84 x 58in (213 x 147cm)

$1,000-1,400   SI

A Bakhtiari rug.
c1910

84 x 64.25in (213 x 163cm)

$5,000-6,000   GH

A Persian Bakhtiari rug.
c1900   124.5 x 75.25in (316 x 191cm)

$4,500-5,000   GH

► A Ghashghai kilim.

104.25 x 64.5in (265 x 164cm)

$1,500-2,000   GY

A Ghashghai rug, from south-west Persia.
c1880

102 x 65.75in (259 x 167cm)

$8,500-9,500   GH

A Ghashghai rug.

81in x 47in (150 x 114cm)

$2,200-2,800   SI

Persian

A Ghashghai rug.
55 x 40in (140 x 102cm)

$750-850 **GY**

A magnificent Ghashghai audience or triclinium carpet, from Fars province, profusely decorated with stylized animals and flowerheads, the main red field with three hooked medallions and spandrels in blue and cream, flanked by panelled borders (kenareh) each with ten hooked blue medallions, and multiple guard bands, similar top panel (kellei) with three hooked medallions and spandrels.

Provenance: Iona Abbey, Argyll, Scotland

A spandrel is a motif placed in the corner of a rug within the border. In a central medallion design the spandrels at the four corners of the rug depict a quarter of the medallion.

505 x 360cm

$9,000-11,000 **L&T**

A section of a Heriz rug, from north-west Persia
c1890
154.75 x 11.25in (393 x 280cm)

$18,000-22,000 **GH**

A Heriz carpet.
c1890
140 x 106.25in (356 x 270cm)

$6,000-7,000 **GY**

A Heriz carpet.
c1890
145.75 x 115.75in (370 x 294cm)

$16,000-18,000 **GY**

A Heriz carpet.
c1910
125 x 96.5in (318 x 245cm)

$6,000-7,000 **GY**

A Heriz rug.
c1920
150 x 108in (381 x 274cm)

$7,500-9,500 **GH**

A Persian silk Kashan rug.
c1920
72.75 x 51in (185 x 130cm)

$10,000-13,000 **GY**

A Heriz carpet.
c1920 106 x 77in (267 x 195.5cm)

$5,000-6,000 **SI**

◀ A Heriz carpet.

c1920
177 x 114in (449.5 x 289.5cm)

$7,000-8,000 **SI**

A pair of Persian Kashan rugs.
c1930 83.5 x 51in (212 x 130cm)

$6,000-7,000 (pair) **GY**

A silk Kashan carpet, from central Persia.

Kashan is an important center for carpet production in Iran. In the 16thC and 17thC it produced magnificent court carpets. Production then declined until the late 19thC and early 20thC when imported Australian wool, spun in Manchester, England, was used in carpet manufacture. These "Manchester Kashans" had a glossy sheen and frequently featured floral designs on a red background. Contemporary Kashans have about 200 knots per sq in (2.5cm). Their primary designs include a diamond-shaped medallion with pendants at the top and bottom.

c1890   144 x 99in (366 x 251.5cm)

$30,000-40,000   SI

A Kashan rug.

Kashan as an area is famous for its brightly colored carpets. The town and city rugs are generally finely woven in either fine wool or silk; tribal designs are mainly wool on wool. City designs are mainly curvilinear and typically floral. Village rugs are woven from memory and, as such, are unique. Any tribal rug from before 1900 is highly valuable.

c1920   60 x 41in (152.5 x 104cm)

$3,000-4,000   SI

A pair of Kashan rugs.
c1940   88 x 48 (213.5 x 122cm)

$6,000-8,000   SI

A Kerman rug.

The city of Kerman is situated in southeast Iran. Kerman rugs were produced from the 16th century, although the major period of production began in the 1890s when there was demand from the American market. Kerman rugs usually have a high knot count of around 150-400 per square inch. Floral motifs, prayer formats, central medallions, panels and pictorial designs are all typically featured in Kerman rugs.

A late 19thC Kermanshah carpet.
221 x 141in (561 x 358cm)

$2,000-2,800   SI

c1900   57 x 30in (145 x 76cm)

$1,800-2,400   GH

An Indo-Kerman carpet.
c1900 178 x 154in (452 x 391cm)

$7,500-8,500   SI

An Indo-Kerman carpet.
c1920 211 x 130in (536 x 330cm)

$3,000-4,000   SI

Persian

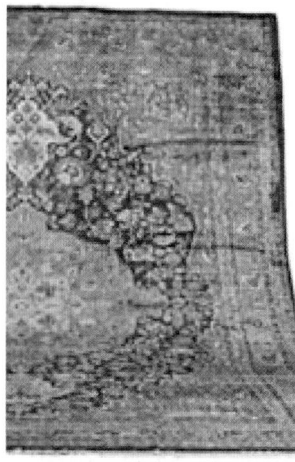

A Kerman carpet.
c1925
217 x 142in (551 x 360.5cm)

$3,500-4,000 SI

A northeast Persian Quchan Kurd carpet.

Quchan *is a city in north-eastern Iran which is inhabited by Kurds.*
c1900 61x 63in (302.5 x 160cm)

$1,500-2,000 SI

A section of a Mahal carpet.
c1900
143.75 x 107.75in (365 x 274cm)

$7,000-8,000 GY

A Kurdish runner.
c1880
122 x 40.5in (310 x 103cm)

$3,000-4,000 GH

A Kurdish long rug.
c1890
123.25 x 58.75in (313 x 149cm)

$4,500-5,500 GH

A Kurdish runner.
c1890
127.25 x 36in (323 x 91cm)

$3,500-4,000 GH

A Persian Mahal rug.
c1920
85.5 x 127.25in (217 x 323cm)

$4,500-5,500 GH

A Kurdish rug.
c1890 85 x 45in (216 x 114cm)

$3,000-4,000 GH

A red Mahal rug.

Mahal *carpets originate in the Arak region of Iran. The name Mahal is also given to rugs from this area which have a medium weave and knot count. The value of Mahal rugs has recently increased due to increased interest among interior designers for the all over patterns and soft colors.*
c1890
82.75 x 56in (210x142cm)

$3,000-4,000 GH

Persian

A Malayer rug, from west Persia.
c1910 80.5 x 52in (204 x 132cm)

$2,200-2,800   **GH**

A Malayer rug.
c1910   92 x 55in (234 x 140cm)

$2,800-3,400   **GY**

A Malayer rug.
c1910 76.5 x 50in (194 x 126cm)

$2,000-2,500   **GY**

A Malayer carpet.
c1920 206 x 169in (523 x 429.5cm)

$7,500-8,500   **SI**

A Persian Qum rug.

Qum is a city in north-west central Iran which is famous for very finely knotted rugs. Production began in the 1930s and designs include floral medallions, trees of life and botehs. Many silk rugs were woven here, and have an average knot count of over 300 knots per sq in (2.5cm).
c1930   78.5 x 54.5in (199 x 138cm)

$3,000-3,500   **GH**

A silk Qum.
     70.75 x 48in (180 x 122cm)

$3,000-4,000   **GY**

A Sarouk rug.
c1890
   72.75 x 48in (185 x 122cm)

$5,000-6,000   **GY**

A Sarouk carpet.
c1900 122 x 87in (310 x 220cm)

$7,500-8,500   **GY**

A Sarouk rug.
c1920 31.5 x 23.75in (80 x 60cm)

$1,000-1,400   **GH**

A Sarouk rug.
c1920 28.5 x 24.5in (72 x 62cm)

$1,200-1,500   **GH**

A Sarouk carpet.

c1920 142 x 104in (360.5 x 264cm)

$5,000-6,000 SI

A Sarouk rug.

c1920 57 x 36in (145 x 91.5 cm)

$1200-1,600 SI

A Sarouk rug.

c1925 79 x 50in (201 x 127cm)

$2,000-3,000 SI

A Sarouk rug, central Persia.

c1935 72 x 51in (195.5 x 129.5cm)

$1,200-1,600 SI

A Sarouk carpet.

c1945 249 x 187in (632 x 475cm)

$8,000-10,000 SI

A Sarouk carpet.

Sarouk *is located in western central Iran. It is well known for it floral rugs produced for the USA market in the 1920s-30s. These typically used a central medallion design until WWI when detached floral sprays on a burgundy or dark pink ground became popular.*

c1945 289 x 185in (734 x 470cm)

$14,000-18,000 SI

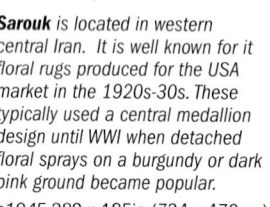

A mid-20thC Sarouk carpet.

279 x 141in (708.5 x 141cm)

$6,000-8,000 SI

A Fereghan rug.

c1890 50 x 77.5in (127 x 197cm)

$4,000-5,000 GH

A late 19thC Fereghan Sarouk carpet.

124 x 85in (315 x 216cm)

$12,000-18,000 SI

A Senneh rug.

Senneh *is a Kurdish city in northwest Iran. It produced very fine rugs and kilims.*

c1890 82 x 53.25in (208 x 135cm)

$5,000-6,000 GH

A Fereghan rug.

c1900 78 x 52in (198 x 132cm)

$1,500-2,000 SI

A Fereghan carpet, with repeating herati and off-centre serrated ivory medallions and corresponding spandrels, within flowerhead border and matched guard bands.

252.75 x 144in (642 x 366cm)

$9,000-11,000 L&T

Persian

A Kurdistan Senneh rug.

c1890   72 x 52in (183 x 132cm)

| **$6,500-7,500** | **GY** |

A late 19thC Serapi carpet, from north-west Persia.

152 x 115in (386 x 292cm)

| **$4,000-5,000** | **SI** |

A late 19thC Serapi carpet

164 x 138in (493 x 350.5cm)

| **$10,000-12,000** | **SI** |

A late 19thC Serapi carpet.

A Serapi is a good quality Heriz carpet that is over 100 years old.

168 x 135in (426.5 x 343cm)

| **$12,000-15,000** | **SI** |

A late 19thC Serapi carpet.

136 x 121in (345.5 x 307.5cm)

| **$15,000-20,000** | **SI** |

A cream Tabriz rug, from north-west Persia.

c1890 78 x 55.25in (198 x 140cm)

| **$6,000-7,000** | **GH** |

A Tabriz carpet.

c1920 225 x 154in (571.5 x 391cm)

| **$15,000-20,000** | **SI** |

A Tabriz rug.

Tabriz *is a city in north-western Iran which has a major weaving tradition dating to the 15th C when its weavers introduced curvilinear designs to the Istanbul Court. Later, in the mid-19thC it established its position as the center for the export of Persian rugs to the West. However, Tabriz weavers have a reputation for copying designs traditional to other areas of Iran, and so the best way to establish the true origin of a Tabriz is to examine its structure. Genuine Tabrizes have double cotton weft threads, cotton warp threads and use Turkish knots. The warp and weft threads are usually not dyed but can be pale blue or light gray. Designs include medallions, hunting patterns, prayer and pictorial rugs. Some superb silk Tabrizes were woven during the late 19th century.*

c1920   170 x 122in (432 x 310cm)

| **$11,000-13,000** | **GH** |

A Tabriz carpet.

c1940 141 x 100in (358 x 254cm)

$4,000-5,000 SI

A Tabriz carpet.

c1945 199 x 144in (505.5 x 366cm)

$9,000-11,000 SI

A northwest Persian Bakshayish rug.

c1880
78.75in x 55in (200 x 140cm)

$5,000-6,000 GY

A Karaja rug.

Karaja *is a town located in the Iranian province of Azerbaijan, close to Heriz. Many runners are woven in this area and they feature a distinctive hooked hexagon medallion.*

c1900
72.5 x 53.25in (184 x 135cm)

$4,500-5,500 GH

A Luri rug, from south-west Persia.

c1900 98 x 44in (249 x 112cm)

$2,000-3,000 SI

A Serab runner, from north-west Persia.

Serab *is a town in northwest and is best known for its runners. Typical designs include repeating diamonds or hexagons on a camel or ivory field.*

c1900
198 x 40in (503 x 101.5cm)

$5,000-6,000 SI

RUGS AND CARPETS

- The earliest Persian carpets can be dated to the second half of the 1stC AD but the most significant period of production was from the 16thC to first half of the 18thC. Carpets from this period are known for harmonious colors and original designs.

- Turkey has been producing carpets for almost as long as Persia, whose carpets have a history of more than 2,500 years. Standard motifs are geometric patterns and animal figures.

- The Prophet Mohammed forbade the representation of animals and humans in art and so Islamic countries such as Persia and India mainly use floral motifs.

- Caucasian and Turkoman carpets typically have geometric designs. Stylized floral patterns are used occasionally.

- Both floral and geometric designs are seen in Turkish rugs, but flowers are more common.

- Chinese carpets feature cranes, bats, peonies, lotus blossoms, dragons and other mythical creatures.

- Prayer rugs can be identified by the arched mihrab (prayer niche) in the centre of the design. This should point towards Mecca when in use. Turkish prayer rugs have densely worked

CAUCASIAN

A Sultanabad rug.

c1890
122 x 61in (310 x 155cm)

$4,500-5,500 GH

▶ A late 19thC Dagestan prayer rug, from the north-east Caucasus.

56 x 41in (142cm x 104cm)

$3,000-4,000 SI

Caucasian

A late19thC northeast Dagestan prayer rug.

71 x 42in (180 x 106.5cm)

$4,500-5,000   **SI**

A late 19thC northeast Dagestan prayer rug.

56 x 49in (142 x 124.5cm)

$2,000-3,000   **SI**

A Karabagh rug, from Armenia.

Karabagh *is an area in the Caucasus known for its large format rugs which feature varied designs including the Cloudband Kazak and Eagle Kazak. Symmetrical knots are generally used and with knot counts of approximately 65 per square inch (2.5cm). The foundation is typically wool.*

1904   100 x 54in (254 x 137cm)

$6,000-7,000   **GH**

A Kazak rug.

c1880 93 x 53.5in (236 x 136cm)

$2,000-3,000   **GH**

An early 20thC Karabagh rug.

85 x 55in (215 x 140cm)

$3,000-4,000   **GY**

A Kazak rug.

c1880   72 x 51in (183 x 130cm)

$4,000-5,000   **GY**

A Kazak rug.

c1880

108.25 x 47.25in (275 x 120cm)

$9,000-11,000   **GY**

A Kazak long rug.

c1885

104 x 41.75in (264 x 106cm)

$3,000-4,000   **GY**

A late 19thC Sewan Kazak carpet.

Sewan Kazak rugs usually have large cross-shaped medallions.

86 x 67in (218.5cm x 170cm)

$4,500-5,500   **SI**

A late19thC Kazak rug.

109 x 58in (277 x 150cm)

$3,000-4,000   **SI**

A late 19thC Kazak rug, from south-west Caucasus

96 x 58in (244 x 147.5cm)

$4,000-5,000   **SI**

Caucasian

A Lori Pambak Kazak rug, inscribed.

c1890   101 x 72in (256.5 x 188cm)

$7,500-8,500   SI

A late 19thC Borjalou Kazak rug.

85 x 46in (216 x 117cm)

$3,000-4,000   SI

A late 19thC southwest Caucasian Kazak rug.

69 x 45in (175.5 x 114.5cm)

$6,000-7,000   SI

A Kazak rug.

c1900

72.75 x 48in (185 x 145cm)

$4,500-5,500   GY

A Kazak rug.

c1910 92 x 74in (233.5 x 188cm)

$4,000-4,500   SI

A Karachopt Kazak rug.

61 x 38 in (155 x 96.5cm)

$1,500-2,000   SI

A late 19thC Karachopt Kazak rug.

79 x 56in (200.5 x 142cm)

$2,200-2,800   SI

▶ A tchichi rug.

A **tchichi** is a Caucasian kuba rug design consisting of a border decorated with diagonal bars alternating with large geometric rosettes. Most tchichi rugs are an average area of 25 ft square

c1880   71 x 49in (180 x 125cm)

$6,000-7,000   GY

A Kuba rug, from east Caucasus.

Kuba is a city in the Caucasus. Kuba rugs are typically of small format and finely woven.

c1890   56 x 47in (142 x 120cm)

$7,000-8,000   GH

A late 19thC Alpan Kuba rug.

62 x 42in (157.5 x 106.5cm)

$3,000-4,000   SI

Caucasian

A Kuba rug.

c1900   77 x 50in (195.5 x 127cm)

$1,200-1,500   **SI**

A Shirvan rug, from east Caucasus.

c1890   79.5 x 56.5in (202 x 143cm)

$4,500-5,500   **GH**

A late 19thC Shirvan rug.

Shirvan *is an important central eastern Caucasian region known for its fine rugs. They average 28 sq ft (853cm) in size and designs include prayer rugs, geometric medallions and animal motifs.*

85 x 69in (216 x 175.5cm)

$9,000-11,000   **SI**

A Shirvan rug.

c1900   75 x 51in (190 x 130cm)

$4,500-5,500   **GY**

A Soumak rug, from east Caucacus.

c1880   107.75 x 88.5in (274 x 225cm)

$6,000-8,000   **GY**

A Caucasian rug, the pale blue paneled field with three hooked medallions and reciprocating borders.

*A **medallion** is a motif usually featured in the centre of the carpet. Designs can be diamonds, circles, stars, octagons, ovals and hexagons.*

81.5 x 41.25in (207 x 105cm)

A very rare Bessarabian Kilim rug, from Moldavia.

Bessarabian kilims come from an area of Romania which is now part of the Ukraine. They typically feature a more formalized floral pattern than is seen in kilims from other parts of southeast Europe.

c1900   139.75 x 39.5in (355 x 100cm)

A Soumak carpet.

101 x 70in (256.5 x 178cm)

$3,000-4,000   **SI**   **$1,000-1,400**   **L&T**   **$7,500-8,500**   **GH**

A Caucasian rug.

c1880

63 x 47.25in (160 x 120cm)

$4,000-4,500 GY

A section of a Caucasian kilim.

Kilim rugs *have no pile, but the design is created by the weft strands.*

c1910 2.75 x 77in (388 x 196cm)

$3,500-4,500 GY

A Caucasian seichur rug.

c1900 69 x 48in (175 x 122cm)

$4,500-5,500 GY

TURKISH

A Yomud Turkoman Okbash, west Turkestan.

Turkestan is a large area of Central Asia. Eastern Turkestan includes the southwestern part of Xinjiang province in western China. Rugs from this region are sometimes referred to as Samarkand. They commonly measure 48 x 96in (122 x 244cm) and popular designs include medallions, pots with flowers and all over geometrics.

Western Turkestan comprises the former Soviet Republics of Tajikistan, Uzbekistan, Kirghizia, Kazakhstan and Turkmenistan. Main weavers in this area are the Turkoman tribes, Khazakhs and Uzbecks. The Yomud are one of the main Turkoman tribes and are known for weaving the most colorful Turkoman tribal rugs. Early Yomud rugs feature guls in vertical columns, while later pieces have them in offset rows. Rugs frequently have ivory borders.

c1900 21 x 24in (53 x 61cm)

$900-1,100 SI

A Turkestan Tekke rug.

c1910 46 x 42.5in (117 x 108cm)

$1,500-2,000 GH

▶ A Tekke Turkoman carpet, from west Turkestan.

c1900 134 x 96 (340.5 x 244cm)

$2,000-2,500 SI

A fine Tekke rug, with rare ivory field.

c1910 59 x 43.25in (150 x 110cm)

$2,000-2,500 GY

European

A 19thC European needlework rug, worked in colored wools with a central diaper flowerhead, with an all over design of scrolling flowers, an outer border of diaper panels and leaves.

Provenance: From the collection of the late The Hon Mrs Daisy Fellowes, Donnington Grove, Berkshire.

133.75in (340cm) wide

$70,000-90,000 **DN**

A late 19thC Aubusson carpet.

126 x 101in (320 x 256.5cm)

$6,000-8,000 **SI**

An early 20thC Bulgarian Sofia pictorial carpet, inscribed That Government of the People, by the People, For the People, Shall Not Perish From the Earth, also inscribed P.P. MOROZOFF and MADE BY B.A. PERSIYSKI. SOFIA.

183 x 122in (465 x 310cm)

$15,000-20,000 **SI**

A Portuguese needlepoint rug.
c1920 72 x 39.5in (183 x 100cm)

$1,200-1,400 **GH**

A 1920s French needlepoint rug.
80 x 78in (203 x 198cm)

$2,000-2,500 **GH**

A Donegal carpet, the green field with Ushak style lattice of flowerheads and corresponding border.

147.25 x 142.5in (374 x 362cm)

$4,000-4,500 **L&T**

A Savonnerie rug.
c1930 59 x 82.75in (150 x 210cm)

$3,000-4,000 **GH**

An 18thC-style hand-woven wool tapestry.

74.5 x 88.5in (189 x 225cm)

$3,000-4,000 **GY**

Samplers

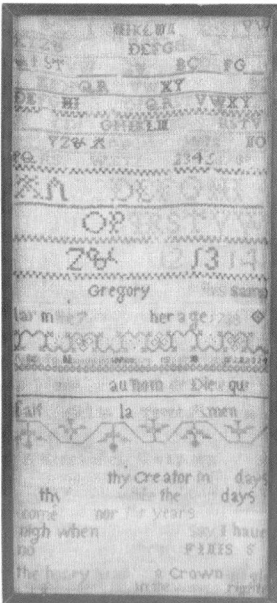

A George II long linen sampler, worked in colored silks, with alphabets and numerals above a stylized floral band and a religious text in French and English, dated.

1738 17.25 x 7.75in (44 x 20cm)

$450-550 **DN**

A George III embroidered picture, worked in colored wools and silks in long and short stitch, depicting a posy of carnations, tulips, rosebuds and other flowers.

14.25 x 11.75in (35 x 30cm)

$600-700 **DN**

A George III silk picture, worked in chenille and colored silks with long and short stitch and knots, depicting a cornucopia filled with flowers, the reverse bearing label of Mr Cove, Hornchurch, in a composition frame.

15.75 x 13.25in (40 x 34cm)

$500-600 **DN**

An American needlework sampler, from New England, worked in silk threads on a linen ground, with rows of the alphabet, flowers, baskets of fruit and the inscription Nancy Sanderson her sampler at 10 years January 21 1793, within a three-sided saw-tooth border and wide outer border of stylized floral motifs.

1793 14 x 21.25in (35.5 x 54cm)

$7,000-10,000 **SI**

◀ A George III linen sampler, by Jane Woodward, worked in crosstitch with three alphabets above stylized fruiting trees and a verse... The Rose, lovely blushing prickly rose..., within a stylized meandering floral border, dated.

1797 17 x 13in (43 x 33cm)

$400-500 **DN**

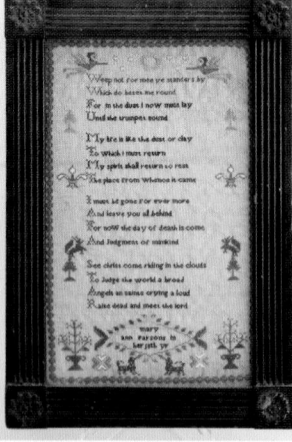

An early 19thC sampler, worked by Ann Parsons in her 10th year, with a verse surrounded by angels, trees, flowers and animals, in contemporary reeded ebonized frame.

11.5 x 7.25in (29 x 18cm)

$450-550 **LFA**

An American needlework picture, entitled Adelaide, worked in chenille yarns, silk thread and watercolor on a silk ground, depicting a shepherdess sitting under a tree with a cottage and hills beyond, with an eglomise mat and gilded frame, inscription at back reads embroidered Henrietta Maria Ghengenise at Mrs. Rivardi's Academy, Philadelphia, PA.

26.5in (10.5cm) high. 1803

$4,500-5,500 **SI**

A pair of early 19thC wool and appliqué embroidered pictures, each worked in colored silks embellished with gilt metal thread, depicting lilies, passion flowers and other flowers, in faux-rosewood frames.

11 x 8.75in (28 x 22cm)

$700-800 **DN**

Samplers

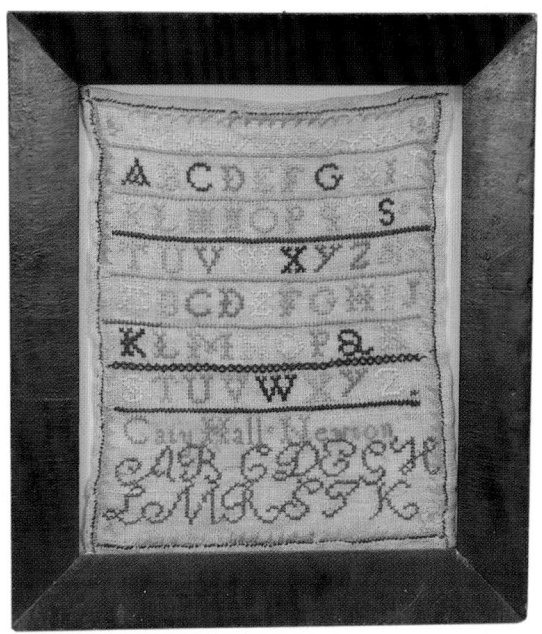

An early 19thC American needlework sampler, by Caty Hall of Newton, New England, worked in silk threads on a linen ground, with rows of alphabet within a saw-tooth border, framed.

9.5in (24cm) high

$700-800   **SI**

An American needlework sampler, worked in silk thread on a wool ground, the central band depicting Adam and Eve with the Tree of Life, a pious verse enclosed by bands of spot motifs and a house flanked by vases of flowers, signed Elizabeth William, aged 13, and dated.

1834   17in (43cm) high

$1,500-2,000   **SI**

An American needlework sampler, worked in wool threads on a linen ground, with bands of alphabets and numerals, signed Ellen S. Karsner/Work 13, dated.

1846   11.25in (28.5cm) high

$450-550   **SI**

A sampler, worked in wool and silk thread on linen, signed Eliza Mitchell, age 10.

1846   23in (58.5cm) wide

$6,000-7,000   **MF&D**

A 19thC American silk needlework picture, worked in silk threads and watercolor on a silk ground , depicting a couple with picnic under a tree, sheep, hills and a country home beyond framed, some spilts, losses.

21in x 25.5in

$6,500-7,500   **SI**

A fine needlework sampler, by Hette Evens, well-worked in shades of green, red, pink, black, ocher silk thread on linen with a strawberry border surrounding a rectangle with a central section of Biblical verse, (Ecclesiastes 12:1) flanked by mirror images of fruit trees with small dogs beneath and signed "Hette Evens her work aged ten years 1798," framed.

Provenance: *By descent from Hette Evens (Morris), mother of Catherinie Evens Morris, daughter-in-law of Governor Morris, to the present generation, Philadelphia, dated.*

1798   15in (38cm) wide

$7,500-8,500   **FRE**

◄ A Victorian canvas needlework picture, by Anne Williams, worked in colored wools, depicting a young girl seated with a dog beside a kennel, within a stylized floral border, dated indistinctly, possibly 1873, framed with an elaborate gilt slip.

20 x 22.5in (51 x 57cm)

$600-700   **DN**

► A fine needlework sampler, by Josephine Lippincott, worked in green, blue, beige, yellow, and black thread on linen, with a geometric floral vine border surrounding an open field with two sections of verse amidst assorted flowers and birds and inscribed "Josephine Lippincott her sampler, rought in the 11th year of her age, 1830" above a stately classical building, framed, some staining.

1830   18.5in (47cm) high

$10,000-11,000   **FRE**

DOLLS ARE UNIVERSALLY POPULAR AND HAVE APPEALED TO BOTH PRIMITIVE AND MODERN CIVILISATIONS. They are a tangible reflection of the culture or period in which they were made and provide a historical record of changing fashions and perceptions of beauty.

Toys and games have always been desirable to collectors as they possess a certain nostalgic value and charm. As well as reflecting the social and technical developments of the day. They chart the change from handmade toys to mass-produced ones and show how wood, paper and lead began to be replaced by steel, tinplate and plastic.

At present the toy market is relatively stable with teddy bears and Hornby and Basset-Lowke trains remaining extremely popular. Plastic toy figures have been selling better than those of lead. However, generally speaking, there has been little fluctuation in the market.

The field of doll collecting has always had a large export market, in particular to Japan. The Japanese have always been big collectors of French dolls and are very specific in their requirements, usually preferring French dolls with blue eyes to English wax and wooden dolls. However the economic decline in Japan has slightly decreased the value of French dolls. English wax and wooden dolls have remained extremely popular with the American and British markets.

When collecting toys or games it is always advisable to buy mint items with their original boxes as these will always hold their value better, or increase in value faster, than the same toy in poorer condition. Also, avoid repainted and restored toys or reproduction boxes as these will seriously detract from the value. Collectors tend to specialize in one area by collecting the key makers or obscure rarities.

When purchasing a doll it is important to note that bisque-head dolls will noticeably deteriorate in value if there is even the tiniest hairline crack or chip. This is because there are so many bisque-head dolls in good condition in circulation. Conversely, wax dolls with crazing will not be so affected as this is an inevitable defect as changes in temperature crack the wax.

DOLLS

An Armand Marseille bisque-head doll, with shoulder length blond hair, sleeping blue eyes, open mouth with teeth and composite jointed body, wearing faded pink velvet bonnet, flower bouquet silk coat with lace trim edging, and pink dress with lace trimming and two leather boots. marked 390 A7M.

Armand Marseille and his son took over a porcelain factory in Thuringia in c1885 and by 1890 had begun to produce bisque-head dolls. Their most prolific period of production was from 1900 to 1930.

23in (57cm) high

$300-400   **HamG**

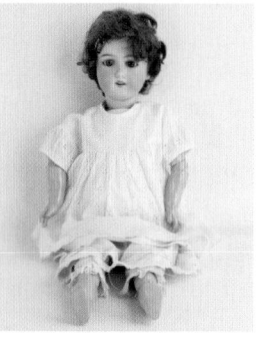

An Armand Marseille bisque-head doll, with sleeping blue eyes and open mouth with teeth, with ball-jointed composition child's body, the head impressed 390 and 7 1-12.

25.5in (65cm) high

$200-300   **DN**

An Armand Marseille black bisque-head baby doll, with sleeping brown eyes and composition body, the head impressed AM Germany 371.-3.K.

12in (30cm) high

$150-200   **DN**

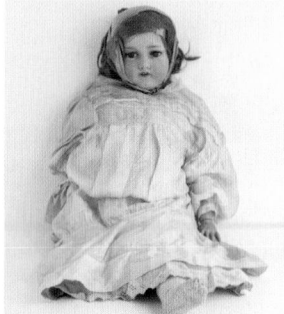

An Armand Marseille bisque-head doll, with sleeping brown eyes and open mouth with teeth, and with ball-jointed composition child's body, the head impressed 390 and 9.

28.5in (69cm) high

$150-200   **DN**

▶ An Armand Marseille painted bisque-head doll, with sleeping blue eyes and open mouth with teeth, wearing a 1930s pink rayon and organza lace trimmed dress, marked A 10 M 996.

20in (51cm) high

$150-200   **DN**

An Armand Marseille bisque-head fairy doll, with composition five-piece body, molded shoes and socks, damage to right leg, all original.

c1910   7in (18cm) high

$70-100   **HB**

Dolls by Named Makers

An Armand Marseille doll, with glass eyes, replacement wig.

So many of these dolls were produced that despite the good quality and condition, this doll does not command as high a price as similar examples.

c1910-15	22in (56cm) high
$300-400	**HB**

A 1920s Armand Marseille doll, with head-on-shoulder plate on a kid body, lower composition limbs, dressed in school uniform.

	19.75in (50cm) high
$450-500	**HB**

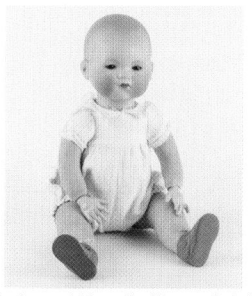

An Armand Marseille "Dream Baby" character doll, with bisque-head, cloth body, and composition hands, the neck is sewn onto the cloth body, perfect condition.

"Dream Babies" *were the most popular dolls produced by the Armand Marseille company and they were mass-produced in a variety of sizes and colors. This doll has a flange head and soft body and is in excellent condition. If the doll has a hairline crack or chip, the value is halved.*

	15in (38cm) high
$450-500	**HB**

A Simon & Halbig bisque-head doll, five-piece jointed composition body, opening and closing eyes, original clothes and box.

Opening and closing eyes are highly desirable in small dolls.

c1880	6.5in (16.5cm) long (box)
$450-500	**HB**

A Simon & Halbig bisque-head girl doll, fully jointed with sleeping eyes, mohair wig and original elaborate clothes.

These elaborately dressed dolls were often made for the French market.

1890-1900	16.5in (42cm) high
$800-900	**HB**

A Simon & Halbig Oriental doll, with open mouth showing teeth, with glass opening and closing eyes.

Simon & Halbig were German manufacturers of dolls from 1869-1930. They specialized in making china and bisque shoulder heads and supplied makers such as Kämmer & Rheinhardt and Jumeau. They also made a large number of ethnic dolls. Their early child dolls had solid domed heads, fixed glass eyes, closed mouths and painted brows and lashes. Later dolls had socket heads, open crown, cardboard pate and an open mouth. Simon & Halbig doll's heads can be identified by marks and the mould numbers.

1900-10	10.25in (26cm) high
$1,000-1,200	**HB**

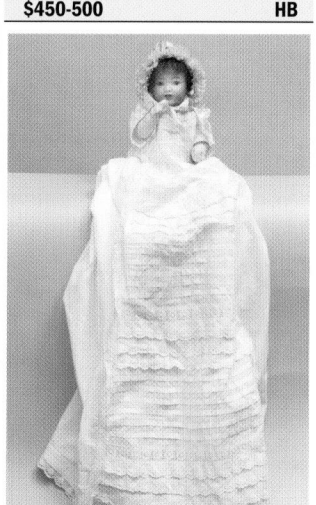

A Simon and Halbig bisque-head doll, with brown hair, character baby face, with brown sleeping eyes, open mouth with teeth and tongue, composite jointed body and limbs, wearing a Victorian lace christening gown and bonnet, marked K star R 126, some color fading and minor damage.

	16.4in (41cm) long
$300-400	**HamG**

▶ A child-size Jumeau doll, with closed mouth, wearing original children's clothes.

c1880	33.5in (85cm) high
$6,000-7,000	**HB**

An early French Jumeau Bebé doll, with closed mouth, blown-glass paperweight eyes, original earrings, honey bee mark, original marked Jumeau shoes and Tête Jumeau stamped in red.

The head size of the doll, in this case size 8, would be marked on the shoe. Many shops scrubbed off the Jumeau label and sold the dolls as their own.

c1880	20in (51cm) high
$3,500-4,500	**HB**

A Simon & Halbig doll, with contemporary dress decorated with pink flowers.

c1915	23.75in (60cm) high
$400-600	**HB**

Dolls by Named Makers

A Jumeau doll, with open mouth and paperweight eyes, dressed in a contemporary sailor suit, hairline crack.

The Jumeau firm was founded by Pierre Francois Jumeau in 1842 at Montreuil-sur-Bois, France, and manufactured dolls until 1899. Jumeau are famous for their bebé doll, or child doll which was recreated in many different forms such as the portrait bebé, and the Jumeau Triste bebé. Other characteristics of the Jumeau doll include a swivel head, applied pierced ears and a closed mouth. They usually have large blue fixed "paperweight" glass eyes. The bodies are typically eight-jointed and made of composition with wooden ball joints and fixed wrists. Jumeau dolls are also noted for their fashionable costumes.

1880-90　　　　　　　19.75in (50cm) high

$900-1,200　　　　　　　　　　　　**HB**

A late Jumeau doll, with open mouth, paperweight eyes, original clothes and paper label stamp.

Jumeau dolls have strong eyebrows which nearly meet in the middle, adding intensity to the eyes. The glass eyes were hand-blown by boys over a bunsen burner; they were often blinded by this work. French dolls had pierced ears so that they could wear earrings.

c1890-1900　　　20.5in (52cm) high

$1,500-2,000　　　　　　　　　**HB**

A Heubach Koppelsdorf bisque-headed baby doll, with blue glass eyes, closed mouth and composite body in contemporary clothing, maker's mark and model number 3502/2.

17in (43cm) high

$200-300　　　　　　　　　　　　**WHP**

A Heubach Koppelsdorf bisque-head doll, with blonde hair, sleeping blue eyes, open mouth with teeth, dimpled chin and composite jointed body, wearing a silk bonnet, silk shawl with lace edging and long silk christening dress also with lace edging, with slight repair work to legs and hands, marked 250-8.

28.4in (71cm) long

$500-600　　　　　　　　**HamG**

A Heubach and Koppelsdorf bisque-head doll, with sleeping brown eyes, open mouth with teeth, and ball-jointed straight limb body.

30in (76cm) high

$150-200　　　　　　　　**DN**

A Montenari poured-wax child doll, with inserted hair, in original clothes.

The Montenari doll makers were Italian immigrants who had made a living making religious figures from wax in their homeland. On their arrival in England in the 1840s they started to make child dolls out of wax to please the commercial market, thus introducing the wax method of doll manufacturing. During Queen Victoria's reign it became fashionable for dolls to be made in the image of her nine children. Therefore these dolls invariably have blue eyes.

c1860　　　22.5in (57cm) high

$700-1,000　　　　　　　　　　　**HB**

▶ A Montenari poured-wax doll, with child's face and blue eyes, clothes are not originals.

c1860　　　21.25in (54cm) high

$700-1,000　　　　　　　　**HB**

▶ A Montenari poured-wax doll, with rooted long hair.

1870-80　　　28.75in (73cm) high

$3,000-4,000　　　　　　　　**HB**

Dolls by Named Makers

A poured-wax doll, possibly a portrait of a real child, unmarked, possibly by Pierotti or Montenari.

During the mid-19thC doll makers were often commissioned to make dolls of real children, perhaps by a wealthy family who wanted a realistic portrait of their child.

c1850-60   29.25in (74cm) high

$1,500-2,000   **HB**

A poured-wax doll, probably by Pierotti, made of unusul honey-colored wax with character face, not in original clothes, but dressed contemporary to the era.

A lot of wax dolls are unmarked.

1860-70   21in (53cm) high

$700-800   **HB**

A Pierotti poured-wax doll, not in original clothes.

Dolls without their original clothes are of less value than those with all the original clothing.

c1860   12in (30cm) high

$600-700   **HB**

A child-size Steiner doll, with closed mouth, impressed mark and hand written "Steiner" mark, dressed in original child's dress.

This doll was the largest that Steiner ever made.

c1870-80   35.5in (90cm) high

$12,000-15,000   **HB**

A 1930s Deans felt doll, in original contemporary clothes.

30in (76cm) high

$450-500   **HB**

▶ A Kammer & Reinhardt character baby, with celluloid head, composition body and flirty glass eyes, no.126.

The Kämmer & Rheinhardt doll company was founded by Ernst Kämmer and Franz Rheinhardt in 1886, in Walterhausen, Germany, where they manufactured dolls until 1940. They were the first company to produce character dolls. These dolls were often named and were available as boys or girls and with either bent-limb bodies or jointed bodies. Those with jointed bodies were the most popular because they were able to stand. They typically have painted eyes, painted, closed mouths and mohair wigs. Kämmer designed the heads until his death in 1901 when Simon & Halbig took over the production using Kämmer's designs.

1920-30   21.25in (54cm) high

$300-400   **HB**

A closed mouth Steiner "A" doll, wearing child's dress.
These later period dolls had softer more realistic expressions than earlier examples.

c1880

$4,500-5,000   **HB**

A lever-eyed Steiner B doll, with open mouth and horse hair wig, in "Figure B" original factory clothes, although an early doll she has a voice box to make her say Mama and Papa with a pull string to operate, stamped Le Petit Parisian Bebé Steiner, with paper label.

Steiner were the innovators of the mechanical doll.

c1880   17in (43cm) high

$6,000-7,000   **HB**

A Kammer & Rheinhardt "Gretchen" character doll, with full-jointed body and painted eyes, series 114.

Kammer & Rheinhardt were innovators of realistic child-dolls. They made a series of dolls numbered 100-126, each representing a portrait of a child.

c1910   9in (23cm) high

$1,500-2,000   **HB**

A 1920s Limoges "Cherie" doll, with jointed elbows and knees, and fixed paperweight eyes.

20in (51cm) high

$600-700   **HB**

A Limoges bisque head doll, dressed as a country gentleman from Brittany, in original clothes.

c1927   18.5in (47cm) high

$600-700   **HB**

Dolls by Unnamed Makers

▲1 A Sonja Henie Doll, with skates and cap with 1939 N.Y. World's Fair button commerating her Gold Medal at the World Championships in Sun Valley. Madam Alexander composition doll with a white velvet skating dress.

$500-600	SI

▲2 A mid 1930s, Shirley Temple Doll, by Ideal Novelty and Toy company.

$250-350	SI

▲3 An Effanbee "Patricia" composition Patsy doll.

$150-200	SI

▲4 A Simon and Halbig Bisque doll, all original (missing crown) brown wig, open mouth, with jointed body, wearing a cotton and lace dress and cameo necklace.

28in (71in) high

$550-650	SI

▲5 An early 20thC, German Bisque head doll, wooden ball joints dressed in handmade clothing, extra shoes and handmade outfits.

$350-450	SI

A early poured-wax "South West highway man" doll.

c1800 16.5in (42cm) high

400-600	HB

A rare Georgian all-wooden doll, with elaborately carved wooden hair with a comb in a plaited bun, the body has a swivel/jointed waist, with painted and jointed arms, in contemporary dress, possibly German.

c1830-40 27.5in (70cm) h

$9,500-10.500	HB

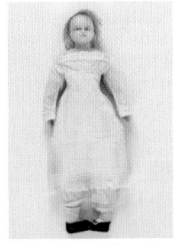

A poured-wax child doll, with turning-in feet.

c1830-40 15in (38cm) h

$700-800	HB

◀ A papier-mâché doll, on kid body with wooden lower arms and legs, dressed as a maid, with molded hair.

c1840-1850 9in (23cm) h

$500-600	HB

A doll, with papier-mâché head, on a kid body with wooden limbs, molded hair and original clothes.

c1840-50 8.75in (22cm) h

$600-700	HB

A rare papier-mâché doll, dressed as a cook in contemporary working clothes, with a kid body and wearing an apron, carrying a whisk, frying pan and cooking pot.

c1840-50 12in (30cm) h

$800-1,000	HB

A wax-over-composition doll, with inset eyes and naïve face, the body is cloth stuffed with horse hair, dressed in original clothes.

1840-50 31.5in (80cm) h

$1,500-2,000	HB

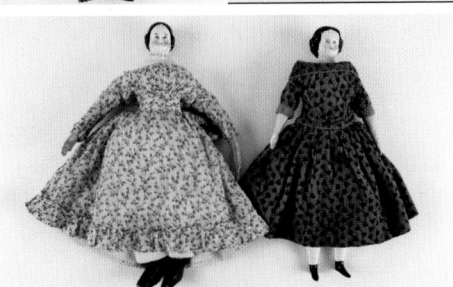

A pair of glazed china dolls, one with glazed limbs, the other with all-kid limbs, the glazed doll is earlier, with original clothes.

c1850-60 11.5in (29cm) high

$400-500 (each)	HB

A wax-over-composition doll, with turning-in feet, dressed in original clothes, very crazed.

c1850 29.5in (75cm) high

$700-800	HB

A wax-over-composition doll, with turned-in feet, leather arms.

1850-60 25.25in (64cm) h

$600-700	HB

PARIAN BISQUE

- Parian bisque is a fine biscuit porcelain that, by the mid-19thC, was often used in doll production.

- Parian dolls have a white, marble-like face, typically with a closed mouth, although an open mouth showing teeth is more desirable.

- The eyes are usually blue and painted; brown or glass eyes are scarce.

- They generally have elaborate hair.

- They often have a kid body.

- Rarely marked.

A Parian-bisque doll, with molded hair, painted eyes, the shoulder-plate head fixed on a kid body, in original clothes.

10.25in (26cm) long	
$200-300	**HB**

A Victorian wax head-and-shoulder plate doll, with composition lower limbs, painted shoes and socks, and filled fabric body, wearing a Victorian painted cotton ribbon and lace trimmed dress.

21.5in (55cm) high	
$300-400	**DN**

A Victorian wax-over-compostion head-and-shoulder plate doll, with blue glass eyes, fabric and straw body, composition limbs and painted shoes and socks, dressed in a Victorian lace-trimmed dress and velvet hat.

18.5in (46cm) high	
$150-200	**DN**

A Victorian wax-over-composition head-and-shoulder plate doll, with blue glass eyes, fabric body and composition lower limbs.

15in (37cm) high	
$100-150	**DN**

A composition baby doll, with cloth body, dressed in contemporary clothes.

c1880   19in (48cm) high

$200-300	**HB**

A wax-over-composition doll, with lower composition arms and legs, clothes are not original, she is dressed in an earlier style (1780-90).

Wax-over-composition dolls are made of card dipped in wax. These dolls are often very crazed as changes in temperature crack the thin layers of wax.

1880   15in (38cm) high

$400-450	**HB**

An early composition doll, with lamb's wool wig and turning-in feet.

c1880 15.5in (39cm) high

$200-300	**HB**

A wax-over-composition doll, with painted boots, wearing an elaborate pearl dress, damage to one foot.

c1890   18.25in (46cm) h

$400-600	**HB**

A late 19thC wax-over-composition head-and-shoulder plate doll, with blue glass eyes and composition lower limbs and fabric body, in pink lace-trimmed cotton clothes.

c1902 16.5in (42cm) high

$200-300	**DN**

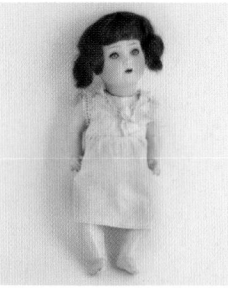

An early 20thC Heubach painted composition head doll, with sleeping eyes and composition body, in original cotton shift.

14in (35cm) high

$150-200	**DN**

A cloth doll, possibly home made, possibly American.

1920-30 17in (44cm) high

$100-150	**HB**

A 1920s ladie's Boudoire doll, smoking a cigarette.

These novelty smoking dolls would have been taken to fashionable parties by ladies as an accessory. They were inspired by the passion of the day for smoking, particularly glamorized in films such as those featuring Marlene Dietrich and Jean Harlow.

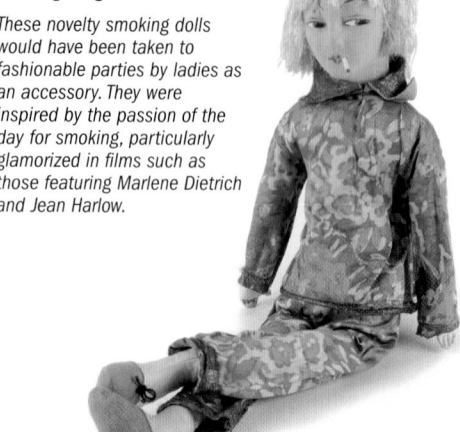

27.5in (70cm) high	
$200-300	**HB**

A pot-head doll, so-called because they are made of pottery.

These dolls are collected for their nostalgic value rather than their quality.

1940-50 20in (50cm) high

$60-80	**HB**

Dolls by Unnamed Makers

A Hancock's bisque-head doll, with blue glass eyes, open mouth with teeth and fabric body with ceramic lower limbs.

18in (46cm) high

$80-120	DN

A German Grodnethal all-jointed wooden doll, in original clothes.

Grodnethal dolls were also known as "tuck-comb" dolls because of the distinctive bun or comb on the top of the head.

c1830   8in (20cm) high

$700-1,000	HB

A German all-jointed small doll, with bisque head and composition body, in box with trousseau of clothes in miniature trunk and miniature ivory powder bowl, with mirror and soap.

c1900   7.5in (19cm) high

$1,000-1,500	HB

A rare German-made Father Christmas character doll.

c1910   11in (28cm) high

$1,000-1,500	HB

A Parisian bisque-head doll, with short blonde wig, sleeping brown eyes, open mouth with teeth and composition jointed body, wearing silk and lace bonnet and christening gown, marked SFBJ "Societe Francaise de Fabrication de Bebes," "60 Paris 6," slight color fading.

23in (59cm) high

$600-700	HamG

A Queen Victoria portrait doll, depicted with open mouth and showing teeth, as if surprised.

This doll was made in the image of Queen Victoria as depicted in a painting of her by Lucy Peck. The painting shows her being woken in the middle of the night by the Archbishop of Canterbury and told that she was to be Queen. The doll has a look of surprise to reflect this moment. These dolls were a special limited edition released after the Queen's coronation.

c1860   31.5in (80cm) high

$20,000-25,000	HB

A pair of Raggedy Anne and Andy dolls, from the famous 1930s children's book.

19.25in (49cm) high

$350-450 (pair)	HB

A rare German five-piece all-bisque character child, with starfish hands, in original Edwardian clothes.

c1920 4.75in (12cm) high

$300-400	HB

An Italian Lenci skier doll, in original clothes.

Lenci were an Italian company who manufactured dolls during the 1920s and 1930s.

9.5in (24cm) high

$300-400	HB

An early 20thC Chinese "Door of Hope" female doll, wearing a navy silk tunic and a black skirt.

11in (28cm) high

$120-180	DN

A Shirley Temple composite doll, open mouthed with six upper teeth, sleeping eyes and applied wig, with original costume by Ideal.

c1935 20.5in (52cm) high

$300-400	WHP

DOLL'S HOUSES

A Georgian white three-storey double-fronted mansion, with pillars supporting balcony over front door, with twin chimney stacks, seven rooms with three staircases, electric lighting, flat roof with pillars and mock gable to front with two small storage drawers under house, minor age wear.

32in (81cm) high

$200-300	W&W

Doll's Houses

A rare 1950s Angel & Sons no. 2 doll's house, with two storys and two rooms, tinplate windows and mock Tudor gable, with garage and three-piece pink and black bathroom suite, fully furnished, central opening front, minor wear.

$200-300   W&W

A 1970s Tri-Ang double-front doll's house, in slot and peg demountable-style with sliding fronts, plastic blue window frames with shutters, red canopy over door, window panes detached but present, all walls white-painted with floral cut-outs to front, lightweight plastic red molded roof, on a green base, minor wear.

24.5in (62cm) wide

$150-200   W&W

A 1960s Mettoy printed tinplate two-storey house, with four rooms and flat roof, electric lighting, nursery, sun terrace, furniture and accessories and eight figures, sun terrace railings missing.

13.5in (34cm) high

$150-200   W&W

A 1960s Tri-Ang doll's house, with two storys, four rooms, hall, stairs and landing, red plastic lightweight detachable roof, tinplate twin sliding front with full height bays, and punched-out windows, with plastic front door frame, door detached, double-fronted and refurbished in white with replacement plant transfers to front walls.

26in (66cm) long

$150-200   W&W

A non-proprietory Veda two story doll's house, two-roomed Tudor stucco front-and-side style house, with single chimney of timber and card construction, internal staircase and low voltage lighting, mounted on textured garden-style baseboard, some restoration required.

20in (51cm) wide

$150-200   W&W

A late Victorian-style town house Rose Cottage, with brick-paper finish to outer walls and gray-paper slate roof, with Regency-style plastic windows and doors, whole front opens to reveal three story kitchen, lounge and bedroom, with internal lighting.

29in (73.5cm) high

$150-200   W&W

◀▲ An early 19thC Federal painted pine house, designed as a flat-roofed red brick two storey building with two pairs of chimney pots at the rear, the symmetrical façade, with central paneled door with a classical architrave and surmounted by a segmental fan-light, flanked on each side by a sliding sash window, with three similar windows above, all on an English basement concealing a drawer, raised on an outset beveled plinth and turned short legs, the hinged facade opening to an interior with a central hall and staircase leading on both doors to a papered room on each side, a fireplace against each rear wall; together with approximately 160 items of miniature furniture, chandeliers, paintings, clocks, hearth accoutrements, china, crockery, candlesticks, pewterware, rugs, two miniature china dolls and other household accessories, many of the items of 19thC date.

42.5 in (108 cm) high

$12,000-15,000   SI

A non-proprietory style Buck House, two storys and four rooms, tinplate windows and door, brick-paper covered external walls, dark-red painted roof with gable extensions over front openings, double-fronted detached, restored.

23.5in (60cm) wide

$200-300	W&W

An early Hirsch doll's house, with one room and single storey, with open-front covered side area, in solid timber and plywood construction, with cream and green-painted window frames, non-opening to front and one side, some wear.

17in (43cm) long

$200-300	W&W

A 1950s-style Mettoy two-storey printed tinplate house, comprising five rooms, with garage to attach to side, minor age wear, chimney missing.

18.5in (47cm) wide

$200-300	W&W

A green and white chalet house, with six rooms and three storys, extended porch with balcony, two staircases, window boxes to ground floor windows, tile-effect roof, electric lighting and double-opening front, minor age wear.

33in (84cm) high

$150-200	W&W

A doll's house doll, with cloth body, china head and original miniature clothes.

c1850-60   3.25in (8cm) h

$60-80	HB

A china doll's house doll, holding original all-bisque baby.

c1850-60 3.75in (9.5cm) h

$100-150	HB

A rare doll's house doll, depicting an Edwardian man-doll chauffeur, with molded hair and moustache.

c1900   7in (18cm) high

$200-300	HB

A doll's house doll, depicting a grandmother, with cloth body, bisque lower limbs and arms.

c1900   6in (15cm) high

$200-300	HB

A doll's house doll, depicting an Edwardian gentleman in evening suit, with molded hands.

1910-1920 5.25in (13cm) h

$150-200	HB

TEDDY BEARS

An early 20thC golden plush teddy bear, with glass eyes, suede pads and paws, and stuffed with wool.

17.5in (44cm) high

$1,000-1,200	DN

A Merrythought bear, with original stud to ear.

c1928   18.4in (46cm) high

$150-200	WHP

A 1930s Chiltern growler teddy bear.

25.5in (64cm) high

$1,300-1,500	OACC

A 1930s Chad Valley teddy bear with button in ear.

20.5in (53cm) high

$1,200-1.500	OACC

A 1940s Steiff terrier, with a button in ear and bell round neck.

3.75in (9cm) high

$50-80　　　　　　**OACC**

A Steiff reindeer.

c1950

$200-250　　　　　　**BCAC**

A 1950s Steiff rabbit.

4.5in (11cm) long

$50-80　　　　　　**OACC**

A 1950s Schuco bear pin.

It is rare to find this bear with the crown and the sash.

3.25in (8cm) high

$150-200　　　　　　**OACC**

DIE-CAST TOYS

A Paddington's Great Aunt Lucy bear, by Gabrielle Designs, in original costume with ticket to rugby match attached.

22.5in (56cm) high

$200-300　　　　　　**WHP**

A rare pre-1940 Dinky Toys De Havilland Albatross Airliner no. 62r G-AEW, complete with gliding hole and metal clip/eye, with box, some damage, minor wear and one propeller blade missing.

4in (10.2cm) long

$200-300　　　　　　**W&W**

A Dinky Guy flat truck with tailboard (513), finished in two tone green, with hook and early version from number plate, in original blue box, slight chipping to paint.

5in (12.7cm) long

$250-300　　　　　　**W&W**

A Dinky Foden regent petrol tanker, in associated box.

7.5in (18cm) long

$100-150　　　　　　**WHP**

A Dinky Bedford End Tipper (410), with box, minor paint chip to body.

4in (10.2cm) long

$200-300　　　　　　**W&W**

Two Dinky Duple Roadmaster coaches (282), with silver detailing, both boxed, minor wear, some pen marking to one box.

4.5in (11.4cm) long

$150-200　　　　　　**W&W**

A Dinky Bedford Heinz van (923), in standard livery, with baked bean can decals to sides, boxed, minor wear.

5.5in (14cm) long

$300-350　　　　　　**W&W**

A Dinky Big Bedford Heinz van (923), in standard livery example, with baked bean can decals, boxed, some wear, minor chipping, retouched.

5.5in (14cm) long

$200-300　　　　　　**W&W**

▶ A mint condition Dinky Big Bedford Heinz van (923), with box.

1955-58　　　5.5in (14cm) long

$1,500-2,000　　　　　　**W&W**

▶ A Dinky Mighty Antar low loader with propeller (986), in red and gray livery, complete with original propeller, boxed with packing, minor marks.

11.75in (30cm) long

$200-300　　　　　　**W&W**

A Dinky Toys Post Office gift set (299), with Royal Mail van, post office telephone, green truck, red telephone booth and two postmen.

c1957-59

$650-750   **W&W**

A rare Dinky Toys sports cars gift set (149), including an Austin Healy, MG Midget, Sunbeam Alpine, Aston Martin and Triumph TR2.

1958-61

$1,500-2,000   **W&W**

A Dinky three-piece BBC outdoor broadcast unit.

largest 6in (15cm) long

$50-80   **WHP**

A Dinky 49 Petrol Pump set, containing four pumps with white rubber hoses and a plain yellow oil bin, all in yellow box with plain cardboard sleeve.

6in (15cm) wide

$200-250   **DN**

A Dinky Hillman Imp rally car (214), finished in dark blue, with Monte Carlo rally decals, in original picture box, some tears to box, slight factory paint defect.

3.25in (8.2in) long

$100-150   **W&W**

A Dinky Cortina Mk 1 rally car (2120), finished in white with black bonnet, with Castrol East African Safari No. 8 decals, in original picture box, slight chipping.

4in (10.2cm) long

$120-180   **W&W**

A French Dinky Citroen ID19 ambulance (556), in light gray with cream roof, light to front, boxed, some minor wear.

4.5in (11.4cm) long

$100-150   **W&W**

Two French Dinky cars, a Fiat 1200 Grande Vue 531, in dark metallic brown and cream roof, and a Borgward Isabella Coupé 549, in pale green with red interior, both boxed, minor wear to Fiat box. Fiat

3.5in (8.9cm) long

$180-220 (pair)   **W&W**

A Dinky lorry-mounted Albion Chieftain (960) cement mixer, with box, some minor wear and chips.

4.75in (12.1cm) long

$100-150   **W&W**

A rare French Dinky Supertoys Grader (886) Profileur 100 Richier, with driver, in original box, slight age wear, minor paint chipping.

6.75in (17.1cm) long

$200-250   **W&W**

▶ A mint condition Dinky Big Bedford Heinz van (923), with box.

c1960   5.5in (14cm) long

$2,200-2,800   **W&W**

▶ A Dinky Lotus Cortina Mk II Rally car (205), finished in white and red, with Monte Carlo Rally No. 7. decals, in original box, slight age wear, lifting to chrome on aerial.

4in (10.2cm) long

$120-180   **W&W**

A Dinky Ford Capri 1.25 (2214) Rally Special finished in red with black bonnet and roof, no. 12 decals, in original bubble pack, damaged, vehicle in mint condition.

6.75in (17.1cm) long

$150-200　　　　　　　　　　　　　　　　　　**W&W**

A Dinky Ford Capri 1.25 (2162), finished in metallic blue with a black roof, original bubble packaging, age wear and damage to bubble pack, slight paint defect to roof.

6.75in (17.1cm) long

$120-80　　　　　　　　　　　　　　　　　　**W&W**

A Dinky Mercedes Benz truck and trailer (917), with box, minor wear, one door mirror missing.

15.25in (38.5cm) long

$100-150　　　　　　**W&W**

Six Dinky Austin covered wagons, in military olive-green, made for the American market, complete set in box tray.

$2,500-3,000　　　　　　**W&W**

A Corgi die-cast Karrier Gamecock, in Decca airfield radar livery.

5.5in (13.5cm) long

$120-180　　　　　　**WHP**

A Corgi Hillman Imp rally car (328), finished in metallic blue with Monte Carlo Rally decals no. 107, with box, part of rear number plate transfer missing.

3.25in (8.2cm) long

$120-180　　　　　　**W&W**

A Corgi 1967 Sunbeam Imp Rally car (340), finished in metallic blue with Monte Carlo Rally front plate no. 77 and rear decal, in 328 box with original factory no. 340 over sticker, VGC rear suspension weak.

3.25in (8.2cm) long

$120-180　　　　　　**W&W**

A mint condition Corgi Monte Carlo Mini Cooper S (318), with no. 52 Rally decals, registration no. AJB 44B, in a no. 317 box.

1965　　　　2.75in (7cm) long

$220-280　　　　　　**W&W**

A mint condition Corgi Monte Carlo Mini Cooper S (321), autographed "Timo Makinen and Paul Easter" in 1966, with no. 2 Rally decals, registration GRX 555D, boxed with factory over sticker.

2.75in (7cm) long

$200-250　　　　　　**W&W**

A mint condition Corgi 1967 Monte Carlo mini Cooper S (339), complete with roof rack and two spare wheels, 1967 Rally plate and decal no. 177, registration no. LBL 6D in 321, box with factory over sticker.

2.75in (7cm) long

$250-300　　　　　　**W&W**

▶ A CIJ Renault Colorale 800 kgs van, with spun silver wheels, with box, minor age blemishes.

3.75in (9.5cm) long

$100-150　　　　　　**W&W**

◀ A CIJ Renault Dauphinoise van (3/67), finished in light sea blue with Postes gold decals to side, with box, minor paint chips.

3.25in (8.2cm) long

$100-150　　　　　　**W&W**

A CIJ Renault Gendarmerie (3/69) Dauphinoise 300kg van, with roof ariel and box.

3.25in (8.2cm) long

$200-250   W&W

A CIJ rare Renault Ambulance, in "Europarc" blue and white livery with blue cross on front doors, and front wing-mounted flag, minor paint blemishes.

1.75in (4.4cm) long

$200-250   W&W

A Tekno VW Philips van, with Philips decals to sides and Philishave to rear panel.

3.25in (8.2cm) long

$200-250   W&W

A Tekno Taunus transit ambulance (415), finished in white with decals to sides, complete with stretcher, patient and blue roof light, with box.

3.25in (8.2cm) long

$150-200   W&W

A Tekno Falck Zonen Taunus transit (415), finished in red with Falck Zonen decals to sides, with box, slight distortion and coloring to rear door.

3.25in (8.2cm) long

$80-120   W&W

A scarce Tekno caravan (815), with folding draw bar, minor chips and wear, number plate transfer worn.

1.5in (3.8cm) long

$150-200   W&W

Two single seat racing cars, to the left a Dalia Maseratti 250 finished in dark red with driver, to the right a Solido Lotus Formula One car in British racing green, complete with driver, both with boxes, slight age wear.

Maseratti 4in (10.2cm) long

$200-250   W&W

Two Solido Grand touring cars, to the left a Mercedes (220) SE (126), finished in metallic red, to the right a Ferrari 250 GT 2+2 123, finished in maroon, both with boxes, some age wear.

Mercedes 4in (10.2cm) long

$200-250   W&W

A rare WWII period Tri-Ang Minic clockwork-powered petrol tank lorry, painted in brown and green camouflage livery with black wheel hubs, in original adapted box, rubber stamped "Camouflaged" at one end, some wear, tyres perished.

5.5in (14cm) long

$400-600   W&W

A rare Tri-Ang Minic clockwork-powered searchlight lorry, in gloss dark green, with red chassis and plated wings, grille bumper and wheel hubs, complete with petrol can, and light bulb, with box, minor wear for age.

5in (12.7cm) long

$400-450   W&W

A Britains die-cast Fordson Major Tractor, in original box.

4in (10cm) long

$300-400   WHP

A 1920s Schieble Roadster, flywheel drive all original.

17.25in

$500-550   SI

► A Shackleton Foden 10 wheel flat back wagon, in dark blue with red wheel arches and gray chassis, clockwork motor, steering mechanism and prop shaft complete and working, together with optimal four wheel trailer, complete with drawbar, with box, some wear.

13in (33cm) long

$250-300   W&W

An American Tootsietoy car.

4in (10cm) long

$50-80   WHP

TINPLATE TOYS

A mint condition Ferdinand Strauss Jazzbo Jim, lithographed tin, reads "Dancer on the Roof" on base, with box.

c1919   10.25in (26cm) long

$1,000-1,500   **Bert**

A Unique Art Manufacturing Jazzbo Jim, lithographed tin, clockwork activated.

c1920   10in (25.5cm) high

$600-800   **Bert**

A Ferdinand Strauss Ham and Sam Minstrel Team, lithographed tin, clockwork mechanism.

1921   6.5in (16.5cm) long

$600-800   **Bert**

A Marx Toys Spic and Span model, lithographed tin, clockwork mechanism.

10in (25.4cm) high

$2,000-2,500   **Bert**

A Louis Marx Charleston Trio, lithographed tin, clockwork activated, box tattered.

9.25in (23.5cm) high

$1,800-2,200   **Bert**

A Ferdinand Strauss Alabama Coon Jigger, lithographed tin, clockwork, base reads "Tombo, the Alabama Coon Jigger".

10.5in (26.6cm) high

$600-800   **Bert**

A Marx Toys Popeye Carrying Parrot Cages, lithographed tin, clockwork mechanism, box reads "Walking Popeye," replaced end flap on box.

8in (20.5cm) high

$600-700   **Bert**

A Louis Marx Popeye and Olive Oyl Jiggers, lithographed tin, clockwork.

9.5in (24cm) high

$750-850   **Bert**

A Louis Marx Popeye Express, lithographed tin, clockwork activated, box reads "Popeye & Baggage".

8.5in (21.5cm) long

$700-900   **Bert**

A Louis Marx Popeye the Pilot, lithographed tin clockwork activated, box reads, "Popeye Eccentric Airplane".

7in (17.5cm) long

$2,000-2,500   **Bert**

A Chein Popeye Heavy Hitter, lithographed tin, clockwork, copy 1932 King Features Synd.

11.5in (29.2cm) high

$3,000-3,500   **Bert**

A Marx Toys Merrymakers Band, lithographed tin, clockwork, some scratching.

$1,000-1,500   **Bert**

A Unique Art Manuafcturing Howdy Doody & Bob Smith Band, lithographed tin, clockwork, box tattered.

c1940   8.25in (20.5cm) long

$1,500-2,000   **Bert**

A mint condition Marx Toys Donald Duck Duet, when clockwork is activated Donald beats the drum while Goofy dances, includes folded box, copy 1946 Walt Disney Prod.

10.25in (26cm) high

$800-1,200   **Bert**

A Unique Art Manuafcturing Lil Abner and His Dog Patch Band, lithographed tin, clockwork mechanism.

1945   9in (22.5cm) high

$800-1,200   **Bert**

A mint condition Marusan 1953 Cadillac, battery operated, with box, made in Japan.

12.25in (31cm) long

$3,500-4,000   **Bert**

An Alps 1953 Cadillac Convertible W/AD, deluxe model, friction powered, trunk features large dealership decal which reads "IRU Sachs for Cadillac's - Philadelphia," with box, made in Japan.

11in (28cm) long

$2,000-2,500   **Bert**

A Marusan 1954 Chevrolet, lithographed tin interior, in popular gray and black, with box, made in Japan, box frayed.

11.25in (28.5cm) long

$2,500-3,000   **Bert**

A Bandai 1955 Ford Ranchero, friction powered, with box, made in Japan.

11.75in (29.5cm) long

$1,000-1,500   **Bert**

A rare Modern Toys 1957 Lincoln, friction powered with siren sounds, with box, made in Japan, box end frayed.

2.5in (31.5cm) long

$5,500-6,000   **Bert**

A rare Alps 1957 Chrysler Newport, friction powered, with box, made in Japan, near mint condition.

14in (35.5cm) long

$7,500-8,500   **Bert**

An ATC 1958 Buick, friction powered with siren sounds, with box, made in Japan.

14.25in (36cm) long

$5,000-6,000   **Bert**

An SSS 1961 Fleetwood Seventy-Five Cadillac, friction powered, with box, made in Japan.

16.5in (42cm) long

$3,000-3,500   **Bert**

A Asahi Toy Co 1961 Chrysler Imperial, friction powered, with box, made in Japan, near mint condition.

16in (40.5cm) long

$25,000-30,000   **Bert**

▶ A Yonezawa Electro Toy Racer, lithographed, battery operated, with box, made in Japan, replaced battery cover, minor scratches.

9.5in (24cm) long

$3,000-3,500   **Bert**

◀ A rare Line Mar Toys Lincoln Mark II Continental, friction powered with electric lights, with box, made in Japan, near mint condition.

11.25in (28.5cm) long

$9,000-10,000   **Bert**

461

MECHANICAL BANKS

▲**1** A Tammany Bank, designed by John D Hall, produced by J & E Stevens Co., patented 12/23/1873.

The bank depicts William Tweed, boss of Tammany Hall, who helped to milk millions of dollars from public funds.

$7,500-8,000   **Bert**

▲**2** An Owl bank, glass eyes, designed by James H Bowen, produced by J&E Stevens Co., patented 9/28/1880.

$25,000-30,000   **Bert**

A Picture Gallery bank, produced by Shephard Hardware Co.

1 Figure deposits coin in the bank.

2 The letters of the alphabet are shown in rotation.

3 The numbers 1 to 26 are shown in rotation.

4 One of 26 animals or objects together with a short word is also shown to correspond with the letter.

The value of this bank can be attributed to the complexity of its mechanism and its overall condition. A mechanism this intricate – and with an educational theme – is highly sought after by collectors of mechanical banks.
c1885

$35,000-40,000   **Bert**

CAST IRON BANKS

Cast iron banks fall into two categories: mechanical, which have a sequence of movements started by depositing a coin and/or pulling a lever, and still banks.

Although savings banks had existed for centuries, the first mechanical bank, the Hall's Excelsior, was patented in 1869. Designed by John Hall of Watertown MA, it was produced by J&E Stevens & Co of Cromwell, CT, who went on to be prolific manufacturers of banks throughout their heyday. This ended c1910 and the company went into decline after the two World Wars when iron was in demand to make weapons.

With coinage in short supply after the Civil War, banks became a popular way to encourage children to save money while entertaining them.

The designs show the humour and stereotypes of the day, as well as the ingenuity of 19thC craftsmen.

● Collectors look for banks in good condition and with the original coin trap. A working mechanism is also important as they are difficult to repair. A bank in good condition can be worth up to ten times more than one in reasonable condition.

● Original paintwork is shiny, with a depth of colour and, perhaps, fine crazing.

● Be aware that banks may have been repainted. Poor restoration can lead to a spotted finish.

● There are many reproductions and fakes. These often have rough surfaces with blurred details, poorly fitting pieces, modern internal components and a rusty, unpainted finish.

A Humpty Dumpty bank, designed by Charles G Shepard & Peter Adams, produced by Shepard Hardware Co., patented 6/17/1884.

1 Place a coin in the hand.

2 Use the thumb-piece behind the left shoulder to raise the arm.

3 As the coin is deposited in the mouth, the tongue falls back and the eyes roll upwards.

$12,000-15,000   **Bert**

A Speaking Dog bank, designed by Charles G Shephard & Peter Adams, produced by Shephard Hardware Co., patented 10/20/1885.

$2,500-3,000   **Bert**

A Darktown Battery bank, designed by James H Bowen, produced by J & E Stevens Co., patented 1/17/1888.

$3,500-4,000   **Bert**

A Mule Entering Barn bank, designed by Edward L Morris, produced by J & E Stevens Co., patented 1/6/1880.

$6,000-6,500   **Ber**

A Professor Pug Frog bank, designed by Charles A Bailey, produced by J & E Stevens Co., new crank, frog repainted.

Charles A Bailey, who patented his first bank in 1880, is thought to have designed 20 per cent of all American cast-iron banks.
c1886

$4,500-5,000   **Ber**

A Chief Big Moon bank, designed by Charles A Bailey, produced by J & E Stevens Co., patented 8/8/1888.

$5,500-6,000   **Ber**

A J&E Stevens cast iron safe bank, with key.

c1890   3.25in (8.5cm) hig

$100-150   **S**

A Jolly Nigger cast iron mechanical bank.

c1890

$200-300	**SI**

An I Always Did Spise A Mule-Bench bank, designed by James H Bowen, produced by J & E Stevens Co., patented 4/27/1897, some fading to left side of base.

$4,000-4,500	**Bert**

A rare octagonal fort bank, manufacturer unknown, but first sold as the Fort Sumpter Bank.

$5,500-6,000	**Bert**

A Bad Accident mechanical money bank, designed by Charles A Bailey, produced by J & E Stevens Co.

c1891

$5,000-6,000	**Bert**

From left: A cast iron "City Bank", a "Leader Safe" bank and a J&E Stevens safe bank. largest

4in (10cm) high

$250-350	**SI**

▲1 An early 20thC AC Williams cast iron bank, in the form of a St Bernard with pack.

▲2 An early 20thC AC Williams cast iron bank, in the form of a seated Indian.

Tallest 5.5in (14cm) high

$150-200 (pair)	**SI**

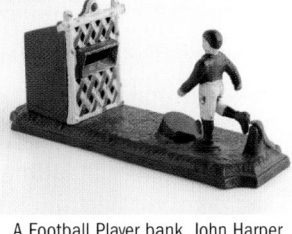

A Football Player bank, John Harper & Co Ltd, registered 1/7/1895.

$6,500-7,000	**Bert**

A cast iron William Tell mechanical bank.

10.5in (26.5cm) high

$1,300-1,700	**SI**

▲1 A lighthouse bank, unknown American manufacturer. *Semi-mechanical with two coin slots. The one on the roof functions as a still bank and the one near the top of the tower takes nickels. The button will permit the bank to open only after the tower has received 100 nickels. The coin stack can be seen through each tower window, and the number of coins deposited is noted above each window.*

c1891

$6,000-6,500	**Bert**

▲2 An Uncle Sam Bank, Shepard Hardware Co., designed by Charles Shepard and Peter Adams, patented 6/8/1886.

$1,500-2,000	**Bert**

An early 20thC AC Williams Darkey, Sharecropper cast iron still bank, toes visible on one foot.

6in (15.5cm) high

$150-200	**SI**

An early 20thC AC Williams cast iron Aunt Jemima still bank.

6in (15.5cm) high

$150-200	**SI**

An early 20thC Hubley 829 cast iron mechanical Monkey Bank, missing bottom plate.

$800-1,000	**SI**

A Boy Scout Bank, designed by Charles A Bailey, produced by J & E Stevens Co.

c1915

$5,500-6,000	**Bert**

A 1930s cast iron Milking Cow mechanical bank. Provenance: From the estate of Ethel Templeton, Jellico, Tenn.

$250-300	**SI**

A Wrenn 00 4-6-2 Duchess of Atholl, model no. WR405 in BR green livery, train no. RN 46231, complete with rail-mounted mahogany display box, with paperwork and certificate, driver and fireman figures added to footplate, minor wear.

This locomotive was limited edition no. 221 of 250.

12.5in (31cm) long

A Hornby 0 gauge goods platform, with crane fixed at one end, litho detailed green tiled roof with brick-colored ridge, brick-effect walls, two windows and two opening sliding doors, mounted on a cream-painted base, with box, some wear.

16.75in (42.5cm) long

A Hornby series no. 2 Windsor Station, complete with side ramps, twin chimneys, opening doors to waiting rooms, surrounding picket fence, with box, some paint scratches and slight rusting.

17in (43.2cm) long

$750-800	W&W	$400-500	W&W	$250-300	W&W

A Hornby series no. 2 Saloon coach, 1st Class LMS No. 402, finished in maroon with gray roof, gold trim to windows, double bogies with plastic wheels, with box, minor wear.

13.5in (34.3cm) long

A Hornby Dublo EDLT20 "Bristol Castle" locomotive and tender, in BR lined green livery, number 7013, with blue-striped box having one taped corner.

A French Hornby 4-4-2 Nord locomotive and tender, finished in dark brown with gold lining no. 31240, with double bogie tender 31801, C/w driven, some retouching.

16.75in (42.5cm) long

$200-300	W&W	$100-150	DN	$250-300	W&W

GAMES AND PUZZLES

An early 19thC English treen boxed set of children's paper covered building blocks, with a colored paper label, "NURSERY RHYME OF "A WAS AN ARCHER", WITH OTHER ALPHABETS ON BLOCKS", in a painted wooden box.

Provenance: From the W.J. Shepherd Collection GP1235.

9in (23cm) wide

$2,000-2,500	PC

▶ A late 19thC English treen dice game.

Provenance: From the W.J. Shepherd collection GP1255.

$200-300	PC

An early 19thC English jigsaw puzzle of the British Isles, in a painted wooden box.

Provenance: From the W.J. Shepherd Collection GP12387.

7in (17.5cm) wide

$200-300	PC

▶ A French rosewood games compendium, by A Giroux & Co, Paris, with two packs of 19thC playing cards (one dated 1816, the other 1853), and bone or ivory counters.

c1825 12in (30cm) wide

$1,500-2,000	Gro

A 19thC painted papier-mâché skittle set, the cabbage-shaped container enclosing nine skittles in the form of various vegetables, each with amusing painted faces.

Cabbage 15.5in (39cm) dia

$1,000-1,200	L&T

Games and Puzzles

A 19thC turned rosewood cup and ball.

5.75in (14.5cm) long

| $250-300 | BonR |

► A Parlor Croquet set, in original brass-bound mahogany box with inset brass plate on the lid, inscribed "Table Croquet", with a set of initials, fitted with a removable velvet-lined tray and containing eight balls, ten lead-weighted hoops (three weights loose), ten leather recovered clamps, and eight mallet heads with seven screw-in handles.

Box 14.25in (36.5cm) wide

| $300-400 | DN |

A Chad Valley official Great Western Railway "GWR Locomotives in the Making" wooden jigsaw puzzle, after a painting by Secretan, contains approximately 200 pieces, with box.

12.5 (31cm) high

| $400-450 | DN |

A Chad Valley official Great Western Railway "The Model Railway" wooden jigsaw puzzle, after a painting by A. Duncan Carse, contains approximately 200 pieces, with box.

12.75 x 15.5in (39cm) high

| $200-300 | DN |

◄ A Chad Valley official Great Western Railway "The Romans at Caerleon" wooden jigsaw puzzle, after a painting by Claude H. Buckle, contains approximately 200 pieces, with box.

13.75 (34.5cm) high

| $100-150 | DN |

A Chad valley official Great Western Railway "The Night Mail" wooden jigsaw puzzle, contains approximately 200 pieces, with box.

10 x 20in (25.1 x 50.4cm)

| $200-300 | DN |

CAP PISTOLS

A boy and bear cap bomb, cast iron, J & E Stevens Co.

13in (33cm) long

| $650-750 | Bert |

▲1 A sambo cap pistol, cast-iron, japanned overall, Ives.

c1883   5in (14cm) long

| $5,000-6,000 | Bert |

▲1 A sea serpent cap pistol, cast iron, ornate details and design, J & E Stevens Co.

| $8000-1,000 | Bert |

▲2 A Punch and Judy cap gun, well cast, excellent condition, Ices

c1882   4in (1ocm) long

| $2,000-2,500 | Bert |

▲2 A Clown on Powder Keg cap pistol, cast iron, Ives

c1880   3.75in (9.5cm) long

| $3,000-4,000 | Bert |

Miscellaneous

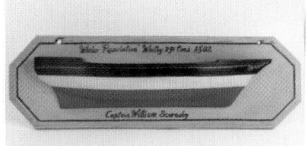

A decorative carved wooden half-hull ship model, mounted on an octagonal pine panel, painted and inscribed "Whaler 'Resolution'", and "Whitby, 291 tons, 1802" and "Captain Scoresby".

22.25in (56.5cm) long

$100-150 **DN**

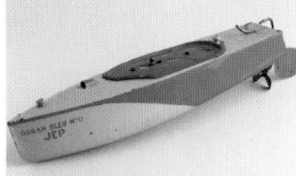

A French clockwork-powered tinplate speedboat, by Jep, Ruban Bleu no. 0, simple stop and go mechanism, large rudder with ratchet fixing, some wear overall, motor in working order.

12.5in (31.5cm) long

$100-150 **W&W**

An American early 20thC cased carved and painted wood model of a ship, the ship with string rigging, the whole set upon cotton baten and set within a glazed case with turned uprights.

25.25in (64cm) long

$450-500 **SI**

▶ A folk art painted farmyard complex, Berks County, Pennsylvania, comprising a two and a half story farmhouse with a filigree wrap around porch, sliding sash windows with classical surrounds, a shingled mansard roof with dormer windows and a roof lantern and a removable, lean to extension; together with three barns, gazebo, corn crib, greenhouse, out-trellises with flowers, water pump and fencing.

c1880 main house 30in (76cm) h

$8,000-10,000 **SI**

A model of the Golden Arrow, marked "Under licence from Sir Henry Seagrove holder of world's speed record".

Henry Seagrove *broke the land speed record in his car the Golden Arrow at Daytona Beach on March 11, 1929 creating a new record of 231.362 miles per hour.*

5.25in (13cm) long

$150-200 **WHP**

A 1930s rare Frog mailplane, in dark-blue Royal Air Mail livery, G-ADGR registration to wings and fuselage, complete and with box, winder and instructions, some damage.

13.5in (34.3cm) long

$400-450 **W&W**

▶ A rare WWII period Meccano set MA Mechanised Army Outfit, comprising parts to produce military toys no.1 to no. 6, including light tank, transport wagon, anti-aircraft guns, etc, all parts painted in olive green, 90% complete, with box and instructions, some damage.

$150-200 **W&W**

A 1940s unusual Frog Vickers Wellesley long range bomber, in balsa wood depicting the record breaking RAF bomber, with box and instructions, one wing repaired, one small wheel missing.

$250-300 **W&W**

Two rare Skybirds Constructional model Aeroplane kits, series n o. 5 Sopwith Camel, and a no. 11 Fokker DR1 triplane, both complete and unused, with original card backing boxes, minor wear to boxes.

$300-450 (pair) **W&W**

Miscellaneous

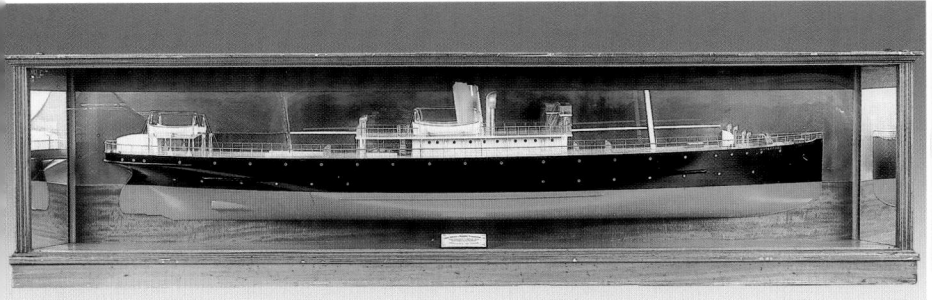

An S S Waterford Edwardian half-hull ships model, mounted on a mirrored backing plate and enclosed within a mahogany glazed case bearing the inscription, "Swan, Hunter & Wigham Richardson Ltd Ship, Engine & Floating Dock Builders and Repairers Walker on Tyne".

87.5in (222cm) long

$6,000-8,000   **L&T**

Three cold-painted bronze miniature Beatrix Potter figures, depicting Benjamin Bunny, Jeremy Fisher, and Pigling Bland.
.

Tallest 1.5in (3.8cm) high

$150-200   **DN**

A Victorian papier-mâché model of a bulldog, with glass eyes, nodding head and hinged jaw, lignum vitae castors.

20.5in (51cm) long

$600-800   **L&T**

◀ A late 19thC painted wooden Noah's Ark, the sliding side panel revealing a quantity of carved and painted wooden animals.

For many families during Victorian times play was forbidden on the Sabbath. A child might read Bible stories with the family, or enjoy a special Sunday toy with a religious theme like Noah's Ark.

$1,000-1,500   **LFA**

▶ A Britains 1654 Snow White and the Seven Dwarfs, all in original orange box with blue label to lid and internal card mount.

9in (23cm) wide

$1,500-2,000   **DN**

A Victorian "rodentomaton" or painted tinplate rodent cage, in the form of a pair of octagonal towers surmounted by carousels which revolve when the connecting wire treadmill is activated, a pair of handles each with a chair wheel can animate the "rodentomaton" when the occupants are sleeping, or when there is a vacancy, each tower has a sliding wire door and a feed tray, well repainted and restored overall, some parts missing.

41in (104cm) wide

$1,000-1,300   **W&W**

A set of early building blocks, paper on wood, excellent condition.

$200-300   **BCAC**

467

ANTIQUITIES Egyptian

INTEREST IN ANTIQUITIES HAS INCREASED DRAMATICALLY OVER THE LAST TEN YEARS. The dusty and boring image has been replaced by widespread interest in these ancient pieces of history. The fact that the objects are often very inexpensive and available has encouraged collectors and non-collectors alike.

Small Egyptian jewelry, amulets and ushabtis are always a popular area, and these have soared in price over the past decade. Roman glass is still an underrated area, but beware of heavily repaired pieces. Greek terracotta vessels, often emanating from collections made during "The Grand Tour" are always in demand due to their highly decorative nature. It has been noted that very recently there has been a significant rise in prices at the lower end of the market, which has been fueled by the enthusiasm of novice collectors. This would indicate that prices in the middle sector of the market are likely to rise in the near future.

Many items from the Ancient World fall into other collecting areas, for instance perfume bottles, wine-related objects and jewelry. Also with the advent of .com auctions and wider availability there will be an increase in demand for all these types of items. Always be aware that there are many forgeries on the market and, as with any antique, it is advisable to buy from a reputable source.

A protective faience amulet, of Ptah the dwarf god, usually depicted naked with a bald head and arm by his side, with a loop through the shoulder for suspension.

Faience is earthenware decorated with colored opaque metallic glazes. It is composed of quartz, lime and natron or plant ash and is coated with a soda-lime glaze. Amulets were carried as a protective talisman or charm and were believed to endow magical properties.

c500 BC   1.5in (3.5cm) high

| $150-200 | AnA |

A Memphis faience triad amulet, showing the young god Horus flanked by Isis and Nephitys, with a loop at the top for suspension, fine glaze remaining.

c684 to 525 BC   1.75in (4.5cm)

| $850-950 | AnA |

An amulet of Thouris, the hippopotamus goddess, with a loop at the back for suspension.

Thouris was the goddess who attended women in childbirth.

c500 BC   2in (5cm) high

| $150-200 | AnA |

An Egyptian pale faience triad amulet, depicting Nepathys, Harpokrates and Isis standing side by side on an integral base, holding hands, Dynasty XXVI.

c664-525 BC   1.5in (3.5cm) high

| $1,500-2,000 | SI |

A faience amulet of a recumbent lamb, sacred to Thoth, with a loop at the top for suspension.

c500 BC   1.5in (3.5cm) wide

| $200-300 | AnA |

A protective amulet, in the form of the knot of Isis.

c500 BC   0.5in (2.5cm) high

| $70-100 | AnA |

Egyptian

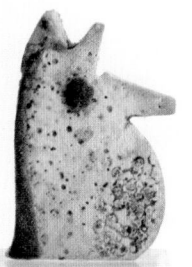

A protective faience amulet, in the form of a sacred eye of Horus.

Horus *is the Falcon-God or "Lord of the sky" and a symbol of divine kingship. The eye of Horus was believed to ward off the evil eye, a popular superstition in the Middle East.*

c500 BC   1.5in (3.5cm) wide

$70-100	AnA

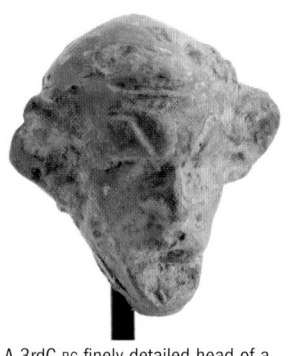

A 3rdC BC finely detailed head of a grotesque, from Tinagra, with protruding ears and gaping mouth.

1in (2.5cm) high

$150-200	AnA

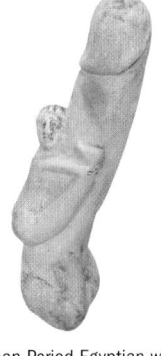

An Roman Period Egyptian white marble erotic figural group, carved to depict a figure of a phallus.

AD *1st-2ndC*   11.5in (26cm) high

$7,500-8,500	SI

A Late Period Egyptian carved stone figure of a cow, striding on a keyhole shaped plinth, its tail falling straight between his legs, the back with incised motifs.

c716-730 BC   3.25in (9cm) wide

$1,400-2,000	SI

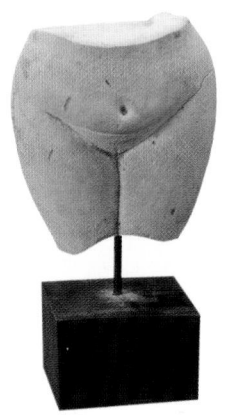

A Late Period Egyptian limestone torso of a woman.

c716-30 BC   3in (8cm) high

$700-800	SI

A Ptolemaic Period Egyptian cartonnage fragment, painted with the goddess Nut with outstretched wings.

The goddess Nut was the ancient Egyptian goddess of the day-time sky.

c304-30 BC   12in (31cm) wide

$2,000-2,500	SI

A Late Period Egyptian faience winged scarab, with separate outstretched wings, the body and wings with incised details and pierced for attachments.

Scarabs *held particular significance for the Egyptians, and they were among the most popular motifs. They were considered to embody the hope of new life and resurrection. This could be enhanced if the article was inscribed or had pictorial representations to its flat underside.*

c715-332 BC   5.5in (14cm) wide

$550-650	SI

A Late Period Egyptian ivory figure of a woman, the slender figure depicted nude and standing with her arms held to her sides, her feet on a rectangular base.

c1085-322 BC   3.75in (9.5cm) high

$225-275	SI

An Egyptian limestone sphinx, seated with the tail curled over the hindquarters and wearing the nemes-headcloth, Ptolemaic Period-Roman Period.

The commanders of Alexander the Great split his empire among themselves after his death and Egypt fell to Ptolemy I. He founded the Ptolemaic state in Egypt that lasted for three centuries.

c50 BC-AD 30   27in (68.5cm) high

$40,000-45,000	SI

Late Period Egyptian carved wood feet, painted in yellow ocher tones, on a plinth.

c716-30 BC   10.5in (27cm) wide

$1,200-1,500	SI

A late Egyptian cartonnage footcase fragment, the rectangular rounded border case painted to depict two feet wearing sandals, framed with double lines and geometric motifs.

AD *1stC*

$1,000-1,500	SI

Egyptian

A pair of Egyptian gilt and gesso-painted linen soles, each with three red and gilt bars on a painted background, Ptolemaic Period.

4th-1stC BC   9in (23cm) wide

$200-300   **SI**

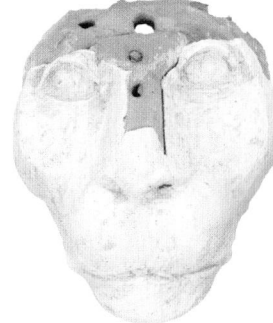

An Egyptian polychrome plaster bust of a woman, with striated coiffure, aquiline nose and full lips, with traces of polychrome on her face.

AD 2ndC   15.75 (40cm) high

$15,000-20,000   **SI**

A Late Period Egyptian polychrome wood head of a baboon, partly gessoed.

c712-30 BC   8in (20cm) high

$750-850   **SI**

A Roman Period Egyptian terracotta head of a woman, with curly coiffure, aquiline nose and full lips, with traces of polychrome.

1stC BC-AD 1stC   0.5in (16.5cm) high

$2,000-2,500   **SI**

A Late Period Egyptian polychrome wood panel from a sarcophagus, painted with the goddess Nut with her wings outstretched.

c716-30 BC   13.5in (34.5cm) wide

$600-700   **SI**

An Egyptian gesso-painted wood Ptah-Sokar-Osiris figure, wearing a tripartite wig, with wooden rectangular base, Ptolemaic Period.

4th-2ndC BC   8in (45.5cm) high

$4,500-5,000   **SI**

A Late Period Egyptian wood figure of a woman, wearing a long dress and a short wig.

c716-30 BC   15.5in (39.5cm) high

$4,000-5,000   **SI**

A Ptolemaic Period Egyptian wood figure of Horus Falcon.

c664-300 BC   14.75in (37.5cm)

$900-1,200   **SI**

An Egyptian gilt-wood head of an ibis, the eyes and bill carefully modeled with projections for attachment to the wrappings of a mummified ibis, Late Period to Ptolemaic Period.

An ibis is a bird with a long thin and curved bill that was worshipped by the ancient Egyptians.

c664-30 BC   19in (48cm) long

$2,000-2,800   **SI**

An Egyptian wood cosmetic spoon, carved in the form of a nude swimming girl, wearing a short wig, her arms outstretched to hold a bowl, New Kingdom.

c1353-1335 BC   8.25in (25cm) long

$12,000-14,000   **SI**

An Egyptian polychrome wood figure of an offering bearer, holding a bird in her right hand and wearing a necklace and bracelets, Middle Kingdom, Dynasty XII.

10in (25cm) high

$18,000-21,000 SI

An Egyptian bronze group of Isis and Horus, depicted wearing a vulture headdress, topped by a modius supporting cow horns framing a solar disc and offering her breast to the divine child whose head she cradles, Third Intermediate Period, Dynasty XXI-XXV.

c1070-664 BC 6.75in (17cm) high

$2,000-2,300 SI

A Roman Period Egyptian bronze oil lamp, cast with three arms radiating from a central circular opening with hinged lid encircled with glyphs.

AD 1st-2ndC 10.75in (26cm) long

$8,000-9,000 SI

A Ptolemaic Period Egyptian granite relief, carved with the head of a king or god wearing tripartite wig, behind him a uaz-scepter.

5th-4thC BC 29in (73.5cm) wide

$30,000-35,000 SI

An Egyptian bronze figure of an oxyrhynchus fish, wearing a modius surmounted by cow horns and a solar disc, with an incised scale pattern, Late Period to Ptolemaic Period.

c664-30 BC 5.75in (14.5cm) long

$2,500-3,000 SI

A Coptic terracotta figure of a woman, molded seated with her hands joined on her lap, and wearing circular earrings.

AD 3rd-6thC 6.25in (16cm) high

$300-350 SI

An Egyptian New Kingdom black stone fragment of a nobleman.

c1,200 BC 6in (15cm) high

$12,000-15,000 AnA

An Egyptian faience figure of a King.

c600 BC 4in (10cm) high

$600-700 SI

An Egypto-Roman basalt bust of a priest, probably from a seated figure with his arms held on his sides, wearing a chiton and a himation with realistic features and almond-shaped eyes inset with glass.

c AD 1stC 13in (33cm) high

$12,000-15,000 SI

NAGADA CULTURES

The pre-dynastic Nagada or Nagada I dates from c4,500 BC, Nagada II dates from c4,000 BC. The Nagada cultures came to form the two kingdoms of Lower and Upper Egypt and were key in building the foundations of this ancient civilization. There is a marked difference between the ceramic industries of Nagada I and II. Nagada I pottery tends to be functional, with few decorative aspects, whereas Nagada II pottery is influenced by organic geometric design, with animal and human motifs. Nagada III pottery is often decorated with patterns.

An Egyptian pre-dynastic black-topped jar, of ovoid form, tapering to a flat bottom with everted rounded lip, Nagada I-II Period.

c3800-3400 BC 6.25in (15.5cm)

$1,300-1,500 SI

An Egyptian pre-dynastic black-top pottery jar of conical form, Nagada I period.

c4000-3600 BC 5in (13cm) high

$1,300-1,500 SI

Egyptian

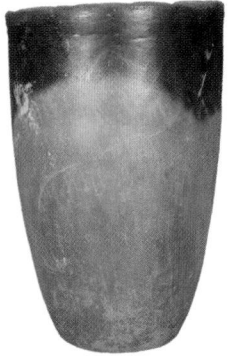

An Egyptian pre-dynastic black-topped pottery jar, of deep tapering and slightly ovoid form with flat base.

c3100 BC   10in (25.5cm) high

$2,000-2,300   **SI**

An Egyptian pre-dynastic red pottery jar, of ovoid form with a short neck and everted rim, Nagada I-II Period.

c4000-3000 BC   7.5in (19cm) high

$450-550   **SI**

An Egyptian pre-dynastic terracotta vessel, of ovoid form, on a flat base with everted rim, the body decorated with a tooled scalloped band.

c3000 BC   7.75in (19.5cm) high

$450-550   **SI**

An Egyptian pre-dynastic terracotta vessel, of slender slightly flaring form with everted rounded rim, the body decorated with a tooled scalloped rim, Nagada III Period.

c3200 BC   10.75in (27.5cm) high

$600-700   **SI**

An Egyptian pre-dynastic terracotta jar, of ovoid form, the body with brown geometric decoration with cylindrical handles and flaring mouth.

c3500 BC   5in (12.5cm) high

$900-1,100   **SI**

An Egyptian limestone canopic jar, of ovoid form, the interior hollowed out, with the lid in the form of one of the four sons of Horus baboon-headed Hapy, the jar with hieroglyphic inscriptions, Dynasty XXVI.

c664-525 BC   15.5in (39.5cm) high

$2,000-2,800   **SI**

An Egyptian pre-dynastic terracotta vessel, of rounded form with a flat everted collar rim and twin lug handles, the body with brown geometric decoration.

c3100 BC   6in (15cm) high

$2,000-2,800   **SI**

Masks were an important part of Ancient Egyptian burials. They were used in conjunction with the anthropoid coffin and provided the dead with a face in the afterlife. They also enabled the spirit to recognize the body.

An Egyptian terracotta part of an anthropoid sarcophagus lid, depicting the face and ears modeled in relief with vivid polychrome decoration, New Kingdom, Dynasty XIX-XX.

c1307-1070 BC   28in (71cm) high

$6,000-7,000   **SI**

A Late Period Egyptian wood mummy mask, with broad round face, slightly aquiline nose with remains of polychrome.

c712-30 BC   9in (23cm) high

$3,000-3,500   **SI**

A Late Period Egyptian wood mummy mask, with broad round face, slightly aquiline nose with remains of polychrome.

c712-30 BC   9in (23cm) high

$900-1,100   **SI**

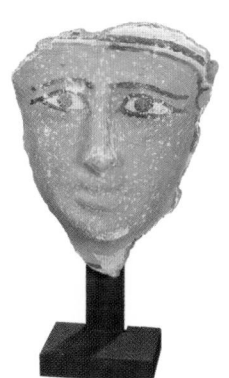

A Late Period Egyptian polychrome wood mummy mask, the face painted, the eyes and eyebrows with long black cosmetic lines.

c716-30 BC 9.5in (26cm) high

$2,000-2,500 **SI**

A Late Period Egyptian polychrome wood mummy mask, the face painted and wearing a striated wig.

c716-30 BC 13.75in (35cm) high

$2,000-2,500 **SI**

A Late Period Egyptian polychrome wood mummy mask.

c1085-322 BC 10.75in (26cm) high

$1,500-2,000 **SI**

A Late Period Egyptian wood mummy mask, carved with a serene expression, with traces of polychrome.

c710-30 BC 12in (30.5cm) high

$2,000-2,500 **SI**

An Late Period Egyptian wood mummy mask, carved with a serene expression, with traces of polychrome.

c710-30 BC 11in (28cm) high

$1,000-1,500 **SI**

A Late Period Egyptian wood mummy mask, with broad round face, slightly aquiline nose with remains of polychrome.

c712-30 BC 9in (22.5cm) high

$750-850 **SI**

A Late Period Egyptian wood mummy mask, with broad round face, slightly aquiline nose with remains of polychrome.

c712-30 BC 10in (25.5cm) high

$900-1,100 **SI**

A Late Period Egyptian wood mummy mask, with broad round face, slightly aquiline nose and remains of polychrome.

c712-30 BC 7in (18cm) high

$800-900 **SI**

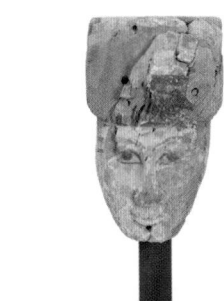

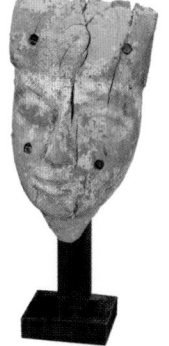

A Late Period Egyptian wood mummy mask, with broad round face, slightly aquiline nose with remains of polychrome.

c712-30 BC 10in (25.5cm) high

$600-700 **SI**

A Late Period Egyptian wood mummy mask with broad round face, slightly aquiline nose with remains of polychrome.

c712-30 BC 11.5in (29cm) high

$600-700 **SI**

A Late Period Egyptian wood mummy mask, carved with a serene expression, with traces of polychrome.

c710-30 BC 10.5in (25cm) high

$600-700 **SI**

A Late Period Egyptian wood mummy mask, carved with a serene expression, with traces of polychrome.

c710-30 BC 10.5in (27cm) high

$600-700 **SI**

A Late Period Egyptian wood mummy mask, with broad round face and slightly aquiline nose with remains of polychrome.

c712-30 BC   11.5in (29cm) high

$600-700   SI

A Late Period Egyptian wood and composite sarcophagus lid, with broad decorative collar and tripartite wig.

c712-30 BC   24in (61cm) high

$7,000-8,000   SI

An Egyptian polychrome wood panel from a sarcophagus, painted with the mummified jackal-headed deity Anubis.

15.5in (48cm) high

$1,400-1,800   SI

An Egyptian faience mummy mask, with fine facial depiction composed of turquoise disc-shaped beads, and with a border of light-blue tubular beads.

c300 BC   6in (15cm) high

$1,000-1,500   SI

An Egyptian bead mummy mask.

c1000 BC   5.5in (14cm) wide

$450-550   AnA

A Late Period Egyptian terracotta part of an anthropoid sarcophagus.

c712-720 BC   10.5in (27cm) high

$2,500-3,000   SI

USHABTIS

Small figurines in the form of manual laborers were placed in graves in ancient Egypt. It was believed that in the next world the dead would be called upon to perform hard labor. It was thought that the buried ushabtis would undertake these tasks on behalf of the dead. The ushabtis are often depicted with crossed arms and exposed hands. Royal ushabtis held a crook and flail, but more commonly ushabtis held a seed bag, hand hoe and mattock.

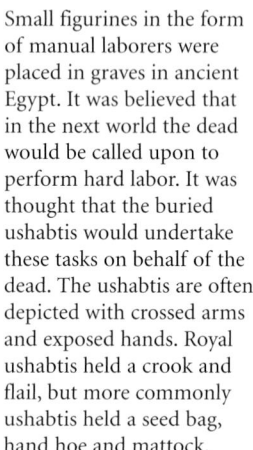

An Egyptian faience ushabti figure, with incised hieroglyphics.

c500 BC   4in (10cm) high

$150-200   AnA

A plain faience Egyptian ushabti figure.

c300 BC   3in (8cm) high

$70-100   AnA

An Egyptian ushabti figure, with panels of hieroglyphics.

c500-300 BC   6.25in (16cm) high

$450-550   AnA

An Ramessine Period Egyptian polychrome terracotta ushabti of Pentaur, yellow-painted with details of broad collar, hoe and mattock and a single column of hieroglyphs.

c1292-1085 BC   7.5in (19cm) high

$750-850   SI

An Egyptian polychrome terracotta ushabti, depicted mummiform, wearing a tripartite wig with the arms crossed on the chest and the body with hieroglyphic text, New Kingdom.

c1307-1070 BC   6.5in (16cm) high

$550-650   SI

A Late Period Egyptian faience ushabti of Sameres, depicted mummiform, wearing a tripartite wig and curved false beard, holding hoes and a seed bag over the left shoulder, decorated with hieroglyphic text.

c1085-322 BC   5in (12.5cm) high

$200-300   **SI**

A Late Period Egyptian faience ushabti, depicted mummiform shape, holding hoes and a seed bag over the shoulder, with hieroglyphic text.

c1085-322 BC   5in (12.5cm) high

$300-400   **SI**

A Late Period Egyptian faience ushabti, depicted in mummiform, wearing a tripartite wig and curved false beard, holding hoes and a seed bag over the left shoulder, decorated with hieroglyphic text.

1085-322 BC 6.75in (17.5cm) high

$1,400-1,800   **SI**

An Egyptian turquoise faience ushabti.

c600 BC   4in (10cm) high

$300-350   **SI**

An Egyptian faience ushabti, with incised hieroglyphics.

c500 BC   4.75in (12cm) high

$150-200   **AnA**

An Egyptian terracotta ushabti figure, with traces of yellow stripe remaining.

c1100 BC   6.25in (15.6cm) high

$350-450   **AnA**

An Egyptian terracotta ushabti, depicted mummiform, wearing a tripartite wig with a line of hieroglyphic inscription, New Kingdom.

c1540-1075 BC   7in (18cm) high

$500-550   **SI**

A Late Period Egyptian linen effigy of Imset, one of the four sons of Horus, tightly wrapped and depicted mummiform with a human head, the wig and broad collar woven in contrasting hues of linen and the features of the face depicted in paint, Dynasty XXVI-XXX.

c664-343 BC   18in (45cm) high

$3,000-3,500   **SI**

A Late Period Egyptian faience ushabti, depicted in mummiform, wearing a tripartite wig, holding a hoe and with a seed bag over the left shoulder, decorated with hieroglyphic text.

c716-30 BC   6.25in (15.5cm) high

$800-900   **SI**

Four Late Period Egyptian faience ushabti of Nestahi, the mummiform figures with arms crossed over the abdomen, each hand holding a hoe and with a single line of hieroglyphic text.

c1085-322 BC   3in (8cm) high

$1,500-1,800   **SI**

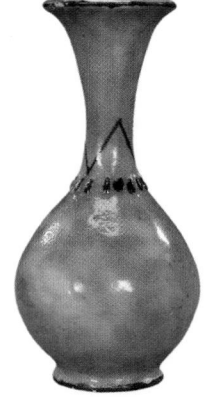

An Egyptian faience ushabti, depicted mummiform with arms crossed over the abdomen, each hand holding a hoe, with a single line of hieroglyphic text inscribed for "Osiris, the scribe", New Kingdom, Dynasty XIX-XX.

c1307-1070 BC 6.25in (16cm) high

$1,000-1,500 **SI**

A Late Period Egyptian faience ushabti, depicted mummiform, wearing a tripartite wig and curved false beard, holding hoes and a seed bag over the left shoulder, with hieroglyphic text.

c1085-322 BC 3.75in (9.5cm) high

$400-500 **SI**

An Egyptian faience ushabti, depicted mummiform, with tripartite wig.

c600 BC 5.5in (14cm) high

$600-700 **SI**

An Egyptian faience vase, of ovoid form, with an elongated neck, with everted rim, with a raised tongue pattern on the shoulders.

8in (20cm) high

$3,000-3,500 **SI**

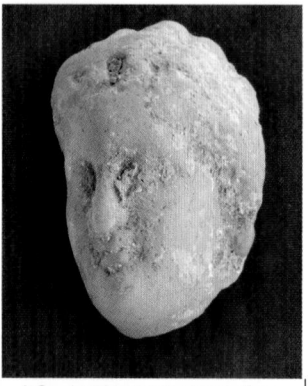

A Greek terracotta head of a youth.

1st-2ndC BC 1in (2.5cm) high

$60-80 **AnA**

A Greek red terracotta head of a youth, with good detail.

1st 2ndC BC 1.5in (4cm) high

$90-120 **AnA**

A Greek terracotta figure of a youth riding a ram.

2ndC BC 3.5 in (8cm) high

$250-300 **AnA**

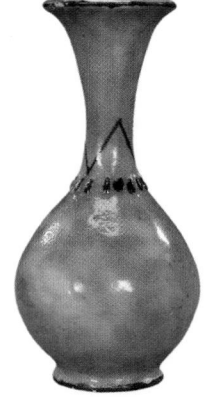

A Coptic polychrome pottery vessel, of ovoid form and conical neck, painted in black and brown with geometric decoration.

The Copts were a Christian descendent of the ancient Egyptians.

AD 4th-6thC 9.5in (24cm) high

$450-550 **SI**

An Islamic Period Egyptian green glass bottle and basket, of globular form with a short neck, in a woven basket with cover.

AD 640-969 4in (10cm) high

$300-350 **SI**

A Roman Period Egyptian glass bottle, with a pear-shaped body and cylindrical neck.

322 BC-AD 395 6in (15cm) high

$200-300 **SI**

An Islamic Period Egyptian green glass bottle, of hexagonal form with a conical neck.

AD 640-969 5.25in (13.5cm) high

$150-200 **SI**

An Islamic Period Egyptian glass stem bowl, of circular bombé-form raised on a conical foot.

AD 640-969 2.5in (6.5cm) high

$300-350 **SI**

A Greek terracotta fragment, from a statue, in the form of a draped female in Helenistic style.

3rdC BC — 4in (10cm) high

$180-220 — **AnA**

A Miletus terracotta scent bottle, in the form of a goose, Aphrodite group.

c575-550 BC — 2.75in (7cm) high

$650-750 — **AnA**

A Greek terracotta protome of a female goddess.

5thC BC — 4in (10cm) high

$300-350 — **AnA**

A Greek terracotta figure of a goddess, probably Demeter.

5thC BC — 7in (18cm) high

$200-300 — **AnA**

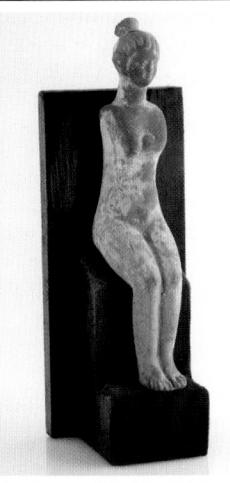

A Greek terracotta figure of a seated woman.

4thC BC — 7in (17.5cm) high

$600-650 — **AnA**

A Greek terracotta statue of a female.

4thC BC — 8.25 in (21cm) high

$1,300-1,800 — **AnA**

An Greek terracotta figure of a priestess, with traces of polychrome.

8thC BC — 6in (15cm) high

$450-550 — **SI**

A late 5thC BC Scythian gold appliqué, the sheet plaque-die-formed as a stag, slightly recessed behind.

The stag, very often recumbent, was one of the most popular Scythian motifs.

2in (5cm) wide

$1,200-1,500 — **SI**

A Greek late Archaic Period head of Persephone.

Persephone was the beautiful daughter of Demeter and Zeus.

c520 BC — 7.5in (19cm) high

$900-1,100 — **SI**

A Greek late Archaic Period terracotta bust of a Koure.

500 BC — 6.25in (16cm) high

$750-850 — **SI**

An 6thC BC Eastern Greek terracotta "plastic" vase, in the form of a crouching dwarf.

7in (17.5cm) high

$1,200-1,800 — **AnA**

A Boeotia Greek terracotta goddess, probably Aphrodite.

4thC BC — 10.25in (26cm) high

$1,400-2,000 — **AnA**

A Magna Graecian lamp filler or Guttos, in burnished blackware.

3rdC BC   3.5in (9cm) high

$300-400   **AnA**

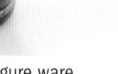

A 4thC BC Magna Graecian red figure ware skyphos or wine cup, with an owl standing.

4thC BC   2.75in (7cm) high

$550-650   **AnA**

A Mycenaean buffware vessel, of ovoid form with two loop handles, painted in brown with circular bands, Mycenaean III.

c1400-1300 BC   6in (15cm) diam

$450-550   **SI**

A Magna Graecian Lekanis, in red ware "lady of fashion" design.

Magna Graecia, or "Great Greece", were the Greek colonies of Southern Italy, founded during the Greek expansion in 8thC BC. They began to decline by 500 BC, probably due to warfare and disease.

4th-3rdC BC   4in (10cm) high

$300-350   **AnA**

A Greek Iron Age terracotta jug, from the Cypro-Archaic Period, with pierced spout resembling a bird.

9thC BC   9.75in (25cm) high

$400-500   **AnA**

A Mesopotamian Terracotta cuneiform foundation cone, with a ten line inscription of Gudea, King of Lagash.

c2100 BC   5in (12.5cm) high

$300-350   **AnA**

SUMERIAN CUNEIFORM

Sumerian cuneiform emerged as the world's first writing system in South Mesopotamia. Cuneiform means "wedge-shaped" and refers to the reed or stylus used to inscribe the clay tablet. Sumerians believed that record keeping was vitally important and only a select few, usually wealthy, boys were permitted to learn the language. Only after twelve years of schooling could they become a scribe.

An old Babylonian tablet in cuneiform writing with Sumerian literature.

c1800 BC   3in (8cm) wide

$2,500-3,000   **AnA**

A Mesopotamian bronze short sword with integral hilt.

c1000 BC   14.5in (37cm) long

$550-650   **AnA**

An old Babylonian cuneiform tablet, written by a scribe in a scribe school.

c1800 BC   3in (7.5cm) wide

$400-500   **AnA**

An old Babylonian administrative document, in cuneiform.

c1800 BC   5.25 in (13cm) wide

$700-800   **AnA**

An Akkadian administrative document, in cuneiform.

c2100 BC   1.5in (3cm) wide

$400-500   **AnA**

An administrative document, in Sumerian cuneiform.

c2000 BC   1.5in (3.5cm) wide

$400-500   **AnA**

A Mesopotamian black stone vessel, with vestiges of lug handle.

c2000 BC   2.75in (7cm) high

$250-300   **AnA**

A Mesopotamian cream stone vessel, with everted lip.

c2000 BC   2.75in (7cm) high

$200-250   **AnA**

A Mesopotamian terracotta head of a Babylonian goddess, with original paint pigment.

c2000 BC   2.25in (5cm) high

$650-700   **AnA**

A Mesopotamian Tel Halaf terracotta figure of a seated female, used for votive purposes, with some restoration.

Mesopotamia was the ancient region located between the Tigris and Euphrates rivers in modern Iraq and Syria. It was the site of several early urban civilizations, including Babylonia.

c5000 BC   3.5in (9cm) high

$300-350   **AnA**

An Akkadian cylinder seal, with contest scene, carved with a "hero" and two horned animals.

c2400-2200 BC   1in (2.5cm) high

$450-550   **SI**

A Sassanian stone cylinder seal, carved with a lion and a hero.

AD 5thC   1.5in (4cm) high

$900-1,100   **SI**

An old Babylonian hematite cylinder seal, showing a king standing between two goddesses and one line inscription.

c2000-1600 BC 0.75in (2cm) high

$400-500   **SI**

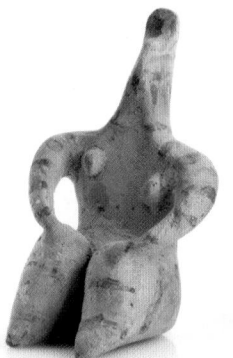

A Mesopotamian Tel Halaf terracotta figure of a seated female, used for votive purposes, with some restoration.

c5000 BC   5.25in (13.5cm) high

$300-350   **AnA**

An old Babylonian hematite cylinder seal, showing a warrior king standing between a suppliant goddess with both hands raised and Ishatar holding a sword.

c2000-1600 BC   0.75in (2cm) high

$400-500   **SI**

A Parthian terracotta figure of a female holding a child and riding a horse.

AD 200   5.25in (13.5cm) high

$200-250

The Pathian Empire spanned from 247 BC to AD 228 in ancient Persia (Iran). The Parthian's conquered most of the Middle East and south-west Asia and became a superpower equivalent to Rome in the west. There is limited historical evidence of the Parthians, and most of what we know has been deduced from their coins.

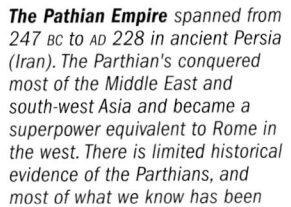

A Syrian Syro Mittite fertility figure, with birdlike features.

c2000 BC   6.75in (17cm) high

$200-300   **AnA**

A Luristan bronze finial, in the form of a two-headed Janiform divinity grasping the throats of confronted monsters.

c8thC BC   4in (10cm) high

$1,200-1,500   **SI**

A Luristan bronze axe head, with curved blade and four prongs on the shaft hole.

c8thC BC　　　　　　8.25in (21cm) high

$700-800　　　　　　　　　**SI**

A Persian terracotta figure of a horse, possibly Luristan or Amlastt.

c1000 BC　　　　　　6.75in (17cm) wide

$400-500　　　　　　　　　**SI**

A Luristan bronze bowl, of circular form with a triangular handle.

c8thC BC　　　　　　　6in (15cm) diam

$200-300　　　　　　　　　**SI**

A northern Indian Ghandara stucco head of a man.

AD 3rdC　　　　　　　2in (5cm) high

$70-100　　　　　　　　　**AnA**

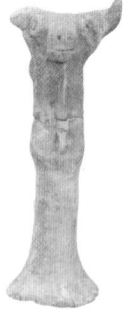

A rare north-west Persian figure of a bull, in the form of a priest sceptor.

c2000 BC　　　　　7.25in (19cm) high

$150-200　　　　　　　　　**SI**

An Anatolian Neolithic terracotta vessel, with applied lotus head.

c3000 BC　　　　　　21in (53cm) high

$1,000-1,500　　　　　　　**SI**

A Near Eastern terracotta vessel, of ovoid form, with two handles, raised on conical foot.

c2200-2300 BC 16in (40.5cm) high

$1,000-1,500　　　　　　　**SI**

A Trans-Jordan Alabaster vessel, with pierced handle.

c2000 BC　　　　　　3in (7.5cm) high

$250-300　　　　　　　　　**AnA**

A Palestine (Holy Land) Iron Age pilgrim flask.

c2000 BC　　　　　　6in (15cm) high

$100-150　　　　　　　　　**AnA**

A Palestine (Holy Land) terracotta "cocked hat" oil lamp.

c2000 BC　　　　　　4in (10cm) diam

$40-70　　　　　　　　　**AnA**

A Palestine (Holy Land) terracotta Abydos ware jug.

c3000-2800 BC　　　　7in (18cm) high

$200-300　　　　　　　　　**AnA**

A Chinese Yuan Dynasty zodiac figure of a snake.

AD c1279-1368　　　　3in (8cm) high

$50-70　　　　　　　　　**AnA**

A Sui Dynasty Chinese straw-glazed female figure.

AD 589-618　　　8.5in (21.5cm) high

$300-350　　　　　　　　　**AnA**

A Chinese straw-glazed female figure, from the Sui Dynasty.

AD 589-618　　　8.75in (22cm) high

$300-350　　　　　　　　　**AnA**

A Chinese Tang Dynasty terracotta figure of a dwarf or medicine man, holding a curly staff.

AD 618-907　　　　6in (15cm) high

$350-400　　　　　　　　　**AnA**

A Northern Qi Dynasty terracotta soldier, with paint pigment.

AD c550-577   9.75in (25cm) high

$350-400   **AnA**

A Sui Dynasty straw-glazed terracotta attendant figure, with traces of paint pigment.

AD c589-618   10.25in (26cm) high

$600-700   **AnA**

A Tang Dynasty terracotta statue of a court lady, with traces of paint pigment.

AD c618-907   9.5in (24cm) high

$250-300   **AnA**

A Sui Dynasty straw-glazed terracotta figure of an attendant soldier.

AD c589-618   11.5in (29cm) high

$700-800   **AnA**

A large Tang Dynasty pottery model of a standing saddled horse, the buff-colored body with traces of original pigment, with some restoration.

China enjoyed a period of consolidation and achievement during the Tang Dynasty, and this is reflected in the realism and assurance of Tang Art. Ceramics of this era show superior craftsmanship and for this reason are often compared to the pottery of the Classical Greeks. This lead glazed earthenware statue is a realistic portrait of a horse with expressive and lifelike features. Horses were revered for their religious significance and were traditionally associated with the dragon, the supernatural and the afterlife. They were also a symbol of military preparedness and diplomacy among Tang rulers and aristocrats.

AD c618-906   24in (61cm) high

$4,000-5,000   **WW**

A Tang Dynasty terracotta attendant figure, with paint pigment.

AD c618-907   38in (97cm) high

$1,000-1,500   **AnA**

A Han Dynasty terracotta miniature soldier, with paint pigment.

206 BC-AD 220   19in (48) high

$500-550   **AnA**

A Northern Qi Dynasty terracotta horse and rider, with paint pigment.

AD c550-577   13in (33cm) high

$1,800-2,200   **AnA**

A Han Dynasty terracotta head of a woman.

206 BC-AD 220 4.5in (11.5cm) high

$260-320   **AnA**

A Schist stone head of Buddah.

AD 3rdC   2.25in (5cm) long

$100-150   **AnA**

A Tang Dynasty terracotta mask of a tomb guardian or demon.

AD c618-907   8in (20cm) diam

$1,700-2,000   **AnA**

A Han Dynasty Sichuan pottery amphora, with spiral decoration.

c200 BC-AD 200   7.5in (19cm) high

$550-600	AnA

A Han Dynasty "cocoon" or "duck egg" jar, in burnished terracotta.

c200 BC   9.75in (25cm) high

$500-550	AnA

A 12thC Song Dynasty granary or dragon jar, with modeled figures.

24in (61cm) high

$300-350	AnA

A 16thC Ming dynasty bronze-gilt head.

4in (10cm) high

$700-800	AnA

A Roman bronze figure of a prancing horse, standing on an integral base.

1stC BC-AD 4thC   2.5in (6cm) high

$700-800	AnA

A Roman bronze figure of a bull, standing on an integral base.

1stC BC-AD 4thC   1.75in (4cm) high

$550-650	AnA

A Roman bronze bust of a man, with superb quality patina.

1stC BC   2.75in (7cm) high

$2,500-3,000	AnA

An ancient Roman bronze appliqué, of the forepart of a horse.

AD 2nd-3rdC   1.25in (3cm) high

$280-320	AnA

A Roman terra sigillata fragment, molded to depict gladiators.

AD c1stC   6.5in (15cm) long

$750-850	SI

A Roman terracotta plaque of Jupiter and Juno.

c1stC BC   4.75in (12cm) high

$900-1,100	SI

A Greco-Roman polychrome terracotta figure of a boy, standing on a square plinth and wearing a pointed hat.

c4thC BC   8.5in (21cm) high

$1,000-1,300	SI

A Greco-Roman terracotta figure of a boy, holding fruits with his left hand.

c1stC BC   11in (28cm) high

$400-500	SI

Two Roman terracotta heads.

c1stC BC   largest 3.5in (9cm) high

$200-300 (both)	SI

A Roman terracotta figure of a dog, with incised details.

AD c2nd C   3.5in (9cm) high

$550-650   **SI**

A Greco-Roman terracotta figure of a bearded man, with one arm raised.

c1stC BC   6.5in (16.5cm) high

$700-800   **SI**

A Greco-Roman terracotta head jar, molded to depict a Satyr head below a waisted neck with loop handle.

AD c1stC   4.25in (11.5cm) high

$1,000-1,300   **SI**

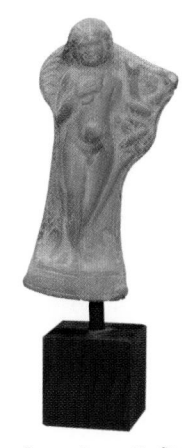

A Greco-Roman terracotta figure of a woman, wearing long robes.

c1stC BC   5.5in (13.5cm) high

$600-700   **SI**

A Roman terracotta figure of a gladiator, holding a shield in his left hand.

1stC BC   25in (11cm) high

$600-700   **SI**

A Roman marble head of a Goddess, after a Hellenistic prototype, wearing a high headdress above an oval face with smiling expression.

AD 2ndC   9in (23cm) high

$2,000-2,500   **SI**

Two Roman terracotta heads.

1stC BC   2.5in (6.5cm) high

$300-350 (both)   **SI**

A Corinthian buff terracotta vessel.

c6thC BC   4.5in (11.5cm) diam

$1,500-2,000   **SI**

An Estruscan Bucchero amphora black-fired clay funerary vessel, with wide openwork handles and incised frieze of animals around shoulder.

6th-5thC BC   14.25in (36cm) high

$2,000-2,500   **SI**

A Greco-Roman terracotta vessel, of ovoid form with a pointed base and waisted neck.

AD c200   6.25in (16.5cm) high

$450-550   **SI**

A Roman terracotta ribbed juglet.

AD c3rd-4thC   5.5in (14cm) high

$70-100   **AnA**

Roman

A Roman stone head of a woman, with her hair parted in the center and swept up from the forehead and temples.

AD 1stC   1.5in (4cm) high

$100-150   **SI**

A Roman marble draped male bust, wearing a tunic and paludamentum.

AD 2nd-3rdC   6.75in (18cm) wide

$1,000-1,500   **SI**

Two Roman white marble Janus Herms, after a Hellenistic prototype, each with a youthful face with small bow-shaped rounded chin and short curly hair with a laurel wreath.

c1stC AD

$7,500-8,500 (both)   **SI**

Provenance: *formerly owned by Paul Horgan, Pulitzer Prize winning author.*

8.5in (21.5cm) pair high

A Roman bronze appliqué disc with the facing head of a river god.

AD 1st-2ndC   5in (13cm) diam

$3,500-4,000   **AnA**

A Roman marble trapezophorus, in the form of a lion's head emerging from a single paw support, the well-modeled lion's head with a mane of thick comma-shaped locks.

AD 2ndC   31in (79cm) high

$35,000-40,000   **SI**

A Roman bronze statue of Zeus flanked by eagles, with inscription on base.

2ndC AD   12in (31cm) high

$42,000-45,000   **AnA**

A Roman marble head of a man, from a lifesize statue or bust, with large deep-set eyes and incised irises.

3rdC AD   9.5in (24cm) high

$24,000-28,000   **SI**

OIL LAMPS

Roman terracotta or "baked-clay" oil lamps were made of fairly coarse, porous clay that assumes a red-ocher color when fired and is usually left unglazed. The wick was of flax that was immersed in vegetable oil or animal fat. Molds were made of stone, clay or plaster. Potters discovered that that forming a spout on the saucer helped to keep the wick in place, which explains the distinctive shape. They were used as a source of light for every household.

A Roman terracotta lamp, with the discus showing a Victory standing on a globe.

AD 2ndC   5.5in (14cm) wide

$500-600   **AnA**

A Roman terracotta lamp, the discus decorated with the head of Zeus Serapis.

AD c1stC   4in (10cm) wide

$650-700   **AnA**

A Roman terracotta lamp, the discus decorated with the scene of Dido burning in Carthage.

AD c2ndC   4.5in (11.5cm) wide

$1,700-2,000   **AnA**

A Roman terracotta lamp, the discus showing Jason and the golden fleece.

AD 2ndC   4.75in (12cm) wide

$550-650   **AnA**

A late Roman terracotta oil lamp, the discus showing a scene from the Bible, of Nebuchadnezzar and the three Hebrews.

                         5.25in (13.5cm) wide

$500-600   **AnA**

A Roman terracotta oil lamp, in buff slip.

AD 1st-2ndC   4in (10cm) wide

$70-100   **AnA**

A Roman terracotta oil lamp, the discus showing a galloping chariot with charioteer.

AD 2ndC   4in (10cm) wide

$400-500   **AnA**

A Roman oil lamp, the discus with a floral pattern.

AD 2ndC   3.25in (8.5cm) wide

$100-130   **AnA**

Roman

ANCIENT GLASS

Glassmakers established themselves Rome during the reign of the Emperor Augustus (27 BC–AD 14). The Romans used more glass than any other ancient civilization and glass vessels became commonplace throughout their empire as far afield as Scandinavia and the Far East. They were used mainly for drinking vessels, perfumes and medicines.

A Roman unguentarium, in honey-colored glass.

AD 1st-3rdC   3.25in (8cm) high

$200-300   **AnA**

A Late Roman glass jar, with trailed decoration around the rim.

AD 4th-5thC   2in (5.5cm) high

$70-100   **AnA**

A Roman unguentarium (tear bottle), in blue glass.

AD 1st-3rdC   2.25in (6cm) high

$200-300   **AnA**

A Roman translucent mold-blown two-handled flask, with decorated square panels.

AD 5thC   4.25in (11cm) high

$1,700-2,000   **AnA**

A Roman translucent, iridescent, mold-blown two-handled jar.

AD c200   4.25in (10cm) high

$900-1,000   **AnA**

A Roman two-handled glass flask, with dimpled body.

AD 4thC   4.75in (12cm) high

$850-950   **AnA**

An iridescent Roman flask, with trefoil mouth and single handle, on pedestal foot.

1stC BC-AD 4thC 6.75in (17cm) high

$2,800-3,200   **AnA**

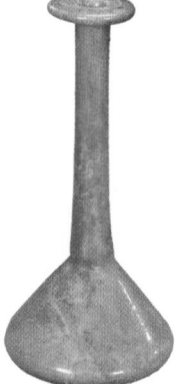

A Roman green glass bottle, of conical form with elongated neck.

AD c2nd-3rdC   9in (23cm) high

$300-400   **SI**

A Roman green glass bottle, of conical form with elongated neck.

AD c2nd-3rdC   9.5in (24cm) high

$350-450   **SI**

TRIBAL ART, ALSO KNOWN AS ART PREMIÈRE OR NON-EUROPEAN ART, refers to genuine objects made in a traditional form, for use in a historic rite, or other purpose of the respective society, as opposed to objects made solely for resale or as tourist souvenirs.

Desirability is increased by the age and beauty of a piece, however these are not the only criteria. A beautiful object that is only 30 years old with evident signs of wear and usage can be equally sought after. Tribal Art with accompanying documented provenance will be of more value.

The strength of form and vision in Tribal Art has influenced many contemporary painters and sculptors. When Picasso first saw African sculptures in the Palais du Trocadero in 1907 he was transfixed and his art transformed. Western eyes have continued to be thrilled by the artistic integrity of authentic Tribal Art. The current fashion for realism extends through art, fashion, film, interiors and architecture. Consequently there has been a resurgence of interest in the bold, uncompromising qualities of masks, sculptures and ethnographic items from Africa, Oceania, South East Asia and the Americas.

A 19thC Salampusu head hunter's knife, with lion's mane.

23.5in (60cm) long

$900-1,000   EL

A mid-19thC Ethiopian Amhara or Amaroo shield, made of Buffalo hide.

26in (66cm) high

$2,500-2,800   EL

From far left: A 19thC Zande spear with large decorated blade, metal binding and metal lower shaft, from the D.R. Congo; a 19thC spear with incised metal tip and carved handle; a 19thC Maasai spear, from Kenya.

$220-280; $90-120; $150-170   EL

An early 20thC Namchi fertility doll, from Cameroon.

10.25in (26cm) high

$1,200-1,500   EL

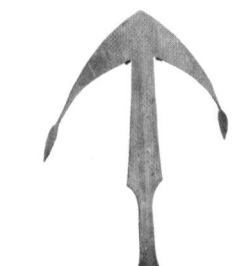

A late 19thC/early 20thC Mandjang iron currency, in the shape of an anchor, from Cameroon.

Metal was used throughout Africa for barter and so most metal objects hover on the edge of being considered currency. Bells, spears, knives or hoes were readily used as "money".

20in (51cm) high

$600-650   EL

A late 19thC/early 20thC currency in an iron bunch.

*These **currencies** were exchanged for rubber or ivory until the beginning of the 20thC when they were abolished by colonials.*

17.5in (44cm) high

$900-1,200   EL

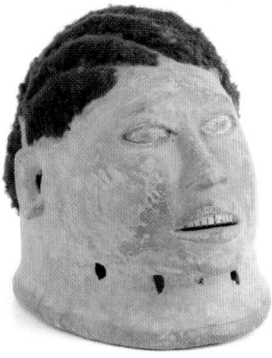

An early 20thC Makonde wooden helmet mask from Tanzania, depicting a European, with human hair.

8.75in (22cm) high

$2,200-2,500   EL

An early 20thC Makonde wooden drum, from Tanzania.

11.25in (29cm) high

$1,500-1,700   EL

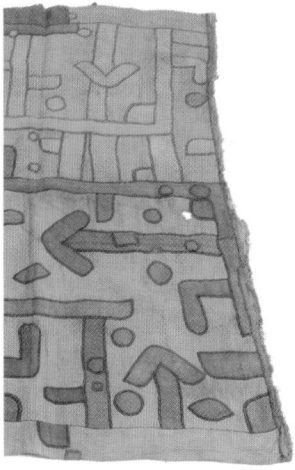

A 19thC Ntchak panel of Kuba fabric, wound from palm fibres, made in D.R. Congo.

28.75in (73cm) wide

$270-300   EL

A 19thC Kuba fabric panel, the border made from palm fibre and the center made from a patchwork of tapa bark cloth, D.R. Congo.

26in (66cm) wide

$1,200-1,800   EL

TEXTILES FROM THE KUBA KINGDOM IN THE DEMOCRATIC REPUBLIC OF CONGO

These lengths of fabric were worn as skirts by both men and women, held up by beaded and woven belts. They were made from beaten palm fibres, which were woven into fabric by men, and embroidered and decorated by women. The amount of time which went into the making of these lengths of fabric made them extremely valuable, and they were traded as dowries and currencies. Skirts with inserts of imported European fabrics were considered a particularly prestige item.

The geometric designs of the Kuba people are not only found in textile designs, but also in body scarifications, wooden carvings, basketwork and pottery. The absence of such decoration was an indication of poverty. The appliquéd patches are thought to have been originally sewn on to repair tears, but gradually these patches took the form of highly stylized patterns. Other decorative techniques included resist dyeing, in which reeds or seeds were bound and stitched onto the textiles before they were dyed with natural pigments and plant dyes; pierced embroidery and the addition of panels of alternate fabric such as bark cloth or imported fabrics. Bark or tapa cloth was made by beating tree bark until it was thin and pliable and then decorating it with a mixture of gardenia juice and charcoal.

A 19thC Kuba fabric panel, made from palm fibre, with a velvet cut pile section in the center.

25.25in (64cm) wide

$1,200-1,800   EL

A 19thC Kuba fabric skirt, with pierced embroidery decoration.

141in (360cm) long

$1,500-1,700   EL

A 19thC Ntchak Kuba fabric panel, wound from palm fibres, made in D.R. Congo.

28.75in (73cm) wide

$270-300   EL

An early 20thC Bambura iron fetish shrine figure, from Mali.

The Bambara masks and sculptures are described as abstract and geometric compared to the naturalistic styles of neighboring tribes around the Guinea Coast or the Congo Basin.

6in (15cm) long

$150-200   EL

An early 20thC Kenyan Maasai buffalo hide shield.

26in (67cm) wide

$1,000-1,500   EL

Two mid-20thC Zulu beer pots, from Southern Africa.

These Zulu pots are from the Northern Nguni region of Southern Africa. They were used for storing and, in the case of pots with rims, transporting beer. It is thought that beer goes sour less quickly in clay pots, and beer drinking is a ritualized activity demanding proper clay vessels as opposed to plastic.

Tallest 14.25in (36cm) high

$600-650, $450-500 EL

A pair of mid-20thC Chiwara male and female antelope headdresses, from Bambara, Mali.

Young men's agricultural societies organize their ceremonies around the sacrifice of chickens and goats and it is through these that the adolescents hope to gain their force, health and working strength. These antelope headdresses are worn attached to a basket weave cap, and are always in pairs of male and female. Before the rainy season, or when a new field has been cleared, a dancer wearing such a headdress will accompany the members of the agricultural society out to the field and supervise the work.

18.5in (47cm) long

$3,000-3,500 EL

Three 20thC Maasai snuff bottles, made from horn, with hide lids.

3in (8cm) long

$90-120 each EL

An early 20thC colonial figure.

7.5in (19cm) wide

$750-800 EL

A 20thC Bambura marionette.

29in (73cm) long

$3,750-4,000 EL

Two pairs of South African Zulu earplugs, made from wood and perspex, with chrome studs.

By the second quarter of the 20thC large disc-like earplugs were increasingly being worn by

women as fashion items. In the 1950s large plain wooden discs known as Marley tiles were decorated with vinyl asbestos. Most of these earplugs were made by Zulu craftsmen in Johannesburg and sold to migrant workers who wore them themselves or took them home as gifts. In the 1960s and 70s the vinyl tiles were replaced by perspex and other plastics. The motifs became simpler and bolder and they were often decorated with large chrome studs.

2.5in (6cm) diam

$150-170 (pair) EL

An African ivory bracelet.

4in (10cm) diam

$675-700 Clv

A Tami Islands wooden food bowl, of elongated form, the exterior with stylized carving.

21in (53.25cm) long

$220-280 SI

A Tanzanian Makonde wood face mask, with protuding chin, bared teeth and prominent ears.

8.25in (21cm) high

$1,800-2,200 SI

A 19thC iron currency, from D.R. Congo.

21in (53cm) high

$550-600 EL

African

A 19thC Ngala or Ngombe ceremonial executioner's knife, from D.R. Congo.

27in (68cm) long

$450-500 EL

A 19thC Lokele Isoko shield, from the Lomani river region of D.R. Congo

19in (48cm) long

$1,500-1,700 EL

A 19thC bunch of five Katanga crosses, used as currencies, with original fibre binding, from the Kasai river region of D.R. Congo.

Katanga crosses were made from the middle of the 18thC until the 1920s, serving as mediums of exchange, regalia, currency, raw material and insignia. The crosses were made by pouring molten copper into molds in the sand. One cross was worth ten kilos of flour, five fowl, three kilos of rubber or six axes. A bride price consisted of fourteen large crosses, one goat, a gun and a female slave.

11in (28cm) wide

$1,200-$1,500 EL

An early 20thC Bena Lulua mask, from D.R. Congo.

12in (30cm) high

$5,200-5,800 EL

An ivory and snakeskin harp, delicately carved in the form of a figure, Nanqbetu, Zaire.

30.5in (77.5cm) long

$1,000-$1,500 SI

UNIQUE ASHANTI GOLD WEIGHTS

Gold was known in Africa even in prehistoric times and revered for its religious or magical properties – it was thought to be pure sun energy that never corrodes. The Akan, which occupied an area of Ghana and the Ivory Coast, developed a weighing system based on Islamic, Portuguese and English systems and introduced weights from 1400. Each weight was made by the lost-wax process, a 5,000 year old method of casting metal objects, and is therefore unique.

Wax is poured into a mold made from the original model and, after cooling, this is further worked before another mold is made around the corrected wax. On heating, the wax melts out of the mold and molten metal is poured in, filling the cavity. After breaking off the mold an exact metal replica of the original remains.

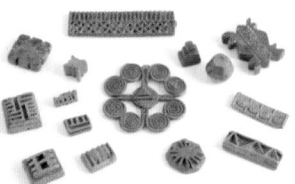

A selection of 15thC Ashanti representational and geometric gold weights, made by the lost wax method.

1.25in (3cm) long

$20-30 (each) EL

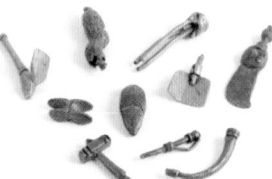

A selection of 18thC Ashanti representational gold weights, made by the lost wax method.

2in (5cm) long

$60-70 (each) EL

A 19thC Senoufu or Dyula bronze Do mask from the Ivory Coast.

*Like wooden masks, metal **Do masks** were used during the funerals of important people or on key Islamic holidays, and involved colorful masquerade dancing. Classical Do masks recall the Kpeli masks from which they are derived, with the decorated lateral extensions of the side of the face, animal horns and "legs" or "locks of hair" at the bottom.*

11in (28cm) high

$10,500-13,000 EL

A 19thC Bamum wooden bush cow mask, from the grasslands in Cameroon.

The buffalo represents strength, courage and power. Initiates were legally obliged to present the heads of all buffalos killed to their ruler. Failure to comply could earn the death penalty.

9in (23cm) wide

$3,700-4,000 EL

African

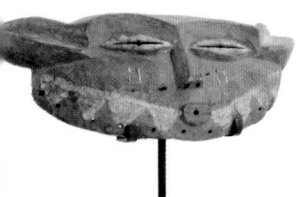

A mid-20thC Pende mask, from D.R. Congo.

6.75in (17cm) long

$1,200-1,500   **EL**

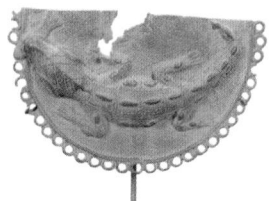

An 18th/19thC Benin bronze plaque, in a half moon shape with an alligator in relief, from Kingdom of Benin, W. Africa.

6.5in (16.5cm) high

$1,000-1,500   **SI**

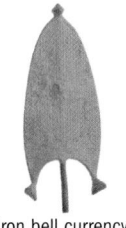

A 19thC iron bell currency, from Bangala, Nigeria.

Bells, *designed to be struck with rubber headed sticks, were traded in the late 19thC in the Congo.*

20.75in (53cm) high

$800-850   **EL**

A 19thC Ashanti chair, of wood, hide and brass, from Ghana.

31.5in (80cm) high

$2,200-2,500   **EL**

Two late 19thC early 20thC manillas, or currencies.

*The word **manilla** means bracelet. Originally these currencies, made from copper, brass or other metals, were open horse-shoe shapes with flared ends, but they evolved into highly decorated and elaborately formed objects. The first manillas may have been bolts from ships wrecked off the West African coast and the earliest pieces date back to 1439. In the 16thC manillas were used in the slave trade and were made in several European countries. Many manillas in use in Liberia and Nigeria were made in Antwerp. For centuries, they were the main currency in West Africa. It is documented that in 1556 the Portuguese paid 40 manillas for an ounce of gold.*
The English started trading in Africa in 1550 using many different styles of manilla, producing them in Birmingham, to pay for gold, ivory and pepper. By 1780 the Birmingham manilla had become a standard form of currency. The French and Dutch traded manilla to purchase palm oil and ivory. From 1902 the import of manillas was prohibited, and in 1911 their use as legal tender was banned. By 1919 foreign traders were prohibited from using manillas to trade with natives. However, they still circulated as currency. In 1948 the government decreed that all manillas should be withdrawn from circulation.

spiral manilla 2.75in (7cm) high

$150-180; $500-550   **EL**

Two late19th/early 20thC Lobi tribe iron serpents, from the Ivory Coast.

These snakes were placed in a shrine to protect against evil spirits.

17in (43cm) long

$225-250 each   **EL**

An early 20thC wooden Punu Okuyi face mask, from the Gabon.

Highly emphasized scarification marks divide the mask at the forehead and cheeks into three areas, which are typical of the Tsangui who live on either side of the D.R. Congo border. Wearers of the Punu mask would officiate at funerals where they danced as embodiments of the spirits of female and male ancestors, wearing stilts up to two meters high.

9in (23cm) high

$4,500-5,000   **EL**

An early 20thC Bambara door from Mali with breast handles, the exterior with weathered patina.

21.75in (55cm) wide

$2,200-2,500   **EL**

A Marke mask from Mali, in wood and brass.

c1940   15.75in (40cm) long

$3,000-3,500   **EL**

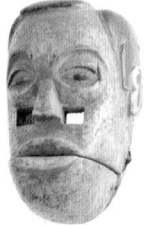

A mid-20thC mask depicting a European, in wood with oil paint, from Nigeria.

10.5in (27cm) high

$1,200-1,500   **EL**

A mid-20thC monkey mask, possibly from Cameroon.

11in (28cm) long

$1,800-2,200   **EL**

A 20thC Dan Gungye mask, in wood with traces of kaolin, from the Ivory Coast.

This mask is from the Northern Dan, demonstrated by its dark patina, smooth interior, high forehead, raised eyebrows and strongly protruding mouth. The large circular eye-holes permit unhindered vision by the wearer, and are characteristic of the masks worn in the racing masquerades, held each week in the dry season.

9.5in (24cm) long

$3,800-4,200   **EL**

491

African

A 20thC Baule mask, in wood with fabric, from the Ivory Coast.

Some baule masks have no ritualistic purpose, but instead are worn for dancing. These masks conform to an ideal of an aesthetically pleasing narrow, well-proportioned face with a high forehead, arching eyebrows, lowered eyelids and a narrow nose. The raised markings on the face are scarifications.

12in (30cm) long

$3,000-3,500	EL

A Baule standing female figure, a spirit mate or otherworld lover (blolo bla), with scarification on the face, from the Ivory Coast.

12.75in (32.5cm) high

$700-1,000	SI

An early 20thC betrothal doll, from the Fali tribe, Cameroon.

Betrothed women are given elaborately decorated carved wooden dolls, made by their fiancés. Worn in a baby carrier on her back, this doll is a symbol of her commitment and is symbolic of a future child. The doll is removed and stored away after the first baby is born.

A Baule heddle pulley, carved with goli masks and coiffure from the Ivory Coast.

Baule weavers, *always men, worked in public in full view of passers-by. The pulleys, from which the two heddles of a loom hang, are some of the most highly decorated Baule items and were intended to draw attention to the weaver and his work.*

c1950   10.25in (26cm) high

$300-350	EL

A Baule heddle pulley, from the Ivory Coast.

c1950   4in (12cm) high

$300-350	EL

10.5in (27cm) high

$900-1,100	EL

An unusual mid-20thC Christian shrine piece, made by the Ashanti tribe in Ghana.

3.5in (9cm) long

$150-170	EL

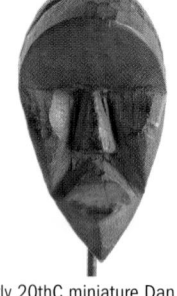

An early 20thC miniature Dan mask, from the Ivory Coast.

These small masks are often referred to as "passport masks" as they are used as an important means of identification for a man when he is traveling outside his immediate community. However, miniature masks have many uses. Any family who owns an important mask is entitled to commission a miniature to be made, so it may be taken to the farm or on long journeys, retaining contact with the mask-spirit even though the original is far away. Women are prohibited from owning full-scale masks, but are allowed miniature masks. The daughter of a family with an important mask may commission a miniature mask at the time of her marriage to retain her connection with the family's spirit.

A mid-20thC mask from Mali, surmounted by "Yasigine", the only female admitted into the Awa male society.

39.75in (101cm) high

$3,700-4,000	EL

3in (8cm) high

$270-320	EL

BEDU PLANK MASK FROM THE IVORY COAST

The Bedu mask is one of the largest African masks with one of the youngest traditions and is used throughout the Bondoukou region of the Ivory Coast. They usually appear in male and female pairs (this example is a male mask). The masks are worn by young men during the month-long harvest festival and represent fertility, healing and protection for the village. The mask is sculpted from the upper part of the roots of the Kapok tree, the largest forest tree of the region, and the accompanying costume is made from the bark of the Baobab tree, which has become a symbol of the African savannah. By removing the log of wood or the "quilt" of bark, neither tree is "killed", they are merely "wounded". Such hunting terminology is often used in connection with sculpting the Bedu mask or making its costume. The making of the mask represents the domestication of a wild animal. The sculpting tames the beast and the painting, carried out by the women of the village, invests it with authority.

A large mid-20thC Bedu plank mask, from the Bondoukou region of the Ivory Coast.

67in (170cm) long

$3,700-4,000	EL

An adult size Nigerian Ibo dance costume.

c1960

$140-180   EL

An Ibibio-Anang Ekpo society face mask, delicately carved with small mouth, downcast eyes, arched eyebrows and high coiffure, from Nigeria.

9in (23cm) high

$450-500   SI

An Igbo (Ibo) monkey mask, with articulated jaw and pronounced nose, with blue-white pigments, from Nigeria.

10in (25.5cm) high

$700-800   SI

An Igbo (Ibo) face mask, with beard, downcast eyes, high coiffure and white pigment, from Nigeria.

10in (25.5cm) high

$700-800   SI

Eastern Nigeria is dominated by the Igbo (Ibo) tribe who have lived there for centuries. The unique masks are made of wood or fabric and are made in honor of the dead in the hope that this will ensure the well-being of the community.

A Baule female figure, with exaggerated feet, the body covered in scarification with a ring neck and incised coiffure, possibly a spirit mate or otherworld lover (blolo bla), from the Ivory Coast.

11.75in (30cm) high

$380-420   SI

A Benin brass cup with handle, for use in Ewana Divination ceremony, from Kingdom of Benin, Africa.

5.25in (13.5cm) high

$600-650   SI

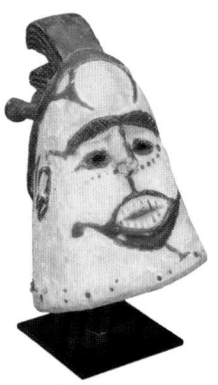

An Igbo (Ibo) wood cap mask, of flared form with a barred mouth and elaborate braids, from Nwanza, Nigeria.

11in (28cm) high

$1,500-2,000   SI

An Igbo (Ibo) dance head crest of a standing female.

21.75in (55cm) high

$1,500-2,000   SI

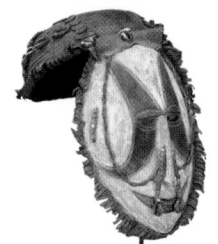

An Igbo (Ibo) Nri-Awka face mask, with raffa, cowrie shells and leather head covering, from Nigeria.

9.5in (24cm) high

$600-650   SI

An Igbo (Ibo) wooden ritual spoon, with a deep bowl and a curved stem, surmounted by a carved head.

22in (56cm) long

$500-550   SI

A small Igbo (Ibo) mask, with backward black-ware turned horns, from Nigeria.

10.5in (16.5cm) high

$380-420   SI

A stylized Senoufo Kpelie face, the a pierced mouth with scarification, from the Ivory Coast.

16.25in (41cm) high

$1,500-1,700   SI

A Mende stool, with a flared seat, the shaft support in the form of a human face, from Sierra Leone.

15in (38cm) high

$300-350 SI

A Sioux beaded child's vest, sewn with triangle and arrow feather designs and lined with early cloth.

c1880   13in (33cm) long

$1,500-2,000 SI

A Plains woven and beaded pipe bag.

26in (66cm) long

$370-450 SI

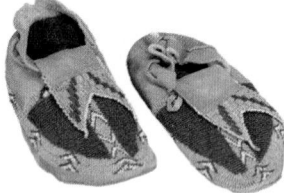

A pair of plain beaded, woven moccasins, with triangular flaps.

9in (23cm) long

$600-650 SI

A Zuni terracotta dough bowl, with geometric and circular motifs.

4.75in (11.5cm) high

$1,200-1,500 SI

A Southwest cylindrical vase, painted with geometric designs, signed Nanequari.

10in (25.5cm) high

$600-650 SI

Two Plains Indian fixed stonehead "skull crackers", of tapering oval form with hide wrapped shafts.

28in (71.25cm) long

$350-400 SI

An Eskimo ivory toy, in the form of a seal with sinew attachments and inset eyes.

7.25in (18.5cm) long

$800-1,000 SI

Seven Eskimo bone and wood implements, including a hook, barbed head, tusk and spear, measurement is of tusk.

Largest 9.5in (24cm) long

$220-280 SI

Three Eskimo wooden food bowls, of flaring oval form with red and black designs.

Largest 12in (30.5cm) long

$450-500 SI

An Eskimo wooden ladle, the bowl with geometric designs on the rim and in the center an anthropomorphic creature in black and burnished red pigment.

18in (46cm) high

$600-700 SI

An Indonesian Dayak Barneo Hampatong sacred standing figure, with the arms held to the chest, Kalimantan.

17.75in (45cm) high

$1,500-1,700 SI

A Colombian female "flat figure", of stylized form, with knobs on the shoulders and wearing an applied necklace and headband with a braid at the back.

c100 BC-AD 300   8in (20cm) high

$220-280 SI

A Colombian male figure, the pronounced mouth with bared teeth, coffee bean-shaped eyes, one ear with circular earspool, with a spout at the top of the head.

c100 BC - AD 250 14in (35cm) high

$2,500-3,000 SI

A Nayarit standing female figure, wearing wrapped garment and holding a bowl in right hand, with a ring necklace and decorated with black and white pigments, Ixtlan del Rio type, Mexico.

c AD 300   14in (35.5cm) high

$1,500-1,700   **SI**

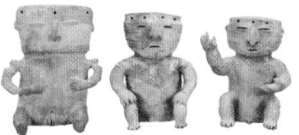

Three Colombian Quimbaya "flat figures", two female and one male, with solid buff ground and traces of pigment.

c AD 500-1,000   Tallest 9in (3cm)

$1,500-1,700   **SI**

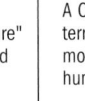

A Colombian Quimbaya "flat figure" of a seated female, the arms and legs ornamented with bands of geometric and dot motifs.

c AD 500-1,000 8.75in (22.5cm) h

$620-680   **SI**

A Colombian Tamalameque terracotta urn, with a ring foot, molded in relief to resemble a human figure.

c AD 500-1,000 12in (30.5cm) high

$850-950   **SI**

Two Colombian Quimbaya terracotta male "flat figures", each with the head perforated for feather attachments, the larger with elaborate black geometric motifs on head.

c AD 500-1,000 Tallest 11in (28cm)

$1,500-2,000   **SI**

Two Mayan bowls, the smaller with indented base, the exterior with colorful polychrome seated deities, the interior with stylized figural bands and avian figures, the deeper bowl with elongated deity and avial designs.

c AD 600   largest 4in (10.25cm)

$700-1,000   **SI**

Two Mayan cylindrical vases, the taller with deep burnished red, black and cream pigments, alternating avial and glyph patterns; the smaller with eroded and faded surface remnants of glyph and avial decoration.

c AD 600   Tallest 8in (21cm) high

$600-700   **SI**

A Mayan two-handled jug with lug handles, together with a terracotta bowl, the base with indented panels, the rim with cream-colored decoration and indented geometric design.

c AD 600   Bowl 4in (11.5cm) high

$450-500   **SI**

A pre-Columbian terracotta figural vessel, depicting a female, the limbs molded in relief.

c AD 1,000   8.25in (21cm) high

$700-1,000   **SI**

A Colombian terracotta globular vessel, in the form of a human, with large pronounced ears, the nose with applied ornaments and traces of black geometric designs.

c AD 1,000   13in (33cm) high

$600-700   **SI**

◄ A large Peruvian terracotta globular vessel, the rim with warrior molded in relief, of stylized form, with incised arrows from the arms to the sides and incised zig-zag and arrow-serrated patterns.

21in (53.5cm) high

$2,200-2,800   **SI**

A Mayan incised cylindrical vase, of gray clay with burnished orange decoration, the rim with a band of geometric designs.

c AD 600-800 8.25in (21cm) high

$300-350   **SI**

A Costa Rican black stone geometric carving with incised decoration.

5.5in (14cm) high

$220-280   **SI**

495

Fireplace Antiques

A provincial Louis XV walnut fire surround, with outset rounded front corners, the frieze centered by a vacant foliate cartouche, the rounded stiles similarly carved and raised on molded brackets above panelled stiles.

59in (150cm) wide

$3,000-5,000 — SI

Three early to mid-19thC American carved and painted mantels, the first with stepped, molded cornice and dental molding over frieze with urns at ends above fluted pilasters on plinth base, the others with molded projecting cornices over flat friezes and squared pilasters with molded plinths, from New England.

largest 71in (180.5cm) wide

$1,000-1,500 — SI

A George III Neo-Classical pine and gesso chimneypiece, the molded and leaf-carved cornice above breakfront frieze, with ribbon-tied husk swags, rosettes and tablets with runs, the molded lugged fire surround flanked by uprights with husk-drops and ram's-head terminals.

53in (135cm) high

$9,000-12,000 — L&T

An Edinburgh George III pine and gesso chimney piece, the molded cornice with festoon and tassel enrichments and acorn frieze, above central concave panel with acanthus arcading and Gothic cathedral at center, flanked by a rustic Georgian church and trees, the side panels with ribbons supporting rose and thistle swags, the uprights with cluster column pilasters.

67in (170cm) wide

$8,000-10,000 — L&T

A George III cast-iron, steel and brass fire grate, the fire basket with an arched and swagged backplate, the frieze with a band of pierced palings and akroteria, and terminating in tapering supports with covered urn finials.

30.5in (77.5cm) high

$1,200-1,500 — SI

An 18thC Continental engraved steel and brass folding fire fender, with a pierced foliate scroll crest, over a band of engraved scrolling and flowering vines centered by an armorial device, flanked at each end by a hinge pin with turned brass finials, possibly German.

34.5in (88 cm) wide

$1,200-1,500 — SI

A George III brass fire fender, the pierced frieze centered by a covered urn, flanked on each side by panels of Greek key fret, surmounted by a paling band and raised on a cavetto-moulded base.

48.5in (123cm) wide

$1,500-2,000 — SI

An early 19thC pair of Federal cast-brass and wrought-iron andirons, with urn-form finials on hexagonal plinth raised on arch-spurred legs and ending on ball feet, probably American.

19in (48cm) high

$600-800 — SI

A pair of 19thC American wrought and cast-iron figural andirons, in the form of a woman's torso on arched legs.

12in (30.5cm high)

$400-600 — SI

▶ A pair of American brass and iron andirons, the ring-turned shafts with conical finials above arched, spurred legs ending on ball feet.
c1840   13.5in (34.25cm) high

$600-800 — SI

A pair of American brass and iron andirons, the ring-turned shafts with conical finials above arched, spurred legs ending on ball feet.
c1840   13.5in (34.25cm) high

$600-800 — SI

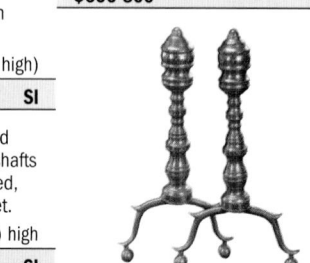

A pair of 19thC Neo-classical gilt-bronze chenets, each surmounted with cast urn finials set with foliate garlands, on shaped bases set with rosettes and Vitruvian scroll frieze on square-shaped bases.

Chenet is the French term for andiron or firedog.

14.75in (37.5cm) high

$1,200-1,500 — L&T

A pair of gilt-metal Louis XV-style chenets, each modeled as an infant reaper beside standing corn, on a pierced rococo plinth.

22.25in (54cm) high

$1,000-1,500   LC

A pair of late 19th-early 20thC American gold-painted cast-iron figural andirons, in the form of Columbia on a shell.

17.25in (44cm) high

$300-500   SI

A pair of late 19th-early 20thC American cast-iron figural andirons, in the form of George Washington.

15in (38cm) high

$200-250 (pair)   SI

An early 19thC lead bucket, painted with royal coat of arms.

20.5in (52cm) high

$500-800   CdK

An early 19thC lead bucket, painted red and with royal coat of arms.

10in (25.5cm) high

$1,200-1,500   CdK

A mid-19thC tole peint oval coal box, painted with flowers on a black ground, the lid with scrolled handle, the base with two handles on scrolled feet.

19.5in (49.5cm) high

$800-1,000   DN

A 19thC octagonal tole peint purdonium, painted with flowers, the hinged lid enclosing a lift-out liner, with cast side handles, pendant finials, on a stepped foot, with registration mark, the paintwork possibly of a later date.

22in (56cm) high

$700-1,000   DN

Two mid to late 19thC American cast-iron garden chairs, each with stylized crest on square-back with scroll-and-urn tracery above a pierced seat, with patterned rail and sabre legs by, marked "Charlotte Hill, Wm. Adams & Dry Co, Philadelphia" and "S. Lunterbacher".

38.5in (98cm) high

$800-1,000   SI

Two mid to late 19thC American cast-iron garden chairs, with scrolling back with foliate tracery on circular seat, shaped foliate rail over molded cabriole legs, marked "L MANK AND ... Phila".

33in (84cm) high

$1,000-1,500   SI

A mid to late 19thC American cast-iron garden armchair, with floriform crest on shaped back with scroll-and-floral swag tracery continuing to arm supports over seat, with geometric tracery and cabriole legs, by Wood and Perot, Philadelphia, some repairs.

35in (89cm) high

$2,000-3,000   SI

A cast-iron garden bench, with scrolling crest rail enclosing a tracery back and arm supports on filigree seat with shaped rails, ending in cabriole legs with scroll feet.

c1900   44in (111.5cm) wide

$2,000-3,000   SI

Garden Furniture

A pair of white painted cast-iron garden seats, with pierced scroll backs and circular pierced seats on four scrolling legs, and a similar cast-iron table.

34in (86cm) high

$500-800　　　**L&T**

A Coalbrookdale over-painted two-seater garden bench, with frond-cast back and arms and slatted wooden seat, in the Fern and Berry pattern.

46.5in (118cm) wide

$800-1,200　　　**L&T**

A pair of wrought-iron garden gates, with arched scroll pediment over twin gates each with scroll panels over galleried base, also a pair of similar side panels.

69.75in (177cm) wide

$1,500-2,000　　　**L&T**

A green-painted single Val d'Osne cast-iron garden seat, with Gothic cast-diamond back and honeycomb seat, on base with pierced stretchers.

$2,000-3,000　　　**L&T**

A patinated-bronze two-tier garden fountain, the graduated reservoirs surmounted by a mermaid and flute-playing putti, raised on three ducks with a wave-cast rectangular base.

82.5in (209.5cm) high

$8,000-10,000　　　**SI**

A Louis XVI-style patinated-bronze wall fountain, the reservoir surmounted by an arched architectural backplate, centered by a ram-head spout and cast with fruit and foliage.

39.5in (100cm) high

$1,000-1,500　　　**SI**

A patinated bronze figural garden fountain, the reservoir surmounted by a Classical maiden with a jar, raised on a standard cast as a herm accompanied by a second Classical maiden, raised on shell-and-leaf cast base.

52in (132cm) high

$1,500-2,000　　　**SI**

A pair of cast-iron terrace urns-on-stands, with inverted rim, lobed body and fluted socle, raised on a molded tapering rectangular plinth cast throughout with foliate decoration.

34in (86.5cm) high diam

$800-1,200　　　**SI**

A pair of patinated-bronze figural terrace urns, with bands of scrolling foliage, applied with a pair of pierced handles incorporating Classical heads and bacchic boar-heads.

39in (99 cm) high diam

$1,500-2,000　　　**SI**

A 17thC-style patinated-bronze figural fountain, two graduated circular reservoirs, all ornamented with winged seahorses, satyr-heads, bacchanalian putti and dolphins.

69.5in (176.5cm) high

$4,000-5,000　　　**SI**

▶ A cast Coade Stone head of a young woman in relief, marked "Coade, London, 1793", nose chipped.

10in (25.5cm) high

$800-1,200　　　**SI**

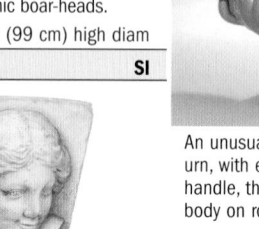

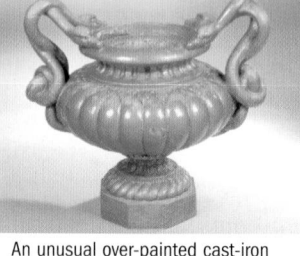

An unusual over-painted cast-iron urn, with entwined swan-neck handle, the leaf-cast gadrooned body on rope-twist octagonal plinth.

26in (66cm) diam

$800-1,200　　　**L&T**

One of a pair of large white-painted twin-handled urns, with deep egg-and-dart borders over trellis-gadrooned tapering bodies with scroll handles and cherub and grape frieze, on rectangular plinths.

40.5in (103cm) high

$1,200-1,500　　　**L&T**

ICONS - RUSSIAN

A late 15thC Russian icon, Mother of God of Vladimir, from Pskov.

12.25in (31cm) high

$15,000-20,000	R&K

A mid-16thC Russian icon, The Ormition and Assumption of the Mother of God, from Moscow.

17.25in (44cm) high

$10,000-15,000	R&K

A 16thC Russian menalogical icon, The Month of April.

13in (33cm) high

$7,000-9,000	R&K

A 16thC Russian icon, The Birth of The Virgin, from Moscow.

12.5in (32cm) high

$12,000-15,000	R&K

A pair of 16thC northern Russian icons, The Presentation of Gifts (Visit of the Magi) and The Presentation of Christ in the Temple, of carved wood and polychrome.

4.75in (12cm) high each

$10,000-14,000 (pair)	R&K

A 16thC north Russian icon, The Resurrecton and Descent into Hell (Anastasis).

18.75in (47.5cm) high

$8,000-10,000	R&K

A 16thC north Russian icon, The Pokrov.

28.25in (72cm) high

$12,000-15,000	R&K

A 16thC Russian icon, Saint Nicholas with scenes from his life, from Tver.

38.5in (98cm) high

$60,000-80,000	R&K

A 16thC south-west Russian icon, The Mother of God the Sign, from the Ukraine/Black Sea area.

31.5in (80cm) high

$12,000-15,000	R&K

A 17thC Russian icon, The Last Judgement.

15.5in (39.5cm) high

$9,000-14,000	R&K

A mid-to late 17thC north-west Russian icon, The Mother of God of Vladimir.

22.25in (56.5cm) high

$7,000-9,000	R&K

Icons

A late 17thC north-west Russian icon, St Nicholas.

22in (56cm) high

$3,000-4,000　　　**R&K**

A 17th/18thC Russian icon, The Resurrection and Descent into Hell (Anastasis).

12.5in (31.5cm) high

$3,000-3,500　　　**R&K**

An early 18thC Russian icon, The Word of God and Festival Scenes.

14in (35.5cm) high

$3,000-4,000　　　**R&K**

An early 18thC Russian Palekh icon, The Decollation of St John the Baptist (The Forerunner).

14in (35.5cm) high

$3,000-4,000　　　**R&K**

An 18thC Russian icon, St Matthew.

21.75in (55.5cm) high

$3,000-4,000　　　**R&K**

An 18thC Russian icon, The Mother of God "Joy of All That Grieve", hall marked silver riza, dated.

1791　　　13.75in (35cm) high

$4,000-4,500　　　**R&K**

An 18thC Russian icon, The Mother of God of the Burning Bush.

12.25in (31cm) high

$2,000-2,500　　　**R&K**

An 18thC Russian icon, Saints Zossima and Sabbati.

14in (35.5cm) high

$2,000-2,500　　　**R&K**

An 18thC Russian icon, St Nicholas with Scenes from his Life, later repainting.

12.25in (31cm) high

$1,500-2,000　　　**R&K**

An 18thC Russian icon , St Matthew.

21.75in (55.5cm) high

$3,000-4,000　　　**R&K**

An 18thC Russian icon, The Presentation of The Virgin in the Temple.

12.25in (31cm) high

$1,000-1,400　　　**R&K**

An 18thC Russian "Old Believer" icon, The Crucifixion, of copper alloy and enamel.

$500-600　　　**R&K**

An 18thC Russian icon, Saints
Julitta and Cyricos with Others (The
Seven Saints), of copper alloy and
enamel.

$600-700   **R&K**

A Russian icon, The Resurection
and Descent into Hell (Anastasis).

c1800   19in (48.5cm) high

$3,000-4,000   **R&K**

An early 19thC Russian icon, The
Bugolupskaya Mother of God.

21.5in (52cm) high

$3,000-4,000   **SI**

A 19thC Russian icon, The All
Seeing Eye.

14.25in (36cm) high

$2,000-3,000   **R&K**

A 19thC Russian triptych, The Deesis, of copper alloy and enamel.

$600-700   **R&K**

A 19thC Russian icon, Christ
Pantocrator.

9.75in (24.5cm) high

$1,100-1,600   **R&K**

A 19thC Russian icon, The
Resurrection and Descent into Hell
(Anastasis).

14in (35.5cm) high

$3,000-4,000   **R&K**

A 19thC Russian icon, The Synaxis
of the Archangel Michael and All
Bodiless Powers.

12.25in (31cm) high

$3,000-4,000   **R&K**

A 19thC Russian icon, St Nicholas
with Scenes from his Life.

14in (35.5cm) high

$3,500-4,000   **R&K**

A 19thC Russian icon, The Mother
of God of Unexpected Joy.

12.25in (31cm) high

$1,800-2,400   **R&K**

A 19thC Russian icon, The
Presentation of The Virgin.

12.25in (31cm) high

$1,000-1,400   **R&K**

► A 19thC Russian icon, Christ
Pantocrator.

14in (35.5cm) high

$1,200-1,500   **R&K**

◄ A 19thC Russian icon, The
Guardian Angel with saints and
various images of the Mother of
God.

21in (53cm) high

$750-850   **SI**

A 19thC Russian icon, The Mother of God of Joy to those who Grieve.

5.25in (13.5cm) high

$1,200-1,600　　　　R&K

A 19thC Russian icon, St Nicholas, of copper alloy and enamel.

$300-400　　　　R&K

A 19thC Russian "Pomorian Old Believer" icon, The Crucifixion, of copper alloy and enamel.

$450-550　　　　R&K

A 19thC Russian icon, The Crucifixion and Four Feasts, of copper alloy and enamel.

$500-600　　　　R&K

A 19thC Russian "Athonite" icon, Saint Parasceva, of carved boxwood.

Mount Athos in north-eastern Greece is the site of 20 independent monastic communes, was established in the 10thC and is still visited today.

4.5in (11cm) high

$450-550　　　　R&K

GREEK

A mid-to late 15thC Italo-Cretan icon, The Mother of God Hodegetria (Madre Della Consolazione).

11in (28cm) high

$18,000-22,000　　　　R&K

A late 15thC Cretan icon, The Mother of God of Tenderness (Eleousa).

10in (25.5cm) high

$20,000-25,000　　　　R&K

An early 16thC Cretan icon, The Seven Sleepers of Ephesus.

10.5in (30cm) high

$8,500-9,500　　　　R&K

An early 16thC Cretan icon, The Mother of God of the Passion.

36.75in (93.5cm) high

$120,000-150,000　　　　R&K

A 16thC Cypriot icon, The Mother of God of Kykkos.

12in (30.5cm) high

$7,500-8,500　　　　R&K

A 16thC Cretan icon, St Anna with The Virgin and St Demetrius.

13in (33cm) high

$20,000-25,000　　　　R&K

A late 16thC Greek/Melchite icon, St Theodore Stratelates. Footnote: A melchite is a member of the Christian church in Egypt or Syria.

11in (28cm) high

$7,000-8,000　　　　R&K

A Greek icon, The Raising of
Lazarus, from Epirus, north-west
Greece, dated.

1611   15.5in (39.5cm) high

$8,000-9,000   **R&K**

An early 18thC Greek provincial
icon, The Raising of Lazarus.

15in (38cm) high

$4,500-5,500   **R&K**

An early 19thC Greek provincial
icon, The Mother of God of the Life
Giving Source.

14.25in (36.5cm) high

$1,000-1,500   **R&K**

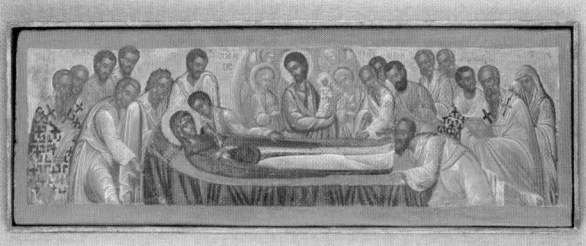

A Greek icon, The Dormition of the Mother of God, probably from the Ionian
Isles.

c1700   25.25in (64cm) wide

$10,000-12,000   **R&K**

An 18thC Greek icon, The Mother of
God Hodegetria.

7.75in (19.5cm) high

$2,000-2,500   **R&K**

A Greek Islands icon, The
Decollation of St John the Baptist.

c1800   11.5in (29.5cm) high

$1,200-1,500   **R&K**

A Greek provinicial icon, The Deesis
with Saints Spiridon and Gerasimus.

c1800   7in (17.5cm) high

$1,300-1,600   **R&K**

A 19thC Greek provinicial icon,
Saints Sophia and Anastasios.

12in (30.5cm) high

$450-550   **R&K**

A Cyclades icon, The Death of the
Good Man (The Archangel Michael),
with contemporary frame, dated.

1817   19.5in (49.5cm) high

$2,500-3,000   **R&K**

A 19thC Greek "German School"
icon, St Barbara.

11.75in (30cm) high

$900-1,100   **R&K**

A Greek Islands reliquary casket or
chrismatory.

*A chrismatory is a vessel
containing blessed oil for use in
religious ceremonies.*

c1700   8.75in (22.25cm) wide

$10,000-12,000   **R&K**

An 18th-19thC Melchite/Greek
Islands icon, The Mother of God of
the Unfading Rose and Saints.

14in (35.5cm) high

$4,000-4,500   **R&K**

A 19thC Greek icon, St Omoiros.

11.25in (28.5cm) high

$900-1,100   **R&K**

Icons

A 19thC Greek triptych icon, The Deesis and Saints.

13.75in (35cm) high

$2,500-3,000   R&K

An early to mid-17thC Macedonian icon, The Deesis.

10in (25.5cm) high

$4,500-5,500   R&K

A mid-17thC Macedonian icon, The Baptist, fragment.

17.25in (44cm) high

$4,500-5,500   R&K

A mid-17thC Macedonian icon, Mother of God Hodegetria (Portaetissa).

9.5in (24cm) high

$4,500-5,500   R&K

A Macedonian icon, The Virgin and St John the Baptist.

c1700   14.75in (37.5cm) high

$4,500-5,500   R&K

An 18thC Balkan icon, The Deesis Surrounded by The Apostles.

19in (48.5cm) high

$7,000-8,000   R&K

A 16thC Central Bulgaria icon, St Marina, from Plovdiv.

14.25in (36.5cm) high

$7,500-8,500   R&K

A late 17thC Dalmatian icon, The Descent from the Cross.

16in (40.5cm) high

$6,000-7,000   R&K

A late 17thC oak plaque, possibly Flemish, The Decollation of St John the Baptist.

12.25in (31cm) high

$700-800   R&K

A 19thC Coptic Ethiopian alabaster icon, The Baptism.

12.5in (31.5cm) high

$1,100-1,400   R&K

An early 17thC Asia Minor collecting box.

5in (12.5cm) wide

$9,000-11,000   R&K

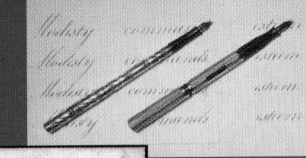
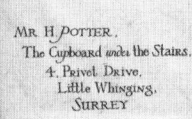

A two-piece suit from "The Private Life of Don Juan", as worn by Don Juan (Douglas Fairbanks Sr), together with a letter explaining the provenance and a still from the film.

1934

$500-600 CO

An Elvis-style jumpsuit from "3000 Miles to Graceland", made by "B & K Enterprises Costume Designs & Embroiders" and worn by Michael Zane (Kurt Russell), together with a pair of ankle boots, a pair of gloves, a pair of "EP" initialled sunglasses and two scarves.

2001

$1,500-2,000 CO

A prop bug from "Indiana Jones and the Temple of Doom", featured in the banqueting scene of the film, mounted with a plaque, framed and glazed.

1984

$600-800 CO

A regulation US Army-style T-shirt from "Saving Private Ryan", as worn by Sgt John Miller (Tom Hanks) with a label inside the collar marked "Miller".

1998

$300-500 CO

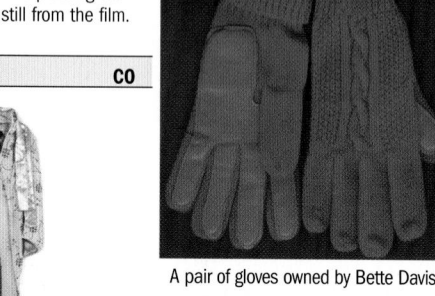

A pair of gloves owned by Bette Davis.

Provenance: *Originally sold at Christies, New York, 19 July 2001.*

$150-200 CO

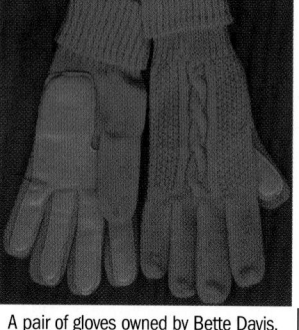

An original Parker puppet from "Thunderbirds are GO", on purpose-built stand signed by David Graham (the voice of Parker).

Provenance: *Originally sold at Phillips on 19 Sept 1995 as part of the Sylvia Anderson Collection.*

1966 21in (53cm) high

$45,000-50,000 CO

A 19thC-style lady's day dress from "Sleepy Hollow".

1999

$500-600 CO

A Samurai costume from "Heaven and Earth".

1990

$500-600 CO

An original Lady Penelope puppet from "Thunderbirds are GO".

Provenance: *Originally sold at Phillips on 19 Sept 1995 as part of the Sylvia Anderson Collection.*

The fur coat can be seen in the dream sequence of the film.

1966 21in (53cm) high

$40,000-45,000 CO

A complete "mummy" costume from "The Mummy Returns".

2001

$1,000-1,500 C•

A section of prop horse armour from "A Knight's Tale".

2001

$150-200 C•

An original FAB 1 Rolls Royce from "Thunderbirds are GO", custom-buil and approved by Rolls Royce Carriage Works.

Provenance: *This car featured in many Thunderbirds exhibitions afte appearing in the film, including the official "World of Gerry Anderson" exhibition in Blackpool, England. Originally sold at Phillips on 12 December 1995.*

1966 101in (256.5cm) lon

$140,000-150,000 CO

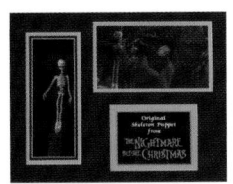

A skeleton puppet from "The Nightmare Before Christmas", mounted with a plaque, framed and glazed.

1993   overall 27in (68.5cm) high

$1,000-1,500   **CO**

A prop copy of the Daily News newspaper from "Superman".

1978

$200-300   **CO**

A prop copy of the Daily Planet newspaper from "Superman".

1978

$400-600   **CO**

A prop copy of the Daily Planet newspaper from "Superman III".

1983

$300-500   **CO**

A prop 13-hour clock-face from "Labyrinth", mounted with a crew Christmas card signed by director Jim Henson, a still of the clock in the film and a plaque, framed and glazed.

1986   20.5in (51cm) wide

$1,000-1,500   **CO**

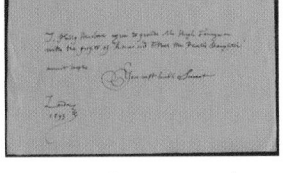

A screen-used prop contract from "Shakespeare in Love".

1998   14in (35cm)

$200-300   **CO**

A screen-used prop letter from "Shakespeare in Love", comprising a wax-sealed envelope addressed to Viola de Lesseps (Gwyneth Paltrow) and containing a copy of the sonnet "Shall I Compare Thee?".

1998

$200-300   **CO**

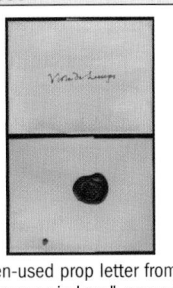

Six screen-used prop manuscript sheets from "Shakespeare in Love".

1998   13.5in (34cm) long

$300-500   **CO**

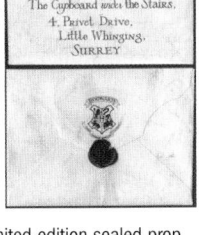

A limited-edition sealed prop Hogwarts acceptance letter from "Harry Potter and the Philosopher's Stone", together with a facsimile of the letter contained inside and a copy of "USA Weekend" featuring Daniel Radcliffe (Harry Potter) with one of the letters on the cover.

This is one of a limited number of letters that were released by Warner Bros.

2001

$4,000-5,000   **CO**

A section of wallpaper from "Moulin Rouge", part of the set decoration, mounted with a plaque, framed and glazed.

2001   32in (81.5cm) high

$1,000-1,500   **CO**

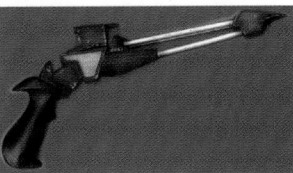

A prop Klingon disrupter from "Star Trek: The Next Generation" and "Star Trek: Deep Space Nine", used as a background prop in a number of episodes.

1980s-90s   19in (48cm) long

$550-650   **CO**

A prop rifle from "Judge Dredd", as used by one of the Aspen guards.

1995

$1,500-3,000   **CO**

A prop gun from "Judge Dredd", as used by one of the judge hunters.

1995

$1,500-3,000   **CO**

A prop katana-style sword and scabbard from the TV series "Highlander", as used by the character Duncan McLeod (Adrian Paul) in one of the episodes, together with a number of behind-the-scene stills from that episode, a signed Adrian Paul photo and a letter of authenticity from the original vendor who was given the sword by the actor.

1990s   sword 42in (106cm) long

$2,500-3,000   **CO**

◄ A limited edition reproduction James Bond "golden gun" No. 493/5000 by SD Studios, licensed replica of the gun featured in "The Man with the Golden Gun", mounted, with letter of authenticity from SD Studios and a still of the original prop, framed and glazed.

$1,000-1,500   **CO**

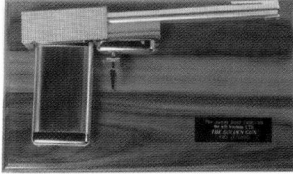

► A prop laser rifle from "Men In Black".

1997   22in (56cm) long

$4,000-6,000   **CO**

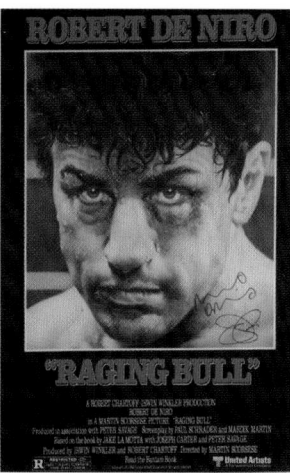

A one-sheet promotional poster for "Raging Bull", signed by Robert De Niro (Jack La Motta) and director Martin Scorcese, framed and glazed.

1980   44in (112cm) high

$600-800   **CO**

A one-sheet promotional poster for "Raiders of the Lost Ark", signed by Harrison Ford (Indiana Jones), Karen Allen (Marion Ravenwood), John Rhys-Davies (Sallah), producer George Lucas, director Steven Spielberg and Colin Williams, framed and glazed.

1981   overall 43in (109cm) high

$2,500-3,000   **CO**

A one-sheet promotional poster for "Pulp Fiction", signed by John Travolta (Vincent Vega), Samuel L Jackson (Jules Winnfield), Tim Roth (Pumpkin/Ringo), Uma Thurman (Mrs. Mia Wallace), Harvey Keitel (Winston Wolf/The Wolf) and director Quentin Tarantino, framed and glazed.

1994   42in (106cm) high

$1,000-1,500   **CO**

A one-sheet promotional poster for "Casino", signed by Robert De Niro (Sam 'Ace' Rothstein), Sharon Stone (Ginger McKenna-Rothstein) and Joe Pesci (Nicholas 'Nicky' Santoro Sr), mounted framed and glazed.

1995   overall 46in (116cm) high

$600-800   **CO**

A one-sheet promotional poster for "Gladiator", signed by Russell Crowe (Maximus).

2000   42in (106cm) high

$1,000-1,500   **CO**

Three stills of Boris Karloff, one signed.

Each 10in (25cm) wide

$200-300   **CO**

A still from "The Invisible Ray", signed by Bela Lugosi (Dr Felix Benet) and Boris Karloff (Dr Janos Rukh), together with three other stills from the same film.

1936   each 12in (30cm) wide

$300-500   **CO**

An Ava Gardner signed photo.

$150-200   **CO**

A John Wayne autograph, together with a Tom Mix autograph.

$500-700   **CO**

A Humphrey Bogart autograph, mounted with a still of the actor, framed and glazed.

$500-800   **CO**

A still from "Batman", signed by Michael Keaton (Batman) and Jack Nicholson (The Joker).

1989   10in (25cm) wide

$200-300   **CO**

A still from "Gladiator", signed by Russell Crowe (Maximus).

2000   10in (25cm) wide

$200-300   **CO**

▶ A Marlon Brando autograph, mounted with a still of the actor, framed and glazed.

$300-500   **CO**

Animation Cels

A Beatles " Yellow Submarine" animation cel, depicting the submarine approaching a shoal of flying fish, peg bar punched near the top edge, framed and glazed.

This cel was prepared as an alternative but not used in the final film. The original vendor of the following "Yellow Submarine" animation cels was the chief animator on that film.

1968   11.5in (29.5cm) wide

$2,500-3,000   **DN**

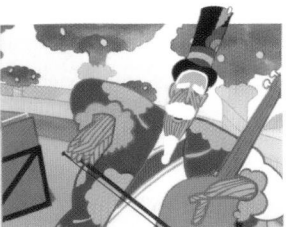

A Beatles "Yellow Submarine" production-used animation cel, depicting the "Mayor of Beatleland", mounted on a watercolour landscape background, framed and glazed.

1968   11.75in (30.cm) wide

$1,500-2,000   **DN**

A Beatles "Yellow Submarine" production-used animation cel, depicting the "Mayor of Beatleland", mounted on a watercolour landscape background, framed and glazed.

1968   11.75in (30.cm) wide

$1,500-2,000   **DN**

A Beatles "Yellow Submarine" animation cel, depicting the four Beatles, peg bar punched near the bottom edge, framed and glazed.

This cel was prepared as an alternative but not used in the final film.

1968   12in (30.5cm) wide

$1,500-2,000   **DN**

A Beatles "Yellow Submarine" animation cel, depicting the four Beatles, peg bar punched near the bottom edge, framed and glazed.

This cel was prepared as an alternative but not used in the final film.

1968   12in (30.5cm) wide

$2,500-3,000   **DN**

A Beatles "Yellow Submarine" animation cel, depicting the four Beatles, peg bar punched near the bottom edge, framed and glazed.

This cel was prepared as an alternative but not used in the final film.

1968   12in (30.5cm) wide

$1,500-2,000   **DN**

A Beatles "Yellow Submarine" animation cel, depicting the four Beatles, peg bar punched near the bottom edge, framed and glazed.

This cel was prepared as an alternative but not used in the final film.

1968   12in (30.5cm) wide

$1,500-2,000   **DN**

A Beatles "Yellow Submarine" colour tracer's and opaquer's model sheet, titled "Final Model sheet 10/1/88", showing the four Beatles and annotated with various instructions, framed and glazed.

The date 10/1/88 on this sheet is incorrect, it should read 10/1/67.

1968   10.75in (27.5cm) wide

$1,500-2,000   **DN**

A Beatles "Yellow Submarine" animation cel, depicting the submarine with the Beatles standing on the aft deck, framed and glazed.

This cel was prepared as an alternative but not used in the final film.

1968   19.75in (50cm) wide

$4,000-5,000   **DN**

A limited edition animation cel no. CJS26-084-022 from "From Hare to Eternity", signed by Chuck Jones together with Warner Brothers certificate of authenticity no. 33115, framed.

1996   20in (51in) wide

$800-1,000   **SI**

◀ Six limited edition animation cels from "How the Grinch Stole Christmas", signed by Chuck Jones together with certificate of authenticity no. 203038, framed.

1999   21in (8.25in) wide

$1,000-1,500   **SI**

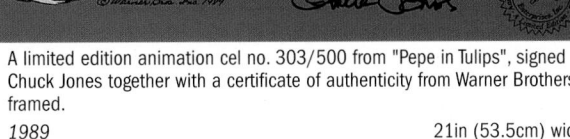

A limited edition animation cel no. 303/500 from "Pepe in Tulips", signed Chuck Jones together with a certificate of authenticity from Warner Brothers, framed.

1989   21in (53.5cm) wide

$700-1,000   **SI**

PENS

THE FIRST PENS WERE PROBABLY THE REED BRUSHES USED BY THE EGYPTIANS TO WRITE ON PAPYRUS. These were developed by the Greeks and then it is thought that the Romans, whose empire was in a different geographical area to that where suitable reeds grew, discovered the quill pen, which dominated writing from the Dark Ages to the 19th century. Then, as literacy grew and technology advanced, the number of pens produced exploded. For example, from 1842 to 1850 the number of nibs produced by Birmingham manufacturer Joseph Gillot rose from 70 million to 180 million.

Quill pens became blunt very quickly and many companies came up with ingenious ways to get around this problem. Joseph Bramah, who patented the first mechanically produced quill pens in 1809, devised a quill cutter that could cut several nibs from one quill. Sold as Bramah's Patent Pens, these nibs were effectively the first disposable pens for when nibs wore out.

From the mid-18th century pressed sheet metal pens became popular. Early fountain pens consisted of a tubular steel shaft containing some ink, but there was no way that the ink flow could be controlled.

The great breakthrough in pen technology came with the development of a pen with a reservoir of ink which produced a continuous and measured flow. There were many steps on the road to its discovery. New York insurance salesman Lewis Edson Waterman is said to have "invented" the modern fountain pen, creating the ink feed for his pens at his kitchen table in 1884. He was aided by new developments such as inks with constant viscosity and wear-resistant nibs.

Mass-marketed fountain pens, in a rainbow of colors and in the new plastics, made a first appearance in the 1920s and 30s. Parker launched its 51 – probably the best fountain pen in the world – in 1941. The first modern cartridge pen was launched by Sheaffer in 1955.

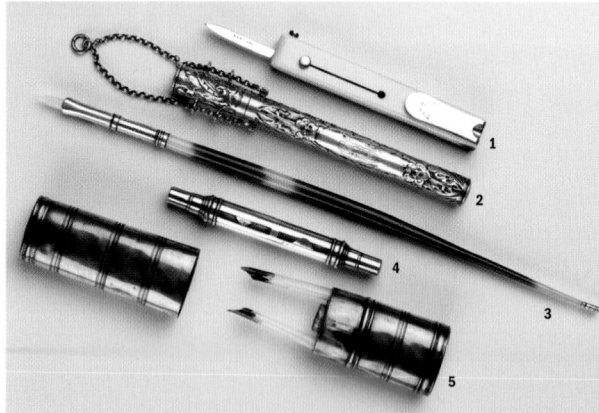

▲1 A rare early/mid 19thC Rodgers ivory pocket quillcutting machine, marked +* RODGERS, with a slide-out extending knife, nibber and anvil, in a red card case.

$250-300

▲2 A Mabie Todd and Bard silver chatelaine pen case, decorated with a repoussé floral design, with pull-off cover and chain.
1911

$250-300

▲3 An early/mid 19thC Mosley porcupine penholder, marked MOSLEY LONDON on the silver Longmore type holder, with quill body and turned silver terminal.

$400-500

▲4 A silver stamp holder and writing compendium, with ribbed bands and a rotating stamp holder/dispenser at each end, one with reversible pen holder, the other with reversible pencil holder.
c1890 – 1920

$350-450

▲5 A late 18thC John & Joseph Mycock brass penner. Stamped MYCOCK on the base, with decorated bands of lines, cover opening to reveal a central glass ink bottle and two holders for quills.

$250-300   GorL

▼1 A W.S. Hicks novelty "owl" magic pencil signed W.S HICKS and PAT MARCH 21. 71, the silver owl with single-cut diamond eyes, a gold plated pencil and ribbon-ring, eyes replaced.
1870s-1880s

$350-450

▼2 A late 19thC silver combination pen, pencil and knife, with barley decorated body, two cast floral and foliate button-slides, and a fold out knife marked LB SHEFFIELD on the blade.

$70-100

▼3 A Mordan three-color pencil, marked S.MORDAN & Co. STERLING SILVER, with plain polished case, three button-slides set with colored glass, and ring-loop.
c1890-1910

$200-250

▼4 An unmarked white metal combination pen-pencil with foliate decoration, cast floral slide-buttons, and shield-shaped seal terminal set with hardstone over a single lead reservoir.
1870s-80s

$70-100

▼5 A late 19thC gold-filled W.S. Hicks combination pen-pencil with chevron and lozenge decoration, slide-out penholder with F. Mordan 5/- nib, extending sleeve and propelling pencil.

$250-300   GorL

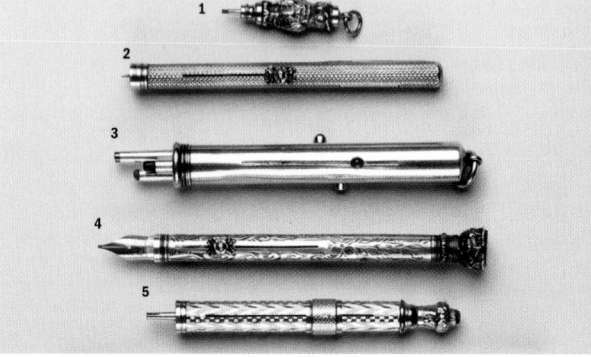

MARKET REPORT

The last 15 years have seen fundamental changes in the nature of pen collecting. Today the market is far larger, with more collectors, and an interest in a greater diversity of brands than ever before. This has occurred in parallel with the revival of the luxury writing instrument in the retail sector and the renaissance of brands, from the long-established Montblanc to the revived Conway Stewart. Collectors of vintage pens were undoubtedly one of the target markets for the wave of "retro" designs that heralded this rebirth, which, in turn, generated interest in vintage models from new collectors.

Prices of vintage fountain pens showed a steady growth throughout the 1990s, while continuing to provide excellent value for money: an original 1920s Parker "Big Red" Duofold, for example, can be bought for less than the retail price of the current Parker Duofold, while quality solid gold vintage pens, including the 1930s Swan Leverless or the 1960s Parker 61, offer even more favorable comparisons with their modern counterparts.

Usability now ranks alongside age or rarity as a determining factor in the value of a pen. The many new collectors, seeking pens suitable for everyday use, increase demand for several classic 1920s and 1930s American pens, particularly precious metal or filigree-overlaid Waterman's and the large or "oversize" Parker Vacumatic, Wahl-Eversharp and Conklin. This has extended to some European brands, including celluloid and plastic Montblanc pens made between the 1930s-1950s, which are currently more valuable than many rarer and more historic models.

Collecting tastes have broadened, and prices have risen, for what were previously considered to be minor or regional brands, including the British manufacturers Conway Stewart and De La Rue, the Italian Aurora and OMAS, and the German Pelikan and Montblanc, all now with an international following. This diversity is due in part to increased knowledge accompanying the publication of books on pen collecting, increased product awareness as mothballed brands are revived, and the rediscovery and spread of repair techniques. However prices have remained stable, or even fallen, for more common pens, and those in less than perfect condition.

Finally, it will be interesting to see how two very different areas develop: limited edition and modern pens are already becoming a distinct collecting area, with an independent price structure reflecting demand and perceived quality among collectors. Early writing instruments from 1700-1850, at the other end of the historical and academic spectrum, are still very affordable, with great discoveries awaiting diligent collectors prepared to assemble impressive collections in a patient, traditional way.

Alexander Crum Ewing

Alexander Crum Ewing is author of 'The Fountain Pen – A Collector's Companion', and can be contacted at Alexander@CrumEwing.fsnet.co.uk

▼**1** A Cartier yellow metal extending ruler-pencil, signed Cartier 14K engraved with one foot ruler in 1-inch divisions marked in sixteenths, scale from 1-120 in divisions of 10 marked in tenths of an inch, and engraved on one face.

1930s-50s

$550-650

▼**2** A Cartier two-color stockbroker's pencil signed CARTIER 5213, white metal with gold-colored stripes with ball-clip and domed button finial, in green Cartier Inc box.

1930s

$200-300

▼**3** An Edward Todd/Hicks style white metal pencil with perpetual calendar marked STERLING with alternating lined and plain design on the body.

Mid-1920s

$100-150

▼**4** A yellow metal "the handy" pencil, marked .750 on body and accommodation clip, with barley-decorated barrel.

1950s

$100-150

▼**5** A yellow metal ballpoint with fine barley decoration, marked .585 on the clip.

Late 1960s

$70-100   **GorL**

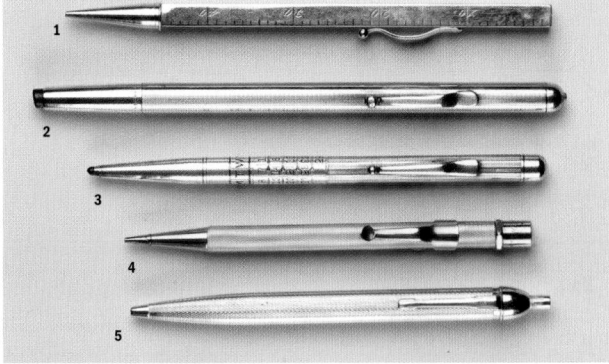

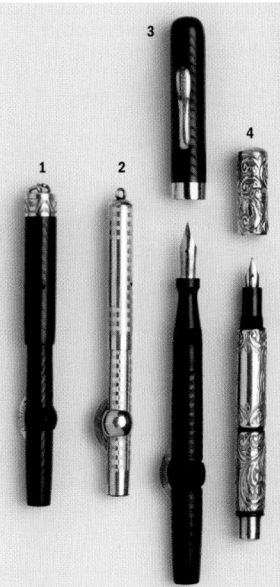

◄**1** A Conklin 25P chased hard rubber ringtop crescent-filler, gold filled cap crown and 2 Toledo nib.

c1918-26

$100-150

◄**2** A Conklin Lady gold filled ringtop crescent-filler, with plain and chequer decoration, threaded section end and 2 Toledo nib.

c1922-26

$100-200

◄**3** A Conklin 3NL chased hard rubber crescent-filler, with Pat Pending clip and 3 Toledo nib.

c1916

$150-200

◄**4** An Edward Baker Moore's Patent type safety pen, 9ct gold repoussé overlay on hard rubber sliding-safety pen, with 14ct nib.

c1900-10

$600-700   **GorL**

Pens

▲**1** A Sterling Fountain Pen Co No3 middle joint eyedropper pen, smooth hard rubber with Sterling Fountain Pen Co 3 nib.

This is a rare pen with an unusual filling system.

c1900

$600-700

▲**2** A half-overlaid taper cap, with gold-filled "chased" ribbon-and-snail decorated barrel sleeve, over hard rubber and Warranted nib.

c1905-10

$100-150

▲**3** An AA Waterman & Co 232C-3 pen, chased hard rubber eyedropper with two decorative gold-filled bands, and AA clip and Warranted nib.

c1915-20

$100-150

▲**4** An AA Waterman & Co 20 Automatic self filling pen, chased hard rubber "The Modern" twist-filler, 14K nib replaced.

c1905-12

$50-90

▲**5** A gold-filled "chased filigree" eyedropper, with Henry Birks & Son nib.

c1910

$100-150

▲**6** A Shreve vermeil bulb-filler, fully covered vest-pocket pen in Hicks/Edward Todd style, marked STERLING 14K-M with Wahl-Eversharp 2 Signature nib.

1920s-30s

$100-150

▲**7** An baby eyedropper, the barrel overlaid with eight alternating panels of abalone and mother-of-pearl and two gold-filled "chased" bands, screw-on cap, Wahl 0 nib replaced.

c1910

$200-300   **GorL**

▼**1** A Wahl-Eversharp Gold Seal "Personal Point", American, coral red, celluloid ringtop, with Wahl 4 nib.

Late 1920s

$100-200

▼**2** A Wahl-Eversharp signature "Personal Point", American, coral red, celluloid, with Gold Seal Flexible nib.

Late 1920s

$200-300

▼**3** A Wahl Oversize Tempoint, American, mottled smooth hard rubber with Wahl 3 nib.

c1918-22

$100-200

▼**4** A Wahl-Eversharp Gold Seal "Deco Band", American, rosewood hard rubber oversize "Personal Point" pen with Gold Seal Manifold nib.

c1929

$100-200

▼**5** A Wahl-Eversharp Gold Seal "Personal Point", American, lapis blue, celluloid with Gold Seal flexible nib.

Late 1920s

$250-300

▼**6** A Wahl-Eversharp Gold Seal "Deco Band", American, lapis blue, celluloid oversize Personal Point pen with rare 18k Gold Seal flexible nib and Eversharp card box.

c1929-32

$700-850

▼**7** A Wahl-Eversharp Gold Seal Oversize Doric, American, Morocco celluloid, with Gold Seal flexible nib.

Early 1930s

$100-200

▼**8** A Wahl-Eversharp Doric pen, American, pearl marble celluloid with Wahl 5 nib, in Wahl-Eversharp presentation box.

Late 1930s

$100-200   **GorL**

Pens

▲1 A Sheaffer Lifetime Masterpiece, American, lever-filler marked 14K on barrel and clip, with line decoration and two bands of hoops, with Lifetime Triumph nib.

c1946-52

$350-450

▲2 A Sheaffer 46 Special pen, American, with 46 Special nib.

1920s

$70-110

▲3 A Sheaffer 5-30 Junior, American, Jade Green, celluloid with white flecks, with 5-30 nib.

Mid 1920s

$150-250

▲4 Two Sheaffer Lifetime Balances, American, one mother-of-pearl inlaid Lady lever filler, with two-color lifetime nib, the other a marble celluloid ringtop vest-pocket with Lifetime nib.

c1935 and 1933

$100-150	**GorL**

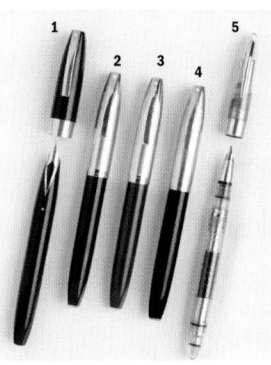

▲1 A Sheaffer PFM III, American, with 14K nib.

1960s

$70-110

▲2 A Sheaffer PFM V, Australian, with 14K nib, in Sheaffer box.

1960s

$100-150

▲3 A Sheaffer PFM V, American, with 14K nib, in Sheaffer box.

Gray is regarded as the rarest color of PFM pens

1960s

$250-300

▲4 A Sheaffer PFM V, Australian, with 14K nib.

1960s

$70-150

▲5 A Sheaffer T.M. Snorkel demonstration pen, American, transparent plastic, with tubular two color Sheaffer nib.

1960s

$300-350	**GorL**

▲1 A Parker Lady Duofold Deluxe pen and pencil, Canadian, pearl green marble permanite ringtops and wide middle caps bands, with Duofold 18ct nib.

c1932

$70-110

▲2 A Parker-Osmia Duofold Senior, German, black, permanite "flat top" Duofold, with PARKER DUOFOLD Sr/Parker-Osmia AG Heidelberg imprint and Duofold Pen "number" nib.

1929-30

$150-200

▲3 A Parker Lucky Curve Duofold Special, Canadian, black, permanite, with Duofold Canada nib.

c1928

$50-90

▲4 A Parker Lucky Curve Duofold Senior, Canadian, permanite with white flecks, and lapis blue Parker Duofold Pen nib.

c1929

$300-350	**GorL**

▲1 A Parker Lucky Curve Duofold Special, American, "Red", permanite, with "large" Lucky Curve banner imprint and Parker Duofold Pen nib.

c1926

$70-110

▲2 A Parker Lady Duofold pen and pencil, Canadian, "Red", permanite ringtops, the pen with additional Juniorette clip and Duofold Pen nib.

c1931 and 1928

$100-150

▲3 A Parker Lucky Curve Deluxe Lady Duofold pen and pencil, American, black, permanite ringtops, with Parker Duofold Pen nib, in Duofold Duo-box.

c1927

$90-120	**GorL**

◀1 A Parker "Thrift-Time", American, celluloid with Parker Pen nib.

This is an unusual variation of celluloid patterning for these attractive Moderne-style pens.

Early-mid 1930s

$70-110

◀2 A Parker Moderne, Canadian, with Parker Pen nib.

1936

$90-150

◀3 A Parker Premiere, Canadian, "mahogany" celluloid with Parker Fountain Pen nib.

c1935

$50-100

◀4 A Parker Premiere, Canadian, "Jet" celluloid with Parker Fountain Pen nib.

c1935

$40-70	**GorL**

◀1 A Parker (Premiere) pen and pencil, 'puddingstone' celluloid.

Early-mid 1930s

$150-250

◀2 A Parker Challenger, celluloid with visometer ink supply.

It is rare to find a "solid color" Challenger as they were usually made from marbled celluloid.

c1939

$90-150

◀3 A Parker Duofold "Geometric", large size "toothbrush" celluloid button filler.

1930s

$250-300

◀4 A Parker Victory MK III, plastic, mint, price band, nib grade stickers.

c1948

$90-150	**GorL**

Pens

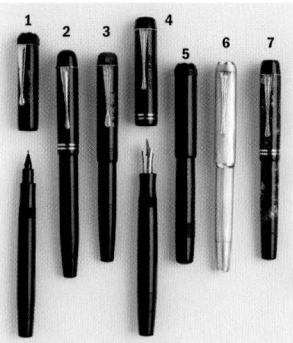

▲**1** A Montblanc Stylo, German, un-numbered celluloid button-filler, with metal teardrop clip.

c1932-34

$100-200

▲**2** A Montblanc 422 Stylo, German, hard rubber push-knob filler, with domed cap top and white star.

c1933-34

$250-300

▲**3** A Montblanc 432 Stylo, German, celluloid piston-filler, with engraved cap bands and "large" red dot on clip screw for large size line.

c1939

$100-200

▲**4** A Montblanc 236, German, celluloid with two-section piston and Montblanc 6 nib.

This is a rare example, the two-section piston was usually only used on the Masterpiece series.
c1939-40

$300-350

▲**5** A Montblanc 6M Safety pen, German, smooth hard rubber, with Montblanc 6 nib.

1920s

$600-700

▲**6** A Montblanc 234½ white metal overlay, German, with barley decoration and Montblanc nib.

These pens were overlaid by Maenner of Stuttgart whose high-quality overlays were used on both Montblanc and Pelikan pens.
c1938

$900-1,000

▲**7** A Montblanc 234½, German, blue and black marbled celluloid piston filler, with Montblanc 4 nib.

c1936

$1,100-1,400   GorL

▲**1** A Montblanc 322, German, blue and black marble celluloid bandless button-filler, with 14 carat "M" nib.

This is an early pen in an extremely rare color and in very good condition.
c1932

$900-950

▲**2** A Montblanc 6-size button-filler, French, plastic button-filler, manufactured in France by C.J. Roseau, with original CJR 16 nib.

1940s

$300-350

▲**3** A Montblanc 204, Danish, plastic button-filler, with 14 karat 4 nib.

1950s

$100-200

▲**4** A Montblanc 214, Danish, plastic button-filler, with rare 18ct Montblanc nib.

1950s

$100-150

▲**5** A Montblanc 246G PL, German, striated celluloid piston filler with Montblanc nib.

c1950

$700-850   GorL

▼ A Mabie Todd & Co. Swan "Lizard" self-filler, English, un-numbered (/90) celluloid, with Swan 3 nib.

This is thought to be only the second lever-filling Swan "Lizard" known to collectors. Mabie Todd reserved this celluloid for the Leverless range and it is therefore extremely rare.
Late 1930s

$300-400   GorL

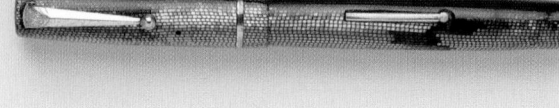

▲**1** A Conway Stewart no.50 button-filler, English, "reversed cracked ice" celluloid with Conway Stewart nib and a "cracked ice" No. 286 with Conway Stewart nib.

c1938

$200-250

▲**2** A Mabie Todd & Co. Swan Leverless demonstration pen, English, with transparent celluloid barrel.

c1948

$100-200

▲**3** A Mabie Todd & Co. Swan self-filler, American, un-numbered marble celluloid, with Swan 6 nib.

1930s

$300-400

▲**4** A Mabie Todd & Co. Gavicta Gigante (Big Blackbird), English for export, mottled hard rubber self-filler with GAVICTA GIGANTE/MANUFACTURA 'SWAN'/LONDRES barrel imprint, with Big Blackbird nib.

c1930

$250-300

▲**5** A Conway Stewart "New Era" no. 555 Lighter, English, pen-shaped petrol lighter in "blue measles" celluloid with ball ended clip, in original cardboard box with instructions.

c1930

$250-350   GorL

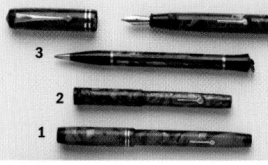

▲**1** Conway Stewart Dinkie no.548, English, multi-colored marble celluloid, with Conway Stewart nib.

1930s

$200-300

▲**2** A Conway Stewart Dinkie no. 540, English, blue marble celluloid, with Conway Stewart nib.

c1925

$200-250

▲**3** A Conway Stewart Dandy no. 728 pen and nippy rotary pencil, English, blue marble celluloid, with Conway Stewart nib.

Late 1930s

$350-450   GorL

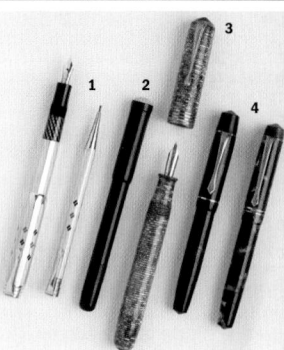

▲**1** A Fend "Partner" pen and pencil set, German, 18k rolled gold faceted piston filling pen and rotary pencil, with enamel Art Deco decoration.

Probably 1930s

$250-300

▲**2** A Napoleon 15-F Safety pen, smooth hard rubber with domed white cap top and warranted nib.

This pen is likely to have been made in Heidelberg, possibly by Osmia or Kawecko, even though the barrel imprint claims it is from the US.
1920s

$40-70

▲**3** A Marco Button-Filler, probably German or Italian, hooped laminated celluloid, senoir size button-filler.

1930s

$40-70

▲**4** Two Kawecko pens, a burgundy marble Special 31M and a pearl/black marble Dia 683F.

1930s and 1940s

$100-200   GorL

ens

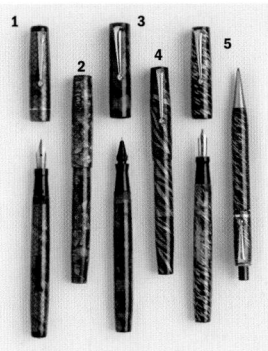

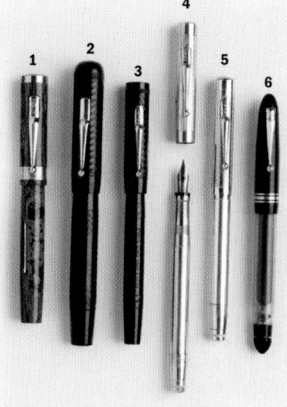

▲1 A Stillnova Extra, Italian, pearl celluloid piston-filler, with transparent ink reservoir and Rodus gold-plated nib.

1930s

$50-100

▲2 A white metal overlaid Safety pen, French, embossed "Versailles" design overlay with French control marks, with accommodation, snake clip and inoperative mechanism.

1920s-30s

$100-150

▲3 Two Stilus pens, Italian, a hard rubber 405 safety with two bands marked 750M and Stilus 5 nib and a black celluloid Automatica 943 with silk tassle and StilusOsmira 13 nib.

c1920s and 1930s

$100-200 GorL

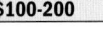

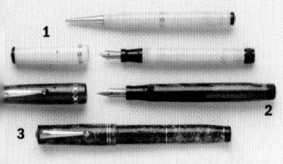

▲1 A Mabie Todd & Co. Swan Leverless [/90] pen and pencil, English, un-numbered "Ivory" (lined cream) celluloid Lady's Leverless with broad oblique Swan 1 nib, with matching Fyne Poynt pencil.

c1937-40

$200-250

▲2 A Mabie Todd & Co. Swan Leverless [-/88], English, un-numbered "Green Lizard" celluloid (Hull type 4 a) with flush gold-plated X-pattern band and Swan 3 nib, in red leather presentation box.

c1940-47

$800-850

▲3 A Mabie Todd & Co. Swan Visofil 340/76, English, green lined celluloid, with Swan 3 nib.

c1937

$200-300 GorL

▲1 A Mabie Todd & Co. Swan self-filler, English, un-numbered [SM205/83] blue snakeskin celluloid with Swan 2 nib.

c1937

$100-150

▲2 A Mabie Todd & Co. unmarked (Blackbird) self-filler English, marble with gold plated lever and Blackbird nib.

Late 1930s-40s

$60-100

▲3 A Mabie Todd & Co. Cygnet self filling Stylo [-/44], English, marble celluloid, with PATENT APPLIED FOR imprint and chrome-plated trim.

Late 1930s

$250-300

▲4 A Mabie Todd & Co. Blackbird Topfiller [BT200/-], English, "ribbon" celluloid spring-plunger-filling pen, with broad Swan 2 nib.

c1936

$350-450

▲5 A Mabie Todd & Co. Blackbird Topfill BT200/81, English, celluloid spring plunger filling pen, with broad oblique Blackbird nib and matching pencil.

c1936

$250-300 GorL

▲1 A Mabie Todd & Co. Swan Leverless pen and pencil, English, plastic Leverless (Hull type 6), with PAT APP FOR imprint, broad gold-plated cap band and Swan 4 nib, with matching Fyne Poynt Pencil.

Possibly a previously unrecorded prototype with broad gold plated band, rather than 18ct gold.

c1949-54

$90-150

▲2 A Mabie Todd & Co. Experimental Swan self-filler (31xx), English, un-numbered plastic lever-filler with broad gold-plated cap band, gold-plated overlaid screw-in section with Swan 1 nib.

This is almost certainly an experimental or prototype model; the metal screw-in section is different from the slip-in friction-fit section found on metal Swan Leverless and the broad gold-plated cap band is also previously unrecorded in this configuration.

c1948-49

$100-150

▲3 A Mabie Todd &Co. Swan Eternal 6, English, un-numbered smooth black hard rubber full-length self-filler, with plain pocket clip and Swan 6 Eternal nib.

1920s

$250-300

◀1 A Parker 51 blue diamond, American, tan (buckskin beige) vacumatic with pearl end jewels, gold filled cap with thin vertical lines and fine nib, in Parker box.

Tan is a rare color for a Parker 51

c1944-45

$300-400

◀2 A Parker 51 blue diamond, Canadian, cordovan brown vacumatic with 'Coin Silver' cap and medium nib, in Parker 51 box.

Late 1940s

$100-150 GorL

▲1 A Mabie Todd & Co. Swan Eternal E644B-61, English, mottled hard rubber midsize self-filler, with Swan Pen Pocket clip and Swan 6 Eternal nib.

1920s

$700-850

▲2 A Mabie Todd & Co. 8-size Swan Safety Screw Cap, English, chased hard rubber eyedropper, with plain pocket clip, "pineapple" feed and Swan 8 nib.

c1915-20

$1,000-1,300

▲3 A Mabie Todd & Co. 4-size Swan Safety Screw Cap, English, chased hard rubber eyedropper numbered 4 on the section, with flat top, "Swan" pocket clip and Swan 4 nib.

1920s-30s

$50-100

▲4 A Mabie Todd & Co. Swan 18 carat gold Leverless [L203/18ct], English, full-length with Design 3 "Chevron" overlay (plain panels alternating with wavy and diagonal panels) and Swan 2 nib, in brown leather presentation case.

1948

$350-450

▲5 A Mabie Todd & Co. Swan Leverless [L203/RG], English, full length, with gold-plated Design 3 "Chevron" overlay (plain panels alternating with wavy and diagonal panels), and Swan 2 nib.

1930s-40s

$100-200

▲6 A Mabie Todd & Co. Swan Leverless Demonstration pen, English, black plastic and see-through Leverless (Hull type 6a), with Swan 2 nib.

c1950-55

$200-300 GorL

Pens

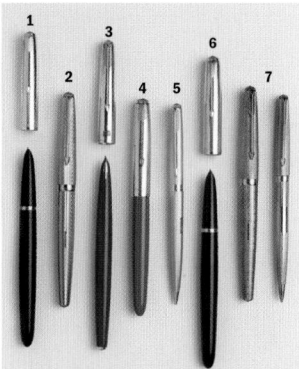

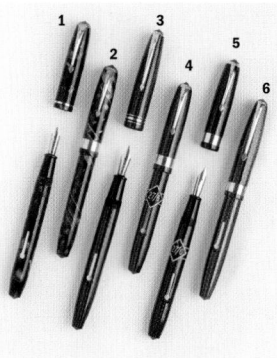

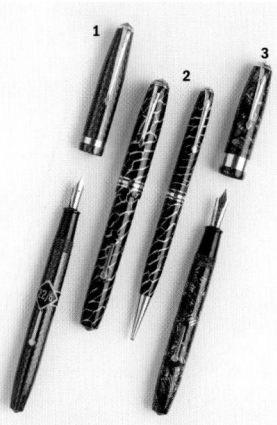

▲1 A Parker 51 custom pen with extra broad nib, English, gold-filled cap with coverging line decoration and extra broad nib, in Parker 51 box.

c1960

$150-200

▲2 A Parker 61 Presidential "Chevron", English, 9ct gold cap, barrel and clip, with convertor and medium nib.

1975

$550-650

▲3 A Parker 61 "Heritage" first edition, American, yellow gold-filled and silver laminated Heritage cap with first edition badge.

1956

$100-150

▲4 A Parker 51 custom, American, with insignia cap and medium-fine nib, with box.

1950s

$90-150

▲5 A Parker 61 Presidential "fine barley" pencil, English, 18ct gold rotary pencil and clip.

1963

$200-300

▲6 A Parker 51 custom, English, with insignia cap and fine nib, with box.

1950s

$90-150

▲7 A Parker Presidential "Waterdrop" pen and ballpoint, English, 9ct gold cap, barrels, and clips, with medium nib, with matching push-cap ballpoint, in brown leather Parker Presidential duo box.

1966 and 1972

$850-950   **GorL**

▲1 An Esterbrook/Relief 12, English, pearl marble celluloid, with gold relief Esterbrook broad oblique nib.

1950s

$90-150

▲2 A Conway Stewart 27, English, "tigers eye" spiral celluloid with broad cap and 5 nib.

1950s

$150-200

▲3 A Conway Stewart 77, English, herringbone celluloid, with three cap bands and Duro 58 nib.

c1955

$100-200

b4 A Conway Stewart 27, English, herringbone celluloid, with wide cap band and medium Conway Stewart 5 nib. *c1955*

$100-150

◄5 A Conway Stewart 27, English, rose herringbone celluloid, with wide cap band and Conway Stewart nib.

c1955

$100-200

◄6 A Conway Stewart 60L, English, herringbone celluloid, with wide cap band and Duro nib.

c1955

$100-200   **GorL**

◄1 A Conway Stewart 85L, English, herringbone celluloid, with medium cap band and fine Conway Stewart 3 nib.

c1955

$90-120

◄2 A Conway Stewart 58 pen and pencil, English, "cracked ice" celluloid, in Conway Stewart box.

1950s

$150-250

◄3 A Conway Stewart Executive 60 English, lined marble celluloid, with wide cap band and Duro nib.

c1951

$150-200   **Gor►**

▲1 A Montblanc Monterosa 042G, German for the Arab market, plastic piston-filler, with oblique Monte Rosa nib.

c1957

$50-90

▲2 A Pelikan 100, German, with marbled celluloid barrel sleeve, celluloid section and Pelikan nib.

c1935-38

$150-200

▲3 A Montblanc Monterosa 0412G, German, plastic, with satin cap and gold Montblanc nib.

Late 1960s

$70-150

▲4 A Pelikan 101N "Lizard", German, lizard (or cobra) celluloid with CN clip and bands, and gold Pelikan nib.

c1938

$400-500

▲5 A Pelikan 100N, German, celluloid with tortoiseshell marbled celluloid barrel and gold Pelikan nib.

c1947

$550-650

▲6 A Montblanc Carrera pen and four-color ballpoint, German, with chrome trim.

1970s

$30-60

▲7 A Montblanc Carrera, German, with GERMANY cap imprint, textured matt cap, medium nib and price tag.

1970s

$70-130

▲8 A Montblanc 254, German, plastic piston-filler with small star and Montblanc "wing" nib.

c1954

$100-200

▲9 A Montblanc 252, German, plastic piston filler with small star and Montblanc "wing" nib. .

c1954

$100-200

▲10 A Montblanc 252, German, plastic piston-filler, with large star and broad semi-oblique Montblanc "wing" nib.

c1954

$100-200   **GorL**

Pens

▼**1** A Lorrick Damascus steel and fossilized mammoth ivory ballpoint, American, made by Rick Hinderer from 240-layer forge welded silver and black Damascus steel (from his own forge in Wooster, Ohio) the cap crown inlaid with fossilized mammoth ivory, and taking standard Lodis-type refills, with certificate and explanatory sheet.

1990s

$500-600

▼**2** A Waterman CF, French, marked ARGENT MASSIF with French control marks, barley decoration and broad oblique 18ct white-gold nib, with box.

1970s

$200-300

▼**3** A Parker Duofold English pearl marble first-series International, with medium two-color 18ct arrow nib.

c1988

$100-150

▼**4** A Parker Duofold English first series International, with fine, two-color 18ct arrow nib.

c1988

$200-250

▼**5** A Montblanc Octavian no.1610/4810, German, silver "Spiderweb" filigree over Montblanc resin, with Octavian nib, box, reply card, personal service card, international service certificate, folder, card box and outer sleeve.

1993

$2,000-2,500

▼**6** An OMAS Marconi '95 Elettra, Italian, two-color Marconi nib, with cloth pouch, wooden box, "Elettra" leaflet, and booklet, in card sales box.

The OMAS Marconi celebrated the 100th Anniversary of Marconi's discovery of the radio wave. It was made in solid gold (340 pieces), solid silver with gold plated trim (2,800 pieces), and blue resin (4,000 pieces). The "Elettra" edition, named after the ship Marconi used for his radio experiments, was an additional special edition of 900 pens reserved for authorized Omas dealers only.

1995

$400-500

▼**7** A Colorado double nibbed pen, Italian, celluloid "scissor" pen, with two plunger-filling half cylindrical barrels, red or white spots by each nib, in card box.

1940s

$1,200-1,500   GorL

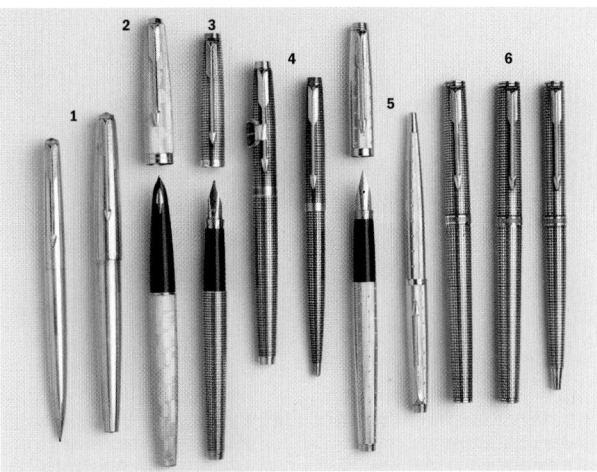

▲**1** A Parker 61 custom insignia pen and pencil, American, rolled gold capillary filling pen with fine nib, and matching rotary pencil, in Parker Duo box.

c1960

$70-110

▲**2** A Parker 61 Stratus, English, gold-plated "cloud" series converter pen, with medium nib and hard Parker box.

c1976

$100-150

▲**3** A Parker 75 "Cisele", American, marked STERLING SILVER and import hallmark, with "Grid" design, flat ends, and broad oblique (75) nib, in Parker box.

c1968

$100-150

▲**4** A Parker 75 "Cisele" pen and ballpoint set, American, marked STERLING CAP AND BARREL with "Grid" design, dimpled ends and fine nib, in hard Parker box.

1970s

$100-200

▲**5** A Parker 75 Place Vendome "Perle" pen and ballpoint, French, gold-plated pen with fine nib and matching ballpoint, in hard Parker box with card outer sleeve.

1980s

$200-250

▲**6** A Parker premiere "Cisele" trio set, French, silver-chequered pen with 18ct fine nib, rollerball and ballpoint, in hard Parker box.

1980s

$650-700   GorL

▲**1** A Bulgari Trifoglio, Italian, silver-plated trefoil-shaped convertor filler, with spring clip and iridium-pointed M nib.

1990s

$100-150

▲**2** A Chaumet Birman, French, marked .925 and with two heads, convertor filler with sprung nib-shaped clip and 18ct Chaumet nib.

1990s

$200-250

▲**3** A Georg Jensen pen, Danish, designed by Torsten Thorup and marked .925, with nib shaped clip and 18ct Georg Jensen nib.

1990s

$250-300   GorL

Pens

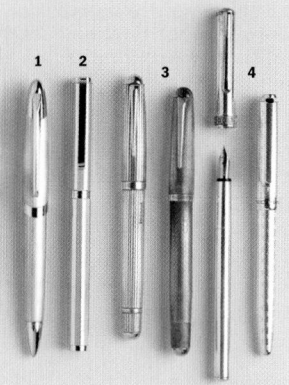

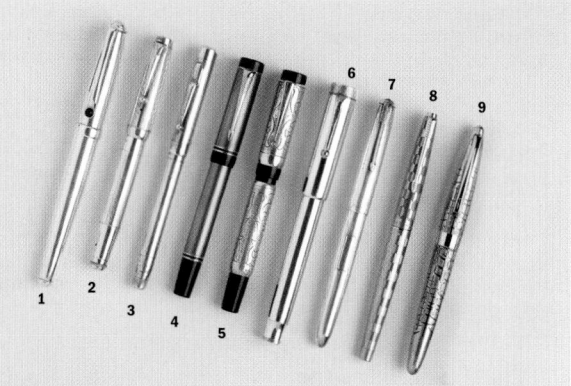

▲**1** A Versace pen, French, polished and brushed steel converter filler, with Versace nib, in box.

1990s

$90-150

▲**2** A Tiffany & Co. Atlas, marked .925 and decorated with alternate polished and frosted panels, with 18k white-gold Tiffany & Co. Atlas nib.

1990s

$100-200

▲**3** Two different Asprey Tregawne, London hallmark 1984 and 1990, a Mk III with barley decoration and a Mk IV with fluted decoration, both silver overlaid piston-fillers with engraved Asprey nib, in boxes.

$200-250

▲**4** Two different Theo Fennell pens, German, one marked .925 with plain polished design and raised THEO FENNELL band, with B&E nib, in box, the other silver hallmarked 1995, with a moire TF design and 18ct nib, both converter-fillers made by Bossert & Erhard.

1990s

| **$100-200** | **GorL** |

▲**1** A Montegrappa prototype, for Harrods, Italian, unmarked, with shaped clip set with lapis lazuli and semi-hooded nib.

A rare Montegrappa prototype, accompanied by letter of authenticity from Harrods.

Late 1990s

$350-450

▲**2** A customized Mabie Todd & Co. L303/RG, English, customized later silver-plated Design 3 "Chevron" Leverless (originally rolled-gold), with Swan 3 nib.

c1938

$500-550

▲**3** A Mabie Todd & Co. L302/RG, English, rolled-gold Design 2 "Lined" Leverless with Swan 3 nib.

c1938

$50-90

▲**4** An L. Michael Fultz Titanium pen no. 100 of 100, American, with extra fine 18k two-color nib, in box.

c1995

| **$450-500** | **GorL** |

▲**5** An L. Michael Fultz "Hand Engraved" No. 94/500, American, marked .925, with extra fine 18k two color nib, in box.

c1993

$450-500

▲**6** A Chris Thompson Lucky Curve Duofold Senior replica, American, aluminium, with period gold filled clip and fine Duofold Centennial two-color 18k nib.

2001

$200-300

▲**7** A Parker 51 rolled silver insignia, English, all rolled silver, with replaced chrome early short flight clip, black shell and fine nib.

Late 1950s

$200-300

▲**8** A Parker 45 gray shield, English, with fine nib.

c1980

$30-50

▲**9** A Pilot Art Craft Silvern "Clump", Japanese, marked STERLING SILVER with fine Pilot Custom 18k nib.

c1969

| **$200-300** | **GorL** |

A Dunhill-Namiki Maki-E balance with Kacho-E by Kohkyo, decorated with an exotic bird flying over flowers in gold, silver, red and blue iroe-hira-maki-e, on a roiro-nuri field with two bands of bokashi-maki and inlaid with aogai, signed KOHKYO with red seal Kao, and NAMIKI-KAN, with rare Pilot 'Falcon' (extra fine) 14K nib.

This is an unusual design for a Dunhill-Namiki pen, drawing on the Kacho-e tradition in Japanese art, where birds and flowers are shown together. The scene is anchored by the design of the barrel: waving flower stems rise up from the ground, where iridescent shell inlay captures the effect of the dew through a gold dust "mist". The eye is drawn upward by the elegant plants to the cap, where Kohkyo has filled the space with movement as the bird's flight lifts it above the flowers. The tail trails near the clip and the eye is drawn to the red-tinged tail feathers, outspread wings, red crest and thrusting head of the bird as it moves into the sky.

1930s

| **$3,000-4,000** | **GorL** |

A Namiki Maki-E lacquer cigarette case, Japanese, signed Namiki-Kan and with Artname and red seal Kao, and decorated with a pair of ducks among stylized grass in red, silver and gold iroe-hiramaki-e on a roiro-nuri ground, with sprung clasp and gilt-wash interior.

A simple, yet beautiful, composition. Ducks, especially the Mandarin duck, mate for life and are so shown together in pairs in Japanese art, as symbols of connubial affection, mutual consideration, love and faithfulness.

Early 1930s

| **$300-350** | **GorL** |

A Sheaffer cartridge pen with a 9ct gold engine-turned case.

$90-150 LFA

▲1 A Waterman's silver overlaid 12VS "plain" American polished overlaid safety pen, with later 2 nib.

1912

$300-350

▲2 A Waterman's 12½S, American black chased hard rubber eyedropper with broad gold-filled barrel band, gold-filled clip cap and 2 nib.

c1910

$100-150

▲3 A Waterman's 18KR overlaid 42, Italian, rolled-overlaid safety pen, with alternating plain and wavy panels, Waterman's Ideal clip and Waterman's 2 nib.

1920s

$100-200

▲4 A Waterman's 18KR overlaid 42, Italian, rolled gold overlaid safety pen, the cap decorated with three imps, with Waterman's 2 nib, in a blue cloth Waterman's box.

1920s

$500-600

▲5 A Waterman's 12½S, American, black chased hard rubber eyedropper, with 2 nib.

c1910

$100-150 GorL

▲1 A Waterman's 542½V "plain", American marked 14KT on the plain polished overlaid ringtop safety, with Waterman's 2 nib.

c1915-1925

$100-200

▲2 A Waterman's 0542½V "etched", American gold-filled overlay with floral "etched" design, and Waterman's 2 nib.

c1910-1920

$70-100

▲3 A Waterman's yellow metal overlaid 42½V, French, overlaid safety pen marked WATERMAN'S OR 18Cts, with barley or line decoration alternating with plain panels, and Waterman's 2 nib.

1920s-1930s

$150-250

▲4 A Waterman's white-metal overlaid 42½V, French, overlaid red ripple hard rubber safety pen marked WATERMAN'S IDEAL AGENT 1er TITRE, with barley or line decoration alternating with plain panels, and Waterman's 2 nib.

1920s-1930s

$100-150 GorL

▼1 A Waterman's model 4, American, smooth hard rubber "second model" straight cap, with two line imprint giving February 12 and November 4 1884 patents only, early three-fissure feed, with c1907 straight-line New York nib.

c1885-1898

$70-110

▼2 A Waterman's (402), English, plain polished fully-covered eyedropper, with replaced warranted nib.

1919

$350-450

▼3 A Waterman's 12 mottle, mottled hard rubber with three-fissure feed and "large star" 2 nib.

c1897

$90-150

▼4 A Waterman's 22, American, smooth hard rubber, with small curved New York 2 nib.

c1903-05

$100-150

▼5 A Waterman's 412 "filigree", American, marked STERLING on the three-leaf filigree overlay, with 2 nib, in an early Waterman's pre-globe.

c1910

$300-350

▼6 A Waterman's 12½ "secretary", American, c1907 chased hard rubber eyedropper with two gold-filled "chased" bands and 2 nib, near mint.

$70-150

▼7 A Waterman's 12½ "secretary", American, black chased hard rubber eyedropper, with 2 nib.

c1907

$100-150

▼8 A Waterman's 412SF "filigree" sleeve-filler, American, marked STERLING on the three-leaf filigree, with Waterman's 2 nib.

c 1910-1915

$750-850

▼9 A Waterman's 17 mottle, American, mottled hard rubber eyedropper, with clip-cap, black feed, and slightly later Waterman's 7 "Account" nib.

c1910

$300-350

▼10 A Waterman's 0512½VP "filigree", American, gold-filled overlaid eyedropper with rare extended floral filigree and Waterman's 2 nib.

c1915

$70-100 GorL

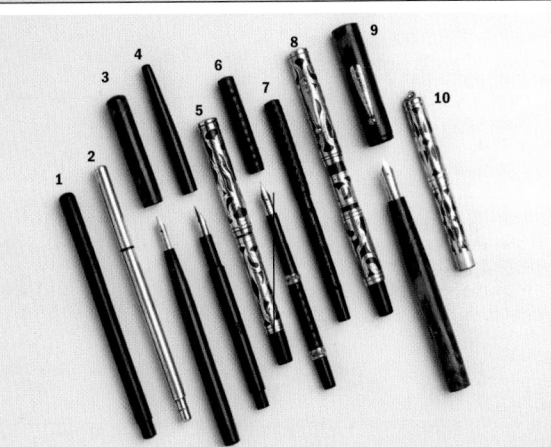

Pens

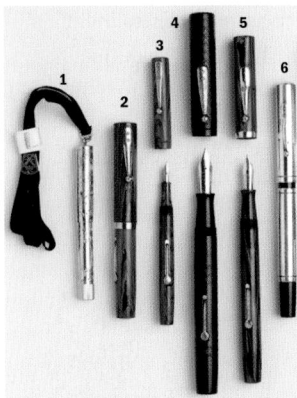

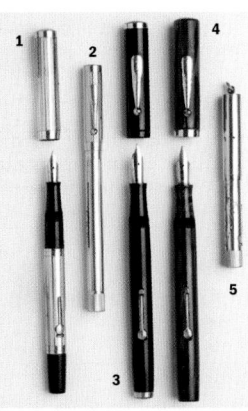

▲**1** A Waterman's 0552½V "etched", American, gold-filled ringtop, with Waterman's 2 nib, and black silk ribbon.

1920s

$100-200

▲**2** A Waterman's 56V, American, ripple hard rubber, with 6 "Account" nib.

c1924-27

$400-450

▲**3** A Waterman's 51V ripple, American, ripple hard rubber with nickel trim, and Waterman's 1 nib.

This small size is very rare.

c1928-30

$200-300

▲**4** A Waterman's 58, American, hard rubber, with nickel lever and Clip-Cap and Waterman's 8 nib.

c1917-23

$750-850

▲**5** A Waterman's 55 Woodgrain, American, "woodgrain" hard rubber, with fine Waterman's 5 nib.

c1923-27

$150-250

▲**6** A Waterman's silver overlaid 52, English, plain polished overlay on hard rubber, with 2 Account nib.

1939

$500-550   **GorL**

▲**1** A Waterman's 0552 "Sheraton", American, gold filled overlaid hard rubber, with Waterman's 2 nib.

1920s

$150-250

▲**2** A Waterman's 0552½ L.E.C. "Sheraton", American, gold filled, with Waterman's 2 nib.

1920s

$100-200

▲**3** A Waterman's 55, American, hard rubber, with 18K gold-filled Clip Cap, plain polished band at each end, and 5 nib.

c1924-27

$100-200

▲**4** A Waterman's 56 Woodgrain, American, "woodgrain" hard rubber, with 18K filled Clip-Cap and Waterman's 6 nib.

1920s

$200-300

▲**5** A Waterman's 0552V "scroll", American, gold filled ringtop, with Waterman's 2 nib.

1920s

$100-150   **GorL**

▼**1** A Waterman's 94 pen and pencil, American, "mahogany" celluloid with keyhole nib.

1930s

$250-300

▼**2** A Waterman's Patrician, American, jet (black hard rubber), with Patrician nib.

c1929-30

$350-450

▼**3** A Waterman's Patrician, American, "nacre" celluloid, with chrome trim and Patrician nib.

1930

$550-650

▼**4** A Waterman's desk pen, American, onyx celluloid "Patrician" style desk pen with brown taper, section and feed, and "brown" Waterman's 7-series nib, with card box and leaflet.

"Brown" was the Waterman's color code for nibs "suitable for general use".

Mid-1930s

$250-300

▼**5** A Waterman's Patrician pen and pencil, American, celluloid, with broad cap bands and Patrician nib.

A rare variation of the classic Patrician design, with distinct differences from the standard protection model, including domed, not stepped cap tops; riveted ball-ended clip; and, broad cap bands. In excellent condition and with outstanding color.

c1935

$1,200-1,500

▼**6** A Waterman's 94, American, "steel quartz" celluloid, with Waterman's 2 nib.

1930s

$50-100

▼**7** A Waterman's 92, Canadian, "lizard" celluloid, with Waterman's 2 nib.

Mid-1930s

$100-200

▼**8** A Waterman's 92V, Canadian, "lizard" celluloid, with broad Waterman's 2 nib.

Mid-1930s

$70-110   **GorL**

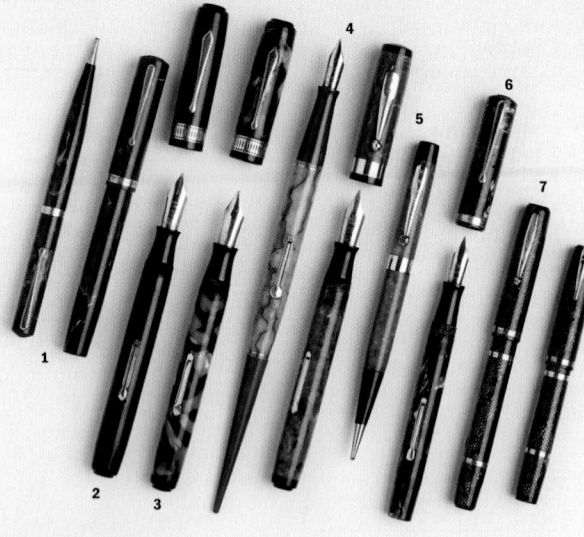

A Waterman's "doll" or "smallest pen in the world" safety pen, American, hard rubber eyedropper safety, with gold nib, in a fitted red morocco leather case.

This is an excellent example of an exceptionally rare pen. Designed to demonstrate Waterman's technical ability, the pen is fully operable despite being only 1.5in (4cm) long.

c1910

$3,000-4,000   **GorL**

DECORATIVE ARTS IS A LOOSE TERM USED TO DESCRIBE A RANGE OF ORNAMENTAL OBJECTS, encompassing furniture, jewelry, ceramics and metalware from c1860 to the 1930s. It includes movements such as Arts and Crafts, and Art Nouveau. In the mid- to late 19thC a number of events influenced the decorative arts; the Great Exhibition of 1851, the first Japanese art exhibition held in Europe, in 1854, the building of William Morris's Red House in 1859 and the Chicago Exhibition of 1893, which was the first international trade show in the US.

CERAMICS

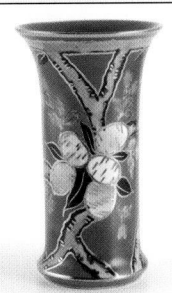

A Carlton Ware sleeve vase, decorated in Honesty pattern 3278, with silver and colors on a blue ground, shape 217.

6in (15cm) high

$80-100   **BAR**

A Carlton Ware pottery vase, of baluster shape, painted with blue-tits amid blackberry canes, a convolvulous spray with an insect verso, gilded rims, brown printed mark, signed Geo. Roberts, dated. 1922

8.25in (21cm) high

$80-120   **BonS**

A Carlton Ware ovoid musical jug, with leaf and flower molded handle, printed and painted with a crinoline lady.

(15cm) high

$80-100   **BAR**

A Carlton Ware vase, of ovoid shape, decorated with Chinese scenes of pavillions and figures in jeweled colors on powder blue ground.

8.75in (22cm) high

$200-250   **BonE**

A CLOSER LOOK AT CLARICE CLIFF

CLARICE CLIFF (1899-1972) became a household name in the 1920s and 30s with her distinctive designs. Colorful, hand-painted tablewares dominated her output for A.J. Wilkinson's Royal Staffordshire Pottery in Burslem, but she also created candlesticks, bookends, figurines and masks.

Cliff is renowned for her distinctive and extensive range of shapes and patterns, although she also produced more traditional designs. Pattern books and contemporary advertisements can be used to identify her work, although different names were sometimes used for the different color combinations chosen for identical patterns.

A team of painteresses worked in a production line, painting her designs on a range of blanks. Cliff designed her patterns to be versatile and suit any number of different shaped items.

Many forms – such as the cone-shaped sugar sifter and beehive honey pot – were highly innovative and futuristic in their design.

Collectors look for bold, geometric patterns, unusual shapes (especially those consisting of separate sections or warped in the kiln) which command a premium over the traditional, common shapes.

A Carlton Ware vase of tapering form, painted with a bird in flight on powder blue ground, printed marks, cracked.

7.75in (20cm) high

$120-160   **BonE**

The enamel paint was applied relatively thickly, leaving behind visible brushstrokes.

Although this conical sugar sifter is a well-known shape, it is extremely rare to find it decorated with the Summerhouse pattern (produced from 1931-1933). In fact, this is one of only three known examples, one of which is badly damaged and in a museum. This sifter is in mint condition.

Stylized country scenes featuring red-roofed houses, distant hills and trees with curved trunks are common.

The earthenware body is covered in a warm, yellow-tinted glaze, resulting in an ivory color.

Most pieces are marked on the base with the Clarice Cliff signature, pattern and factory name. Impressed dates may indicate date of production rather than that of the decoration or design.

A Clarice Cliff conical sugar sifter, painted in colored enamels, printed marks.

5.5in (14cm) high

$10,000-12,000   **L&T**

Ceramics – Clarice Cliff

A Clarice Cliff Bizarre breakfast set, comprising teapot and a cover, two cups and saucers, a single plate, a milk jug and a sucrier, each geometrically modeled and painted in the Nasturtium pattern, printed marks.

$3,000-4,000   **L&T**

Two of a set of four Clarice Cliff Bizarre Fantasque coffee cans and saucers, in Umbrellas and Rain pattern, two damaged cans.

$3,000-4,000 (set of 4)   **BAR**

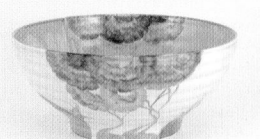

A Clarice Cliff Bizarre ribbed bowl, in Aurea pattern.

9.5in (24cm) diam

$400-500   **BAR**

A Clarice Cliff Bizarre planter, of twin-handled oval shape, painted with the Aurora pattern, shape no. 450, black printed mark.

Cliff designed the Bizarre range between 1928 and 1936. The Art Deco patterns use bold geometric, abstract and figural forms in bright, often clashing, colors.

13.25in (33.5cm) wide

$400-450   **Chef**

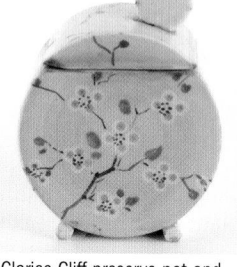

A Clarice Cliff preserve pot and cover, in the Bonjour shape, with May Blossom pattern, slight damage.

4in (10cm) high

$75-95   **BAR**

A Clarice Cliff Bonjour shape sugar sifter, painted in the Idyll pattern.

5in (12.5cm) high

$900-1,100   **GorL**

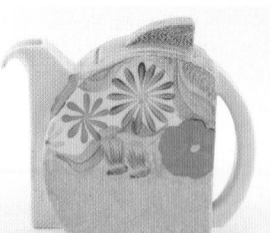

A Clarice Cliff Stamford shape teapot, in the Canterbury Bells pattern.

4.75in (12cm) high

$650-700   **GorL**

A Clarice Cliff plate, designed by Laura Knight ARA, decorated in the Circus pattern, factory marks and artist's facsimile signature.

9.5in (23cm) diam

$1,000-1.300   **DN**

A Clarice Cliff Lotus jug, the ribbed body painted in colored enamels in the Orange Trees and House pattern, printed Fantasque marks.

11.5in (29cm) high

$3,500-4,000   **L&T**

A large Clarice Cliff charger, painted in colored enamels in the Autumn pattern, printed marks.

There are several reasons why this piece has such a strong appeal.

- Chargers are popular because they show the pattern so clearly, and you get a lot of pattern for your money.
- They are easy to display, and make a bold impact, more so than, say, bowls or tea cups.
- This piece is in perfect condition, without even a scratch.
- The pattern is very good – a real hallmark of Clarice Cliff.

13.5in (34cm) diam

$4,500-5,500   **L&T**

A Clarice Cliff conical sugar sifter, of typical form, painted with the Crocus pattern.

5.5in (14cm) high

$600-700   **DN**

A pair of Clarice Cliff vegetable tureens and covers, each of drum form, painted in the Sungleam Crocus pattern, the cover with button finial, the base applied with segment handles, printed Bizarre marks.

9.75in (24.5cm) diam

$400-500   **HamG**

A Clarice Cliff preserve jar and cover of drum form, painted in the Sungleam Crocus pattern, the cover with drum finial, printed Bizarre marks, two chips to inner rim.

4in (10cm) high

$350-400   **HamG**

A Clarice Cliff Fantasque beaker, painted with the Blue Chintz pattern.

3in (7.5cm) high

$300-400   **DN**

A Clarice Cliff beehive honey pot and cover, of typical form, painted with the Crocus pattern.

Clarice Cliff designed the Crocus pattern in 1929. It was an instant success, and became her signature design. The pattern consists of simple, deft brushstrokes and came in a number of different colorways.

4in (10cm) high

$350-450   **DN**

A Clarice Cliff Daffodil shape bowl, painted in the Petunia pattern no.450, small chip to base rim.

13in (33cm) wide

$400-500   **GorL**

A Clarice Cliff Harvest molded preserve jar.

$60-90   **GorB**

A Clarice Cliff flower vase, the conical bowl painted with stylized flowers, printed mark in black, cracked, central flower holder chipped and repaired.

6.75in (17cm) high

$1,200-1,500   **BonE**

DOULTON & CO (est. 1815) was one of the first major companies to take commercial advantage of the opportunities offered by collaboration with Arts and Crafts designers, in particular with the students of the Lambeth School of Art. In c1870, using the profits made from its successful stoneware sanitation pipe business, it set up an art pottery that produced decorative hand-thrown, salt-glazed stoneware vessels. The objects were decorated by the students, using a number of different techniques, to produce distinctively complex yet restrained designs. The art stoneware varied from stylized Victorian patterns, to high quality Art Nouveau pieces. Some of the most successful designs were executed by the Barlow family – Hannah (1859-1913), Florence (d1909) and their brother Arthur (d1909).

- Carved, incised and molded decoration

- Barlow often embellished his pieces with applied florets

- Muted color palette of brown, gray and blue glazes

A Doulton Lambeth stoneware vase, by Arthur B Barlow, incised with flowering plants, no. 983, oval date mark.

1875

18in (45.5cm) high

$750-1,000   **BAR**

A Doulton Lambeth tankard, with silver mounts, incised with a frieze of stags and hinds in a landscape, impressed and incised marks for Hannah Barlow.

4.5in (11.5cm) high

$550-600   **L&T**

A Doulton Lambeth vase, with continuous incised hay-making scene, by Hannah Barlow.

16.5in (42cm) high

$750-1,000   **GorL**

A Doulton Lambeth vase, incised with a continuous band of cattle, by Hannah Barlow.

The muted palette, use of sgraffito decoration over a colored slip and the decorative borders are typical of the work produced by Hannah Barlow for Doulton.

1883   12in (30.5cm) high

$750-900   **GorL**

A Doulton Lambeth vase, with incised decoration of horses and cattle within stylized scrolling foliage bands, by Hannah Barlow and Eliza Simmance.

16in (40.5cm) high

$1,000-1,500   **GorL**

A Royal Doulton stoneware jug of Marshall Foch, decorated with a portrait medallion among floral swags and inscribed "Armistice, signed Nov. 11th 1918", on blue ground, impressed marks.

7in (18cm) high

$250-300   **HamG**

A Doulton Lambeth stoneware jug and two beakers, commemorating Queen Victoria's Diamond Jubilee, molded with cameos of the young and old Queen, with the words "She wrought her people lasting good", impressed and incised marks.

Jug 5in (12.5cm) high

$550-650   **L&T**

A Doulton Lambeth stoneware jug, decorated with green sprigging and with portrait medallion and inscription "Hero of Heroes, Governor General, General Gordon", impressed marks.

7.25in (18.5cm) high

$300-400   **HamG**

A Doulton Lambeth stoneware motto jug, decorated with Neo-classical medallions and the words "He that buys land, buys stone, He that buys flesh, buys bones, He that buys eggs, buys shells, He that buys good ale, buys nothing else", handle cracked.

7.5in (19cm) high

$100-150   **BonS**

A Doulton Lambeth commemorative jug, for Queen Victoria's Diamond jubilee, decorated with portrait medallions of the young and old Queen, and with the words "She wrought her people lasting good".

1897   6.5in (16cm) high

$100-150   **BonS**

A pair of Royal Doulton stoneware commemorative jugs, each depicting the Coronation of King Edward VII in 1902, and showing portraits of King George and Queen Alexandra.

8.5in (20cm) high

$320-370   **LC**

A Doulton Lambeth stilton bell and cover, decorated with incised and applied scroll and leaf work, bell with incised monogram ES and HH, stand with incised and impressed marks.

9.5in (24cm) high

$1,500-2,000   **L&T**

A Royal Doulton Lambeth bibelot, the dish surmounted by a figure of a koala, impressed and incised marks.

4.5in (11cm) high

$300-350   **L&T**

A Royal Doulton Lambeth bibelot, the circular dish surmounted by the figure of a night heron, impressed and incised marks for Maud Bowden.

5.75in (14.5cm) high

$4050-550   **L&T**

A Doulton Lambeth biscuit barrel, with plated mounts, cover and swing handle, with applied foliate decoration, impressed and incised marks AS.

1880   5.5in (13.5cm) high

$140-200   **L&T**

A Doulton Lambeth salad bowl and servers, with plated rim, applied and incised decoration, incised marks for Kate M. Davis, and dated, with salad servers (not ensuite), plated mark for Mappin and Webb.

1882   9.5in (24cm) diam

$350-400   **L&T**

A Doulton Lambeth bowl, with silver rim, applied and incised beadwork, decorated externally and internally, incised marks for Elizabeth M. Small, Mary Aitken (possibly) and Lilian Curtis, dated, rim hallmarked Birmingham.

1879   8in (20cm) diam

$700-800   **L&T**

A Doulton Lambeth mantel clock, with applied and incised decoration, two lion masks to sides, incised mark for Emily M.R. Welsh, impressed date.

1883   9in (22.5cm) high

$850-950   **L&T**

A Doulton Lambeth cruet set, comprising an open salt, covered mustard and pepper on a silver fitted stand, all with applied scroll and flower decoration, incised monogram for Emily M.R. Welsh and Alice Longhurst, silver hallmaked Birmingham 1883.

1883

$550-650   **L&T**

A Doulton Lambeth egg epergne, with applied and incised beadwork decoration, incised marks for Georgina Burr and Margaret Aitken, and date.

1884   6.75in (17cm) high

$750-850   **L&T**

A Doulton Lambeth stoneware ewer, by Mary Ann Thomson, with stiff leaves on a floret ground with bands of beads, leaves and trefoils above, round mark.

1876   9in (30cm) high

$300-350   **BAR**

A pair of Doulton Lambeth moon flasks, with applied and pierced work, incised marks for Edith Green and Annie Cupitt.

$1,000-1,500   **L&T**

A Doulton Lambeth patented inkwell, decorated with floral and foliate applied friezes, impressed and incised marks "Manufacture for Thos de la Rue & Co. London, The Isobath, patd. resevoir inkstand"

5.5in (15cm) high

$450-500   **L&T**

A Doulton Lambeth Isobath inkwell, glazed in green, impressed marks.

4.75in (12cm) high

$450-500   **L&T**

A Doulton Lambeth "owl" jar and cover, with heavily incised and applied decoration, cover with incised mark for Clara Baker, base with incised mark for Jane S Hurst.

8in (20cm) high

$1,500-2,000 L&T

A Royal Doulton stoneware jardinière, with shoulder band of applied green flowerheads under green marbled wave rim, no.6512.

7.25in (18.5cm) high

$120-180 BAR

A Doulton Lambeth jardinière and stand, with applied floral and foliate motifs, impressed and incised marks.

32in (81cm) high

$700-800 L&T

A Doulton Lambeth jardinière and stand, with applied foliate and floral motifs, impressed and incised marks.

47.25in (120cm) high

$700-800 L&T

A Doulton Lambeth lemonade jug and two matching beakers, with applied incised beadwork decoration by George Tinworth, incised GT initials, impressed and incised marks.

1880 Jug 9.75in (24.5cm) high

$900-1,000 L&T

A pair of Doulton Lambeth tapered cylindrical oil jugs, with stylized leaf molded decoration, by Emily Stormer.

9in (23cm) high

$900-1,300 GorL

A Royal Doulton Lambeth matchstand and ashtray, the stand cast as a man smoking a pipe and leaning on a barrel, impressed and incised marks.

4in (10cm) high

$600-700 L&T

A Doulton Lambeth matchstand and bell cover, with incised and beaded floral decoration, impressed and incised marks AEB, no. 680.

1882 3.25in (8cm) high

$400-500 L&T

A Doulton Lambeth mug, with incised lovat leaves, incised monogram for Florence C Roberts.

1879 5in (13cm) high

$400-500 L&T

◄ A Doulton Lambeth Slaters Patent owl oil lamp, formed in two parts, the removable resevoir molded as the head, with applied eyes, beak, wings and feet and overlapping applied feathers, on cast gilt-metal base, impressed marks to resevoir.

18in (46cm) high

$2,800-3,400 L&T

A 20thC Doulton Lambeth ring tray, modeled as a bird seated on a stump issuing from a flanged base, impressed mark and numerals 11497 to base.

4.25in (11cm) high

$400-500 BonS

A Doulton Lambeth brass-mounted oil lamp, the painted body applied and incised with winged dragons, impressed and incised marks for Mark V Marshall, Francis C Pope and Emma Martin, date mark.

1882   24.25in (61.5cm) high

$1,200-1,500   **L&T**

A pair of Royal Doulton stoneware vases, of slightly waisted form, the rims molded and applied with flowerheads and pendants.

13.25in (33.5)cm high

$260-300   **J&H**

A Doulton Lambeth vase, with stylized leaf molded decoration, possibly by Edith Lupton.

1886   18in (46cm) high

$750-950   **GorL**

► A Doulton Lambeth spirit barrel, painted with floral and foliate decoration, impressed mark for Jane Rumbol, no. 8039.

12.5in (32cm) long

$2,000-2,500   **L&T**

A Doulton Lambeth tea caddy, with silver cover, bears cartouches with inscription "Honest Tea is the Best Policy", incised marks for Ellen Palmer and Harriette EE Knight, no. 3401, lid hallmarked Chester 1896.

1896   4in (10cm) high

$450-500   **L&T**

A Royal Doulton stoneware cauldron vase, with three short feet and shoulder handles, chine decorated and flower painted.

4.5in (11.5cm) high

$50-70   **BAR**

A Royal Doulton Stoneware three-handled tyg, with applied Art Nouveau plant forms on a streaky treacle ground, impressed and incised marks.

7in (18cm) high

$200-250   **L&T**

► A pair of early 20thC Royal Doulton stoneware vases of waisted cylindrical form, tubelined with sprays of cabbage roses painted, impressed marks, numerals 7816D, incised JH.

10.25in (26cm) high

$200-250   **BonS**

A Doulton Lambeth tazza, the dish with central molded medallion enclosed by incised and beaded foliate decoration, incised marks for Eliza Simmance and one other.

9.25in (23.5cm) diam

$700-800   **L&T**

Royal Doulton Slaters Patent three-handled pot-bellied urn.

5in (12.5cm) high

$60-80   **AS&S**

◄ A pair of Royal Doulton stoneware vases, of square baluster form, decorated with a continuous landscape, incised FJ, impressed numerals 75577.

6.75in (17cm) high

$150-200   **BonS**

A pair of Doulton Lambeth vases, with relief-molded floral panels, one chipped.

11in (38cm) high

| $250-300 | GorL |

One of a pair of Doulton Lambeth vases, relief-molded with birds on a vermicelli ground, by Frank Butler, no. 922.

11in (28cm) high

| $1,000-1,400 (pair) | GorL |

A tall pair of Doulton Lambeth Slaters patent baluster vases, each impressed with floral frieze and decorated in gilt and colored glazes.

17.75in (45cm) high

| $900-1,200 | L&T |

A Doulton Lambeth water filter, the main body with applied frieze of cavorting putti, original charcoal filter, impressed and incised marks for Emily J. Partington and others.

14.5in (37cm) high

| $550-650 | L&T |

A pair of Doulton Burslem vases, of globular form, each painted and gilded with flowers on a celadon green ground, the neck applied with gilt strap handles, incised shape no.596, green printed mark, slight wear to gilt.

6.25in (16cm) high

| $300-350 | HamG |

A Doulton Burslem Morrisian biscuit barrel and cover, with electroplated mounts, printed and painted with a frieze of dancing maidens, printed impressed and painted marks, D479.

6.75in (17cm) high

| $300-350 | L&T |

A Doulton serpentine flower trough, decorated in gilt with floral sprigs beneath a waved rim, printed marks, retailer's mark for Phillips Oxford Street, rim chip.

c1890   14.25in (36cm) wide

| $75-100 | DN |

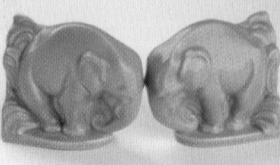

A pair of rare Royal Doulton elephant bookends by Gertrude Bayes, impressed marks.

5.5in (14cm) high

| $1,100-1,400 | L&T |

A pair of Royal Doulton sea lion bookends.

7.75in (19.5cm) high

| $550-650 | L&T |

A Royal Doulton brown salt-glazed jug.

9in (22.5cm) high

| $200-250 | Chef |

A Royal Doulton Kingsware jug, decorated with a monk in a cellar with glass and bottles, printed mark, incised Noke and a Royal Doulton figure of "The Jovial Monk", HN 2144, printed mark.

9in (23cm) high

| $150-200 | BonE |

A Royal Doulton jug, of bellied form, relief-molded with stylized flowers and leaves, by Frank Butler, incised no.717.

7.25in (18.5cm) high

| $600-700 | GorL |

A Royal Doulton plate, painted with a distant view of Ludlow Castle within gilt rim, painted by J. Hughs, printed mark and mark of New York retailers Messrs Collamore.

1901 9in (22.5cm) diam

$180-220 **Chef**

A pair of Royal Doulton shoulder vases, the ground applied with looped beads, flowerheads and leaves, no. 6621.

13.75in (34.5cm) high

$400-450 **BAR**

A pair of Royal Doulton Impasto ware bottle vases, decorated with wild roses, impressed factory marks and incised RK, probably Rosa Keen, chipped foot.

1881 11.75in (29.5cm) high

$200-250 **BonS**

A pair of Royal Doulton vases, with applied Art Nouveau foliate and beadwork designs, incised mark for Ethel Beard, no. 8425.

13in (33cm) high

$550-600 **L&T**

A Royal Doulton baluster vase, with jeweled neck, painted with a continuous frieze of sheep crossing a river, signed F Dancock.

7in (18cm) high

$200-300 **L&T**

A pair of Royal Doulton stoneware baluster vases, each decorated with beaded swags and with streaked glazes, impressed mark.

9.5in (24cm) high

$250-300 **L&T**

A large pair of Royal Doulton vases, tubelined decoration with a scrolling foliate band, impressed and incised marks for Florrie Jones.

13.5in (34cm) high

$550-600 **L&T**

One of a pair of Royal Doulton vases, decorated with galleons, impressed 8532, with MB signature.

8in (20.5cm) high

$150-200 (pair) **AS&S**

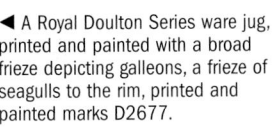

◀ A Royal Doulton Series ware jug, printed and painted with a broad frieze depicting galleons, a frieze of seagulls to the rim, printed and painted marks D2677.

7.75in (19.5cm) high

$150-200 **L&T**

A Royal Doulton Series ware tobacco jar and cover, of waisted cylindrical form, printed and painted in colors with a galleon in full sail and a bust of Sir Walter Raleigh, the rim with frieze of sailing ships, printed marks.

8in (20cm) high

$260-300 **L&T**

A Royal Doulton Heraldic and Grotesque Animal Series jug, with transfer decoration of cats "Rampant" and "Passant", with the motto "May we never break a joke to crack a reputation", no. D2441.

8in (20.5cm) high

$260-300 **Clv**

Ceramics – Royal Doulton

A Royal Doulton Series ware Secessionist-shaped jar and cover, depicting medieval girls at play, some staining and hairline cracks.

5in (12.5cm) high

$85-100   **AS&S**

A Royal Doulton Series ware bowl, "Jesters".

7in (17.5cm) diam

$30-60   **AS&S**

A pair of Royal Doulton flambé wood-cut pattern bottle vases, no.1618.

9.25in (23.5cm) high

$300-350   **GorL**

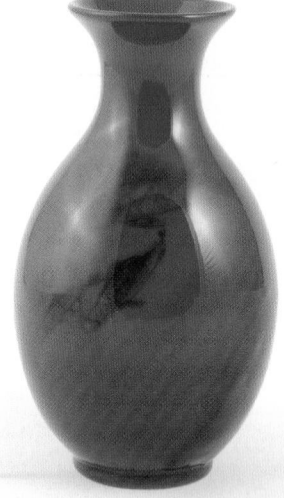

A Royal Doulton Sung vase, decorated with fish against a flambé ground, signed Noke and initialled FM.

6.5in (16.5cm) high

$400-500   **GorL**

A Royal Doulton Sung ware flambé vase decorated with red streaks, and a Royal Doulton flambé bowl, decorated with sunflowers after a design by Noke Tallest

10.25in (26cm) high

$400-500 (both)   **WW**

► A Royal Doulton Chang vase, of ovoid form, thickly covered with multi-colored crackle glazes, the red and ocher flambé ground painted with stylized plant forms, painted marks and monograms for H Nixon, C Noke and F Andrews.

9in (23cm) high

$1,500-2,000   **L&T**

A Royal Doulton flambé vase, of shouldered ovoid form, by Harry Nixon, printed marks, painted monogram.

8.25in (21cm) high

$600-700   **L&T**

A Royal Doulton flambé vase, of shouldered ovoid form, decorated with flying rooks above a cloud, by Harry Nixon, printed marks with HN monogram.

7in (18cm) high

$1,100-1,400   **L&T**

A Royal Doulton Chang vase, of beaker form with bulbous rim, thickly crackle-glazed over a flambé ground, by Harry Nixon and Charles Noke (Noke joined the Doulton Pottery and Porcelain factory in 1889 and was the Art Director from 1914-1936), printed marks, painted monograms.

This piece is particularly special because of its unusual shape and eyecatching colors. Flambé is a high-fired glaze that sometimes flows in the kiln. This causes these flame-like streaks of color. Here the glaze is even all the way round the vase, and the overall condition is superb.

4.5in (11cm) high

$1,800-2,200   **L&T**

A Royal Doulton figure of a rough-haired terrier, green printed factory mark and Ch.Scotia signature to one foot, painted no. HN1036.

9.5in (24cm) long

$550-600   **BonS**

A Royal Doulton figure of a smiling fox, printed and molded marks.

5in (12.5cm) high

$400-450   **L&T**

A Royal Doulton figure of a night heron, impressed and incised marks for Harry Simeon and Florrie Jones.

6in (15cm) high

$900-1,100   **L&T**

A Royal Doulton figure, "Derrick" HN1398, produced 1930-1938.

8in (20.5cm) high

$400-450   **Clv**

A Royal Doulton figure, "The Pied Piper" HN2102, by Leslie Harradine, produced 1953-1976.

8.5in (21.5cm) high

$90-120   **DN**

A Royal Doulton figure, "The Huntsman", HN2492, printed marks and "Copr 1973".

8in (20cm) high

$150-200   **Chef**

A Royal Doulton figure, "Sir Henry Doulton" HN3891, Limited Edition No.907/1997.

1997

$200-250   **GorL**

A Royal Doulton figure,"Bluebeard" HN2105, by Leslie Harradine.

10.5in (26.5cm) high

$250-300   **DN**

Four Royal Doulton Dickens figures, "Little Nell", "Fat Boy", "Tony Weller" and "Dick Swiveller".

$250-300   **GorB**

A Royal Doulton figure, "Henry VIII" HN 3350, printed marks, with certificate.

10in (25cm) high

$680-720   **BonE**

A Royal Doulton figure, "Lucy Ann" HN1502, printed mark.

5.5in (13.5cm) high

$300-350   **BonE**

Ceramics – Royal Doulton

A Royal Doulton figure, "The Puppetmaker" HN 2253, printed mark.

8in (20.5cm) high

$225-300   BonE

▶ A Royal Doulton figure, "The Newhaven Fishwife", designed by Harry Fenton, produced from 1931-1938, printed and painted marks.

The date, rarity and named designer are what make this piece so desirable. Figures from the 1930s are always popular, and Fenton is an especially sought after designer. Interestingly, it is often the pieces that were not very successful when they were first produced, and therefore not produced in great quantities, that are valuable today. In addition, this figure is in excellent condition.

7.75in (19.5cm) high

$4,500-5,000   L&T

A Royal Doulton figure, "Grossmith's Tsing Ihang, Perfume of Thibet", printed marks.

11.5in (29cm) high

$700-800   L&T

A Royal Doulton figure, "All O'Bloomin'" HN 1466, printed and painted marks.

6.25in (16cm high)

$1,400-1,800   L&T

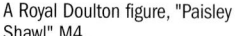

A Royal Doulton figure, "Paisley Shawl" M4.

$500-600   GorL

A Royal Doulton figure, "Fortune Teller" HN2159.

$300-350   GorL

A Royal Doulton figure, "The Parsons Daughter" HN564.

$225-300   GorL

A Royal Doulton figure, "Fanny" or "Angela" HN1204, extensive restoration.

$420-500   GorL

Royal Doulton

A Royal Doulton figure, "The Jovial Monk" HN2144.

$300-350   **GorL**

A Royal Doulton figure, "A Victorian Lady" HN728.

$150-200   **GorL**

A Royal Doulton figure, "Miss Demure" HN1402, chipped.

$150-200   **GorL**

A Royal Doulton figure, "Veronica" HN1517, fitted as a lamp.

$150-200   **GorL**

A Royal Doulton figure, "Mary Had a Little Lamb" HN2048, green printed marks.

3.5in (8.5cm) high

$85-100   **Chef**

A Royal Doulton figure, "Fair Maiden" HN2211, green printed marks.

5in (13cm) high

$60-80   **Chef**

A Royal Doulton figure, "Alice" HN2158, green printed marks.

4.75in (12cm) high

$120-150   **Chef**

A Royal Doulton figure, "Wendy" HN2109, green printed marks.

5in (13cm) high

$70-90   **Chef**

A Royal Doulton figure, "Cherie" HN2341, green printed marks.

5.5in (14cm) high

$85-100   **Chef**

A Royal Doulton figure, "Peggy" HN2038, green printed marks.

5in (13cm) high

$100-140   **Chef**

A Royal Doulton figure, "Rose" HN1368, green printed marks.

4.75in (12cm) high

$90-120   **Chef**

A Royal Doulton figure "Valerie" HN2107, green printed marks.

5in (13.5cm) high

$100-140   **Chef**

A Royal Doulton figure, "Choir Boy"
HN2141, green printed mark.

5in (12.5cm) high

$70-90   **Chef**

A Royal Doulton figure, "Suzette"
HN1487, green printed marks.

8in (20cm) high

$260-300   **Chef**

 A large Elton pottery jug,
with frilled rim and applied
handle, decorated with
applied and incised flowering
branches, painted marks.

*The Elton pottery was set up
by Sir Edmund Harry Elton
(1846-1920), in Cleveden,
Somerset. Elton was an art
potter and his wares were distinguished by their unusual
shapes and floral relief decoration, and in particular for
their streaky metallic glazes.*

10.25in (26cm) high

$300-350   **L&T**

A late 19thC Elton pottery tyg, with
mask terminals to the handles, the
body slip-decorated with flowers
and a bird on a streaked ground,
Elton signature.

8.25in (21cm) high

$120-150   **Chef**

An Elton pottery vase, of globular
form with tall cylindrical neck,
decorated in colored slips with
exotic flowers and foliage, Elton
signature to base.

15in (38cm) high

$500-550   **DN**

An Elton pottery oviform vase,
decorated in colored slips with
stylized roses and foliate stems,
against streaked glazed body, Elton
signature to base.

10.25in (26cm) high

$330-390   **DN**

A late 19thC Elton pottery vase,
with applied handles and streaked
glaze, Elton signature.

9.25in (23.5cm) high

$75-100   **Chef**

A late 19thC Elton pottery jug, with
trefoil lip and the handle in a
sweeping curve, streaky glaze, Elton
signature.

10.5in (27cm) high

$150-200   **Chef**

A late 19thC Elton pottery vase, the
ovoid body slip-decorated with a
branch of red flowers on a mottled
and streaked ground, Elton
signature.

9.75in (24.5cm) high

$225-300   **Chef**

A large Elton pottery vase, of tapered
globular form with tapering rim, applied
and incised sunflower decoration, the
whole covered in a polychrome
streaked glaze, painted mark.

10.5in (26.5cm) high

$530-550   **L&T**

An Elton pottery vase, with metallic
luster.

c1910   4.5in (11.5cm) high

$280-320   **ADE**

A Lladro bisque figure, depicting a fisher woman with basket.

14.5in (36.8cm) high

$600-650 SI

A Lladro porcelain figural group, depicting a Dutch family.

14.75in (37.5cm) high

$375-425 SI

A Lladro figurine, no. 1394, depicting Holy Mary.

14in (35.6cm) high

$700-800 SI

A Lladro figural group, no. 1445, depicting "Springtime in Japan".

13in (33cm) long

$1,000-1,400 SI

MAJOLICA IS A TYPE OF EARTHENWARE, often elaborately modeled with brightly colored, thick lead glazes. The word "majolica" is derived from the Italian "maiolica", the term for tin-glazed pottery. It was first developed at Minton in the mid-19thC, but was also produced by Wedgwood and George Jones & Sons, at Staffordshire among others. It also became popular with European, and later American factories.

Italian Renaissance pottery was one of many influences to have inspired majolica wares. The French Huguenot potter Bernard Palissy (c1510-90), produced realistically painted wares applied with reptiles, plant life and crustacea, and his work is clearly reflected in majolica. Thomas Whieldon and Ralph Wood, makers at the Staffordshire factories were also influential.

The typical majolica palette is blue, turquoise, green, yellow, orange, black and brown. Wares include jardinières, vases, teapots, tureens and dishes, and many of these pieces are decorated with eccentric and bizarre motifs, which are highly collectable.

A George Jones majolica game tureen and cover, molded with a border of stiff leaves and fronds, the cover modeled with a game bird on fronds, raised mark on base, pattern no.1758, chips to side and cover.

12in (30cm) wide

$1,500-2,000 BonE

A George Jones majolica dessert plate, molded in relief with a young girl wading through the sea with a shrimping net, painted with colored glazes, some surface staining.

c1870

$1,000-1,300 DN

▶ A George Jones majolica stilton dish and cover, molded with lotus flowers, with lotus flower finial to cover, turquoise interior, painted numerals in black to base, indistinct impressed diamond registration mark, cover with hairline cracks and small chips.

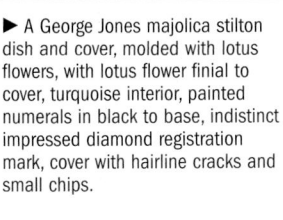

12.5in (32cm) high

$7,000-8,000 BonS

A George Jones majolica game pie dish, cover and liner, the cover modeled with a woodcock and her seven chicks among ferns, 3370 painted in black, molded registration mark for 27 Dec 1873, the liner with a restored rim.

George Jones was an employee at Minton until he opened his own factory at Trent Potteries, Stoke on Trent, in 1861. It made good quality earthenwares, which combined humor, even eccentricity, with elegance. His majolica is known for its glowing colored glazes. From 1872, the firm also produced bone china. Almost all of his majolica is marked with the maker's name and a date code. The first mark was a monogram of the initials GJ with "& Sons" added from December 1873 and a crescent shape from 1874. George Jones died in 1893, but the factory continued until 1951.

1873

14.25in (36cm) wide

$20,000-30,000 WW

A Minton majolica cheese dish and cover, molded in high relief with lilies, bullrushes and insects, patent office mark, pattern no. 3412/111, restorations.

11in (28cm) diam

| $1,500-2,000 | LC |

A 19thC majolica Minton-style salt or bon-bon dish, modeled as a putto seated atop a conch shell, unmarked.

6.25in (16cm) high

| $500-600 | PH |

Two Minton majolica sweetmeat dishes, modeled as oak leaves and acorns with blue tits perched to one end, impressed marks, date ciphers, both with some damage.

1879 8.75in (22cm) wide

| $1.000-1,300 | WW |

A Minton majolica nut dish, molded as a leaf surmounted by a squirrel, some damage.

9.5in (24cm) wide

| $500-600 | GorL |

A CLOSER LOOK AT MINTON MAJOLICA

PAUL COMOLERA (1818-1897) was a very fine and influential French sculptor known mainly for his models of birds. He taught Jules Moigniez, one of the most important sculptors of the Animalier school. He worked in bronze but is also known as a ceramicist. This important piece for Minton shows the quality of the factory's majolica, and the skill of the artist.

● The size of the piece contributes to its overall desirability.

● The whole piece is extremely well modeled, from the graceful lines of the bird's pose, to the variety of textures, from feathers to foliage to rockwork that the artist has captured.

● The figure is not decorated in the typical Minton majolica palette, however the superb glowing glazes denote the finest quality. They are well controlled, without any hint of blurring or dribbling.

● Colors are subtle, naturalistic and painstakingly applied, with subtle shading and sensitive yet confident brushwork.

● Comolera's birds are highly realistic. Note the attention to detail on the heron's legs.

A large Minton majolica model of a gray heron with a fish in its beak, modeled by Paul Comolera, the artist's signature molded to the base, 1917 and Minton impressed, date cipher for 1876, minor damages.

1917 39.5in (100cm) high

| $12,000-14,000 | WW |

A Minton majolica game dish and cover, the body ozier-molded with oak leaf garland, the cover decorated with hare and game birds on a leaf molded ground, crabstock handles, turquoise interior, impressed factory mark and date code, minor losses to cover.

Ozier *is a pattern simulating basket weave. It was devised at Meissen in the 1730s.*

1871 14.5in (36.5cm) long

| $1,500-2,000 | BonS |

A large Minton majolica jardinère, modeled as a nautilus shell resting on coral branches, bowl restored.

27.5in (70cm) high

| $3,000-3,500 | BonE |

A Minton majolica Palissy plate, painted in colored glazes, impressed marks, date code.

1863	10in (25cm) dia
$700-800	**DN**

► A large Minton majolica garden seat, modeled as a crouching blackamoor supporting a square tasseled cushion, impressed marks and date code for 1867, chips to base, corner of base repaired.

	19.25in (49cm) high
$5,000-6,000	**BonE**

A large Minton majolica vase, with ring handles, molded with two classical mask panels, the ground decorated with bows and olive branches, impressed marks, restored.

	13.5in (34.5cm) high
$600-700	**BonE**

A Minton majolica rectangular flower trough, the sides molded as a plank fence growing with strawberry leaves, impressed marks and date code.

1871	11in (27.5cm) wide
$250-300	**WW**

A Minton majolica teapot and cover, modeled as a monkey clutching a coconut, Minton and 1844 impressed and date code for 1878, the pot with an invisible crack across the handle, the cover with knop re-glued, small chip to ear.

During the latter half of the 19th century, the firm of Minton, manufacturers of fine porcelain, appointed Léon Arnoux, a ceramicist from Sèvres, as art curator. Among his innovations was the development of majolica in the Renaissance style. Majolica was used for all kinds of objects, including elaborately modeled novelty teapots. Classic designs such as the Chinaman, the tortoise and the monkey, originally produced by Minton in the 1870s, are now rare and highly sought after.

1878	8.5in (21.5cm) high
$3,500-5,000	**WW**

A late 19thC majolica game dish, the oval body molded with hanging game and swags of fruiting vine, on a brown glazed ground, impressed marks.

	10.75in (27cm) wide
$45-70	**Chef**

A majolica figure, modeled as a young grape harvester.

	8.75in (22cm) high
$550-600	**LC**

An unusual Worcester majolica trefoil-shaped bowl, modeled as three scallop shells, on writhing dolphin supports, and with shell-cast platform base, impressed mark, rim with glaze firing imperfection, minor flakes and chips.

c1876-91	6.75in (17cm) high
$2,500-3,000	**L&T**

A 19thC majolica jardinière, modeled as an elephant with a conch-shaped howdah.

16cm (40.5cm) high

$750-950	Clv

A Joseph Holdcroft majolica jardinière, molded with female mask handles and leaf-molded bosses suspending floral swags, some small chips, deterioration to interior.

c1880   11in (28cm) diam

$600-700	DN

A mid-Victorian Wedgwood majolica jug, the rustic handle with blackberry terminals flowering and fruiting onto the barked body, impressed marks.

7.75in (19.5cm) high

$300-350	Chef

A "Volunteers" majolica jug, molded in relief with figures representing "Our Army and Navy and Brave Volunteers", flanking a profile portrait medallion of Queen Victoria, registration mark, some restoration work to medallion.

This design was originally registered by the Sandford Pottery of Wareham, Dorset to commemorate reviews of The Volunteer Rifles, held in London and Edinburgh during 1860, but made in buff-colored earthenware.

10.75in (27cm) high

$200-250	HamG

A 19thC majolica gurgling-fish pitcher, probably by Thomas Forester & Sons.

10in (25.5cm) high

$140-200	Clv

A 19thC majolica dish, the center molded with a figure picking corn encircled by a mottled band and molded wheat ears.

12.75 (32.5cm) diam

$75-125	WW

A Victorian Burmantoft majolica jardinière and stand, molded with sunflower decoration, impressed monogram mark, 1948B.

26.5in (67.5cm) high

$400-450	GorL

A Continental majolica jardinière, the bowl with lion-mask handles and incised stylized maize, cornflower, and foliate decoration, the pedestal with figural decoration of a man in Elizabethan dress.

44in (112cm) high

$600-700	SI

A mid-Victorian Majolica garniture, comprising two jugs and a two-handled vase, each molded and painted with foxgloves and acorns on a brown bark ground.

Tallest 8.25in (21cm) high

$300-350	Chef

Majolica

Three 19thC American majolica vessels, from left: a pineapple-form pitcher, a tobacco jar modeled as a Chinaman's head and a pineapple-form syrup pitcher with pewter lid.

Pitcher 7in (18cm) high

$480-520   **SI**

A pair of late 19thC majolica dessert plates, molded as lily leaves flanking a central flowerhead, impressed registration marks.

9in (23cm) diam

$140-180   **Chef**

A late 19thC majolica dessert plate, with mottled glazes within a floral molded border.

7.75in (19.5cm) diam

$50-70   **Chef**

A majolica garden seat, modeled as a blackmoor among bullrushes below a square cushion, restored.

18in (46cm) high

$1,500-2,000   **BonE**

A 19thC Wedgwood majolica stand, molded with four groups of dancing putti divided by angels, the reverse with a mottled green and brown glaze, impressed marks, two rim chips.

12.25in (31cm) diam

$300-350   **WW**

A 19thC majolica teapot and cover, molded as a pineapple, some damage.

8.75in (22cm) long

$260-300   **WW**

A 19thC majolica teapot and cover, modeled as a Chinaman holding a face mask that forms the spout, his head forming the cover, some repair to cover.

8.25in (21cm) long

$700-800   **WW**

A 19thC majolica teapot and cover, possibly Rye potteries, modeled as a monkey with hands clasped before the snake spout, the tail forming the handle, the hat forming the cover.

11in (28cm) high

$200-250   **Chef**

► A 19thC majolica three-piece set, of hexagonal section molded with flowerheads, comprising teapot and cover, sugar basin and cover and milk jug, the jug damaged.

$1,200-1,800   **WW**

► A 19thC American three-piece majolica tea service, comprising teapot, covered sugar bowl and creamer, all of squat form, the ground impressed with a Renaissance Revival pattern overlayed with leaves and berries, the handles modeled as branches.

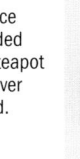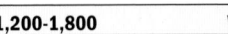

Teapot 4in (10cm) high

$240-300   **SI**

A late 19thC majolica hanging vase, molded with flowerheads and leaves and with a berry terminal, the rim pierced with three suspension holes.

12.25in (31cm) diam

$250-300   **WW**

A Minton Secessionist vase, tube-lined with stylized tulips and swags, between angular handles, printed mark Minton Ltd and no.1.

The avant garde shape of this piece, along with the strong vertical lines of the decoration reflect the influence of Viennese Art Nouveau designers.

12.25in (31cm) high

$600-700   **BonS**

A Minton Secessionist vase, decorated with flowers and foliate stems with tube-lined detail, printed mark Mintons Ltd and no. 32.

7in (17.5cm) high

$200-250   **DN**

A pair of Minton Aesthetic candlesticks, each decorated with linear, floral and beaded bands beneath the glaze, impressed with Minton and Rd No. 101464.

6.5in (16.5cm) high

$140-180   **DN**

A Minton Secessionist oviform vase, with tube-lined decoration of stylized plant forms and vertical stems linked by foliate swags, maker's marks on base.

12.5in (32cm) high

$380-440   **DN**

A Minton Secessionist vase No.1, rim restored.

13in (32.5cm) high

$350-400   **AS&S**

A Minton Secessionist vase.

c1910   5.25in (13.2cm) high

$200-250   **ADE**

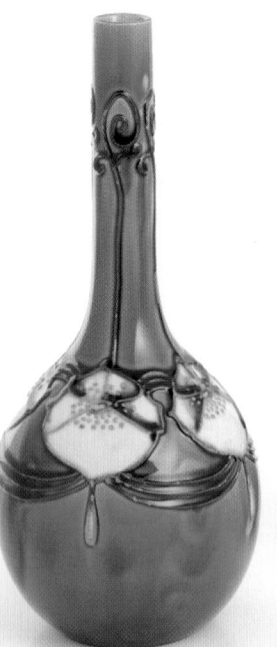

A Minton bottle vase, of onion form on circular foot, glazed in bleu celeste and decorated in the Japanese style with tooled gilt insects, impressed mark, shape no. 1626, date code, bruise to the glaze.

1872   14.5in (36.5cm) high

$350-400   **BonS**

A Minton Secessionist oviform vase, applied with twin twig handles and transfer-printed with stylized flowers and foliage, globe mark and Minton England on base.

10.5in (26.5cm) high

$300-350   **DN**

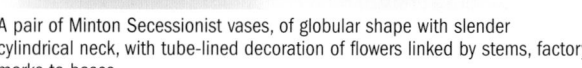

A pair of Minton Secessionist vases, of globular shape with slender cylindrical neck, with tube-lined decoration of flowers linked by stems, factory marks to bases.

10.75in (27.5cm) high

$600-700   **DN**

Moorcroft

WILLIAM MOORCROFT'S (1872-1945) involvement in art pottery began when he was 12 years old. He later worked as a designer for James Mcintyre & Company in Burslem where he first produced the popular "Aurelian" series. This ware was produced for only a short period. It can be distinguished by its ironed and blue enameled and transfer-printed decoration of highly stylized floral motifs, frets and diapers set against a white ground. A forerunner of British Art Nouveau ceramics, Moorcroft later produced the "Florian" range; inspired by Middle and Far Eastern ceramics as well as Classical forms, these wares are painted with floral motifs, foliage and peacock feathers and brought the process of tube-lined decoration to a new level.

In 1913 Moorcroft set up his own factory with financial backing from Liberty & Co. and on William's death in 1945, his son Walter took over the running of the company. There he produced the famous Lily, Magnolia and Hibiscus designs. Moorcroft pottery has enjoyed continued success, winning many gold medals, awards and Royal appointments and is still running today. Early pottery can be found throughout the world, including the Victoria and Albert Museum in London and with the exception of some pieces made during the late 1970s and early 1980s all Moorcroft is sought-after with the most desirable being a matter of personal taste.

A Moorcroft baluster vase, with inverted rim, decorated in the Anemones pattern, printed and painted marks.

7.75in (19.5cm) high

$150-200 | **L&T**

A Moorcroft baluster vase, with everted rim, painted in Anemones pattern, painted and impressed marks.

2.25in (6cm) high

$200-250 | **L&T**

A Moorcroft circular bowl, tube-lined with Anna pattern on a cream and cobalt blue ground, printed and painted marks.

10.25in (26cm) diam

$225-300 | **Chef**

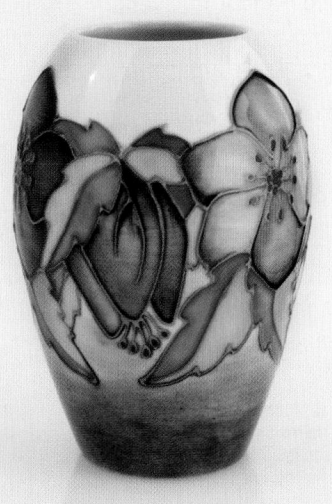

► A Moorcroft oviform vase, designed by Rachel Bishop for the Moorcroft Collectors Club, tube-lined with stylized clematis and leaves in naturalistic colors, impressed factory marks, club marks for 1995 and signed in gold Rachel Bishop des.

Tube-lining was used extensively in Moorcroft ceramics. It is a form of ceramic decoration, in which a thin line of slip is applied to the surface to outline areas of colored glaze.

A Moorcroft shouldered ovoid vase, with inverted rim, decorated with balloons, painted marks.

7in (18cm) high

$180-220 | **L&T**

A Moorcroft oviform vase, designed by Rachel Bishop, tube-lined and painted with flowers against a shaded blue ground, factory marks and signed in gold Rachel Bishop des.

5.25in (13.5cm) high

$80-140 | | **DN**

5.25in (13.5cm) high

$180-220 | **DN**

Ceramics – Moorcroft

This biscuit barrel caused a great deal of interest when it came up for sale recently. Although the Claremont pattern is not rare, there are a number of reasons why the piece proved so popular with buyers.

- A rare shape is always one of the key factors that determines desirability. This barrel, with its slightly rounded cube form is unusual.
- Overall the condition is good, but the piece does have a tiny firing fault to the neck rim. On a common object, this would affect the value dramatically, but in this case buyers were not deterred.
- The Claremont pattern comes in a number of slightly different colorways, and this piece has a particularly striking blend of shades that compliments the pattern beautifully.
- Inevitably, fashion plays its part. This is a commercially successful design that has always been popular, but the subtle, earthy colors, and the intriguing "other-worldly" quality of the pattern are in vogue now.

A Moorcroft "Cobridge" stoneware vase, incised and painted with canals, narrowboats and buildings in a rural setting, factory marks, edition no. 30/100 and signed in gold Philip Gibson 2.10.99.

1998　　　10in (25.5cm) high

$680-740　　　**DN**

A Moorcroft blue cornflower vase, on mottled blue ground, remains of paper label to base.

7in (18cm) high

$1,300-1,800　　　**GorL**

A Moorcroft "Claremont" biscuit box and cover, decorated with toadstools, impressed Moorcroft Made in England and signed W.M. in green.

c1910　　　6.5in (16.5cm) high

$3,000-3,500　　　**DN**

A Moorcroft ginger jar and cover, decorated in the Fairy Rings pattern, with toadstools against a blue/green ground, lid broken.

6in (15.2cm) high

$1,400-1,700　　　**GorL**

A Moorcroft Macintyre Florian ware comport, with dark and pale floral decoration.

8in (20.3cm) diam

$350-400　　　**GorB**

A large Macintyre Florian ware ovoid vase, brightly decorated with large tulips and swirling leaves, green facsimilie signature, brown printed mark.

c1900　　　11.25in (28.5cm) high

$6,000-6,500　　　**WW**

A Moorcroft Florian ware jardinière, with frilled rim, painted with yellow poppies, printed marks 326471, signed in green.

7.75in (20cm) high

$1,500-2,000　　　**L&T**

A pair of Moorcroft Florian ware baluster vases, printed mark 347807, initialled in green.

9.5in (24cm) high

$2,400-3,000　　　**L&T**

A pair of Moorcroft Florian ware bottle vases, with everted rim, decorated in the Florian 404017 pattern, painted in gilt and green on an olive ground, printed marks, signed in green.

10.5in (27cm) high

$1,500-2,000　　　**L&T**

A Moorcroft Florian ware vase, of slim baluster form, decorated with a frieze of poppies on a white ground, printed marks, signed in green.

5in (13cm) high

$900-1,000 **L&T**

A Moorcroft Florian ware twin-handled vase, of ovoid form with everted rim, decorated with forget-me-nots on a white ground, printed marks, signed in green.

5in (12.5cm) high

$1,500-2,000 **L&T**

A Moorcroft Florian ware vase, with dark blue cornflowers against a pale blue ground, W. Moorcroft des in green script to base and no.7753.

5in (12.5cm) high

$850-950 **GorL**

A Moorcroft small footed bowl, in Freesia pattern on shaded green/blue background, impressed marks.

4.25in (11cm) diam

$90-120 **BAR**

A William Moorcroft teapot, decorated in shades of yellow and red with freesias on a mottled green ground, impressed marks.

6in (15cm) high

$225-300 **Chef**

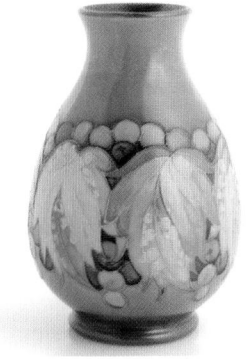

A Moorcroft Grape and Leaf oviform vase, tube-lined and painted in autumnal colors, impressed W. Moorcroft, Potter to H.M. the Queen and signed in blue, W. Moorcroft.

9.75in (25cm) high

$1,500-2,000 **DN**

A Moorcroft vase, of baluster shape, tube-lined with the Gypsy pattern on a dark green ground, printed and painted marks.

8in (20.5cm) high

$120-150 **Chef**

A Moorcroft vase, of flowering cylindrical shape, tube-lined with the Hepatica pattern on a cream ground, impressed and painted marks.

6in (15.5cm) high

$90-120 **Chef**

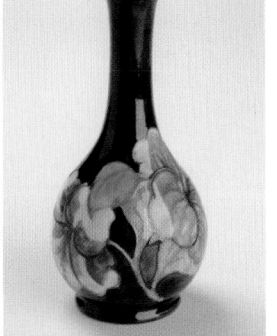

A Moorcroft bottle vase, decorated with hibiscus on a blue ground, impressed and painted marks, paper label.

10.25in (26cm) high

$375-450 **WW**

A tall Moorcroft baluster vase, decorated in the Hibiscus pattern, impressed mark, initialled in blue.

8.25in (21cm) high

$165-200 **L&T**

▲1 20thC Moorcroft vase, of squat form, with hibiscus flowers and puce leaf decoration on green ground, incised MOORCROFT and MADE IN ENGLAND.
▲2 20thC Moorcroft vase, of ovoid form tapering to an elongated neck, similarly decorated and incised MOORCROFT and MADE IN ENGLAND.

Tallest 5.5in (14cm) high

$500-600 (both) **SI**

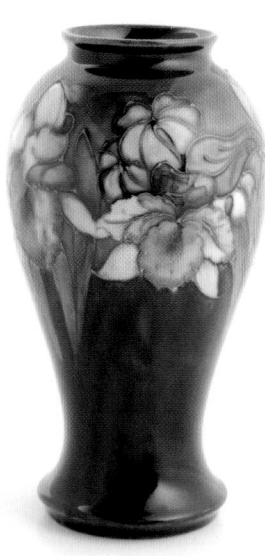

▲1 A 20thC Moorcroft Hibiscus pattern vase, the squat ovoid body tapering to a long neck, impressed MOORCROFT and MADE IN ENGLAND.
▲2 A 20thC Moorcroft Hibiscus pattern vase, the ovoid body tapering to a flaring neck.

Tallest 9.5in (24cm) high

$700-800 (2 items) | **SI**

A Moorcroft Macintyre vase, of baluster form with swollen upper portion, finely tube-lined and painted with swags of flowers, foliate motifs on spreading foot, gilded rims, factory marks and signed W. Moorcroft in green.

7.75in (19.5cm) high

$550-600 | **DN**

A Moorcroft shallow dish, tube-lined with Oberon pattern on a dark green ground, impressed and painted marks.

10in (25.5cm) diam

$120-150 | **Chef**

A Moorcroft baluster vase, decorated with orchids and irises, facsimile signature Made in England and W.M. initials in blue.

9.75in (25cm) high

$550-600 | **DN**

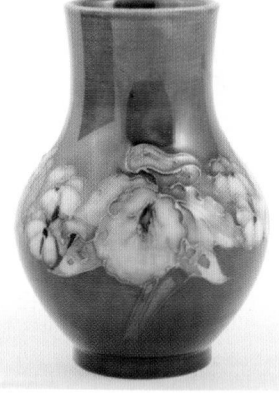

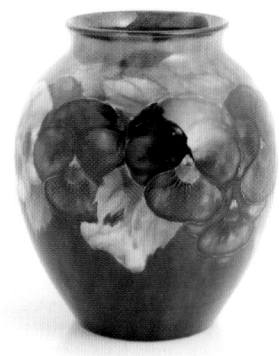

A Moorcroft vase, decorated with orchids against a green/blue ground.

4.75in (12cm) high

$260-300 | **GorL**

A Moorcroft ovoid vase, decorated with orchids against a blue ground.

6.5in (16.5cm) high

$550-600 | **GorL**

A Moorcroft Pansies vase, painted in naturalistic colors with pansies amid foliage, impressed Moorcroft Burslem England, signed in green W. Moorcroft.

8.25in (21cm) high

$550-600 | **DN**

A William Moorcroft fruit bowl, decorated with pansies on a dark blue ground.

9.5in (24cm) diam

$450-500 | **GorB**

▲1 A 20thC Moorcroft covered dish, of ovoid form with pansies on a pale green ground, impressed MOORCROFT/MADE IN ENGLAND.
▲2 A 20thC Moorcroft vase, similarly decorated and impressed MOORCROFT/MADE IN ENGLAND. Vase

Vase 8in (20.5cm) high

$700-800 (2 items) | **SI**

A Moorcroft biscuit barrel, with electroplated cover and mounts, in Pomegranate pattern, on a shaded green/blue ground, painted green initials.

7in (18cm) high

$600-700 | **BAR**

A large Moorcroft oviform vase, decorated with pomegranates, leaves and berries, impressed Moorcroft Burslem England and signed in green W. Moorcroft.

16.25in (41cm) high

$1,500-2,000 | **DN**

A Moorcroft vase, of pear shape, decorated with pomegranates, grapes and foliage, impressed factory marks and signed in green W. Moorcroft, small repaired chip to neck.

9.75in (25cm) high

$400-500 | **DN**

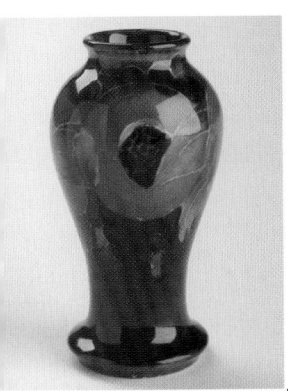

A Moorcroft miniature baluster vase, painted in the Pomegranate pattern, impressed mark, initialled in green.

4in (10cm) high

$250-300 **L&T**

A Moorcroft Pomegranate pattern vase, of squat form decorated with fruit and foliage on cobalt ground, impressed MADE IN ENGLAND, signature W Moorcroft.

c1932 7.5in (19cm) high

$750-950 **SI**

A Moorcroft Pottery pomegranate ginger jar and cover, decorated with pomegranates, leaves and berries on a mottled blue ground, signed W. Moorcroft in green and impressed MADE IN ENGLAND/769, cover impressed MOORCROFT.

c1918-1929 11in (28cm) high

$2,200-2,800 **SI**

A Moorcroft Pottery Pomegranate pattern bowl, the flaring rimmed bowl decorated with pomegranates, berries and leaves on a mottled blue ground, signed W. Moorcroft in green and impressed MOORCROFT/BURSLEM/ENGLAND/M6B.

c1916 12in (31.8cm) diam

$1,000-1,500 **SI**

A Moorcroft urn, decorated with pomegranates against a mottled green ground, Moorcroft signaure to base in green, stamped Made for Liberty & Co, impressed 996.

6in (15cm) high

$2,000-2,500 **GorL**

A Moorcroft baluster vase, decorated in the Pomegranate and Grape pattern, on a dark blue ground.

9.25in (23.5cm) high

$750-950 **GorL**

A Moorcroft vase, of baluster shape, tube-lined and painted with the Queen's Choice pattern on a cobalt blue ground, impressed and painted marks.

6in (15.5cm) high

$260-300 **Chef**

A Moorcroft tall baluster vase, decorated with roses and chrysanthemums, impressed and painted marks.

8.25in (21cm) high

$150-200 **L&T**

A Moorcroft vase, of gourd shape, tube-lined with sweet briar on a salmon pink ground, impressed and painted marks.

11.25in (28.5cm) high

$150-200 **Chef**

A Moorcroft simple vase, designed by Sally Tuffin, of onion shape, tube-lined with a lattice pattern of stylized florets and foliage, impressed factory marks and I.S.F. sample written on paper label on base.

4.25in (10.5cm) high

$150-200   **DN**

A Moorcroft plate, designed by Sally Tuffin as a limited edition of 300 for Richard Dennis, London, tube-lined with a tabby cat against a ground of stylized leaves, factory marks on base and 52/300.

1992/3   10.25in (26cm) diam

$400-500   **DN**

A Moorcroft miniature baluster vase, designed by Sally Tuffin, decorated with violets, impressed and painted marks.

4in (10cm) high

$90-120   **L&T**

A Moorcroft Waving Corn twin-handled vase, of compressed globular shape, tube-lined, impressed W. Moorcroft, Potter to H.M. the Queen and signed in blue W. Moorcroft.

7.75in (20cm) high

$1,000-1,500   **DN**

A Moorcroft Weeping Willow landscape vase, of baluster shape finely tube-lined, impressed W. Moorcroft, Potter to H.M. the Queen and signed in blue W. Moorcroft.

9in (23cm) high

$1,500-2,000   **DN**

A Moorcroft jug, the broad-bellied form decorated with tube-lined fish and seaweed on a mottled blue-green ground, impressed MOORCROFT and MADE IN ENGLAND.

c1920-30   8.5in (22cm) high

$700-900   **SI**

A Moorcroft vase, of flared cylindrical shape, tube-lined with stylized flowers after a Charles Rennie Macintosh design, on a cobalt blue ground, impressed and painted marks.

10in (25.5cm) high

$250-300   **Chef**

A Pilkington's Lancastrian luster pear-shaped vase, by Gordon Forsythe, painted with foliage and berries against a blood-red ground, impressed Bees mark, date code, painted artist's rebus

1906   6.25in (16cm) high

$200-250   **DN**

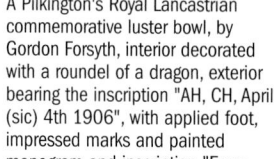

A Pilkington's Royal Lancastrian commemorative luster bowl, by Gordon Forsyth, interior decorated with a roundel of a dragon, exterior bearing the inscription "AH, CH, April (sic) 4th 1906", with applied foot, impressed marks and painted monogram and inscription "From M.B.C. & P.W.C. April 4th 1916".

8.75in (22cm) diam

$350-400   **L&T**

A Pilkington's luster vase, by William S. Mycock, painted with a frieze of galleons in full sail, impressed mark, painted monogram, dated.

1907   8in (20cm) high

$750-950   **L&T**

A large Pilkington's Lancastrian vase, by Gordon Forsyth, with motto "Ave Maria Gratia Plena", cut from sheet clay, imprinted factory mark, rebus mark Gordon Forsyth, dated.

1907   11in (28cm) high

$2,500-3,000   **WW**

ilkington

A pair of Pilkington's baluster vases, the ribbed bodies covered in a streaking turquoise glaze, impressed mark, dated.

1912   8.75in (22cm) high

$450-500   **L&T**

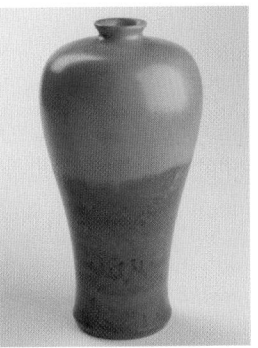

A Pilkington's shouldered baluster vase, with everted rim thickly glazed in bands of orange and green, impressed mark 3017, dated.

1913   12.5in (32cm) high

$350-400   **L&T**

A Pilkington's Royal Lancastrian luster vase, by William S. Mycock, painted with ducks flying over the sea, impressed marks, painted initials.

6.25in (16cm) high

$250-300   **L&T**

A Pilkington's Royal Lancastrian vase, thrown by E.T. Radford.

c1930   15.5in (39.5cm) high

$700-800   **ADE**

A large Pilkington's Royal Lancastrian twin-handled luster vase, by William S. Mycock, of shouldered ovoid form, decorated with panels of flowering lilies, impressed marks, painted monogram, dated.

1921   9.5in (24cm) high

$1,700-2,000   **L&T**

A Pilkington's Royal Lancastrian luster bowl, decorated by William S. Mycock, with foliate buds on a turquoise and royal blue background, painted monogram, impressed factory marks.

13.75in (35cm) diam

$2,800-3,500   **L&T**

A large Pilkington's Royal Lancastrian footed bowl, painted by Richard Joyce with an overall scale pattern, impressed mark, painted monogram.

13.5in (34cm) diam

$120-150   **BonE**

A Pilkington's Royal Lancastrian vase, painted by Richard Joyce with stylized leaves and zigzag border on gray ground, impressed mark, painted monogram.

9in (23cm) high

$80-100   **BonE**

A Pilkington's shouldered ovoid vase, with everted rim, covered in a streaked blue glaze, impressed marks.

10.5in (27cm) high

$250-300   **L&T**

A Pilkington's Royal Lancastrian shouldered vase, covered in an orange, green and yellow streaked and crystalline glaze, impressed marks.

10.5in (27cm) high

$250-300   **L&T**

A Pilkington's Royal Lancastrian shouldered vase, with everted rim, covered in a sparkling crystalline bronze glaze, impressed marks.

12.25in (29.5cm) high

$600-700   **L&T**

Ceramics – Poole

CARTER, STABLER AND ADAMS

Carter, Stabler and Adams was established in 1873 as Carter and Co. in Poole in Dorset. In 1921 it expanded under the names of its partners, Charles Carter, Phoebe Stabler and John Adams.

The items produced in the 1920s and 30s successfully combined artistic merit with commercial viability, and this period is considered the factory's golden age. Most of Poole's wares from this time, which include decorative tiles, vases, urns, and tableware, consists of hand-thrown stoneware with a matt grayish white glaze. Pieces were decorated by hand in a range of bold, highly distinctive patterns, in a palette that was both subtle and eye-catching. Although they produced some plain and two-colored pieces, most use a combination of rich hues in similar tones.

Carter, Stabler and Adams became officially known as Poole Pottery in 1963, although earlier wares are often referred to by the later name. The firm used a variety of marks and if the base of a piece is unmarked it is almost certainly not Poole. The earliest examples from 1873-1921 are marked "Carter & Company" or "Carter Poole". From 1921 they are marked "Poole England". Most earlier pieces also bear the decorator's monogram, and some have a pattern number. From 1963 they are simply marked "Poole Pottery Ltd". The firm is still in production today.

A CLOSER LOOK AT POOLE

- As with most ceramics, rare patterns and shapes are usually more valuable than standard pieces.
- Designs from Poole's heyday in the 1920s and 30s are generally the most sought after, and are often collected by pattern.
- Look for strong Art Deco designs combining geometric and floral motifs. Patterns that include stylized images of birds or animals are particularly desirable.
- Larger pieces have greater impact and always sell well.
- To determine whether or not a piece was hand-thrown, put your hand inside and feel for the tell-tale ribbing.
- The abstract designs of the 1960s and 70s, often in shades of bright orange, yellow and brown were popular in their day, but quickly became passé. As a result, many were discarded. Today, ceramics that define their era are highly collectable, and the last few years has seen the prices soar (see Contemporary).

A pair of Carter & Co. Poole Pottery candlesticks.

1906　　　16.25in (41.5cm) high

$2,000-2,500　　　**ADE**

A 1920s Carter, Stabler and Adams Ltd. Poole Pottery vase.

8.75in (22.5cm) high

$900-1,000　　　**ADE**

A 1920s Carter, Stabler and Adams Ltd. Poole Pottery vase.

10.5in (27cm) high

$450-500　　　**ADE**

A 1920s Carter, Stabler and Adams Ltd. Poole Pottery vase, with the Fuchsia pattern.

11.25in (28.5cm) high

$1,200-1,400　　　**ADE**

A 1920s Poole Pottery sculpture, by Harold and Phoebe Stabler, of child on a bull.

$3,500-4,000　　　**ADE**

A Carter, Stabler and Adams Ltd. two-handled Poole Pottery red earthenware vase, hand-painted with lesser known pattern 995/CS, designed by Truda Carter.

1928-34   8.75in (22cm) high

$1,700-2,000   **ADE**

A Carter, Stabler and Adams Ltd. Poole Pottery red earthenware vase, hand-painted with lesser known pattern 999/DR, with a tinted glaze, designed by Truda Carter.

1928-34   7.75in (20cm) high

$1,700-2,000   **ADE**

A 1930s Carter, Stabler and Adams Ltd. Poole Pottery cylindrical jug, pattern by Truda Carter, painted with fuchsias and other flowers by Ruth Pavely, impressed Poole England and marked 321_ED, painters mark.

4.75in (12cm) high

$130-170   **DN**

A Carter, Stabler and Adams Ltd. Poole Pottery vase, unusual pattern.

c1930   10.25in (26cm) high

$1,500-2,000   **ADE**

A Carter, Stabler and Adams Ltd. Poole Pottery jardinière, with rare pattern.

c1930   7in (17.5cm) high

$1,700-2,000   **ADE**

A 1930s Carter, Stabler and Adams Ltd. Poole Pottery jug, decorated with a rare pattern.

7.75in (19.5cm) high

$1,200-2,500   **ADE**

A 1930s Carter, Stabler & Adams Ltd. Poole Pottery vase.

The Victoria and Albert Museum, London, has the same vase in it's collection

6.5in (16.5cm) high

$600-700   **ADE**

A 1930s Carter, Stabler and Adams Ltd. Poole Pottery vase.

9.75in (24.5cm) high

$1,200-1,500   **ADE**

A 1930s Carter, Stabler and Adams Ltd. Poole Pottery vase.

4.5in (11.5cm) high

$170-200   **ADE**

A 1930s Carter, Stabler and Adams Ltd. Poole Pottery vase.

7.25in (18.5cm) high

$900-1,100   **ADE**

A 1930s Carter, Stabler and Adams Ltd. two-handled Poole Pottery vase.

9in (23cm) high

$1,100-1,400   **ADE**

A 1930s Carter, Stabler and Adams Ltd. Poole Pottery vase.

5.75in (14.5cm) high

$900-1,100   **ADE**

A 1930s Carter, Stabler and Adams Ltd. Poole Pottery vase.

5in (13cm) high

$500-550   **ADE**

A 1930s Carter, Stabler and Adams Ltd. Poole Pottery vase.

6.75in (17cm) high

$450-500   **ADE**

A 1930s Carter, Stabler and Adams Ltd. Poole Pottery Sylvanware vase.

$250-300   **ADE**

A Carter, Stabler and Adams Ltd. Poole Pottery earthenware vase, with Leaping Deer pattern 599/TZ, designed by Truda Carter.

1934-37   8.25in (21cm) high

$1,200-1,500   **ADE**

A Carter Stabler and Adams Ltd. Poole Pottery earthenware vase, with Persian Deer pattern 684/SK, designed by Truda Carter, hand-painted by Gwen Haskins, an interesting reworking of the pattern from the twenties.

c1949-50   14.25in (36cm) high

$2,500-3,000   **ADE**

A Carter, Stabler and Adams Ltd. Poole Pottery earthenware vase, designed by Truda Carter, superbly decorated with Art Deco pattern 333/KN.

1934-37   9.75in (24.5cm) high

$2,500-3,000   **ADE**

A Carter, Stabler and Adams Ltd., Poole Pottery vase, with Comic Bird pattern.

1920-30   10.25in (26cm) high

$600-700   **ADE**

A Carter, Stabler and Adams Ltd. Poole Pottery vase, painted to a design by Truda Carter, decorated with highly-stylized foliage and geometric forms, impressed mark Poole England, 208/YE, and indistinct painters mark.

3.25in (8.5cm) high

$120-150   **DN**

A Rookwood pottery double-handled vase, of ovoid form with angular inverted u-shaped handles, pale yellow cream hi glaze, impressed factory mark and no. 68875.

1945   5.25in (13.5cm) high

$300-350   **SI**

A Rookwood Pottery pitcher, probably by Matt Daly, with sprig-molded bumblebees around neck and an applied small c-form handle, the whole painted in the Japanese style with a bird in flight and a wispy pine tree branch, impressed "ROOKWOOD/1885/239 W2".

1885   7in (18cm) high

$250-300   **SI**

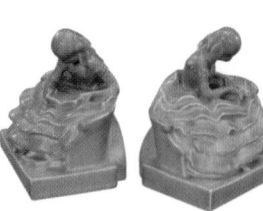

A pair of Rookwood Pottery figural bookends, each modeled as a seated girl wearing a broad ruffled skirt and reading a book, pink and green matte glaze, 6037 impressed mark, backs of the figures impressed with "M" in a circle.

1930   6.25in (16cm) high

$300-350   **SI**

A pair of Rookwood pottery bookends, modeled as reclining panthers in matte blue/gray glaze, designed by William McDonald, impressed mark and 2564, impressed "Mc" on back.

1922   6in (15cm) high

$400-500   **SI**

A Royal Copenhagen porcelain Oriental Fairy Tale figure group, of a turbaned man seducing a reclining nude, designed by Gerhard Henning.

8.5in (21.6cm) high

$700-800   **Clv**

A Royal Copenhagen porcelain figure group, depicting two Oriental lovers on oval base.

10in (25.4cm) high

$850-950   **Clv**

A Royal Copenhagen porcelain figure, depicting a kneeling girl holding a horn shaped trumpet, base inscribed Kristine Svendsdatter.

9.5in (24.1cm) high

$400-500   **Clv**

A Royal Copenhagen porcelain figure group, depicting two standing Oriental figures gazing skyward, on rectangular base.

8in (20.3cm) high

$550-650   **Clv**

DERBYSHIRE, IN THE NORTH OF ENGLAND, HAS A LONG HERITAGE OF PORCELAIN PRODUCTION and a number of factories were based there, with the first established around 1750, one of the earliest in Britain.

In 1876 William Litherland and Edward Phillips established the Derby Crown Porcelain Co., at Osmaston Road. The works still occupy this site today and a second factory was established nearby in 1953.

In 1890 the company was renamed Royal Crown Derby Porcelain following the award of a Royal Warrant by Queen Victoria and this warrant has been subsequently renewed. The company made, and still makes, richly decorated pieces of a very thin porcelain, heavily gilded with elaborate patterns, the majority based on Japanese and Rococo designs. They are best know for their high-quality tableware, which has graced the tables of some of the finest country houses in England.

Some Royal Crown Derby artists to note are Albert Gregory, for his exquisite floral designs and Cuthbert Gresley, known also for his flowers and landscapes. The finest all-round decorator was Sevres-trained Désiré Leroy who was responsible for an exceptionally high standard of painting, jeweling, gilding and burnishing. His dedication to his art means that his work, which is usually signed, is now keenly collected and very valuable.

A small Royal Crown Derby vase, decorated with flowers on vertical pompadour panels, green mark.

c1865   5in (12.5cm) high

$350-400   **WW**

A Royal Crown Derby ewer, richly decorated with raised gilt, flowers and scrolls on a blue and yellow ground, red factory mark.

c1895   8.25in (21cm) high

$200-250   **WW**

A small Royal Crown Derby campana vase, painted with flowers in a scrolling cartouche on a pink ground, gilding detail, red factory marks, date code.

1901   4.75in (12.2cm) high

$150-200   **WW**

A small Royal Crown Derby vase, painted with flowers in enamels and gilt on a blue ground, red mark, date code.

1902   4.25in (10.7cm) high

$300-350   **WW**

A Royal Crown Derby ovoid vase and domed cover, body painted with floral swags and applied with two gilt foliate handles, gilt detail, iron-red printed marks, date code, small flaked area to one handle, possible small hairline to base of vase.

1903   75in (25cm) high

$400-500   **DN**

A small pair of Royal Crown Derby flared campana vases, decorated with Imari pattern no.1128, factory marks and date codes, one neatly glued through the stem.

1907   5.25in (13.3cm) high

$500-600   **WW**

A pair of Royal Crown Derby porcelain candlesticks, the flared drip pans above a squat baluster sconce upon a fluted everted trumpet stem and shaped square foot, decorated in Imari colors with 4591 pattern, red printed mark and date code, minor wear to gilding.

1909   6.25in (16cm) high

$600-650   **BonS**

A Royal Crown Derby octagonal porcelain bowl, decorated in Imari colors with 1128 pattern, red printed mark and date code.

1921   7.5in (19cm) diam

$300-350   **BonS**

Two from a set of twelve 20thC Royal Crown Derby porcelain dessert plates, decorated with floral and geometric motifs in the Imari palette, printed in red ROYAL CROWN DERBY/MADE IN ENGLAND/ (BONE CHINA)/2451/, the whole enriched in gilt.

8.5in (21.5cm) diam

$1,200-1,500 (set)   **SI**

◄ A 20thC Royal Crown Derby porcelain vase and cover, decorated with chrysanthemums, pattern no. 2153, shape no. 1048, cover repaired, wear to gilding.

$300-350   **BonS**

A Royal Crown Derby porcelain three-handled goblet, the flared conical bowl encircled by three high loop foliate handles, upon socle stem and circular foot, Imari coloration with green highlights, pattern no. 6299, shape no. 1255, also incised to the foot, red printed mark and indistinct date code, minor wear to gilding.

7in (18cm) high

$400-500   **BonS**

A pair of large Royal Crown Derby twin-handled vases, of Middle Eastern design, with narrow flared necks and pierced loop handles over baluster body, the ground painted with Turkish quatrefoil panels and scrolls, black printed mark, incised no. 227, some rubbing to gilt and minor chips.

6.25in (41cm) high

$550-600   **L&T**

In 1860, the town of Dux (or Duchcov), in what was Bohemia, became the site of a famous porcelain factory. It used local raw materials to produce pieces styled on Royal Worcester, in its matt ivory and bronze finishes. The company continued to grow and despite Dux becoming part of Czechoslovakia in 1918, it continued to use the same Royal Dux Bohemia as its trademark, with an acorn within a triangle mark.

The factory is noted for its 1930's Art Deco figures and continues to trade today as the Porcelain Manufactory Royal Dux Bohemia a.s.

►1 A Royal Dux porcelain figure group, modeled as a pair of suitors, the man in Roman dress, on shaped naturalistic plinth with impressed mark Hampel, pink triangular mark and impressed no. 1559, base with star crack extending through to the man's foot, his wrist with hairline, his gown with an area of tiny chips.

19.52in (49cm) high

$400-400   **L&T**

►2 A Royal Dux figure group, of Pax et Labor, the man modeled as a woodcutter, on naturalistic plinth with post, pink triangular mark and number mark.

c1944   19.75in (50cm) high

$1,000-1,300   **L&T**

An early 20thC Royal Dux porcelain vide poche, modeled as two woman in the style of Alphonse Mucha and glazed in white.

13 in (33cm) high

$900-1,100   **SI**

A Royal Dux centerpiece, of shaped outline embellished with waves, flowers and foliage and centered with a nymph in wrapped robe, resting on rockwork, bearing pink triangle mark and the no. 468 on base.

11.5in (29cm) high

$1,200-1,500   **DN**

A pair of Royal Dux figures, each modeled as a standing figure beside a column, he playing pan pipes attended by sheep, she listening with goats at her feet, on circular rockwork bases, green triangular pad mark, impressed shape no.s 678 and 677.

16.25in (41.5cm) high

$900-1,100   **BonS**

A Royal Dux figure, of a shepherdess wearing a tunic draped with a sheepskin, on leaf-encrusted base, triangular pad with impressed mark, impressed no. 272, sheep's ear missing, other slight chips, crook replaced.

16.5in (42cm) high

$1,000-1,300   **BonE**

A Royal Dux figure group, of a courting couple, by Hampel, both wearing classical-style dress, standing on grassy base, incised on back of base HAMPEL, triangular pad with impressed mark, impressed no. 1559.

9in (48cm) high

$1,200-1,500   **BonE**

A Royal Dux figure, of a young girl wearing a tunic and reclining on a rocky base, triangular pad with impressed mark, impressed no. 206.

16.5in (42cm) high

$1,000-1,300   **BonE**

A pair of Royal Dux porcelain figurines, of fisherman and a water carrier.

20in (50.8cm) high

$2,000-2,500   **SI**

Ceramics – Royal Worcester

In 1852, W.H. Kerr joined the Worcester factory and the firm was briefly named Kerr & Binns, but became known as the Worcester Royal Porcelain Company from 1863. The most influential sculptors at the factory were James Hadley (1837-1903) and George Owen (1845-1917). Hadley is known for his range of Japanese or "Eastern" subjects, which won universal praise. Pieces that imitate Indian carved ivory and Middle Eastern metalwork are especially impressive. George Owen made outstanding copies of pierced ivory in reticulated porcelain, with each tiny hole cut out whilst the porcelain was still wet. The Japanese, Indian, Middle Eastern ware are typically in soft colors with rich gilding. Decoration includes piercing, enameling and jeweling.

The 1930s and 1940s saw a period of success with the production of a series of ceramic sculptures.

The firm merged with Spode in 1978 and continues to produce high quality porcelain today.

A pair of Royal Worcester figures, modeled as a boy gardener and his girl companion, printed puce mark and code no. 1875, boy with repaired crack and chip to hat brim, girl with chip to flower pot.

10.25in (26cm) high

$550-600 L&T

A Royal Worcester figure, "My Favorite", by F.G. Doughty, a small child sits surrounded by white rabbits, holding one in her arms, printed and painted marks in puce, no. 3014, indistinct date code.

5.5in (14cm) high

$260-300 BonE

A pair of Royal Worcester porcelain figures, of An Irishman (1835) and An Irish girl (1874), standing on rectangular plinth with cut corners, by James Hadley.

Man 6.75in (17.1cm) high
Girl 6.5in (16.5cm) high

$1,000-1,300 GorL

A pair of Royal Worcester porcelain figures, modeled as two young girls, painted in flesh colors and ivory, with naturalistic plinths, impressed mark, both with minor base chips.

c1876-91

$300-350 L&T

A Royal Worcester figure, of John Bull from James Hadley's figures representing the world, his clothes edged in gilt, impressed marks.

c1880 7in (18cm) high

$100-130 Chef

A Royal Worcester figural sweet basket, the boy dressed in Kate Greenaway style with gilt edged clothes, he sits on a tree looking into the ozier basket, printed and impressed marks, date code.

1883 7in (17.5cm) high

$180-220 Chef

A pair of Royal Worcester Double early English comports, of Hadley type, each formed as a tree supporting two circular dishes, a boy and a girl beneath on a circular rockwork base, gilded highlights, impressed factory mark and shape no. 936 and 937, one with green printed mark and date code, restoration to one basket.

1883 7.5in (19cm) high

$1,200-1,500 BonS

A pair of Royal Worcester figural baskets, circular palisades to one side of the tree trunks with a girl siting on one and a boy on the other, both wearing straw hats, printed marks, date code.

1890   6.75in (17cm) high

$550-600   **Chef**

A pair of Royal Worcester figures, each dressed in Kate Greenaway style with gilt-edged clothes, printed marks and registration diamond, date code.

1890   9in (22.5cm) high

$700-800   **Chef**

A Royal Worcester "ivory ground" figure of a female water carrier, painted in matt colors and gilt, puce printed marks, model no. 637, date code, hairline crack through back foot, slight wear to gilding.

1895   5.5in (14cm) high

$300-400   **DN**

A set of four Royal Worcester figures, of officers, depicting "Officer of the 17th Light Dragoon Guards, 1814", "...Of the 3rd Dragoon Guards, 1806", "...Coldstream Guard, Field Order" and "Admiral circa 1780", printed marks and retailer's mark of Waring and Gillow, date codes.

1917 & 1918   tallest 11.5in (29cm) high

$1,500-2,000   **Chef**

A pair of Royal Worcester figures, each dressed in Kate Greenaway style with gilt-edged clothes, printed marks and registration diamond, date code.

1890   9in (22.5cm) high

$700-800   **Chef**

A small 20thC Royal Worcester figure, designed by F.G. Doughty, modeled as an Oriental child seated eating from a bowl of rice, printed mark and indistinct date code.

2.25in (6cm) high

$120-150   **BonS**

A pair of 20thC Royal Worcester white glazed busts of Night and Day, each raised on a tall wood plinth, impressed and printed marks.

14.25in (36cm) high

$450-500   **WW**

A Royal Worcester flatback jug, decorated with flowers on an ivory ground, puce mark.

c1892   7in (17.5cm) high

$250-300   **WW**

A pair of Royal Worcester Tusk jugs, blush ivory coloration, printed and painted with summer flowers, the handle formed to simulate an antler, green printed mark, shape no. 1116.

6in (15cm) high

$450-500   **BonS**

A Royal Worcester globular vase, with a molded mouth, the body decorated with flowers on an ivory ground, puce mark.

c1884   9in (23cm) high

$350-400   **WW**

A Royal Worcester vase, with gilt handles, decorated in raised gilt with a fruiting branch, green factory mark.

c1886   7in (17.5cm) high

$300-350   **WW**

A Royal Worcester flatback jug, decorated with flowers on an ivory ground, puce mark.

c1889   5in (12.5cm) high

$225-250   **WW**

A Royal Worcester tapering cylindrical jug, decorated with flowers on a blush ground, shape 1047, puce printed mark.

c1889   10.25in (26cm) high

$350-400   **WW**

A Royal Worcester flatback jug, decorated with flowers on an ivory ground, puce mark.

c1890   7in (17.5cm) high

$225-250   **WW**

A small Royal Worcester jug, with a compressed circular body, painted with flowers on an ivory ground, puce mark.

c1895   3.5in (9cm) high

$300-350   **WW**

A Royal Worcester vase, with a tall cylindrical neck and globular body, decorated with flowers on an ivory ground.

c1895   6.5in (16.5cm) high

$150-200   **WW**

A Royal Worcester tapering vase, with scroll side handles, decorated with flower sprays on a shaded ground, puce mark.

c1895   9.5in (24cm) high

$300-350   **WW**

A tall Royal Worcester vase, decorated with flowers on a shaded ground, shape 1775, puce mark.

c1896   12.75in (32.5cm) high

$375-425   **WW**

A large Royal Worcester ovoid vase, with scroll side handles, decorated with flowers on a blush ground, shape 1969.

c1899   12in (30.5cm) high

$600-700   **WW**

A Royal Worcester ovoid vase, with gilt side handles, decorated with flowers on a shaded ground, puce mark.

c1903   6.75in (17cm) high

$250-300   **WW**

A Royal Worcester conical vase, with gilt side handles, decorated with thistles and flowers on a shaded ground, brown mark.

c1903   9.75in (25cm) high

$450-500   **WW**

A Royal Worcester cylindrical tyg, decorated with flowers on a shaded ground, puce mark.

c1904   5in (13cm) high

$550-600   **WW**

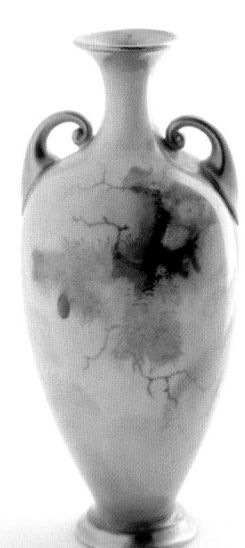

A Royal Worcester jug, with a gilt coral handle and decorated with flowers on a shaded ground, puce mark.

c1907   8.75in (22cm) high

$300-350   WW

A Royal Worcester vase, signed R. Austin, ovoid form with trumpet neck and circular foot, painted decoration with ground color of graduated green tones, between gilded rams horn handles, printed mark and date code, shape number H287.

1910   6.75in (17cm) high

$200-250   BonS

A large Royal Worcester vase, decorated with colorful flowers on shaded ground, shape 1692, puce mark.

c1906   13.5in (34cm) high

$450-500   WW

A small Royal Worcester quatrelobed vase, with a reticulated cover, decorated with flowers on a blush ground, shape 291/H puce mark.

c1915   5in (12.5cm) high

$300-350   WW

A Royal Worcester gold ground plate, the center painted with fruit, signed Telford, the ground acid etched with panels and scrolling flowers and foliage, gold mark, pattern Z2711.

10.75in (27.5cm) diam

$360-400   WW

A Royal Worcester cabinet plate, painted with grapes and peaches, by Freeman, gilded gadrooned border.

9.5in (24.1cm) diam

$300-350   GorL

One of a pair of Royal Worcester vases, of cylindrical form with pierced rims and fruit decoration, one signed P. English, the other Leaman, on four acanthus scroll feet, no. G42L/S.

8.5in (21.6cm) high

$1,200-1,500   GorL

A large Royal Worcester two-handled vase and cover, with a fluted waisted neck, the body painted with fruits and leaves, shape 1439, the knop re-glued.

1890   16.5in (42cm) high

$750-850   WW

A Royal Worcester comport, indistinctly signed J (**?**) Austin, the bowl painted with roses upon a waisted circular stem, molded with foliated lambrequins, green printed marks, Hadley shape code H280 B/10.38, dated.

1899   7.75in (20cm) high

$850-950   **BonS**

A Royal Worcester jardinière, of fluted globular form with molded scroll border, painted with sprays of roses by R. Austin, signed on ivory ground, printed mark, shape no. 191/H/10.154, date code.

1912   7in (17cm) high

$1,000-1,300   **BonE**

A small Royal Worcester vase, decorated with roses on a blush ground, gilt handles and base, shape 202, puce mark.

c1918   5.5in (14cm) high

$225-300   **WW**

A Royal Worcester square section vase, painted with roses on a shaded ground, signed F. Harper, puce mark.

c1920   7.25in (18.5cm) high

$450-500   **WW**

A Royal Worcester jardinière, signed Sedgley (Walter), the flattened globular body molded with foliate scrolls beneath the pierced gallery rim, well painted decoration on a blush ivory ground, printed mark, dated and shape no. H295.

1923   7.25in (18.5cm) high

$1,000-1,300   **BonS**

A Royal Worcester comport, painted by T. Lockyer, with fruit in elaborate gilt borders, printed puce mark, date code, restored foot.

1924   12.25in (31cm) wide

$700-800   **DN**

A Royal Worcester lobed globular vase, painted with roses, signed Hunt, puce mark.

c1925   3.25in (8cm) high

$150-200   **WW**

◀ A small Royal Worcester teacup and saucer, signed A.G Moseley and H Everett, painted with fruit on a naturalistic ground, exterior of cup and saucer gilded, printed mark and date code.

1927   saucer 3.75in (9.8cm) diam

$350-400   **BonS**

A small Royal Worcester vase, with a tapering cylindrical neck, painted with roses, signed Hunt, puce mark.

c1929   5.25in (13.5cm) high

$150-200   **WW**

A Royal Worcester plate, painted with fruit against a naturalistic ground within a gilded scallop and gadrooned rim, printed mark and date code.

1934   9in (23cm) diam

$550-650   **BonS**

A Royal Worcester cabinet plate, by E. Townsend, painted with fruit in a naturalistic setting, within a gilt edge, puce printed mark and date code.

1938-43   9.25in (23.5cm) diam

$400-450   **HamG**

A Royal Worcester plate, painted by H. Price, with fruit in gilt gadrooned border, blue printed mark, date code.

1939   9.5in (24cm) diam

$750-850   **DN**

A 20thC Royal Worcester coffee cup and saucer, signed H. Ayton and H.N. Price, painted with fruit against a naturalistic ground, interior of cup and exterior of saucer gilded, printed marks and indistinct date code.

Saucer 3.75in (9.8cm) diam

$350-400   **BonS**

A Royal Worcester plate, painted by H. Ayrton, with decoration within gilt gadrooned rim, black printed mark, date code.

1951   8.75in (22cm) diam

$700-800   **DN**

A Royal Worcester ivory vase, the trumpet-shaped neck bound by a ribbon and bow, above a lappet molded shoulder, the body decorated with a pattern of flowers and gilt foliage, green printed mark.

7.5in (19cm) high

$120-150   **HamG**

A pair of Royal Worcester ivory vases, of cornucopia form, glazed and highlighted in gilt, the quatrefoil neck bound by a serpent trailing to form a handle, supported by a winged ram, the body terminating in a bird finial, on a triform base, impressed marks and registration mark, bird terminals restored.

c1868   7.5in (19cm) high

$225-300   **HamG**

A Royal Worcester ivory candlestick, in the form of a ram's horn surmounted by a sconce, gilt borders, puce printed mark and date code.

1888   9in (23cm) high

$200-250   **HamG**

A Royal Worcester coffee cup and saucer, signed Jas. Stinton, painted with a vignette of a hen and cock pheasant within gilded line rims, printed mark and date code.

1911 Saucer 3.75in (9.5cm) diam

$200-250   **BonS**

A Royal Worcestershire coffee cup and saucer, signed H. Stinton, painted with vignettes of highland cattle in a moor land setting, interior of cup and exterior of saucer gilded, printed mark and date code.

1912 Saucer 3.75in (9.7cm) diam

$440-500   **BonS**

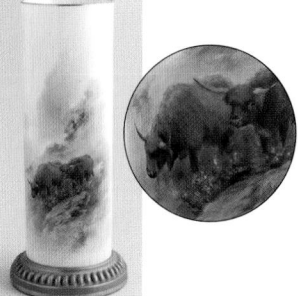

A Royal Worcester cylindrical vase, painted with highland cattle signed John Stinton, shape 2147, puce mark, some good restoration to base.

c1912   10in (25.5cm) high

$900-1,100   **WW**

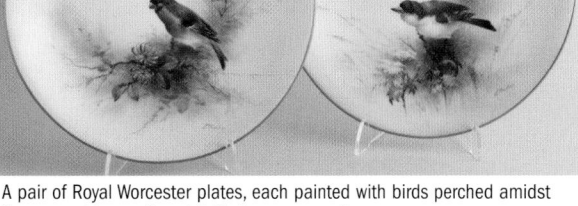

A pair of Royal Worcester plates, each painted with birds perched amidst flowers and trees, signed E. Barker, puce marks.

c1913   9in (23cm) diam

$450-500   **WW**

A Royal Worcester coffee cup and saucer, signed Jas. Stinton, painted with ducks on a pale ivory ground, interior of the cup and exterior of saucer gilded, printed mark and date code.

1914 Saucer 3.75in (9.7cm) diam

$300-350 **BonS**

A Royal Worcester teapot, painted with sheep beneath a flowering fruit tree, signed E Barker, puce mark, handle restored.

c1919 8.75in (22.5cm) wide

$350-400 **WW**

A Royal Worcester vase, painted with highland cattle, signed H Stinton, gilded neck and foot, puce mark, shape 661, repaired at the base of neck.

c1920 9in (23cm) high

$750-850 **WW**

A Royal Worcester plate, painted by Harry Stinton, decorated with Highland cattle, gilt gadrooned rim, black printed marks, date code.

1954 10.75in (27.5cm) diam

$1,000-1,200 **DN**

A Royal Worcester porcelain figure of an elephant, modeled by Hadley, with gilt, green and ink tasseled howdah and headdress.

8.5in (22cm) high

$225-300 **J&H**

A Royal Worcester Crown Ware coffee pot and cover, designed by Scottie Wilson, with black banding on a brown ground.

7.75in (19.5cm) high

$60-80 **BAR**

A Royal Worcester Crownware bowl, decorated with a galleon at sea.

11in (27.9cm) diam

$2225-300 **GorB**

A Royal Worcester Crown Ware vase, decorated with gilt bands of grapes and vine leaves against a mottled ground with areas of greeny luster, factory marks on base.

10.5in (27cm) high

$140-170 **DN**

A Royal Worcester milk jug, with gilded reticulated decoration and mock bamboo handle.

5in (12.7cm) high

$1,200-1,500 **GorL**

A pair of mid- to late 19thC Royal Worcester Parian ware inkwells, with covers and liners, each modeled with three Sphinx monopodium on a triform base, damage to the lids and liners.

5.25in (13.5cm) diam

$200-250 **WW**

A Royal Worcester vase, decorated with a figure of Ceres standing on a plinth, gilded details, printed mark.

c1873 4in (10cm) high

$150-200 **WW**

Royal Worcester/Wedgwood

A Royal Worcester two-handled vase, of urn shape, with mask handles and molded scroll borders, painted with a spray of flowers on ivory ground, within blue and gilt borders, printed mark, shape no. 1632, date code.

1895	8.75in (22cm) high

$200-250   **BonE**

A pair of Royal Worcester plates, puce marks.

c1908	9.25in (23.5cm) diam

$375-425   **WW**

A Royal Worcester shell vase, the large nautilus shell supported by coral and seaweed, the base decorated with shells, covered with blush ivory glaze with details in gilt, printed mark, shape no. 4/94, date code.

1910	8.25in (21cm) high

$165-200   **BonE**

A Royal Worcester ewer, of squat globular shape, molded with basket weave, with bamboo handle, applied with a lizard, gilt interior, printed mark, shape no. 1714, date code.

1910	6.25in (16cm) high

$225-300   **BonE**

A pair of Royal Worcester amphora shaped porcelain vases, finely painted on a rose pompadour ground, with enameled beading and gilding, signed Phillips, printed mark.

c1911	7in (18cm) high

$1,000-1,300   **SI**

A Royal Worcester Sabrina ware vase, painted by Walter Powell, depicting a pair of storks wading among grasses, factory marks on base.

c1911	9in (23cm) high

$700-800   **DN**

One of a pair of Royal Worcester porcelain vases, each decorated on one side with a tall bush with golden foliage, colored florets and a pair of bluebirds, factory marks, date code and numbered "2472".

1917	9.25in (23.5cm) high

$500-600   **DN**

A Royal Worcester bowl, painted by Cole, with a still life of fruit, within small circular cartouche surrounded by scrolls, reserved on powder blue ground, signed, printed mark in blue, shape no. 2769, date code.

1931	10.5in (26.5cm) diam

$400-500   **BonE**

DAISY MAKEIG-JONES (1881-1945) was one of the first notable female ceramic designers of the 20thC. Born in South Yorkshire, her family moved to Torquay in 1899 and after showing a great aptitude for art at boarding school, she later studied at the School of Art in Torquay.

Makeig-Jones joined Wedgwood and Sons in 1909 and by 1914 was employed as a Wedgwood designer with her own studio. She became interested in luster decoration and developed her own lusters, which were first used in the Ordinary Luster series launched in 1915. Her most famous work is the "Fairyland Luster" range, which portrays magical landscapes with fairies, goblins and pixies, in several types of color and glazes and printed in gold.

Her pieces rarely bear her initials, but the patterns are usually numbered and pre-fixed with a Z, which was the Wedgwood factory code for china ornaments.

A Wedgwood Flame Fairyland Luster bowl, designed by Daisy Makeig-Jones, interior printed in gilt and painted with Woodland Bridge pattern, about a central roundel of a mermaid, exterior with Poplar Trees pattern, flame luster ground, gold printed Portland Vase mark and pattern number Z5360.

c1930	11in (28cm) diam

$5,500-6,500   **BonS**

A Wedgwood Fairyland Luster punch bowl, designed by Daisy Makeig-Jones, interior with Woodland Bridge design with daylight background, about a central mermaid roundel, exterior with Black Fairyland Poplar Trees design, gold printed Portland Vase mark and Z4968.

c1930 — 10.5in (26.5cm) diam

$3,500-4,000 — **BonS**

A Wedgwood Fairyland Luster bowl, decorated with elves and other creatures in continuous landscape inside, outside with decoration on dark blue ground, pattern no. Z4963, printed mark in gilt.

$4,600-5,000 — **BonE**

A Wedgwood Luster bowl decorated in the Goblin pattern against a maroon ground, Z5200.

4in (10.2cm) diam

$600-650 — **GorL**

A Wedgwood Luster Lahore pattern bowl, Z5266.

8in (20.3cm) diam

$700-800 — **GorL**

A Wedgwood Alphabet mug, designed by Eric Ravilious, transfer-printed with the letters of the alphabet on two horizontal bands, alternating with images relating to each individual letter, the letters Y and Z in an oval inside the mug, marked Wedgwood, made in England and Designed by Eric Ravilious on base.

3.25in (8cm) high

$400-500 — **DN**

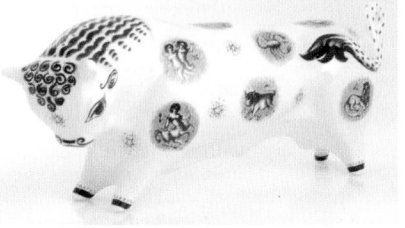

A Wedgwood Luster bowl, decorated with dragons and hookah birds, extensively cracked and restored.

8in (20.5cm) diam

$120-160 — **AS&S**

A pair of 19thC Wedgwood green glazed leaf-shaped dishes, impressed marks.

9in (23cm) long

$30-50 — **WW**

◀ A Wedgwood Taurus the Bull, designed by Arnold Machin, decorated with dark brown details and transfer-printed signs for the zodiac, interspersed with stars, marked "Wedgwood Barlston England".

15.25in (39cm) long

$225-250 — **DN**

A Wedgwood vase, by Norman Wilson.

c1930 — 9.25in (23.5cm) high

$1,300-1,500 — **ADE**

A Wedgwood vase, designed by Keith Murray, of ovoid ribbed form and Moonstone glazed, full signature mark.

1934-36 — 5.5in (14.2cm) high

$350-450 — **BAR**

An Art Deco Ashstead Pottery figure, of The Corn Girl, with brown and green striped headdress, seated holding a sheaf of corn, on a glazed pillow, the black glazed base dated and marked Allan G. Wyon, printed marks, raised no. M72.

1927   7.75in (20cm) high

$450-500   **J&H**

An Art Deco earthenware figure, by S. Nicholson Babb, of a naked female figure poised beside a sinuous tree, incised mark S. Nicholson Babb FRBS.

1929   10.5in (27cm) high

$300-350   **L&T**

A 20thC Kevin Francis Beach Belle figure, of a woman with a beach ball, seated on a rock wearing a swimming costume and hat, painted in colored glazes.

9.75in (25cm) high

$100-130   **DN**

A Goldscheider Art Deco figure, by Lorezl, modeled as a young woman wearing a costume with shaped cloak-like edges resembling the wings of a butterfly, above a circular base with printed factory marks, facsimile artists signature near her feet, restoration on one hand.

17.75in (45cm) high

$5,000-6,000   **DN**

A Griselda Hill Pottery Wemyss-style figure of a cat, painted with black and pink on white, glass eyes, painted marks.

12.25in (31cm) high

$150-200   **L&T**

A Hutschenreuther porcelain figure, by K. Tutter, modeled as a female dancer, wearing a dress with black florets, a white shirt, and shoes and hat to match, factory marks on base and K. Tutter on edge of base, restoration on lower legs.

10in (25.5cm) high

$450-500   **DN**

A Harry Parr pottery figure, of a lady with a basket and a bunch of flowers wearing a mottled blue shawl, mottled blue dress with white apron, the octagonal base dated and with impressed mark.

1931   10in (25.4cm) high

$850-900   **Clv**

A Rosenthal porcelain group, Cappriccio, designed by Ferdinand Liebermann, of a naked young boy, sitting astride a male goat, taunting the creature by rubbing his toes against its horns, poised on a pedestal base, factory marks on base.

12in (30.5cm) high

$1,200-1,500   **DN**

◄ An Ernst Wahliss Art Nouveau figure, modeled as a Mucha-style maiden, her hair dressed with flowers, wearing loosely wrapped robes and jeweled belt, on a scrolling base embellished with chrysanthemums, and gilt detailing, impressed Made in Austria/Ernst Wahliss / Turn Wien, no. 4583 - 22.

17.25in (44cm) high

$1,500-2,000   **DN**

► A Wiener Werkstatte terracotta figure group, depicting a woman holding a fan in diaphanous robe, with her child, dressed in Chinese costume and holding a bird, on rectangular plinth base, painted in colored glazes, impressed factory marks, broken and repaired.

15in (38cm) high

$1,300-1,700   **L&T**

Ceramics

A Zsolny-Pecs figure group, depicting a mythical female figure, seated on a rock by an urn, covered in iridescent glaze, molded marks Zsolny Pecs.

9in (23cm) high

$700-800   **L&T**

An Austrian porcelain figure, of a woman holding a large Secessionist jardinière, resembling bronze and basketwork, impressed Made in Austria.

16.25in (41cm) high

$250-300   **DN**

A 20thC Continental porcelain figure, of a Spanish dancer, wearing a dress with layered skirt, and white gloves, her hair dressed with a comb, on oval base.

10.5in (27cm) high

$100-130   **DN**

A pottery figure of a Rangers footballer, the figure standing with his right foot resting on a ball, circular base, painted mark Rd. Patt. 366136.

14.25in (36cm) high

$750-850   **L&T**

An Austrian Art Nouveau figure, possibly by Ernst Wahliss, of a naked nymph standing on a rockwork base lapped by waves and punctuated with shells, flanked by large waterlily leaves and flowers in bud, with gilt detailing, impressed Made in Austria and no. 4638.

16.25in (41cm) high

$1,600-1,900   **DN**

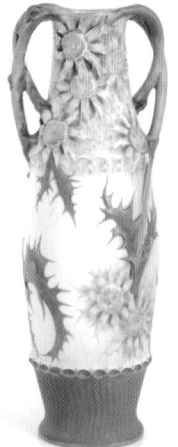

◄ An Amphora oviform vase, molded in relief with thistles and spiky foliage, the stems of which extend to form handles linking to the neck, picked out in naturalistic colors and heightened with gilding, marked Amphora, Made in Czechoslovakia.

17in (43cm) high

$225-300   **DN**

An Amphora oviform vase, decorated with bands of stylized flowers and foliage against a marbled ground, marked Amphora Made in Czechoslovakia.

10.25in (26cm) high

$250-300   **DN**

A monumental Amphora baluster vase, with everted rim, incised with a frieze depicting a vulture seated amongst scrolling foliage and branches, decorated in colored enamels on a mottled matt ground, impressed and painted marks 508016080.

19.25in (49cm) high

$260-300   **L&T**

An Amphora vase, with four lug handles and lion decoration on a turquoise ground.

11in (28.9cm) high

$180-220   **GorL**

A Barnstable vase, by C.H. Brannam.

c1888   7.75in (19.5cm) high

$200-240   **ADE**

A Crown Ducal "Manchu" vase, designed by Charlotte Rhead, the slightly baluster ridged body decorated with a dragon and flaming pearl, printed marks, signed C Rhead, impressed no. 12.

8.5in (21.5cm) high

$250-300   **J&H**

A Crown Ducal ribbed squat vase, by Charlotte Rhead, in Golden Leaves pattern, no. 4921.

4.75in (12cm) high

$90-120   **BAR**

One of a pair of Charlotte Rhead Crown Ducal tube-lined baluster vases, with floral decoration.

7.5in (19.1cm) high

$350-400 (pair)   **GorL**

A pair of Eichwald Pottery Art Nouveau vases, the waisted cylindrical bodies with square necks, molded with flowers, stylized handles.

9.75in (25cm) high

$100-130   **J&H**

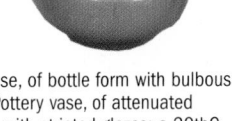

From left to right: A 20thC Fulper Pottery vase, of bottle form with bulbous base, with striated glazes; a 20thC Fulper Pottery vase, of attenuated cylindrical form, raised on a pedestal base, with striated glazes; a 20thC Fulper Pottery vase, of urn form with C scroll handles, striated glazes.

Tallest 6.75in (17cm) high

$250-300 (3 items)   **SI**

A Keller & Guerin luster pottery vase, of flared cylindrical shape, painted in a bluey-silver luster with oak leaves and acorns against a field of ruby-tinted dashes and dark blue ground, signed K & G, Luneville, no. 1855 and with initial F, dated.

1895   9.75in (24.5cm) high

$750-850   **DN**

Left: A Royal Lancastrian vase, by Gwladys Rodgers, impressed factory marks, incised E.T.R and painted artist's monogram. Right: A Royal Lancastrian Lapis ware vase, by Gwladys Rodgers, of globular shape decorated with arched panels of stylized foliage.

Tallest 6.75in (17cm) high

$350-450   **DN**

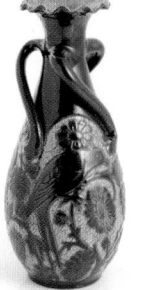

A Lauder pottery oviform vase, tapering to a frilled neck, with three twisted handles, scraffito decorated with variegated glazes, with panels of birds perched on flowering branches, impressed Lauder Barum on base.

11.5in (29.5cm) high

$250-300   **DN**

A large Linthorpe Pottery oviform vase, with flared cylindrical neck and spreading foot, painted in thick enamels with decoration of branches of blossom, impressed Linthorpe and no. 477, restored on foot.

14.75in (37.5cm) high

$180-220   **DN**

Ceramics

Three hand-painted Limoges porcelain vessels, comprising two urn-form vases, one with slender applied angled handles, and a flattened ovoid-form vase, mounted as a lamp, each hand-painted by Clara N. Stewart with woodland scenes, one including a view of the Washington Monument, and another depicting a view of sailing boats on the Potomac River, one dated 1908, each marked J.P.L. France and signed CNS.

Clara N. Stewart *owned a china painting studio on P street in Washington D.C. during the first decades of the 1900s.*

c1908   Lamp vase 8in (20cm) high

$500-600 (3 items)   **SI**

A 20thC early Martinware oviform vase, decorated with vertical bands of short incised lines, beneath a shaded glaze, signed Martin London.

$300-350   **DN**

A Mort Lake vase, by George Cox.

c1912   6.5in (16.5cm) high

$700-800   **ADE**

A Roseville Pottery vase, of trumpet form, in the Laurel pattern, signed with HP of Hester Pillsbury; A Rosewood Pottery vase, of inverted trumpet form, with applied bracket handles, in Montacello pattern; A Rosewood Pottery vase, of tapering ovoid form with applied C-scroll handles, in Baneda pattern.

Left: 1934; center: 1931; right: 1933   Tallest 6.75in (17cm) high

$1,200-1,500 (3 items)   **SI**

▲**1** A Rosewood Pottery vase, of broad cylindrical form, in paneled design, with molded flowers and leaves in matte glazes, ink "R" mark.
▲**2** A Rosewood Pottery vase, of tapering cylindrical form, with contiguous angled handles, in Laurel pattern.

c1934   max 7.25in (18.5cm) high

$400-450   **SI**

A Ruskin baluster vase on stand, with everted rim, covered in a mottled cream and cornflower blue streaked and crystalline glaze, impressed marks.

13in (33cm) high

$350-400   **L&T**

A Rye Pottery posy vase, of pinched basket form, one side applied in low relief with a rose spray, the other with green hops, covered in a mottled brown glaze.

7.5in (19cm) wide

$120-150   **LC**

A mid-20thC Shelley vase, the cone shape with recess above the foot, streaked with horizontal bands, printed marks.

9.5in (24cm) high

$170-200   **Chef**

A Studio stoneware ovoid vase, with bronze everted rim, painted with stylized foliage on a pitted gray ground, impressed monogram mark.

10.25in (26cm) high

$100-130   **L&T**

A Wardle Art Nouveau shouldered baluster vase, with everted rim and spreading base, painted with a frieze of elongated flowering plants, impressed marks.

17in (43cm) high

$400-450   **L&T**

Ceramics

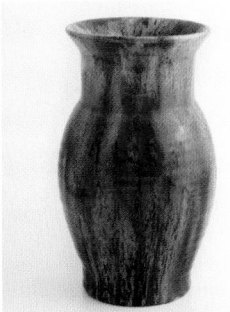

A Reginald Fairfax Wells "Soon" vase.

c1919-51   7.25in (18.5cm) high

$450-500   **ADE**

A Michael Cardew Winchcombe Pottery vase.

c1930   5.75in (14.5cm) high

$450-500   **ADE**

A 20thC Zsolnay luster oviform vase, painted with a butterfly among flowers, in ruby, blue and silvery pink lusters against a deep blue ground, with factory marks and Made in Hungary.

5in (12.5cm) high

$300-350   **DN**

A French "Primavera" pottery vase, of globular form supported on a spreading circular foot, covered with a streaked glaze implying stylized flowerheads and vertical stems, the glaze parting to reveal the "dry" body beneath, impressed Primavera, Made in France and no. 8806.

7.25in (18.5cm) high

$120-150   **DN**

An Austrian pottery oviform vase, attributed to Gmundner Keramik and Schleiss, painted with stylized flowers and foliage against a crackled gray ground, painted fish mark and initials S and G.

12.25in (31cm) high

$90-120   **DN**

An electric blue vase.

c1930   7in (17.5cm) high

$260-300   **ADE**

A Zsolnay luster vase, designed by Sandor Apati Abt, of broad tapering shape, decorated with a stylized landscape, with trees of eosine green luster foliage, partly glazed and partly matt against a muted luster sky, raised circular makers mark on base and no. 7334.

6.75in (17cm) high

$3,000-3,500   **DN**

An early 20thC Artus Van Briggle Pottery flower bowl and frog, the oval bowl with irregular rim, molded at one end with a young maiden kneeling on a rock, the conforming frog (flower-holder) modeled as a turtle atop a rock, both glazed, incised conjoined "A"s within a rectangle and signed Van Briggle/Colo. Spgs.

14in (36cm) diam

$1,000-1,400   **SI**

A C.H. Brannam tyg, of tapering cylindrical form with three long handles, the body incised with peacocks, incised mark F.B. 1908, repairs.

1908   9in (23cm) high

$200-250   **L&T**

A Bristol Cat and Dog Pottery chamberstick, painted in black with a cat and dog, titled "It's years since last we met", signed Louis Wain, printed and impressed marks.

6in (15cm) high

$600-700   **Chef**

A Burleigh Ware octagonal bowl in Sylvan pattern, no. 4100.

9.75in (24.5cm) diam

$250-300   **BAR**

Ceramics

A Burleighware jug of cricketing interest, the handle molded as a cricketer, the body decorated with pavilion, printed and painted marks, CCG.

7.5in (19cm) high

| $350-400 | | L&T |

A Burmantofts faience umbrella stand, of cylindrical form, molded and decorated in tube-line with irises, impressed marks 2026, painted mark Col.No.80.2.

24.5in (62cm) high

| $950-1,100 | | L&T |

A Chameleon ware Persian-style flask, the shaped body with mottled blue and green glaze, painted with panels of stylized flowers and raised panels of Eastern design, No. 350.

| $60-80 | | J&H |

A Susie Cooper 4-piece Moons and Mountains part tea set, comprising a teapot, teacup, plate and cream jug, blue enamel worn.

Teapot 3in (7.5cm) high

| $1,000-1,200 | | GorL |

A pair of Compton Pottery bookends, each of disc shape supported on a rounded base, embellished in relief with the kneeling figure of a naked male archer, picked out in soft cold-painted colors, unmarked but one bearing old paper label with 17_6.

7in (18cm) high

| $300-350 | | DN |

JOSEPH CRAWHALL (1821-1896) was a distinguished English woodcut engraver. Copies of his most amusing verse were painted on china. According to C.S. Felver, Crawhall's work, "carries the same freshness of color and boldness and informality of touch that was so much a part of the work of William Nicholson and James Pryde, the Beggarstaff brothers, at the turn of the (20th) century. They in turn derived much of their inspiration for working in bold colors and broad lines from Joseph Crawhall." In his work he often collaborated with his son Joseph, who in turn influenced and was influenced by his contemporaries E.A. Walton, George Henry, and the other Glasgow Boys.

1   2

▲1A Joseph Crawhall earthenware platter, painted with the figure of Guy Fawkes and bearing the inscription "The lively portraiture of the truly pious, learned and judicious gentleman Guido Fawkes... etc" painted mark verso "Jos Crawhall Jan '79" with bearded man monogram.

12.25in (31cm) dia

| $750-850 | | L&T |

▲2 A Joseph Crawhall earthenware platter, painted with a portrait Captain Lemuel Gulliver and bearing inscription "Drake and Columbus long att th' unknown Shoar, Vespucci, at his best - but half seas o'er... etc" inscribed verso Joseph Crawhall, Newcastle on Tyne Jan 1879, with bearded man monogram.

12.25in (31cm) diam

| $750-850 | | L&T |

A William De Morgan plate, painted in the Isnik style, with radiating foliate design eminating from a raised central boss, painted with a flower, the reverse painted with concentric bands of turquoise and blue.

9.25in (23.5cm) diam

| $1,800-2,000 | | L&T |

A William de Morgan dish, decorated in red and yellow luster with Winged Lions Fishing design 1178, 24 impressed marked, invisible hair crack.

| c1890 | 2.25in (5.5cm) diam |
| $4,500-5,500 | | WW |

An unusual 20thC Foley "Intarsio" teapot and cover, the design attributed to Frederick Rhead, modeled in the form of a crown, with molded detail, the domed drop-in cover with an orb finial, factory marks, no. 3183 and registration no. 356481, restoration to cover.

6in (15.5cm) high

$1,200-1,500   **DN**

An early 20thC Gustavsburg Argenta Ware ashtray, of mottled green glaze, decorated in silver, the central well with a rampant lion and the surrounding well impressed with a radiating chequerboard pattern, the whole banded in silver, marked GUSTAVSBURG/ARGENTA/MADE IN SWEDEN.

7in (18cm) diam

$600-700   **SI**

Three 20thC Gustavsburg Argenta Ware dishes, all mottled in green matte glaze decorated in silver, the scalloped dish with scattered foliate sprigs, the square dish with a central foliate spray, and the bowl with an interior band of tapering drops, each marked GUSTAVSBURG/ARGENTA/MADE IN SWEDEN in gilt.

Bowl 4.25in (11cm) diam

$600-700 (3 items)   **SI**

A pair of Aesthetic Movement pottery ewers, appearance and design attributed to Linthorpe Pottery and Christopher Dresser, of globular form, with "humped" middle, flared neck and exaggerated loop handle, the red clay bodies with streaked beige beneath a clear glaze, unmarked.

7.25in (18.5cm) high

$260-300   **DN**

A Linthorpe Pottery shallow bowl, designed by Christopher Dresser, the clay body decorated in slip with flowers and foliage beneath a streaked glaze, supported on a circular foot resembling a Chinese carved wooden stand, impressed Linthorpe with designer's facsimile signature, no. 451, restored.

9.75in (25cm) diam

$200-250   **DN**

An Art Nouveau Losol Ware part dinner service, decorated in the Tulip pattern and comprising a soup tureen, cover and stand, two graduated oval ashets, ten side plates, eleven meat plates, eight pudding plates, twelve soup plates, a sauce boat and stand, each printed and painted with stylized flower motifs and gilt embellishments, printed and painted marks, 1646.

$1,400-1,800 (service)   **L&T**

A Scottish porcelain box and cover, by J Loudon, the cylindrical Rosenthal blank, painted with a young woman tending a pot of basil and with inscription to the rim "Hung over her sweet basil ever more and moisten'd it with tears unto thee," the interior with core painted inscription, "Isabella or the Pot of Basil," painted marks, J. Loudon, Studio, Ayr, dated.

1927   5.5in (14cm) diam

$400-450   **L&T**

A large Lurcat pottery jug, of broad oviform with flared neck and pinched spout with arched grip below and strap handle, painted with stylized foliate forms, painted on base "dessin J. Lurcat, Sant-Vincens, AK 20/80".

14.25in (36cm) high

$750-850   **DN**

A Mafra Caldas pottery ewer, cover and stand, of squat baluster form with lizard handle, decorated with mosswork and further applied with a frog and glazed beetles, frog finial to the cover, impressed mark to underside of jug, some losses.

11in (28cm) high

$500-600   **BonS**

A Maling luster ovoid jar, in Anemone Rose pattern, no. 6386.

6.25in (16cm) high

$120-150   **BAR**

Ceramics

A Maling luster large bowl, decorated in pattern no. 4075, with gilt and black scroll and conforming border with fruit panels, castle mark.

10.25in (26cm) diam

$200-250 **BAR**

A Mettlach porcelain two-handled oval bowl, of Art Nouveau design, each side decorated with a mermaid with fish in pâte-sur-pâte style.

14in (35.6cm) wide

$150-200 **Clv**

A Continental stoneware jardinère on pedestal, jardinière with molded profile of Victorian lady and molded bird beak loose ring handles, pedestal with molded armorial crest surrounded by pinecone and vine.

43in (109.2cm) high

$2,300-2,800 **SI**

Five pieces from a rare Maling luster coffee service, decorated in pattern no. 5698, comprising coffeepot, hot milk jug and cover, sugar bowl, and six cans and saucers, the green ground with gilt spider's web and black and orange prunus blossom, castle mark.

c1932-34 Pot 6in (15cm) high

$2,500-3,000 (service) **BAR**

A Morris Ware rose bowl, by George Cartlidge, of squat ovoid form with inverted rim, decorated with a band of flowers, printed marks, signed in green.

8.75in (22cm) diam

$1,500-2,000 **L&T**

A 20thC Austrian Art Nouveau pottery box and cover, in the form of a Mucha-style maiden's head, her face embellished with a band dressed with flowers and pendant medallions, and colored to resemble cold painted bronze.

5.25in (13.5cm) high

$200-280 **DN**

A Martin Brothers stoneware beaker, decorated with a heron resting amid bulrushes and irises with ducks in flight nearby, signed RW Martin and Bros, London & Southall, dated 2.1.90.

1890 4.75in (12cm) high

$350-400 **DN**

A Martin Brothers stoneware cachepot, of lobed square section with shaped and molded rim, decorated in shallow relief with newts in speckled naturalistic colors, signed Martin Bros, London & Southall, and dated 12.1900, restoration on one corner.

4.75in (12cm) high

$750-850 **DN**

A Ruskin West Smethwick Pottery plate, with leaf and florette band on the rim beneath the green glaze, scissor and impressed mark, dated.

1906 8.25in (21cm) diam

$300-350 **Chef**

A late 19thC owl jug, possibly Rye potteries, the bird applied with brown button eyes, the clay body dipped in green slip, with combed detail.

10.25in (26cm) high

$120-150 **Chef**

▶ An American 20thC Margaret Tafoya blackware pot, of bulbous form with carved Avanyu design and polished surface, signed "Margaret."

3.5in (8.5cm) high

$600-700 **FRE**

An early American Maria Martinez (1887-1980) black-on-black bowl, of flaring form with design of an Avanyu water serpent encircling basin, signed "Marie," San Ildefonso, scratch to edge.

c1920-1925

$2,000-3,000 **FRE**

Ceramics – Fulper

Aᴿᵀ ᴘᴏᴛᴛᴇʀʏ ʜᴀꜱ ᴀʟᴡᴀʏꜱ ʙᴇᴇɴ ᴛʜᴇ ꜱᴀꜰᴇꜱᴛ ᴄᴏᴍᴍᴏᴅɪᴛʏ, enjoying a broad collecting base spread over the 200 companies and studios that produced the ware 100 years ago. The more people learn about American Arts and Crafts, the more they've come to appreciate decorative ceramics by makers such as George Ohr from Biloxi, Mississippi, William Grueby of Boston, Massachusetts, and the relatively obscure work of Redlands, California.

Accordingly, works by these potters, and others of similar quality, have risen to record levels in the past year. A tall Grueby vase, with yellow quatrefoils on a green matte ground, sold at auction for $92,000, breaking the previous record for the ware by 50%. A small Redlands pot and a tapering cylinder, with embossed sharks under a burnished rust finish, more than doubled its previous high in selling for over $31,000. The work of George Ohr, in the wake of the announcement that architect Frank Gheary is designing the museum that will house some of his work, has doubled in value in a single year. At a recent auction, four diminutive pieces sold for nearly $120,000.

It seems likely that the scarcity of such high-end work, coupled with its inherent fragility, ensures a trickle of supply for a burgeoning demand.

David Rago

An early Fulper centerbowl, embossed with fish and waves under a Copper Dust and green crystalline glaze, abrasion to interior, rectangular ink mark.

11.25in (28.5cm) diam

$900-1,000	**CR**

A fine Fulper vase, with two angular buttressed handles, covered in a fine leopard skin crystalline glaze, rectangular ink mark.

11in (28cm) high

$1,000-1,300	**CR**

A Fulper squat bowl, covered in Flemington green flambé glaze over a matte mustard ground, rectangular ink mark.

10in (25.5cm) diam

$800-900	**CR**

A CLOSER LOOK AT FULPER

A fine and rare Fulper wallpocket, embossed with a link band and covered in a leopard skin crystalline glaze, small chips around edge, rectangular ink mark.

7in (17.5cm) high

$350-450	**CR**

A rare Fulper ovoid wallpocket, embossed with a Greek key band under a café-au-lait glaze, rectangular ink mark, two bruises to rim.

8.25in (21cm) high

$200-250	**CR**

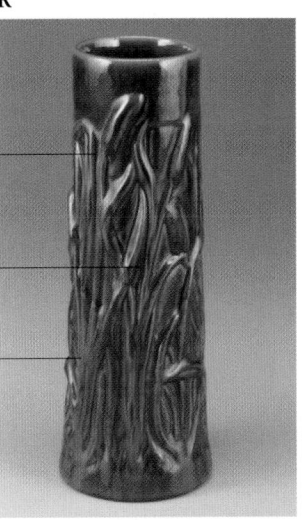

This vase is very high quality, with crisply embossed details.

Note the glossy blue-gray and moss flambé glaze. This was one of Fulper's specialities.

Although molded and not hand-modeled, this piece displays vibrancy and an almost three-dimensional quality.

A Fulper "Cattail" vase, embossed with intertwined cattails and covered in a gloss blue-gray and moss flambé glaze, rectangular ink mark.

13in (33cm) high

$4,000-4,500	**CR**

A Fulper vessel with two buttressed handles, covered in café-au-lait glaze, rectangular ink mark.

9.5in (24cm) high

$700-800   CR

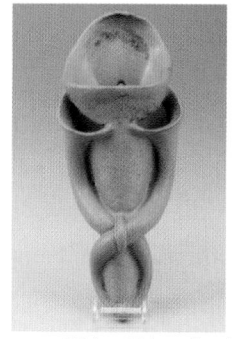

An unusual Fulper triple wallpocket, covered in matte blue glaze, remnant of rectangular ink mark.

11.5in (29cm) high

$400-500   CR

A fine and early Fulper hemispherical bowl on cross feet, covered in an ivory and mahogany flambé glaze, no visible mark.

4in (10cm) high

$500-600   CR

A Fulper tapering two-handled vase, with excellent mouse-gray to blue flambé glaze, raised racetrack mark.

10in (25.5cm) high

$750-850   CR

FULPER

Fulper pottery was established at Flemington, New Jersey, in 1815. They produced practical, simple wares in the early period which are unmarked. Fulper began making artistic wares from about 1910, specializing in matt or crystalline glazed vessels in Japanese Arts and Crafts form.

- Fulper made a variety of household items including jugs, bowls, lamps, desk accessories and tobacco jars.

- Fulper never achieved the same acclaim as companies such as Grueby and Rookwood. Their dependence on glazes meant that no two pieces were the same which lead to inconsistency in production. Fulper art pottery ceased production in 1935.

- Today Fulper pottery is highly collectable. Value is determined by form and glaze. The rarer and more vibrant pieces and also Fulper pottery with inset stained glass are the most collectable.

- The most desirable is the Vasecraft line produced prior to World War I. This was inspired by a German potter J M Stangl, and reflected a medieval revival.

- Fulper's production was very varied and care should be taken to avoid poor shapes and inconsistent glazes.

- The bodies grew lighter from the 1910s to the 1930s when the Art Deco influence was evident. Much of this ware is of poor quality.

An unusual and early Fulper two-handled bulbous vase, covered in aqua and olive flambé glaze, raised racetrack mark.

8.5in (21.5cm) high

$450-600   CR

A rare Fulper collared urn, with two angular handles, covered in a sheer olive green crystalline glaze, raised racetrack mark.

9.25in (23cm) high

$700-950   CR

A Fulper three-handled bulbous vase, with a dynamic cucumber crystalline glaze, raised racetrack mark.

6in (15cm) high

$1,100-1,300   CR

A Fulper bulbous vessel, covered in a copper dust crystalline glaze, raised racetrack mark.

5.5in (14cm) high

$1,000-1,300   CR

An unusual and early Fulper ovoid vase, with an exceptional frothy medium brown and olive flambé glaze, raised racetrack mark.

9.5in (24cm) high

$850-950   CR

A tall Fulper tear-shaped vase, covered in a mirror black glaze, incised racetrack mark, base has restoration to drill hole, and minor (grinding) chip.

13in (33cm) high

$800-900   CR

AMERICA'S OLDEST AUCTION HOUSE

Fine Silver & Jewelry

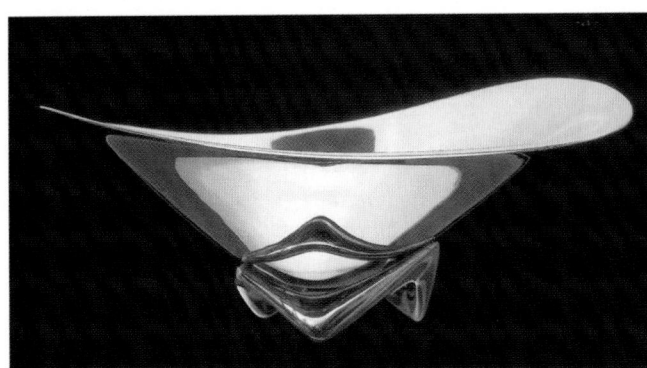

American Silver
Samuel M. Freeman II
Peter C. Thomson

English & Continental Silver
Phillip Knapper
Peter C. Thomson

Jewelry
Virginia Salem

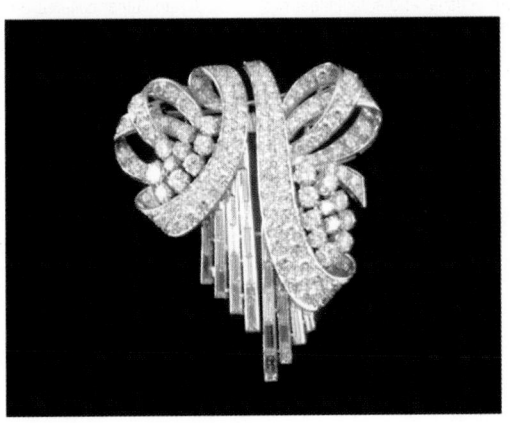

Top: A Danish Silver Centerpiece Bowl by Henning Koppel for Georg Jensen.
hammer price - **$20,000**

Bottom: A Pair of Diamond and Platinum Leaf-form Clips.
hammer price - **$38,000**

FREEMAN'S

1808 Chestnut Street
Philadelphia, PA 19103
(215) 563-9275

w w w . f r e e m a n s a u c t i o n . c o m

Ceramics - Fulper

DATING TIPS FOR FULPER

An important point to note is that all Fulper marks overlapped somewhat and hence the dates are approximate.
Commonly found marks:

- Vertical rectangular ink stamp: (1910-1915)
- Incised racetrack mark: (1915-1920)
- Raised racetrack mark: (1915-1920)
- Ink racetrack mark: (1920-1925)

A CLOSER LOOK AT A FULPER VASE

A well-defined strong shape is always popular with collectors

This shape also allows the glaze to be seen in its full splendour

Fulper was well known for rich varied glazes; mattes, crystalline and deep colors such as this

Although this piece would have been molded, a trained decorator individually glazed each piece

A Fulper gourd-shaped two-handled vase, covered in a blue and amber crystalline glaze, incised racetrack mark.

7.5in (19cm) high

$500-600   **CR**

A rare and early Fulper peacock bowl, embossed with panels of peacock feathers in olive green, blue and ivory flambé glaze, incised racetrack mark.

10in (25.5cm) high

$550-650   **CR**

A large Fulper bullet-shaped vase, covered in a fine and frothy mirrored Chinese blue flambé glaze, incised racetrack mark.

10.25in (26cm) high

$900-1,000   **CR**

A Fulper classically-shaped vase, covered in a Chinese blue crystalline flambé glaze, ink racetrack mark.

12in (30.5cm) high

$550-650   **CR**

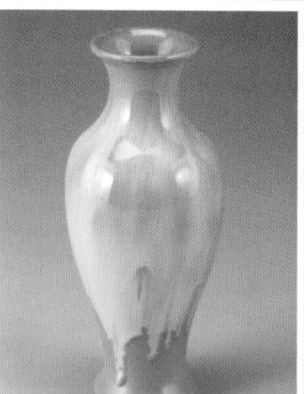

A Fulper classically-shaped vase, with ivory flambé glaze dripping over a mustard matte ground, ink racetrack mark.

10.5in (26.5cm) high

$800-900   **CR**

A Fulper baluster vase, with an excellent olive to Chinese blue flambé glaze, ink racetrack mark.

5.25in (13cm) high

$700-800   **CR**

A fine Fulper baluster vase, with an exceptional turquoise glaze, ink racetrack mark, incised D.

9in (23cm) high

$500-600   **CR**

A fine and early Fulper baluster vase, with an ivory to sky blue flambé glaze, ink racetrack mark.

9.5in (24cm) high

$500-600   **CR**

Grueby

A Grueby vase, with subtle leaf and bud design and Grueby green glaze.
c1900-1910

$3,500-4,000 **LG**

A bulbous Grueby vase, with tooled and applied rounded leaves alternating with buds, under a medium matte green glaze, small nick to one leaf edge, mark obscured by glaze.

7.5in (19cm) high

$2,800-3,000 **CR**

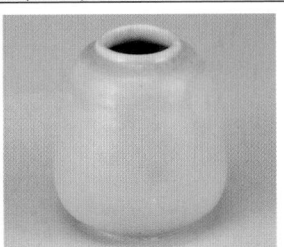

An unusual high-fired Grueby vessel covered in a dripping matte mustard glaze, stamped Grueby Pottery.

3.75in (9.5cm)

$650-700 **CR**

A squash-shaped Grueby vase, with green glaze.
c1900-1910

$3,500-4,000 **LG**

A rare and large bulbous Grueby vase, with tooled and applied rounded leaves alternating with irises under a curdled medium green matte glaze, restoration to small drilled hole near base, minor glaze slip at top, stamped circular mark / paper label / $18.00 price tag.

13.75in (34.5cm) high

$9,000-10,000 **CR**

A bulbous Grueby vase, by Florence S Liley, decorated with tooled and applied broad leaves under a spectacular leathery matte green glaze, small chip to one leaf tip, circular faience mark / 144 / FSL.

8in (20.5cm) high

$4,000-4,500 **CR**

A CLOSER LOOK AT GRUEBY

This bud design is archetypal Grueby.

The matte green ground is the finest in American art pottery.

The leaves are tooled and applied – these are modeled not molded.

This piece is large in size for Grueby.

A rare and large bulbous Grueby vessel, by Marie Seaman, with tooled and applied leaves applied to a ridge, floriform base and covered in a superior organic matte green galze, a couple of very minor nicks to edges, stamped Grueby Faience circular mark/ incised MS/152.

12.5in (31.5cm) high

$11,000-14,000 **CR**

GRUEBY

The American potter William H Grueby founded the Grueby Faience Company in 1884, in Boston. Although successful the company was not profitable and in 1908 it went bankrupt. Most Grueby pottery was produced between 1892 and 1907. Grueby continued potting with the Grueby Faience and Tile Company.

● The company specialized in handmade tiles and slip-cast vessels with thick matt glazes, the pieces are organic and highly stylized.

● Grueby is famous for his fine matt green glaze.

● His work often featured details such as petals and these works tend to be more valuable than plainer pieces.

● Polychrome wares are also more sought after, as are single colour pots with deep tooling.

An ovoid Grueby vase, decorated with crisply tooled broad leaves, covered in a leathery dark green glaze, some nicks to high points of leaves, circular pottery mark.

5.5in (14cm)

$2,800-3,000 **CR**

A rare gourd-shaped Grueby vase, by Ruth Erickson, with tooled and applied leaves under a green matte ground, glaze misses and 0.5in bruise to rim, firing chip to base, circular pottery mark / 101 /RE.

8in (5.4cm) high

$2,000-2,500 **CR**

GRUEBY TILES

Grueby tiles are were incredibly popular at the beginning of the 20thC. They were found in hotels, restaurants and also on the walls of many stations in the New York Subway.

Gustav Stickley used only these tiles to complement his furniture. The tiles are of superb quality and highly sought after by collectors.

Approximately 200 Grueby hexagonal and 40 half-hexagonal floor tiles, covered in matte green glazes (mostly dark green), unmarked.

3in (7.5cm) diam

$4,000-4,500 **CR**

A Grueby tile, decorated in cuenca by Marie Seaman, with a pink tulip on a green matte ground, mounted in a bronze Tiffany trivet base, light wear to surface, fine original patina to mount, tile marked MS, mount is unmarked.

Cuenca is a Spanish tile-making process whereby wet tiles are impressed with raised outlines before firing.

6in (15cm) wide

$8,000-10,000 **CR**

Two Grueby floor tiles, both with white backgrounds one with hart in red clay, the other with knight on horseback in indigo, both stamped Grueby / Boston.

6in (15cm) wide

$900-1,200 **CR**

A CLOSER LOOK AT GRUEBY TILES

This tile is highly desirable due to the small amount of advertising tiles produced.

It is extremely clean and crisp and in good condition.

It displays the dark green glaze resembling the skin of a cucumber.

The secondary colour, yellow, is crisp (on some pieces it runs).

A rare Grueby advertising tile, decorated in cuenca with a half-burnt yellow candle in green chamberstick under the words "Grueby Tile", very minor glaze flake to top, signed MD/retail paper label.

6in (15cm) high

$11,000-14,000 **CR**

A large and rare Grueby architectural faience plaque, carved and molded with a family of elephants, glazed in black against a blue-gray ground, mounted in a black box frame, two firing lines to the body, restoration to one, and small chip to one corner, stamped Grueby Boston.

A similar plaque is in the collection of The Smithsonian.

23in (58.5cm) wide

$10,000-13,000 **CR**

MARBLEHEAD

Marblehead Pottery was set up in 1904 as part of a sanatorium in Marblehead, Mass. Run by Arthur Baggs, it soon became a business. It mainly produced enamel-glazed, hand-thrown wares, as well as decorated pieces and tiles. It closed in 1936.

An early Marblehead experimental gourd-shaped vase, carved with flying geese in black against a dark green matte ground, unmarked.

6in (15cm) high

$3,000-3,500 **CR**

A Marblehead ovoid vase, decorated with grapes and leaves in blue, green and brown against a speckled gray ground, impressed ship mark.

6.5in (16.5cm) high

$4,000-5,000 **CR**

A Marblehead tapering vase, decorated with a wreath of stylized leaves in amber and brown, against a speckled gray ground, impressed ship mark.

4.5in (11.5cm) high

$3,000-3,500 **CR**

A Marblehead cabinet vase, decorated with grapes and leaves in blue on a speckled gray ground, impressed ship mark.

3.5in (9cm) high

$2,500-3,000 **CR**

A CLOSER LOOK AT MARBLEHEAD

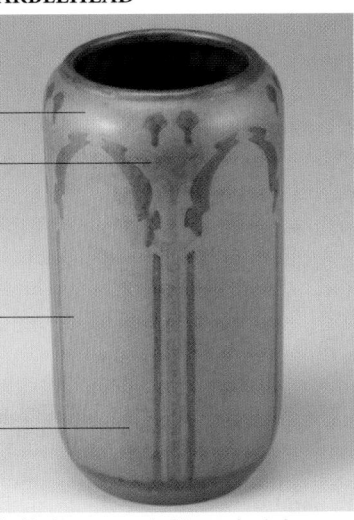

This hand thrown pot uses the palette of the Arts and Crafts period.

The stylized poppy, combined with the elongated geometric design is highly prized by collectors.

Although simple, the gently incised decoration adds interest as at least 90% of Marblehead pieces use a single glaze.

The vase is taller, and hence more valuable than the standard production.

A fine and early Marblehead cylindrical vase, carved with poppies in brown and indigo on a speckled olive green ground, opposing hairlines to rim, impressed ship mark and script, "MT".

9.25in (23.5cm) high

$10,000-12,000   **CR**

A fine, large and early Marblehead corseted pitcher, by Hannah Tutt, with incised panels incorporating stylized flowers in brown, green and indigo on a speckled matte green ground, stamped ship mark / H T.

8.75in (22cm) high

$5,500-6,500   **CR**

A pair of Marblehead triangular bookends, each embossed with a triptych of a sailing ship in green, red and white on an indigo ground, minute glaze fleck to corner of one, stamped ship mark and paper label.

5.5in (14cm) high

$2,000-2,500   **CR**

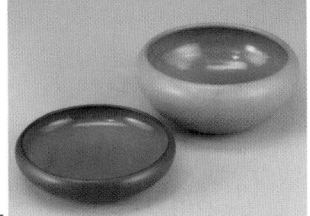

Two Marblehead low bowls, one with a blue matte exterior, the other in speckled gray (opposing hairlines to rim), impressed ship mark.

8in (20.5cm) diam

$400-500   **CR**

A Marblehead bulbous vase, covered in matte gray glaze, illegible mark.

5.5in (14cm) high

$450-550   **CR**

A Marblehead small ovoid vase covered in matte gray glaze, impressed ship mark.

4in (10cm) high

$350-450   **CR**

A large Marblehead ovoid vase, covered in smooth dark blue, matte glazed drilled hole to base, impressed ship mark and paper label.

8.5in (21.5cm) high

$400-500   **CR**

NEWCOMB COLLEGE POTTERY

In 1895 Ellsworth Woodward founded an Arts and Crafts workshop at Newcomb College, New Orleans, with the proviso of teaching the mainly female students how to make a living from producing bookbindings, metalwork, needlework and pottery.

- The pottery was hand-thrown by men and then decorated by women. It is feminine with soft curving lines and has incised, typically floral decoration with a blue glaze.
- Early wares are the most sought after and can be identified by their highly glazed finish.
- By 1910, this had been replaced by a transitional "waxy" finish.
- The pottery was generally associated with the soft matte-glazed finish, which was introduced in 1914.
- 1935 saw a brief return to the high-glazed finish, but these pieces lack the subtle shapes and designs of the originals.

An unusual Newcomb College squat vessel, carved by Sadie Irvine, with blossoms under an overall lavender matte glaze. NC / SI / JM / JK8.

1918   *1.5in (4cm) high*

$900-1,000   **CR**

An early and large Newcomb College high-glaze ovoid vase, by Roberta Kennon, deeply carved and incised with irises in shades of indigo against a pale blue ground, very short, very tight line to rim. NC/RBK/N30/JM/U

1902   *12.5in (31.5cm) high*

$18,000-22,000   **CR**

A unusual Newcomb College bulbous vase, carved by Sadie Irvine, with stylised blossoms under an all-over lavender glaze, tight line to rim. NC / SI / FQ46 / JM.

1913   7.5in (19cm) high

$1,500-2,000   **CR**

A Newcomb College carved bulbous vase, by Anna Frances Simpson, decorated with wreath of pink flowers on a medium blue ground. NC / JM / AFS / 315 / NT33.

1924   4.5in (11.5cm) high

$3,000-3,500   **CR**

A Newcomb moon and moss vase, decorator unknown, dated 1923.

The moon through Spanish moss design depicts an archetypal Southern scene. It shows how a sense of place influenced American Arts and Crafts potters. This can also be seen in the restrained glazes of the north, such as those used by Grueby in Boston MA.

1923

$4,500-5,000   **LG**

A CLOSER LOOK AT NEWCOMB COLLEGE POTTERY

The carved detailing tooled onto the surface of the vase gives the piece three-dimensionality.

The sharp carving adds value – some pieces have exceptionally fine carving and are more valuable.

The use of color is good – extra colors such as mint green and yellow are desirable.

This piece is by one of the main artists, the others being Sadie Irvine and Henrietta Bailey.

This vase has all over decoration, which adds to the value.

A Newcomb vase, decorated with jonquils by Anna Frances Simpson.

1928

$5,000-6,000   **LG**

A fine Newcomb College scenic matte ovoid vase, probably by Sadie Irvine, crisply carved with willows, Spanish moss, and a full moon on a denim blue ground. NC/RA?/JM/19/artists cipher, plus original paper label.

6in (15cm) high

$4,500-5,500   **CR**

A fine and rare Newcomb College scenic matte bulbous vase, by Sadie Irvine, crisply carved with live oaks and Spanish moss on a denim blue ground. NC/RX25/JM/24/ artists cipher, plus original paper label.

1929   5.25in (13cm) high

$4,000-5,000   **CR**

▶ A fine and rare Newcomb College scenic matte covered jar, by Anna Frances Simpson, carved with livr oaks and Spanish moss on a denim blue ground, half-inch firing line to rim of base. NC/RU3?/ JM/29/artists cipher, plus original paper label.

1929   5in (12.5cm) high

$8,000-9,000   **CR**

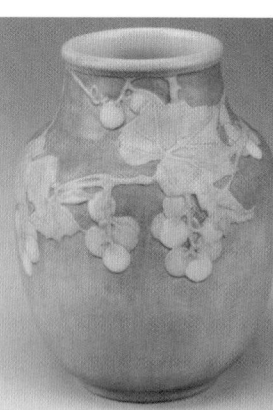

A Newcomb College carved matte bulbous vase, by Sadie Irvine, crisply decorated with grapes and leaves on a medium blue ground. NC / KG45 / 178, and paper label.

1919   8.25in (21cm) high

$5,000-6,000   **CR**

A Newcomb College carved matte vase, by Sadie Irvine, with live oaks, moon, and Spanish moss, short, tight line to rim and some glaze running. NC / UA42 / SI / 50.

1932   3.25in (8cm) high

$2,500-3,000   **CR**

A Newcomb vase, decorated by Sadie Irvine, marked 1933.

$3,500-4,500   **LG**

Newcomb Pottery

Left to right: low bowl by Sadie Irvine, 1933, 3¾" h, Jonquil vase by
Anna Frances Simpson, 1928, 8½" h; landscape vase with original label, 1923, 6½"h

LEAH GORDON

Manhattan Art & Antiques Center
1050 Second Ave. (55th St.)
New York, NY 10022

Gallery 18
Tel: 212 872-1422
Fax: 212 355-4403

GEORGE OHR

- George E Ohr was born in 1857 in Biloxi, Mississippi, where he spent most of his life. His friend Joseph Meyer offered to teach him the art of potting and in 1879 he travelled to New Orleans to do so.

- He returned to Biloxi where he set up the "Pot-Ohr-E" and started to experiment with thinly potted vessels with distorted shapes and dark iridescent glazes. In 1886 he married Josephine Gehring.

- The pottery, along with the family home, was destroyed by fire in 1894 and Ohr built the Biloxi Art Pottery Unlimited almost immediately after. Despite exhibiting at a number of international expositions, and even winning a silver medal at one, his work was not popular with buyers.

- He was known as the mad potter of Biloxi and called his pots his "little mud babies."

- In 1903 he moved away from glazed wares and produced only bisque pieces until he stopped potting altogether.

- On his death in 1918, two of his sons took over the pottery and turned it into an auto repair workshop. Ohr's remaining stock was stored in the attic until it was sold to a New Jersey antiques dealer in 1968, who then offered it for sale.

- Ohr's temperament and unusual style, which is only now appreciated, meant that almost all of his work was unsold, totalling nearly 10,000 pieces.

A CLOSER LOOK AT GEORGE OHR POTTERY

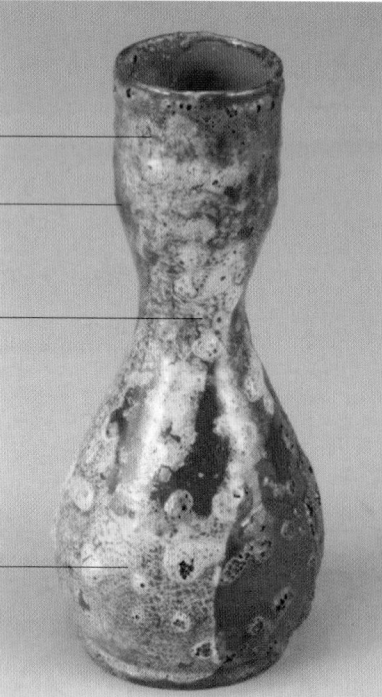

Taller pieces are always more desirable.

This simple tapered form is the perfect backdrop for the interesting use of the glaze.

The unusual raspberry and white volcanic glaze on blue adds to the value. Ohr experimented with vibrant color glazes during the 1890s and combined with a vibrant form these are some of his most valuable pieces.

Ohr's skill was in producing a very fine pottery in increasingly weird shapes.

A fine George Ohr bulbous vase, covered in an unusual raspberry and white volcanic glaze (some loss) on a glossy blue ground, underglazed firing line inside neck, stamped.

6in (15cm) high

$14,000-15,000   **CR**

A George Ohr Joe Jefferson mug, dedicated to H R Durant, Atlanta GA, covered in a sheer olive glaze, stamped GEO E OHR / BILOXI, MISS, and dated 3-18-96.

1896   3.75in (9.5cm) high

$2,000-2,500   **CR**

A George Ohr puzzle mug, with snake handle covered in a mottled brown and gunmetal glaze, stamped G E OHR / Biloxi, Miss.

3.5in (8.5cm) high

$1,800-2,200   **CR**

A George Ohr squat vase, with flaring and folded rim covered in a raspberry and amber glossy glaze, stamped GEO E OHR, tight line base.

3.25in (8cm) high

$2,000-2,500   **CR**

A George Ohr vase.

This is a vase rather than a sculpture, but severe manipulation means it is no longer functional.

c1900

$4,000-4,500   **LG**

A George Ohr bulbous vase, with lobed rim and in-body twist, covered in green and amber speckled glaze, unmarked.

The vase comes with letter of provenance from James Carpenter.

4in (10cm) high

$5,500-6,500   **CR**

A unusual George Ohr baluster cabinet vase, covered in a mottled forest green glossy glaze, stamped, touch-up to rim, minor abrasion to base.

4.75in (12cm) high

$3,000-3,500   **CR**

George Ohr

A George Ohr small hour-glass shaped pitcher, covered in mirror black and eggplant glaze, stamped.

5.5in (14cm) high

$6,000-7,000   **CR**

A George Ohr bulbous cabinet vase, with folded rim, covered in fire sparking gunmetal glaze, stamped G E OHR / Biloxi, Miss., minor nick to rim.

3in (7.5cm) high

$2,500-$3,000   **CR**

A George Ohr panther inkwell, covered in a colbalt-blue glaze, firing line to base, Incised "Biloxi" in script.

3.5in (9cm) high

$2,300-2,500   **CR**

A George Ohr small ovoid pitcher, covered in gunmetal glaze, stamped G E OHR / Biloxi, Miss.

4in (10cm) high

$2,000-2,500   **CR**

A large George Ohr vase, with straight sides, notched shoulder, and folded rim, covered in gunmetal brown glaze, incised Biloxi.

5.5in (14cm) high

$3,800-4,200   **CR**

A George Ohr small pinched pitcher, with three lobed openings, covered in a speckled gunmetal glaze, stamped G E OHR/Biloxi Miss., repairs to handle and rim edge.

4.25in (10.5cm) high

$5,500-6,000   **CR**

A vase by George Ohr. c1900

$1,500-2,000   **LG**

A George Ohr bulbous bisque vase, of red clay with deep in-body twist and closed-in rim, fired to a dark brown sheen, stamped.

$2,600-2,800   **CR**

A large George Ohr bulbous bisque vase, of white clay with dimpled shoulder and folded rim, script signature, four small chips inside rim.

5.5in (14cm) high

$4,000-4,500   **CR**

A George Ohr squat bisque vase, of red clay with folded sides and closed-in rim, script signature.

3.75in (9.5cm) high

$2,800-3,000   **CR**

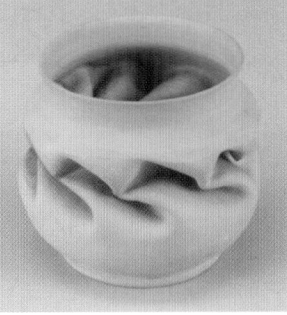

A George Ohr bisque vessel, with deep in-body twist, with script signature.

This unglazed pottery was George Ohr's final development in potting and was at the essence of the Arts and Crafts Movement, where the material is the art form. Ohr said, "God put no color in souls, and I'll put no color on my vases".

3in (7.5cm) high

$4,200-4,500   **CR**

ROOKWOOD POTTERY

Maria Nichols originally founded the Rookwood Pottery in Cinncinnati in 1880 as an amateur pottery club, but it grew to be one of the most successful and diverse American factories.

This was largely due to the business acumen of William Watts Taylor who joined the company in 1883 and took over its running in 1890 when Maria Nichols remarried and moved abroad.

He hired a German chemist, Karl Lagenbeck, to produce original glazes, including their unique matte glaze. He also employed a number of professional artists, including Kataro Shirayamadani, and many Rookwood pieces have an oriental feel to them.

As a result of their ingenuity and attention to detail, the pottery won a number of awards including the Exposition Universelle in Paris in 1889 and the World Columbian Exposition in Chicago in 1893.

After Taylor's death in 1913, the board continued to run the pottery with new owners taking over after World War II. Arthur Townley currently runs Rookwood and produces a limited number of pieces each year from the original molds.

A large Rookwood Sea Green vase, modeled with aquatic plants in brown and blue on a green ground, drilled hole on bottom, seconded mark for no apparent reason, flame mark/ 578B/ remnant of artist's cipher obscured by drilled hole/X.

The prices for Rookwood Sea Green have seen a rapid rise over the last 30 years. A desirable 8in. vase which would have sold for $250 in the 1970s could now sell for in excess of $4,000.

1898	16in (40.5cm) high
$3,000-3,500	**CR**

A fine and rare Rookwood Sea Green spherical vessel, by Albert Valentien, painted with seagulls flying over waves. four short hairlines from rim, firing lines around base, flame mark / 346B.

1895	7in (17.5cm) high
$450-500	**CR**

A tall Rookwood Iris glaze ovoid vase, by O G Reed, with golden blossoms on a shaded ground, seconded mark, possibly for crazing, minor touch up to rim 4in (10cm) Y-shaped line to interior only (does not go through), flame mark / III / 901B / O G R W / X.

1903	11.75in (29.5cm) high
$900-1,000	**CR**

A Rookwood Iris glaze vase, by Frederick Rothenbusch, decorated with blue crocus on a shaded celadon ground, hairline to rim, small bruises to base, overall crazing, flame mark / IV / 941 / C / W / FR.

1904	9.5in (24cm) high
$1,500-2,000	**CR**

A Rookwood Vellum bulbous vase, with branches of white and gray apple blossom, flame mark/IV/30EZ/V/artists cipher.

1904	4.25in (10.5cm) high
$750-950	**CR**

A fine Rookwood Vellum tapering vase, by Lenore Ashbury, painted with pink waterlilies on a shaded teal and ivory ground, 1in bruise near the rim, fine overall crazing, flame mark IV / 646Z / V / LA.

1904	10in (25.5cm) high
$650-700	**CR**

A fine and tall Rookwood carved matte vase, by William Hentschel, decorated with stylised flowers under an indigo and caramel flambé glaze, flame mark/XIV/856B/WEH and original paper price tag.

1914	16.5in (42cm) high
$5,500-6,000	**CR**

A fine and large Rookwood Scenic Vellum plaque, by Sara Sax, "Lake Louise", with trees framing the blue-green lake, fine overall crazing, in original quarter-sawn oak frame, flame mark, signed Sax on surface.

1914   plaque 12in (30.5cm) high

$6,500-7,000 **CR**

A Rookwood banded scenic Vellum classically-shaped vase, by Ed Diers, decorated with a hillside landscape with trees, some peppering to decoration, flame marks / XV / 1920 / V / ED.

1915   10in (25.5cm) high

$1,400-1,800 **CR**

A Rookwood vase, decorated with a winter scene by Sally Coyne.

1918   10in (25cm) high

$3,200-3,500 **LG**

A Rookwood Scenic Vellum "Early Day" plaque by Lorinda Epply, mounted in original frame, flame mark / XIX / LE.

plaque 8in (20.5cm) high

$3,000-3,500 **CR**

▲1 A Rookwood landscape decorated pottery vase, of slender baluster form, allover landscape decoration by E D Biers, the base incised with the date and artist's monogram.

1918   8.75in (22cm) high

$1,200-1,500 **FRE**

▲2 A Rookwood Vellum glazed pottery vase, by Frederick Rothenbusch, dated 1923, a pastoral landscape scene executed in blues, pinks and greens adorns the slender baluster vase, incised artist's monogram and impressed date code.

1923   7.25in (18cm) high

$1,000-1,500 **FRE**

A Rookwood vase, decorated by Sally Coyne.

1921   7.25in (18cm) high

$2,800-3,200 **LG**

A fine Rookwood Scenic Vellum "The Pine Tree" plaque, by Lenore Asbury, depicting a river landscape in pastel tones, uncrazed, in its original gilded frame, signed L A on surface.

11.5in (29cm) high

$6,000-6,500 **CR**

A fine Rookwood Standard Glaze bulbous vase, by Constance Baker, with flaring rim painted with orange and yellow carnations, flame mark / 353 / artists cipher.

1895   11.5in (29cm) high

$1,500-2,000 **CR**

A Rookwood Standard Glaze bulbous vase, by Constance Baker, with flaring rim painted with orange popies.

1897   10.5in (26.5cm) high

$1,500-2,000 **CR**

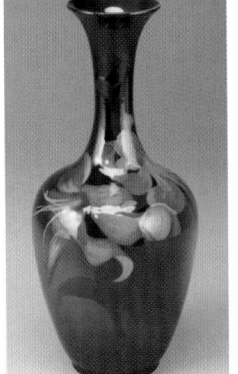

A tall Rookwood Standard Glaze baluster vase, painted by Sallie Toohey, with orange day lilies, one-inch scratch near base, seconded for minor underglaze smudge, flame mark/803A.ST/X.

1899   15in (38cm) high

$800-1,000 **CR**

A Rookwood Standard Glaze puzzle mug, painted by Sturgis Lawrence, Grutzner's portrait of a monk, seconded mark for no apparent reason, a few scratches, flame mark/711/SL after Grutzner/X.

1899   4.75in (12cm) high

$600-650 **CR**

An unusual Rookwood Standard Glaze ovoid vase, painted by Carl Schmidt, with mushrooms, flame mark / 534C/artists cipher.

1900   7in (17.5cm) high

$1,600-1,800 **CR**

A Rookwood vase, by Kataro Shirayamadani.

While the designs, tecniques and colors have their roots in the 19thC, Shirayamadani's treatment is much influenced by the Art Nouveau movement.

1925   8.5in (18.5cm) high

$4,000-4,500   LG

A Rookwood Incised Matt bottle-shaped vase, by C S Todd, decorated with lotus flowers in pink, bule and green on a pink butterfat ground, flame mark/XX/763C/CST/.

1920   6.5in (16.5cm) high

$650-700   CR

An unusual Rookwood Wax Matt vase, by Elizabeth Lincoln, decorated with panels of red cherry blossoms on a black and raspberry butterfat ground, flame mark /XXII/819/LNL.

1922   5.75in (14.5cm) high

$1,200-1,500   CR

A Rookwood wax matt vase, decorated by Catherine Crabtree.

1923   7in (17.5cm) high

$1,000-1,300   LG

A Rookwood wax matt vase, decorated by Jens Jensen.

1930   5.25in (13cm) high

$1,000-1,300   LG

A Rookwood Wax Matte vase, by Jens Jensen, decorated with magnolia on a turquoise butterfat ground, flame mark / XXXIV / S / artist's cipher.

1934   6.5in (16.5cm) high

$1,200-1,500   CR

A Rookwood Wax Matte bulbous vase, by E T Hurley, decorated with yellow crocus and green leaves on a yellow butterfat ground, flame mark / XXXIV / S artists cipher.

1934   5.5in (14cm) high

$1,000-1,500   CR

A Rookwood Wax Matt squat vase, by Jens Jensen, with abstract floral forms in black and green on a dark teal ground, flame mark / XXX/ 1929 / artist's cipher.

1930   4.5in (11.5cm) high

$900-1,100   CR

A fine, large and rare Rookwood faience tile, molded with peacocks at a fountail in matte ivory, celadon and blue glaze, chip to back top edge, stamped Rookwood Faience / 1879Y.

12in (30.5cm)wide

$3,200-3,800   CR

A rare Rookwood bisque plaque by Grace Young, "Portrait of Carl Malery, after Van Dyke", depicting a cavalier, restoration to hairline from side to center, framed, with linen liner, signed and titled on side, impressed flame mark (illegible date).

c1903   plaque 10in (25.5cm) high

$2,800-3,000   CR

A Rookwood production ware vase, designed by Kataro Shirayamadani.

This vase is an unusually large production piece, most Rookwood production pieces were 6-7in (15-17.5cm) high.

1929   11.25in (28.5cm) high

$1,400-1,600   LG

A fine Rookwood Jewel Porcelain bulbous vase, by Jens Jensen, decorated with exotic green birds on a cobalt ground, flame mark / XXXIV / artist's cipher.

1934   6in (15cm) high

$2,000-2,500   CR

A Roseville Futura vase.

These vases can be dated precisely as the pottery changed its designs frequently.

1928

$900-1,200   **LG**

ROSEVILLE POTTERY

The Roseville Pottery was begun by George F Young in Roseville, Ohio, in 1890 where it produced utilitarian stoneware and decorated flowerpots. In 1898 the company moved to Zanesville, Ohio.

Slip-painted artware began to be produced under the direction of John Herold in 1900 with the name Rozanne. The pottery competed directly with a number of other potteries including Rookwood and Weller. A number of Weller employees joined Roseville and many designs were variations on Weller's lines.

Despite being mass-produced, the production ware is the most popular with collectors, but due to the volume available to the market, damaged examples are worth considerably less.

A Roseville Baneda bowl.

1933   6.5in (16cm) diam

$300-400   **LG**

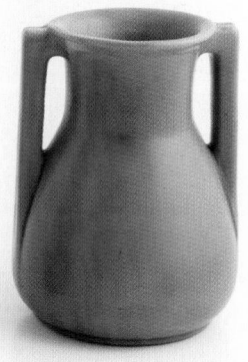

A Roseville Futura vase.

1928

$800-1,000   **LG**

A Roseville sunflower vase.

c1930

$1,200-1,500   **LG**

TECO POTTERY

William Gates founded a pottery in Terra Cotta, Illinois in 1881 and launched the Teco line in 1902.

There are two main types of wares, an angular, geometric design with a matte, typically green, glaze and a flowing, organic range, again with green matte glazes.

Gates had a strong love of architecture and many of his designers had an architectural background, which can be seen in the style of wares the pottery produced.

A rare Teco Pottery America catalog, copyright by the Gates Potteries, with color illustrations and attributions to the original artists, good condition, some foxing to cover, some tears to interior, Japan paper label.

1906   6in (15cm) high

$1,8800-2,000   **CR**

A Teco Pottery vase.

c1905-1910

$2,000-2,500   **LG**

A Teco Pottery vase.

This vase displays elements of Teco's geometric range with the angular buttressed handles but with a gently curving body and characteristic matte green glaze.

c1905-10

$2,000-2,500   **LG**

A fine and unusual Teco double gourd-shaped vase, designed by W B Mundie, with four buttressed handles, covered in a charcoaled matte green glaze, stamped Teco.

6.75in (17cm) high

$4,000-5,000   **CR**

A Teco spherical vase, covered in a smooth matte green glaze, stamped Teco.

4.5in (11.5cm) high

$650-750   **CR**

An unusual Teco small pitcher, embossed with stylized leaves and covered in sheer matte green and brown glaze, minor nick to spout, illegible mark.

3.25in (8cm) high

$400-450   **CR**

An early Van Briggle tall vase, embossed with iris under a matte ochre glaze, incised AA / Van Briggle / 1903.

1903   13.75in (34.5cm) high

$8,000-9,000   **CR**

A Van Briggle bulbous vase, embossed with leaves and covered in shaded turquoise matte glaze, incised AA/Van Briggle/Colo Spgs.

8.5in (21.5cm) high

$200-250   **CR**

An early Van Briggle cylindrical vase, embossed with thistles under a fine green crystalline glaze, 1in kiln kiss near rim. Incised AA / Van Briggle / Colo. Spgs / 105.

This example has particularly fine molding.

1908-11   9in (23cm) high

$1,500-2,000   **CR**

A Van Briggle bottle, covered in a mustard and dark blue leathery matte glaze, complete with x-rays of mark.

1914   8.5in (21.5cm) high

$450-500   **CR**

A Van Briggle "Siren of the Sea" centerbowl, with flower frog, covered in a shaded turquoise matte glaze, several dark crazing lines under bowl, glaze flanking under flower frog, incised AA/Van Briggle/ Colo. Spgs on dirty bottom.

1920s   7.5in (19cm) high

$650-700   **CR**

VAN BRIGGLE

Artus Van Briggle was an artist at the Rookwood Pottery, when in 1893 he went to study in Paris for three years. While there he encountered Anne Gregory to whom he became engaged. He also became inspired by the matte or "dead" glazes of the Chinese Ming Dynasty.

He returned to Cincinnati with the intention of rediscovering the lost technique of matte glazing. Tuberculosis forced Artus to move to the warmer climes of Colorado Springs and a year later, in 1900, he set up his own pottery. One of the first pieces he produced was his now famous slip-cast "Lorlei" vase, which is decorated with a flimsily clad woman draped round the body. Production standards in those early years were such that output was limited. In 1902 Artus and Anne married, but two years later Artus was dead and his widow took over the running of the business.

She continued production from her husband's molds and also started a range of tiles, decorated with her own designs, which proved popular with local builders and architects.

The company still exists today, making pieces from Artus' molds, however a number of molds and formulas were lost in a flood in 1935.

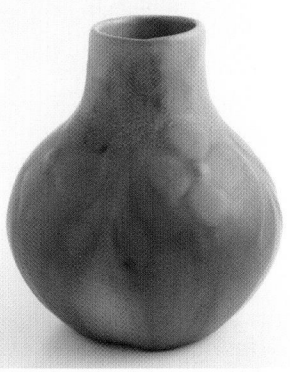

A early Van Briggle squat vessel, embossed with birds in flight under a fine green and blue leathery matte glaze, incised AA / Van Briggle / Colo Springs / 1907 / 512.

1907   4.75in (12cm) high

$1,500-2,000   **CR**

▶ A Van Briggle vase, decorated with daisies.

This vase is one of Artus' designs which Anne made after his death in 1904. The Van Briggles used an atomiser to spray glaze onto their pots, resulting in the speckled effect seen here.

c1920   9in (22.5cm) high

$800-1,000   **LG**

A Van Briggle low bowl and flower frog, the bowl embossed with dragonflies, incised AA/Van Briggle/Colo Spgs. bowl

8in (20.5cm) diam

$250-300   **CR**

Ceramics

An early Arequipa gourd-shaped vase, covered in matte olive green glaze, painted Arequipa/California/in blue on white glaze.

1912   6in (15cm) high

$700-800   **CR**

A tall and unusual Arequipa baluster vase, from the Salon period, carved under a sheer green and turquoise glossy glaze, hand-incised GC/Arequipa/illegibla markings.

c1916   13.5in (34cm) high

$3,200-3,800   **CR**

A 1940s bisque tile, by Batchelder of Los Angeles.

6in (16cm) high

$800-1,000   **LG**

A pair of Calco vertical tiles, molded with blackbirds against a full moon in polychrome, small chips around edges, unmarked.

16in (40.5cm) high

$2,000-2,500   **CR**

A rare Clifton "Tirrube" vase, with stovepipe neck and squat base, decorated with yellow and orange nasturtium on a terracotta ground, marked Clifton / Tirruba / 254.

12in (30.5cm) high

$800-900   **CR**

A Clifton "Tirrube" bottle-shaped vase, decorated with white nasturtium, stamped Clifton / 140.

8.5in (21.5cm) high

$1,500-2,000   **CR**

A rare Denver Denaura column-shaped vase, with flaring rim and base, covered in shaded semi-matte green glaze, stamped Denaura and numbered.

9.25in (23.5cm) high

$1,800-2,000   **CR**

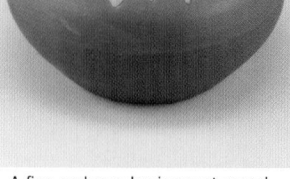

A fine and rare Jervis squat vessel, incised with stylized leaves in green and white on a blue dead-matte ground, incised Jervis.

4.75in (12cm) high

$1,800-2,000   **CR**

A Jugtown ware vase, with Persian blue glaze.

c1940-1950   6in (15cm) high

$600-800   **LG**

◄ A large Louise McLauglin spherical vase, decorated in barbotine with large roses on a gray ground, several glaze chips around rim and base, a couple of firing lines at base, incised L/NCL/Cincinnati/ 1878/16A and butterfly cipher.

1878   13in (33cm) high

$3,300-3,500   **CR**

A rare and unusual North Dakota School of Mines reticulated flowerpot, by I Kelman, decorated with dogwood and covered in a lavender and celadon glaze, tight line to rim circular ink stamp, signed and dated.

1952   5.5in (14cm) wide

$700-900   **CR**

A North Dakota School of Mines spherical vessel, by Margaret Cable, "Covered Wagon" covered in a smooth matte brown glaze, circular ink mark, signed, titled and numbered 186.

6.5in (16.5cm) high

$1,000-1,500   **CR**

A North Dakota School of Mines Bentonite clay vessel, decorated with Native Indian motifs in yellow and black on a red ground, small glaze flakes around rim, circular ink stamp, and L J.

4in (10cm) high

$200-250   **CR**

A rare Overbeck squat vessel, carved with panels of stylized Art Deco flowers under a matte green glaze. Stamped OBK / EH.

4in (10cm) high

$3,500-4,000   **CR**

A Pewabic classically shaped vase, covered in a fine lustered, dripping blue, green, and gold mottled glaze, stamped and ink marks.

c1950   8.75in (22cm) high

$700-800   **CR**

A fine Pewabic bulbous vase covered in a thick Persian blue glaze dripping over a gunmetal base, circular paper label.

5.75in (14.5cm) high

$900-1,000   **CR**

A fine, rare and early Pewabic dinner plate, decorated in squeezebag with a band of rabbits and trees in black and green, on a crackled ivory ground, a few minor glaze nicks, stamped Pewabic.

9.25in (23.5cm) diam

$2,800-3,000   **CR**

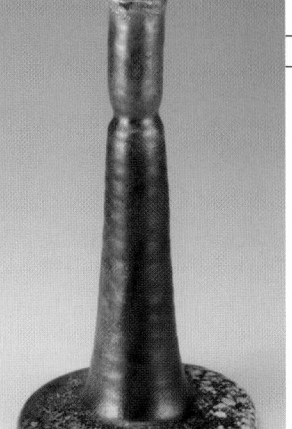

 ◄ A rare Pewabic tall candlestick, covered in a lustered blue and black glaze with volcanic base, one hairline to base, circular stamp and paper label.

12in (30.5cm) high

$1,000-1,100   **CR**

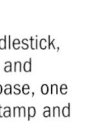

A Pewabic bulbous vase, covered in an unusual mustard and lavender iridized glaze, small chip at base, circular stamp.

6.25in (15.5cm) high

$550-600   **CR**

A fine and rare spherical porcelain vase, by Adelaide Robineau, covered in frothy blue-green and white glaze dripping over a crackled olive-green glaze, very short hairline to side carved 2/AR/1921. 1921

5.5in (14cm) high

$7,000-8,000   **CR**

Ceramics

SATURDAY EVENING GIRLS' CLUB

The Saturday Evening Girls' Club, also known as the Paul Revere Pottery, was established in 1899 in Boston. The pottery's members were predominately Italian and Jewish immigrant girls who were drawn to art pottery rather than the prospect of factory work or unemployment. In 1908 the club moved to a new location in Boston and became the Paul Revere Pottery. The start of World War I meant that trade lines to Europe were closed and the pottery began making doll's heads, but the project was unsuccessful. The pottery continued to be funded by Mrs Storrow, its founder, until its closure in 1942.

- Saturday Evening Girls' wares are typified by the distinctive designs of flowers, farmyard animals and stylised landscapes, often within banded decoration.
- Pieces tend to have porous matte glazes. Colors are usually soft and pretty.
- The abundance of practical wares made by the club meant that collectors prefer the vase forms. A design that covers the whole piece will command three times the price of a border or band design. Wares with a dull finish, rather than a gloss one, are also of more value.

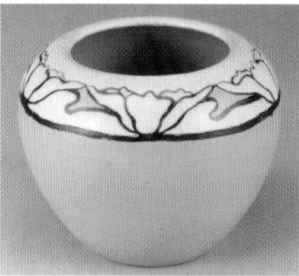

A Paul Revere jardinière, with closed-in rim, decorated in cuerda seca with black-outlined white lotus blossoms on a yellow ground, firing lines around rim and at base, restoration to two chips at rim, stamp marked 9-24.

7in (17.5cm) high

$1,500-2,000   **CR**

A 1940s rare Shearwater vase.

The Shearwater pottery, in Mississippi, was run by the Anderson family. Since it was a family business, production was low and relatively little of it circulated outside the South.

7.25in (18cm) high

$1,000-1,300   **LG**

◄ A Weller Pottery vase, made by Jacques Sicard, with an irridescent glaze.

The Weller Pottery was based in Zanesville, Ohio. Jacques Sicard trained as a potter in France under Clement Massier and was recruited by the Weller Pottery in 1901. He only worked in America for six years, returning to France in 1907.

c1905   9in (22.5cm) high

$1,200-1,600   **LG**

A plate by the Saturday Evening Girls' Club, Greek key design, decorated by Sarah Galner.

1916   7.5in (18.5cm) diam

$600-800   **LG**

A W J Walley squat vessel, with flat sholder covered in a rich brown and green matte glaze, stamped WJW.

2.5in (6.5cm) high

$500-600   **CR**

A W J Walley squat vessel, covered in a green flambé galze over red clay, rare WSH mark (Worchester State Hospital).

3in (7.5cm) high

$350-450   **CR**

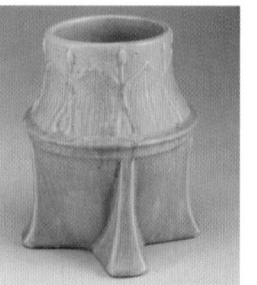

A Wheatley architectural vase, with four buttressed feet and embossed leaves and buds, under a matte ochre glaze, chip to one foot, WP mark.

10.5in (26.5cm) high

$1,100-1,300   **CR**

A fine Saturday Evening Girls' Club ovoid vase, decorated in cuerda seca with a band of oak leaves and acorns in green, brown and turquoise on a blue-green ground, in ink, SEG/AM/12-17.

1917   6.25in (15.5cm) high

$3,800-4,200   **CR**

A fine and rare Walrath corseted vase, matte-painted with stylized trees in brown and green on a matte green ground, two short tight hairlines from rim, small stilt-pull chip, incised Walrath Pottery.

7in (17.5cm) high

$4,500-5,000   **CR**

A large Wheatley vessel, with squat base, crisply decorated with stylized flowers and tooled leaves, covered in a partially-feathered light green matte glaze, restored base, incised WP.

10.25in (26cm) high

$1,000-1,500   **CR**

FURNITURE

An Arts and Crafts copper-framed wall mirror, the frame applied with four heart-shaped pottery plaques of Ruskin type, with beveled plate.

30in (75cm) high

$1,000-1,200　　　**J&H**

An Edwardian oak smoker's cabinet, with carved top above a pair of glazed doors, enclosing a fitted interior with four small drawers, having embossed Arts and Crafts brass handles and a silver presentation plaque.

4.25in (41cm) wide

$130-170　　　**J&H**

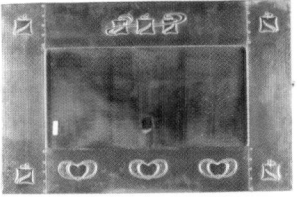

An Arts and Crafts Scottish School copper wall mirror, the broad frame repoussé-decorated with stylized plant motifs on a beaten ground.

42in (107cm) wide

$1,400-1,800　　　**L&T**

An Arts and Crafts oak sideboard, by Harris Lebus Ltd, the projecting cornice above central mirror flanked by pierced supporting brackets and inlaid panels, the base with asymmetric arrangement of two drawers, single door and an open shelf with decorated copper hinges and handles, raised on turned feet.

c1901　　65.75in (167cm) high

$900-1,100　　　**L&T**

▶ An Arts and Crafts stained beech corner cabinet, the ogee-molded cornice above single door with leaded and glazed panel enclosing shelf, flanked by open shelves above a shaped apron with heart-shaped piercing, the canted and pierced sides enclosing an open void below.

79in (201cm) high

$900-1,100　　　**L&T**

An Arts and Crafts oak bookcase, in the manner of E.A. Taylor, the reverse breakfront molded cornice above three open shelves with horizontal tongue and groove back board, over a paneled fall opening to reveal a fitted interior, the base with single shelf on molded reciprocal breakfront plinth base.

71in (181cm) high

$1,400-1,800　　　**L&T**

An Arts and Crafts oak bureau bookcase, the molded cornice with three quarter gallery, the sloping fall with decorative leaf embossed and pierced decorative hinges and drop handles, opening to reveal a fitted interior.

77in (196cm) high

$1,400-1,800　　　**L&T**

An Arts and Crafts oak hall cupboard by Liberty & Co., the projecting cornice set with a heart-shaped turquoise ceramic mount above a hinged panel door and curtained hanging space, the sides fitted with coat pegs and to one side with stick stand, the other with a folding shelf, all raised on bracket feet, bears maker's mark.

76in (195cm) high

$2,000-2,400　　　**L&T**

An Arts and Crafts oak-framed stick stand, the shaped surmount with open shelf above arched copper panel, repousse decorated with stylized fruiting plants, above a green tiled panel and ring-turned and blocked stick supports with drip tray below.

50in (128cm) high

$800-1,000　　　**L&T**

591

A satin birch side cabinet by George Walton, decorated with chevron banding, the surmount with opposing mirrored doors centered by two drawers, above a rectangular top and an arrangement of four short over two long drawers, each with cut out handles and beaten silvered backplates, the whole raised on bracket feet.

This cabinet shows characteristics of furniture produced at Elm Bank, York by Walton in 1898 for Sidney Leetham. It is inlaid with bold geometric chevron banding, which had been revived and popularized by George Jack at Morris & Co., however the enlargement of this decoration at Elm Bank was more expansive.

67in (172cm) high

$7,000-8,000   **L&T**

A Charles Rennie Mackintosh green painted Windsor chair, the later inscribed top rail above a slatted back on molded seat and turned tapering legs united by stretchers, designed for the Dutch Kitchen, Argyle Street Tearooms, Glasgow.

This chair was donated to the Glasgow "Ours" Club by the secretary and the top rail is carved "Secretary's chair, Ours". The Ours Club was set up in 1871 by a group of schoolmasters to study philology. The club's first name, "The Philological Society of Glasgow", was found too cumbrous and perhaps somewhat pretentious and was changed to Ours.

c1906   29in (73cm) high

$3,000-4,000   **L&T**

An Arts and Crafts ebonized beech ladderback armchair.

$250-300   **GorL**

A large Arts and Crafts oak armchair, the curved top rail flanked by rectangular uprights and with splat-filled back pierced with lozenges, the slatted open arms with upholstered seat and pierced seat rail.

9.5in (24cm) high

$450-500   **L&T**

A pair of Charles Rennie Mackintosh stained oak side chairs, each with serpentine top rails with cut-out carrying handles above slatted backs and drop-in upholstered seats, raised above arched seat rails on square tapering legs linked by stretchers, designed for the Argyle Street Tea Rooms, Glasgow.

1887   39.25in (99.5cm) high

$11,000-14,000   **L&T**

An Arts and Crafts oak lug armchair, the back with upholstered panel above pierced rail flanked by pierced arms and an upholstered seat with pierced apron on shaped legs, with pot castors.

$1,200-1,500   **L&T**

An Arts and Crafts stained oak love seat, the arched spindle-filled back flanked by shaped side supports with reeded arms enclosing a bowed solid seat.

37in (95cm) high

$1,200-1,500   **L&T**

A pair of oak Arts and Crafts tub chairs, the curved back and arms above pierced splat and spindle supports, the drop-in rush seats on square tapered legs united by stretchers.

$1,000-1,200   **L&T**

A mahogany "Brussels" armchair by George Walton, the molded serpentine top rail above tall baluster splat inlaid with a marquetry penwork design of wild flowers, the shaped arms on ring-turned baluster supports enclosing an upholstered panel seat on turned and tapering legs with flared feet.

This chair was first designed for the Brussels showroom of Kodak in 1899.

47in (120cm) high

$5,500-6,000   **L&T**

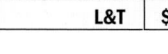

A pair of Arts and Crafts ash side chairs, each with a heart-pierced broad-shaped top horizontal backsplat between canted square section uprights, over woven seagrass seat on conforming stretchered supports.

35.75in (90.5cm) high

$150-200   **BAR**

One of a pair of Arts and Crafts oak open-arm dining chairs, with pierced bar backs, on square tapered legs.

$1,200-1,500   **GorB**

An Arts and Crafts stained beech brass-studded and embossed mounted jardinière trough, on shaped end standards with uniting platform.

28in (71cm) high

$450-500   **GorL**

A pair of oak side chairs by Hans Ofner, each with lozenge lattice panels to the backs, above upholstered seats on square section legs linked by stretchers.

$1,500-2,000   **L&T**

One of a pair of 19thC Gothic Revival oak chairs, designed by A.W.N. Pugin for the House of Lords, London, each with rectangular upholstered backs with decorative studs and chamfered uprights, the upholstered seats similarly decorated on faceted legs linked by tuned faceted and blocked stretchers.

$900-1,200   **L&T**

One of a pair of 19thC Gothic Revival oak side chairs, each with upholstered pad backs with crossed chamfered frames, the upholstered seats on cross frame legs linked by stretchers.

$450-500 pair   **L&T**

An Edwardian mahogany framed sofa, covered in "Tulip and Rose" woven woollen fabric by Morris & Co.

Tulip and Rose was designed by William Morris and registered as a fabric on 20th January 1876.

59.5in (151cm) wide

$400-450   **L&T**

A stained beech side chair, in the manner of Morris & Co., with spindle-filled rectangular back above upholstered panel seat on bobbin-turned legs with domed and reeded feet, with hidden castors.

$450-500   **L&T**

A late 19thC Scottish Arts and Crafts oak chest, designed by Sir Robert Lorimer and made by Wheeler's of Arncroach, the rectangular molded top above a panel inlaid with a hunting scene above two short and one long drawer with raised panels and turned handles, on stile feet, with modern slate insert.

Provenance: *By descent from Sir David and Janet Chalmers.*

There was an oak writing desk made by Wheeler and included in the 1896 Arts and Crafts Exhibition which had a pink marble slab on top. It may be that this piece was intended to be finished in this manner.

42in (107cm) wide

$2,500-3,000   **L&T**

An Arts and Crafts walnut chest of drawers, the rectangular top with exposed dovetails, above two short and two long graduated paneled drawers, with turned handles raised on a molded base with flattened bun feet. Designed by Sir Robert Lorimer, and made by Whytock & Reid, Edinburgh.

Provenance: *Earlshall, Fife.*

34in (87cm) high

$4,000-5,000   **L&T**

A Heals oak "Letchworth" tallboy chest, the rectangular top with square finials to the angles, above an asymmetric arrangement of two doors with circular applied panels, three short drawers and a single paneled door, all above two long drawers on block feet.

58.75in (149cm) high

$2,200-2,600   **L&T**

A Scottish School Arts and Crafts fire surround, in mahogany with the projecting mantel above a stained and leaded glass door, flanked by an open shelf above an arched pierced apron, flanked by square columns on a plinth with copper fire surround.

60in (152cm) high

$900-1,100   **L&T**

Furniture – Arts and Crafts

The settle was designed by Robert Lorimer for his sister Janet. They constitute part of a group of furniture designed by Lorimer in a self-consciously Arts and Crafts manner in the last decade of the 19thC. This furniture was mostly made by William Wheeler, the master of a small cabinet making firm in Arncroach in Fife. Arncroach was the nearest village to Kellie Castle, Lorimer's parents' home and one of his great inspirations, and he clearly felt it was appropriate he should be using these local joiners. The marquetry panels were apparently made by Whytock & Reid of Edinburgh. Lorimer had exhibited a highly commended blanket chest made by Wheeler at the Arts and Crafts Exhibition in London in 1893. The same exhibition included a walnut armoire made by Morison & Co. of Edinburgh, which was finished in their typical sophisticated and polished manner. This had also been made for Janet.

The settle is directly comparable to one made for R.W.R. Mackenzie of Earshall, and dated 1893. Lorimer had been restoring the ruined 17thC tower of Earlshall, at Leuchars in Fife, since 1890. It was one of his most romantic restorations, for which he provided a range of furniture in an Arts and Crafts or slightly self-consciously vernacular manner. The Studio critic when writing for the exhibition of 1896 sung the praises of Lorimer's earlier work, recounting that "the furniture designed by (him) at the last exhibition was so good that this time one refers to his contributions with some degree of certainty that they will be admirable". Certainly, the oak furniture made by Wheeler in the last decade of the 19th century is amongst some of the most charming of Lorimer's output.

There are several pieces still at Kellie from this period which incorporate similar marquetry panels. The 1896 Exhibition included an oak chest with a marquetry scene of a huntsman and his hounds, which is broadly identical to that used on Janet's chest, and also on the dresser made for Earlshall.

A Scottish Arts and Crafts oak settle, made by Wheeler's of Arncroach, the top rail carved with initials DPC and JAC centered by the date, above three panel back, the center panel inlaid with decorative roundel depicting a bird in a tree, above solid hinged seat enclosing void, and solid paneled sides and arms, the front with marquetry panel inlaid with rabbits being chased by a hound, on sled feet designed by Sir Robert Lorimer and dated.

Provenance: *By descent from Sir David and Janet Chalmers. Janet was Robert Lorimer's sister.*

1892   66in (168cm) wide

$15,000-18,000   **L&T**

An Arts and Crafts oak hall settle, the molded cornice above ogee canopy supported by curved brackets above three stained and leaded panels, the back with floral and foliate inlaid fielded panels above a squab cushion and enclosed by curved arms on barley-twist supports and molded stretcher base, with flattened bun feet.

65in (167cm) high

$6,000-7,000   **L&T**

An oak and chequer inlaid sideboard, after H.M. Baillie Scott, the ledge back above rectangular top and central drawer flanked by two paneled doors, each carved with a pewter and ebony roundel and enclosing an open shelf, raised on turned tapering legs linked by an undertier.

47.25in (120cm) high

$1,100-1,400   **L&T**

An Arts and Crafts oak sideboard, the projecting cornice above central mirror flanked by astraglazed doors with decorative copper hinges, the base with two drawers above central carved panel flanked by two doors with decorative hinges, the whole raised on bracket feet.

71in (181cm) high

$2,000-2,400   **L&T**

An Arts and Crafts oak sideboard, the simple ledge back above molded rectangular top supported by curved brackets, the three central drawers of tapering rectangular outline flanked by doors with long carved panels, on shaped bracket feet, supported by curved brackets.

42in (109cm) high

$1,500-1,800   **L&T**

An Austrian black-lacquered center table, the circular top above molded frieze painted blue, and four pierced supports linked by a cross stretcher.

29in (74cm) high

$550-600   **L&T**

A satin birch occasional table by George Walton, with chevron banded decoration, the rectangular top with copper frame and glazed panel raised on a square section tapering legs linked by a lower tier.

32in (82.5cm) high

$4,500-5,000   **L&T**

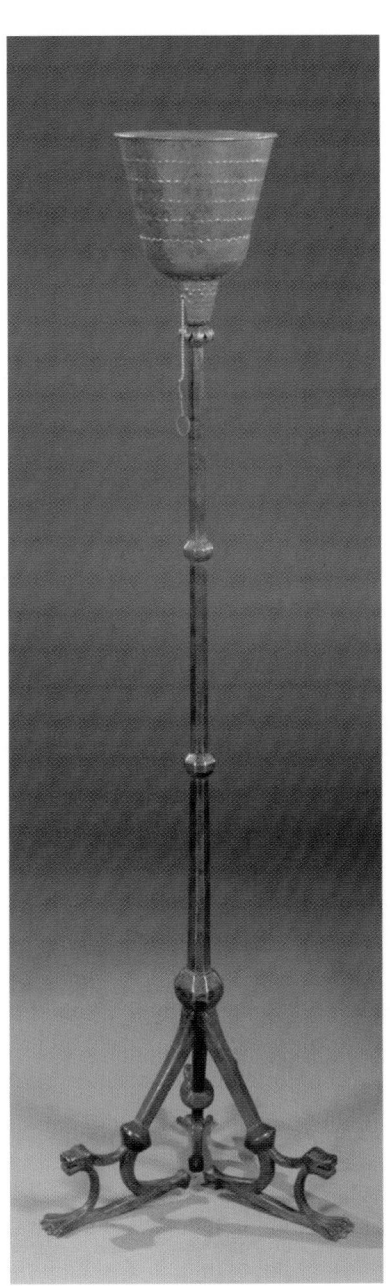

A Charles Rennie Mackintosh white painted oak table, the rectangular top with rounded edge above two opposing drawers with pine linings and turned finial, above a waved apron on rectangular section supports linked by stretchers, designed for the Main Bedroom, Windyhill, Kilmalcolm.

Two tables of this type were quoted for Windyhill by Francis Smith, and he was paid £1 13 0d and £1 5 0d for the tables. Only one table is shown in contemporary photographs and it is assumed that this example was the more expensive. The other table is now in the collection of Glasgow University.

30in (77cm) high

$15,000-18,000	L&T

A 19thC Gothic Revival oak writing desk, in the manner of Alfred Waterhouse, the rectangular top with inset leather scriver and dentil edging above arcaded frieze with two drawers to the front, raised above turned and blocked supports with decorative crossed, turned and blocked brackets and linked by chamfered stretchers.

30in (76cm) high

$4,000-5,000	L&T

An Aesthetic Movement ebonized side cabinet, with central cowled fabric panel flanked by spindle gallery above a central mirror and applied fret panels, the surmount supported by cluster columns, the base with central mirrored door flanked by open shelves and raised above turned legs.

65in (165cm) high

$220-280	L&T

An Arts and Crafts mahogany wardrobe, the center section with two panel doors with tongue and groove paneling having plant-form cut outs, the canted sides with glazed and leaded doors with open shelves and four drawers with beaten copper fittings, raised on a plinth, bears maker's label, designed by Barry Parker and Sir Raymond Unwin and made by Goodall, Lamb & Heighway Ltd, Manchester.

This wardrobe once belonged to the ceramics designer Clarice Cliff and stood in the bedroom of her house "Chetwynd" in Northwood, Staffordshire. Designed by Parker & Unwin between 1899-1902 for C.F. Goodfellow the house was bought and renamed in 1926 by Coney Shorter who first lived here with his first wife Nancy and two daughters until his marriage to Clarice Cliff in 1940. She lived at "Chetwynd" until her death in 1972.

70in (180cm) high

$6,000-7,000	L&T

An Aesthetic Movement walnut ebonized and gilt corner cabinet, by Gillows and designed by Bruce Talbert, with a single drawer above door with inset and gilt-tooled leather panels flanked by open shelves and raised on turned and tapering legs, bears retailer's label.

37.75in (96cm) high

$1,500-1,800	L&T

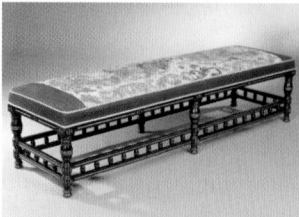

A late Victorian Aesthetic Movement ebonized long stool, with incised decoration, the floral woolwork needlework seat raised on six turned legs joined by galleried stretchers.

$4,000-4,500	L&T

An Aesthetic Movement ebonized parlor chair, probably E.W. Godwin for William Watt, the upholstered top rail above lattice sides and stuff-over seat, raised on square section outswept legs linked by stretchers.

24in (61cm) high

$1,500-2,000	L&T

A pair of oak Aesthetic Movement chairs by E.W. Godwin, each with flower-carved top rails and upholstered panel, the upholstered seats raised above ring-turned and blocked legs linked by H stretchers.

c1880

$1,000-1,200	L&T

◄ Two of a set of six Italian Aesthetic Movement carved, painted and parcel-gilt side chairs, with curved panels "wrapped" around the posts and centered by a sunken tondo painted with portraits in the Italian Renaissance style, the tapering legs headed by carved florets and terminating in lion paw feet.

c1880

$10,000-12,000 (set)	SI

An Aesthetic Movement ebonized and gilt-incised Davenport desk, the hinged stationery lid with fretwork gallery above sloping fall with inset leather writing surface, enclosing a maple-lined and fitted interior, the sides with opposing flower-carved panels and door enclosing drawers, the front with carved rosette flanked by fretwork bracelets.

c1860   36.5in (92.5cm) high

$750-850   **L&T**

An 19thC cast-iron fire surround in the Aesthetic taste, cast with sunflower motifs and set with tiles painted in colors with stylized roses, the sides set with tiles decorated with leafy orange branches.

34.5in (87.5cm) high

$150-200   **L&T**

◄ An Aesthetic Movement mahogany two-tier work table, attributed to E.W. Godwin, with two graduated circular rotating tiers, separated by a turned column, raised on ring-turned and knopped legs with outswept ends, and centered by a lower tier.

There are no surviving drawings for this table; however it resembles Godwin's Sheraton-inspired designs of the 1870s. The design is based on English dumbwaiters of the 17th and 18th centuries and the tripod form and lower-tier configuration can be found in some Godwin sketches.

37in (94cm) high

$2,500-3,000   **L&T**

An Art Nouveau oak bookcase cabinet, the projecting dentil cornice above three open shelves flanked by pierced decorative brackets supporting open shelves, the twin doors with stained and leaded glass panels enclosing adjustable shelves.

76in (195cm) high

$3,000-4,000   **L&T**

An Art Nouveau mahogany hallstand, the shaped molded surmount fitted with repousse copper panel bearing the legend "East, West; Hame's Best", above a rectangular beveled mirror and frieze of pierced plant motifs, the base section with stick stand and seat, having square section supports with flared feet, by Wylie & Lochhead, Glasgow.

87in (222cm) high

$900-1,000   **L&T**

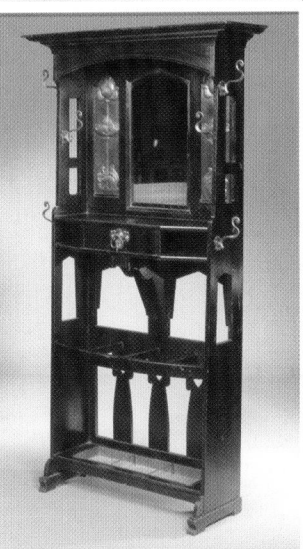

An Art Nouveau stained oak hallstand, by Wylie and Lochhead, Glasgow, the molded cornice above central beveled plate flanked by repousse copper panels and above single glove drawer with compartments for sticks below.

77.5in (197cm) high

$1,500-1,700   **L&T**

An Art Nouveau Scottish School mahogany display cabinet, the broad molded cornice above twin astragal glazed doors enclosing shelves flanked by two pairs of turned and tapering columns, the lower section with four open shelves.

66.5in (169cm) high

$3,000-4,000   **L&T**

◄ An Art Nouveau mahogany and inlaid display cabinet, the super-structure with molded cornice above twin doors glazed with convex panels, the sides similarly glazed, above arched and slatted supports and beveled mirror back, the pierced sides enclosing twin glazed doors with central marquetry foliate motifs, the whole raised on square section tapering legs.

75in (190cm) high

$1,800-2,200   **L&T**

▶ An Art Nouveau mahogany and inlaid display cabinet, the shaped ledge back with pierced sides and molded finials to the angles, having whiplash foliate and floral marquetry inlay above twin leaded and stained glass panel doors enclosing similar marquetry panels, the whole raised on square section tapering legs with molded feet.

64.5in (164cm) high

$2,800-3,200   **L&T**

▶ A pair of beech and elm side chairs, designed by Harry Napper, each with curved top rails above spindle-filled tall backs, on solid seats with slightly curved front rails, raised on square section legs, tapering and flared to the feet.

Harry Napper is best known for his involvment with the Silver Studios, founded by Arthur Silver in 1880. Napper was employed in 1890 and his work, mainly in textile design, can be seen as a continuation of the work of William Morris. The Silver Studios produced an enormous variety of designs for a wide range of manufacturers including Wylie & Lochead in Glasgow and Liberty & Co. in London. As director of the sudios in the 1890s Napper favored bold colors and Art Nouveau forms. The bold and linear style of these chairs reflect this taste.

A pair of German Art Nouveau oak chairs, by Unbekannter Hersteller, Munich, each with asymmetric back having upholstered panel above upholstered paneled seat on shaped legs linked by a strut.

c1900

50in (129cm) high

| $600-700 | L&T | $7,500–8,500 | | L&T |

An Edwardian Liberty-style mahogany open arm elbow chair, with a tapered high back panel inlaid with stylized flowers, a padded panel below with triangular-shaped padded seat on tapered square front supports terminating in stepped blocks.

47.25in (120cm) high

A late 19thC Continental Art Nouveau armchair or bergere, with original fabric.

39in (103cm) high

A Goodyears mahogany Art Nouveau armchair, the back with upholstered panel and shaped horizontal slats, the uprights with turned finials, above open arms and upholstered panel seat with square tapering legs.

Two of a set of six Continental Art Nouveau mahogany dining chairs, each with entwined whiplash back, the tapering pierced splat continuing below the seat to form a pierced knot, the drop-in seats on turned legs united by stretchers and with flaring feet.

| $600-700 | Clv | $3,000-3,500 | CdK | $300-350 | L&T | $2,000-2,500 (set) | L&T |

An Art Nouveau mahogany writing desk by Shapland and Petter, the heart-pierced super structure with curved open shelf and spindle-filled back above a rectangular top with inset leather skiver, above an asymmetric arrangement of four drawers with kneehole and open shelf below, raised above swollen square section supports with block feet.

39in (100cm) high

An Art Nouveau three fold draft screen, possibly Liberty & Co., each fold with stained and leaded glass panel, decorated with stylized foliate and floral designs, above two double-sided fabric panels and enclosed within white painted frame, the central panel with finial surmounts.

75in (191cm) high

An Art Nouveau occasional table by J.S. Henry, London, the shaped top above an elaborate fretwork frieze on slender tapering cabriole legs, linked by a lower tier and terminating on fronted pad feet, bears maker's label.

28in (72cm) high

An Art Nouveau macassar ebony inlaid games table, the square top with parquetry inlay of tortoiseshell and mother-of-pearl pieces forming a chess board and raised above pierced and tapering supports linked by a concave lower tier.

26in (66cm) high

| $1,500-1,800 | L&T | $1,300-1,600 | L&T | $900-1,100 | L&T | $1,200-1,500 | L&T |

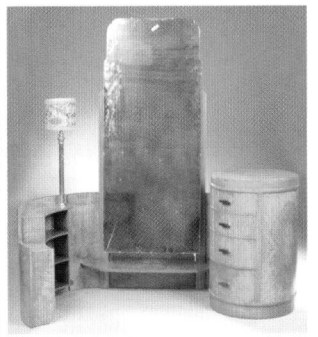

An Epstein Art Deco burr walnut and maple cocktail cabinet, with two breakfront fluted doors flanked by recessed drawers, on U-shaped underframe.

58in (147cm) high

$4,000-5,000   **GorL**

Part of an Art Deco walnut dining room suite, the sideboard with the breakfront top above three drawers flanked by cupboard doors raised on a plinth, a side table, the rectangular crossbanded top above two drawers fitted for cutlery and a coal box of rectangular outline with single pull-out lined compartment for coal.

Sideboard 35in (91cm) high

$2,000-2,500 suite   **L&T**

An Art Deco walnut dressing table, of semi-circular form, the shaped rectangular hinged mirror flanked by curved open shelves and a chromium-plated light fitting and by a cylindrical pedestal with four graduated drawers, also a matching stool and tallboy.

65in (167cm) high

$750-850   **L&T**

An Art Deco style rocket-shaped display cabinet, the circular center flanked by fin-tailed support.

$750-850   **BW**

An Art Deco amboyna wood commode, the stepped rectangular top over a front with two drawers veneered a-deux faces, the front drawer fronts mounted with pyramidal bronze-dore pulls and centered by a bronze-dore disc, raised on square-section tapering legs.

c1930 31in (80cm) wide

$3,000-3,500   **SI**

A 1930s Art Deco calamander wood tray-top pastry wagon, the rectangular tray with rounded corners, lug handles and a glass bottom, the conforming wagon with glazed bottom-hinged sides opening to a mirrored under-tier, the bracketed stile legs terminating in brass caps with spoked wheels.

20.5in (51.5cm) wide

$3,000-3,500   **SI**

One of a pair of 1930s armchairs, (re-upholstered).

29in (74cm) high

$1,500-1,800 pair   **CdK**

◀ A pair of Art Deco satin birch bedside tables, with gilded decoration, the square tops with carved edging above simple drawers and waved aprons, raised on slender molded cabriole legs with stylized leaf moldings terminating in flared feet.

28in (73cm) high

$450-500   **L&T**

A 20thC French Art Deco walnut and burr oval extending dining table, the well-figured, segmentally-veneered top with a stepped edge, the conforming frieze raised on slightly curved, channeled, square section legs, with one finished leaf and three unfinished leaves.

29.25in (74.5cm) high

$1,500-1,800   **SI**

599

Arts and Crafts Furniture – Limbert

THE STATE OF THE AMERICAN ARTS AND CRAFTS FURNITURE MARKET IS QUITE COMPLEX. On one hand, major pieces in perfect condition have never sold for more than they are now, even middle-range pieces with fine original finishes are finding strong support at auctions nationwide. Yet good examples, with even minor excuses, appeal to a limited market at best. In truth, the buyers for the best work by makers such as Gustav Stickley or Charles Rohlfs are still very, very concerned with condition. An early Gustav Stickley sideboard, for example, with chamfered sides and faceted wooden pulls, might bring $75,000 in pristine condition, yet the same form, with some wear to the finish, the scuff marks associated with a century of normal use, will be lucky to realize half of that. At a recent sale, a unique Gustav Stickley bookcase, probably custom made or purely experimental in design, had problems stemming from benign neglect. Though bearing its original finish, the piece failed to reach an opening bid of $70,000 when the general consensus was that, if perfect, it might have brought $250,000.

This suggests that the greatest bargains in Arts and Crafts furniture are the best forms in anything but the best condition. While there are enough great pieces coming on to the market to meet the demands of a selective few, this too will change as the collecting base continues to expand over the next decade.

Another positive note for present day collectors is that even good, clean middle range pieces like bookcases are down about 20% over the last year. This is probably a matter of supply and demand, as the large footprint of a case piece allows for only so many in a home. Bookcases and china cabinets of similar size are selling for about $6,000 compared with $8,000 a year ago.

David Rago

A Limbert armchair with two vertical backslats and brown leather-covered seat cushion, new finish and leather, branded mark.

42in (106.5cm) tall

$1,000-,1500   **CR**

A set of six Limbert dining side chairs, each with two vertical backslats and inset seat, reupholstered in green vinyl (tear to one), original finish, branded marks, some looseness.

36.25in (92cm) high

$2,500-3,000   **CR**

A rare and oversized Limbert, with angled back, corbels under flat paddle arms, scooped apron, and drop-in spring seat recovered in black leather, cleaned original finish, unmarked.

33in (84cm) high

$4,500-5,000   **CR**

A Limbert single-door china cabinet, with arched backsplash, overhanging rectangular top, and three adjustable interior shelves, excellent original finish, branded mark /1397.

29.75in (75.5cm)

$2,300-2,800   **CR**

▶ A large Limbert sideboard, with mirrored backsplash, two over three drawers flanked by cabinets, and large linen drawer, all with brass drop pulls, stencilled number on back, refinished, missing interior hardware for cabinet locks.

60in (152.5cm)

$4,000-6,000   **CR**

A fine and rare Limbert magazine stand, with five shelves and square cut-outs of flaring legs, branded mark.

40in (101.5cm) high

$3,500-4,000   **CR**

CHARLES P. LIMBERT

Charles P Limbert (1894-1944) produced oak furniture in New Holland, near Grand Rapids, Michigan. He began his career as a furniture salesman but opened up his own showroom for other furniture manufacturers in 1889 with his partner Philip J Klingman.

Limbert and Klingman soon began producing their own line of chairs, and by 1894 Limbert was manufacturing on a bigger scale in his own firm.

- His work shows influences from Scottish designer Charles Rennie Mackintosh (1868-1928) and the Glasgow School, Gustav Stickley and Harvey Ellis.

- Pieces are usually made in pale oak and crafted to a high standard.

- Limbert furniture will most commonly be marked with a large brand featuring a craftsman at work.

- Interest in Limbert high-quality furniture has grown recently following an exhibition in New York in 1995.

A Limbert server with plate rial, single drawer with pyramidal hammered copper pulls, arched aprons, and recessed lower shelf, original finish, some wear to feet, delamination of back panel, branded mark.

40in (101.5cm) wide

$2,000-2,500 CR

A Limbert single-drawer library table, with overhanging rectangular top covered in original brown Japan leather with copper tacks, faceted copper pulls, and lower shelf, branded mark, finish redone some time ago, old repair to top, some missing tacks.

42in (107cm) wide

$1,000-1,500 CR

A Limbert magazine stand, with arched apron around a flush top, broad slat to each side, and four shelves, original finish with overcoat, branded mark.

20in (51cm) wide

$2,000-2,500 CR

A Limbert two-drawer desk, with flush top, faceted copper pulls, long corbels, and lower shelf, branded mark, original finish, some stains to top.

48in (122cm) wide

$1,700-2,000 CR

A Limbert extension dining table, with circular top and apron on a buttressed pedestal base, includes two 12in leaves, branded mark, faded original finish. closed

48.5in (123cm) wide

$2,000-2,500 CR

A Limbert octagonal chalet table, no.120, with cross-stretchers mortised through spade-shaped cut-out legs with keyed through-tenons, original finish, unmarked, minor chips to feet.

29.5in (75cm) tall

$4,000-4,500 CR

A Limbert oval library table no. 146, with cut-out sides, long corbels, and lower shelf, new finish, some replaced wood on aprons, splits to sides, unmarked.

44in (111.5cm) wide

$1,800-2,000 CR

A large Limbert sideboard, with plate rail, two-over-two drawers flanked by cabinets over a linen drawer, with hammered copper pulls, original finish, branded mark, some water damage to top, small chip to plate rail.

66in (167.5cm) wide

$3,500-4,000 CR

▶ A Limbert server with arched backsplash and apron, single drawer with square hammered copper pulls, and lower shelf, original finish, branded mark, overcoat and minor wear to top, some looseness.

36in (91.5cm) wide

$2,000-2,500 CR

◀ A Limbert lamp table, with circular top, square lower shelf, and tapering legs, overcoat to original finish, branded mark and numbered.

18in (45.5cm) dia

$2,800-3,800 CR

A Gustav Stickley twin-size spindled bed, on casters, good new finish, branded mark.

79in (200.5cm) wide

$2,000-2,500	CR

A Gustav Stickley ladderback rocker, with scooped crest rail and leather-covered seat, new finish, red decal mark.

33in (84cm) high

$2,000-2,500	CR

▶ A Gustav Stickley cube chair, with spindled back and sides, its cushions upholstered in new dark brown leather, excellent new finish, remnant of decal.

29in (73.5cm) high

$9,500-10,500	CR

GUSTAV STICKLEY

Gustav Stickley (1858-1942) was a prominent US Arts and Crafts furniture-maker in New York. He began making chairs with his brothers at his uncle Jacob Schlager's chair factory, but was converted to the Arts and Crafts style after a visit to England. He founded the Gustav Stickley Company in 1898, which came to be named The Craftsman Workshops in 1901.

- Gustav Stickley furniture is typically solid, geometric and comfortable, without decoration or ornament.

- The furniture was usually made of quarter-sawn white oak with the mortise and tenon joints exposed.

- Panel and frame construction was also used, and typical forms include slat-back chairs, benches, dining and writing tables, bookcases, umbrella stands and mirrors.

- Although some of his work exhibits influences from 17thC colonial furniture, the most collectable of his pieces are those that are modern in design.

- Gustav Stickley furniture tends to have a distinct, warm patination. This is from the process of fuming the oak for preservation. Original patination will add to the value to a piece, as will rarity of design.

- Gustav Stickley pieces are marked with a medieval joiner's compass and are usually inscribed "Als ik kan" which roughly translates as "The best that I can" from the Flemish.

- He filed for bankruptcy in March 1915 and in 1916 his brothers, Leopold and John George, took over and ran the company as L&JG Stickley. The company is still running today under the Stickley name, but it passed out of the family's hands in 1974.

A CLOSER LOOK AT GUSTAV STICKLEY

Notice the structure of the piece. Stickley's work increasingly became "angular, plain and severe."

The chest is rectangular, simple in style, of bold construction and undecorated.

A fine and rare Gustav Stickley blanket chest, with paneled top and sides joined by wrought-iron strap hardware, signed with "02-03" red decal mark.

This chest demonstrates Stickley's philosophy of "returning to the plain principles of construction and making simple, strong, comfortable furniture.

34.75in (88cm) wide

$30,000-35,000	CR

▶ A Gustav Stickley drop-front desk no. 729, with gallery top, full gallery interior, two short drawers over three wide ones with hammered copper drop pulls, fine new finish, unmarked.

36.5in (92.5cm) wide

$3,500-4,000	CR

A fine and rare Gustav Stickley vice cabinet, with dovetailed hinged lid enclosing two copper-lined shelves, the single drawer and lower cabinet with hammered copper hardware, and interior fitted with pipe and bottle holders, original finish with light overcoat to top only, retains all interior accessories, remnant of decal and Craftsman paper label, veneer crack across door.

24in (61cm) wide

$3,500-4,000	CR

A rare and unusual Gustav Stickley music cabinet, probably custom-designed, with gallery top, single door with twelve panes of "hammered" amber glass, and adjustable glass panel (perfect match), hole drilled in back of panel, branded mark and evidence of paper label.

20in (51cm) wide

$15,000-17,000	CR

Gustav Stickley

A Gustav Stickley drop-front desk no. 732, with gallery interior and two small drawers over two large ones, with wrought-iron V-pulls, paper Craftsman lable and red decal, original finish, a few chips, missing lock, escutcheon and pencil holders.

32in (81cm) wide

$3,000-3,500 — **CR**

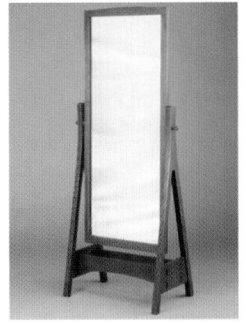

A fine and rare Gustav Stickley cheval mirror no. 914, with wishbone legs, arched stretched mortised through sides, and iron hardware, large red decal mark, fine original finish, four small repaired holes on corners.

69in (175cm) high

$21,000-23,000 — **CR**

A Gustav Stickley hanging wall mirror, with arched top rail, iron hardware and hanging chains, original finish, branded Stickley.

23.5in (59.5cm) high

$1,500-2,000 — **CR**

A Gustav Stickley magazine stand, with D-shaped handles, four shelves, and arched base, red decal mark, original finish, some stains to top.

13.75in (34.5cm) wide

$2,000-2,500 — **CR**

An early Gustav Stickley footstool, with arched sides and crossed-stretchers, tacked-on burgundy leather (replaced), and tapering feet, cleaned and waxed original finish, faint signature.

17in (43cm) high

$5,500-6,000 — **CR**

A Gustav Stickley magazine stand, designed by Harvey Ellis, with overhanging rectangular top over arched aprons, three shelves, and arched sides, original finish, unmarked.

21.5in (54.6cm) wide

$2,500-3,000 — **CR**

A rare Gustav Stickley maple veneer drop-leaf sewing stand, designed by Harvey Ellis, with copper and fruitwood inlay to leaves and to three drawer-fronts, circular pulls, and tapering legs, cleaned finish, remnant of red decal mark, restoration to several small veneer chips, replaced piece of copper inlay.

18in (45.5cm) wide

$6,000-6,500 — **CR**

A Gustav Stickley lamp table, with clip-corner top, lower shelf and arched cross-stretchers mortised through the legs, original finish, minor seam seperation to top and shelf, Craftsman paper label.

24in (60.9cm) wide

$1,500-2,000 — **CR**

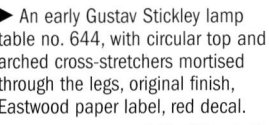

A Gustav Stickley five-legged extension dining table, with circular top and apron, includes four 12in leaves, with holder, original finish, normal wear and seam separation to top, unmarked, wear to legs, missing screws for center leg.

30.75in (78cm) high

$4,500-5,500 — **CR**

A Gustav Stickley tabouret, with circular top and arched cross-stretchers, new finish, unmarked.

16in (40.5cm) high

$650-750 — **CR**

► An early Gustav Stickley lamp table no. 644, with circular top and arched cross-stretchers mortised through the legs, original finish, Eastwood paper label, red decal.

30in (76cm) dia

$1,800-2,200 — **CR**

A CLOSER LOOK AT GUSTAV STICKLEY

Notice the mortise-and-tenon joints, secured by dowels. Stickley specified that the tops of the tenons should stand proud of the tops of the front posts and should protrude through the mortise.

This table has the original finish. This is important when looking at Stickley furniture as it will dramatically affect the value.

An early Gustav Stickley lamp table, with flush circular top and corseted cross-stretchers mortised through the legs, topped by a finial, original finish, decal mark.

1902-03   28in (71cm) high

$5,500-6,000 — **CR**

An L & J G Stickley mahogany spindle-back side chair, with reupholstered seat, original finish, unmarked.

41.25in (104.5cm) high

$400-450   **CR**

A set of six L & J G Stickley side chairs, with arched crestrail, five vertical backslats, and drop-in seat cushions recovered in tan leather, refinished, some bear branded mark.

38.5in (97.5cm) tall

$4,000-4,500   **CR**

An L & J G Stickley open-arm rocker, with six vertical backslats and drop-in seat cushion, original finish with overcoat, bears "The Work of..." label, chip to one rocker.

40in (101.5cm) high

$1,500-1,800   **CR**

An L & J G Stickley two-door china cabinet, with arched gallery top, six glass panes per door, copper hardware, arched toeboard and three interior shelves, original finish, branded mark inside door, some delamination to back.

47.75in (121cm) wide

$4,000-4,500   **CR**

L & J.G. STICKLEY

In 1900 Leopold Stickley (1869-1957) left the workshop of Gustav Stickley, his brother, and joined with his other brother, John George Stickley, and founded the L & J.G. Stickley firm, in Fayetteville, New York, also known from 1904 as the Onondaga Shops and from 1906 as Handcraft.

- Their designs include bookcases, serving-tables, settles, and spindle chairs, all most commonly finished in oak.

- They incorporate many of Gustav's structural details such as pegs, mortise and tenons, and the use of quartered oak. The "Handcraft" range typically features hand-hammered copper hardware, and their most modern designs were influenced by those of The Prairie School.

- Their pieces are popular with collectors because they are more widely available than those of Gustav.

An L & J G Stickley/Onondaga Shops sideboard, with large mirrored backsplash with shelf, four drawers flanked by paneled cabinets with strap hardware, over a linen drawer, with hammered copper hardware, good new finish, unmarked.

53.25in (135cm) wide

$4,500-5,000   **CR**

An L & J G Stickley sideboard with plate rail, three center drawers flanked by cabinets, over a large linen drawer, with hammered copper pulls, good original finish, branded mark.

48in (121.9cm) wide

$4,500-5,000   **CR**

A L & J G Stickley server with backsplash, overhanging top, arched apron, and two lower shelves, refinished, unmarked.

40in (101.5cm) wide

$3,000-3,500   **CR**

A large L & J G Stickley trestle library table, with rectangular top and lower shelf keyed through the sides, original finish, remnant of Handcraft label, some screw holes, two feet cut off.

72in (183cm) wide

$1,700-2,000   **CR**

An L & J G Stickley drop-leaf occasional table, with circular top and footed base, unmarked, refinished, replaced stretcher.

28in (71cm) dia

$700-900   **CR**

An L & J G Stickley drink stand, with circular copper-covered top and flared legs with arched cross-stretchers, red Handcraft decal mark, excellent original condition, some stains to top.

28.25in (71.5cm) tall

$7,000-7,500   **CR**

◄ An L & J G Stickley extenstion dining table, with circular top and five-post pedestal base with shoe feet, includes four 12in leaves in storage rack, good original finish, bears "The Work Of...." decal, normal wear to top.

29in (73.5cm) x 48in (122cm) dia

$3,500-4,000   **CR**

► An early L & J G Stickley trestle library table, with rectangular top, harp-shaped legs, and lower shelf, unmarked, missing some tacks along edge of tabletop.

40in (101.5cm) wide

$2,000-2,500   **CR**

A Stickley Brothers ladderback rocker with open arms, its seat cushion reupholstered in brown vinyl, original finish, partial paper label.

33.5in (85cm) high

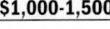

$1,000-1,500   **CR**

A Stickley Brothers bookrack with gallery top, three spindles to each side, and four shelves, original finish, unmarked, minor stains to top shelf, a little loose.

26.5in (67.5cm) wide

$1,500-2,000   **CR**

A Stickley Brothers chest, with pivoting mirror, and two small drawers over four larger ones, with circular wooden pulls, original finish, with Quaint metal tag, some veneer lifting on bottom.

36in (91.5cm) wide

$2,000-2,500   **CR**

▶ An unusual Stickley Brothers lamp table no. 2505, with circular top, covered in its original black leather with embossed tacks, overhanging a square apron, and lower shelf ,and tapering feet original condition, stenciled 6729, with remnant of paper label.

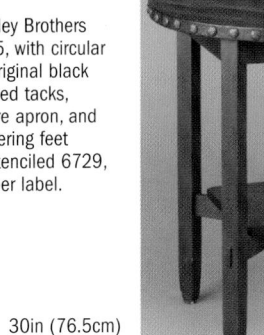

30in (76.5cm)

$2,500-3,000   **CR**

A Stickley Brothers two-door china cabinet no. 8852, with backsplash, mirrored top to paneled interior, three shelves, and single-pane doors with hammered copper hardware, good original finish, branded mark and stenciled number.

46.25in (117.5cm) wide

$2,200-2,800   **CR**

A Stickley Brothers two-door bookcase, with paneled sides and eight-pane faux-mullion lattice to each door, original finish, overcoat to top only, Quaint metal tag, small drilled hole to left door.

48in (122cm) wide

$3,000-3,500   **CR**

JOHN STICKLEY

John George Stickley helped his brother Albert set up the Stickley Brothers Company in 1891, in Michigan. Albert's designs were influenced by Scottish and English designs, and he named his version of mission furniture "Quaint," attributing his ideas to the ideals William Morris and Burne-Jones. Albert's furniture is typically more decorative than that of the other brothers, with designs incorporating inlay of various woods and metal, tapering legs, curving boards, carving and elaborate metalwork. The Stickley Brothers furniture is acclaimed for its unique and distinctive expression of British Arts and Crafts influences.

▶ A Stickley Brothers lamp table with rectangular overhanging top, straight apron, mortised lower shelf, and tapered legs, original finish, unmarked.

26in (66cm) wide

$1,000-1,500   **CR**

A Stickley Brothers lamp table, with circular top covered in tacked-on brown leather, square lower shelf, and tapering legs, new finish and leather, remnant of paper label.

30in (76cm) high

$1,200-1,500   **CR**

A Stickley Brothers mahogany tea table, with circular top and arched cross-stretchers mortised through the legs, with metal tag, good original finish to base, top refinished.

28in (71.1cm) high

$600-700   **CR**

A rare Roycroft wall-hanging rectangular mirror, with six iron hooks, and hanging chains. unmarked.

30in (76cm) high

$2,700-3,000   **CR**

A Roycroft architectural bookcase, from the Roycroft Inn in East Aurora, NY, with overhanging cornice top, glass-paned door and four adjustable shelves over a single drawer, with copper hardware, carved Roycroft and stamped with Inn registration number RO84, chip to back of top.

34in (86.5cm) wide

$18,000-22,000   **CR**

A Roycroft armchair, with single broad backslat, short curved arms, and tacked-on black hard leather seat, original leather and tacks, new finish, carved orb and cross mark on apron.

40.75in (103.5cm) high

$18,000-22,000   **CR**

A Roycroft desk chair, with single broad backslat and original tacked-on black leather seat, on a swivel base, light overcoat to original finish, carved orb and cross mark on side.

26.5in (67.5cm) high

$1,000-1,500   **CR**

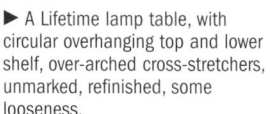

A Roycroft slipper chair, with two horizontal backslats, tacked-on back hard leather seat, and tapering legs with Mackmurdo feet, original finish and leather, carved Roycroft on apron.

35in (89cm) high

$2,500-3,500   **CR**

Early Roycroft library table, with overhanging top and lower shelf double-keyed through the legs, new finish, seam separation, minor cupping, small edge chips, carved Roycroft on apron.

50in (127cm) wide

$2,800-3,200   **CR**

▶ A rare Roycroft vanity, with pivoting bevel-edged mirror, single drawer with copper drop pulls, on tapering legs with Mackmurdo feet, original finish, excellent condition, carved orb and cross mark.

The simple construction and the hammered copper hardware on this oak piece are typical Roycroft designs. The prominent position of the orb-and cross mark at the top of the leg is also characteristic as is the distinctive tapered leg terminating in a bulbous foot.

39in (99cm) wide

$4,000-6,000   **CR**

▶ A Lifetime lamp table, with circular overhanging top and lower shelf, over-arched cross-stretchers, unmarked, refinished, some looseness.

29.25in (74cm) high

$700-800   **CR**

◀ A Lifetime three-door bookcase, with flush top, eight-pane faux-mullion lattice per door, copper hardware, and interior shelves, original finish, unmarked, two small drilled holes on back post.

62in (157.5cm) wide

$6,500-7,000   **CR**

A Lifetime bookcase, with single drawer over door with faux-mullion latticework, and three interior shelves, original finish, remnant of paper label.

32in (81cm) wide

$2,500-3,000   **CR**

A J.M. Young settle, with square posts and vertical slats to the back and under the arms, its drop-in seat recovered in green leather, original finish, unmarked.

78in (198cm) wide

$2,800-3,000   **CR**

A "Dryad" wicker reclining garden chair, the rectangular adjustable back above arms with compartments for drinks and magazines, on turned legs and with pull out foot rest, bears makers label.

40in (104cm) high

$700-800   **L&T**

A 1930s four-fold lacquer screen, painted to one side with an exotic palm tree landscape, populated by flying birds and reptiles and enclosed within a meandering floral border, the reverse painted with all over floral decoration.

70in (178cm) high

$2,200-2,800   **L&T**

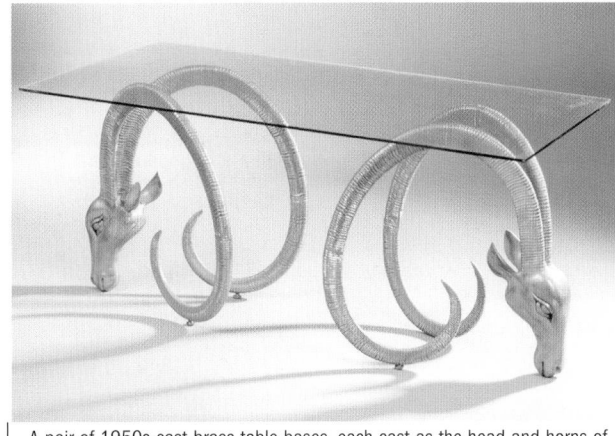

A pair of 1950s cast brass table bases, each cast as the head and horns of an antelope, (glass top not included).

19.5in (49.5cm) high

$3,000-3,500   **L&T**

GLASS

A cameo glass vase, of exhibition quality, signed Baccarat, dated 2nd January 1867 (Paris Exhibition).

The Compagnie des Cristalleries de Baccarat was founded 1765 and became a major European manufacturer of lead crystal glass.

24in (61cm) high

$30,000-40,000   **AL**

A Baccarat cameo crystal vase, with stencilled base mark.

c1900   14.25in (36cm) high

$850-950   **L&T**

A Baccarat ruby cameo crystal vase, acid-etched with flowering datura branches on a frosted ground and highlighted with gilding, stencilled base mark.

c1900   12in (30cm) high

$1,000-1,300   **L&T**

A Daum cameo glass bowl, with gilt signature.

c1895   6.25in (16cm) high

$1,500-2,000   **AL**

A De Vez cameo glass vase, decorated with an extensive landscape, signed.

14.5in (36.5cm) high

$850-950   **BAR**

A De Vez cameo glass vase, acid-etched with poppies.

6.5in (16cm) high

$400-450   **L&T**

A Stourbridge brilliant-cut cameo scent bottle, probably Stuart & Sons, carved with a panel of convolvulus, with silver vermicular screw-cap, hallmarks for London 1887, chip.

10.25in (26cm) long

$1,800-2,200   **DN**

Cameo Glass

Left: An Emile Gallé cameo glass vase, of ovoid form with everted rim, with acid-etched decoration of flowering wysteria, cameo signature.

10.75in (27cm) high

$3,000-3,500

An Emile Gallé cameo glass vase, decorated with flowers and leaves.	An Emile Gallé acid-cut cameo glass vase, decorated with thistles.	An Emile Gallé cameo glass vase, with acid-etched decoration, Gallé cameo mark.
3.75in (9.5cm) high	c1900 5.5in (14cm) high	7in (18cm) high
$600-700 GorL	**$1,000-1,400** AL	**$750-850** L&T

CAMEO GLASS

Cameo glass was first made in Roman times, but the technique was all but forgotten until the 19thC when it was revived by a number of manufacturers in many countries.

It is made by producing a "blank" consisting of two or more layers of colored glass. The upper layers are cut away from the base of the piece by hand, leaving the subject standing proud of the surface. Most cameo glass consists of a colored base and white overlay, but examples with up to four colors can be found. A good quality piece will feature a smooth ground with the subject showing fine and intricate details and well-defined outlines.

The blanks were made by local glassworks and then carved by skilled craftsmen working for companies such as Stevens and Williams, Thomas Webb, B&J Richardson and W.H., who were all based in the British Midlands. The most renowned maker was George Woodall who worked for Thomas Webb & Sons.

As the different colors cool at different rates, the glass layers sometimes cracked. This means it is possible to find unfinished pieces, identified by the blurred edges of the design. Unfinished items are collectable but much less valuable than finished ones.

Pieces with a signature are worth up to 25 percent more than unsigned ones, however there are fakes, so it is important to ensure the quality of the cameo matches the reputation of any mark or signature.

Internal cracks decrease the value of a piece dramatically. Examine carefully by holding the glass up to a strong light.

Restoration to disguise chips or other damage may include grinding down a piece at the top or base. Check for this by making sure patterns are complete.

The Thomas Webb Chinese-style double-gourd cameo vase opposite, carved by F. Kretschman and colored by Jules Barbe, is a superb example of the glass carver's art. It is an unusual shape and color and its quality is such that it may have been made for an exhibition; it represents many hundreds of hours work on behalf of the craftsmen who made it and would have been a very expensive luxury item when new. Sotheby's sold an almost identical vase in 1970 and a third example is in the collection of the Corning Museum of Glass in New York State.

A Thomas Webb Chinese-style double-gourd cameo vase, occasional minute surface chips.

c1888   8.75in (22.5cm) high

$60,000-70,000   DN

Lalique

After his success with jewelry, the French designer René Lalique turned his hand to glass-making in 1910. He had already experimented with glass for his jewelry, but began manufacturing on a large scale when he was commissioned by François Coty to make scent bottles. In 1921 he took over a glassworks at Wingen-sur-Moder in Alsace. There he produced a range of items including vases, lamps, ashtrays, car mascots, clocks and architectural panels.

Lalique glass is usually opalescent or clear with a frosted or partly frosted surface. Lalique used metal molds and because these had to be broken to remove the glass, each cast is unique. Lalique oversaw almost all the pieces from the glassworks and as a result the vast majority of items are of high quality.

- There are fakes around, so check pieces carefully. Look out for post-war Lalique with a pre-war signature.
- Pieces made after 1927 have "France" added to the main signature.
- Pieces made after 1945 do not include the initial "R".
- Fake Lalique tends to be relatively lightweight.
- With Lalique's opalescent glass, the opacicty is controlled and becomes part of the design, with fakes, the opalescence tends to be uniform.

A 20thC René Lalique blue opalescent glass vase, of trumpet form, with molded wheat ears in eight radiating sections, etched R. Lalique, France to base.

6.75in (17cm) high

$375-425 | **BonS**

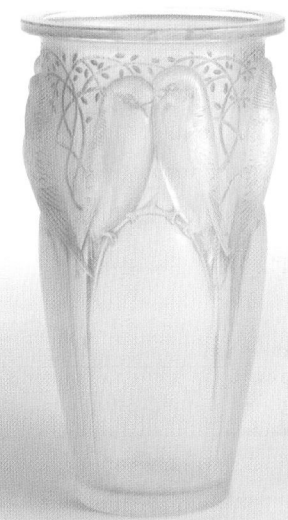

René Lalique Love Birds vase, with R. Lalique France mark, some stain loss.

c1925 | 9.5in (24cm) high

$6,000-6,500 | **AS&S**

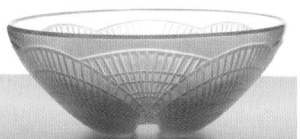

A large René Lalique coquille scalloped bowl.

c1925 | 9.5in (24cm) dia

$700-1,000 | **AL**

A rare pair of René Lalique Chamonix vases.

c1933 | 5in (13cm) diam

$3,000-4,000 | **AL**

A René Lalique clear and frosted Aras glass vase, molded with parakeets among thorny branches, traces of blue staining, molded R. Lalique mark, etched France mark.

9in (23cm) high

$4,000-4,500 | **L&T**

A René Lalique Montmorency vase, with etched R. Lalique France mark, original blue stain.

8in (20.5cm) high

$8,500-9,500 | **AS&S**

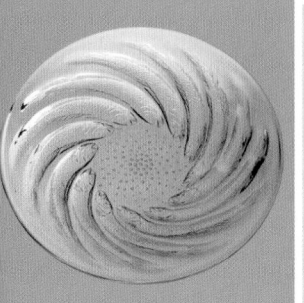

A mid-20thC René Lalique glass dish, molded with sardines arranged about a central well, molded R. Lalique mark.

11.5in (29cm) dia

$400-450 | **BonS**

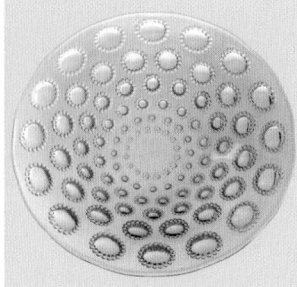

A mid-20thC René Lalique opalescent glass dish, molded with rows of concentric beaded circles, acid-etched R. Lalique France mark.

10in (25cm) dia

$350-400 | **BonS**

A René Lalique car mascot, Victoire, molded R Lalique France mark.

10.5in (26.5cm) long

$8,500-9,500 | **L&T**

609

MONART GLASS

Monart glass was made by the Moncrieff Glassworks (1865-1996) in Perth, Scotland, in the 1920s and 30s. The name Monart is a combination of Moncreiff and Ysart, the Spanish family employed by the Moncreiffs to make glass in the 1920s.

The most common Monart vases come from its production range of Oriental shapes which were often made in mottled pink and green glass with swirling colored and aventurine inclusions. In general they fetch $200-700. Special shapes and color combinations can fetch well over $1,500.

After World War II, three of the Ysart brothers began producing their own Vasart glass. Teachers whisky took over Vasart in 1964 and began producing Strathern glass. The value of the three types of glass decreases the later it was produced; Monart is therefore the most valuable.

Monart glass has a polished pontil mark and the rim of the foot is often polished flat. There may be evidence of the paper label that covered the pontil mark, although this has often been removed.

Vasart feet tend to be rounded rather than polished flat and are often etched with the company name in a copperplate script. The colors are more pastel in shade.

With Strathern glass, the pontil mark bears an impressed mark of a leaping salmon.

A Monart glass bowl.

c1920-25   9.5in (24cm) diam

$650-750   **ADE**

A Monart glass vase, shape B, made 1924-61.

10.5in (26.5cm) high

$300-350   **NBen**

A Monart glass vase, with yellow swirled body and polychrome rim, made 1924-61.

4in (10cm) high

$180-220   **NBen**

A Monart vase, with herringbone design, shape RA, made 1924-61.

5in (13cm) high

$170-200   **NBen**

A Monart green glass vase, with black, red and aventurine decoration to the rim, made 1924-61.

5in (13cm) high

$160-180   **NBen**

A Monart orange and brown vase.

c1925   9.75in (24.5cm) high

$350-400   **PC**

A Monart blue/green flared vase.

c1925   8in (20cm) high

$500-600   **PC**

A Monart glass vase, with pale blue body and aventurine rim, made 1948-61.

7.75in (19.5cm) high

$260-300   **NBen**

A Monart glass basket.

8.25in (21cm) high

$110-140   **NBen**

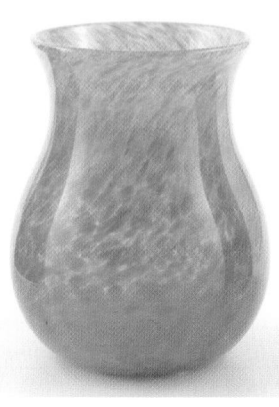

► A Monart glass vase of baluster form, with green mottled included decoration, bearing original paper label and marked SA. VI.

8in (20.5cm) high

$220-280   **HamG**

A Monart glass vase, with bubble inclusions, paper label on base.

7.75in (19.5cm) high

$220-280   **BonE**

A Monart glass vase, mottled blue and pink with purple and aventurine whorls.

8in (20cm) high

| $300-350 | BonE |

A Monart glass vase, of bulbous shape with wide neck and everted rim, with aventurine inclusions.

7in (17.5cm) high

| $380-420 | BonE |

A Monart glass vase, of squat ovoid form with everted rim, blue mottled body joining the green rim with a band of swirls.

6.25in (16cm) high

| $450-500 | L&T |

A large Monart glass vase, with bubble and swirl inclusions.

10.5in (26.5cm) high

| $800-900 | L&T |

▶ A rare Monart vase, of tapering cylindrical form with everted rim, the red body with vertical white striped decoration.

This Monart vase is rare three times over: it is a rare color (red), with a rare pattern (the stripes) and a rare shape. Monart glass was made by melting strong, dramatic enamels into the molten glass. The later produced Vasart glass used softer pastel shades which reflected the tastes of the 1940s and 50s.

11in (28cm) high

| $1,500-1,800 | L&T |

A Monart glass vase, the pale jade-green body with random and swirling inclusions.

9in (23cm) high

| $700-800 | L&T |

A Monart glass vase, of baluster form, the amethyst bands with bubble inclusions.

8in (20cm) high

| $450-500 | L&T |

A Monart glass vase, of ovoid form with everted rim, the mottled body with aventurine inclusions.

8.5in (21cm) high

| $600-700 | L&T |

A Monart glass vase, of shouldered cylindrical form, the mottled ground with allover aventurine inclusions.

8.75 (22cm) high

| $400-450 | L&T |

A Monart glass vase, of slender shouldered form with everted rim, the mottled body with aventurine inclusions.

11.5in (29cm) high

| $750-850 | L&T |

A Vasart glass vase, with white body and lilac rim, made 1947-64.

9.75in (24.5cm) high

| $180-220 | NBen |

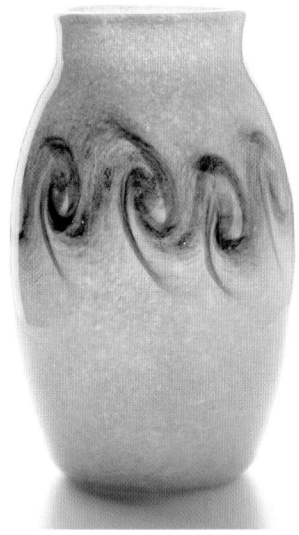

A Vasart glass vase glass, with swirl decoration, made 1947-64.

10in (25cm) high

$190-220 **NBen**

A thistle-shaped Vasart glass vase, made 1947-64.

7in (18cm) high

$130-150 **NBen**

A Vasart glass bowl, made 1947-64.

11in (27.5cm) diam

$150-180 **NBen**

A Vasart glass bowl, made 1947-64.

10in (25cm) dia

$130-150 **NBen**

A Vasart glass vase, made 1947-64.

3.25in (8cm) high

$30-40 **NBen**

A Vasart glass vase, with broad frilled rim, the body with aventurine inclusions, etched marks.

9.5in (24cm) high

$150-200 **L&T**

A Vasart glass vase, the body with bubble inclusions, the rim with aventurine inclusions, applied foot.

9in (23cm) high

$450-500 **L&T**

A 1930s Nazeing mulberry swirl glass bowl.

8in (20.5cm) diam

$110-140 **NBen**

A 1930s Nazeing white jug, with clear glass handle.

6.5in (16.5cm) high

$40-60 **NBen**

A 1950s Nazeing glass vase, with clear foot.

4.75in (12cm) high

$30-50 **NBen**

A 1950s Nazeing glass ashtray.

5in (13cm) diam

$30-35 **NBen**

A 1950s Nazeing glass bowl.

9.5in (24cm) diam

$50-80   **NBen**

A 1930s Nazeing glass vase.

10in (25cm) high

$110-150   **NBen**

A Powell amethyst glass vase, pattern no. 3000.

c1919-1940

$210-250   **JH**

WHITEFRIARS GLASSWORKS

Whitefriars Glassworks, founded in the 17th century, was acquired by James Powell (1774-1840) in 1834 and traded under the name of James Powell & Sons until 1962 when it returned to it's original name. In the 19thC it was renowned for its traditional hand blown glass, and its simple, elegant designs for William Morris. During the 20thC the factory was best known for its fashionable art glass.

A 1930s Powell sapphire glass "Lily" bowl, with fold-over rim.

14.5in (37cm) diam

$100-130   **NBen**

A 1930s small aubergine glass bowl, possibly Whitefriars, applied with spiral trail.

$40-70   **Chef**

A large 1930s aubergine glass vase, possibly Whitefriars, applied with spiral trail.

$60-90   **Chef**

A 1930s Powell glass vase.

7in (17.5cm) high

$90-120   **NBen**

A 1930s Powell Ribbon Ware amber glass bowl, with trail decoration.

10.5in (26.5cm) diam

$120-150   **NBen**

A 1930s Powell sea-green glass vase, in the Curtain or Drapery ware pattern.

12.25in (31cm) high

$70-100   **NBen**

A Whitefriars gold amber glass vase, pattern no. 9032, designed by William Watson. **Provenance:** Cargin Morley Collection.

1935-37   8in (20cm) high

$550-600   **JH**

A Whitefriars gold amber glass vase, pattern no. 9043, designed by William Wilson.

Provenance: *Cargin Morley Collection.*

c1935-37

$550-650   **JH**

A Whitefriars gold amber glass vase, pattern no. 9020, designed by William Wilson.

Provenance: *Cargin Morley Collection.*

c1935-37   7.5in (19cm) high

$550-600   **JH**

A Whitefriars sapphire glass bowl, pattern no. 9034, designed by William Wilson. **Provenance:** Cargin Morley Collection.

1935-1937

$550-600   **JH**

A Powell ruby glass vase, in the Ribbon ware pattern, with trailed decoration, produced 1940-1966.

The ruby color was developed in late 1930s but went into general production after World War II.

c1940   8in (20cm) high

$70-90   **NBen**

A Whitefriars glass vase, with bubble decoration and pull-up rim, designed by Geoffrey Baxter.

c1954.   8in (20cm) high

$60-80   **NBen**

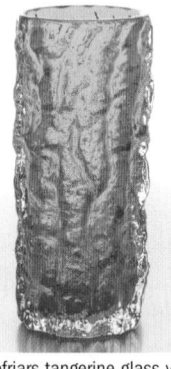

A Whitefriars tangerine glass vase, with textured bark decoration, designed by Geoffrey Baxter in 1966, produced from 1967-80.

7.5in (19cm) high

$45-60   **NBen**

A Whitefriars cinnamon glass "Shoulder" vase, designed by Geoffrey Baxter in 1966.

9.75in (24.5cm) high

$220-280   **NBen**

A kingfisher-blue Whitefriars glass vase with green ribbon trail, designed by Geoffrey Baxter in1969.

8.75in (22cm) high

$120-150   **NBen**

A Whitefriars ruby glass vase, with textured bark and fleck decoration, designed by Geoffrey Baxter in 1972.

7.25in (18.5cm) high

$60-80   **NBen**

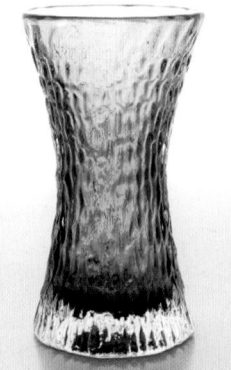

A Whitefriars sage-green glass vase, of waisted form, with fleck decoration, designed by Geoffrey Baxter in 1974.

5.75in (14.5cm) high

$45-65   **NBen**

An aubergine glass molded bowl, possibly Whitefriars.

$45-60   **Chef**

Glass

A Baccarat plate with molded scalloped border, the base hobnail-cut and overlaid in cobalt-blue.

c1860   7.5in (19cm) diam

$450-600   **AL**

A Françoise Decorchemont paté de crystal bowl, marked Decorchemont in horseshoe and B819 on base.

c1929   5.5in (14cm) diam

$4,500-6,000   **AL**

An American Mount Washington brides bowl.

Mount Washington was one of the leading glass manufacturers of art glass the1880s. Their "Burmese" range was particularly popular and is characterized by by subtle graduations of shading, from light lemon to delicate pink.

$3,500-4,500   **JJ**

A Continental Art Nouveau glass vase, of organic form, with trailed iridescent decoration, possibly made by Loetz, rim ground.

8in (20.3cm) high

$150-200   **GorL**

A Legras "Indiana" glass vase, the interior enameled red, the exterior acid-etched with poppies and foliage on a textured ground, the rim gilded, printed marks.

6in (15.5cm) high

$1,000-1,300   **L&T**

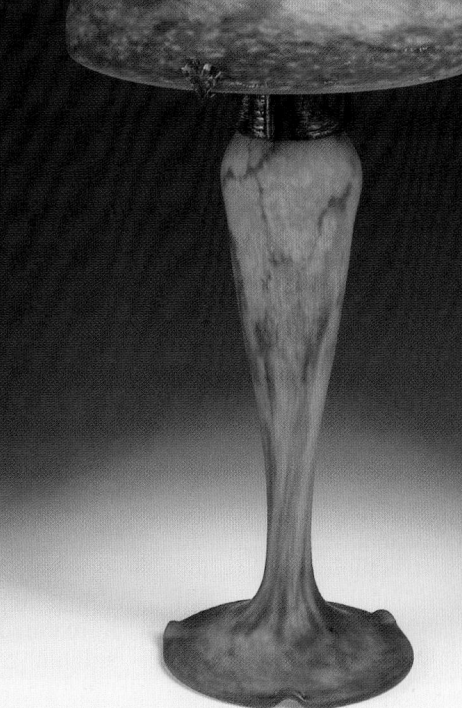

A Loetz iridescent vase, with applied butterflies.

6.5in (16cm) high

$500-600   **L&T**

A Loetz iridescent glass vase, of squat ovoid form with frilled rim, with applied floral rosettes.

5in (13cm) high

$250-300   **L&T**

A large Müller Frères frosted glass lamp, with mushroom shade, etched mark Mller Fres Luneville.

25in (63cm) high

$1,200-1,500   **BonE**

A very rare piece of Henry Navarre furnace-worked studio glass, with four typical applied medallions, signed H Navarre.

Henry Navarre *was a follower of Maurice Marinot but his work is more difficult to find.*

c1930   6.75in (17cm) high

$3,500-4,500	AL

An Orient and Flume iridescent glass vase, of baluster form with everted rim, decorated with a frieze of feathered motifs and leafy tendrils on an iridescent ground, etched mark.

6in (15.5cm) high

$260-300	L&T

A Sabino frosted glass figure of a feeding bird, molded marks Sabino Paris.

6.75in (17cm) wide

$250-300	L&T

A clear glass vase, with air-trap bubble decoration, designed by G. Nynan for Nuutäjarvi Notsjo, Finland.

1947   4.75in (12cm) high

$180-220	NBen

A Tiffany Jack in the Pulpit glass vase, with broad undulating rim and twisted neck with flattened bulbous body, the Favrile glass with peacock iridescence, etched marks L.C. Tiffany - Favrille.

Favrile glass *was developed by Louis Comfort Tiffany in 1884. It has a lustrous iridescent finish and was used for a range of Art Nouveau glassware. The word "favrile" derives from the now obsolete "fabrile", which relates to a craftsman.*

12.25in (31cm) high

$3,000-3,500	L&T

A Tiffany favrile glass and patinated bronze table screen, the three rectangular panels depicting cherry blossoms and a spider's web, with confetti and striated glass, no marks.

c1899-1920   Each panel 8.5in (21.5cm) high

$10,000-12,000	SI

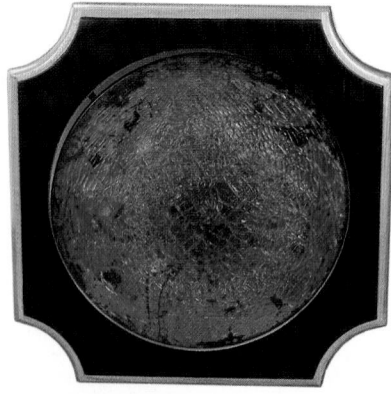

A Tiffany favrile glass panel, inscribed L.C.T/Spec, the circular panel in amber iridescent glass with craquelured surface, in an ebonized and giltwood frame.

The term "craquelure" refers to the fine cracking that occurs in the varnish or pigment of old paintings. Both glass and ceramic artists imitated this pattern for decorative effect.

c1920   panel 10.5in (26.5cm) diam

$750-850	SI

A G. Vallon opalescent glass bowl, with molded decoration of three groups of cherries forming the tripod, molded marks.

9.25in (23.5cm) diam

$150-200 **Chef**

A mid-20th century French glass bowl, the underside molded with rosettes on a leaf ground, the glass with milky opalescence, molded mark Made in France.

12.5in (31.5cm) diam

$150-200 **Chef**

A Thomas Webb iridescent glass bowl, in the Art Nouveau style, of globular shape with wide flared rim, printed mark.

4.25in (10.5cm) diam

$150-200 **BonE**

A Scottish Monart-style footed glass bowl.

6in (15.5cm) diam

$220-280 **GorL**

A CLOSER LOOK AT MUCHA GLASS

A stained glass and painted leaded glass panel, La Plume, after the original design by Alphonse Mucha.

c1899 39in (99cm) high

Alphonse Mucha (1860-1939) was Czech-born graphic artist who trained in Munich, Vienna and Paris. He designed wallpaper, furniture, jewelry and clothes, but is best known for his posters, which often featured romantic images of women. These designs are now considered the epitome of the Art Nouveau style. In 1904 he moved to New York where he worked with Louis Comfort Tiffany.

Organic, interlacing shapes and stylized flower motifs epitomise the Art Nouveau style

The idealized female figure, often in medieval dress, is typical of Mucha's style

Many of Mucha's posters depict women representing the four seasons, and the beauty of nature is a recurring theme in his designs

$2,700-3,000 **L&T**

► A Thomas Webb "Bronze" glass vase, of tapering oviform with flared neck, supported on a circular foot, the black appearance relieved by violet, kingfisher-blue and golden iridescence.

5.5in (14cm) high

$200-240 **DN**

An Art Deco-style overlay glass vase, of tapering cylindrical form, the body cut through with a design of stylized poppies, engraved mark.

12.75in (32.5cm) high

$700-800 **BonS**

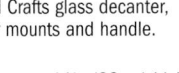

An Arts and Crafts glass decanter, with pewter mounts and handle.

11in (28cm) high

$150-200 **AS&S**

LIGHTING

An Arts and Crafts brass hall lantern, the ventilated pagoda above swollen cage sides of tapering outline on sphere feet.

15.75in (40cm) high

$850-950 **L&T**

A pair of Arts and Crafts silver candlesticks, with broad dished drip trays and tall tapering columns terminating in broadly flaring bases with rivet decorated straps to the angles, each marked G & S Co., London 1908 twice.

1908 9in (23cm) high

$2,000-2,500 **L&T**

A wrought iron three branch candelabrum, each scrolling arm supported circular drip trays raised on a base with applied leaves.

18in (46cm) high

$400-500 **L&T**

A pair of Tudric candlesticks, designed by Archibald Knox, each with broad drip trays and tapered supports, with three flared brackets on a broad base cast with entwined tendrils, stamped mark 0221.

5.75in (14.5cm) high

$1,500-1,800 **L&T**

A pair of Tudric candlesticks, the scrolled drip trays above molded tapering columns on circular spreading bases cast with leaves and set with turquoise enamel roundels, stamped marks 023.

5.5in (14cm) high

$1,200-1,500 **L&T**

A pair of Arts and Crafts copper candlesticks, of tapering form, with broad pie crust drip trays and applied handles, repoussé decorated with stylized seed heads on a beaten ground.

4in (10cm) high

$300-350 **L&T**

An early 20thC Arts and Crafts hammered copper three-light candelabra, the scalloped edge tray with candle nozzles raised on a standard with two supporting arms and set upon a scalloped edge foot, the whole with hammer marks, the joints riveted together.

5.75in (14.7cm) high

$400-450 **SI**

A bronze Art Nouveau ceiling light fitting, the green glass shade with iridescent wash contained within a basket cast as stylized fruiting plant forms, with beaten domed cover and turned finial with ring, with ceiling fitment, chain lacking.

15in (38cm) diam

$1,000-1,200 **L&T**

A set of four tin ceiling light fittings, after original designs by Charles Rennie Mackintosh, each with domed covers above square section bodies, pierced with leaded and stained glass fomed as stylized flower buds in amethyst glass.

These lights are reproductions of the fittings designed by Mackintosh for his home at 120 Mains Street, Glasgow in 1900 and at 78 South-park Avenue, Glasgow six years later.

13.5in (34cm) diam

$700-800 **L&T**

DIRK VAN ERP

Dirk Van Erp (1860-1953) was a Dutch immigrant who came to the US and settled in California in 1886. He was an active Arts and Crafts metalworker from 1908, and his son William Van Erp continued his work in his studio until 1944.

- He specialized in meticulously hand-hammered copper with exposed riveting and strapwork decoration.

- Typical wares include vases, decorative hollow-wares and table lamps with conical shades of mica panels, which are highly collectible today.

- There are authentic reproductions on the market, although these are not to the high standard of Erp originals. Reproductions will usually be stamped with modern marks, but beware of forgeries as originals are rare.

- Lamps will be marked with the Van Erp name below a windmill.

A fine Dirk Van Erp hammered-copper table lamp, with bulbous base and four panel mica shade, with two original sockets, new patina, original mica, open box mark.

Work by San Francisco master Dirk van Erp has always brought large sums at auction and in private sales. Recently a fine and early lamp established a new high of $172,000 at auction

18in (45.7cm) high

$10,000-13,000   **CR**

A fine and unusual Prairie School bronze lantern, with flat overhanging top, four leaded glass panels with amber Glasgow roses over frosted glass, original patina, a couple of short hairlines to glass, unmarked.

Lantern 12in (30cm) high

$2,000-2,500   **CR**

An Old Mission Kopperkraft hammered copper table lamp, with a flaring three-panel mica shade over a bulbous base with riveted trim, original mica, normal wear to original patina on base, die-stamped mark.

12in (30cm) high

$3,500-4,000   **CR**

◀ A rare Charles Rohlfs oak candelabra, with seven copper candle holders, original finish, splits to two feet, branded.

10.25in (26cm) wide

$1,000-1,500   **CR**

A Roycroft hammered copper desk lamp, dome shade with riveted acanthus leaf straps, fine original patina, orb and cross mark.

14.5in (37cm) high

$3,000-4,000   **CR**

An unusual Roycroft pierced copper chandelier, from The Roycroft Inn, the triangular strap support base with cut-out hearts and three pendant fixtures, each with enameled amber glass shade decorated in stylized floral motif, complete with triangular ceiling plate and hanging chains, shades are period but not original to piece, orb and cross mark.

10.5in (27cm) long

$2,000-2,500   **CR**

A Gustav Stickley hammered copper chandelier, cross-form riveted bracket, four pendant lanterns with clear "hammered" yellow glass panels' complete with original 8ft 8in hanging chain and ceiling plate, original patina and glass, 'Als Ik Kan' stamped mark to ceiling plate.

21in (53.5cm) long

$18,000-22,000   **CR**

A rare hammered copper table lamp, shade by Elizabeth Burton incorporating five inset abalone shells surrounded spade-shaped appliques, riveted four-strap by base by Christopher Tornoe, fine original red patina, unmarked.
Provenance: *Purchased from the Christopher Tornoe estate in Santa Barbara in the late 1980s.*

22in (56cm) high

$22,000-25,000   **CR**

A Tiffany style stained and leaded glass light shade, of tapering ten-sided section, with foliate pierced dome crown and stylized floral frieze.

17.75in (45cm) diam

| $1,300-1,600 | L&T |

A large Handel stained and leaded hanging light shade, of domed form with everted lip, depicting a random floral design, bears factory monogram.

20.5in (52cm) diam

| $1,100-1,400 | L&T |

A Handel stained and leaded hanging light shade, of domed form, depicting an allover floral design, bears factory monogram.

12in (30.5cm) diam

| $500-600 | L&T |

A Handel stained and leaded hanging light shade, of domed form, depicting a fruiting vine design, bears factory monogram.

12.5in (31.5cm) diam

| $1,600-2,000 | L&T |

A stained and leaded glass hanging light shade, of bulbous form, tapering to an everted detachable crown and depicting a frieze of bullrushes and water lilies.

19.75in (50cm) diam

| $500-600 | L&T |

An American slag glass hanging lamp, with crowned octagonal drop-apron dome shade, with eight triangular glass inserts, apron decorated with overlaid floral swag decoration, and curved glass inserts.

25in (63.5cm) diam

| $1,200-1,500 | SI |

An American leaded glass hanging lamp, drop-apron conical shade with eight triangular panels of four-petal flowers amidst foliage, alternating with eight narrow triangular panels.

24.5in (62.2cm) diam

| $1,300-1,600 | SI |

An American table lamp, by Charles Parker, in slag glass and copper patinated metal, dome shaped with six panels of glass, with irregular border and curved glass inserts of flowers amidst stylized Art Nouveau design, base with relief dragon decoration and impressed mark CHARLES PARKER CO/ MERIDEN CONN.

22.5in (57.1cm) high

| $1,300-1,600 | SI |

An American flashed glass and painted metal table lamp, by H.E. Rainaud, the octagonal shade cast with floral motif, comprised of eight finely painted and curved glass inserts, base cast with similar floral motif, base stamped 27/H.E. Rainaud.

24in (60.9cm) high

| $700-800 | SI |

An American slag glass and cast metal table lamp, the shade cast with floral and foliate motif and pierced lattice work design, fitted with eight glass inserts, the base cast with ribbed shaft and stylized foliate motif.

22.75in (57.7cm) high

| $250-300 | SI |

An American leaded glass and patinated bronze table lamp, with drop-apron shade with eight rows of geometric tiles terminating into irregular floral border comprised of five-petal blossoms amidst foliage, the base cast with three organic loop handles resembling flower stems.

22in (55.8cm) high

| $4,000-5,000 | SI |

▶ A Handel metal overlay desk lamp, the rose-coloured slag glass shade overlaid with bronze-coloured metal depicting oriental-style trees and grass, the adjustable bronze finish base weighted and signed with cloth label, small scuff to bronze finish.

16in (40.5cm) high

$3,000-4,000   JDJ

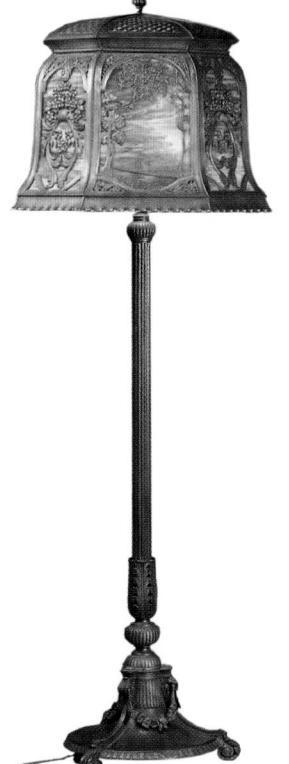

A monumental Handel "Four Seasons" slag glass and pierced brass floor lamp, mansard shaped shade with four panels cast to depict landscape scenes, alternating with four narrow panels cast with floral and foliate motif, all fitted with curved glass panels, supported by fluted base with floral swag decoration at bottom, raised on three scrolled feet, base and shade each with impressed mark P. HANDEL MERIDIAN CONN.

76in (193cm) high

$30,000-35,000   SI

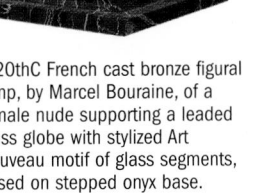

A 20thC French cast bronze figural lamp, by Marcel Bouraine, of a female nude supporting a leaded glass globe with stylized Art Nouveau motif of glass segments, raised on stepped onyx base.

36.75in (93.3cm) high

$18,000-22,000   SI

A Daum cameo glass lamp, yellow shading to orange background with cameo and enameled ships and rocks. Signed on base "DAUM NANCY 65".

14in (35.5cm) high

$15,000-18,000   JDJ

A Daum winter scene lamp, acid cut and enameled glass. Signed on base "DAUM NANCY" and carries a paper label "DELVAUX RUE ROYALE, PARIS". Both the base and the shade illuminate when lit.

12.5in (32cm) igh

$15,000-18,000   JDJ

▶ A Tiffany table lamp, linenfold glass set in a bronze bordered Tiffany shade, resting on a patinaed slender bronze base. Base signed "TIFFANY STUDIOS NEW YORK 615". Three of the large Linenfold panels are cracked and several of the small border panels are also cracked.

19.5in (49.5cm) high

$6,000-8,000   JDJ

An American Art Nouveau patinated bronze and nautilus shell table lamp, modeled as a flower on leaf-form base, impressed DH/576.

c1900   16.25in (41.5cm) high

$4,500-5,500   SI

A Tiffany Studios patinated bronze desk lamp base, the ribbon cushion-form base rising to a slender stem applied with wire scrolls and set upon ball feet, green-brown patination, impressed TIFFANY STUDIOS/NEW YORK.

1899-1928   9.75in (25cm) high

$2,000-2,500   SI

Silver

METALWARE

An Art Deco three-piece silver coffee service, comprising a coffee pot with reeded rim and foot, the hinged lid with applied turned wood finial, a sugar bowl and cream jug, marks for London 1935.

Coffeepot 5.5in (14cm)

$150-200 **L&T**

A sterling silver cocktail shaker, by Arthur and Bond, cast and chased with irises on a hammered ground, stamped marks Arthur & Bond, Yokohama, Sterling.

10in (25cm) high

$500-600 **L&T**

A Continental Art Nouveau silver plated centerpiece, one side repousse with a reclining maiden, within flowers and foliage on four scroll feet.

16in (41cm) long

$150-200 **SI**

A silver twin-handled comport, by Albert Edward Jones, with beaten finish, the bowl of eliptical form pierced to the ends and chased with leafy branches, on spreading square section base with riveted decoration, marks for Birmingham

1916.

12.5in (31.5cm) wide

$1,500-2,000 **L&T**

A Kayserzinn electroplated tea service, comprising a teapot, milk jug, sucrier and cover and a twin-handled tray, each piece cast with stylized foliage and buds, cast marks 4402.

teapot 6.75in (17cm) high T

$300-350 **L&T**

An Art Nouveau electroplated strut mirror, the beveled plate enclosed with pierced whiplash frame cast with a maiden reaching up to a floral cresting.

20in (50cm) high

$1,200-1,500 **L&T**

An electroplated claret jug, in the manner of Christopher Dresser, the body with frieze and opposing chased cartouche, with hinged lid, stamped marks to base W.W.H. & Co. EP.

10.25in (26cm) high

$150-250 **L&T**

◄ A five-piece German Art Deco silver tea and coffee service, comprising a teapot, coffeepot, cream jug, sugar bowl with cover and an oval tray, each vessel of lobed oval section with beaded rim, the ebony finials with stylized acanthus decoration.

Tray (18.5in) 47cm	
$1,500-2,000	**SI**

A Mappin & Webb table center piece, with the deep circular bowl supported by three sinuous stems issuing from a domed circular base,

25.5 cm d, 21cm h,	
$1,000-1,500	**BonS**

A German presentation goblet, made by G. Hermeling, decorated with lapis lazuli and enamel and inscribed "Bibite cum laetitia."

c1910	8.75in (22cm) high
$1,500-2,000	**JBS**

An American sterling silver jug.

c1920	16.5cm high
$1,000-1,500	**JBS**

A Continental silver bowl with handles,

c1950	6in (14.5cm) wide
$120-160	**JBS**

A silver menu holder with butterfly in blue and green enamel.	

A silver ashtray by Mappin and Webb, London,

1905	9cm diam at base
$225-275	**JBS**

A silver bowl with handles by George Lawrence Connell, Birmingham,

1913	25.5cm wide at handles,
$800-900	**JBS**

A sliver menu holder with butterfly in blue and green enamel.

c1911	4.5cm high
$225-275	**JBS**

A silver and glass claret jug by Hodd and Hodd, London,

1894	21cm h
$1,200-1,600	**JBS**

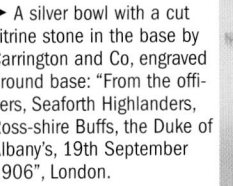

▶ A silver bowl with a cut citrine stone in the base by Carrington and Co, engraved around base: "From the officers, Seaforth Highlanders, Ross-shire Buffs, the Duke of Albany's, 19th September 1906", London.

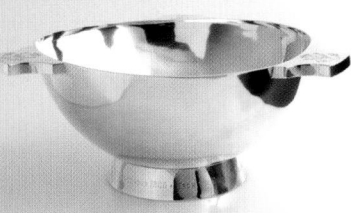
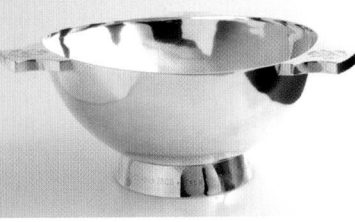

1902	31cm diam
$3,500-4,500	**JBS**

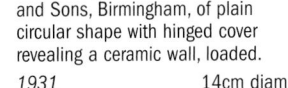

A silver capstan inkwell by W. Neale and Sons, Birmingham, of plain circular shape with hinged cover revealing a ceramic wall, loaded.

1931	14cm diam
$150-200	**Chef**

Silver

ROBERT JARVIE (1865-1940) was an Arts and Crafts metalworker in Chicago. He operated the Jarvie Shop, an independent workshop from 1904, specializing in candlesticks. His designs were typically simple and elegant in form and made from cut brass or turned copper. It is rarer to find silver objects by Jarvie. Pieces are usually marked with the name "Jarvie" in script.

A Jarvie hammered sterling silver four-piece coffee and tea service, the pots with ivory finials and detail, the bottom of teapot also engraved "Ruth Langworthy / From / Elizabeth and Benjamin Becker / January 10 / 1914," with applied initial "L," die-stamped mark and numbered, small dent to body of tea pot and to creamer.

1914   coffee pot 10in (25.5cm) high

$6,500-7,000   **CR**

A Kalo Shops hand-wrought sterling silver syrup dispenser and underplate, both with applied initial "L," die-stamped mark, and numbered, a couple of small dents to dispenser.

4.5in (11.5cm) high

$2,500-3,000   **CR**

A Kalo Shops hand-wrought sterling silver octagonal pitcher, with angular initial "L", the bottom engraved "January 10, 1914" die-stamped mark and numbered, small dent to one panel.

1914   9.5in (24cm) high

$4,000-4,500   **CR**

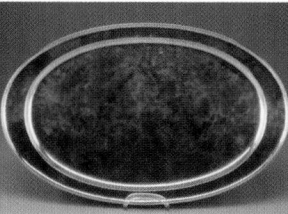

A large Kalo Shops hand-wrought sterling silver oval serving platter, monogrammed "RLL" and engraved on reverse "Ruth Langworthy Levinson / from Sol / October 9, 1921," die-stamped mark and numbered, some minor scratches and pitting to surface.

24.5in (62cm) wide

$2,300-2,500   **CR**

THE KALO SHOPS

The Kalo Shops in Park Ridge, Illinois, produced Arts and Crafts silver between 1900 and 1940. Their wares, including jewelry, candlesticks and small items for the desk or dressing table, are typically simple in design. The Kalo Shops continued producing silver until 1970, but it is the early Arts and Crafts pieces that are the most collectible.

A set of three Kalo Shops hand-wrought sterling silver graduated circular trays, with scalloped rim, die-stamped mark and numbered, minor scratches to surface.

largest 12in (30.4cm) dia

$1,500-2,500   **CR**

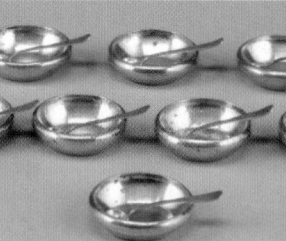

A set of eight Kalo Shops hand-wrought sterling silver salt cellars and spoons, die-stamped mark, salts also numbered, some wear and pitting.

2.5in (6.5cm) diam

$1,500-2,000   **CR**

A Kalo Shops hand-wrought sterling silver serving bowl and underplate, each with scalloped rim, die-stamped mark, numbered.

8in (20.3cm) diam

$1,000-1,500   **CR**

A Kalo Shops hand-wrought sterling silver scalloped ladle, die-stamped mark, numbered.

8in (20.5cm) long

$350-400   **CR**

Georg Jensen

GEORG JENSEN (1866-1935) is recognized as one of the greatest ever silversmiths, founding his factory in his native Copenhagen in 1904. He was heavily influenced by the Art Nouveau and the Arts and Crafts movements and this, coupled with his own sculptural approach to design, high standards of craftsmanship and use of design talent from different fields helped to secure his success. Initially producing small pieces of jewelry, his output soon grew to hollow-wares and then flatwares, often incorporating ivory, semi-precious stones and other materials. He was also innovative, producing pieces with distinctive oxidized satiny surfaces. The company he built is still thriving today – waiting lists can be up to five years for some new pieces.

A Georg Jensen Blossom vegetable tureen, design no.2, hand-hammered.
This Art Nouveau pattern was the first significant design to come out of Georg Jensen Silversmiths.

c1904   12in (30.5cm) wide

$10,000-12,000   SF

A Georg Jensen Blossom jam pot, design no.2C, Baccarat glass.

c1904   3.5in (9cm) wide

$1,800-2,400   SF

A Georg Jensen five-piece Blossom set on tray, design no 2 with ivory handles.

c1904   tray 22in (56cm) wide

$30,000-35,000   SF

A Georg Jensen Grape vegetable tureen, design no.408.

This 1910 pattern takes the same form, only with a different motif, as the Blossom pattern.

c1910   13in (33cm) wide

$10,000-12,000   SF

A Georg Jensen three-light candelabra, design no.3.

c1915   11in (28cm) high

$22,000-28,000   SF

A Georg Jensen compote with lid, design no.17C.

c1920s   6.5in (16.5cm) high

$20,000-25,000   SF

A Georg Jensen two-light Pomegranate candelabra, design no.324.

1918   8in (20.5cm) high

$22,000-28,000   SF

A Georg Jensen Grape comport, design no.264.
This comport was made in four different sizes.

c1918   10in (25.5cm) high

$7,500-8,500   SF

A Georg Jensen Grape candlestick, design no.263A.

c1920s   5.5in (14cm) high

$3,000-3,500   SF

A Georg Jensen Grape goblet, design no.296D.

c1918   4in (10cm) high

$22,000-28,000   SF

A Georg Jensen water pitcher, incorporating hammered finish, design no.319.

c1940s   8in (20.5cm) high

$6,000-7,000   **SF**

A Georg Jensen small sweet dish, design no. 347B.

1920s   4.5in (11.5cm) wide

$450-550   **SF**

A pair of Georg Jensen compacts, by Harold Nielson, left: design no. 150A, right: 277D with dolphin motif and mirrors inside.

c1920s   largest 3.5in (9cm) diam

$300-400 (each)   **SF**

A Georg Jensen centerpiece bowl, by Johan Rohde.

c1920s   9in (23cm) hig

$9,000-11,000   **S**

A Georg Jensen vegetable tureen, design no.290, with ebony finial, hammered finish

c1920s   9in (23cm) diam

$3,000-4,000   **SF**

A Georg Jensen five-piece Cosmos tea and coffee set on tray, designed by Johan Rohde, design no.5861, with ebony handles.

13.75in (35cm) high

$22,000-25,000   **SF**

A Georg Jensen cigar box, design no.195, with flower motif, hammered finish.

c1930s   7in (7in (18cm) wide

$25,000-30,000   **S**

A Georg Jensen small jewelry box, by Harald Nielsen, with filigree work.

c1920s   4in (10cm) wide

$3,000-4,000   **SF**

A Georg Jensen triple vegetable dish, design no.290.

c1920s   9in (23cm) wide

$6,000-7,500   **SF**

A Georg Jensen inkwell, design no.442.

c1920s   5.5in (14cm) high

$4,500-5,500   **SF**

A Georg Jensen Cosmos water pitcher, designed by Johan Rohde, design no.45J, with ebony handle.

c1920s   9in (23cm) high

$7,500-8,500   **SF**

Georg Jensen

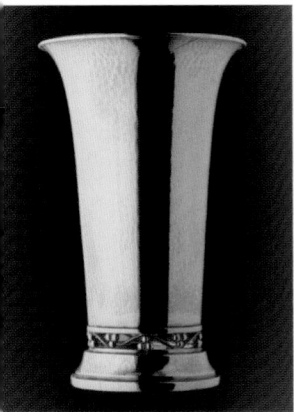

A Georg Jensen vase, design no.469B.

c1925　　　7in (18cm) high

$1,000-1,500　　　**SF**

A Georg Jensen water pitcher, designed by Johan Rohde, design no. 432, with ebony handle, designed 1920.

9.5in (24cm) high

$6,000-7,000　　　**SF**

A Georg Jensen Pyramid covered bowl, designed by Harold Nielson.

1928　　　6in (15.5cm) wide

$3,000-4,000　　　**SF**

A Georg Jensen Cactus serving dish, designed by Gundolph Albertus, design no.629, hammered finish.

c1930s　　　10in (25.5cm) wide

$4,500-6,500　　　**SF**

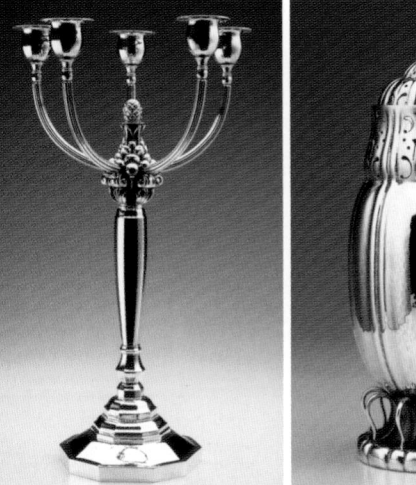

A Georg Jensen five-light Acorn candelabra, designed by Johan Rohde, design no.474.

c1930s　　　17in (43cm) high

$15,000-20,000　　　**SF**

A Georg Jensen sugar caster, design no.4.

5.5in (14cm) high

$4,500-5,500　　　**SF**

A Georg Jensen two-handled cigarette box, design no.829.

c1930s　　　8in (20.5in) wide

$22,000-28,000　　　**SF**

A Georg Jensen bowl, design no.778, with Grape foot.

c1930s　　　4.5in (11.5cm) high

$1,800-2,200　　　**SF**

A Georg Jensen side-handled dish, design by Harald Nielsen, design no.681.

c1930s　　　7in (18cm) wide

$4,000-5,000　　　**SF**

A Georg Jensen three-light candelabra, designed by Gundolph Albertus, design no.537C.

c1930s　　　9in (23cm) high

$4,500-5,500　　　**SF**

A Georg Jensen three-piece coffee set, designed by Sigvard Bernadotte, design no.1015, coffee pot with wicker handle.

1930s   9.5in (24cm) high

$6,000-7,000   SF

A single Georg Jensen candlestick, design no. 604B.

c1930s   3in (7.5cm) high

$2,200-2,800   SF

A small Georg Jensen caddy, designed by Sigvard Bernadotte, design no. 849.

c1930s   6in (15.5cm) high

$3,000-4,000   SF

A Georg Jensen bowl, designed by Harald Nielsen.

1930s   8in (20cm) diam

$3,000-4,000   SF

A Georg Jensen three-piece coffee set, design no.37, coffee pot and cream jug with ebony handles, hammered finish.

pre-1945   pot 8.75in (22cm) high

$4,000-5,000   SF

A Georg Jensen sauce boat, design no.896, with ebony handle.

c1940s   7in (18cm) wide

$1,800-2,200   SF

A Georg Jensen Louvre bowl, design no.180.
The bowl was named after the museum in Paris, France, when it purcased one for its collection.

pre-1945   6.75in (17.25cm)

$5,000-6,000   SF

A Georg Jensen fish platter, designed by Johan Rohde, design no.335.

pre-1945   18.5in (47cm) wide

$4,500-5,500   SF

A Georg Jensen centerpiece bowl, designed by Henning Koppel, design no. 7284.

pre-1945   13.75in (35cm) diam

$16,000-18,000   SF

Georg Jensen

A Georg Jensen selection of acorn servers, comprising;
A cheese plane

	8.25in (21cm) long

$1,500-2,000

A tomato server

	8.25in (21cm) long

$2,200-2,800

A set of salad servers

	9.5in (24cm) long

$1,500-2,000   **SF**

A large Georg Jensen cannister, design no.530.

c1940	8in (20.5cm) high

$7,500-8,500   **SF**

A Georg Jensen silver paper knife.

c1950	8in (20cm) long

$225-275   **JBS**

A Georg Jensen dish, design no. 620C.

	9.5in (24cm) wide

$900-1,100   **SF**

A Georg Jensen covered centerpiece vegetable tureen, designed by Henning Koppel, design no.1155.

c1950s	18in (45.75cm) wide

$30,000-40,000   **SF**

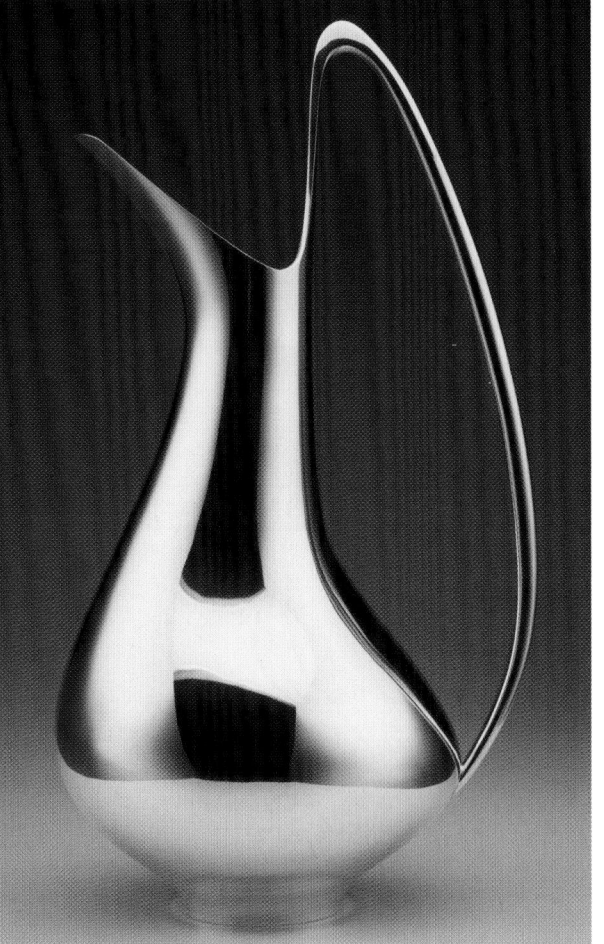

A Georg Jensen Goose water pitcher, by Henning Koppel, design no.1052.

c1950s	16.5in (42cm) high

$15,000-20,000   **SF**

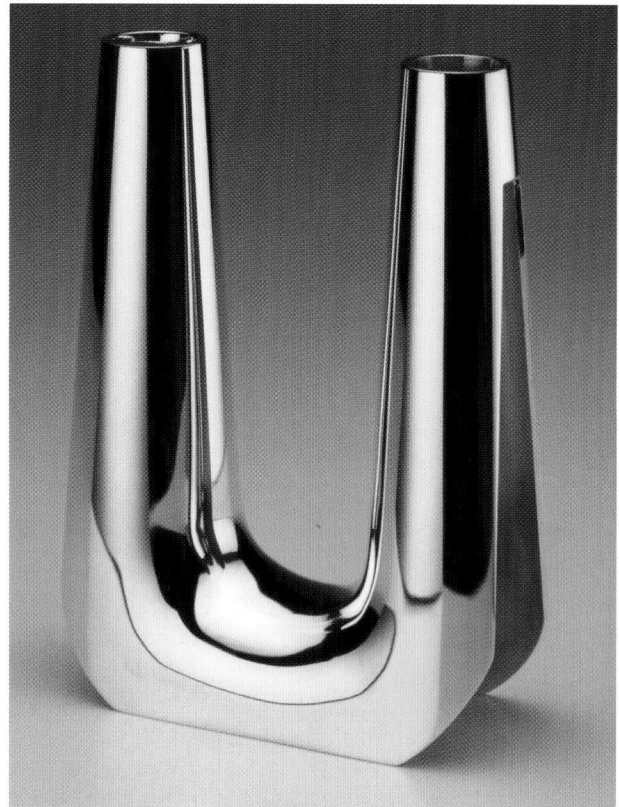

A Georg Jensen two-light candelabra, designed by Soren Jensen, design no.1087.

c1960s   7in (18cm) high

$4,500-5,500   **SF**

A Georg Jensen three-light candelabra, designed by Henning Koppel, design no.1075.

c1950s   10in (25.5cm) high

$10,000-12,000   **SF**

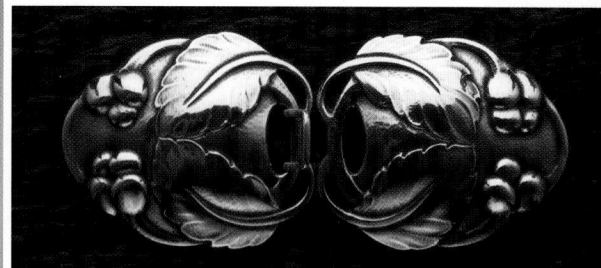

A Georg Jensen belt buckle.

c1906

$2,200-2,600   **SF**

A very rare Georg Jensen pin, set with three amber stones.

c1908

$4,000-5,000   **SF**

A Georg Jensen 18ct gold brooch, design no.172, with filigree work and pearls.

1920s   1.5in (4cm) wide

$2,200-2,800   **SF**

A Georg Jensen oval pin, with silver ball decoration, design no. 23.

c1908

$3,000-4,000   **SF**

A Georg Jensen cuff bracelet, design no. 55.

c1930s

$1,800-2,200   **SF**

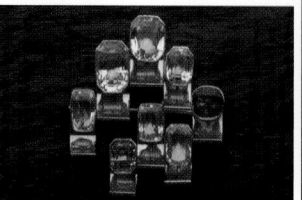

A Georg Jensen 18ct gold pin set with tourmalines.

c1960s

$6,000-7,000   **SF**

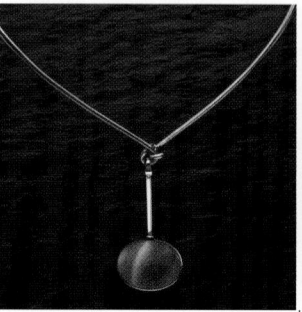

A Georg Jensen necklace, designed by Vivienne Bülow Torun.

1960s

$2,200-2,500   **SF**

A Georg Jensen 18ct gold bangle, designed by Nana Dizel.

1960s   3in diam

$3,500-4,000   **SF**

An Art Nouveau ring, set with four diamonds.

$600-700   **JHB**

A French Art Nouveau diamond set ring.

$900-1,100   **JHB**

► An Art Deco dress ring, claw-set with an emerald-cut amethyst, the stirrup-shaped shoulders each set with five diamonds enclosing a panel of carved jade, on a channeled white gold shank, signed "Boucheron, Paris".

stone 0.75 (2cm)

$3,000-4,000   **Duk**

An Art Deco platinum ring, set with emeralds and diamonds.

$5,000-6,000   **JHB**

An Art Deco platinum-set oblong ruby and diamond ring.

$4,000-5,000   **JHB**

An Art Deco-style yellow sapphire and diamond dress ring, set with a central emerald-cut yellow sapphire flanked on either side by a line of three brilliant-cut diamonds, on an 18ct yellow gold shank.

stone 0.5in (1.5cm)

$3,000-4,000   **Duk**

An Art Deco tourmaline, sapphire and diamond cluster ring, with a central circular-cut tourmaline enclosed by a band of onyx, with brilliant-cut diamonds and baguette-cut sapphires on a white metal shank.

setting 0.5in (1.5cm)

$1,500-2,000   **Duk**

◄ An Art Deco-style aquamarine and diamond dress ring, set with a a large rectangular-cut aquamarine, the shoulders set with baguette-cut diamonds, on a white metal shank.

stone 0.75in (2cm)

$1,300-1,600   **Duk**

A diamond and demantoid garnet-set dragonfly pin, with en tremblant wings and ruby-set eyes.

En tremblent is a type of setting where the central part of the piece is set on a spring to produce a trembling motion when the wearer moves.

An Art Nouveau silver pin, set with amethysts and moonstones.

c1920

$120-180   **PC**

An Art Deco diamond "bow" pin, set in white metal with numerous brilliant and circular-cut diamonds.

2in (5cm) wide

$3,500-4,500   **Duk**

$12,000-15,000   **L&T**

► An Art Deco-style emerald and diamond clip pin, with a central rectangular-cut emerald surrounded by numerous brilliant and baguette-cut diamonds.

2in (5cm) wide

$6,000-7,000   **Duk**

◄ An Art Deco pin, set with amethyst glass and marcasite.

c1925

$45-55   **PC**

Jewelry

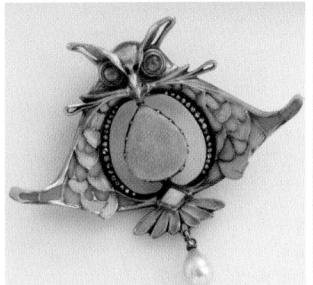

An Art Nouveau-style owl pin, with plique-à-jour enamel wings, an opal body and gold head.

c1970   3in (8cm) wide

$6,000-7,000   **NBlm**

A contemporary dragonfly clip, set with Madagascan sapphires and diamonds in an oxidized gold mount.

4in (10cm) wide

$22,000-26,000   **NBlm**

An Art Deco bracelet, with enamel silver panels, depicting Egyptian scenes divided by cornelian hoops.

c1920   7.75in (19.5cm) long

$900-1,100   **NBlm**

An Art Deco bracelet, set with diamonds (est 8ct), in platinum mounts.

$12,000-18,000   **JHB**

An Art Deco Cartier platinum charm bracelet.

c1925   (19.5cm)

$9,000-11,000   **NBlm**

A French Art Deco platinum, mixed-cut diamond (est 20ct) and carved emerald (est 25ct) bracelet.

c1925   7.75in (20cm)

$60,000-70,000   **NBlm**

An Austrian Art Deco 14ct gold bracelet, with domed onyx links.

c1930   7.25in (18.5cm)

$800-900   **NBlm**

An Art Deco-style diamond bracelet, with three principal pierced geometric panels, set with numerous brilliant-cut diamonds divided by subsidiary pierced "buckle" sections, set with brilliant and baguette-cut diamonds.

6.75in (17cm) long

$3,000-4,000   **Duk**

A set of three Art Nouveau plique-à-jour enamel choker panels, each with gold floral motifs.

c1900   13.75in (35cm) long

$22,000-24,000   **NBlm**

A French Art Nouveau silver locket, with amber glass.

$150-200   **PC**

A French Art Nouveau silver mirrored locket, with silver chain.

$225-275   **PC**

◄ A 20thC multi-strand small cultured pearl necklace, with jade and diamond Art Deco clasp.

15.75in (40cm) long

$4,500-5,500   **NBlm**

► A pair of Art Deco aquamarine and diamond drop earrings, each set with an emerald-cut aquamarine within a border of circular-cut diamonds.

2in (5cm) long

$2,200-2,500   **Duk**

ARCHIBALD KNOX (1864-1933), a designer from the Isle of Man, was a pioneer of the Celtic interpretation of the Arts and Crafts and Art Nouveau Movements. His Tudric ware designs for Liberty & Co. epitomized this style with decoration of entrelac motifs, vitreous enamels and stylized leaves and flower heads.

An Archibald Knox Tudric pewter tea service, for Liberty & Co, each piece cast with whiplash foliage and fruiting buds on a hammered ground, comprising a teapot, two hot water jugs, a milk jug, a sugar bowl and a twin-handled tray, stamped marks Tudric 0231.

water jug 9in (23cm) high

$1,800-2,200   **L&T**

One of a pair of Archibald Knox Tudric pewter glass holders, each diagonally pierced and cast with entwined foliage and leaves, stamped marks 0534.

3in (7.5cm) high

$90-120 (pair)   **L&T**

An Archibald Knox Tudric pewter jug, with hinged lid and large thumbpiece, the body cast with stylized leafy plants, stamped mark 0967.

6.25in (16cm) high

$150-200   **L&T**

An Archibald Knox Tudric beaker holder, cast with stylized whiplash frieze, stamped marks 0324, later glass liner.

2.75in (7cm) high

$2,200-2,800   **L&T**

A Tudric pewter inkwell, the sides decorated with applied buds, stamped marks 021.

3.75in (9.5cm) high

$220-280   **L&T**

An Archibald Knox Tudric pewter tazza, the bowl pierced and cast with flowerheads, on three shaped supports and circular base, stamped marks 0276, liner lacking.

5in (13cm) high

$200-300   **L&T**

An Archibald Knox Tudric pewter biscuit barrel and cover, cast with a chequer pattern of stylized leaves and flowers, stamped marks 0194.

4.75in (12cm) wide

$800-900   **L&T**

An Archibald Knox Tudric plate, cast with whiplash foliage and seedheads, with a central enameled panel, stamped marks 0162.

8.75in (22cm) diam

$750-850   **L&T**

A pair of Archibald Knox Tudric pewter vases, each of bullet form with three applied brackets, cast with a frieze of stylized flowerheads, stamped marks 0226.

7.25in (18.5cm) high

$900-1,100   **L&T**

◄ A pair of Tudric pewter spill vases, of waisted cylindrical form, with applied wrythen handles, inset with turquoise stones, stamped marks 030.

7.25in (18.5cm) high

$300-350   **L&T**

An Archibald Knox Tudric pewter twin-handled bowl, the pierced sides cast with stylized leaves and tendrils, stamped marks 0320, liner lacking.

9in (23cm) diam

$150-200 **L&T**

An Orivit Art Nouveau pewter liqueur set, comprising a pewter-mounted bottle-shaped decanter, cut with sinuous tendrils, a set of four glasses and a shaped twin-handled tray, stamped marks.

decanter 8.75in (22cm) high

$350-400 **L&T**

A WMF pewter siphon stand, in Art Nouveau style, with tendril handles, pierced and embossed with leaves, impressed marks.

8in (20.5cm) high

$200-250 **LFA**

A pewter inkwell, cast in the form of a grotesque bird, with ceramic body, stamped marks.

4.5in (11cm) high

$500-600 **L&T**

A pewter tankard with applied turquoise roundels, stamped Germany.

3.5in (9cm) high

$450-550 **L&T**

An unusual pewter box and cover, the lid with four applied enamel panels, the sides with applied pairs of cast panels with scroll motifs, stamped marks 0165.

$225-275 **L&T**

Pewter inkwell made by Ramsden and Carr, inscribed around rim "I was wrought for E.N. by desire of R.E. and V.M.K. to mark her wedding day 1916, on base: "Omar Ramsden et Alwyn Carr me fecerunt".

1916 15.5cm diam

$1,200-1,400 **JBS**

◀ A Scottish School wrought iron-framed standing clock, the single train movement with arched rectangular copper dial, repoussé-decorated with stylized flowerheads and seedpods with whiplash foliage, enclosing a circular dial and set with green enamel, on a beaten ground, the case with arched hood and wrought finials above the square section uprights with swollen knops, linked by an oval lower stretcher and terminating in pad feet to the front and curved brackets to the rear.

67.5in (171cm) high

$6,000-8,000 **L&T**

A Roycroft hammered copper squat vessel, original patina, orb and cross mark.

6.5in (16.5cm) wide

$650-750 | **CR**

A fine Marie Zimmermann hammered copper flaring vase, lobed body, cleaned patina, a few minor dents to body and bends to rim, die-stamped mark.

10.75in (27cm) high

$500-600 | **CR**

Two Gustav Stickley hammered copper bowls, cast, riveted feet and rolled rim, some cleaning to patina, unmarked.

largest 7in (17.5cm) diam

$700-800 | **CR**

A Glasgow School copper frame, repoussé-decorated with pomegranates, with rivetted straps to the angles.

30.5in (77cm) wide

$1,000-1,500 | **L&T**

Two small Tiffany Studios patinated bronze trays, each cast with radiating ribs and serrated rim, intaglio finish, both impressed TIFFANY STUDIOS/NEW YORK.

1899-1928 5.75in (14.5cm) diam

$300-400 | **SI**

▶ A brass and copper spirit kettle and stand, designed by Christopher Dresser for Benham and Froud, raised above a burner and supported by a wrought-iron stand with wrythen tendril decoration and tripod base, with copper weight, stamped factory marks.

30in (76cm) high

$1,100-1,400 | **L&T**

One of a set of four Roycroft hammered copper vessels, each with stamped Roycroft logo, comprising a vase, two dishes with concave rims and one small patinated copper dish, the cylindrical vase banded with a silver geometric pattern.

Vase 6.5in (16.5cm) high

$1,300-1,600 (set) | **SI**

A Weiner Werkstatte white metal flower vase, designed by Joseph Hoffman, of rectilinear outline and latticed basket construction with loop handle, separate glass liner, stamped monogram and factory marks.

9.5in (24cm high)

$3,500-4,500 | **L&T**

▶ A WMF white metal liquor set, modeled as a figure holding a drum-shaped receptacle with a cut glass decanter and stopper (not pictured), the batwing-shaped base molded with six wells for drinking glasses, wear throughout, lacking three glasses.

9in (23cm) high

$350-450 | **BonS**

A WMF Art Nouveau electroplated jardinière, cast as a lily pond, with applied leaves and lizard and surmounted to the rim with the figure of a mermaid on a conch shell, impressed marks.

12.25in (31cm) high

$1,200-1,600   L&T

A WMF patinated bronze bottle vase, engraved with leafy branches on a verdigris ground, stamped mark.

10.25 (26cm) high

$150-200   L&T

A Continental white metal goblet and cover, the cover with applied decorative straps and with beaded and cagework finial, the body supported to the turned stem with similar straps, on a circular beaded base with rivetted bracket supports, stamped Dutch import marks.

14.75in (37.5cm) high

$450-550   L&T

A wrought-iron twin-handled jardinière, in the manner of the Guild of Handicrafts, with scrolling rim and applied spiralling and twisted open handles.

13.5in (39cm) wide

$300-400   L&T

A late 19thC ornate French cast iron coal bin, of tapered oval form with shell and mask decorated hinged lid and cast makers mark "Godin - Lemeire a Guise, Aisne".

15.75in (40cm) wide

$500-600   L&T

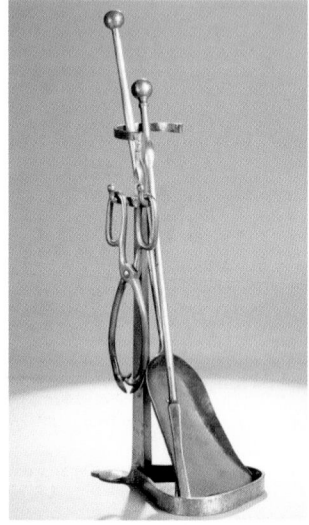

A steel fireside companion set, designed by Sir Robert Lorimer and made by Thomas Hadden, the tapering column with scrolled support for poker and ash shovel, with applied hooks for oval nippers, the shaped and galleried base tray with shaped foot.

20.5in (52cm) high

$1,200-1,600   L&T

An Art Nouveau brass standard lamp, the turned adjustable column with armed brackets, the base with applied brackets cast with whiplash tendrils and flowers.

64in (163cm) high

$650-750   L&T

A Continental gilt-metal and champlevé enamel table jewelry casket, the rectangular stepped lid with inset pietra dura panel of birds on a branch, folding side handles, the whole with applied champleve enamel mounts, velvet lined interior.

9in (30cm) wide

$2,500-3,000   L&T

A late 19thC brass helmet-shaped coal scuttle, with pressed Neo-classical decoration, hinged lid, raised handle centered by turned ebony grip and integral shovel with similar handle.

18in (46cm) high

$750-850   L&T

An Austrian Art Nouveau brass and copper chamber candlestick, the broad drip tray above four knopped supports, on spreading square section base, with applied handle.

6.75in (17cm) high

$500-600   L&T

◀ A late 19thC repoussé brass coal bin, a drum-form decorated with cartouches with griffin supporters and lion mask ring handles.

19cm (48cm) diam

$900-1,100   L&T

Metalware

An Art Nouveau brass-mounted inkwell, the iridescent pink glass reservoir with pierced waterlily and whiplash foliate cage, surmounted by a molded hinged lid.

3.25in (8cm) across

$225-275   **L&T**

An Art Nouveau brass and luster glass inkwell, the base cast as a lily pad surmounted by a lustrous pink glass reservoir, with cast flowerbud lid.

3.5in (9cm) high

$450-550   **L&T**

A Scottish School brass jardinière, with broad repoussé-decorated rim, the sides with opposing stylized floral panels and opposing mottled turquoise roundels.

9in (23cm) wide

$650-750   **L&T**

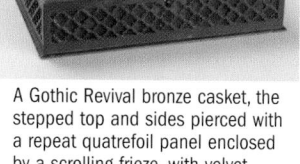

A Gothic Revival bronze casket, the stepped top and sides pierced with a repeat quatrefoil panel enclosed by a scrolling frieze, with velvet-lined interior.

8.75in (22cm) wide

$150-200   **L&T**

An Arts and Crafts copper box, the hinged lid with strapwork decoration centered by a peacock iridescent roundel, the sides set with similar roundels, the angles supporting riveted brackets.

8in (20cm) wide

$450-550   **L&T**

A Huntley & Palmer painted biscuit tin, in the form of an Arts and Crafts lantern, stamped marks.

9.5in (24cm) high

$100-140   **L&T**

A pair of late 19thC American Aesthetic Movement brass and forged steel andirons, in the form of leaf-capped, twist-turned Corinthian columns rising from a diaperwork Romanesque columns.

Provenance: *The Society of the Cincinnati*

38in (96.5cm) high

A 19thC enameled desk set, comprising an inkpot and two dwarf candlesticks.

$70-120   **AS&S**

$4,500-5,000   **SI**

A white metal inkwell, in the form of a spaniel's head, with a hinged mouth, on oak footed base, stamped WWH & Co.

$60-90   **AS&S**

An Arts and Crafts brass and copper casket, the lid with riveted decoration centered by a rainbow enamel panel below lattice tree motif, the sides with branch motifs, the angles with riveted supports, lined interior.

4in (10cm) wide

$250-300   **L&T**

CLOCKS

A French Art Nouveau gilt-metal mantel clock, the twin-train movement with circular porcelain dial painted with poppies enclosed within a waisted case, cast with flowers and a central panel of a maiden in a garden.

15.75in (40cm) high

$400-500   **L&T**

A Liberty pewter clock, shaped lozenge outline, embossed with stylized Arabic numerals and inlaid with abalone panels, the shaped hands similarly inlaid, minute hand missing.

An American Arts and Crafts oak longcase clock, the single-train movement with square oak dial and applied brass numerals, enclosed within case with four square section supports and with slats to the sides and back above an astragal glazed door enclosing a shelf.

78.5in (199cm) high

$1,000-1,400   **L&T**

An Art Nouveau patinated bronze mantel clock, the single-train movement with circular silvered dial, the broadly tapering case cast with tendrils above a shaped opening enclosing a seated fairy in diaphanous robes.

11in (28cm) high

$650-750   **L&T**

10.5in (26.5cm) high

$12,000-15,000   **L&T**

BRONZES

► A Glasgow-style brass wall clock, the circular dial repoussé-decorated with a band of entwined thorny branches and roses, with repoussé-decorated weights and pendulum.

A bronze group of reveling Bachante, by Claude Michael Clodion.

A bronze figure, cast as the Callipygian Venus, after the Antique, on a turning base.

16.5in (41.5cm) diam

$1,500-2,000   **L&T**

c1800   10.5in (27cm) high

$3,000-3,500   **RGA**

c1820   17in (44cm) high

$2,200-2,800   **Gro**

A 19thC bronze figure group, cast as two naked male wrestlers, after the Antique, with verdigris patination.

17.75in (45cm) high

$3,000-3,500 **L&T**

A mid-19thC bronze figure, cast as a convivial friar, possibly doubling as a night-light, with detachable tonsure to fill reservoir, on a later yew socle.

10.5in (26.5cm) high

$1,200-1,600 **RGA**

A large bronze figure, David and the head of Goliath, by Marcus Jean Antoin Mercié (1845-1916).

37in (94cm) high

$12,000-14,000 **RGA**

A finely detailed bronze figure, cast as the returning fisherman with net and gaff, with original parcel gilding.

870 6in (15cm) high

$1,200-1,500 **RGA**

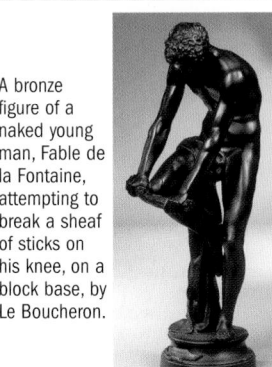

A bronze figure, "Pandora Assise", after Eugene Aizelin (1821-1902), incised "Aizelin", foundry mark of F Barbedienne, Achille Collas reduction mecanique seal.

c1870 17.75in (45cm) high

$3,500-4,500 **Gro**

RUSSIAN HENRI TRODOUX was born in St Petersberg of French parents and trained and worked in the city between 1835-55, in particular on the decoration of the Winter Palace. He later moved to France and exhibited works at the Salon during the 1870s.

A bronze figure of a naked young man, Fable de la Fontaine, attempting to break a sheaf of sticks on his knee, on a block base, by Le Boucheron.

35in (89cm) high

$3,200-3,800 **L&T**

A bronze figure, cast as a classical lady with her jewel casket, after Trodoux and incised "Trodoux", with dark brown and green patina.

c1870 13.75in (35cm) high

$1,500-2,000 **Gro**

A 20thC cast of a bronze bust, "Buste de jeune fille souriante", after Jean Antoine Injalbert (1845-1933), signed "A Injalbert", foundry stamp of Siot, Paris.

19.75in (50cm) high

$3,000-3,500 **Gro**

A bronze bust, entitled "Suson", by Auguste Rodin, signed and inscribed.

c1890 10.75in 27cm high

$20,000-25,000 **RGA**

Bronzes

A bronze panel of a maiden in profile, by Charles Pierre van der Stappen (1843-1910) "For Auld lang Syne" signed and with foundry marks.

The foundry mark is "J Petermann Fondeur Bruxelles". An identical plaque is fitted above one of the chimneypieces in the members room of the Glasgow Art Club at 185 Bath Street, Glasgow. The club was extended in 1890 under the stewardship of the well known firm of Honeyman and Keppie for whom Charles Rennie Mackintosh was working. Mackintosh was largely responsible for the interiors of this room.

30.75in (78cm) high

| $2,000-3,000 | L&T |

A Charles Raphael Peyre bronze of an Assyrian maiden, partly gilded with verdigris patination, the semi-clothed figure with long skirt and peacock headdress, holding a snake and leaning on a hermed pedestal, raised on a later-stepped marble plinth.

Verdigris *is the green powdery deposit that forms naturally on the surface of brass and copper. It is also produced artificially and used as a pigment.*

40in (102cm) high

| $6,500-7,500 | L&T |

A bronze of "The Dying Gaul", after the Antique, on a shaped marble plinth and inscribed Chiaruzzi, Naples.

21.5in (55cm) wide

| $4,000-4,500 | L&T |

An early 20thC bronze figure of male tobogganist, lying prone on his sledge. mounted on a quartz rock.

6.25in (16cm)

| $900-1,200 | L&T |

Three early 20thC bronzed figures of mountaineers, in various poses climbing a quartz rock.

6in (15cm) high

| $750-850 | L&T |

An Art Deco bronze bust of Beethovan, by M. Temporal, signed on the bronze with La Stele foundry mark.

19.5in (50cm) high

| $1,300-1,600 | L&T |

A bronze figure of Salome holding a sword, by Charles Levy, on a plinth base.

34in (86cm) high

| $5,500-6,500 | L&T |

A pair of American early 20thC patinated bronze figural bookends, each modeled as a putto leaning against drapery.

5in (12.5cm) high

| $450-500 | SI |

A bronze figure of a Pierrot, entitled "Au Clair de la Lune", by Bouret.

19.25in (49cm) high

| $2,500-3,000 | L&T |

A bronze bust of a child, by E. Whitney Smith, on a verde antico marble base, signed and dated.

1923   13in (33.5cm) high

| $1,200-1,500 | L&T |

A bronze figure, cast as a recumbent terrier, with good detail and rich brown patination, raised on a rectangular base, by Demas.

c1840   4.25in (11cm) high

$1,000-1,400   **RGA**

A bronze figure, cast as a tethered dog, by Christophe Fratin, signed and with Vittoz foundry inscription.

c1840   5.5in (14cm) high

$2,500-3,000   **RGA**

A bronze figure, cast as a recumbent dog.

c1840   6.75in (17cm) wide

$600-700   **Gro**

A small bronze figure group, cast as a farmyard scene, by Paul Comolera, stamped with his foundry mark.

1818-1897   5in (12.5cm) high

$1,500-1,800   **RGA**

A bronze figure group, cast as a boy with his horse, by Arthur Waagen. 1833-1898

9.5in (24cm) high

$5,000-6,000   **RGA**

A 19thC bronze, cast as an ostrich hunt, by Alfred Dubucand.

14in (36cm) high

$6,000-7,000   **RGA**

A 19thC bronze figure, cast as a crowing cockerel, on a marble base, by Emmanuel Fremiet.

5.75in (14.5cm) high

$750-850   **RGA**

A 19thC bronze portrait group of a family of deer, entitled "Cerf, Biche et Faon" , by Antoine L Barye, with seal mark.

Antoine-Louis Barye *was one of the finest sculptors of the French Animalier school. Barye's animal figures are characterized by violent movement and tense stances.*

9.25in (23.5cm) high

$15,000-20,000   **RGA**

A pair of 19thC seal bronzes, modeled as bulls entitled "un taureau cadre" and "un taureau se defendant", by Antoine L Barye.

8.75in (22.25cm) high

$30,000-40,000   **RGA**

A bronze cast of a standing basset, with rich green patination, by Antoine L Barye, signed with Barbedienne foundry stamp.

1870   6in (15.5cm) wide

$7,500-8,500   **RGA**

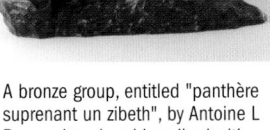

A bronze group, entitled "panthère suprenant un zibeth", by Antoine L Barye, signed and inscribed with the Peyrol foundry mark.

c1870   12.5in (31.5cm) high

$15,000-20,000   **RGA**

Bronzes

A bronze standing pheasant, with good color and detail, by Antoine L Barye, signed and inscribed F Barbedienne.

1870   4.75in (12cm) high

$4,000-5,000   **RGA**

An Austrian bronze owl, with glass eyes, perched on a book with hinged lid.

9in (23cm) high

$1,200-1,500   **DN**

A bronze paperweight, cast as a recumbent putti, in the manner of Francoise Dequesnoy.

c1860   5in (13.5cm) long

$700-800   **RGA**

A bronze setter and rabbit, by Jules Moigniez, on an oval and naturalistic base.

c1870   8in (20cm) high

$4,000-5,000   **RGA**

A French gilt bronze, "lion qui marche", with intricate detail, raised on a rectangular naturalistic base, signed Jules Moigniez.

c1870   3in (8cm) high

$750-850   **RGA**

ISIDORE JULES BONHEUR was born in 1827. The Hippolyte Peyrol, founded by his brother-in-law, cast the majority of his works and these bronzes are of exceptionally good quality. Bonheur became part of the group of late 19thC animal sculptors known as "Les Animaliers". Although Bonheur made studies of many animals, he will always be revered for his horse sculptures. This is one of the earliest and most important Polo sculptures of the 19thC. It exhibits exceptional anatomical accuracy and has captured the spirit of the animal. As such this is an extremely rare and highly sought after piece.

A pair of bird groups, by Jules Moigniez, with fine detail and rich golden patina.

c1870   9.75in (25cm) high

$7,500-8,500   **RGA**

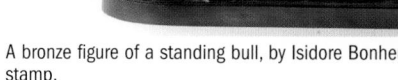

A bronze figure of a standing bull, by Isidore Bonheur with Peyrol foundry stamp.

c1870   15.25 (39cm) high

$15,000-18,000   **RGA**

A pair of bronze figures of huntsmen on horseback, by John Willis Good, signed and dated.

1874   11.75in (30cm) high

$20,000-25,000   **RGA**

A bronze group of a mounted polo player, by Isidore Bonheur, signed and with Peyrol foundry stamp.

c1875   13in (33cm) high

$30,000-35,000   **RGA**

A bronze, cast as a pointer guarding game by a tree stump, by Pierre Jules Mêne, signed.

1850   11in (28cm) high

$11,000-14,000   RGA

A superb quality figure, cast as a King Charles spaniel, by Pierre Jules Mêne, on naturalistic carpet base.

c1860   3in (8.5cm) high

$2,500-3,000   RGA

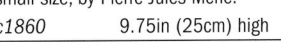

A bronze figure, "Vanquer de Derby", cast as a horse and jockey, of rare small size, by Pierre Jules Mêne.

c1860   9.75in (25cm) high

$10,000-12,000   RGA

A bronze cast of a cow suckling a young calf, by Pierre Jules Mêne.

c1860   8.75in (22cm) high

$10,000-12,000   RGA

A bronze figure, cast as a seated griffin, highly detailed with rich brown patination, signed Pierre Jules Mêne.

The griffin is not widely known but was one of the foremost hunting breeds in 19th century Europe.

1860   7in (17.5cm) high

$3,000-3,500   RGA

A rare and unusual bronze figure, cast as a standing ewe, on a naturalistic base, signed Pierre Jules Mêne.

1864

$4,500-5,500   RGA

A bronze figure, "Chien Braque Seul", cast as a small pointer, by Pierre Jules Mêne.

c1870   3.5in (9cm) high

$1,300-1,600   RGA

A bronze figure, "Fabio", cast as a retriever, by Pierre Jules Mêne.

c1870   7in (17cm) high

$4,000-5,000   RGA

▶ A bronze figure, "Sylphe", cast as a setter, with rubbed brown patina and excellent detail on a naturalistic base, signed Pierre Jules Mêne.

c1870 8.5in (21.5cm) high

$4,500-5,500   RGA

A bronze group, cast as a pair of hunting dogs, by Pierre Jules Mêne, signed.
c1870   5.75in (14.5cm) high

$2,500-3,000   RGA

A late 19thC Coalbrookdale bronze, "Djinn, cheval à la barrière", by Pierre Jules Mêne.

11.75in (30cm) high

$6,000-7,000   RGA

Bronzes

A bronze figure of a stallion, on a naturalistically cast base, inscribed "H and C Macarty 9787".

13.5in (34cm) high

$2,000-2,500   **DN**

An bronze eagle, "Aigle les Ailes étendues se ouvsry", by Antoine L Barye, from the Barbedienne foundry.

c1900

$6,500-7,500   **RGA**

A small bronze figure of a bull, with the Barbedienne foundry stamp.

c1880   5.5in (14cm) high

$1,200-1,600   **RGA**

An unusual bronze figure of a pigeon, by Eugene Delaplance.

c1880   10.5in 27cm high

$4,500-5,500   **RGA**

A bronze figure of two hunting dogs, by Prosper Lecourtier.

c1889   24in (61cm) high

$15,000-20,000   **RGA**

An Austrian cold-painted bronze bull with lowered head.

c1900   2in (5.3cm) high

$750-850   **RGA**

A bronze figure of a reclining deerm, by Clovis Masson.

c1900   5.5in (14cm) high

$1,100-1,400   **RGA**

An Austrian cold-painted bronze figure of a bird.

c1920   0.75in (2cm) high

$250-300   **RGA**

An excellent bronze figure of a bear, entitled "ours assis", by Georges Gardet , signed and with Delaville foundry stamp and number.

c1900   7in (17.5cm) high

$3,000-3,500   **RGA**

A 20thC "standing elephant" from the Bermann foundry in Austria, with fine quality naturalistic cold-painted detail, this is the original casting model.

c1920   5in (13cm) high

$1,500-2,000   **RGA**

A cold-painted bronze inkwell, in the form of a stag's head mounted on a bed of oak leaves, the hinged face enclosing small ceramic well.

6.25in (16cm) high

$900-1,100   **L&T**

A bronze of a Native American on horseback, with rich-brown, olive-green, mid-brown and golden patinas, by Edouard Droust with Etling foundry stamp.

c1910   20.75in (53cm) high

$7,500-8,500   **RGA**

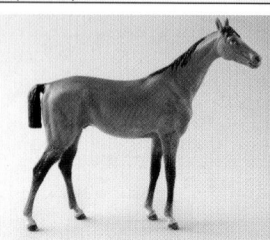

A "small standing horse" from the Bermann foundry in in Austria, with fine quality cold-painted detail, original casting model.

c1920   5.5in (14cm) high

$1,200-1,600   **RGA**

An P. Phillipe Art Nouveau patinated bronze figure, entitled "Le Reveil", cast as a naked girl stretching, raised on faceted onyx base and signed on the base.

15.5in (39.5cm) high

$750-850   **L&T**

The Art Deco years saw the rebirth of bronze sculpture, and it became an art form for the masses. Women are the most common subjects, often represented as Amazonian or athletic. Also frequently featured are futuristic or theatrical figures, sporting subjects and children. Erotic figures are particularly collectable. Figures are usually signed, however, there are many fakes on the market. Genuine sculptures will show natural signs of wear, being not too bright or too rusty.

▲ **1** A bronzed Art Deco table lamp, cast as a naked girl reclining and holding a vessel, with frosted glass fan shaped shade behind, held in a bronze frame, the whole raised on onyx base.

17in (43cm) long

$800-1,000

▲ **2** A bronzed Art Deco table lamp, cast as a naked girl, holding aloft a glass globe, raised on a spherical marble base on a plinth.

32in (82cm) high

$1,200-1,600   **L&T**

An painted bronze and ivory Art Deco figure, mounted on an onyx-cased clock.

9.75in (25cm) long

$5,000-6,000   **L&T**

A 1920s Gerda Iro Gerdago patinated and painted bronze and ivory figure, cast as a dancer.

14.5in (37cm) high

$7,000-8,000   **L&T**

▶ **1** An H Kerk bronze and ivory figure, cast as an exotic dancer, her tunic colored in blue and red enamels, on a circular base supported by three crouching elephants with ivory tusks, signed on the base.

12in (31cm) high

$1,500-2,000

▶ **2** A bronze and ivory figure, cast as a young girl, dressed as a Pierrette on an oval stepped plinth, signed on foot, one hand lacking and the other with some damage.

9.75in (25cm) high

$150-200

▶ **3** A silvered brass and ivory figure, cast as a young woman standing and raised on a stepped square section onyx plinth.

$2,500-3,500   **L&T**

An Art Deco ivory figure, carved as a naked female figure with arms outstretched, raised above a stepped onyx base.

5.75in (14.5cm) high

$400-500   **L&T**

Bronze and Ivory Figures

A patinated bronze Art Deco figure group, cast as a lady in flowing dress flanked by two hounds, raised on green and white stepped onyx base, signed on the base.

28in (73cm) wide

$3,500-4,000	L&T

A pair of Art Deco bronze bookends, each cast as a seal balancing an onyx ball on its nose, raised on a stepped triangular base.

5in (12.8cm) high

$200-250	L&T

A pair of Pierre Laurel bronze figures, entitled "Autumn and Spring Dancers" , cast as dancing girls wearing diaphanous tunics, one holding flowers in her hands, the other grapes, on stepped demi-lune onyx bases, signed P Laurel.

Tallest 11in (28cm) high

$3,000-3,500	L&T

A CLOSER LOOK AT BRONZE AND IVORY FIGURES

The Art Deco movement brought about a renaissance in sculpture at the beginning of the 20thC with pieces being mass-produced for the first time. France, Germany and Austria were the main centers of production and the greatest designers included Ferdinand Preiss, Demetre Chiparus, Claire-Jeanne-Roberte Colinet, Marcel Bouraine, Joseph Lorenzl and Bruno Zach.

The most common subject for these artists were athletic – even Amazonian – women, often shown performing "modern activities" such as smoking and playing sport, dancers, as Diana the Hunter, or in erotic poses. Sporting poses, animals, children and historical figures were also created, although the latter are not so highly sought after today.

The main materials used were bronze or a mixture of bronze and ivory known as chryselephantine which became popular in the 1920s. Chryselephantine figures lead the market today, and fetch more than figures made from bronze or ivory alone. As a general rule, the more ivory in the figure, the higher its value.

The bronze was often patinated: gilt and silver were popular, and green was the most common color. Bases were usually made from green onyx, black slate or cream marble.

Condition is of paramount importance when buying bronze and ivory figures. Ivory dries out as it ages, leaving behind hairline cracks and fissures, particularly on the figures' faces, and the patinated and enameled bronze often becomes rubbed and scratched.

Most figures by the German artist Ferdinand Preiss (1882-1943) are made from chryselephantine, although he did make a few all-ivory ones. On this patinated bronze and ivory figure, entitled "Stile" (above right), both the ivory and bronze are in perfect condition. Otherwise the value would reduce by 25 percent. The subject also has a lovely 1930s period look and the face is beautifully modeled, adding to the appeal.

Preiss figures are usually less than 14in (35.5cm) high and are always anatomically correct.

Most figures bear the PK monogram (from the Preiss-Kassler foundry where they were made) and the signature F. Preiss.

Parts were carved separately before being screwed to the bronze and finished.

Genuine bases, made from green and/or black Brazilian onyx, sometimes banded with black Belgian slate, are of simple form.

A Ferdinand Preiss patinated bronze and ivory figure, entitled "Stile".

$20,000-25,000	L&T

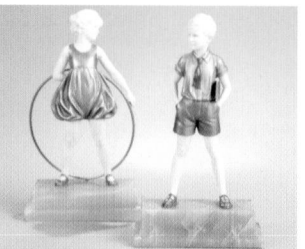

A pair of Ferdinand Preiss patinated bronze and ivory figures, Hoop Girl and Sonny Boy, raised on molded green onyx plinths, with etched signature on plinths.

8.5in (21.5cm) high

$7,000-8,000	L&T

A Ferdinand Preiss patinated bronze and ivory figure, entitled "Lighter than air".

This figure has its original glass ball. They are very easily broken and so have often been replaced.

$9,000-11,000	L&T

► A Joseph Lorenzl bronze figure, cast as a young girl in a shawl and tunic playing a mandolin, on a circular base and faceted pink marble plinth, marked on the base "Lorenzl 5113-5".

A Le Verrier patinated bronze figural lamp base, cast a naked female holding aloft a light fitting and standing on a stepped circular base with green marble plinth, signed in bronze.

An Joseph Lorenzl Austrian Art Deco gilt bronze figure, cast as stylized dancer, on onyx base, signed .

13in (34cm) high	18.5in (47cm) high	12.25in (31cm) high
$3,500-4,500 RGA	$1,200-1,800 L&T	$1,200-1,500 L&T

MISCELLANEOUS

► A Liberty & Co compostition sundial, the later brass gnomon and dial above top cast with owls and inscriptions East, West, North & South, above a facetted column with scrolling brackets, the base cast with the legend "Time is but a shadow that shall cease - Eternity will bring us perfect peace", bears cast mark Designed and manufactured by Liberty & Co.

An Arts and Crafts oak jewelry casket, with mother-of-pearl inlay, the interior fitted with three lift-out trays.

A set of six William De Morgan earthenware tiles, each painted with red luster with flowering foliage, and set into walnut firescreen frame.

9in (22.5cm) wide	Each tile 8in (20.5cm) sq	44.5in (113cm) high
$400-450 L&T	$1,500-2,000 L&T	$1,800-2,400 L&T

Blackthorn, a watercolor design for wallpaper by Morris & Company, numbered 6516, and marked in pencil with a list of color variations, inscribed on the reverse "Blackthorn 32 Morris & Co Merton Abbey Works Surrey", bearing two company stamps for Morris and Company 17 George Street, Hanover Square.
Provenance: Arthur Halcrow Verstage, Godalming, Surrey.

William Morris (1834-96) was a foundation stone of the British Arts and Crafts Movement. A designer, writer, romantic socialist and printer, he was a major campaigner for the crafts revival and deeply opposed to factory production. He co-founded Morris, Marshall, Faulker & Co in 1861 and it made furniture and furnishings for domestic interiors until 1940 (the company was renamed Morris & Co in 1875).

His fame as a designer is based on his carpet, textile and wallpaper designs, which show a complete understanding of the nature of pattern and its creation.

40in (101.5cm) wide
$60,000-70,000   L&T

MODERN CLASSICS Furniture

MODERN DESIGN HAS ONLY BECOME POPULAR WITHIN THE LAST 10 OR 20 YEARS, and as a result is viewed as a very young market within the antiques trade. However, it is an area that is continuing to expand year by year, and we could see it reaching its full potential within the next couple of decades.

Modern design tends to attract a younger generation than traditional antiques; main buyers are under 40 and often involved in arts and media circles.

Within this market, buyers' tastes have a tendency to follow current fashion trends. However, in recent years, those who have been following the market for some time have started to become more educated and informed, and as a result are becoming more selective in what they buy. This allows the market to mature by developing alongside the tastes of the customer base.

The buyers' market is still quite conservative when it comes to Modern design. There is a tendency to opt for "safer" pieces, which echo the values of traditional antiques, such as good craftsmanship, functionality and use of natural materials. This accounts for the popularity of many Modern Scandinavian designers.

As a rule, innovative designers such as Le Corbusier, Charles Eames and Alvar Aalto always sell well. However, there have been a number of developments this year, which may help predict how the market will advance in the near future. The American market is beginning to show an interest in Post-war British designers. Particular emphasis is given to early 50s furniture by Robin Day and 40s pieces by Ernest Race. The popularity of Scandinavian designers will also continue, with names such as Arne Jacobsen, Hans Wegner, Hans Brattrud, Poal Kjaerholm and Yrjo Kukkapuro leading the field. This is likely to be reflected in the retail market by the availability of reproduction furniture.

Judging by present interior trends, the demand for Perspex furniture will also be high, although this may fade once the current fashion has run its course.

In glassware, Tapio Wirkkala will remain very collectable, as will good quality Italian glass such as Venini & Co. Czechoslovakian glass has a huge growing potential, which has yet to be tapped into; it could be one of *the* areas to look out for this year.

FURNITURE

ALVAR AALTO (1898-1976), a Finnish architect and designer, is considered one of the great pioneers of 20thC design. His designs, although distinctly Modernist in approach, also displayed a marked sensitivity to the environment which they inhabited. In his furniture, this can be seen in his use of natural materials such as laminated birch plywood, which he felt more sympathetic to the human condition, than other more modern materials

- Studied Architecture at the Helsinki Polytechnic, Finland, from 1916-1921.
- Designed both the building and interiors for the Paimio Sanitorium for Tuberculosis in Finland from 1929-1933.
- Patented a method for bending wood for stools, used famously in his "Stacking Stool" in 1933.
- Set up the company Artek to manufacture and distribute his furniture designs in 1935.
- Designed a range of vases for the Savoy restaurant in Turku, Finland, in 1937.

One of a set of four Alvar Aalto stools, retailed by Finmar Ltd, each having round seat with ebonized edging, on three L-shaped plywood uprights.

$530-600 (set)   **BonBay**

An Alvar Aalto "No.31" chair, the paimio painted molded plywood seat on laminated birch cantilever frame, designed 1931-32.

$2,000-2,400   **BonBay**

A Jacques Adnes nest of tables, produced by C.A.F., the tinted mirror glass top on chrome-plated steel base.
c1930

$4,000-4,500   **BonBay**

A set of four Gijs Bakker slatted chairs, produced by Castelijn, the angular wood slat construction slung with black-fabric straps.
c1965

$2,3000-2,600 (set)   **BonBay**

HARRY BERTOIA (1915-1978), an Italian born sculptor and furniture designer, emigrated to America in 1930 and worked alongside Charles Eames during the 1940s. In contrast to Eames's plywood and molded plastic, Bertoia favored the use of wire mesh to give a lightness to his designs, which are often thought to reflect his sculptural background.

Bertoia's "Diamond Chair", was one of Knoll's most successful designs. The chair was produced in a number of versions, including a high-back, a dining-room chair, and a child's version. It is still in production today.

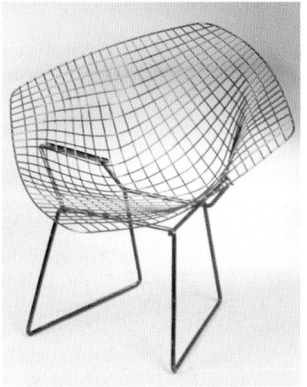

One of a set of four chairs, designed by Gijs Bakker for Castelijn, each of laminated plywood in plank sections of continuous form, designed 1977.

31.5in (80cm) high

Three Mario Bellini "Amanta" rigid plastic and leather modular lounge chairs.

27.5in (70cm) high

One of a pair of Harry Bertoia diamond mesh armchairs, for Knoll Associates, each painted with black enamel.

| $600-700 (set) | **BonBay** | $450-550 (set) | **CA** | | $220-280 (pair) | **L&T** |

A Max Bill three-legged chair, retailed by Wohnbedarf, Switzerland, with turned beech and plywood elements.

c1949

One of a pair of Cini Boeri "Bobo" lounge chairs.

c1970   23.5in (60cm) high

A Cini Boeri & Tomu Katayanagi "Ghost Chair", produced by Fiam, Travula, single piece molded glass construction, designed 1987.

c1988.

One of a set of four Cees Braakman dining-chairs, for Pastoe, the teak faced seat and back on dowel uprights.

c1960   31.5in (80cm) high

| $2,400-2,800 | **BonBay** | $200-250 (pair) | **CA** | $2,300-2,800 | **BonBay** | $750-1,000 (set) | **BonBay** |

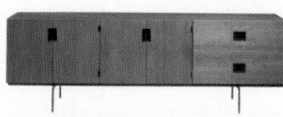

An Osvaldo Borsani desk and chair, produced by Tecno, the rosewood-veneered body on pedestal supports, the matching chair with leather upholstered seat and back, on cast aluminium frame.

c1965

A Cees Braakman tall side cabinet, produced by Pastoe, with birch plywood carcass, comprising shelves and fall-front section with writing surface and drawers, on curved U-shape supports.

c1955

A Cees Braakman U+N sideboard, produced by Pastoe, the teak carcass with a series of doors enclosing the shelved interior, on enameled metal uprights, designed 1959.

90.25in (229cm) wide

| $2,600-3,000 | **BonBay** | $850-950 | **BonBay** | $1,100-1,300 | **BonBay** |

Furniture

WHAT TO LOOK FOR WHEN BUYING:

- Always check on condition. Don't assume that because an item is relatively new, it won't have damage. As with older antiques, condition will dramatically affect the value.
- Try to buy pieces that are as close to their original state as possible. If a piece has been re-upholstered, it will be worth considerably less, particularly if the style is unsympathetic to the original design.
- Don't be put off by items that require superficial restoration. Wood or leather that appears dry and dusty can be easily cleaned with furniture wax.
- Never buy plastics that are cracked or chipped – they cannot be restored.
- Look for pieces that are innovative, either in their design, process or aesthetics.
- Don't be afraid to buy designs that are still in production today. If they were produced around the period they were designed, they will be more desirable.
- Be aware of the retail market as well as the auction market. Many popular designs are re-released at a later stage.
- Never underestimate the importance of provenance. Pieces that have been owned by popular icons or have appeared in cult films will always sell well.
- Check on the production period of a design. An item will always be more appealing if it was individually commissioned or part of a limited edition series.
- Look out for designers who excelled in several areas. There is a market for collecting around the designers themselves, rather than in one area such as furniture.
- Do your research – read up on the period, this will familiarize you with the designers and their styles, it will also begin to educate your eye.
- Don't be afraid to mix old with new – classic modern pieces can go very well in a setting with older antiques.

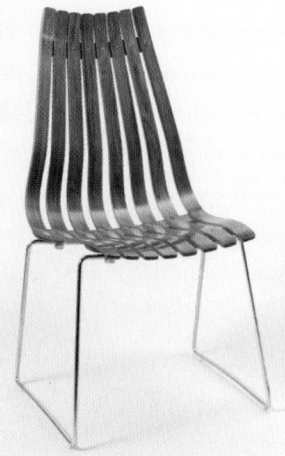

A set of six Hans Brattrud chairs, produced by Hove Møbler, each with vertical slatted rosewood-faced seat and back, on steel rod understructure.

c1970

$900-1,000 (set)   **BonBay**

A stool, the design attributed to Marcel Breuer, produced in Estonia for Isokon Ltd, molded and pierced plywood with detachable seat, remains of original Made in Estonia paper label to underside.

c1935

$250-300   **BonBay**

A Marcel Breuer "B10" dining table, produced by Thonet, Frankenberg, with painted top, on tubular steel frame, paint retouched.

1927-30

$3,000-3,500   **BonBay**

A Marcel Breuer "B9" occasional table/stool, produced by Thonet, the ebonized top on tubular steel frame.

c1927-30

$300-350   **BonBay**

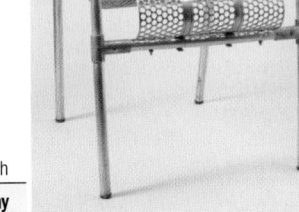

A 1950s Adrien Claude steel and aluminium chair, produced by Meubles Artistiques Modernes, Paris, the scrolling perforated steel seat on aluminium frame joined by pipe-clamps, with rubber feet, designed 1950.

31in (79cm) high

$3,500-4,000   **BonBay**

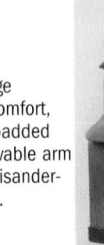
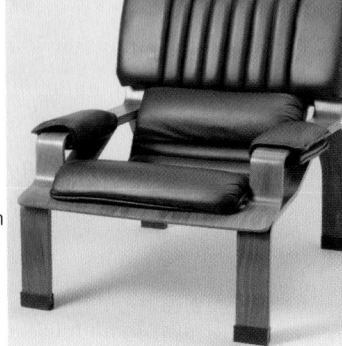

A rare Joe Colombo "Supercomfort" lounge chair, produced by Comfort, the leather-covered padded seat, back and removable arm rests on unusual Pallisander-faced plywood frame.

c1964

$3,000-3,500   **BonBay**

A Joe Colombo "Tubo" modular seating system, made by Flexform Prima.

c1969

$10,000-11,000		**BonBay**

A Hans Coray "Landi" chair, produced by Metallwarenfabrik Blattmann, bent and pressed aluminium construction, with stained seat, designed 1938, this example produced before 1962.

$550-600	**BonBay**

A set of four Robin Day chairs, of pierced plastic and tubular metal construction.

27in (68.5cm) high

$130-170 (set)	**CA**

ROBIN DAY (b.1915), a British furniture designer from High Wycombe, Buckinghamshire, has recently become one of *the* names to look out for in Post-war British design. He is known for his innovative approach to the design of low-cost production furniture, particularly through the use of new materials. The "Hillestak" chair of 1950 and the "Poly" molded plastic polypropolyne chair of 1963, both stacking chairs, are among his most famous pieces.

● Attended the Royal College of Art, London, in 1934-38.
● Set up a design company with his wife, the textile designer, Lucienne Day, in 1948.
● Joined Hille as a design consultant in 1949.
● Became the Design Director at Hille in 1950.
● Was commissioned to design the seating for the Royal Festival Hall as part of the Festival of Britain, in 1951.

A Robin Day form group seating unit, produced by Hille, the painted metal frame supporting a seating unit with back, a seating unit without back and formica-veneered table top, the cushioned seats upholstered in tweed fabric, designed 1960.

$1,100-1,400	**BonBay**

A pair of Robin Day "Royal Festival Hall 661" chairs, produced by Hille, the molded teak-faced plywood back on black stove enameled uprights, the seat re-covered in vinyl fabric, designed 1951.

c1956

$1,200-1,500 (pair)	**BonBay**

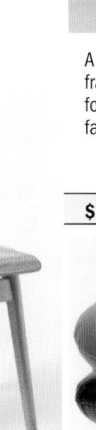

A set of four Robin Day chairs, the beech-faced plywood seat and back on similar supports, designed c1953.

c1956 29.5in (75cm) high

$600-700 (set)	**BonBay**

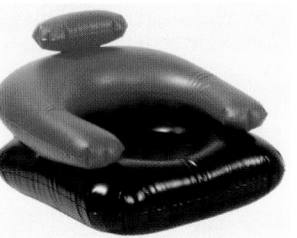

An inflatable "Blow" chair, by Gionatan De Pas, after Donato D'Urbino, Paolo Lomazzi & Carla Scolari, produced by Zanotta, Milan, made of PVC, radio-frequency-welded.

c1967

$120-170	**BonBay**

A pair of Nana & Jorgen Ditzel side chairs, produced by MK, the shaped teak X-frame with vinyl rope-bound pierced backrest to be employed as carry handle.

c1960

$300-350 (pair)	**BonBay**

Furniture

One of a pair of Nana & Jorgen Ditzel side chairs, produced by MK, each with shaped teak frames with pierced handles bound with nylon twine, manufacturer's metal badge to underside.

c1965

$450-500 (pair)   **BonBay**

CHARLES EAMES (1907-1978), an American architect, designer and film-maker, is considered one of the leading lights of the American Modern Movement. He was instrumental in developing the idea that the shell and base of a chair should be considered separately in the production process. In furniture design, Eames and his wife, Ray, are responsible for some of the modern classics of the mid-20thC, including the lounge chair with ottoman (which won a gold medal in the 1960 Milan XII Triennale) and the fibreglass shell chair, made by Zenith Plastics for Herman Miller in 1950.

- Studied architecture at Washington University, St. Louis from 1924-1926.
- Became head of the department of experimental design at Cranbrook Academy of Art from 1937-1940.
- Won the Organic Design in Home Furnishings competition at New York's Museum of Modern Art in 1941 (along with Eero Saarinen).
- Supplied leg splints to the US Navy from 1942.
- Set up his own design company in 1944.
- Joined the progressive furniture manufacturer, Herman Miller in 1948.

A Charles Eames group duraluminium and leather-cloth desk chair.

2ft 33.5in (85cm) high

$280-340   **CA**

A Charles Eames lounge chair (670) and matching ottoman (671), for Herman Miller, each with leather upholstery and rosewood-veneered undersides raised on aluminium pedestals, bearing maker's labels.

c1956

$2,000-2,500   **L&T**

Always check the condition of Eames's lounge chair with ottoman thoroughly. The rubber shock mounts that were used to fix the back plywood shell to the seat shell disintegrate over time, leaving the piece unstable.

An early Charles & Ray Eames "RAR" rocking chair, produced by Zenith Plastics/Herman Miller, the fibreglass shell with embedded-cord edge and wide diameter shock-mounts on zinc-wire understructure and wooden rocker, early square red, black and white transfer label to underside, designed 1950.

1950-1955

$1,500-1,800   **BonBay**

The Eames "RAR" rocking chair made for Herman Miller has had a long production span. An easy way to distinguish an early model is to check the lip of the fibreglass shell. Designs made before the mid-50s were reinforced with cord under the lip, later designs were made from more advanced fibreglass and did not need such support. Early designs will also carry the red, black and white Zenith label, while later examples will be stamped with the manufacturer's mark.

▶ One of a set of four Charles & Ray Eames "DCM" chairs, for Herman Miller, with walnut-faced molded-plywood seat and back shell, on chrome-plated tubular steel frame, designed 1945-46.

$1,200-1,500 (set)   **BonBay**

◀ A Charles & Ray Eames "RAR" rocking chair, produced by Herman Miller, the fibreglass shell on wire and wood understructure, manufacturer's labels to underside, designed 1950.

c1980

$700-800   **BonBay**

Furniture

A Yngve Eckstrom lounge chair, the shaped oak frame with wool upholstery.

c1970

$850-950   **BonBay**

A rare Egon Eiermann desk chair, produced by Wilde u. Spieth GmbH, the molded plywood seat and back on cast metal pedestal with height mechanism.

c1950

$750-850   **BonBay**

A pair of Egon Eiermann side chairs, produced by Wilde u. Spieth GmbH, the plywood seat and back on metal frame, designed 1948.

$750-850 (pair)   **BonBay**

A 1950s Jorge Ferrari-Hardoy, Juan Kurchan & Antonio Bonet "Butterfly" chair, produced by Knoll Associates, the leather slung seat on enameled tubular steel frame, designed 1938.

$550-600   **BonBay**

A side chair, attributed to Marcel Gascoin, produced by Amentagement Rational De L'habitation Art Des Collectives, the interwoven vinyl seat and back on angular construction wood frame.

c1950

$600-700   **BonBay**

A Wilhelm H. Gispen side chair, produced by Gispen, Holland, the ebonized molded plywood seat and back on undulating chrome-plated tubular steel frame.

c1930

$900-1,000   **BonBay**

WILHELM H. GISPEN (1890-1981), a Dutch designer, attended the Academy for Visual Arts and Technical Sciences in Rotterdam, Holland, in 1913. He was the founder of Gispen International, a Dutch furniture manufacturer, specializing in office furniture. He was the first to start the mass-production of tubular steel furniture in the Netherlands. His designs are characterized by a balance between form and function. Gispen also designed and manufactured lighting, through GISO; his pieces shown at the 1927 "Die Wohnung" exhibition, in Stuttgart, brought him international acclaim.

A Pierre Guariche side chair, the molded birch-faced plywood seat shell on painted steel uprights.

$450-500   **BonBay**

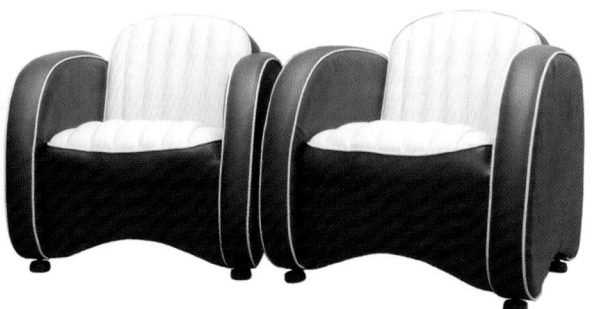

A pair of Max Greenall cream and black upholstered "Leatherlux" leather "Chummy" armchairs.

32.25in (82cm) high

$2,500-2,800   **CA**

A pair of Geoffrey Harcourt "042" lounge chairs, made by Artifort.

c1970

$750-1,000   **BonBay**

Furniture

A Marc Held "Culbuto" chair and ottoman, with high-back fibreglass seat shell, upholstered in wool fabric, designed 1967, produced from 1970, this example produced c1975 by Knoll International, New York.

This design was the first French-designed chair to be produced by Knoll International, New York.

| $4,000-5,000 | BonBay |

A late 1970s Iseo Hosoe plastic side chair, produced by Bilumen, of cantilever stacking construction, designed 1973.

| $250-300 | BonBay |

One of a pair of Peter Hvidt & Orla Nielsen "AX" chairs, for Fritz Hansen, the molded plywood seat and back on laminated birch frame, manufacturer's marks to underside, designed 1950.

| $600-700 (pair) | BonBay |

One of a set of four Arne Jacobsen "3101" armchairs.

29in (74cm) high

| $400-450 (set) | CA |

One of a set of five Arne Jacobsen "3105" stacking chairs, produced by Fritz Hansen, each with ebonized beech plywood seat shell on tubular steel uprights, designed 1955.

This version of the "Ant" chair is no longer in production.

| $800-900 (set) | BonBay |

▶ A Wilhelm Kienzle free-standing shelf system, produced for Embru and retailed by Wohnbedarf, Switzerland, with series of untreated beech shelves, on textured enameled sheet steel frame.

c1930   65.5in (166cm) high

| $900-1,100 | BonBay |

One of a set of six Arne Jacobsen "3103" chairs, produced by Fritz Hansen, each with teak-faced plywood seat shell, on plastic coated tubular metal legs, designed 1955.

| $1,000-1,300 (set) | BonBay |

A rare Arne Jacobsen "Swan" sofa, produced by Fritz Hansen, the tweed fabric covered seat and back on cast aluminium frame.

| $3,000-3,500 | BonBay |

A Florence Knoll conference/dining table, produced by Knoll Associates, walnut top of boat-shaped form with beveled edge, on square section painted metal frame, designed c1958, this example produced c1970.

112in (284cm) wide

| $2,500-3,000 | BonBay |

Furniture

LE CORBUSIER (1887-1965), born Charles Edouard Jeanneret, is one of the most famous French architects and designers. His *Les 5 Points d'une Architecture Nouvelle*, published in 1926, is generally though to have laid the foundations for modern architecture as we know it. Among his many innovations, he is credited with introducing the concept of an open-plan living and working environment. In 1929 he began to design furniture alongside Charlotte Perriand. His "Chaise Longue" and "Fauteuil Grand Comfort" are considered to be design classics.

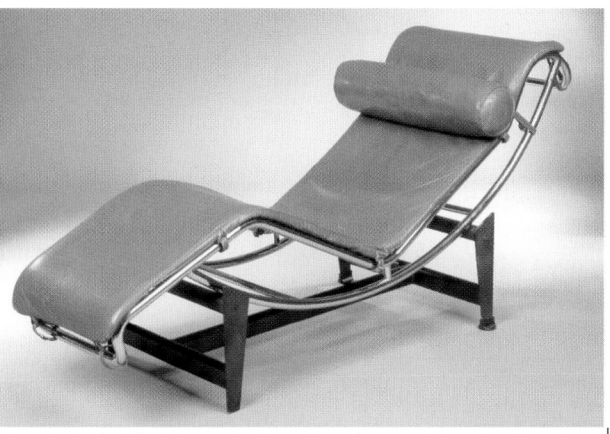

A Le Corbusier, Charlotte Perriand and Pierre Jeanneret chromium-framed LC4 lounger, the buff leather cover and adjustable bolster on black enameled base, bears paper label.

65.25in (166cm) wide

| $1,800-2,200 | | L&T |

One of a pair of late 1960s Le Corbusier, Pierre Jeanneret and Charlotte Perriand basculant armchairs, manufactured by Aram, the chrome-plated tubular steel frame slung with leather, the back rail of chair stamped Le Corbusier LC/1 – 5674 and Le Corbusier LC/1 – 5675.

| $1,000-1,200 (pair) | BonBay |

A Raymond Loewy cocktail cabinet, produced by DF2000, the formica-veneered carcass with sliding top enclosing three drawers (one of double depth), above door enclosing sliding bottle drawer, manufacturer's label to inside of drawer.
c1970

| $750-850 | BonBay |

A Hans & Wassili Luckart "Siesta Medizinal Chaise", produced by Thonet, of beech and birch plywood and solid articulated wood frame with tension adjustment bracket to one side, manufacturer's pre-1939 label to underside.

| $1,300-1,500 | BonBay |

A Vico Magistretti "Vicario" chair, with molded ABS plastic body.
c1970

| $150-200 | BonBay |

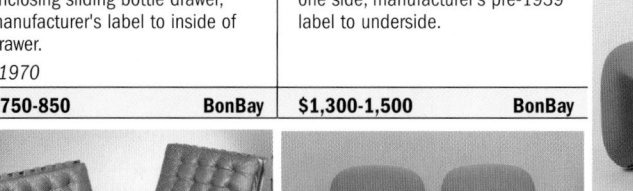

A 1950s Willi van der Meeren desk, produced by Tubax, the birch-faced plywood top on welded stove-enameled steel understructure, designed 1952.

| $700-800 | BonBay |

A pair of Ludwig Mies van der Rohe "Barcelona" lounge chairs, each with chromium cross frames supporting leather upholstered and buttoned cushions.

| $2,200-2,500 | L&T |

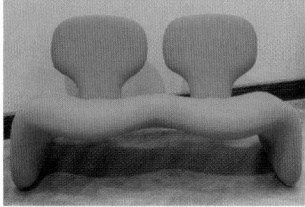

An Olivier Mourgue "Djinn" sofa, the urethane and metal frame upholstered with jersey stretch fabric, the whole on metal runners, designed 1965.

| $2,500-2,800 | BonBay |

An Olivier Mourgue "Djinn" chair, produced by Airborne, the urethane and metal frame upholstered with jersey stretch fabric, the whole on metal runners, designed 1965.

Oliver Mourgue's red "Djinn" chair featured in the film "2001: A Space Odyssey" in 1968.
c1970

| $2,500-2,800 | Bonbay |

One of a set of four Vittorio Nobili "Medea" chairs, each having molded plywood seat and back, on enameled tubular metal uprights, designed 1955.

| $2,000-2,400 (set) | BonBay |

Furniture

GEORGE NAKASHIMA (1905-1990), a Japanese descendant, was born in Spokane, Washington.

● Nakashima studied architecture at the University of Washington and Massachusetts Institute of Technology, graduating with a Masters degree in architecture in 1930.

● He began making furniture during time spent in India and Japan, where he learnt his craft from traditional woodworkers. His attraction to woodwork had been a lifelong interest, and combined with his architectural abilities, he produced innovative and progressive designs.

● His style was further developed whilst being detained in an internment camp during World War II. There he trained under a master Japanese carpenter, using salvaged wood for material.

● He was released through the sponsorship of Antonin Raymond and founded his workshop in Bucks County in 1945.

● Subsequently Nakashima achieved international acclaim, his style reflecting the simplicity of the Shakers as well as the Arts and Craft Movement. He received numerous commissions and awards, including the Gold Craftsmanship Medal of the American Institute of Architects in 1952.

● Nakashima's daughter, Mira, who has a Masters degree in architecture, collaborated with her father on many of his designs. After his death she took over the backlog of orders and has since been head of the Nakashima Studio.

A George Nakashima large figured walnut credenza and cabinet, the bookcase top with adjustable shelves and sliding walnut and grass-cloth grilled doors, the credenza base with three sliding doors exposing three compartments, adjustable shelves and flatware drawer in two flanking compartments, central space with six drawers.

This piece is accompanied by copy of original 1967 commissioned receipt.
1967   top 48in (122cm) wide

$14,000-16,000   **FRE**

A Verner Panton "Cone" swivel chair, for Fritz Hanson, with steel cross frame base.

$450-500   **L&T**

One of a pair of Verner Panton bachelor chairs, produced by Fritz Hansen, each with steel frame slung with suede leather, suede-covered padded seat and back cushions, designed 1955.

$1,000-1,300 (pair)   **BonBay**

A rare pair of Verner Panton side chairs, produced for Ikea, of cantilever form, the wood laminated in formica sheets.

c1980

$1,000-1,300   **BonBay**

A Hans Pieck laminated birch lounge chair, produced by Lawo Design, cut and folded from a single laminated sheet, with metal brackets to affix seat at rear, underside stamped "1579", designed 1944.

c1946   30in (76cm) high

$3,300-3,600   **BonBay**

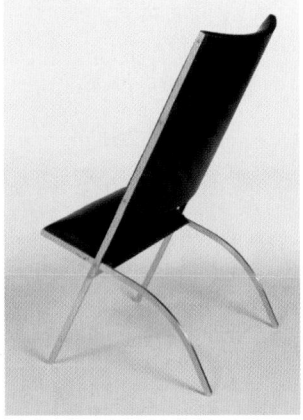

A Gio Ponti "Gabriela" side chair, made by Walter Ponti.

c1970

$1,200-1,700   **BonBay**

One of a set of six standard model dining chairs, design attributed to Jean Prouvé, produced by Ateliers Jean Prouvé, the molded plywood seat and back on painted tubular steel frames, with rubber bung feet.

c1950

$2,000-2,500 (set)   **BonBay**

An early Jean Prouvé wooden chair, produced by Vauconstante, plywood and solid wood frame.

c1942

$3,500-4,000   **BonBay**

A Gerrit Thomas Rietveld crate chair, produced by Metz & Co, Amsterdam, composed of 18 rectangular sections of stained pine, joined by screws.

c1934

$2,000-2,500   **BonBay**

GERRIT THOMAS RIETVELD
(1888-1964), a Dutch architect and designer, is most famous for his "Red Blue" chair, designed in 1918. In this chair, Rietveld rejected all previous notions of Modern design and created an abstract sculpture based around complicity of design and structure. The "Red Blue" chair, with its strong primary colors and straight lines, pre-dates Mondrian paintings.

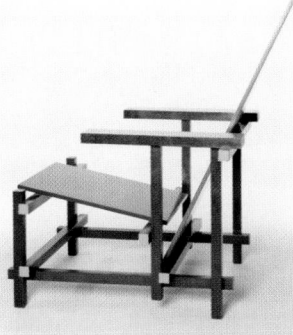

A Gerrit Rietveld "Red Blue" chair, originally made by Gerard A Van de Groenekan, Utrecht, this example made under license by Cassina.
c1980

$1,000-1,300	BonBay

One of a set of four late 1970s Richard Rogers and Renzo Piano limited edition "Biblioteque" dining chairs, with wire mesh and leather seat and back.

Only 20 examples of this design were produced, for the Pompidou Center in Paris.

$2,000-3,000 (set)	BonBay

A white enameled dining suite, designed for Form International after Eero Saarinen, comprising a marble-top table and six "tulip" chairs, of molded form, with flared pedestals.

Table 52.75in (134cm) dia

$1,500-1,800	L&T

An Adolf G. Schneck "Die Billige Wohnung" side chair, produced by Deutsche Werkstatten Hellerau, with wood frame and original canework seat.
c1926

$600-700	BonBay

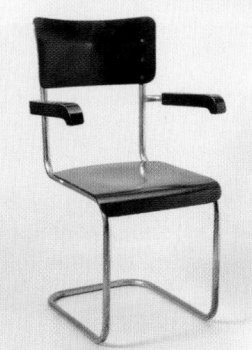

A 1940s Herman A. Sperlich painted steel and wood health chair, produced by Ironite Inc. USA, the hinged plywood back above plywood seat, on enameled band steel frame, designed 1938.

$350-400	BonBay

A rare Mart Stam side chair, produced by Thonet, the ebonized molded plywood seat and back on chrome-plated tubular steel cantilever frame, with ebonized beech armrests.
c1930

$900-1,000	BonBay

A Mart Stam side chair, produced by Goed Wohnen, the woven ropework seat on angular wood frame, with three branch woven back rest.
c1947

$850-1,050	BonBay

◄ A limited edition Hein Stolle easy chair, comprising a series of square section planks of pine, joined by wood dowels, signed by the designer on the underside of the runner and numbered 2 out of 25, executed by the architect.

This piece was one of Hein Stolle's first designs to be translated from the drawing board to the workshop. The chair design was devised in 1988. Stolle made 25 examples by hand, each numbered and signed. One is in the Stedlijk Museum in Amsterdam.
c1990

$1,000-1,300	BonBay

One of a set of four Hans Wegner dining chairs, for Carl Hansen & Sons, the laminated rosewood seat on solid rosewood frame, manufacturer's ink stamp to underside, designed 1958.

$850-1,050 (set)	BonBay

Furniture

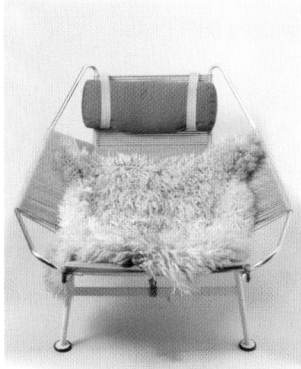

A Hans Wegner "Flaghaylard" lounge chair, produced by Getama, the tubular steel frame slung with flagline, together with the original sheep skin cover and cotton head cushion, designed 1950.

$5,000-6,000	**BonBay**

A pair of unique Hans Wegner bespoke day beds, each with original wool fabric covered padded seat on rectangular pine and oak sprung frames, with similar optional wall mounted back rest.

These sofas were designed specifically by Hans Wegner for Ove Arup's office at 13 Fitzroy Street, London.
c1955

$1,000-1,300 (pair)	**BonBay**

A pair of tubular steel armchairs, the arched side panels clad with wooden slats forming the arms and legs, the back and seat covered with ribbed rubber sheeting.

36.5in (93cm) high

$900-1,100	**L&T**

A leather-upholstered "Globe" armchair, with black piping.

34.5in (88cm) high

$1,000-1,300	**CA**

A Pirelli rosewood leather-upholstered armchair, with registration and patent numbers.

31.5in (80cm) high

$500-600	**CA**

Four Danish laminated bentwood leather upholstered easy chairs.

32in (81cm) high

$85-950 (set)	**CA**

One of a set of four rigid plastic and chrome Modern Movement bar stools.

40.25in (102cm) high

$200-250 (set)	**CA**

A prototype rocking chair, designer unknown, the orange fibreglass shell on hand-welded metal frame.

$500-550	**BonBay**

One of a pair of stacking dining chairs, produced by Artek, the circular seat and pierced plywood back on L-shaped plywood uprights, birch plywood, designed 1932.

$450-550 (pair)	**BonBay**

A René Herbst "Sandows" chair, produced by Establissements René Herbst, Paris, the tubular steel frame slung with elasticated sprung straps, designed 1928-29.

$4,000-5,000	**BonBay**

A French stool, designer unknown, with yellow painted top, on black enameled tubular steel frame.
c1930

$200-250	**BonBay**

A Torn Peman mahogany-framed coffee table, the square top enameled with a free-form design in crackled orange and crimson, the top inscribed Torn Peman, XLV11/200 1967.

35.5in (90cm) wide

$230-280   **L&T**

A crate table, of angular construction with pine planks, designer unknown.

c1930

$350-450   **BonBay**

A bronze coffee table, the base configuration cast into the form of a stylized Prunus tree, the tinted toughened glass top with irregular edge, designer unknown.

c1970

$700-800   **BonBay**

An "Attica Chair", by Studio 65, made by Guffram, with polyeurethane shell.

c1972

$750-1,000   **BonBay**

GLASS

A "Savoy" vase, by Alvar Aalto, produced by Iittala, mold-blown, of undulating free-form section, underside engraved "ALVAR AALTO 3030".

This Savoy vase was part of a series of vases Aalto designed for the Savoy restaurant in Turku in 1937. The curvilinear form of the vase reflects Aalto's organic approach to design as a whole.

1949-1954   6in (15cm) high

$700-800   **BonBay**

VENINI & CO, a glass-making company founded by Paolo Venini in 1925, was one of the top Post-war Italian glassworks. It is known for its high quality glass and use of strong colors and abstract designs. Since 1988, it has traded as Venini S.p.a.

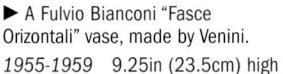

▶ A Fulvio Bianconi "Fasce Orizontali" vase, made by Venini.

1955-1959   9.25in (23.5cm) high

$4,500-5,500   **BonBay**

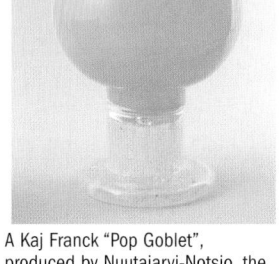

A Kaj Franck "Pop Goblet", produced by Nuutajarvi-Notsjo, the foot specked with opaque white glass particles, designed 1956.

8.25in (20.5cm) high

$150-180   **BonBay**

A Kaj Franck ovoid vase, produced by Nuutajarvi-Notsjo, free-blown underside engraved "Kaj Franck Nuutajarvi Notsjo 64", designed 1960.

1964   8.25in (21cm) high

$225-280   **BonBay**

An Edvard Hald bottle and stopper, produced by Orrefors, the surface wheel-engraved with figural scene, engraved marks to underside.

c1970   9.5in (24cm) high

$700-800   **BonBay**

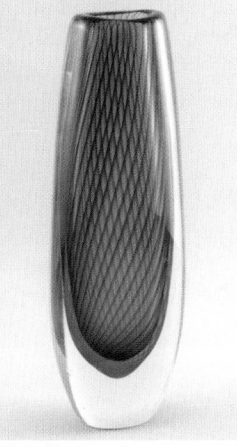

A Vicke Lindstrand net vase, made at Kosta, the green and blue sommerso with swirling inclusions, cased in clear glass, engraved marks to underside.

c1955   11in (28cm) high

$850-950   **BonBay**

A Vicke Lindstrand vase, produced by Kosta, of heavy cased clear glass, the outer surface with incised decoration, against a texture wheel-engraved and acid-treated ground surface, engraved marks to underside.

c1955   6.75in (17cm) high

$2,500-3,000   **BonBay**

Glass

An Ingeborg Lundin "Ariel" vase, produced by Orrefors, with trails of trapped air bubbles forming a series of irregular squares, of shaded glass cased in clear glass, engraved marks to underside and numbered "No. 4476", dated.

1972   5.5in (14cm) high

$900-1,100   **BonBay**

A large Per Lutkin bubble vase, produced by Holmgaard, of globular form, engraved manufacturer's mark to underside.

c1960   9.6in (24.5cm) high

$200-250   **BonBay**

A Gunnel Nyman clear vase, produced by Nuutajarvi-Notsjo, of undulating cylinder form, designed 1946.

6.5in (16.5cm) high

$400-500   **BonBay**

A Gunnel Nyman pearl band vase, produced by Nuutajarvi-Notsjo, of tear-drop form, with trailed air bubbles cased in clear crystal, designed 1946.

7in (17.5cm) high

$300-350   **BonBay**

▶ A 1960s Edvin Öhrström "Ariel" vase, produced by Orrefors, with trails of trapped air bubbles, depicting stylized female figure and dove, heavily cased in clear glass, engraved maker's marks to underside and numbered 7057913.

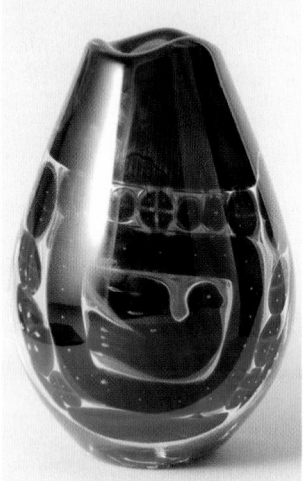

An Edvin Öhrström "Ariel" vase, produced by Orrefors, decorated with trails of trapped air bubbles forming squares, heavily cased in clear glass, engraved maker's marks to underside and numbered 1920E.

7.75in (20cm) high

$1,300-1,500   **BonBay**

c1960   4.25in (11cm) high

$2,000-2,400   **BonBay**

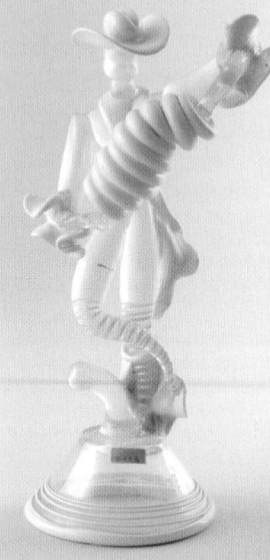

▲ A 1930s Flavio Poli figure of an accordion player, made at Seguso Vetri D'Arte, hand-blown and worked clear glass with opalescent surface and opaque white glass, manufacturer's paper label to foot.

10.75in (27.5cm) high

$1,200-1,500   **BonBay**

A Timo Sarpaneva "Archipelago" vase, for Iittala, the spun mold-blown clear glass engraved TIMO SARPANEVA 01214, designed 1978.

The "Archipelago" series demonstrates the first use of the technique of forming glass by spinning the metal in the mold to form a cylinder.

4.5in (11.5cm) high

$400-500   **BonBay**

A Timo Sarpaneva "Cardinal's Hat" bowl, for Iittala, of stick-blown glass, the underside engraved TIMO SARPANEVA - IITTALA - 56, designed 1956.

1956   8.5in (21.5cm) diam

$600-700   **BonBay**

◀ A tall Timo Sarpaneva carafe, for Iittala, the deep indigo glass cased in clear, underside engraved TIMO SARPANEVA - 3288, designed 1957.

15.25in (40cm) high

$450-500   **BonBay**

Glass

An Irene Stevens vase, produced by T Webb Corbett, of cylinder form, with undulating miter-cuts intersected by a series of concave discs.

c1940

$250-300 **BonBay**

A Wilhelm Wagenfeld glass vase, produced by VLG Weisswasser, of mold-blown smoky tinted clear glass, the outer surface with wheel-cut decoration by E. Jachmann.

c1938 6.25in (16cm) high

$300-360 **BonBay**

A Tapio Wirkkala large "Foal's Foot" vase, for Iittala, of turned mold-blown crystal with line-cut surface decoration, underside engraved Tapio Wirkkala-Iittala.

1951-59 9.75in (24.5cm) high

$220-280 **BonBay**

A Tapio Wirkkala "Art Object 3538", for Iittala, still mold-blown crystal, with comb-cut surface decoration, underside engraved Tapio Wirkkala - Iittala - 56, designed 1952.

1956

$500-550 **BonBay**

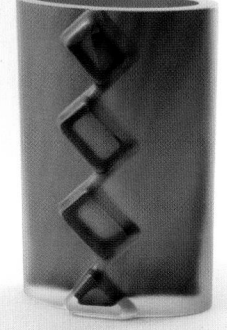

A Tapio Wirkkala "Turned Leaf" vase, for Iittala, in line-cut crystal, underside engraved Tapio Wirkkala-Iittala, designed 1953.

1953-59

$500-550 **BonBay**

A Tapio Wirkkala vase, produced by Iittala, mold-blown, deep-red glass cased in clear with three polished, embossed squares to one side, sand-blasted and acid-treated texture to outer surface overall, engraved maker's marks to underside.

c1955 7in (18cm) high

$400-450 **BonBay**

A Tapio Wirkkala, "Iceberg" vase, produced by Iittala, mold-blown clear crystal, designed 1950.

7in (18cm) high

$700-800 **BonBay**

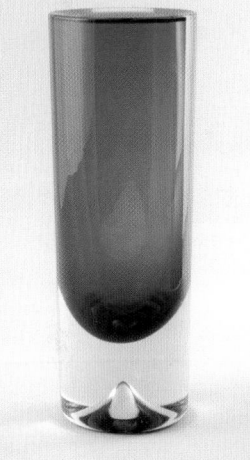

A Tapio Wirkkala cylinder vase, blue glass cased in clear, with engraved marks to underside.

c1955 8in (20.5cm) high

$120-170 **BonBay**

A large Heilbronn glass bowl, produced by V.L.G. Weisswasser, in smoky-tinted clear glass, press-molded, underside with molded mark "XX".

c1937 13.25in (33.5cm) diam

$400-500 **BonBay**

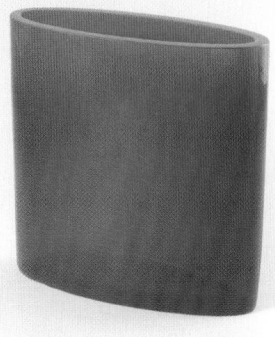

A rare Tapio Wirkkala ovalis vase, produced by Iittala, of compressed cylinder form, in ruby-red glass.

6.5in (16.5cm) high

$750-800 **BonBay**

A rare Tapio Wirkkala Q-color vase, produced by Iittala, of organic form, in milky glass cased in clear.

$700-800 **BonBay**

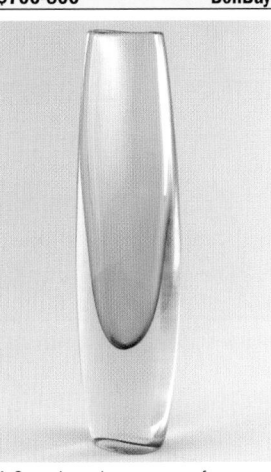

A Strombergshyttan vase of teardrop form, in pale green glass cased in clear.

c1955 13.5in (34cm) high

$200-250 **BonBay**

661

CERAMICS

A Theodor Bogler large tureen and cover, produced by Keramikfabrik Velten Vordamm, with a pierced hole in the lid for ladle, designer's painted marks to underside.

c1925   10.25in (26cm) high

$1,000-1,200   **BonBay**

A Werner Burri bowl, produced by Keramikfabric Velten Vordamm, stamped and painted manufacturer's mark to underside.

c1928   9in (23cm) diam

$600-700   **BonBay**

A Werner Burri footed ceramic bowl, produced by Keramikfabrik Velten Vordamm.

c1928   9in (23cm) diam

$600-700   **BonBay**

A Marguerite Friedlander vase, produced by Burg Giebichenstein, KPM, of Hallesche form, painted marks to underside.

c1930   8in (20.5cm) high

$350-400   **BonBay**

A Guido Gambone vase.

$1,100-1,400   **BonBay**

A Margarete Heymann-Marks vase, the bulbous body with raised neck, on rim foot, shaded glaze body, painted manufacturer's marks to underside.

c1929   9.5in (24cm) high

$300-350   **BonBay**

A Janet Leach vase.

c1970   7.75in (20cm) high

$550-600   **ADE**

A Bernard Leach vase, with tenmoko glaze.

c1960   5.5in (14cm) high

$1,300-1,500   **ADE**

A David Leach teapot, from Lowerdown Pottery.

c1960   5.75in (14.5cm) high

$300-350   **ADE**

A Stig Lindberg cat, produced by Gustavsberg, the molded stoneware with shaded glaze and incised surface decoration, manufacturer's paper label to underside.

c1960   13in (33cm) wide

$350-400   **BonBay**

A 1950s Gunnar Nylund "Nymolle" vase.

10.75in (27.5cm) high

$250-300   **ADE**

A Gunnar Nylund stoneware bowl, produced by Rorstrand, incised manufacturer's marks to underside.

c1955   10.5in (27cm) diam

$375-425   **BonBay**

An Eva Stricker-Zeisel decanter and plate, produced by Schramberg Majolika, inkmaker's mark and stamp to underside.

c1929   10.25in (26cm) high

$500-600   **BonBay**

A Portmeirion Potteries Ltd jug, in the Tivoli pattern.

c1966   5.75in (14.5cm) high

$85-125   **ADE**

A 1960s Portmeirion Potteries Ltd coffee set, in the Magic City pattern.

12.25in (31cm) high

$150-200   **ADE**

PABLO PICASSO (1881-1973), one of the greatest painters of the 20th century, was also influential in the field of ceramics. His interest in the medium dated back to the early 1900s when he was introduced to the ceramic work of Paul Gauguin. However, it was not until 1947, when he began work at the Madoura Pottery in Vallauris, France, that he started to produce work on a large scale. Throughout 1947 and 1948, Picasso devoted his time to Madoura, producing many original pieces such as statuettes and human figures along with traditional wares such as plates and vases. Although his focus was to return to painting in the 1950s, he continued to work with clay, undertaking a number of large scale projects in the 1960s, including a set of thirteen dessert plates given to Rita Hayworth as a wedding gift.

A Pablo Picasso oval pottery dish, "Visage De Femme", "Madoura Plein Feu" and "Edition Picasso" impressed, in an edition of 400, dated.

1953   15in (38cm) wide

$5,000-5,500   **WW**

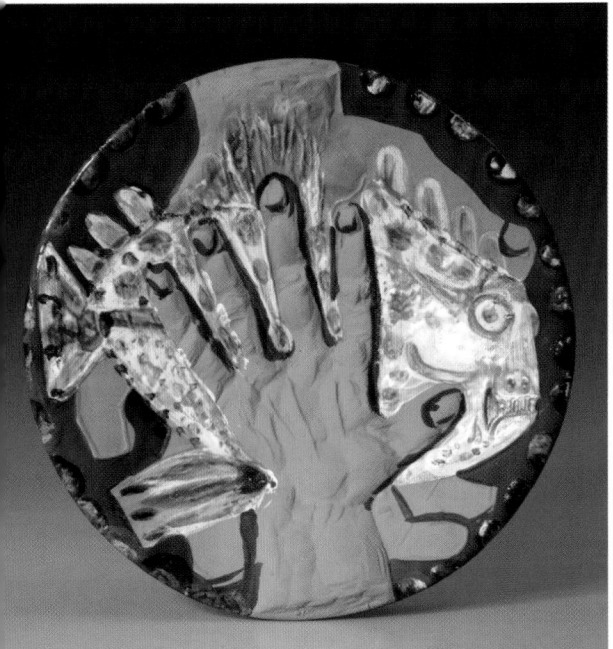

A Pablo Picasso terracotta plate, stamped "Madoura Plein Feu, Empreinte Originale de Picasso 4/250".

c1953   11.75in (30cm) diam

$3,000-4,000   **WW**

A Mari Simmulson bowl, for Upsala Ekeby.

1951   13.25in (33.5cm) wide

$750-850   **ADE**

A 1950s Mari Simmulson dish, for Upsala Ekgby.

7.75in (20cm) wide

$120-150   **ADE**

Ceramics

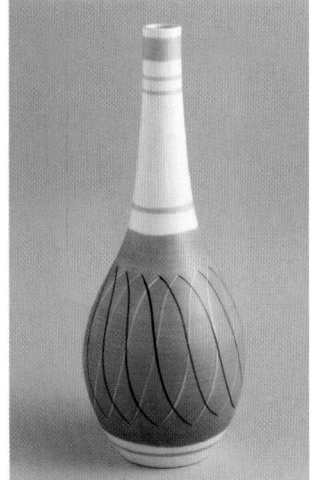

A Poole Pottery vase, in the
Contemporary style.

c1952-55   10.5in (27cm) high

$200-250   **ADE**

A Poole Pottery vase, in the
Contemporary style.

c1952-55   7.75in (19.5cm) high

$200-250   **ADE**

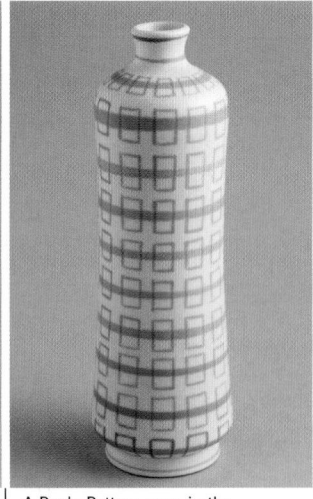

A Poole Pottery vase, in the
Contemporary style.

c1952-55   7.75in (19.5cm) high

$200-250   **ADE**

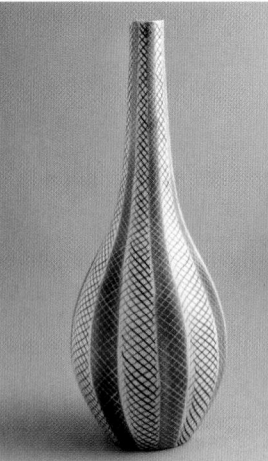

A large Poole Pottery vase, in the
Contemporary style, with criss-cross
hatching.

c1952-55   15.25in (38.5cm) high

$800-900   **ADE**

A Poole Pottery vase, in the
Contemporary style, with Spiral Leaf
pattern 185/Y.F.P, designed by Alfred
B Read.

c1952-55   9.75in (25cm) high

$350-400   **ADE**

A Poole Pottery vase, in the
Contemporary style, designed by
Alfred B. Read.

c1952-55   10in (25.5cm) high

$450-500   **ADE**

A Poole Pottery peanut earthenware
vase, in the Contemporary style,
with Leaf pattern 700/PG.T,
designed by Alfred B. Read.

c1953-55   10.75in (27.5cm) high

$450-500   **ADE**

A large 1950s Poole Pottery carafe,
in the Contemporary style.

                11.75in (30cm) high

$550-650   **ADE**

A large Poole Pottery skittle vase, in
the Contemporary style.

c1952-55   14.25in (36.5cm) high

$750-800   **ADE**

A Poole Pottery bowl, in the
Freeform style, decoration designed
by Ruth Pavely.

c1955-59   7.75in (20cm) high

$200-250   **ADE**

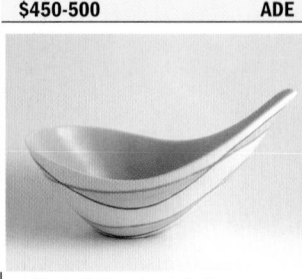

A Poole Pottery bowl, in the
Freeform style, decoration designed
by Ruth Pavely.

c1955-59   7.25in (18.5cm) high

$160-200   **ADE**

A Poole Pottery vase, in the
Freeform style.

c1955-59   12.25in (31cm) wide

$400-450   **ADE**

A Poole Pottery vase, in the Freeform style.

c1955-59 12.25in (31cm) wide

$700-750 ADE

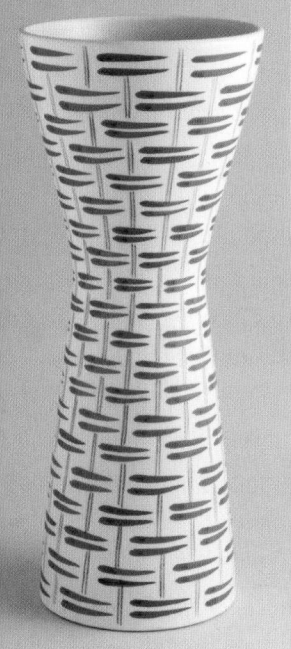

A Poole Pottery vase, in the Freeform style, with Basket Leaf pattern, designed by Ann Read.

c1955-59 12.5in (31.5cm) high

$900-1,100 ADE

A 1950s Poole Pottery jardinière, in the Freeform style.

9in (22.5cm) high

$700-800 ADE

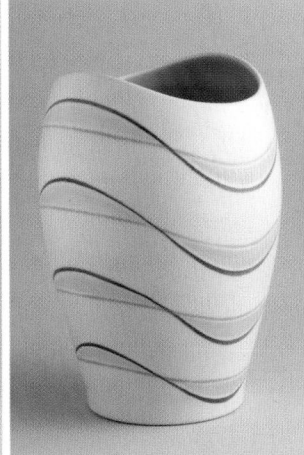

A Poole Pottery vase, in the Freeform style, with Loop pattern.

c1955-59 9.75in (24.5cm) high

$1,200-1,400 ADE

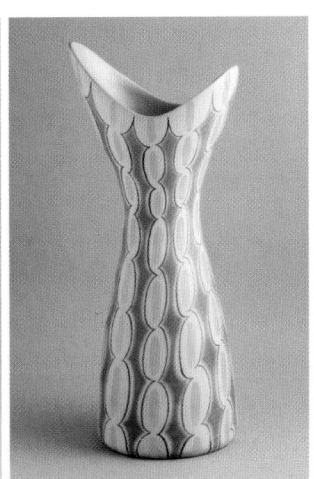

A Poole Pottery double-horned vase, in the Freeform style, with Bamboo pattern.

c1955-59 14.25in (36cm) high

$900-1,100 ADE

A 1950s Poole Pottery vase, with Rope pattern.

9.25in (23.5cm) high

$450-500 ADE

A Poole Pottery vase, in the Freeform style.

c1955-59 7.5in (18.5cm) high

$330-380 ADE

A 1950s Poole Pottery vase, with Harlequin pattern.

7.75in (19.5cm) high

$1,000-1,200 ADE

Ceramics

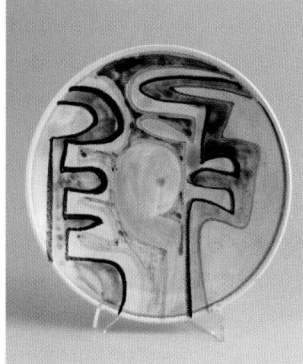

A Poole Pottery plate, from the Delphis range.

c1960   8in (20.5cm) diam

$200-250   **ADE**

A Poole Pottery plate, from the Delphis range.

1960-70   8in (20.5cm) diam

$200-250   **ADE**

A 1970s Poole Pottery plate, from the Aegean range.

8in (20.5cm) diam

$90-120   **ADE**

A 1970s Poole Pottery plate, from the Aegean range.

10.5in (26.5cm) diam

$120-160   **ADE**

A 1970s Poole Pottery vase, from the Atlantis range, hand-thrown and decorated by Beatrice Bolton.

7in (18cm) high

$500-600   **ADE**

A 1970s Poole Pottery vase, from the Atlantis range, hand-thrown by Jennie Haigh.

8in (20.5cm) high

$400-450   **ADE**

A 1970s Poole Pottery vase, from the Atlantis range, by Guy Sydenham.

7in (17.5cm) high

$500-600   **ADE**

GUY SYDENHAM (b.1916) is one of the most renowned figures in the history of Poole Pottery. He joined Carter, Stabler and Adams Ltd in 1931 as a thrower. In 1949 he progressed to foreman in the clay shape department, moving on to designer and studio potter during the 1960s. He worked closely with Alfred B. Read and Robert Jefferson, and was responsible for some of the most innovative shapes and patterns to be produced at Poole, in particular his designs for the Atlantis range (1966-67) and his red earthenware lamps in the 1970s. He retired in 1977.

A rare Poole Pottery vase, by Guy Sydenham and Beatrice Bolton, with applied molded monkey heads, signed on underside.

c1970   11.75in (30cm) high

$3,000-3,500   **ADE**

MISCELLANEOUS

MARIANNE BRANDT (1893-1983) attended the Bauhaus in Germany, one of the most important design schools of the 20thC. Brandt's metal and glass lamps were some of the most successful designs to come out of the Bauhaus. Her geometric teapots and metal ashtrays were also among her most celebrated designs.

Traditionally, Bauhaus designs, particularly from the 1920s and 30s, sell very well. However, the last year has seen a decline in the demand for such early pieces.

A rare Marianne Brandt silver-plated napkin holder, produced by Ruppelwerk, Gotha, of sheet metal, on disc foot, manufacturer's stamp to underside.

c1930

$750-800　　　　　　　**BonBay**

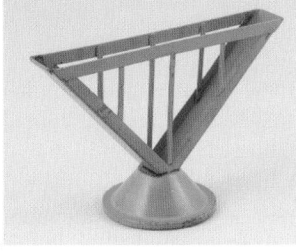

A Marianne Brandt napkin holder, produced by Ruppelwerk, Gotha, lacquered metal, with printed underside mark "mehrfach geschutzt" and "ruppel".

c1930　　　　5in (13cm) high

$450-500　　　　　　　**BonBay**

A pair of Marianne Brandt coaster holders, produced by Ruppelwerk, Gotha, of sheet metal, the underside marked "ruppel geschuzt" and marked with a star.

c1930　　　　5in (13cm) dia

$700-800　　　　　　　**BonBay**

A Marianne Brandt cigarette box, produced by Ruppelwerk, Gotha, lacquered in black with chrome-metal stripe decoration.

c1930　　　4in (10cm) wide

$450-500　　　　　　　**BonBay**

A Marianne Brandt bookstand, produced by Ruppelwerk, Gotha, of sheet steel, the outer surface painted in chequerboard pattern of orange paint and polished bare steel surfaces.

c1930　　　5.75in (14.5cm) high

$300-350　　　　　　　**BonBay**

Three 1930s Fritz August Breuhaus eggcups, produced by WMF, the white metal cups on spherical feet, each piece displaying a different step in the product's development.

$150-200　　　　　　　**BonBay**

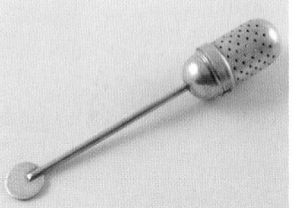

A Christian Dell tea infuser, unknown manufacturer, of electroplated brass, the infuser with pierced holes, the handle with circular finger holder.

c1924　　　5in (13cm) long

$750-850　　　　　　　**BonBay**

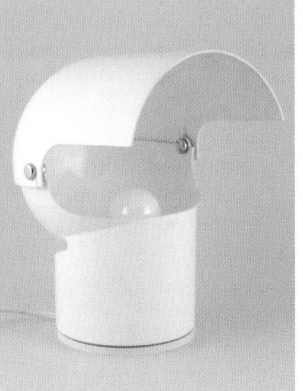

A Gae Aulenti "Pileo" desk lamp, produced by Artemide the articulated metal shade on ABS plastic foot, stamped manufacturer's marks to underside.

Provenance: *This was the property of seminal 1960s designer Max Clendinning*

c1975　　　9.75in (25cm) high

$220-280　　　　　　　**BonBay**

A Helen Von Boch "La Bomba" picnic set, produced by Villeroy and Boche from the Avant Garde programme, comprising ABS picnic box which breaks down to provide plates, cups and cutlery.

c1975　　　　15.25in (39cm) high

$1,000-1,300　　　　　　　**BonBay**

A Jean Perzel brass and copper desk lamp, with conical shade and high pedestal.

25.25in (64cm) high

$900-1,100　　　　　　　**BonBay**

Miscellaneous

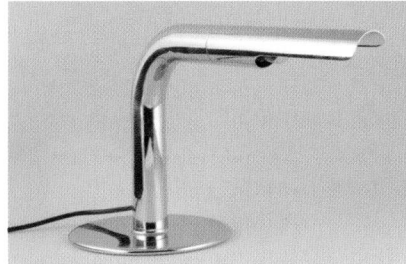

A Ingo Maurer desk lamp, of L-shaped cylindrical section.

c1970   9.5in (24cm) high

$225-275	BonBay

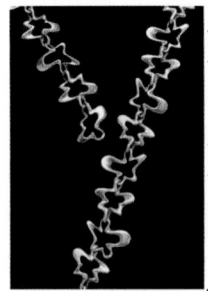

A Henning Koppel silver necklace and bracelet, produced by Georg Jensen, each link cast and individually shaped, designer's monogram and "88" stamped to underside of each, designed 1946.

$900-1,000	BonBay

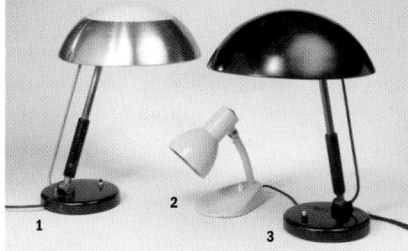

▲1 A Karl Trabert deluxe no.6580 super table lamp, produced by Schanzenbach, the spun metal shade with glass top section, raised on adjustable steel arm, with ebonized wood handle.

c1933   18in (45.5cm) high

$1,000-1,300	BonBay

▲2 A night stand lamp, produced by Kandem, of painted metal shell, with articulated shade.

c1928   9in (23cm) high

$600-700	BonBay

▲3 A Karl Trabert adjustable no.6580 super table lamp, produced by Schanzenburg, the painted metal domed shade raised on steel arm with ebonized wood handle.

c1933   18in (45.5cm) high

$375-425	BonBay

▲1 A Christian Dell polo popular table lamp, produced by Bünte & Remmier, with early enameled metal shade, together with another desk lamp by Christian Dell, with painted steel shell, on unusual base configuration, each marked ORIGINAL JDELL.

c1931

$550-600	BonBay

▲2 A rare Christian Dell DK 37 table lamp, produced by Gebruder Kaiser & Co. Neheim-Husten, this example of early production featuring early painted steel shade, on adjustable chromed metal stem, with ribboned ebonized wood handle, the switch on stepped plinth, cast maker's mark ORIGINAL JDELL molded to top of lamp.

c1934   17in (43cm)

$550-600	BonBay

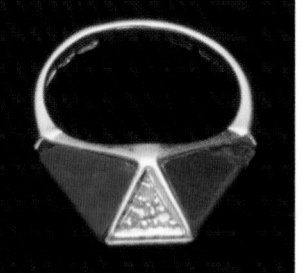

An 18ct gold and tourmaline ring, the freeform organic body, set with cut-tourmaline, stamped maker's marks and assay mark to underside.

$600-700	BonBay

A diamond and lapis lazuli silver ring, stamped maker's marks to underside.

1976

$220-280	BonBay

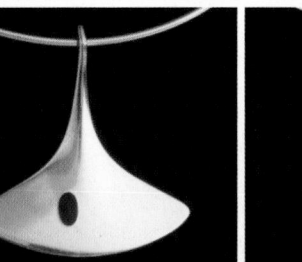

A Hans Hansen white metal necklace, the pendant inlaid with black enamel, on white metal wire band, stamped manufacturer's marks to underside.

c1955

$270-320	BonBay

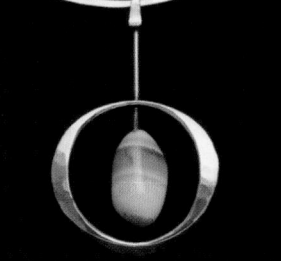

A necklace, crafted by Plus Jewellery, Norway, white-metal and semi-precious stone, together with original presentation box, stamped manufacturer's marks to body.

c1960

$270-320	BonBay

BJÖRN WECKSTRÖM (b.1935), a Finnish goldsmith and sculptor, is highly regarded within the field of jewelry. One of his "Space Series" pieces, a necklace entitled "Planetary Valleys", was worn by Princess Leia in the 1977 film *Star Wars*. In the late 1960s, he produced a series of jewelry called "Flame Bronze", which was discontinued after a short period due to technical difficulties. As a result they are highly sought after, particularly the "General Motors" and "Star Fighter" pendants and the "Krupp" and "Maginot" bracelets.

▲1 A Björn Weckström "Big Drop" necklace, made from acrylic and silver.

c1970

$750-1,000	BonBay

▲2 A 1970s Björn Weckström "Heart Pendant" made from acrylic and silver.

$350-440	BonBay

▲3 A Björn Weckström "Iguana" necklace made from acrylic and silver.

c1975

$300-400	BonBay

▲4 A 1970s Björn Weckström ring made from acrylic and silver.

$300-400	BonBay

Marine Antiques

THE INVENTION OF THE STEAM ENGINE SAW AN EXPLOSION IN SHIPBUILDING TECHNOLOGY DURING THE MID-19TH CENTURY. Initially the main function of the ocean liner was to transport mail, but by the beginning of the 20th century it had become a well-established means of travel. The opulence and master-craftsmanship of the vessels were a measure of prestige and power and they emerged as nationalist symbols, with countries striving to produce the best liners in the world.

There was another boom in the shipping industry during the post-war optimism of the 1920s and this was carried through to the next decade when the Normandie and the Queen Mary were built. By 1960 ocean liners began to lose their revenue to airlines and went into decline and today only the Queen Elizabeth II remains in transatlantic service.

Ocean liner memorabilia is a growing collectors market, both in the United States and Britain, with few dealers and rising demand. Recently there has been an increased interest in memorabilia as more people are traveling on cruise ships. The 1998 film *Titanic* also fired the public imagination and rekindled nostalgia for the past glamor of the liners.

Ephemera, chinaware, silver plate, maritime books, souvenirs, ship's instruments and even old steamer blankets are all highly collectable.

A 1970s silver plate tankard from the Ambassador.

5in (12.5cm) high

$30-40   COB

A 1950s RMS Andes tea strainer.

6in (15cm) long

$30-40   COB

A photograph of the ship Aquitania in "The Floating Dry Dock".

c1920   11.75in (30cm) wide

$30-40   COB

A surgeon's mortar for mixing medicines, from the wreck of HMS Association, sunk 22nd October 1707.

c1700   4.25in (11cm) high

$630-700   COB

An RMS Australia pin cushion, a rare item from this ship.

c1900   5.25in (13.5cm) wide

$80-120   COB

Two silver napkin rings from the 1996 Canberra world cruise.

1.25in (3cm) wide

$80-120   COB

Three 1950s tea caddy spoons, left: RMMV Capetown Castle, center: RMS Arundel castle, right: RMMV Athlone castle.

2.75in (7cm) long

$20-40 each   COB

A 1950s Cunard Line White Star ashtray in the shape of a shell.

3.25in (8.5cm) high

$20-30   COB

A 1950s Cunard Line matchbox.

2in (5cm) wide

$6-10   COB

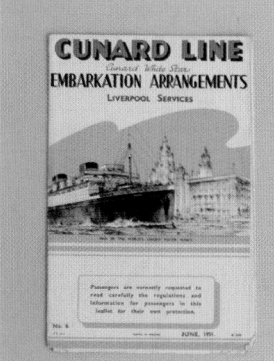

A Cunard Line embarkation list.

1951   7.75in (20cm) high

$20-30   **COB**

A napkin ring from RMSF SS Deseado.

1911-1934   1in (2.5cm) high

$30-50   **COB**

A brass bell from the Dilwara steam tug.

1930   8in (21cm) high

$400-500   **COB**

An SS Finland spelter box.

c1910   3.75in (9.6cm) wide

$50-70   **COB**

A 1950s French Line ashtray.

4in (10.5cm) diam

$50-70   **COB**

An SS France fold-out plan of the ship's interior, French Line.

1962   12.5in (32cm) high

$80-120   **COB**

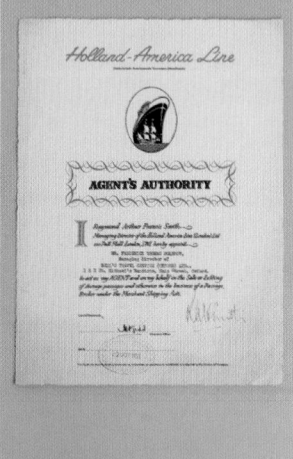

An agent's certificate from the Holland America Line.

1953   11.75in (30cm) long

$50-70   **COB**

An Imperator Line wallet.

c1914   5.5in (14cm) long

$70-100   **COB**

An Italian sailing list.

1927   9in (23cm) long

$20-40   **COB**

A 1930s pot and cover, with the Normandie on the cover.

5in (13cm) wide

$150-200   **COB**

A ceramic dish from the Normandie.

c1935   5in (13cm) diam

$80-120   **COB**

A 1950s pack of Orient Line SS Oreades playing cards.

3.5in (9cm) long

$20-30   **COB**

Marine Antiques

A 1930s SS Oronsay brass spoon.

4.5in (11.5cm) long

$30-40   **COB**

A fruit bowl with Royal Yacht Osborne monogram printed on the inside.

The Royal Yacht Osborne was Queen Victoria's favorite yacht.

c1900   10.75in (27.5cm) diam

$350-400   **COB**

A QE2 Scotch whisky bottle, from the maiden voyage.

1969   5in (12.5cm) high

$12-15   **COB**

A 1950s sweet tin with a picture of the Belgian State Mail boat, Ostend-Dover line, printed on the lid.

7.75in (20cm) long

$20-30   **COB**

A P&O glass decanter, with P&O engraved on the front.

c1910   7in (18cm) high

$70-100   **COB**

A 1930s pack of P&O playing cards.

3.5in (9cm) long

$30-40   **COB**

A 1980s QE2 single malt Scotch whisky jug.

8.25in (21cm) high

$30-40   **COB**

A rare limited edition QE2 globe, with certificates. Only 100 of these were made.

1999   2.5in (6.5cm) diam

$200-240   **COB**

Three napkins from the Queen Elizabeth Ship, Cunard Line.

1947   5in (12.5cm) wide

$12-15   **COB**

A menu from the Queen Elizabeth.

1968   10.5in (16.5cm) high

$15-20   **COB**

RMS QUEEN MARY, standing at 1,019.5ft and weighing 81,237 tons, is generally regarded as one of the finest ocean liners of all time. Launched in 1934, the Queen Mary was hostess to the world's rich and famous including Greta Garbo, Clark Gable and Mary Pickford. She was also known as "The Gray Ghost" and had carried more than 800,000 troops by the end of World War II, playing a significant role in the Allied campaign. Today the Queen Mary is a tourist attraction and hotel in Long Beach, California.

A 1930s powder compact, with TS Queen Mary II on the cover.

2in (5cm) high

$50-70   **COB**

A 1950s Queen Mary Cunard Line hymn book.

7in (18cm) high

$15-20   **COB**

A rare embossed Queen Mary tin.

1936   10in (25.5)cm wide

$80-120   **COB**

A lamp from the Queen Mary, presented to a crew member by his colleagues.

1936   25.25in (64cm) high

$550-600   **COB**

A Queen Mary mirror.

1936   10.5in (26.5cm) wide

$40-50   **COB**

A Queen Mary condiment set.

1950s   8.25in (21cm) high

$140-170   **COB**

A 1960s Queen Mary sailor toy.

8.75in (22cm) high

$50-70   **COB**

A 1960s Hornby model of the Queen Mary, with original box.

12.25in (31cm) long

$70-100   COB

A 1930s Royal Mail Line advertising blotter.

13in (33.5cm) long

$20-30   COB

A 1950s pack of Shaw and Saville playing cards.

3.5in (9cm) long

$40-50   COB

A 1930s Southhampton Docks millk jug, from a cafe on the docks.

4.25in (11cm) high

$70-100   COB

A 1930s RMS Stratnaird spoon.

4.5in (11.5cm) long

$30-40   COB

THE TITANIC was built by Harland and Wolff for the White Star Line and was the largest passenger ship of her day. She was unequalled in opulence and was designed to attract the rich. When she sank during her maiden voyage at 2.20am 15th April 1912, only 703 of the 2207 people on board survived. There has been an upsurge in interest in Titanic-related memorabilia since James Cameron's epic film was released in 1998.

A White Star line *Olympic & Titanic* book.

1911   9.75in (25cm) long

$500-550   COB

A Titanic *in memoriam* picture, with a shell frame.

These were made in memory of those who died on board.

1912   6in (15cm) diam

$170-200   COB

An *in memoriam* Titanic tissue.

1912   14in (36cm) wide

$280-320   COB

A set of five 8mm plastic film reels for the 1958 film *A Night to Remember* with Kenneth Moore, with a picture of the Titanic on the cover.

c1960s   7in (18cm) wide

$70-100   **COB**

A limited edition Titanic teddy bear, with original box.

This mohair bear is a reproduction of a German teddy that was rescued with a child from the sinking Titanic. The bear was donated to the Museum of Childhood, in Golders Green, London. 5,000 of these bears were produced for the 80th anniversary of the sinking of the Titanic in 1992.

6in (15.5cm) high

$180-200   **COB**

An 1950s former United States Line plate.

6.25in (16cm) diam

$50-60   **COB**

A china cup and saucer film prop for the 1998 film *Titanic*.

Saucer 6in (15cm) diam

$100-140   **COB**

A plate with Victoria and Albert HM Yacht monogram printed in the center.

c1910   10.25in (26cm) diam

$350-400   **COB**

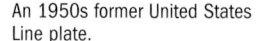

A 1950s Union Castle ship's blanket.

$30-40   **COB**

A 1940s ship's phone, with wheel house dial.

6.5in (16.5cm) high

$100-150   **COB**

A pair of 1940s ship's binoculars.

7in (18cm) wide

$80-120   **COB**

A bronze porthole key.

c1900   6.2w5in (16cm) high

$30-40   **COB**

◄ A pair of German ship's binoculars, with original case.

c1910   4.5in (11.5cm) wide

$70-90   **COB**

Portrait Miniatures

MINIATURE PORTRAITS ORIGINATED IN 16TH CENTURY ENGLAND AND CONTINUED TO BE FASHIONABLE UP UNTIL THE 19TH CENTURY, BOTH IN ENGLAND, on the Continent and in the Americas. They were intended as a memento of a loved one, or several were commissioned to portray a potential bride or groom to prospective spouses. Miniatures of this kind might contain a lock of the sitter's hair to enhance the intimate nature of the painting. They were also exchanged as gifts among the aristocracy or given as a symbol of political allegiance.

Portraits of ladies, children and officers were the most popular and fashionable subjects, and are still the most valuable today. The popularity of an artist will increase a painting's worth, as will a portrait of a well-known sitter. The condition of a painting can dramatically affect its worth, so always check for restoration.

A silhouette is an outline of an object or person that is filled with solid shadow. They derive their name from the cheapskate French Finance Minister Etienne de Silhouette (1709-1767) who cut profiles from black paper rather than spend money on portraits. They were particularly popular in the 18th and early 19th centuries.

Both miniatures and silhouettes are gaining popularity with American collectors.

A portrait of a lady, Mrs Holland, by Isaac Oliver, on vellum in a gilt metal frame with pierced spiral cresting.

ISAAC OLIVER was a miniaturist to Queen Elizabeth I's court. His work can be seen in the Victoria and Albert Museum, London and in the Clevedon Museum, Clevedon.

1593	2in (5cm) high
$36,000-40,000	**CH**

A portrait of a lady, believed to be Anne Clifford, Countess of Pembroke and Montgomery, by Alexander Cooper.

ALEXANDER COOPER was the brother of Samuel Cooper, also a famous miniaturist. He was a painter at the court of Queen Christina of Sweden.

c1633-35	2in (5cm) high
$24,000-26,000	**CH**

A portrait of a Knight of the Bath, by Samuel Cooper, wearing a brown doublet and white lawn collar, painted on vellum and set in a gilt-metal frame with gold ropework mounts chased and enameled with four foliate clusters, signed with monogram and dated.

SAMUEL COOPER was one of England's finest miniaturists. He painted many famous Englishmen and showed great skill in his use of light and color. His work is in the collections of the Duke of Devonshire and the Duke of Buccleuch; at Windsor Castle; in the V&A Museum and in the Metropolitan Museum of Art, New York.

1655	1in (2cm) high
$17,000-20,000	**CH**

A portrait of an officer, by Richard Gibson, wearing armor plate and a white lawn collar, painted on vellum and set in a gilt-metal frame with pierced spiral cresting.

c1650	2.5in (6.5cm) high
$13,000-15,000	**CH**

A fine quality portrait of a gentleman, by Gaspard Smitz, in oil on copper.

c1660	2in (5cm) high
$2,500-3,000	**CH**

A portrait of a gentleman called John Evelyn, by F. Smiadecki, in oil on copper.

c1670	2.25in (6cm) high
$4,200-5,000	**CH**

A portrait of a gentleman by Christian Richter.

c1710	1.5in (4cm) high
$2,500-3,000	**CH**

A portrait of a gentleman, by Jean André Rouquet, on enamel.

c1730	1.75in (4.5cm) high
$2,800-3,200	**CH**

Portrait Miniatures

A portrait of Prince Frederick, son of George II, by Bernard Lens, painted in oil on ivory.

c1740	2in (5cm) high
$1,400-2,000	**CH**

A German 18thC portrait of Frederick the Great, Emperor of Prussia (1740-1786), set in a gold ring, artist unknown.

	0.75in (2cm) high
$1,000-2,000	**CH**

A portrait of a vicar, by Ozias Humphrey, in a garnet frame.

c1760	1.5in (3.5cm) high
$1,400-2,000	**CH**

A portrait of a young boy, by Samuel Finney, in a ruby frame.

c1760	1.25in (3cm) high
$1,000-1,400	**CH**

A portrait of a gentleman, by Nathanial Hone, in a garnet frame, signed and dated.

1761	1.25in (3cm) high
$1,400-2,000	**CH**

A superb portrait of a lady, by Richard Crosse.

c1770	1.5in (4cm) high
$2,000-2,800	**CH**

A portrait of a lady, by Patrick McMoreland, in original gold frame.

c1770	1.75in (4.5cm) high
$1,000-1,400	**CH**

A rare portrait by Charles Forrest, signed with initials and dated.

1776	1.75in (4.5cm) high
$1,400-1,700	**CH**

A portrait of Elizabeth James, daughter of Frederick Ratling Rasch of Denmark, by Samuel Shelley.

c1780	1.75in (4.5cm) high
$2,000-2,800	**CH**

A portrait of Sir Charles Cockrell, by Richard Cosway.

RICHARD COSWAY (1742-1821) was a renowned miniaturist in his day. Having gained the friendship of the Prince of Wales, he was given an appointment as a court painter and there is a collection of his work in Windsor Castle. His self-portrait can be seen in the National Portrait Gallery, London.

c1780	2in (5cm) high
$11,000-$12,000	**CH**

A portrait of a lady, by Richard Cosway.

c1790	1.75in (4.5cm) high
$7,500-8,500	**CH**

A portrait of Queen Charlotte, the wife of George III, by Richard Cosway.

c1760	1.5in (4cm) high
$5,600-6,000	**CH**

A portrait of three children, by Samuel Shelley.

c1790   3.5in (9cm) high

$12,000-13,000   **CH**

A preparatory sketch, by John Smart.

c1780   2.25 (6cm) high

$3,500-4,000   **CH**

A portrait of a gentleman by W. Read, in a gold frame with Brazilian link, signed and dated.

1784   1.75in (4.5cm) high

$1,000-1,700   **CH**

A portrait of Colonel Blair, by George Place.

c1790   2.25in (6cm) high

$2,200-2,800   **CH**

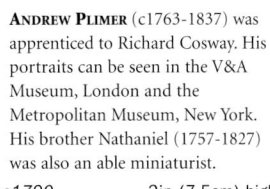

A portrait of a gentleman, by Andrew Plimer, in a gold frame.

ANDREW PLIMER (c1763-1837) was apprenticed to Richard Cosway. His portraits can be seen in the V&A Museum, London and the Metropolitan Museum, New York. His brother Nathaniel (1757-1827) was also an able miniaturist.

A portrait of a gentleman, by the Irish artist Thomas Robinson.

c1790   2.5in (6.5cm) high

$1,400-2,000   **CH**

A portrait of an officer, by Charles Sherriff.

c1790   2.25in (6cm) high

$800-1,200   **CH**

c1790   3in (7.5cm) high

$3,800-4,200   **CH**

A portrait of James Hamilton, by Mrs Ann Mee.

c1790   3in (7.5cm) high

$2,800-3,200   **CH**

A portrait of a gentleman, by John Bogle, signed and dated.

1794   2in (5cm) high

$2,200-2,800   **CH**

A portrait of a young lady, by Jeremiah Meyer.

c1795   1.75in (4.5cm) high

$2,800-3,200   **CH**

A portrait of a lady, by W. Thicke.

c1795   3in (7.5cm) high

$2,200-2,800   **CH**

A portrait of a child dressed in blue, by Thomas Hazlehurst, signed.

c1800   2.25in (6cm) high

$3,500-4,000   **CH**

Portrait Miniatures

A portrait of a child holding cherries, by Thomas Richmond.

c1800   3in (7.5cm) high

$3,200-3,800   **CH**

A portrait of a lady, by Henry Jacob Burch.

c1800   3in (7.5cm) high

$1,000-1,700   **CH**

A portrait of a gentleman by Henry Jacob Burch.

c1800   2.75in (7cm) high

$1,000-1,700   **CH**

A portrait of L.T. Cork, by Richard Collins, signed and dated.

1802   3in (7.5cm) high

$1,400-2,000   **CH**

A portrait of a gentleman by George Engleheart, signed with initials, in a gold frame.

GEORGE ENGLEHEART (1752-1829) was a court miniaturist during the reign of George III and is known for the expression and charm of his paintings. His nephew John Cox Dillman Engleheart was also a miniaturist.

c1800   3in (7.5cm) high

$4,500-5,500   **CH**

A portrait of Miss Douglas Walker, by John Cox Dillman Engleheart, signed and dated.

1815   3in (7.5cm) high

$3,500-4,000   **CH**

A portrait of a gentleman, by William Wood.

c1805   2.75in (7cm) high

$4,500-5,500   **CH**

A portrait of of Mrs Powyer, by Isaac Wane Slater, signed with initials and dated.

1808   3in (7.5cm) high

$2,200-2,800   **CH**

A pair of portraits of gentlemen, by William John Thompson, on ivory.

c1815   3.5in (8.9cm) high

$2,200-2,800   **CH**

A portrait of John Clements, by Henry Bone, signed and dated.

1817   3in (7.5cm) high

$4,500-5,000   **CH**

A portrait of a lady, by Karl Von Saar.

c1820   2.5in (6.5cm) high

$2,800-3,200   **CH**

A portrait of two children, by G.E. Lami, in the original ormolu frame, signed and dated.

1821　　　　3in (7.5cm) high

$2,500-3,000　　　　**CH**

An American School portrait of a young woman, in watercolor on paper, depicting the sitter wearing a tortoiseshell comb, with applied gilt paper necklace, in a veneered frame.

c1830　　　　5in (13cm) high

$550-650　　　　**SI**

A portrait of a gentleman, by Charles le Brown, of Massachusetts, USA.

1850　　　　2.75in (7cm) high

$700-1000　　　　**CH**

A portrait of Queen Alexandria, wife of Edward VII, by Alyn Williams.

c1904　　　　3.5in (9cm) high

$1,400-2,000　　　　**CH**

JOHN MIERS (1756-1821) is generally considered to be one of the greatest and most successful profilists of the 18th and 19th centuries. He painted on card, but his most renowned works were those on plaster. Miers achieved incredible likenesses of his subjects, with the black being thinned to diaphonous grays to pick out the details of hair and veils.

A portrait of a lady, by C.S. Wiltscher.

1951　　　　4in (10cm) high

$1,000-1,700　　　　**CH**

A silhouette of the actress Sarah Siddons, by John Miers, painted on plaster.

c1787　　　　3.25in (8cm) high

$3,800-4,200　　　　**CH**

A silhouette of a lady, by John Miers, painted on plaster.

c1789　　　　3in (7.5cm) high

$2,200-2,800　　　　**CH**

A silhouette of a gentleman, by John Miers, painted on plaster.

c1790　　　　3.5in (8.5cm) high

$1,400-2,000　　　　**CH**

A silhouette of a boy, by John Field, painted on plaster.

c1805　　　　3.5in (9cm) high

$1,000-1,700　　　　**CH**

One of a pair of silhouettes of Mr and Mrs John Wollaston, by John Field, bronzed on plaster.

1809　　　　3in (7.5cm) high

$2,200-2,800 (pair)　　　　**CH**

Two 19thC framed silhouettes, the smaller of a young woman with the details of clothing highlighted in gold ink, the larger of an older woman.

4.25in (12cm) high
8.75in (19.5cm) high

$220-280　　　　**SI**

LIGHTING

A pair of Regency bronze and gilt-bronze table candelabra, each with leaf-cast scrolling branches with cut-glass feather surmounts, supporting turned nozzles and with anthemion-pierced and luster-hung decoration, the whole above an eagle support raised on square section leaf and anthemion-cast base with stepped plinth below.

12.5in (32cm) high

$3,000-4,000	L&T

► A garniure of three George IV gilt-brass and bronzed table lusters, comprising; a two-branch candelabrum with foliate scroll arms supported on a reed column, mounted with an eagle with round step-molded base, and two similar candlesticks, adapted.

Largest 15in (38cm) high

$2,200-2,800	DN

A pair of 19thC bronze candelabra, each formed as a patinated cherubic satyr seated on a tree stump and holding twin branch leaf-cast candelabra in each hand, on shallow-cast brass socle base with marble plinth.

16.5in (42cm) high

$4,000-5,000	L&T

A pair of early 19thC gilt-metal and bronzed two-branch candelabra, each with scrolled arms and prism drops, a turned column molded with acanthus and a square base with bun feet, incomplete.

11in (28cm) wide

$1,000-1,400 (pair)	DN

A pair of mid-19thC French bronze candelabra, after Clodion, each in the form of a faun, supporting two ormolu vine-chased branches, on a fluted base with ormolu laurel border.

17.25in (43.5cm) high

$6,000-7,000	DN

A pair of French patinated bronze ormolu marble-vert three-branch candelabra.

c1880   21.75in (55cm) high

$7,500-8,500	RG

A pair of early 19thC Empire bronze and ormolu table candelabra, each cast as an Ancient Egyptian female figure, supporting three candle sconces, raised on a turned tapering base with molded collar on a plinth.

24in (61cm) high

$12,000-15,000	L&T

A late Victorian ormolu candelabrum centerpiece, the two luster candle nozzles flanking amethyst vase, all on foliate rocaille tripod foot, one foot missing.

16.5in (42cm) high

$700-800   Chef

A pair of French Louis XV-style porcelain and glass-mounted gilt-bronze three-light candelabra, the trifid scrolling framework issuing three scrolling candlearms, mounted with porcelain flowers and amber, amethyst, green and clear glass drops, surmounted by a glass spire-form finial, electrified, impressed mark.

17.75in (45cm) high

$600-700   SI

A 20thC five-branch press-molded glass chandelier, with three baluster sections, the lower dished section supporting five S-shaped arms terminating with flared sconces and serrated rim drip pans suspending facet drops.

23.75in (60cm) high

$400-450   DN

A pair of 18thC brass candlesticks, with banded baluster stems on chamfered rectangular bases.

6.5in (17cm) high

$75-85   J&H

► A pair of George III mahogany candlesticks, each with leaf-cast brass nozzle on lifting adjustable rod, the stick of turned and fluted columnar form with spirally fluted base and turned saucer foot.

16.5in (42cm) high

$2,000-3,000   L&T

▲1 A pair of mahogany table candlesticks, each with brass drip trays above turned nozzles and tapering stop-fluted columns on spreading circular bases.

17in (43cm) high

$700-800   L&T

▲2 A pair of early 19thC mahogany table candlesticks, each with leaf-cast turned nozzles above fluted and spirally fluted turned column on spreading circular base.

14.5in (37cm) high

$1,500-2,000   L&T

◄ A pair of 19thC Neo-classical-style ormolu candlesticks, with stiff acanthus and beaded sconces, fluted columns set in acanthus seats, the circular-stepped bases with floral and fruiting vine decoration.

13in (33cm) high

$750-850   BonS

A pair of Regency candlesticks.

8.5in (22cm) high

$1,200-1,500   Gro

A pair of bronze candlesticks, with glass lusters.

c1825   12in (30cm) high

$2,200-2,800   Gro

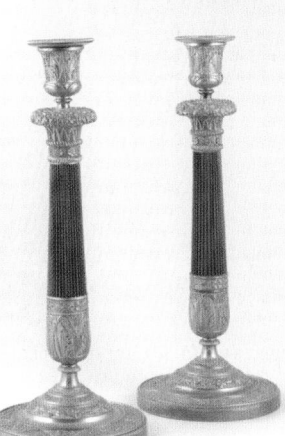

Lighting

A 19thC brass and iron adjustable candlestick on stand, with two candlecups and scrolled arm on an urn shaft with reel-form finial, with brass snuffer.

23in (58.5cm) high

$1,400-1,800   **SI**

A pair of Victorian Gothic-style gilt-brass extending candlesticks, the stems and bases cast with Gothic arches, with trefoil decoration to the edges, with matching candle snuffers with foliate-cast finial.

10in (25.5cm) high

$500-600   **BonS**

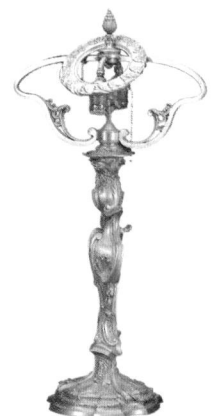

A late 19thC early 20thC French Louis XV-style gilt-bronze candlestick, the spiralling baluster form standard-cast with scrollwork and cartouches on a circular domed base similarly cast with cartouches, a butterfly and scrollwork, mounted as a lamp.

18.5in (47cm) high

$3,500-4,500   **SI**

Two 20thC French gilt-bronze bouillotte lamps, with tole-painted shades, one with three C-scroll candlearms, each terminating in bird-heads and a pierced circular tray base, the other with three scrolling candlearms in the form of swans and a four-footed circular base.

26in (66cm) high

$900-1,100   **SI**

▶ A pair of pale-blue-dip Jasper cut-glass and gilt-metal mounted candlesticks, with thistle-shaped sconces suspending prism drops, broad floriform drip-pans suspending prism drops above a facet-cut ovoid central section, on gilt-metal mounted plinth bases with cylindrical Jasper sections carved and molded in white relief with typical classical scenes.

12.25in (31cm) high

$1,300-1,600   **DN**

▶ A pair of Neo-Rococo-style bronze table candlesticks, with triform plinth rising to a baluster stem with foliate sconce, some damage to one.

9in (22cm) high

$200-300   **LC**

A pair of French Louis XV-style gilt-bronze candlesticks, each with a spiral foliate candle holder above a baluster support cast with scrolling flowers and foliage on a circular domed base with applied flowering branches and bracket feet.

13in (32.5cm) high

$800-900   **SI**

A pair of gilt-bronze candlesticks, each with beaded drip pan above bucranea and grape clusters on spiral vintage wrapped standards, raised on three leaping lion feet.

12.75in (32.5cm) high

$1,200-1,600   **SI**

A Sheffield Argand lamp, with cut-glass globe above a turned shaft, domed cylindrical plinth and circular foot flanked by scrolled arms holding cylindrical burners with pierced tops and pendants, base with applied gadrooning and floral borders, old repairs.

c1800   17.75in (45cm) high

$3,000-4,000   **SI**

A pair of 19thC gilt-brass storm lights, each with a cut-glass shade with brass rim, the bases cast with scrolls and vases of flowers, indistinctly stamped.

19in (48cm) high

$1,500-2,000   **DN**

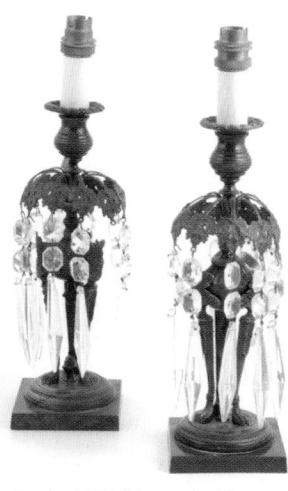

A pair of gilt and cast-bronze and cut-glass Argand lamps, with cut-crystal urn-form font with knop finial, on a cylindrical and leaf-ornamented vasiform standard and domed acanthus-leaf ornament base, the horizontal columnar arm with feline head holds burner tube with pendant and shaped bobeche, maker's stamped plate, Johnston Brookes & Co, Manufacturers London.

c1825

| **$6,000-7,000** | **SI** |

A pair of 19thC bronzed table lusters, cast with vine leaves and supported on three tapering legs with paw feet on round base, converted to electricity, showing signs of rusting.

12in (30cm) high

| **$800-900** | **DN** |

A No 2 Hinks oil lamp, with cranberry glass shade.

c1860   28in (71cm) high

| **$350-400** | **OACC** |

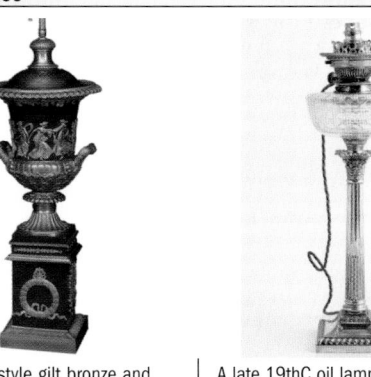

A Louis XVI style gilt bronze and patinated metal campana form urn, decorated with classical figures of dancing figures in relief, fitted as lamp.

23in (58.4cm) high

| **$6,000-7,000** | **SI** |

A late 19thC oil lamp, the hobnail-cut clear glass receiver supported on electroplate Corinthian column and gadrooned square foot, the column by Hawksworth Eyre and Co.

19.75in (50cm) high

| **$450-550** | **Chef** |

► A Victorian gilt-brass three-branch oil lamp, cast overall with strapwork, the lobed finial above a goblet-shaped reservoir, the three tubular branches supported by foliate scrolls, cornucopia and male torso, their arms uplifted to support the lights, on a round stepped base, by Whitfield and Hughes, London.

33.75in (85.5cm) high

| **$1,500-2,000** | **DN** |

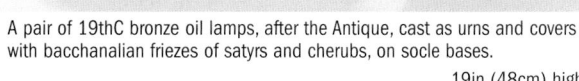

A pair of 19thC bronze oil lamps, after the Antique, cast as urns and covers with bacchanalian friezes of satyrs and cherubs, on socle bases.

19in (48cm) high

| **$2,200-2,800** | **L&T** |

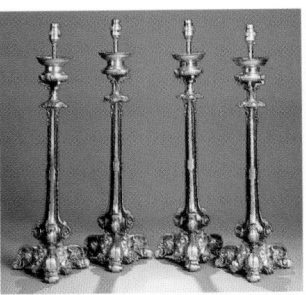

A set of four part-bronzed brass lamp stands, of columnar form clasped by three fins with shaped circular top on consoled supports, spreading scrolling leaf-cast tripod base with masks.

23in (58cm) high

$6,000-7,000		L&T

A set of four 19thC gilt-bronze wall sconces, each with ribbon-tied supports entwined by oak leaves, the electrified lamps former crossed torches.

39.75in (101cm) wide

$10,000-12,000		L&T

A late 19thC Irish cranberry glass and gilt-brass oil lamp, the receiver, column and plinth of facetted glass, the collars separating the three, cast with leaves, all on square red and gray mottled base, by D Sheehan, 109 and 110 Patrick St Cork.

20in (51cm) high

$1,500-2,000		Chef

A pair of early 20thC bronze-mounted marble table lamps, each with light fitting and adjustable ruched shades surmounted by a butterfly, issuing from marble urn with Neo-classical mounts supported by three cherubic caryatids linked at the wrists by chains, with single hoof feet, on stepped circular marble plinth with lambrequin mounts and turned feet, circular shades. overall

39.75in (101cm) high

$6,000-7,000		L&T

A CLOSER LOOK AT A WALL LIGHT

These lights are of grand proportions and were not made for a small house. This increases their value.

The chasing and gilding incorporate interesting design elements, such as the trumpets, winged figure and the bugle.

The quality of casting is substantially better than many of 20thC reproduction pieces which tend to be insipid and a bit ragged round the edges.

The acanthus scroll is classical and crisp, giving an almost three-dimensional effect.

A pair of late 19thC ormolu and bronze wall lights, each cast with acanthus scrolls, with three trumpet-shaped branches supported by a bronze winged figure with arms aloft, on a stylized leaf and palmette bracket, stamped 11029.

19in (48cm) high

$12,000-15,000		DN

A CLOSER LOOK AT ORMOLU CANDELABRA

All elements of the pair are very decorative.

There are interesting design elements such as the ram's masks and pomegranate.

The ormolu casting is exceptionally crisp.

The fact that the candelabra are a pair increases their value.

A pair of late 18thC French ormolu candelabra, each with pomegranate finial and basket of fruit, above a blued steel urn with three leaf-scrolled candle branches, the engine-turned sconces and drip pans supported by cockerel heads, the urn on a central vine-entwined support and a classical tripod headed with ram masks supporting three further candle branches, the tripod terminating with sphinxes, on a later gilt-metal round base with projecting plinths.

Provenance: from the collection formed by the late The Hon Mrs Daisy Fellowes, Donnington Grove, Bershire.

40.5in (103cm) high

$50,000-60,000		DN

▶ One of a pair of bronze and gilt-brass five-branch wall lights, each with foliate scroll arms supported on winged figured cast with anthemions.

26.5in (67.5cm) high

$3,000-4,000 (pair)		DN

BOXES

▶ An 18thC enamel snuffbox, probably South Staffordshire, decorated with raised white enameling of diaper asymmetric panels, flowers and scrolls on a light-blue tinted ground, gilt-metal mounts, the interior with a painted portrait of a woman with spindle.

c1780   3.5in (8.8cm) wide

$750-850   **BAR**

▶ An 18thC French enamel box, with bronze hinge and framing, the lid depicting a pair of lovers and a sheep in a rustic lakeside setting, the sides painted with floral sprays, painted mark to underside SCEOULX.

6.25in (16cm) wide

$400-500   **L&T**

An 18thC French enamel box, with silver-metal hinge and frame, decorated with raised gilt-work.

3.25in (8cm) wide

$400-500   **L&T**

An 18thC German enamel snuffbox, with gilt-metal mounts, decorated with an urn on a plinth before majestic ruins, the interior with one similar panel and turquoise enamel.

3.25in (8cm) wide

$100-160   **L&T**

An 18thC gilt-metal mounted enamel box, the lid decorated with figures in a landscape and the sides with landscape panels.

3.5in (9cm)

$600-700   **GorL**

An 18thC enamel box and cover, with classical landscape lid and floral paneled sides.

3.75in (9.5cm)

$600-700   **GorL**

A Bilston enamel small circular pillbox, with "A Token of Regard" and motif printed in black on white cover with turquoise base.

Enameled wares were produced in the town of Bilston, West Midlands, from the 1750s. During it's heyday, from 1760 to 1790, it was the largest enamel factory in England. Decorative enameling declined, probably as a result of the Napoleonic wars and developments in making small items using ceramics, but industrial enameling continued to be produced in the town into the 20thC. As Bilston enamels are never signed and the colors used were not unique, it is very difficult to identify and provenance is usually the only reliable method of authentication.

1in (2.2cm) dia

$200-250   **BAR**

A late 18thC Battersea enamel-on-copper patch-box.

Provenance: *Given as a wedding present by Robert Cay of North Charlton (1754) to his wife Elizabeth Hall of Otterburn and Catelugh. Bequethed to Isabella Cay, Robert Cay's great grand-daughter and then to her niece Margaret Dunn in 1935.*

The Battersea Enamel Factory was founded by Stephen Theodore Janssen in London in 1753. The factory was the first to use transfer-printing on enamels and its manager, John Brooks, invented a technique for enameling on a copper base. Typical wares are puce on a white ground, often imitating Meissen porcelain, and common motifs include landscapes and flowers. The factory closed in 1756 but influenced a number of other factories including those in Birmingham and Staffordshire, England.

2in (5cm) wide

$700-800   **Gro**

A 19thC enamel box, with molded gilt-brass frame and leaf-cast spandrels to lid, painted with courtiers in historical dress.

5.5in (14cm) wide

$180-220   **L&T**

A 19thC Continental enamel box and cover, with a figural panel lid and floral paneled sides.

5.25in (13.5cm) dia

$600-700   **GorL**

◀ A 19thC German enamel and gilt-metal mounted box and cover, with gilded Oriental figures.

4in (10cm) wide

$500-600   **GorL**

Enamel Boxes

A 19thC gilt-metal mounted Limoges enamel box with domed cover, decorated with portrait medallions of saints, within "jeweled" borders.

Enameled wares were produced in Limoges, France during the 16thC and 17thC and are considered the finest European examples of that period. Most of the work was done by a small number of families and early designs include Gothic-style religious scenes, Renaissance motifs and monochrome designs. Bright rather than harmonious colors dominated later production.

5in (9cm) dia

$700-800   **GorL**

A 19thC Continental enamel and gilt-metal mounted box and cover, with gilded floral decoration.

3.25in (8.5cm) wide

$400-500   **GorL**

A 19thC German enamel box and cover, the lid gilded with musicians.

4in (10cm) wide

$500-600   **GorL**

A 19thC French enamel box and cover, the lid with drinkers in a tavern on a gilded guilloche ground.

3.75in (9.5cm) wide

$500-600   **GorL**

A 19thC French enamel and gilt-metal mounted box and cover, the lid with ladies at a fountain, and floral sides.

3.5in (9cm)

$700-800   **GorL**

A large 19thC French enamel and gilt-metal mounted box and cover, the lid decorated with a harbor view and boats at anchor, floral swagged sides.

5in (12.5cm)

$800-900   **GorL**

A 19thC Continental enamel box and cover, the lid decorated with a Venetian harbor, the sides and base with flowers and mayflies.

3.5in (9cm) wide

$700-800   **GorL**

A large 19thC French enamel and gilt-metal mounted box and cover, the lid painted with figures drinking and playing cards in a barn, floral sides and base.

5.5in (14cm) wide

$1,000-1,200   **GorL**

A 19thC French enamel and gilt-metal mounted box and cover, the lid decorated with gentlemen playing cards, floral sides and base.

3.25in (8.5cm) wide

$400-500   **GorL**

A 19thC French enamel and gilt-metal mounted box and cover, the lid with naval battle scene, floral sides.

5.25in (13.5cm) dia

$800-900   **GorL**

A Continental enamel and sterling silver box, the base engine-turned, maker's mark A K stamped 925.

3.25in (8cm) dia

$700-800   **BonS**

A Continental gilt-metal and champleve-enamel table jewelry casket, the lid inset with a pietra dura panel of birds on a branch, folding side-handles, the whole with applied champleve-enamel mounts, velvet-lined interior.

11.75 (30cm) wide

$2,700-3,000   **L&T**

A silver and tortoiseshell snuffbox, by Charles Ombreissett, the lid with an embossed portrait of Charles II.

c1720   3in (8cm) diameter

$1,200-1,500   **MB**

A silver snuffbox, made in Birmingham.

1827   2.5in (6.5cm) wide

$400-500   **JBS**

A silver-gilt snuffbox, by John Bettridge, Birmingham.

1827   2.75in (7cm) wide

$800-1,000   **JBS**

A silver snuffbox, by Nat Mills, Birmingham.

1827   2.25in (5.5cm) wide

$250-350   **JBS**

A book vinaigrette, made in Birmingham.

1831   1.5in (4cm) long

$800-1,000   **JBS**

A silver vinaigrette, made in Birmingham.

1833   1.5in (4cm) long

$600-700   **JBS**

A silver vinaigrette, made in Birmingham.

1835   1.5in (4cm) long

$500-600   **JBS**

A Victorian table snuff-box, by Joseph Willmore, Birmingham, the ogee sides engine-turned with closed floral scroll borders, the gilt interior with contemporary inscription "John Moore to James Cross, a token of friendship etc".

1841   3in (8cm) wide

$500-600   **BonS**

An embossed silver ladies' compact mirror, in the shape of a book, made in London.

1874   2.75in (7cm) wide

$800-1,000   **JBS**

A French silver cigarette case, the enamel cover depicting two dogs lying on a rug.

1880   3.25in (8.5cm) long

$3,000-3,500   **JBS**

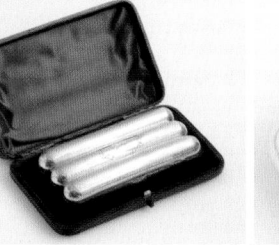

A silver cigar case, made in Birmingham, in original box.

1883   4.75in (12cm) long

$750-850   **JBS**

A silver perfume bottle, decorated with enamel flowers and foliage, made in Birmingham.

1887   3in (7.5cm) long

$1,000-1,200   **JBS**

A Russian silver enamel box, by Khlebnikov, Moscow, enameled with flowers and foliage, the rims enameled with stylized flowers and hearts on gilt-matted ground, the handles in the form of roosters, the hinged cover opening to reveal a gilt interior, on four ball-and-claw feet.

Ivan Khlebnikov started a family company of jewelers in Moscow, in the middle of the 19thC. As well as jewelry and objets d'art, his company was famous for the iconostases and decorative items it made for a number of important cathedrals in Moscow. The company closed in 1917 due to the revolution. Khlebnikov's work can be found in the Kremlin museum, Moscow and the State Hermitage.St Petersburg.

A Russian silver and enamel cigarette box, applied with stylized flowers and two owls on a branch, with gilt interior, monogrammed.

c1900   4.5in (11cm) wide

$2,500-3,000   **SI**

A silver case for three cigars, made in Birmingham.

1901   5.5in (14cm) long

$250-300   **LFA**

A silver vesta, made in Birmingham.

1910   2in (5.5cm) long

$150-200   **JBS**

1891   6.5in (16.5cm) long

$3,000-4,000   **SI**

A silver vesta, made in Chester.

1902　　　　1.5in (4cm) long

$100-150　　　　**JBS**

A silver sovereign and half-sovereign holder, made in Birmingham.

1914　　　　2in (5cm) wide

$200-250　　　　**JBS**

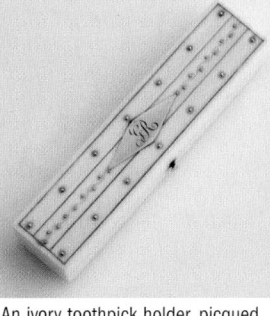

An ivory toothpick holder, picqued with gold.

c1790　　　　3.5in (8.5cm) wide

$300-400　　　　**RdeR**

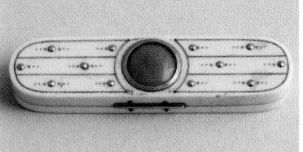

A George III ivory toothpick case, the hinged lid inlaid with gilt-metal and a circular panel.

3.5in (9cm) wide

$250-350　　　　**Clv**

A George III ivory toothpick box, decorated with gold-colored metal dots.

3.25in (8.5cm) wide

$300-400　　　　**BonS**

A George III ivory toothpick box, the hinged cover with raised gold-metal flowerheads and wirework detail.

2.5in (6cm) wide

$250-350　　　　**BonS**

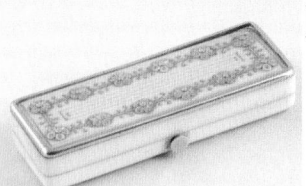

An Indian ivory-veneered box with etched and black-stained foliate bands and sandalwood interior.

7.5in (19cm) wide

$400-500　　　　**BonS**

A Regency ivory box, signed M Seguin, with miniature of the Prince Regent.

c1820　　　　4.25in (10.5cm) dia

$600-800　　　　**RdeR**

A French shell box.

c1860　　　　5.5in (14cm) wide

$200-250　　　　**SS**

A French shell box.

c1860　　　　7in (18cm) wide

$200-250　　　　**SS**

A shell box.

c1860　　　　6in (15cm) wide

$150-200　　　　**SS**

A French shell box.

c1920　　　　6.5in (17cm) wide

$150-200　　　　**SS**

A Scottish horn with nickel-mounted snuff mull.

c1820　　　　3.5in (8.5cm) long

$300-400　　　　**MB**

▶ A 19thC horn snuff mull, with simple silver clasp and mount engraved Duncan Cameron.

Snuff-taking first became popular at the beginning of the 18thC and snuff boxes from that time tend to be similar to tobacco boxes but with a hinged lid. Larger examples are known as table snuff-boxes and would probably been used to offer snuff to guests around the dinner table. By the mid 19thC snuff-taking had begun to decline and the manufacture of snuff-boxes declined with it. Snuff mulls have a ridged interior so that a plug of tobacco could be ground against it to produce snuff. Early mulls were made from horn, but later examples were engraved silver, gilt-metal or tortoiseshell.

2.5in (6.7cm) high

$450-500　　　　**L&T**

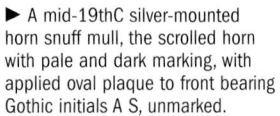

▶ A mid-19thC silver-mounted horn snuff mull, the scrolled horn with pale and dark marking, with applied oval plaque to front bearing Gothic initials A S, unmarked.

3.75in (9.5cm)

$250-350　　　　**BonS**

A 19thC pressed-horn snuffbox, in the form of a French officer's hat, decorated with a figure of Napoleon, and titled "Napoleon A' St. Helene".

3in (8cm) wide

$300-400   **LFA**

A Victorian horn snuffbox, the hinged cover with parquetry tortoiseshell inlay on an ivory ground.

3in (8cm) wide

$100-150   **BAR**

A French carved and painted bone prisoner of war domino box set, with an erotic painting on inner lid.

Prisoner of War *work was predominately carved from bone by French prisoners from the Napoleonic War while imprisoned on ships off the coast of Plymouth, England. They include ships models and were often sold to improve conditions.*

c1790   5.5in (14cm) long

$300-400   **RdeR**

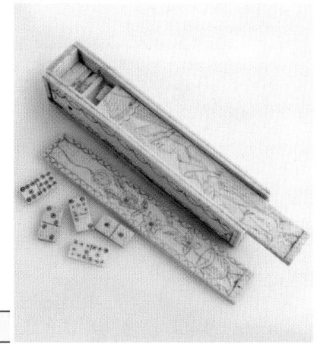

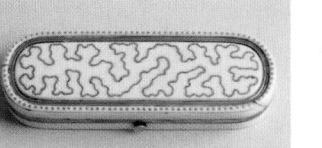

A George III toothpick case, the hinged cover with inlaid gilt-metal decoration and reeded border, interior with inset mirror.

3.5in (9cm) wide

$400-500   **Clv**

A George III tortoiseshell and silver inlaid twin scent bottle case, lid restored.

$300-400   **HamG**

A 19thC Continental gilt-copper box, the hinged lid and box cast with scenes of peasant life, the whole set upon turned, beaded feet.

8in (20.5cm) long

$1,000-1,200   **SI**

A Scottish table snuffbox with glass bottom and stone-set top.

c1870   3in (7.5cm) dia

$150-200   **MB**

MISCELLANEOUS

A Russian gold cigarette box, maker's mark for Henri Wegstrom, also bears a Fabergé mark, the cover repoussé-decorated with double-headed imperial eagle within foliate decoration, with cabochon sapphire push piece, in fitted box.

3.5in (9cm) wide

$1,500-2,000   **SI**

A Dutch silver miniature cabinet, decorated with a romantic rural scene.

1890   4in (10.5cm) high

$700-800   **JBS**

A Dutch silver miniature piano.

1890   3.25in (8cm) long

$700-800   **JBS**

A Dutch silver ornamental piece, depicting two figures dancing in front of a band playing above.

1890   4in (10cm) high

$750-850   **JBS**

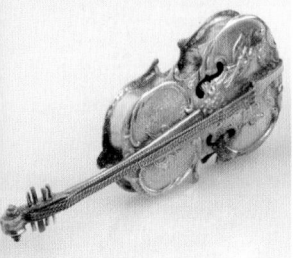

A Dutch silver miniature cello.

c1900   3.75in (9.5cm) long

$300-400   **JBS**

A late 18thC Continental silver and mother-of-pearl eyeglass case, engraved with flowers, leaves and C-scrolls.

2.5in (6.5cm) long

$150-200   **LFA**

A silver belt-buckle, by William Comyns, London.

1899   5in (12.5cm) long

$100-150   **JBS**

A silver shoe-shaped ring holder, embossed with leaf scrolls, made in Birmingham.

1901   6.25in (16cm) long

$450-550   **LFA**

Miscellaneous

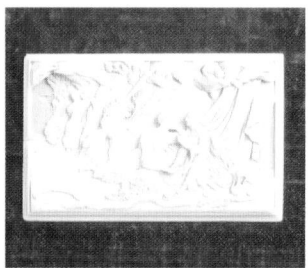

An 18thC French ivory plaque, in the Turkish taste, carved in relief with a scene of lovers in a cave and mounted on a velvet table.

4in (10cm) wide

$700-800	L&T

A pair of 19thC Continental ivory figures, possibly German.

8.25in (21cm) high

$3,000-4,000	Gro

A late 19thC Black Forest carved-bone group depicting a poacher with stag being challenged by two gamekeepers and a dog in a woodland setting.

4.5in (11.4cm) high

$300-400	Clv

A Continental ivory cross, mounted with cherubim, fitted in shadowbox frame.

6.5in (16.5cm) high

$1,000-1,500	SI

A French gold and abolone aide-mémoire.

Abolone comes from a tropical mollusc, which produces mother-of-pearl. An aide mémoire (memory aid) was a small decorative case containing sheets of ivory leaves or paper, which were used for note taking. They were popular throughout the 18thC and 19thC.

▲1 An enamel aide-mémoire, the front with gold dots, the central panel hand-painted with flowers, the rear with gold dots, side opening and ivory pencil.

c1860   3.5in (9cm) long

$450-550	PC

▲2 A turquoise-blue porcelain aide-mémoire, with one side decorated with hand-painted flowers on white panels, reverse with silver and gold gilding, red silk interior.

c1860   3.5in (9.8cm) long

$600-800	PC

▲3 A porcelain aide-mémoire, with hand-painted flowers, silver mounting, side opening, beige cloth interior, pencil missing.

c1860   3.75in (9.6cm) long

$600-800	PC

A Victorian horn beaker, by Joseph Bett, London.

c1862   4in (10.5cm) high

$100-150	MB

A Georgian horn beaker with coaching scene.

The scene on the beaker refers to an incident in the village of St. Hinder, England in 1819 where a coaching party were set upon by a lion.

4in (10.5cm) high

$300-400	MB

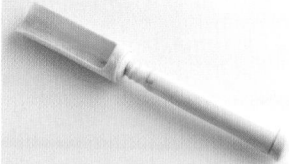

A Regency ivory Stilton scoop.

c1820   7.75in (19.5cm) long

$300-400	RdeR

A French ormolu and marble poodle paperweight.

c1860   5in (13cm) wide

$1,000-1,200	Gro

c1840   3.5in (9cm) long

$250-300	RdeR

A miniature chiffonier, decorated with shells.

1860   9in (23cm) high

$350-450	SS

A late 19thC nut, inscribed "Peruvian Ashore at Seaford, Feb 8th 1899" with naive inkwork decoration depicting a three-masted ship at anchor with various figures standing on the shore.

2in (5cm) wide

$80-120	Clv

A collection of opals and other semi-precious stones set in a glass-topped, blue john surround.
Blue john is a violet-blue banded hardstone indigenous to the Castleton area of Derbyshire, England. It has been used in ornamentation for centuries.

2.5in (6.5cm) dia

$300-400	Clv

A pair of Russian Fabergé-style silver-gilt mounted hardstone cassolettes and covers, on concave tripartite hardstone base with paw-feet.

Cassolettes are vases with reversible lids that could be used to hold candles.

$1,500-2,000	L&T

AFTER AN INITIAL UNCERTAINTY, IN THE WAKE OF THE TERRORIST ATTACKS, the American painting market has rallied, and we have seen a stream of record prices for American artists. Any painting with the Stars and Stripes has quite literally 'flown off the wall'. Most notable is Norman Rockwell's 1943 "Rosie the Riveter" selling for 4,959,500 at Sotheby's New York in May 2002. In this section of our guide we have chosen to look in some depth at Western Art. This is a particularly strong area with a devoted following, with artists such as Remington and Russell doing exceptionally well, along with contemporary artists of this genre. Currently there is a lot of interest in the Modernist artists, especially the Stieglitz

Circle, particularly Marsden Hartley (whose Kandinsky-influenced "Painting No. 6" sold at Sotheby's for in excess of $2,700,000). Many collectors are starting to look for 'edgier' material than the Impressionists, although having said that, Pennsylvania and California Impressionists are in great demand, particularly in the former group Garber and Redfield (whose "The Village of Carversville" sold for a record price of $519,500 at Freemans in December 2001). Old stalwarts such as the Hudson River School, Luminists and Sargent are still very popular. Also well worth checking out are Trompe L'Oeil Still Life and Black Artists and subject matter such as Jacob Lawrence and Romare Bearden.

Alasdair Nichol

WESTERN ART

Roy Andersen "The Horsetail Lance". mixed media. signed.
30 x 30in (76.2 x 76.2cm)

$10,000-20,000	RENO

ROY ANDERSEN was born in 1930 and grew up on a horse farm in New Hampshire. He studied at the Chicago Academy of Fine Art and the Art Center School of Los Angeles, and subsequently became an illustrator for National Geographic, Time magazine and Sports Illustrated, living in New York and Chicago.

Andersen's paintings focus primarily on Crow, Cheyenne and Apache Indians. He is renowned for his acute accuracy, uncanny sense of composition and color harmony. Andersen was admitted to the Cowboy Artists of America in 1989 and in 1990, at the 25th Annual CAA Exhibition, Andersen's "We Hunt Them" won the coveted Gold Medal for Oil award. In 1991, he received the Silver Medal for Oil for his piece "The Silent Blanket."

Roy Andersen currently resides on a horse ranch in Cave Creek, Arizona, where he raises horses that often feature in his paintings.

Roy Andersen "Where the Sacred Bird Leads", oil on canvas, signed bottom right.

of this painting Andersen writes, "The Thunder Bird, ruler of the air, the war eagle epitomised by the golden eagle, carried the power of great vision. The owner of a sacred eagle medicine bundle dreams of a place that his band of Absaroka (Crow) people should move to. In great faith they set out to fulfill the unknown promise of that dream".

48 x 72in (122 x 183cm)

$60,000-90,000	RENO

Clyde Aspevig "Mt. Rundle". Oil on canvas.
40in (101.5cm) wide

$18,000-26,000	RENO

Roy Andersen "Breakfast in the Bighorns", oil on canvas, signed bottom left.
24 x 48in (61 x 122cm)

$55,000-65,000	RENO

691

Clyde Aspevig "Grand Canyon of the Yellowstone". Oil on canvas.

Provenance: *Grand Central Art Galleries, Inc., New York City. Property of Rockwell International Corporation, Pittsburgh, Pennsylvania, purchased 1995.*

24in (61cm) wide

$6,000-12,000	RENO

CLYDE ASPEVIG was born in 1951 on a farm near Rudyard, Montana. He was introduced to painting as a child whilst convalescing after an accident which left him with a broken leg. In 1969, Aspevig moved to Billings, Montana where he majored in art at Eastern Montana College. He then moved to Sandy, Oregon, where he taught art at Sandy Union High School.

His paintings reveal his deep attachment to the Western landscape, featuring the wide, open horizons of Wyoming and Montana. He established his national reputation as a prominent artist during the 1970s and 80s. In 1997, his "Rocky Mountains Colorado" won the "Prix de West "award from the National Cowboy Hall of Fame in Oklahoma City.

Clyde Aspevig "Glacier Basin Hike". Oil on canvas. signed.

24 x 30in (60.9 x 76.2)

$10,000-15,000	RENO

James Bama "Pawnee Indian". Oil on board. Footnote: the model for "Pawnee Indian" is Wes Studi, who starred in "Dances with Wolves" and "The Last of the Mohicans".

13in (33cm) wide

$8,000-12,000	RENO

Albert Bierstadt, (1830-1902), "Buffalo Herd", oil on board.

18in (46cm) wide

$70,000-80,000	RENO

Albert Bierstadt, "King's Canyon",oil on canvas.

18in (45.5cm) wide

$90,000-110,000	RENO

Ralph Albert Blakelock, (1847-1919), "Indian Camp",oil on board.

11in (28cm) wide

$25,000-30,000	RENO

Edward Borein, (1872-1945), "Navajo Horsemen", watercolor.

11in (28cm) wide

$25,000-30,000	RENO

Edward Borein,"Cattle Drive", watercolor, signed.

7 x 10in (17.7 x 25.4cm)

$22,000-26,000	RENO

Vestern Art

Edward Borein, "Driving a Herd", watercolor, signed.

5 x 11in (12.7 x 27.9cm)

$20,000-23,000   **RENO**

EDWARD BOREIN (1873-1945) was born in San Leandro, California. At the age of seventeen he began working for a saddlemaker, going on to work as a cowboy, whilst continuing his passion for sketching and illustration. He later spent a month at the San Francisco Art Association, leaving to join a ranch in Santa Barbara and then Mexico as a cowboy. The owner admired Borein's sketches and asked him to take part in a tour of Mexico as a staff artist. During the tour, Borein began painting in watercolor.

After many years without success, he began illustrating for magazines including, "Harpers," "Colliers," and "Western World." He subsequently became one of the most famous artists in America, achieving national acclaim in 1921.

Borein married in 1921 and settled in Santa Barbara, where he stayed for the rest of his life.

James Boren, (1921-1990), "Yesterday Was Like Spring", watercolor, signed.

21 x 29in (53.3 x 73.6cm)

$19,000-22,000   **RENO**

Ken Carlson, (b.1940), "Valley of the Past", oil on board.

of this painting Carlson writes: "Valley of the Past" resulted from my observations of these great beasts and imagining the vastness of their once great habitat. I borrowed this title from a line penned by Charles "Badger" Clark, the famed first Poet Laureate of South Dakota".

45in (114.5cm) wide

$50,000-60,000   **RENO**

JOHN CLYMER (1907-1989) was born in Ellensburg, Washington. He studied in Canada at the Vancouver School of Art and the Ontario College of Art, before embarking on his career as an artist. His travels to Alaska, Canada and the American Northwest, largely provided the inspiration for his big game and wildlife paintings. The Northern plains Indians, fur trappers, animals and the history of the Pacific Northwest all feature strongly in his work. He was considered one of the most "realistic" painters of his time, depicting the struggles and triumphs of the early pioneers.

He worked as an illustrator for over forty years for, amongst others "Saturday Evening Post" and "Field and Stream." He also won many prestigious wards and was a member of numerous galleries and Arts associations.

John Clymer's work is represented in the permanent collections of the National Cowboy Hall of Fame, Oklahoma City and the Whitney Gallery of Western Art, Cody, Wyoming

John Clymer, (1907-1989), "Grizzly Mother and Cubs", oil on canvas.

40in (101.5cm) wide

$60,000-70,000   **RENO**

John Clymer, "Snow Line", oil on canvas.

36in (91.5cm) wide

$45,000-60,000   **RENO**

693

John Clymer, "Indians and Buffalo", oil on board, signed.

36in (91.4cm) wide

$110,000-130,000   **RENO**

Michael Coleman, (b.1946), "The Watchers", gouache, signed.

10.5in (26.5cm) wide

$8,500-9,500   **RENO**

John Clymer, "Colockum Trail", oil on board, signed.

20 x 30in (50.8 x 76.2cm)

$50,000-60,000   **RENO**

Michael Coleman, "Blackfeet Sunset", oil on board, signed.

20in (51cm) wide

$13,000-15,000   **RENO**

▶ Eanger Irving Couse, (1866-1936), "Moonlight", oil on board.

accompanied by two letters from the artist's son, Kibbey Couse, regarding his father's painting techniques and the purchase of "Moonlight".

12in (30.5cm) wide

$40,000-50,000   **RENO**

Eanger Irving Couse, "Moonlight Spring", oil on board, signed.

9 x 12in (22.8 x 30.4cm)

$20,000-23,000   **RENO**

Thomas Aquinas Daly, (20th C), "Fox Trapper", watercolor, signed.

6 x 11in (15.2 x 27.9cm)

$4,500-5,000   **RENO**

Western Art

Donald Crowley, (b. 1926), "Mountain Trail", oil on canvas, signed.
24in (60.9cm)

$36,000-40,000　　　　　　　　**RENO**

Charlie Dye, (1906-1972), "The Chase", oil on board, signed.
7 x 9in (17.7 x 22.8cm)

$17,000-20,000　　　　　　　　**RENO**

Joe DeYong, (1894-1975), "Men of the Open Range", oil on canvas, signed. "Men of the Open Range" is dated 1921 and bears a strong resemblance to Chales Russell's painting of the same title dated 1923. On the reverse is a repoduction of Russell's painting with the notion, "Did Russell copy DeYong, "Men of the Open Range, 1923?"

$15,000-18,000　　　　　　　　**RENO**

Robert Duncan, (b.1952), "Forest Trail", oil on board, signed.
20 x 28in (51 x 71cm)

$10,000-13,000　　　　　**RENO**

Charlie Dye, "Morning Round-Up", oil on board, signed.
7 x 9in (17.7 x 22.8cm)

$15,000-18,000　　　**RENO**

W Herbert Dunton, (1878-1936), "The Frontiersman", oil on canvas, signed.
30 x 16in (76.2 x 40.6cm)

$35,000-40,000　　　**RENO**

Charlie Dye, "Morning Round-Up", oil on board, signed.
7 x 9in (17.7 x 22.8cm)

$15,000-18,000　　　　　　　　**RENO**

Western Art

Charlie Dye, "Pay Day", mixed media, signed. This is a study for the larger version of "Pay Day".

1961   11in (28cm) wide

$32,000-35,000   **RENO**

John Fery, (1859-1934), Mt.Wilbur - Glacier Park, oil on canvas.

72in (183cm) wide

John Fery, "Glacier Elk", oil on canvas, signed.

36in (91.5cm) wide

$17,000-20,000   **RENO**   **$9,000-11,000**   **RENO**

Luke Frazier, (20thC.), "After the Chase", oil on board, signed.

48in (121.9cm) wide

$23,000-26,000   **RENO**

Eugene C.Frank, (1844-1941), "Buffalo Grazing at Sunset", oil on canvas, signed "E.C. Frank" bottom right.

35.7in (91cm) wide

$10,000-12,000   **FRE**

Charles Fritz, (20th C.), "The Mystic", oil on canvas, signed.

50in (127cm) wide

$50,000-55,000   **RENO**

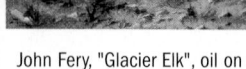

Elling William Gollings, "Tall In The Saddle", oil on canvas, signed and dated "1925".

14in (35.6cm) wide

$45,000- 50,000   **FRE**

E WILLIAM GOLLINGS (1878-1932) was born in a mining camp at Pierce City, Idaho. He was educated in Chicago before moving West in 1896. He worked his way towards his brother Dewitt's ranch in Montana. There he borrowed a horse and joined what was known as the "grub-trail," roaming the range, fur trapping, branding cattle and looking for gold.

In 1905 Gollings returned to Chicago and studied at the Royal Academy of Fine Arts where he was awarded a scholarship. Despite this he left, preferring to return to the west. He moved to Sheridan, Wyoming, where he settled and built a studio. He devoted himself to his painting of western scenes, using "Gollings" and a pony track symbol to sign his work. He died in Sheridan in 1932.

Elling William Gollings, (1878-1932), "Range Riders", oil on board, signed bottom left.

10in (25.5cm) wide

$68,000-74,000   **RENO**

Elling William Gollings, "Indian Scouts", oil on canvas.

1921   18in (45.5cm) wide

$40,000-45,000   **RENO**

Elling William Gollings,"Showing Off", oil on canvas, signed.

11 x 17in (27.9 x 43cm)

$8,000-11,000   **RENO**

Elling William Gollings, "Driving Cattle", watercolor, signed.

11.5 x 9.5in (29.2 x 24cm)

$7,000-9,000   **RENO**

Ernest Martin Hennings, (1886-1956) "In Taos Canyon", oil on board.

14in (35.5cm) wide

$68,000-75,000   **RENO**

Thomas Hill, (1829-1908), "The Elusive Quarry", oil on canvas, signed.

30 x 44in (76.2 x 111.7cm)

$ 45,000-60,000   **REN**

Frank Tenney Johnson, (1874-1939), "The Stillness of Night", watercolor.

16in (40.5cm) wide

$62,000-65,000   **RENO**

Frank Tenney Johnson, "The Meeting", oil on canvas.

17in (43cm) wide

$24,000-28,000   **RENO**

Harvey William Johnson, (b1920),"Fur Bridge on the Move (Spring)", oil on canvas.

50in (127cm) wide

$20,000-25,000   **RENO**

Frank Tenney Johnson, "Morning Ride", oil on canvas, signed.

12in (30.4) wide

$20,000-25,000   **RENO**

Bob Kuhn, (b1920),"Ursa Major", acrylic on board.

36in (91.5cm) wide

$75,000-85,000   **RENO**

Bob Kuhn, "Cape Buffalo", acrylic on board.

Thomas Kinkade, (b1947), "The Company Store", oil on board, signed.

10in (25.4cm) wide

$18,000-20,000   **RENO**

36in (91.5cm) wide

$45,000-50,000   **RENO**

William R. Leigh, (1866-1955) "At the Water-Hole", oil on board, on the reverse is a receipt from Grand Central Galleries, New York City, indicating a price of $200, as well as a description that reads: "An unmarried girl of Zuni, New Mexico: these people - first cousins to the Aztec - have had always the purest form of communistic (sic) government; a president and a high-priest, both subject to recall, the houses are owned by women, who make the matrimonial propositions, the farming and hunting done by all equally".

8in (20.5cm) wide

$90,000-110,000   RENO

◆ 225

William R Leigh, (1866-1955) "Grand Canyon", oil on canvas, signed.

1909   9in (22.8cm) wide

$24,000-28,000   RENO

Tom Lovell, (1909-1997), Study for "Five Miles Ahead of the Column", pastel, signed bottom left.

5 x 7.75in (13 x 19.5cm)

$7,000-9,000   RENO

Tom Lovell, Study for "Flannel Shirt Flag", oil on board, signed bottom right.

5.5in (18 x 14cm)

$13,000-16,000   RENO

TOM LOVELL (1909-1997) was born in New York City. He received a bachelor of Fine Arts from Syracuse University in New York. He began his career as a freelance illustrator for many well-established magazines including "Colliers," "McCalls," and "National Geographic." He moved to Santa Fe, New Mexico in 1975 and pursued his career as a full-time artist. In the same year he was elected to the prestigious Cowboy Artists of America. His paintings are renowned for their attention to detail and poignant subjects, focusing mainly on the relationship between white men and Indians and early expeditions.

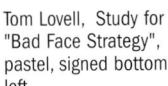

Tom Lovell, Study for "Bad Face Strategy", pastel, signed bottom left.

8.75in (22cm) wide

$5,000-7,000   RENO

Tom Lovell, "Study for Tumbleweed Serenade", oil on board, signed.

8.5in (21.5cm) wide

$13,000-16,000   RENO

▶Tom Lovell, "Study for Hard Crossing", oil on board, signed.

9.5in (24cm) wide

$15,000-18,000   RENO

▶ Frank McCarthy, ((b1924), "Apache Threat", oil on canvas,

1987   11in (28cm) wide

$10,000-12,000   RENO

699

Frank McCarthy, "His Death Song", oil on board.

18in (45.5cm) wide

$10,000-12,000	**RENO**

Robert Meyers, (1919-1970), "Wagon Train and Dog", gouache, signed.

12.5 x 19in (31.7 x 48.2cm)

$4,000-6,000	**RENO**

Dan Mieduch, (b1947), "West of the Little Laramie", oil on board, signed.

48in (121.9) wide

$35,000-40,000	**RENO**

Terry Mimnaugh, (20th C), "Jig's Team Along the Flathead", oil on board.

36in (91.5cm) wide

$18,000-20,000	**RENO**

Gary Niblett, (b.1943), "Downpour at Castle Rock", oil on canvas.

40in (101.5cm) wide

$19,000-21,000	**RENO**

EDGAR SAMUAL PAXSON (1852-1919) was born in upstate New York and worked for his father who was a sign painter and decorator of carriages. Apart from the training he was given by his father it appears he had no formal artistic training.

At the age of 25, inspired by the novels of James Fenimore Cooper and the Battle of the Little Big Horn, he moved to Montana. Working on ranches and as a government scout he absorbed the frontier life of the vanishing West.

His subject matter ranges from Native Americans to historical battles, hunting scenes to early exploration. His aim was to immortalize the Old West he knew so well before it changed beyond recognition.

His best known work is "Custer's Last Battle on the Little Big Horn," which contains more than 200 figures locked in battle and is revered for its attention to detail.

The expedition of Lewis and Clark was one of his major subjects, completed as a mural, but his small watercolours are his most sought after works.

Paxson's works are historically important within late 19th and early 20thC art, while also being nostalgic, romantic and sentimental.

Edgar S. Paxson, (1852-1919), "Portrait - Nag-A-Shaw", oil on canvas, signed bottom right.

According the his grandson, William Edgar Paxson Jr., "One of Edgar's favourite subjects was Nag-A-Shaw, chief of the Lemhi Bannock-Shoshone band. He had served as a scout for Generals Terry and Crok against the Sioux in 1876-77...He made reference to the Indian in a 1901 entry in his journal: "...He is very intelligent and knows just what is wanted. He often gets down a gun or tomahawk, or some pieces of Indian dress and strikes a pose with such grace and dignity as to make one wish he could do him in each and every one. He will sit all day for $1.00/hr. I often give him two-bits for simply drawing him in a five minute sketch".

13in (33cm) wide

$28,000-30,000	**RENO**

▶ Edgar S Paxson, "California Joe, Custer's Chef of Scouts", watercolor, signed.

1902   14in (35.5cm) wide

$23,000-26,000	**RENO**

◀ Edgar S Paxson, "Indians in Canoe", oil on board, signed.

11in (27.9cm) wide

$17,000-20,000	**RENO**

Edgar S Paxson, "Halt", oil on board, signed.

17 x 12in (43 x 30.4cm)

$7,000-10,000　　**RENO**

Clark Kelley Price, (20thC), "Knower of the Unknown", oil, signed.

40in (101.6cm) wide

$18,000-20,000　　**RENO**

Kenneth Pauling Riley, (b1919), "Camp Site", oil on canvas.

12in (30.5cm) wide

$12,000-15,000　　**RENO**

Carl Rungius, (1868-1959), "Mt. Cascade", oil on canvas.

20in (51cm) wide

$60,000-70,000　　**RENO**

Edgar Payne, (1882-1947), "Saddled Horse", oil on board, signed.

10 x 10in (25.4 x 25.4cm)

$11,000-13,000　　**RENO**

Donald L. Perceval, (1908-1979), "Cattle Drive", oil on canvas.

80in (203cm) wide

$28,000-30,000　　**RENO**

◀ Winold Reiss, (1886-1953), "Many White Horses and Eagle Calf", oil on canvas.

of this painting Reiss wrote, "Chief Eagle Calf posed for me in handsome traditional regalia in Glacier National Park when he was 56. He was one of the first full-blood Blackfeet educated at the Carlisle Indian School, Carlisle, Pennsylvania. His companion Many White Horses (Acapogotosa) was 38.

1927　　　36in (91.5cm) wide

$200,000-250,000　　**RENO**

Carl Rungius, "Lost Timber", oil on board, signed.

36 x 56in (91.4 x 142.2cm)

$140,000-160,000　　**RENO**

Carl Rungius, "Bull Elk", oil on canvas.

33 x 24in (83.8 x 60.9cm)

$75,000-90,000　　**RENO**

Western Art

Carl Rungius, "On the Upper Yukon Caribou at the Junction of the Pelly and MacMillian Rivers, Yukon Territory", oil on canvas.
45in (114.5cm) wide

$250,000-300,000   **RENO**

Charles M. Russell, (1864-1926), "Meat for Wild Men", watercolor.
1916   24in (61cm) wide

$1,200,00-1,500,00   **RENO**

Charles M. Russell, "Blackfeet Indian with Capote", watercolor,
1896.   9in (23cm) wide

$45,000-50,000   **RENO**

Charles M. Russell, "War Party", watercolor,
1890.   12in (30.5cm) wide

$45,000-50,000   **RENO**

Charles M. Russell, "Indian on Horseback", watercolor.
6in (15cm) wide

$40,000-50,000   **RENO**

Charles M Russell, "Waiting", watercolor, signed.
1897   28in (71cm) wide

$140,000-170,000   **RENO**

CHARLES MARION RUSSELL (1864-1926), was born in St Louis, Missouri. Russell's childhood dreams were about the American West. At sixteen his family enrolled him in Burlington Military Academy in New Jersey in an attempt to dissuade him, but he left after a year and so his parents agreed to let him go west. In 1881, Russell signed up with the Judith Ranch, where he stayed for seven years. Whist learning the cowboy's life Russell continued to paint and draw, and became immersed in both cowboy and Indian cultures. He lived with the Blood Tribe, a sect of the Blackfoot Nation, in Canada, for a short time, witnessing all the ceremonies and traditions of the tribe.

Russell moved to the Great Falls, Montana, in 1893, where the community became the first collectors of his work. In 1896 Russell married Nancy Cooper. It was Nancy who pushed Russell to further his career, and determined to make him famous, she tirelessly promoted his work through publishers and art galleries. In 1898, Russell cast his first bronzes at the Roman Bronze Works foundry in New York, and in 1899 he published the Pen Sketches, a collection

Charles Schreyvogel, (1861-1912), "Mountain Man", watercolor. signed.
13,5 x 11in (34.2 x 27.9cm)

$12,000-14,000   **RENO**

Olaf C. Seltzer, (1877-1957), "Blackfeet War Party", watercolor.
15in (38cm) wide

$25,000-30,000   **RENO**

OLAF CARL SELTZER (1877-1957) was born in Copenhagen, Denmark. After his father's death his mother moved the family to the Great Falls, Montana. Seltzer became a railway and locomotive repairman, and continued in this industry for over twenty-five years. During the early years of his employment he met the artist Charles Russell, who encouraged him to paint. In 1921 Seltzer was laid off from the railway, but found he was able to make a living from his art. In 1926 and during the following years, Seltzer made many trips to New York where he studied paintings in the galleries and museums and made contacts with buyers. He began to receive recognition and acclaim, although, not to the same extent of his mentor Charles Russell. However, recent years have seen an increase in appreciation for the prolific artsist, who produced over 2,500 paintings. A large collection of Seltzer's work is owned by the Gilcrease Institute in Tulsa, Oklahoma.

Olaf C. Seltzer, "Crow Scout", oil on board.
14in (35.5cm) wide

$55,000-60,000   **RENO**

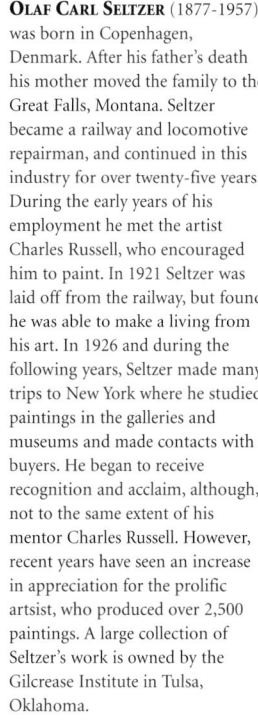

Olaf Carl Seltzer, "The Sentinel", oil on canvas, signed.
20in (50.8) wide

$55,000-60,000   **RENO**

Joseph Henry Sharp, (1859-1953), "Encampment in the Foothills", oil on canvas, signed.
18in (46cm) wide

$55,000-60,000   **RENO**

Olaf C Seltzer, "C M Russell on Monte", oil on board. signed.
6 x 4.5in (15.2 x 11.4cm)

$19,000-21,000   **RENO**

Olaf C Seltzer, "Mounted Brave", oil on board, signed.
6.5 x 5.5in (16.5 x 13.9cm)

$14,000-16,000   **RENO**

► Joseph Henry Sharp, "Evening-Toas Valley", oil on board, signed.
6.5 x 8.5in (16.5 x 21.5cm)

$19,000-21,000   **RENO**

Oleg Stavrowsky, (b.1927), "Last Hill Before Sundown", oil on canvas, signed.

52.5in (133.3cm) wide

| $16,000-18,000 | RENO |

Don Stivers, "Sergeant of the Line", oil on board, signed.

19 x 22in (48.2 x 55.8cm)

| $6,000-8,000 | RENO |

Susan Terpning, (20thC), "Scouting the High Country", oil on canvas,

36in (91.5cm) wide

| $11,000-13,000 | RENO |

▼ Gregory Sumida, (20thC.), "Earth People", oil on canvas, signed.

18 x 24in (45.7 x 60.9cm)

| $9,000-11,000 | RENO |

Bettina Steinke, (b.1913), "Navajo Mother and Daughter", signed "Bettina Steinke" bottom right, oil on canvas.

| $12,000-15,000 | FRE |

HOWARD TERPNING was born in 1927 in Oak Park, Illinois. He was educated at the Chicago Academy of Fine Arts and the American Academy of Art. He later gained employment as a commercial illustrator after moving to New York. He also became involved as an artist in movies, his assignments including The Guns of Navarone, Dr Zhivago, The Sound of Music and Cleopatra.

In the 1970s Terpning moved to Arizona where he began his first Western painting and after just three years was elected to the National Academy of Western Art and also to the Cowboy Artists of America. His work focuses on the Native American people of the Great Plains during the nineteenth century. Howard Terpning continues to live and work in Arizona today.

Don Stivers, (20thC.), "Deputy", oil on board, signed.

26 x 15in (66 x 38cm)

| $7,000-9,000 | RENO |

Howard Terpning, (b.1927), "Allegiance to the Crown", oil on canvas,

20in (51cm) wide

| $110,000-130,000 | RENO |

Howard Terpning, "Readin' Sign", oil on canvas.

23in (58.5cm) wide

$90,000-100,000   **RENO**

Howard Terpning, "Transfer of Power", oil on board, signed.

10in (25.4) wide

$90,000-100,000   **RENO**

OLAF WIEGHORST (1899-1975) was born in Jutland, Denmark. He emigrated to America when he was nineteen, landing in New York. Subsequently he joined the United States Cavalry, working on the Mexican border. Following his service he spent some time as a cowboy, and traveled around the southwest. He later returned to New York to paint and his work caught the attention of Grand Central Galleries, who exhibited his paintings. In1944, Wieghorst settled in El Cajon, California, where he began painting full time. His paintings depict cowboys, horses, and Indians, although his horse paintings were the most prolific. His works are in several private collections as well as The Eisenhower Library, Kansas and the Whitney Gallery, Wyoming.

Howard Terpning, "Entering the Apache Stronghold", oil on canvas.

24in (61cm) wide

$150,000-170,000 RENO

Olaf Wieghorst, (1899-1988), "Nez Perce", watercolor, signed.

9.5 x 8in (24 x 20.3cm)

$9,000-11,000   **RENO**

Olaf Wieghorst, "Bronc Rider", oil on canvas.

24in (61cm) wide

$50,000-60,000   **RENO**

Olaf Wieghorst, "Apaches on the Trail", oil on canvas.

30in (76cm) wide

$75,000-80,000   **RENO**

Jim Wilcox, (20thC) "Elk Refuge Rainbow", oil on board, signed.

24 x 36in
(60.9 x 91.4cm)

$12,000-14,000   **RENO**

Nat Youngblood, (20thC), "Winter, Taos Pueblo", watercolor, signed.

22 x 29in (55.8 x 73.6cm)

$7,500-8,500   **RENO**

WESTERN BRONZES

George Carlson, "The Fiddler", bronze.

1976   24.5in (62.5cm) high

$6,000-8,000   **RENO**

George Carlson, "Spear Fisherman", bronze.

1975   20in (51cm) high

$7,000-8,000   **RENO**

Earl e Heikka, (1910-1941) "The Unexpected". Bronze.

1939   15.5in (39.3cm) high

$8,000-9,000   **RENO**

Harry Jackson, "Bronc Stomper", bronze.

1959   18in (45.7cm) high

$4,000-5,000   **RENO**

► Frederic Remington, (1861-1909), "The Bronco Buster", bronze, stamped on the bottom.

"The Bronco Buster" was Remington's first sculpture. Capturing the balance between horse and rider was a difficult task for even an experienced sculptor, yet this work received immediate praise for its artistic merit. After 190, castings of "The Bronze Buster" were completed by the Roman Bronze Works employing the lost-wax method of casting. Throughout the rest of his career, Remington continued his association with this foundry.

23in (58.5cm) high

$90,000-110,000   **RENO**

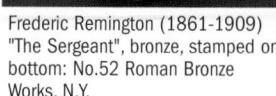

Frederic Remington (1861-1909) "The Sergeant", bronze, stamped on bottom: No.52 Roman Bronze Works, N.Y.

a copy of a letter from noted Remington bronze authority Rudolf G. Wunderlich authenticating this bronze accompanies the lot.

10.5in (27cm) wide

$26,000-28,000   **RENO**

Charles M. Russell (1864-1926) "Smoking Up No.29", bronze, signed on base: Roman Bronze Works NY.

Provenance: *The Latendorf Bookshop, New York City. Earl C. Adams, purchased*

1962.   11.75in (30cm) high

$15,000-25,000   **RENO**

Charles M Russell (1864-1926) "Sleeping Thunder". Bronze. signed on base; Roman Bronze Works NY.

7in (17.7cm) high

$5,000-10,000   **RENO**

Charles M Russell (1864-1926) "Enemy Tracks". Bronze. signed on base; Roman Bronze Works Inc. NY.

13in (33cm) high

$4,000-6,000   **RENO**

Robert M Scriver, (1914-1999), bronze, "Herd Bull",

20in (50.8cm) high

$8,000-10,000   **RENO**

PENNSYLVANIA ACADEMY OF THE FINE ARTS

Thomas Pollock Anshutz (1851-1912). "An Oarsman Rowing From The Jetty", watercolor, signed bottom right.

14in (35.6cm) wide

$4,000-6,000　　　　**FRE**

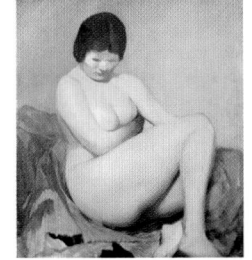

Arthur Beecher Carles, "Nude With Mask", oil on canvas.

36in (92cm) wide

$46,000-50,000　　　　**FRE**

Arthur Beecher Carles, (1882-1952), "Flowers", signed "Carles" bottom left, oil on panel. .

12.5 x 16in (32 x 40.5cm)

$30,000-40,000　　　　**FRE**

Nancy Mabin Ferguson, (1872-1967), "The House with Red Shutters", signed "Nancy Mabin Ferguson" and inscribed with title verso, oil on canvas.

20 x 24in (51 x 61cm)

$5,000-6,000　　　　**FRE**

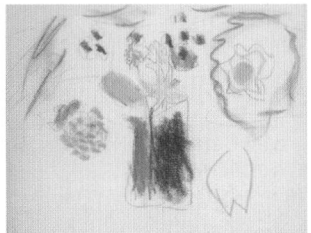

Arthur Beecher Carles, "Abstract Flowers", oil pastel.

24in (61.5cm) wide

$11,000-13,000　　　　**FRE**

Frank F. English, (1854-1922), "Homeward Bound", signed "F.F.English" bottom left, watercolour.

18 x 27.5in (46 x 70cm)

$6,000-7,000　　　　**FRE**

James Hamilton (1819-1878), "Breakers Crashing On the Rocks, Sunset", signed "J. Hamilton" bottom right, signed and dated "Jas Hamilton 1873" verso, oil on canvas.

36in (91.5cm) wide

$3,000-4,000　　　　**FRE**

George Cochran Lambdin, (1830-1896), "Roses", signed "Geo.C.Lambdin" bottom left signed, inscribed and dated "Geo.C.Lambdin, Germantown, Phila.1877" verso oil on canvas.

14in (35.5cm) wide

$24,000-28,000　　　　**FRE**

Pennsylvania Academy of the Fine Arts

Edmund Darch Lewis, (1835-1910), "Figure on a Path by an Extensive River Landscape", oil on canvas, signed and dated "Edmund D. Lewis 1883" bottom right.

70in (178cm) wide

$13,000-15,000   **FRE**

EDMUND DARCH LEWIS (1835-1910) was born into Philadelphia's elite society and is best known for the marine watercolors he painted later in his life, although he was also a prolific landscape painter.

He lived and worked in Philadelphia, studying under the direction of Paul Weber for five years and showing his first works at the Pennsylvania Academy of Fine Arts in 1854, then later at the National Academy of Design in New York and the Boston Athenaeum.

Lewis' artistic career can be divided into three: he was a painter first, then worked as an illustrator and finally as a watercolorist.

His early landscapes of Pennsylvania, the Delaware Water Gap in New Jersey and New York, were very popular and made him a wealthy man.

His spectacular landscapes were designed to inspire awe and reverence for nature. However, once he had found a panoramic composition which encapsulated the supreme divinity of nature he would transpose it to other scenes, simply altering specific details to make each one unique to its setting. This allowed him to maintain his output.

Lewis painted up to three watercolors a day, and at times sold more paintings than any other artist in America. As a result he was the most financially successful artist of the 19thC. At the height of his watercolor career he would give dealers 60 to 70 works at a time, exchanging them for works by Old Masters, or using the money to build his furniture and ceramics collections.

Edmund Darch Lewis, "Lake Como", signed and dated, oil on canvas.

30 x 50in (76.2 x 127cm)

$10,000-14,000   **SI**

Frank Bentley Ashley Linton (1871-1943), "An Evening's Reminiscence", oil on canvas, signed bottom right, inscribed on verso label.

27in (68.6cm) wide

$9,000-12,000   **FRE**

Antonio Pietro Martino, (1902-1989), "Still Life", oil on canvas, signed and dated "32" bottom left, signed and inscribed on stretcher verso.

16in (40.6cm) wide

$12,000-15,000   **FRE**

◀ Antonio Pietro Martino, "Early Snow" signed and dated "A P Martino 1927" bottom right, signed and inscribed on label verso, oil on canvas.

32.25in (82cm) wide

$36,000-40,000   **FRE**

▶ Giovanni Martino,(b.1908), "A view of Manayunk", signed "Giovanni Martino" bottom left, oil on canvas.

23.75 x 36in (60.5 x 91.5cm)

$9,000-11,000   **FRE**

Jane Piper, (d.1992), "Pink Still Life", signed and dated "Jane Piper '82" bottom left, oil on canvas.

42 x 44ikn (107 x 112cm)

$7,500-8,500   **FRE**

Joseph Sacks, (1887-1973), "Children Playing On The Beach, Ventnor", oil on board.

12in (30.5cm) wide

$4,000-5,000   **FRE**

Violet Oakley, (1874-1960), "The Creation and Preservation of the Union" Abraham Lincoln delivering The Gettysburg Address. Oil paint over printed base, with printed inscription "It Is For Us The Living Rather To Be Dedicated To The Unfinished Work".

Provenance: *Pennsylvania Manufacturer's Association. Philadelphia, Pennsylvania. Until recently this work hung in Oaks Cloister, the home of Joseph Huston, architect of the Pennsylvania State Capitol.*

This work appears to be a working study for murals Oakley was commissioned to paint following the death of the previous muralist Edwin Austin Abbey in 1911. This commission was to be her great life's work, taking some 16 years, and for which she was paid the then huge sum of $100,000.

24in (60.9cm) wide

$30,000-35,000	FRE

William T. Richards, (1833-1905), "In the Woods", oil on canvas. *1872*   14in (35.5cm) wide

$60,000-70,000	RYG

Francis Speight, (1896-1989), "Main and Cotton" (Manayunk) signed and dated "F.Speight '50", oil on canvas. *1951.* 24.25 x 30in (61.5 x 76cm)

$9,500-11,500	FRE

Walter Stuempfig, (1914-1970), "Figure in an Italian Landscape", oil on canvas.

20 x 30in (51 x 76.5cm)

$4,000-5,000	FRE

WILLIAM TROST RICHARDS (1833-1905) was born in Philadelphia and attended school until the age of 14, when his father died and he was forced to drop out to help support his family. He took a job as a commercial draftsman, and in his spare time he pursued the fine arts. He began exhibiting at the Pennsylvania Academy of the Fine Arts in 1852 and was elected an Academician in 1863. Richard's subject matter included many popular touring sites such as the Catskills, Airondacks and White Mountains as well as the Coastal areas of New Hampshire, Rhode Island and New Jersey.

Richard's meticulous attention to the depiction of flora stems from his involvement with the American Pre-Raphaelite movement during the late 1850s and early l860s. The artist had begun to execute detailed drawings of nature as early as the 1850s.

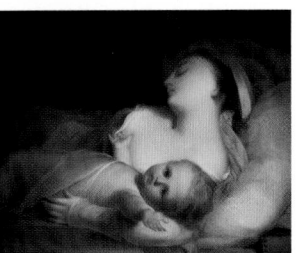

Thomas Sully (1783-1872), "Mother and Child". Oil on canvas.

30in (76cm) wide

$120,000-130,000	RYG

Shortly after his return from study in London in 1810, **THOMAS SULLY** (1783-1872) became recognized as the finest portrait painter in Philadelphia, a reputation that followed him the remainder of his long, prolific career. Certainly, the quintessential romantic portrait of the nineteenth century is Sully's 1818 "Portrait of Eliza Ridgely" commonly known as "The Lady with Harp," whose elongated body and classical garb defined the ideal of beauty for a generation.

The artist's thematic figure paintings, such as "Mother and Child," were often idealizations as well. Here, Sully's facile brushwork and use of warm, harmonious color coalesce, creating an image of maternal contentment and newborn innocence.

Paulette Van Roekens, (b.1896), "Seashore Days", oil on board, signed bottom right, inscribed on lable verso.

12in (30.4cm) wide

$17,000-20,000	FRE

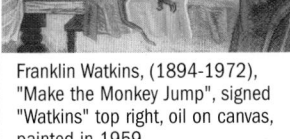

Franklin Watkins, (1894-1972), "Make the Monkey Jump", signed "Watkins" top right, oil on canvas, painted in 1959.

36 x 48in (92 x 122cm)

$60,000-80,000	FRE

Frederick Judd Waugh, (1861-1940), "Swirling Surf", signed "Waugh" bottom right, oil on board.

24 x 30in (61 x 76cm)

$10,000-12,000	FRE

Pennsylvania Impressionists

Walter Emerson Baum, (1884-1956), "Lafayette College Hill, Easton", signed "W E Baum" lower left, inscribed verso , oil on canvas.

25 x 30in (64 x 76cm)

$14,000-17,000　　　**FRE**

Walter Emerson Baum, (1884-1956), "Pennsylvania Winter", signed, also titled on reverse and with "still life study" on reverse, oil on canvas laid on board.

16 x 20in (41 x 50.8cm)

$9,000-11,000　　　**SI**

Fern Isabel Coppedge, (1888-1951), "Screen of Gold", signed "Fern I Coppedge", lower centre left, signed and inscribed with title on stretcher in pencil, oil on canvas.

24in (61cm) wide

$60,000-70,000　　　**FRE**

Fern Isabel Coppedge,"The House with Blue Shutters", signed " Fern I. Coppedge" bottom right, oil on canvas.

24in (51 x 61cm)

$53,000-58,000　　　**FRE**

FERN ISABEL COPPEDGE (1883-1951) was born in Decatur, Illinois. She studied art at the Art Institute of Chicago before moving to New York to study at the Art Students League. She then went to Pennsylvania and took classes at the Pennsylvania Academy of the Fine Arts. She settled in Pennsylvania, moving between Philadelphia and New Hope, where she painted many of the winter scenes for which she is renowned. In 1920 she moved to New Hope in Bucks County but continued to travel between there and her studio in Philadelphia. She also spent many summers painting in Gloucester and Rockport, Massachusetts.

Coppedge's distinctive style of impressionism has become celebrated for its bright, contrasting colors, often being compared to the Fauves and European Post-Impressionists. She exhibited for many years with the women's collective the "Ten Philadelphia Painters."

Fern Isabel Coppedge, (1888-1951), "Lumberville, October", oil on canvas, signed " Fern I. Coppedge" bottom centre right, inscribed with title on stretcher verso.

30in (76.5cm) wide

$130,000-160,000　　　**FRE**

John Fulton Folinsbee, "Rockport Harbour", oil on canvas, laid down on panel, signed "John Folinsbee" bottom left, inscribed with title on label verso.

10in (26cm) wide

$24,000-28,000　　　**FRE**

John Fulton Folinsbee, (1892-1972), "Robert's Mill, Lambertville", oil on canvas, signed "John Folinsbee" bottom right,

24in (61cm) wide

$26,000-28,000　　　**FRE**

Daniel Garber, "A Solebury Farm", oil on canvas, signed bottom left, inscribed with title on stretcher verso.

1943　　　28in (71.1cm) w

$160,000-180,000　　　**FRE**

▶ Daniel Garber, (1880-1958), "Jericho", signed "Daniel Garber" bottom centre left, signed and inscribed with title verso, oil on board.

20in (51cm) wide

$120,000-140,000　　　**FRE**

William Langson Lathrop, (1859-1938), "Autumn Landscape", signed "W.L.Lathrop" bottom left, oil on canvas.

15.5 x 21.25in (39.5 x 54cm)

| $12,000-15,000 | FRE |

Kenneth R. Nunamaker, (1890-1957), "An Old Stone Mill in the Snow", oil on board, signed "K R Nunamaker" bottom left,

Edward Willis Redfield, "Sunlight And Shadow", signed "E. W. Redfield" bottom left, signed and inscribed twice on stretcher verso, oil on canvas.

26 x 32in (66.5 x 81cm)

| $19,000-22,000 | FRE | $160,000-180,000 | FRE |

EDWARD WILLIS REDFIELD (1869-1965) is the premier painter of the New Hope School of American Impressionism, and in his day was the most famous landscape painter in the country.

Born in Bridgeville, DE, he moved to Center Bridge, near New Hope, PA, in 1898. His presence lured many younger artists to Bucks County, making it a nucleus for the American Impressionist movement and he is a continuing influence on New Hope painters.

From 1885 to 1889 Redfield studied with Thomas Anshutz and Thomas Hovendon at the Pennsylvania Academy of the Fine Arts, also becoming a close friend of Robert Henri. He then travelled to Europe for four years, studying at the Academie Julian in Paris and painting in France, Italy, and England.

On his return he lived in the Philadelphia area for a short time before moving to Center Bridge, where, apart from a trip to France in 1899, he spent the rest of his life. He continued to paint landscapes in the Delaware Valley until 1953.

Redfield is best known for his lavish winter and spring landscape scenes – especially snow scenes – of Bucks County. He usually completed his paintings on location and in one sitting, sometimes strapping his canvas to a tree on windy days. In the summers, Redfield painted at Boothbay Harbor, Maine.

He won more awards than any other American artists except John Singer Sargent. These include a Bronze medal from the 1900 Paris Exposition; Fischer Prize and Gold Medal from the Corcoran Art Gallery, Washington D.C., 1908; Palmer Gold Medal, Chicago Art Institute, 1913; and Pennsylvania Academy of the Fine Arts Temple Medal in 1903 and Gold Medal of Honor in 1907.

Edward Willis Redfield, (1869-1965), "The Village of Carversville", oil on canvas, signed "Edward Redfield" bottom right, signed and inscribed with title on stretcher verso, in a carved, gilded frame signed "Harer".

50in (127cm) wide

| $520,000-600,000 | FRE |

PHILADELPHIA ARTISTS

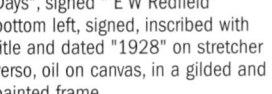

Edward Willis Redfield, "Balmy Days", signed " E W Redfield" bottom left, signed, inscribed with title and dated "1928" on stretcher verso, oil on canvas, in a gilded and painted frame.

Edward Willis Redfield, "French Countryside", signed "EW Redfield" bottom left, oil on canvas.

21in (54cm) wide

Ben Austrian, (1870-1921), "Chicks", oil on canvas, signed and dated "1908", bottom right.

12in (30.5cm) wide

| $170,000-200,000 | FRE | $35,000-50,000 | FRE | $14,000-17,000 | FRE |

Philadelphia Artists

Franklin Dullen Briscoe, (1844-1908), "In the Tropics", signed and dated "FD Briscoe 74" bottom right, signed, inscribed with title and dated verso, oil on board.

12in (31cm) wide

$4,000-6,000	**FRE**

Harry Leith-Ross, (1886-1973), "Stony Brook", signed "Leith-Ross" bottom left, watercolour with scratching out.

20.25 x 28.25in (51.5 x 72cm)

$2,000-2,500	**FRE**

Robert Riggs, (1896-1970) "Chemical Plant, Michigan", Tempera on panel, signed, This painting was reproduced in an advertisement for the Wyandotte Chemicals Corporation, Wayandotte, Michigan. It depicts a giant limestone kiln at one of Wyandotte Chemicals' plants.

26.5in (67.3cm) wide

$30,000-35,000	**SI**

Robert Riggs, "Chemical Plant, Michigan", Tempera on panel, signed. This painting is believed to depict a scene at the Wyandotte Chemicals Corporation.

26.5in (67cm)

$32,000-35,000	**SI**

Henry Bayley Snell, (1858-1943), "Pink Barn", signed "Henry B. Snell" bottom left, oil on board.

3.25in (29 x 33.5in)

$4,000-5,000	**FRE**

IMPRESSIONISTS

Roy H. Brown, (1879-1956), "Southegan Valley", signed "Brown" bottom right, oil on canvas.

40x 50in (101.5 x 127cm)

$20,000-23,000	**FRE**

Charles Philipp Weber, (1849-1921), "In the Adirondacks" signed and dated "1880", oil on canvas.

22 x 36in (55.9 x 91.4cm)

$12,000-15,000	**SI**

Mary Cassatt (1844-1926), "Sara and Her Mother with the Baby (no.1)", pastel on paper.

c1901   24in (61cm) wide

$1,250,000+	**RYG**

John Edward Costigan, (1888-1972), "Girls in an Autumn Landscape", oil on board, signed.

22.5in (57cm) wide

$15,000-18,000	**FRE**

William Merritt Chase (1848-1916), "Shinnecock Hills", oil on canvas.
c1895   20in (51cm) wide

$600,000-700,000   **RYG**

Animated by virtuoso brushwork and bright colors, the Shinnecock landscapes are the most prized works by **WILLIAM MERRITT CHASE** (1848-1916), the pre-eminent master of American Impressionism. The gentle diagonal of the path leads the viewer into the picture, where the shady tree and the low shrubs frame the quiet intimacy of the foreground while the horizon shimmers in the summer light. "Shinnecock Hills" was painted during Chase's tenure at the Shinnecock Hills Summer Art School, which he began in 1891. Specializing in outdoor landscape painting, the school quickly became the largest and most famous outdoor painting school in America.

Edmund William Greacen, (1877-1949), "A Wooded Lakeland Landscape", signed, inscribed and dated , oil on board.
15.75 x 11.5in (40 x 29cm)

$7,500-8,500   **FRE**

LANDSCAPE ARTISTS

Louis Aston Knight, (1873-1948), "A Venetian Canal", oil on canvas, signed and inscribed bottom right.
32 x 26in (81.2 x 66cm)

$10,000-13,000   **FRE**

Walter Launt Palmer, 1854-1932, "The Bridge, Winter", signed "W.L. Palmer" bottom left gouache on paper, laid down on card.
12in (31cm) wide

$8,000-10,000   **FRE**

Albert Bierstadt, (1830-1902), "Mountain Peaks", oil on paper laid on panel, signed,
16.6in (42cm) wide

$35,000-40,000   **SI**

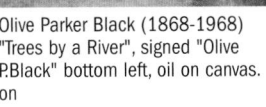

Olive Parker Black (1868-1968) "Trees by a River", signed "Olive P.Black" bottom left, oil on canvas. on
20 x 30in (51 x 76cm)

$6,000-8,000   **FRE**

John Ford Clymer, (1907-1989), "Kids Walk on Tree", signed "John Clymer" bottom left. inscribed "September, Wenas, Washington" in pencil verso, signed, inscribed and dated "2/5/57" in brown ink on Saturday Evening Post label verso.
27in (68.5cm) wide

$36,000-40,000   **FRE**

John Stuart Curry, (1897-1946), "Fording the River", signed "John Stuart Curry" bottom left, oil on canvas.
22.25 x 33in (56.5 x 84cm)

$60,000-65,000   **FRE**

Henry Golden Dearth, (1864-1918), "River in a Landscape", signed, inscribed and dated "H. Dearth, Rothenburg 86" bottom right, oil on canvas.

51in (129.5cm) wide

$9,000-11,000   **FRE**

Ben Foster, (1852-1926), "Country Pasture" signed, oil on canvas.

25 x 30in (63.5 x 76.2cm)

$6,500-7,000   **SI**

Ben Foster, (1852-1926), "Moonlight Road", signed "Ben Foster" bottom right, inscribed with title on label verso, with estate stamp, oil on canvas.

30.25 x 35in (77 x 89cm)

$5,000-6,000   **FRE**

Charles Henry Gifford, (1839-1904), "Lake George", signed and dated "C.H. Gifford 1876" bottom left, inscribed in pencil and ink on stretcher.

12 x 20in (30 x 51cm)

$17,000-19,000   **FRE**

Emile Albert Gruppe, (1896-1978), "Autumn Landscapes with Stream" signed, oil on canvas.

30 x 36in (76.2 x 91.4cm)

$13,000-15,000   **SI**

Aldro Thompson Hibbard, (1886-1972), "Covered Bridge, Late Autumn", signed "A.T. Hibbard" bottom left, artist's label verso, oil on canvas.

24 x 30in (61 x 76cm)

$10,000-14,000   **FRE**

Garnet W Jex, (1895-1979), "The Dead Canal Schaeffer's Lock", signed and dated "1927"and also titled on stretcher label, oil on canvas.

6 x 20in (40.6 x 50.8cm)

$4,500-5,000   **SI**

Garnet W Jex, (1895-1979), "Harper's Ferry from Jeffersons Rock, 1925" signed, oil on canvas.

24 x 28in (60.9 x 71cm)

$7,000-8,000   **SI**

Paul King, (1867-1947) painting, entitled "Autumn", signed "Paul King" bottom right, oil on canvas.

25 x 30in (63.5 x 76cm)

$4,000-5,000   **FRE**

Landscape Artists

Charles Wilson Knapp, (1822-1900), "Fishing in the Catskills", signed and dated "1868", oil on canvas.

14 x 22in (35.6 x 55.9cm)

$4,500-5,500   **SI**

Sydney Laurence, "Summer Cache", watercolor.

10in (25.5cm) wide

$20,000-23,000   **RENO**

Sydney Laurence, (1865-1940), "Mt. McKinley Winter", oil on canvas.

20in (51cm) wide

$30,000-40,000   **RENO**

SYDNEY LAURENCE (1865-1940) was born in Brooklyn, New York. He studied at the Arts Students League in New York, and was exhibiting regularly there by the late 1880s. He and his wife, New York artist Alexandrina Dupre, then traveled to Europe, eventually settling in England where they lived in the artists' colony of St. Ives, Cornwall. Over the next decade he exhibited at the Royal Society of British Artists and was included in the Paris Salon. Laurence moved to Alaska in 1904. By 1920 he was Alaska's most prominent painter, the first professionally trained artist to settle there.

Laurence is known for his depictions of Alaskan landscapes, including steamships, totem poles, cabins and caches, Native Alaskans, miners and trappers, often in an Impressionist style. However, his trademark has become his paintings of the view of Mount Mckinley, which for many, personifies Laurence and his work.

Laurence remarried in 1928 and spent most of his winters in Los Angeles and Seattle, returning to Alaska to paint in the summers. Sydney Laurence died in Anchorage, Alaska, in 1940.

Sydney Laurence, "Autumn Morning", oil on board.

14in (35.5cm) wide

$22,000-25,000   **RENO**

Sydney Laurence, "Cabin", oil on board.

16in (40.5cm) wide

$10,000-15,000   **RENO**

Sydney Laurence, "Mt McKinley", oil on board, signed.

7.5 x 5.5in (19 x 13.9cm)

$10,000-12,000   **RENO**

Hayley Leaver, N A (1876-1958) "Belleville, New Jersey 1930" signed, oil on canvas

20.2 x 24in (51.5 x 61.3cm)

$10,000-12,000   **SI**

A Levi Wells Prentice, (1851-1935), "Sunset", oil on canvas, signed "LW Prentice" bottom right.

9in (22.5cm) wide

$11,000-14,000   **FRE**

Charles H. Seaton, (1865-1926), 'Rock Creek in Winter', signed and dated, "C. H. Seaton 1918" , oil on canvas.

16 x 20 in (40.6 x 50.8 cm)

$2,000-3,000   **SI.**

George Henry Smillie,(1840-1921), "Gathering Blossoms", oil on canvas, signed,

30in (76.2cm) wide

$3,000-4,000   **SI**

Julius Gari Melchers, (1860-1932), "The Studio, Snow" signed, oil on canvas. The painting depicts "Belmont", Melchers' first studio in Falmouth, Virginia.

23.5 x 27.5in (60.3 x 69.9cm)

$20,000-25,000   **SI**

Julius Gari Melchers, "Camp Meeting" signed in pencil, watercolour on paper laid on paperboard.

12.2 x 19.7in (31.1x 50.2cm)

$20,000-25,000   **SI**

ERIC SLOANE (1905-1985) was born Everard Jean Hinrichs in New York City. An early interest in art led to his starting a career as a sign painter. His early customers included aviators, one of whom taught him to fly. During his first flight Sloane fell in love with the sky and clouds and these became central to his work as an artist.

He left home in 1925 after falling out with his family, and worked and traveled throughout the Northeast. Here, he identified with and became devoted to the history, culture and symbols of early American architecture but realised they were going to disappear forever. For the rest of his life he would write and paint from this point of view.

In 1926 he joined an artists' colony in Taos, New Mexico, and worked with painters such as Leon Gaspard and the members of Taos Society of Artists.

Sloane returned to New York and studied at the Art Students League under John Sloan. He changed his name in honour of his mentor, his first name coming from the word America.

A prolific artist of the Hudson River School tradition, it is estimated he painted nearly 15,000 works – mostly oil on masonite, a method he pioneered. He also wrote 38 books.

The greatest testimony to his skill at painting skies and clouds is the specially-commissioned mural he created at the National Air and Space Museum at the Smithsonian, Washington D.C.. Painted when he was 71 years old, the work measures seven stories high and half a city block long, but took him less than two months to complete.

Eric Sloane,(1910-1985), "Old Still River Bridge 1838", signed and inscribed "Old Still River Bridge 1838 Eric Sloane" bottom left, signed and inscribed "Eric Sloane Cornwall Bridge Conn." verso, oil on masonite.

24 x 36in (61 x 91.5cm)

$10,000-14,000   **FRE**

Landscape Artists/Marine Artists

William Allen Wall, (1801-1885), "Whaling Captain's House, Acushnet, New Bedford, Mass.", watercolour and gouache with traces of pencil on paper, signed "WA Wall" bottom right, inscribed in pencil verso, unframed.

24.7in (62cm) wide

£10,000-13,000 FRE

Paul Weber, (1823-1916), "Cattle Grazing by a River", signed and dated "Paul Weber, 1901", oil on canvas.

19in (48.5cm) wide

$6,000-8,000 FRE

John Williamson, (1826-1885), "On the Platte Near Castle Rock" signed with initials "JW 71" bottom left, inscribed and signed "J. Williamson NY 1871" verso, oil on canvas.

15.5 x 19.75in (39 x 50cm)

$65,000-75,000 FRE

Robert Wood (1889-1979) "Autumn". Oil on canvas. signed and inscribed "Autumn" on scretchers verso.

30in (76.5cm) wide

$2,000-3,000 FRE

Carl Wuermer, (1900-1982), "Birches in Winter", signed and also inscribed "no 446" in pencil on stretcher. oil on canvas.

25 x 30in (63.5 x 76.2cm)

$4,500-5,000 SI

MARINE ARTISTS

◀ Reginald E Nickerson, (b 1915), "The Four Masted Scooner "Marie Palmer", oil on canvas, signed and dated "1941" bottom right.

36.2in (92.1cm) wide

$6,000-8,000 FRE

M A Thomas, (19thC) ,"The Catherine Jackson of Baltimore Under Full Sail" signed and dated 1844, watercolour heightened with white on paper, in eglomise frame.

21.7 x 26.5 (55.3 x 67.3cm)

$3,500-4,000 SI

▶ Charles Robert Patterson, (1878-1958), "Clipper Ship 'Westward Ho'", signed "Charles Robert Patterson", bottom right, oil on canvas, executed in 1931, the clipper ship "Westward Ho" was built in 1851 by Donald McKay of East Boston, Massachusetts. The ship measured 210ft x 40ft 6in x 23ft 6in. In 1864, the ship caught fire at anchor in the harbour of Callo.

20 x 24in (51 x 61cm)

$9,000-11,000 FRE

Frank Vining Smith, (1879-1967), "The Clipper Ship-red Jacket", signed "Frank Vining Smith" bottom right, dated "1939" and inscribed with title verso, oil on canvas, laid down on board. "Red Jacket" was built in 1853 by George Thomas of Rockland, Maine. It measured 251ft 2in x 44ft 31ft. In 1854, it set the record, which remains to this day, for sailing from New York to Liverpool in 13 days, 1 hour and twenty-five minutes.

$5,000-7,000   **FRE**

James Gale Tyler, (1855-1931), "A Sailing Boat with Row Boats in Tow, signed "James G. Taylor" bottom left, oil on canvas.

24 x 20in (61 x 51cm)

$6,000-8,000   **FRE**

Emile Albert Gruppe, (1896-1978), "Dock Scene", oil on canvas, signed,

19.7 (45.7cm) wide

$6,000-8,000   **SI**

Emile Albert Gruppe, "Morning, Gloucester Harbour", oil on canvas, signed "Emile A. Gruppe" bottom right, signed and inscribed with title and dated "1959" on stretcher.

24in (61cm) wide

$12,000-14,000   **FRE**

Arthur Vidal Diehl, (1870-1929), "Fisherfolk Along The Shore", oil on canvas, signed,

24in (61cm) wide

$2,000-2,500   **SI**

EMILE A GRUPPE (1896-1978), son of landscape artist Charles Paul Gruppe, was born in Rochester, New York. He studied at The Hague in the Netherlands and in New York City at the National Academy of Design and The Arts Students League, and subsequently lived throughout his painting career in Gloucester, Massachusetts.

By 1930 he was known for his Post-Impressionist style American landscapes, and Gloucester boating views. His style was largely influenced by French Impressionist Claude Monet. Gruppe's prolific career brought him many awards and memberships. His popular painting "Winter, Vermont," won the Richard Mitton Award at the Jordan Marsh Exhibition in Boston in 1943.

► George Tompson Pritchard,(1878-1962), "Harbour Scene", oil on canvas, signed,

30in (76.2cm) wide

$3,000-4,000   **SI**

◄ Ferdinand Kaufman, (1864-1942), "Morning at Lumbar Wharf", signed and also titled and located, "Los Angeles-Harbour- Calif" on reverse, oil on canvas.

20 x 24in (50.8 x 61cm)

$5,000-6,000   **SI**

Marine Artists/Still Life

Harry Aiken Vincent, American 1864-1931, "Port Scene" signed and dated "20", watercolour.

23.5 x 18.5in (60 x 47cm)

$2,500-3,000	FRE

James Perry Wilson,(1889-1976), "Dock Scene", oil on canvas, signed,
24in (61cm) wide

$800-1,200	SI

Jay Hall Connaway, N A (1893-1970), "A Big Sea" ,signed and dated "Connaway" l.r; also signed and titled on reverse, oil on canvasboard.

16 x 20in (40.6 x 50.8cm)

$4,000-5,000	SI

Emile Albert Gruppe, "Bass Rocks" signed also signed and titled on reverse, oil on canvas.

17 x 36in (43.2 x 91.4cm)

$6,000-8,000	SI

Jonas Lie, (1880-1940), "Tug Boats in Icy River", oil on canvas, signed and dated "Jonas Lie '21" bottom right,

16in (41cm) wide

$8,000-10,000	FRE

Alice Kent Stoddard, (1893-1976), "Monhegan, Maine" inscribed, "Surf/Alice Kent Stoddard/ owned by Walter E Baum" on reverse, oil on canvas.

25 x 30in (63.5 x 76.2cm)

$3,500-4,500	SI

Henry S Talbot, (19thC) "Morning in Mid-Ocean Steamers Signaling", signed and dated, "H S Talbot 80" l.r; also inscribed on stretcher "Morning in Mid-Ocean Steamers Signalling/ by H S Talbot painted 1880"; oil on canvas.

12 x 20in (30.5 x 63.5cm)

$3,000-3,500	SI

STILL LIFE

Matilda Browne,(1869-1947), "Tabletop Still Life Of Mixed Flowers In A Vase", oil on canvas, signed and dated "1920",

25in (63.5cm) wide

$9,000-10,000	SI

Richard La Barre Goodwin, (1840-1910), "Still Life with Irises and Hydrangea", oil on canvas, signed "R. La Barre Goodwin", lower right.

18in (45.5cm) wide

$9,000-11,000	FRE

Ben Kamahira (b 1925) "Still Life",signed bottom right, oil on board.

20.2in (51.5cm) high

$3,000-4,000	FRE

Still Life/Figural Paintings

August Laux, (1853-1921), "Apples By A Basket", oil on canvas, signed.
20in (50.1cm)

$5,000-7,000 FRE

Herman Dudley Murphy, (1867-1945), "Golden Scarf", signed "H. Dudley Murphy" top right, signed and inscribed on label verso, oil on canvas, in a carved giltwood frame.
30 x 35in (76 x 89cm)

$22,000-25,000 FRE

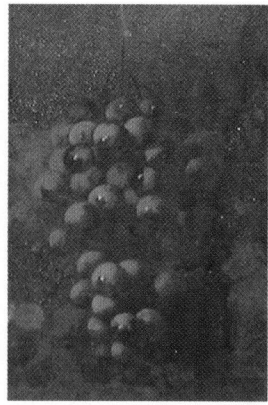

Cardicus Plantagenet Ream, (1836-1917), "Hanging Black Grapes", signed "C P Ream" bottom right, oil on board.
12 x 8.25in (30.5 x 21cm)

$3,000-3,500 FRE

FIGURAL PAINTINGS

John Koch, (1910-1978), "Pink Poinsetta", oil on canvas, signed and dated "70" bottom right.
16in (40.6cm) wide

$20,000-23,000 FRE

Robert Brackman, (1898-1980), "Early Chores", oil on canvas, signed and inscribed.
28in (71cm) wide

$10,000-12,000 FRE

Emile Albert Gruppe, (1896-1978), "Nude at Forest's Edge" signed, oil on canvas.
17 x 13in (43.2 x 33cm)

$4,000-5,000 SI

Louis Ritman, A N A (1889-1963), "Nude in an Interior", signed, oil on canvas.
25.5 x 31.8in (64.9 x 81cm)

$14,000-16,000 SI

John Ramsay Conner (1869-1952) painting, entitled "Music", signed J.R.Conner bottom left, stamped "EX PAFA" on stretcher, oil on canvas, unframed.
63.5 x 76in (122 x 138cm)

$8,000-10,000 FRE

Edith Lucille Howard, (1885-1960), "At the Piano", signed "E Howard" bottom left, oil on canvas.
40.25 x 35.5in (102 x 90cm)

$9,000-11,000 FRE

A Sigurd Skou, (d.1929),"Captain Louis", signed and dated "Sigurd Skou 1924", lower left, oil on canvas, laid down on panel.
32 x 34in (81.5 x 86.5cm)

$10,000-12,000 FRE

Figural Paintings

Louis Comfort Tiffany, (1848-1933), "The Gate Keeper", oil on panel, signed "Louis C. Tiffany" bottom right, 14in (35.5cm) wide

$13,000-16,000 **FRE**

Philip Evergood (1901-1973), "The Dog Bite Clinic", oil on canvas. *1933* 50in (127cm) wide

$170,000-180,000 **RYG**

Ferdinand Harvey Lungren, (1866-1950), "Cafe Scene", oil on canvas, signed. 24in (61cm) wide

$12,000-15,000 **FRE**

Harry Roseland, (1866-1950), "The Crystal Ball", oil on canvas, signed. 20in (50.8cm) wide

$9,000-12,000 **FRE**

PHILIP EVERGOOD (1901-1973) was born into an artistic family in New York City. He entered the Slade School of Art at the University of London and completed his certificate in drawing in 1923. Eager to return to New York City, he enrolled in the Art Students League and was greatly influenced by the lessons he received from Ashcan artist George Luks.

Back in New York City in the early 1930s, Evergood became committed to working as a Social Realist, painting scenes from contemporary urban life. He spent a bitter cold night with a group of homeless men in an empty lot near West and Christopher Streets in Greenwich Village. He was so impressed by the men, huddled around their small fire, that he ran home to spend the rest of the night drawing images of the scene.

Evergood believed the sketches from that evening to be among his best work, and he incorporated aspects of them into larger oil paintings for years to come. "Dog Bite Clinic" draws heavily on the sketches, both in character delineation and composition. "Dog Bite Clinic" also exemplifies the artist's preference for vivid color, a lasting influence of Gaugin and Matisse, whose paintings he encountered while in Europe.

The painting is based on Evergood's personal experience. In the thirties, he had a pet pit-bull named Sheeba. When the dog bit him, Evergood went to Bellevue hospital for treatment. Dog Bite Clinic resulted from the artist's clear-eyed observation of the scene.

Norman Rockwell, (1894-1978), Study for "After the Prom", oil on card with traces of pencil, signed with initials "NR" lower right,

"After the Prom" is one of Rockwell's best known and most enduring images. It was reproduced as the cover for the May 25, 1957 issue of the Saturday Evening Post. The above work was a study done by the artist for the finished piece. 10.5in (26.5cm) wide

$25,000-35,000 **FRE**

Walter Gay, (1856-1937), "The Green Bed", signed "Walter Gay" bottom right, signed and inscribed twice on labels, verso, oil on canvas. *c1909-11* 26 x 21.5in (66 x 54.5cm)

$17,000-20,000 **FRE**

▶ Susan Catherine Waters, (1823-1900), "Squirrels Eating Strawberries Watched by a Cat", oil on canvas, signed "S.C.Waters" bottom right. 16in (40.5cm) wide

$20,000-24,000 **FRE**

William Meade Prince, (1839-1951), "The Newsboy and the Blind Fiddler", oil on canvas, signed and dated "Wm. Meade Prince 1924" lower right, inscribed in pencil verso. 21in (53.5cm) wide

$6,000-8,000 **FRE**

Edward Hopper, (1882-1967), Study for "People in the Sun", charcoal on paper. *c1960* 10in (25.5cm) wide

$160,000-170,000 **RYG**

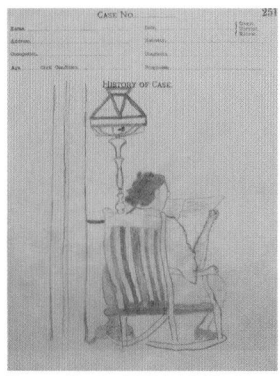

Horace Pippin, (1888-1947), "Ora Jennie Pippin seated in a rocking chair reading a newspaper", pencil on paper.

this work bears the following inscription verso: "Dear Dave, This original drawing of Ora Jennie Pippin, the wife of Horace Pippin, was made by the artist from life. I got this drawing direct from Horace, and owned it up until this date when I sold it to you.
Bob Carlen, Phil., PA 19102, 11-17-68"

8in (21cm) wide
$11,000-15,000   **FRE**

John Marin, "Autumn, New Jersey", watercolor on paper.
1913   17in (43cm) wide
$60,000-70,000   **RYG**

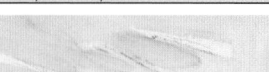

John Marin, "Coast, Trees, Deer Isle, Maine", watercolor on paper.
1919   16.5in (42cm) wide
$140,000-150,000   **RYG**

Andrew Wyeth, (b 1917), "Kuerner's House", watercolor, executed on the frontispiece of the book "Andrew Wyeth" published by Houghton Mifflin, Boston, 1968. signed and dedicated "Painted for Mrs. John Milton by Andrew Wyeth". approx. image size
10.5in (26.7cm) wide
$22,000-25,000   **FRE**

John Marin, "The Little Maple Tree, Castorland, New York", oil on canvas.
1913   22in (56cm) wide
$165,000-180,000   **RYG**

John Marin, "Grain Elevator, Weehawken", watercolor on paper.
1914   14.5in (37cm) wide
$30,000-40,000   **RYG**

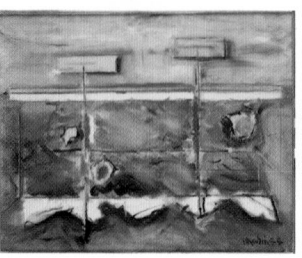

John Marin, "Related to Hurricane", oil on canvas.
1944   28in (71cm) wide
$500,000-700,000   **RYG**

MODERNISTS

John Marin (1870-1953), "The Tyrol", watercolor on paper.
1910   18.5in (47cm) wide
$40,000-50,000   **RYG**

John Marin, "Weehawken Sequence", oil on canvas mounted on board.
c1916   14in (35.5cm) wide
$50,000-60,000   **RYG**

John Marin, "Telephone Building, Lower New York", watercolor on paper.
1926   21in (53.5cm) wide
$1,100,000-1,300,000   **RYG**

JOHN MARIN (1870-1953) was born in Rutherford, New Jersey. Marin began sketching as a child, enthralled by the American landscapes. In 1893, he established himself as a practicing architect, but after eleven years, decided to become a professional artist. He studied for a short time at the Pennsylvania Academy of the Fine Arts, Philadelphia and at the Art Students League, New York.

Marin developed a style of watercolor sketching, often compared to the late Impressionists. Marin left for Paris, where he spent the next five years. There, he met the American photographer Alfred Stieglitz, whose contact led to Marin's first serious exhibition in America in 1910. He spent some time in New York, painting the architectural monuments, but by 1914 was drawn towards the landscapes of Maine.

In the following years Marin made many studies of Maine, his work embracing some Cubist elements. In 1948 "Look" magazine announced that Marin had been chosen by artists and museum directors as the most pre-eminent artist working at the time.
John Marin died in 1953 at the age of eighty-two.

John Marin, "Movement in Red,Yellow and Green", oil on canvas.

1947   28in (71cm) wide

$300,000-400,000   **RYG**

David Burliuk,(1882-1967), "The Harbour, Gloucester, Massachusetts", signed, dated and inscribed "Burliuk 1927 Gloucester Mass" bottom right, oil on canvas.

13 x 18in (33 x 45.75cm)

$6,000-8,000   **FRE**

Earl Horter, (1881-1940), "Barn by a River", watercolour, signed and dated "E Horter 39" bottom right.

28.7in (73cm) wide

$8,000-9,000   **FRE**

Ida Ten Eyck O'Keeffe, (1889-1961), "Tulips", oil on canvas.

1936   13in (33cm) wide

$60,000-70,000   **RYG**

John Marin, "Movement: Tunk Mountains", oil on canvas.

1950   28in (71cm) wide

$350,000-450,000   **RYG**

Charles Demuth, (1883-1935) ,"Father's Day 1". signed and inscribed, gouache and graphite on paper.

9.2in (23.5cm) wide

$15,000-17,000   **FRE**

Karl Knaths, (1891-1971), "The Barker",oil on canvas, signed "Karl Knaths" lower right, signed, inscribed and dated "Provincetown 1968" on stretcher.

1968   50in (127cm) wide

$9,000-11,000   **FRE**

Joseph Stella, "Fountain". Oil on canvas.

1929   40in (124.5cm) wide

$750,000-800,000   **RYG**

Milton Avery, (1885-1965), "Gloucester Docks", gouache on black paper, signed. This painting is accompanied by a letter from the Milton Avery Trust dated September 27, 1996 stating: "This is to certify that "Glouester (sic) Docks", 17 x 12, gouache on black paper was painted in the 1930's by my father, March Avery Cavanaugh."

36.2in (91cm)

$6,000-7,000   **FRE**

David Burliuk, (1882-1967), 'Mimi', signed, "Burliuk" l.l.; titled l.c.; dated 1948 l.r. also dated, titled with "Harold M. Levy Fine Art, Brooklyn, New York" stamp on reverse, oil on canvas board.

9 7/8 x 7 7/8 in. (25.1 x 20 cm.)

$1,800-2,000   **SI**

Joseph Stella, (1877-1946), "Palms", oil on canvas.

TheTropics provided important inspiration for Joseph Stella throughout his career. His trips to North Africa, southern Italy and, later Barbados gave him a chance to study tropical flora and fauna firsthand. The fullness of the coconut palms in this canvas suggest that it was inspired by the luxuriant climate of Barbados, which he visited for five months in 1937-38 and which provided him with tropical imagery for the years to come.

1938   43 x 24in (109 x 61cm)

$170,000-180,000   **RYG**

KEY TO ILLUSTRATIONS

Every antique illustrated in *Antiques Price Guide 2003* by Judith Miller has a letter code that identifies the dealer or auction house that sold it. The list below is a key to these codes. In the list, auction houses are shown by the letter Ⓐ and dealers by the letter Ⓓ. Some items may have come from a private collection, in which case the code in the list is accompanied by the letter Ⓟ. Inclusion in this book in no way constitutes or implies a contract or a binding offer on the part of any of our contributors to supply or sell the goods illustrated, or similar items, at the prices stated.

A Ⓓ
Arca Stand 351-3, Grays Antique Market, South Molton Lane, London W1Y 2LP UK
Tel: 00 44 (0)20 7629 2729

AA Ⓓ
Albert Amor 37 Bury Street,
St James, London UK
Tel: 00 44 (0)20 7930 2444
Fax: 020 7930 9067

AD Ⓓ
Andrew Dando 34 Market Street,
Bradford-on-Avon BA15 1LL UK
Tel: 00 44 (0)1225 422 702
andrew@andrewdando.co.uk
www.andrewdando.co.uk

ADE Ⓓ
Art Deco Etc 73 Upper Gloucester Road,
Brighton, Sussex BN1 3LQ UK
Tel: 00 44 (0)1273 329 268
Fax: 00 44 (0)1273 329 268
Mob: 07971 268 302
johnclark@artdecoetc.co.uk

AL Ⓓ
Andrew Lineham Fine Glass The Mall,
Camden Passage, London N1 8ED UK
Tel: 00 44 (0)20 7704 0195
Fax: 00 44 (0)20 7704 0195
Mob: 07767 702 722
Andrew@AndrewLineham.co.uk
www.andrewlineham.co.uk

AM Ⓓ
Arthur Millner 2 Campden Street,
(Off Kensington Church Street),
London W8 7EP UK
Tel: 00 44 (0)20 7229 3268
info@arthurmillner.com
www.arthurmillner.com

AnA Ⓓ
Ancient Art 85 The Vale,
Southgate,
London N14 6AT UK
Tel: 00 44 (0)20 8882 1509
Fax: 00 44 (0)20 8886 5235

AS&S Ⓓ
Andrew Smith & Son Hankin's Garage,
47 West Street, Alresford, Hampshire UK
Tel: 00 44 (0)1962 842 841
Fax: 01962 863 274

B Ⓐ
Bracketts Fine Art Auctioneers Auction Hall,
The Pantiles, Tunbridge Wells, Kent TN2 5QL UK
Tel: 00 44 (0)1892 544 500
Fax: 00 44 (0)1892 515 191
sales@bfaa.co.uk www.bfaa.co.uk

BAR Ⓐ
Bristol Auction Rooms St John's Place,
Apsley Road, Clifton, Bristol BS8 2ST UK
Tel: 00 44 (0)117 973 7201
Fax: 00 44 (0)117 973 5671
info@bristolauctionrooms.co.uk
www.bristolauctionrooms.com

BCAC Ⓓ
Bucks County Antique Center
Route 202, Lahaska, PA 18931
Tel: 215 794 9180

BD Ⓓ
Barry Davies Oriental Art Ltd,
1 Davies Street, Mayfair, London
W1K 3DB UK
Tel: 00 44 (0)20 7408 0207
Fax: 00 44 (0)20 7493 3422
bdoa@btinternet.com
www.barrydavies.com

Ber Ⓓ
Bertoia Auctions 2141 Demarco Drive,
Vineland NJ 08360
Tel: 856 692 1881 Fax: 856 692 8697
bill@bertoiaauctions.com
www.bertoiaauctions.com

BM Ⓟ
Barrie Macey Private Collector

BonBay Ⓐ
Bonhams 10 Salem Road,
London W2 4DL
Tel: 00 44 (0)20 7313 2727
Fax: 00 44 (0)20 7313 2701
info@bonhams.com www.bonhams.com

BonE Ⓐ
Bonhams 65 George Street,
Edinburgh EH2 2JL UK
Tel: 00 44 (0)131 225 2266
Fax: 00 44 (0)131 220 2547
www.bonhams.com

BonS Ⓐ
Bonhams, 49 London Road,
Sevenoaks, Kent TN13 1 AR UK
Tel: 00 44 (0)1732 740310
Fax: 00 44 (0)1732 741842
info@bonhams.com www.bonhams.com

BW Ⓐ
Biddle & Webb of Birmingham
Icknield Square, Ladywood, Middleway,
Birmingham B16 0PP UK
Tel: 00 44 (0)121 455 8042
Fax: 00 44 (0)121 454 9615
antiques@biddleandwebb.freeserve.co.uk
www.invaluable.com/biddle&webb

CA Ⓐ
Chiswick Auctions 1-5 Colville Road,
London W3 8BL UK
Tel: 00 44 (0)20 8992 4442
Fax: 00 44 (0)20 8896 0541

CdK Ⓓ
Caroline de Kerangal
Mob: 0787 9400 344
kerangal@aol.com

CH Ⓓ
Claudia Hill (By appointment only)
7 Ledborough Wood, Beaconsfield,
Buckinghamshire HP9 2DJ UK
Tel: 00 44 (0)1494 678 880

Chef Ⓐ
Cheffins The Cambridge Saleroom,
2 Clifton Road, Cambridge CB1 4BW UK
Tel: 00 44 (0)1223 213343
Fax: 00 44 (0)1223 413396
fine.art@cheffins.co.uk www.cheffins.co.uk

Clv Ⓐ
Clevedon Salerooms Herbert Road,
Clevedon, Bristol BS21 7ND UK
Tel: 00 44 (0)1275 876699
Fax: 00 44 (0)1275 343765

CO Ⓐ
Cooper Owen, 10 Denmark Street,
London, WC2H 8LS UK
Tel: 00 44 (0)20 7240 4132
Fax: 00 44 (0)20 7240 4339
info@cooperowen.com
www.cooperowen.com

COB Ⓓ
Cobwebs 78 Old Northam Road,
Southampton SO14 OPB UK
Tel/Fax: 00 44 (0)2380 227 458
www.cobwebs.uk.com

CR Ⓐ
Craftsman Auctions
333 North Main Street, Lambertville,
NJ 08530 USA
Tel: 609 397 9374
info@ragoarts.com
www.craftsman-auctions.com

Cris Ⓓ
Cristobal 26 Church Street,
London NW8 8EP UK
Tel/Fax: 00 44 (0)20 7724 7230
steve@cristobal.co.uk www.cristobal.co.uk

DN Ⓐ
Dreweatt Neate Donnington Priory Salerooms,
Donnington, Newbury, Berkshire RG14 2JE UK
Tel: 00 44 (0)1635 553 553
Fax: 01635 553 599
fineart@dreweatt-neate.co.uk
www.auctions.dreweatt-neate.co.uk

DR Ⓓ
Derek Roberts Fine Antique Clocks
& Barometers 25 Shipbourne Road,
Tonbridge, Kent TN10 3DN UK
Tel: 00 44 (0)1732 358986
Fax: 00 44 (0)1732 771842
drclocks@clara.net
www.qualityantiqueclocks.com

Duk Ⓐ
Dy. Duke and Son The Dorchester Fine Art
Salerooms, Weymouth Avenue, Dorchester,
Dorset DT1 1QS UK
Tel: 00 44 (0)1305 265 080
Fax: 00 44 (0)1305 260 101
enquiries@dukes-auctions.com
www.dukes-auctions.com

EL Ⓓ
Elms Lesters Painting Rooms, Flitcroft Street,
London WC2H 8DH UK
Tel: 00 44 (0)20 7836 6747
Fax: 00 44 (0)20 7379 0789
gallery@elms-lesters.demon.co.uk

FLA Ⓓ
Fayne Landes Antiques
Fayne Landes, 593 Hansell Road,
Wynnewood, PA 19096 USA
Tel: 610 658 0566
fayne@comcast.net

FRE Ⓐ
Freeman's 1808 Chestnut Street,
Philadelphia, PA 19103 USA
Tel: 215 563 9275 Fax: 215 563 8236
info@freemansauction.com
www.freemansauction.com

GH Ⓓ
Gideon Hatch 1 Port House, Plantation Wharf,
Battersea, London W11 3TY UK
Tel: 00 44 (0)20 7223 3996
Fax: 00 44 (0)20 7223 3997
info@gideonhatch.co.uk

GorB Ⓐ
Gorringes Terminus Road, Bexhill-on-Sea,
Sussex TN39 3LR UK
Tel: 00 44 (0)1424 212994
Fax: 00 44 (0)1424 224 035
bexhill@gorringes.co.uk
www.gorringes.co.uk

GorL Ⓐ
Gorringes, 15 North Street, Lewes, BN7 2PD UK
Tel: 00 44 (0)1273 472 503
Fax: 00 44 (0)1273 479 559
auctions@gorringes.co.uk www.gorringes.co.uk

Gro Ⓓ
Mary Wise and Grosvenor Antiques
27 Holland Street, London W8 4NA UK
Tel: 00 44 (0)20 7937 8649
Fax: 00 44 (0)20 7937 7179

GY Ⓓ
Gallery Yacou 127 Fulham Road,
London SW3 6RT UK
Tel: 00 44 (0)20 7584 2929
Fax: 00 44 (0)20 7584 3535

H&G Ⓓ
Hope and Glory
131A Kensington Church Street
London W8 7LP UK
Tel: 00 44 (0)20 7727 8424

HamG Ⓐ
Hamptons, Baverstock House,
93 High Street, Godalming, Surrey GU7 1AL UK
Tel: 00 44 (0)1483 423 567
Fax: 00 44 (0)1483 426 392
fineart@hamptons-int.com
www.hamptons.co.uk

HB Ⓓ
Victoriana Dolls 101 Portobello Rd,
London, W11 2BQ UK
Tel: 00 44 (0)1737 249 525
Fax: 00 44 (0)1737 226 254
heather.bond@totalserve.co.uk

JBS Ⓓ
John Bull Silver 139A New Bond Street,
London W1Y 9FB UK
Tel: 00 44 (0)20 7629 1251
Fax: 00 44 (0)20 7495 3001
elliot@jbsilverware.co.uk
www.jbsilverware.co.uk

JDJ Ⓐ
James D Julia Inc PO Box 830, Fairfield,
Maine 04937 USA
Tel: 207 453 7125
Fax: 207 453 2502
jjulia@juliaauctions.com
www.juliaauctions.com

J&H Ⓐ
Jacobs and Hunt Fine Art Auctioneers
26 Lavant Street, Petersfield,
Hampshire GU32 3EF UK
Tel: 00 44 (0)1730 233 933
Fax: 00 44 (0)1730 262 323
auctions@jacobsandhunt.co.uk
www.jacobsandhunt.co.uk

JH Ⓓ
Jeanette Hayhurst Fine Glass
32A Kensington Church Street,
London W8 4HA UK
Tel: 00 44 (0)20 7938 1539

JHB Ⓓ
Joseph H Bonnar, 72 Thistle Street,
Edinburgh UK
Tel: 00 44 (0)131 226 2811
Fax: 00 44 (0)131 225 9438

L&T Ⓐ
Lyon and Turnbull Ltd. 33 Broughton Place,
Edinburgh EH1 3RR UK
Tel: 00 44 (0)131 557 8844
Fax: 00 44 (0)131 557 8668
info@lyonandturnbull.com
www.lyonandturnbull.com

LC Ⓐ
Lawrence's Fine Art Auctioneers South Street,
Crewkerne, Somerset TA18 8AB UK
Tel: 00 44 (0)1460 73041
Fax: 00 44 (0)1460 74627
enquiries@lawrences.co.uk
www.lawrences.co.uk

LFA Ⓐ
Law Fine Art Ltd. Firs Cottage, Church Lane,
Brimpton, Berkshire RG7 4TJ UK
Tel: 00 44 (0)118 971 0353
Fax: 00 44 (0)118 971 3741
info@lawfineart.co.uk www.lawfineart.co.uk

LGA Ⓓ
Leah Gordon Antiques. Gallery 18, Manhatten
Arts and Antiques Centre, 1050 Second
Avenue, New York, NY 10022
Tel: 212 872 1422 Fax: 212 355 4403
info@lawfineart.co.uk www.lawfineart.co.uk

MB Ⓓ
Mostly Boxes 93 High Street, Eton, Windsor,
Berkshire, SL4 6AF UK
Tel: 00 44 (0)1753 858 470
Fax: 00 44 (0)1753 857 212

MF&D Ⓓ
M Finkel and Daughter 936 Pine Street,
Philadelphia, PA 19107 USA
Tel: 215 627 7797 Fax: 215 627 8199
antiquesamplers@aol.com www.samplings.com

Key to Illustrations

MIB Ⓓ
Michael's Boxes Stand L 14-15,
Grays Mews, 1-7 Davies Mews,
London W1K 5AB UK
Tel: 00 44 (0)20 7629 5716

NBen Ⓓ
Nigel Benson 20th Century Glass, 58-60
Kensington Church Street, London W8 4DB UK
Tel: 00 44 (0)20 7938 1137
Mob: 07971 859848

NBlm Ⓓ
N. Bloom & Son Ltd. 12 Piccadilly Arcade,
London, SW1Y 6NH UK
Tel: 00 44 (0)20 7629 5060
Fax: 00 44 (0)20 7493 2528
nbloom@nbloom.com
www.nbloom.com

OACC Ⓓ
Otford Antiques and Collectors Centre
26-28 High Street, Otford, Kent TN15 9DF UK
Tel: 00 44 (0)1959 522025
Fax: 00 44 (0)1959 525858
www.otfordantiques.co.uk.

OG Ⓓ
Ormonde Gallery
156 Portobello Road, London W11 2EB UK
Tel: 00 44 (0)20 7229 9800

PC Ⓟ
Private Collection

R&GM Ⓓ
R & G McPherson Antiques at
Stockspring Antiques 114 Kensington Church
Street, London W8 4BH UK
Tel: 00 44 (0)20 7727 7995
Fax: 00 44 (0)20 7727 7995
www.orientalceramics.com

R&K Ⓓ
Richardson & Kailis 65 Rivermead Court,
Ranelagh Gardens, London SW6 3RY UK
Tel: 00 44 (0)20 7371 0491
chris.richardson1@virgin.net

RdeR Ⓓ
Rogers de Rin 76 Royal Hospital Road,
Paradise Walk, Chelsea, London SW3 4HN UK
Tel: 00 44 (0)20 7352 9007
Fax: 00 44 (0)20 7351 9407
rogersderin@rogersderin.co.uk
www.rogersderin.co.uk

Reno Ⓐ
The Cour'Alene Art Auction
PO Box 310, Hayden, ID 83835
Tel: 208 772 9009 Fax: 208 772 8294
drumgallery@nidlink.com
www.cdaartauction.com

RGA Ⓓ
Richard Gardner Antiques
Market Square, Petworth,
West Sussex GU28 0AN UK
Tel: 00 44 (0)1798 343 411
rg@richardgarderenantiques.co.uk
www.richardgardener.co.uk

RYG Ⓓ
Richard York Garllery
21 East Street,
New York, NY 10021
Tel: 212 772 9155 Fax: 212 288 0410
www.artnet.com/ryork.html

SA Ⓓ
Stockspring Antiques
114 Kensington Church Street,
London W8 4BH UK
Tel: 00 44 (0)20 7727 7995
Fax: 00 44 (0)20 7727 7995
stockspring@antique-porcelain.co.uk
www.antique-porcelain.co.uk

SC Ⓓ
Sheila Cook, 283 Westbourne Grove,
London, W11 2QA UK
Tel: 00 44 (0)20 7792 8001
Fax: 00 44 (0)20 7229 3855
sheilacook@sheilacook.co.uk
www.sheilacook.co.uk

SCT Ⓓ
Sara Covelli Mob: 07971 043916
sara_petre@hotmail.com

SF Ⓓ
The Silver Fund 40 Bury Street,
London, SW1Y 6AU UK
Tel: 00 44 (0)20 7839 7664
Fax: 00 44 (0)20 7839 8935
dealers@thesilverfund.com
www.thesilverfund.com

SI Ⓐ
Sloan's 4920 Wyaconda Road,
N Bethesda, MD 20852 USA
Tel: 301 468 4911 Fax: 301 468 9182
www.sloansauction.com

SI (FI) Ⓐ
Sloan's Coral Gables 2516 Ponce de Leon
Blvd, Coral Gables, FL 33134,
Tel: 305 447 0757 Fax: 305 444 2944
www.sloansauction.com

SS Ⓓ
Spencer Swaffer Antiques
30 High Street, Arundel,
West Sussex BN18 9AB UK
Tel: 00 44 (0)1903 882 132
Fax: 00 44 (0)1903 884 564
spencerswaffer@btconnect.com

TEM Ⓓ
Tempus Union Square, The Pantiles,
Tunbridge Wells, Kent UK
Tel: 00 44 (0)1932 828 936
tempus@antiquesweb.co.uk
www.tempus-watches.co.uk

W&W Ⓐ
Wallis and Wallis West Steet Auction Galleries,
Lewes, East Sussex BN7 2NJ UK
Tel: 00 44 (0)1273 480 208
Fax: 00 44 (0)1273 476 562
grb@wallisandwallis.co.uk
www.wallisandwallis.co.uk

WHA Ⓐ
Willis Henry Auctions 22 Main Street,
Marshfield, MA 02050
Tel: 781 834 7774 Fax: 781 826 3520
wna@willishenry.com
www.willishenry.com

WHP Ⓐ
WH Peacock 26 Newnham Street,
Bedford MK40 3JR UK
Tel: 00 44 (0)1234 266366
Fax: 00 44 (0)1234 269082
info@peacockauction.co.uk
www.peacockauction.co.uk

WW Ⓐ
Woolley and Wallis 51-61 Castle Street,
Salisbury, Wiltshire SP1 3SU
Tel: 00 44 (0)1722 424500
Fax: 00 44 (0)1722 424508
enquiries@woolleyandwallis.co.uk
www.woolleyandwallis.co.uk

NOTE

For VALUATIONS, it is advisable to contact the dealer in advance to confirm that they will perform this service and whether any charge is involved. Telephone valuations are not possible, so it will be necessary to send details, including a photograph, of the object to the dealer, along with a stamped addressed envelope for response. While most dealers will be happy to help you with an enquiry, do remember that they are busy people. Please mention *Antiques Price Guide 2003* by Judith Mille when making an enquiry.

KEY TO ADVERTISERS

CLIENT	PAGE NO	CLIENT	PAGE NO
James D. Julia Inc	291	Leah Gordon	579
Doan's	16, 394	Willis Henry Auctions Inc	299
Freeman's	188, 402, 573, 595	Cooper Owen	505
Bertoia Auctions	449	Craftsman Auctions	583

DIRECTORY OF AUCTIONEERS

THIS IS A LIST OF AUCTIONEERS THAT conduct regular sales. Auction houses that would like to be included in the next edition should contact us by February 2003.

Alabama

Flomaton Antique Auction
PO Box 1017, 320 Palafox Street, Flomaton 36441
Tel: 334 296 3059
Fax: 334 296 3710
www.flomatonantiqueauction.com

Jim Norman Auctions
201 East Main St, Hartselle, 35640
Tel: 205 773 6878

Vintage Auctions
Star Rte. Box 650, Blountsville, 35031
Tel: 205 668 0204
Fax: 205 429 2457

Arizona

Dan May & Associates
4110 N. Scottsdale Road, Scottsdale, 85251
Tel: 602 941 4200

Old World Mail Auctions
671 Highway 179, St 2C, Sedona, 86334
Tel: 928 282 3944
marti@oldworldauctions.com
www.oldworldauctions.com

Star Auction Inc
P. O. Box 1232, Dolan Springs, 86441-1232
Tel: 602 767 4774
Fax: 602 767 3900

Arkansas

Ponders Auctions
1504 South Leslie, Stuttgart, 72160
Tel: 501 673 6551

Hanna-Whysel Auctions
3403 Bella Vista Way, Bella Vista, 72714
Tel: 501 855 9600

California

Butterfield & Butterfield
7®601 Sunset Blvd, Los Angeles, 90046-2714
Tel: 323 850 7500
Fax: 323 850 5843
info@butterfields.com
www.butterfields.com

Butterfield & Butterfield
220 San Bruno Ave, San Francisco, 94103-5018
Tel: 415 861 7500
Fax: 415 861 8951
info@butterfields.com
www.butterfields.com

I.M. Chait Gallery
9330 Civic Center Drive, Beverly Hills, 90210
Tel: 310 285 0182
Fax: 310 285 9740
imchait@aol.com
www.chait.com

Cuschieri's Auctioneers & Appraisers
863 Main Street, Redwood City, 94063,
Tel: 650 556 1793
Fax: 650 556 9805
peter@cuschieris.com
www.cuschieris.com

eBay, Inc
2005 Hamilton Ave, Ste. 350, San Jose, 95125
Tel: 408 369 4839
staff@ebay.com
www.ebay.com

L. H. Selman Ltd
123 Locust St, Santa Cruz, 95060
Tel: 800 538 0766
Fax: 408 427 0111
lselman@got.net
www.paperweight.com

San Rafael Auction Gallery
634 Fifth Avenue, San Rafael, San Rafael, 9490
Tel: 415 457 4488
Fax: 415 457 4899
srauction@aol.com
www.sanrafael-auction.com

Slawinski Auction Co
6192 Hwy 9, Felton, 95018
Tel: 831 335 9000
wjantqs@znet.com
www.slawinski.com

Colorado

Pacific Auction
9138 North 95th, Longmont, CO 80501
Tel: 303 772 9401

Pettigrew Auction Company
1645 S. Tejon Street, Colorado Springs, 80906
Tel: 719 633 7963

Priddy's Auction Galleries
5411 Leetsdale Drive, Denver, CO 80222
Tel: 800 380 4411

Stanley & Co
Auction Room,
395 Corona Street, Denver
Tel: 303 355 0506

Connecticut

Norman C. Heckler & Company
79 Bradford Corner Rd, Woodstock Valley, 06282-2002
Tel: 860 974 1634
heckler@neca.com
www.hecklerauction.com

Lloyd Ralston Toys
350 Long Beach Blvd, Stratford, 06615
Tel: 203 386 9399
www.lloydralstontoys.com

Winter Associates, Inc.
Auctioneers & Appraisers,
21 Cooke St, P. O. Box 823, Plainville, 06062
Tel: 860 793 0288

Delaware

Remember When Auctions, Inc
42 Sea Gull Rd, Swann Estates, Selbyville, 19975
Tel: 302-436-8869
sales@history-attic.com
www.history-attic.com

Washington DC

Weschler's
909 E St. NW, Washington, 20004-2006
Tel: 202 628 1281/
800 331 1430
www.weschlers.com

Sloan's Auction Galleries
4920 Wyaconda Rd, N Bethesda 20852
Tel: 310 468 4911/
800 649 5066
sloans@sloansauction.com
www.sloansauction.com

Florida

Auctions Neapolitan
995 Central Avenue, Naples 34102
Tel: 941 262 7333
www.auctionsneapolitan.com

Burchard Galleries/Auctioneers
2528 30th Ave N, St. Petersburg, 33713
Tel: 727 821 11667/
727 823 4156
burchard@atlantic.net
www.burchardgalleries.com

Dawson's
P.O. Box 646, Palm Beach 33480
Tel: 561 835 6930
info@dawsons.org
www.dawsons.org

Directory of Auctioneers

Arthur James Galleries
615 E. Atlantic Ave,
Delray Beach
Tel: 561 278 2373

Kincaid Auction Company
3214 E. Hwy 92,
Lakeland, 33801
Tel: 800 970 1977
kincaid@kincaid.com
www.kincaid.com

Albert Post Galleries
809 Lucerne Ave,
Lake Worth 33460
Tel: 561 582 4477
a.postgallery@juno.com
www.albertpostgallery.com

Sloan's Auction Galleries
8861 NW 18th Terrace, Ste. 100,
Miami, 33172
Tel: 305 751 4770/
800 660 4524
sloans@sloansauction.com
www.sloansauction.com

Georgia

Arwood Auctions
26 Ayers Ave, Marietta, 30060
Tel: 770 423 0110

Great Gatsby's
5070 Peachtree Industrial Blvd,
Atlanta,
Tel: 770 457 1905/
800 428 7297

My Hart Auctions Inc
P. O. Box 2511, Cumming, 30028
Tel: 770 888 9006

Red Baron's Auction Gallery
6450 Roswell Rd,
Atlanta, 30328
Tel: 404 252 3770
rbarons@onramp.net

Southland Auction Inc.
3350 Riverwood Parkway, Atlanta
Tel: 770 818 2418

Idaho

The Coeur d'Alene Art Auction
P. O. Box 310, Hayden, 83835
Tel: 208 772 9009

Indiana

Curran Miller Auction
& Realty, Inc
4424 Vogel Rd, Ste. 400,
Evansville, 47715
Tel: 800 264 0601/
812 474 6100
auctionx@evansville.net
www.cmillerauctions.com

Kruse International
P. O. Box 190, Auburn, 46706
Tel: 219 925 5600/
800 968 4444

Lawson Auction Service
923 Fourth St, Columbus, 47265
Tel: 812 372 2571
dlawson@lawson-auction.com
www.lawson-auction.com

Majolica Auctions
Michael G. Strawser, 200 N. Main,
P. O. Box 332, Wolcotville, 46795
Tel: 219 854 285
michael@strawserauctions.com
www.strawserauctions.com

Schrader Auction
209W. Van Buren St,
Columbia City, 46725
Tel: 219 244 7606

Slater's Americana
5335 N. Tacoma Ave, Suite 24,
Indianapolis, 46220
Tel: 317 257 0863

Stout Auctions
11 W. Third St, Williamsport,
47993-1119
Tel: 765 764 6901

Illinois

Butterfield & Dunning
755 Church Rd, Elgin, 60123
Tel: 847 741 3483
info@butterfields.com
www.butterfields.com

Hack's Auction Center
Box 296, Pecatonica, 61063
Tel: 815 239 1436

Hanzel Galleries
1120 South Michigan Ave,
Chicago, 60605-2301
Tel: 312 922 6247

Susanin's Auction
228 Merchandise Mart,
Chicago, 60654
Tel: 888 787 2646/
312 832 9800
info@susanins.com
www.susanins.com

Joy Luke Auction Gallery
300 E. Grove St, Bloomington,
61701-5232
Tel: 309 828 5533
robert@joyluke.com
www.joyluke.com

Iowa

Gene Harris Antique
Auction Center
2035 18th Ave, P. O. Box 476,
Marshalltown, 50158
Tel: 641 752 0600/
800 862 6674
ghaac@marshallnet.com
www.geneharrisauctions.com

Jackson's Auctioneers &
Appraisers
2229 Lincoln St, P. O. Box 50613,
Cedar Falls, 50613
Tel: 319 277 2256
jacksons@jacksonsauction.com
www.jacksonsauction.com

Tubaugh Auctions
1702 8th Ave, Belle Plaine, 52208
Tel: 319 444 2413/
800 368 1292
www.tubaughauctions.com

Kansas

AAA Historical Auction Service
P. O. Box 12214, Kansas City,
66112
www.manions.com,

CC Auction
416 Court, Clay Center, 67432
Tel: 913 632 6511

Spielman Auction
2259 Homestead Rd, Lebo,
66856
Tel: 316 256 6558

Kentucky

Hays & Associates, Inc.
120 South Spring St,
Louisville, 40206-1953
Tel: 502 584 4297

Steffen's Historical Militaria
P. O. Box 280, Newport, 41072
Tel: 606 431 4499

Louisiana

Estate Auction Gallery
3374 Government St,
Baton Rouge, 70806
Tel: 504 383 7706

Morton M. Goldberg
Auction Galleries
547 Baronne St,
New Orleans, 70113
Tel: 504 592 2300

New Orleans Auction
Galleries, Inc.
801 Magazine St,
New Orleans, 70130
Tel: 504 566 1849

Maryland

DeCaro Auction Sales, Inc.
8133 Elliott Rd, Easton,
21601-7184
Tel: 410 820 4000
info@decaroauctions.com
www.decaroauctions.com

Hantman's Auctioneers &
Appraisers
P. O. Box 59366, Potomac,
20859-9366
Tel: 301 770 3720
hantman@hantmans.com
www.hantmans.com

Isennock Auctions &
Appraisals, Inc.
4203 Norrisville Rd, White Hall,
21161-9306,
Tel: 410 557 8052
isennock@starix.net
www.isennockauction.com

Richard Opfer Auctioneering, Inc.
1919 Greenspring Dr, Lutherville,
Timonium, 21093-4113
Tel: 410 252 5035
info@opferauction.com
www.opferauction.com

North Carolina

Robert S. Brunk Auction
Services, Inc.
P. O. Box 2135, Asheville, 28802
Tel: 828 254 6846
auction@brunkauctions.com
www.brunkauctions.com

Historical Collectible Auctions
P. O. Box 975, Burlington, 27215
Tel: 336 570 2803
info@hcaauctions.com
www.hcaauctions.com

South Carolina

Charlton Hall Galleries, Inc.
912 Gervais St, Columbia,
29201
Tel: 803 799 5678
info@charltonhallauctions.com
www.charltonhallauctions.com

North Dakota

Curt D. Johnson Auction Company
RR1 Box 135, Grand Forks, 58201
Tel: 701 746 1378
merfeld@rrv.net
www.curtdjohnson.com

Directory of Auctioneers

South Dakota

Fischer Auction Company
238 Haywire Ave, P. O. Box 667,
Long Lake, 57457-0667
Tel: 800 888 1766/
605 577 6600
gofish@valleytel.net
www.fischerauction.com

Maine

James D. Julia Auctioneers Inc.
Rt. 201, Skowhegan Rd, P. O. Box
830, Fairfield, 04937
Tel: 207 453 2502
jjulia@juliaauctions.com
www.juliaauctions.com

**Thomaston Place Auction
Galleries**
P. O. Box 300, Business Rt. 1,
Thomaston, 04861
Tel: 207 354 8141
johnh@kajav.com
www.kagav.com

Massachusetts

Douglas Auctioneers
Rte. 5, South Deerfield, 01373
Tel: 413 665 3530
www.douglasauctioneers.com

Eldred's
P. O. Box 796, East Dennis,
02641-0796
Tel: 508 385 3116
info@eldreds.com
www.eldreds.com

Grogan & Company Auctioneers
22 Harris St, Dedham, 02026
Tel: 781 461 9500
grogans@groganco.com
www.groganco.com

Shute Auction Gallery
850 W. Chestnut St,
Brockton, 02401
Tel: 508 588 0022/
508 588 7833

Skinner, Inc.
357 Main St, Bolton, 01740-1104
Tel: 978 779 6241
info@skinnerinc.com
www.skinnerinc.com

Willis Henry Auctions, Inc.
22 Main St, Marshfield, 02050
Tel: 781 834 7774/
800 244 8466
wha@willishenry.com
www.willishenry.com

Michigan

DuMouchelle Art Galleries Co.
409 East Jefferson Ave, Detroit,
48226
Tel: 313 963 6255
info@dumouchelles.com
www.dumouchelles.com

Minnesota

Buffalo Bay Auction Co.
5244 Quam Circle, Rogers, 55374
Tel: 612 428 8480
buffalobay@aol.com

Tracy Luther Auctions
2548 E. 7th Ave, St. Paul, 55109
Tel: 612 770 6175

Rose Auction Galleries
2717 Lincoln Dr, Roseville, 55113
Tel: 612 484 1415
www.rosegalleries.com

Missouri

Ivey-Selkirk
7447 Forsyth Blvd,
Saint Louis, 63105
Tel: 314 726 5515
www.iveyselkirk.com

**Simmons & Company
Auctioneers**
40706 E. 144th St,
Richmond, 64085
Tel: 816 776 2936/
800 646 2936
simmons_auction@raycounty.com
www.raycounty.com/simmons

Montana

Stan Howe & Associates
4433 Red Fox Dr, Helena,
59601-7561
Tel: 406 443 5658/
800 443 5658

New Hampshire

Northeast Auction
694 Lafayette Rd, P. O. Box 363,
Hampton, 03483
Tel: 603 926 9800

New Jersey

Bertoia Auctions
2141 Demarco Dr, Vineland,
08360
Tel: 856 692 1881
bill@bertoiaauctions.com
www.bertoiaauctions.com

Craftsman Auctions
333 North Main Street,
Lambertville, 08530
Tel: 609-397-9374
mtucker@ragoarts.com
www.ragoarts.com

Dawson's
128 American Rd,
Morris Plains, 07950
Tel: 973 984 6900
info@dawsons.org
www.dawsons.org

Greg Manning Auctions, Inc.
775 Passaic Ave,
West Caldwell, 07006
Tel: 973 883 0004/
800 221 0243
info@gregmanning.com
www.gregmanning.com

Rago Modern Auctions, LLP
333 North Main Street,
Lambertville, 08530
Tel: 609-397-9374
mtucker@ragoarts.com
www.ragoarts.com

New York

Framefinders
454 East 84th Street,
New York 10028
Tel: 212 396 3896
framefinders@aol.com
www.framefinders.com

Christie's
502 Park Ave, New York, 10022
Tel: 212 546 1000
info@christies.com
www.christies.com

Christie's East
219 E. 67th St, New York, 10021
Tel: 212 606 0400
info@christies.com
www.christies.com

Samuel Cottone Auctions
15 Genesee St,
Mount Morris, 14510
Tel: 716 658 3119
William Doyle Galleries
175 E. 87th St, New York,
10128-2205
Tel: 212 427 2730
info@doylegalleries.com
www.doylegalleries.com

Guernsey's Auction
108 East 73rd St,
New York, 10021
Tel: 212 794 2280
catalogues@guernseys.com
www.guernseys.com

Mapes Auction Gallery
1729 Vestal Parkway,
West Vestal, 13850-1156
Tel: 607 754 9193
davidmapes@compuserve.com
www.mapesauction.com

Phillip's, De Pury & Luxemburg
23 West 57th Street,
New York, 10019
Tel: 212 940 1200
carole.bellidora@phillips-dpl.com
www.phillips-dpl.com

Sotheby's
1334 York Ave,
New York, 10021
Tel: 212 606 7000
info@sothebys.com
www.sothebys.com

Swann Galleries, Inc.
104 E. 25th St, New York,
10010-2977
Tel: 212 254 4710
swann@swanngalleries.com
www.swanngalleries.com

Ohio

**Cowan's Historic
Americana Auctions**
673 Wilmer Avenue,
Cincinnati, 45226
Tel:513-871-1670
info@historicamericana.com
www.historicamericana.com

DeFina Auctions
1591 State Route 45,
Austinburg, 44010
Tel: 440 275 6674
info@definaauctions.com
www.definaauctions.com

Garth's Auction, Inc.
2690 Stratford Rd, P. O. Box 369,
Delaware, 43015
Tel: 614 362 4771/614 369
5085 info@garths.com
www.garths.com

Oklahoma

C & C The Auction Company
4801 MacKelman Dr,
Oklahoma City, 73135-4135
Tel: 405 670 1705

Pennsylvania

Alderfer Auction Company
501 Fairground Rd, P. O. Box 640,
Hatfield, 19440-0640
Tel: 215 393 3000
auction@alderfercompany.com
www.alderfercompany.com

Directory of Auctioneers

Noel Barrett
P.O. Box 300, Carversville,
18913
Tel: 215 297 5109
toys@noelbarrett.com
www.noelbarrett.com

Dargate Auction Galleries
5607 Baum Blvd.,
Pittsburgh, 15206
Tel: 412 362 3558
dargate@dargate.com
www.dargate.com

Freeman's
1808 Chestnut St,
Philadelphia, 19103
Tel: 610 563 9275/
610 563 9453
info@freemansauction.com
www.freemansauction.com

Pook & Pook, Inc.
P. O. Box 268, Downington,
19335-0268
Tel: 610 269 0695/
610 269 4040
info@pookandpook.com
www.pookandpook.com

Skinner's Auction Company
3807 Margate Rd, Bethlehem,
18020
Tel: 610 868 985
skinnauct@aol.com
www.skinnerauct.baweb.com

Stephenson's Auction
1005 Industrial Blvd,
Southampton, 18966-4006
Tel: 215 322 6182
info@stephensonsauction.com
www.stephensonsauction.com

Rhode Island

Gustave White Auctioneers
37 Bellevue, Newport,
02840-3207
Tel: 401 841 5780

Tennessee

Berenice Denton Estates
4403 Murphy Road,
Nashville, 37209
Tel: 615 292 5765
lnichols66@home.com

Kimball M. Sterling Inc.
125 W. Market St,
Johnson City, 37601,
Tel: 423 928 1471
kimsold@tricon.net
www.sterlingsold.com

Texas

Austin Auctions
8414 Anderson Mill Road, Austin,
78729-5479
Tel: 512 258 5479
austinauction@cs.com
www.austinauction.com

Utah

America West Archives
P. O. Box 100, Cedar City,
84721-0100
Tel: 435 586 9497/435 586
7323
awa@netutah.com
www.americawestarchives.com

Vermont

Eaton Auction Service
RR 1, Box 333, Fairlee, 05045
Tel: 802 333 9717

Virginia

The Auction Gallery
3140 W. Cary St, Richmond,
23221
Tel: 804 358 0500/
804 359 0688
knightm@mindspring.com

Ken Farmer Auctions & Estates
105A Harrison Street,
Radford, 24141
Tel: 540 639 0939
info@kfauctions.com
www.kenfarmer.com

Phoebus Auction Gallery
14-16 E. Mellen
St, Hampton, 23663
Tel: 757 722 9210
bwelch@phoebusauction.com
www.phoebusauction.com

Wisconsin

Krueger Auctions
P. O. Box 275, Iola, 54945-0275
Tel: 715 445 3845

Milwaukee Auction Galleries
1919 N. Summit Ave,
Milwaukee, 53202
Tel: 414 271 1105

Schrager Auction Galleries, Ltd.
P. O. Box 10390, 2915 North
Sherman Blvd, Milwaukee, 53210
Tel: 414 873 3738

DIRECTORY OF SPECIALISTS

SPECIALISTS THAT WOULD LIKE TO BE INCLUDED in the next edition, or have a change of address or telephone number, should contact us by February 2003.

Readers should contact dealers by telephone before visiting them to avoid a wasted journey.

American Paintings

James R. Bakker Antiques Inc.
248 Bradford Street,
Provincetown, MA 02657
Tel: 508 487 9081

Jeffrey W. Cooley
The Cooley Gallery, Inc. 25 Lyme
Street, Old Lyme, CT 06371
Tel: 860 434 8807
cooleygallery@snet.net

Richard York Gallery
21 East Street, New York,
NY 10021
Tel: 212 772 9155

Americana and Folk Art

Bucks County Antique Center
Route 202, Lahaska, PA 18931
Tel: 215 794 9180

The Splendid Peasant
Route 23 and Sheffield Road,
P. O. Box 536, South Egremont,
MA 01258
Tel: 413 528 5755
folkart@splendidpeasant.com
www.splendidpeasant.com

**J. M. Flanigan American
Antiques,** 1607 Park Avenue,
Baltimore, MD 21217
Tel: 800 280 9308
jmf745i@aol.com

Augustus Decorative Arts
Ltd, Box 700,New York, NY 10101
Tel: 212 333 7888
elle@portrait minatures.com

Judith and James Milne Inc.
506 East 74th Street, New York
NY 10021
Tel: 212 472 1481
milne@aol.com

Jeffrey Tillou Antiques
33 West Street & 7 East Street,
PO Box 1609, Litchfield, CT 06759
Tel: 860 567 9693
webmaster@tillouantiques.com

Marion Robertshaw Antiques
PO Box 435, Route 202, Lahaska,
PA 18931 Tel: 215 295 0648

Monkey Hill
6465 Route 202, New Hope, PA
18938 Tel: 215 862 0118
Fax: 215 862 3436
info@monkeyhillantiques.com

The Stradlings
1225 Park Avenue, New York,
NY 10028
Tel: 212 534 8135

Thomas and Julia Barringer
26 South Main Street, Stockton,
NJ 08559 Tel: 609 397 4474
Fax: 609 397 4474
tandjb@voicenet.com

Pantry & Hearth
121 East 35th Street,
New York, NY 10016
Tel: 212 532 0535
gail.lettick@prodigy.net

Paul and Karen Wendhiser
PO Box 155, Ellington, CT 06029

Cheryl and Paul Scott
PO Box 835, 232 Bear Hill Road,
Hillsborough, NH 03244
Tel: 603 464 3617

Frank Gaglio, Inc
56 Market St., Suite B,
Rhinebeck NY 12572
Tel: 845 876 0616

Olde Hope Antiques Inc.
P.O. Box 718, New Hope,
PA 18938
Tel: 215 297 0200
Fax: 215 297 0300
info@oldehopeantiques.com
www.oldehopeantiques.com

Raccoon Creek Antiques
PO Box 457, 20 Main Street
Bridgeport, NJ 08014
Tel: 856 467 3197

J. B. Richardson
6 Partrick Lane, Westport,
CT 06880
Tel: 203 226 0358

**Pat and Rich
Garthoeffner Antiques,**
122 East Main Street, Lititz,
PA 17543
Tel: 717 627 7998
Fax: 717 627 3259
patgarth@voicenet.com

Allan Katz Americana
25 Old Still Road, Woodbridge,
CT 06525
Tel: 203 393 9356
alkatze@concentric.net

Nathan Liverant and Son
168 South Main Street,
PO Box 103, Colchester,
CT 06415
Tel: 860 537 2409
nliverantandson@biz.ctol.net

Sharon Platt
1347 Rustic View,
Manchester, MO 63011
Tel: 636 227 5304
sharonplatt@postnet.com

Antiquities

Frank & Barbara Pollack
1214 Green Bay Road,
Highland Park,
IL 60035
Tel: 847 433 2213
FPollack@compuserve.com

Architectural Antiques

Garden Antiques
Katonah, NY 10536
Tel: 212 744 6281
gardenantiques@pipeline.com
www.bi gardenantiques.com

Cecilia B. Williams
12 West Main Street,
New Market, MD 21774
Tel: 301 865 0777

Carpets and Rugs

D. B. Stock Antique Carpets
464 Washington Street,
Wellesley, MA 02482
Tel: 781 237 5859

John J. Collins
Jr. Gallery, PO Box 958,
11 Market Square,
Newburyport, MA 01950
Tel: 978 462 7276
bijars@att.net

Karen and Ralph Disaia
Oriental Rugs Ltd., 23 Lyme Street,
Old Lyme, CT 06371
Tel: 860 434 1167
orientalrugs@snet
www.orientalrugsltd.com

Ceramics

Philip Suval, Inc.
1501 Caroline Street,
Fredericksburg, VA 22401
Tel: 540 373 9851

Mellin's Antiques
PO Box 1115, Redding,
CT 06875
Tel: 203 938 9538
remellin@aol.com

Mark & Marjorie Allen
6 Highland Drive, Amherst,
NH 03031
Tel: 603 672 8989
mandmallen@antiquedelft.com
www.antiquedelft.com

Charles & Barbara Adams
289 Old Main St,
South Yarmouth, 02664
Tel: 508 760 3290
adams_2430@msn.com

Clocks

Kirtland H. Crump
387 Boston Post road,
Madison, 06443
Tel: 203 245 7573
kirt@crumpclocks.com

Decorative Arts
Sumpty Priddy,
601 South Washington Street,
Alexandria, 22314 4109
Tel: 703 299 0800
sumpterpriddy@sumpterpriddy.com

Lillian Nassau
220 East 57th Street
New York, NY 10022
Tel: 212 759 6062
lilnassau@aol.com
www.lilliannassau.com

Leah Gordon Antiques
Gallery 18, Manhattan Art and
Antiques Center, 1050 Second
Avenue, New York, NY 10022
Tel: 212 872 1422

Directory of specialists

Furniture

Carswell Rush Berlin, Inc.
P.O. Box 0210, Planetarium
Station, New York,
NY 0024 0210
Tel: 212 721 0330
carswellberlin@msn.com
www.americanantiques.net

Israel Sack
730 Fifth Avenue, Suite 605,
New York, NY 019
Tel: 212 399 6562

James L. Price Antiques
831 Alexander Spring Rd.,
Carlisle, PA 17013
Tel: 717 243 0501
jlpriceantiques@earthlink.net

John Keith Russell Antiques Inc.
110 Spring Street, PO Box 414,
South Salem, NY 10590
Tel: 914 763 8144
jkrantique@aol.com

Lilcoln and Jean Sander
235 Redding Road, Redding,
CT 06896
Tel: 203 938 2981
sanderlr@aol.com

Milly McGehee,
P.O. Box 666, Riderwood,
21139 MD 0666
Tel: 410 653 3977
millymcgehee@home.com

Peter H. Eaton Antiques Inc.
39 State Street, Newburyport,
MA 01950
Tel: 978 465
2754peter@petereaton.com
www.petereaton.com

R. Jorgensen Antiques
502 Post Road (US Route 1),
Wells, ME 04090
Tel: 207 646 9444
rja@cybertours.com

Susie Burmann
23 Burpee Lane, New London,
NH 03257
Tel: 603 526 5934
rsburmann@tds.net

**Van Tassel/Baumann
American Antiques**
690 Sugartown Road,
Malvern, PA 19355
Tel: 610 647 3339

American Spirit Antiques
PO Box 11152, Shawnee Mission.
KS 66207
Tel: 913 345 9494
Tedatiii@aol.com

Gart and Martha Ludlow Inc.
5284 Golfway Lane, Lyndhurst,
OH 44124,
Tel: 440 449 3475,

Bettina Krainin
289 Main Street, Woodbury.
CT 06798
Tel: 203 263 7669

Leigh Keno American Antiques
127 E. 69th Street, New York,
NY 10021
Tel: 212 734 2381
leigh@leighkeno.com
www.leighkeno.com

Artemis Gallery
Wallace Road, North Salem,
NY 10560
Tel: 914 669 5971
artemis@optonline.net
www.artemisantiques.com

**Kathy Schoemer American
Antiques**
PO Box 429, 12 McMorrow Lane,
North Salem, NY 10560
Tel: 914 277 8464

RJG Antiques
PO Box 60, Rye, NH 03870
Tel: 603 433 1770
antiques@rjgantiques.com
www.rjgantiques.com

Samuel Herrup Antiques
35 Sheffield Plain Road (Route 7),
Sheffield, MA 01257
Tel: 413 229 0424
ssher@ben.net

Brian Cullity
18 Plesant Street, PO Box 595,
Sagamore, MA 02561
Tel: 508 888 8409
bcullity@capecod.net

Jack and Ray Van Gelder
Conway House, 468 Ashfield Road,
Conway, MA 01341
Tel: 413 369 4660

Joan R. Brownstein
Daniel Hightower, 2068 Ellis
Hollow Road, Ithaca, NY 14850
Tel: 607 539 6507
jrb.antqs@clarityconnect.com

Stephen H. Garner Antiques
PO Box 136, Yarmouthport,
MA 02675
Tel: 508 362 8424

William E Lohrman
248 Route 208, New Paltz,
NY 12561
Tel: 845 255 6762

H. L. Chalfant Antiques
1352 Paoli Pike, West Chester,
PA 19380
Tel: 610 696 1862
chalfant@gateway.net

**Gordon and Marjorie
Davenport Inc.**
4250 Manitou Way, Madison,
WI 53711
Tel: 608 271 2348
GMDaven@aol.com

American Antiques
161 Main Street, PO Box 368,
Thomaston, ME 04861
Tel: 207 354 6033
acm@midcoast.com

Ron and Penny Dionne
55 Fisher Hill Road, Willington,
CT 06279
Tel: 860 487 0741

Joanne and Jack Boardman
522 Joanne Lane, DeKalb,
IL 06115 Tel: 815 756 359
boardmanantiques@aol.com

Thomas Schwenke Inc.
50 Main Street North, Woodbury,
CT 06798 Tel: 203 266 0303
tgs@schwenke.com
www.schwenke.com

Barbara Ardizone
PO Box 433, 62 Main Street,
Salisbury, CT 06068 Tel: 860 435
3057

Jackson Mitchell Inc.
5718 Kennett Pike, Wilmington,
DE 19807
Tel: 302 656 0110
JacMitch@aol.com

Glass

Paul Reichwein
2321 Hershey Avenue, East
Petersburg, PA 17520
Tel: 717 569 7637

Jewelry

Arthur Guy Kaplan
P.O. Box 1942, Baltimore,
MD 21203
Tel: 410 752 2090

Marine Antiques

Hyland Granby Antiques
PO Box 457, Hyannis Port,
MA 02647
Tel: 508 771 3070
gmarine@capecod.net

Metalware

Wayne and Phyllis Hilt
RR 1, Haddam Neck, CT 06424
3022 Tel: 860 267 2146
philt@snet.net

Silver

Jonathan Trace
P.O. Box 418, 31 Church Hill Road,
Rifton, NY 12471
Tel: 914 658 7336

Textiles

Stephen & Carol Huber
40 Ferry Road, Old Saybrook,
CT 06475 Tel: 860 388 6809
hubers@antiquesamplers.com
www.antiquesamplers.com

M. Finkel & Daughter
936 Pine Street, Philadelphia,
PA 19107 6128
Tel: 215 627 7797
mailbox@finkelantiques.com
www.samplings.com

Cora Ginsburg
19 East 74th Street New York,
NY 10021
Tel: 212 744 1352

Colette Donovan
98 River Road, Merrimacport,
MA 01860
Tel: 978 346 0614

Fayne Landes Antiques
593 Hansell Road, Wynnewood,
PA 19096
Tel: 610 658 0566

Tribal Art

**Marcy Burns American
Indian Arts**
PO Box 181Glenside, PA 19038
Tel: 215 576 1559
mbindianart@home.com

Elliot & Grace Snyder
P.O. Box 598, South Egremont,
MA 01258
Tel: 413 528 3581

GLOSSARY

A

acanthus A popular leaf motif found carved and inlaid.

acid etching A technique using acid to decorate glass to produce a matt or frosted effect.

appliqué Decoration that is formed separately and then applied to a piece. In textiles, decoration that is made from a different material and then applied to the main ground, often with braids or decorative stitching.

apron/skirt The piece of wood underneath the seat rail of a chair or settee, or beneath the legs of a table or chest.

architrave The molding around a door or aperture on a piece of furniture.

articulated A doll or figure's body with jointed limbs.

astragal Small architectural molding with a semi-circular section.

B

bakelite An early form of plastic which was popular in the 1920s and 1930s.

balance A type of escape mechanism that is used in clocks without pendulums.

ball-jointed Limbs that are attached to a doll's body with a ball and socket.

baluster A curved form with a bulbous base and a slender neck.

beading A type of decoration, usually in a band or border, and in the shape of small beads.

bébé The French term for a doll that represents a baby rather than an adult.

bergère The French term for an armchair with an upholstered back and sides, and a deep seat.

bezel The groove or rim on the inside of the cover or lid on vessels such as coffeepots or teapots.

biscuit Porcelain that has been fired once and has a characteristic matt white body.

bisque A type of unglazed porcelain used for making dolls heads from 1860 to 1925.

blowing A method of shaping glass by blowing a blob of molten glass through a tube.

bob The metal weight at the end of a pendulum rod.

body The material from which ceramics are made, such as pottery, porcelain, earthenware, or stoneware.

bombé A swollen curving form.

bone china A type of porcelain which has dried ox bone added to the body to produce a very white china. Produced extensively in Britain from 1820.

boulle case A type of marquetry that includes tortoiseshell and metal.

bow front An outwardly curving shape typically found on case furniture.

bracket clock A spring-driven clock originally designed to stand on a wall bracket and later on a shelf or table.

bracket foot A square-shaped foot often found on case furniture from the 18thC.

break/broken arch The arch at the top of longcase and bracket clocks.

C

cabriole leg A leg formed of two slight curves that create an S-shape.

cameo Hardstone, coral, or shell that has been carved in relief to show a design in a contrasting color.

cameo glass Decorative glass made from two or more differently colored layers, which are then carved or etched to reveal the color beneath.

cannetille Filgree formed from silver or gold wire coiled into scrolls or rosettes.

canterbury A small stand with dividers for storing sheet music.

capital The end of a column on the hood or trunk of a longcase clock.

carriage clock A small, spring-driven clock, designed for traveling.

cartouche A framed panel, often in the shape of a paper scroll, the side of which can be inscribed.

caryatid An architechtural column in the form of a woman, also found on 17th and 18thC furniture.

cast metal Metalware formed by pouring molten metal into a cast or mold.

celluloid An early plastic invented in 1869 and used for making dolls heads and bodies.

centre seconds hand A seconds hand that is pivoted at the centre of the dial.

champlevé A type of decoration where enamel is applied to stamped hollows in metal.

chapter ring The ring of hour and minute numbers applied to a clock dial.

character dolls A doll with a face that resembles a real child rather than an idealised one.

chassis The base of a toy vehicle including the wheels and fender.

chinoiserie Oriental-style lacquered or painted decoration featuring figures, buildings, and fauna.

chronometer Precision timekeeper designed for use at sea to calculate longitude.

clock garniture A matching set comprising of a clock and candelabra.

closed back A jewelry setting where the back of the gem is covered with metal.

collet setting A jewelry setting where the gem sits on a circular mount.

commode A decorated low chest of drawers with a bombé or serpentine shape.

composition A mixture including wood pulp, plaster, and glue and used as a cheaper alternative to bisque in the production of dolls heads and bodies.

core forming An early form of glass-making where trails of molten glass are wound around a mud or clay core.

cornice The projecting molding on the top of tall furniture.

crackle A deliberate crazed effect found in the glaze of Chinese Song dynasty and later porcelain.

craze A network of fine cracks in the glaze caused by uneven shrinking during firing.

creamware A cream-colored earthenware with a lead glaze. Produced by Wedgwood in the 1760s and then by other factories.

credenza The Italian term for a side cabinet with display shelves at both ends.

crewelwork An embroidery technique using wool thread on a linen ground.

cultured pearl A pearl formed when an irritant is artifically introduced to the mollusc.

D

damask Fabric woven from silk, linen, or cotton with the decoration formed from the contrasting warp and weft threads.

davenport A large parlour sofa and, in the UK, a small writing desk with drawers.

dentils Small teeth-like blocks that form a border under a cornice.

diaper A repeating pattern of diamond or other geometric shapes.

diecast Objects made by pouring molten metal into a closed metal die or mold.

drop-in seat/slip-in A removable, usually upholstered seat.

E

earthenware A type of porous pottery that requires a glaze to make it waterproof.

épergne A metal or glass center-piece with a bowl at the center and other detachable bowls.

Glossary

escapement The mechanical part of a clock that regulates the transfer of energy from the weights or spring to the movement.

estucheon The protective shield-shaped plates fixed over keyholes.

excelsior A stuffing for teddy bears made from wood shavings.

F

faïence The French name for tin-glazed earthenware.

fashion doll A mid- to late-19thC French doll, usually with a bisque head and elaborate, fashionable clothing.

finial A decorative knob at the end of a terminal or on the cover of silver or ceramic vessels.

firing The baking of ceramics in a kiln.

flashing The covering of a glass vessel with a thin layer of differently colored glass which can then be carved.

flatware A general term of any type of cutlery.

flirty eyes Dolls' eyes that move from left to right as well as open and close.

foliate Leaf and flower motifs.

footrim The projecting circular support at the base of a plate or vessel.

fretwork Geometric pierced decoration.

frieze A long ornamental piece of wood underneath table top or cornice.

frit Powdered glass added to white clay to produce a type of soft-paste porcelain.

fusee A grooved metal cone that offsets the force of the spring as it runs down to ensure accurate timekeeping.

G

gadroon A decorative border of flutes or reeds.

gesso A plaster-like base applied to timber and then carved and gilded.

gilding Applying a gold coating to silver or other metals or materials.

gimbals The rotating rings attached to a chronometer to keep it level in its case.

glaze The glassy coating applied to porous ceramics to make them stronger and waterproof.

googly eyes Dolls' eyes that are large and round and glance to one side.

grosse point A needlepoint stitch that crosses two warp and two weft threads.

ground The base or background color of ceramics on which decoration is applied.

growler A mechanism found in teddy bears from the early to mid 20thC that makes a growling noise.

guilloché enamel Translucent enamel applied over engraved metal.

H

hard-paste porcelain Porcelain made from kaolin, petuntse, and quartz.

hyalith Opaque black or sealing-wax red glass produced in Bohemia from c1818.

I

inclusion Naturally occuring flaws within gemstones.

intaglio Cut or engraved decoration on glass.

J

jasperware A hard and refined stoneware produced by Wedgwood c1775. Can be colored blue, green, yellow, or claret.

K

kaolin A fine white china clay used as the main ingredient in hard-paste porcelain.

kapok A lightweight fiber made from the seeds of the kapok tree and used to stuff teddy bears.

knop The decorative knob on lids and covers and also the bulge on the stem of a candlestick or glass.

L

lamé Silk or synthetic woven fabric shot through with metal threads.

lantern clock A mostly brass weight-driven wall clock shaped like a lantern.

lead glass or crystal A particularly clear type of glass with a high lead oxide content.

lead glaze A clear glaze that includes a lead based component.

lithography A method of printing where a design is drawn in ink on to a stone surface and then transferred to the object.

longcase clock A weight-driven, free-standing clock.

lustre An iridescent finish found on pottery and produced using metallic oxides.

M

maiolica Italian tin-glazed earthenware produced from the 14thC.

majolica 19thC heavily modeled earthenware with thick lead glazes.

mantel clock A small bracket or table clock designed to stand on a shelf or mantelpiece.

marquetry A decorative veneer with the design made up from colored woods and other materials.

mohair plush Used to make teddy bear fur and produced from angora fleece.

monochrome Single color decoration.

mold blowing A method of shaping glass objects by blowing molten glass in a mold.

molding Geometric decoration formed as strips from wood, metal, or plaster.

movement The entire time-keeping mechanism of a clock or watch.

N

niello A black alloy of lead, silver, sulphur, and copper, which is applied to metal and engraved.

O

ogee An S-shaped shallow curve.

opaline glass A translucent white glass made with the addition of oxides and bone ash.

open back A jewelry setting where the back of the gemstone is exposed.

open work Pierced decoration.

ormolu Bronze gilded by the mercury or fine gilding processes, and used in 18thC and early 19thC France as decorative mounts.

overglaze Enamel or transfer-printed decoration on porcelain, which is applied after the glaze has been fired.

ovolo A quarter-circle shaped molding.

P

paisley A soft woollen fabric with a stylized design based on pinecones.

palette The range of colors used in the decoration of ceramics.

parian A semi-matt type of porcelain produced with feldspar, and that does not require a glaze.

parure/demi-parure A jewelry set usually comprising a matching necklace, earrings, a pair of bracelets, and a brooch. A demi-parure is typically just two items such as a necklace and earrings.

pashmina A fine shawl made from the fine underbelly hair of a Himalayan mountain goat.

paste The mixture of ingredients that make up porcelain. Also a compound of glass used to make imitation gemstones.

patera An oval or circular motif often with a floral or fluted center.

pâte-sur-pâte A form of cameo-like low relief decoration produced by carving through layered slip.

pearlware Fine English earthenware developed by Wedgwood. Identified by its blue tinted glaze.

pedestal clock A large bracket clock designed to stand on a matching pedestal.

Glossary

pediment The gabled form on top of a cornice.

pembroke table A small table with two flaps and four legs.

pendulum A wood or metal rod with a weighted end that controls the timekeeping of a clock.

penny toys Small and simple toys made from a variety of materials and designed to be sold for a penny.

petit point Finely worked embroidery with stiches that only cross one warp or weft thread.

petuntse The Chinese name for china stone. A feldspar that is mixed with kaolin to form hard-paste porcelain.

pinion A small toothed wheel that acts a gear within a clock movement.

piqué Form of decoration where metal is inlaid into tortoiseshell or ivory.

plinque-à-jour Technique where translucent enamel is set into an openwork metal frame to create an effect similar to stained glass.

plush A fabric with a long cut pile used to make teddy bear fur.

polychrome Decoration in more than two colors.

prattware A type of creamware decorated with a high-fired palette of blue, green, and yellow.

press-molded Ceramics formed by pressing clay into a mold. Press-molded glass is made by pouring molten glass into a mold and pressing it with a plunger.

Q

quatrefoil A motif incorporating four lobes or leaves.

R

regulator A precision timekeeper used to regulate other clocks.

repoussé Embossed relief decoration on metal.

S

Sabot The metal "shoe" on the end of cabriole legs.

sabre leg A leg shaped like the curved blade of a sabre.

salt glaze A thin glaze used on stonewares and made with the addition of salt during firing.

sautoir A long chain with gems or pearls set at intervals along the length.

seat rail The horizontal bar that joins the chair legs directly below a chair seat.

serpentine A curved form with a projecting middle used in case furniture.

silver gilt Silver with a thin layer of gold.

skiver The sheepskin leather inset found in the top of writing tables and desks.

slip A smooth mixture of clay and water used to decorate pottery and in the production of slip-cast wares.

slip-casting Method of manufacturing thin-bodied vessels by pouring slip into a mold.

socle A plain block that forms the base of a sculpture, vase, or column.

soda glass Formed by the addition of soda to the batch to produce a light glass with a yellow or brown tint.

soft-paste porcelain Porcelain made from kaolin, powdered glass, soapstone, and clay.

spandrel The triangular bracket found at the top of legs.

splat The central upright in a chair back.

sprigged ware Pottery decorated with ornaments applied with slip.

staining (glass) A method of coloring glass with metal oxides which are painted on and then fired.

stoneware A type of ceramic similar to earthenware and porcelain and made of high-fired clay mixed with stone, such as feldspar, which makes it non-porous.

stretchers The bar between two legs on tables and chairs used to stablise the structure.

stuff-over seat A chair with an upholstered seat rail.

stumpwork Raised embroidered needlework.

subsidiary dial A secondary dial set in the main dial that indicates seconds or the date.

swags Decorative ornaments similar to a festoon made up of fruit, flowers, husks, or nuts, or a loop of cloth.

swan-neck cresting or pediment Formed when two S-shaped curves almost meet.

T

tallcase clock *See* longcase clock

tantulus A lockable frame holding cut-glass spirit decanters.

tazza A shallow bowl or cup on a pedestal foot.

terracotta A red earthenware that is lightly fired and usually unglazed.

thrown ware Hollow vessels made by hand on a wheel.

tin-glaze An opaque, white glaze used on earthenware such as delftware, faïence, and maiolica and produced using tin oxide.

tinplate Toys made from thin steel covered with a coating of tin to guard against rust, which could then be painted or decorated with lithography.

toile Cotton fabric printed with a monochrome design.

torchère A portable stand with a table top to support a candle or lamp.

train A set of interconnected wheels and pinions that transfers energy from the spring or wheel to the escape mechanism.

transfer printing A method of decorating ceramic objects. An image is transferred to paper from an inked engraving and then to the vessel.

trefoil A motif incorporating three lobes or leaves.

U

underglaze The color or decoration painted on to a biscuit body before the glazing and firing.

W

wax doll Dolls with heads and occasionally bodies made from either molded or carved wax.

INDEX

Index

Index

Index

Index

Index

Index

Index

INDEX